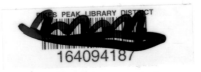

BAKER's Biographical Dictionary of

POPULAR MUSICIANS SINCE 1990

BAKER's Biographical Dictionary *of*
POPULAR MUSICIANS SINCE 1990

INTRODUCTION BY
David Freeland

SCHIRMER REFERENCE™

New York • Detroit • San Diego • San Francisco • Cleveland • New Haven, Conn. • Waterville, Maine • London • Munich

Baker's Biographical Dictionary of Popular Musicians Since 1990

For permission to use material from this product, submit your request via Web at http://www.gale-edit.com/permissions, or you may download our Permissions Request form and submit your request by fax or mail to:

Permissions Department
The Gale Group, Inc.
27500 Drake Rd.
Farmington Hills, MI 48331-3535

Permissions Hotline:
248–699–8006 or 800–762–4058

LIBRARY OF CONGRESS CATALOGING-IN-PUBLICATION DATA

Baker's biographical dictionary of popular musicians since 1990.
    p. cm.
    Includes bibliographical references, discographies, and indexes.
    ISBN 0-02-865799-3 (set : alk. paper) -- ISBN 0-02-865800-0 (v. 1) -- ISBN 0-02-865801-9 (v. 2)
    1. Popular music--Bio-bibliography--Dictionaries. 2. Musicians--Biography--Dictionaries.
ML102.P66 B35 2003
781.64'092'2--dc21

                                                        2003013956

Printed in the United States of America
10 9 8 7 6 5 4

Editorial & Production Staff

SENIOR EDITOR	Stephen Wasserstein
PROJECT EDITOR	Ken Wachsberger
ASSOCIATE EDITOR	Tanya Laplante
COPYEDITORS	Tony Coulter, Bill Kaufman, Gina Misiroglu
PRODUCT DESIGN	Michelle DiMercurio
IMAGING & MULTIMEDIA	Dean Dauphinais, Sara Frischer, Lezlie Light, Daniel Newell, Dave Oblender
PERMISSIONS	Lori Hines
COMPOSITION	Evi Seoud
MANUFACTURING	Rita Wimberley
INDEXER	Julia Marshall
PUBLISHER	Frank Menchaca

Contents

Contributors

RAMIRO BURR is a *San Antonio Express-News* syndicated columnist and arts and entertainment reporter who covers rock, pop, country, and Latin music. He is the author of *The Billboard Guide to Tejano and Regional Mexican Music* (Billboard Books). His freelance articles have been published by *Pulse, Rhythm Music, Cashbox,* and *New Country Music* magazines. Burr was assisted in his *Baker's Biographical Dictionary* contributions by Doug Shannon.

SEAN CAMERON studies law at the University of Virginia. He has profiled Belle and Sebastian, Wilco, Steve Earle, and other artists for *Black Book* magazine and *Spin Online.*

DARA COOK has worked in television on MTV shows including *TRL* and *DFX*. Her writings on hip-hop music and culture have appeared in *The Source, VIBE,* and other publications. She lives in the Bronx, New York.

DAVID FREELAND is the author of *Ladies of Soul* (University Press of Mississippi), which treats the lives and careers of female rhythm and blues musicians of the 1960s. His writings on music and American culture have appeared in *Relix, Goldmine, Blues Access.* and *South Dakota Review.* He lives in New York.

SHAWN GILLEN teaches American literature, journalism, and popular music's relation to literature at Beloit College in Wisconsin. He has published in the *Colorado Review, New Hibernia Review, Isthmus, Henry James Review,* and *Highbeams.* In the 1980s and 1990s Gillen was a freelance music critic for *City Pages,* the Minneapolis *StarTribune,* and the *Minnesota Daily.*

MARK GUARINO has been the music critic for the *Chicago Daily Herald,* the state's third largest daily newspaper, since 1997. He has written for *SPIN, Blender, Chicago Reader, virginmega.com,* and *Gene Simmons Tongue magazine.*

CARRIE HAVRANEK has written about music for the *Village Voice, In Touch Weekly, Salon.com, Spin.com,* and *Sonicnet.com,* and about women's issues for *Cosmopolitan* and *First for Women.* She lives with her husband in Easton, Pennsylvania.

STAN HAWKINS is Associate Professor in Music at the University of Oslo, Norway. He is the author of *Settling the Pop Score: Pop Texts and Identity Politics* (Ashgate), and is widely published in the research field of popular musicology.

MATT HIMES writes the weekly *Hip-Hop Countdown,* among other shows, for MTV2. He wrote all 50 episodes of *Sisqo's Shakedown* for MTV, and has profiled artists including Britney Spears and Snoop Dogg. He lives in Brooklyn, New York.

HUA HSU has written about art and politics for the *Village Voice, VIBE,* and *The Wire.* He is in the midst of his dissertation on American democracy and the Trans-Pacific imagination, due to Harvard University's History of American Civilization program sometime this century.

GIL KAUFMAN is a freelance writer and editor who contributes frequently to *Rolling Stone, Wired, MTV.com, VH1.com, Cincinnati Enquirer,* and *iD* magazine. He lives in Cincinnati, Ohio.

ARCHIE LOSS is Professor of English and American Studies at Penn State Erie, the Behrend College. His American Popular Culture course focuses on the 1960s, especially the popular arts. His books include *Of Human Bondage: Coming of Age in the Novel* (Twayne) and *Pop Dreams: Music, Movies, and the Media in the 1960s* (Harcourt Brace College Publishers).

DONALD LOWE has written humor, editorial, and feature pieces for a variety of Connecticut publications in addition to articles in Upper Midwest regional magazines such as *Horizons and North Dakota Outdoors*. His writings have included a memoir of a 400-mile hike across the state of North Dakota. He is currently recording original songs that he performs in coffee house and club venues. He lives in Sherman, Connecticut.

HOWARD MANDEL has written since the mid-1970s about jazz, blues, and new and unusual forms of music for the *Village Voice, Washington Post, Down Beat, Jazziz, The Wire, Swing Journal,* and *Musical America.* He also produces reports for National Public Radio. A former editor of *Down Beat, Ear,* and *RhythmMusic* magazines, Mandel is an associate adjunct professor at New York University and president of the Jazz Journalists Association (www.Jazzhouse.org). He is the author of *Future Jazz* (Oxford University Press).

DOUGLAS MCLENNAN is a critic and arts reporter and the editor and founder of *ArtsJournal.com,* the Seattle-based arts news website. He is a graduate of Mannes College and the Juilliard School with degrees in piano performance.

CAROLINE POLK O'MEARA is a graduate student in musicology at the University of California, Los Angeles. She has published on the British all-female punk rock band the Raincoats, and is writing a dissertation on the genealogy of noise in American popular music since 1968.

DENNIS POLKOW is co-creator of the *Chicago Musicale,* an experimental music and arts publication, as well as *Spotlight,* the arts and entertainment section of the Press Publications newspaper chain. His "Face the Music" column pioneered the notion of a single columnist covering all forms of music—rock, jazz, pop, folk, rap, hip-hop, world music, early music, classical, opera, musical theater, and new music—all in a single venue with a single voice. Polkow has been a regular contributor to *Musical America, Grammy Magazine, Clavier, The Instrumentalist, Chicago Tribune, Chicago Reader,* and *Chicago Jazz Weekly,* among others. He produced the Grammy Award-winning Chicago Pro Musica's *The Clarinet in My Mind* (1992) and is on the adjunct faculties of Lewis University and Oakton Community College.

DAVE POWERS is a New York-based writer and producer, who has worked in television production since 1997 for music channels including VH1, MTV, and MTV2. He has produced *Chart 2 Chart,* a weekly look at the popular music charts, and *Subterranean,* a forum for new and underground music. His writing has appeared in *Time Out New York, CityPaper* (Washington, DC), and *3wk.com.*

MICHAEL SELVERNE is a trained musician as well as the founder and managing partner of Selverne, Mandelbaum & Mintz, LLP, an entertainment, technology, and media law firm headquartered in New York. His clients include entertainers, recording artists, and media companies.

JOE SCHLOSS is a lecturer in music at Tufts University. He holds a Ph.D. in ethnomusicology from the University of Washington and was the recipient of the Society for Ethnomusicology's Charles Seeger Prize in 2000. His writing has appeared in *VIBE, The Seattle Weekly, The Flavor,* and the anthology *Classic Material.* Schloss is the author of *Making Beats: The Art of Sample-Based Hip-Hop* (Wesleyan University Press).

SCOTT TRIBBLE is an Ohio-based writer who has contributed to *Musician.com, Guitar.com, Musician's Friend,* and the *St. James Encyclopedia of Popular Culture.* A graduate of Harvard College, Tribble plays rhythm guitar and keyboards in the Chicago-area band Liam.

OLIVER WANG is a radio and club DJ, the editor of *Classic Material: The Hip-Hop Album Guide* (ECW Press), and a frequent contributor to *SF Bay Guardian, LA Weekly, Source,* and *Popmatters.Com.* He is completing a dissertation at the University of California, Berkeley, in the Ethnic Studies department, on the social history of the Filipino American DJ community in the San Francisco area.

SIMON WARNER is Senior Teaching Fellow in the School of Music at the University of Leeds, England, where he directs the bachelor of arts program in Popular Music Studies. He is the author of *Rockspeak: The Language of Rock and Pop* (Blandford) and *Popular Music for Beginners* (Writers and Readers). He is working on a new volume, *Text and Drugs and Rock 'n' Roll: The Beats and Rock from Kerouac and Ginsberg to Dylan and Cobain,* to be published by Continuum in New York.

WYNN YAMAMI is a musician and writer working on a Ph.D. in historical musicology at New York University, where he organized two interdisciplinary conferences: *The Postmodern Inheritance* (2001) and *The 1980s: Popular Music and Culture* (2003). He has performed at the Metropolitan Museum of Art, the Brooklyn Museums of Art, Birdland, and the FringeNYC.

Introduction

Any biographical volume of contemporary personalities faces an inherent problem; such works are dated from the moment they appear. To a certain extent, attempting to encapsulate the state of popular music "since 1990," the period on which *Baker's Biographical Dictionary of Popular Musicians* focuses, is to aim at a moving target. Given the fleeting nature of stardom—and the evanescence of pop culture as a whole—some "hot new performers" of 2003 likely will be forgotten within five years, others as soon as six months. Ongoing developments in technology and the music industry have accelerated this process, so that artists sometimes release one album and, unable to hold their own amid so many competing outlets for entertainment—DVDs, video games, the Internet—are not heard from again. Trends rise and disappear with equal unpredictability.

For example, the popularity of "divas," a term previously reserved for only the most venerable female performers but bestowed in the late 1990s upon newcomers such as Shania Twain and Brandy, had largely played out by the early 2000s, as one-time divas Mariah Carey and Whitney Houston released albums that proved critically and commercially disappointing.

Selection and Inclusion of Artists

The question of which performers to include required a substantial degree of judgment. Targeting the top tier, or "most popular," performers—Eminem, Madonna, Michael Jackson, Nirvana, and others—was simple; choosing the next level and the one below it proved more difficult. The selection process was always challenging and often thorny. The value of an entry on rock and R&B star Tina Turner, for instance, is clear: Not only did Turner set a standard for energy and tenacity that continues to be an inspiration for younger performers, she also retained her hit-making prowess into the 1990s. At the same time, other talented performers of Turner's generation—Patti LaBelle, Gladys Knight—are omitted because their commercial success in the 1990s did not reach the same heights. They still perform concerts and sell recordings among a core group of fans, but their appeal is largely confined to those with esoteric tastes. Like Bob Dylan and the Rolling Stones, two "veteran" acts also included, Turner has proven consistently relevant from a commercial perspective. When considering entries for younger performers—newcomers who have invigorated pop by presenting old styles in a different way—*Baker's Biographical Dictionary of Popular Musicians Since 1990* has targeted those artists who are likely to have staying power in the years to come, with the understanding that the vagaries of the music business render long-term predictions impossible.

The bulk of the book is devoted to rock, pop, country, R&B, and hip-hop. For entries in these categories, the book's goal is to spotlight artists who are popular in the current period, those who have established their success with hit recordings, CD sales, and radio airplay. When considering entries for other genres—classical, world, Latin, Broadway, blues, folk, New Age, and jazz—and determining the right balance of entries for each category, the criteria for inclusion were slightly different, but commercial success remained as one factor. In the field of jazz, for instance, the critical attention given to performers often outdistances their "success" from a commercial standpoint. Although the 1990s saw young jazz musicians such as

Diana Krall moving into the pop mainstream, the bulk of jazz artists continued to work far outside the confines of hit radio and music television. The jazz entries, therefore, represent a survey not only of "crossover" artists such as Krall but also of established performers—Keith Jarrett, Wynton Marsalis—who seldom achieve hits on the Top 40 pop charts. At the same time, classically inclined readers may be surprised that an orchestra such as the London Symphony is included while the Berlin Philharmonic, considered one of the most accomplished in the world, is not. In a larger collection both would have warranted inclusion. In this collection, the London Symphony was selected because it epitomizes what contributor Douglas McLennan calls the "entrepreneurial spirit that has made it one of the most recorded orchestras in the world." The goal in presenting entries for non-pop or rock genres is to provide readers with a sample survey of the field. Although not every worthy artist or group is included, the present collection will give readers a solid base from which to explore these styles further.

Changes in Pop Since 1990

The concept of "crossover," the transition of an artist from a "niche" or "cult" status into the mainstream of popular recognition, is a recurring theme within the entries, one that has notably characterized the state of pop music since the 1990s. Latin artists Marc Anthony and Ricky Martin, blues guitarist Kenny Wayne Shepherd, and classical performer Andrea Bocelli are just a few of the performers whose careers have benefited from this movement. Crossover, of course, has been a goal of pop performers for decades—the success of the 1960s record company Motown, for example, was built upon crossover from R&B into the pop market—but the 1990s witnessed the enactment of crossover to an unprecedented degree. It became not merely a goal, but a necessity for economic survival. Commercial radio formats in the 1990s grew more conservative, with little attention devoted to new or untested artists; at the same time, the music industry continued to issue new product at a steady pace. As Michael Selverne discusses in his essay within the appendix, approximately 6,500 albums are released each year in the United States. Of these, only two percent are judged successful by attaining "gold" or "platinum" status. Further, the standard channel for music distribution, the CD, has been threatened by the increased number of ways fans can hear music by their favorite artists: MP3 file sharing, audio streaming, and websites. As a result, by 2003 the entire industry was in the midst of one of its worst slumps in history, battling music downloads on the one hand while pushing CDs with the all-time high price of $19.99 on the other.

In this shaky climate, artistic risk-taking, even among those known for their iconoclasm, has become rare.

Former music "rebels" such as Randy Newman, while continuing to issue solid material, firmly joined the 1990s Hollywood establishment, composing family-friendly scores for hit movies. In country music, "traditional" artists such as Mark Chesnutt have smoothed out the rough edges in their sound, bringing it into line with the accessible standards of hit radio, in which "playlists"—song sets given regular rotation at stations—are determined by market research strategies such as focus groups and surveys. Similarly, hip-hop artists such as R. Kelly and Mary J. Blige added pop elements—soaring choruses, inspirational lyrics—to their recordings as the 1990s progressed, although, despite the odds, they often succeeded in preserving the integrity of their original artistic vision. Kelly's "I Believe I Can Fly" (1996), one of the biggest hits of the decade, gained its power from traditional gospel vocalizing combined with a slick pop production, while Blige crafted one of the most appealing albums of her career, *Mary* (1999), by setting her grainy voice against a bed of lush strings and elegant orchestrations.

As Kelly and Blige prove, crossover is not necessarily a negative force. It has, for instance, allowed rap music to retain its commercial potency throughout the 1990s and into the new millennium, as rappers such as Will Smith, Ja Rule, and Eminem have earned lasting favor among a pop audience. If the tenacity of a style is any indication of its value, rap has emerged as one of the most important musical developments of the late twentieth century. As rap has evolved over the course of a 25-year recorded history, it has displayed remarkable staying power and resilience, adapting to new trends by filtering into pop, rock, hip-hop, and R&B. By the early 2000s, rap had enjoyed a longer hit-making life than those of antecedent styles in African-American music such as soul, funk, or disco. Coming to terms with the ongoing development and vitality of rap, a style initially disregarded by the critical establishment as "nonmusical" or "talky," is one of the most exciting elements of this volume, proof that innovation is not necessarily stifled by the presence of commercial success.

A development separate from, but related to, crossover has been the rise of pluralism within pop music since the 1990s. As pop continues to evolve, a greater number of artists have incorporated elements from outside genres into their work. By the end of the 1990s this musical breadth had become a mark of erudition on the part of the artist, pointing to an awareness of the disparate styles that blend into pop's musical brew. In previous decades, it was common for performers to remain within a single, definable stylistic pattern. The albums of 1970s singer Carole King, for example, vary little in terms of sound from one to the next. When folk-rock artist Joni Mitchell experimented with jazz on her mid-1970s albums, the effort was viewed as a bold stylistic move. Such initiatives were the norm by the 1990s, when digital technology and musical "sampling" made it easy for an artist to insert a riff from the past or a snippet of an African polyrhythm into a modern song. Contemporary artists such as Wyclef Jean, Annie Lennox, and David Byrne have made eclecticism their trademark, delving into new musical terrain with each successive release. While it can be argued that many of these explorations are more concerned with style than with substance, it is undeniable that contemporary musicians are more aware than ever of the array of options, or "sound bites," available for use in their music.

In addition to crossover and pluralism, the entries reflect other changes that occurred within the pop world of the 1990s. In support of the maxim that trends never disappear but are instead recycled and updated, "boy bands"—a staple of pop music in the early 1970s with groups like the Jackson 5 and the Osmonds—returned in the 1990s. Acts such as Hanson, the Backstreet Boys, and *NSYNC attained idol status among one of the pop industry's primary target markets: teenage girls. At the same time, another branch of pop music appealed to a more mature, music-savvy audience, with older artists such as Santana, Aerosmith, Tony Bennett, and Frank Sinatra gaining a renewed fame that rivaled their success in the past, particularly in terms of record sales (Sinatra's 1993 *Duets* album became the biggest seller of his career). In a sense, the pop audience's attentions have always been balanced between a craving for the "new" and a nostalgic yearning for the past; the most successful pop music looks both forward and backward. Music fans of the 1990s took pride in their eclecticism, and it was not uncommon for purchasers of the latest album by Sheryl Crow or Alanis Morissette also to buy a "traditional" CD such as the 1997 crossover hit *Buena Vista Social Club*, which showcased a number of Cuba's finest, yet most neglected, musicians.

With the expanding selection of choices in pop music, audiences by the early 2000s began to fall into segmented categories associated with their interests: Southern Rock, Speed Metal, Gangsta Rap. These fans found kindred musical spirits through Internet websites and chat rooms tailored to their needs. Traditional marketing initiatives began to seem out of date as more music fans learned about new artists through word-of-mouth and online recommendations. In a mark of the dichotomy that has always characterized popular culture, however, segmented audiences also possessed a greater capacity to branch out into other musical areas. The range of musical subgenres is now wider than ever, but, due to technology and the cross-pollination of pop music styles, the gaps separating one listener from another have grown smaller. Acknowledging this development by featuring entries on a diverse range of styles, the contributors have sought to capture the complex, variegated nature of current popular music.

Format and Style

Within the entries, contributors have represented bands and artists on their own terms; a rock performer such as Bruce Springsteen is not depicted as "greater" or "lesser" in value than Broadway theater composer Stephen Sondheim. Both have been active since 1990, and in this way have contributed immeasurably to the current musical landscape. At the same time, the contributors have exerted critical assessment within each style. Unlike many musical reference works that describe the subject's work with technical, dispassionate language, the new *Baker's* offers judgment without entirely discarding the ideals of objectivity and distance with which such volumes are informed.

In this way *Baker's Biographical Dictionary of Popular Musicians Since 1990* departs from the Ninth "Centennial" Edition of *Baker's Biographical Dictionary of Musicians* (2001), edited by Nicolas Slonimsky and Laura Kuhn. The emphasis in that six-volume work is classical, and its guiding principles are biographical and bibliographical. Furthermore, it does not attempt to assess the recording achievements of its subjects. Slonimsky's entry on Ludwig van Beethoven, for example, contains more than ten columns devoted to the composer's complete output, including orchestral works, chamber works, works for piano, for voice, and for solo instruments and orchestra. Yet *Baker's Biographical Dictionary of Musicians* does not mention any famous Beethoven recordings by the conductors Wilhelm Fürtwangler, Leonard Bernstein, or Carlos Kleiber; the pianists Wilhelm Kempff or Alfred Brendel; or sopranos such as Christa Ludwig and Barbara Bonney. Such a listing would have proved overwhelming, and invariably the question of which recordings are still in print would need to be answered.

In contrast, and as the book's cover image implies, *Baker's Biographical Dictionary of Popular Musicians Since 1990* focuses largely upon the recordings. This is fitting, since the recorded album or single track, unlike a musical score, can be considered a finished work of art. The book assumes that readers will get to know the subject not through formal study of piano, guitar, or voice, but through repeated exposure to recordings. Although the interests of fans and inveterate music lovers have been considered, the book is tailored for general readers, those without formal training in music. Each entry, therefore, strives to provide a general overview while delving deeply enough to seize upon the inherent worth of its subject. On the whole, contributors have not been concerned with assessing an artist's career on a strict album-by-album basis. Rather, they have employed a selective approach that limns an artist's special contribution—the elements making that artist worthy of inclusion.

It is hoped that the book's balance—critical yet inclusive—will be useful for placing each performer's work in its proper context. Entries on pioneering artists such as James Brown and George Jones are presented as "appreciations" as much as biographies. Neither performer can be accurately described as a "hot" artist in a contemporary sense. Both have remained active performers since 1990, but their commercial success peaked decades earlier. Without an understanding of the ways in which they have influenced the course of contemporary music, however, the work of their descendants in rhythm and blues and country cannot adequately be assessed. Likewise, the Beatles, a group that has not existed officially since 1970, are given a substantial entry due to the enormous influence they have exerted upon every rock band that has followed them. The volume's mission, therefore, is to appeal to two different audiences. One can be described as an older reader familiar with the Beatles and James Brown, but for whom developments since 1990 in rock and R&B—grunge, rap, hip-hop—have gone largely unnoticed. The second is a reader born after 1980, aware of young artists such as Mary J. Blige and Britney Spears but oblivious to pop music's longstanding relation to Broadway, jazz, and Tin Pan Alley. Through categorical inclusiveness, *Baker's* seeks to bridge the gap between these audiences.

Through its format, structure, and content, *Baker's* hopes to complement, rather than compete with, the Internet. While the editors and contributors understand that a great deal of biographical information is available on the Web, they also believe in the value of two concise volumes that can be browsed and consulted through multiple encounters. Further, given the transitory nature of material on the Web, *Baker's* will provide readers with a long-lasting, dependable alternative. Acknowledging the importance of Internet research, contributors have included Web links for performers and bands wherever possible. They have also strived for accuracy with regard to the biographical information at the beginning of each entry: birthplace, birth date, best-selling album since 1990, and hits since 1990; although it has not always been possible to unearth more arcane data such as the birth dates of musicians who long ago left a group. The albums listed at the end of each entry reflect the contributor's assessment of which works are significant—the recordings that best represent an artist's contributions as a whole—rather than a complete discography.

Selected sidebars, called "spotlights," target the recordings, events, and movements that have defined popular music since 1990. There are spotlights on special events and cultural moments (such as Farm Aid or Gilberto Gil being named Brazil's minister of culture); hit songs (Hanson's "MMMBop"); and pivotal albums (Nirvana's *Nevermind*). The genre index at the end of Volume 2 supplements the general index and is designed for browsing. Only the largest genre categories are included in this index. Examples include rock and pop, classical, country, jazz, Latin, rhythm and blues, and world. No attempt has been made to separate rock from pop or to divide rock into its fragmented components. Artists and bands in the genre index appear only once, each within a single category, even though the genre description that appears beneath a subject title in the book may list multiple categories. For example, the subject "Elvis Costello" appears in the genre index under rock; the genre line under Costello's article lists rock, pop, and country.

Four interpretive essays in the appendix have been commissioned to help expand the use and depth of the book, providing historical context for many of the subjects. The essays address themes of particular importance to popular music in the United States since 1990: the rise and fall of grunge (the dominant popular rock genre at the start of the 1990s); rap music's emergence within the commercial mainstream; the impact of corporate radio since the mid-1990s and its effects upon musical content; and the role of the Internet and the crisis of the music industry in the early 2000s.

Attempting to Define "Popular"

In conclusion, the term "popular music" can be challenging to define, as it begs the question, "What is popular?" In his book *The Rise and Fall of Popular Music* (1994), music historian Donald Clarke equates "popular" with "commercial." In contrast to classical music, the creation and performance of which is often aided by governmental or private subsidies, "popular music" is associated with business and enterprise. In general, a symphonic, operatic, or chamber composer creates music irrespective of commercial considerations. A popular music writer, on the other hand, must score some kind of "hit"—whether on the Top 40 charts, in a Hollywood film, or on the Broadway stage—in order to enjoy a full-time career in music. This is not to say that creators of pop music are not simultaneously interested in making "art"; rather, that popular art is often created with commercial considerations in mind. At the same time, the lines between "popular" and "classical" are not always clear-cut. The years since 1990 have witnessed classical performers moving into the cultural mainstream to an unprecedented degree. Opera singers such as Renée Fleming are marketed like pop stars, via advertising campaigns that emphasize their good looks and sex appeal. This development notwithstanding, "classical" and "popular" are still widely perceived as separate areas of appreciation. The difference between the two can be detected through a trip to a local CD store. While the pop, rock, and R&B aisles will be thronged with crowds, the classical section is often empty, an oasis of quiet amidst the hubbub and cacophony that surrounds it.

Moving past categorical divisions, the concept of popular music can perhaps best be described through its entry in the *Collins English Dictionary*: "music having wide appeal." It is this definition that most accurately expresses the philosophy of this book and its editor, Stephen Wasserstein. Over the course of almost 600 entries, the two volumes comprising this new addition to *Baker's* seek to address the question of which musicians have been popular at some point since 1990, regardless of genre or style. For this reason, classical artists such as Fleming, as well as classical "bands" such as the Boston Pops and the Chicago Symphony Orchestra, are included; their appeal is so widespread that they can be described as "popular" in their reach and influence. As the first book of its kind to spotlight all forms of music since 1990, it targets and surveys those artists who have made a significant impact on current popular culture. Although the book's emphasis is contemporary, the decision to use 1990 as a starting point gives it the historical perspective common to a reference work. Popular music has changed dramatically since 1990; in these volumes, the editorial team and contributors aim to capture the varied, complex nature of today's pop within a readable, concise format.

DAVID FREELAND
NEW YORK

A^a_A

AALIYAH

Born: Aaliyah Haughton; Brooklyn, New York, 16 January 1979; died Abaco, Bahamas, 25 August 2001

Genre: R&B

Best-selling album since 1990: *Aaliyah* (2001)

Hit songs since 1990: "Try Again," "More Than a Woman"

A teenage star who never reached her adult potential, Aaliyah Haughton blazed a bright trail through the world of contemporary rhythm and blues during the middle to late 1990s, until her untimely death at the age of twenty-two in a plane crash in the Bahamas.

Haughton was born in New York and raised in Detroit. (Her name, pronounced Ah-LEE-yah, a transliteration from Swahili, means "exalted one"). She was inspired by her mother, Diane, a singer, and her uncle, a lawyer briefly married to Gladys Knight, the R&B legend best known for the 1970s ballad "Midnight Train to Georgia." Haughton got her first break performing with Knight at the age of eleven and released her debut album, *Age Ain't Nothing but a Number*, in 1994, at the age of fifteen. The preternaturally mature singer scored several Top 10 hits from the album with the sing-songy, hip-hop-flavored "Back & Forth" and the Isley Brothers's "At Your Best (You Are Love)."

But her marriage to her producer, the Chicago singer R. Kelly, threatened to overshadow her debut. Kelly wrote most of the songs on the album, which mixed street-savvy R&B with rapping and a few unexceptional ballads. The songs, such as "Throw Your Hands Up," feature lyrics that

match Aaliyah's early image, which blended street-tough baggy pants and bandannas with a sly, girl-next-door smile ("Straight from the streets / Is where I'm coming from / Straight out the streets / With a touch of jazz in me").

Because Haughton was underage at the time of the marriage, the union generated controversy and was quickly annulled; it did nothing, however, to slow the singer's meteoric rise. Her second album featured even stronger compositions and touches that prefigured her later signature style, thanks to a close collaboration with the producer, Timbaland, and the rising star rapper/producer, Missy "Misdemeanor" Elliott. Their combination of skittering, minimalist space-age beats and Haughton's rich yet ethereal vocals set the stage for their most distinguished future collaborations. The 1996 album *One in a Million* produced another pair of hits, including the languid title track and the seductive "If Your Girl Only Knew." "One in a Million" finds Haughton evolving from the inexperienced, shy teen of her debut into a more mature, enigmatic seductress.

Haughton continued to grow artistically with every single she released, most notably in her 1998 single, "Are You That Somebody," from the *Dr. Dolittle* soundtrack. Again buoyed by Timbaland's crisp, futuristic beats, the song is built around an infectious sample of a baby's cry. "Journey to the Past," a track from the animated Disney film *Anastasia,* was nominated for an Academy Award for Best Song that same year, and Haughton performed it on the Academy Awards.

Unlike so many of her contemporaries, Haughton kept her private life off-limits, furthering her slightly mysterious image. Known for her close familial relationships, a tireless work ethic, and a pleasant disposition, the singer gained fans among profanity-spewing rap artists and suburban teens alike with an image that was both streetwise and classy. With a preference for black leather, dark sunglasses, and a tuft of hair covering her left eye, the singer exuded an air of effortless cool that extended to her fluid, languid dance moves. It was that enigmatic style that earned Haughton her first movie role, co-starring with the Asian martial arts star Jet Li in *Romeo Must Die* (2000).

The single "Try Again," from the film's soundtrack, further cemented the creative and commercial symbiosis between Haughton and Timbaland; this stutter-stepping, up-tempo R&B affirmation helped push the album, which Haughton executive-produced, to more than 2 million in sales. With positive reviews for her work in *Romeo Must Die* Haughton signed on to appear in a co-starring role in the two sequels to the science fiction film *The Matrix* and a lead part in the vampire drama *Queen of the Damned*.

Superstardom Cut Short by a Tragic Accident

While filming her gothic role in the Anne Rice–inspired *Queen of the Damned*, Haughton recorded her self-titled third album, which further expanded her sound, adding touches of blues, jazz, and salsa to a group of songs exploring themes of abusive relationships, sex, and betrayal. Tracks such as the propulsively funky "More Than a Woman" and the Caribbean-flavored "Rock the Boat" are infused with Haughton's increased confidence and control.

Just one month after the album's release, Haughton was returning from the Bahamas after filming a video for *Rock the Boat* when her promising career was cut short. The charter airplane she and eight of her entourage were on crashed after takeoff. Haughton's elaborate funeral in downtown New York City, which featured a horse-drawn carriage pulling her casket, was fit for royalty. A ceremony for friends and family following the funeral featured a photo of Haughton with the inscription "We were given a Queen, We were given an Angel." The singer was buried in Westchester County, New York.

An album of outtakes, remixes, and previously unreleased songs with contributions from many of the singer's contemporaries and fans, *I Care 4 U*, was released in late 2002.

SELECTIVE DISCOGRAPHY: *Age Ain't Nothing but a Number* (Blackground, 1994); *One in a Million* (Blackground, 1996); *Aaliyah* (Blackground, 2001); *I Care 4 U* (Blackground, 2002).

SELECTIVE FILMOGRAPHY: *Queen of the Damned* (2002); *Romeo Must Die* (2000).

GIL KAUFMAN

AC/DC

Formed: 1973, Sydney, Australia

Members: Brian Johnson, vocals (born Newcastle, England, 5 October 1947); Phil Rudd, drums (born Melbourne, Australia, 19 May 1954); Cliff Williams, bass (born Essex, England, 14 December 1949); Angus Young, guitar (born Glasgow, Scotland, 31 March 1959); Malcolm Young, guitar (born Glasgow, Scotland, 6 January 1953). Former members: Mark Evans, bass (born Melbourne, Australia, 2 March 1956); Ronald Belford "Bon" Scott, vocals (born Kirriemuir, Scotland, 9 July 1946; d. London, England, 20 February 1980); Chris Slade, drums (born Pontypridd, Wales, 30 October 1946); Simon Wright, drums (born Alden, England, 19 June 1963).

Genre: Rock

Best-selling album since 1990: *The Razor's Edge* (1990)

Hit songs since 1990: "Moneytalks"

AC/DC blended power chords, hard-rock beats, and searing vocals with a theatrical stage presence that featured the ceaseless cavorting of lead guitarist Angus Young in his trademark school uniform. Blatant sexual innuendo was proudly displayed in their songs, from "Big Balls" to "You Shook Me All Night Long." After the release of *Highway to Hell* (1979) and the sudden death of singer Bon Scott, AC/DC returned triumphantly with *Back in Black* (1980) and *For Those About to Rock We Salute You* (1981). Through subsequent decades AC/DC continued to release albums using a pat formula.

AC/DC was formed by the brothers Malcolm and Angus Young in 1973. Playing at local pubs with Dave Evans (vocals), Larry van Knedt (bass), and Colin Burgess (drums), the group gained notice for their bombastic sound and energetic stage presence. At the suggestion of his sister, Angus began to wear his school uniform onstage, a gimmick that rapidly became his trademark. Evans and the Young brothers relocated to Melbourne, where bassist Mark Evans and drummer Phil Rudd joined the group. After Dave Evans refused to sing at a performance in September 1974, the group's chauffeur, Bon Scott, stepped in for the night and soon replaced Evans as the group's lead singer.

After recording two albums released only in Australia, the group was signed to Atlantic Records, which offered selections from these albums under the title *High Voltage* (1976). Mark Evans quit the group after lengthy tours, and Cliff Williams was recruited as the new bassist. Upon moving to London, AC/DC gained a cult following and was soon touring with such groups as KISS, Aerosmith, Styx, and Cheap Trick. The group's April 1978 performance at the Apollo in Glasgow, Scotland, was recorded and later released as *If You Want Blood, You've Got It* (1978).

During this time AC/DC released *Let There Be Rock* (1977), which include the perennial favorite "Whole Lotta Rosie," and *Powerage* (1978). Gaining international attention, the group recorded *Highway to Hell* (1979) with the producer Robert John "Mutt" Lange. The title track begins with a blistering guitar riff that characterizes all of the verses. This riff is balanced by a chorus with the memorable line, "I'm on a highway to hell." Bon Scott presents the melody in a characteristically forceful tone that verges on screaming.

Soon after the album's release, AC/DC incurred a tragic setback with the sudden death of Bon Scott, who choked on his own vomit after a night of heavy drinking. Many critics and fans assumed that the band would fold, but Brian Johnson was quickly recruited as the new lead singer. After two months in the studio, AC/DC released *Back in Black* (1980), whose title and black cover paid tribute to Scott. The title track opens with a straightforward guitar riff that concludes with a syncopated rhythm. Johnson belts out the melodic line, which is limited in pitch movement but effective in its extremely high register. In "You Shook Me All Night Long," Johnson employs a string of sexual innuendoes beginning with the first line, "She was a fast machine, she kept her motor clean."

With *Back in Black* and *Dirty Deeds Done Dirt Cheap* (originally recorded with Bon Scott in 1976 and released in 1981), AC/DC occupied the charts simultaneously with two albums featuring two different singers. Following the release of *For Those About to Rock We Salute You* (1981) and *Flick of the Switch* (1983), Rudd left the group and was replaced by Simon Wright. In the mid-1980s, the group was implicated in a bizarre controversy that centered on Richard Ramirez, a serial killer who claimed that their song "Night Prowler" inspired him to commit numerous murders. This negative publicity eventually dissipated, and AC/DC continued to record albums and tour. After the release of *Blow Up Your Video* (1988), Simon Wright left the group to join Dio and was replaced by Chris Slade.

After a series of mildly successful albums in the late 1980s, AC/DC released *The Razor's Edge* (1990), which eventually charted at number two on the *Billboard* chart. "Money Talks" begins with a guitar riff that echoes the melodic line. Although the song is humorous at times, with the tongue-in-cheek chorus, "C'mon, c'mon, love me for the money," it lacks energy and momentum. While exploring some new musical territory with extended introductions and prominent backup vocals, the album is uneven and uninspired. "Mistress for Christmas," with its line, "Want to be in heaven with three in a bed," sounds like a failed joke, and "Let's Make It" recalls a weaker version of "Back in Black."

AC/DC then released *Live* (1992) and *Bonfire* (1995), a box set memorial to Bon Scott. Phil Rudd rejoined the group, and with their next album, *Ballbreaker* (1995), AC/DC regained some of its energy. "Cover You in Oil" begins with a strong introduction and a medium-tempo rock groove. The lyrics in the chorus are effective, although the rhyme scheme in the verse is awkward and forced: "Pull on the zip, she give good lip (service)." The song "The Honey Roll" begins with a strong guitar riff that leads into a straightforward verse. The guitar solo is followed by a short bridge and extended choruses.

With *Ballbreaker* and *Stiff Upper Lip* (2000), AC/DC uses a different style of guitar riff with a single-note drone set against a melodic line. In "Stiff Upper Lip," the introductory guitar sounds lithe and blues-tinged rather than raucous. Brian Johnson begins the verse in a low register, singing "I was born with a stiff, stiff upper lip" with an effective pause halfway through the line. "All Screwed Up" explodes with an oscillating guitar riff and includes a surprisingly melodic interlude before the chorus.

Throughout their career AC/DC were intensely loyal to their musical formula: riff-driven rock replete with power chords, blistering vocals, and constant allusions to sexual acts. They eschewed popular manifestations of hard rock, from the imagery of glam-metal and hair-bands to the power ballads of arena rock. For these same reasons their recent material sounds derivative, recycled, and at times lethargic. While AC/DC gained little ground in the U.S. singles charts, their albums enjoyed tremendous sales internationally. In 2003 they were inducted into the Rock and Roll Hall of Fame, a fitting tribute to their uncompromising spirit and tireless musical activity.

SELECTIVE DISCOGRAPHY: *High Voltage* (Atlantic, 1976); *Let There Be Rock* (Atlantic, 1977); *Powerage* (Atlantic, 1978); *If You Want Blood, You've Got It* (Atlantic, 1978); *Highway to Hell* (Atlantic, 1979); *Back in Black* (Atlantic, 1980); *Dirty Deeds Done Dirt Cheap* (Atlantic, 1981); *For Those About to Rock We Salute You* (Atlantic, 1981); *Flick of the Switch* (Atlantic, 1983); *'74 Jailbreak* (Atlantic, 1984); *Fly on the Wall* (Atlantic, 1985); *Who Made Who* (Atlantic, 1986); *Blow Up Your Video* (Atlantic, 1988); *The Razor's Edge* (Atco, 1990); *Live* (Atco, 1992); *Live (Special Collector's Edition)* (Atco, 1992); *Ballbreaker* (EastWest, 1995); *Bonfire* (EastWest, 1997); *Stiff Upper Lip* (EastWest, 2000).

WEBSITE: www.ac-dc.net.

WYNN YAMAMI

ACE OF BASE

Formed: 1990, Gothenburg, Sweden

Members: Jenny Berggren, lead vocals (born Gothenburg, Sweden, 19 May 1972); Jonas Berggren, producer (born

Gothenburg, Sweden, 21 March 1967); Malin "Linn" Berggren, lead vocals (born Gothenburg, Sweden, 31 October 1970); Ulf "Buddha" Ekberg, producer (born Gothenburg, Sweden, 6 December 1970).

Genre: Rock

Best-selling album since 1990: *The Sign* (1993)

Hit songs since 1990: "All That She Wants," "Don't Turn Around," "The Sign"

With a bright, danceable sound reminiscent of 1970s disco, Ace of Base enjoyed a string of hits in the early 1990s and proved that the Seattle grunge movement could not keep pop music down for long.

The sisters Jenny and Linn Berggren began their singing careers in a church choir in their native Gothenburg, Sweden. Their older brother Jonas was also involved in music, playing synthesizers and writing songs with his friend Ulf Ekberg. The four joined forces in 1990 and formed Ace of Base. The fledgling band began playing local dance clubs and, within a year, the Scandinavian label Mega Records signed Ace of Base to a recording contract.

After Ace of Base achieved early chart success in Scandinavia, Metronome Records, based in Germany, signed Ace of Base to a distribution deal and released the band's first European single, "All That She Wants." The song's jaunty rhythm, peppy keyboards, and infectious sing-along chorus ("All that she wants is another baby") made the song a hit on radio and in dance clubs throughout Europe. The tune reached number one on the pop charts in ten countries.

Arista Records signed Ace of Base to a U.S. distribution deal and released "All That She Wants" in the fall of 1993. The song's breezy European feel, coupled with the overwhelming popularity at the time of brooding, "grunge" songs from acts such as Nirvana and Pearl Jam, made "All That She Wants" an unlikely contender for mass appeal, but the track became a Top 10 hit. Ace of Base's follow-up single, "The Sign," was even more successful, reaching number one on the U.S. pop charts. "The Sign" epitomizes Ace of Base's relentless optimism and enthusiasm; over an upbeat, pulsing groove, the Berggren sisters trade vocals, exulting in a recent breakup: "I got a new life, you would hardly recognize me, I'm so glad / How can a person like me care for you? / Why do I bother, when you're not the one for me? / Oo-hoo-hoo-oo-oo." "The Sign" also benefited from heavy rotation on MTV, which embraced the good-looking Swedes and their promotional videos. By the end of 1994, Ace of Base's U.S. debut album, *The Sign*, had sold more than 8 million copies and had charted three Top 10 singles. The band also received three Grammy nominations, including one for Best New Artist.

Ace of Base released its sophomore album, *The Bridge*, in 1995. The single "Beautiful Life" features a more intense, club-centric beat, but it still resonated with mainstream audiences, reaching number fifteen on the *Billboard* charts. The album was a commercial disappointment, as was its follow-up, *Cruel Summer* (1998), despite the latter's charting of another Top 10 hit, the band's cover of the Bananarama title track. While Ace of Base's popularity in the United States sagged, the band remained wildly popular in Europe, scoring several number one hits with songs largely ignored by U.S. radio.

Though the band's stay at the top of the U.S. charts was brief, Ace of Base created some of the more enduring pop hits of the 1990s.

SELECTIVE DISCOGRAPHY: *The Sign* (Arista Records, 1993); *The Bridge* (Arista, 1995); *Cruel Summer* (Arista, 1998); *Greatest Hits* (Arista, 2000).

SCOTT TRIBBLE

BRYAN ADAMS

Born: Kingston, Ontario, 5 November 1959

Genre: Rock

Best-selling album since 1990: *Waking Up the Neighbours* (1991)

Hit songs since 1990: "(Everything I Do) I Do It for You," "Please Forgive Me," "Have You Ever Really Loved a Woman?"

After entering the pop music scene in the early 1980s, Canadian singer/songwriter Bryan Adams quickly gained notoriety with a catchy, easily definable mainstream rock sound. However, that definition has gotten murky through the years, as his soft love ballads, some of which are movie soundtrack hits, have commercially triumphed.

Early Years

As far back as he can remember, Adams was interested in music, but this passion flew in the face of his dominating father's wishes. The father was a military man, later a diplomat to the United Nations, and the family lived all over the world. When Bryan's parents divorced, his mother, a schoolteacher, took him and his younger brother to settle in Vancouver, British Columbia. Adams quit high school at age sixteen and began performing and writing songs for a local rock group called Shock and another named Sweeney Todd, with which he cut two albums. Adams sought out the songwriter/producer Jim Vallance in 1980, and they began co-writing songs, some of which were recorded by the Canadian supergroups Bachman-Turner Overdrive and Loverboy as well as by Bonnie Tyler and KISS.

The Making of a Superstar

In 1981 Adams decided on a solo career and signed a now-famous contract with A&M Records in Toronto for the sum of one dollar. His first release went nowhere, but his second, *You Want It, You Got It* (1981), sold well in Canada and made way for *Cuts Like a Knife* (1983). This album went platinum in the United States and introduced Adams's husky-voiced, passionate rock with agreeable hits like "This Time," "Straight from the Heart," and the title track, "Cuts Like a Knife." Adams followed with *Reckless* (1984), which soared to the top spot on the U.S. record charts. It features six major hit singles, including "Run to You," "Summer of '69," and a red-hot duet with singing legend Tina Turner, "It's Only Love." The handsome Adams seemed to have found a perfect balance with his pliable foot-stomping rock. He became one of rock's bona fide superstars.

In 1991, after Adams and his band toured the world playing sold-out stadiums at every stop, he recorded a dulcet ballad by the veteran film composer Michael Kamen "(Everything I Do) I Do It for You" for the soundtrack to the film *Robin Hood: Prince of Thieves* starring Kevin Costner. The song was a megahit and went number one immediately in the United States, Canada, and England, where Adams now lives. It sold over 8 million copies as a single. The song's success paved the way for *Waking Up the Neighbours* (1991), which contains "(Everything I Do) I Do It for You" in addition to the bouncy hit "Can't Stop This Thing We Started." *Waking Up the Neighbours* sold almost 6 million copies in its first two months of issue.

Adams continued to succeed with ballads and movie soundtracks, adding the gorgeous "Please Forgive Me," another chart topper, to a greatest hits album, *So Far So Good* (1993). The album sold 13 million copies worldwide. Later that year he recorded the song "All for Love" with his fellow superstars Rod Stewart and Sting for the film *The Three Musketeers*. The film was a flop but the song went to number one, as did "Have You Ever Really Loved a Woman?," which he recorded for the film *Don Juan DeMarco* (1995), starring Johnny Depp. In the meantime, Adams continued to tour worldwide, developing a massive following in Europe and Asia in addition to the United States.

Rock music success and all of its trappings has claimed its fair share of casualties, but seems to have had few adverse effects on Adams. By all accounts down-to-earth, Adams has used his celebrity to promote and raise money for an impressive list of personally favored humanitarian causes, including Live Aid, Net Aid, Amnesty International, Greenpeace, cancer research, environmental causes, Ethiopian famine, and freedom for Nelson Mandela. He is a devout vegetarian, an avid equestrian, and has never been married. Adams has a strong passion for photography and has snapped shots in privileged photo sessions with such luminaries as the queen of England and Paul McCartney. His work has appeared in galleries, books, and magazines worldwide.

Placated by live and compilation albums, fans had to wait five years for Adams to follow-up the colossal *Waking Up the Neighbours*. In 1996 he released *18 'til I Die* (1996). The album used the same formula as *Neighbours* by adding an already-released soundtrack hit. This time it was "Have You Ever Really Loved a Woman?" Adams's fans were beginning to split down the middle. One side longed for the raw rock of his earlier days, the other for Adams's recent ballads; most of Adams's later work is saddled with the challenge of satisfying both camps. The following year he answered with a collection of songs, including some of his heaviest rockers, in a live acoustic set on MTV as part of its *Unplugged* series.

Accolades and Staying Power

Adams has sold more than 50 million albums throughout a career that shows no sign of slowing down. He has been showered with awards, including sixteen wins out of twenty-four Juno nominations (the Canadian version of a Grammy), and three Grammy Awards out of thirteen nominations. He has also won two MTV Music Awards and had three Academy Award nominations for soundtrack songs. In 2002 he was nominated for a Golden Globe Award for the song "Here I Am" from the soundtrack to DreamWorks's animated epic, *Spirit: Stallion of the Cimarron*. He also released an album of the film's music under the same title. The ballad-heavy recording features a duet with fellow Canadian Sarah McLachlan on "Don't Let Go." The album as a whole displays Adams's songwriting growth and his innate ability to infuse his songs with satisfying hooks. "Get Off My Back," from *Spirit*, was one return on the album to his rock sound. He toured most of 2002 with the bare-bones trio of Keith Scott on guitar, Mickey Curry on drums, and Adams on bass guitar, a departure from his usual role as rhythm guitarist.

The pride of Canada, Bryan Adams has earned a top spot in contemporary music with relentless touring and an ability to appeal consistently to a mainstream audience.

SELECTIVE DISCOGRAPHY: *Bryan Adams* (A&M Records, 1980); *You Want It, You Got It* (A&M Records, 1981); *Cuts Like a Knife* (A&M Records, 1983); *Reckless* (A&M Records, 1984); *Into the Fire* (A&M Records, 1987); *Waking Up the Neighbours* (A&M Records, 1991); *So Far So Good* (A&M Records, 1993); *So Far So Live* (Alex Records,

1994); *18 'til I Die* (A&M Records, 1996); *MTV Unplugged* (A&M Records, 1997); *On a Day Like Today* (A&M Records, 1998); *Greatest Hits* (A&M Records, 1999); *The Best of Me* (Polygram Records, 2001); *Spirit: Stallion of the Cimarron* (Universal Records, 2002).

BIBLIOGRAPHY: B. Adams, *Bryan Adams: The Official Biography* (Toronto, 1995).

DONALD LOWE

JOHN ADAMS

Born: Worcester, Massachusetts, 15 February 1947
Genre: Classical

John Adams's evocative scores and provocative projects helped make him one of the most prominent American composers of the final decades of the twentieth century. In 1991 a survey of major American orchestras by the American Symphony Orchestra League showed Adams to be the most frequently performed living American composer that year.

Adams grew up in the northeastern United States and earned bachelor's and master's degrees from Harvard University, where he studied conducting, played the clarinet, and composed. His prominent teachers included Leon Kirchner, David Del Tredici, and Roger Sessions. In 1971 he moved to San Francisco, California, to teach and conduct at the San Francisco Conservatory of Music (1972–1983) and to be composer-in-residence for the San Francisco Symphony (1978–1985). It was here that some of his most important works—including *Shaker Loops* (1978, 1983), *Harmonium* (1980–1981), *Harmonielehre* (1984–1985), and *Grand Pianola Music* (1982)—were commissioned and performed.

Adams's music fit neatly with the minimalist style of composition that was shaking off the complexities of atonality in the 1970s and 1980s and gaining something of a popular following. Minimalism reduced the complexities of harmony and melody to their most basic form, repeating chord progressions and melodic fragments and simplifying the musical language. Adams's brand of undulating minimalism always seemed to have more going on, and his writing quickly evolved into a distinctive postmodernist blend of styles. Right from the first composition, his music had an expressive bent that seemed to want to develop beyond the repetitions of the minimalist style.

These expansive musical sensibilities were channeled into provocative projects, such as his widely debated first opera based on President Richard Nixon's historic trip to China, *Nixon in China*. The piece was startling when it premiered at the Houston Grand Opera in 1987. At a time when contemporary opera—particularly American contemporary opera—was something of a rare undertaking, Adams and his A-list creative team of director Peter Sellars, librettist Alice Goodman, and choreographer Mark Morris tackled a contemporary subject and sparked a new genre of postmodernist music for the theater. A recording of the piece won a Grammy Award in 1989 for Best Contemporary Composition, and the original production was restaged at opera houses throughout Europe and America in the 1990s.

Though not as well known as a conductor, Adams has championed his own and other contemporary composers' work from the podium. From 1987–1990 he was "creative chair" of the St. Paul Chamber Orchestra, serving as part of the orchestra's experimental creative leadership team, conducting four weeks of concerts, and overseeing the orchestra's contemporary music programs. He has also conducted the Cleveland Orchestra, Chicago Symphony, Philadelphia Orchestra, New York Philharmonic, San Francisco Symphony, Los Angeles Philharmonic, Concertgebouw, London Symphony, and BBC Orchestra, and has recorded his own music conducting the San Francisco Symphony.

Adams's second opera—an even more controversial work than *Nixon*—was *The Death of Klinghoffer*. The opera is built around the story of the 1984 hijacking of the Italian cruise ship *Achille Lauro* in the Mediterranean Sea by Palestinian terrorists, and the subsequent murder of a wheelchair-bound American tourist Leon Klinghoffer.

The opera debuted in March 1991 in Brussels, Belgium, as the Persian Gulf War was coming to a close, and the performances were picketed and condemned for the opera's subject matter. *Klinghoffer* employed the same creative team (Goodman/Sellars/Morris) as *Nixon*, but many of the reviews, both in Europe and at the American premiere in San Francisco later that year, were scathing, mostly because of the subject. A subsequent production planned by the Los Angeles Music Center Opera (one of the co-commissioners) was canceled, and the opera was not performed again during the next ten years, despite the fact that the score offers some of Adams's most lyrical and luminous music. A third stage piece, a "song" play, a kind of staged story set to music titled *I Was Looking at the Ceiling and Then I Saw the Sky* (1995), failed to generate the kind of intense interest of Adams's previous efforts.

If the 1980s established Adams as a major voice in American music, the 1990s secured his position. As his compositional style evolved beyond the simplified musical structures of minimalism and into a new take on the expressive qualities of Romanticism, Adams's eclectic style encompassed a wide range of twentieth-century idioms and references, from Russian-born American composer Igor Stravinsky to swing music. He produced a series of chamber and orchestral works, including *Violin Concerto* (1994), which was commissioned by an unusual partnership between the Minnesota Orchestra, the London Symphony, and the New York City Ballet. City Ballet director Peter Martins choreographed a dance to the work and it was presented during the 1994–1995 season. The *Concerto* won the 1995 Grawemeyer Award for Contemporary Music.

The *Chamber Symphony* (1993) is typical of Adams's wit: It sets up a musical duel between the rigorously intellectual style of serialism, in which each note is determined by strict formulas, and the inflated freneticism of cartoon soundtrack music. Adams also has a love of musical puzzles and odd titles, chosen sometimes just because he likes the sounds of the words, as witnessed in titles such as *Slonimsky's Earbox* (1996), *Gnarly Buttons* (1996), and *Naïve and Sentimental Music* (1997–1998).

Yet it was because of his ability to express deep sentiment that the New York Philharmonic chose Adams to write a work commemorating the September 11, 2001, attacks on the World Trade Center. Adams's *On the Transmigration of Souls* opened the New York Philharmonic's 2002 season.

As the twenty-first century began, Adams emerged as one of the leading composers of the day, as close as anyone since the iconic quintessential American composer Aaron Copland to being considered a "national" American composer. His ability to synthesize musical styles and create music of freshness opened up a new vein of American music.

SELECTIVE DISCOGRAPHY: **Stage:** *Nixon in China* (1985–1987); *The Death of Klinghoffer* (1990–1991); *I Was Looking at the Ceiling and Then I Saw the Sky* (1995); *El Niño Nativity Oratorio* (1999–2000). **Chamber:** *Grand Pianola Music* (1982); *Chamber Symphony* (1992). **Orchestra:** *Harmonium* (1980–1981); *Shaker Loops* (1983); *Harmonielehre* (1984–1985); *Fearful Symmetries* (1988); *Violin Concerto* (1993).

DOUGLAS MCLENNAN

RYAN ADAMS

Born: David Ryan Adams; Jacksonville, North Carolina, 5 November 1974

Genre: Rock

Best-selling album since 1990: *Gold* (2001)

Hit songs since 1990: "New York, New York," "When the Stars Go Blue," "Answering Bell"

Ryan Adams, the solo singer/songwriter, combines the cocky cacophony of garage rock with the sweet and sad aspects of country music. Adams started out as the lead singer and songwriter of Whiskeytown, a band that rode the wave of alternative-country in the mid- to late 1990s. Formed in 1994, the group officially broke up around 2000, shortly before the release of Adams's debut album *Heartbreaker* (2000). In just two years, the prolific Adams released three albums.

For someone who dropped out of high school after tenth grade, Adams has proved to be a success. Guest appearances by country singers Kim Richey and Emmylou Harris make *Heartbreaker* no ordinary debut. It is an introspective tearjerker, an earthy, spare production, with Adams's cracked, worldly voice holding it together, while the pianos, banjos, harmonicas, and acoustic guitar play in the background. First-person songs examine failed romantic relationships. A sorrowful, wailing harmonica accompanies cry-in-your-beer tunes such as "Sweet Carolina," a duet with Emmylou Harris, and the desperate, waltzy ballad "Why Do You Leave?"

Adams quickly signed to Lost Highway, the country-rock imprint of Universal Music Group. *Gold* (2001), which Adams wrote while living in Los Angeles, brought him some attention. The video for "New York, New York," the album's first track, showed the downtown skyline of Manhattan and was recorded just a few days before the terrorist attacks of September 11, 2001. It became an unintended anthem. Adams called "New York, New York" his love letter to the city, but did not mean it to be patriotic. In the chorus he sings, "Love don't play any games with me like she did before / The world won't wait so I better shake / That thing right through the door / Hell I still love you though, New York." With its Hammond organ, chugging beat, and a guitar lick worthy of the Rolling Stones, "New York, New York" is *Gold*'s most inspirational moment. *Gold*'s other fifteen tracks are mostly mid-tempo musings on city life, relationships, and late nights at bars. "La Cienega Just Smiled" is lovely. "When the Stars Go Blue" was covered by Bono of U2 and the Corrs shortly after the album's release.

With a chameleonlike voice, Adams conjures the raw grit and rebellious spirit of Steve Earle one minute, and the sweetness and desperation of a folksinger the next. He has the disheveled, devil-may-care demeanor of a true punk rocker and the heart of a die-hard romantic troubadour unafraid to wear his heart on his sleeve. As a musician, his instincts are more varied than any single genre could convey.

SELECTIVE DISCOGRAPHY: *Heartbreaker* (Bloodshot Records, 2000); *Gold* (Lost Highway/Universal, 2001); *Demolition* (Lost Highway/Universal, 2002).

CARRIE HAVRANEK

KING SUNNY ADÉ

Born: Sunday Adéniy; Oshogbo, Nigeria, 1946
Genre: World
Best-selling album since 1990: *Odu* (1998)

Sunny Adé, son of a royal Yoruban family—his father was a Methodist minister-church organist and his mother was leader of the choir—was interested in percussion instruments as a child, but his parents opposed a career in music: A Nigerian prince was meant to pursue law. At age seventeen Adé quit school to go to Lagos, teach himself to play guitar, and join the Rhythm Dandies, a high-life band run by Moses Olaiya (subsequently famous throughout Africa as Baba Sala, a comic and filmmaker). So began Adé's commercial empire, based on a tradition-based but futuristic, polyrhythmic West African guitar-orchestra dance style called "juju music."

The term *juju* may be imitative of the sounds of a small hexogonal tambourine. Others believe that it is a disparagement (like "mumbo jumbo") that musicians turn topsy-turvy or a variant of *jojo*, Yoruban for "dance." The post–World War II Nigerian singer/songwriter Tunde Nightingale and bandleader I. K. Dairo pioneered the style and influenced Adé, as did American soul stars James Brown and Brook Benton and the country singer Jim Reeves. Adé established his first band, the Green Spots (referring to Dairo's Blue Spots) in 1966, emphasizing Yoruba religious rhythms performed on hand-held percussion devices and two-head "talking drums," pulsating through interlocking layers of electric guitar riffs. He used this format in twelve albums recorded through 1974, reissued on CD as *The Best of the Classic Years* (2003).

Adé and juju music thrived during an era of oil-industry profitability and overall optimism in independent Nigeria. His subtle but energized and positive songs, with lyrics conveying social lessons through ancient Yoruban proverbs and parables, reflected a sophisticated Africa looking forward. When legal problems beset his arrangement with the Nigeria-Africa Song label, Adé formed his own firm, connected to the major U.S. label Decca Records, to back his new band, the African Beats. In 1982 the internationally distributed label Island Records signed King Sunny to a recording contract, hoping he would become the next black star to reach the heights of the recently deceased reggae singer/songwriter Bob Marley.

Adé's American debut album, *JuJu Music* (1982), and his follow-up, *Syncro-system* (1983), were well received, and he embarked on tours of the United States, Europe, and Japan with a troupe of some thirty members, including female background singers, interweaving electric guitarists and bassists, three talking drummers, a trap-set drummer, other percussionists, and players of electric keyboards, synthesizers, pedal-steel guitars, vibes, xylophones, and accordions. The singers shake beads and shells and netted gourds; the talking drummers ape speech patterns, hammering out fast phrases with curved sticks against drumheads, stretched taut or slackened to produce various tones. The guitarists play catchy, repetitive, sparkling grooves. The odd soloist dashes across the ensemble's steady state of sonic flux. The rhythms are irresistible, seemingly ancient and profound yet funky; they compel the body to move.

French producer Michael Messonier collaborated on Adé's third U.S. album, *Aura* (1984), with Stevie Wonder as harmonica soloist on the title track. But the mix muted the African Beat's power, and sales were disappointing. Though Adé performed in and contributed music to Robert Altman's film *O. C. and Stiggs* (1985), he was dropped by Island in 1988. In one well-publicized incident his band quit in the midst of a Japanese concert. Through the rest of the 1980s and early 1990s Adé continued to release albums in Nigeria—his catalog there numbers more than a hundred—and appeared irregularly, purportedly to "combat rumors of my demise," usually in world music circuit venues. *King Sunny Adé and His African Beat: Live at Montreux*, a concert video released by Island Visual Arts in 1990, was shot during a 1983 performance.

In the early 1990s Adé sharpened his aim. Though he remained in the Yoruban tradition of praise singer rather than gadfly or polemicist like his friend and rival, the late Fela Kuti, he wrote more pointed lyrics, including a song about family planning, an ironic subject for a father of twelve.

Adé has invested his superstar earnings wisely and participates in the running of an oil firm, a mining company, a nightclub, and film and video production houses, among other concerns. Named the first president of the Musical Cooperative Society of Nigeria in 1982, Adé continues as chairman of the society's Advisory Council and as "patron" of the Juju Bandleaders' Association. He chairs the Musical Copyright Society of Nigeria, and founded the King Sunny Adé Foundation with other Nigerian civic and business leaders.

Mesa recorded and released *E Dide/Get Up* (1995), Adé's first American studio album in over a decade. Adé also convened an African supergroup to record "The Way Forward," his composition advocating political unity among Nigerians of diverse ethnic strains. His next U.S. album, *Odu* (1998)—recorded in Louisiana—was celebrated as his return to top form. With management from the Seattle-based world music producer Andy Franklin, Adé has mounted new tours of Europe and the United States.

Adé remains a heroic entertainer, a lean, closely cropped man with a tight smile and great reverb, and the most elegant imaginable duckwalk-with-instrument. Adé slings his guitars low over his shoulder down to his hip or knees. He is a musician of nuance, not overkill—a master of chord placement rather than a single-note line wonder. He understands tempi and pacing, and he often performs sets of an uninterrupted two or three hours. His immediately identifiable sound is a beacon of Afro-pop, influencing Caribbean dance styles, including reggae, soca, calypso, the music of African exiles in Europe, world music hybrids like Afro-Celt Sound System, and U.S. jam bands.

SELECTIVE DISCOGRAPHY: *Live at the Hollywood Palace* (I.R.S., 1992); *E Dide (Get Up)* (Mesa, 1995); *Odu* (Mesa, 1998); *Seven Degrees North* (Mesa, 2001); *The Best of the Classic Years* (Shanachie, reissued 2003).

WEBSITES: www.artandculture.com/arts/artist?artistId= 546; www.afropop.org/explore/show_artist/ID/25; www.artistdirect.com/showcase//contemporary/king sunnyade.html.

HOWARD MANDEL

AEROSMITH

Formed: 1970, Sunapee, New Hampshire

Members: Tom Hamilton, bass (born Colorado Springs, Colorado, 31 December 1951); Joey Kramer, drums (born Bronx, New York, 21 June 1950); Joe Perry, lead guitar (born Lawrence, Massachusetts, 10 September 1950); Steven Tyler, lead vocals (born Steven Victor Tallarico, Yonkers, New York, 26 March 1948); Brad Whitford, rhythm guitar (born Winchester, Massachusetts, 23 February 1952). Former members: Jimmy Crespo, lead guitar (born, Brooklyn, New York, 5 July 1952); Rick Dufay, guitar (born Richard Marc Dufay, Paris, France, 19 February 1952).

Genre: Rock

Best-selling album since 1990: *Get a Grip* (1993)

Hit songs since 1990: "Cryin," "I Don't Want to Miss a Thing," "Jaded"

Since the early 1970s Aerosmith has been one of the most popular bands in rock music and synonymous with a lusty, bad-boy persona. Buoyed by a remarkable comeback in the late 1980s, a cleaner, sober version of the band went on to even greater success. Ironically, the rock titans owe a portion of their rebound to rap music.

From Unknowns to Superstars

Singer Steve Tyler and guitarist Joe Perry formed Aerosmith in 1970 in the resort town of Sunapee, New Hampshire, where their families both owned summer homes. Tyler was already a veteran of the band Chain

Reaction, which had recorded with Verve Records and was an opening act for the Yardbirds and the Beach Boys. Tyler had admired Perry's playing in a rock group called Jam Band and they decided to form Aerosmith. They added guitarist Brad Whitford, bass player Tom Hamilton, and drummer Joey Kramer, moved to Boston, and began competing for gigs in the local area. Aerosmith's reputation as an exciting club band spread fast across the northeast and in 1972 they managed to secure a record deal with Columbia Records.

Their debut album, *Aerosmith* (1973), was a success in the Boston area but nationwide sales were only lukewarm, despite the band's hitting the charts with their ballad "Dream On." In pursuit of more exposure, they began to extensively tour, taking time off to record a second album, *Get Your Wings* (1974). This album sold better as the band's audience had expanded and Aerosmith was hitting full stride, with critics hailing them as an American version of the Rolling Stones. Their flamboyant concerts featured a swaggeringly raw, muscular rock. Perry's guitar hung low off his pelvis like an afterthought, an extra appendage that chunked chords and seared blistering solos while Tyler strutted from one side of the stage to the other. Pouting his oversized lips to the crowd, whipping them into frenzy with his lurid strut, Tyler was quickly gaining a reputation as one of hard rock's greatest lead singers. Furthermore, Tyler's voice could hop two octaves into a melodic scream. His vocal work on "Dream On" is an example. Whitford, Hamilton, and Kramer provided a fierce rhythm usually based around Perry's pulsating guitar riff with Tyler's rapid-fire lyrics spewing rhyming chronicles of sexual conquests and related misbehavior.

Aerosmith was turning into America's rock and roll icon and their next album, the mega-selling *Toys in the Attic* (1975), cemented that image. It contains the sassy "Sweet Emotion" and rock anthem "Walk This Way." *Toys in the Attic* remained a top seller for years and dramatically increased the sales of the first two releases, leading the way to Aerosmith's superstardom. They began headlining stadium-sized venues all over the world and subsequent albums, especially *Rocks* (1976), sold extremely well.

However, just like their indulgent image onstage, the members of Aerosmith were also indulging offstage in every excess that rock superstardom offers. Particularly rowdy were Tyler and Perry, who digested such a variety of drugs that they were labeled "The Toxic Twins." By 1979 fatigue and craziness from seven straight years of touring and recording caused tremendous turmoil within the band. Perry finally left to go solo and journeyman guitarist Jimmy Crespo replaced him. Two years later disgruntled rhythm guitarist Whitford departed to start a band with Ted Nugent's disgruntled rhythm guitarist Derek St. Holmes. Rick Dufay took Whitford's place. Their subsequent recordings sold poorly and in 1981 Tyler suffered a serious motorcycle accident that required more than six months of recovery. He returned and Aerosmith continued, but many wrote them off as finished.

The Comeback

In 1984 Perry and Whitford, unsuccessful in their ventures, rejoined the other members, putting Aerosmith back in its original form—but by no means was the band reformed. Drug and alcohol consumption was even more prevalent as they stumbled through two tours and one album, *Done with Mirrors* (1985). Finally, each member surrendered to rehabilitation for substance abuse and a sober Aerosmith emerged. Their first post-rehab effort was in collaboration with the rap group Run-D.M.C. on a rap version of "Walk This Way." The single was an enormous seller, went high on the charts, and was just the push that Aerosmith needed. Their next album, *Permanent Vacation* (1987), continued in a commercial vein and produced three chart hits, most notably "Dude Looks Like a Lady," which was featured in the hit movie *Mrs. Doubtfire* (1993). The album went triple platinum and Aerosmith was once again riding high, albeit sober.

After roaring out of the 1980s in a storm of success, Aerosmith began the 1990s on hiatus in preparation for the recording of their next album, *Get a Grip* (1993). The album lacked some of the rawness that older fans had come to expect, but Aerosmith was sensing that music tastes were changing from a harder rock/blues sound to what would later be called alternative rock and they understood firsthand from their work with Run-D.M.C. how a change in style could pay off. In contrast to the plunder of their previous work, the newer songs made note of what all that plunder really meant. While still carrying their trademark swagger, several of the songs, such as "Get a Grip," "Living on the Edge," and "Fever," speak of the depths of drug misery and a newfound peace in sobriety. The lyrics "Now I'm feeling low down, even slow seems way too fast, and now the booze don't work and the drugs ran out of gas" sung in "Fever" reveal some of this. *Get a Grip* contains three power ballads, "Amazing," "Crazy," and "Cryin,'" all of which landed high on the charts, and the album was a giant, selling 12 million copies. An MTV video of "Crazy" introduced the world to Tyler's then sixteen-year-old daughter, Liv Tyler, as she and actress Alicia Silverstone played the video's main characters. Ms. Tyler later became a major movie star and the video represented Tyler's return to responsible fatherhood. "Crazy" won a 1995 Grammy Award for Best Performance by a Group, as did "Living on the Edge" in 1994.

Aerosmith spent much of the mid-1990s on another world tour, during which the band silenced skeptics who did not think they could still deliver the snarling rock of their past. After the tour, they recorded *Nine Lives* (1997), which scored a Grammy nomination in 1998 for Best Rock Album. *Nine Lives* was recorded amidst unfounded rumors that the band was doing drugs again and the ensuing chaos within the group resulted in them firing their manager. The hard-rocking album is a hearkening back to the band's early days with heavy riffs driving a frolicking spirit. A rock ballad in the style for which Aerosmith is reknown, the sweeping "Hole in My Soul" is one of the album's highlights. A European printing of *Nine Lives* features two extra songs. One of them, "I Don't Want to Miss a Thing," written by Dianne Warren, is among the four songs that Aerosmith contributed to the movie soundtrack *Armageddon* (1998). The film stars Liv Tyler and the song became Aerosmith's first number one hit. By 1999 *Nine Lives* reached 6 million in sales and scored the band another Grammy for "Pink."

Many felt that Aerosmith would slow down in the new millennium as the band members had reached or were close to reaching their fifties, but they came blasting back. Intermittently that year Aerosmith sequestered itself in an old farmhouse creating material for their next record, *Just Push Play* (2001), which they would also produce. In January 2001 they pre-released a ballad off the album, "Jaded," and promoted it with a memorable appearance at halftime of the 2001 Super Bowl, billed with pop sensations *NSYNC and Britney Spears. They appeared shortly after in Los Angeles at the American Music Awards and followed that with their fourth appearance on the television show *Saturday Night Live*. *Just Push Play* was released on March 19, 2001, the same day that the group was inducted into the Rock and Roll Hall of Fame. The artist Kid Rock introduced them at the Hall of Fame ceremonies and joined them in a performance of "Sweet Emotion." Aerosmith then teased the crowd with their gentle "Jaded" before segueing into the powerhouse classic, "Train Kept a Rollin.'" The crowd, mostly music industry insiders, was electrified. By April, *Just Push Play* had gone platinum in sales and Aerosmith was at the start of a sold-out worldwide tour. The terrorist attacks on September 11, 2001, interrupted the tour, but only for six days. Tyler strongly advocated the healing powers of rock music and the importance of the United States resuming its normal activities. In October they performed a Washington, D.C., concert to benefit victims of the tragedy.

Aerosmith released another successful compilation album, *O' Yeah! Ultimate Aerosmith Hits* (2002) and moved to Hawaii in 2003 to record their next studio release. In August they kicked off a world tour with KISS, another band of surviving rock legends. On February 7, 2003, Aerosmith performed with myriad top artists to celebrate and benefit the Blues Music Foundation at New York's Radio City Music Hall in what was billed as the music event of the year.

Aerosmith set out in the 1970s with the goal to become the greatest rock band in the world. In some assessments, they achieved that goal and then surpassed it with massive staying power in the pop rock scene later on. Aerosmith was first identified by their boisterous rock sound, but may be remembered longer for their powerful rock ballads.

SELECTIVE DISCOGRAPHY: *Aerosmith* (Columbia, 1973); *Get Your Wings* (Columbia, 1974); *Toys in the Attic* (Columbia, 1975); *Rocks* (Columbia, 1976); *Draw the Line* (Columbia, 1977); *Live Bootleg* (Columbia, 1978); *A Night in the Ruts* (Columbia, 1979); *Aerosmith's Greatest Hits* (Columbia, 1980); *Rock in a Hard Place* (Columbia, 1982); *Done with Mirrors* (Geffen, 1985); *Permanent Vacation* (Geffen, 1987); *Gems* (Columbia, 1988); *Pump* (Geffen, 1989); *Pandora's Box* (Geffen, 1991); *Get a Grip* (Geffen, 1993); *Box of Fire* (Geffen, 1994); *Nine Lives* (Columbia/Sony, 1997); *A Little South of Sanity* (Geffen, 1998); *Just Push Play* (Columbia/Sony, 2001). **Soundtrack:** *Armageddon* (Sony, 1998).

BIBLIOGRAPHY: M. Huxly, *Aerosmith: The Fall and Rise of Rock's Greatest Band* (New York, 1995); C. Foxe-Tyler and D. Fields, *Dream On: Living on the Edge with Steven Tyler and Aerosmith* (New York, 2000); E. Anjou, *Aerosmith* (Broomall, PA, 2002).

DONALD LOWE

AFROCELTS

Formed: 1995, London, England

Members: Ronan Browne, uilleann pipes (born 7 August 1965, Dublin, Ireland); Kauwding Cissakho; Massamba Diop; Simon Emmerson, producer, guitar, mandolin, bouzouki, programming, keyboards (born 1950, Wolverhampton, England); Johnny Kalsi, dhol drum, tabla (born Leeds, England); N'Faly Kouyate, kora, balaphon, vocals (born in Guinea); Mass, drum programming; Emer Maycock, uilleann pipes; James McNally, keyboards, whistle, bamboo flute, bodhran, accordion; Myrdhin, Breton harp; Ayub Ogada, nyatiti (born Kenya); Iarla O'Lionaird, vocals (born Cúil Aodha, County Cork, Ireland, 1964); Martin Russell, keyboards; Moussa Sissoko, djembe, talking drum; Dave Spillaine, uilleann pipes. Former members: Jo Bruce, keyboards (born 9 February 1969; died 8 October 1997). Guest artists: Jah Wobble, bass; Peter Gabriel, Nina Mirando, Sinéad O'Connor, Robert Plant, vocals; Jesse Cook, flamenco guitar; Martin Hayes, Eileen Ivers, fiddles.

Genre: World, Fusion

Best-selling album since 1990: *Volume 3: Further in Time* (2001)

Hit songs since 1990: "When You're Falling" (2001)

AfroCelts is the name taken by the ensemble formerly known as Afro-Celt Sound System upon the release of its fourth album, *Seed* (2003). The band's conceits and charms remain the same: AfroCelts is a recording and concertizing troupe creating a fantasy fusion. In it, African drums accent keening U.K. pop and traditional singing, electric guitars, studio keyboards, and strings, and identifiably Gaelic instruments such as uilleann pipes, bodhran, and Breton harp are also blended into the band's technically slick and sophisticated mix.

Over the course of a selective performance schedule initiated at Peter Gabriel's July 1995 WOMAD (World of Music Art and Dance) festival in Reading, England, and the release of four albums, AfroCelts has realized the original inspiration of Simon Emmerson. Emmerson first toyed with the multicultural notion of mixing African and Celtic signature sounds by introducing uilleann pipes into an album he produced for Senegalese singer/bandleader Baba Maal in the late 1980s. Emmerson was at the time also a producer of Afro-pop and active in the experimental dance world. He drew on both circles of contacts to convene musicians from West Africa and the British Isles for the WOMAD sojourn, though he claimed his collaborators were merely fellow residents of his London neighborhood, a hotbed of musicians, mixers, and sound studios.

James McNally of the Irish band the Pogues and Martin Russell of the hard-core Irish hip-hop band Marxman have become Emmerson's co-producers and co-composers. The intricate arrangements require creative input from kora player N'Faly Kouyate and percussionist Moussa Sissoko and uilleann pipists, including Ronan Browne, from the touring cast of the theatrical event "Riverdance." Early on, Emmerson was encouraged by visual artist Jamie Reid, who created his work "Afro Celts: Music from the Light Continent: Sound Magic" especially for the cover of Afro-Celt Sound System's debut album, *Volume 1: Sound Magic* (1996), prior to its production.

Afro-Celt Sound System made its U.S. concert debut in July 1997, after having established itself as a U.K. success through a repeat WOMAD festival performance in 1996. It gained attention at well-received concerts at the Cambridge Folk Festival, Tribal Gathering (attended by a dance crowd), and at the Lowlands Festival in the Netherlands (cablecast on MTV). The band made its WOMAD USA festival debut in 1999, and Gabriel sang with it at WOMAD USA 2001, making his first American performance since 1992.

Though AfroCelts spotlights the undiluted talents of traditionalists, it is not a purist folk unit. Afro-Celt Sound System recordings always have glossy pop formulas and at least one mainstream rock ballad at their cores. One description of the compositional equation as "jigs and reels atop global percussion and rave rhythms" ignores Emmerson's heroic guitar lines and proud balladry that in *Volume 3: Further in Time* (2001) was given voice by Gabriel (on "When You're Falling"), Sinéad O'Connor (on the title track), and Robert Plant, of Led Zeppelin fame (on "Life Begin Again").

McNally concurs, saying, "Our style of writing and playing music does not pretend to adhere to any particular traditional style except our own . . . music rooted in the past that's reaching into the future." On *Seed* (2002), AfroCelts departs from its central African and Celtic sources to include a flamenco guitar solo and a Brazilian singer. The album is promoted as AfroCelts's new beginning, and something of a regrouping after the death in 1997 of keyboardist Jo Bruce, son of Jack Bruce, bassist for the legendary British blues-rock band Cream.

Emmerson, discussing the ensembles' name change, explained, "We're not a sound system anymore. . . . We've developed a very defined sound which has come from us playing together. It's not about a DJ and programs and samples. It's taken a long time, but we've finally become a band." Presumably a pinch of hardship is necessary to leaven cleverness and virtuosity in the achievement of such musical status.

SELECTIVE DISCOGRAPHY: *Volume 1: Sound Magic* (Real World, 1996); *Volume 2: Release* (Real World, 1999); *Volume 3: Further in Time* (Real World, 2001); *Seed* (Real World, 2003).

HOWARD MANDEL

CHRISTINA AGUILERA

Born: Christina Maria Aguilera; Staten Island, New York, 18 December 1980

Genre: R&B, Pop, Latin, Rock

Best-selling album since 1990: *Christina Aguilera* (1999)

Hit songs since 1990: "Genie in a Bottle," "What a Girl Wants"

After becoming one of the most popular teen pop singers of the late 1990s, Christina Aguilera sought to break out of the squeaky-clean image and sound that she had helped popularize along with the teen queen Britney Spears. With a strong, expressive voice that set her apart from other carefully packaged pop acts, the singer underwent a public image makeover that saw her reemerge as a streetwise, salacious sex bomb.

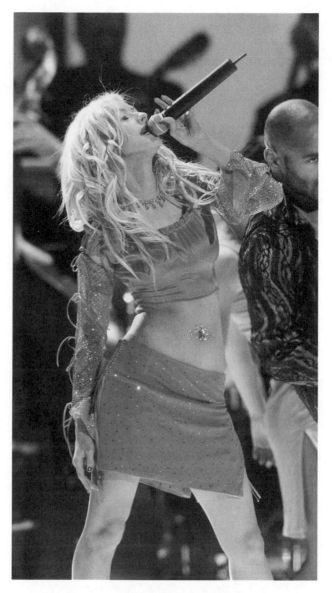

Christina Aguilera [AP/WIDE WORLD PHOTOS]

Born in New York to parents of Irish and Ecuadorian descent, Aguilera endured a peripatetic childhood because of her father's military career. When the family landed in Philadelphia, Aguilera began her performing career by appearing in local talent shows at age six. The minidiva graduated to a losing appearance on the televised talent show *Star Search* in 1988, later joining the cast of the Disney Channel's *The New Mickey Mouse Club* in 1992; the cast featured Spears as well as Justin Timberlake and JC Chasez, future members of the boy band *NSYNC.

In 1994 Aguilera moved to Japan, recording a duet, "All I Wanna Do," with Japanese pop star Keizo Nakanishi. She returned to the United States in 1998 to record the song "Reflection" for the Disney animated film *Mulan*. The song helped secure a recording contract with RCA, which issued Aguilera's self-titled debut in the summer of 1999.

Released seven months after Spears's debut, *Christina Aguilera* hewed closely to the pop formula employed by the singer's fellow Mickey Mouse Club alum: saccharine ballads mixed with catchy pop and slickly produced rhythm and blues songs. With a stable of some of the music industry's most able songwriters behind her, Aguilera was able to concentrate on her vocals, which climbed to Whitney Houston–like pop gospel heights on tracks such as "I Turn to You."

The album spawned the instantly hummable, number one hit "Genie in a Bottle," a slinky dance-pop confection on which the squeaky-clean, blonde-haired teenager sings the controversial lines, "If you want to be with me, baby there's a price to pay / I'm a genie in a bottle / You gotta rub me the right way." Despite its smash number one charting success, the song's burbling keyboards and generic electronic drumbeats did little to distinguish Aguilera from her peers. The album also spawned the hits "What a Girl Wants" and "Come On Over Baby (All I Want Is You)." Aguilera took home a Grammy in 2000 for Best New Artist.

Hopping onto another trend of the moment, Aguilera released a Spanish-language album in September 2000. Though half-Ecuadorian, Aguilera did not speak Spanish, which required that she learn how to sing the album's songs phonetically. A combination of Spanish versions of her hits ("Genio Atrapado") and new tracks, the album was quickly followed by the Christmas offering, *My Kind of Christmas*. The holiday album mixes renditions of traditional Christmas tunes such as "Have Yourself a Merry Little Christmas" with a handful of songs written by Aguilera.

A Controversial Career Makeover

An unsanctioned album of demos recorded by Aguilera when she was fourteen and fifteen, *Just Be Free*, was released to the singer's chagrin in June 2001. After a short period out of the spotlight, Aguilera emerged as part of a female supergroup to cover Patti Labelle's disco hit "Lady Marmalade" for the *Moulin Rouge* movie soundtrack. Dressed in lingerie, a large gold nose ring, and thick makeup, Aguilera took her place alongside singers Pink and Mya and rapper Lil' Kim in the video for the song, which became one of the biggest hits of 2001 and won a Grammy in 2002 for Best Pop Collaboration with Vocals. The new look was the beginning of a makeover for the singer, who seemed desperate to break out of her girl-next-door image and distance herself from other pop-divas-in-the-making such as Jessica Simpson and Mandy Moore.

Just three years after bursting onto the scene, a barely recognizable Aguilera emerged in 2002 with *Stripped*, a col-

lection of intensely personal songs co-written and co-produced by the singer. Along with the album's cover, which features a topless Aguilera in low-slung pants with only her hair covering her breasts, the video for the album's first single, "Dirrty," made it clear that this was a new Aguilera. Joined by rapper Redman in the clip for the lascivious, high-energy R&B dance song, a barely clothed, heavily pierced and dreadlocked Aguilera—now preferring the name X-Tina—shimmies amid a panoply of gritty and bizarre characters, from masked female boxers and bodybuilders to mudwrestlers and fire-eaters.

Heavily influenced by rap and rock music, *Stripped* is full of defiant lyrics in which Aguilera derides her glossy pop image and strikes out at ex-lovers and an abusive father while painting a portrait of the complex, conflicted woman behind the hype. Showcasing her more mature, wider range, Aguilera shines on the album's sweeping ballads, including the smoky, jazzy "Walk Away," in which she sings "I was naïve, your love was like candy / Artificially sweet, I was deceived by the wrapping / Got caught in your web and I learned how to bleed / I was prey in our bed and devoured completely."

Though a critical and commercial backlash greeted the perhaps too-transgressive "Dirrty," Aguilera accomplished the rarest of feats for a teen pop act: a second act. Successfully breaking out of and remaking her manufactured image, Aguilera's powerful voice and emerging songwriting style showed promise for the former Mouseketeer's career prospects.

SELECTIVE DISCOGRAPHY: *Christina Aguilera* (RCA, 1999); *Mi Reflejo* (RCA, 2000); *My Kind of Christmas* (RCA, 2000); *Stripped* (RCA, 2002).

GIL KAUFMAN

AHRENS AND FLAHERTY

Members: Lynn Ahrens (born New York, New York, 1 October 1948); Stephen Flaherty (born Pittsburgh, Pennsylvania, 18 September 1960).

Genre: Musical Theater

Best-selling album since 1990: *Ragtime* [Original Cast Recording] (1998)

The team of lyricist Lynn Ahrens and composer Stephen Flaherty found a marked degree of success within the musical theater world of the 1990s, writing with enough complexity to please critics while retaining a cheery tunefulness that appealed to mainstream audiences. Stylistically, the pair falls between legendary composer Stephen Sondheim, whose work has been critically praised but often popularly ignored, and

Frank Wildhorn, whose hook-laden pop scores gained 1990s commercial success but critical derision. Ahrens and Flaherty are unique in their ability to write in many different styles; the sound of their work is largely shaped by the setting and subject matter of the material. While they gained recognition in the late 1990s for film scoring, Ahrens and Flaherty remain devoted to the musical theater form, with several of their shows ranking among the most recognizable Broadway theater productions of the decade.

Lynn Ahrens came to musical theater after a distinguished career in television writing and production. During the 1970s she contributed songs such as "Interplanet Janet" and "Do the Circulation" for the popular children's *Schoolhouse Rock* television series. In 1982 she attended the prestigious BMI Musical Theatre Workshop, where she met Flaherty, who had written musicals since his teenage years. Soon the pair began working on a theatrical version of the 1967 film, *Bedazzled,* but were forced to abandon the project after failing to obtain the stage rights. Fortunately, the musical captured the interest of Playwrights Horizons, a New York off-Broadway theater company known for its development of new writers and their work. At Playwrights Horizons, Ahrens and Flaherty developed their next two projects, *Lucky Stiff* (1988) and *Once on This Island* (1990), the latter the musical that would establish their commercial and artistic reputation. Sporting a lush score that combined gentle Afro-Caribbean rhythms with bright, cheerful melodies, *Once on This Island*—a compelling love story notable for its entirely African-American cast—sold out at Playwrights Horizons and soon moved to a larger Broadway theater, where it ran for more than a year.

By the early 1990s, Ahrens and Flaherty were widely recognized as up-and-coming talents within the theatrical community. After premiering the Broadway musical *My Favorite Year* (1992), which was dismissed by critics as overblown and unfocused, they rebounded with *Ragtime* (1996), a musical based on author E. L. Doctorow's acclaimed 1975 novel of early-twentieth-century history. One of ten writing teams considered for the project, they succeeded in composing four songs for an audition tape in less than two weeks. Winning the contract, the pair created a rich, varied score that includes standouts such as the exuberant "Gettin' Ready Rag" and "Back to Before," a powerful, rousing ballad. Opening in 1996 in Toronto, *Ragtime* arrived two years later on Broadway, where it ran until 2000.

Featuring a high-profile cast, the Broadway production starred such notable stage actors as Marin Mazzie, Audra McDonald, and, in the performance that made him a Broadway star, Brian Stokes Mitchell, portraying an entertainer who takes the fight for racial justice into his own hands. Writing for Mazzie's character of "Mother," a well-to-do white woman who comes to a gradual awareness of inequality and racial injustice, Ahrens crafted some of her most compelling lyrics: "Each day the maids trudge up the hill / the hired help arrives / I never stopped to think they might have lives beyond our lives." Successfully interweaving plot lines featuring a wide range of historical characters—from famed magician Harry Houdini to architect Stanford White and his scandalous lover, Evelyn Nesbit—*Ragtime* captures the narrative feel of an epic. In 1997 Ahrens and Flaherty scored another commercial triumph when they contributed songs to the hit animated film, *Anastasia.*

In 2000 the pair completed *Seussical,* a musical based on the stories of famous children's author Dr. Seuss. Starring noted comedian and clown David Shiner, the show was largely rejected by critics as forced and overproduced, bearing a flashy, high-tech production but few distinctive or memorable songs. The replacement of Shiner with famous comedian and talk show host Rosie O'Donnell in January 2001 did little to help sales. *Seussical* was a rare commercial and artistic misfire for Ahrens and Flaherty, closing after a six-month Broadway run. In 2002 the pair premiered *A Man of No Importance,* based on the 1994 film about a middle-aged bus driver coming to terms with his homosexuality, at New York's Lincoln Center Theater.

Ahrens and Flaherty rank as one of contemporary musical theater's most versatile composing teams, crafting accessible, intelligent works that draw upon source material ranging from children's stories to award-winning novels. With Ahrens providing sharp lyrics and Flaherty creating melodic songs, the pair has established a long-lived and successful creative partnership.

SELECTIVE DISCOGRAPHY: **Original Cast Recordings:** *Once on This Island* (RCA, 1990); *My Favorite Year* (RCA, 1993); *Lucky Stiff: A Musical Comedy* (Varese Sarabande, 1994); *Ragtime* (RCA, 1998); *Seussical* (Polygram, 2001). **Soundtrack:** *Anastasia* (Atlantic, 1997).

WEBSITE: www.ahrensandflaherty.com.

DAVID FREELAND

AIR

Formed: 1995, Versailles, France

Members: Jean-Benoît Dunckel, Rhodes piano, organ (born Versailles, France, 7 September 1969); Nicolas Godin, bass, mini-Moog, tambourine (born Paris, France, 25 December 1969).

Genre: Electronica

Best-selling album since 1990: *Moon Safari* (1998)

Hit songs since 1990: "Sexy Boy," "Playground Love"

The French duo Air, composed of a former architect, Nicolas Godin, and a mathematician, Jean-Benoît Dunckel, are closely associated with the ambient-electronica dance music trend of the mid- to late 1990s. Air's innovative music often combines moody vocals in French and English, atmospheric keyboard flourishes, and elements of jazz. Ironically, given the band's nomenclature, Air grounds an otherwise lofty and airy music form by playing its own instruments and using programmed samples, loops, and effects. The approach makes it part of a growing movement in electronica music, rooted in the 1990s, in which bands employ both organic and synthetic musical effects. The British trip-hop groups Morcheeba, Massive Attack, and Portishead exemplify this trend.

Dunckel and Godin, both originally from Versailles, France, met at university in Paris. In the early 1990s Dunckel played with the band Orange and was introduced to Godin through Alex Gopher, the other member of Orange. Godin joined Orange, and the three formed a trio that lasted until the mid-1990s, when Gopher decided to leave the band and produce music for the Paris-based dance labels Source and Solid. Godin and Dunckel teamed up to form Air in 1995, creating what the press called "ambient-kitsch electric French pop," a clumsy but effective description of the group's sound.

After some forays into recording, including the EPs *Modular Mix for Source* (1995) and *Casanova '70* (1996), Air eventually released four EPs under the album title *Premiers Symptomes*; that work helped the duo gain the attention of French and European DJs. For their first full-length album, *Moon Safari* (1998), the pair recorded in an eighteenth-century chateau outside Paris. The album features mini-Moog keyboards, the warm vibey feel of Rhodes keyboard, and ethereal strings to back up songs that are sung in a mix of French and English, often meander for five minutes or more, and tend toward the instrumental. The title track is tinged with hand claps, Rhodes' keyboard, and splashes of keyboard noise; "La Femme D'Argent" is a laid-back, jazzy, space-age, improvisational jam; the instrumental "Ce Matin La" features Burt Bacharach–like trumpets and acoustic guitar. The single "Sexy Boy" features an equally spacey mini-Moog, guitar, drums, and minimal lyrics that alternate between French and English.

Air released several albums after *Moon Safari*, including its unofficial follow-up, the haunting soundtrack to the film *The Virgin Suicides* (2000). Thanks to the precision of its music, with its signature loops, esoteric instrumentation, and experimental jazz, Air carved out a unique niche in the 1990s.

SELECTIVE DISCOGRAPHY: *Premiers Symptomes* (Source/Virgin, 1997; reissued Virgin, 1999); *Moon Safari* (Source/Virgin, 1998); *The Virgin Suicides* (Virgin, 2000); *10,000 Hz Legend* (Astralwerks, 2000); *Everybody Hertz* (Astralwerks, 2002).

CARRIE HAVRANEK

ALABAMA

Formed: 1969, Fort Payne, Alabama; Disbanded 2003
Members: Jeff Cook (born Fort Payne, Alabama, 27 August 1949); Teddy Gentry (born Fort Payne, Alabama, 22 January 1952); Mark Herndon (born Springfield, Massachusetts, 11 May 1955); Randy Owen (born Fort Payne, Alabama, 14 December 1949).
Genre: Country, Rock
Best-selling album since 1990: *Pass It on Down* (1990)
Hit songs since 1990: "I'm in a Hurry (and Don't Know Why)," "Reckless," "Sad Lookin' Moon"

Combining country songwriting with the easy percussive sound of pop and rock, Alabama emerged as the most commercially successful country band of the 1980s, scoring twenty-seven number one singles over the course of the decade. Often dismissed by critics because of their slick style, Alabama deserve credit for popularizing the concept of the musical *group* within mainstream country, a genre in which most stars had been single vocalists during the 1960s and 1970s.

The key to Alabama's enduring appeal was its consistency. Although its albums of the early 1990s made a few concessions to the tougher neotraditionalist sound popular during the era, Alabama's musical foundation of electric bass, hard drums, and cheerful harmony singing did not change. Likewise, the durable appearance of its members—long hair, beards, and blue jeans—cultivated a "just folks" image that appealed to the band's working-class fan base. Blending predictability with professionalism, Alabama continued to score sizable hits throughout the 1990s.

The first cousins Randy Owen and Teddy Gentry, who grew up on separate cotton farms on Alabama's Lookout Mountain, formed the first incarnation of the group in 1969, naming it Young Country. Adding a third cousin, Jeff Cook, to its lineup, Young Country won first prize at a high school talent contest, performing a song by country star Merle Haggard. In 1972, after their members graduated from college, the band adopted the name Wildcountry and began attracting a loyal following through appearances in bars in the southeastern United States. Making one final name change to Alabama in

1977, the group achieved a minor country hit, "I Wanna Be with You Tonight," for the small GRT label. Unfortunately, GRT declared bankruptcy soon after, and, because of hidden contractual obligations, the band was prevented from recording for the next two years.

After addding the talents of the rock drummer Mark Herndon, Alabama reemerged in 1979 with the hit "I Wanna Come Over," released on the small MDJ label. The following year Alabama was signed by the major label RCA and quickly earned a number one country hit, "Tennessee River" (1980).

During the 1980s Alabama issued a slew of albums, each divided thematically between devotional ballads and nostalgic odes to the band's southern upbringing. Of these albums, *Mountain Music* (1982) is often cited by critics as the finest. The title track, sporting the steady kick of Herndon's drums, became a crossover pop hit because of its smooth, radio-groomed sound. Meanwhile, the string-drenched "Close Enough to Perfect" extols traditional marital values, a theme that resurfaced in the band's later work. Although none of the band's members were especially strong vocalists, their voices blended well together, creating an appealing harmony sound that recalled 1970s pop groups such as Three Dog Night. Despite the group's unprecedented chart success, critics were, for the most part, unkind. The 1982 edition of the *Rolling Stone Record Guide*, for example, characterized the band's music as "flaccid country-rock." Although albums such as *The Touch* (1986) and *Just Us* (1987) sounded even slicker than their predecessors, the band returned to form with *Southern Star* (1989). Featuring production assistance from R&B keyboardist Barry Beckett, the album is enlivened by traditional-sounding harmonica and banjo on tracks such as "High Cotton."

By the early 1990s Alabama's albums were incorporating a slightly harder-edged sound that reflected neo-traditionalism, a popular movement that returned country to a more basic, roots-oriented sound built upon fiddles, drums, and acoustic guitar. "I'm in a Hurry (and Don't Know Why)" (1992) uses this style to achieve a loose, free-spirited quality that contrasts favorably with the band's earlier recordings. At the same time Alabama continued to hit with syrupy ballads such as "Once upon a Lifetime" (1993), in which a father speculates on how his "first born" views the world: "through the innocence you see/the value of a family." Often the group's members displayed their true talent on nonhit album tracks, which allowed them a greater sense of freedom from the dictates of formula. Although *In Pictures* (1995) promotes the band's standard combination of religion and romance on the hit "The Maker Said Take Her," it also contains "I've Loved a Lot More Than I've Hurt," a rewarding slice of down-home philosophy. Set against gently strumming guitar and rustic-

sounding barrel-house piano, the song conveys the wise, seasoned perspective of an aged romantic: "I've hurt a little now and then / But once you're broke you learn to bend." Likewise, "A Better World for Love," from *Cheap Seats* (1993), is a restrained, ruminative ballad, an anomaly within Alabama's catalog.

By 2001 Alabama no longer scored as high on the charts as it had in the 1980s and 1990s, but they continued to release successful albums such as *When It All Goes South* (2001). By this time critics observed that the group's lyrical emphasis on nostalgia and southern values was sounding dated, even inappropriate, within the modern climate of multicultural awareness. The album's title track, for example, seems to extol southern Confederate ideology with lines such as "Get yourself some rebel pride." Elsewhere, the song culls slogans that have often been used by racist and segregationist groups: "It really don't matter what state you're in / Some day the South's gonna rise again." While of dubious sensitivity in a thematic sense, "When It All Goes South" benefits from a rhythmic, funky supporting band. The album also features a strong track in "Wonderful Waste of Time," a breezy song whose gentle, Caribbean feel is enhanced by a full-bodied horn section. In 2003, after enjoying more than twenty-five years of success, Alabama's members made the decision to disband.

Alabama's rock-influenced sound and radio-friendly harmonies paved the way for the success of 1990s groups such as Lonestar and the Mavericks. Maintaining a reputation for consistency and professionalism, Alabama deviated little from the successful formula they developed during the 1980s and 1990s, performing songs of tradition and devotion with an assured, polished sound.

SELECTIVE DISCOGRAPHY: *My Home's in Alabama* (RCA, 1980); *Mountain Music* (RCA, 1982); *Southern Star* (RCA, 1989); *Pass It on Down* (RCA, 1990); *American Pride* (RCA, 1992); *Cheap Seats* (RCA, 1993); *In Pictures* (RCA, 1995); *Twentieth Century* (RCA, 1999); *When It All Goes South* (RCA, 2001).

DAVID FREELAND

ALICE IN CHAINS

Formed: 1987, Seattle, Washington

Members: Jerry Cantrell, guitar (born Tacoma, Washington, 18 March 1966); Mike Inez, bass (born California, 14 May 1966); Sean Kinney, drums (born Seattle, Washington, 27 March 1966); Layne Staley, vocals (born Kirkland, Washington, 22 August 1967; died Seattle, Washington, 5 April 2002). Former member: Mike Starr, bass (born Honolulu, Hawaii, 4 April 1966).

Genre: Rock

Alice in Chains. L-R: Layne Staley, Mike Starr (original bassist), Jerry Cantrell, Sean Kinney [PAUL NATKIN/PHOTO RESERVE]

Best-selling album since 1990: *Dirt* (1992)

Hit songs since 1990: "Man in the Box," "Would?"

Renowned nearly as much for their inactivity as their musical style, Seattle's Alice in Chains was one of the premier heavy metal bands of the early 1990s. Though hobbled by singer Layne Staley's fatal drug addiction, the group created a body of dark, brooding hard rock and intense visual imagery that set the standard for a new generation of heavy metal bands.

Early Years

The enigmatic, rail-thin Staley formed the group while still in high school in Seattle in the mid-1980s, dubbing it Alice N Chains. Like several other pioneering Seattle bands of the time, Alice N Chains melded the primping, gender-bending posturing of glam rock with catchy, noisy heavy metal. When Staley met Diamond Lie guitarist Jerry Cantrell in 1987, the pair began rehearsing at a warehouse called the Music Bank along with a pair of mutual acquaintances, bassist Mike Starr and drummer Sean Kinney. Though they considered several names at first, including Mothra, they settled on Alice in Chains, a slightly different version of the name of Staley's previous band. Staley said the name evoked an image of a speed metal band that dressed in women's clothing.

A Major-Label Deal

Honing their mix of heavy crunching guitar chords and thick, psychedelic blues, the group set itself apart from many of its Seattle peers by relying almost exclusively on a bleak, menacing sound that owed more to heavy metal than the punk-derived sound of such grunge rock peers as Nirvana. Unlike some of their fellow grunge bands, the group spent no time on an independent label proving themselves; instead they quickly inked a recording deal with a major label, Columbia Records, in 1989 on the strength of recordings they made in 1987 and 1988. *We Die Young*, a three-song promotional album, was released in July 1990, followed by the group's full-length debut, *Facelift*, two months later.

The metallic, colorized cover of *Facelift*, featuring all four members' faces superimposed onto one face, set a precedent for the group's pervasively dark imagery. The album is a tour de force of bleak, forceful hard rock. Mixing the over-the-top guitar excess of the 1980s with thick, grinding tempos, tracks such as "Love, Hate, Love" and "I Can't Remember" marked the emergence of a confident if morbid new voice in rock. Staley's vocals are low and rumbling, ominously expressing sentiments such as the following, from the song "Confusion": "Love, sex, pain, confusion, suffering / You're there crying / I feel not a thing/ Drilling my way deeper in your head / Sinking, draining, drowning, bleeding, dead."

The album also produced a bona fide hit with "Man in the Box," a song that bears the band's soon-to-be hallmark style. Inspired by a story Staley had overheard about how veal came from sheep penned in small spaces, the harrowing song combines Staley's haunted, menacing vocals with Cantrell's distorted, choppy guitar lines and the rhythm section's pounding backing. The inclusion of songs such as "Bleed the Freak," "Sea of Sorrow," and "We Die Young" set the template for what became Staley's signature creative voice, that of a morbidly disaffected, diseased pariah struggling to survive on the outskirts of mainstream society.

The group mounted its first U.S. tour in 1990 and followed it up with a multigroup summer 1991 tour—dubbed "Clash of the Titans"—with fellow heavy metal bands Anthrax, Slayer, and Megadeth. Having established themselves as a premier metal band, they returned in March 1992 with the largely acoustic four-song *Sap* release, which features guest stars Ann Wilson of Heart and Soundgarden singer Chris Cornell.

Growing Popularity

With the breakout success of Nirvana's smash grunge album *Nevermind* and the inclusion of their song "Would?" on the soundtrack to the popular mainstream film *Singles* in the summer of 1992, Alice in Chains was suddenly marketed as both a heavy metal and alternative rock act, broadening their fan base considerably. The group began work on their 1992 album, *Dirt*, in Los Angeles on the day the Los Angeles riots erupted; they waited out the violence for two weeks in nearby Venice, California. The bleak album is an unabashed look at the tortured lives of the now commercially successful, Grammy-nominated group, with Staley singing several songs about drug addiction and self-destruction ("Junkhead," "God Smack," "Sickman," and "Angry Chair") and Cantrell seeking to heal wounds with his father on the Vietnam-themed song, "Rooster."

While the songs are unabashedly catchy amid the dim themes, there is no hiding Staley's pain. "I want to taste dirty, a stinging pistol / In my mouth, on my tongue / I want you to scrape me from the walls / And go crazy like you've made me," he wails on the album's molasses-thick, sludgy title track. Following the album's release, Starr was replaced by former Ozzy Osbourne bassist Mike Inez. While rumors of Staley's drug addiction dogged the band, they successfully completed a headlining stint on the third multiact Lollapalooza summer tour in 1993, helping the album sell more than 3 million copies. Another short album of mostly acoustic songs, *Jar of Flies* (1994), features two of the band's most beloved songs, the string-laden power ballad "I Stay Away" and "No Excuses," both of which shone a dim light amidst the usual dark imagery.

Staley mounted a short tour with a Seattle supergroup, the Gacy Bunch, featuring Pearl Jam's Mike McCready, the Screaming Trees's Barrett Martin, and John Saunders. The band, named for the serial killer John Wayne Gacy, later changed their name to Mad Season and released their debut, *Above*, in 1995. The album is a somber hybrid of Staley's dark vocals and McCready's sometimes meandering guitar lines. Alice in Chains returned later that year with a self-titled album that debuted at number one on the charts. They did not tour to promote the album, again raising rumors of Staley's drug addiction that had surfaced after a similar failure to tour to promote *Jar of Flies*. A long period of inactivity followed.

Fadeout

For their first concert in three years, the group gave an intense performance on MTV's *Unplugged* show in

1996. An album of the event was released in July of that year. Though gaunt, Staley sounded fine; however, barring a few dates opening for their heroes in KISS that summer, it would be one of the band's final performances. Cantrell released his solo debut, *Boggy Depot* (1998), several years later, with contributions from Inez and Kinney, and Staley was replaced by Screaming Trees singer Mark Lanegan on Mad Season's second album.

A four-disc commemorative box set featuring rare and previously released material, *Music Bank*, was released in 1999, and a live album, *Live*, followed in 2000. Though rumors of his demise were rampant throughout the late 1990s, Staley's death at thirty-four from a lethal overdose of heroin and cocaine in April 2002 came as a shock to the band's longtime fans, providing confirmation that the band would never return to form.

Though their period of creativity was short-lived, Alice in Chains helped to change the face of heavy metal in the 1990s, bringing a poetic, nihilistic edge to a genre that had fallen into parody only a decade earlier. Along the way, they inspired a new generation of bands such as Creed, Puddle of Mudd, and Godsmack, the last taking its name from one of Alice in Chains's songs.

SELECTIVE DISCOGRAPHY: *We Die Young* (Columbia, 1990); *Facelift* (Columbia, 1990); *Sap* (Columbia, 1992); *Dirt* (Columbia, 1992); *Jar of Flies* (Columbia, 1994); *Alice in Chains* (Columbia, 1995); *MTV Unplugged* (Columbia, 1996); *Music Bank* (1999); *Nothing Safe: Best of the Box* (Columbia, 1999); *Live* (Columbia, 2000); *Greatest Hits* (Columbia, 2001).

GIL KAUFMAN

THE ALLMAN BROTHERS BAND

Formed: 1969, Macon, Georgia

Members: "Gregg" Lenoir Allman, lead vocals, keyboards (born Nashville, Tennessee, 8 December 1947); Oteil Burbridge, bass (born Washington, D.C., 24 August 1964); Warren Haynes, lead guitar, vocals (born Asheville, North Carolina, 6 April 1960); Jaimoe "Jai" Johanny Johanson, drums (born John Lee Johnson, Ocean Springs, Mississippi, 8 July 1944); Butch Trucks, drums (born Claude Hudson Trucks Jr., Jacksonville, Florida, 11 May 1947); Derek Trucks, lead guitar (born Jacksonville, Florida, 8 June 1979). Former members: Howard "Duane" Allman, lead guitar (born Nashville, Tennessee, 20 November 1946; died 29 October 1971); Forrest Richard "Dickie" Betts, guitar, vocals (born West Palm Beach, Florida, 12 December 1943); David "Rook" Goldflies, bass; Chuck Leavell, keyboards (born Birmingham, Alabama, 28 April 1952); Raymond "Berry" Oakley, bass guitar (born Chicago, Illinois, 4 April 1948; died 11 November 1972); Jack Pearson, guitar, vocals (born Nashville, Tennessee); Marc Quiñones, drums (born Bronx, New York); Dan Toler, guitar (born Connersville, Indiana, 23 September 1948); David "Frankie" Toler, drums (born Connersville, Indiana, 28 June 1951); Lamar Williams, bass (born Hansboro, Mississippi, 14 January 1947; died 25 January 1983); Douglas "Allen" Woody, bass (born 1956; died Queens, New York, 28 August 2000).

Genre: Rock, Blues

Best-selling album since 1990: *An Evening with the Allman Brothers* (1992)

Credited for fashioning the southern rock sound, the Allman Brothers gained hasty notoriety at the turn of the 1970s with their muscular blues-based rock, paving the way for numerous other southern rock bands. They continue to rekindle the spirit of those early glory days through signature live shows featuring inventive improvisation and robust rhythms driven by two drummers.

The Original Band

The band's name derives from original members Duane Allman and his younger brother Gregg. They grew up in Nashville, Tennessee, and a tragedy early in their lives would be a harbinger for things to come. Their father, an army sergeant, home on Christmas leave from the Korean War, was murdered by a hitchhiker. In 1958 their mother, Geraldine, moved the family to Daytona Beach, Florida, where the brothers became interested in music and formed several bands, most notably the Allman Joys. Recognized as a guitar prodigy, Duane Allman became a renowned studio player at the famed Muscle Shoals studio in Alabama. A major record company offered him a contract to form a band so he left the studio to rejoin his brother, Gregg, who played keyboards and sang lead vocals with raspy emotion that belied his age. They recruited guitarist Dickie Betts, bassist Berry Oakley, and drummers Jai Johanny Johanson and Butch Trucks. They called themselves the Allman Brothers.

Their first two albums, *The Allman Brothers Band* (1969) and *Idlewild South* (1970), did not sell particularly well, but their concert reputation as an exciting act who improvised jazz-influenced blues spread fast. From late 1969 until the fall of 1971, they gave over 500 performances, culminating in a live album recorded in New York City, *Live at the Fillmore East* (1971). The double album became a hit and is still regarded as one of rock music's best records. However, the band suffered a huge setback when Duane Allman was killed on October 29, 1971, after he crashed his motorcycle while swerving to miss a truck. The band recovered enough to finish recording a fourth album, *Eat a Peach* (1972), but suffered the loss of another member, bassist Berry Oakley, when he was killed in a motorcycle mishap on November 11, 1972, eerily close to where Duane had died.

The Allman Brothers continued touring and recording into the middle of the 1970s although each member was also branching off into solo projects. They managed to produce several of their most popular songs during this period, including their biggest hit, "Ramblin' Man," which was written and sung by Betts. However, personal distractions, including ongoing heavy drug use, debilitated the band and in 1976 the Allman Brothers were caught up in a swell of narcotics investigations. Gregg Allman eventually testified against a former Allman Brothers road manager, who as a result received a stiff prison sentence for distributing narcotics. Greatly dismayed over what they viewed as Allman's betrayal, the band split up. Throughout, Allman was in an up-and-down relationship with pop diva Cher, marrying her twice before their split in 1979. In the meantime, Betts and Allman made amends and decided to reform the Allman Brothers in 1978 with a line-up that featured brothers Dan and Frankie Toler on guitar and drums. They toured successfully to packed stadium-sized venues and recorded three albums. Nevertheless, they broke up again in 1982 over creative squabbles and rampant drug use.

Picking Up the Pieces

In 1990 the Allman Brothers re-formed after releasing a four-album box set of their past music, *Dreams* (1989). Led by Allman and Betts, each cascading off solo-career failures, there was little expectation that the band had much of the old spark. The release of *Seven Turns* (1990), a remarkable comeback album, erased that doubt. The Allman Brothers borrowed guitarist Warren Haynes and bassist Allen Woody from a group called Government Mule to accompany the four original members. Haynes's slide guitar talents reminded many of Duane Allman's style and he worked well with the multitalented Betts. Betts's reputation and individuality suffered through the years in the shadow of Duane Allman and later in the shadow of Allman's legend. However, many critics regard Betts, who incorporates a generous blend of country and melodic pop influences into his blues-based guitar work, as one of the best players of his time. He also did a sizable share of the band's vocal work although the voice that fans most identify with the Allman Brothers belongs to Gregg Allman. Recognized as one of the great blues voices, Betts is a master of deep, expressive singing, perfectly suited for wrenching up all the tribulations that life has handed him.

In the next three years the new Allman Brothers Band released two more highly regarded recordings, *Shades of Two Worlds* (1991) and *Where It All Begins* (1994), proving that the band was back to stay. Yet, their spirited live shows continued to bring the band most of its praise. New

Spot Light | The Firing of Dickie Betts

Following a vote by the three founding members of the Allman Brothers, longtime guitarist Dickie Betts, the other living founder, was informed by fax in May 2000 of his firing from the band. The reason for his sudden ouster, according to band members, was his erratic playing on recent concert dates. Betts had been laid off from the band once before, in 1994, due to drug and alcohol treatment. Deeply depressed over this last firing and the lack of communication with his former band mates, Betts turned erratic in his behavior and he was checked into a clinic for psychiatric evaluation shortly after. Weeks later, he filed suit against the Allman Brothers over issues regarding his termination, steadfastly claiming that drugs were not the issue. That fall he was arrested and jailed for spousal battery. Although the firing was first thought to be only temporary, there is no indication that Betts will return to the Allman Brothers. The following year Betts recorded *Let's Get Together* (2001), his first solo album in thirteen years.

York City's Beacon Theatre became a regular stop and in some years they extended their stay for as long as one month. Two live recordings, *An Evening with the Allman Brothers* (1992) and a sequel called *2nd Set* (1995), capture their live approach, which is trademarked by spontaneous freeform jams. In 1995 the Allman Brothers Band was inducted into the Rock and Roll Hall of Fame.

More changes occurred in 1997 as Haynes and Woody amicably left to concentrate on Government Mule. The Allman Brothers continued to tour with guitarist Jack Pearson (who replaced Haynes) and released another live album, a tribute to the Beacon Theatre called *Peakin' at the Beacon* (2000). It mostly contains selections from their *Live at the Fillmore East* glory days, but is notable for featuring the first appearance of nineteen-year-old guitar whiz Derek Trucks. A nephew to drummer Butch Trucks, the younger Trucks amazed the audience with his bottleneck slide playing and his likeness to Duane Allman. *Peakin' at the Beacon* turned out to be Betts's final recording appearance as he was unceremoniously given a termination notice shortly after the record's release.

In conjunction with a ten-day stay in March 2003 at the Beacon Theatre, the Allman Brothers released their first new album of songs in nine years, titled *Hittin' the Note* (2003). The returning Haynes along with young Trucks share the guitar work.

Through four decades of making music, the Allman Brothers Band has faced constant comparison to a few celebrated years at their beginning. Whether the specter of that past has been help or hindrance to the band's musical life may never fully be understood. As members of the Allman Brothers stomped through the minefield of life in rock and roll, it is significant that they produced great music with every step.

SELECTIVE DISCOGRAPHY: *The Allman Brothers Band* (Polygram, 1969); *Idlewild South* (Polygram, 1970); *Live at the Fillmore East* (Polygram, 1971); *Eat a Peach* (Polygram, 1972); *Brothers and Sisters* (Polygram, 1973); *Win, Lose, or Draw* (Polygram, 1975); *Wipe the Windows, Check the Oil, Dollar Gas* (Polygram, 1976); *Enlightened Rogues* (Polygram, 1979); *Reach for the Sky* (Polygram, 1980); *Seven Turns* (Sony, 1990); *Shades of Two Worlds* (Sony, 1991); *An Evening with the Allman Brothers* (Sony, 1992); *Where It All Begins* (Sony, 1994); *2nd Set* (Sony, 1995); *Peakin' at the Beacon* (Sony, 2000), *Hittin' the Note* (2003).

BIBLIOGRAPHY: S. Freeman, *Midnight Riders: The Story of the Allman Brothers Band* (New York, 1996).

DONALD LOWE

TORI AMOS

Born: Myra Ellen Amos; Newton, North Carolina, 22 August 1963

Genre: Rock, Pop

Best-selling album since 1990: *Under the Pink* (1994)

Hit songs since 1990: "Silent All These Years," "God," "Cornflake Girl"

Singer, songwriter, and pianist Tori Amos is one of the most unusual and acclaimed performers to have emerged from the 1990s. With her 1991 debut album, *Little Earthquakes,* Amos took listeners by storm with achingly honest songs drawn from her personal experience growing up in the South. Throughout the 1990s Amos toured exhaustively, built up a large international fan base, and released more than half a dozen albums with aggregate sales of several million copies. Quirky, idiosyncratic, fearless, and sensual,

the flame-haired Amos appeals equally to men and women.

From the age of four, Amos was gifted at the piano; by the time she was a teenager, she knew that she wanted to pursue a career in music. The daughter of a homemaker and a Methodist minister, she was born in North Carolina but grew up in Maryland and attended the prestigious Peabody Conservatory in Baltimore from 1968 to 1974. While attending Peabody, Amos became more interested in rock music, especially Led Zeppelin. In her late teens she moved to Los Angeles to pursue her musical career, playing in bars. Atlantic Records signed her in 1987; oddly, Amos's first professional recording featured her pop-heavy-metal band Y Kant Tori Read. It was a flop, but Atlantic kept her. It was a wise decision—all but one album Amos has released since then for Atlantic have gone platinum, and she has received eight Grammy Award nominations.

Amos's career breakthrough came with her second album, *Little Earthquakes* (1991). Its inspired, intensely personal, piano-based compositions prompted comparisons to Joni Mitchell and Kate Bush. The album spawned two hits: "Crucify," a plea for self-acceptance, and "Silent All These Years," about a woman trying to find her voice, literally and figuratively. Both songs were successful singles on college and adult album alternative stations. "Me and a Gun," the penultimate track on *Little Earthquakes,* also commanded attention for its harrowing, a cappella tale of Amos's own experience with rape.

Amos's live shows at this time were a stunning sight: She wriggled, writhed, and pounded away on the piano as if it were equivalent to an electric guitar as a symbol of rock-and-roll prowess and sexuality. *Little Earthquakes* peaked at number fifty-four on the *Billboard* Top 200 and reached number one on the Heatseekers chart.

Amos's follow-up album, *Under the Pink* (1994), is a similarly vulnerable but more eclectic collection that examines everything from female jealousy ("The Waitress") to relationships ("Baker, Baker"). As a minister's daughter she deals compellingly with religious disillusionment in the stirring, chilling "Icicle" and in her duet with Trent Reznor in "Past the Mission." This has been her most successful release, and it produced a few hits, including "Cornflake Girl," a song about prostitution. In the soulful "God," punctuated with squalling guitars in between verses, Amos poses the following question in the first verse: "God sometimes you just don't come through/ Do you need a woman to look after you?"

Never one to worry about offending people, Amos made waves with her next album, *Boys for Pele* (1996), the cover of which depicts a pig sucking her breast. Her most ambitious and difficult record, it yielded the classic single "Caught a Lite Sneeze." *Boys for Pele* debuted at the number two spot and quickly went platinum.

During most of 1997, Amos dealt with personal changes, including a miscarriage and a marriage, while working on her fourth album, *From the Choirgirl Hotel* (1998), which also went platinum. Two years later Amos kicked off a tour with Alanis Morissette with the release of *To Venus and Back*, a two-CD set with one disc of new material and the other of live concert recordings. The new material is full of harder-edged songs that are epic in scope and owe much to her friendship with the industrial artist Trent Reznor.

Amos switched from Atlantic to Epic Records after the release of her collection of covers, *Strange Little Girls* (2001), which received mixed reviews. Her first release for Epic, *Scarlet's Walk* (2002), was recorded in the shadow of the terrorist attacks on the World Trade Center in New York City on September 11, 2001. The album charts the psychological and geographical terrain of her travels throughout every state in the United States. The result is a thoughtful, seemingly effortless collection of eighteen tracks that mark a welcome return to the strong story-songs of her earlier albums, most notably in the first single, "Sorta Fairytale." The work upholds Amos's stature as an uncompromising artist whose quirky feminist musings on religion and sexism have earned her a legion of loyal fans and a secure niche among the creative forces in contemporary American music.

SELECTIVE DISCOGRAPHY: *Little Earthquakes* (Atlantic, 1991); *Under the Pink* (Atlantic, 1994); *Boys for Pele* (Atlantic, 1996); *From the Choirgirl Hotel* (Atlantic, 1998); *To Venus and Back* (Atlantic 1999); *Strange Little Girls* (Atlantic, 2001); *Scarlet's Walk* (Epic, 2002).

CARRIE HAVRANEK

FELA ANIKAPULAPO-KUTI

Born: Abeokuta, Nigeria, 15 October 1938; died Lagos, Nigeria, 2 August 1997
Genre: World
Best-selling album since 1990: *Red Hot + Riot* (2002)

Fela Anikapulapo-Kuti wielded political criticism and opposition to the Nigerian government in the form of hard-hitting, high-life-derived "Afro-beat" music from the late 1960s until his death from an AIDS-related illness in 1997. His birthplace had been established by the British in 1800 as a home for freed slaves and had a heritage of creative activism. Kuti's Yoruban grandfather was a celebrated composer, his father was a pianist and preacher, and his mother was a leading figure in the Nigerian nationalist struggle.

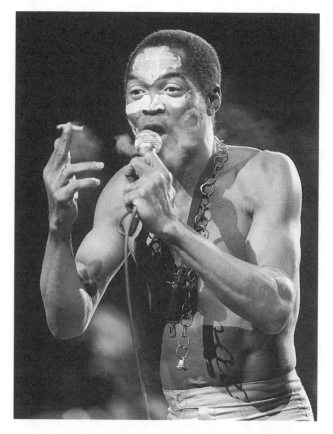

Fela Anikapulapo-Kuti [AP/WIDE WORLD PHOTOS]

Kuti began his career in 1954 as singer in the Cool Cats high-life band in Lagos. Even then he had his own style, which he called high-life jazz. By the early 1960s, after four years of musical study at Trinity College of Music, London, he was back in Lagos, an apprentice radio producer playing alto and tenor saxophone, and handling keyboards for a band called Koola Lobitos, which was influenced by James Brown and Geraldo Pino, a singer from Sierra Leone. He announced his new Afro-beat style in 1968 and then spent ten months in the United States in 1969, during which time he met members of the Black Panther Party. Kuti's hard-edged music was further shaped by avant-garde techniques and the black-nationalist rhetoric of some American jazz musicians, and he recorded a succession of singles decrying the poverty and oppression suffered by the Nigerian population. He enjoyed considerable success on a tour of Europe, acknowledged for his insistent ire and fiercely individualistic Pan-African ideology. Upon returning to Nigeria, he opened the Shrine nightclub to showcase his band Africa 70 (later called Egypt 80), featuring drummer Tony Allen.

Kuti's troupes were typically composed of as many as forty-five players: singers and dancers, reeds and brass players, drummers, hand percussionists, and guitarists. His songs were equally expansive; a single piece often filled the entire side of an album, and in performance he directed sprawling, noisy jams over militantly stiff rhythms unsuitable for most dancing. He also disliked performing songs once he had recorded them, a preference that, along with his lengthy diatribes from the stage, hampered his success in the United States. However, his use of pidgin English rather than a tribal tongue made his work accessible—and popular—throughout Anglophone Africa.

Performing bare-chested, usually smoking a spliff of igbo (Nigerian marijuana), Kuti exhorted his audiences with chants and rants about the corruption of politicians, the brutality and stupidity of the Nigerian military (which ruled his country during much of his career), and the plight of the disenfranchised, including women. In 1975 he changed his middle name, Ransome, which he considered a slave name, to Anikapulapo, so that his entire name translated into "he who emanates greatness, having control over death, death cannot be caused by human entity."

The bluntness of Kuti's criticisms of African elites and bourgeoisie led to nearly constant conflict with those in power. In 1977 the Nigerian military staged a heavily armed attack on his private, walled compound, which he called the Kalakuta Republic. Kuti was beaten, his eighty-two-year-old mother thrown out of a window, and his home set afire. He went into voluntary exile in Ghana, where he continued to attack with music, then was deported back to Nigeria. Upon arrival, to affirm his African roots, he married twenty-seven women, all of whom he divorced in 1986, declaring "No man has a right to own a woman's vagina."

In 1979, during a period of civilian government, Kuti established his own political party, MOP (Movement of the People), but when the military returned to power in 1983, he was charged with currency violations and sentenced to a five-year jail term. International protest led a new government to release him in 1986. But while Kuti was incarcerated, the New York–based producer Bill Laswell completed work on his *Army Arrangement* (1986); out of prison, Kuti collaborated with producer Wally Badarou on *Teacher Don't Teach Me Nonsense* (1987). Both of these albums, and the distribution of some 133 songs from Kuti's seventy-seven albums, sustained international interest in and acclaim for his music and political stance.

Kuti was arrested in Nigeria again in 1994 on drug charges and agreed to undergo counseling for substance abuse, but he then sued the government for pressing those charges. The case was still pending when Kuti fell into a coma in 1997, having refused either Western or traditional Yoruba treatment as "a matter of principle." Fela's son Femi carries on the Kuti name and Afro-beat sound, though in a less overtly political, more musically solicitous manner.

SELECTIVE DISCOGRAPHY: *Underground System* (Kalakuta, 1992); *Red Hot + Riot* (MCA, 2002)

WEBSITE: www.ghotek.com/fela/.

HOWARD MANDEL

MARC ANTHONY

Born: Marco Antonio Muñiz; New York, 16 September 1969

Genre: Latin

Best-selling album since 1990: *Marc Anthony* (1999)

Hit songs since 1990: "Hasta Que Te Conocí," "I Need to Know," "You Sang to Me"

In a decade Marc Anthony had three careers encompassing divergent styles. He started out as a freestyle dance maniac, moved on to salsa, and became huge as a pop crooner.

Marc Anthony was raised in New York's Spanish Harlem. His father was a musician who gave him the same name as a prominent Mexican balladeer of the 1960s. In the late 1980s Marc Anthony got into freestyle music, a stripped-down style influenced by techno and hip-hop that grew out of New York's Latino community. He wrote "Boy, I've Been Told" (1988), a hit for Sa-Fire, and had a few dance-club hits of his own in 1991 with "Rebel" and "Ride on the Rhythm."

Upon hearing Mexican balladeer Juan Gabriel sing the dramatic "Hasta Que Te Conocí" on the radio, Marc Anthony was inspired to move into Spanish-language music, where brazen sentimentality is the order of the day. Many other former freestyle artists, including Sa-Fire, Brenda K. Starr, and India, made the same leap.

His Spanish-language debut, *Otra Nota* (1993), features a soulful, salsa version of "Hasta Que Te Conocí." Salsa is a popular Latin dance rhythm with elements of Cuban *son* and Latin jazz. The album was produced by Sergio George, an expert musician who likes to fuse Latin rhythms with R&B-influenced vocals.

His follow-up album, *Todo a Su Tiempo* (1995), is another treat for dancers, as Marc Anthony's passionate tenor adds tension to George's percolating arrangements, especially on standout cuts "Se Me Sigue Olvidando," "Te Conozco Bien," and "Nadie Como Ella." Unsure of his Spanish abilities, Marc Anthony relied on composer Omar Alfanno for much of his material. For that reason he also avoids the vocal improvisation that characterizes the coda of many salsa tunes.

Contra la Corriente (1997) continues in the same vein and earned Marc Anthony a Grammy for best tropical Latin album. That year he also starred in the Paul Simon musical *The Capeman*. It flopped, but Marc Anthony received good notices for his acting and went on to appear in the Martin Scorsese film *Bringing Out the Dead* (1999), though it, too, flopped.

Anthony returned to the English language in a big way with *Marc Anthony* (1999). But this time, instead of hanging out in the free-style subgenre, he aimed for mass success. He comes across as a traditional pop balladeer who adds subtle R&B and Latin elements. Producer Cory Rooney was an important contributor. Anthony said that Rooney was the first collaborator with whom he's felt chemistry—they finish each other's hooks and lyrical ideas. The single "I Need to Know," written by the pair, uses a stripped-down arrangement featuring piano and synthesized brass, borrowing from the old free-style days. But the tempo recalls classic Afro-Cuban ballroom fare. Despite sounding like nothing else on Top 40 radio, the song shot to number three on the Hot 100. The ballad "You Sang to Me" became one of the biggest recent pop hits to feature an accordion solo.

In 2000 Anthony married the former Miss Universe Dayanara Torres. She gave birth to their first son, Christian, in early 2001. Marc Anthony also has a daughter Arianna, born in 1994 to his former girlfriend, Debbie Rosado, a New York City police officer.

Anthony built a home studio in order to stay closer to his new family and finally released *Libre* (2001), his first Spanish album in four years. A complex work co-produced by Marc Anthony and his longtime keyboardist Juanito Gonzalez, the album does not have the danceable hooks that his salsa fans wanted. However, Marc Anthony viewed the effort as a maturation, since he co-wrote all but one song.

Mended (2002) again tapped Rooney as a producer. However, the album never ignites the fire of his salsa material. The ballad "I Need You" is expertly crafted adult contemporary, with pretty synthesizers and acoustic guitar, but is weighed down by a Muzak-y blandness. "I've Got You," with its samba feel, is more energetic. But lyrics about hanging out with models and world travel do not resonate with most CD buyers. The album also includes "Tragedy," one of the strongest tracks. Columbia did not attempt to re-release the single in the United States, instead promoting a Spanish version in Latin America. Upon the album's release, Anthony said it expresses his contentment with family life. Unfortunately, a few weeks later he and Torres separated, just as he embarked on a grueling U.S. tour. However, the couple insisted they were not seeking a divorce and were trying to work things out.

Though far from a flop, *Mended* did not reach the heights of *Marc Anthony*. And the esoteric nature of *Libre* dimmed his star with salsa fans. However, with his singing talent, on-stage charisma, and eclectic musical tastes, Marc Anthony is likely to re-emerge with more interesting fusions and danceable concoctions.

SELECTIVE DISCOGRAPHY: *Otra Nota* (Sony, 1993); *Todo a Su Tiempo* (Sony, 1995); *Contra la Corriente* (Sony, 1997); *Marc Anthony* (Columbia, 1999); *Libre* (Sony, 2001); *Mended* (Columbia, 2002).

RAMIRO BURR

ANTHRAX

Formed: 1981, New York, New York

Members: Charlie Benante, drums (born Bronx, New York, 27 November 1962); Frank Bello, bass (born Bronx, New York, 7 September 1965); John Bush, vocals (born Los Angeles, California, 24 August 1963); Rob Caggiano, guitar (born New York, New York); Scott Ian, guitar (born Scott Rosenfeld, Queens, New York, 31 December 1963). Former members: Joey Belladonna, vocals (born Oswego, New York, 30 October 1960); Dan Lilker, bass (born Queens, New York, 18 October 1964); Dan Spitz, guitar (born Queens, New York, 28 January 1963); Neil Turbin, vocals (born Brooklyn, New York, 24 December 1963).

Genre: Heavy Metal, Rock

Best-selling album since 1990: *Sound of White Noise* (1993)

Hit songs since 1990: "Bring the Noise" (featuring Public Enemy), "Only"

Anthrax emerged as one of the top thrash/speed metal bands of the 1980s along with Metallica, Megadeth, and Slayer. While most vocalists in the genre effected coarse growls, Anthrax's synthesis of hardcore punk's blistering rhythmic aggression and heavy metal's technical precision stood out due to Joey Belladonna's polished vibrato. With no assistance from mainstream radio and minor support from MTV, the group developed a substantial underground following of both skateboarders and headbangers. In the early 1990s, they helped launch the rap-metal movement, but gradually found their audience wane after changing vocalists.

Mutual interest in comic books, skateboarding, and aggressive music brought guitarist Scott Ian and bassist Dan Lilker together to form Anthrax in 1981 in New York City. They were soon joined by drummer Charlie Benante, guitarist Dan Spitz, and several vocalists, until they settled on Neil Turbin. With the band's chugging heavy metal attack and Turbin's superhuman howls they sounded like a neophyte version of Judas Priest or Iron Maiden. Persistent pursuit of Megaforce Records led to a deal and the release of *Fistful of Metal* (1984). That same year Lilker quit and Turbin was fired. They were replaced by bassist Frank Bello, the group's roadie at the time, and vocalist Joey Belladonna, and the group moved in a new direction.

With blitzkrieg double-bass percussion, lightning-fast riffs, Belladonna's powerful wail, and trademark backing vocal grunts, Anthrax developed a unique sound that captured both heavy metal's virtuosity and hardcore's minimalism. An understated use of guitars distinguished them as thrash, while bands that implemented blistering, classically influenced guitars were more often labeled speed metal. After signing a major-label deal with Island Records, Anthrax released the full-length albums *Spreading the Disease* (1985), *Among the Living* (1987), and *State of Euphoria* (1988) in the 1980s. Throughout the albums, Belladonna narrates stories about comic book and mythical characters, as well as protagonists in several Stephen King works. Their cartoon-like fascination with popular culture is balanced by the dark subject matters involved.

Among the Living's scathing commentary on America's treatment of Native Americans in "Indians" introduced the more political direction the band was heading. On *State of Euphoria*, in addition to humorous rants about plagiarism and televangelism, they tackled the plight of New York City's homeless in "Who Cares Wins." MTV claimed the realistic images and statistics in the song's video were too depressing for their viewers, but a few months later put Phil Collins's similarly themed "Another Day in Paradise" into heavy rotation. Collins's video was revered for the same reason Anthrax's was shunned.

Undaunted by the lack of mainstream support, Anthrax forged ahead with their darkest, most socially conscious, and consistent effort to date: *Persistence of Time* (1990). Leaving their lighthearted side behind, the group repeatedly spoke out against prejudice, hatred, and corruption, and rallied for freedom and change. With several of the tracks measuring six to seven minutes, it was an epic tour de force. It was quickly certified gold and nominated for a Best Metal Performance Grammy Award.

With its new agenda in place, Anthrax teamed up with rap's most political group, Public Enemy, on "Bring the Noise." The highly influential song appeared on *Attack of the Killer B's* (1991), a b-sides and rarities collection with some new tracks, which, unlike most albums of a similar nature, was not just for die-hard fans. The format enabled them to show a playful side with cover songs, an updated version of their first foray into rap, a parody of sappy heavy metal ballads, and the hilariously foul-mouthed, anti-censorship rant "Startin' Up a Posse."

As the band's creative output peaked, personal friction between Belladonna and the other members led to his departure. He was replaced by John Bush, longtime vocalist of Los Angeles metal veterans Armored Saint. With a significantly lower growl than Belladonna, his arrival marked a distinctly new course. The band's mesmerizing speed often slowed to a more bludgeoning pulse, while keeping the angrier, more serious direction of *Per-*

Spot Light | "Bring the Noise"

In 1991, when Anthrax and Public Enemy teamed up to revamp the latter's 1988 song "Bring the Noise," they ignited rap-metal. Over chunky, rhythmic guitar riffs Public Enemy frontman Chuck D rapped the first two verses, and Anthrax guitarist Scott Ian rapped the last two verses with assistance from bandmates Charlie Benante and Frank Bello. The song's video received steady airplay on MTV and generated a substantial underground buzz in rap, heavy metal, and alternative rock circles. As a result, the groups embarked on a co-headlining tour that broke down musical and racial barriers. The concept of rap lyrics and rock guitars in the same song was not new. Run-D.M.C. introduced the style on "Rock Box" and "King of Rock" in the mid-1980s; artists like the Beastie Boys and the Red Hot Chili Peppers followed suit. Combining rap and metal also had a precedent—Anthrax's "I'm the Man," Faith No More's "Epic," and some Ice-T tracks. Each of these fusions stood out as a novelty but failed to spawn a movement, particularly Run-D.M.C.'s 1986 landmark collaboration with Aerosmith on "Walk This Way." While the "Bring the Noise" single and tour were singular events, 1992 saw three major rap-metal debut albums from Body Count, Biohazard, and Rage Against the Machine. The following year the soundtrack for the thriller *Judgment Night* was an entire album's worth of heavy metal artists collaborating with rap artists. At the same time, new bands such as Korn, P.O.D., and Limp Bizkit would join Papa Roach, Kid Rock, and Linkin Park to sell millions of records as part of the rap-metal explosion of the late 1990s and early 2000s. Most artists and fans point to "Bring the Noise" as the original inspiration.

sistence of Time. Despite the changes, the first album with Bush, *The Sound of White Noise* (1993), was Anthrax's only Top 10 release and went gold faster than all previous efforts. Support for the follow-up, *Stomp 442* (1995), was drastically less. Without Belladonna, the band's sound began to blend in with most conventional metal and the group's audience quickly shrunk. With minimal fan interest for *Volume 8: The Threat Is Real* (1998) and *We've Come for You All* (2003), seemingly only Belladonna's return could restore the former support for the band.

Anthrax's 1990s work influenced both the rap-metal and nu metal movements that rose to prominence in the late 1990s. They are most revered, though, for their consummate version of thrash metal, which influenced many contemporaries in the 1980s, but was rarely imitated.

SELECTIVE DISCOGRAPHY: *Spreading the Disease* (Megaforce/Island, 1985); *Among the Living* (Megaforce/Island, 1987); *I'm the Man* EP (Megaforce/Island, 1987); *State of Euphoria* (Megaforce/Island, 1988); *Persistence of Time* (Megaforce/Island, 1990); *Attack of the Killer B's* (Island, 1991); *The Sound of White Noise* (Elektra, 1993).

WEBSITE: www.anthrax.com.

                                    DAVE POWERS

FIONA APPLE

Born: Fiona Apple Maggart; New York, New York, 13 September 1977

Genre: Rock, Pop

Best-selling album since 1990: *Tidal* (1996)

Hit songs since 1990: "Shadowboxer," "Criminal"

The self-proclaimed "Sullen Girl," Fiona Apple was viewed as a contradiction when she burst onto the music scene in 1996 at the age of nineteen. The blue-eyed singer/songwriter with the bee-stung lips, throaty voice, and quirky piano-playing style wrote headstrong songs about the wars of the sexes; but she also stripped down to her underwear in the risqué video for her breakthrough single, "Criminal." It was a pattern the volatile singer followed over the next five years, mixing righteous indignation, cruel self-doubt, and public breakdowns with bitter send-offs of lovers and recording a second album whose title made history before it was even released.

Discovered on the cusp of a popular revolution in rock music that put female-fronted acts at the vanguard of pop music in the wake of the male-dominated heavy grunge rock scene of the early 1990s, nineteen-year-old Fiona Apple quickly distinguished herself. The daughter of the singer/dancer Diane McAfee and actor Brandon Maggart (*Dressed to Kill, The World According to Garp*), Apple began playing piano at age eight and writing her own compositions by the time she was twelve.

Traumatized by the separation of her parents when she was four and a rape at age twelve in the Upper West Side apartment she shared with her mother and sister—chronicled in the seething "Sullen Girl"—Apple left New York City for Los Angeles at age sixteen.

The singer gave a rough tape of three of her songs to a friend who babysat for a music industry publicist, who, in turn, passed it on to producer/manager Andrew Slater. The tape helped Apple land a recording contract with Sony Music, which released her debut, *Tidal*, in 1996. Produced by Slater, the album heralds the arrival of a strong, uncompromising new female singer/songwriter who is not afraid to spill her emotions, no matter how painful, uplifting, or confused. Like fellow cathartic singer/songwriters Tori Amos and Alanis Morissette, Apple was unafraid to sit at a piano and unfurl intensely personal poetry; she often seemed on the verge of breaking down in mid-song. Apple's voice veers from a breathy, growling low end reminiscent of jazz singer Nina Simone to a quavering falsetto. Coupled with a reliance on arrangements owing more to jazz torch singers than to rock or pop music, Apple's richly textured songs distanced her from contemporaries.

Tidal's opening track, "Sleep to Dream," is a model of the musical economy employed throughout the album. Compounded of an ominous, booming drum sound; ebb-and-flow piano figures; and Apple's mocking, yet vulnerable vocals, the song is a statement of purpose and defiance, summed up by the line, "So don't forget what I told you / Don't come around / I've got my own hell to raise." The backing musicians on the album—drummer Matt Chamberlin, pianist Patrick Warren, multi-instrumentalist Jon Brion, and pedal steel guitarist Greg Leisz—emerged as some of the most versatile, in-demand session players of the late 1990s. The video for "Shadowboxer" became a staple on both MTV and VH1, while the clip for the song "Criminal" generated instant controversy. Reminiscent of a widely panned series of 1995 Calvin Klein ads that were criticized for sexualizing seemingly underage children, the clip featured the lithe singer crawling in her underwear amid hollow-eyed, young-looking models in a grimy bedroom.

Rants, Raves, and a History-Making Album Title

In 1997 Apple won the Best New Artist award at MTV's Video Music Awards, confounding many in the audience with an anti-entertainment-industry rant that came to be known as the "go with yourself" speech. Apple won a Grammy for Best Female Rock Vocal Performance in 1998 for "Criminal" and recorded a dreamy cover of the Beatles's "Across the Universe" for the soundtrack to the 1998 film *Pleasantville*.

Not known for doing things the easy way, it was hardly shocking that in 1999 Fiona Apple chose to release her second album with a ninety-word title that is believed to be among the longest in pop music history. The run-on sentence, foreshortened by space-sensitive publications to *When the Pawn . . .*, reads, in full, *When the Pawn Hits the Conflicts He Thinks Like a King What He Knows Throws the Blows When He Goes to the Fight and He'll Win the Whole Thing 'Fore He Enters the Ring There's No Body to Batter When Your Mind Is Your Might So When You Go Solo, You Hold Your Own Hand and Remember That Depth Is the Greatest of Heights and If You Know Where You Stand, Then You Know Where to Land and If You Fall It Won't Matter, 'Cuz You'll Know That You're Right.*

Apple's second album, *When the Pawn . . .* (1999), drew attention not just for the length of the complete title, but also for its expansion of her signature jazzrock sound. Tracks such as "On the Bound" and "Get Gone" add lush strings and twisted carnival keyboard sounds to her repertoire. On the album's single, "Limp," an aggressive rock arrangement melds with the sounds of warped metal and junkyard percussion to create yet another bitter kiss-off tirade to an unkind lover. "So call me crazy, hold me down/ Make me cry, get off now, baby / It won't be long 'til you'll be / Lying limp in your own hands," she sings.

In March 2000 Apple had an onstage meltdown at New York's Roseland Ballroom in front of a sold-out audience, leaving the stage after forty-five minutes. Complaining about not being able to hear herself, Apple began crying and stormed off the stage, but not before cursing at furiously scribbling music critics. The appearance marked the beginning of a self-imposed exile from the spotlight for the singer, who was slated to release her third album in 2003.

Fiona Apple opened her diaries for the world to hear, and the results were not always tidy, for the singer or her audience. Her talent and singular voice rose above the willful exploitation of her image to create the indelible image of a gifted singer who was at once sexy and slightly menacing.

SELECTIVE DISCOGRAPHY: *Tidal* (Clean Slate/WORK, 1996); *When the Pawn . . .* (Clean Slate/Epic, 1999).

WEBSITE: www.fiona-apple.com.

GIL KAUFMAN

MARTHA ARGERICH

Born: Buenos Aires, Argentina, 5 June 1941
Genre: Classical

Martha Argerich is one of the most sought-after piano virtuosos of our time. That she seems to treat her career playing the piano as an imposition rather than a reward only seems to make her more appealing to fans. Her concert schedule is pocked with cancellations, often at the last minute, but her cachet is so strong that, in a business that typically books its artists years in advance she is often able to schedule performances on short notice.

Born in Buenos Aires, Argerich made her concert debut at the age of five and performed at the Teatro Astral and Teatro Colon while still a child. At the age of fourteen, she moved with her mother to Vienna, where she studied with Friedrich Gulda, Nikita Magaloff, and, briefly, Arturo Benedetti Michelangeli.

In 1957, at the age of sixteen, Argerich handily won the Geneva International Piano Competition and the Busoni Piano Competition; the resulting recognition led to a whirlwind of European concerts. In 1960 she made her first recording, a collection of pieces by Chopin, Liszt, Brahms, Ravel, and Prokofiev; critics favorably compared the album to historic Horowitz recordings. But, just as her career was taking off, Argerich took a break, complaining of fatigue.

She moved to New York and stopped playing the piano for a year, emerging in 1965 to make her London debut and compete in the Warsaw International Chopin Competition, which she easily won. Winning one of the world's top piano competitions put her squarely back into the international concert circuit. Resuming her concert and recording career, she made her Carnegie Hall debut in 1965 and has been at the top of the piano world ever since.

Argerich's volatility has loomed large in both her career and personal life. She was married to conductor Pierre Dutoit from 1969 to 1974, and the two have been longtime musical collaborators. She has three children by three different men. She stopped performing solo in the early 1980s, and, in the middle of the decade, she took a two-year break from all performing. When she returned

Martha Argerich [ALEX VON KEOTTUTZ/ANGEL RECORDS]

SELECTIVE DISCOGRAPHY: *Tchaikovsky Piano Concerto No. 1; Rachmaninov Concerto No. 3* (Philips, 1995); *Prokofiev, Ravel: Piano Concertos* (Deutsche Grammophon, 1996).

DOUGLAS MCLENNAN

ARRESTED DEVELOPMENT

Formed: 1988, Atlanta, Georgia; Disbanded 1995

Members: Timothy "Headliner" Barnwell, vocals (born New Jersey, 26 July 1967); Rasa Don, drums (Donald Jones; born New Jersey, 22 November 1968); Montsho Eshe, dancer, choreographer (Temelca Garther; born Georgia, 23 December 1974); Dionne Farris, vocals (born Bordentown, New Jersey, 1969); Baba Oje, spiritual advisor (born Laurie, Mississippi, 15 May 1932); Aerle Taree, vocals (Taree Jones; born Wisconsin, 10 January 1973); Todd "Speech" Thomas, vocals (born Milwaukee, Wisconsin, 25 October 1968).

Genre: Hip-Hop

Best-selling album since 1990: *3 Years, 5 Months, and 2 Days in the Life of . . .* (1992)

Hit songs since 1990: "Tennessee," "People Everyday," "Mr. Wendel"

to the stage, it was with orchestras and chamber music collaborators. The cutback in her performances only made each concert more prized as an event. When she finally performed solo again—at Carnegie Hall on March 25, 2000—the concert was the talk of the music world. It had been nineteen years since she had performed solo.

Though she seems to dislike performing in concerts, Argerich has recorded extensively: Her resume boasts more than fifty albums for Deutsche Grammophon, Teldec, RCA, EMI, Philips, and Sony. Her recordings, highly prized by collectors, cut across the piano repertoire: solo pieces and collaborations with full orchestra and chamber ensembles. In 1999 her recording of Prokofiev's Concertos Nos. 1 and 3 and Bartok's Concerto No. 3 with Charles Dutoit and the Montreal Symphony won a Grammy. In 2001 she was named Musical America's Musician of the Year.

Argerich's appeal is not difficult to understand. Her performances are charismatic, but in a way that draws attention to the music rather than herself. A listener feels her connecting to the music, exploring novel expressive paths rather than retreading familiar ones. Her musical instincts are harnessed to a prodigious technique that allows her the freedom to explore.

Southern hip-hop collective Arrested Development burst onto the popular music scene in 1992 with a quadruple platinum debut album, three Top 10 singles, and two Grammy Awards. Although they failed to build upon their phenomenal early success, in their short career Arrested Development was influential in expanding the geographic, demographic, and thematic scope of hip-hop. Their many references to life in the rural South prefigured such later southern "alt-rap" groups as Goodie Mob and Nappy Roots, while their introspective lyrics and eclectic inclusion of gospel, blues, and soul elements helped paved the way for artists such as the Fugees and Lauryn Hill.

The founders of Arrested Development, Todd "Speech" Thomas and Timothy "DJ Headliner" Barnwell, met in the late 1980s while students at the Art Institute of Atlanta. Although they initially formed a "gangsta" rap group called Disciples of Lyrical Rebellion, the music of Public Enemy inspired them to reinvent themselves as a more socially conscious, politically minded group. Renaming themselves Arrested Development, Speech and DJ Headliner gradually added new members to their growing collective, including dancers Montsho Eshe and Aerle Taree, percussionist Rasa Don, singer Dionne Farris, and eventually "spiritual advisor" Baba Oje, whom Speech had known from his childhood. The group moved into the same house and began recording music together. In March 1992 they released their debut album, *3 Years, 5 Months, and 2 Days in the Life Of . . .*, reportedly named after the amount of time it took the group to secure a record deal.

Spiritual Breakthrough

3 Years, 5 Months, and 2 Days in the Life Of . . . was an instant critical and commercial sensation, thanks in large part to the album's first single, "Tennessee." An unabashedly spiritual and personal song inspired by the deaths of Speech's brother and grandmother, "Tennessee" finds the narrator addressing God, who directs him to seek the self-knowledge and peace of mind he craves by returning to his old family home in Ripley, Tennessee. Bolstered by the refrain's upbeat, heartfelt chorus asking God to "Let me understand your plan," Speech connects his own personal grief and confusion to the larger historical grief of African Americans: "Now I see the importance of history / Why people be in the mess that they be / Many journeys to freedom made in vain / By brothers on the corner playin ghetto games." "Tennessee"'s combination of vulnerability and gentle wisdom was a marked departure from the more confrontational political rap of artists like Public Enemy and KRS-One, and critics and listeners quickly embraced Arrested Development as a group whose "positive" message sought to unify a troubled and racially divided culture.

3 Years, 5 Months, and 2 Days in the Life Of . . . tackles a variety of high-profile issues, from feminism ("Mama's Always on the Stage") and the environment ("Children Play with Earth") to homelessness ("Mr. Wendel"). On the album's second single, "People Everyday," Arrested Development explicitly distance themselves from the "gangsta" posturing then popular in mainstream hiphop. Taking its tune and chorus from the old Sly and the Family Stone hit "Everyday People" (1968), the track depicts the narrator reluctantly yet successfully defending himself and a female companion from a group of thuggish "brothers" drinking "the 40 ounce" and "holdin' their crotches and bein' obscene." The album further distinguishes itself from the hip-hop of the day by departing from its traditional grounding in inner-city culture. Instead, it draws from the black folk traditions of the rural South, adding bluesy vocals and gospel-tinged call-and-response singing to its raps.

3 Years, 5 Months, and 2 Days in the Life Of . . . ended up being one of the most successful albums of 1992. It scored three major hits, and went on to sell some 4 million copies, and the group was named Band of the Year by *Rolling Stone* magazine. In late 1992 the band contributed the song "Revolution" to the soundtrack of the highly anticipated movie *Malcolm X*. In February

1993 Arrested Development won Best Rap Performance by a Duo or Group for "Tennessee" and became the first hip-hop act to win a Grammy for Best New Artist. A month later, Arrested Development released *Unplugged*, a live recording of all the tracks from their debut (with the exception of "Tennessee"), along with a few remixes and three new tracks. Although the album failed to sell as well as its predecessor, it sold well enough to keep the group in the public eye, and the group spent the summer of 1993 headlining the popular Lollapalooza alternative music tour.

Growing Pains

By the time Arrested Development released their second studio album, *Zingalamaduni*, in the summer of 1994, the original group was beginning to fall apart. Emboldened by the attention her vocals on "Tennessee" had won her, singer Farris had left to pursue a solo career. Meanwhile, Speech had rearranged the group's lineup, making Headliner a co-rapper and adding a few new members.

In keeping with its Swahili title (meaning "beehive of culture"), *Zingalamaduni* both lyrically and musically expanded upon the Afrocentric philosophy hinted at in Arrested Development's debut. Unlike *3 Years, 5 Months, and 2 Days in the Life Of . . .*, however, *Zingalamaduni* failed to make much of an impact with critics, who found it unfocused, shrilly political, and lacking any song on par with "Tennessee." Commercially, the album was also a bit of a letdown, selling half a million copies. Arrested Development broke up in 1996.

That same year Speech went solo with a self-titled album, which, although it resulted in the minor hit "Like Marvin Gaye Said (What's Going On)," sold poorly. Speech followed up with *Hoopla* in 1999. Although his solo career never brought him the same level of success as Arrested Development did, Speech continued to perform and record, releasing the critically acclaimed *Spiritual People* in late 2002.

Despite having one of the biggest breakthrough albums of 1992, Arrested Development never parlayed their initial success into a long-term career. Nonetheless, their rootsy, southern-influenced instrumentation and spiritual, positive raps proved influential on the popular music of the decade.

SELECTIVE DISCOGRAPHY: *3 Years, 5 Months, and 2 Days in the Life Of . . .* (Chrysalis, 1992); *Unplugged* (Chrysalis, 1993); *Zingalamaduni* (Chrysalis, 1994); *Classic Masters* (Capitol, 2002). **Soundtrack:** *Malcolm X* (Warner Bros., 1992).

WEBSITE: www.speechmusic.com.

MATT HIMES

ASHANTI

Born: Ashanti S. Douglas; Glen Cove, New York, 13 October 1980

Genre: R&B, Hip-Hop

Best-selling album since 1990: *Ashanti* (2002)

Hit songs since 1990: "Always on Time," "Foolish"

The guest-appearance cameo has long been a means of introducing a new voice into the worlds of rhythm and blues and rap. Few artists, however, so quickly and successfully capitalized on the strength of a handful of smartly placed guest spots as New York-born Ashanti Douglas, whose recordings eventually sold millions.

Trained as a dancer at New York's renowned Bernice Johnson Cultural Arts Center, Ashanti had harbored dreams of pop stardom since her childhood in Glen Cove, New York, in the home of a singing father and a dancing mother. After honing her chops in a gospel choir beginning at age six, the singer signed her first recording contract at age thirteen with Jive Records. Nothing came of the contract, and it took nearly eight more years before Ashanti made a name for herself.

In the meantime, Ashanti danced in a variety of settings: as part of the Senior Pro Ensemble at Carnegie Hall, the Apollo Theater, and the Brooklyn Academy of Music, and in Disney's television musical *Polly*. The singer also danced in several music videos and appeared in the hip-hop comedy *Who's Da Man* and Spike Lee's *Malcolm X*.

While focusing on her schoolwork, Ashanti, a talented runner, was offered track scholarships to Hampton and Princeton Universities, which she turned down in order to pursue her singing career. Two more record deals fell through before Ashanti was discovered in 2001 by Irv Gotti, the CEO of a rising record label. Mining a formula that he used to make his record label, Murder Inc., one of the most successful of the early 2000s, Gotti paired the girlish singer with the late Latin rapper Big Pun on the 2001 hit single "How We Roll," giving Ashanti her big break via a cameo vocal on the rapper's song.

Like many of her future hits, the song mixed Pun's street-themed, sometimes profane boasting with Ashanti's smooth, elegant vocals on the song's chorus, a formula that shrewdly appealed to both male and female hip-hop fans. Gotti tried the "gangsta and the lady" trick with Ashanti a few more times, pairing her with rapper Fat Joe, on the smash hit "What's Luv?" and with the Murder Inc. cornerstone Ja Rule on "Always on Time," which hit number one on the *Billboard* singles chart in early 2002. Ashanti also sang backup on the remix of the number one hit from Jennifer Lopez, "Ain't It Funny."

An Instant Hit Debut

With several hit singles under her belt working for Gotti in a freelance role, Ashanti was officially signed by him as the first R&B act in the label's nearly all-male, testosterone-heavy lineup. In addition to her facility with singing a song's "hook"—the catchy portion of the chorus between verses—Ashanti proved to be a deft lyricist, penning singles for Lopez and singer Christina Milian.

It was no surprise then that the singer wrote all twelve songs—many on the spot—on her self-titled debut (2002), which broke first-week sales records for a debut from a female R&B artist. The album easily topped the *Billboard* charts as her debut solo single, the obsessive love tale "Foolish," reigned on the singles chart. Owing to her sudden ubiquity, in a single week in March prior to the album's release, "Foolish," "Always on Time," and "What's Luv?" all sat in the Top 10 on the singles chart.

Ashanti songs such as "Happy" (featuring Ja Rule), "Baby," and "Rescue" explore the ups and downs of relationships with a mix of preternatural maturity and high school-crush sincerity, all delivered in the singer's understated, seductive style. In "Leaving (Always on Time Part II)," another tale of infidelity, Ashanti pleads, "When you was cheating you was probably thinking I won't sense a thing / But love got a funny way of catchin' up to lies."

"Foolish" relied on a sample of the same El Debarge song ("Stay with Me") used by the late rapper Notorious B.I.G. in his hit of the same name. A sample of a Notorious B.I.G. rap is included on the equally popular remix of the song, "Unfoolish."

Ashanti's mix of hip-hop rhythms, a girlish, sensual voice, and ties to a credible, street-tough label set the stage for the singer to quickly catapult into the same rarefied air as one of her idols, the "queen of hip-hop soul," Mary J. Blige. It also opened doors for the hip-hop community by finding a way to appeal simultaneously to male and female audiences.

SELECTIVE DISCOGRAPHY: *Ashanti* (Murder Inc./Universal, 2002).

GIL KAUFMAN

ASLEEP AT THE WHEEL

Formed: 1970, Paw Paw, West Virginia

Members: Ray Benson, guitar, vocals (born Philadelphia, Pennsylvania, 16 March 1951); David Miller, bass guitar (born Torrance, California); Jim Murphy, steel guitar, sax (born Jefferson City, Missouri); Jason Roberts, fiddle, vocals (born Richmond, Texas); Dave Sanger, drums (born Coronado, California); John Michael Whitby, piano (born

Austin, Texas). Selected former members: Chris Booher, piano, fiddle; Cyndi Cashdollar, pedal steel, dobro; Floyd Domino, piano (born Jim Haber); Michael Francis, saxophone; Danny Levin, piano; Lucky Oceans, steel guitar (born Reuben Gosfield, 22 April 1951); Christine O'Connell, vocals (born Williamsport, Maryland, 21 March 1953); LeRoy Preston, rhythm guitar, drums.

Genre: Country

Best-selling album since 1990: *A Tribute to the Music of Bob Wills* (1993)

Hit songs since 1990: "Keepin' Me Up Nights," "Roly Poly"

Known to fans simply as "The Wheel," Asleep at the Wheel is one of country music's most durable bands, having survived numerous personnel changes since its inception in the early 1970s. Led by vocalist and guitarist Ray Benson, the band is a leader in the contemporary revival of "Western Swing," a style that combines traditional country fiddling with jazz and blues elements. The result is an exuberant, danceable sound that lends Asleep at the Wheel's records a pleasing consistency. Each of the band's albums provides a solid example of its appealing style: up-tempo rhythms, accompanied by pounding piano, nimble fiddles, and Benson's unwavering bass-baritone vocals. Having come close to country stardom on major labels at various points during their career, the group by the early 2000s had signed with a small record company, thus freeing themselves from the pop-oriented dictates of modern country.

Although nearly eighty members have passed through the band's ranks since the early 1970s, "the Wheel" has held together through the endurance of Benson, its founder and sole original member. Raised in Philadelphia, Pennsylvania, Benson grew up a fan of big-band music, an orchestrated jazz style that peaked in popularity during the 1940s with bandleaders such as Glenn Miller and Artie Shaw. Playing bass in his high school band, Benson discovered the music of the great jazz bandleader Count Basie and further refined his musical education by listening to folk, blues, and country music. As a teenager, Benson met steel guitarist Ruben ("Lucky Oceans") Gosfield, and the pair began performing together. In 1970, after Benson's graduation from high school, they moved to a farm in West Virginia with pianist Danny Levin and drummer LeRoy Preston. The four musicians, forming the core of the original band, began to secure gigs in local clubs. With pianist Jim (Floyd Domino) Haber replacing Levin, the group in 1971 started performing in Washington, D.C., where the rock and country artist Commander Cody introduced them to their first manager.

After moving to the West Coast and adding more members, the band performed with African-American country artist Stoney Edwards before signing with United Artists Records in 1973. In 1974 the group moved to the music-rich city of Austin, Texas, where they have remained. By the end of the 1970s, the band had enjoyed a string of country hits, including "The Letter That Johnny Walker Read" (1975), their only single to reach the top ten.

Asleep at the Wheel experienced a difficult period during the early 1980s, when their members discovered they were more than $200,000 in debt. By the middle of the decade, Benson had turned to producing records for others, working with the country singer Willie Nelson and smooth R&B/pop vocalist Aaron Neville. Well-suited to the tougher, "neotraditionalist" sound emerging in late 1980s country music, the band enjoyed a resurgence in 1987, signing with Epic Records and scoring hits such as "House of Blue Lights" (1987). In 1990 the group moved to Arista Records for *Keepin' Me Up Nights*, a rousing album that achieved minor hits with "Dance with Who Brung You," "That's the Way Love Is," and the title track. Produced by veteran R&B keyboardist Barry Beckett, *Keepin' Me Up Nights* pairs the band's celebratory style with a polished, assured sound.

After undergoing another lineup change, the band moved to Liberty Records in 1993 and released one of their most fulfilling projects, *A Tribute to the Music of Bob Wills and the Texas Playboys*. Featuring a roster of high-profile guest artists, including country stars Brooks & Dunn and Dolly Parton, the album celebrates the music of Benson's idol Bob Wills, often considered the founder of western swing. Famed for his onstage clowning and spoken interjections to band members within songs, Wills formed the Texas Playboys in 1933, finding a distinctive lead vocalist in Tommy Duncan. Duncan's smooth, crooning style—heavily influenced by that of legendary pop singer Bing Crosby—was a major influence upon Benson's own vocalizing. The connection is particularly evident on "Dusty Skies," one of *Tribute*'s most effective tracks. Detailing a western plains family forced from its home by a dust storm, the song is notable for its unflinching social realism. Benson and his fellow western swing revivalists Riders in the Sky sing the poetic lyrics with straightforwardness and restraint: "The blue skies have failed / We're on our last trail / Underneath these dusty skies." Elsewhere on the album, Parton's rendition of "Billy Dale" (recorded by Bob Wills as "Lily Dale") achieves a lilting purity, presaging the bluegrass style she pursued in the late 1990s.

Returning to Epic Records, Asleep at the Wheel released a live album, *Back to the Future Now* (1997), which reunites the band with past members such as Gosfield and

Preston. On the free-spirited "House of Blue Lights," Benson performs with the McGuire Sisters, one of the most popular pop vocal groups of the 1950s. Moving to the DreamWorks label, the band released a second Bob Wills tribute, *Ride with Bob* (1999), which features the talents of country stars such as Reba McEntire, the Dixie Chicks, and Dwight Yoakam. By the late 1990s, however, traditional-sounding bands such as Asleep at the Wheel no longer found acceptance within the pop-oriented world of mainstream country radio. Tellingly, the band's next album, *Take Me Back to Tulsa* (2003), was recorded for Evangeline, a small, independent label based in the U.K. In 2003 Benson released a solo album, *Beyond Time*, for another small label, Audium.

Overcoming countless personnel revisions, label changes, and shifts in public taste, Asleep at the Wheel have persevered largely through the efforts of Ray Benson, whose revival of western swing began a full decade before George Strait and other country neotraditionalists popularized the style. Having celebrated their thirtieth anniversary in 2000, "the Wheel" continue to perform their spirited brand of dance music for a loyal cadre of fans.

SELECTIVE DISCOGRAPHY: *Comin' Right at Ya* (United Artists, 1973); *Asleep at the Wheel* (Epic, 1974); *Texas Gold* (Capitol, 1975); *10* (Epic, 1987); *Western Standard Time* (Epic, 1988); *Keepin' Me Up Nights* (Arista, 1990); *A Tribute to the Music of Bob Wills & the Texas Playboys* (Liberty, 1993); *Back to the Future Now—Live at Arizona Charlie's* (Epic/Sony, 1997); *Ride with Bob* (DreamWorks, 1999); *Take Me Back to Tulsa* (Evangeline, 2003).

WEBSITE: www.asleepatthewheel.boz.

DAVID FREELAND

PATTI AUSTIN

Born: New York, New York, 10 August 1948

Genre: R&B, Jazz, Pop

Best-selling album since 1990: *Love Is Gonna Getcha* (1990)

Hit songs since 1990: "Through the Test of Time," "Givin' in to Love"

One of the most versatile singers in popular music, Patti Austin can handle pop, rhythm and blues, and jazz with equal mastery. A protégée of the great mid-century vocalist Dinah Washington, Austin evokes a style that harks back to the 1940s and 1950s, when the commercial division between pop, blues, and jazz was less rigid and

singers routinely performed material from all three genres. Although she has enjoyed some Top 40 success, Austin has fallen short of pop stardom. Her versatility has often worked against her, making her difficult for record companies to categorize. Nonetheless, Austin's fine 1990s and post-2000 recordings establish her as a mature, intelligent artist who can withstand comparison with great vocalists of the past such as Sarah Vaughan and Ella Fitzgerald.

A native New Yorker, Austin began performing professionally at age five. During the 1950s she worked not just with Washington but also with famed pop singer Sammy Davis Jr. By the late 1960s she was recording as a solo artist, scoring her first rhythm and blues hit in 1969 with "Family Tree." The 1980s were her most commercially successful decade: She released the romantic pop hit, "Baby, Come to Me," and issued a series of albums on the Qwest label, owned by producer/arranger Quincy Jones. Austin's 1988 Qwest release, *The Real Me*, in which she deftly interprets a collection of classic "standard" songs, is a career highlight. Austin shines on material ranging from the jazzy, up-tempo, "I Can Cook Too," to the beguiling "Lazy Afternoon," on which she caresses the lyrics in a mood of romantic mystery. Other albums of the 1980s, however, failed to capture her full talent, promoting her as an easy-listening pop singer.

In 1990 Austin switched to the smaller GRP label and recorded a series of albums that explored the contrasting sides of her musical personality. *That Secret Place* (1994) is one of her most representative works, an album in which she moves convincingly from jazz to reggae to gospel and, finally, to pop balladry. Throughout the album Austin's voice is technically perfect, stretching effortlessly over several octaves. What's most impressive about *That Secret Place*, however, is that Austin's perfection never obstructs the songs' emotional content. Rather, her virtuosity gives her the freedom to explore emotional subtleties within the lyrics. On one of the album's most moving songs, "Somebody Make Me Laugh," she paints a vivid portrait of loneliness, mining sadness without slipping into self-pity: "Somebody make me laugh, somebody make me cry / Somebody take me by the hand, and look me in the eye."

For Ella, Austin's 2002 tribute to the late jazz legend Ella Fitzgerald, is perhaps the most satisfying album of her career. Singing with a large orchestra, she shows no sign of vocal strain at age fifty-four. While Austin's voice may be less distinctive than Fitzgerald's, the two singers have much in common. Like Fitzgerald, Austin is blessed with perfect pitch and precise articulation, never pushing her voice harder than the songs require. When she *does* choose to push, however, the results are startling. In the album's boldest move, Austin reinterprets "Miss Otis Regrets," a song about the lynching of a society woman, as a powerful gospel number. Austin sings with cool precision at first, but slowly builds to a hard shout as she recounts the horror: "When the mob came and got her / You know, they dragged her from the jail." Beautifully structured, her performance captures a sense of outrage, turning a song usually treated with delicate irony into a hard-hitting indictment of hypocrisy.

Whether singing jazz, pop, or gospel, Patti Austin approaches each song with sensitivity and assurance. Through exploration of her wide-ranging talent, she has honored the traditions of the past while forging her own vision for the future.

SELECTIVE DISCOGRAPHY: *End of a Rainbow* (CTI, 1976); *Every Home Should Have One* (Qwest, 1981); *The Real Me* (Quest, 1988); *That Secret Place* (GRP, 1994); *On the Way to Love* (Warner Bros., 2001); *For Ella* (Playboy Jazz, 2002).

WEBSITE: www.pattiaustin.com.

DAVID FREELAND

B

BABYFACE

Born: Kenneth Edmonds; Indianapolis, Indiana, 10 April 1959

Genre: R&B, Pop

Best-selling album since 1990: *For the Cool in You* (1993)

Hit songs since 1990: "For the Cool in You," "When Can I See You," "Every Time I Close My Eyes"

As a guiding force behind the hit recordings of artists such as Whitney Houston, Boyz II Men, Toni Braxton, and Madonna, Kenneth Edmonds—known professionally as "Babyface"—became one of the most recognizable and distinctive producers of the 1990s, his smooth but engaging sound bridging the gap between pop and R&B. Babyface's success as a producer has often threatened to obscure his considerable performing talents. While his solo recordings have not scaled the commercial heights of his outside productions, they are consistent, solid examples of contemporary R&B, plush enough for relaxed listening but musically challenging and complex.

From Funk to Stardom

Raised in the Midwestern city of Indianapolis, Indiana, Edmonds began playing guitar and keyboards in local rhythm and blues bands as a teenager. In the mid-1970s he worked with famed soul and funk artist Bootsy Collins, who jokingly nicknamed the young performer "Babyface" because of his handsome, boyish appearance. After spending the late 1970s performing with Manchild, an

R&B and funk band, Babyface formed the group the Deele with fellow artist Antonio "L.A." Reid. The pair continued to work together during the 1980s, producing records for R&B group the Whispers and pop singer Sheena Easton before forming the LaFace label in 1989.

Babyface's solo album *Tender Lover* (1989) features the hit singles "It's No Crime" and "Whip Appeal," but its success was soon eclipsed by his excellent work for others. On hits such as Madonna's "Take a Bow" (1994) and Boyz II Men's "End of the Road" (1993), Babyface displays an unerring ability to bring out the best in his artists, highlighting their vocal strengths in productions that, for all their slickness, retain an aura of warmth. Occasionally his work crossed the line into bland, overly arranged pop, but even his most ornate creations were saved by a solid underlying groove. As the 1990s progressed Babyface became known for his intuitive, sensitive work with female performers, through capturing the personality and vocal contours that made them unique. These strengths are evident in one of his finest works, the soundtrack to the film *Waiting to Exhale* (1995).

Solo Recordings

In the 1990s Babyface found time to record his own albums, although due to his busy production schedule they came at intervals of several years. While his voice is rather modest in terms of range and quality, he showcases it to great advantage within the context of his recordings. *For the Cool in You* (1993) is a high point in his solo career, its title track a successful blend of breezy jazz and pop. Unlike more aggressive performers such as R. Kelly and D'Angelo, Babyface shuns sexual explicitness in favor of old-fashioned romance, wooing his lover with gentle pleas

Spot Light | *Waiting to Exhale*

In 1995 Kenneth "Babyface" Edmonds was hired to score and write songs for a film version of author Terry McMillan's best-selling 1992 novel, *Waiting to Exhale* (1995), about four young African-American women dealing with the challenges of love and friendship. Respected for his talents in capturing the warmth and vitality of the female voice, Babyface conceived the project as a showcase for a range of great R&B women, from legends such as Aretha Franklin and Patti LaBelle to younger performers such as Mary J. Blige. After watching a rough version of the film, Babyface began writing songs and matching them to each artist according to her vocal qualities. The results are exhilarating: Aretha Franklin's performance on "It Hurts Like Hell" smolders with a lifetime of tough knowledge and pain. On "Exhale (Shoop Shoop)" 1990s superstar Whitney Houston exhibits a new soulfulness, while 1970s and 1980s star Chaka Khan proves her skills as a jazz singer on a fiery rendition of the popular standard, "My Funny Valentine." For relative newcomer Mary J. Blige, Babyface wrote "Not Gon' Cry," a bluesy song that Blige performs with a vocal bite and acuity absent in her previous work. Taken as a whole, *Waiting to Exhale* is a testament to the ongoing vitality of the female tradition in R&B and an artistic peak in Babyface's career.

out sacrificing the gentle, approachable quality for which he is known. Recalling his early years as a funk performer, "Outside In/Inside Out" pulsates with a hard, steady groove, one of the deepest he has put on record. The hit single "There She Goes" is pushed along by an insidious, affecting synthesizer riff, while the reflective ballad "What If" builds gradually to a climax in which vocals and orchestration merge in a rich canvas of sound. Elsewhere on the album Babyface delves into varying musical styles with successful results. The supple horn lines and deep-sounding organ of "I Keep Calling" suggest the churchy influence of southern gospel music, while "How Can U Be Down" features a swaying jazz rhythm upon which Babyface applies an off-hand, relaxed vocal. Overall, critics found *Face2Face* to be a compelling summation of Babyface's talents, wide-ranging yet personal and heartfelt.

In his work with Whitney Houston, Toni Braxton, Madonna, and others, Babyface has crafted some of the most consistently appealing music in contemporary pop and R&B. While his low-key voice could not be described as powerful, Babyface imbues his own recordings with warmth and intelligence, creating albums layered with technical assurance and imagination.

SELECTIVE DISCOGRAPHY: *Tender Lover* (Solar/Epic, 1989); *For the Cool in You* (Epic, 1993); *The Day* (Epic, 1996); *Face2Face* (Arista, 2001). **Soundtrack:** *Waiting to Exhale* (Arista, 1995).

WEBSITE: www.babyfaceonline.com.

DAVID FREELAND

BACKSTREET BOYS

Formed: 1993, Orlando, Florida

Members: Nick Carter (born Jamestown, New York, 28 January 1980); Howie Dorough (born Orlando, Florida, 22 August 1973); Brian Littrell (born Lexington, Kentucky, 20 February 1975); Alexander James ("AJ") McLean (born West Palm Beach, Florida, 9 January 1978); Kevin Richardson (born Lexington, Kentucky, 3 October 1971); all vocalists.

Genre: Rock, Pop

Best-selling album since 1990: *Millennium* (1999)

Hit songs since 1990: "Quit Playin' Games (with My Heart)," "I Want It That Way," "Shape of My Heart"

and a soft voice. "When Can I See You," a tender ballad built upon Babyface's acoustic guitar playing and sweet vocal, augurs the smooth style of late 1990s performers such as Maxwell.

After a three-year hiatus Babyface returned with *The Day* (1996), an album featuring well-crafted ballads such as "Every Time I Close My Eyes." Despite its quality, *The Day* was a commercial disappointment, perhaps because Babyface by this point was better known in the eyes of the public as a producer. After another long break, Babyface released *Face2Face* (2001), one of his most satisfying efforts. With assistance from the hot production team the Neptunes, Babyface achieves a new sonic toughness with-

In 1993 in Orlando, Florida, three young men and a mere boy were on the make for show-business careers. Two of them knew each other from high school, and a third had recently moved there from Kentucky. They got together with the idea of forming a group, invited a fifth member from back home, and, taking their name from a local flea-market site, named themselves the Backstreet Boys. Four years passed before they became popular in America, but before then they became major players on the world scene as boy bands became the craze. The Backstreet Boys created the kind of music and personalities that pressed all the right buttons in adolescent females.

Beginnings

AJ McLean and Howie Dorough, both Florida natives, were friends in high school. The Kentuckians were Kevin Richardson and Brian Littrell. The boy—then only twelve years old—was Nick Carter. With a musical model derived primarily from African-American groups like Boyz II Men and the promotional acumen of their manager, Lou Pearlman, who saw them as another New Kids on the Block, the Backstreet Boys began their career singing in schools and malls in the Orlando area. Soon they were touring in the United Kingdom and Europe and developing a major following in France, Germany, Italy, and England. By 1997, when their debut album was released in America, they were ready to explode.

The Music Scene

Nothing about the music scene in the early 1990s was especially hospitable to the sort of music the Boys specialized in. The year they formed and went under Pearlman's wing, grunge was dominating the rock scene, and Nirvana was the group of the moment. Romantic ballads with sentimental lyrics were hardly the recipe for instant musical success. Yet the audience for melodic, soft-edged music is always there. In the late 1980s the white boy band New Kids on the Block emulated early rap and break dance music, while black groups like Boyz II Men proved that soul could still be popular. Building on the kind of songs Boyz II Men were noted for, embellished with dance moves that suited the music, the Backstreet Boys were poised to reach listeners that grunge could never speak to.

A great part of their success resulted from the promotional skills of their management, but it was also obvious that the Boys themselves were very musical. They were not simply a group of good-looking guys who could sing and dance. They harmonized well, they had good performance sense, and they knew how to reach an audience.

The Chemistry of the Group

Howie Dorough and AJ McLean formed the group, adding Nick and Kevin after encountering them in the Orlando area. Despite the five-year difference in their ages, Howie and AJ knew each other from their high school days and sensed early on that a band like theirs had the potential to become popular by playing a subdued and romantic version of R&B. Howie became known as the peacemaker of the group, and AJ took on the role of bad boy. Kevin is the oldest and is known for having his feet on the ground and a strong business sense. Brian—the puritan of the group—carried the standards of his family and culture into the glitzy world of the boy bands. Nick Carter is the youngest and by reputation the most volatile and unpredictable. Anchored by the older members of the group, he often complained that he never had the chance to do the normal things boys do in growing up. From early in his life he pursued a career in music, and, after joining the Boys at twelve, his life, like theirs, became that of a celebrity in a fish bowl.

The Pearlman Era

Elvis Presley had his Colonel Tom Parker, the Beatles their Brian Epstein, and the Backstreet Boys had Lou Pearlman. Any entrepreneur in the entertainment world takes major risks, but it is a credit to Pearlman's judgment that he saw how far the Boys could go before they had gone anywhere. Initially he pitched them to the European market, where they quickly met with their first great success.

Their first release, the single "We've Got It Goin' On," an urban-style pop song, became a hit in Europe in 1995 and was followed by their first album, also a success via a similar release pattern. In 1996 the Boys were named the number one international group by TV viewers in Germany, and their single "I'll Never Break Your Heart" became a chart topper there and in Austria. Their second album—*Backstreet's Back*—appeared the same year and became a smash in the same countries where the first had been issued. Their third album, made up of tracks from the first two and self-titled, was released in America in 1997, and the success of the single, "As Long as You Love Me," put the Backstreet Boys on the map. From that point on, under Pearlman's management, they were a number one act. However, their romance with Pearlman was about to end.

Shortly after breaking into the market in America, the Boys discovered that Pearlman was taking most of their considerable earnings while developing a competing boy group with the name *NSYNC. The Boys reached a settlement with Pearlman limiting him to one-sixth of the band's earnings. The bitterness of the dispute lingered on, however.

Millennium and After

The Boys broke with Pearlman as they were about to record *Millennium* (1999), their most important album to that time. Produced primarily in Stockholm, the album features one of their greatest hits, "I Want It That Way." On the first day of its release, *Millennium* sold half a million copies in the United States, entered the *Billboard*

Spot Light | Boy Bands

The Beatles were the first major white boy band, and, like all the bands that followed them, they were influenced by African-American music. The Backstreet Boys became the preeminent white boy band of the 1990s through their combination of musicianship, performance sense, and shrewd management. But their place was soon challenged by a group, *NSYNC, that was developed by the same entrepreneur who discovered them, Lou Pearlman. At first *NSYNC looked like they would be in the shadow of the Backstreet Boys, but their 2000 release, *No Strings Attached,* and the popularity of their sexy lead vocalist Justin Timberlake, put them in first place with album sales of 2.4 million in the first week, breaking the record set by *Millennium.* Imitators in the boy-band craze included groups like 98 Degrees and the TV-created O' Town, none of which had a long shelf life. By the beginning of the new century, it appeared that the boy-band craze—a recurring phenomenon in American popular music—may have peaked. The Backstreet Boys—now men—were facing internal problems of alcoholism and stress; their anticipated follow-up album to *Black and Blue* (2000) had not appeared by the spring of 2003. Nick Carter, like Justin Timberlake, has gone solo, though with less success, and popular music has moved to hip-hop, rap, and a revival of rock in various forms.

doors to get people to play our music, play our videos on MTV." Hurt by comparisons to groups like New Kids on the Block, the Boys had to be recognized for what they were: "We're a vocal group," he went on. "We'd like people to look at us like Boyz II Men or New Edition, only we're white."

The Boys specialized in romantic ballads influenced by soul music and church choirs. Although often verging on formula and cliché, the Boys's music remained fresh thanks to the fine musicianship of the five members and their skillful arrangements. In addition, the Boys varied their song book with other sounds, including touches of rap and hip-hop.

By the end of the 1990s, the Backstreet Boys were the preeminent boy band in the music business, though by then the competition had intensified. *NSYNC was vying with the Backstreet Boys for popularity, and a white rapper from Detroit with the stage name Eminem had recorded his first big album. With the ascendancy of hip-hop and rap, the boy bands seemed to have reached their peak. Their 2000 release, *Black and Blue,* its title echoing the Rolling Stones's album of 1976, topped the chart for only two weeks, and it did less well than *NSYNC's album released at the same time.

In one decade's time, the Backstreet Boys moved from the obscurity of their beginnings to become one of the most successful musical groups in the history of pop music. Their albums set records in sales, and their tours took their place among the top grossers of all time.

SELECTIVE DISCOGRAPHY: *Backstreet Boys* (Jive, U.K., 1996); *Backstreet's Back* (Jive, 1997); *Millennium* (Jive, 1999); *Black and Blue* (Jive, 2000).

BIBLIOGRAPHY: D. Coates and J. Delisa, *Backstreet Boys: The Hits (Chapter One)* (Miami, 2002); A. Csillag, *Backstreet Boys: The Official Book* (New York, 2000); S. Hughes, *Backstreet Boys: The Illustrated Story* (New York, 2001).

ARCHIE LOSS

album chart at number one, and broke the record for first-week sales previously held by Garth Brooks. The album took the number one spot in twenty-five other countries as well and produced four smash singles. It went twelve-fold platinum in the United States and spent more than seventy-seven weeks on the chart.

Acceptance by the music world took longer, however. The Boys were regarded as little more than lip-synchers, despite their obvious talents at harmonizing *a cappella.* Gradually, however, they began to command respect from music professionals. As Kevin Richardson once remarked to an interviewer, "We had to break down

BAD RELIGION

Formed: 1980, Los Angeles, California

Members: Jay Bentley, bass; Brett Gurewitz, guitar; Brian Baker, guitar; Pete Finestone, drums; Greg Graffin, vocals; Greg Hetson, guitar; Brooks Wackerman, drums.

Genre: Rock

Best-selling album since 1990: *Stranger Than Fiction*

Hit songs since 1990: "Stranger Than Fiction," "Infected," "Sorrow"

Forming at the tail end of punk's first explosion, Bad Religion spent years honing its sound and flying under mass-audience radar—until the early 1990s, when the alternative-rock juggernaut finally struck middle America.

Bad Religion has always maintained punk's ethic of simplicity, speed, and protest, but the group's principal songwriters, Gurewitz and Graffin, create hummable melodies and dramatic harmonies. Their aggressive but catchy sound has influenced recent alt-rockers such as Cake and System of a Down.

Gurewitz founded Epitaph Records to release the band's material, starting with 1982 debut album *How Could Hell Be Any Worse?* The album featured the raw "F---Armageddon, This Is Hell," with the sixteen-year-old Graffin singing raspy, Sex Pistols-influenced vocals. Little did he know that Epitaph was a name that would figure prominently into alt-rock's 1990s ascendance. In their first few years the group underwent frequent lineup changes and finally took a hiatus during the mid-1980s but returned triumphantly in 1987 with the catchy but angry-as-ever album *Suffer.* Though punk music was far from most music fans' minds during that era, Bad Religion was sowing the seeds of its latter-day commercial renaissance by sticking it out through punk's wilderness years.

Bad Religion kicked off the 1990s with *Against the Grain,* whose sarcastic "21st Century Digital Boy," penned by Gurewitz, skewered middle-class apathy. Graffin's voice had matured into a passionate but lucid shout, and he enunciated his lyrics with a precision uncharacteristic of punk. The members also tweaked the punk rulebook by incorporating some spirited vocal harmonies. During the early 1990s Graffin also did graduate work in paleontology at Cornell University in New York.

With *Stranger than Fiction* (1994), Bad Religion confronted the punk rocker's dilemma: The group was finally big enough for a major label, but would such a move represent a sellout? The CD was the group's first on Atlantic Records, but Gurewitz was uncomfortable losing business control. Meanwhile, his label's young prospect Offspring was breaking out of nowhere to define punk's next generation. Gurewitz decided to leave the band and was replaced by Brian Baker. With his departure the band lost not only its guitarist but also the songwriter of half its material. But no one could deny Atlantic's distribution muscle—*Stranger than Fiction* was the group's first album to make the *Billboard* charts, peaking at number 87. The album contained a new version of Gurewitz's "21st Century Digital Boy" and also featured the title track, a pessimistic song proclaiming that "life is the crummiest book I ever read, there isn't a hook, just a lot of cheap shots, pictures to shock and characters an amateur would never dream up." Graffin picked up the slack for the rest of the decade, taking over nearly all the songwriting chores for the subsequent *The Gray Race* (1996), *No Substance* (1998), and Todd Rundgren-produced *New America* (2000).

The group figuratively hit a "reset" button in 2002 with the return of Gurewitz. Back on Epitaph Records, Bad Religion finally enjoyed both commercial success and full control. *The Process of Belief* made number forty-nine on the *Billboard* 200, and the idealistic, harmony-filled "Sorrow" peaked at number thirty-five on *Billboard*'s Modern Rock Tracks.

Bad Religion has always been a group with plenty on its mind, but its longevity comes from its ability to express itself concisely and melodically.

SELECTIVE DISCOGRAPHY: *Suffer* (Epitaph, 1988); *Against the Grain* (Epitaph, 1990); *Generator* (Epitaph, 1992); *Recipe for Hate* (Epitaph, 1993); *Stranger than Fiction* (Atlantic, 1994); *The Gray Race* (Atlantic, 1996); *The Process of Belief* (Epitaph, 2002).

RAMIRO BURR

ERYKAH BADU

Born: Erykah Wright; Dallas, Texas, 26 February 1972
Genre: R&B
Best-selling album since 1990: *Baduizm* (1997)
Hit songs since 1990: "On & On," "Tyrone"

With her towering headdresses, dignified stance, and a vocal style that echoes that of a jazz legend, Erykah Badu emerged in the mid-1990s as the voice of a new breed of rhythm and blues singer steeped in the smooth soul sounds of the 1970s yet thoroughly versed in the attitudes of 1990s hip-hop music.

Born in Dallas, Texas, and raised in a single-parent home, Badu attended Booker T. Washington High School of the Arts as a child and began her performing career at age four, when she shared the stage with her mother, the actress Kolleen Wright. Trained as a dancer and known in Dallas for her cameos on a local hip-hop radio show under the pseudonym MC Apples, Badu studied theater at Louisiana's Grambling State University. After dropping out to focus on her music career, she was discovered while working as a schoolteacher and part-time dance and drama teacher in Dallas.

In 1994 the singer—who had taken the name Badu as an homage to jazzy, scat phraseology—got her break when she opened for a fellow new soul crooner, D'Angelo, at a Dallas show. D'Angelo's manager, Kedar Massenberg, was impressed with her talent and signed Badu to his newly

Erykah Badu [PAUL NATKIN/PHOTO RESERVE]

formed label, Kedar Entertainment, and paired her with D'Angelo for a cover of the Marvin Gaye/Tammi Terrell duet "Your Precious Love" for the *High School High* (1996) soundtrack.

When Badu's debut album, *Baduizm*, was released the next year, it was hailed as a breath of fresh air in the rhythm and blues world for its innovative mix of jazzy vocals, vintage soul, rap-influenced beats and language, and positive, conscious message. With a supple, sultry voice and mellifluous phrasing, Badu could not avoid comparisons to the jazz great Billie Holiday. Her work with the pioneering, instrument-playing Philadelphia rap group the Roots helped place Badu at the forefront of the Philadelphia-based "neo-soul" movement, a loose aggregation of singers, producers, session players, and rappers centered in the Philadelphia area who looked to classic 1970s soul for inspiration.

Such tracks as "Next Lifetime" and the album's breakthrough hit, "On & On," mix bass-thumping funk and hip-hop-style beats and lyrics with Badu's signature personal mysticism, which touches on aspects of pacifism, Afrocentrism, and Egyptian iconography. Often, Badu, who wrote all but one of the songs on the album, mixes these influences within the span of just a few lines, such as in "On & On," when she languidly sings, "My cipher keeps movin' like a rollin' stone / On & on and on & on / Alright 'til the break of dawn / I go on & on and on & on."

A Live Album Quickly Follows

Badu did not waste time following up the chart success of *Baduizm*, giving birth to both a live album and her first child, Seven, on the same day, just nine months after the February 1997 release of her debut album. In addition to revisiting a number of songs from *Baduizm*, the live album introduces two new tracks, most notably the showstopper "Tyrone," which Badu is said to have improvised during a London show. An audience favorite, the sassy slow-jam soul song is a tirade against an unkind lover who cannot seem to find quality time for his mate. "I just want it to be you and me / Like it used to be, baby / But you don't know how to act," Badu sings, suggesting her time-pressed beau call his friend Tyrone to help him collect his possessions—but not on her phone.

Paying homage to her idols, Badu also covers classic soul songs by Roy Ayers ("Searching") and Rufus and Chaka Khan ("Stay") on the album, which again mixes her earthy, conscious attitude with a streetwise flair. In addition to solid sales, Badu reaped critical awards in 1998, taking home honors at the American Music Awards, the Soul Train Lady of Soul Awards, the NAACP Image Awards, Soul Train Music Awards, and the Grammys.

Badu's versatility allowed her to tour with both hardcore hip-hop group the Wu-Tang Clan and the female-centric Lilith Fair. Badu also filmed a cameo for *Blues Brothers 2000* and a well-received supporting part in the film *The Cider House Rules*. In early 2000, Badu won another Grammy for her collaboration with the Roots on their song, "You Got Me."

While appearing as a guest on a host of albums from rap artists (Guru, Outkast, Rahzel, the Roots), Badu continued work on her second studio effort, *Mama's Gun* (2000). The album is an artistic leap for Badu, retaining her jazzy, soulful flavor while incorporating elements of hard-edge funk and psychedelic rock on songs such as the album opener, "Penitentiary Philosophy." With credits that read like a who's who of neo-soul, *Mama's Gun* finds Badu weaving her tales of self-reliance and strength with a more clear-eyed view of the world. "If you're looking for a free ride, you better run chile / Or you sure won't get too far/ You'd better dance a dance / To make the rain come down/ If you want to be a star," she sings on the bouncy jazz/soul song "My Life." The album's full, vivid funk sound is enriched further by the presence of the legendary jazz vibraphone player Roy Ayers and the jazz trumpeter Roy Hargrove, who plays on the slinky homage to Badu's sexual wiles, "Booty."

From the 1990s and into the new millennium, Erykah Badu was instrumental in sparking a renewed interest in introspective, socially conscious soul music.

SELECTIVE DISCOGRAPHY: *Baduizm* (Kedar/Universal, 1997); *Live* (Kedar/Universal, 1997); *Mama's Gun* (Motown, 2000).

SELECTIVE FILMOGRAPHY: *The Cider House Rules* (1999).

GIL KAUFMAN

ANITA BAKER

Born: Toledo, Ohio, 20 December 1957

Genre: R&B, Pop

Best-selling album since 1990: *Rhythm of Love* (1994)

Hit songs since 1990: "Body & Soul," "I Apologize"

One of the most successful rhythm and blues performers of the 1980s and early 1990s, Anita Baker excelled at what the Washington, D.C., disc jockey Melvin Lindsey termed "quiet storm," a style of music that creates a romantic mood through lush instrumentation and smooth vocalizing. More than any other popular performer of the era, Baker brought a jazz music sensibility to her work, claiming as her inspiration great jazz vocalists such as Billie Holiday and Sarah Vaughan.

Born in Toledo but raised in Detroit, Baker was singing in a local Baptist church choir by age twelve, and in her late teens she joined the Detroit rhythm and blues band Chapter 8. After several small hits with Chapter 8, Baker left the music business for the security of a nine-to-five job, but by 1982 she was working her way back into the industry as a solo artist. Her first solo album, *The Songstress* (1983), brought her some attention, but it was her second album, *Rapture* (1986), that made her a household name. *Rapture* is different from other rhythm and blues recordings of the 1980s in eschewing a synthesizer-based sound in favor of more traditional instrumentation such as guitar, saxophone, and drums. *Rapture's* most distinctive feature, however, was Baker's voice: rich, deep, and creamy, it recalled Sarah Vaughan but also had a contemporary, urban edge. The album sold 6 million copies in the United States and won a Grammy for Best R&B Female Performance in 1987.

In 1990 Baker released *Compositions*, an ambitious, personal album that featured five of her own compositions. Stylistically, *Compositions* is similar to Baker's previous work, but unfortunately the material is not as melodic or distinctive as anything on *Rapture*, and sales were disappointing. Her next album, *Rhythm of Love* (1994), contained more of Baker's own material as well as updated versions of older, "standard" songs such as "My Funny Valentine" and "The Look of Love." By this time critics were beginning to complain of overstylization in Baker's vocals. The writer Goeffrey Himes claimed that "*Rhythm of Love* . . . is so embellished with slides, moans and trills it's often difficult to find the songs underneath it all." Others felt that, given Baker's remarkable voice, she should move away from the mainstream and record jazz music instead.

Baker herself was getting tired of the fast-paced music industry and decided to take time off to raise a family. After suffering several miscarriages, she gave birth to healthy sons in 1993 and 1994, settling down into home life with her husband in the Detroit suburb of Grosse Pointe. In 2000 she signed with Atlantic Records and began work on a new album but wound up in an extended lawsuit, claiming the recording equipment had been defective and the tapes therefore unusable. In 2002 Baker announced plans to return to recording, launching a concert tour in December of that year and promising a new album in 2003.

Anita Baker's relaxed, fluid, and engaging style made her a pioneer of contemporary rhythm and blues and a profound influence on younger performers such as Toni Braxton. Her best music flows with the creativity of one who understands the subtle art of vocalizing and links Baker with a long line of legendary singers.

SELECTIVE DISCOGRAPHY: *The Songstress* (Beverly Glen Music, 1983); *Rapture* (Elektra, 1986); *Givin' You the Best That I Got* (Elektra, 1988); *Compositions* (Elektra, 1990); *Rhythm of Love* (Elektra, 1994).

BIBLIOGRAPHY: Nathan, D., *The Soulful Divas* (New York, 1999).

DAVID FREELAND

BUJU BANTON

Born: Mark Anthony Myrie; Kingston, Jamaica, 15 July 1973

Genre: World, Reggae

Best-selling album since 1990: *Voice of Jamaica* (1992)

Hit songs since 1990: "Murderer"

Rude boy reggae singer/songwriter, the youngest of fifteen siblings raised in a slum, Buju Banton managed a 180-degree turnaround in social attitudes over his decade-long career. From the scandal he caused at age nineteen, calling in his song "Boom Boom Bye Bye" (1992) for violence and death to be reigned upon Jamaica's homosexuals, Banton has become a spokesperson for AIDS education, composer of the first Jamaican song advocating condom use, and advocate of religion.

The parents of Mark Myrie (as Banton was named at birth) were impoverished street vendors, but claimed direct descent from the Maroons, Jamaican blacks who carried on a long fight against the colonizing British for freedom and independence. Mark Myrie's nickname "Buju" means breadfruit; it refers both to his baby fat and the weight of his patrimony. He took the name Banton, a word for a skilled dancehall storyteller, from Burro Banton, another dancehall performer he admired. At age thirteen Banton wielded a mike behind a dancehall sound system, and he began recording thereafter, starting with "The Ruler" (1986). Even then his hoary voice belied his youth, and he had a wild, wooly nihilism to match them both. His album *Mr. Mention* (1991) broke all Jamaican sales records, including those set by famous Jamaican singer Bob Marley.

Banton's conversion to greater tolerance and social consciousness has been gradual, and while it was surely the wise, if not necessary, response to the outpouring of criticism leveled at him for "Boom Boom Bye Bye," he appears to be genuine in his commitment to a shift of position. That most offending song, upon its release, was just another in his series of harshly worded, sexually explicit, and provocative songs such as "Bogle," "Love Me Browning," "Love Black Woman," and "Big It Up," all co-written with his then-engineer/producer, David Kelly. Raw language delivered with breathless articulation over nonstop reggae beats advanced Banton to the head of his dance floor class.

However, protests from gay organizations in the United States and tourist boards throughout the Caribbean islands resulted in Mercury Records asking its artist to write a statement about the song. He did so, but justified his antigay sentiments with reference to the Bible and his religious beliefs.

Banton evidently rethought his readings and conclusions following the incident. He became a Rastafarian and subsequently his lyrics exhibited more interest in love than sex, more generosity and consideration behind his positions, and concrete devotion to his causes. For instance, proceeds from his pro-condom song "Willy (Don't Be Silly)" from his album *Voice of Jamaica* (1993) were donated to fund his Project Willy, created to help AIDS-afflicted children.

Banton's subject matter and his music have both matured. On "Murderer" he delivers an unflinching dia-

tribe against exploitive and destructive elements of dancehall culture as exemplified in the shooting deaths of two aspiring reggae performers. The song reached the top of the charts in Jamaica; its success inspired imitation, and may have influenced some DJs to stop playing gun-happy songs. His mixes are complex, often pitting his hoarse gargle against lighter, more melodic male voices. *'Til Shiloh* (1995) shook up the assumptions of the dancehall genre, formerly an exclusively synthesized and computer-generated music, by returning to the use of a live-in-the-studio band with horn section. Banton's success is not confined to Jamaica; *'Til Shiloh* was cited as one of the Top 20 albums of the year by *Spin* magazine, and Banton is reputed to be the first dancehall DJ to sell out New York City's 5,600-seat Paramount Theater.

Banton consciously courts a crossover audience. On *Unchained Spirit* (2003) he ventures beyond his dancehall purview to sing ska, gospel, soul, and African highlife-inspired tunes, with guests including his reggae rival Luciano and punk rockers Rancid.

SELECTIVE DISCOGRAPHY: *Mr. Mention* (Penthouse, 1992); *Voice of Jamaica* (Mercury, 1993); *'Til Shiloh* (Loos Cannon, 1995); *Inna Heights* (Loos Cannon, 1997); *Rudeboys Inna Ghetto* (Jamaican Vibes, 2000); *Dubbing with the Banton* (Germaine, 2000); *'Til Shiloh* [Expanded] (Universal, 2002); *The Voice of Jamaica* [Expanded] (Universal, 2002); *Want It* (NYC Music, 2002); *Friends for Life* (Atlantic, 2003); *Unchained Spirit* (Epitaph/Anti-Gravity, 2003).

WEBSITE: www.bujubanton.net/biography.html.

HOWARD MANDEL

BARENAKED LADIES

Formed: 1988 in Scarborough, Ontario

Members: Jim Creeggan, bass (born Canada, 12 February 1970); Kevin Hearn, keyboards; Steve Page, vocals/guitar (born Scarborough, Canada, 22 June 1970); Ed Robertson, guitar/vocals (born Scarborough, Canada, 25 October 1970); Tyler Stewart, drums (born Canada, 21 September 1967).

Genre: Rock

Best-selling album since 1990: *Stunt* (1998)

Hit songs since 1990: "Brian Wilson," "One Week," "Pinch Me"

The erudite Barenaked Ladies appeal to fans who think lyrics are just as important as music. Not affecting a punk pose, the group used gentle humor to sing about growing pains and middle-class ennui.

Barenaked Ladies. L-R: Tyler Stewart, Jim Creeggan, Steve Page, Ed Robertson, Kevin Hearn [PAUL NATKIN/PHOTO RESERVE]

The lead vocalist, Steve Page, came from a music-business family—his father was a concert promoter and owned a publishing company. He and Robertson were childhood friends who had played together in a Rush cover band. The duo recorded the Barenaked Ladies's first cassette, *Buck Naked* (1989), and went on tour with the Canadian alternative act Corky and the Juice Pigs. The duo added the Creeggan brothers Andy and Jim for *Barenaked Lunch* (1990) and completed their lineup with the addition of Steward for *The Yellow Tape* (1991).

The latter cassette's release gained notoriety that year when the Toronto mayor, June Rowlands, denied the band permission to play at the city-owned Nathan Phillips Square because she considered the band's name sexist. *The Yellow Tape* went on to go gold in Canada, with sales reaching 85,000 there. The following year Sire Records signed the band on the steps of Toronto's City Hall in a publicity stunt that tweaked Rowlands's stance.

The group's major-label debut, *Gordon* (1992), showcases the band's wit and gentle irony. Page and Robert-son contributed the bulk of the songwriting. The album included "Brian Wilson," "Be My Yoko Ono," and "If I Had $1,000,000," favorites from *The Yellow Tape*. Relying heavily on the folk-rock instrumentation of acoustic guitar and fretless bass, *Gordon* produced a campfire, sing-along vibe. The uptempo "Brian Wilson" muses on whether listening to the Beach Boys's experimental *Smiley Smile* would be any more mind-opening than Wilson's infamous treatment by his psychologist, Eugene Landy. The slightly corny "If I Had $1,000,000" became a live spectacle, with Page thinking up ridiculously childish ways of spending the fortune: "But we would eat Kraft dinner / Of course we would, we'd just eat more. And buy really expensive ketchups with it." Live, fans would shower the band with uncooked macaroni upon hearing that line. *Gordon* went on to sell over 1 million copies in Canada.

The group signed a management contract with Terry McBride of the renowned Nettwerk management group. McBride worried about the group's flakiness. The members wore plaid pants and suspenders and looked a little too much like a novelty group. Noting that few novelty acts enjoy long careers, he convinced the group to dress more conservatively and showcase their considerable instrumental and songwriting talent. He also convinced the band to start touring in the United States, even though it meant giving up lucrative gigs in front of loyal Canadian fans.

The work bore fruit slowly. While *Gordon* was a Canada-only phenomenon, the follow-up album, *Maybe You Should Drive* (1994), showed a glint of U.S. success, peaking at number 175 on the *Billboard* 200. More musically colorful than its predecessor, *Maybe* incorporated touches of soulful organ and jazzy chords. It was produced by Ben Mink, known for his work with k.d. lang. "A" spoofs the children's alphabet game of "A is for apple, B is for book . . ." by endlessly riffing on the letter A, incorporating ever-sillier puns and topical references. However, most of the material is more serious than that on *Gordon*. The midtempo rocker "Jane," with its three-part harmonies, wistfully eulogizes a relationship with a woman who's constantly fending off suitors.

The group got a mainstream boost in 1995, when its "Shoe Box" was included on the soundtrack to the hit NBC sitcom *Friends*. Andy Creeggan left the band to return to college and was replaced by Kevin Hearn, of Corky and the Juice Pigs.

Barenaked Ladies self-produced the album *Born on a Pirate Ship* (1996); U.S. sales continued a slow climb—the album peaked at number 111. Another album with more serious themes, it features "When I Fall," which empathizes with the fears of a skyscraper window-washer. The country-influenced "Straw Hat and Old Dirty Hank" tells a dark tale of a farmer driven to controlling rage. The CD was one of the first to double as a CD-ROM with multimedia content. It is also one of the first whose lyrics mention the Internet.

The band reprised its best material from its last three albums for the live set *Rock Spectacle* (1996), the group's first to be certified gold in the United States. The disc conforms to McBride's desire to showcase the group as an instrumental powerhouse, minus the members' improvised banter. It contains the definitive version of "Brian Wilson" and "The Old Apartment," which became the group's first two singles on the Hot 100. The *Beverly Hills 90210* star and Barenaked booster Jason Priestley directed the video for "The Old Apartment."

As the group wrapped up *Stunt* (1998), Hearn was diagnosed with leukemia. After six months of treatment, he made a complete recovery. The album features a bigger, more electric sound that finally got the group noticed on Top-40 radio, even though it turned out to be a novelty tune, the free-association "One Week," that really

Spot Light | "One Week"

Stars in their native Canada since 1991, the Barenaked Ladies seemed destined to appreciation in the United States only by a few college-music connoisseurs, the kind of smart, earnest fans who would like They Might Be Giants or Rusted Root. But these intellectual, aw-shucks musicians found their way to hipsters' hearts in 1998 with the left-field single "One Week." Brimming with pop culture references, the song features Jim Creeggan's monotone, ragamuffin-inspired rap. Though almost impossible to follow in real-time, the tongue-twisting song sends shouts out to Harrison Ford and his movie *Frantic*, the country-pop singer LeAnn Rimes, and even the 1960s orchestra leader Bert Kaempfert. Then, in another stylistic departure for the theretofore low-key band, the chorus plunges into hard-rock bombast and knowing musings about the stubborn predictability of a squabbling couple. The song's sunny disposition and topical references were perfect for a year that saw a booming economy and a news media fixated on Monica Lewinsky. "One Week" made it all the way to number one on the *Billboard* Hot 100. In a self-deprecating nod to the song's mention of TV drama *The X Files,* one of the show's stars, David Duchovny, sang backing vocals during the band's 1999 appearance on *The Tonight Show with Jay Leno.*

broke barriers and soared to number one on the Hot 100. Something about the pop-culture references, the ragamuffin melody, and the hard-rock chorus connected with mainstream America. In a self-deprecating nod to the song's reference to the TV drama *The X Files,* the show's costar David Duchovny sang backing vocals during the band's 1999 appearance on *The Tonight Show with Jay Leno.* The second single, "It's All Been Done," is also among the group's best material, boasting more muscular guitar than previous efforts and a sunny 1960s Motown rhythm. But despite the doors opened by "One Week," the song peaked at number forty-four. Some wondered if McBride's misgivings about the dreaded novelty connection were all too prescient. However, the album was easily the band's greatest commercial success, selling more than 4 million copies in the Unites States.

The band appeared in the Priestley-directed documentary *Barenaked in America* (1999), which chronicles its tour in support of the album *Stunt*. The good-natured film portrays the members as courteous, ordinary guys, the antithesis of stereotypical rock stars. The same year, Toronto finally gave the group their due with a presentation of the keys to the city.

For once in the band's history, commercial expectations were high. *Maroon* (2000) did not match *Stunt*, only reaching the 1 million mark in the United States, but it did overcome the novelty jinx once and for all, with the single "Pinch Me" making number fifteen on the Hot 100. The respected rock/blues producer Don Was came on board, determined to highlight the band's increasingly soulful percussion and bass. He was reportedly still frustrated that his own late-1980s funk-rock project, Was (Not Was), did not get taken seriously because of tunes like "Walk the Dinosaur" and "I Feel Better Than James Brown." With the subsequent singles "Too Little Too Late" and "Falling for the First Time" offering ambivalent takes on romance, the group became a staple at adult Top 40 radio.

Hosting the 2002 Juno Awards, Canada's equivalent of the Grammys, the group returned to their roots as a skit-based music-and-comedy revue.

Although they earned nearly overnight fame in Canada, the Barenaked Ladies persisted on a long mission to bring smart rock lyrics and self-deprecation to the American airwaves. They found plenty of followers among Gen Xers alienated by sullen hip-hop stars but by no means ready to accept adult contemporary pop.

SELECTIVE DISCOGRAPHY: *Gordon* (Sire, 1992); *Maybe You Should Drive* (Sire/Reprise, 1994); *Born on a Pirate Ship* (Reprise, 1995); *Rock Spectacle* (Reprise, 1996); *Stunt* (Reprise, 1998); *Maroon* (Reprise, 2000).

RAMIRO BURR

CECILIA BARTOLI

Born: Rome, Italy, 4 June 1966
Genre: Classical

One of the most popular mezzo-sopranos to have emerged in the 1990s, Cecilia Bartoli has a brilliant vocal technique and radiant personality that have propelled her to international renown as an accomplished recitalist and opera singer. Nevertheless, her career is considered unconventional by traditional diva standards.

Born in Rome, Italy, to a family of professional singers, Bartoli was coached by her mother and father while getting her musical training at the Conservatorio di Santa Cecilia. She made her first opera appearance at the age of nine as a shepherd boy in a production of *Tosca* in Rome.

At nineteen she was spotted by conductor Riccardo Muti on an Italian TV talent show and offered an audition at La Scala. Herbert von Karajan invited her to sing at the 1990 Salzburg Festival (he died before the concert could take place), and Daniel Barenboim saw her performing in a tribute to Maria Callas on French television. The meeting with Barenboim led to an important collaboration with Barenboim and the conductor Nikolaus Harnoncourt that focused on Mozart.

Known as an immaculate interpreter of Mozart and Rossini, Bartoli is also renowned for her performances of Cherubino (with Harnoncourt at the Zurich Opera), Zerlina (with Muti at La Scala and Barenboim at the Salzburg Festival), Cenerentola (with Chailly at the Bologna Opera and Houston Grand Opera), Despina (with Muti at the Vienna Opera and Levine at the Metropolitan Opera in New York City).

Though she made a name for herself singing Mozart and Rossini, she has a passion for music of the eighteenth century and earlier and has actively explored the music of Pergolesi, Vivaldi, Gluck, and Monteverdi. Her interest in the repertoire has resulted in the rediscovery of a number of neglected pieces. It is a repertoire that suits the size of her voice and her formidable vocal technique, but not one that fits the meatier expectations of the full-fledged diva.

Although blessed with both an agile voice and a commanding presence, she is not so well suited temperamentally and vocally for bigger dramatic operatic roles. Indeed, she is at her best in operas that feature ensemble casts rather than big star roles.

Singing opera is not the major focus of Bartoli's career, in fact. She appears in only a few productions a year. She is a busy recitalist and has collaborated with numerous partners, including Barenboim, Adras Schiff, Jean-Yves Thibaudet, Myung-Wha Chung, and James Levine. Her interest in Early Music has led to collaborations with some of the world's leading period instrument ensembles and Early Music specialists, including Les Art Florrissants, the Orchestra of the Age of Enlightenment, Concentus Musicus Wien, and others.

Bartoli won four Grammy awards for Best Vocal Performance—in 1993, 1997, 2000, and 2001. Her recordings were among the best-selling in classical music during the 1990s. At one point five of her recordings appeared on *Billboard*'s top-fifteen classical recordings chart at one time.

SELECTIVE DISCOGRAPHY: *Cecilia Bartoli: A Portrait* (Polygram, 1995); *Cecilia Bartoli—An Italian*

Songbook (Bellini, Donizetti, Rossini) (Polygram, 1997); *Cecilia Bartoli—The Vivaldi Album, with Il Giradino Armonico* (Polygram, 1999).

BIBLIOGRAPHY: M. Hoelterhoff, *Cinderella and Company: Backstage at the Opera with Cecilia Bartoli* (New York, 1999).

DOUGLAS MCLENNAN

KATHLEEN BATTLE

Born: Portsmouth, Ohio, 8 August 1948

Genre: Classical

Best-selling album since 1990: *Baroque Duet* (1992)

Kathleen Battle emerged from humble beginnings to become a world-renowned opera diva. Once regarded as the most promising lyric soprano in the world, her erratic behavior in the later periods of her career cast a shadow over what she had previously accomplished. However, she continues to attract a large concert and recital audience with her ample classical abilities, and through her performances of spirituals and jazz works.

Battle grew up as the youngest of seven children in Portsmouth, Ohio. Her father was a steel worker who sang in a gospel group and her mother introduced the children to spiritual music through the Methodist Church. Although her extraordinary vocal gift was recognized and developed during her youth, Battle decided to attend the University of Cincinnati to major in mathematics. However, she graduated with a master's degree in music education in 1971 and afterward taught sixth grade in Cincinnati's gritty inner city. She also auditioned for classical singing roles and the heralded conductor, Thomas Schippers, selected Battle to perform Brahms's "Requiem" at the Spoleto Festival in Italy. Following excellent reviews, Battle began getting opera roles at the best houses in the world and her career rose fast. She managed a wide range of classical music and was especially noted for her roles in Mozart and Strauss operas. Battle's debut with the New York City Opera came in 1976 and two years later conductor James Levine brought her to the New York Metropolitan Opera where she went on to play numerous leading roles until her abrupt dismissal from the venerated opera institution on February 7, 1994.

As her career progressed the tales of her abusive treatment of fellow cast members, sporadic rehearsal attendance, and unreasonable demands became legendary opera gossip fodder. After her dismissal from the Met, Battle found it difficult to get work in any of the world's major opera houses and her career depreciated to mostly recitals and concerts. She was no longer the critic's dar-

ling by any stretch; however, her public audience was larger than ever.

Battle's uniquely high voice is regarded for its striking charisma, pure timbre, and superior technical edge. While not considered strong by opera standards, it is genuine and aided by her acting skills and strong physical presence. Battle's numerous recordings have documented her busy schedule of opera and concert performances and she has released eleven albums since 1991.

Battle recorded the works of Bach, Handel, Scarlatti, and other baroque composers in collaboration with trumpet genius Wynton Marsalis in the popular *Baroque Duet* (1992). The results are spectacular as Marsalis's horn skills perfectly complement Battle's incredible artistry. A documentary film on the recording of this album produced by the Public Broadcasting Channel won her an Emmy Award for Outstanding Individual Achievement in a Classical Program on Television in the USA. Battle followed with a much anticipated crossover album of jazz and spirituals, *So Many Stars* (1995), in which she recorded with distinguished jazz artists Grover Washington Jr. and Cyrus Chestnut. She continued the crossover with classical guitar virtuoso, Christopher Parkening, in an intimate collection of Christmas and rarely heard folk songs titled *Angels' Glory* (1996). In 2002 she released *Classic Kathleen Battle: A Portrait*. This compilation album features some baroque favorites in addition to spiritual and ethnic folk songs that she has enjoyed singing through the years. The album contains four previously unreleased selections including her rendering of Puccini's "Omio bibbino Caro" and Duke Ellington's "Prelude to a Kiss."

Battle has been awarded five Grammy Awards and has been the recipient of honorary degrees from six major American colleges. In 1999 Battle was inducted into the NAACP (National Association for the Advancement of Colored People) Image Award Hall of Fame for her remarkable achievements as an African-American woman.

Although Battle's perfectionist ways altered her opera career, she remains vastly popular throughout the world for her pure voice and distinctive style.

SELECTIVE DISCOGRAPHY: *Kathleen Battle Sings Mozart* (Sony, 1990); *Baroque Duet* (Sony, 1992); *Kathleen Battle at Carnegie Hall* (Sony 1992); *Bel Canto* (Sony, 1993); *Kathleen Battle in Concert* (Sony, 1995); *Battle amd Domingo Live* (Sony, 1995); *French Opera Arias* (Sony, 1996); *Angels' Glory* (Sony, 1996); *Grace* (Sony, 1997); *Classic Kathleen Battle: A Portrait* (Sony, 2002).

DONALD LOWE

BEASTIE BOYS

Formed: 1981, New York, New York

Members: Michael Diamond/Mike D, lead rapper, drums (born New York, New York, 20 November 1965); Adam Horovitz/King Ad-Rock, lead rapper, guitar (born New York, New York, 31 October 1966); Adam Yauch/MCA, lead rapper, bass (born Brooklyn, New York, 15 August 1967).

Genre: Rap, Alternative Rock

Best-selling album since 1990: *Ill Communication* (1994)

Hits songs since 1990: "So What'cha Want," "Sabotage"

The Beastie Boys proved to be the most unlikely force in pop culture twice in their relatively sprawling career. Originally, they were the first white rap group of note, and for a period, regardless of their race, the most popular and controversial. The second time around, they reinvented themselves as the soul of genre-bending mid-1990s pop. Their chart presence seemed all but depleted at the start of the 1990s, the result of a backlash against their explosive popularity and drunken frat boy antics. Then seemingly out of nowhere, they re-emerged as a more sensitive and organic band with the release of their third album, *Check Your Head* (1992). They brought together an audience that liked hip-hop just as much as rock, and dabbled in disco kitsch to kick-start the 1990s fascination with the 1970s. This potent mixture made the group party favorites once again, but with a new social conscience that brought politics to the mainstream in an otherwise apathetic decade.

Rock to Rap to Riches

The Beastie Boys grew up in middle-class New York families, and like other kids of their age and class, they immersed themselves in the city's eclectic underground music scene. Diamond and Yauch formed the Beastie Boys as a hardcore punk band in 1981, and released *Polly Wog Stew* (1982) before Horovitz joined the band the following year. Exhibiting an early knack for absorbing influences, the band released the rap-inflected *Cooky Puss* in 1983, which caused a minor stir in the downtown scene. As a result, the band decided to shift gears and concentrate on the hip-hop sound. They attracted the attention of Def Jam Records founder Rick Rubin, who signed them to the label and produced their first notable single, "She's on It" (1985). The single solidified their high-concept sound and image: prankster rappers, who combined the beats and rhyming of hip-hop with the heavy metal guitars of white suburbia.

Beastie Boys. L-R: King Ad-Rock (Adam Horovitz), Mike D (Michael Diamond), MCA (Adam Yauch) [PAUL NATKIN/PHOTO RESERVE]

After tour stints opening for Madonna and Run-D.M.C., the Beastie Boys were unleashed on an unsuspecting mainstream with the release of *Licensed to Ill* (1986), which quickly became the best-selling album in rap history. The record features witty raps that satirize frat boys and B-boys alike, all set to Rubin's hard-rocking beats. Sales were driven largely by the single "Fight for Your Right (to Party)," a knuckleheaded anthem driven by crude raps and blaring guitars. The irony of their music was largely lost on their audience, who simply found it great to get drunk and party to. The Beastie Boys responded by becoming the kind of people they set out to mock, mounting a tour that celebrated rock star excess and gross behavior. They were attacked from all sides, accused of demeaning women, corrupting youth, and lampooning black culture. By the time the tour ended, the band was burned out, and retreated from public view.

The New Style

Over the next two years, the group seemed to further self-destruct; in actuality, they began laying the groundwork for their return to mass appeal. First, they split with

Def Jam after a feud with Rubin. Then they signed to Capitol Records and released *Paul's Boutique* (1989), a sprawling album built on the inventive sampling strategy of their new production team, the Dust Brothers. Their fan base balked at the album's sophisticated collage of old-school funk and psychedelia, and the more subtle (but no less comic) raps, which lacked the shock value of *Licensed to Ill*. The album failed commercially, but its sonic template proved to be wildly influential—the Dust Brothers went on to produce best-selling albums for Beck, White Zombie, and the Rolling Stones.

In 1992 the Beastie Boys returned to prominence with *Check Your Head*, a loose and diverse album that saw them combining the wild sampling of *Paul's Boutique* with live instrumentation. In the three years since its release, *Paul's Boutique* had found favor with hipsters and college radio DJs, and the Beastie Boys were suddenly hip, not merely popular. Their new image reflected their move to California, complete with 1970s-inspired clothing and a new commitment to women's rights and Buddhist spirituality. Their music was similarly inspired, running the gamut from party funk to old school rap to classic rock and hardcore punk. *Check Your Head* has something for everyone, all filtered through the Beastie Boys's come-one-come-all party aesthetic. This egalitarian attitude is the glue that holds together its wildly eclectic tracks; thus, the old school thump of "Pass the Mic" flows seamlessly into the Zeppelin-esque rock of "Gratitude." "So What'cha Want" emerges as the definitive track, with the fuzz-distorted Boys rapping goofily over a primal arena-rock drumbeat, and jittery scratches and horn samples providing irresistible texture. *Check Your Head* is at once catchy and soul stirring, and paved the way for genre-straddling hitmakers like Beck, Kid Rock, and Rage Against the Machine.

The group followed up *Check Your Head* with the similarly paced *Ill Communication* (1994). The album debuted at number one on the strength of the single "Sabotage," an infectious rock workout that features the muscular guitar and manic vocals of Ad Rock. The Spike Jonze-directed video for the song, which features the Boys mocking the testosterone-fueled cop shows of the 1970s, proved to be just as popular. The album, by comparison, feels a little too comfortable, especially after the freshness of *Paul's Boutique* and *Check Your Head*, but it is just as catchy and worthy in its own right. "Sure Shot" kicks off the album with a slinky flute sample, and includes an apology by MCA for the boorish behavior of their past: "I gotta say a little something that's long overdue / The disrespect to women has got to be through." The raps and backing tracks are more refined, deeper, and less amateurish than those on *Check Your Head*. They offer classic Beastie humor and weirdness on "B-Boys Makin' with the Freak Freak," and hold their own with the legendary rapper Q-Tip on the hard-bouncing "Root Down."

Spot Light | The Tibetan Freedom Concerts

Despite its classification as an angry youth movement and its punk/independent rock pedigree, the alternative music explosion of the early 1990s was strangely apolitical. The Beastie Boys attempted to correct this by raising awareness of political and social issues at their shows and through their *Grand Royal* magazine. Their most enduring political act came in 1996 with the massive Tibetan Freedom Concert benefit. Buddhism convert Adam "MCA" Yauch co-founded the Milarepa Fund, a charity devoted to supporting Tibetan liberation from Chinese rule, after witnessing the plight of Tibetan Buddhists firsthand while traveling in the country. The first festival, held in San Francisco on June 15 and 16, 1996, raised funds for the charity, and attracted the participation of wildly diverse acts like De La Soul, Pavement, Sonic Youth, and the Fugees. Concerts in Washington, D.C., and New York followed in subsequent years, culminating with a worldwide event that took place in Chicago, Amsterdam, Tokyo, and Sydney on June 12 and 13, 1999. The concerts raised millions of dollars for the Tibetan cause and treated hundreds of thousands of music fans to the best in forward-thinking pop, rock, and hip-hop. The fifth Freedom Concert never got off the ground, but the Milarepa Fund remained active, most notably organizing the New Yorkers against Violence benefit in the wake of the September 11, 2001 attacks. Yauch continues to work closely with the organization, helping to spread their nonviolence ethos throughout the world.

The Beastie Boys spent the next few years working on side projects and touring, including a headlining stint on the fourth Lollapalooza festival. They earned a reputation as a hard-working live unit, playing their instruments and commanding the stage like true professionals, effectively erasing the memory of their mid-1980s booze-fueled antics. They released a mini-album of hardcore tunes titled *Aglio e Olio* (1995), and a collection of their funk-jazz instrumental tracks, *The In Sound from Way Out!* (1996). They expanded the operation of their record label and magazine, both named Grand Royal. In addition, MCA dedicated himself to the plight of Tibetan Monks, and organized a yearly concert event, the Tibetan Freedom Concert, to raise money and awareness. Throughout their performances, the band spoke about international events and injustice, and encouraged their fans to get involved with causes ranging from Greenpeace to the anti-death penalty movement. The band attempted to bring issues to their audience in a nondidactic way, avoiding the earth-saving earnestness associated with the bands U2 and Rage Against the Machine. In this way, their messages did not obscure the music, and they effectively chipped away at the political apathy of their audience.

In 1998 the band released their fifth album, *Hello Nasty*. After a split with their longtime disc jockey Hurricane, the band hired Mixmaster Mike of the techno-"turntablist" crew Invisibl Scratch Piklz to refine their sound. The result is an album steeped in the electronic grooves of the 1980s, effectively returning the group to the sounds that prompted their move into hip-hop. The songs reflect this new energy, with the Boys dropping their expert rhymes over supercharged rhythms. "Intergalactic" sets the tone; the Boys's complicated three-part flow coasts on a lock-step backing track. The album evokes video games, old school style, and the giddy thrill of hearing the simple yet futuristic beats of rap for the first time. "Body Movin'" is a classic Beasties rump shaker, and "Three MC's and One DJ" proclaims their ongoing mission to rock the party with class and style. *Hello Nasty* may not be as outwardly manic as earlier, but it shows the Beastie Boys aging gracefully, and keeping their forward-looking souls intact.

The Beastie Boys continue to perform with integrity and enthusiasm. Despite their seemingly condemnable beginning, they have revealed themselves to be genuine artists.

SELECTIVE DISCOGRAPHY: *Polly Wog Stew* EP (Southern, 1982); *Cooky Puss* EP (Southern, 1983); *Rock Hard* EP (Def Jam, 1985); *Licensed to Ill* (Def Jam, 1986); *Paul's Boutique* (Capitol, 1989); *Check Your Head* (Grand Royal, 1992); *Some Old Bullshit* (Grand Royal, 1994); *Ill Communication* (Grand Royal, 1994); *Aglio e Olio* EP (Grand Royal, 1995); *The In Sound from Way Out!* (Grand Royal, 1996); *Hello Nasty* (Grand Royal, 1998); *The Sounds of Science* (Grand Royal, 1999).

WEBSITE: www.beastieboys.com.

SEAN CAMERON

THE BEATLES

Formed: 1957, Liverpool, England; Disbanded 1970

Members: George Harold Harrison, lead guitar, vocals (born Liverpool, England, 25 February 1943; died Los Angeles, California, 29 November 2001); John Winston (later changed to Ono) Lennon, rhythm guitar, harmonica, vocals (born Liverpool, England, 9 October 1940; died New York, 8 December 1980); James "Paul" McCartney, bass, vocals (born Liverpool, England, 18 June 1942); Ringo Starr, drums (Richard Starkey Jr., born Dingle, England, 7 July 1940). Former members: Peter "Pete" Best, drums (born Liverpool, England, 24 November 1941); Stuart "Stu" Sutcliffe, bass (Stuart Fergusson Victor Sutcliffe, born Edinburgh, Scotland, 23 June 1940; died Hamburg, West Germany, 10 April 1962).

Genre: Rock, Pop

Best-selling album since 1990: *The Beatles 1* (2000)

Hit songs since 1990: "Free As a Bird," "Real Love"

The Beatles were the most innovative, emulated, and successful music group of the twentieth century. The Beatles set in motion both the creative and marketing paradigms of the modern rock era—through transforming hairstyles and fashion; evolving attitudes about youth, politics, and drug culture; writing their own songs and making the first music videos to accompany them; performing the first arena rock concerts; creating the first unified rock albums alongside hit singles; and being the first rock performers who were truly considered groundbreaking artists in their own time.

British Invasion

In January 1964 New York disc jockeys such as "Murray the K" began playing the Beatles' "I Want to Hold Your Hand" virtually nonstop, introducing it with the cryptic adage, "The Beatles are coming." The record went to number one on the music charts in early February, and a fascination developed for this new "British" sound with its raw energy, wild electric guitars, and syncopated clapping. The next month, on February 7, 1964, a plane carrying the Beatles arrived at New York's Idlewild—soon to be renamed Kennedy—Airport. More than 3,000 screaming fans were there to greet the lads from Liverpool, England, as they got off the plane and waved, quickly to be ushered into a room of waiting reporters and photographers who were assigned to cover what was then negatively referred to as the "British Invasion."

The big news at the time was the group's "mop top" hairstyle. Men's crew cuts were still common and reporters had tremendous difficulty telling one Beatle from the other. Editors thought it was a funny story: the screaming girls, the foreign lads with the insectlike group name, and the long hair. Some forty-eight hours later, 73 million curious television viewers tuned in to Sunday night's *Ed Sullivan Show* to watch the Beatles perform live. The next day there was hardly a teenager in the country who did not want to go out and buy a guitar and scarcely a parent around who was not horrified at the prospect of his or her son emulating, or his or her daughter loving, the Beatles. The phenomenon, pejoratively dubbed "Beatlemania," would only grow and by the time of the group's departure back to England in late February 1964, over 60 percent of all records sold in America were Beatles records.

Liverpool Roots and Early Recordings

The group's roots extend back to the Liverpool of the late 1950s, when then teenagers John Lennon and Paul McCartney had a chance meeting at a church fete. Lennon was performing with his group the Quarrymen and McCartney was brought by a mutual friend to hear them. McCartney loved that Lennon had a band, and Lennon loved that McCartney knew more than three guitar chords. McCartney's younger schoolmate George Harrison was soon recruited as another guitarist, as was Lennon's art college friend Stu Sutcliffe, to play bass. The group broke through the Liverpool club scene and eventually made its way to Hamburg, West Germany, to play clubs there, but not before hiring drummer Pete Best to accompany them. Liverpool record shop owner Brian Epstein was getting orders for a single of "My Bonnie" (1961) that the band had made with British rock pioneer Tony Sheridan and that had charted in West Germany, and decided to check out the Beatles at Liverpool's Cavern Club. Sutcliffe, who never really learned how to play bass, remained in Hamburg, where he later died of a brain hemorrhage related to a head injury; after his departure, McCartney began playing bass. Epstein was charmed by the quartet's charisma, energy, and humor, and took them on as a manager, immediately trading in their leather look for tailored suits and long, thin ties and helping the band to polish its overall presentation.

Epstein secured studio auditions for the Beatles, but these were unsuccessful until the record label EMI decided to sign them in 1962. Comedy and novelty producer George Martin agreed to work with the group, but wanted to use a session drummer rather than Pete Best. The band then fired Best, and Liverpool drummer Ringo Starr of Rory and the Hurricanes was successfully recruited for the spot. As the group began to record, the struggle was on to convince producer Martin that its own material was as good as the cover material it was recording. Martin, for instance, thought that the group's first attempt at a number-one hit should be a song by Mitch Murray called "How Do You Do It" and the Beatles did record that number—it was never released, but did show up on *Anthology 1* (1995)—but the group wanted one of their own songs to be their first big hit. Martin was skeptical, but told them that if they came up with something as good, he would consider it. The number they gave him was "Please, Please Me," which did indeed become the

Beatles's first number one single, and subsequently the title of their first album (1963).

New Material, New Sounds

Martin kept his ears open, and as material warranted inclusion, the number of Beatles originals put to record kept expanding. *A Hard Day's Night* (1964) was the first Beatles album—indeed the first rock album by anyone—to be made up entirely of original compositions. Several had been written for the Beatles's film of the same name, which established the distinctive personalities and offbeat humor of the group in the public consciousness. The field scene of the group horsing around in fast and slow motion to "All My Loving" established a new visual language to accompany rock music that anticipated the heyday of MTV by two decades. For the acoustic ballad "Yesterday" on *Help!* (1965), Martin suggested the use of strings, and an arrangement for string quartet was made. This inaugurated a process in which the group took an unusual interest in the *sound* of its music: a constant drive to come up with new sounds, new textures. An Indian sitar, for instance, dominates "Norwegian Wood (This Bird Has Flown)" on *Rubber Soul* (1966), the Beatles's memorable take on the popular folk rock movement of the time. *Revolver* (1966), which many consider the Beatles's masterpiece, features the melancholic "Eleanor Rigby" accompanied by a bouncy string octet with no Beatles playing whatsoever, while "Got to Get You into My Life" features a soulful brass band; "Tomorrow Never Knows" incorporates the then common technique in avant-garde "serious" music circles of taking recorded bits of random sounds, committing them to tape, and then "looping" the bits of tape together into tape loops that could play the sound at will.

The developing complexity of the Beatles's music made it increasingly difficult for the band to reproduce what it was doing in the studio in live performance. This, combined with the incessant screaming and general chaos that accompanied Beatlemania, made the group give up touring in 1966 after setting box office records everywhere it played. The first Shea Stadium Concert (1965) was not only a record setter, but a prototype of the megaconcert spectaculars that are still commonplace among rock music's biggest acts.

No longer having to worry about reproducing their music live, the Beatles reached a climax in studio creativity with the groundbreaking *Sgt. Pepper's Lonely Hearts Club Band* (1967), which took the drive for new sounds and textures to new heights. Expanding the same recording techniques that had been used on *Rubber Soul* and *Revolver*, *Sgt. Pepper* even incorporated a full orchestra rising to a psychedelic wall of sound in the climax of the urban melodrama "Day in the Life," banned by the BBC (British

Broadcasting Company) because of its supposed drug references. *Sgt. Pepper* ushered in a new era not only for the Beatles, but for popular music in general with its colorful cover, double-sleeve printed song lyrics, and band cut-outs. It was not only the first rock concept album, but also the first rock album that was widely considered to be "art" by those outside the genre.

The Break-Up

The death of Beatles manager Brian Epstein in 1967 was a blow from which the group was never able to recover. Although the band continued to evolve artistically, business concerns that Epstein had always taken care of so efficiently were now left for the four to fight over. By the time of *The Beatles* (1968) double album, which came to be known as the "White Album" because of its plain white cover, the beginning of the end was clearly in sight. The Lennon-McCartney songwriting team was mostly writing apart, and George Harrison's own compositional style had evolved to a point where one or two tracks per album were no longer adequate to contain his talents. The creation of Apple Records, which was so mismanaged that the Beatles began hemorrhaging money, and Lennon's refusal to be anywhere—including Beatles recording sessions—without his future wife Yoko Ono, all added significantly to group tensions.

The low point came in early 1969 with sessions for the film *Let It Be* (1970), which showed the group literally coming apart at the seams. The band came back together that summer to record *Abbey Road* (1969), which turned out to be the last time the group would work together. John Lennon had privately indicated his intention to leave the group, but had hoped that the band members could continue to pool their individual creative efforts as Beatles projects. Without Lennon as a direct collaborator and with the group still unwilling to perform live, McCartney wanted to move on completely, and beat Lennon to the punch in "officially" quitting the group the following spring with the release of his *McCartney* (1970) album. Lennon was livid, as were Harrison and Starr, that the album was released mere weeks before the Beatles' long-dormant *Let It Be* (1970) was due out. Bitter litigation began, which lasted nearly a decade beyond Lennon's 1980 assassination by an obsessed fan outside of his New York apartment, and which effectively prevented any real possibility of a group reunion even while Lennon was still alive.

Compact Disc Configurations, a Reunion, and an Ongoing Feud

One of the burning issues of the 1980s involved deciding in which configurations Beatles albums should be re-released in the then-new compact disc (CD) format. In England, the Beatles had originally released material during the vinyl era on EMI singles, short albums (EPs), and long-playing albums (LPs) that rarely included the same songs. This was a bold move, as it meant that new Beatles albums were not dependent on previously known hit singles, which was in direct opposition to standard industry practice at the time. When the same Beatles piece did appear as a single and an album, the mixes—and sometimes even the takes, solos, or arrangements—would be slightly different. The original American Capitol releases of Beatles material, however, often combined material from singles and albums and sometimes in configurations that, although shorter than the British albums, were often more logically organized. The longer British LP configurations won out in the end, along with leftover single and EP material released as two separate *Past Masters* collections (both 1988). The initial re-release of Beatles albums on CD in the mid- and late 1980s became an event that created booms in the purchase of CD players and helped propel CD sales across the board. Few considered the CD little more than a novelty until the Beatles catalog was finally available in the format.

When Northern Songs, the publishing company that owned the entire Lennon-McCartney song catalog, came up for sale in 1984, McCartney saw a unique opportunity to finally have control over his own music. While he was still attempting to set up a bid with Lennon's widow Yoko Ono, pop icon Michael Jackson made an offer of $47.5 million with the enormous profits from his *Thriller* (1984) album that in effect put him in control of how and when Beatles songs would be used. The result has been an influx of Beatles songs being used for commercial purposes. Although McCartney publicly complains about this, he continues to make a 25 percent profit from the licensing of any Lennon-McCartney song.

The speculation that a Beatles reunion might take place at the group's induction into the Rock and Roll Hall of Fame in 1987 was dashed when McCartney was a conspicuous no-show. Harrison, Starr, Ono, and Lennon's sons, Julian and Sean, accepted the award together, but McCartney issued a statement that said that, with all of the unsettled legal matters that still existed between the surviving Beatles, he thought it would be hypocritical to participate in a "fake reunion."

The soundtrack to the film *Imagine* (1988) included all Lennon-penned Beatles numbers alongside Lennon's best post-Beatles solo material in a move clearly designed by Ono to minimize the McCartney side of the Lennon-McCartney equation. McCartney responded by going out for the first time ever as a solo artist performing McCartney-penned Beatles material live alongside Wings and McCartney solo material on a gargantuan world tour that broke box office records everywhere, and which was subsequently released as a film (*Get Back!*, 1990) and a live

SpotLight | The Beatles Reunion

"There will be no Beatles reunion as long as John Lennon remains dead," read George Harrison's much-publicized statement made in 1990, responding to Paul McCartney's media speculation that the surviving Beatles might get back together. Yet, ironically, it would be Harrison and Lennon's widow, Yoko Ono, who would come up with the means to musically raise Lennon from the dead, so to speak. After Roy Orbison died of a heart attack in 1988, Harrison and fellow Traveling Wilbury band mates Tom Petty, Bob Dylan, and Jeff Lyne investigated using some solo tracks of Orbison's voice to complete a Wilbury album when an even more bizarre idea hit Harrison: to use the voice of Elvis Presley. Presley's estate loved the idea and was willing to allow the Wilburys to strip his voice electronically from some unreleased tracks and have the Wilburys record around it. Presley himself was to have been credited as "Aaron Wilbury." In the end, the band decided it was too gimmicky of an idea, but when Harrison shared the story with Yoko Ono, she indicated that she possessed unreleased Lennon songs that were so bare that they would not

need to be stripped down. In the wake of the phenomenal success of Natalie Cole's "Unforgettable" (1992) duet with her dead father Nat "King" Cole, the option of using Lennon demos that would be reworked by the other Beatles began to take on greater appeal. In February 1994, behind locked doors, McCartney, Harrison, and Ringo Starr—along with the electronic presence of John Lennon—reunited in the studio to record "new" Beatles tracks. The first of these, "Free as a Bird," had its much-anticipated unveiling at the conclusion of the first part of the 1995 prime-time weeklong television airing of *The Beatles Anthology,* the Beatles's own documentary that had been called *The Long and Winding Road* while it was a work in progress for more than two decades. Secrecy was paramount, as screeners and advance releases of *The Beatles Anthology* did not contain the song, which was released as part of *Anthology 1* a few days later and as a single. Another spruced-up Lennon demo, "Real Love," appears at the conclusion of the series and was released on *Anthology 2* (1996) and as a single. All of this was a far cry from the elaborate Beatles reunion that fans and promoters had desperately hoped for throughout the 1970s when Lennon was still alive, but in light of Harrison's death in 2001, it becomes the final chapter of the Fab Four, for better or worse.

---

double album (*Tripping the Live Fantastic*, 1990). All legal matters between the former Beatles having finally been settled after nearly two decades of wrangling, McCartney began speculating during the tour on the possibility of getting the Fab Three back together.

A reunion of sorts did finally occur in the mid-1990s when the surviving Beatles created music "around" some Lennon demos that were released to much anticipation and fanfare as part of *The Beatles Anthology* television documentary miniseries (1995) and the three-volume double CD *Anthology* sets (1995, 1996), which saw the group finally profiting from unreleased material, alternate takes, and demo recordings that had been available in bootleg form for years. A print account of *The Beatles Anthology* appeared just in time for Christmas 2000 and an expanded DVD version appeared in 2003 with unreleased footage of the truncated trio jamming together.

Harrison's death in late 2001—the first Beatle to die of natural causes—was a sobering moment for aging baby boomers. As with Lennon's death in 1980, entire magazines and television specials were devoted to the late Bea-

tle and the Fab Four, and Beatles albums sold out seemingly everywhere. This followed upon the enormous success of *The Beatles 1* (2000), a collection of all of the Beatles's number one hits packaged together, which saw new generations of listeners discovering Beatles music. McCartney's postmillennial contribution to the long-standing Lennon-McCartney feud was to reverse the order of the songwriting credits for nineteen Beatles songs on his *Back in the U.S.* album (2002), from the traditional "Lennon-McCartney" to "Composed by Paul McCartney and John Lennon." In 2003 long-missing stolen tapes from the *Let It Be* sessions were recovered in Holland, revealing a trove of "lost" Beatles performances and uncovering even more group bitterness than the film had. The ongoing interest in this material served as a reminder that nearly four decades after they first appeared on the scene, the public appetite for anything Beatles-related continued to be insatiable.

In 1964 composers Richard Rodgers and Leonard Bernstein were among the few to see the Beatles not merely as captivating performers, but as great songwriters as well.

Though the Lennon-McCartney song catalog is standing the test of time and continues to enchant generations of new listeners with an undiminished freshness, its overwhelming presence set a new standard in pop and rock music by which artists were suddenly expected to write—as well as perform—their own music, for better or worse. The six-year period when the Beatles were at the peak of their powers was one of those rare, brief, and wonderful moments when popular culture and high art converged. Their ultimate influence can be seen in the fact that no subsequent act has even remotely captured the public imagination as the Beatles did, and that the creative and cultural revolution that the group helped launch remains a work in progress.

SELECTIVE DISCOGRAPHY: *Past Masters, Volume One* (Capitol, 1988); *Past Masters, Volume Two* (Capitol, 1988); *Please, Please Me* (Capitol re-release, 1990); *With the Beatles* (Capitol re-release, 1990); *Beatles for Sale* (Capitol re-release, 1990); *Rubber Soul* (Capitol re-release, 1990); *Revolver* (Capitol re-release, 1990); *Sgt. Pepper's Lonely Hearts Club Band* (Capitol re-release, 1990); *Magical Mystery Tour* (Capitol re-release, 1990); *The Beatles* (Capitol re-release, 1990); *Abbey Road* (Capitol re-release, 1990); *Live at the BBC* (Capitol, 1994); *Anthology 1* (Capitol, 1995); *Anthology 2* (Capitol, 1996); *Anthology 3* (Capitol, 1996); *The Beatles 1* (Capitol, 2000). **Soundtracks:** *A Hard Day's Night* (Capitol re-release, 1990); *Help!* (Capitol re-release, 1990); *Let It Be* (Capitol re-release, 1990); *Yellow Submarine* (Capitol re-release, 1999).

BIBLIOGRAPHY: H. Davis, *The Beatles: The Authorized Biography* (New York, 1968); G. Martin with J. Hornsby, *All You Need Is Ears* (New York, 1979); P. Norman, *Shout! The Beatles in Their Generation* (New York, 1981); M. Lewisohn, *The Beatles Live* (New York, 1986); M. Lewisohn, *The Beatles Recording Sessions* (New York, 1988); G. Martin with W. Pearson, *With a Little Help from My Friends: The Making of Sgt. Pepper* (New York, 1995); A. Kozinn, *The Beatles* (New York, 1995); The Beatles, *The Beatles Anthology* (New York, 2000).

WEBSITE: www.thebeatles.com.

DENNIS POLKOW

THE BEAUTIFUL SOUTH

Formed: 1989, Hull, England

Members: Paul Heaton, vocals (born Birkenhead, Merseyside, England, 9 May 1962); David Hemmingway, vocals (born Hull, England, 20 September 1960); David Rotheray, guitar (born Hull, England, 9 February 1963); David Stead, drums (born Huddersfield, West Yorkshire, England, 15 October 1966); Sean Welch, bass (born Enfield, England, 12 April 1965); Briana Corrigan, vocals (born Londonderry, Northern Ireland); Jacqueline Abbot, vocals (born Whiston, Merseyside, England, 10 November 1973).

Genre: Rock

Best-selling album since 1990: *0898 Beautiful South* (1992)

Hit songs since 1990: "You Keep It All In," "A Little Time," "We Are Each Other"

The British independent rock band the Beautiful South formed from the remains of the Housemartins in 1989 after vocalist Paul Heaton and drummer David Hemmingway joined forces. The Beautiful South is known for sophisticated, jazz-pop melodies that serve as a stark and often jarring contrast to their cynical, sly, and at times macabre lyrics. Whereas the Housemartins's wry lyrics and jangly guitars were more closely influenced by the seminal band the Smiths, the Beautiful South took a sophisticated, jazz-pop approach. The band enjoyed far more success and a greater following in their native United Kingdom than in the United States, where they had a mild hit with the song "We Are Each Other," a celebration of partnership.

Heaton and Hemmingway formed the Beautiful South right after the breakup of the Housemartins, one of Britain's most popular guitar-pop bands of the mid-1980s. The duo hired Briana Corrigan, whose crystalline, childlike voice lent an eerie innocence to the band's sound in the early days; bassist Sean Welch; drummer David Stead; and guitarist David Rotheray, who became Heaton's primary collaborator for the new band. Their debut album, *Welcome to the Beautiful South* (1989), brought them moderate success and good reviews; a single from the album, "You Keep It All In," is an upbeat love song addressed to a lover who is not quite emotionally forthcoming. Their next album, *Choke* (1990), features the lovely ballad "A Little Time."

The band's third album, *0898 Beautiful South* (1992), with its slightly macabre illustrations in the lyric booklet, spawned the hit "We Are Each Other," notable for its celebration of the suffocation of a love relationship in lyrics like "Said we'd be close / Said we'd work perfectly/ Said that we'd toast / Beautiful company." The song at times sounds like a joyful tribute to love, but its very title acknowledges the occasionally suffocating qualities of a partnership. Other songs round out the appeal, from the opener, "Old Red Eyes Is Back," a thoughtful but warning look at an old man who probably drinks too much, to the piano- and harmonica-tinged ballad "Something That

You Said," which chronicles the love-hate nature of a destructive relationship. ("The perfect love song has no words / It only has death threats / And you can tell a classic ballad / By how threatening it gets.") These are unlikely themes for a pop album, but the Beautiful South is a band skilled at dressing dispiriting, dark images in a bright palette of chiming guitars and sunny melodies.

A greatest hits collection, *Carry Up on the Charts*, was issued at the end of 1994; it entered the U.K. charts at number one and has since gone platinum several times over. By the middle of the 1990s, the Beautiful South's albums were not consistently released in the United States, leaving devoted fans in search of imports and offering the band scant opportunity to make an impact on American pop music. Despite this contraction of the band's reach, few rivals, whether British or American, can match the Beautiful South's marriage of bitter and sweet in pop music.

SELECTIVE DISCOGRAPHY: *Welcome to the Beautiful South* (Elektra, 1989); *Choke* (Elektra, 1990); *O898 Beautiful South* (Elektra, 1992); *Miaow* (1994); *Carry Up on the Charts* (1995); *Blue Is the Colour* (1996); *Quench* (1998); *Painting It Red* (2000); *Solid Bronze: The Very Best of Beautiful South* (2001).

CARRIE HAVRANEK

BECK

Born: Beck Hansen; Los Angeles, California, 8 July 1970

Genre: Rock

Best-selling album since 1990: *Odelay* (1996)

Hit songs since 1990: "Where It's At," "Devil's Haircut," "New Pollution"

The talented chameleonlike singer/songwriter who calls himself Beck has been keeping his fans and critics guessing ever since the debut of his tongue-in-cheek, catchy, but elusive single "Loser" in 1993. Beck has released a handful of albums in just seven years, each one a cohesive unit but different from the others in scope, genre, inspiration, and tone. Some dismiss his lyrics as nonsensical gibberish, while others detect irony, sarcasm, cynicism, and hope. His multiplatinum-selling album *Odelay!* (1996) brought Beck into the mainstream pop world.

Beck is adept at combining elements of every genre of music that has influenced him into complete songs. He exemplifies the best of the folk tradition because his songs are well-constructed and based on roots music such as blues, jazz, and folk. But what separates Beck is the fear-

lessness with which he blends whatever moves him, whether it is James Brown–influenced soul music, the agile rhymes and rhythms of hip-hop, or the synthetic programming tools that allow him to weave and splice samples, beats, blips, loops, and other noises into postmodern songs in which everything is fodder for inspiration

Musical Background

Born in California, Beck grew up the son of a bluegrass street musician, David Campbell, and an office worker, Bibbe Hansen. He grew up in East Los Angeles, a section of the city known, at the time, for its crime problems. East L.A., however, was fraught with colorful characters and musical influences from all around the world, including Spanish, Caribbean, African, and Mexican. Beck credits his youth in Los Angeles as a huge musical influence. Beck also spent some time living with his grandparents in Kansas as a child and became deeply influenced by church hymns and gospel music; his grandfather was a Presbyterian minister.

At the age of sixteen, after spending most of his teen years working odd jobs, Beck bought a guitar and became a street musician, like his father. He played on the city buses, on the street, and in coffeehouses. He eventually caught the attention of an executive with BMG music, who connected him with Karl Stephenson, a hip-hop producer. The end result was the genre-spanning single "Loser," which put Beck on the map as a quirky new talent. Radio stations were infatuated with the song, and MTV played the video constantly. In the self-deprecating, tongue-in-cheek song, Beck sings half in Spanish and half in English in the refrain, "*Yo soy perdido* / I'm a loser baby / So why don't you kill me?" During the verses he raps over scratchy beats and a repeated acoustic guitar riff. While some critics initially dismissed him as a one-hit wonder, this unusual song barely scratched the surface of his talents. The song's non sequitur lyrics caused some critics to believe they were just random, nonsensical words strung together; others recognize Beck's intent to play with language and create a jumbled, free-form poetry over guitar, drum machines, keyboards, and any other instrument.

From Loser to Multiplatinum Success

With major-label album debut *Mellow Gold* (1994), Beck was poised for an interesting and varied career. *Odelay!* (1996) proved to Beck's skeptics that "Loser" was no accident. Co-produced with the Dust Brothers, well known for their work with hip-hop and electronica artists, nearly every song on *Odelay!* offers something slightly different. With the lead single "Where It's At," which mixes elements of rap, blues, and other musical forms, Beck hit number five on the *Billboard* Modern Rock tracks chart and sixty-one on the *Billboard* Top 100. The song also earned him a Grammy Award for Best Male Rock Vocal Performance (1996). The second single, "Devil's Haircut," with its spy-thriller guitar riff and sped-up, chunky beat-box drum loop in the chorus, is basically a funked-up blues song. No one knows what Beck really means when he says "I've got a devil's haircut / In my mind / got a devil's haircut / in my mind," but what the sound and the imagery together convey is more important than any literal reading of the words. Cribbing from a Rolling Stones tune and creating a loop of the guitar riff gave Beck inspiration for the self-deprecating song "Jack-Ass," in which he sings, "I've been creeping along in the same, stale shoes / Loose ends tying the noose in the back of my mind." Tunes like "Jack-Ass" prove that Beck could be literal and create easily understood metaphors.

After the huge success of *Odelay!*, Beck toured in support of the album and produced an album that was completely different, *Mutations* (1998). He wrote the songs, recorded them quickly, and pointed out in interviews with reporters that it was not an official follow-up but merely something he wanted to do. *Mutations*, with its slow ballads and country waltzes, launched the bossa nova–flavored single "Tropicalia" and achieved platinum status. Beck followed up with *Midnight Vultures* (1999), which borrows heavily from soul and funk. With Beck having covered just about every genre, critics wondered if he could keep up the impressive and exhaustive pace.

A Change of Pace

Following his breakup with his longtime girlfriend, Leigh Limon, Beck released the somber, beautiful, and introspective album *Sea Change* (2002), a musical diary of a journey through heartbreak. A mostly acoustic affair, with sad, wailing guitars, hollowed-out vocals, and lyrics loaded with themes of loss, *Sea Change* signals Beck's consistent versatility and proved he could be both sincere and ironic. Notable tracks include the tearjerkers "Guess I'm Doin' Fine" and "Lost Cause." Beck was uncertain as to whether or not he ought to release such a downtrodden set of tunes, but *Sea Change* was met with critical acclaim and positive sales, peaking at number eight on the *Billboard* Top 200 chart. It also landed in the number-two slot, behind Wilco's *Yankee Hotel Foxtrot*, on the *Village Voice* Critics' Poll of the best albums of 2002.

Singer, songwriter, experimental genius, Beck made his mark in the mid-1990s with a cheeky hit but has grown into a skilled, versatile, and accomplished postmodern musician.

SELECTIVE DISCOGRAPHY: *Mellow Gold* (1994, DGC); *Odelay!* (DGC, 1996); *Mutations* (DGC, 1998); *Midnight Vultures* (DGC, 1999); *Sea Change* (DGC, 2002).

CARRIE HAVRANEK

JEFF BECK

Born: Wallington, England, 24 June 1944
Genre: Rock
Best-selling album since 1990: *Who Else* (1999)

Revered by many as a "guitar god," Jeff Beck is one of the legendary rock guitarists. At every step, Beck pioneered advances in guitar technique, from his waves of roaring feedback overtones in the early days to an innovative techno-guitar style later on. He has traveled a long distance musically from his rock/blues beginnings. Yet for all his technical mastery and tasteful note phrasing, Beck has had a curiously spotty career.

Beginnings

Born in Wallington, England, Beck studied violin and cello as a child. He received a strong foundation in classical and jazz music from family members, and he attended the Wimbledon School for the Arts in London in the 1960s. His first gig as a guitar player was as the opening act for Jimmy Page's band. Later the two played together with the Yardbirds, a group famous for a string of hits in the 1960s, including "For Your Love" and "Heart Full of Soul."

Yardbirds and After

After toiling around London in the 1960s as a guitar player for hire, Beck received an invitation in 1965 to join the well-established Yardbirds as a replacement for Eric Clapton. A few months later Page joined the band. The group disbanded in 1967, never having taken full advantage of harboring two guitar virtuosos on each side of the stage. Page went on to form Led Zeppelin, and Beck went searching for a singer, a recurring theme in his career. He settled on Rod Stewart. He also added guitarist Ron Wood, who shifted reluctantly over to bass. The Jeff Beck Group, as they were named, recorded two classic albums, *Truth* (1968) and *Beck-Ola* (1969). Both albums are power rock/blues primers and demonstrate Beck's remarkable ability to arrange other people's songs into his own mold. They also show his capacity to take the guitar to new heights, particularly with the use of feedback. With the volume turned ear-splittingly high, Beck would hit a note and then move the guitar close to the amplifier. The ensuing cacophony was something that any amateur could achieve; Beck, however, learned to manipulate this screeching sound into entrancing, harmonious tones. The only other guitar player pushing those same boundaries was Jimi Hendrix, to whom Beck was soon compared. Hendrix's famous version of "The Star-Spangled Banner" is a good example of these controlled overtones.

New Departures

On November 2, 1969, Beck nearly died in an automobile accident that left him hospitalized for months. During his long recovery he discovered that Stewart and Wood had left him to join a band called Faces. (Stewart went on to a megastar solo career and Wood has enjoyed many years with the Rolling Stones.) Beck began touring and recording with several musician assemblies, but none of them were quite what he was looking for—especially the singers. In 1975 he decided that the voice could be replaced by inventive guitar work. His next release, *Blow by Blow*, (1976), was his first in a series of instrumental albums. While this breakthrough album contains remnants of Beck's rock/blues past, it also featured a funky melodic jazz sound, or, as it is sometimes labeled, jazz/rock fusion. The stunning "Cause We Ended as Lovers," from *Blow by Blow*, was Beck's fitting tribute to Roy Buchanan, a guitar player whom Beck admired. The track exemplifies one of Beck's trademark guitar "tricks": With the volume knob of his guitar turned completely off and his amplifier full up, he would strike a chosen string and at the same time twist up the guitar's volume by wrapping his little finger around the volume knob. The effect is a long sustaining note that builds in force somewhat in the way a train whistle sounds as it approaches fast into a station. Beck followed up with *Wired* (1976), another successful effort sans singer, in which he collaborated with jazz keyboard maven Jan Hammer. *Wired* was a further journey down the rock/jazz fusion path and enough of a success to justify Beck's turning down opportunities to play with the Rolling Stones and Elton John, both of whom sought his services at various times.

Throughout his career, Beck has obsessively avoided being pigeonholed into any one type of musical form. He reasoned that playing with new people for each recording would force him to keep striving to make inventive and challenging music. Working selectively through the 1980s, Beck managed to win a Grammy Award for Best Rock Instrumental with "Escape," from the album *Flash* (1985). Different from other efforts, the album has a pop music style and includes guest vocalists. It also reunited him with Rod Stewart on "People Get Ready," which became a hit.

Beck toured with blues-guitar great Stevie Ray Vaughan in the 1990s before entering a period of semi-retirement, during which he got a chance to tinker with his collection of vintage cars, something that has always been his passion. He returned by teaming with the Big Town Playboys, a 1950s novelty group with a local London following, and recorded *Crazy Legs* (1993). On this album, Beck moves from the blues and jazz/rock of his past work into a world of three-chord sock-hop ditties. *Crazy Legs* contains eighteen previously written rockabilly songs and is Beck's tribute to Cliff Gallup, the guitarist with singer Gene Vincent and the Blue Caps who once had a hit song called "Be Bop A-Lula." His guitar sound, usually fat and sustained, was pure tin as he painstakingly recreated authentic rockabilly solos that scurry up and down the guitar's fret board. A departure from anything else he had done, Beck drew raves on *Crazy Legs* for his fast and clean playing.

Despite having no record to promote, *Crazy Legs* being a niche recording, Beck went on tour with another distinguished guitarist, Carlos Santana, in 1995 and continued to tour throughout the 1990s. Finally, he released the long-awaited *Who Else* (1999), his first album of new material in almost a decade. Once again, Beck's choice of material surprised his listeners with songs featuring electronic backgrounds and a pounding technobeat. The chunky "Space for the Papa" and the hard rock "What Mama Said" sound like disco or club music leavened by Beck's searing guitar riffs. "Declan" features an interesting New Age music style as flutes trade phrases with Beck's guitar. The album, which is completely instrumental, also features a traditional blues, "Brush with the Blues." *Who Else* was nominated for a Grammy.

Beck waited just two years to release *You Had It Coming* (2001). The album features the Grammy winner for best rock instrumental, "Dirty Mind." He teases a mixture of wailing tones from his supercharged guitar and rips through the album's wide-ranging musical styles. "Nadia" is a gorgeous Middle Eastern ballad, and "Earthquake" vibrates with thrashing rock. Beck fashioned the idea for "Blackbird" by recording a bird that was chirping outside his home and then trying to recreate the sound on his guitar. *You Had It Coming* is an instrumental album with the exception of "Rollin and Tumblin." Beck has singer Imogen Heap lend a rich vocal interpretation to his masterful arrangement of the Muddy Waters classic.

Beck is an agile musical arranger, although not a particularly strong songwriter. His shortcomings as a composer and singer have lowered the ceiling on his commercial success. Nevertheless, whereas many of his contemporaries merely rest on their decades-old laurels, Beck moves forward, always pushing the musical envelope. An icon to his musical peers, he will long be considered one of the top guitarists in the history of rock music.

SELECTIVE DISCOGRAPHY: *Truth* (Epic, 1968); *Beck-Ola* (Epic, 1969); *Rough and Ready* (Epic, 1971); *Jeff Beck Group* (Epic, 1972); *Blow by Blow* (Epic, 1975); *Wired* (Epic, 1976); *Jeff Beck with the Jan Hammer Group LIVE* (Epic, 1977); *There and Back* (Epic 1980); *Flash* (Epic 1985); *Jeff Beck's Guitar Shop* (Epic, 1989); *Frankie's House* (Epic, 1992); *Crazy Legs* (Epic, 1993); *Who Else!* (Epic, 1999); *You Had It Coming* (Epic, 2001).

BIBLIOGRAPHY: A. Carson, *Jeff Beck: Crazy Fingers* (San Francisco, 2001).

DONALD LOWE

THE BEE GEES

Formed: 1958, Brisbane, Australia; Disbanded 2003

Members: Barry Gibb (born Manchester, England, 1 September 1946); Maurice Gibb (born Isle of Man, England, 22 December 1949; died Miami, Florida, 12 January 2003); Robin Gibb (born Isle of Man, England, 22 December 1949).

Genre: Rock, Pop

Best-selling album since 1990: *Still Waters* (1997)

Hit songs since 1990: "Alone," "Still Waters (Run Deep)"

A family vocal group known for its talent and durability, the Bee Gees enjoyed a long, colorful career before disbanding in 2003. Initially finding success during the mid- to late 1960s as a pop outfit inspired by rock pioneers the Beatles, the group recorded in a soulful ballad style before switching in the mid-1970s to R&B-influenced dance music, becoming a leading force behind the era's disco phenomenon. Although the Bee Gees were no longer a hit-making force by the early 1980s, they remained dedicated performers, launching a comeback near the end of the decade that sustained them throughout the 1990s. Due to the group's strong associations with disco—a style often dismissed by serious music fans—the Bee Gees never earned strong critical praise, although certain reviewers have noted the musicality and versatility of their work. By 2001 the Bee Gees were recording albums that qualify as solid examples of pop craftsmanship.

Composed of fraternal twin brothers Robin and Maurice, as well as their older brother Barry, the Bee Gees (a modification of "Brothers Gibb") began performing as children in Manchester, England, inspired by African-American vocal groups of the 1930s and 1940s such as the Mills Brothers. Encouraged by their father, a bandleader, the brothers began performing at movie theaters in 1955. Moving to Brisbane, Australia, in 1958, they began writing songs and singing on television, eventually releasing a single, "Three Kisses of Love" (1962). Returning to England in 1966, the Bee Gees joined forces with producer Robert Stigwood, who arranged for their recordings to be distributed in the United States by the Atlantic/Atco label.

While early hits such as "To Love Somebody" (1967) and "I've Gotta Get a Message to You" (1968) were inspired by the Beatles's easy pop sound, their emotional feel also suggested a strong R&B influence. After enjoying further hits with "Lonely Days" and the lovelorn ballad, "How Can You Mend a Broken Heart" (both 1971), the Bee Gees floundered briefly before latching onto disco, recording in the R&B hotbed of Miami, Florida, and releasing classics such as "You Should Be Dancing" (1976), "Night Fever" (1978), and their most famous song, "Stayin' Alive" (1978). All three songs were featured on the multimillion-selling soundtrack to the 1977 film *Saturday Night Fever*. Having reached a pinnacle of fame in the late 1970s, the group endured a host of problems throughout the 1980s—particularly the commercial decline of disco and the drug-related death of younger brother Andy in 1988.

Always tenacious, the Bee Gees launched a comeback in the late 1980s, scoring a Top 10 pop hit with "One" in 1989. Proving their ability to stay in touch with the latest trends, they released *Size Isn't Everything* (1993), incorporating light hip-hop rhythms on the minor hit "Paying the Price of Love." Like much of the group's earlier work, the album is marked by Barry's high falsetto vocals. In 1997 the group members were inducted into the Rock and Roll Hall of Fame, an important recognition of their endurance and influence. This honor led to the recording of a new album, *Still Waters* (1997). The minor hit "Alone" contains all of the ingredients that ensured the group's ongoing popularity: tuneful melody, smooth harmony vocals, and a likable, accessible sound. The title track "Still Waters (Run Deep)" was also a small hit, its easygoing R&B grooves providing strong support for the brothers' still-potent voices.

After releasing a live album, *One Night Only* (1999), the Bee Gees returned with *This Is Where I Came In* (2001), an album encompassing the many styles in which the group has recorded, from Beatles-inspired pop to tough rock. On "Technicolor Dreams," they add a clarinet and shuffling rhythm that suggest the "Dixieland" style of jazz music. Tragedy struck in early 2003, when Maurice died unexpectedly during surgery for an intestinal blockage. Devastated, the two surviving brothers announced their intention to disband.

Largely associated in the minds of listeners with disco, the Bee Gees were a unique, versatile outfit that recorded in a broad range of styles during their nearly forty-year career. Falling out of popular favor in the early 1980s, the group rebounded in the 1990s, releasing diverse, enjoyable albums before Maurice's death forced early retirement in 2003.

SELECTIVE DISCOGRAPHY: *Bee Gees First* (Atco, 1967); *Odessa* (Atco, 1969); *Main Course* (RSO, 1975); *Children of the World* (RSO, 1976); *Spirits Having Flown* (RSO, 1979); *One* (Warner Bros., 1989); *Size Isn't Everything* (Polydor, 1993); *Still Waters* (Polydor, 1997); *This Is Where I Came In*

(Uptown/Universal, 2001). **Soundtrack:** *Saturday Night Fever* (RSO, 1977).

WEBSITE: www.beegeesonline.com.

DAVID FREELAND

BELLE AND SEBASTIAN

Formed: 1996, Glasgow, Scotland

Members: Isobell Campbell, vocals, tambourine, viola, cello, guitar; Richard Colburn, drums; Mick Cooke, trumpet; Stuart David, bass; Chris Geddes, keyboards; Sarah Martin, violin; Stuart Murdoch, singer.

Genre: Rock

Best-selling album since 1990: *If You're Feeling Sinister* (1998)

Hit songs since 1990: "Stars of Track and Field," "If You're Feeling Sinister," "The Boy with the Arab Strap"

The Scottish octet Belle and Sebastian takes its name from a French children's story about a boy named Sebastian and his dog, Belle. The esoterically named, reluctant pop stars who comprise Belle and Sebastian owe much of their cheeky, knowing approach to fellow British superstars the Smiths and to the acoustic, pastoral sounds of folksinger Nick Drake. The band peaked in popularity in the late 1990s, culling special favor with college radio stations and fans of independent ("indie") rock. This charming band is often classified as part of the British "twee" genre of artists, characterized by their delicate and somewhat precious sound and appearance, and their personal, ruminative, and often melancholic lyrics. The instrumentation—hushed piano rumblings, soft brush drumming, and gentle wafts of trumpet or clarinet—is an apt accompaniment to their unique lyrics.

Belle and Sebastian began with singer/songwriter, and guitarist Stuart Murdoch and bassist Stuart David in January 1996, at a cafe in Glasgow, Scotland. Belle and Sebastian soon grew to eight members, and the band was invited by a scout from the British label Jeepster to record. Even though the band had not been together for very long, they already had enough material to fill an entire album. They released *Tigermilk* in 1996. (It became available in the United States in 1999.)

Belle and Sebastian's saucily titled *If You're Feeling Sinister* was released in 1997 on a now-defunct label, Enclave. Belle and Sebastian's territory is adolescent confusion, both sexual and interpersonal, relayed with a laconic delivery by primary singer Stuart Murdoch. "If you are feeling sinister / Go off and see a minister / He'll try in vain to take away the pain of being a hopeless unbeliever" sings Murdoch over an acoustic guitar, plain brush drumming, and the strains of children playing in a schoolyard. In 1998 Belle and Sebastian won the Brit Award for Best New Band, much to their surprise, as they are reclusive, often refusing to be photographed and to release personal information about themselves.

Belle and Sebastian, for all their mystery and privacy, are prolific. In the six short years between 1996 and 2002, the band compiled four albums and seven EPs. David departed in 2000 to publish his first novel and concentrate on his side project Looper. Campbell left in 2002 after Belle and Sebastian's release of *Storytelling*, the soundtrack to a film directed by Todd Solondz. He went on to form Gentle Waves.

The music of Belle and Sebastian is somewhat of an acquired taste, but those who enjoy their uniquely British, laid-back observations, Murdoch's laconic delivery, and the shimmering, chamber pop arrangements remain their ardent supporters.

SELECTIVE DISCOGRAPHY: *Lazy Line Painter Jane* (Matador re-release, 1997); *If You're Feeling Sinister* (Enclave/Virgin, 1998); *The Boy with the Arab Strap* (Matador, 1998); *Tigermilk* (Matador re-release, 1999); *Fold Your Hands, Child, You Walk Like a Peasant* (Matador, 2000). **Soundtrack:** *Storytelling* (Matador, 2002).

CARRIE HAVRANEK

BELLY

Formed: 1991, Newport, Rhode Island; Disbanded 1996

Members: Members: Tanya Donelly, vocals and guitar (born Newport, Rhode Island, 14 July 1966); Thomas Gorman, lead guitar (born 20 May 1966); Christopher Toll Gorman, drums (born 29 August 1967); Gail Gorman, bass (born 3 October 1960).

Genre: Rock

Best-selling album since 1990: *Star* (1993)

Hit songs since 1990: "Gepetto," "Feed the Tree," "Now They'll Sleep"

Tanya Donelly, later the honey-voiced lead singer of alternative rock band Belly, initially performed brief stints with other musical outfits: the art-rock band Throwing Muses and the Breeders, a punk-infused guitar-fuzz band that she founded with Kim Deal. Unhappy because these bands did not perform her own songs, Donelly sought the help of musician brothers Tom and Chris Gorman, and Throwing Muses bassist Fred Abong. Together they formed the band Belly.

Like a belly, the group's music could be soft—but it could also be macabre and guttural, with fuzzy, distorted guitars in some songs and waltzy, chiming acoustic guitars in others. With lyrics that were often cryptic and surreal, the band found overnight success in indie and alternative rock circles. Despite their dark tendencies, many of Belly's songs are melodic and usually adhere to the constraints of pop music. Belly's debut album, *Star* (1993), earned two Grammy Award nominations for Best New Artist and Best Alternative album.

Star was certified gold within a year of its release, thanks largely to Belly's extensive touring schedule and success with college radio, which prompted larger radio stations to play their singles "Gepetto" and "Feed the Tree" (southern slang for "death"), with the latter peaking at number one on the *Billboard* Modern Rock Tracks chart. Its spunky chorus, "Take your hat off boy when you're talking to me / And be there when I feed the tree," is indeed cryptic but vaguely feminist. It struck a chord with high school and college-age women searching for a no-nonsense female role model in the form of a pop star who chose not to exploit her beauty in exchange for fame.

Belly was a strong part of the alternative rock scene in the mid-1990s. In 1993 Gail Greenwood joined the band on bass and performed more than 200 dates in just a little more than a year with the band. The surprise success of their first album prompted them to ask Glyn Johns to produce their follow-up. Their second album, *King* (1995), is straightforward and aggressive where *Star* is languid and dreamy, but it retains the band's signature oblique lyrics, swirling guitars, and surrealism. Despite its more consistent sound and radio-friendly hooks, such as in "Now They'll Sleep" and "Super-Connected," *King* was greeted with mixed reviews by the press and the fans. *King* peaked at fifty-seven on the *Billboard* chart and never reached the sales of Belly's debut.

Donelly left the band in 1996 and started a solo career. By the end of 1996, she released her solo debut album, *Sliding and Diving*. Greenwood joined the all-female punk rock band L7. Sadly, Belly never fully reached its potential. At the band's peak, their memorable blend of strengths—Donelly's big voice, quirky songs with shifting time signatures, and a strong, determined persona—showed that even a group with an unconventional approach could achieve mainstream success.

SELECTIVE DISCOGRAPHY: *Star* (Sire/Reprise, 1993); *King* (Sire/Reprise, 1995).

CARRIE HAVRANEK

TONY BENNETT

Born: Anthony Dominick Benedetto; New York, New York, 3 August 1926
Genre: Vocal
Best-selling album since 1990: *MTV Unplugged* (1994)
Hit songs since 1990: "Steppin' Out with My Baby"

The renewed popularity of Tony Bennett across multiple generations crowns a remarkable career that has spanned more than half a century of American popular music. A vocalist in the Sinatra tradition where word meaning, phrasing, and mood are paramount, Bennett's jazz sensibility contributes to the swing and swagger that he brings to his interpretations as well as to the use of his voice as a vocal instrument. He remains one of the last of the seminal artists who came to prominence in the post–World War II pre-rock era who is still successfully performing in the new millennium.

Neighborhood Origins and Early Successes

Born to Italian-born immigrants in the Astoria section of Queens, New York City, Bennett displayed considerable talent and affinity for singing and painting from an early age. A neighborhood grocer, Bennett's father had been a singer in Collabra, Italy, where it was said he had a voice so beautiful that he could stand on a mountaintop and mesmerize an entire valley below. Bennett's mother was left to raise her three children alone during the Great Depression by working as a seamstress after her husband passed away.

The young Bennett began singing in school, at home, and at parties, even taking a job as a singing waiter after graduating from high school. After a stint in the army during the last days of World War II, Bennett began a struggling career in Long Island clubs supporting visiting stars of the day such as Al Cohn and Tyree Glenn.

The lean years came to an end in 1949 when the unknown Joe Bari—the stage name Bennett was using at the time—was heard by Bob Hope in a Pearl Bailey revue at the old Greenwich Village Inn. Hope invited Bennett to sing at the Paramount Theatre with him, but not before shortening Anthony Benedetto to Tony Bennett so that his name would fit on the theater marquee.

A year later, Bennett successfully auditioned for producer and arranger Mitch Miller at Columbia Records, and soon scored his first hit with "The Boulevard of Broken Dreams" (1950). This success was followed by a string of hit singles—"Because of You" (1951), "Cold, Cold Heart" (1951), "Stranger in Paradise" (1953), "Rags to Riches"

(1953), and "Just in Time" (1956), among others—and culminated in Bennett's international hit and signature tune, "I Left My Heart in San Francisco" (1962), which won three Grammy Awards, including Best Solo Vocal Performance—Male and Record of the Year. During his peak period from the mid-1950s to the mid-1960s, Bennett recorded no less than three albums a year and was in constant demand in the most posh clubs and concert halls in the country.

Shunned, Then Celebrated

After the British Invasion took hold and a new style of pop music emerged, Bennett was viewed as a dinosaur by a new breed of record executive who now saw rock music as the only meal ticket and Bennett as out of step with the times, because of his insistence on remaining with a repertoire made up of classic American popular songs. Bennett left Columbia Records rather than compromise his material by singing covers of songs by rock artists.

Equally unwilling to compromise his stage act by adding the glitz and paraphernalia so common to stage acts of the 1970s, Bennett soon found himself shut out of Las Vegas as well, despite having been one of the earliest regular solo performers to help establish that desert town as an oasis of entertainment. Bennett retreated to England for a time, and even formed his own record label during the disco era, though all the while Bennett's hardcore public remained as loyal to him as he remained to them.

By the mid-1980s, a new generation of performers such as Michael Feinstein and Harry Connick Jr. began making careers by singing American popular songs of yesteryear. Additionally, standards were now being recorded by many of the same pop stars whom a decade or two before had been singing the same rock material that Bennett had refused to record. Suddenly, posh music was fashionable again, and Bennett, who embodied the genre, once again found himself in high demand.

Bennett returned to his old label for a series of albums and firmly re-established himself as a consummate communicator of the classic American popular song. His albums from this period include *The Art of Excellence* (1986), *Bennett/Berlin* (1987), *Astoria: Portrait of the Artist* (1990), and his Grammy Award-winning tribute to his mentor Frank Sinatra, *Perfectly Frank* (1992).

Managed by his media-savvy son Danny, Bennett made a guest voice appearance on an episode of *The Simpsons*, appeared with the Red Hot Chili Peppers on the *MTV Music Awards*, and became a regular guest on popular media outlets such as shows hosted by David Letterman and Howard Stern. Such appearances served to introduce Bennett to a new generation of admirers, while never compromising Bennett's art form.

Spot Light | Tony Bennett on MTV's *Unplugged*

Tony Bennett's groundbreaking music video of Irving Berlin's "Steppin' Out with My Baby" was released in 1993 in collaboration with Bennett's Fred Astaire tribute album of the same name. Much to virtually everyone's surprise and thanks to the persistence of Bennett's manager/son Danny Bennett, the swinging video was shown on MTV and subsequently entered the regular MTV playlist rotation. The stage was set for an MTV *Unplugged* appearance with Bennett on April 14, 1994. Snapping his fingers and taking a few dance steps with young models against the backdrop of elaborate visual effects in a highly stylized music video was one thing, but could the then-sixty-eight-year-old postwar matinee idol of the bobby socks era really deliver the goods to their Generation X grandchildren in a no-frills live performance? Most doubted it, as the whole concept had absolutely no precedent. And so, as Bennett took a bare stage with his longtime pianist and arranger Ralph Sharon at the Steinway grand piano along with acoustic bassist Doug Richeson and drummer Clayton Cameron and began crooning "Old Devil Moon," Bennett knew a lot was at stake. The young crowd went wild listening to Bennett sing songs by legendary songwriters George Gershwin, Cole Porter, Kurt Weill, Irving Berlin, Victor Herbert, and others, as did a cross-generational nation of home viewers. The love affair between Bennett and his adoring young fans continued on throughout the evening, ironically faltering only slightly when k.d. lang and Elvis Costello came out and each sang a duet with Bennett. But in the end, the evening was Bennett's, and fans responded by eagerly snapping up MTV's *Unplugged* in both audio and video formats. Even Bennett's colleagues in the recording industry stood up and took notice, awarding the album two Grammy Awards, including Record of the Year.

In 1993 Bennett shattered all boundaries when his music video of Irving Berlin's "Steppin' Out with My Baby" charted on MTV and began appearing in regular rotation alongside standard MTV fare. This success culminated in Bennett's extraordinary appearance on MTV's *Unplugged*; the resulting album earned Bennett a Grammy Award for Record of the Year.

Bennett's MTV performance was followed by the A&E television special *By Request . . . Tony Bennett*, in which callers phoned in song requests to Bennett live. The success of this venture won Bennett a Cable ACE Award and an Emmy Award, as well as making the format a regular A&E staple.

An avid and respected painter, Bennett continues to paint under his own name and was "discovered" by no less than artist David Hockney. Bennett has regular exhibitions of his paintings in the country's major art galleries, where they sell from $5,000 to $40,000.

Bennett's extraordinary longevity as a vocalist is in no small part due to his refusal to compromise his material or his musical integrity. Bennett's mentor Sinatra had advised the singer to not compromise when Bennett came to him for advice early in his career, and Bennett never forgot. Bennett has always been at home performing for audiences of every age, a tradition that stems back to childhood Sunday family get-togethers that had him performing for relatives of every age. This, together with Bennett's consistent eagerness to please his public and his uncanny ability to both energize and be energized by an audience, is part of why Bennett has flourished when most of his contemporaries have long since disappeared.

SELECTIVE DISCOGRAPHY: *Forty Years: The Artistry of Tony Bennett* (Columbia, 1991); *Perfectly Frank* (Columbia, 1992); *Steppin' Out* (Columbia, 1993); *MTV Unplugged* (Columbia, 1994); *Here's to the Ladies* (Columbia, 1995); *On Holiday (A Tribute to Billie Holiday)* (Columbia, 1997); *At Carnegie Hall June 9, 1962* (Columbia re-release, 1997); *The Playground* (Columbia, 1998); *Hot and Cool: Bennett Sings Ellington* (Columbia, 1999). **With Count Basie:** *Basie Swings, Bennett Sings* (Columbia, 1958). **With Bill Evans:** *The Tony Bennett Bill Evans Album* (Columbia re-release, 1991). **With various artists:** *Playin' with My Friends: Bennett Sings the Blues* (Columbia, 2001). **With k.d. lang:** *What a Wonderful World* (Columbia, 2002).

BIBLIOGRAPHY: T. Bennett, *What My Heart Has Seen: Tony Bennett* (New York, 1996); M. Hoffman, *Tony Bennett: The Best Is Yet to Come* (New York, 1997); T. Bennett with W. Friedwald, *The Good Life* (New York, 1998).

WEBSITE: www.tonybennett.net.

DENNIS POLKOW

GEORGE BENSON

Born: Pittsburgh, Pennsylvania, 22 March 1943
Genre: Jazz
Best-selling album since 1990: *Best of George Benson* (1995)

A brilliant jazz guitarist who smoothly crosses into other musical genres, George Benson earned pop music fame in the 1970s after placing greater emphasis on his singing. In the later years of his career, he has increasingly revisited his jazz guitar beginnings.

While growing up in Pittsburgh, Pennsylvania, Benson won a talent contest at the age of four as a singer. He continued making his mark as a singer throughout his teenage years with several rock and R&B groups. His stepfather, a major influence in his formative years, presented him with a guitar when he was eight years old and promised the child prodigy that learning the instrument would pay off. The styling of saxophone pioneer Charlie Parker, in addition to guitarists Charlie Christian and Grant Green, fascinated Benson early on and in 1961 Benson, just eighteen years old, joined bandleader and organist "Brother" Jack McDuff. He elevated McDuff's music for four years with his hot jazz guitar work before leaving in 1965 for New York to pursue his own musical interests.

Benson arrived in New York with a solid reputation, having already worked as a sideman for other jazz luminaries such as Herbie Hancock, Billy Cobham, and Miles Davis. It was there that he met his most important influence, now-legendary jazz guitarist Wes Montgomery. The self-taught Montgomery impressed Benson with his ability to move comfortably from jazz to other styles and Benson began emulating Montgomery's soft touch and penchant for playing octave solos, improvisational note patterns in which a second string, the octave of the chosen note, is struck simultaneously. This technique is a staple component in Benson's guitar style. At times, Benson adds a third and even a fourth string, making it a chord solo.

Benson's first recordings were well received by the jazz community. When Montgomery died in 1968 Benson was looked upon as the heir apparent to his style and he did not disappoint. Benson recorded several critically acclaimed jazz works in the early 1970s, yet repeatedly switched record labels in search of a broader appeal and began playing pop interpretations of tunes like "California Dreamin" and "Unchained Melody." He also sang more and gradually developed the "scat" style soon to become his signature sound.

Warner Bros. producer Tommy LiPuma convinced Benson to add pop style string arrangements to *Breezin* (1976) for a more commercial touch and the mostly instrumental album became a multiplatinum Grammy Award–winning sensation. It made Benson a pop superstar on the strength of the album's one vocal, the hit single "Masquerade." Written by Leon Russell, "Masquerade" features Benson scat singing to his guitar solos, matching the instrument note for note with his voice. On later recordings, he varies the technique and sings an octave apart or lets his voice harmonize with the guitar. Critics note Benson's velvety high singing tone seems to have no limit when he lets it follow the heights reached by his guitar notes.

He continued recording successful pop albums throughout the 1970s and 1980s, spawning hits on the strength of his singing, such as "Give Me the Night" and "Turn Your Love Around." He also caught plenty of flak along the way from the pure jazz world, which saw Benson as a commercial sellout. However, most others recognized Benson as an artist who adroitly infused pop music with his jazz genius. He returned to a pure jazz sensibility in the 1990s with *Tenderly* (1989) and continued to avoid being pigeonholed by recording *Big Boss Band* (1990) with the Count Basie Orchestra. *Big Boss Band* is a departure from all previous work and Benson sounds like he belongs in the big band swing era as he croons classics such as "Without a Song" and "Walkin' My Baby Back Home."

An eight-time Grammy Award winner, Benson subsequently released recordings in the 1990s that mix jazz guitar instrumentals with a light blend of pop, Latin rhythms, soul, and R&B. They typify the smooth jazz sound that emerged as an extension of Benson's similarity to Wes Montgomery. Benson surprised the music world with the mostly instrumental *Absolute Benson* (2000), again letting his listeners know that he had not forgotten his beginnings. His pure jazz guitar grooves are marked by trademark octave and chord solos and there is a strong Latin influence. One of the three songs that he sings on the album is Ray Charles's "Come Back Baby."

From his time as a young man playing Pittsburgh nightclubs to the present, Benson has ultimately focused on being a crowd pleaser, an artist whose primary concern was getting his music out to as many listeners as possible. He nonetheless maintains respect in the jazz world for never letting go of his roots, and holds an honorary doctorate of music from the esteemed Berklee College of Music in Boston, Massachusetts.

SELECTIVE DISCOGRAPHY: *George Benson/Jack McDuff* (Prestige, 1965); *Benson Burner* (Columbia, 1965); *It's Uptown* (Columbia, 1965); *The George Benson Cookbook* (Columbia, 1966); *Giblet Gravy* (Verve, 1967); *The Shape of Things to Come* (A&M, 1968); *The Other Side of Abbey Road* (A&M, 1969); *Beyond the Blue Horizon* (CTI, 1971); *White Rabbit* (CTI, 1972); *Bad Benson* (CTI, 1974); *Breezin'*

(Warner Bros., 1976); *In Flight* (Warner Bros., 1977); *Weekend in L.A.* (Warner Bros., 1978); *Livin' Inside Your Love* (Warner Bros., 1979); *Give Me the Night* (Warner Bros., 1980); *In Your Eyes* (Warner Bros., 1983); *20/20* (Warner Bros., 1984); *Twice the Love* (Warner Bros., 1988); *Tenderly* (Warner Bros., 1989); *Big Boss Band: With the Count Basie Orchestra* (Warner Bros., 1990); *Love Remembers* (Warner Bros., 1993); *Best of George Benson* (Warner Bros., 1995); *That's Right* (GRP, 1996); *Standing Together* (GRP, 1998); *Absolute Benson* (Polygram, 2000).

DONALD LOWE

BJÖRK

Born: Björk Gundmundsdottir; Reykjavik, Iceland, 21 November 1965.

Genre: Rock

Best-selling album since 1990: *Debut* (1993)

Hit songs since 1990: "Human Behaviour," "Big Time Sensuality," "Army of Me"

Eclectic, iconoclastic, idiosyncratic, and melodic are useful adjectives when describing the Icelandic singer and songwriter Björk, one of the most unusual singers to emerge during the 1990s. She has managed to keep critics and fans guessing with each new and increasingly adventurous release since her split in 1992 from the Icelandic punk-pop band she fronted, the Sugarcubes. Björk's albums have sold several million copies, but it is difficult to pigeonhole her as an artist; her music incorporates elements of rock, pop, electronica, and dance. With her kewpie-doll looks, multioctave voice that can be at once girlish and arresting, and unpredictable sense of style, Björk's avant-garde appeal has resulted in platinum-sales success and a loyal following among college students and adults.

Björk grew up as an only child; her father, Gudmundur, was an electricians' union chief, and her mother, Hildur, was a homeopathic doctor and martial-arts instructor. Her parents divorced when she was only a year old, and she lived with her mother, who enrolled the youngster at age five in music school. By the time she was eleven, she had released her first self-titled solo album, a collection of Icelandic pop music tunes. Her arrival as singer for the new wave-meets-punk-rock band the Sugarcubes in the 1980s was not terribly surprising to those in her native country who remembered her as a child singer, and soon the rest of the world became captivated by her quirky, honest music.

Björk [PAUL NATKIN/PHOTO RESERVE]

nous synthesizer. In the chorus Björk warns, "And if you complain once more / You'll meet an / Army of Me." Every lyric uttered by Björk is given an odd inflection, perhaps the unique result of singing in a language that is not her native tongue.

In another surreal track on *Post,* Björk contemplates a relationship from the edge of a cliff. In "Hyper-Ballad," which reached number one on the *Billboard* dance chart, she explains, "Every morning / I walk toward the edge and throw little things off / Like car parts, bottles and cutlery." It takes a rare voice to pull off such a random, stream-of-consciousness lyric without giving the impression of insanity. Two tracks later, "It's So Quiet," a jazzy pop tune reminiscent of 1940s and 1950s Broadway musicals— complete with blasts of trumpets—finds Björk moving from a hushed whisper to a joyful scream.

Homogenic (1997) was well received, although the textures are heavier, darker, and more industrial, the lyrics and imagery more abstruse, than those of her previous recordings. The singer was also cast as the lead in *Dancer in the Dark* (2000), a dark, musical-like drama directed by Lars von Trier. Björk surprised the critics when she received an acting award at the Cannes Film Festival (2000) for her turn as Selma, a Czech mother who finds comfort in musicals as she toils away to try to save her son from an inherited disease that causes blindness. Björk herself composed the soundtrack for this blend of fantasy and reality, musical and drama.

SELECTIVE DISCOGRAPHY: *Debut* (Elektra, 1993); *Post* (Elektra, 1995); *Homogenic* (Elektra, 1997); *Selmasongs: Music from the Motion Picture* Dancer in the Dark (Elektra, 2000); *Vespertine* (Elektra, 2001); *Björk's Greatest Hits* (Elektra, 2002).

CARRIE HAVRANEK

Björk has suffered through many difficulties: the divorce of her parents when she was young, her rocky marriage to Thor Eldon, and her pregnancy at the age of twenty. She gave birth to a son named Sindri and divorced Thor in 1988, shortly after their band, the Sugarcubes, was signed to Elektra records; the band then recorded three albums hailed for their eccentricity and innovation. When the band broke up in 1992, Björk moved to London and started to work on a solo album.

Debut (1993) sold more than 2.5 million copies and includes several hits: "Venus as a Boy," "Human Behaviour," "Big Time Sensuality." Her lyrical inspiration came from her diaries; she has often described her songwriting as private and intimate. However intimate her songwriting may be, it is conveyed often in a cryptic, elliptical style. Her follow-up album, *Post* (1995), is one of her best. The album's lead-off track, "Army of Me," begins with an omi-

CLINT BLACK

Born: Long Branch, New Jersey, 4 February 1962

Genre: Country

Best-selling album since 1990: *Put Yourself in My Shoes* (1990)

Hit songs since 1990: "A Better Man," "Loving Blind," "Easy for Me to Say"

Clint Black was the first in a wave of fresh-faced artists to emerge from the early 1990s as part of the "new country" music revolution. By infusing his traditional country songwriting with a pop-influenced performing style, he got off to one of the fastest career starts in country music history. Black's career slowed later in the 1990s as similar artists traveled faster on the road that he had paved.

Although born in New Jersey, Black was raised in Katy, Texas, a suburb of Houston. The youngest of four boys in a musically influenced family, he learned both harmonica and guitar in his teens. Black dropped out of school in 1978 to play in a band formed by one of his brothers and two years later began playing extensively throughout the local Texas club circuit. In 1987 he met fellow guitarist/songwriter Hayden Nicholas, who owned a home recording studio, and they began writing songs together. Their demo tape impressed Bill Ham, the manager of Texas rock icons ZZ Top, and he introduced Black to RCA Records in Nashville, Tennessee. RCA immediately signed the charismatic twenty-five-year-old to a contract and Black's first album, *Killin' Time* (1989), was a smash success. The debut album astounded country music with five number one hits and won numerous awards, including ones from both the Country Music Association (CMA) and the Academy of Country Music (ACM) for Best Male Vocalist.

The following year he released *Put Yourself in My Shoes* (1990), which also sold well and contained four Top 10 hits including a number one single, "Loving Blind." Ambitious to a fault, Black appeared on scores of television and radio shows in addition to performing extensive concert tours. He infused his live appearances with a natural charm and a fan-friendly energy, often signing autographs until the last person left. The songs, usually co-written with Nicholas, who also played lead guitar in the band, carried easily relatable themes of the traditional country mode. Yet, he was setting groundbreaking standards in a style that was soon followed by other country newcomers such as Garth Brooks and Alan Jackson. His live shows featured expensive production values not previously associated with country music and the music was performed with a gusto and sex appeal more akin to rock or pop music. While it wrinkled the brows of country music traditionalists, much of the public loved it and Black's career was red hot. Along with more awards, he was inducted into the Grand Ole Opry in 1991 and that same year Black married actress Lisa Hartman.

Black was ready to capitalize on this success with a third album but its release, along with his career, became bogged down in a legal struggle with his manager Ham. After nearly seven months of court battles, he finally released *The Hard Way* (1992), which produced another number one hit, "We Tell Ourselves." Though the album was successful in both country and pop music charts, subsequent record sales declined. In the developing conflict between "new" and "traditional" country music, many felt that Black's increased pop music appeal was turning away traditional country fans. However, the sales decline was probably more the result of other artists claiming their mar-

ket share of the burgeoning new country field than it was due to any failing on Black's part.

Subsequent recordings over the next ten years proved Black's amazing ability to write songs that land high on the charts. His albums have produced over twenty Top 10 hits and, while they have not reached the sales height of his first two releases, Black's place in the forefront of country music is solid. He has also enjoyed collaborating with other country stars of every style. In 1991 he sang with the legendary Roy Rogers at the Grand Ole Opry and toured the summer of 1993 with country music diva Wynonna Judd, with whom he recorded the hit duet "A Bad Goodbye." That same year he lent his interpretation to the classic Eagles hit, "Desperado," for their tribute album *Common Threads* (1993). Often compared to country icon Merle Haggard, they collaborated on writing the hit, "Untanglin' My Mind" in 1994.

Black took on the role of producer for his all-acoustic, *D'Lectrified* (1999). The album featured guest appearances by Kenny Loggins, Bruce Hornsby, and others including Black's wife. Black and Hartman perform a duet on the hit ballad, "When I Said I Do," and she sings background on two other songs. Two years later, Black and Hartman produced another hit single, "Easy for Me to Say," which was one of the four previously unreleased songs from *Greatest Hits II* (2001). The celebrity couple enjoyed the birth of a daughter, Lily Pearl, in 2000.

Black's records have sold over 18 million copies and his numerous performer awards include a Grammy. He has also been honored nine times by the Nashville Songwriters Association, and the St. Jude Children's Research Hospital named him 2001 Celebrity of the Year for his relentless charity fundraising on their behalf. In 1996 he received a star on Hollywood's Walk of Fame. Black is a down-to-earth superstar who loves his fans and continues to find wonder in the process of writing a song and helping it develop.

SELECTIVE DISCOGRAPHY: *Killin' Time* (RCA, 1989); *Put Yourself in My Shoes* (RCA, 1990); *The Hard Way* (RCA, 1992); *No Time to Kill* (RCA, 1993); *One Emotion* (RCA, 1994); *Looking for Christmas* (RCA, 1995); *The Greatest Hits* (RCA, 1996); *Nothin' but the Taillights* (RCA, 1997); *D'Electrified* (RCA, 1999); *Greatest Hits II* (RCA, 2001).

DONALD LOWE

THE BLACK CROWES

Formed: 1984, Atlanta, Georgia; Disbanded 2002

Members: Audley Freed, guitar; Eddie Harsch, piano, keyboards (born Toronto, Ontario, 27 May 1957); Andy Hess, bass; Chris Robinson, vocals (born Atlanta, Georgia, 20 December 1966); Rich Robinson, guitar (born Atlanta, Georgia, 24 May 1969). Former members: Jeff Cease, guitar (born Nashville, Tennessee, 24 June 1967); Johnny Colt, bass (born Cherry Point, North Carolina, 1 May 1966); Marc Ford, guitar (born Los Angeles, California, 13 April 1966); Steve Gorman, drums (born Muskegon, Michigan, 17 August 1965).

Genre: Rock

Best-selling album since 1990: *Shake Your Money Maker* (1990)

The history of brotherly rock and roll singer/guitarist combos, which includes the Davies brothers from the Kinks, Don and Phil Everly of the Everly Brothers, Oasis's Gallagher brothers, and Rich and Chris Robinson of the Black Crowes, is riddled with acrimony and conflict. Though the battling Robinson brothers—nicknamed the "Rotten Twins" by band mates—were able to set aside their differences to release a string of successful Southern-fried blues rock albums, the familial tension proved to be the undoing of the group by the early 2000s.

The Black Crowes began life as Mr. Crowe's Garden, formed by the Robinson brothers in Atlanta, Georgia, in 1984. The only children of Nancy and Stan Robinson—the latter an ex-musician who hit number eighty-three on the charts in 1959 with the song "Boom-a-Dip-Dip" before retiring from the music business to run a clothing business—the Robinsons seemed destined to follow the family muse.

Heavily influenced by the hard-charging 1960s and 1970s sounds of bands such as the Rolling Stones, Faces, and early Aerosmith, the Black Crowes arrived on the music scene in 1990 with a look and sound that was at odds with the tastes of the day.

Though their retro blues rock sound, long hair, flouncy, velvet frocks, bell bottom jeans, and shaggy appearance failed to fit in with the glam look of the early 1990s hard rock scene or the slouchy, ripped jeans aesthetic of the rising grunge movement, the Black Crowes struck gold with the classic rock of their 1990 debut, *Shake Your Money Maker*.

Making the Blues New Again

Combining Rich Robinson's raucous slide guitar with singer Chris Robinson's cigarette-stained, Southern blues man vocals, the group scored hits with the ragged boogie-woogie blues song "Jealous Again" and the acoustic ballad "She Talks to Angels." The first album also spawned what would be the Crowes' signature hit, a cover of Otis Redding's southern blues song "Hard to Handle," given a

hard rock edge by Rich Robinson's thick guitar lines and Allman Brothers–style stinging guitar solos.

With an unabashed fondness for indulging in illicit substances, the Crowes sowed the seeds of chaos while touring behind the album in 1991. Singer Chris Robinson caused the group to be fired from their stint opening up for ZZ Top on a Miller beer–sponsored tour after making disparaging comments about commercial sponsorship. The gaunt singer was arrested for assault and disturbing the peace midyear after an argument with a female fan in Denver following the group's show and was later hospitalized for malnutrition and exhaustion during a British tour.

With guitarist Marc Ford recruited to replace Jeff Cease, the Black Crowes returned in 1992 with *Southern Harmony and Musical Companion*, which advanced their signature mix of 1970s boogie rock and aspects of gospel, rhythm and blues, and soul. Named after an antebellum gospel hymnal, the album entered the *Billboard* charts at number one and signaled a career-long turn towards more introspective, conflicted material.

Though still relying on the same classic rock touchstones, the album mixes the band's dark blues rock with more gospel touches, nowhere more than on the opening track, "Sting Me." As a loose funk/soul beat burns in the background, Robinson sings, "If you feel like a riot, then don't you deny it / Put your good foot forward / No need for heroics, I just want you to show it / Now's the time to shine," with a gospel duo backing his vocals. The album spawned the hit single "Remedy," a five-minute, midtempo blues that melds the raunchy rock of midperiod Rolling Stones with gritty Southern soul.

With album tracks that frequently clocked in at five minutes or more and a live show that highlighted extended instrumental passages, the Black Crowes stood at the vanguard of a new group of American rock acts dubbed "jam bands." The loose aggregation of groups, many acolytes of the improvisatory rock masters the Grateful Dead, allowed fans to tape record their concerts—which were often traded through an underground network—and placed a premium on concerts that expanded the parameters of their recorded music.

A Darker Turn

The group's 1994 album, *Amorica*, generated controversy for its cover, which depicted a woman in a bikini with her pubic hair exposed—an homage to a cover of the pornographic magazine *Hustler*. The art was quickly airbrushed and changed after some retail chains refused to stock it.

Though the hard-edged album did not spawn any hit singles and did not sell as well as their previous efforts, it moves further into a darker, more introspective direction and is both homage to rock heroes and unmistakably original. Songs such as "High Head Blues" add Latin percussion into the mix, while "Wiser Time" is spiced with country-flavored pedal steel guitar. Chris Robinson's lyrics again focus on failed relationships, the search for meaning in a troubled existence, and salvation from a vividly painted purgatory.

Three Snakes and One Charm (1996) adds an additional helping of Led Zeppelin–style hard rock bombast to the group's sound, again augmented by pedal steel player Bruce Kaphan, as well as the Dirty Dozen horn section and banjo player Rick Taylor. With the exception of the Beatles-inspired psychedelic pop number "One Mirror Too Many," though, the album was not an artistic leap forward for the group.

By Your Side (1999) reigns in the band's more expansive songs for succinct three- and four-minute tracks that recapture the energy of their debut, though without the more instantly hummable melodies. The Crowes joined former Led Zeppelin guitarist Jimmy Page for a mid-2000 tour, which yielded a well-received live double album, *Live at the Greek* (2000), featuring a mixture of Zeppelin songs and blues standards. The group again clashed with retailers, this time over the album's exclusive online distribution through the website Musicmaker.com.

A greatest hits album, *Greatest Hits 1990–1999*, was released in mid-2000 and Chris Robinson married actress Kate Hudson, daughter of actress Goldie Hawn, on New Year's Eve of that year. Still relying on the combination of Rich Robinson's bombastic, blues-inspired guitar riffs and Chris Robinson's ragged vocals, *Lions* (2001) is the sound of a leaner, more straightforward Black Crowes. "Lickin'" is a pile-up of fuzz-toned guitar licks, while the Robinsons pay homage to their rock star status in the hard-driving "Soul Singing" with the lyrics "I've been down / Cascading and blue without a sound / Now I've traded my black feathers for a crown."

An outing with the battling Gallagher brothers of Oasis, cheekily called the "Brotherly Love" tour, followed in June 2001. By January 2002, though, the strain had proven too much, as the group announced an indefinite hiatus. Following the release of a live album, Chris Robinson emerged with his solo debut, *New Earth Mud*, in the fall of 2002, while Rich Robinson worked on his solo debut, indicating in interviews that the hiatus was permanent.

Though tagged as classic rock fetishists/revivalists at first, the Black Crowes grew into their sound, proving they were interested not merely in aping the beloved music of their youth, but in emulating it in order to bring it into a new century.

SELECTIVE DISCOGRAPHY: *Shake Your Money Maker* (American, 1990); *The Southern Harmony and Musical Companion* (American, 1992); *Amorica* (American, 1994); *Three Snakes and One Charm* (American, 1996); *By Your Side* (Columbia, 1999); *Lions* (V2, 2001); *Live* (V2, 2002).

GIL KAUFMAN

MARY J. BLIGE

Born: Bronx, New York, 11 January 1971
Genre: R&B, Hip-Hop
Best-selling album since 1990: *Share My World* (1997)
Hit songs since 1990: "You Remind Me," "Real Love," "Not Gon' Cry"

During the 1990s Mary J. Blige helped usher rhythm and blues music into the hip-hop era, becoming known as "The Queen of Hip-Hop Soul." Blige's longevity was due in part to producers who crafted complex, distinctive, and likable rhythms behind her vocals, but a more important key to her success was the personal artistic current that ran through her work. While her contemporaries such as Whitney Houston and Toni Braxton largely confined their work to love ballads, Blige used music to explore the travails of her life, bringing a new degree of honesty to rhythm and blues. As a result, she became an idol to young African-American women who identified with her toughness, pain, and perseverance. The opening line of "Where I've Been" (2001) sums up her appeal: "To all the youth in the world," she says, "the thing nobody understands; well, I understand." With each album Blige grew more assured, creating music that is all the more enjoyable for its depth of feeling.

Early Years

Although she spent her summers living with family in Savannah, Georgia, Blige was raised in the Schlobohm Gardens housing projects in Yonkers, New York. Growing up in a neighborhood full of drugs and crime, Blige fell in with a rough crowd and dropped out of high school during her junior year. In interviews she later alluded to the troubles that plagued her during these years. Discussing her childhood with *Rolling Stone* in 2001, she said, "In the ghetto, I didn't want to be nothing. I didn't want to be *anything* . . . when you're younger, you like the ignorance. You love the ignorance."

Despite her troubles, Blige was exposed to the positive influence of music through her father, a performer who lived in Michigan but visited her occasionally.

Mary J. Blige [PAUL NATKIN/PHOTO RESERVE]

While still a teenager, Blige recorded herself at a local mall singing a karaoke version of "Rapture," a hit song by the pop-soul vocalist Anita Baker. The tape eventually found its way to Andre Harrell of Uptown Records, who enlisted Blige to sing backup vocals for the artists on his label. In 1991 Blige began working with producer Sean "Puffy" Combs, who spearheaded the production of her first album, *What's the 411?* (1992). The album, a success on the pop and rhythm and blues charts, was an important step in bringing hip-hop and rap into the mainstream. With its catchy riffs, sturdy beats, and melodic songs, *What's the 411?* helped define rhythm and blues in the 1990s, paving the way for later groups such as TLC and Destiny's Child. "Real Love," the album's most popular single, was an infectious dance number that juxtaposed Blige's girlish, somewhat unsteady vocals against a bouncy rhythm track. Distinguished by a pounding piano part, "Real Love" was instantly recognizable on the radio, where it received extensive play during the early years of the decade.

Rhythm and Blues Stardom

Blige's third album, *Share My World* (1997), marked a turning point in her career; it features a slicker, more polished sound than previous efforts and places an increased emphasis on her vocals. Designed for mainstream appeal, *Share My World* became Blige's most successful album to date, debuting at number one on the pop charts. The album's high point is "Not Gon' Cry," a ballad written by producer Kenneth "Babyface" Edmonds that was also featured on the soundtrack to the 1995 film *Waiting to Exhale*. On "Not Gon' Cry" Blige uses the dark, bluesy contours of her voice to tell the story of a fallen relationship. Sounding less youthful and winsome than on previous recordings, she brings a chilling matter-of-factness to such lines as "Eleven years I've sacrificed, and you can leave me at the drop of a dime." The song demonstrates the specific, detailed way in which Blige probes her emotions, a skill that overcomes any vocal shortcomings. Comparing her to the 1960s "Queen of Soul," the Baltimore *City Paper* asserted in 1999, "[Blige's] raspy voice is weak and it often cracks. . . . Having said that, she's also her generation's Aretha Franklin. . . . You swear you *know* Blige, and you *feel* what she's singing."

A New Maturity

With *Mary* (1999), Blige took the mature style developed on *Share My World* and pushed it further, creating a sophisticated, assured album that showed how much she had developed as a singer and artist. On the album's cover, Blige is shown in profile, the scar under her eye prominently displayed. With the music Blige seems to be stating, "this is who I am," as she delves into a wide range of influences and styles. "All That I Can Say," produced by fellow hip-hop performer Lauryn Hill, features a complex melody and multiple key changes that Blige navigates with ease. On "Deep Inside," featuring pop singer Elton John on piano, Blige opens up about the difficulties of being a star. "The problem is," she sings, "for many years I've lived my life publicly / So it's hard for me to find a man I trust." One of the album's most potent songs is the dark, moody "Time." Backed with a funky rhythm track, Blige rails against narrow-mindedness: "People nowadays so shady / Now what is wrong with them / Something cast a spell up on their minds / And they always wanna condemn." Overall, *Mary* gives the impression of an artist secure and comfortable with her talents, intelligent enough to deliver music both danceable and thought-provoking.

Blige's maturity is fully evident on her 2001 album, *No More Drama*. On one level the album works as solid party music, but it also provides a framework for presenting Blige's emotional and spiritual orientation, taking listeners into the far reaches of her psyche. On "PMS," for example, she is both penetrating and funny: "My lower back is aching/ and my clothes don't fit." On the autobiographical "Where I've Been," one of her most uplifting songs, Blige relates how she has turned trauma into triumph: "At the age of seven years old / A strange thing happened to me. . . . And I've got the mark to show / And it became a thing of beauty." The album's biggest hit, "Family Affair," is a dance number that benefits from a tight, dense groove supplied by the producer, Dr. Dre. The playful lyrics, written by Blige and her own family members, coin new terms to emphasize unity: "Don't need no hateration, holleration." The title track, "No More Drama," which incorporates the theme song to the soap opera *The Young and the Restless*, reflects Blige's upbeat state of mind and new confidence: "It feels so good / When you let go / Of all the drama in your life / Now you're free from all the pain." Extending her positive message beyond her music, Blige became a spokesperson for AIDS awareness and the rights of battered women and children.

A major trendsetter in contemporary R&B, Mary J. Blige remained on top at the start of a new millennium by constantly updating her image, message, and style. Exploring her life's experiences with honesty and humor, she created music that challenges as it entertains.

SELECTIVE DISCOGRAPHY: *What's the 411?* (MCA, 1992); *My Life* (MCA, 1994); *Share My World* (MCA, 1997); *Mary* (MCA, 1999); *No More Drama* (MCA, 2001).

WEBSITES: www.mjblige.com; www.maryjbligeonline.com.

DAVID FREELAND

BLIND MELON

Formed: 1989, Los Angeles, California

Members: Shannon Hoon, vocals (born Lafayette, Indiana, 26 September 1967; died New Orleans, Louisiana, 21 October 1995); Roger Stevens, guitar (born West Point, Mississippi, 31 October 1970); Christopher Thorn, guitar (born Dover, Pennsylvania, 16 December 1968); Brad Smith, bass (born West Point, Mississippi, 29 September 1968); Glen Graham, drums (born Columbus, Mississippi, 5 December 1968).

Genre: Rock

Best-selling album since 1990: *Blind Melon* (1992)

Hit songs since 1990: "No Rain"

By the early 1990s, music videos were a well-established means of creating excitement over and awareness of a group's music. Few bands from that era were as defined by their music videos as Blind Melon of Los Angeles. Though the group's career was cut short by the drug overdose death of vocalist Shannon Hoon in 1995, their time in the spotlight was defined by the hippieish, classic-rock-inspired sound of their signature song and video "No Rain."

Formed in Los Angeles in 1989, Blind Melon looked backward for inspiration for their music. Whereas popular grunge-rock bands such as Nirvana and Soundgarden drew inspiration from the aggressive, harsh punk and post-punk movements of the decade before, and the heavy metal bands of the era focused on trashy, pop-inspired sounds, flashy clothes, and make-up, Blind Melon looked to the earthy southern rock and folk of the 1970s for their motivation.

Built around the whiny falsetto of the Indiana-born singer Shannon Hoon and the Allman Brothers–inspired guitar playing of Roger Stevens and Christopher Thorn, the group caught the attention of Capitol Records thanks to a four-track demo recording dubbed *The Goodfoot Workshop*, recorded in 1989, just one week after the band had formed. Lacking sufficient material to record a full-length album, Blind Melon set to work on a mini-album with veteran producer David Briggs (Neil Young), but the results were scrapped when the band feared the songs were too polished.

It was through music videos that Blind Melon reached a mass audience. While the group pondered their next move, Hoon rekindled a relationship with fellow Indiana native and Guns N' Roses singer Axl Rose, who invited the long-haired Blind Melon singer to lend backing vocals to a number of tracks on the Guns N' Roses 1991 double album, *Use Your Illusion*. Hoon sang on and appeared in the video for the hit song "Don't Cry."

With buzz from the Guns N' Roses cameo, but still without an album, the group appeared on the 1992 MTV 120 Minutes Tour in the spring alongside several more established acts, helping to build anticipation for their self-titled debut, which was released in September of that year.

A Landmark Video

Produced by Rick Parashar (Pearl Jam), songs such as "Soak the Sin" explore hard-charging Led Zeppelin–style rock, while the tracks "Change" and "Tones of Home" mix elements of wistful acoustic folk with Hoon's mostly upbeat, nature-inspired lyrics about growing up and searching for meaning in life. With the excitement from the Guns N' Roses cameo and the MTV tour diminished, and their songs not garnering attention on radio or on MTV, the group took to the road. In addition to opening for Guns N' Roses, Blind Melon shot a video for the simple acoustic ballad "No Rain" with director Samuel Bayer, best known for his pioneering direction of videos by Nirvana.

Bayer brought to life the cover image from the group's album: a photo of drummer Graham's sister in a bumblebee costume. The imagery of the video came to define the band. Floated on a sprightly acoustic guitar figure and Hoon's high, cracked vocals, "No Rain" is a simple song about trying to find sanity in an insane world. "All I can say is that my life is pretty plain / I like watching the puddles gather rain / All I can do is just pour some tea for two / And speak my point of view, but it's not sane, it's not sane," Hoon sings. The video, in which the group performed in a vast green field while a chubby, bespectacled girl danced around them in a bee costume, became a smash hit, helping the album sell more than 3 million copies. Despite critical indifference, the group found itself opening for such superstar acts as the Rolling Stones, Pearl Jam, Lenny Kravitz, and Neil Young.

A pair of Grammy nominations for Best New Artist and Best Rock Performance followed, but the group was unable to celebrate its success because of Hoon's increasing drug use, which forced the cancellation of their 1994 headlining tour. They performed a strong set at Woodstock '94 and opened several dates for the Rolling Stones before entering the studio with producer Andy Wallace (Nirvana) in the fall to begin work on their second album. Hoon was arrested for a drunken brawl with an off-duty police officer during the sessions and later entered into a rehab facility upon the album's completion. Hoon's girlfriend gave birth to a daughter one month before the September release of *Soup* (1995).

The album is much darker than the group's debut, with a harsher, more aggressive sound and lyrics about drug dependency, thoughts of suicide, and soul weariness. The exception is "New Life," in which Hoon practically pleads for the answer to the question, "When I look into the eyes of our own baby / Will it bring new life into me?"

Though *Soup* was an artistic success, helping to dispel Blind Melon's reputation as a lightweight one-hit wonder, audiences and critics did not respond to the sound and sales foundered. Against the advice of his rehabilitation doctors, Hoon joined the band for a promotional tour, dismissing a drug counselor less than two months into the outing. Several days later, the twenty-eight-year-old Hoon was found dead of a cocaine overdose on the band's tour bus in New Orleans.

An album of unfinished tracks, demos, rarities, and unreleased material, *Nico* (named after Hoon's daughter), was released in November 1996, accompanied by a home video, *Letters from a Porcupine*. The remaining members attempted to recruit a new lead singer, but eventually called it quits and split to pursue several side projects.

Though Blind Melon brought a playful, bright edge to the mostly dim, pessimistic rock scene of the early 1990s with "No Rain," the group was torn apart by those same dark forces that felled many of their grunge peers.

SELECTIVE DISCOGRAPHY: *Blind Melon* (1992, Capitol); *Soup* (1995, Capitol); *Nico* (1996, Capitol).

GIL KAUFMAN

BLINK-182

Formed: 1993 as Blink, Poway, California

Members: Travis Barker, drums (born San Diego, California, 14 November 1975); Tom Delonge, guitar, vocals (born San Diego, California, 13 December 1975); Mark Hoppus, bass, vocals (born San Diego, California, 15 March 1972). Former member: Scott Raynor, drums (born San Diego, California, 23 May 1979).

Genre: Rock, Punk, Pop

Best-selling album since 1990: *Enema of the State* (1999)

Hit songs since 1990: "All the Small Things," "What's My Age Again?"

Injecting a healthy dose of scatological humor and teen angst into the prefabricated world of late-1990s pop, Southern California's Blink-182 brought ultra-catchy, humorous pop punk to the top of the charts with their 1999 album, *Enema of the State*. The potty-mouthed trio infiltrated the music mainstream with a string of slapstick videos and bathroom-humor-filled concerts, paving the way for countless of their peers to follow them up the *Billboard* charts.

Taking Off

Formed near San Diego in 1993, Blink began life as a skateboarding punk trio obsessed with playing fast, melodic songs about teen angst and the fruitless search for love. After playing dozens of live shows—which invariably featured wet T-shirt and wet shorts contests—the group self-released an eight-track album entitled *Fly Swatter* (1993), which featured several songs that later appeared on *Buddha* (1994) on the Kung Fu label.

Lacking the polish of the band's later work, *Buddha* songs such as "Carousel" and "Fentoozler" show signs that the group knows how to use melody amid the furious punk-rock assault. The lyrics to "Carousel" ("I talk to you every now and then / I never felt so alone again / I stop to think at a wishing well / My thoughts send me on a carousel") also display a poetic sensibility that would later help the band reach a mass audience. With whiplash rhythms and bored, snotty vocals, the album is a rough template of things to come.

Cheshire Cat (1995) features more refined versions of several songs from *Buddha*, as well as the twisted, homo-erotic "Ben Wah Balls." Along with their penchant for performing barely clothed or nude, "Ben Wah Balls" was typical of the group's boyish bathroom humor. By the time they released their third proper album, *Dude Ranch* (1997), the group had changed their name to Blink-182 after the threat of a lawsuit by an Irish band named Blink, toured the world with such popular punk groups as Pennywise and

Tom Delonge of Blink-182 [PAUL NATKIN/PHOTO RESERVE]

NOFX, appeared on the Vans Warped punk rock package tour several times, and had their music in a series of popular skating and snowboarding videos.

Crossing Over

Picking up the mantle of another successful punk rock group that learned how to inject melody into its songs, Northern California's Green Day, *Dude Ranch* spawned the radio track "Dammit (Growing Up)," which was a harbinger of the group's crossover into the music mainstream. Built on the same loud, aggressive punk rhythms of their earlier songs, "Dammit" slows down the pace a bit and allows room for a more deliberate, traditional rock arrangement. Delonge plays a speedy, distorted guitar riff over a lyric that glumly states, "And it's happened once again / I'll turn to a friend / Someone that understands / Sees through the master plan / But everybody's gone / And I've been here for too long." Produced by local punk drummer Mark Trombino, the album weds a pop sheen to Delonge's and Hoppus's snotty, nasal vocals, highlighting their strong lyrical vision.

A founding member, Raynor, was replaced by former Aquabats drummer Travis Barker following the album's release. Barker's precise yet acrobatic drumming is in evidence on the band's breakthrough album *Enema of the State*

(1999). A brilliant mix of Blink-182's punk energy and pop smarts, the album spun off a series of hit songs and videos, eventually selling more than 6 million copies.

Their gleeful homage to immaturity, "What's My Age Again?" ("Nobody likes you when you're 23 / And are still more amused by prank phone calls"), was accompanied by a wildly popular music video in which they famously ran down the streets of San Diego naked. But the song and video that rocketed the group to superstardom was the pure pop confection "All the Small Things." Dressed as the boy band the Backstreet Boys, the group mocked mainstream pop music even as they performed it themselves with a head-bobbingly catchy ditty complete with a "na-na-na-na" chorus.

Both hits find singers Delonge and Hoppus practically crooning and singing in two-part harmony over Barker's bashing drums and alternately furious and delicate guitar strumming. While songs such as "Dysentery Gary" revel in grade-school humor, the sensitive ballad "Adam's Song" tackles the horrors of teenage suicide with sober seriousness and a thrilling ebb-and-flow arrangement complete with a dramatic piano solo. In a further nod to their mainstream acceptance, Hoppus and Delonge were asked to record a version of 1960s surf duo Jan and Dean's "Dead Man's Curve" for the CBS miniseries *The History of Rock 'n' Roll*.

The live album *The Mark, Tom, and Travis Show (The Enema Strikes Back)* (2000) is a snapshot of the group's typically crude, lewd live show, highlighted by bathroom and sexual humor and copious foul language. Barker (Famous Stars and Straps) and the combo of Delonge and Hoppus (Loserkids.com) launched youth-oriented clothing and accessories companies during this period. Secure in their pop stardom, the trio returned in 2002 with the pruriently titled *Take Off Your Pants and Jacket*. Though still approaching their music with the same aggression and punk energy, the trio had clearly matured, tackling such subjects as broken homes and emotional abuse, along with the usual litany of failed love affairs and teenage angst.

Barker's drumming shows an almost jazzlike efficiency and precision, while Hoppus and Delonge trade vocals on tracks about young love ("First Date"), goofing off with friends ("The Rock Show"), and, in their most accomplished song to date, divorce ("Stay Together for the Kids"). Juxtaposing spare, elegantly strummed guitar, lean drums, and sensitive singing on the verses with choruses of snarling vocals, ominous walls of guitar, and bashing drums, the song is an example of the band growing up without losing their edge.

Delonge and Barker formed the side project Box Car Racer in 2001 with guitarist David Kennedy and bassist Anthony Celestino. The group's self-titled 2002 debut was in a more traditional hard, bleak punk vein than Blink-

182's albums. Barker teamed with Rancid front man Tim Armstrong for the self-titled 2002 debut from the Transplants, a hard-edged album that mixes punk, reggae, rapping, and programmed drum-machine beats for a raucous, multigenre explosion of noise and fury.

Blink-182 became famous by never underestimating the value of a catchy chorus and a juvenile bathroom joke. With their carefree attitude and increasingly sophisticated arrangements, the trio proved to be much more than a one-note joke band.

SELECTIVE DISCOGRAPHY: *Buddha* (Kung Fu, 1994); *Cheshire Cat* (Cargo/Grilled Cheese, 1995); *Dude Ranch* (Cargo/MCA, 1997); *Enema of the State* (MCA, 1999); *The Mark, Tom, and Travis Show (The Enema Strikes Back)* (MCA, 2000); *Take Off Your Pants and Jacket* (MCA, 2001); **With Box Car Racer:** *Box Car Racer* (MCA, 2002).

BIBLIOGRAPHY: A. Hoppus (ed.), *Tales from Beneath Your Mom* (New York, 2001).

WEBSITES: www.blink182.com; www.loserkids.com; www.famoussas.com.

GIL KAUFMAN

BLUES TRAVELER

Formed: 1987; Princeton, New Jersey

Members: Brendan Hill, drums (born London, England, 27 March 1970); Chandler "Chan" Kinchla, guitar (born Hamilton, Ontario, 29 May 1969); Tad Kinchla, bass (born Princeton, New Jersey, 21 February 1973); John Popper, vocals, harmonica (born Cleveland, Ohio, 29 March 1967); Ben Wilson, keyboards (born Chicago, Illinois, 17 November 1967). Former members: Bobby Sheehan, bass (died New Orleans, Louisiana, 20 August 1999).

Genre: Rock

Best-selling album since 1990: *four* (1994)

Hit songs since 1990: "Run-Around," "Hook," "But Anyway"

Blues Traveler took chances by updating steeped-in-tradition blues. But the group gradually won respect for its original way of incorporating R&B, jazz, and flower-power influences to create a spicy, danceable fusion, and it became one of America's top touring groups.

Tough Beginnings

Vocalist John Popper, one of seven children, made no secret of his upper-middle-class background. His father was an information technology consultant and his mother was a lawyer. Despite the comforts of a middle-class lifestyle, he did experience his share of misery growing up. Obese since childhood, Popper referred to food as his "drug." Naturally, he endured his share of bullying. To deal with the teasing, he considered becoming a comedian. He enjoyed John Belushi and Dan Aykroyd's Blues Brothers sketches on *Saturday Night Live*. He did not feel like he had enough material to do stand-up every night, though his love for the medium would show up in his witty lyrics later on. As it turned out, watching the Blues Brothers gave him a love for blues and harmonica. Purists did not think much of the way young Popper was introduced to the venerable American genre, but he pursued it with admirable gusto and sincere appreciation.

In high school and immediately after, he began jamming with drummer Brendan Hill, guitarist Chan Kinchla, and bass player Bobby Sheehan. Popper, Hill, and Sheehan studied at the New School of Jazz in New York. They jelled through their mutual love of blues and relocated to Brooklyn, New York, performing in blues and R&B clubs. Blandly christened the Blues Band at first, the band wisely adopted its better-known moniker after Gozer the Traveler, a character in the film *Ghostbusters* (1984). Fusing blues with hippie rock and alternative rock, the band found itself unwelcome in a few traditional clubs.

The group got a major boost when legendary rock promoter Bill Graham became a fan and took the group under his wing. Noticing the group's propensity for extended jams, he gave it an opening slot for the Jerry Garcia Band. By 1990 the group was one of New York's top club attractions and inked a deal with A&M Records.

The band's debut album, *Blues Traveler* (1990), does not capture the mesmerizing energy of the group's gigs, but it does show some fine songwriting and intergenerational rock eclecticism. It leads off with "But Anyway," an up-tempo number that highlights many of the strengths that would lead the group to bigger and better things. In the forefront are Popper's forceful but intricate harmonica riffs, his raspy blues-man singing, and Hill's funky backbeat. "Gina" alludes to the group's bar-band roots with earthy guitar and pleading lyrics. The bleak ballad "100 Years" mulls over the evanescent nature of human existence. The instrumental "Mulling It Over" is pure 1960s narcissism, with a noodling harmonica solo and a quasi-psychedelic, cymbal-overloaded drum solo. There is plenty of variety, especially in the first half of the album, proving that the group has songwriting talent and is more than just a jam band.

The band wasted no time in releasing sophomore set *Travelers and Thieves* (1991), which features guest keyboardist/vocalist Gregg Allman on "Mountain Cry." The whole band pitches in on songwriting, with Popper taking most of the load. The word "travelers" took on a new meaning in the band's context, referring to fans who follow the group around from gig to gig, much like Deadheads followed the Grateful Dead. In 1992 the band founded the H.O.R.D.E. (Horizons of Rock Developing Everywhere) Tour to give exposure to other jam bands. The tour ran every summer for five years.

With *Save His Soul* (1993), Blues Traveler began to finally break out of its regional box, earning a modest rock-radio hit with "Conquer Me." Mindful that a label like A&M would not put up with modest-selling efforts forever, the band keeps its jamming tendencies under control for the most part, though two of fourteen tracks clock in at over seven minutes.

For Blues Traveler, the fourth time was a charm. The band's *four* (1994) received scant attention upon its early fall release, but after the new year the irresistibility of first single "Run-Around" worked its magic first on alternative-rock radio, then on Top 40. In a departure from the group's sometimes complex music, "Run-Around" is based on a facile two-bar, four-chord motif. What keeps the tune from seeming boring is the way Popper works himself into a frenzy of indignation over a girlfriend's behavior, and his cathartic "yeeeah" at the beginning of each chorus. Popper furiously blasts away at his harmonica as the single fades out. The song reached number eight on the Hot 100 and spent forty-nine weeks on the chart. The midtempo "Hook," whose title describes its Top 40 appeal, is notable for its funky, silver-tongued breakdown. It spent over eight months on the Hot 100.

Captured Live

In an attempt to lessen the inevitable pressure of following up a major success with another hit-filled studio collection, the group released its double album *Live from the Fall* (1996), recorded over six months of touring. This set finds the group in its solo-happy element; six tracks last over eight minutes. "But Anyway," from the debut album, reappears and became a middling hit on alternative-rock radio.

For *Straight on Till Morning* (1997), a title full of suggestive meanings, the group tries to capture its improvisational vibe, worrying less about keeping songs hook-filled and radio-friendly. However, by the end of the sessions Popper felt like he had nearly run out of songs. Popper attempts a confessional, Barenaked Ladies–style story-song with "Canadian Rose," and adds a Latin feel to the flirtatious boogie "Felicia." Though the playing is excellent as usual, the album was a commercial and critical disappointment, lacking the energy and hunger of *four*.

A dream gig presented itself later in 1997—the group got the opening slot for part of the Rolling Stones's tour. It would have been a perfect opportunity to win stadiums full of new, if older, fans. Unfortunately, Sheehan almost caused the band to lose the gig when he was arrested for cocaine possession in Canada. Fortunately for the band, his detention was brief. However, it foreshadowed tragic events. In August 1999 Sheehan, thirty-one, died of a drug overdose. After mourning his death and doing some soul searching, Blues Traveler decided to carry on. Chan Kinchla's younger brother Tad joined as bass player in November 1999.

The group slowly got back on its feet in 2000, adding a new member, keyboardist Ben Wilson. The move was designed to take some of the emphasis off Popper's harmonica and create a more varied sound. Popper lost a significant amount of weight during that time, and on *Bridge* (2001) it is obvious that his new physique changed his voice as well, making it sound a little more mellow and less angst-ridden. The group brings the funk, with Wilson conjuring soul legend Stevie Wonder on "You Reach Me" and coloring "Rage" with electric piano. "Pretty Angry" uncompromisingly expresses the band's grief over Sheehan's death. While the album explores promising new horizons, it was not a hit and the band redoubled its focus on its strength—live performances.

While never attaining the heady mix of cult status and mainstream acceptance of groups like the Dave Matthews Band, Blues Traveler became an important band among hippies young and old, blues fans, alternative rockers, and others who enjoyed sunny grooves and a communal atmosphere.

SELECTIVE DISCOGRAPHY: *Blues Traveler* (A&M, 1990); *four* (A&M, 1994); *Live from the Fall* (A&M, 1996); *Straight On Till Morning* (A&M, 1997); *Bridge* (A&M, 2001).

RAMIRO BURR

BLUR

Formed: 1989, Colchester, England

Members: Damon Albarn, vocals (born Whitechapel, London, England, 23 March 1968); Graham Coxon, guitar (born Rinteln, Hannover, Germany, 12 March 1969); Alex James, bass (born Bournemouth, Dorset, England, 21 November 1968); Dave Rowntree, drums (born Colchester, Essex, England, 8 May 1964).

Genre: Rock

Best-selling album since 1990: *Blur* (1997)

Hit songs since 1990: "There's No Other Way," "Girls and Boys," "Song 2"

The British guitar-based rock band Blur started off in the 1990s in the alternative rock scene. They saw their popularity peak in the United States with their eponymous fifth album in 1997. Blur's cheeky sense of humor, often pointed at

England's class structure, interpersonal relationships, and the vagaries of life, is their hallmark, along with the clever wordplay and psychedelic swaths of guitar found in their music. During its heyday, Blur wrote great dance music, evident in songs such as "She's So High," "Girls and Boys," and "Number 2."

Band members Damon Albarn, Graham Coxon, and Alex James met at Goldsmiths College in the late 1980s; they met drummer Dave Rowntree, whose father was a sound engineer for the Beatles at the British Broadcasting Company, in London after college. Blur developed a small following in the United States among British pop enthusiasts, thanks to the song "She's So High" (1990), which found its way into the U.K. charts. Many of Blur's songs adeptly and cleverly skewer class stratification, politics, and pop culture, but much of their guitar-driven material also deals with the typical pop music fare of love and relationships. At this time, their music was guitar-driven and accented with a Hammond organ. Blur became a popular choice for deejays at dance clubs known for playing alternative music. The band was also a large part of the Manchester rock scene, which was comprised of other similar bands such as Charlatans U.K., Ride, and Lush. "There's No Other Way," another melodic and danceable guitar-heavy single, hit number eight on the U.K. charts in the spring of 1991. Both tracks appeared on their debut *Leisure* (1991) and helped the album sneak into the U.K. Top 50. Their follow-up, the cheekily titled *Modern Life Is Rubbish* (1993), emerged after the band struggled in 1992 to present an album that pleased their record label. A typical example of the sophomore slump, *Modern Life Is Rubbish* sold less than their debut.

Parklife (1994), Blur's third album, brought greater record sales both in the United Kingdom and the United States; it borrows heavily from just about every great British pop band of the twentieth century, including the Kinks, the Who, and the Beatles. The album's Euro-disco tune "Girls and Boys" is Blur at its best and seems to celebrate, or make fun of, sexual ambiguity. In his unmistakable Cockney accent, Albarn sings the circular chorus, "Girls who are boys / Who like boys to be girls / Who do boys like they're girls / Who do girls like they're boys / Always should be someone you really love." *Parklife* earned Blur a nomination for the prestigious Mercury Music Prize, and they won Best Band and Best Album at the 1995 Brit Awards.

After these musical coups, the famously incendiary British press schemed to create an Oasis versus Blur campaign. Oasis, a rock band heavily influenced by the Beatles and comprised mostly of the notoriously misanthropic brothers Liam and Noel Gallagher, had released a single the same day as Blur in August 1995. The fans caught on, and for the most part, Blur kept quiet as Oasis, cocksure and aggressively ambitious, gained constant headlines. The feud was more or less nonexistent on American shores, and in truth Blur and Oasis are completely different pop bands. Oasis thrives on the notoriety of its feuding brothers. Blur was always the sly, detached observer interested in creating sonic textures and social commentary, while Oasis was the instigator.

Blur never reclaimed the critical success they found after *Parklife*. However, their self-titled fifth album (1997) became their best-selling record in the United States, thanks to the thrashy song "Number 2." The song inspired teenagers to jump up and down, crash into each other, and occasionally hoist someone up in the air to ride the crowd in a practice known as moshing. In 1999 they released the electronica-heavy *13*, produced mostly by William Orbit and recorded without Coxon, who unofficially left to release his own material in 1998. Albarn released an album with hip-hop producers under the moniker the Gorillaz, and it is uncertain whether Blur will record an album together again.

In the 1990s, guitar band Blur was a significant player in what critics and music industry types were calling a "British Invasion," à la the Beatles in the 1960s. With their cerebral, dispassionate lyrics and knack for creating melodic hooks that stick in the listener's head, Blur managed to succeed, despite stiff competition from fellow Brits Oasis throughout most of the 1990s.

SELECTIVE DISCOGRAPHY: *Leisure* (Virgin, 1991); *Modern Life Is Rubbish* (Virgin, 1993); *Parklife* (Virgin, 1994); *The Great Escape* (Virgin, 1995); *Blur* (Virgin, 1997); *13* (Virgin, 1999).

BIBLIOGRAPHY: S. Maconie, *Blur 3862 Days: The Official Story* (London, 2002).

CARRIE HAVRANEK

ANDREA BOCELLI

Born: Lajatico, Italy, 22 September 1958
Genre: Classical

The world has long had a fascination with the celebrity tenor. Dashing voices from Enrico Caruso to Mario Lanza to Luciano Pavarotti have captured the popular imagination. A worthy addition to that list is the Italian tenor Andrea Bocelli, who, in the 1990s, established himself as an international singing sensation with a repertoire of classical and soft pop songs.

Born in Tuscany, he grew up in a close-knit farming community, studying piano, flute, and saxophone and listening to opera. At the age of twelve, he lost his sight because of glaucoma and a soccer accident. He studied law at the University of Pisa and, for a year after graduation, practiced as a defense attorney before deciding to quit and pursue music full time. He approached the renowned tenor Franco Corelli for lessons and supported himself playing piano and singing in bars and nightclubs. It was in one of these clubs that he met his future wife, Enrica.

In 1992 he auditioned for Italian pop star Zucchero, who was looking for a tenor to make an audition tape of his duet "Miserare" in an attempt to convince Pavarotti to record it. Convinced by the demo, Pavarotti sang on the recording, and it became a hit in Europe. For the next Zucchero tour, Bocelli was hired to sing the song, and he took over a solo spot in the show.

Pavarotti invited Bocelli to sing with him at his annual charity gala, and this performance led to a series of appearances and TV broadcasts across Europe. In 1994 Bocelli won the top prize in the popular San Remo Song Festival; his performance of the song "Il Mare Calmo della Sera" made him a sensation. His debut album, *Il Mare Calmo della Sera*, was the first in a series of pop hits, and led to *Bocelli*, his follow-up album.

His breakout European hits were "Con Te Partiro" and a duet arrangement of the same song with Sarah Brightman, "Time to Say Goodbye (Con Te Partiro)." The solo version topped the French pop charts, and the duet sold 3 million copies in Germany, sitting atop the pop charts there for fourteen weeks.

The album *Romanza* (1996) became a hit in Europe and the United States, selling 15 million copies. After *Sogno* was released in 1999, Bocelli had four albums on the U.S. pop charts at one time; he became the first artist since Garth Brooks in 1992 to accomplish the feat. His duets with Celine Dion at the Grammys and Academy Awards launched sold-out tours of the United States. In 2000 Bocelli sang at the Vatican, the Eiffel Tower, and the base of the Statue of Liberty. He also sang the official concert of the Euro 2000 soccer tournament in Rotterdam and helped carry the Olympic torch into Sydney Harbor.

Although secure in his success in the pop world, Bocelli has craved legitimacy in the classical realm as well. In the late 1990s he released a series of classical recordings: *Viaggio Italiano* (1997), a collection of popular arias and Neapolitan songs; *Aria* (1998); and *Sacred Arias* (1999). Each was a best-seller, and for a while, these albums occupied the top three top spots on the classical charts.

The classical music press has been less kind to Bocelli than his legions of fans. His voice, unamplified, is not very large and has trouble filling a concert hall without a microphone. His voice can produce a gorgeous tone, and his sincerity and emotive ability are impressive. But he is stylistically unsophisticated, his phrasing is clumsy, and his early attempts to sing opera—a Verdi album, a recording of *La Bohème*, and a performance in Detroit of *Werther*—have elicited mostly negative critical reviews.

Critical reservations notwithstanding, Bocelli commands the unflagging loyalty of a mass of paying customers: He has sold more than 40 million CDs, is the top-selling classical artist of the 1990s, sells out his tours, and has inspired fans in a way that few pure classical artists have.

SELECTIVE DISCOGRAPHY: *Romanza* (Philips, 1997); *Viaggio Italiano* (Philips, 1998); *Sogno* (Philips, 1999).

WEBSITE: www.bocellionline.com; www.andreabocelli.com.

DOUGLAS McLENNAN

MICHAEL BOLTON

Born: Michael Bolotin; New Haven, Connecticut, 26 February 1953

Genre: Rock, Pop

Best-selling album since 1990: *Time, Love, and Tenderness* (1991)

Hit songs since 1990: "How Am I Supposed to Live without You," "Love Is a Wonderful Thing," "When a Man Loves a Woman"

Michael Bolton gained fame in the 1980s and 1990s by applying his powerful, weighty vocal pipes to big-sounding pop ballads. Although Bolton had performed extensively in a hard-edged rock style during the 1970s under his real name, Michael Bolotin, he did not break through commercially until he simplified his surname and began singing romantic-themed songs in the mid-1980s. Never a critical favorite, Bolton nonetheless proved himself a skilled songwriter and performer with a sharp eye for gauging the taste of the record-buying public. His dramatic vocal style, leonine mane of hair, and sturdy, handsome image won him legions of female fans, while his far-ranging musical interests spurred a commercially successful foray into opera. Although Bolton stepped away from the spotlight during the late 1990s and early 2000s, he returned in 2002 with an album that brought his sound up to date with the latest trends in pop and rock.

Raised in Connecticut, Bolton began performing at the age of thirteen, singing blues songs in local nightclubs. By the mid 1970s, he had embarked upon a career as a singer and songwriter, signing to RCA Records and releasing his debut album, *Michael Bolotin* (1975), on which he sings in a tough style heavily influenced by rock singer Joe Cocker. While critics dismissed his singing as overblown, they applauded the intelligence of his songwriting; soon he had written an engaging song, "How Am I Supposed to Live without You," which became a 1983 hit for the pop singer Laura Branigan. After a stint fronting a heavy metal band, Blackjack, Bolton reemerged as a solo artist and released the hard-rock-oriented *Michael Bolton* (1983). His commercial breakthrough did not come until 1987, however, when he revamped his style and released *The Hunger*, a set of blustery pop ballads including the self-penned hit, "That's What Love Is All About." The album initiated what became a career trademark for Bolton: covers of R&B classics that bore distinct resemblances, in terms of arrangements and vocal phrasing, to the original versions. On *The Hunger*, Bolton scored a number-eleven pop hit with "(Sittin' On) The Dock of the Bay," a 1967 signature song for the late R&B legend Otis Redding.

Soul Provider (1989), an album recorded in a similar style to its predecessor, made Bolton a star. This time, the R&B cover was a version of "Georgia on My Mind," a song associated with music pioneer Ray Charles. By the end of 1990, five of the album's singles had hit the Top 40, among them a strong version of "That's What Love Is All About." Although Bolton was often criticized for pilfering the rugged, soulful sound of great but neglected R&B singers, R&B pioneer Irma Thomas recorded a moving rendition of "That's What Love Is All About" in 1991, an indication that artistic influence often works both ways.

In 1991 Bolton returned with *Time, Love, and Tenderness*, another multi-million-selling album that featured his hit rendition of "When a Man Loves a Woman," a cover of the 1965 hit recording by Percy Sledge. By this time, Bolton had begun to receive substantial flak from the critical community. After performing the song at the 1992 Grammy Award ceremony, he was cornered by an angry group of journalists who faulted him for not giving artists such as Charles and Sledge proper credit. A nettled Bolton responded to the group with a suggestion that would be unprintable in most publications.

After his 1997 album *All That Matters* performed disappointingly on the charts, Bolton switched gears by recording *My Secret Passion* (1998), a collection of opera arias that reached the top position on the classical charts, causing many of Bolton's detractors to admit that he performed this material with more finesse than had been expected. Taking a self-imposed sabbatical from the music industry for the next several years, Bolton continued his deep involvement with charity work, lending his support to the fight against child abuse. In 2002 he released a comeback album, *Only a Woman Like You*, in which he

updated his sound with slick, Latin-style rhythms and a new sense of vocal restraint.

After an unsuccessful career as a hard-rock artist, Bolton reinvented himself in the 1980s as a torchy balladeer of classic R&B songs and glitzy pop. Although his derivative style brought critical disdain, it pushed sales of his albums over the 40 million mark. Proving himself adaptable to new ideas, Bolton made a successful venture into opera before returning to streamlined pop music in the early 2000s.

SELECTIVE DISCOGRAPHY: *Michael Bolotin* (RCA, 1975); *Michael Bolton* (Columbia, 1983); *The Hunger* (Columbia, 1987); *Soul Provider* (Columbia, 1989); *Time, Love and Tenderness* (Columbia, 1991); *All That Matters* (Columbia, 1997); *My Secret Passion* (Columbia, 1998); *Only a Woman Like You* (Jive, 2002).

DAVID FREELAND

BON JOVI

Formed: 1983, Sayreville, New Jersey

Members: Jon Bon Jovi, vocals, guitar (born John Bongiovi, Perth Amboy, New Jersey, 2 March 1962); David Bryan, keyboards (born Edison, New Jersey, 7 February 1962); Richie Sambora, guitar (born Woodbridge, New Jersey, 11 July 1960); Tico Torres, drums (born New York, New York, 7 October 1953). Former member: Alec John Such, bass (born Perth Amboy, New Jersey, 14 November 1956).

Genre: Rock

Best-selling album since 1990: *Crush* (2000)

Hit songs since 1990: "It's My Life," "Bed of Roses," "Always"

After a commercial downturn for much of the 1990s, Bon Jovi returned with a bang in 2000 and reestablished themselves as America's preeminent commercial rock band.

John Bongiovi had an inglorious start to his musical career, working as a "go-fer" at New York's legendary Power Station recording studio. After hours he began recording his own songs and soon had amassed a collection of demos. One song in particular, "Runaway," attracted the attention of a local radio station, WAPP, which included the song on a compilation of local music. "Runaway" became a huge local hit and even began to pick up national airplay. Bongiovi, lacking a band, quickly called upon fellow New Jerseyans David Bryan (keyboards), Richie Sambora (guitar), Tico Torres (drums), and Alec John Such (bass), dubbing his new band Bon Jovi and changing his own name to Jon Bon Jovi.

Bon Jovi signed with Mercury Records, which released the band's self-titled debut album in 1984. "Runaway" was included on the album and, backed by the marketing power of Mercury Records, landed in the Top 40 in its second life. With their big, teased hair and tight leather pants—the standard look of hard rock acts of the day—the band quickly became an MTV favorite.

The band's second album, *7800 Fahrenheit* (1985), was a commercial disappointment and put pressure on the band to release a hit third album. Bon Jovi did not disappoint—the resulting *Slippery When Wet* (1986) spent ninety-four weeks on the *Billboard* album charts, including eight at number one; the album sold 9 million copies in the United States and featured two number one singles: "You Give Love a Bad Name" and "Livin' on a Prayer."

The band toured relentlessly in support of *Slippery When Wet* and, when the tour finally ended, the band rushed back into the studio to record *New Jersey* (1988), a big-sounding pop-rock record that featured four Top 10 singles, including the chart toppers "Bad Medicine" and "I'll Be There for You." *New Jersey* sold 5 million copies.

Physically exhausted from years of constant touring and recording, the band members went their separate ways at the beginning of the 1990s. The producers of the movie *Young Guns II* wanted to use Bon Jovi's cowboy anthem "Wanted Dead or Alive" as the movie's theme song, but Jon Bon Jovi ended up recording the entire soundtrack album for the film—his first solo effort—and also made his film debut in the movie. The soundtrack featured the single "Blaze of Glory," which reached number one on the pop charts and earned Jon Bon Jovi a Golden Globe for Best Song from a Motion Picture. Sambora also released his own solo album, the bluesy *Stranger in This Town* (1991), which features guitar legend Eric Clapton.

In 1992 the band reunited to record *Keep the Faith*. The album was a commercial disappointment by Bon Jovi's standards, selling only 2 million copies in the United States. Though the band had come to rely less on its keyboard-driven, 1980s-style sound in favor of a more complex and varied hard-rock presentation, Bon Jovi suffered from their past success and reputation; in large part, American commercial hard rock had shifted away from the band's pop-metal style and more toward the raw, grunge sounds of bands such as Nirvana. *Keep the Faith* did spawn the top ten ballad "Bed of Roses," which features a soft piano prominently in the mix and sports a slick, adult contemporary sound, punctuated by the romantic chorus hook: "I want to lay you down in a bed of roses / For tonight, I sleep on a bed of nails / I want to be just as close as the Holy Ghost is / And lay you down on a bed of roses."

With Bon Jovi's contemporary music stalling, Mercury Records chose to release *Cross Road*, a greatest hits collection, in 1994. *Cross Road* featured the new song

"Always," another tender ballad. "Always" sold more than 3 million copies as a single and suggested that a Bon Jovi comeback was in the offing. The band's renewed success was tempered somewhat by the loss of their original bass player, Alec John Such, whom the band fired in 1994.

The band's much-anticipated new album, *These Days* (1995), was a major commercial disappointment for Bon Jovi, selling only 650,000 copies. The album's slick adult contemporary pop-rock sound disappointed the Bon Jovi faithful, which longed for the band's trademark working-class rock anthems such as "Livin' on a Prayer." The band's future seemed in doubt as well, with Jon Bon Jovi and Richie Sambora each focusing on second solo albums. Jon Bon Jovi also became more involved in cinema, starring in the film *Moonlight and Valentino* (1996).

In 2000 Bon Jovi released their seventh studio album, *Crush*. The album found the band embracing its roots, revisiting the big arena-rock sound that had established the band in the 1980s—a sound that also was enjoying major retro appeal at the time. The lead single "It's My Life" was a major hit. "It's My Life" features a crunching rock sound punctuated by the same talk-box guitar that Sambora had employed on "Livin' on a Prayer"; the song's lyrics find the band celebrating the here-and-now and addressing adversity, perhaps in recognition of the band's own difficulties: "It's my life / It's now or never / I ain't gonna live forever / I just want to live while I'm alive." *Crush* debuted on the *Billboard* album charts at number seven and sold more than 7 million copies worldwide. In support of the album, the band did a sold-out arena tour of Europe, Japan, and the United States, culminating in two homecoming concerts at Giants Stadium in New Jersey; the concerts, broadcast on VH1, broke the music television station's ratings records.

The band's plans for a hiatus following the *Crush* tour changed with the terrorist attacks of September 11, 2001. Bon Jovi appeared at the Tribute to Heroes telethon and at the Concert for New York that fall, raising money for victims of the tragedy. Bon Jovi also returned to the studio to record *Bounce*, a tribute to the nation's resiliency in the face of the terrorist attacks. Released in 2002, the album featured the hard-charging lead single "Everyday," which, like "It's My Life," celebrated the band's live-in-the-moment philosophy: "I've had enough of cryin' / Bleeding, sweatin', dyin' / Hear me when I say / Gonna live my life every day." *Bounce* debuted at number two on the Billboard album charts.

Bon Jovi emerged from a commercial void in the 1990s and launched a major comeback by returning to their musical roots. Launching a "second career" with "It's My Life," Bon Jovi entered the new millennium once again atop the charts.

SELECTIVE DISCOGRAPHY: *Bon Jovi* (Mercury, 1984); *7800 Fahrenheit* (Mercury, 1985); *Slippery When Wet* (Mercury, 1986); *New Jersey* (Mercury, 1988); *Keep the Faith* (Mercury, 1992); *These Days* (Mercury, 1995); *Crush* (Island, 2000); *Bounce* (Island, 2002).

                                    SCOTT TRIBBLE

BONE THUGS-N-HARMONY

Formed: 1993, Cleveland, Ohio

Members: Anthony "Krayzie Bone" Henderson, vocals (born Cleveland, Ohio, 3 June 1974); Byron "Bizzy Bone" McCane, vocals (born Columbus, Ohio, 12 September 1976); Steve "Layzie Bone" Howse, vocals (born Cleveland, Ohio, 23 September 1977); Charles "Wish Bone" Scruggs, vocals (born Cleveland, Ohio, August 1977); Stan "Flesh-N-Bone" Howse, vocals (born Cleveland, Ohio).

Genre: Hip-Hop

Best-selling album since 1990: *E 1999 Eternal* (1995)

Hit songs since 1990: "Thuggish Ruggish Bone," "1st of tha Month," "Tha Crossroads"

In the mid-1990s, Cleveland rappers Bone Thugs-N-Harmony became the first major hip-hop artists to emerge from the Midwest, achieving near-instant success with a fresh variation of the then-dominant G-funk sound. Alternating reggae-inflected, rapid-fire emceeing, and interwoven vocal harmonies over G-funk's typical funk-based, synth-laden melodic grooves, Bone Thugs-N-Harmony quickly scored a pair of hits, a cult favorite EP, and a blockbuster debut album that is one of the milestones of the 1990s. Following their impressive debut, however, they managed to do little more than repeat their signature sound. Underperforming solo projects and the disappointing commercial and critical reception of their ambitious second album weakened Bone Thugs-N-Harmony's cohesion as a group. Nonetheless, they remained together, releasing their fourth album in 2002.

The five founding members of Bone Thugs-N-Harmony (Krayze Bone, Layzie Bone, Bizzy Bone, Wish Bone, and Flesh-N-Bone) began rapping together in Cleveland, Ohio, in the early 1990s, a time when hip-hop was dominated by artists based either in New York or Los Angeles. Realizing the improbability of getting noticed from their hometown, in 1993 the group traveled to Los Angeles and auditioned for Eric "Eazy-E" Wright, founder of the influential "gangsta" rap group N.W.A. Impressed, Eazy-E signed them to his label, Ruthless Records, which released Bone Thugs-N-Harmony's debut EP, *Creepin' On Ah Come Up,* in the summer of 1994. The album's first single, "Thuggish Ruggish Bone," showcased the group's novel combination of high-speed, reggae-influenced rapping and sung vocal harmonies over a typically synthesizer-heavy, funk-based "G-funk" groove. "Thuggish Ruggish Bone" quickly became a huge rap hit, particularly in the Midwest, and crossed over to the pop charts. A second single, "Foe Tha Love of $," also did well, driving sales of *Creepin' On Ah Come Up* to 2 million. Bone Thugs-N-Harmony promptly returned to the studio with their executive producer, Eazy-E, to record a full-length album.

Released in the summer of 1995, *E 1999 Eternal* skillfully expands the sound established in *Creepin' On Ah Come Up* to album length. *E 1999 Eternal* is not groundbreaking; it competently follows the then-successful G-funk template, combining slow grooves and heavy bass with whiny synthesized melodies. Moreover, much of its lyrics cover the standard "gangsta" rap themes of pot-smoking, drinking, and crime. The album is notable chiefly for the unique rapping style and the consistently masterful interweaving of Bone Thug-N-Harmony's five voices. Bone Thugs-N-Harmony further distinguished themselves with the album's first single, "1st of Tha Month," which slyly comments on urban poverty by celebrating the day welfare checks come. The song helped to drive the album to the top of the R&B and Pop charts, but it was the album's second single that turned Bone Thugs-N-Harmony into superstars. Released in May 1996, "Tha Crossroads" is at once a somber meditation on mortality and a heartfelt pledge never to forget dead loved ones, including the band's mentor, Eazy-E, who died suddenly from AIDS-related complications a few months before the album's release. "Tha Crossroads" connected with listeners, topping the pop charts and winning a Grammy for Best Rap Performance by Duo or Group in early 1997. Its massive success helped drive sales of *E 1999 Eternal* to 4 million.

Bone Thugs-N-Harmony—minus Flesh-N-Bone, who was off pursuing a solo career—followed up their debut with the double album *The Art of War* in July 1997. Although the album yielded the hit singles "Look My Eyes" and "If I Could Teach the World" and eventually sold 4 million copies, many regarded it as a disappointing and overlong retread of *E 1999 Eternal*. The members of Bone Thugs-N-Harmony spent the remainder of the 1990s releasing solo albums and launching the spin-off group Mo Thugs Family, which consisted of Bone Thugs-N-Harmony and various artists signed to the group's Mo Thugs label.

None of these projects attracted lasting attention, however, and in early 2000 Bone Thugs-N-Harmony released their third album, *BTNHResurrection*. Although touted as a "comeback" album, *BTNHResurrection* neither

Bone Thugs-N-Harmony, July 1997. L-R: Bizzy Bone, Wish Bone, Krayzie Bone, Layzie Bone. Member Flesh-N-Bone was in jail at the time. [AP/WIDE WORLD PHOTOS]

matched the sales of its predecessors nor generated any significant hits. In October 2002 Bone Thugs-N-Harmony released *Thug World Order*, which featured a collaboration with pop singer Phil Collins. In early 2003 Bone Thugs-N-Harmony announced that Bizzy Bone was no longer with the group, citing personal differences.

Bone Thugs-N-Harmony's fresh vocal style made them the first Midwestern rap act to achieve widespread success, further loosening the grip of New York and Los Angeles on hip-hop culture. Although their career never again achieved the heights at which it began, their debut album and its breakout single, "Tha Crossroads," are major works of 1990s pop music.

SELECTIVE DISCOGRAPHY: *Creepin' On Ah Come Up* (Ruthless, 1994); *E 1999 Eternal* (Ruthless, 1995); *The Art of War* (Ruthless, 1997); *BTNHResurrection* (Ruthless, 2000); *Thug World Order* (Ruthless, 2002).

WEBSITE: www.bonethugsnharmony.com.

MATT HIMES

BOSTON POPS ORCHESTRA

Formed: 1885, Boston, Massachusetts

Genre: Classical, Pop

The Boston Pops is one of the oldest and most venerable musical institutions in the United States. Founded in 1885 for a Promenade Series by the Boston Symphony Orchestra, the Pops promised Bostonians programs of "light music of the best class." It also promised Boston Symphony musicians employment during the six months of the year they were normally unemployed.

Begun in the summer as an attempt to recreate the ambience of the concert gardens of Vienna, the Pops Orchestra won immediate popularity and quickly evolved into its comfortable Americana persona. The orchestra's timing coincided with the development of a distinctive American music in the 1890s, especially that of march king John Philip Sousa, whose music the orchestra frequently performed. By 1899 the orchestra had adopted Sousa's

"Stars and Stripes Forever!" as the traditional finale for its concerts. More than a century later, the Pops format is essentially the same: programs of three sections divided by two intermissions.

From the start the orchestra championed music by composers of its time. As long as the music was fun the audiences were loyal. In 1890 the orchestra—still essentially the Boston Symphony musicians—formally adopted the name of the Boston Pops Orchestra. By the 1920s, the Pops was running out of steam. The Italian composer and pianist Alfred Casella, appointed music director in 1927, tried to deepen the orchestra's programming, performing heavier and more cerebral music. Audience complaints led to the termination of Casella's contract at the end of 1929.

That set the stage for Arthur Fiedler, then a thirty-five-year-old violist who had been a member of the orchestra for fifteen years. Fiedler took over as music director and began one of the longest and most successful musical partnerships in American music history. Fiedler had a keen business sense, knew his audience, and infused his programs with a sense of fun. He redecorated the concert hall (installing a big crystal chandelier over the stage) and revamped the music, concentrating on the best light music of the day (his first program included Ravel's "Bolero," which had been composed only the year before), including music by Gershwin and Romberg. He also refocused the orchestra's repertoire on American music, programming what at the time was called "symphonic jazz" and including music from current Broadway hits. Fiedler's changes were an instant pick-me-up for the orchestra, and audiences returned.

In 1935 the orchestra made its first recordings, among them "Jalousie" by Jacob Gade. The song became a big hit, the first orchestral recording to sell 1 million records. The recording also established the orchestra's identity for a vast new audience. For the ensuing fifty years under Fiedler's baton, the Boston Pops became the most recorded orchestra in the world, selling millions of records. In 1962 the orchestra began regular national broadcasts and in 1969 landed on public television in the *Evening at Pops* series. The orchestra's July 4, 1976, bicentennial concert on the Boston Esplanade drew an audience of 400,000, the biggest in orchestral history. Through TV, radio, and recordings, the orchestra became an American ambassador, touring both inside and outside the United States. Fiedler engaged some of the best performers of the day as soloists, but he was the Pops's charismatic star until his death in 1979.

The Pops was so identified with Fiedler that it was difficult to imagine the orchestra without him; the inspired choice to succeed him was John Williams, well known for his orchestral music for blockbuster Hollywood movies such as *Star Wars*, *Superman*, and *Close Encoun-*

ters of the Third Kind. Williams brought in a new generation of fans, broadened and updated the orchestra's repertoire, and led the orchestra in a series of best-selling recordings. Williams's movie celebrity helped sell the orchestra's tours.

In 1993 Keith Lockhart took over as music director. Lockhart broadened the orchestra's touring activities, taking the Pops to concert halls and sports arenas across the country. The Pops makes a half-dozen appearances on national television each year, tours internationally, and, in 1998, was nominated for a Grammy in the Classical Crossover category for *The Celtic Album*. In February 2002 the Pops performed in the pregame show at the Super Bowl in New Orleans, the first time an orchestra has been featured at a Super Bowl.

The Boston Pops is a living national monument that attracts fans and visitors from all over America. Its musical standards—as you might expect from musicians of the Boston Symphony—are high, and its repertoire, though lightweight, is performed with zest. In the late twentieth century, most American orchestras performed regular pops concerts, but none did it with the flair of the Bostonians.

SELECTIVE DISCOGRAPHY: *Fiedler's Greatest Hits* (RCA, 1991); *American Visions* (RCA, 1997); *Cinema Serenade, Vol. 2* (Sony, 1999).

BIBLIOGRAPHY: H. Dickson, *Arthur Fiedler and the Boston Pops: An Irreverent Memoir* (New York, 1984); J. Fiedler, *Arthur Fiedler: Papa, the Pops, and Me* (New York, 1994).

WEBSITE: www.bso.org.

DOUGLAS MCLENNAN

BOUKMAN ESPERYANS

Formed: mid-1980s, Port-au-Prince, Haiti

Members: Daniel Beaubrun, lead and backup vocals, lead guitar, bass, drum programming; Theodore "Lolo" Beaubrun Jr., lead and backup vocals, keyboards, piano, tambou; Mimerose "Mize" Beaubrun, lead and backup vocals; Marjorie Beaubrun, backup vocals; Eddy "Samba Agua" Francois, lead and backup vocals, rhythm guitar, bass; Evens Seney, backup vocals, maman toubou (lead mother drum); Gary Seney, backup vocals, tambou, kata, percussion; Frantz "Ti Crabe" Seney, backup vocals, percussion; Patrick St. Val-Demorcy, backup vocals, percussion; Henry Bernard D, backup vocals, katabou, percussion; Maggy Jn-Louis, backup vocals.

Genre: World

Best-selling record since 1990: *Vodou Adjae* (1991)

Hit songs since 1990: "Ke'-m Pa Sote," "Wet Chenn," "Kalfou Danjare"

The brothers Theodore, known as "Lolo," and Daniel Beaubrun were raised as members of the Protestant elite in Haiti, the poorest country in the Western Hemisphere. During their childhood their mother separated from their father, a satirical comic who headed the National Theatre in Haiti and who introduced his sons to the music of James Brown. They went to live with her in Brooklyn, New York, where they heard soul and rock and roll hits, including the music of Jimi Hendrix, Carlos Santana, and Bob Marley on the radio.

In 1978 Lolo and his wife, Mimerose Beaubrun, an anthropologist, joined a Haitian "lakou," a commune organized around a central courtyard after an African model, in order to investigate their cultural and spiritual roots. Their search led them to the vodou religion, long an opposition force to the dominant Catholic Church and oligarchic government of Haiti, and they began leading a drum ensemble in local performances. With Daniel adding rock and roll elements (foremost, electric guitar lines), Even Seney at the center of the percussion section, and Eddie Francois as the charismatic lead singer, they named themselves after Boukman Dutty, a legendary Jamaican-born vodou priest who fought for Creole freedom from French colonialism and slavery in the revolution of 1804.

Minidaz bands, spurring a "roots-music-fusion" movement, were then on the rise in Haiti, along with rara groups, bands of men blowing one-pitch wooden or metal vaskins. They asserted the raw music of freed slaves against the frothy "compas" dance style favored by the Duvalier family dictatorship that had governed Haiti for some thirty years. However, roots bands ignored pressing social issues in their lyrics, a failing Lolo corrected. His song "Wett Chenn" ("Remove the Chains") won the third Konkou Mizik (Pop Music Competition) in 1989 with the words "Get angry . . . break the chains that keep us from uniting . . . ever since Africa we've been suffering / it's so much harder here. . . ."

Boukman Experyans's songs were banned from Haitian radio but were broadcast on pirate stations and disseminated via self-recorded cassettes. Their second enormous hit, "Ke'-m pa sote" ("My heart doesn't leap / I'm not afraid") (1990), challenged the Duvalier government outright with music drawn from a chant to the vodou war god. They won the year's competition at Carnival, only the second Carnival celebration the government had allowed since 1985, and "Ke'-m pa sote" became an anthem of the presidential campaign by professed reformer Jean-Bertrand Aristide; Boukman performed at his inauguration in 1991. But by the end of 1990, Francois, Seney, and guitarist Vladimir (Jimmy) Jean-Felix left the Beaubruns to form their own mizik rasin group, Boukan Ginen.

In 1991 Boukman Esperyans released the album *Vodou Adjae*, a collection of its competition-winning songs. Its title was the name given the band's dance style, borrowed from a temple dance following a vodou ritual. The band toured the United States, but their success was hampered at home by the resurgence of the brutal Haitian military after a coup deposing Aristide. At one concert in Haiti, Lolo was stopped by soldiers from singing the forbidden title track of Boukman's Grammy-nominated album *Kalfou Danjare* ("Dangerous Crossroads"; 1992); when the audience members began to sing the song, they were bombarded with tear-gas. Though Boukman's popularity afforded the band members some protection from the violence taking hold of their society, they were affected by the American embargo imposed on Haiti and the death of their bassist, Oliche Lynch, whose emergency medications for meningitis mysteriously went missing at the Port-au-Prince airport.

In the summer of 1994 Boukman Experyans embarked on a European tour but were denied permission to perform as scheduled in the United States because of new visa restrictions. They were not allowed to return to Haiti, either, and so took refuge in Jamaica, where they eventually obtained legal status and produced a third album, *Liberté (Pran Pou'l!) / Liberty (Let's Take It!)*, at Bob Marley's Tuff Gong studio in Kingston. After resecuring Haitian residence, they recorded the album *Revolution* in the New Jersey studio of the rock band the Fugees, with repertoire incorporating, for the first time, English lyrics and Japanese folk melodies.

Some reviewers contend that Boukman Espyeryans have lost their spark, but other critics wrote glowingly of the band's late 1990s performance at Fete de Piyan. One critic noted Beaubrun's devotion to twin goals: "to reinstate Haitian culture and to resist the waves of politically motivated, anti-Haitian propaganda." The band continues to reach out, adapting Jamaican reggae bass lines and American funk guitar fills.

SELECTIVE DISCOGRAPHY: *Vodou Adjae* (Mango, 1991); *Kalfou Danjare* (Mango, 1992); *Liberté* (Pran Pou'l!) / *Liberty* (Let's Take It!) (Island, 1995); *Revolution* (Lightyear, 1999); *Live at Red Rocks* (Lightyear, 1999); *Kanaval Rasin-Vodou Adja* (TropicSimbi, 2000).

HOWARD MANDEL

PIERRE BOULEZ

Born: Montbrison, France, 26 March 1925

Genre: Classical

Best-selling album since 1990: *Pierre Boulez Edition:* Stravinsky, *Pétrouchka/Le Sacre du printemps*

Pierre Boulez is arguably one of the twentieth century's most innovative composers. A conductor, author, and lecturer of international renown, he helped reshape the course of music after World War II.

Early Innovations and Conductor by Accident

Coming of age during the Nazi occupation of his native France, Boulez initially studied mathematics. His first important compositions date from the mid-1940s, when he emerged from compositional studies at the Paris Conservatory with French composer and mystic Olivier Messiaen and René Lebowitz, who had been a pupil of Schoenberg and Webern. Boulez's Second Piano Sonata (1947-8) marked his own radical and mature adaptation of the atonal twelve-tone method pioneered by Schoenberg, Berg, and Webern. Boulez would go on to apply serial principles to rhythm, register, dynamics, and all other aspects of music in his *Structures I* for two pianos (1951–2), fully developing that style in two large-scale works with strong literary references: *Le marteau sans maître* ("The hammer without a master") (1953-5), after the poems of surrealist René Char, and *Pli selon pli* ("Fold upon fold") (1957-62), set to poems of Mallarmé.

Attending a rehearsal prior to a performance of *Marteau* in the late 1950s, Boulez noticed that the conductor and musicians were completely lost trying to make sense of the music, and so Boulez stepped in. Boulez's subsequent conducting was initially devoted to performing new works that otherwise would not have been heard, but over time his repertoire expanded to include music of the recent past as well. Boulez was chosen by George Szell in 1969 to become the Cleveland Orchestra's principal guest conductor so that Szell's audiences would be able to hear large doses of twentieth-century music that Szell himself felt unable to present convincingly. Boulez's Cleveland Orchestra recording of Stravinsky's *The Rite of Spring* had a transparency and power that forever changed the way the public thought about the work. In 1971, Boulez went on to simultaneously accept the music directorships of London's BBC Symphony and the New York Philharmonic. The New York years were particularly stormy ones, with Boulez constantly taxing the ears, minds, and endurance of post-Bernstein audiences with experimental and unpopular scores and with what more than one critic labeled his "French arrogance."

After a stunning success with Wagner's *Parsifal* at the composer's own theater in Bayreuth (in Germany), Boulez was invited by Wagner's grandson to conduct his first *Der Ring des Nibelungen* (a cycle of Wagner operas) for the *Ring* centennial in 1976. A controversial contemporary staging of the work by Patrice Chéreau caused an uproar among Wagnerian traditionalists.

New Materials, New Music

In 1974, French president George Pompidou was courting Boulez to come back to the land he had left in self-imposed exile because of what Boulez considered to be government limitations on artistic freedom. Boulez insisted that he would return only if the conditions could be set up for researching the most advanced technology available that could be applied to the composition of new music. To that end Boulez founded the Paris-based IRCAM—The Institute for Research of Coordination between Acoustics and Music—in 1976. IRCAM's goal has been to enlarge the domain of materials used for music, a goal that has been embraced by musicians of all genres, including rock artists such as Frank Zappa.

According to Boulez a crisis had emerged in the late twentieth century because composers' imaginations had gone beyond the tools that were then available. To illustrate his point, he noted how architecture had been completely transformed when the new materials of concrete, glass, and steel replaced stone and wood as building materials.

A Greek Temple or a Gothic Cathedral, Boulez argued, could no more be built with steel and concrete than a skyscraper could be built with marble or sandstone. Likewise, composers had been using the same acoustic instruments for centuries, and the possibilities of music making that existed with them had been exhausted. Electronic media, still in its infancy, opened up a new frontier for an entirely new type of music where new tuning systems and new sounds not achievable through traditional means would be possible.

Boulez has written a handful of works incorporating the cutting-edge technology that had been developed at IRCAM, excerpts from one of which—*Répons* (Responses) (1981–1988)—was the centerpiece of an extraordinary and groundbreaking series of concerts when Boulez's L'Ensemble InterContemporain toured the United States in 1986. "The sound," as Boulez himself described it at the time, "was everywhere yet nowhere." Entire ripples of sound made up of digital transformations of conventional instrumental timbres made in real time engulfed the listener from every direction. Unlike early electronic music pieces, which had to be created layer by layer on tape, the transformations for *Répons*—the recording of which won a Grammy Award in 1999 and pushed the limits of recording technology—were made in real time. This same effect is employed for a large-scale stage work that Boulez was working on as the new millennium began.

Since the 1990s Boulez has been more visible as a conductor than as a composer. In addition to seminal concerts and recordings with the Vienna and Berlin Philharmonics, in 1995 Boulez became the principal guest conductor of the Chicago Symphony Orchestra following years of sold-out Boulez-led concerts and a string of landmark Grammy Award–winning recordings Boulez made with that ensemble (Boulez has won twenty-three Grammy Awards since 1967). Ironically, these awards highlighted recordings of earlier twentieth-century masterpieces by other composers. In fact, the Chicago Symphony Orchestra's music director, Daniel Barenboim, has actually conducted more of Boulez's music with the CSO than Boulez himself has.

Formerly a radical and outspoken *enfant terrible* who advocated that concert halls and opera houses be burnt to the ground as dead monuments to an irrelevant past, Boulez would paradoxically spend the twilight of his career primarily as an interpreter of that past. His provocative statements—which in the spirit of Boulez's philosophical mentor Friedrich Nietzsche were intended metaphorically—came back to haunt him in the weeks after September 11, 2001, when, while on tour at a music festival in Basle, Switzerland, the seventy-six-year-old Boulez was dragged out of his hotel bed in the middle of the night by police, handcuffed, and held for three hours as a terrorism suspect before a formal apology was made. Notoriously late for commission deadlines, including a decade-old CSO commission, and a composer who frequently returns to older works to revise them, Boulez admits that he has difficulty predicting the amount of time it will take him to enter into a work and, harder still, how long it will take to escape out of a new work once it has come into being: "To me, each of my compositions is like a labyrinth, and a labyrinth can go on forever."

SELECTIVE DISCOGRAPHY: *Boulez Conducts Zappa: The Perfect Stranger and Other Works* (EMI, 1984); Boulez, *Rituel/Éclat Multiples* (Sony re-release, 1991); Debussy, *Pelléas et Mélisande* (Sony re-release,1991); Ravel, *The Orchestral Works* (Sony re-release, 1991); Varèse, *Arcana/Ameriques/Ionization/Density 21.5/Offrandes/Integrales/Octandre* (Sony re-release, 1991); Webern, *Complete Works* (Sony re-release, 1991); Bartók, *The Wooden Prince/Cantana profana* (Deutsche Grammophon, 1992); Stravinsky, *Pétrouchka/Le Sacre du printemps* (Deutsche Grammophon, 1992); Debussy, *Images* (Deutsche Grammophon, 1992); Schoenberg, *Die Glückliche Hand/Variations for Orchestra/Verklärte Nacht* (Deutsche Grammophon,1993); Schoenberg, *Gurre-Leider/Four Songs* (Sony re-release, 1993); Schoenberg, *Pierrot lunaire/Lied der Waldtaube/Erwartung* (Sony re-release, 1993); Stravinsky, *The Firebird/Fireworks/Four Studies* (Deutsche Grammophon, 1993); Boulez, *Structures [I, II]* (Wergo, 1993); Bartók, *Concerto for Orchestra/Four Orchestral Pieces* (Deutsche Grammophon, 1994); *Boulez Conducts Ligeti* (Deutsche Grammophon, 1994); Ravel, *Boléro/Ma mère l'oye/Miroirs* (Deutsche Grammophon, 1994); Debussy, *Orchestral Works* (Sony re-re-release, 1995); Bartók, *Divertimento/Dance Suite* (Deutsche Grammophon, 1995); Berg, *Altenberg Lieder/Early Songs* (Sony re-release, 1995); Berg, *Chamber Concerto/Three Orchestral Pieces/Violin Concerto* (Sony re-release, 1995); Boulez, *Pli selon pli/Livre pour cordes* (Sony re-release, 1995); Carter, *A Symphony of Three Orchestras/Varèse, Deserts/Ecuatorial/Hyperprism* (Sony re-release, 1995); Messiaen, *Et exspecto resurrectionem mortuorum/Couleurs de la cité céleste* (Sony re-release, 1995); Messiaen, *Chronochromie/La Ville d'en haut* (Deutsche Grammophon, 1995); Stravinsky, *Pétrouchka/Le Sacre du printemps* (Sony re-release, 1995); *Boulez, Schoenberg, Berio, Carter, Kurtàg, Xenakis* (Erato, 1995); Boulez, *Le visage nuptial/Dérive I/cummings ist der Dichter* (Erato re-release, 1995); Debussy, *La Mer/Nocturnes* (Deutsche Grammophon, 1995); Ravel, *Daphnis et Chloé/La valse* (Deutsche Grammophon, 1995); Mahler, *Symphony No. 6* (Deutsche Grammophon, 1995); Boulez, *Piano Sonata No. 2* (Deutsche Grammophon re-release, 1995); *Boulez Conducts Boulez . . . . explosante-fixe . . . Notations I-XII/Structures II* (Deutsche Grammophon, 1996); Bartók, *The Miraculous Mandarin/Music for Strings, Percussion, and Celesta* (Deutsche Grammophon, 1996); Birtwistle, *Secret Theatre/Tragoedia* (Deutsche Grammophon, 1996); Mahler, *Symphony No. 7* (Deutsche Grammophon, 1996); Schoenberg, *Moses und Aron* (Deutsche Grammophon, 1996); Berg, *Wozzeck* (Sony re-release, 1997); Berlioz, *Symphonie fantastique/Tristia* (Deutsche Grammophon, 1997); Mahler, *Symphony No. 5* (Deutsche Grammophon, 1997); Messiaen, *Poémes pour Mi/Sept Haikai/La Réveil des oiseaux* (Deutsche Grammophon, 1997); Bartók, *Bluebeard's Castle* (Deutsche Grammophon, 1998); Mahler, *Symphony No. 9* (Deutsche Grammophon, 1998); Schoenberg, *Pierrot lunaire/Herzgewächse/Ode to Napoleon* (Deutsche Grammophon, 1998); Bartók, *Violin Concerto No. 2/Rhapsodies* (Deutsche Grammophon, 1999); Boulez, *Répons/Dialogue de l'ombre double* (Deutsche Grammophon, 1999); Ravel, *The Piano Concertos* (Deutsche Grammophon, 1999); Mahler, *Symphony No. 1* (Deutsche Grammophon, 1999); Scriabin, *Poeme de l'extase/Piano Concerto/Promethée* (Deutsche Grammophon, 1999); R. Strauss, *Also sprach Zarathustra/Mahler, Totenfeier* (Deutsche Grammophon, 1999); Boulez, *Orchestral Works and Chamber Music* (Col Legno, 2000); Boulez, *Trois sonates pour piano* (Disques

Montaigne, 2000); Boulez, *Sur Incises/Messagesquisse/Anthèmes 2* (Deutsche Grammophon, 2000); Bruckner, *Symphony No. 8* (Deutsche Grammophon, 2000); *Complete Webern* (Deutsche Grammophon, 2000); Mahler, *Symphony No. 4* (Deutsche Grammophon, 2000); Messiaen, *80th Birthday Concert* (Disques Montaigne, 2000); Stravinsky, *Symphony of Psalms/Symphony in Three Movements* (Deutsche Grammophon, 2000); Boulez, *Domaines* (Harmonia Mundi, 2001); Berg, *Lulu* (Deutsche Grammophon re-release, 2001); *Boulez Conducts Varèse* (Deutsche Grammophon, 2001); *Boulez Conducts Stravinsky* (Deutsche Grammophon, 2001); Mahler, *Das Lied von der Erde* (Deutsche Grammophon, 2001); Schoenberg, *Piano Concerto* (Deutsche Grammophon, 2001); Wagner, *Der Ring des Nibelungen* (Philips re-release, 2001); Boulez, *Pli selon pli* (Deutsche Grammophon, 2002); Mahler, *Symphony No. 3* (Deutsche Grammophon, 2003).

BIBLIOGRAPHY: J. Peyser, *Boulez: Composer, Conductor, Enigma* (New York, 1976); P. Boulez, *Boulez on Music Today* (London, 1979); P. Griffiths, *Boulez* (London, 1985); H. Barth, *Wagner: A Documentary Study* (Preface by Pierre Boulez) (London, 1986); P. F. Stacey, *Boulez and the Modern Concept* (Lincoln, NE, 1987); P. Boulez, *Orientations: Collected Writings* (Cambridge, MA, 1990); L. Koblyakov, *Pierre Boulez: A World of Harmony* (London, 1990); P. Boulez, *Stocktakings from an Apprenticeship* (London, 1991); J. J. Nattiez and R. Samuels, *The Boulez-Cage Correspondence* (Cambridge, MA, 1993); G. Born, *Rationalizing Culture: IRCAM, Boulez, and the Institutionalization of the Musical Avant-Garde* (Berkeley, CA, 1995); J. Vermeil, *Conversations with Boulez: Thoughts on Conducting* (Portland, 1996); J. Peyser, *To Boulez and Beyond: Music in Europe Since the Rite of Spring* (New York, 1999); R. Di Pieto, *Dialogues with Boulez* (Lanham, MD, 2001).

WEBSITES: www.ircam.fr/index-e.html; www.cso.org/conductors_pboulez.taf.

DENNIS POLKOW

BOUNTY KILLER

Born: Rodney Basil Price; Trenchtown, Jamaica, 12 June 1972

Genre: Rap, Reggae

Best-selling album since 1990: *My Xperience* (1996).

Hit songs since 1990: "Living Dangerously," "Benz and Bimma"

Bounty Killer is one of the most popular and controversial dancehall singers in contemporary popular music. His songs, a conflicting mix of belligerent and conciliatory lyrics, give him a depth and texture rarely found in other artists.

Much of Bounty Killer's lyrical content is shaped by his poor and violent upbringing. He was born Rodney Basil Price in poverty, one of nine children. In his early childhood his mother moved the family to a literal dump in Kingston, the capital and largest city in Jamaica. Inspired by the reggae and dancehall music (a dance-oriented form of reggae) he heard in the neighborhood, Price began to sing, or DJ, as it is called in reggae and dancehall, at the age of nine. His skills won him a string of local talent competitions. When his family moved to another housing community, two events altered the trajectory of his career. First, his talent show record enabled him to perform at dances with his idol, the dancehall artist Shabba Ranks. Second, at the age of twelve he was caught in the crossfire of a politically charged gunfight and was shot. Spurred to exact vengeance against his assailants, Price adopted the name Bounty Hunter.

Bounty Hunter sought to achieve acclaim on the scale of Shabba Ranks and asked the veteran artist King Jammy for a "riddim," or a reggae beat, for use in a song. Bounty Hunter recorded "Coppershot." The lyrics chronicle his brutal past, and King Jammy thought it too stark for release. Nevertheless, King Jammy's brother Uncle T noticed the power of the song and aided its release to a welcoming audience, first in Jamaica and then in Europe and the United States. Largely based on his graphic verses, fans began to call Bounty Hunter by a new name: Bounty Killer.

Bounty Killer's subsequent songs were just as explicit, as evidenced in titles like "New Gun" and "Gun Thirsty." His rivalry with the more commercially successful dancehall artist Beenie Man enabled him to increase his international profile. The feud mirrored that of rap artists Notorious B.I.G. and Tupac Shakur. Bounty Killer and Beenie Man soon realized that their song feud could easily devolve into physical combat and signed a peace treaty in 1996, the same year in which Tupac Shakur was murdered.

Bounty Killer made some strategically prudent moves. He started a production company and record label. His breakout album, *My Xperience* (1996), features collaborations with big-name hip-hop artists the Fugees, Busta Rhymes, and Wu-Tang Clan, assuring him of a wide audience. Nevertheless, the biggest hit on the album, with his fellow Jamaican Barrington Levy, is a pure dancehall concoction. The juxtaposition of Bounty Killer's gruff voice and the sing-songy Levy on "Living Dangerously" made the track a nightclub staple. The album topped the reggae charts for half the year and spent two months at number one on the *Billboard* R&B albums chart.

Consistently solid albums followed, although many of his singles were banished from Jamaican radio, probably because of their political content. For example, his song "Down in the Ghetto" questions the origins of destructive forces in the community and implies a government conspiracy: "Who give the guns, who give the crack / No-one to take the blame." The Jamaican politician/activist Edward Seaga even wanted to use Bounty Killer's song "Fed Up," from My Xperience, in his election campaign, but Bounty Killer refused. Jamaican communities lauded Bounty Killer for his benefit concerts to aid disadvantaged children, and he earned the moniker "The Poor People's Governor."

In the early 2000s, Bounty Killer's career hit new zeniths. His album Ghetto Dictionary: The Mystery (2002) received a 2003 Best Reggae Album Grammy nomination but lost to Jamaican E.T, helmed by Lee "Scratch" Perry, Bob Marley's producer. Bounty Killer managed a high-profile collaboration with the multiplatinum pop-ska band No Doubt on the title track to their Grammy award-winning album Hey Baby (2002).

Bounty Killer's success suggests new heights to come. He has surmounted political opposition and earned respect from disenfranchised people, all while steadily augmenting his audience.

SELECTIVE DISCOGRAPHY: *Roots, Reality, and Culture* (VP, 1994); *Face to Face* (VP, 1994); *Down in the Ghetto* (VP, 1995); *No Argument* (Greensleeves, 1996); *My Xperience* (VP, 1996); *Ghetto Gramma* (Greensleeves, 1997); *Next Millennium* (TVT, 1998); *The 5th Element* (TVT, 1999); *Ghetto Dictionary: The Art of War* (VP, 2002); *Ghetto Dictionary: The Mystery* (VP, 2002).

DARA COOK

DAVID BOWIE

Born: David Robert Jones; London, England, 8 January 1947

Genre: Rock

Best-selling album since 1990: *Heathen* (2002)

One of rock's most prolific stars, singer/songwriter David Bowie is a steadfast innovator with a keen eye for staying ahead of the music scene; he is not content to merely rekindle aspects of his glorious past. Throughout his storied career, Bowie's commitment to his performance personae has crept into his off-stage life, making his actual self somewhat unrecognizable. Over the course of five decades, Bowie has been at the vanguard of glitter/glam rock, disco, technorock, electrofunk, and other musical variations; has unabashedly presented himself in various sexual and political identities; and has made successful forays into acting, producing, and art. Bowie is the first rock star to market a song's release exclusively over the Internet and to let his identity "go public" over the stock market. He embraces both the avant-garde and sheer commercialism.

Identity Oddity

Bowie was born David Robert Jones into a working-class family in the Brixton section of London, England. His leading musical influence was a half-brother, Terry, who introduced him to jazz, R&B, and artists from early American rock such as Elvis Presley and Little Richard. He learned both guitar and saxophone in his rather unhappy youth, which found him withdrawing further into music and other art forms. As a harbinger of the artistic variety Bowie later brought to his professional life, he acted in plays, studied mime for three years, and painted. He even seriously considered becoming a Buddhist monk. After graduating with a degree in commercial art from a technical school, Bowie worked for a short time in a London ad agency while playing music with local bands. As his music aspirations grew, he changed his name to David Bowie to avoid being mistaken for Davey Jones, the London theater star who gained fame in the late 1960s as the lead singer for the band the Monkees.

Although he enjoyed marginal recording success in London for nearly five years with various bands, Bowie's first work of prominence came in 1969 when he introduced the world to his thin, haunting voice with the release of the hit single, "Space Oddity." His first official solo album, *Man of Words, Man of Music* (1969), later re-released as *Space Oddity* (1969), contains the single of the same name, the tale of an all-American astronaut named Major Tom who chooses to disconnect from orbit and drift off into space rather than return to his ideal life on earth. Inspired by Stanley Kubrick's film *2001: A Space Odyssey*, the song was intended as an allegory for America's space program, which many counterculturalists viewed as a symbol of America's overachieving bravado. The rest of the album's songs are folk-style, psychedelic ramblings and give little notice of what was to come.

Bowie reached superstardom in the 1970s as he explored various rock music phases by reinventing himself three times: as the tragic glam rocker Ziggy Stardust; the fragile, androgynous Aladdin Sane; and the Euro-fascist Thin White Duke. This creativity generated several hit albums and many of his signature songs, including, "Changes," "Young Americans," "Rebel, Rebel," "Golden Years," and a precursor to disco recorded with his friend, John Lennon, titled "Fame." Whether it was a delusional reaction from heavy drug use or calculated self-promotion, Bowie lived these stage personae in his off-stage life. This fascinated the public, as did Bowie's declarations that he was homosexual and/or bisexual. (He married Angela Barnet in 1970 and they had a son, Zowie, in 1971.) Although much of post-1970s rock blurred the lines of gender dress codes, Bowie took cross-dressing several steps further than any other musical artist.

His most notable stage persona was Ziggy Stardust, and his album, *The Rise and Fall of Ziggy Stardust and the Spiders from Mars* (1972), counts as one of rock's classic recordings. Similar in attitude to the Restoration comedy fop, the character Ziggy, created in 1972, was an overblown parody of a rock star who took himself and his stardom too seriously. However, as Bowie prophesied on the album, Ziggy met his demise barely a year after he emerged. Even his band mates were flabbergasted when Bowie suddenly announced to a London audience in June 1973 at the Hammersmith Odeon on the last date of the Ziggy Stardust Tour that Ziggy would be retiring forever that evening. Incidentally, a DVD and double CD set of that historic concert, which includes Ziggy's farewell speech, was released in 2003.

By 1977 after several years of excessive drug abuse, Bowie moved to Berlin in order to put his life back together. This also marked another bizarre chapter for the rock chameleon as he embodied the persona of an eerie, clean-cut Anglo aristocrat called the "Thin White Duke." Bowie, during this phase, alarmed many of his fans as he spoke flatteringly of Hitler and many extreme far-right causes. One of the albums from this period, *Station to Station* (1976), contained the megahit "Golden Years."

Bowie also found time to produce and play on albums for Lou Reed, Iggy Pop, and Mott the Hoople, for whom he wrote the hit song "All the Young Dudes." For a short period in 1977, Bowie toured somewhat anonymously as Pop's piano player. Additionally, he acted in a several films and began the 1980s by joining the cast of the Broadway hit *The Elephant Man* in the demanding role of John Merrick, a man beset with a grotesque birth defect. Bowie's performance surprised skeptics and garnered excellent reviews.

The 1980s marked Bowie's most commercial period. His first two album releases, *Scary Monsters* (1980) and *Let's Dance* (1983), featured electronically informed, funky rock that spawned several of the decade's biggest hit singles, among them "Fashion," "Modern Love," "China Girl," and "Let's Dance." He also publicly announced his sobriety and that he was neither homosexual nor bisexual. Bowie continued mixing film acting with an active recording schedule that saw him release two more studio albums while also recording songs with Tina Turner and Mick Jagger. He and Jagger recorded a pop version of Mar-

---

Spot Light | Bowie Banks on His Future Success

In 1997 David Bowie issued $55 million worth of bonds against the future royalty payments on his massive catalog of music. The move prompted the *Guinness Book of World Records* to categorize Bowie as "the most valuable music artist on the stock market." He enlisted the help of investment guru David Porter to issue the ten-year, asset-backed "Bowie Bonds," which pay 7.9% interest to their holder. The entire issue was sold to the Prudential Insurance Co., providing Bowie with immediate millions and preventing him from having to wait for royalty earnings to trickle in over the years. The shrewd and successful financial maneuver was viewed negatively by many of Bowie's fans, who accused him of overt capitalism. However, the business world applauded and has since used it as a model that has been followed by many other entertainment artists and entities, including sports stars.

---

vin Gaye's "Dancing in the Streets" that received major airplay. If Bowie was playing characters throughout the 1980s, then one of them was certainly that of a successful and wealthy pop star.

Bowie Portrays Himself

In 1990 Bowie seemed to shed the success of the previous decade and revert to exploring the musical fringe by touring with a low-profile group of his assemblage called Tin Machine. They released two recordings, *Tin Machine* (1989) and *Tin Machine II* (1991), which gained little attention before the group broke up so that Bowie could resume his solo career. He released his first solo recording in six years, *Black Tie, White Noise* (1993), which contained many of the songs that Bowie wrote for his wedding in 1992 to Iman, a world-famous model who was born in Somalia. The album attempted to recreate the sound and hit success of *Let's Dance*, but sales fizzled.

Bowie enlisted producer/musician Brian Eno, with whom he had worked during his Berlin period, to assist him on his next recording, *Outside* (1995). Bowie also employed a market research team to discern what the public wanted to hear. The result was a concept album that featured a nebulous narrative casting a web of indiscernible, shady characters against the backdrop of the high art world. He followed the album's release by touring with the band Nine Inch Nails.

In 1996 Bowie was inducted into the Rock and Roll Hall of Fame. That same year he portrayed his late friend, Andy Warhol, in the film *Basquiat*. That role was Bowie's fifteenth film-acting appearance. He also broke new ground by becoming the first artist to release a song, "Telling Lies," exclusively over the Internet. A year later Bowie formed an Internet provider service called BowieNet that made, among other services, music and art information available to its paid subscribers. He also broke new ground when he floated a $55 million bond issue against his music royalties.

Inspired by his touring mates, Nine Inch Nails, Bowie explored the modern industrial beat and sifted his evocative baritone through studio electronics to win high critical acclaim on *Earthling* (1997). He followed that with an equally hip but introspective and cryptically styled solo effort, *Hours* (1999). Bowie once again set the music industry on its ear with the successful release of *Heathen* (2002), his twenty-fourth solo album. The album's stark simplicity brought it strong sales, and critics lauded the effort, claiming that it let Bowie be Bowie.

The line between impulsive artist and manipulative entrepreneur gets fuzzy over the multihued career of David Bowie. Never resting on his laurels, striving desperately forward with the times, he is undeniably one of the most influential and clever performers in rock music history.

SELECTIVE DISCOGRAPHY: *Space Oddity* (Mercury, 1969); *The Man Who Sold the World* (Mercury, 1970); *Hunky Dory* (RCA, 1971); *The Rise and Fall of Ziggy Stardust and the Spiders from Mars* (RCA, 1972); *Aladdin Sane* (RCA, 1973); *Diamond Dogs* (Virgin, 1974); *Young Americans* (RCA, 1975); *Station to Station* (RCA, 1976); *Low* (RCA, 1977); *Heroes* (RCA, 1978); *Lodger* (RCA, 1979); *Scary Monsters* (RCA, 1980); *Let's Dance* (EMI, 1983); *Tonight* (EMI, 1984); *Never Let Me Down* (EMI, 1987); *Tim Machine* (EMI, 1989); *Tin Machine II* (Victory, 1991); *Black Tie, White Noise* (Savage, 1993); *Outside* (Virgin, 1995); *Earthling* (Virgin, 1997); *Hours* (Virgin, 1999); *Heathen* (Columbia, 2002).

BIBLIOGRAPHY: D. Buckley, *Strange Fascination: David Bowie: The Definitive Story* (London, 2001).

DONALD LOWE

BOYZ II MEN

Formed: 1988, Philadelphia, Pennsylvania

Members: Nathan Morris (born Philadelphia, Pennsylvania, 18 June 1971); Wanya Morris (born Philadelphia, Pennsylvania, 29 July 1973); Michael McCary (born Philadelphia, Pennsylvania, 16 December 1971); Shawn Stockman (born Philadelphia, Pennsylvania, 26 September 1972). Former member: Marc Nelson.

Genre: R&B, Pop

Best-selling album since 1990: *II* (1994)

Hit songs since 1990: "End of the Road," "I'll Make Love to You," "On Bended Knee"

Excelling at tight, four-part harmony layered over sweet melodies, Boyz II Men became the most successful vocal group of the 1990s, selling more records than any group in rhythm and blues history. Building upon the sophisticated vocal interplay of 1960s groups such as the Temptations, as well as the energy and flash of 1980s superstars New Edition, Boyz II Men crafted smooth ballads that glorified sex and romance without venturing into explicitness. Their creamy sound was showcased on tuneful material supplied by hot 1990s record producers such as Babyface and Jimmy Jam and Terry Lewis. Well dressed and respectable, the group transcended boundaries of age, race, and sex. Although Boyz II Men's winning streak ran out by the end of the decade, a 2002 comeback album proved that its vocal sophistication and talent remained intact.

Beginnings

Formed in 1988 by five teenagers at the High School of the Creative and Performing Arts in Philadelphia, Pennsylvania, Boyz II Men initially billed itself as Unique Attraction. After performing a successful Valentine's Day concert sponsored by the school, the group honed a well-timed and executed act modeled upon New Edition. Sneaking backstage during a 1989 concert, the young men met Michael Bivins, a former New Edition member then making a transition into the business side of the music industry. Impressed with the performers' a cappella rendition of the New Edition hit, "Can You Stand the Rain," Bivins arranged for a recording contract with Motown Records, the label that launched famed 1960s groups such as the Supremes and the Temptations. Prior to entering the studio, member Marc Nelson dropped out of the group due to personal difficulties.

Reduced to a quartet, Boyz II Men evinced a subtle sense of harmony and swing on its debut album for Motown, *Cooleyhighharmony* (1991). Its title taken from the popular film, *Cooley High* (1975), the album sports a pleasing cross-section of 1990s R&B approaches, from the jumpy, up-tempo style known as "New Jack Swing" to glossy ballads. It was on the latter that the group excelled, its perfectly blended vocals grounded in McCary's low bass and Wanya Morris's pleading, slightly pinched high notes. "It's So Hard to Say Goodbye to Yesterday," the first of many number one R&B hits for the group, provides an example of Boyz II Men's unique style. Singing a cappella, without instrumental accompaniment, the members let their voices coast on a rich bed of sound supported by complex harmonies. Plush yet engaging, "It's So Hard" balances genuine feeling with vocal glitter such as melisma, the singing of multiple notes within a syllable. Such flourishes became Boyz II Men's trademark, evident in its smash hit of 1992, "End of the Road."

Stardom

With "End of the Road" securing the group's popularity through 1993, Boyz II Men did not record a follow-up album until 1994. Building upon the group's success with ballads, *II* was a well-structured collection of aching slow songs interrupted by the occasional upbeat number, all performed with a combination of grit and polish. "I'll Make Love to You," similar in sound and spirit to "End of the Road," surpassed the popularity of its predecessor, spending fourteen weeks at the number one pop position. Although the lyrics reach a new level of sexual forthrightness, with promises such as "I submit to your demands," they retain a feel of sweetness due to the group's gentle vocalizing. Like many of Boyz II Men's finest songs, "I'll Make Love to You" gains an added dimension through McCary's bass, which provides the music with a compelling through-line.

"On Bended Knee," another massive hit from *II*, is perhaps even more successful from an artistic standpoint. A swelling, old-fashioned ballad recalling the lush work of 1970s Philadelphia soul producers Kenneth Gamble and Leon Huff, "On Bended Knee" is supported with assured, tender vocals that balance the over-the-top lyrics: "I'll never walk again / Until you come back to me." The most impressive moment on *II*, however, is an a cappella rendition of the Beatles' hit, "Yesterday." Here, the group's deft sense of timing and interaction create a unity of purpose rare in contemporary pop music. Shifting vocal layers with each verse, adding rhythmic bass notes, and playing with volume and texture, Boyz II Men created what critics and fans agree is one of their finest performances. Like the great vocal "doo-wop" groups of the 1950s, Boyz II Men understands how individual sacrifice is built into the collaborative ethos; on "Yesterday" not one element sounds out of place.

Decline

In the mid-1990s Boyz II Men was at the peak of its popularity, but difficult times were ahead. After Motown angered the group by issuing a rehashed album of old mate-

"End of the Road"

By 1992 Boyz II Men had built a reputation as an exciting young vocal group on the basis of its *Cooleyhighharmony* album, released the previous year. Since the group's busy concert schedule prevented an immediate follow-up album, it quickly recorded a contribution for the soundtrack to the film *Boomerang* (1992). The song, "End of the Road," was a soft ballad written by Kenneth "Babyface" Edmonds, who would become one of the most successful producers of the 1990s. During an era in which many R&B groups were pushing the boundaries of sexuality, the song is notable for its old-fashioned profession of devotion. Trading lead vocals with dexterity, the singers build tension with a series of yearning pleas: "I can't sleep at night without holding you tight / Each time I try I just break down and cry." The bass recitative, recalling the spoken love ballads of 1970s singer Barry White, only adds to the song's romantic urgency. Although the record features the kind of slick, polished sound popular in the early 1990s, its heart-tugging feel of protestation saves it from blandness. Melodic and universal in its appeal, "End of the Road" shot to the top of the pop charts, remaining there for a record-breaking thirteen weeks. Armed with one of the longest-running hits in history, Boyz II Men had, by the end of 1992, achieved pop stardom.

rial, *The Remix Collection* (1995), relations with the label became strained. In spite of its title the group's 1997 album *Evolution* sounds similar to its earlier work, without the advancement of concept and idea that would have signified artistic development. In 2000 the group left Motown and moved to Universal Music for its next album, *Nathan Michael Shawn Wanya*. By now, Boyz II Men was writing much of its own material, with results less distinctive than the catchy love songs of its recent past. Another setback occurred when Michael McCary developed scoliosis and was forced to perform most of his live performances sitting down. In addition, the group's reliance on traditional love balladry had begun to seem old-fashioned, in comparison to the raunchy style of newer artists such as Sisqó and Next. Speaking to *Vibe* magazine in 2000, group member Nathan Morris expressed dismay over the new explicitness: "Someone says 'thong.' We say 'lingerie.'" Tellingly, none of the singles from *Nathan Michael Shawn Wanya* became substantial hits, and Boyz II Men, the most popular vocal group in the business only five years earlier, began to slip out of view.

In 2002, newly signed to Arista Records, Boyz II Men released *Full Circle*, an album that again showcased the group's impeccable harmonies. On the Babyface-penned ballad, "The Color of Love," the voices blend beautifully, alternating high and low notes and repeating the title in a gentle manner that recalls the soft pop music of the early 1970s. Although most of the album is built upon the group's standard ballad style, the thumping "Ain't a Thang Wrong" provides a nice change of pace, featuring a tough, heavy beat that resembles the sound of hip-hop artist Mary J. Blige. However, critics felt that the remainder of the material on *Full Circle*, most of it penned by the group, lacked distinction. The romantic style that once seemed so natural for Boyz II Men now sounded calculated; as a result the album did not fare well commercially or critically. In its review the U.K. *Guardian* complained that "everything is shoehorned into place with ruthless efficiency." In early 2003 McCary left the group, turning his attentions to the restaurant business.

Although its peak was brief, Boyz II Men left a deep imprint on pop and R&B of the 1990s, proving that old-fashioned harmony and love balladry could remain viable in the sophisticated world of modern pop. While other 1990s groups such as Destiny's Child were frequently pulled apart by infighting, Boyz II Men remained cohesive in spirit and sound, its relaxed, collaborative vocals pointing to group confidence and security. Sporting a wide range of voices, from bass to high tenor, the group honored the sound of the past while adding a sleek contemporary sheen. At its best, Boyz II Men created music that was both easy on the ears and artistically satisfying.

SELECTIVE DISCOGRAPHY: *Cooleyhighharmony* (Motown, 1991); *II* (Motown, 1994); *Evolution* (Motown, 1997); *Nathan Michael Shawn Wanya* (Universal, 2000); *Full Circle* (Arista, 2002). **Soundtracks:** *Boomerang* (La Face, 1992).

WEBSITE: www.boyzIImen.com.

DAVID FREELAND

BILLY BRAGG

Born: Steven William Bragg; Barking, Essex, England, 20 December 1957
Genre: Rock

Best-selling album since 1990: *Mermaid Avenue* (with Wilco, 1998)

Hit songs since 1990: "Sexuality," "You Woke Up My Neighborhood"

Always political, always outspoken, and always witty, British singer/songwriter Billy Bragg counts the Clash and Bob Dylan as equal influences on his folk rock protest songs. Bragg started off as a brash singer in the 1980s, admiring the Clash for their outspoken, do-it-yourself ethos and unabashed political beliefs, and infused his own music with barbed wit and picayune observations of life, class stratification, irresponsible governments, and male-female relationships. Bragg's music has historically sold well in his native country, but he mostly enjoyed a cult following in the United States during the early part of his career.

Bragg grew up in the East London suburb of Barking, a working-class neighborhood that accounts for his Cockney accent and his approach to songwriting. At age sixteen Bragg left school and started a spate of odd jobs, including working as a goat herder and a bank messenger, and bought a cheap guitar. His guitarist friend Wiggy, with whom Bragg still plays, taught him how to play, and the two formed a band called Riff Raff in 1977. The band split by 1981, and Bragg became a solo artist. Galvanized by the reelection of Margaret Thatcher, Bragg found his muse: political injustice. Angered by Thatcher's cuts to social services, and the miners' strike of 1984 in England, Bragg wrote some political songs and produced an EP that eventually landed him a deal with Charisma Records' Utility label. Through a series of record label shuffles, Bragg wound up at Go!Discs, after which his song "A New England" reached the top spot on Britain's independent charts in January 1984. The refrain of the song sums up Bragg's lyrical skills: "I don't want to change the world / I'm not looking for a new England / I'm just looking for another girl." It also shows his ability to mesh the political and the personal within a song.

Many years and several albums later Bragg broke through in the United States with the humorously titled *Don't Try This at Home* (1991), his most pop-minded, accessible album to date. The album even garnered him a number two hit on the *Billboard* Modern Rock chart with the sly, witty "Sexuality," which pokes fun at sexual mores and politics with its chorus "Sexuality / Young and warm and wild and free / Sexuality / Your laws do not apply to me." Thanks to "Sexuality," with the jangly guitar work of former Smiths member Johnny Marr, and the country-tinged love song "You Woke Up My Neighborhood," the album was his first to appeal to American radio. It also

Spot Light

Mermaid Avenue and Mermaid Avenue, Vol. 2

In the spring of 1995 Woody Guthrie's daughter Nora invited Billy Bragg to visit the Guthrie Archive in New York. Sensing a kinship, and hoping he might be the person to provide the musical context, she showed Bragg thousands of unpublished lyrics her father had written prior to his death. Bragg told the British publication *The New Statesman,* "We've had similar influences. But the political angle really binds me to Woody. I'm writing songs about unions, too, and there's not many of us about." Bragg recruited the Chicago alternative country rock band Wilco to collaborate with him on a Guthrie tribute, and the two proved an apt pairing: Bragg, for his Socialist, literate songwriting, and Wilco, for its keen understanding of American roots music. The album *Mermaid Avenue* (1998), with Bragg and Wilco songwriter Jeff Tweedy sharing composing credits, was recorded in Dublin, Ireland, and has sold more than 500,000 copies. Named for the street on Coney Island, New York, where Guthrie lived with his family after World War II, *Mermaid Avenue* is a timeless folk rock classic, from the bawdy "Walt Whitman's Niece" to the cavernous yearning of "California Stars" and the nonsense rhyming lyrics in the children's song "Hoodoo Voodoo." A follow-up, *Mermaid Avenue, Vol. 2* (1999), was recorded shortly thereafter, and both albums were nominated for Grammy Awards. A companion documentary on the project's genesis, *Billy Bragg & Wilco: Man in the Sand* (1999), offers a more intimate look. The *Mermaid Avenue* project boosted the career of both parties and sparked a renewed interest in a seminal American folksinger.

missioned Bragg, who in turn sought out Wilco, the alternative country band, to write and perform music for unreleased Woody Guthrie lyrics. The ensuing *Mermaid Avenue* project helped boost Bragg's visibility in the United States and secured his position as one of pop music's more unusual talents: a singer/songwriter with a biting, witty intelligence who manages to work everything from class inequality and global warming to the politics of interpersonal relationships into consistently engaging pop tunes that are never boring or preachy.

SELECTIVE DISCOGRAPHY: *Life's a Riot* (Charisma/Utility, 1981); *Talking with the Taxman about Poetry* (Elektra, 1986); *Don't Try This at Home* (Elektra, 1991); *Reaching to the Converted* (Rhino, 1999). **With Wilco:** *Mermaid Avenue* (Elektra, 1998); *Mermaid Avenue, Vol. II* (Elektra, 1999). **With the Blokes:** *England, Half English* (Elektra, 2002).

BIBLIOGRAPHY: A. Collins and B. Bragg, *Billy Bragg: Still Suitable for Miners—the Official Biography* (London, 2002).

WEBSITE: www.billybragg.co.uk.

CARRIE HAVRANEK

BRANDY

Born: Brandy Rayana Norwood; McComb, Mississippi, 11 February 1979
Genre: R&B, Pop
Best-selling album since 1990: *Full Moon* (2002)
Hit songs since 1990: "I Wanna Be Down," "Have You Ever?," "The Boy Is Mine"

A rhythm and blues performer with a wholesome, girl-next-door image, Brandy gained stardom in the mid-1990s with a series of well-crafted hits that emphasized her youthful, winsome voice. More than a singer, Brandy became an all-around media celebrity, starring on television in the hit series *Moesha,* which she also helped produce. Leaving the business at the peak of her fame in 2000, she returned to music two years later with a more mature, adventurous sound.

Born in the small Mississippi town of McComb, Brandy began singing in her family's church at the age of two. Two years later she moved with her parents to Carson, California, where her father worked as a church music director. Influenced by the dramatic vocal style of pop star Whitney Houston, Brandy began entering local talent contests during the late 1980s. In 1993 she was cast in the

warmed up American audiences to his political leanings, which became prized later in the decade.

Bragg's political views and his ability to turn them into insightful melodic songs no doubt appealed to Nora Guthrie, daughter of Woody Guthrie, the American folksinger who had performed at Communist Party rallies in support of their fight against fascism. Guthrie com-

short-lived television series *Thea,* but her real break-through came the next year, when an audition led to a recording contract with Atlantic Records.

Her self-titled debut album appeared in 1994 and featured four rhythm and blues hits, including "I Wanna Be Down" and "Baby." While lacking the vocal power of her idol Houston, Brandy has a sweet voice with an attractive, smoky lower register. On the album's best tracks, such as "I Wanna Be Down," her singing combines a girlish quality with the assertiveness of an adult. Riding the song's steady hip-hop beat Brandy is completely at home, skirting her way around the rhythms with ease. On the album's ballads, however, she often sounds tentative, unable to summon the vocal or emotional variety to make the material interesting. Unlike Houston, who possesses the vocal reserves to meld herself into any type of material or style, Brandy requires a carefully built and controlled production, one that highlights her voice's strengths.

In 1995 Brandy was cast in *Moesha,* a sitcom that became television network UPN's most-watched program. She spent the next several years out of the recording spotlight, focusing her energies on the show and other television projects, such as a 1997 version of the classic television musical *Cinderella,* in which she performed opposite Houston. Brandy's second album, *Never Say Never,* appeared in 1998 and features the smooth, driving hit "The Boy Is Mine," a duet with fellow vocalist Monica. With its tough beat and catchy melody, the song is Brandy's most successful recording to date, selling over 3 million copies and becoming the best-selling female duet in pop history. Elsewhere on *Never Say Never* Brandy shows signs of artistic growth, sounding more assured and confident than on her debut. The album marks her first collaboration with hot R&B producer Rodney Jerkins, who brings to Brandy's music a new street-wise toughness, although her respectable, sweet-tempered image remains unchanged. By 2000, however, there were signs of cracks beneath the upbeat façade: Weighing only 105 pounds, she was hospitalized for dehydration and exhaustion after walking off the set of *Moesha.* In addition, rumors swirled of an ongoing feud with co-star Countess Vaughn. As a result, aside from a few modeling and television appearances, Brandy largely fell out of sight during the next two years.

By the time she returned to the scene in 2002 Brandy was a grown woman, capable of making her own decisions in music and life. Discussing her self-imposed sabbatical on the television program *20/20,* she admitted that during the grueling filming of *Moesha* she had suffered from an eating disorder as well as an abusive romantic relationship. In a bold move she severed her professional relationship with her mother, who had managed her career from its beginning. Tellingly, Brandy's first album after her newfound independence, *Full Moon* (2002), emerged as her strongest, most compelling work to date. Although her voice continues to have shortcomings, including a tendency to become thin in its upper register, it is well served by the production genius of Rodney Jerkins. On the excellent single "What About Us?" he buoys the singer with an array of unusual sonic devices, including a stomping beat that resembles the hammering sound of a pickaxe. Surprisingly the single's glossy ornamentation, featuring an array of electronic blips and scratches, never gets in the way of its underlying groove; it manages to sound elaborate and minimalist at the same time. With their slightly off-kilter sensibility, "What About Us?" and similarly styled tracks such as "I Thought" incorporate the kind of synthesized, electronic sound associated with 1980s new wave music. Infusing this sound with a modern sense of groove, Brandy and Jerkins create a bold style of R&B that looks to the future. In keeping with her upbeat state of mind, Brandy during this period studied metaphysics, became a vegetarian, and married record producer Robert Smith, with whom she gave birth to a daughter, Sy'rai, in 2002.

Beginning her music career at the age of fifteen, Brandy quickly forged her own identity as a well-rounded entertainer, achieving remarkable success as a singer and actress. As she matured from shy teenager into confident woman, her music took on a new sophistication and depth, reflecting her ability to select producers who understood and amplified her vocal strengths.

SELECTIVE DISCOGRAPHY: *Brandy* (Atlantic, 1994); *Never Say Never* (Atlantic, 1998); *Full Moon* (Atlantic, 2002).

WEBSITE: www.foreverbrandy.com.

DAVID FREELAND

TONI BRAXTON

Born: Severn, Maryland, 7 October 1967
Genre: R&B, Pop
Best-selling album since 1990: *Toni Braxton* (1993)
Hit songs since 1990: "Breathe Again," "Another Sad Love Song," "Un-break My Heart"

Toni Braxton brought a new degree of sultry sophistication to rhythm and blues music of the 1990s. Unlike her contemporaries such as Mary J. Blige, Braxton had no trouble reaching a mainstream pop audience; her records were equally popular on youthful hip-hop radio stations and "adult contemporary" stations aimed at middle-aged listeners. Braxton's across-the-board success was a combined result of songs that were catchy without being formulaic, good looks, and a distinctive, husky voice that managed to sound both vulnerable and tough. Since most of her songs dealt with the universal subject of love, she was able to transcend boundaries of race, class, and gender in her audience. Her most famous records, steamy ballads such as "Breathe Again" (1993) and "Un-Break My Heart" (1996), received constant radio play and made Braxton a household name.

Born in a small Maryland town to conservative, religious parents who at one point did not allow her to wear pants, Braxton grew up listening to gospel music with her four sisters. Over time, her parents relaxed their strictures and she developed a love of secular vocalists, especially rhythm and blues singers such as Luther Vandross and Anita Baker. After being discovered by producer Bill Petteway, Braxton and her sisters were signed to Arista Records as the Braxtons. Braxton released one single with her sisters, but was soon pulled out of the group by the hot young producers Kenneth "Babyface" Edmonds and Antonio "L. A." Reid, who signed her to their new LaFace label, affiliated with Arista. Although rumor had it that Arista chief Clive Davis was not satisfied with Braxton's vocal ability, any fears were allayed when her debut album, *Toni Braxton* (1993), became a sensation, eventually selling more than 8 million copies. Braxton and her producers spent a great deal of time working on the album, and the effort showed. Nearly every track is first-rate, and six of its eleven songs became hits. But the album's biggest asset is Braxton herself: On songs like "Another Sad Love Song," "Seven Whole Days," and "You Mean the World to Me," she burrows into the tuneful melodies with her deep, profound voice, and then belts at the top of her range when the music reaches peak moments of intensity. Throughout the album her vocals meld themselves perfectly to the arrangements, creating the feel of a unified, cohesive work. Like Anita Baker's *Rapture* (1986), it is a perfect mood album, designed for romance by candlelight. In 1994, Braxton won a much-deserved Grammy Award for Best New Artist.

Braxton's second album, *Secrets*, was released in 1996 and repeated the commercial and artistic success of its predecessor. On *Secrets* Braxton began to experiment with her sound, developing a tougher, more sexually aggressive persona on the hit "You're Making Me High." With producer Babyface playing a lean, muscular guitar part, Braxton settles assuredly into the song's danceable groove. Because of its references to masturbation and its overall sensual feel, "You're Making Me High" qualifies as perhaps the most torrid moment of her career. Another highlight of the album is "Let It Flow," which also appeared on the soundtrack to the film *Waiting to Exhale* (1995). Here, Braxton uses the haunting low end of her voice to deliver a powerful message about strength and perseverance. The lyrics are some of the finest Babyface has written: "First thing early Monday morning / I'm gonna pack my tears away." However, the biggest-selling single on *Secrets* was "Un-break My Heart," a big, dramatic ballad that spent eleven weeks at number one on the pop chart. The song features all the ingredients—lilting melody, strong vocal, subtle but sophisticated orchestration—that marked her previous hits, but it gains extra distinction through an acoustic guitar part that suggests Spanish flamenco music.

In 1997 Braxton was at the top of her game commercially and artistically, but there was trouble on the horizon. Late that year, she filed suit against LaFace Records, claiming that her contract no longer reflected the high sales of her records or the profit she was bringing to the company. When LaFace countersued, Braxton promptly filed for bankruptcy, a move that stalled any further legal action. Appearing on "The Oprah Winfrey Show," Braxton claimed that, despite her massive record sales, she was over $1 million dollars in debt because of poor accounting of bills and expenses. During the lengthy legal battle that ensued, she fell out of the pop music spotlight, working instead on Broadway in the Disney musical *Beauty and the Beast*. By the time the dispute was finally resolved in 1999, Braxton's career had lost some of its momentum.

Remaining with LaFace Records, she released her third album, *The Heat*, in 2000. Although *The Heat* contained the type of slow ballads for which Braxton had become famous, it also threw in doses of urban-sounding hip-hop in an attempt to update her sound. Unfortunately, the songs were not as strong as those on previous releases, and a further album, *More Than a Woman* (2002), pushed Braxton even further into a contemporary hip-hop sound. For the most part critics were not pleased, claiming that Braxton's unique voice had been eclipsed. Comparing Braxton's new sound to that of the teen pop star Britney Spears, *USA Today* called the album "predictable and so painfully trendy." Despite signs of creative confusion, Braxton seemed happy, announcing that she and her husband, keyboardist Keri Lewis, were expecting their second child.

Her career difficulties notwithstanding, Braxton is one of the freshest, most distinctive singing talents to emerge in the 1990s. More than her excellent voice and sexy appearance, the root of her success is her talent for exploiting contradictions: She offers music that encompasses both middle-of-the-road pop and hard rhythm and blues, a persona both tough and sweet, and singing that skillfully balances calculation with genuine emotion.

SELECTIVE DISCOGRAPHY: *Toni Braxton* (LaFace, 1993); *Secrets* (LaFace, 1996); *The Heat* (LaFace,

2000); *Snowflakes* (Arista, 2001); *More Than a Woman* (Arista, 2002).

WEBSITE: www.toni-online.com.

DAVID FREELAND

MICHAEL BRECKER

Born: Philadelphia, Pennsylvania, 29 March 1949

Genre: Jazz

Best-selling album since 1990: *Nearness of You: The Ballad Book* (2000)

Hit songs since 1990: "African Skies," "Chan's Song," "Naima"

By 1990 Michael Brecker, a seven-time Grammy winner, had established himself as one of the most technically accomplished and widely heard tenor saxophonists in popular music. He spent the 1990s seeking to shore up his credentials as a jazz player. Brecker was among the first reed players of the jazz-rock era as a co-founder of the vocals-horns-guitars-rhythm band Dreams. Brecker gained name recognition when he and his older sibling, the trumpeter Randy, recorded as the Brecker Brothers in 1975. Their father was a part-time jazz pianist, and their sister is a classical pianist. From 1973 to 1974, Michael earned mainstream jazz credits in the group helmed by jazz pianist Horace Silver, but the commercial success of the Brecker Brothers' urbane electric funk style—dubbed "heavy metal bebop"—and Michael's burgeoning career as a studio session player and guest soloist in performance (for Frank Sinatra, Frank Zappa, Joni Mitchell, Bruce Springsteen, and Steely Dan, among others) delayed him from recording an album under his own name until he was thirty-eight years old.

By then the saxophonist was the owner, along with his brother, of the Manhattan jazz club Seventh Avenue South. He had been an influential member of the virtuosic ensemble Steps Ahead, whose members employed the newest instrumental technology; he had championed the Akai Electric Wind Instrument (EWI), a breath-controlled synthesizer. But Brecker was best known for his unwavering saxophone tone, crisp articulation, and dexterity, which allowed him to finger unusually complex melodic lines. These skills were on display on albums featuring the elite of progressive jazz, including *Don't Try This at Home* (1988) (for which he won his first Grammy) and *Now You See It . . . Now You Don't* (1990), efforts that gained Brecker an enthusiastic following among saxophone students.

There were dissenting notes in the choir of praise, however. Some critics and hard-core jazz fans dismissed Brecker as purveying technique over expressiveness. While attempting to refute that charge, he remained tirelessly eclectic. He toured with Paul Simon's Afro-Brazilian-steeped tour in support of the album *Rhythm of the Saints* in 1991 and 1992 and then rejoined Randy for two new Brecker Brothers albums. These garnered multiple Grammy nominations, and *Out of the Loop*, with Brecker's South African–inflected tune, "African Skies," won a Grammy for Best Contemporary Jazz Performance Instrumental in 1994. The Brothers toured internationally in 1995, introducing contemporary jazz to the People's Republic of China with sold-out performances in Shanghai and Beijing.

Thereafter, Brecker turned his attention to the aggressive acoustic jazz that had excited him in his youth, especially as expressed in the work of the late John Coltrane. He recorded *Infinity* (1995) with a trio led by Coltrane's piano collaborator McCoy Tyner; the album won a Grammy for Best Instrumental Jazz Performance, Individual or Group (1995). Tyner repaid the favor, playing an unplugged version of "African Skies" on Brecker's Grammy-winning (for Best Instrumental Jazz Performance, Individual or Group) album *Tales from the Hudson* (1996). On *Time Is of the Essence* (1999) Brecker worked with Coltrane's drummer, Elvin Jones. He also forged collaborations or strengthened existing creative ties with pianist Herbie Hancock, guitarist Pat Metheny, bassists Dave Holland and Charlie Haden, and drummer Jack DeJohnette.

By the age of fifty, Brecker had clearly harnessed his prodigious energy and facility to eloquent ends. His release *Nearness of You: The Ballad Book* (2000) was inspired by Coltrane's 1962 album *Ballads*. Brecker was awarded the Jazz Instrumental Solo Grammy for his poetic statement on Hancock's composition "Chan's Song," while James Taylor won Best Male Pop Vocal Performance for a wistful reprisal of his old hit "Don't Let Me Be Lonely Tonight," around which Brecker wrapped a tender obligatto.

Brecker recorded and toured with Hancock and trumpeter Roy Hargrove in a production called *Directions in Music* (2002), revisiting repertoire associated with Coltrane and Miles Davis. He was nominated for a Grammy for his unaccompanied rendition on that album of Coltrane's challenging ballad "Naima," and he was favorably cited for his unadorned but exalted chorus of "America the Beautiful" on Charlie Haden's *American Dreams* (2002). From fusion roots Michael Brecker has developed into an ardent upholder of American standards.

SELECTIVE DISCOGRAPHY: *Now You See It . . . Now You Don't* (Impulse!, 1990); *Return of the Brecker Brothers* (GRP, 1992); *Out of the Loop* (GRP, 1994);

Tales from the Hudson (Impulse!, 1996); *Two Blocks from the Edge* (Impulse!, 1997); *Time Is of the Essence* (Verve, 1998); *Nearness of You: The Ballad Book* (2000); *Directions in Music* (Verve, 2002).

HOWARD MANDEL

THE BREEDERS

Formed: 1990, Boston, Massachusetts

Members: Kim Deal, guitar, vocals (born Dayton, Ohio, 10 June 1961); Kelley Deal, guitar, vocals (born Dayton, Ohio, 10 June 1961); Mando Lopez, bass; Jose Medeles, drums; Richard Presley, guitar. Former members: Tanya Donelly (born Newport, Rhode Island, 14 July 1966); Shannon Doughton, drums (born Britt Walford, Louisville, Kentucky); Nate Farley, guitar (born Dayton, Ohio, 13 May 1971); James Macpherson, drums (born Dayton, Ohio, 23 June 1966); Josephine Wiggs, bass (born Letchworth, Hertfordshire, England, 26 February 1965).

Genre: Rock

Best-selling album since 1990: *Last Splash* (1993)

Hit songs since 1990: "Cannonball," "Divine Hammer"

Formed out of mutual frustration by two members of leading alternative rock bands of the late 1980s, the Breeders were an erratic, but popular band that never quite lived up to the initial promise of its 1993 hit, "Cannonball." Led by the ex-Pixies bassist Kim Deal, the band crafted a distinctive combination of dissonance and finely honed rock songs, but personal problems and a severe case of writer's block crippled the group for nearly a decade following their most popular release.

Identical twin sisters Kim and Kelley Deal grew up in Dayton, Ohio, near Wright Patterson Air Force base, where their father worked as a physicist. In addition to their love for classic rock groups such as Led Zeppelin and AC/DC, the twins were popular athletes at their high school. Kim attended seven different colleges before dropping out to join the Boston alternative music stars the Pixies in the late 1980s.

Feeling underappreciated in their respective bands, Deal and Throwing Muses guitarist Tanya Donelly joined forces in 1990 to form the Breeders. Taking their name—a slang term used by homosexuals to describe heterosexual parents—from a group formed by the Deal sisters in their youth, the two recruited bass player Josephine Wiggs of England's Perfect Disaster to record their debut album, *Pod* (1990), during a Pixies tour of England.

See-sawing between the ponderously slow, thick sound of songs such as "Glorious" and the frantic, throbbing punk rock of "Doe," the album is a showcase both for Deal's wounded, angelic vocals and Wiggs's prominent, thrumming bass lines. Slint drummer Britt Walford played drums under the pseudonym Shannon Doughton on the album, which was recorded by the renowned alternative rock producer Steve Albini. Bringing with her the patented Pixies's sound—a chaotic swirl of noise that often gelled into curiously off-kilter, catchy pop rock songs—Deal was clearly the creative force of the group. Deal was fired from the Pixies in 1992, allowing her to focus all her energies on the Breeders.

Pod earned the Breeders a loyal group of fans. To satisfy them and tide them over until the Breeders's next full-length album, 4AD/Elektra released a four-song mini-album, *Safari*, in 1992. It features a more melodic but still bottom-end-heavy sound, especially on a cover of the Who's "So Sad About Us." The untrained musician Kelley Deal joined the group for the recording of *Safari*, playing guitar and doubling the vocals of sister Kim; she replaced Donelly, who quit the group to form her more pop-oriented group, Belly. Jim Macpherson was added as the band's drummer.

The Breeders played their first major concerts in 1992, opening for Nirvana on a European tour, which was followed by the sessions for their second album, *Last Splash*. Released in the summer of 1993, the album thrust the group into a surprisingly bright mainstream spotlight courtesy of the breezy pop hit "Cannonball," for which a whimsical video was created by Spike Jonze, then on the brink of renown as a video and film director.

A perfectly crafted blend of funk-inspired bass, jazzy drumming, and repetitive, distorted guitar lines, "Cannonball" layered the noisy rock sound of the Pixies with a relentless pop sensibility and Kim Deal's compelling vocals. An amalgamation of nonsense syllables and oblique lyrics ("Spitting in a wishing well / Blown to hell / Crash, I'm the last splash / I know you, little libertine"), the song secured sales of 1 million for the album and a slot on the 1994 alternative rock festival, Lollapalooza. Alternating between feedback-drench surf-inspired rock ("No Aloha," "Invisible Man"), abstract, noisy punk songs ("Roi," "S.O.S.") and plodding, dark ballads ("Do You Love Me Now?"), *Last Splash* signaled the rise of a new, powerful female voice in rock.

Unfortunately, the sudden success and nonstop touring and promotion took its toll on the group. The Breeders went on hiatus in late 1994, and Kelley Deal was arrested for drug possession in early 1995; she was sent to court-mandated drug rehabilitation. Kim Deal began work on a solo album, but eventually recruited Macpherson, guitarist Nathan Farley, and bassist Luis Lerma for her short-lived side project, the Amps. The group's only album, *Pacer* (1995), is a more aggressive, distorted take on the

Breeders's sound, though with traces of the surf and punk music that inspired the latter.

A Failed Attempt to Regain the Spotlight

Following rehab, Kelley Deal self-released an album from her new band, the Kelley Deal 6000, *Go to the Sugar Altar* (1996), a wide-ranging collection of shambling punk songs in a Breeders vein, with several addressing the horrors of addiction. Wiggs departed from the dormant group in 1996 to form her own band, the Josephine Wiggs Experience, followed by Macpherson.

Afflicted with writer's block and stymied in an abortive attempt to record a new Breeders's album in the late 1990s, Kim Deal retreated from the spotlight to concentrate on learning how to play drums. In 1998, rejoined by Kelley, the group recorded a cover of the 3 Degrees's "Collage" for *The Mod Squad* soundtrack, signaling the rebirth of the band. The entire lineup changed once again before a third album was finally delivered in 2002. Bassist Mando Lopez, guitarist Richard Presley, and drummer Jose Medeles joined the Deals on *Title TK*.

Though eagerly anticipated, the album failed to live up to fans' expectations. Downbeat and mostly mid-tempo, *Title TK* goes for low-key introspection ("London Song," "Off You"), adding touches of droning farfisa organ and off-kilter drumming on tracks such as "The She." The shambling "Too Alive" and "Put on a Side" feel like unfinished, impromptu garage recordings, whereas the sprightly "Son of Three," with its grinding guitars, insistent beat, and the Deals' intertwined vocals, is one of the few tracks to recapture the band's former glory.

The Breeders's initial success and promise fell victim to personal problems and creative indolence, transforming the uniquely talented Deal sisters into one of the strangest punk one-hit wonders in rock history.

SELECTIVE DISCOGRAPHY: *Pod* (4AD/Rough Trade, 1990); *Safari* (4AD/Elektra, 1992); *Last Splash* (4AD/Elektra, 1993); *Live in Stockholm* (Breeders Digest, 1994); *Title TK* (Elektra, 2002).

WEBSITES: www.4ad.com/artists/breeders.

GIL KAUFMAN

JIM BRICKMAN

Born: James Brickman; Cleveland, Ohio, 20 November 1961

Genre: New Age

Best-selling album since 1990: *Picture This* (1997)

Hit songs since 1990: "Valentine," "The Gift," "You"

Composer/performer Jim Brickman mines the taste for romance with his pop-influenced, sentimental piano instrumentals. His discerning use of guest vocalists helped propel him further into the world of pop music. After enjoying success as a composer of commercial jingles, Brickman's dogged determination, strong marketing acumen, and gift for creating melodies enabled his pop music success.

While growing up in Cleveland, Brickman began studying music early after his mother put him in piano lessons at the age of four. He showed a propensity for improvising pop songs early on and he later studied music at the Cleveland Institute of Music while taking classes in business at another nearby institution. After college, he formed Brickman Arrangements, which focused on creating music for advertising campaigns, known in the industry as "jingles." Throughout the 1980s and early 1990s, Brickman wrote music for a variety of national advertising accounts such as McDonalds, the Gap, AT&T, Miller beer, Revlon, and Standard Oil. Brickman eventually tired of the jingle business and cut some piano instrumentals, which he actively marketed to radio stations and record companies. Most were unreceptive but Brickman was undeterred. Finally, Windham Hill, a label known for producing a variety of instrumental artists such as George Winston and Yanni, offered Brickman a record contract.

His first release, *No Words* (1994), sold well, partly due to the mood-creating acoustic piano melodies and partly due to Brickman loading his car with *No Words* CDs and personally distributing them to radio stations all across the country. A single from the album, "Rocket to the Moon," was the first solo instrumental song to ever land on the adult contemporary music chart. He built on that success the following year by releasing *By Heart: Piano Solos* (1995), which surpassed most recordings in its genre by landing on the *Billboard* 200 chart. What ensued was a flurry of successful recordings starting with *Picture This* (1997), his most successful seller, and *The Gift* (1997), a Christmas album on which Kenny Loggins sings the title song.

Brickman stepped into the role of producer with *Visions of Love* (1998), a compilation of twelve songs written and performed by a variety of established artists such as Stephen Bishop, Janis Ian, and Peabo Bryson. Brickman composed one instrumental for the album and plays piano accompaniment on select songs.

Love Songs and Lullabies (2002), Brickman's ninth solo release since 1994, contains eight solo piano pieces mixed with four songs that feature guest vocal appearances from the group All-4-One and actress Jane Krakowski of television's *Ally McBeal*, who displays her ample singing skills on the ballad "You."

In addition to recording and keeping up with a 150-city touring schedule each year, Brickman hosts a three-hour weekly radio program, *Your Weekend with Jim Brickman*. The show features Brickman doing celebrity interviews and presenting music from the adult contemporary hit list. It airs on over 170 radio stations across the United States. He also collaborated with writer Cindy Pearlman on the self-help book, *Simple Things* (2001). The book focuses on how to gain appreciation for all that life offers in the face of today's hurried existence. It became a bestseller in its category.

From his productive days of writing advertising jingles, Brickman discovered how to create melodies that sell, an art he now applies to his catalog of romantic pop music.

SELECTIVE DISCOGRAPHY: *No Words* (Windham Hill, 1994); *By Heart: Piano Solos* (Windham Hill, 1995); *Picture This* (Windham Hill, 1997); *The Gift* (Windham Hill, 1997); *Visions of Love* (Windham Hill, 1998); *Destiny* (Windham Hill, 1999); *If You Believe* (Windham Hill, 1999); *My Romance* (Windham Hill, 2000); *Simple Things* (Windham Hill, 2001); *Love Songs and Lullabies* (Windham Hill, 2002).

DONALD LOWE

SARAH BRIGHTMAN

Born: Berkhampstead, England, 14 August 1960
Genre: Vocal
Best-selling album since 1990: *Timeless* (1997)
Hit songs since 1990: "Time to Say Goodbye," "Deliver Me"

Often linked with her work in musical theater, Sarah Brightman for most of her career has been a determined recording artist in a variety of musical styles whose delicate soprano has touched millions of listeners.

Brightman was born and raised in Berkhampstead, England, where she began voice lessons and ballet training at an early age. She debuted theatrically in 1973 on London's West End at the Piccadilly Theatre in Charles Strouse's regally themed musical, *I and Albert*, and performed as a dancer in the British television series *Pan's People* in 1976. Two years later, she danced and sang as a member of the British pop group Hot Gossip and scored a Top 10 single in the United Kingdom with the disco hit, "I Lost My Heart to a Starship Trooper." In 1981 she won the role of Jemina in Andrew Lloyd Webber's musical *Cats* and performed the long-running musical in its initial London resurrection.

Brightman and Lloyd Webber were married on March 22, 1984, the second marriage for both. Brightman's first marriage was in 1978 to rock manager Andrew Graham Stewart, from whom she was divorced 1983. Her nuptial to Lloyd Webber, who was already a superstar composer, received major media scrutiny and was a double-edged sword for the young soprano. Lloyd Webber placed her in several of his projects and Brightman gained international notoriety for her singing. However, doggedly stalking her career was the suggestion that she merely married well. In 1985 Lloyd Webber cast her alongside renowned tenor Plácido Domingo in his politically controversial *Requiem* and she scored a Grammy Award nomination for Best New Classical Artist. Later, Brightman starred in his London and Broadway productions of *Phantom of the Opera*, which opened in 1988. She followed that by headlining the world concert tour, *The Music of Andrew Lloyd Webber: A Concert Spectacular*. She also starred on Broadway in another Lloyd Webber show, *Aspects of Love*, in 1991, although they were no longer a couple. Their marriage had amicably dissolved in 1990 and some of Brightman's harsher critics felt that her career might dissolve along with it. They were mistaken.

Recordings of her theatrical roles, previous solo albums, and concert tours had already made millions of fans of Brightman's silky, mesmerizing voice. In 1992 her duet with opera singer Jose Carreras, "Amigos Para Siempre," the anthem of the 1992 Olympics, landed high on the charts in England. The next year she released *Dive* (1993), a foray into bouncy pop and the first record produced by a new romantic companion, Frank Peterson, who also wrote many of the album's songs. They followed with *Fly* (1995), whose re-release in 1996 added her blockbuster duet with Italian tenor Andrea Bocelli, "Time to Say Goodbye." Except for the epic duet, the other songs on *Fly* had more of a 1980s electronic pop fusion sound. Both albums did well; however, the release of "Time to Say Goodbye" as a single eclipsed them. The song sold more then 10 million copies worldwide and is the biggest-selling single ever in Germany. Consequently, Brightman and Peterson decided to include it on their next album, *Timeless* (1997). This popular recording is titled *Time to Say Goodbye* (1997) for the United States release. Along with a strong return to operatic work, including Puccini's "O Mio Babbino Caro," the album also contains several pop efforts and firmly established Brightman as a versatile crossover artist.

Brightman's international presence results in varying titles and song listings on her albums depending on the locale of the release. She also sings in several languages, most notably Spanish, Italian, Hebrew, and her native English. Brightman's concerts are known to feature mood-creating theatricality that enthralls her fans, but is sometimes loathed by serious classical lovers. In 2001 Brightman released a compilation album, *Classics*, containing songs off her previous three releases in addition to seven new songs that mix pop, neo-classical, and new age styles. Her follow-up, *Encore* (2002), is another compilation of previous recordings, including many of Lloyd Webber's songs from her days in musical theater.

Brightman's fearless crossovers from one style to the next have often put her at the mercy of the critics. Yet, in every invention of herself, she has attracted legions of fans and established herself as one of the most prominent sopranos in the world.

SELECTIVE DISCOGRAPHY: *The Trees They Grow So High* (EMI, 1986); *The Songs That Got Away* (Polygram, 1989); *As I Came of Age* (Polygram, 1990); *The Music of Andrew Lloyd Webber* (Phantom, 1992); *Dive* (A&M, 1993); *Surrender* (Polygram, 1995); *Fly* (Wea International, 1996); *Timeless* (Angel Classics, 1997); *Eden* (EMI International, 1998); *La Luna-La Luna* (Wea, 2000); *Classics* (Angel Classics, 2001); *Encore* (Universal, 2002).

DONALD LOWE

JONATHA BROOKE

Born: Boston, Massachusetts, January 1964
Genre: Folk
Best-selling album since 1990: *Steady Pull* (2001)
Hit songs since 1990: "Crumbs," "Steady Pull"

Singer/songwriter Jonatha Brooke thought she would become a dancer until she reached college. She lived with her parents, Nancy and Robert Nelson, in London, where she studied ballet at an all-girls school. It is unsurprising that Brooke started off as a dancer because her songs often have an unusual rhythmic sensibility. Brooke decided against dancing and started to write songs while studying English at Amherst College in Massachusetts. Brooke met Jennifer Kimball in 1982 and formed the folk-pop duo the Story about a year later.

With their unusual melodies and strong storytelling style, the Story found a home with folk music lovers and singer/songwriter enthusiasts. Their first album, *Grace and Gravity*, was released on the small label Green Linnet, and was eventually picked up by Elektra in 1992. The duo's second album, *The Angel in the House* (1993), an Elektra release, enjoyed steady play on college radio, thanks to its unusual arrangements, poetic lyrics, and almost off-kilter harmonies.

Before the release of *The Angel in the House*, Brooke married jazz pianist Alain Mallet, who co-produced the album, played piano on some tracks, and provided some of the arrangements. Personal differences surfaced among the two performers, and after touring and critical accolades had helped to build a loyal fan base, Brooke and Kimball parted ways in 1994. Brooke went solo and, billing herself somewhat misleadingly as Jonatha Brooke and the Story, released the album *Plumb* (1995), under the MCA imprint Blue Thumb Records.

Because Brooke wrote most of the duo's songs, *Plumb* does not stray too far from the familiar territory of insightful, clever lyrics and complex, soaring melodies. Her second solo release, *Ten Cent Wings* (1997), feels more like a pop music pastiche; it, too, was produced by her husband but was mixed by the renowned Bob Clearmountain. Every track maintains her straightforward delivery and thoughtful lyrics, but the single, "Crumbs"—an angry, mid-tempo rock song with electric guitar, double-tracked vocals, and even a string section—marked the largest departure from her previous, contemplative folk sound.

Ten Cent Wings was the last album Brooke released with MCA; they dropped her from their roster as major labels consolidated and retained only those artists whose records would make them the most money. It also seems that Brooke and Mallet parted ways around this time; it is her last album with his participation. Indeed, some of its songs suggest an emotional impasse, especially "Landmine," with the sad lyrics "I give my love to you/And you walk away too soon."

Brooke created her own label, Bad Dog Records, and released a live album in 1999. Soon after, Brooke brought in Bob Clearmountain to produce her fourth album, *Steady Pull* (2001), a spirited, funky effort with touches of R&B (as in the title track) and straight-ahead rock and roll, thanks to squalling guitars on "Red Dress." It was her best-selling album, and many of her fans followed her along in this new direction. Brooke married her longtime manager, Patrick Rains, in the south of France in 2002. Although she has been compared to Joan Baez and Joni Mitchell, Brooke has become more of a rock-and-roll artist than either of these iconic folk singers.

SELECTIVE DISCOGRAPHY: **With the Story:** *The Angel in the House* (1993). **As Jonatha Brooke and the Story:** *Plumb* (Blue Thumb/MCA, 1995). **As Jonatha Brooke:** *Ten Cent Wings* (MCA, 1997); *Jonatha Brooke Live* (Bad Dog Records, 1999); *Steady Pull* (Bad Dog Records, 2001).

CARRIE HAVRANEK

GARTH BROOKS

Born: Tulsa, Oklahoma, 7 February 1962
Genre: Country

Best-selling album since 1990: *Ropin' the Wind* (1991)

Hit songs since 1990: "Friends in Low Places," "The River," "We Shall Be Free"

The most commercially successful country singer of the 1990s, Garth Brooks was largely responsible for the massive crossover success country enjoyed during the decade. Brooks was the first country performer to treat his live shows like rock concerts, incorporating into his act lighting effects, wireless microphones, pyrotechnics, and harnesses (allowing him to take flying leaps over the audience). These "arena-rock" aesthetics appealed to rock and pop fans who were otherwise indifferent to country music. Through songs such as "We Shall Be Free," Brooks also injected a tone of liberalism into country's largely conservative world. By 1991, when his album *Ropin' the Wind* debuted at number one on the pop charts—the first country album to do so—Brooks was an international star, having brought country music to a new level of mainstream acceptance. While some critics complained that he had severed ties with country's roots, others applauded his ingenuity, also noting the compelling emotional current running through his work. By the early 2000s, Brooks's popularity had faded slightly, hurt by the unsuccessful promotion of his "rock-star" alter ego, Chris Gaines, and his own increasingly ambivalent attitude toward stardom.

Getting Started

Although Brooks achieved success with a rock-oriented style, his upbringing in Oklahoma points to more traditional forms of country music. Colleen Carol Brooks, his mother, was a part-time country singer who recorded several unsuccessful singles for Capitol Records during the 1950s. Although Brooks loved country music as a child, he also pursued athletics, playing football and basketball during high school and entering Oklahoma State University on a track and field scholarship. While attending college, he performed at local clubs before graduating with a degree in advertising. Deciding to pursue a music career full time, he made an abortive trip to the country music capital of Nashville, reportedly staying in the city only twenty-three hours before cowering home to Oklahoma. In 1986 he married his girlfriend, Sandy Mahl, and the couple returned to Nashville, determined to make it in the music business. The newly tenacious Brooks was turned down by several record labels before Capitol/Liberty signed him in 1988. His self-titled debut album appeared in 1989 and was an immediate hit, sporting a number one country hit single with the tender ballad "If Tomorrow Never Comes."

Garth Brooks [PAUL NATKIN/PHOTO RESERVE]

In 1989 Nashville was still in the midst of the "neo-traditionalist" movement, which overthrew the lush strings and vocal choruses of 1970s "countrypolitan" for a more basic sound honoring country's past. In keeping with this style, *Garth Brooks* features tough, "honky-tonk" songs such as "Not Counting You," a swinging, up-tempo number that gives no indication of the pop sound Brooks would soon pursue.

Country Stardom

In 1990 Brooks released his breakthrough album, *No Fences*, which eventually sold more than 10 million copies. The album received a strong advance push through the hit single "Friends in Low Places." A rowdy and humorous account of a country brawler wreaking havoc on a black-tie party, the song earned constant airplay on both country and pop stations, buoyed by a catchy melody and Brooks's rambunctiously likable performance. *No Fences* spawned three additional number one country hits, including "Two of a Kind, Workin' on a Full House," a light-hearted portrayal of marriage that retains a traditional country feel through prominent fiddles, a tinkling piano, and the exaggerated twang in Brooks's singing. The album's other hits, such as the brooding, atmospheric "The Thunder Rolls" and the sentimental ballad "Unanswered Prayers," sport blaring electric guitars and slick strings, marking Brooks's initial foray into a pop and rock sound. As a vocalist, Brooks's great strength is his sincerity. Delivering his songs with an appealing catch in his voice, he cultivates a straightforward, nice-guy persona—an everyman whose approachability attracts listeners from diverse social and economic backgrounds.

Now a major star, Brooks returned in 1991 with *Ropin' the Wind,* an album that equaled the commercial success of its predecessor. Despite containing a humorous country tune, "We Bury the Hatchet (but Leave the Handle Sticking Out)," the album solidified Brooks's rock reputation with a hit version of "Shameless," a ballad first recorded by the pop artist Billy Joel. By this time Brooks was becoming famous for his live performances. In addition to the flying contraptions and flashy lights, he surrounded his band with large ramps that allowed him to career back and forth among various areas of the stage. Many writers lambasted his overblown style; a notable exception was the esteemed music critic Robert Christgau, who claimed Brooks possessed "the most voracious emotional appetite of anyone to hit pop music since R&B star Aretha Franklin." Critics edged further toward Brooks's camp with his next album, *The Chase* (1992), which features the adventurous song "We Shall Be Free." Perceptively noting gospel music's historic ties to the struggle for civil rights, Brooks imbues the arrangement with a stirring piano and gospel-flavored choir. Making a plea for unity among humanity, Brooks advances racial equality and—in a mainstream country first—gay rights: "When we're free to love anyone we choose / When this world's big enough for all different views . . . we shall be free."

Artistic and Commercial Uncertainty

Despite its artistic success, *The Chase* was far less popular than Brooks's previous two releases, prompting a return to safer themes on his next album, *In Pieces* (1993). In what critics decried as a hypocritical pandering to country's conservative audience, and as a means of defusing the mild controversy "We Shall Be Free" had generated, Brooks recorded "American Honky-Tonk Bar Association," a mildly jingoistic song that criticizes welfare recipients. After releasing two more albums, *Fresh Horses* (1995) and *Sevens* (1997), Brooks began to set his sights on goals outside of music. In 1998 he tried out, unsuccessfully, for the San Diego Padres pro baseball team, and soon after began expressing an interest in film acting. After much lobbying, he won the role of fictional rock star Chris Gaines in *The Lamb,* a thriller to be produced by the famed R&B

artist Kenneth "Babyface" Edmonds. In a measure of his excitement over the role, Brooks developed a persona for Gaines in advance of shooting the film, reinventing himself as a tough, leather-sporting rock star and releasing an album titled *Greatest Hits* (1999). The record-buying public, largely unaware of the forthcoming film, treated the album with puzzlement. Once *Greatest Hits* fizzled and record stores began selling it at cut prices, plans for the film were scrapped. The imbroglio hurt Brooks's credibility, keeping him out of the studio for the next two years.

After enduring a divorce from his wife and the loss of his mother, Brooks released *Scarecrow* near the end of 2001, announcing the album would be his last. Applauded by critics as a welcome return to form, *Scarecrow* features a broad range of material, from "Beer Run," a rousing, humorous duet with country legend George Jones, to the breezy, pop-influenced "Wrapped Up in You." Brooks strikes a personal chord on several of the tracks, particularly the ruminative ballad "Pushing Up Daisies," in which the narrator's father becomes helpless after his wife's death: "Now Dad turns his back on each day that he's given / Because he'd rather be pushing up daisies." Heralding his return, the *Houston Chronicle* advised Brooks to "stop pretending to retire and make more albums like this."

During the early 1990s, Brooks led country music's crossover into the pop mainstream, paving the way for the success of artists such as Tim McGraw, Shania Twain, and Faith Hill. While he benefited from good timing and a listening public receptive to new, rock-oriented trends, Brooks also succeeded on the strength of his memorable material and a direct, engaging singing style. After enduring personal and career problems in the late 1990s and early 2000s, Brooks continued to record successful, vital work.

SELECTIVE DISCOGRAPHY: *Garth Brooks* (Liberty, 1989); *No Fences* (Liberty, 1990); *Ropin' the Wind* (Liberty, 1991); *The Chase* (Liberty, 1992); *In Pieces* (Liberty, 1993); *Fresh Horses* (Liberty, 1995); *Sevens* (Liberty, 1997); *Scarecrow* (Capitol, 2001); **As Chris Gaines:** *Greatest Hits* (Capitol, 1999).

WEBSITE: www.garthbrooks.com.

DAVID FREELAND

BROOKS & DUNN

Formed: 1990, Nashville, Tennessee

Members: Leon Eric "Kix" Brooks (born Shreveport, Louisiana, 12 May 1955); Ronnie Dunn (born Coleman, Texas, 1 June 1953).

Genre: Country

Best-selling album since 1990: *Steers and Stripes* (2001)

Hit songs since 1990: "Brand New Man," "She's Not the Cheatin' Kind," "The Long Goodbye"

Composed of two veteran vocalists who had pursued solo careers with little success, Brooks & Dunn became one of the most popular acts in country music in the 1990s. Key factors in their ongoing success are versatility and flexibility. By the early 1990s, they had proven themselves adept in handling a variety of modern country styles, from "western swing"–styled dance numbers to pop-influenced ballads. Although both members play guitar and sing leads, Ronnie Dunn is generally considered the stronger vocalist, while Kix Brooks is described as the crowd pleaser, performing the "duckwalk," a dance move inspired by rock great Chuck Berry, during live concerts. As songwriters, they display an ability to update classic country themes with wit and humor, particularly on their earlier albums. Brooks & Dunn continued recording into the early 2000s with little sign of commercial decline, although later albums tended to smooth over the duo's sound with a glossy finish, in keeping with the slickness of contemporary country.

Beginnings

Brooks was raised in Shreveport, Louisiana, not far from the family of Johnny Horton, a popular country singer who died in 1960. Brooks made his singing debut at the age of twelve with Horton's daughter; later, in high school, he began performing his own songs in local clubs. After graduation, Brooks worked on the Alaskan pipeline and then moved to Maine, where he often performed in ski resorts. By the early 1980s he had relocated to the country music hub of Nashville, Tennessee, and begun writing hits for artists such as John Conlee and Highway 101. In 1989 Brooks released a self-titled solo album that made little commercial impact. Dunn's route to Nashville was quite different. Initially planning to become a Baptist minister, he studied theology at Abilene Christian College in his home state of Texas. Having learned to play the bass during high school, Dunn became increasingly interested in music during his college years, spending much of his free time in local music bars. Leaving college to move to Tulsa, Oklahoma, with his family, he soon found work within the house band at a popular nightclub, Duke's Country. Having scored two minor country hits for a small label, Dunn moved to Nashville after winning a talent contest. Through the influence of producer Scott Hendricks, he met Arista Records vice president Tim DuBois, who encouraged him to write songs and perform with Brooks.

1990s Success

Impressed with the pair's first writing collaboration, "Brand New Man," DuBois offered the newly formed Brooks & Dunn a recording contract. "Brand New Man," with its tight, close harmonies and lyrics celebrating rebirth and love, was a smash hit, reaching the number one country chart position in 1991. Many critics have judged *Brand New Man* (1991), Brooks & Dunn's first album, as their finest. A pleasing blend of up-tempo swing numbers and heartfelt ballads, the album is smooth and radio-friendly without succumbing to blandness. "My Next Broken Heart," another number one hit, is a rousing western-swing number, enlivened by Dunn's high, keening voice, one of the most impressive instruments to emerge within 1990s country. The song features woebegone lyrics that mine the best of classic country humor: "I thought all along you'd be the death of me / But I met one tonight who wants what's left of me." "Neon Moon" is more pop-oriented: an easy, percussive ballad on which Dunn's vocals convey a sense of wistful longing. "Boot Scootin' Boogie," another number one hit, is one of the album's most enjoyable tracks. Driven by a lean guitar rhythm and a pounding piano, the song recalls the spirited, rowdy, "honky-tonk" country hits of the 1950s. With four number one hits in all, *Brand New Man* established Brooks & Dunn as major country stars, the most successful vocal duo since 1980s country act the Judds.

Throughout the 1990s, Brooks & Dunn's string of number one country hits continued unabated. Sometimes described as country's answer to 1980s rock group Hall & Oates, the duo gradually moved in a pop direction as the decade progressed. Hits such as "She Used to Be Mine" (1993) and "That Ain't No Way to Go" (1994) feature a polished production that adheres to the increasingly slick dictates of 1990s country. On rocking up-tempo songs such as "Hard Workin' Man" (1993), Brooks & Dunn retained more of the verve displayed on their debut. While extolling virtues of traditional masculinity, "Hard Workin' Man" reflects the socially sensitive attitude of the early years of the Clinton administration. After singing lines such as "I can ride, rope, hammer, and paint, do things with my hands that most men can't," Dunn ends the song with the spoken interjection, "and women too." While giving the appearance of an amusing afterthought, the line nonetheless illustrates the social changes that had permeated country during the early 1990s.

By the mid-1990s, Brooks & Dunn had settled upon a standard formula for album releases: several large ballad and up-tempo hits, surrounded by less distinctive tracks, or "filler." *Waitin' on Sundown* (1994) contains what critics have described as one of the duo's finest hits, "She's Not the Cheatin' Kind." An account of a spurned wife who goes out for a night of dancing in order to forget her husband's unfaithfulness, the song features lyrics with a strong female point of view: "She's not the cheatin' kind/ She's been cheated one too many times." The impassioned quality of Dunn's singing—smooth, but capable of a tough shout when pushed—gives the song an added dimension of truthfulness. Elsewhere on *Waitin' for Sundown*, Brooks & Dunn display their keen songwriting ability. Penned by both members, "Whiskey under the Bridge" sports the kind of witty title—a popular saying rephrased in a humorous way—that characterized country music writing of the past. While the duo's late 1990s albums are less satisfying from an artistic perspective, they often feature inspired vocal performances. Criticized by reviewers as overly produced, *Borderline* is enhanced by Dunn's energetic delivery of the 1970s pop hit "My Maria." Soaring into a gliding falsetto on the song's chorus, Dunn displays further development as a singer.

Ongoing Popularity after 2000

In 2001 Brooks & Dunn released one of their most commercially successful albums, *Only in America*. Reflecting a trend of the early 2000s toward flag-waving conservatism in country, the number one hit "Only in America" features a mildly patriotic message, one underscored with lyrics that display little of the duo's past ingenuity: "If we all get a chance / Everybody gets to dance." "The Long Goodbye," another number one hit, is a pop ballad lacquered with synthesized aural effects such as the sound of wind blowing. While well arranged and orchestrated, the song deviates far from Brooks & Dunn's roots, the only discernable country influence being the twang in their voices. Veering from the hard rock of "See Jane Dance" to the Latin rhythms of "My Heart Is Lost to You," *Only in America* manages to display the versatility for which the duo is known.

One of the most enduringly popular of all 1990s country groups, Brooks & Dunn hit upon a successful formula and retained it through the early 2000s, making adjustments for the pop-oriented influences that overtook country in the mid- to late 1990s. While the wit and bite of their early lyrics disappeared on later albums, Brooks & Dunn continued to deliver vocal performances full of energy and charisma.

SELECTIVE DISCOGRAPHY: *Brand New Man* (Arista, 1991); *Hard Workin' Man* (Arista, 1993); *Waitin' on Sundown* (Arista, 1994); *Tight Rope* (Arista, 1999); *Steers and Stripes* (Arista, 2001).

WEBSITE: www.brooks-dunn.com.

DAVID FREELAND

GREG BROWN

Born: Ottumwa, Iowa, 2 July 1949

Genre: Folk

Best-selling album since 1990: *Covenant* (2000)

Folksinger Greg Brown is not only precious to his home state of Iowa, but he qualifies as a national treasure as well. Since the 1970s, the singer/songwriter has given the impression that he is a drifting musical Johnny Appleseed, haphazardly tossing out the seeds of his earthy, wisdom-filled songs. In actuality, Brown is one of the hardest workers in music—an artist whose impressive canon of songs and compelling voice allow him to forge a living in the financially frustrating world of folk music.

Brown was born in rural southeastern Iowa (local Iowans refer to the region as the "Hacklebarney" section of the state) into a musically inclined family with roots back to Appalachia. His father was a traveling Pentecostal preacher and Brown sojourned America's heartland with his father, who conducted Bible studies in various churches throughout Iowa, Kansas, and Missouri. After high school, Brown took off to New York City where he immediately found work hosting open-mic nights at Gerdes Folk City in Greenwich Village. In the 1970s he eventually returned to Iowa, which has been his home base ever since. Brown caught a break when radio host Garrison Keillor asked him to be part of his Prairie Home Companion radio broadcast. The regular exposure on National Public Radio increased his fan base and allowed Brown to form his own record company, Red House Records. This began a long string of critically acclaimed albums that positioned Brown as an extremely popular artist in regional pockets of the United States, although overall he sits only on the fringe of the mainstream.

One of Brown's most distinctive characteristics is his voice, which floats expressively out of him in a deep, low rumble. Playing an acoustic guitar for accompaniment, he sings his bluesy folk material in an uncomplicated style that communicates his overall unpretentiousness. Brown's songs are poetic tales ripe with irony, and contain detailed imagery often reflective of his rural Iowa upbringing. Willie Nelson, Carlos Santana, Shawn Colvin, and Mary Chapin Carpenter number among those artists who have performed his songs.

In the 1990s his album sales began increasing progressively as an aggressive concert schedule—Brown played 100 to 150 gigs per year throughout the 1990s—added to his popularity. *Slant 6 Mind* (1997) sold nearly 60,000 copies and *Covenant* (2000) has fared even better. Both albums contain Brown's raw, pleasing mix of blues and folk ballads. He also shows a strong country influence as heard on *Down in There* (1990), which features a bluegrass-styled tribute to the locale of his youth in "Hacklebarney Time."

Greg Brown [CRAIG HARRIS/RED HOUSE RECORDS]

His career has gone well enough for him to purchase 200 acres of land once owned by his grandparents in that same area of southern Iowa.

In 2002 a tribute album honoring Brown's music, *Going Driftless* (2002), was released. It contains renderings of fourteen songs by sixteen different female performers, including his three daughters, who perform "Ella Mae," which Brown wrote in honor of his grandmother. Other performers include Lucinda Williams, Gillian Welch, Ani DiFranco, and Iris Dement. All proceeds from *Going Driftless* go toward the Breast Cancer Fund.

The new millennium saw Brown scale down his feverish concert schedule as his well-deserved upswing of success allowed him to rest and take stock of his career. Among his many ambitions is to get more involved in writing for independent films. Brown remains one of the most important artists in contemporary folk music.

SELECTIVE DISCOGRAPHY: *Iowa Waltz* (Red House, 1983); *44 and 66* (Red House, 1984); *In the Dark with You* (Red House, 1985); *Songs of Innocence and of Experience* (Red House, 1986); *One More Goodnight Kiss* (Red House, 1988); *One Big Town* (Red House, 1989); *Down in There* (Red House, 1990); *Bathtub Blues* (Red House, 1993); *The Poet Game* (Red House, 1995); *The Live One* (Red House,

1995); *Further In* (Red House, 1996); *Slant 6 Mind* (Red House, 1997); *Over and Under* (Trailer 20, 2000); *Covenant* (Red House, 2000); *Milk on the Moon* (Red House, 2002).

DONALD LOWE

JAMES BROWN

Born: Barnwell, South Carolina, 3 May 1928
Genre: R&B
Best-selling album since 1990: *Love Over-Due* (1991)
Hit songs since 1990: "Move On," "Can't Get Any Harder"

Known variously as "The Godfather of Soul," "Soul Brother Number One," and "The Hardest Working Man in Show Business," James Brown is perhaps the most inventive and influential musician in rhythm and blues. Many critics have ranked him with rock pioneer Elvis Presley as a pioneering force in American popular music. Beginning his recording career in the mid-1950s, Brown helped usher in the soul era of the 1960s, spicing R&B with the sanctified cries of gospel music. By the middle to late 1960s, he was experimenting with dense, polyrhythmic structures and stripping lyrics to their barest essentials, thereby pioneering a new R&B musical style: funk. His rhythm grooves of the early 1970s were so sinuous and complex that, decades later, they helped define the sound of rap and hip-hop music. Through it all, Brown maintained the tightest, most professional band in R&B, whose ranks he oversaw with a Spartan sense of discipline. Continuing to perform his trademark dance moves and spine-chilling screams even at an age when many singers think of retiring, Brown was one of the great showmen of his era, his kinetic, dramatic stage style copied by pop stars such as Michael Jackson and Prince. After losing his commercial footing in the late 1970s, Brown rebounded in the 1980s and 1990s, less vigorous but still one of the most dynamic entertainers in music.

Early Years

Born in South Carolina but raised in Augusta, Georgia, Brown spent his early years living with relatives in a shack rented for seven dollars a month. Possessed of a steely determination that later served him well in his music career, Brown as a youth picked cotton, shined shoes, and attended school barefoot—all the while competing in local amateur shows. During the early 1950s, having served a prison sentence for robbery, Brown sang gospel music before setting his sights on developing an R&B band. Known eventually as James Brown and the Famous Flames, the band enjoyed its first R&B hit in 1956 with "Please Please Please," a ballad marked by Brown's hortatory, gospel-infused shouts. Throughout the 1960s Brown was never off the R&B charts, his sound becoming tougher and more frenetic as the decade progressed.

1960s and 1970s Triumphs

In 1963, against the wishes of his record company, the Cincinnati-based King Records, Brown released *Live at the Apollo*, a recording of one of his concerts at the famed Harlem showplace for African-American entertainment. The album, capturing Brown's high-voltage energy and brilliant interplay with his audience, was a huge seller, changing the way in which R&B—previously sold mostly through singles—was marketed. Lean, razor-sharp hits such as "Papa's Got a Brand New Bag," "I Got You (I Feel Good)" (both 1965), and "Cold Sweat" (1967) ushered in Brown's most productive period. Expressing solidarity with the civil rights movement, Brown also recorded stirring declarations of African-American pride such as "Say It Loud—I'm Black and I'm Proud" (1968).

In the early 1970s Brown became even more energized and frantic, discarding traditional vocalizing for a series of screams, coughs, and grunts. Helped by the rhythmic exactitude of his band, Brown transformed songs such as "Hot Pants" (1971) and "Get on the Good Foot" (1972) into sexually charged exercises in tension and release. Throughout these years Brown's band never failed him, although it defected temporarily in 1969, having grown tired of his rigid control. Known as a hard taskmaster, Brown regularly fined band members for playing a note out of tune or missing a beat.

Renewed Attention in the 1980s and 1990s

Like many R&B stars of the 1950s and 1960s, Brown was hurt by the disco explosion of the late 1970s. Nevertheless, he continued to record and perform, scoring a comeback hit with "Living in America" (1986). Beginning in 1989 he served a much-publicized jail sentence for assault and battery, charges brought by his wife. Released from prison after two years, Brown again found himself at the center of musical attention—his danceable, percussive grooves were being sampled by scores of rap and hip-hop artists. In one of many examples the rap artist Rob Base incorporated pieces of "Think (About It)," a 1972 track Brown had produced and arranged for the R&B singer Lyn Collins, into his hit "It Takes Two" (1988).

By the early 1990s this wave of interest in Brown led many critics, who previously had dismissed much of his 1970s work as tedious and repetitive, to elevate him into the highest ranks of American popular musicians. This new

prominence also allowed Brown to record strong albums such as *Love Over-Due* (1991). On a version of R&B group Hank Ballard and the Midnighters' 1959 hit, "Teardrops on Your Letter," Brown proves that he still has plenty of his old fire, spicing the song's final moments with his trademark screams. Working with the longtime Famous Flames tenor saxophonist St. Clair Pinckney, Brown recaptures his classic sense of groove on "Standing on Higher Ground" and the hit "(So Tired of Standing Still We Got to) Move On."

Critics pointed out that Brown was now following trends rather than leading them and that his 1990s albums lacked the passion of his greatest work. These criticisms notwithstanding, Brown in his sixties sounded vital and alive. In 1995 he returned to the scene of some of his greatest triumphs—the Apollo Theatre—to record *Live at the Apollo 1995*. Although his voice has lost some of its youthful expressiveness, Brown sounds powerful and in command on revved-up versions of former hits such as "Cold Sweat" and "Papa's Got a Brand New Bag." While uneven, Brown's 1998 album *I'm Back* sports trenchant funk tracks such as "James on the Loose" and "Funk on Ah Roll," presented in three different mixes. Now past seventy, Brown maintained his arduous performance schedule, touring and releasing albums such as *The Next Step* (2002), on which he is reunited with longtime associate, keyboardist and vocalist Bobby Byrd.

The top-selling performer in R&B history, James Brown set new standards for endurance, stagecraft, and musical innovation throughout the 1960s and 1970s. In the 1990s he gained renewed fame as a chief influence on rap and hip-hop. Never losing his sense of professionalism or power over an audience, Brown remained an influential presence in the new millennium.

SELECTIVE DISCOGRAPHY: *Live at the Apollo* (King, 1963); *Papa's Got a Brand New Bag* (King, 1965); *Cold Sweat* (King, 1967); *Say It Loud, I'm Black and I'm Proud* (King, 1969); *Hot Pants* (Polydor, 1971); *Get on the Good Foot* (Polydor, 1972); *I'm Real* (Scotti Bros., 1988); *Love Over-Due* (Scotti Bros., 1991); *Live at the Apollo 1995* (Scotti Bros., 1995); *I'm Back* (Mercury, 1998); *The Next Step* (Red Ink, 2002).

DAVID FREELAND

JEFF BUCKLEY

Born: Jeff Scott Buckley; Orange County, California, 17 November 1966; died Memphis, Tennessee, 29 May 1997

Genre: Rock

Best-selling album since 1990: *Grace* (1994)

Hit songs since 1990: "Last Goodbye"

The life of singer/songwriter Jeff Buckley is fraught with sadness and tragedy. Buckley's mastery of guitar and his fragile-sounding tenor earned him comparisons to veteran rockers Robert Plant and Van Morrison, and his bittersweet lyrics and early death at the age of thirty earned him comparisons to British folksinger Nick Drake, who suffered a similar fate. Although Buckley had released only a live EP and one full-length studio album, *Grace* (1994), before his untimely death in 1997, his death saddened thousands of fans and friends in the music industry. At the time of his death, Buckley had recorded much of his second full-length album, which was released in 1998 under the guidance of his mother, Mary Guibert, who is the executor of his estate.

Buckley had the uncanny misfortune of following the legacy of his father, Tim Buckley, an eccentric folksinger known by critics and the folk music community for the innovation he showed in the melding of jazz, folk, and rock in the 1960s and 1970s. Tim Buckley also suffered a tragic death; he died, penniless, of a heroin overdose when Jeff was only eight years old. Despite the impressive lineage, Jeff Buckley never really knew his father. His Panamanian-born, classical pianist mother divorced Tim when Jeff was very young. Buckley grew up in Orange County, California, and was uprooted constantly throughout his childhood as his mother struggled against poverty.

He began to perform in the early 1990s and released an EP, *Live at Sin-e*, named after a club in New York City where Buckley had been playing steadily. Ironically, Buckley first caught the attention of music industry executives when he performed at a tribute concert for his father in April 1991, at St. Ann's Church in Brooklyn. On *Live at Sin-e*, with grace and fire equally present, Buckley shifts from a cover of French cabaret singer Edith Piaf to Van Morrison without missing a beat. It caught the attention of music critics, industry veterans, and fans for its rawness, passion, and deft guitar playing.

When Buckley released his full-length debut *Grace* (1994), critics could not stop praising him as a virtuoso and an original. Richly textured, ambitious, and marked by spiritual and emotional examinations, *Grace* is so coherent and moving it shows that Buckley possessed the wisdom, romanticism, and the skill of someone much older. On the rollicking "Last Goodbye," he sings "This is our last embrace / Must I dream and always see your face?" The string instruments soar along with his voice; it is impossible to miss his utter devastation. Though his friends and his mother avow that Buckley during those years was happy and not depressed, it is impossible to miss the despair in his lyrics. Another standout track "Lover, You Shouldn't Have Come Over," with its romantic ruminations, showcases his emotional range.

There are a few covers on the album, which are as varied as they are lovely. Buckley imbues Leonard Cohen's "Hallelujah" with a sad joyfulness, accompanied solely by a meandering electric guitar. With his angelic, soulful falsetto, Buckley hits the upper register in his cover of "Corpus Christi Carol," a sixteenth-century madrigal arranged by composer Benjamin Britten.

After the success of his debut, Buckley took a break from recording. It was during this break that he died from drowning in the Mississippi River after deciding to go for a swim with his boots on. His body was found on June 4, 1997. His death was deemed an accidental drowning.

After Buckley's death, his mother met with executives from Columbia, and they decided to release an album he had been working on. In the liner notes to the posthumous album, *Sketches for My Sweetheart the Drunk,* a title that Buckley had chosen himself, Bill Flanagan writes that it was not out of character for Buckley to spontaneously jump in the river for a swim. Buckley was a passionate individual who had scarcely begun what was sure to be a storied and varied musical career. He will be remembered for his powerful, pained voice, sturdy command of the guitar, and achingly honest songwriting.

SELECTIVE DISCOGRAPHY: *Live at Sin-e* EP (Columbia, 1993); *Grace* (Columbia, 1994); *Sketches for My Sweetheart the Drunk* (Columbia, 1998). *Mystery White Boy: Live Recordings 1995–1996* (Columbia, 2000).

BIBLIOGRAPHY: D. Browne, *Dream Brother: The Lives and Music of Jeff and Tim Buckley* (New York, 2001).

CARRIE HAVRANEK

BUENA VISTA SOCIAL CLUB

Formed: 1996, Cuba

Members: Ry Cooder, acoustic and electric slide guitars, dobro, oud, bolon, marimba, percussion (born Los Angeles, California, 15 March 1947); Ibrahim Ferrer, vocals, bongos, clave (born Santiago, Cuba, 1927); Juan de Marcos Gonzalez, conductor, vocals, guiro (born Havana, Cuba, 1954); Ruben Gonzalez, piano (born Cuba, 1920); Pio Layva, percussion (born Cuba, 1917); Orlando "Cachaito" Lopez, bass (born Cuba, c. 1940s); Eliades Ochoa, vocals, guitar (born Santiago, Cuba, 1946); Omara Portuondo, vocals (born c. late 1920s); Compay Segundo, vocals, guitar, congas (born 1908; died 15 July 2003).

Genre: World

Best-selling album since 1990: *Buena Vista Social Club Soundtrack* (1997)

Spot Light | Buena Vista Social Club Documentary

The Cuban musicians who comprise the Buena Vista Social Club in Wim Wenders's 1999 documentary film were part of the golden era of popular Cuban music. Musician Ry Cooder and Wenders worked together when Cooder scored Wenders's film *Paris, Texas* (1984). The documentary, shot on digital video by Wenders and later transferred to film, is a humble, uncluttered look at the individuals, their lives, and their stories. The film and its soundtrack introduced the music to the world, and enabled these musicians to play at Carnegie Hall in New York City. The Club toured the world; their shows were impassioned, sellout successes. The players kept up a demanding tour schedule, and several members put together their own releases and corresponding tours. The film was nominated for an Academy Award for Best Documentary in 1999.

wanted to tell their story and share their music with the rest of the world. He visited Cuba in 1996 and met with singer Ferrer, whose soft, smooth, and airy voice Cooder describes as sounding like a Cuban Nat King Cole. There are contributions such as "Chan Chan" from guitarist Compay Segundo and a cover of "De Camino a la Veranda," a 1950s song by seventy-two-year-old composer Ferrer. The group's romantic sound and excellent musicianship transcend language; the album's liner notes provide an English translation of lyrics. The music is bittersweet, stirring; the musicians' love for their culture's guitar-based music is unmistakable.

The album and film's stunning success paved the way for the release of the back catalogs of many of the musicians involved, bringing the music of Cuba to a much larger audience.

SELECTIVE DISCOGRAPHY: *Buena Vista Social Club* (Nonesuch, 1997); *Introducing . . . . Ruben Gonzalez* (Nonesuch, 1997); *Buena Vista Social Club presents Ibrahim Ferrer* (Nonesuch, 1999); *Buena Vista Social Club Presents Omara Portuondo* (Nonesuch, 2000).

SELECTIVE FILMOGRAPHY: *Buena Vista Social Club* (1997).

CARRIE HAVRANEK

Buena Vista Social Club is a group of musicians named for a Havana, Cuba, club that was a cultural, musical hub in the late 1940s and 1950s. The musicians who comprised the group in the 1990s came together thanks to the work of American musician Ry Cooder. Cooder's interest in the group of aging Cuban maestros, many of them in their sixties, seventies, and even older, resulted in a Grammy Award for Best Tropical/Latin Album and a self-titled documentary, directed by German filmmaker Wim Wenders. In their native homeland, the men are well known and respected, but their international performing careers were cut short with the rise of Communist leader Fidel Castro in the 1960s. Consequently, musicians such as Ibrahim Ferrer, Eliades Ochoca, and Compay Segundo were largely unknown outside their country prior to the album and documentary. The album was an unexpected commercial and critical smash hit, achieving gold status in a little over two years after its release and going platinum by 2000.

The eclectic and curious guitarist and producer Cooder was fascinated with this group of musicians and

JIMMY BUFFETT

Born: Pascagoula, Mississippi, 25 December 1946
Genre: Country, Folk, Rock
Best-selling album since 1990: *Boats, Beaches, Bars, and Ballads* (1992)

Singer/songwriter Jimmy Buffett specializes in relaxed, country-influenced musical tales with a humorous twist. He has set himself apart from hoards of similar artists by parlaying his image—as a pleasure-seeking tropical-beach slacker—into tremendous commercial success. No artist has profited as much from one song as Buffett has from his 1977 hit, "Margaritaville," which spawned an entire entrepreneurial empire and made him one of music's wealthiest performers. Buffett also enjoys a successful second career as a writer.

Buffett grew up along the Gulf of Mexico near Mobile, Alabama, and his roots in the sea extend many generations back. His father was a naval architect and his grandfather a sailor. He chronicled his maritime heritage and attitude in the title song of his release *Son of Son of a Sailor* (1978). Buffett traveled to the eastern edge of Alabama to study journalism at Auburn University, where he began writing his own songs and performing in coffeehouses and clubs. As many country and folk singer/songwriters at that time did, Buffett traveled to Nashville, Tennessee, to begin a music career. However, instead of toiling in menial occupations while waiting for a break, as is the common practice, Buffett used his journalism experience to land a job with *Billboard* magazine. He rose to assistant editor at the publication while continuing to push his own songwriting and performing career. It turned out to be the only nine-to-five job Buffett ever worked.

Although he had two previous releases, Buffett's first major album success arrived after he began living on his own boat, soaking up and writing songs about the sights, sounds, characters, and lifestyle of Key West, Florida. His third album, *A White Sport Coat and a Pink Crustacean* (1973), was a charm and started a sequence of successful albums that brought Buffett into prominence. "Come Monday" from *Living and Dying in 3/4 Time* (1974) received extensive airplay, and other songs such as "Cheeseburger in Paradise," "Why Don't We Get Drunk," and "My Head Hurts, My Feet Stink and I Don't Love Jesus" became infamous, especially in rowdy college circles. However, "Margaritaville," his first and only major hit, defined Buffett. The song is about a happy-go-lucky beachcomber who sorts through the harebrained details of an alcohol-blurred summer to reach the gradual realization that his relationship problems are his own fault. While the three-chord song's subject matter is the stuff of country music tragedy, "Margaritaville" comes across as an appealing calamity, and it jump-started the phenomenon of Buffett's fans wearing tropical gear and perching stuffed parrots on their shoulders at his concerts. Consequently, Buffett's fans earned the label Parrotheads. The album containing "Margaritaville," *Changes in Latitudes, Changes in Attitudes* (1977), went platinum, and Buffett became a major star. Soon after, he used the Margaritaville branding for a series of stores that sell song-related items, a chain of Margaritaville Cafes, an on-line radio station called *Margaritaville Radio*, and even a fictional paradise in his first book, *Tales from Margaritaville* (1989). Within Buffett's laid-back beach dude persona rests a cunning businessman.

Like many contemporary songwriters possessing humor and substance, Buffett suffered a career slump in the 1980s. He abated this by arranging a concert sponsorship with Corona Beer, which hiked popularity for both entities. Buffett's live release, *Feeding Frenzy* (1990), went platinum, and he maintained his strong album sales without scoring major hits. Almost all of his work has a tropical theme, and the comical and catchy wordplay of his song and album titles sets the mood even before one hears the music. In the 1980s he released albums titled *Last Mango in Paris* (1985) and *Off to See the Lizard* (1989). The platinum-selling *Banana Wind* (1996) contained "Jamaica

---

Spot Light | Buffett as Author

Despite his many-faceted life, Jimmy Buffett somehow finds time to write books. His first, *Tales from Margaritaville: Fictional Facts and Factual Fictions* (1989), a collection of fictional and autobiographical short stories, remained on the *New York Times* best-seller list for seven months. He scored another *New York Times* best-seller with his first novel, *Where Is Joe Merchant?* (1992). Buffett's highly acclaimed memoir, *A Pirate Looks at Fifty* (1998), also earned best-seller status and in its second week hit the number one spot in the nonfiction genre. Buffett became one of only six writers in history to have reached number one on both the fiction and nonfiction bestseller lists of *The New York Times*. Additionally, he collaborated with his daughter, Savannah Jane, to pen two children's books, *The Jolly Mon* (1998) and *Trouble Dolls* (1991).

Mistaica," "Mental Floss," and "Happily Ever After (Now and Then)." *Beach House on the Moon* (1999) featured a song about pregnancy in "Permanent Reminder of a Temporary Feeling" and the title, "Altered Boy," from *Far Side of the World* (2002), may have reflected Buffett's Catholic school upbringing.

In concert Buffett usually accompanies himself on guitar and his folksy, midrange voice is more that of a storyteller or song interpreter than that of a classic country singer. He is a master showman, and few performers handle a live audience more deftly than Buffett. In 2003 he released a thirty-eight-song compilation album, *Meet Me in Margaritaville* (2003), which chronicled thirty years and thirty-three albums of work. The album's accompanying information sheds light on Buffett's life, which incorporates a concert and recording schedule, business responsibilities, the championing of environmental causes, world travel via his yacht or seaplanes (which he pilots), a passion for family responsibilities, and a career as a best-selling author.

Few musical artists manage to combine Buffett's balance of leisure and commercial success. Yet, while many herald his entrepreneurial accomplishments, it is the sincerity and wisdom found in his massive volume of songs that earn him a rank of distinction among American song-writers of the past quarter century.

SELECTIVE DISCOGRAPHY: *Down to Earth* (Barnaby, 1970); *A White Sport Coat and a Pink Crustacean* (Dunhill, 1973); *Living and Dying in 3/4 Time* (Dunhill, 1974); *Havana Daydreamin'* (ABC, 1976); *Changes in Latitudes, Changes in Attitudes* (ABC, 1977); *You Had to Be There: Jimmy Buffett In Concert* (MCA, 1978); *Son of a Son of a Sailor* (ABC, 1978); *Volcano* (MCA, 1979); *Coconut Telegraph* (MCA, 1981); *Riddles in the Sand* (MCA, 1984); *Last Mango in Paris* (MCA, 1985); *Floridays* (MCA, 1986); *Hot Water* (MCA, 1988); *Off to See the Lizard* (MCA, 1989); *Fruitcakes* (Margaritaville/MCA, 1994); *Barometer Soup* (Margaritaville/MCA, 1995); *Banana Wind* (Margaritaville/MCA, 1996); *Christmas Island* (Margaritaville/MCA, 1997); *Don't Stop the Carnival* (Margaritaville/Island, 1998); *Beach House on the Moon* (Margaritaville/Island, 1999); *Far Side of the World* (Mailboat, 2002); *Meet Me in Margaritaville* (Mailboat/MCA, 2003).

BIBLIOGRAPHY: J. Buffett, *Tales from Margaritaville: Fictional Facts and Factual Fictions* (San Diego, 1989): J. Buffett, *Where Is Joe Merchant?* (San Diego, 1992); J. Buffett, *Daybreak on the Equator* (New York, 1997); J. Buffett, *A Pirate Looks at Fifty* (New York, 1998); S. Eng, *Jimmy Buffett: The Man from Margaritaville Revealed*, (New York, 1997); M. Uscher, *Jimmy Buffett* (Kansas City, 2001).

DONALD LOWE

BUILT TO SPILL

Formed: 1992, Boise, Idaho

Members: Doug Martsch, lead vocals, guitar (born Idaho); Brett Nelson, bass guitar; Scott Plouf, drums. Former members: Andy Capps, drums; Brett Netson, bass guitar; Ralf Youtz, drums.

Genre: Rock

Best-selling album since 1990: *Ancient Melodies of the Future* (2001)

Built to Spill is the brainchild of singer/guitarist/songwriter Doug Martsch, who changed the band's lineup many times during its first years. Martsch demonstrated his songwriting chops in the early 1990s on Built to Spill's several well-received, independently released albums. Since signing to Warner Bros. in 1996, Built to Spill has honed their combination of eccentric vocal melodies and intricately formed guitar riffs, while increasingly adding the polish of the studio.

Martsch formed Built to Spill in Boise, Idaho, after leaving his first band Treepeople in 1992. After having a fluctuating lineup on the first few releases (including, confusingly, first Brett Netson and later Brett Nelson on bass guitar), the band finally settled into Martsch, Nelson, and Scott Plouf by the late 1990s. With the release of *There's Nothing Wrong with Love* (1994) on the independent label Up, the band began to receive increased critical attention. Martsch then signed Built to Spill to Warner Bros. in 1996. Their first major label release, *Perfect from Now On* (1997), initially sold under 50,000 copies. However, Warner Bros. kept the band on board, releasing two subsequent albums and Martsch's solo debut *Now You Know* (2002).

Early Built to Spill albums, especially *There's Nothing Wrong with Love*, are filled with catchy, personal songs alternating between Martsch's quirky melodic invention and brief bursts of guitar artistry. The lyrics complement the melody's unlikely turns, as in the track "Big Dipper," where Martsch concludes the choruses with "Should've been here last night and heard what the Big Dipper said to me." *There's Nothing Wrong with Love* also marks the beginning of Built to Spill's longstanding relationship with producer Phil Ek. On *Perfect from Now On* the band stretches out the songs into six-minute tracks that remain rooted in Martsch's blend of catchy tunes and strong guitar.

With their second major label release, *Keep It Like a Secret* (1999), many declared Built to Spill on the verge of commercial success. Although this proved elusive, the album's shorter songs were full of memorable tunes and a new level of studio technique that matched the band's increasing instrumental polish. Rather than simply reigning in the sprawling forms of *Perfect from Now On*, the band compressed moments of instrumental finesse into brief outbursts. From the opening of the first track, "The Plan," the album confronts the listener with a powerful, guitar-driven sound. Their next release, *Ancient Melodies of the Future* (2001), continues where *Keep It Like a Secret* left off, increasing the stylistic diversity. Regular collaborators Sam Coomes and Netson (now of Caustic Resin) contribute additional instruments throughout both *Ancient Melodies of the Future* and *Keep It Like a Secret*.

By striving for new sounds without venturing too far from their stylistic foundation, Built to Spill has managed to hold onto their record contract without achieving blockbuster success. They have been consistently well received by critics, and maintain the respect of the independent ("indie") rock community from which they emerged.

SELECTIVE DISCOGRAPHY: *Ultimate Alternative Wavers* (C/Z, 1993); *There's Nothing Wrong with*

Love (Up, 1994); *Perfect from Now On* (Warner Bros., 1997); *Keep It Like a Secret* (Warner Bros., 1999); *Ancient Melodies of the Future* (Warner Bros., 2001).

WEBSITE: www.builttospill.com.

CAROLINE POLK O'MEARA

T BONE BURNETT

Born: John Henry Burnett; St. Louis, Missouri, 14 January 1948

Genre: Country, Rock

Best-selling album since 1990: *The Criminal under My Own Hat* (1992) (as a performer); *O Brother, Where Art Thou?* (2000) (as a producer)

T Bone Burnett's career began in the 1960s where he carved out a stylistically eclectic career as an offbeat musical handyman. His career shifted more to producing and, in the 1990s and 2000s, his creative touch enabled music's biggest names to enjoy tremendous recording success. Burnett is a much respected and well-liked figure within the music industry and is the driving force behind a revived fascination for bluegrass music in the new millennium.

John Henry Burnett received the nickname "T Bone" when he was five years old while growing up in Fort Worth, Texas. After high school, Burnett tried college but quit to run his own recording studio in Fort Worth. He also performed in various blues bands before relocating to Los Angeles, California, where he recorded his debut album, *The B-52 Band and the Fabulous Skylarks* (1972). That same year he hooked up and toured with the folk rock duo, Delaney and Bonnie. In 1975 Bob Dylan hired him to play guitar on his Rolling Thunder Review Tour. When the tour ended, he joined forces with tour mates, guitarist/singer Steve Soles and the multitalented David Mansfield, to form the Alpha Band. Alpha Band recorded three critically acclaimed but only marginally successful albums before they broke up. Burnett began a solo career and released six albums in the 1980s, again scoring high marks with the critics but failing to achieve commercial success.

Burnett is a keen songwriter whose music wavers between a Texas-inflected country folk and British-styled pop rock. His lyrics are often political in nature and can be heavy-handedly moralistic at times. Burnett is unusual in contemporary music for unabashedly proclaiming his Christian beliefs. Yet many of his songs harangue fundamentalist preachers and conservative politicians, furthering his multifaceted image and "everyman" appeal. After his 1992 release, *The Criminal under My Own Hat* (1992), Burnett began to focus more of his energy on producing other artists' albums.

Throughout the 1970s and 1980s Burnett's work as a producer/engineer gained momentum and his strong sense of artistic integrity made him a favorite of many artists as he produced albums for Los Lobos, Leo Kottke, Marshall Crenshaw, Elvis Costello, the legendary Roy Orbison, and other top performers. He also served as musical director for the televised concert tribute to Roy Orbison *A Black and White Night* (1989), which featured numerous stars as special guests, including Bruce Springsteen and Elvis Costello. Burnett produced *The Turning* (1987) for Christian singer Leslie Phillips, which helped Phillips make inroads into secular pop music. Burnett and Phillips (who changed her name to Sam Phillips) married, and Burnett went on to produce all of her later efforts into the 1990s.

Except to the cultlike followers of his recording career, Burnett remained largely unknown into the 1990s. However, music industry insiders considered Burnett a major force. He continued to produce successful work, most notably albums for Counting Crows, the Wallflowers, k.d. lang, Tony Bennett, and Gillian Welch. Although he has produced more than seventy albums, it was the Grammy Award–winning soundtrack, *O Brother, Where Art Thou?* (2000), that brought Burnett special notoriety.

O Brother, Where Art Thou? features Emmylou Harris, Alison Krauss, Gillian Welch, Ralph Stanley, and others performing traditional country and bluegrass songs, many from the 1930s and before. The album sold more than 6 million copies and started a bluegrass revival of sorts in the United States. It also scored a 2001 Grammy Award for Album of the Year and gave Burnett a 2001 Grammy Award for Producer of the Year.

In 2002 Burnett used the same idea for the soundtrack to the film *Divine Secrets of the Ya-Ya Sisterhood* (2002). He spent considerable time combing Louisiana's rural locales in search of authentic Cajun blues and traditional pieces. The album is a mixture of soft jazz and Cajun-influenced southern songs. It features performances by Bob Dylan, Lauryn Hill, Tony Bennett, and Ray Charles, among others.

After a nearly ten-year hiatus from songwriting, Burnett started composing music for the theater, specifically Sam Shepard's play, *The Late Henry Moss* (2000). Burnett remains a throwback to an era when the music industry was about the music, and not the stardom.

SELECTIVE DISCOGRAPHY: *The B-52 Band and the Fabulous Skylarks* (UNI, 1972); *Truth Decay*

(Takoma, 1980); *Trap Door* (Warner Bros., 1982); *Proof through the Night* (Warner Bros., 1983); *Behind the Trap Door* EP (Demon, 1984); *T Bone Burnett* (MCA, 1986); *The Talking Animals* (Columbia, 1988); *The Criminal under My Own Hat* (Columbia, 1992). **With the Alpha Band:** *The Alpha Band* (Arista, 1976); *Spark in the Dark* (Arista, 1977); *The Statue Makers of Hollywood* (Arista, 1978). **As producer:** *Delbert and Glen* (Atlantic, 1971); *Time Step* (Chrysalis, 1983); *How Will the Wolf Survive?* (Warner Bros., 1985); *Downtown* (Warner Bros., 1985); *King of America* (Columbia, 1986); *In Dreams* (Virgin, 1987); *Cruel Inventions* (Virgin, 1991); *August and Everything After* (DGC, 1993); *Dart to the Heart* (Columbia, 1994); *Revival* (Almo Sounds, 1996); *A Wonderful World* (Sony, 2002). **Soundtracks:** *O Brother, Where Art Thou?* (Universal, 2000); *Divine Secrets of the Ya-Ya Sisterhood* (Sony, 2002).

DONALD LOWE

BUSH

Formed: 1992, London, England

Members: Robin Goodridge, drums (born Crawley, Sussex, England, 10 September 1966); Dave Parsons, bass (born Uxbridge, London, England, 2 July 1962); Gavin Rossdale, vocals, guitar (born Kilburn, London, England, 30 October 1967). Former member: Nigel Pulsford, guitar (born Newport, Gwent, Wales, 11 April 1963).

Genre: Rock

Best-selling album since 1990: *Sixteen Stone* (1994)

Hit songs since 1990: "Everything Zen," "Comedown," "Machinehead"

The year 1994 witnessed the end of grunge's first wave, as the movement's spiritual leader, Nirvana's Kurt Cobain, committed suicide and, in so doing, ended what many considered a musical revolution. It also saw a new wave of grunge acts, like the British band Bush, whose landmark album *Sixteen Stone* (1994) polished up the genre's raw and abrasive edges and made it acceptable to the masses.

Gavin Rossdale and Nigel Pulsford formed Bush in 1992 after a chance meeting at a London pub. The pair found common musical ground in their affection for the Pixies, whose raucous pop-noise albums from the 1980s had inspired many of the acts currently spearheading the Seattle grunge revolution, including Nirvana. Rossdale and Pulsford hooked up with local bass player Dave Parsons and drummer Robin Goodridge; after a few short months

of playing live, Bush scored an American recording contract with Interscope Records.

Interscope released Bush's debut album *Sixteen Stone*. The lead single "Everything Zen" quickly captured the attention of MTV viewers, landing in the television station's "Buzz Bin," a spot reserved for hip, emerging acts. The driving "Everything Zen" draws heavily upon stock grunge production "tricks": The guitars drop out for the verses, while a brooding bass carries the tune, and the song increases in intensity as it approaches the chorus, at which point the guitars reach a crunching climax, punctuated by Rossdale's howl. Though Bush borrowed from Nirvana sonically, the band tidied up its predecessor's sound, eschewing dark, murky lo-fi sounds for a crisp and fleshed-out production more friendly to mainstream radio ears. Bush's Nirvana-influenced presentation extended to its lyrics as well, such as on "Everything Zen," which offers this odd and slightly disarming wordplay: "There's no sex in your violence."

The follow-up singles employed similar tactics. The ballad "Comedown" offers an instrumental analogue to "Everything Zen," with bass and guitars intermittently dropping in and out of the mix. "Glycerine" spotlights a solo Rossdale for much of the song; in a style close to Cobain, Rossdale chops at a simple four-chord progression on his electric guitar, while delivering tortured lyrics: "It must be your skin I'm sinkin' in / Must be for real, 'cause now I can feel."

On the strength of five hit singles, *Sixteen Stone* sold 3 million copies. While the public embraced Bush, critics were far less approving. They delivered scathing reviews of *Sixteen Stone*, charging that the songs were soulless Nirvana facsimiles. For some critics Rossdale's striking good looks seemed incompatible with his "grunge" music.

Bush sought artistic credibility by hiring noted grunge producer Steve Albini to oversee the recording of its follow-up album, *Razorblade Suitcase* (1996). Upon release, *Razorblade Suitcase* debuted at number one on the album charts and earned a smattering of positive reviews, but Bush's image was beyond rehabilitation with most critics. The bad press inevitably hurt the band's momentum, and *Razorblade Suitcase* scored only one hit single in "Swallowed."

Bush's subsequent two albums, *The Science of Things* (1999) and *Golden State* (2001), likewise stalled on the charts. Original guitar player Pulsford left the band during the tour for the latter album. Though its albums generated little enthusiasm, Bush remained in the public eye during Rossdale's high-profile romance with Gwen Stefani, lead singer of No Doubt. After a long courtship, the pair married in 2002.

While Bush may not weather comparison to Nirvana, nevertheless it did produce a series of memorable grunge-lite hits in the late 1990s and helped to solidify the genre's standing in the popular culture.

SELECTIVE DISCOGRAPHY: *Sixteen Stone* (Trauma/Interscope, 1994); *Razorblade Suitcase* (Trauma/Interscope, 1996); *The Science of Things* (Trauma/Interscope, 1999); *Golden State* (Atlantic, 2001).

SCOTT TRIBBLE

BUSTA RHYMES

Born: Trevor Smith Junior; Brooklyn, New York, 20 May 1972

Genre: Rap

Best-selling album since 1990: *Extinction Level Event* (Elektra, 1998)

Hit songs since 1990: "Woo Hah!," "What's It Gonna Be?" (featuring Janet Jackson), "Pass the Courvosier" (with P. Diddy)

Busta Rhymes is notable for his energy and his quirky, superanimated rapping. He is one of hip-hop's most dependable artists, with each of his albums receiving considerable commercial attention.

Trevor Smith Jr. was born to a family of Jamaican roots in the East Flatbush section of Brooklyn, New York, a multicultural community. The Smiths moved to Long Island, New York, where young Busta Rhymes met a fellow lyricist, Charlie Brown. They formed a group called Leaders of the New School. The ensemble was considered part of hip-hop's Native Tongues subgenre, an earthy bohemian movement popular in the late 1980s and early 1990s. The band was discovered by the rap supergroup Public Enemy, who agreed to nurture the act after seeing them perform at a talent show. Leaders of the New School expanded to include the rap artists Dinco D. and Cut Monitor Milo, and recorded songs at Public Enemy's studio. They secured a deal with Elektra Records and released their debut album, *A Future without a Past . . . .* (1991). The album spawned the bouncy hits "Case of the P.T.A." and "Sobb Story," and critics and a cult following of fans hailed them as a refreshing, vital force within the Native Tongues scene. Nevertheless, that album failed to make a dent with consumers.

Although his group's commercial viability was in question, Busta Rhymes was emerging as a superstar. His wild, upward-combed hair and tall, lanky frame created a memorable image. Busta Rhymes's breakout moment occurred

Busta Rhymes [AP/WIDE WORLD PHOTOS]

on the song "Scenario" (1991), by A Tribe Called Quest. The song also features Charlie Brown and Dinco D., but it is Busta's closing verse that attracted the fans. Here he debuts his sound-effect style of rapping, somewhere between rhyming and beat boxing, which became his signature. His frenetic flow, coupled with vigorously enacted lyrics like "rroaw rroaw like a dungeon dragon," have made him a unique voice in hip-hop.

Busta Rhymes's rising star did little to save his group's follow-up effort, *T.I.M.E.* (1993), from obscurity. The group disbanded, and Busta Rhymes embarked on a solo career marked by a flamboyant image. His hair was a fountain of dreadlocks and he dressed in loud, cartoonish costumes. Thanks to another magnetic cameo appearance, this time on the 1995 remix of Craig Mack's "Flava in Ya Ear," Busta Rhymes experienced a resurgence with diehard rap fans. He collaborated with the video director Hype Williams, whose bold treatments emphasized Busta Rhymes's colorful, attention-grabbing style. Busta Rhymes's first solo single, "Woo-Hah," and first solo album, *The Coming* (1996), were platinum smashes.

Busta Rhymes developed his partnership with Hype Williams, making videos as fast-paced and frenzied as his delivery and beats. Their clips were hip-hop's most inventive. The video "Put Your Hands Where My Eyes Can See" received three MTV Video Music Award nominations. The song, from the album *When Disaster Strikes* (1997), is built on a tribal beat and a clever rhyme sequence, in which the first lines all end with the slang term "yo."

Each of Busta Rhymes's solo albums went platinum, and he recorded a dizzying array of songs with other artists. His biggest collaboration, "What's It Gonna Be?!," with Janet Jackson, is another highlight. The song sold more than 1 million copies, and the high-tech video cost more than $2 million to produce. The album behind it, *Extinction Level Event* (Elektra, 1998) also includes a duet with Ozzy Osbourne, endearing Busta Rhymes to new rock audiences. His slot on Puff Daddy's 1998 No Way Out arena tour showcased his expressive performing style.

Along with selling records, Busta Rhymes found steady work as a film actor. His first significant role was in the John Singleton movie *Higher Learning* (1995). He also appeared in *Shaft 2000, Finding Forrester* (2002) and *Halloween: Resurrection* (2002). Busta Rhymes started another group, Flipmode Squad, of which he is the lead member, and a record label of the same name.

In 2001 Busta Rhymes severed his long relationship with Elektra and signed to the newly formed J-Records, headed by the music industry legend Clive Davis. His first J-Records release, *Genesis* (2001), seemed to lag in sales in its first months of release, but thanks to a club remix of the marketing mantra "Pass the Courvosier," featuring P. Diddy, it joined his other albums in the platinum club. His second J-Records album, *It Ain't Safe No More* (2002), boasts a dancehall-tinged single "Make It Clap" and the smooth "I Know What You Want" with Mariah Carey and the Flipmode Squad.

Unlike artists who need to reinvent themselves over time, Busta Rhymes maintains a formula that remains constant and relevant to his fans. Futuristic and frenetic, his dynamic rapping style pulses with a vitality seldom matched by his peers.

SELECTIVE DISCOGRAPHY: *The Coming* (Elektra, 1996); *When Disaster Strikes* (Elektra, 1997); *Extinction Level Event* (Elektra, 1998); *Anarchy* (Elektra, 2000); *Genesis* (J-Records, 2001); *It Ain't Safe No More* (J-Records, 2002). **With Leaders of the New School:** *A Future without a Past . . . .* (Elektra, 1991); *T.I.M.E.* (Elektra, 1993).

DARA COOK

DAVID BYRNE

Born: Dumbarton, Scotland, 14 May 1952
Genre: Rock, World

Best-selling album since 1990: *Look into the Eyeball* (2001)

Hit songs since 1990: "She's Mad," "Angels"

As lead singer for the new wave rock band Talking Heads, David Byrne was a musical pioneer of the 1970s and 1980s, combining punk music's energy and bite with the polyrhythmic beats of world music. Emerging as a solo artist in the late 1980s, Byrne continued experimenting with musical pluralism, drawing together alternative rock, Latin music, worldbeat, and R&B with an off-kilter sensibility. Never losing his quirky diction and slightly goofy persona, Byrne brought a detached air of intellectualism to his work, often collaborating with celebrated avantgarde theater artists such as Robert Wilson. While critics sometimes perceived his songwriting as ponderous and trite, most celebrated Byrne's unique ability to create vivid, complex sonic landscapes. In contemporary pop, where eclecticism is often prized for its own sake, Byrne has made tasteful and adroit musical choices; his far-ranging explorations are unified through the strength and integrity of his vision.

Born in Scotland but raised in Baltimore, Maryland, Byrne played in various bands as a teenager before attending the Rhode Island School of Design. Feeling dissociated from the school's mostly upper-class student body, Byrne dropped out after one year but continued to live and perform in Rhode Island. In the early 1970s he joined forces with his fellow students Chris Frantz and Tina Weymouth to form the Artistics, later renamed Talking Heads after the band relocated to New York in 1974. Signing with Sire Records in 1977, Talking Heads initially recorded in an edgy, new wave rock style, in evidence on the minor 1978 hit, "Psycho Killer." But through the influence of their producer, the experimental rock artist Brian Eno, they soon began adding electronic instruments and African percussion. As early as 1981 Byrne began to pursue solo work, teaming with Eno for *My Life in the Bush of Ghosts* (1981), an album that, through its incorporation of sonic elements such as Muslim chanting and Lebanese mountain singing, anticipated the "world music" explosion of the late 1980s. Byrne also worked on collaborations with Wilson, acted in and directed the film *True Stories* (1986), and won an Academy Award for his work scoring *The Last Emperor* (1989), an acclaimed film by the Italian director Bernardo Bertolucci.

While critically acclaimed, Byrne's solo albums—perhaps overshadowed by his work with Talking Heads—have never produced many hits. Leaving the group in 1988, Byrne released *Rei Momo* (1989), an engaging collection underscored with Latin rhythms, and *Uh-Oh* (1992), on which he explored styles as diverse as R&B/funk and Jamaican reggae. While critics were largely disappointed with *David Byrne* (1994), complaining that the album's stripped-down musical setting accentuated the puzzling obliqueness of Byrne's lyrics, they responded positively to *Feelings* (1997), featuring a prominent guest appearance by the electronic, "trip-hop" dance band Morcheeba. Sonically adventurous, Byrne's albums of this period resist critical analysis, demanding acceptance on their own idiosyncratic terms.

In 2001 Byrne released what many view as his finest solo album, *Look into the Eyeball*. While lyrics such as "Jesus is cool / Jesus is scared / Baby you're the only car I drive" (from the album's opener, "U.B. Jesus") evince Byrne's trademark opacity, the album as a whole succeeds by employing a muted, restrained style. Songs such as "The Accident" recall the sonorous work of modern classical composers such as Steve Reich, while "The Revolution" sports an affectingly spare arrangement of acoustic guitar and strings. Two highlights are "Like Humans Do" and "Neighborhood," arranged by the noted 1970s soul producer Thom Bell, who underscores Byrne's eccentric vocal style with a lush, rhythmic groove. In a move emphasizing his separation from mainstream pop music, Byrne spices "Walk on Water" with a biting critique of the shallowness of rock stardom: "He can walk on the water / But he can't stop fallin' in." The sting, however, is softened by the giddiness of the rest of the lyrics: "Get up, you men and women / Walk on, like fishes swimming."

Beginning his career with the influential rock band Talking Heads, Byrne in the 1980s and 1990s led forays into diverse music from many cultures. Esoteric, challenging, and sometimes frustrating, Byrne's solo work is striking in its refusal to abide by the strictures of any particular school of music. Like avant-garde artists such as Wilson and Laurie Anderson, Byrne commands a limited yet significant following among an artistically educated audience.

SELECTIVE DISCOGRAPHY: *The Catherine Wheel* (Luaka Bop, 1981); *Rei Momo* (Luaka Bop/Sire, 1989); *The Forest* (Luaka Bop, 1991); *Uh-Oh* (Luaka Bop, 1992); *David Byrne* (Luaka Bop, 1994); *Feelings* (Luaka Bop, 1997); *Look into the Eyeball* (Virgin, 2001).**With Talking Heads:** *Talking Heads: 77* (Sire, 1977); *Remain in Light* (Sire, 1980); *Speaking in Tongues* (Sire, 1983); *Stop Making Sense* (Sire, 1984). **Soundtrack:** *The Last Emperor* (Virgin, 1987).

WEBSITE: www.davidbyrne.com.

DAVID FREELAND

C

c
c

CAKE

Formed: 1991, Sacramento, California

Members: Vincent DiFiore, trumpet, keyboards; John McCrea, vocals, guitar; Xan McCurdy, guitar; Pete McNeal, drums; Gabriel Nelson, bass. Former members: Greg Brown, guitar; Victor Damiani, bass; Frank French, drums; Sean McFessel, bass; Todd Roper, drums.

Genre: Rock

Best-selling album since 1990: *Fashion Nugget* (1996)

Hit songs since 1990: "The Distance," "Rock 'n' Roll Lifestyle"

Rock and roll history is littered with the carcasses of oddball, one-hit wonder bands that were able to capture the public's imagination for a moment, then quickly fade into obscurity. Sacramento's Cake, however, were able to launch quirky hit after quirky hit with songs such as "The Distance" and "Short Skirt/Long Jacket," driven by an unusual combination of country waltzes, trumpet solos, and founder John McCrea's deadpan vocals and oddball lyrics.

The brainchild of veteran musician John McCrea, Cake was founded in Sacramento in 1991, after McCrea spent several fruitless years in Los Angeles playing coffeehouses while attempting to launch his music career. Upon moving back to Sacramento, McCrea recruited the band's first lineup and released Cake's self-produced, self-financed debut, the offbeat *Motorcade of Generosity* (1993). With 1950s-inspired graphics and a sound that owes more to Mariachi, classic country, and lounge music than to the aggressive, guitar-based alternative rock and roll of the time, the group was an anomaly.

The album introduces the soon-to-be familiar combination of McCrea's deadpan, often inscrutable vocals and lyrics, Vincent DiFiore's brassy trumpet solos, and the liberal use of the rattlesnake-sounding vibraslap percussion instrument. The airy, playful arrangements are matched by songs with bizarre, often humorous lyrics, such as the jazzy, spoken word piece "Mr. Mastadon Farm," in which McCrea sings/talks an homage to birds plummeting from window ledges.

Capricorn records signed the group in 1994 and re-released the album in its original form. The album produced a bona fide radio hit with the novelty song "Rock 'n' Roll Lifestyle," a sarcastic jab at the excesses of rock stars that became a staple of alternative radio two years after the album's release. "How much did you pay for the chunk of his guitar / The one he ruthlessly smashed at the end of the show? / And how much will he pay for a brand new guitar / One which he'll ruthlessly smash at the end of another show?" McCrea sings as a combination of rattlers, bluesy guitar, and cocktail drums play behind him. Despite its unusual, cocktail lounge arrangement and a sarcastic tone that mocked some of the very fans who bought the album, the song set the standard for the group's future success.

French and Nelson were replaced by Todd Roper and Victor Damiani after a distribution deal with Capricorn records was completed; it would be the first of many lineup changes for the group.

In addition to their own off-kilter originals, *Fashion Nugget* (1996) features an odd cover that would become

113

a staple of the band's live show. In typically deadpan style, McCrea sings/talks the lyrics to Gloria Gaynor's disco classic "I Will Survive," re-imagined here as a sarcastically bluesy rock number with Neil Young–style classic rock guitar solos by Greg Brown, nimble, jazzy bass lines from Damiani, and a Tijuana Brass–like trumpet solo from DiFiore.

Among a trio of automobile-themed tracks on the album is "The Distance," which would be one of the group's biggest hits. Combining elements of bleating, urgent jazz horns, white boy funk, and chunky rock guitar lines, the song tells the story of a race car driver hellbent for speed. "Reluctantly crouched at the starting line / Engines pumping and thumping in time / The green light flashes, the flags go up / Churning and burning the years for the cup," McCrea sings, his poker-faced vocals purposely not rising to meet the excitement of the lyrics.

With songs honoring Frank Sinatra, a Willie Nelson cover ("Sad Songs and Waltzes"), and a pseudo-rap/beat poetry song ("Nugget"), though more aggressively rock in parts, *Fashion Nugget* continues Cake's disregard for the trends of the day—be they mainstream pop, thuggish hip-hop, or the tail end of thrashing grunge rock—in favor of McCrea's singular vision.

Prior to the release of *Prolonging the Magic* (1998), the band's lineup shuffled again, with Nelson returning in place of Damiani, and Brown, author of "The Distance," departing to start the group Deathray with Damiani. The album, which trades some of the group's signature smirking irony for more sincere sentiment, again taps into McCrea's defining influences, sad country waltzes ("Mexico"), acoustic, jammy funk ("Guitar"), and absurdist jazz rock story songs ("Alpha Beta Parking Lot," "Sheep Go to Heaven"). In the latter, a funk-inspired meditation on death, McCrea sings, "And the gravedigger puts on the forceps / The stonemason does all the work / The barber can give you a haircut."

The album spawned two songs that became minor radio hits, the Latin-jazz-meets-funk "Never There," which adds elements of retro 1970s keyboard sounds to the group's repertoire, and the twitchy, midtempo rock song of unworthiness, "Hem of Your Garment."

Guitarist Xan McCurdy joined the group following the album's release and was on board when they recorded *Comfort Eagle* (2001). Safely clear of one-hit wonder status, the group embellished their sound on their fourth album with keyboards and drum machines. Still partial to jokey funk rock songs about oddball characters ("Opera Singer"), *Comfort Eagle* retains the band's quirky sensibility while it turns down the irony.

Jack-of-all-trades McCrea directed a low-budget video for "Short Skirt/Long Jacket" that looked like an infomercial in which people on the street were asked their unrehearsed opinions of the song. The honest reactions to the driving, disco rock song about the search for the perfect woman spawned yet another radio hit for the group.

With a consistent, yet unconventional sound and sardonic attitude that might normally have doomed them to a "whatever happened to . . . ?" career in one-hit wonderland, Cake managed to bend the ears of listeners time and again by sticking to their guns.

SELECTIVE DISCOGRAPHY: *Motorcade of Generosity* (Capricorn, 1994); *Fashion Nugget* (Capricorn, 1996); *Prolonging the Magic* (Capricorn, 1998); *Comfort Eagle* (Columbia, 2001).

GIL KAUFMAN

CAM'RON

Born: Cameron Giles; New York, New York, 4 February 1976

Genre: Hip-Hop

Best-selling album since 1990: *Confessions of Fire* (1998)

Hit songs since 1990: "357," "Horse and Carriage," "Let Me Know"

Harlem-based rapper Cam'ron's streetwise yet witty rhymes and edgy charisma seemed to mark him as the late 1990s heir to one of his earliest mentors, fellow New York MC the Notorious B.I.G. (alternately known as Biggie Smalls). He made his solo debut in 1998 with an album delivering the polished, pop-friendly rap then enjoying prominence thanks to another Cam'ron ally, producer and rapper Sean "Puff Daddy" Combs. Label difficulties, however, stalled Cam'ron's career, and he would have to wait until the early twenty-first century for major success.

Born in Harlem, Cameron Giles attended Manhattan Center High School, where he played on the basketball team with future hip-hop star Mason "Ma$e" Betha. Although his basketball skills were enough to earn him college scholarships, his poor academic record led him to a small school in Texas. He soon dropped out and returned to Harlem, where he became a drug dealer for a time before encountering Betha again and beginning to pursue a rap career. Adopting the name "Killa Cam," Giles and his cousin, Derek "Bloodshed" Armstead, joined Betha and another neighborhood rapper, Lamont "Big L" Coleman, to form the group Children of the Corn. When the death of Armstead in a car accident prompted Children of the Corn to disband, the remaining members began pursuing solo careers. In 1995 Big L became the first to succeed, and he featured Giles, then still known as Killa Cam, on a track on his debut album. It was Ma$e, however, who provided Giles with the break that launched his career.

In 1996 Ma$e had signed with Combs's Bad Boy label, home to one of the time's most popular and respected rappers, the Notorious B.I.G. In 1997 Ma$e got Giles an audition with the Notorious B.I.G., who was impressed enough to introduce Giles to his partner, Lance "Un" Rivera. Cam'ron, as he was by then known, became the first artist signed to Rivera's Untertainment label.

Cam'ron got his first airplay in May 1998 with "Pull It," a collaboration with rapper DMX. He followed this with "357," a track from the soundtrack to the movie *Woo* (1998) that wrapped Cam'ron's boasts of his drug-dealing past around a catchy sample of the theme song to 1980s television drama *Magnum P.I.* While "357" barely cracked the R&B/hip-hop charts, Cam'ron's next single, the Latin-tinged "Horse and Carriage," became a Top 10 R&B/hip-hop hit in the summer of 1998. Reteaming Cam'ron with Ma$e, the track introduced listeners to the menacing yet tongue-in-cheek bravado that characterized the debut album from which it was taken: "Aiyyo, you might see Cam in designer underwear / New reclining leather chair, reminders everywhere / How we pull up in whips, the minors stop and stare."

Released in July 1998, *Confessions of Fire* presents nineteen tracks laying Cam'ron's celebratory tales of gangsta life over slick, pop-friendly production, interspersed with cameos from the likes of Ma$e, Noreaga, Jermaine Dupri, and Cam'ron's mother. The album's second single, "Feels Good," tempers Cam'ron's thuggishness with a hook sung by R&B crooner Usher and lyrics honoring long-term romantic commitment. "Feels Good" became a minor hit, helping *Confessions of Fire* sell some 500,000 copies and reach the Top 10 of the R&B and pop album charts.

In June 1999 Cam'ron released "Let Me Know," the first single from his second album, *S.D.E.*, which stands for "Sports, Drugs, and Entertainment." Just before *S.D.E.* was to be released, Untertainment lost its distribution deal with Epic, causing the album to be shelved for more than a year. *S.D.E.* debuted in September 2000 to little fanfare. In 2002 Cam'ron signed with Jay-Z-led industry powerhouse Roc-A-Fella records, which put out his third album, *Come Home with Me*, in May of that year. *Come Home with Me* became Cam'ron's biggest success to date, spawning a series of Top 40 hits and going platinum.

Well-connected supporters such as Ma$e and the Notorious B.I.G., along with a knack for combining gritty street-oriented attitude with shrewd pop savvy, allowed Cam'ron to make a bid for hip-hop stardom in the late 1990s. Although Cam'ron's 1990s career failed to make good on his early promise, it set the stage for his success in the early 2000s.

SELECTIVE DISCOGRAPHY: *Confessions of Fire* (Untertainment/Epic, 1998); *S.D.E.* (Epic, 2000); *Come Home with Me* (Roc-A-Fella, 2002). **Soundtrack:** *Woo* (Sony, 1998).

WEBSITE: www.rocafella.com/company.htm.

MATT HIMES

CANADIAN BRASS

Formed: 1970, Toronto

Members: Ryan Anthony, trumpet (born Santiago, California, 17 May 1969); Josef Burgstaller, (born Chicago, Illinois, 27 April 1971); Charles Daellenbach, tuba (born Rhinelander, Wisconsin, 12 July 1945); Jeffrey Nelsen, French horn (born Edmonton, Alberta, 11 December 1969); Eugene Watts, trombone (born Sedalia, Missouri, 22 February 1936). Former members: Chris Cooper, French horn; Martin Hackleman, French horn; Stuart Laughton; Jens Lindemann, trumpet; Fred Mills, trumpet; David Ohanian, French horn; Graeme Page, French horn; Bill Philips, trumpet; Ron Romm, trumpet.

Genre: Classical, Pop

When trumpeter Fred Mills and tuba player and trombonist Gene Watts came up with the idea for the Canadian Brass in 1968, there were no working professional brass quintets. The group was formed two years later with tuba player Chuck Daellenbach, trumpeters Bill Phillips and Stuart Laughton, and horn player Graeme Page (Mills had other commitments and joined the group two years later).

With a limited number of works for brass ensemble available, the players had to invent both a viable sound and repertoire. With its quirky personality, sense of play, and virtuosic musicianship, the group quickly won a wide following. A measure of the group's success is the mob of brass quintets that sprang up after the Canadian Brass were formed, establishing the brass quintet as a standard ensemble.

In the beginning the group helped support itself by serving as the brass section of the Hamilton (Ontario) Philharmonic Orchestra. The players also developed an ambitious educational program for Ontario schoolchildren; the need to appeal to younger audiences helped develop the group's humorous presentations. The players spoke to audiences between pieces, engaged in good-natured kidding, and performed musical skits. The shows were hugely entertaining, and the players found that the routines that worked best with kids also worked on adults.

If comedy was all the Brass were offering, the group's musical career would not have lasted long. But along with humor, the Brass served up brilliant ensemble work, a tight sound, and formidable technical ability and musicianship. The group created its own repertoire, transcribing, arranging, and commissioning more than 200 works. Music ranged from Baroque (particularly Bach) to the Beatles, jazz, ragtime, and pop songs. In the 1990s the Brass even performed a Western "Brass Opera" called "Hornsmoke" by composer Peter Schickele, a melodrama in which the players dress up in costumes, move about the stage, and "sing" their parts on their instruments.

In the 1990s, despite personnel changes, the Brass embarked on ambitious projects, performing and recording arrangements of two of Bach's most musically challenging works: the *Goldberg Variations* and *Art of the Fugue*.

Many of the Canadian Brass arrangements—both serious classical works and lighter popular fare—have become staples of the repertoire for brass groups all over North America and Europe. The members work with young chamber groups, and they have served as quintet-in-residence at several summer festivals, including the Banff Festival and the Music Academy of the West in Santa Barbara.

The Brass have recorded more than fifty albums and perform more than a hundred shows a year, both solo and with symphony orchestras. They have appeared frequently on television shows such as *The Tonight Show*, *Today*, and *Entertainment Tonight*, along with numerous PBS, CBC, and Christmas specials. They have also produced eight videos.

SELECTIVE DISCOGRAPHY: *Bach: The Art of the Fugue* (Sony, 2001); *The Essential Canadian Brass* (Polygram, 1992); *The Canadian Brass Greatest Hits* (RCA, 1990).

BIBLIOGRAPHY: R. Walters, *The Canadian Brass Book: The Story of the World's Favorite Brass Ensemble* (Milwaukee, 1992).

WEBSITE: www.canbrass.com.

DOUGLAS MCLENNAN

MARIAH CAREY

Born: Long Island, New York, 27 March 1970

Genre: Pop, Disco, Rock

Best-selling album since 1990: *Music Box* (1993)

Hit songs since 1990: "Hero," "Dreamlover," "Fantasy"

As one of the most successful artists of the 1990s, Mariah Carey has reached the same pop star status as other females such as Celine Dion, Janet Jackson, and Whitney Houston.

Known for a singing style that draws on soul and rock, Carey has had a number of dance-pop hits.

Raised in a musical family, with a mother who was a former opera singer and voice coach, Carey started her career at a young age by singing on R&B sessions while still at school. Having moved from Long Island, New York, to New York City at the age of seventeen, she started writing songs with arranger Ben Margulies. Her songs fused pop, gospel, and soul in a way that maximized her vast vocal range. Carey's break came when she signed with Columbia Records and started on her debut album, *Mariah Carey*, in 1990. With a string of top hits, "Vision of Love," "Love Takes Time," "Someday," and "I Don't Wanna Cry," the album became a great success, winning her Grammy Awards for Best Female Artist and Best New Artist.

Carey's talent as a singer became obvious to millions of fans. With a strong soul vocal style that exuded exuberance through its wide register, and a stylishly sexy image, she continued to produce albums that sold well. Her next two releases included *Emotions* in 1991 and *MTV Unplugged* in 1992. The latter included a live performance recorded for MTV within an intimate setting where the audience was able to respond to her spontaneously. Backed by a group of talented musicians, Carey managed to pull off a mannered and reflective performance that was epitomized by tracks such as the Jackson 5's "I'll Be There."

In 1993 she released her best-selling album, *Music Box*, with which she went on tour. This album consists of two of her most memorable hits, "Hero" and "Dreamlover," which reached the top of the charts all around the world. In both of these songs Carey's delivery is overdramatic and impassioned with her squeezing out every drop of sentimentality in a style not unlike that of Barbra Streisand. While the songs on the album are stylishly performed and well produced, there is a lack of imagination in the lyrics, which mainly deal with themes of love and yearning. In addition, Carey's vocal parts are not profiled enough in the mixes of these songs. As a result, the songs lack a sense of conviction and direction. It was perhaps the oversentimentality and excessive performance that resulted in mixed reviews during her first tour.

Following her marriage to producer Tommy Mottola in 1993, her next album, *Merry Christmas*, was released, featuring the number one single "All I Want for Christmas Is You." The appeal of this song lies in its clever production with catchy chords, overdone bell sounds, and sleighbell connotations. Even more success was enjoyed by Carey with her next hit single, "Fantasy," from her 1995 album *Daydream*. The other big hit from this album was "One Sweet Day," a collaboration with Boyz II Men, which topped the U.S. charts for sixteen weeks. For many, the material on this album signified a maturity in her style, not least for an adult-oriented public impressed by her musical craftsmanship.

In 1997, having separated from Mottola (whom she later divorced), Carey released her next album, *Butterfly*, which showed a determination to succeed alone. All sorts of references are found in the songs that relate to the theme of her survival and freedom at the breakup of her marriage. Not as up-tempo as her previous dance-style hits, these songs are intended for listening, hence their ballad style. Tracks such as "Butterfly," "Babydoll," "Break Down," and the Prince cover "The Beautiful Ones" are all poignantly delivered in a controlled and sensual manner. With this album, Carey finally sealed her credibility as pop diva.

Her star status was evidenced by the recording of a duet with Whitney Houston in 1998, "The Prince of Egypt (When You Believe)," for her forthcoming greatest hits album, *#1's*. The chemistry of these two stars visible in the promo video was enough to confirm Carey's standing as pop diva. In fact, Carey's peak in terms of fame came at the end of the 1990s. With the hit "Heartbreaker," from her 1999 album *Rainbow*, she became the only artist to ever have topped the charts each consecutive year of a decade. Stylistically, this hit is a blend of hip-hop and R&B, with a melodramatic expression forcing its sassy delivery. In contrast, the duet with Snoop (Doggy) Dogg on the track "Crybaby" shows off the groove-based panache of Carey's material and represents one of the high points on this album.

During the early 2000s Carey's popularity waned. Her next album, *Glitter* (2001), the soundtrack for the film of the same name, in which she starred, struggled to achieve its intended commercial success. As it was her Virgin Records debut, a breakdown between artist and record company resulted. She subsequently formed her own label, MonarC. With her ninth album, *Charmbracelet*, released in 2002, there was little sign of a comeback as a disappointing collection of tracks characterized a notable decline through a jaded performance.

Having become one of the best-selling female artists of the 1990s, Carey's success at the beginning of the new millennium dwindled. Negative critical response to *Glitter* and *Charmbracelet* did not help her career, and only time will tell whether she can make a comeback to her previous superstar status.

SELECTIVE DISCOGRAPHY: *Mariah Carey* (Columbia, 1990); *Emotions* (Columbia, 1991); *Music Box* (Columbia, 1993); *Merry Christmas* (Sony, 1994); *Daydream* (Columbia, 1995); *Butterfly* (Columbia, 1997); *#1's* (Columbia, 1998); *Rainbow* (Columbia, 1999); *Charmbracelet* (Mercury, 2002). **Soundtrack:** *Glitter* (Virgin, 2001).

BIBLIOGRAPHY: M. Cole, *Mariah Carey* (Bear, Delaware, 1997); C. Nickson, *Mariah Carey Revisited: Her Story* (New York, 1998); M. Shapiro, *Mariah Carey* (Ontario, 2001).

STAN HAWKINS

MARY CHAPIN CARPENTER

Born: Princeton, New Jersey, 21 February 1958
Genre: Country, Folk
Best-selling album since 1990: *Stones in the Road* (1994)
Hit songs since 1990: "He Thinks He'll Keep Her," "Shut Up and Kiss Me"

The commercial success of Mary Chapin Carpenter points to the increased diversity of country music in the early 1990s. Raised in the North, politically liberal, and largely influenced by folk music, Carpenter was an anomaly within country's southern, mostly conservative environment. Like fellow performers Reba McEntire and Martina McBride, Carpenter tapped into a current of feminism running through 1990s country. In the hit "He Thinks He'll Keep Her" (1992), she details the gradual awakening and liberation of a woman trapped in an unhappy marriage, while "I Feel Lucky" (1992) and "Shut Up and Kiss Me" (1994) exude a bold confidence far removed from the long-suffering image of female country singers of the 1960s and 1970s. An understated performer, Carpenter appealed to audiences through her relaxed bearing and warm, throaty voice. By the end of the 1990s, with commercial country music veering in a smooth pop direction, Carpenter continued to hew her own path, recording challenging albums that could not be categorized within any particular style.

Folk Beginnings

The daughter of an executive for *Life* magazine, Carpenter grew up in the university town of Princeton, New Jersey, spending an additional two years of her childhood in Japan, where her father oversaw the Asian edition of *Life*. Carpenter began playing guitar at an early age, influenced by her mother's love of folk performers such as Woody Guthrie and Judy Collins. Moving with her family to Washington, D.C., when she was sixteen, Carpenter became involved in the city's active folk music scene before attending prestigious Brown University, where she received a degree in American Civilization. Returning to Washington after graduation, Carpenter began performing with guitarist John Jennings, selling a homemade demo

Spot
Light

Spot Light | Come On Come On

The release of *Come On Come On* (1992) signaled Mary Chapin Carpenter's progression from up-and-coming performer with folk leanings to full-fledged country star. Although the album sports an array of styles, Carpenter's strong personality and the smooth guidance of producer Steve Buckingham ensure a warm, cohesive sound. Containing no less than seven hit singles, the album features one of Carpenter's best-known hits, "He Thinks He'll Keep Her," a compelling tale of a frustrated wife who leaves her husband. Presented as stages of aging and maturity in the woman's life, the song captivates listeners with a strong narrative through-line: "When she was twenty-nine, she delivered number three / And every Christmas card showed a perfect family." The album's other hits are equally impressive: "I Feel Lucky" is a rousing, humorous number in which a woman declares her optimism in the face of a bad horoscope, while the driving "Passionate Kisses" captures a sensuousness and longing that echo in Carpenter's subsequent work. While "I Feel Lucky" and "I Take My Chances" depict a tough feminine spirit that would inform the confident image of late 1990s singers such as Shania Twain, the quiet, restrained, "I Am a Town" recalls Carpenter's early folk influences. A rich, detailed snapshot of small-town life, the song displays Carpenter's gift for lyrical imagery: "I'm a town in Carolina, I am billboards in the fields / I'm a old truck up on cinder blocks, missing all my wheels." Earning Grammy Awards for both "I Feel Lucky" and "Passionate Kisses," Carpenter emerged with *Come On Come On* as one of the most influential country performers of the 1990s.

country hits, gentle ballads such as "Just Because" revealed Carpenter as a performer of subtlety and charm. After the commercial success of her second album, *State of the Heart* (1989), Carpenter left her day job at a Washington philanthropic organization to pursue her music career full time.

Country Stardom

Carpenter's next album, *Shooting Straight in the Dark* (1990), integrated her folk impulses within a polished country setting, an infusion that resulted in the hits "Going Out Tonight" and "You Win Again." On the latter, built upon the concept of a woman calling her lover from a pay phone, Carpenter displays her talent for sharp, intelligent songwriting: "I just start crying, 'cause it makes so sense / To waste these words and twenty-five cents on a losing game / Baby, you win again." The album's biggest hit, however, is "Down at the Twist and Shout," an exuberant dance number sporting the shuffling, loping rhythms of Louisiana Cajun music. Recorded with the Cajun group Beausoleil, the song's success paved the way for Carpenter's 1992 breakthrough album, *Come On Come On*.

Riding the success of *Come On Come On*, Carpenter's next release, *Stones in the Road* (1994), became her best-selling album. However, aside from the catchy hit, "Shut Up and Kiss Me," *Stones in the Road* lacked the impact and influence of its predecessor. On *A Place in the World* (1996), the disparity between Carpenter's country and folk styles is more marked than on previous releases. Veering from the flashy, horn-driven R&B sound of "Let Me into Your Heart" to the wistful, romantic, "What If We Went to Italy," the album failed to garner any Top 10 country hits. While Carpenter's eclecticism was satisfying from an artistic standpoint, it began to hamper her ongoing success within the increasingly streamlined, pop-oriented world of late 1990s country radio.

By the release of *time*sex*love**(2001), which contained only one minor hit, "Simple Life," it had become clear that Carpenter's idiosyncratic talents no longer fit the strictures of mainstream country. Exploring themes of aging and remembrance, Carpenter uses the album as a showcase for her deepened voice and new songwriting maturity. On songs such as "Someone Else's Prayer," she tinges her romantic perspective with a sense of loss, exploring how concrete objects are linked with ephemeral feelings of longing and desire. A highlight of the album is "Late for Your Life," a probing study of life at midstream. Reinforced with gentle, flowing instrumentation, the song's theme of missed chances and opportunity is captured in Carpenter's philosophical lyrics: "No one knows where they belong / The search just goes on and on and on / For every choice that ends up wrong / Another one's right." Ignored by mainstream radio,

tape of her songs at concerts. After hearing a copy of the tape, a Columbia Records executive offered Carpenter an audition that led to a recording contract in 1987. Carpenter's debut album, *Hometown Girl* (1987), spotlighted her skills as a folk singer, songwriter, and guitarist. While its folk-oriented approach was too laidback to produce any

time*sex*love* nonetheless contains some of Carpenter's deepest, most powerful work.

Carpenter rose from the world of folk music to become a major country star of the 1990s, finding success with her warm voice and lyrical, intelligent songwriting. Although she had difficulty maintaining her stardom within the late 1990s country music industry, Carpenter demonstrated the talent to grow with her fans, moving from the thirty-something wife of "He Thinks He'll Keep Her" to the middle-aged truth seeker of "Late for Your Life" with power and conviction.

SELECTIVE DISCOGRAPHY: *Hometown Girl* (Columbia, 1987); *State of the Heart* (Columbia, 1989); *Shooting Straight in the Dark* (Columbia, 1990); *Come On Come On* (Columbia, 1992); *Stones in the Road* (Columbia, 1994); *A Place in the World* (Columbia, 1996); *time*sex*love** (Columbia, 2001).

WEBSITE: www.marychapincarpenter.com.

DAVID FREELAND

DEANA CARTER

Born: Nashville, Tennessee, 4 January 1966

Genre: Country

Best-selling album since 1990: *Did I Shave My Legs for This?* (1996)

Hit songs since 1990: "Strawberry Wine," "How Do I Get There"

The daughter of the session guitarist Fred Carter, Jr., Deana Carter struggled for years to find a niche in the country music industry before her 1996 debut album, *Did I Shave My Legs for This?*, made her a star. Like singers Faith Hill and Lee Ann Womack, Carter came to represent the new pop sound of 1990s country, even though her folk-oriented style also suggested the 1990s rock star Sheryl Crow. After spending nearly five years out of the spotlight because of personal problems and conflicts with her record company, Carter returned in 2003 sporting a new sound that owed an even greater debt to pop. Carter's voice, sweet and girlish with a hint of grit, has been well served by her intelligent, uncluttered songwriting.

Although she grew up in the country music capital of Nashville, Tennessee, Carter was introduced to a diverse array of music through the influence of her father, who played guitar on the recordings of many country and rock stars of the 1960s and 1970s. With his help Carter first tried to secure a recording contract at age seventeen. After

that attempt failed, she entered the University of Tennessee and received a degree in rehabilitation therapy. Carter spent several years working in hospitals before deciding to make another stab at a music career, cleaning bathrooms and selling china door-to-door while honing her songwriting and guitar playing. In 1994 the country-music legend Willie Nelson heard one of her demo tapes and hired her to perform in his annual Farm Aid concert. That appearance led to a recording contract with Capitol Records.

Carter's debut album, *Did I Shave My Legs for This?*, appeared in the summer of 1996 and, thanks to its appealing melodies and personal lyrics, became an immediate hit. On songs such as "Love Ain't Worth Making" and the tongue-in-cheek title track, Carter displayed the ability to craft compelling songs with clear through-lines, capturing key ideas while avoiding the trite details that sometimes hamper modern country songwriting. In keeping with the popularity of 1990s rock performers such as Sheryl Crow and Alanis Morissette, Carter's songs evince a feminist slant; her infectious humor and working-class perspective, however, secure her ties to traditional country. On the title track, for example, she mocks a husband who prefers beer to romance: "Here I stand / Over this frying pan / And you want a cold one again." But the album's most memorable hit comes with a song Carter did not write, "Strawberry Wine," a sensitive coming-of-age ballad with a lilting melody. The album provides a showcase for Carter's appealing voice and straight-from-the-hip personality. In keeping with her trademark forthrightness, Carter often performed barefoot and wore a fifty-dollar halter dress to the elegant People's Choice Awards in 1997.

Carter's follow-up album, *Everything's Gonna Be Alright* (1998), edged more toward a pop-rock sound. Despite strong material the album lacks a distinctive identity, Carter's sharp-edged personality sounding diffused. The album was a surprise commercial failure, with only two of its songs hitting the lower reaches of the country charts. The years that followed were marked by trouble. Although Carter released a Christmas album for a small label in 2001, she was otherwise inactive on the recording front, fighting with Capitol Records over the songs to be included on a prospective album. In 2002, recovering from a divorce, she pled guilty to a conviction for driving under the influence (DUI). Despite her problems, Carter retained her sunny personality and re-emerged in 2003 with *I'm Just a Girl*, her first album for Arista Records. Composed of songs Carter had been working on for three years, *I'm Just a Girl* largely eschews country for a California pop-rock sound heavily influenced by the 1960s group the Beach Boys. While the breezy title track is tuneful and appealing, critics complained that product-heavy lyrics such as "I'm a Chevy girl" sound fabricated and shallow. "Cover of a Magazine" has the feel of personal experience, as the narrator criticizes supermarket tabloids while stating her desire to appear on the cover of a *Cosmo*-style publication. Reviewers observed that the album's pop approach is not always successful. For example, the otherwise fine ballad "Wildflower" is marred by a loud guitar part that turns the song into hard rock overdrive midway through. These flaws aside, *I'm Just a Girl* signals a welcome return for a likable performer.

Deana Carter's personal songwriting and sweet, dusky voice brought an individualized edge to late-1990s country. Although she failed to follow her impressive debut with additional hits, Carter remains a strong talent who combines country's twang and humor with the accessibility of pop.

SELECTIVE DISCOGRAPHY: *Did I Shave My Legs for This?* (Capitol, 1996); *Everything's Gonna Be Alright* (Capitol, 1998); *Father Christmas* (Rounder, 2001); *I'm Just a Girl* (Arista, 2003).

WEBSITE: www.deanacarter.net.

DAVID FREELAND

JOHNNY CASH

Born: J. R. Cash; Kingsland, Arkansas, 26 February 1932; died Nashville, Tennessee, 12 September 2003

Genre: Country

Best-selling album since 1990: *American Recordings* (1994)

Hit songs since 1990: "Rusty Cage," "Delia's Gone"

Johnny Cash always defied easy categorization, his chugging rhythms and vivid stories of murder and heartache falling just outside the boundaries of folk, country, and rock and roll. This, coupled with his "Man in Black" outlaw persona, ensured that a new generation discovered him in each decade of his nearly fifty-year career. The 1990s were no exception: After a string of slick and uninspired records, he joined forces with rock and hip-hop producer Rick Rubin for the *American Recordings* series. The records focused on his haunting baritone and introduced him to an audience weaned on the dark balladry and traditional stylings of alternative country.

Toughness and Rebellion

Johnny Cash began writing songs as a teenager in Arkansas, but did not immediately set off on a music career. He went to college, worked in a factory, and served in the U.S. Air Force before moving to Memphis in 1954 for a radio broadcasting course. He began to play in a country trio with guitarist Luther Perkins and landed a recording contract with the legendary rock and roll label Sun Records the following year. His first single, "Cry Cry Cry," an immediate success, kicked off a frenzied schedule of touring and recording that lasted until the mid-1960s. His songs combine the immediacy of rock and roll with the blunt honesty of country, as well as deep respect for the traditions of American music. Cash crossed over onto the pop charts, angered the Nashville establishment with his rebelliousness, and won the hearts of the downtrodden classes often venerated in his songs.

By the mid-1960s, alcohol and amphetamines had taken a toll on his creativity, and Cash was considered washed up. He was saved by June Carter, a singer who co-wrote his comeback hit "Ring of Fire." She helped him to beat his addictions and convert to fundamentalist Christianity; the pair married in 1968. With his soul and career recharged, Cash entered another fertile period, releasing his two most popular albums, the live prison recordings *Johnny Cash at Folsom Prison* (1968) and *Johnny Cash at San Quentin* (1969). His popularity surging, he found favor with a younger rock audience as a guest on Bob Dylan's *Nashville Skyline* (1969), and burst headlong into the mainstream with *The Johnny Cash Show*, a television program for ABC that ran for two years.

Cash remained a presence on the country charts with a string of hits throughout the 1970s. The 1980s, however, found him at odds with his record company over the direction of his music—they preferred the slick, pop-oriented Nashville style, and his voice never fit that mold. Despite minor success with the Highwaymen (a supergroup formed with fellow country singer/songwriters Waylon Jennings, Willie Nelson, and Kris Kristofferson), fans and critics generally agree his recorded output from the period lacks the vibrancy of his prior work.

The Man Comes Around

In 1994 Cash signed to American Records, the label owned by Rick Rubin, a legendary figure credited with co-founding the first major hip-hop label, Def Jam Records, and producing edgy rock bands like Red Hot Chili Peppers and Slayer. Rubin stripped away the sheen of Cash's later work, and encouraged him to return to the tough storytelling of his early hits. The result, titled *American Recordings* (1994), features Cash's roughhewn voice, a lone acoustic guitar for accompaniment, and a strong collection of stark and often brutal songs. The spare production recalls a wind-blown road in a ghost town, creating an atmosphere that heightens the rich and haunting baritone of the singer. "Delia's Gone," a novelistic tale of love and murder gone wrong, was a minor hit on college radio and introduced Cash to an audience that preferred the hard-edged authenticity of punk and alternative rock to current pop and country music. The record won a Grammy

Award for Best Contemporary Folk Album, and the latest Cash renaissance kicked off in earnest.

Cash and Rubin followed up the somber *American Recordings* with *Unchained* (1996), a more full-bodied affair that found the singer backed up by Tom Petty and the Heartbreakers. The result is a looser album, with Cash running through an array of styles, from muscular traditional country tunes like "The Kneeling Drunkard's Plea" to angsty heavy metal on "Rusty Cage." Continuing in this playful vein, Cash teamed up with Willie Nelson for *VH1 Storytellers* (1998), a live album recorded for the cable music network. The set finds the pair running through their most beloved songs, relating the story of their respective origins. The album is a warm and relaxed affair, with each performer nicely accompanying the other.

Cash and Rubin returned to their ongoing project in 2000 with *American III: Solitary Man*, which merged the approaches of the first two albums. Here, the bleak and lonely ballads are partnered with rocking band-oriented material. Once again, the more striking songs are the covers of recent material, including an interpretation of U2's soaring "One," and a devout version of the hymnal "I See a Darkness," sung with its writer, Will Oldham of Palace. He also uncovers the distress and doubt lurking beneath the title track, originally a hit for its writer, singer/songwriter Neil Diamond. More than any album in the series, *American III* displays Cash's strengths as the ultimate outsider, able to interpret a musical form and make it his own. As always, his themes of faith, loss, and revenge leave no doubt that he is a master singer.

American IV: The Man Comes Around was released in 2002 amid reports of Cash's failing health. His voice sounds weary on the record, which intensifies the anguished delivery of covers like Depeche Mode's "Personal Jesus" and Simon and Garfunkel's "Bridge Over Troubled Water." The pop standard "We'll Meet Again" closes the record, signaling a kind of defiance in the face of death that only Cash is capable of pulling off convincingly. The song emphasizes why Cash is among the most American of musical figures—his only truly defining characteristics are his resolute toughness and rebellion. The *American Recordings* series provides a perfect cap to his career, charting the obsessions of emotion and music that make him one of this country's most valuable musicians. He died September 12, 2003.

SELECTIVE DISCOGRAPHY: *Johnny Cash with His Hot and Blue Guitar* (Sun, 1957); *Hymns by Johnny Cash* (Columbia, 1959); *I Walk the Line* (Columbia, 1964); *Ballads of the True West* (Columbia, 1965); *Johnny Cash at Folsom Prison* (Columbia, 1968); *Johnny Cash at San Quentin* (Columbia, 1969); *Hello, I'm Johnny Cash* (Columbia, 1969); *A Man in Black* (Columbia, 1971); *One Piece at a Time* (Columbia, 1976); *American Recordings* (American, 1994); *Unchained* (American, 1996); *VH1 Storytellers: Johnny Cash and Willie Nelson* (Universal,1998); *American III: Solitary Man* (American, 2000); *American IV: The Man Comes Around* (American, 2002). **With the Highwaymen:** *Highwayman* (Columbia, 1985); *Highwayman 2* (Columbia, 1990); *Highwaymen: The Road Goes on Forever* (Liberty, 1995).

WEBSITE: www.johnnycash.com.

SEAN CAMERON

NICK CAVE AND THE BAD SEEDS

Formed: 1984, London, England

Members: Nick Cave, vocals, piano (Nicholas Edward Cave, born Wangaratta, Victoria, Australia, 22 September 1957); Warren Ellis, violin; Mick Harvey, guitar (born Rochester, Australia, 20 September 1958); Jim Sclavunos, drums; Blixa Bargeld, guitars (Christian Emmerich, born Berlin, Germany, 12 January 1959); Thomas Wydler, percussion.

Genre: Rock

Best-selling album since 1990: *Murder Ballads* (1996)

Hit songs since 1990: "Where the Wild Roses Grow," "Bring It On"

Conjuring the despair of Johnny Cash, the vocal quiver of Elvis Presley, and the volatility of Jim Morrison, Nick Cave and the Bad Seeds enjoyed a long career as cult favorites. Their black humor and death-obsessed songs did not subscribe to the cheesy satanism of metal bands, but to the older Anglo-American folk ballad and story-song tradition.

In 1977 Nick Cave and Mick Harvey formed the punk band Boys Next Door in Melbourne, Australia. Hoping to make it big, they trekked to London in 1980 and founded the Birthday Party. Cave suffered the hardscrabble existence endemic among struggling artists. However, the band began to get attention with Cave's cathartic, almost possessed vocals. The group split in 1983 and Cave decided to go forward as a solo artist backed by a band whose lineup could be fluid. At this point, Nick Cave and the Bad Seeds were born. Harvey remained a constant, and founding guitarist Blixa Bargeld stayed on until shortly after the release of *Nocturama* (2003).

Their debut album, *From Her to Eternity* (1984), displays a group that is too theatrical and eccentric for radio but perfect for the underground. Cave delivers seething vocals on the Elvis Presley cover "In the Ghetto," which foreshadows Cave's obsession with songs about death.

The follow-up, *The Firstborn Is Dead* (1985), is informed by rural American blues. But Cave sings with a creepy, almost maniacal baritone while the Bad Seeds create foreboding guitar riffs and whooshing percussion effects. "Tupelo" uses apocalyptic biblical imagery of plagues and floods to dramatize the birth of "the King," Elvis Presley. Cave's voice becomes a haunting wail on "Knockin' on Joe," an eight-minute saga of a condemned killer's final moments.

The band performed in the Wim Wenders motion picture *Wings of Desire* (1987) and Cave wrote and acted in *Ghosts of the Civil Dead* (1988), playing a prisoner named Maynard. Cave later disparaged his foray into acting, saying it did not feel natural. He published a novel, *And the Ass Saw the Angel* (1990), a weird tale full of allegory and symbolism. Though far from a best-seller, it became a cult favorite, like his music.

Known for their foursquare, simple rhythms, Nick Cave and the Bad Seeds grew more sophisticated by the early 1990s, incorporating jazzy piano and violin arrangements. *Let Love In* (1994) reflects the improvement, with the ballad "Nobody's Baby Now" featuring creative interplay between piano and guitar. But the band's dangerous side is still in effect, with "Red Right Hand" portending doom and "Loverman" examining the ugly extremes of male lust. The latter track was covered by Metallica for *Garage Inc.* (1998).

Cave indulged in his vocal histrionics for *Murder Ballads* (1996), almost a self-parody of his reputation for gloomy subject matter. He growls like blues rocker George Thorogood on "Song of Joy," which details the damage wrought by a serial killer. The story-song "Where the Wild Roses Grow" is a left-field duet with pop diva Kylie Minogue, where the Australian popster plays an innocent maiden who ends up bludgeoned to death.

Murder Ballads seems to have served as a purgative, as Cave lightens up on subsequent releases. *The Boatman's Call* (1997), perhaps the band's most accessible album, rests on Cave's subtle piano textures and sentimental lyrics. "Into My Arms" sounds inspired by Negro spirituals, with Cave praying that his true love will remain with him forever. The dirgelike "People Ain't No Good" approaches sixties pop singer Bobby Goldsboro–level pathos with its eulogy to a broken marriage. The album spent one week on the *Billboard* 200 chart, hitting number 155 and giving Cave his first U.S. chart album six months before his fortieth birthday.

Nocturama (2003) signals an unusually laid-back approach. Cave and his band recorded the album in one week. Instead of applying his usual workaholic perfectionism to the lyrics, Cave trusts his instinct. This leads to a few jarring moments for longtime fans. The first single, "Bring It On," utilizes a vibrating bass line akin to Curtis Mayfield's "Superfly" and is accompanied by an uncharacteristic video full of booty-shaking dancers. Talented as the Bad Seeds are, funk is not their specialty, and ultimately the effort seems awkward. Cave sounds almost sweet on the ballads that lead off the album—"Wonderful Life," propelled by piano and a meandering bass line, "He Wants You," with its solemn violin and Cave's almost crooning vocals, and "Right Out of Your Hand," a pulsating soft-rocker that almost sounds like a live recording. However, *Nocturama* ends with the bizarre, bombastic "Babe, I'm on Fire." It rambles on for fifteen minutes and features Cave calling out seemingly random categories of people ("the athlete with his hernia," "the corporate flunky") and informing listeners that they all say, "Babe, I'm on fire." It is a track sure to exasperate new fans and old, and the mischievous Cave would likely have it no other way.

Though Cave returned to Melbourne to record *Nocturama*, he continued to reside full time in the temperate beach town of Brighton, England, saying it was easier for him to be himself and live in relative anonymity in his adopted country. Understandably absent from commercial radio, Cave and the Bad Seeds are an acquired taste, but ultimately rewarding for those who believe in rock music as a form of lyricism and exorcism.

SELECTIVE DISCOGRAPHY: *From Her to Eternity* (Mute/Elektra, 1984); *The Firstborn Is Dead* (Mute, 1985); *Let Love In* (Mute, 1994); *Murder Ballads* (Mute/Reprise, 1996); *The Boatman's Call* (Mute/Reprise, 1997); *Nocturama* (Anti, 2003).

SELECTIVE FILMOGRAPHY: *Wings of Desire* (1987); *Ghosts of the Civil Dead* (1988).

RAMIRO BURR

STEVEN CURTIS CHAPMAN

Born: Paducah, Kentucky, 21 November 1962
Genre: Christian Rock
Best-selling album since 1990: *Speechless* (1999)

Steven Curtis Chapman's songs profile his professed Christian beliefs and he combines that testament with the energy of rock music. One has to listen hard to discern the difference between Chapman and the grassroots rock of Bryan Adams or the ballads of Michael Bolton; only the songs' religious themes reveal that Chapman's music is not mainstream radio fare. His last album went beyond devotion to a higher deity and chronicled his views on relationships through the filter of his own longstanding marriage.

Chapman grew up in western Kentucky in the town of Paducah. His father, once an aspiring country-western songwriter, went on to own a music store and influenced Chapman to play several instruments. Guitar and piano were the two that caught most of his interest. After high school, Chapman enrolled in the premed program at Indiana's Anderson College, but dropped out to pursue music full time in Nashville. Once there, he performed at the Grand Ole Opry—a dream that his father held for years. Chapman also had some success as a songwriter and drew the interest of several record labels.

Despite his father's wishes to the contrary, Chapman signed with a Christian music label, Sparrow. His first album, *First Hand* (1987), displayed Chapman's ability to write and perform appealing rock music with a Christian message. His subsequent recordings built on that success and enabled Chapman to become a repeated winner at the Dove Awards, Gospel Music's most prestigious award show. After more than fifteen years in the Christian rock genre, Chapman has far outdistanced any other performer by winning forty-seven Dove Awards. He has also garnered four Grammy Awards, each for Best Contemporary Gospel Album with *For the Sake of the Call* (1990), *The Great Adventure* (1992), *The Live Adventure* (1993), and *Speechless* (1999).

After a one-year hiatus for personal introspection, Chapman recorded *Speechless* as a response to the death of a close friend's eight-year-old daughter and the nationally spotlighted school shooting in his high school alma mater, Heath High School in Paducah. The album features 1980s-sounding hard rock with funky and driving rhythms mixed with Chapman's slightly raspy vocals. The snappy lyrics sound especially contemporary as they glorify a Christian higher power. Chapman also used inspiration from the album to co-author a book with pastor and friend, Scotty Smith, *Speechless: In Awe of the Power of God's Disruptive Grace*, which dealt with giving a message of hope to people who suffer tragic occurrences in their lives.

Chapman built on the success of *Speechless* with a similar effort, *Declaration*, featuring the rocker "Live Out Loud." The song became another number one hit single on the contemporary Christian charts to help Chapman take his place as the king of Christian music with thirty number one hits throughout his career. His signature song, "I Will Be Here," an ode of faithfulness to his wife, Mary Beth, has become a staple wedding song for couples all over the world. Chapman contributed "I Will Not Go Quietly" for the soundtrack to *The Apostle* (1998), and also recorded "Soldier" (changed from an earlier title "When You Are a Soldier") for the soundtrack to *When We Were Soldiers* (2002).

Chapman flirted nearer to pop mainstream with *All About Love* (2003). The album, his thirteenth studio release, is inspired by his marriage of seventeen years and explores the various aspects of love and relationships. Having sold more than 5 million albums in the Christian marketplace, there is little question that Chapman could have achieved comparable results in rock's mainstream markets had he chosen to follow that path.

SELECTIVE DISCOGRAPHY: *First Hand* (Sparrow, 1987); *Real Life Conversations* (Sparrow, 1988); *More to This Life* (Sparrow, 1989); *Great Adventure* (Sparrow, 1992); *Live Adventure* (Sparrow, 1993); *Heaven in the Real World* (Sparrow, 1994); *Signs of Life* (Sparrow, 1996); *Speechless* (Sparrow, 1999); *Declaration* (Sparrow, 2001); *All About Love* (Sparrow, 2003). **Soundtracks::** *The Apostle* (Rising Tide, 1998); *When We Were Soldiers* (Sparrow, 2002).

DONALD LOWE

TRACY CHAPMAN

Born: Cleveland, Ohio, 20 March 1964
Genre: Folk, Pop
Best-selling album since 1990: *New Beginning* (1995)
Hit songs since 1990: "Give Me One Reason," "Telling Stories"

Tracy Chapman burst into the pop music scene in the late 1980s as a uniquely styled singer/songwriter whose straightforward songs chronicled diverse social problems. Chapman's rhythmic folk music features poetic lyrics framed in catchy, simple melodies while expressively sung in her rich alto. As her popularity dipped following her initial mega-success, Chapman's song topics became less about social crusades and more about love and personal issues. Chapman is a participating advocate in a variety of human rights causes.

Chapman was born in Cleveland, Ohio, and raised in lower-middle-class means by her mother. Her older sister, Aneta, gave her a guitar when she was eight and Chapman began writing songs soon after. Later, she won a scholarship to a private high school in Danbury, Connecticut, and went on to study anthropology and African culture at Tufts University in Boston, Massachusetts. Struggling financially at Tufts, Chapman was persuaded into playing her guitar and singing songs on the streets and later in coffeehouses around Boston. She earned a strong local following and recorded some demo tapes. After a series of rejections, she signed with Elektra Records and released the debut album, *Tracy Chapman* (1988), whose raw, acoustic sound contrasted greatly with the general radio fare of the 1980s.

Tracy Chapman was one of the most remarkable album debuts in music history. On the strength of her hit "Fast Car," the album sold more than 10 million copies, and Chapman immediately became a superstar and gained prominence as a voice for the voiceless. Her songs, tales about the hopelessness of growing up poor, racism, corporate greed, male dominance, and a plethora of other socially charged topics, struck a resonant chord with the burgeoning, upwardly mobile "yuppie" generation. Months after the release of her debut album, Chapman was in the forefront of social relevancy as she performed in a satellite-linked concert at London's Wembley Stadium in celebration of Nelson Mandela's seventieth birthday. Soon after, she headlined the Human Rights Now Tour with Sting, Bruce Springsteen, and Peter Gabriel. It was a long way from the coffeehouses of Boston.

Chapman's image as a social crusader was further enhanced with her following efforts, *Crossroads* (1990) and *Matters of the Heart* (1991). The songs on these two recordings continue in the honest, issue-conscious vein of the debut album. However, Chapman became a victim of her own success as critics, expecting her to build on her extraordinary first effort, were harsh over the sameness of *Crossroads* and *Matters of the Heart*. Sales fell dramatically as fans grew weary of the melancholy material. Exhausted and disenchanted with stardom, Chapman, reticent by nature, entered a reclusive period. Yet she continued performing for causes such as AIDS Awareness, Farm Aid, Nelson Mandela's Freedomfest, Neil Young's Bridge School concerts, civil liberties, minority rights, environmental causes, gender equity, sexual freedom, and many others. She also performed in 1992 at New York's Madison Square Garden with a lineup of stars in the thirtieth anniversary tribute concert for Bob Dylan. She performed his "The Times They Are a Changin'."

In late 1995 Chapman released her fourth album, *New Beginning*. As in her debut album, *New Beginning* was helped by a hit single. "Give Me One Reason," a chunky, twelve-bar pop-blues showcasing Chapman's honeyed belt, became her largest hit and won a Grammy Award. Unlike earlier albums, her attention to social issues was blunted in favor of songs focused more on personal issues and relationship intimacies. With more than 4 million in sales, *New Beginning* is her best commercial effort since the debut recording. Backed by a new band, the usually solo-performing Chapman promoted the album in a series of tours that took her all over the world. She also recorded a duet with blues legend B.B. King on his album *Deuces Wild* (1997). The album has King performing duets with a number of stars and Chapman sings his signature "The Thrill Is Gone."

Chapman waited almost five years to release her next album, *Telling Stories* (2000). The title song was released as a single, and its lyric, "there is fiction in the space between you and me," speaks to an uncommitted lover or possibly to a larger entity such as the media. Only one song on *Telling Stories*, an ode to the unimportance of materialism called "Paper and Ink," resembles the socially relevant songs of her earlier albums.

Chapman lives in the San Francisco area, where she recorded her sixth album, *Let It Rain* (2002). In 2003 she toured western Europe, beginning in France. She remains active in a variety of causes.

Folk music has never been regarded as a particularly commercial genre; nevertheless, Chapman raised the bar considerably. Although many fans feel that critics unfairly held her to the standards of her spectacular debut, Chapman is an uncompromising artist who resists trends and sets her own standards.

SELECTIVE DISCOGRAPHY: *Tracy Chapman* (Elektra, 1988); *Crossroads* (Elektra, 1989); *Matters of the Heart* (Elektra, 1992); *New Beginning* (Elektra, 1995); *Telling Stories* (Elektra, 2000); *Let It Rain* (Elektra, 2002).

DONALD LOWE

THE CHEMICAL BROTHERS

Formed: 1990, London, England

Members: Tom Rowlands, programming, keyboards (born Henley-on-Thames, Oxfordshire, England, c. 1971); Edward Simons, programming, keyboards (born Dulwich, London, England, c. 1970).

Genre: Electronica, Dance

Best-selling album since 1990: *Dig Your Own Hole* (1997)

Hit songs since 1990: "Block Rockin' Beats," "Setting Sun"

For a time in the mid-1990s, the music industry launched a campaign to convince consumers that anonymous young men with keyboards and digital sampling devices were going to replace rock bands with guitars and charismatic front men. A pair of unassuming musicians from England called the Chemical Brothers came closest to that goal, creating a body of relentlessly catchy, uplifting futuristic dance anthems such as "Setting Sun" and "Block Rockin' Beats," which stood at the vanguard of a genre dubbed "electronica."

Middle-class kids Tom Rowlands and Ed Simons met while sharing a history course at Manchester Polytechnic Institute in the late 1980s, both drawn to the city by music, but of a different sort. Rowlands was interested in being

Chemical Brothers. L-R: Ed Simons, Tom Rowlands [MICK ROCK/ ASTRALWERKS]

instrumental debut, *Exit Planet Dust* (1995). With the aim of keeping England's ravenous, drug-fueled ravers—a large subset of dance fans who attended all night, hedonistic parties—moving, as well as taking them to ever-higher peaks of ecstasy, the music employs electronic beats that build to frenzied crescendos before beginning the process anew, as well as wide swaths of futuristic synthesizer, backward tape loops, and repetitive drum machine beats.

Combining elements of psychedelic sound effects, deep, pounding beats, expertly placed samples of old songs, and catchy, repetitive keyboard phrases, songs such as "Leave Home" and "Chico's Groove" helped to usher in a new type of music, called variously "big beat" and "electronica." The album also features another signature of the duo's albums, guest vocals from some of England's most popular artists. Charlatans singer Tim Burgess lends his lyrics and vocals to the driving original electronic rock song "Life Is Sweet." Little-known folk chanteuse Beth Orton adds a ghostly vocal to the slinky, Middle Eastern-tinged "Alive Alone."

Though their live show consisted of the duo punching buttons and spinning records, they became a credible live draw at rock and dance festivals throughout Europe and America, putting a face—Rowland's lanky frame, colored glasses, and long, blonde hair and Simons's short-haired, clean-cut visage—on the generally anonymous genre.

Modern Dance-Floor Pop Meets the Beatles

Having gained a fan in Noel Gallagher, musical mastermind of English rock band Oasis, the Chemical Brothers tapped him to sing the vocals on their psychedelic dance anthem "Setting Sun," a tribute to the Beatles's "Tomorrow Never Knows" from their second album, *Dig Your Own Hole* (1997). The wildly popular album also launched "Block Rockin' Beats," one of the most popular big beat hit singles of all time. The track combines a bouncy bass line, live-sounding jazzy drums, and a sample of a vocal from a pioneering American rap artist, Schooly D, chanting "Back with another one of those block rockin' beats!"

The single, like the rest of the album, is heavily influenced by American rap music, mixing that genre's aggressive rhythms with big beat's ecstatic peaks and valleys and techno music's futuristic keyboard sounds and mind-numbing repetition. *Dig Your Own Hole* landed the duo near the top of the American album charts, spawned a number one British hit with "Setting Sun," which, despite the guest vocal, garnered a Grammy for Best Rock Instrumental and found them featured on a multitude of big-beat compilation albums.

It also made the Chemical Brothers a popular headlining act around the world. As with previous and future

near the city's legendary hedonistic Hacienda dance nightclub, while Simons had an interest in studying in the home of two of his favorite English new wave rock groups of the 1980s, the Smiths and New Order.

When not performing with the dance group Ariel, Rowlands spent time with Simons working on music under the name the Dust Brothers—an homage to the American producers responsible for the hip-hop group the Beastie Boys's landmark, sample-heavy album *Paul's Boutique* (1989). The duo performed at dance clubs such as Naked Under Leather, building a solid reputation for their original music and prowess as music mixing disc jockeys. The pair's popularity convinced them to record the track "Song to the Siren" (1993) in their bedroom studio, a tip of the hat to the Baleraic style of the time, which mixed funk, hip-hop, dance, and groove-oriented jazz with European disco and the repetitive house beats pioneered by Chicago musicians in the 1980s.

A Fine and Proper *Exit*

Rowlands quit Ariel and the duo moved to London and got steady gigs performing at such popular clubs as Heavenly Sunday Social, as well as jobs remixing material for such notable bands as Primal Scream, Prodigy, and the Charlatans. After a threatened lawsuit from America's Dust Brothers in 1995, the pair changed their name to the Chemical Brothers and released their mind-bending, mostly

albums, several mini albums with a number of remixes and new tracks were released before and after the appearance of *Dig Your Own Hole*. Along with English techno acts Prodigy and Underworld, the Chemical Brothers were tagged in the music press as the next big thing in popular music.

The pair released a mix album of their favorite tracks, *Brothers Gonna Work It Out* (1998), followed by their third full-length album, *Surrender* (1999). Again working with a number of guest vocalists, the album broke little creative ground, save for allowing the pair to work with their reclusive hero, New Order singer Bernard Sumner, on the electronic pop song "Out of Control." Gallagher again lends vocals to a slice of Beatlesque psychedelica, "Let Forever Be," while Mazzy Star singer Hope Sandoval sings on the delicate ballad "Asleep from Day."

Their fourth album, *Come with Us* (2002), scales back the guest vocalists and looks to obscure French pop and American soul for sample material. With warmer, more organic sounds mixed in with the usual relentless, programmed beats, tracks such as the tribal "It Began in Afrika" and "Galaxy Bounce" incorporate the energy of the duo's lauded debut with the revivalist French disco sound of such popular groups as Daft Punk. Orton is again featured on the folky "The State We're In," while ex-Verve singer Richard Ashcroft sings the vocals for the album-ending transcendental dance epic "The Test."

Though their popularity waned after the fall of the electronica genre in America in the late 1990s, with their pioneering sound and creative use of modern musical technology, the Chemical Brothers proved that superstar pop groups do not need a singer, a band, or even conventional instruments to reach the top.

SELECTIVE DISCOGRAPHY: *Exit Planet Dust* (Freestyle Dust/Astralwerks, 1995); *Live at the Social, Vol. 1* (Heavenly, 1996); *Dig Your Own Hole* (Freestyle Dust/Astralwerks, 1997); *Brothers Gonna Work It Out* (Freestyle Dust/Astralwerks, 1998); *Surrender* (Freestyle Dust/Astralwerks, 1999); *Come with Us* (Freestyle Dust/Astralwerks, 2002).

WEBSITE: www.thechemicalbrothers.com.

GIL KAUFMAN

CHER

Born: Cherilyn Sarkisian LaPierre; El Centro, California, 20 May 1946

Genre: Pop, Rock

Best-selling album since 1990: *Believe* (1998)

Hit songs since 1990: "Believe," "Strong Enough"

Few performers have earned the label "survivor" more deservedly than Cher. Constantly reinventing herself during a forty-year career, the indomitable performer has triumphed over fluctuations in popular taste to become an American institution, one of the few singers more famous for who she is than for her music. Cher's celebrity persona has sometimes obscured the appealing quality of her recordings. While her voice often sounds awkward and her phrasing excessively blunt, Cher puts tremendous energy and strength of spirit into her music. Never one to err on the side of subtlety, she infuses her performances with an aggression and straightforwardness that transcend technical limitations. Focusing mostly on acting during the 1980s, she re-entered the music spotlight in the late 1990s to release one of the most successful albums of her career. By 1999, at age fifty-three, Cher had won an entirely new generation of fans.

Sonny and Cher

Born in El Centro, California, Cher was raised by a struggling actress mother with few financial means, her father having left the family when Cher was three years old. At sixteen, Cher moved alone to Los Angeles, where she worked as a background singer in order to support her acting ambitions. The next year she met Salvatore "Sonny" Bono, a songwriter and protégé of hit pop producer Phil Spector. The pair soon married and formed a professional alliance as the singing duo Caesar and Cleo. As Sonny and Cher, they scored a smash hit in 1965 with "I Got You Babe," a charming pop confection featuring clumsy but sincere vocals and a lilting, sing-song arrangement. Unfortunately, Sonny and Cher's popularity faded near the end of the 1960s after they starred in two poorly received films. Plagued by subsequent troubles with the Internal Revenue Service, they decided to embark upon a television career. Their TV program, *The Sonny and Cher Comedy Hour*, was a huge success and ran in various forms from 1971 to 1976. At the same time Cher pursued a career as a solo artist, recording in a more adult, yet equally intense, style. Songs such as "Gypsies, Tramps, and Thieves" (1971) and "I Saw a Man and He Danced with His Wife" (1974) dealt with themes of teen pregnancy and adultery, and, along with her trend-setting fashion sense, contributed to Cher's bold, daring image during this period.

Splitting from husband Bono in the mid-1970s, Cher recorded a disco hit, the promiscuously themed "Take Me Home" (1979), before returning to her first love, acting. Fine performances followed in films such as *Silkwood* (1983) and *Mask* (1985). In 1988 she won an Academy

Spot Light | *Believe*

In 1998 Cher had not had a major hit in nine years, although her albums continued to sell among a core group of fans. That year she worked with a young, relatively unknown production and songwriting team, Mark Taylor and Brian Rawling, in their small, low-tech London studio. The result was *Believe,* an album that brought Cher's thirty-five-year career to new heights. The title track, featuring an electronic dance rhythm suggestive of 1970s disco music, became the best-selling single of 1998 and remained on the charts through the next year. Although the energetic beat recalls disco's good-time party atmosphere, Cher's haunting vocals and the bittersweet lyrics—"Do you believe in life after love?"—point to the sadness of the post-AIDS era. The song's most unusual element is the use of an electronic vocoder, an instrument that makes Cher's voice sound distorted and robotic. Rather than ruining her performance, the vocoder adds a spiky layer of character in keeping with the singer's unconventional personality. Impressively, Taylor and Rawling sustain the single's enthusiasm throughout the album's remaining nine songs, taking Cher through a series of catchy tunes, hook-laden tracks, and infectious beats. For all their sophistication, songs such as "The Power" and "All or Nothing" reveal a gritty, homemade quality that captures Cher's fighting spirit and tough essence. Attesting on *Believe* that, "I know that I'll get through this / Cause I know that I am strong," Cher sings with the knowledge and experience of a true show-business survivor.

Award for her funny, touching performance in the romantic comedy *Moonstruck* (1987).

1990s Stardom

By the late 1980s and early 1990s Cher was balancing a dual acting and singing career, recording hits and shooting music videos that emphasized her outrageous taste. In 1989 her video for the song "If I Could Turn Back Time" was banned by music video network MTV after viewers complained about her revealing costume. While many of Cher's late-1980s and early-1990s songs were hard-rock-influenced "power ballads," with heavy drums and blaring electric guitar, she displayed a softer, warmer side on the 1996 album, *It's a Man's World.* On the opening track, "One by One," she sings with a breathiness that recalls 1960s pop vocalist Dusty Springfield, while "Not Enough Love in the World" conveys a sweetness that is out of character with her brash earlier recordings. "The Sun Ain't Gonna Shine (Anymore)" is another highlight, a well-orchestrated song that Cher sings with soaring exuberance. Taken as a whole, *It's a Man's World* presents a subtler Cher whose awareness of her vocal strengths has deepened. While her voice could not be described as pretty in the conventional sense, it is nonetheless distinctive and powerful. Like that of pop singer Barbra Streisand, it is immediately recognizable and uniquely her own. Still, Cher's mid-1990s recordings were often overshadowed by her ongoing presence in tabloid newspapers, whose writers speculated on her bouts with chronic fatigue syndrome and the extent of her plastic surgery. In 1998, however, she found herself back in the musical spotlight with the album *Believe,* which brought her a degree of popular acceptance she had not experienced in years. During this period Cher became an activist for gay rights after her daughter with Bono, Chastity, came out as a lesbian. The late 1990s were also marked by loss: Former husband and longtime friend Sonny was killed in a skiing accident in 1998.

In early 2002 Cher released *Living Proof,* another collection of techno-disco dance songs emphasizing themes of unity and strength. Although not as compelling as *Believe, Living Proof* succeeds through Cher's undiminished energy and professionalism. When the album's first single, the inspirational "Song for the Lonely," entered the Top 100 hit charts, Cher set a new record in pop music: Her hits have spanned thirty-seven years, the longest period for any artist. Soon after *Living Proof*'s release she announced plans for a farewell tour in 2002, but later extended the dates into 2003. Cher pulled out all of the stops for these live performances, creating a circuslike atmosphere through a host of larger-than-life stage devices. Starting the show by riding a giant chandelier onto the stage amidst dancers and acrobats, she then disappeared and returned on top of a large puppet elephant. The show's theatricality helps explain Cher's enduring appeal. As much performance artist as singer, Cher makes each appearance an event.

Remaining a star through five decades of changing trends, Cher is more than a pop singer; she is a force, an all-around performer with a canny sense of style and publicity. Recording in virtually every pop musical style since the 1960s, from teen ballads to disco, she has set a standard for endurance and energy. Never a subtle vocalist, Cher succeeds through her sweeping sense of drama and astute understanding of the dynamics of performance. Despite the ever-changing musical backdrops, she retains her individuality and spirit.

SELECTIVE DISCOGRAPHY: *With Love, Cher* (Imperial, 1967); *Gypsies, Tramps, and Thieves* (Kapp, 1971); *Take Me Home* (Casablanca, 1979); *Heart of Stone* (Geffen, 1989); *It's a Man's World* (Warner Bros., 1996); *Believe* (Warner Bros., 1998); *Living Proof* (Warner Bros., 2002).

SELECTIVE FILMOGRAPHY: *Silkwood* (1983); *Mask* (1985); *Moonstruck* (1987); *Faithful* (1995); *If These Walls Could Talk* (1996); *Tea with Mussolini* (1999).

WEBSITE: www.cher.com.

DAVID FREELAND

KENNY CHESNEY

Born: Knoxville, Tennessee, 26 March 1968

Genre: Country

Best-selling album since 1990: *No Shirt, No Shoes, No Problems* (2002)

Hit songs since 1990: "She's Got It All," "How Forever Feels," "The Good Stuff"

Although his music bears a strong pop and rock influence, Kenny Chesney is at heart a fine country balladeer in the manner of famed 1950s and 1960s singers such as Eddy Arnold and Bill Anderson. His voice, a flexible, assured instrument that ranges higher than most of his male contemporaries, has a built-in twang that carries a strong emotional pull. Chesney's inherent sweetness allows him to tackle material that would sound hokey in other hands; his rendition of the sentimental, half-spoken ballad, "A Lot of Things Different" (2002), for instance, ranks as a highlight of his career. While in appearance Chesney resembles the numerous country "hunks in a hat" who proliferated in the 1990s, his fine sense of pitch, sensitive phrasing, and appealing honesty reveal an artist of genuine talent. For all his ability, however, Chesney sometimes sounds as if he is skirting the emotional borders of his songs, preferring sensitivity to soulful exploration and depth.

Raised in the East Tennessee town of Luttrell, Chesney grew up surrounded by the influence of country music, although his own tastes leaned closer to rock. While working on a marketing degree at East Tennessee State University, Chesney heard veteran country performer Merle Haggard on the car radio and decided to shift his musi-

cal focus. Soon he was practicing guitar and performing frequent gigs around campus. In 1991 Chesney moved to the country music hub of Nashville and found a steady gig at the Turf, a rough and tumble bar in the city's seedy lower Broadway district. Chesney's appearances at the Turf led to a recording contract with Capricorn Records, a small label best known for its rock acts during the 1970s. Although Chesney released one album for Capricorn, his career did not take off until he moved to the larger BNA label, a division of music conglomerate BMG. Chesney's debut album for BNA, *All I Need to Know* (1995), was a well-crafted set that spotlighted his high, quavering voice on a range of up-tempo and ballad material. On songs such as "Fall in Love" and "Grandpa Told Me So," Chesney established his nice-guy image, eschewing old-fashioned country rowdiness to proclaim virtues of family and tradition.

Chesney released several albums during the remainder of the 1990s, frequently displaying signs of artistic growth. On songs such as "When I Close My Eyes" and "It's Never Easy to Say Goodbye" (both 1996), Chesney paints vivid portraits of love and loss, confirming his status as one of the finest ballad singers of his generation. Elsewhere, on the silly novelty hit "She Thinks My Tractor's Sexy" and the pop-influenced ballad "You Had Me from Hello" (both 1999), he sounds burdened with the weight of his own professionalism, singing with smooth efficiency but little depth.

In 2002 Chesney released his most commercially successful album, *No Shoes, No Shirt, No Problems*. Although the cut-off T-shirt he sports on the album's cover points to a new, sexier image, Chesney sings with his familiar warmth and tenderness. The album's biggest hit, "The Good Stuff," perfectly sums up his appeal. After a fight with his wife, he walks into a bar and asks for "the good stuff." In the days of Haggard and his hell-raising contemporary George Jones, the set-up would be an excuse for a booze-drenched exploration of pain and heartache. In Chesney's song, however, the bartender responds by refusing a drink, instead telling him: "It's the first long kiss on a second date, mama's all worried when you get home late . . . that's the good stuff." More than any song in Chesney's canon, "The Good Stuff" illustrates the difference between tough country music of the 1960s and its clean, modern equivalent. It perfectly embodies Chesney's well-scrubbed persona, although he clearly possesses the vocal capacity to deliver more adventurous work.

Like fellow performer John Michael Montgomery, Chesney helped guide country music toward pop and rock in the 1990s. Unlike Montgomery, however, Chesney has the vocal power and range to communicate both country and pop material with honesty and effectiveness. Although from an emotional standpoint he sometimes sounds less than engaged, Chesney never fails to suffuse his recordings with technical assurance and warmth.

SELECTIVE DISCOGRAPHY: *In My Wildest Dreams* (Capricorn, 1994); *All I Need to Know* (BNA, 1995); *Me and You* (BNA, 1996); *I Will Stand* (BNA, 1997); *Everywhere We Go* (BNA, 1999); *Greatest Hits* (BNA, 2000); *No Shoes, No Shirt, No Problems* (BNA, 2002).

WEBSITE: www.kennychesney.com.

DAVID FREELAND

MARK CHESNUTT

Born: Beaumont, Texas, 6 September 1963

Genre: Country

Best-selling album since 1990: *Almost Goodbye* (1993)

Hit songs since 1990: "Too Cold at Home," "I'll Think of Something," "I Don't Want to Miss a Thing"

Mark Chesnutt's smoky, textured voice and taste for tough, "honky-tonk" country made him one of the finest "neotraditionalists" of the early 1990s. Like his fellow neotraditionalists Randy Travis and George Strait, Chesnutt cast aside the slick, pop-oriented sound of 1970s and early 1980s country for a simplified approach built on fiddles, drums, and steel guitar. When country returned to a smoother, less gritty pop style later in the 1990s, Chesnutt proved his adaptability by recording rock-influenced numbers such as "I Don't Want to Miss a Thing." Chesnutt's talents were better suited to traditional country, however, and by the turn of the century, his singles were no longer hitting the charts with regularity.

Mark Chesnutt entered country music through the influence of his father, Bob, an amateur vocalist who achieved local popularity in Texas but later gave up singing to work in the used-car business. Influenced by soulful country vocalist George Jones, the younger Chesnutt began singing in nightclubs at the age of fifteen. During the 1980s he performed as part of the house band at Cutters, a club in his hometown of Beaumont, Texas, and recorded for a variety of small labels. In 1990 one of his recordings, "Too Close to Home," earned him a contract with MCA Records. "Too Close to Home," a classic country ballad built upon strong, ironic lyrics and a theme of heartbreak, became his first major country hit when he re-recorded it for MCA. Chesnutt's second MCA album, *Longnecks & Short Stories* (1992), was one of his best, featuring slow, heart-tugging ballads such as the hits "I'll Think of Something" and "Old Country." In 1993 he moved in a slicker

pop direction with "Almost Goodbye," a number one hit arranged with sugary strings. Compared to the nice-guy sensitivity of late-1990s artists such as Kenny Chesney, Chesnutt sounded like a holdover from country's hell-raising past on "Thank God for Believers" (1997). Here, Chesnutt's character is an old-school boozer with a long-suffering wife.

Building upon the crossover pop success of country in the late 1990s, Chesnutt scored his last number one hit in 1999 with a strong version of "I Don't Want to Miss a Thing," a ballad first recorded by rock group Aerosmith the previous year. The song's success notwithstanding, Chesnutt's rough-edged persona seemed like an anachronism by 2000, when disappointing sales of his album, *Lost in the Feeling,* caused him to be dropped by MCA. Chesnutt's self-titled debut for Columbia appeared in 2002 and was marked by Nashville songwriting's new lyrical conservatism, increasingly in evidence in the wake of the September 11, 2001, terrorist attacks. Like Kenny Chesney's 2002 hit, "The Good Stuff," "I'm in Love with a Married Woman" takes a time-worn country theme—adultery—and renders it toothless by making the "married woman" the narrator's own wife.

In the 1990s Mark Chesnutt found commercial success with his tough neotraditionalist sound. In keeping with the changes in modern country, Chesnutt recorded smoother, pop-influenced music toward the end of the 1990s. Although his later recordings lacked the fire and bite of his early work, Chesnutt's rich, burnished voice remains one of the most appealing in country.

SELECTIVE DISCOGRAPHY: *Too Cold at Home* (MCA, 1990); *Longnecks & Short Stories* (MCA, 1992); *Almost Goodbye* (MCA, 1993); *I Don't Want to Miss a Thing* (MCA, 1999); *Lost in the Feeling* (MCA Nashville, 2000); *Mark Chesnutt* (Columbia, 2000).

WEBSITE: www.markchesnutt.com.

DAVID FREELAND

CHICAGO SYMPHONY ORCHESTRA

Formed: 1891, Chicago, Illinois

Genre: Classical

With more than 900 recordings and fifty-eight Grammy Awards, the Chicago Symphony Orchestra is one of the best-known, most prolific orchestras in the world. For most of its history, the Chicago Symphony has been considered one of the top five orchestras in the United States. In the closing decades of the twentieth century many critics considered the orchestra's brass section to be unequaled anywhere in the world.

The orchestra was founded in 1891, when Theodore Thomas, then one of America's leading conductors, was invited by a Chicago businessperson to put together an orchestra of "the highest quality." Thomas served as the orchestra's music director for thirteen years, until his death in 1905.

Frederick Stock, who had been a violist in the orchestra, took over as music director and performed that role for thirty-seven years. He helped firmly establish the orchestra at the center of the city's cultural life, and also established a training orchestra and music education program. Other music directors include Desire Defauw (1943–1947), Artur Rodzinski (1947–1948), Rafael Kubelik (1950–1953), Fritz Reiner (1953–1963), Jean Martinon (1963–1968), Sir Georg Solti (1969–1991), and Daniel Barenboim (1991–). Principal guest conductors include Carlo Maria Giulini (1969–1972), Claudio Abbado (1982–1985), and Pierre Boulez (1995–).

The orchestra has recorded since 1916, but it was during the Reiner years of the 1950s and 1960s that some of its most significant recordings were made. Many became prized collector's items and in the twenty-first century are still considered important historical performances.

Solti's twenty-two-year tenure at the head of the orchestra built on Reiner's legacy, and he made more that 100 recordings with the orchestra, selling more than 5 million copies. Solti took the orchestra on its first international tours, beginning in 1971, helping cement an international reputation.

In 1991 pianist/conductor Barenboim took over as music director. Barenboim deepened the orchestra's repertoire and expanded its touring, including the orchestra's first tour of South America. Though the classical music recording industry largely collapsed in the 1990s, the Chicago Symphony often found itself on the classical bestseller charts. It was one of the last major American orchestras to lose its recording contract (in 2001), and in the 1990s the orchestra won eleven Grammy Awards.

A sign of its strength was the range of music for which the orchestra won Grammys in the 1990s: Gustav Mahler's Symphony No. 9, Bela Bartok's *Bluebeard's Castle*, John Corigliano's Symphony No. 1, Johann Bach's Mass in B Minor, and Dmitry Shostakovich's Symphonies Nos. 1 and 7.

Though it is difficult to declare a "best American orchestra," the Chicago Symphony belongs on any potential list for consideration. With one of the orchestra world's biggest budgets, a loyal audience, and an energetic music director, the Chicago Symphony was one of the most successful orchestras of the 1990s.

SELECTIVE DISCOGRAPHY: *Collector's Choice: Chicago Symphony Orchestra in the Twentieth Century* (CSO, 2000).

WEBSITE: www.cso.org.

DOUGLAS MCLENNAN

THE CHIEFTAINS

Formed: 1963, Dublin, Ireland

Members: Derek Bell, harp, timpani, dulcimer, harpsichord, organ, piano, oboe, keyboard, synthesizer (born Belfast, Northern Ireland, 1935; died 17 October 2002); Kevin Conneff, bodhran, vocals, percussion (born Dublin, Ireland, 8 January 1945); David Fallon (born Ireland); Martin Fay, fiddle, bones (born Ireland, circa 1937); Sean Keane, fiddle, tin whistle (born Dublin, Ireland, 12 July 1946); Matt Molloy, flute, tin whistle (born Ballaghaderreen, Roscommon, Ireland, 12 January 1947); Paddy Moloney, uilleann pipes, bodhran, tin whistle (born Donnycarney, Dublin, Ireland, 1 August 1938). Former members: Peadar Mercier, bones, bodhran (born, Cork, Ireland, 1914); Sean Potts, tin whistle, bones, bodhran (born Dublin, Ireland, 1930); Michael "Mick" Tubridy, flute, concertina, tin whistle (born Kilrush, Clare, Ireland, 1935).

Genre: World

Best-selling album since 1990: *Bells of Dublin* (1991)

Hit songs since 1990: "Have I Told You Lately That I Love You," "Factory Girl," "Over the Sea to Skye"

The supergroup the Chieftains were one of the first bands from Ireland to bring their country's music to the rest of the world. Hard work and dedication to Irish traditional music and other musical forms, an ambitious approach to collaboration with musicians of every stripe, and a tireless approach to touring and recording account for their success. In their forty years together the Chieftains recorded dozens of albums, won six Grammy Awards, and performed all over the world, including numerous appearances at Carnegie Hall in New York City.

The Chieftains' classic sound stems from Paddy Moloney's uilleann pipes. The group was formed as a mostly professional outfit, culled from the top tier of the country's folk musicians. The early incarnation of the Chieftains came from Moloney, who had worked with a group called Ceoltoiri Cuallann, which specialized in instrumental music and consisted of Sean Potts (tin whistle), Martin Fay (fiddle), David Fallon (bodhran), Mick Tubridy (flute and concertina), and Sean O'Riada.

The Chieftains [PAUL NATKIN/PHOTO RESERVE]

Ironically, the Chieftains came together at a time when most Irish musicians were putting down their traditional instruments in favor of guitars, saxophones, and other sounds of rock and roll. The band was successful nearly from the start in Ireland and England, and within ten years, they were known worldwide. Their first few albums were reissued in the United States through Island Records.

From the late 1970s through the 1980s, the Chieftains achieved the peak of their success with American audiences. O'Riada and Fallon left after the first album, Peadar Mercier came in on bodhran, and fiddle champion Sean Keane joined them for the second album. After they recorded *Chieftains 4*, Ronnie McShane joined as a percussionist, and Derek Bell came on board as harpist, oboist, and timpanist.

Like their fellow Irish musicians Clannad, the Chieftains' first break with American audiences came through a film. They were commissioned to provide the music for Stanley Kubrick's *Barry Lyndon* (1975). One song in particular, "Women of Ireland," gained airplay on radio stations with adventurous play lists, which gave them the confidence they needed to mount a full-scale tour of the States. They also won an Academy Award for the soundtrack.

With a new contract with Island Records, the Chieftains were free to be as prolific and productive as they could, and they released albums nearly annually through 1980, when they switched to Columbia Records. Their album *Chieftains 9* was the first to feature vocals by Kevin Conneff; at this time Tubridy and Potts departed, and Matt Molloy came in to play whistle and flute. Their 1981 release, *Chieftains 10: Cotton-Eyed Joe*, expanded their sound; one critic called the title track "Texas meets the Chieftains."

From the late 1980s through the 1990s, the Chieftains's albums were available on the American label Shanachie, known for its strong stable of folk and traditional musicians. Comfortably ensconced in the folk-Celtic world, the Chieftains started collaborating with other musicians, most notably Eric Clapton, Paul McCartney, and the Rolling Stones. Perhaps their most successful and natural collaboration was with the Irish musician Van Morrison, on the album *Irish Heartbeat* (1988), which features two disparate though equally Irish musical acts at the top of their game; the album earned a Grammy Award nomination for Best Folk Recording.

A few years later, in 1991, the group recorded a Christmas album, *The Bells of Dublin*, which features many popular musicians, including Elvis Costello, Marianne Faithfull, Rickie Lee Jones, and Jackson Browne. During this time the Chieftains drew on a connection to Brittany, a Celtic region in northwest France. They also acknowledged their northwest country's connection with Celtic Spain, producing the 1996 album *Santiago,* which acknowledges Spanish music with Celtic roots.

After several nominations in their twenty years together, the Chieftains finally earned a Grammy Award by 1992 for Best Traditional Folk Recording and brought home six by 1998, in traditional and contemporary folk categories as well as world music and pop vocal collaboration. In 2002 the Chieftains created *Down the Old Plank Road,* an album that acknowledges the kinship between American Appalachian/folk/roots music and Celtic music; in a display of the group's multigenre appeal, the album reached number 21 on *Billboard*'s Country chart, number ninety-one on the *Billboard* 200, and number one in the World Music Chart.

The Chieftains did much to change the previously held view of Irish folk musicians as either carousing and boisterous like the Irish Rovers or sentimental and nostalgic like Mary O'Hara. The Chieftains's longevity is due to an adventurous spirit, exceptional musicianship, and the beauty and timelessness of the Irish music they perform.

SELECTIVE DISCOGRAPHY: *The Chieftains 1* (Shanachie, 1964); *The Chieftains 2* (Shanachie, 1969); *The Chieftains 3* (Shanachie, 1971); *The Chieftains Live* (Shanachie 1977); *The Chieftains 9: Boil the Breakfast Early* (Columbia, 1980); *The Chieftains 10: Cotton-eyed Joe* (Shanachie, 1981); *The Chieftains in China* (Shanachie, 1985); *Celtic Wedding: Music of Brittany Played by Irish Musicians* (RCA, 1987); *Irish Heartbeat* (Mercury, 1988); *The Bells of Dublin* (RCA, 1991); *The Best of Chieftains* (Legacy, 1992); *Santiago* (RCA, 1996); *The Chieftains: Claddagh Years* (RCA, 1999); *Water from the Well* (RCA, 2000); *The Chieftains: Claddagh Years Volume 2* (RCA Records, 2000); *Down the Old Plank Road: The Nashville Sessions* (RCA, 2003).

CARRIE HAVRANEK

CHARLOTTE CHURCH

Born: Cardiff, Wales, 21 February 1986

Genre: Classical

Best-selling album since 1990: *Charlotte Church* (1999)

Classical singer Charlotte Church proved to be one of the unexpected stars of the late 1990s with the success of her debut album *Voice of an Angel* (1998), recorded and released when she was only twelve years old. Church's albums showcase her soprano voice in a variety of musical contexts, including opera arias, folk songs, art songs, and show tunes, all accompanied by world-class orchestras. Church is as much a product of the classical music industry struggling to maintain its shrinking market position as it is a product of her own drive toward success. As a crossover artist, Church has successfully brought her voice, and the music she sings, to a large audience.

An only child from a middle-class Welsh Catholic family, Church began singing publicly at an early age, making a name for herself in local karaoke competitions. Her mother, a former classical guitarist who worked in city government prior to Church's rise to fame, supported her daughter's singing. However, Church herself was responsible for many of her early breaks. She was famously discovered while introducing her aunt (also a singer) on a televised talent show. Her first manager, Jonathan Shalit, quickly arranged for an audition with Sony U.K., which offered her a generous five-album contract.

Church's albums chronicle her development as a singer. *Voice of an Angel* features songs in three languages—English, Latin, and Welch—carefully chosen to display her voice's best assets while appealing to a wide audience. Her signature song, the "Pie Jesu" from Andrew Lloyd Webber's play *Requiem,* showcases her voice's finest qualities: clear high notes, light vibrato, and an often mature sense of phrasing. *Charlotte Church* (1999) expands her repertoire with carefully selected Italian arias, including "O mio babbino caro" from Puccini's opera *Gianni Schicchi.* Like *Voice of an Angel,* it includes a range of folk and show tunes, such as "Summertime" from George Gershwin's opera *Porgy and Bess.* With her youthful voice, Church shifts the narrative position of "Summertime" from the mother to the child, and what was once a dispirited lullaby loses its melancholy.

Her next album, *Enchantment* (2001), is a stylistic departure from earlier albums, with a much greater focus on show tunes rather than opera. Released on the Sony Music imprint (instead of Sony Classical), this album represents Church's concerted effort to shift her focus to pop repertoire.

Church's critics have been many and vocal. While some will grudgingly admit the appeal of her voice, most are quick to lament its inevitable destruction. Others have accused her parents and Sony U.K. of child abuse. Unlike instrumental child protégés, who are often praised for their interpretive abilities, many have declared Church not old enough to understand what she sings. When critics point out that many other children have good (or even better) voices, they either ignore or downplay Church's charisma and stage presence. Many of her fans find her voice a refreshing change from older opera singers too deeply steeped in convention. Church's repertoire of familiar favorites matches their expectations as much as her sweet voice appeals to their ears.

SELECTIVE DISCOGRAPHY: *Voice of an Angel* (Sony Classical, 1998); *Charlotte Church* (Sony Classical, 1999); *Enchantment* (Sony Music, 2001).

WEBSITES: www.charlottechurch.com; www.charlottechurchfans.com.

CAROLINE POLK O'MEARA

CLANNAD

Formed: 1970, County Donegal, Ireland

Members: Ciaran Brennan, vocals, guitar, bass, keyboards (born Gweedore, Ireland, 1951); Márie Brennan, vocals, harp (born Gweedore, Ireland, 4 August 1952); Noel Duggan, guitar, vocals (born Gweedore, Donegal, Ireland, February 1949); Padráig Duggan, vocals, mandolin, harmonica (born Gweedore, Donegal, Ireland, February 1949). Former members: Enya Brennan, vocals (born Gweedore, Donegal, Ireland, 17 May 1961); Paul Brennan, guitar, percussion, flute, vocals (born Gweedore, Donegal, Ireland, 1957).

Genre: World, Celtic

Best-selling album since 1990: *Anam* (1992)

Hit songs since 1990: "Harry's Game," "In a Lifetime," "Lore"

Clannad has achieved gradual success and spawned modestly selling albums throughout the world, despite the band's rich and long history as a beloved act in Ireland. Clannad is one of the few Irish bands to bridge the gap between the traditional sounds of their homeland and the more accessible pop music, without compromising their roots or their musical integrity. Early fans were exposed to their ethereal vocals, stellar musicianship, and love of traditional Irish folksongs and ballads through the use of one of their songs in a Volkswagen commercial in 1993, more than twenty years after they formed. Clannad, however, is probably best known for their famous soprano Enya Brennan, who left the band in 1982 to pursue a highly successful solo career.

Clannad formed when siblings Paul, Ciaran, and Márie Brennan started performing with their twin uncles, Padráig and Noel Duggan, at a family member's pub. The Brennan siblings began with Paul on tin whistle and flute, Ciaran on double bass and vocals, and Márie singing with her hauntingly lovely soprano, a voice that, coupled with

her sister Enya's, seemed to typify the mystical, beautiful, and otherworldly qualities of Ireland itself. Uncles Padráig and Noel joined on mandolin, guitar, and other assorted instruments, and the group named themselves Clannad, which is derived from the phrase "an clann as Dobhar," which roughly translates as "family from Dore" in Irish. Initially they did not stray from the traditional music they loved and which defined them. This staunch commitment to their homeland meant that they sang in Irish, a testament to their upbringing in the west of Ireland where Irish is more commonly heard than English.

Clannad began their career performing in folk festivals through Ireland, and after a few years of gathering a loyal following released an album. Their self-titled debut, with songs in Irish, was released in 1973, but they did not achieve wider success in Europe until they toured in 1975. Although they began to play traditional songs with a slightly more contemporary style by adding harmonies and a full band, they were torn between pleasing Irish music purists and winning over the masses.

However, Clannad continued with their signature folk-based arrangements and beautiful vocals. The addition of Enya to the band in 1979 marked a turning point. During Enya's tenure, Clannad released a live album and toured the United States for the first time. With Enya on keyboards and vocals the band's sound, perhaps influenced by the popular trend at the time, became more electronic and less based on guitar and mandolin.

Clannad recorded albums and remained popular even as Enya's success began to overshadow them. Clannad became sought after for television and film scores. They were commissioned to write the theme song for a television show *Harry's Game* (1982). Ironically, it is their most popular song ever; it broke through to the United Kingdom Top 10 sales chart, and won the Ivor Novello Award, Britain's equivalent to the Grammy Award.

By the start of the 1990s, the band had enough material for a retrospective album, and they began recording for the Atlantic label. They released *Pastpresent* (1990), their last album for RCA. Around this time individual members began to release solo albums, including Márie Brennan, who was now the primary vocalist. In 1992 they released their best album in years, *Anam*, and included for the United States audience the tracks "In a Lifetime " (a duet with U2's lead singer Bono) and "Harry's Game." Inclusion of the latter proved to be a wise move, because it was picked up for use in a Volkswagen Passat commercial and as a song on the *Patriot Games* (1992) soundtrack.

Anam became Clannad's first gold record in America and their best-selling work. Clannad also contributed to the soundtrack to *The Last of the Mohicans*. In 1993 Clannad released *Banba*, which marked their twentieth anniversary together. *Banba* fared well with critics and audiences, a testament to the band's rich musical history and spare, careful inclusion of more contemporary sounds.

For three decades, Clannad has stuck together as a family of versatile musicians who are proud of their heritage and committed to remaining true to their roots, whether or not their music is commercially successful.

SELECTIVE DISCOGRAPHY: *Clannad* (Phillips, 1973); *Clannad 2* (Shanachie, 1975); *Clannad in Concert* (Shanachie, 1979); *Fuaim* (Atlantic, 1981); *The Legend* (RCA, 1984); *Pastpresent* (RCA, 1990): *Anam* (Atlantic, 1992); *Banba* (Atlantic, 1993); *Lore* (Atlantic, 1996); *Rogha: The Best of Clannad* (Atlantic, 1997). **Soundtracks:** *Patriot Games: Music from the Original Motion Picture Soundtrack* (RCA,1992); *The Last of the Mohicans: Original Motion Picture Soundtrack* (Morgan Creek, 1992).

CARRIE HAVRANEK

ERIC CLAPTON

Born: Eric Clapp; Ripley, England, 30 March 1945

Genre: Rock

Best-selling album since 1990: *Unplugged* (1992)

Hit songs since 1990: "Tears in Heaven," "Change the World," "Layla" (from *Unplugged*)

Guitarist/singer/songwriter Eric Clapton became one of music's biggest superstars in the late 1960s. He has maintained that status throughout his career despite suffering tremendous personal chaos at many junctures of his life. Although successful in a variety of musical styles, Clapton keeps returning to the blues, a musical form that inspired him from the onset and seems to mollify the up-and-down circumstances of his life.

Clapton grew up in post–World War II Ripley, England. At nine years old, he discovered that his parents were, in fact, his grandparents; that his sister was actually his mother, and that his brother was his uncle; and that his mother had turned the newborn Clapton over to her parents after giving birth at age sixteen following an affair with a married soldier. The emotional fallout from the discovery of his illegitimate birth fueled Clapton's insecure and enigmatic behaviors throughout his life.

Clapton Is God

As a preteen, Clapton enjoyed all music but was exhilarated by the blues. He received a guitar from his grand-

parents at thirteen and practiced so obsessively that it interfered with schooling. Clapton finally dropped out of Kingston College of Art in 1962 to pursue music professionally. He joined the Yardbirds in 1963. They recorded two albums before Clapton fled the pop-driven band (fellow guitar icon Jeff Beck replaced him) to immerse himself in the blues with John Mayall and the Bluesbreakers. Soon he impressed critics and fellow musicians alike with his blues-rooted, imaginative guitar improvisations, swelling his popularity. The worshipful phrase "Clapton is God" became a standard chant at live performances and commonly appeared as graffiti. Clapton left Mayall after a year and formed the power trio Cream, with drummer Ginger Baker and bassist Jack Bruce, in 1966. Egos clashed from the start and their substance abuse was rampant, but Cream managed to last until 1968. They produced some of rock's most prolific songs, including "Sunshine of Your Love" and "White Room."

After Cream Clapton fleetingly jumped in and out of various band formations leaving behind a scattered trail of classic songs and albums. Clapton played for a short time with close friend and Beatle George Harrison. In addition, he journeyed with another Beatle, John Lennon and his Plastic Ono Band. Clapton joined Traffic's Steve Winwood and formed Blind Faith in 1969. Blind Faith recorded one album and enjoyed a sold-out world tour before breaking up. At that point, Clapton decided to record his first solo album and he chose friends, Delaney and Bonnie, who had backed up Blind Faith, as his playing mates. It spawned the classic "After Midnight" but Clapton left Delaney and Bonnie to form another short-lived, legendary group, Derek and the Dominoes. Here he worked and formed a deep friendship with famed guitarist Duane Allman. His signature "Layla" along with many other dynamic songs came about during this time, as did a heroin addiction. Drugs and an obsessive love affair with George Harrison's wife, Patti Boyd, whom he later married, began to consume Clapton. Additionally, he was staggered by the 1971 deaths of Allman and fellow guitar mate Jimi Hendrix. Derek and the Dominoes tried to record again but anguish coupled with drug use left Clapton emotionally paralyzed and he disappeared into seclusion.

He resurfaced three years later, drug-free, and his solo albums *461 Ocean Boulevard* (1974) and *Slowhand* (1977) offer a glimpse into his musical eclecticism. They feature the reggae-styled "I Shot the Sheriff" from *461 Ocean Boulevard* and the chunky rock of "Cocaine" and easy groove of "Lay Down Sally" from *Slowhand*. Incidentally, Slowhand is a nickname that still sticks to Clapton from the "Clapton is God" era when the audience would patiently wait for him to change a broken guitar string by clapping in a slow, rhythmic manner.

Although he had kicked hard narcotics, alcoholism debilitated Clapton throughout the early 1980s. He continued to tour, release solo albums, and score soundtracks to the *Lethal Weapon* films, but his personal life and his health were in a shambles. In 1986 his union with Italian model Lori Del Santo produced a son, Conor, and his tumultuous relationship with Boyd ended in divorce in 1988. Along the way, Clapton received treatment for alcoholism and issues stemming from his disjointed childhood, both of which were destroying his career. In 1990 Clapton emerged in strong physical and mental health and looked forward to becoming an active parent to his son. A four-CD career retrospective, *Crossroads* (1988), and the roots-oriented *Journeyman* (1989) were big successes, plus he won his first Grammy Award in 1990 from *Journeyman* for "Bad Love." The cloud looming over Clapton seemed to be lifting. However, a series of numbing tragedies waylaid this comeback period.

In August of that year, Clapton's close friend and virtuoso guitarist Stevie Ray Vaughan died in a helicopter accident after the two had performed together in concert. Additionally, two members of Clapton's touring entourage, also his close friends, lost their lives in the mishap. Clapton was devastated. Vaughan, also an alcoholic in recovery, was at the high point of his career. However, there was barely time to grieve. On March 20, 1991, Conor died after falling to the street from a high-rise Manhattan apartment through a window that had been left open accidentally.

Striving On

Numbed with heartache, a secluded Clapton received an outpouring of love from fellow musicians. He continued to stay sober through Alcoholics Anonymous and used music to channel his sorrow. Clapton wrote several songs about Conor and one of those, "Tears in Heaven," became a hit. The song appeared on the soundtrack for the movie *Rush* (1991) and was included on his Grammy Award-sweeping acoustic effort, *Unplugged* (1992). The album, performed live, also features a reworked version of his signature "Layla," and a variety of old blues classics such as "Rollin and Tumblin" and "Before You Accuse Me." The success of the raw *Unplugged* furthered Clapton's decision to record *From the Cradle* (1994), an album comprised solely of old blues classics. Recorded live in the studio with almost no overdubs, the album was a huge success and Clapton showed that his electric blues guitar skills were still comparable to his days with Mayall and Cream. Additionally, Clapton was finally gaining recognition for his vocal skills. A reluctant singer, Clapton began focusing on singing in his days with Delaney and Bonnie. He honed his singing in subsequent solo efforts and surfaced as a likable pop voice in mainstream hits "Wonderful Tonight," "Forever Man," "She's Waiting," and many others. Many younger fans, unfamiliar with his "Guitar God" status, primarily consider Clapton a singer.

He scored a Grammy Award in 1997 with the single "Change the World," written by Kenneth "Babyface" Edmonds for the soundtrack to the film *Phenomenon* (1996). The song inspired his introspective *Pilgrim* (1998), an impressive departure from the unprocessed blues of *From the Cradle*. Driven by rhythm and blues flavorings and techno-electronic influence, *Pilgrim* presents Clapton's voice as soulful and meditative. The autobiographically styled songs chronicle the mindset of an artist who has endured great pain. The song "Circus" deals with his son's death as does "My Father's Eyes," which also alludes to issues regarding Clapton and his own father, whom he has never met.

When Clapton was inducted into the Rock and Roll Hall of Fame in 2000 for his work as a solo performer, he became the only performer in music history ever triple honored. Previously he was inducted with the Yardbirds in 1992 and Cream in 1993. *Riding with the King* (2000)—on which Clapton collaborates with the celebrated "King of the Blues," B.B. King—marked a strong return to the blues. The two bluesmen trade guitar and vocal licks on twelve classics that come mostly from King's repertoire. *Riding with the King* won a Grammy for Best Traditional Blues Album.

Sorrow greeted Clapton again when his uncle Adrian, his mother's brother with whom he was raised, passed away during the recording of *Reptile* (2001). He dedicated the album to Adrian, whom he had believed to be his brother throughout the early days of their childhood. *Reptile* serves as a career montage of sorts for Clapton with nearly every musical style that he has played through the years embodied within the fourteen songs. He followed *Reptile*'s release with a world tour, reportedly to be his last, and chronicled the tour with the live, *One More Car, One More Rider* (2002).

Although hailed for a lengthy portion of his career as "God," Clapton's understated demeanor suggests none of it. He usually performs dressed in comfortably casual attire with eyeglasses adding to his relaxed and modest manner. The aura is more of a sage survivor who has learned plenty along the way. However, when the spirit moves, usually stimulated by the familiar chug of a twelve-bar blues backdrop, Clapton ascends to the playing that brought about all the worship in the first place.

SELECTIVE DISCOGRAPHY: *Delaney & Bonnie & Friends on Tour with Eric Clapton* (Atlantic, 1970); *Eric Clapton's Rainbow Concert* (Polygram, 1973); *461 Ocean Boulevard* (Polygram, 1974); *There's One in Every Crowd* (Polygram, 1975); *E.C. Was Here* (Polygram, 1974); *No Reason to Cry* (Polygram, 1976); *Slowhand* (Polygram, 1977); *Backless* (Polygram, 1978); *Just One Night* (Polygram, 1980); *Another Ticket* (Polygram, 1981); *Money and*

Cigarettes (Warner Bros., 1983); *Behind the Sun* (Warner Bros., 1985); *August* (Warner Bros., 1986); *Journeyman* (Warner Bros., 1989); *24 Nights* (Warner Bros., 1991); *Unplugged* (Warner Bros., 1992); *From the Cradle* (Warner Bros., 1994); *Pilgrim* (Warner Bros., 1998); *Blues* (Polygram, 1999); *Riding with the King* (Warner Bros., 2000); *Reptile* (Warner Bros., 2001); *One More Car, One More Rider* (Warner Bros., 2002). **With B.B. King:** *Riding with the King* (Duck/Reprise, 2000). **Soundtracks:** *Lethal Weapon: Original Soundtrack* (Warner Bros., 1986); *Lethal Weapon 2: Original Soundtrack* (Warner Bros., 1989); *Homeboy* (EMI International, 1989); *Rush* (Warner Bros., 1991); *Lethal Weapon 3: Original Soundtrack* (Warner Bros., 1992); *Lethal Weapon 4: Original Soundtrack* (Warner Bros., 1998); *Phenomenon* (Warner Bros., 1996).

BIBLIOGRAPHY: R. Coleman, *Clapton!: An Authorized Biography* (New York, 1986); E. Clapton with M. Robarty, *Eric Clapton: In His Own Words* (London, 1995); C. Sandford, *Clapton: On the Edge of Darkness* (New York, 1999).

DONALD LOWE

ROSEMARY CLOONEY

Born: Maysville, Kentucky, 23 May 1928; died Beverly Hills, California, 29 June 2002

Genre: Vocal

Best-selling album since 1990: *Mothers and Daughters* (1996)

One of the most distinctive vocal stylists of the twentieth century, Rosemary Clooney enjoyed a highly successful career, even though her periods of greatest success were spaced decades apart. Beginning in 1950, she released a long string of hits for Columbia Records, where her work often fell under the guidance of pop producer Mitch Miller. Her hits of this period are composed largely of light-hearted "novelty" numbers such as "Come On-a My House" (1951) and "Mambo Italiano" (1954). Beginning in the late 1970s, however, after suffering a harrowing emotional breakdown, Clooney returned to the scene as a sensitive, intelligent jazz interpreter, imbued with a subtle sense of swing and a dry, textured voice. Clooney earned her greatest critical attention during this period—the late 1970s through the early 2000s—when she issued a series of strong albums for the small Concord Jazz label.

Always working with excellent supporting musicians, she performed continuously until six months before her death.

Born in Maysville, Kentucky, in 1928, Clooney was raised in an unstable, shifting home. After moving several times, the family settled in Cincinnati, where Clooney and her sister, Betty, found steady work during the early 1940s singing for radio stations. In the mid-1940s she performed as lead vocalist for bandleader Tony Pastor, signing with Pastor's label, Columbia, as a solo artist in 1950. At Columbia, her recordings were overseen by Miller, whose work is often derided by modern jazz critics for its lowbrow pop leanings. Although Clooney recorded some fine jazz work at Columbia, she became a star on the basis of novelty numbers such as "Come On-a My House"—a song she initially did not want to record. Sustaining her stardom throughout the 1950s, Clooney acted in films such as *White Christmas* and *Red Garters* (both 1954). By the late 1960s, however, Clooney's life and career had unraveled. In 1968, addicted to pills, distraught over her failed marriage to actor Jose Ferrer and the assassination of her friend Senator Robert Kennedy (Clooney was present when Kennedy was killed), Clooney broke down after ranting at an audience during a performance. Released from a psychiatric ward after a four-week stay, Clooney worked to rebuild her career with the help of her friend, legendary vocalist Bing Crosby. By the late 1970s, she had re-emerged as a jazz stylist of the first rank.

During the 1980s and 1990s, Clooney, under contract to the Concord Jazz label, recorded many fine albums, often presented as "songbooks" honoring a particular composer. While critics and fans observed that her voice no longer possessed the suppleness of its youth, all agreed that her skills as an interpreter had sharpened. On songs such as "We'll Be Together Again" (from the album *Do You Miss New York?* [1992]), she underscores her performance with a rich yet subtle current of emotion, extending words with a smoky vibrato and then cutting them off for dramatic emphasis. Like pop legend Frank Sinatra, Clooney never allows emotion to push a song out of control; instead, she plumbs depths of feeling through quiet power.

Another highlight of the 1990s was *Dedicated to Nelson* (1995), an album tribute to gifted 1950s arranger Nelson Riddle, with whom Clooney worked and, at one point, shared a romantic relationship. Backed by re-creations of Riddle's original arrangements, Clooney applies her finely shaded voice and astute rhythmic sense to classic songs such as "Do You Know What It Means to Miss New Orleans" and "Come Rain or Come Shine." *Demi-Centennial* (1995), an album of new performances celebrating Clooney's fifty years as a singer, ranks with her finest recordings. Here, delivering songs associated with various periods in her life, Clooney captures an honesty and warmth rare in contemporary music.

In November 2001, Clooney gave her final performance at the Blaisdell Concert Hall in Honolulu, Hawaii. The recording of the evening, released after her death as *The Last Concert* (2002), is notable for Clooney's voice—shakier and less potent than it had been in the 1980s and 1990s, but still impressive—and undiminished sense of timing. On "Happiness Is a Thing Called Joe," first performed by the legendary entertainer Ethel Waters in the 1943 film *Cabin in the Sky,* Clooney distills romantic affection with sincerity and directness. After a long battle with lung cancer, Clooney died in June 2002.

Infusing her performances with honesty and emotional commitment, Clooney became one of the most beloved American vocalists, her consistency and taste rivaled only by her tenacity. Overcoming personal conflicts after her initial popularity declined, Clooney returned in the late 1970s with renewed force, giving listeners impeccable jazz recordings for the next two decades.

SELECTIVE DISCOGRAPHY: *Rosemary Clooney with Harry James* (Columbia, 1952); *Clap Hands! Here Comes Rosie!* (RCA Victor, 1960); *Love* (Reprise, 1963); *Here's to My Lady* (Concord Jazz, 1978); *Sings the Music of Cole Porter* (Concord Jazz, 1982); *Do You Miss New York?* (Concord Jazz, 1993); *Demi-Centennial* (Concord Jazz, 1995); *Dedicated to Nelson* (Concord Jazz, 1995); *Mothers & Daughters* (Concord Jazz, 1996); *Sentimental Journey* (Concord Jazz, 2001); *The Last Concert* (Concord Jazz, 2002).

WEBSITE: www.rosemaryclooney.com.

DAVID FREELAND

BRUCE COCKBURN

Born: Ottawa, Ontario, 27 May 1945

Genre: Folk

Best-selling album since 1990: *The Charity of Night* (1997)

Canadian singer/songwriter Bruce Cockburn is a many-textured musical journeyman whose iconic popularity in Canada began with his first album in 1970 and has grown in the United States and the rest of the world with his twenty-five subsequent album releases. His music has encompassed many genres at various junctures in his career and his lyrics often reflect a passion for political and environmental issues. Cockburn has taken his music all over the world and has a keen interest in the music and cultures of Third World

nations. He is credited with being a brilliant guitarist.

Cockburn (pronounced Coe'-Bern) grew up on a farm near Ottawa, and took an early interest in the guitar. He played in high school groups and later sojourned to Europe where he performed as a street musician in Paris. He returned from Europe and attended the Berklee College of Music in Boston in 1964 to pursue a formal musical education. He stayed there nearly three years but grew impatient and left before graduating. (In 1997 Berklee College awarded Cockburn with an honorary degree.)

After his first release, *Bruce Cockburn* (1970), Cockburn gained immediate attention in his home country after being named Folk Singer of the Year at the 1971 Juno Awards (Canada's equivalent to the Grammy Awards). However, due to a marketing mix-up, the album was barely released elsewhere. He continued through the 1970s gaining a reputation as an earnest and outspoken folksinger. Cockburn's persona was difficult to nail down—a trait that would continue throughout his career—as he mixed progressive social views with his newfound Christianity. Most of his albums in the later 1970s reflect his Christian beliefs. In the 1980s he changed to a more electric sound, adding varieties of rock to his music, which was growing increasingly political and angry. He was particularly concerned with matters in Central America.

Although Cockburn remains an unwavering voice on issues regarding land mines, animal rights, and environmental concerns, the 1990s marked a return to music that was more reflective. His first album of the decade, *Nothing but a Burning Light* (1991), is tinged with blues and serves as a reminder of Cockburn's tremendous guitar skills. Additionally, his glass-clear chameleon voice adjusts to any style that he plays and expressively highlights his vivid lyrics. His other releases within the decade, *Dart to the Heart* (1994), *The Charity of the Night* (1997), and *Breakfast in New Orleans, Dinner in Timbuktu* (1999), continue in a similar vein.

Cockburn has won several Juno Awards, including Best Album for *Breakfast in New Orleans, Dinner in Timbuktu.* In 2000 he was inducted into the Canadian Music Hall of Fame. He released a new studio album, *You've Never Seen Everything* (2003), and Cockburn continues exchanging and exploring musical ideas with musicians in third world regions such as Nepal, Mozambique, and Central America.

Many critics have wondered why Cockburn, an agile songwriter and a monumentally talented performer, has not become more successful commercially. Some reason that his left-wing politics in combination with his devout Christianity confuse listeners; others feel that he has been too wide-ranging in his musical styles. In the meantime, Cockburn is well respected within the industry and he continues to provide his loyal fan base with progressive, thought-provoking material.

SELECTIVE DISCOGRAPHY: *Bruce Cockburn* (Epic, 1970); *High Winds, White Sky* (True North, 1971); *Night Vision* (True North, 1973); *Salt, Sun & Time* (True North, 1974); *Joy Will Find a Way* (True North, 1975); *Circles in the Stream* (True North, 1977); *Dancing in the Dragon's Jaws* (Millennium, 1979); *Humans* (Millennium, 1980); *Mummy Dust* (True North, 1981); *Inner City Front* (Millennium, 1981); *The Trouble with Normal* (Gold Castle, 1983); *Stealing Fire* (Gold Mountain, 1984); *Waiting for a Miracle* (Gold Mountain, 1987); *Nothing but a Burning Light* (Sony, 1991); *Dart to the Heart* (Sony, 1994); *The Charity of Night* (Rykodisc, 1997); *Breakfast in New Orleans, Dinner in Timbuktu* (Rykodisc, 1999); *You've Never Seen Everything* (Rounder, 2003).

DONALD LOWE

LEONARD COHEN

Born: Montreal, Quebec, 21 September 1934

Genre: Folk

Best-selling album since 1990: *Ten New Songs* (2001)

Leonard Cohen was in his mid-thirties and had already established himself as a poet and best-selling author before he released an album of his own musical compositions in 1968. Over the next three decades, he made nine more studio albums of strikingly original and sometimes masterly blendings of word and song, delivered in an unsentimental, vibratoless, mournful baritone that has grown raspier and grittier with age and untold numbers of cigarettes.

Cohen was born and raised in Montreal, by his mother; his father died when he was only nine. Encouraged by his mother to pursue his artistic interests, Cohen attended McGill University in Montreal, where his poetry and fiction writing garnered award-winning notice. Cohen listened to country music in his youth and, while attending McGill, played rhythm guitar in a traditional square-dance band called the Buckskin Boys. He published his first poetry collection, *Let Us Compare Mythologies*, in 1956, when he was twenty-one years old. In addition to several more published volume of poetry, Cohen became famous for his two novels, *The Favorite Game* (1963) and *Beautiful Losers* (1966). Each book has sold more than 1 million copies worldwide.

In 1966 Cohen met folksinger Judy Collins. Collins showed great interest in his songs and recorded some of them, including his most famous composition, "Suzanne." He ends the first verse with the lyric, "And you know that she will trust you, for you've touched her perfect body with your mind." Other artists also began recording Cohen's music before he decided to release his own album, *Songs of Leonard Cohen* (1968), which became a college campus musical staple as well as a critical and commercial success. The album contains his version of "Suzanne" and other famous Cohen songs such as "Sisters of Mercy" and "So Long, Marianne," whose chorus repeats, "Now so long Marianne, it's time that we began to laugh and cry and cry and laugh about it all again."

Cohen continued releasing albums and remained popular into the early 1980s. His music—melancholy odes to lost love, flatly delivered ironic social commentaries, and chronicles of his diverse travels—fell out of favor in the 1980s. However, Cohen made a comeback of sorts with *I'm Your Man* (1988), an album that sold well around the world, especially in the Scandinavian countries.

Cohen's songs have been recorded by musical artists as stylistically diverse as Diana Ross, Joe Cocker, Joan Baez, Rita Coolidge, and Neil Diamond. In 1991, as a tribute to Cohen, eighteen young rock groups including REM, Nick Cave and the Bad Seeds, and the Pixies combined on an album of his songs titled *I'm Your Fan* (1991). In 1995 another tribute album, *Tower of Song* (1995), was released. It features established stars such as Elton John, Billy Joel, Bono, Don Henley, Sting, Peter Gabriel, and many others performing renditions of Cohen's songs.

In his customary trait of creating albums methodically, Cohen's follow-up release to *I'm Your Man* was more than four years in the making. *The Future* (1992) is a collection of astringent social and political songs, some of them starkly bleak in a prophetic vein, a melding of the indignation of 1960s protest music with a dark, foreboding existentialism. In the album's title song Cohen offers a harbinger of things to come with the lyric, "Get ready for the future: It is murder."

Although the album sold reasonably well, Cohen was in no hurry to release another. He chose instead to spend most of the remaining decade at Mount Baldy, a Zen retreat in southern California. He became an ordained Zen Monk and earned the name Jikan, which means "silent one." Cohen eventually began assembling songs for his next album, *Ten New Songs* (2001). He collaborated with the singer/songwriter Sharon Robinson on the album, on which she sings background to Cohen, his voice seldom rising above a faint, croaky whisper in characteristically brooding explorations of love and regret. His lyric, "The ponies run, the girls are young, the odds are there to beat," pushes the point forward in Cohen's "A

Thousand Kisses Deep," a cynical lament to love from the perspective of a man growing older and one of the album's highlights.

In 2002 *The Essential Leonard Cohen* was released. It contains thirty-one songs and chronicles his recording career from 1968 through 2001. The album displays Cohen's gift for writing songs that are at once topically relevant, emotionally gripping, and intellectually challenging.

When Cohen first began playing guitar and singing his poetry in various folk gatherings, most of the performers were dressed in the hippie garb of that time. Cohen set himself apart by wearing tailored suits. This is merely one characteristic of many that separates Cohen from the typical folksinger. Immune to the passing dictates of fashion, unswervingly true to his quirky creative impulses, Cohen has recorded in song a visionary quest that is among the most enduring and important to have emerged from the realm of popular music in the late twentieth century.

SELECTIVE DISCOGRAPHY: *Songs of Leonard Cohen* (Columbia, 1968); *Songs from a Room* (Columbia, 1969); *Song of Love and Hate* (Columbia, 1971); *Live Songs* (Columbia, 1973); *New Skin for the Old Ceremony* (Columbia, 1974); *Death of a Ladies Man* (Warner Bros., 1977); *Various Positions* (Columbia, 1984); *I'm Your Man* (Columbia, 1988); *The Future* (Columbia, 1992); *Ten New Songs* (Sony, 2001); *The Essential Leonard Cohen* (Sony, 2002) .

BIBLIOGRAPHY: D. Sheppard, *Leonard Cohen* (New York, 2000).

DONALD LOWE

COLDPLAY

Formed: 1998, London, England

Members: Chris Martin, vocals/piano (born Devon, England, 2 March 1977); Will Champion, percussion (born Hampshire, England, 31 July 1978); Guy Berryman, bass (born Kirkcaldy, Fife, Scotland, 12 April 1978); Jon Buckland, guitar (born London, England, 11 September 1977).

Genre: Rock

Best-selling album since 1990: *A Rush of Blood to the Head* (2002)

Hit songs since 1990: "Yellow," "In My Place," "Clocks"

In an American pop scene that flirted with but quickly turned on hyped British bands like Blur, Oasis, and the Prodigy, Coldplay reached the hearts of middlebrow America with a down-to-earth persona, feel-good lyrics, and stately, atmospheric pop.

Chris Martin, of Coldplay [PAUL NATKIN/PHOTO RESERVE]

Chris Martin learned piano as a youngster and began playing in bands at fifteen, with music serving not only as a passion but also as a way of facing down his shyness. The foursome met at University College London in the mid-1990s. Martin and Jon Buckland started writing songs together and from the start believed their artistic synergy would take them far. Guy Berryman joined later, as did Will Champion, a guitarist who moved to drums to accommodate Buckland, also a guitarist.

The group released a pair of independent-label EPs, *Safety* (1998) and *Brothers and Sisters* (1999). Their touring in England and promising material caught the attention of Parlophone, which released the group's next EP, *Blue Room* (1999). The disc contains "Such a Rush" and "High Speed," which would show up on their debut album, *Parachutes* (2000).

Parachutes makes ample use of Buckland's breezy, sometimes twangy guitar chords. Martin offers comforting words, singing "I'll be there by your side" on "Shiver," and "I promise you this / I'll always look out for you" on "Sparks." With a pronounced accent and a relaxed tenor, Martin sounds a little like Dave Matthews. "Don't Panic" recalls the tagline from the sci-fi novel *The Hitchhiker's Guide to the Galaxy* by British author Douglas Adams.

With a shuffle beat and whimsical falsetto vocals, the song also shares the book's fatalism about the state of the universe.

But the album's highlight is the soothing "Yellow," which, despite its dreamy tempo and sentimental lyrics, became a sleeper hit on Top 40 radio. The ballad's invasion of rock radio was surprising, and some critics dismissed it as easy-listening music for young professionals. But the album's superb melodies and original fusion of acoustic and electronic rock won over the group's peers, who awarded *Parachutes* the 2001 Grammy for best alternative music performance.

However, the sudden demands of constant gigs caught up with Martin, who had to cut short a U.S. tour in 2001 with throat problems. The group retreated to the studio to work on a follow-up. The result was *A Rush of Blood to the Head* (2002), in which the group avoided the sophomore slump that affected so many of its compatriots who sought international success.

Like its predecessor, the album sold more than 1 million copies. This album features a larger dose of Martin's piano, but with co-producer Ken Nelson returning, it maintains the group's trademark ethereal groove. The ballad "In My Place" uses abstract lyrics but manages to be moving nonetheless with the rousing coda, "Come on and sing it out, now, now." The majestic "Politik" begins with piano chords before kicking into an intense, guitar-and-drum-propelled anthem. Martin indulges in falsetto wailing and simple piano arpeggios on second single "Clocks," whose pulsating beat made it an unlikely dance-club hit. Another standout, the Beatle-esque "The Scientist," highlights Martin's echoing piano and cryptic but seductively delivered lyrics.

Confirmation of Coldplay's surprising U.S. success came with its 2003 tour, which included several dates in the Midwest. The band members kept ticket prices reasonable, between thirty and thirty-five dollars, aimed for mid-size venues, and made themselves available to the press and sponsors. On tour the group unveiled a new song, "Moses," that became a favorite and raised hopes for future work.

Meanwhile, like their fellow Atlantic-crosser Bono of U2, Martin became involved in political causes, attaching himself to Oxfam, which believes that saving small Third World farmers requires an international effort to raise the price of many basic foodstuffs.

Coldplay helped make the case that soft music does not have to be treacly or banal. The group also showed that British bands can still appeal to mainstream America if they're willing to start modestly and engage in the necessary back-slapping.

SELECTIVE DISCOGRAPHY: *Parachutes* (Parlophone/EMI, 2000); *A Rush of Blood to the Head* (Capitol/EMI, 2002).

RAMIRO BURR

NATALIE COLE

Born: Los Angeles, California, 6 February 1950
Genre: R&B
Best-selling album since 1990: *Unforgettable: With Love* (1991)
Hit songs since 1990: "Unforgettable," "Take a Look"

The daughter of legendary pop crooner Nat "King" Cole, Natalie Cole has enjoyed a distinguished, if erratic, recording career. Issuing her first recordings in the mid-1970s, Cole initially pursued a spirited, gospel-infused sound heavily influenced by R&B legend Aretha Franklin. Overcoming a host of personal problems during the early 1980s, Cole continued performing in a pop and R&B vein before switching in the early 1990s to orchestrated pop tinged with jazz—the type of sophisticated music associated with her late father. In spite of this new focus on pop styles of the past, Cole maintained her commercial success, earning multiple Grammy Awards for an album dedicated to her father's memory, *Unforgettable: With Love* (1991). Although writers have sometimes criticized her latter-day style as too sedate, Cole has preserved her warm, expressive voice and phrasing. In 2002 she broadened her artistic horizons further, recording an album for the jazz-oriented Verve label that some critics regard as her finest.

R&B Beginnings

Raised in a luxurious neighborhood in Los Angeles, Cole made her stage debut performing with her father as a child in 1962. In her teens she longed to embark upon an artistic career but was deterred by her mother, singer Maria Cole, who insisted that she attend college. After graduating with a degree in child psychology from the University of Massachusetts at Amherst in 1972, Cole worked as a waitress and performed in nightclubs. During a 1974 engagement at the Chicago club Mr. Kelley's, Cole met producers Marvin Yancey and Chuck Jackson, who oversaw writing and production work on her debut album, *Inseparable* (1975). Featuring the joyous, piano-driven hit, "This Will Be," as well as the creamy title ballad, the album staked Cole's claim as an impassioned soul singer rooted in Franklin's flamboyant gospel tradition. Marrying

Spot Light | *Unforgettable: With Love*

By the early 1990s, after nearly two decades of hit recordings, Natalie Cole had established a reputation as a respected, successful R&B singer. Still, her career had long been hampered by critical comparisons to other R&B vocalists—notably Aretha Franklin and Chaka Khan—as well as the shadow of her famous father, pop legend Nat "King" Cole. Ironically, it was through delving into her father's work that Cole was finally able to forge her own identity as a vocalist. *Unforgettable: With Love* (1991), a collection of songs made famous by her father, became the most successful album of Cole's career, climbing to the top of the Pop Albums chart. On lushly arranged songs such as "The Very Thought of You" and "Mona Lisa," Cole reveals herself as a first-rate stylist, her diction, pitch, and lyrical interpretation confident and mature. On rhythmic songs such as "Route 66" she displays a finely honed sense of swing and timing. The album is especially notable, however, for the title track, on which Cole "duets" with her father, electronically layering her vocal over his original performance. A measure of how far recording technology has advanced since the elder Cole originally hit with "Unforgettable" in 1952, the performance garnered much publicity and spurred sales of the album past the 5 million mark. Although some critics complained that the album's string arrangements were watery and without distinction, *Unforgettable: With Love* revived Cole's career, earning Grammy Awards for Album of the Year and Best Traditional Pop Recording.

Yancey, Cole continued having hits into the 1980s, although her career was curtailed during this period by a severe drug dependency—described in honest, unsettling detail in her 2000 autobiography, *Angel on My Shoulder*. By 1984 Cole had conquered drugs and resumed her recording career, entering her second marriage with musician Andre Fischer. Fischer spearheaded Cole's musical shift toward jazz and pop, producing her breakthrough album, *Unforgettable: With Love* (1991).

Gaining Stardom through Pop and Jazz

Having found a distinct musical voice through the success of *Unforgettable: With Love*, Cole continued on the same path, recording another set of pop and jazz standards with *Take a Look* (1993). In many respects *Take a Look* qualifies as the equal of its predecessor, with Cole displaying intelligence in song selection and ease in navigating a range of pop styles. One of the album's most impressive moments is Cole's treatment of the title song, first recorded by her one-time musical idol, Aretha Franklin, in 1964. A biting critique of the human capacity for cruelty, "Take a Look" builds slowly through Cole's interpretation, reaching a powerful climax in which her emotiveness draws out the song's outrage and sadness. Although Cole spent the majority of the 1990s recording in the same pop-jazz style, *Snowfall on the Sahara* (1999) is a notable exception, a collection of blues and soul-based material. Tackling classics such as rock pioneer Bob Dylan's frequently recorded "Gotta Serve Somebody" and soul singer Lorraine Ellison's dramatic 1966 classic "Stay with Me," Cole again demonstrates her range and versatility.

Cole's signing with the reputed jazz label, Verve, in 2002 suggests a desire to delve deeper into jazz territory, to stake her claim as a stylist on a par with famed singers of the past such as Billie Holiday and Dinah Washington. While *Ask a Woman Who Knows* (2002) does not approach the finest work of those performers, it ranks as one of Cole's richest and most rewarding efforts, a collection that finds the singer in total command of her voice and craft. Featuring a billowing horn arrangement, the title track—a song often associated with Washington—is one of the album's strongest. Cole's thoughtful, incisive interpretation is balanced by the precision of an all-star quintet that includes pianist Joe Sample and bassist Christian McBride. While some critics observed that the album's string arrangements often veer toward bland "cocktail jazz," *Ask a Woman Who Knows* emerges as an admirable, impressive new artistic direction for Cole, proving that, at age fifty-two, the singer remains in her vocal prime.

Over the course of a long career, Cole has witnessed her share of triumph and loss—both professional and personal. Beginning as an R&B vocalist molded in the manner of Aretha Franklin, Cole evolved by the early 1990s into a jazz and pop singer of the highest order, honoring her father's memory with her successful album *Unforgettable: With Love*. In the early 2000s Cole embarked upon a deeper exploration of jazz terrain with satisfying results.

SELECTIVE DISCOGRAPHY: *Inseparable* (Capitol, 1975); *Thankful* (Capitol, 1977); *Everlasting* (Elektra, 1987); *Unforgettable: With Love* (Elektra, 1991); *Take a Look* (Elektra, 1993); *Stardust* (Elektra, 1996); *Snowfall on the Sahara* (Elektra, 1999); *Ask a Woman Who Knows* (Verve, 2002).

BIBLIOGRAPHY: N. Cole with D. Diehl, *Angel on My Shoulder: An Autobiography* (New York, 2000).

WEBSITE: www.nataliecole.com.

DAVID FREELAND

PAULA COLE

Born: Rockport, Massachusetts, 5 April 1968

Genre: Rock

Best-selling album since 1990: *This Fire* (1996)

Hit songs since 1990: "Where Have All the Cowboys Gone?" "I Don't Want to Wait," "Me"

The classically trained multi-instrumentalist Paula Cole is perhaps best known for writing the song "I Don't Want to Wait," which became the theme song for the popular Warner Bros. network teen soap opera *Dawson's Creek*.

Cole had a somewhat unconventional childhood; her mother was a visual artist and her father an entomologist who also played bass in a polka band. She officially started her musical career in Boston at the prestigious Berklee College of Music, studying voice. Initially, she thought she would become a jazz singer, but she began writing songs. After graduating, she moved to San Francisco and eventually played her songs for Terry Ellis, the president of the now-defunct Imago Records. He quickly signed her, passed on her album to Peter Gabriel, and she was asked to tour with him in 1992–1993 in support of his album *Us*.

After the release of her thoughtful, introspective debut album *Harbinger* (1994), which received some airplay on the country's Adult Album Alternative stations, the piano-playing former choirgirl Paula Cole broke through with the multiplatinum album *This Fire* (1996), which earned her seven Grammy nominations, including the distinctive Producer of the Year. It was the first time a woman received that honor in Grammy Award history. Cole also won a Grammy for Best New Artist, disproving the dreaded sophomore slump. "I Don't Want to Wait," a single from the album, was picked up as the theme song for *Dawson's Creek* shortly after its release. *The New York Times* called her "a rising talent with tremendous artistic potential," while *Entertainment Weekly* praised Cole as "a feisty poet with a soaring voice and a funky groove."

Sultry, feminist, and dramatic, with a powerful voice that can climb from a whisper to a near scream, Cole exercises the full range of the piano's capabilities, creating percussive, explosive songs on *This Fire*. Cole's sense of freedom and spirituality pervades her songs. In the personal anthem "Me," she admits that she is her own worst enemy, a sentiment that many young women can relate to, and sings, "It's me who is too weak / And me who is too shy / To ask for the thing I love." Lyrics such as those earned her a spot on the groundbreaking Lilith Fair tour in the mid-1990s.

The release of her third album, *Amen* (1999), which she also produced, suffered from overwrought, didactic songwriting that was not nearly as commercially successful and did not come close to the overwhelming beauty of *This Fire*.

Paula Cole is an unusual talent, with an uncompromising streak, a powerful voice, and a maestrolike command of the piano.

SELECTIVE DISCOGRAPHY: *Harbinger* (Columbia, 1994); *This Fire* (Columbia, 1996); *Amen* (Columbia, 1999).

WEBSITE: www.paulacole.com.

CARRIE HAVRANEK

COLLECTIVE SOUL

Formed: 1993, Stockbridge, Georgia

Members: Ross Childress, guitar (born Stockbridge, Georgia, 8 September 1970); Shane Evans, drums (born Stockbridge, Georgia, 26 April 1970); Dean Roland, guitar (born Stockbridge, Georgia, 10 October 1972); Ed Roland, lead vocals, guitar (born Grandview, Texas, 3 August 1963); Will Turpin, vocals, bass (born Fairbanks, Alaska, 8 February 1971).

Genre: Rock

Best-selling album since 1990: *Collective Soul* (1995)

Hit songs since 1990: "Shine," "World I Know," "December"

Collective Soul earned a reputation in the mid-1990s as a hard rock band with driving guitar riffs and striking melodies. After the success of their hit song "Shine" from the album *Hints, Allegations, and Things Left Unsaid* (1994), Collective Soul gained widespread attention by performing at Woodstock '94 and touring with Aerosmith and Van Halen. Their second album, *Collective Soul* (1995), contains the hits "The World I Know" and "December"; the latter was named Album Rock Song of the Year by *Billboard*. Ed Roland, the principal songwriter for the band, resurrected guitar rock of the 1970s with contemporary textures. Although the band's popularity diminished after their initial splash of success, Collective Soul continued to experiment with a hard-rock aesthetic.

The group's songwriter, Ed Roland, grew up in a strict household and was discouraged from pursuing a musical career. Nevertheless, Roland moved away from his hometown of Stockbridge, Georgia, in order to study guitar at the Berklee College of Music. Plagued by financial difficulties, Roland returned to Stockbridge, where he worked at a local recording studio and formed a band that performed for many years without any major success.

In 1993 the song "Shine" was picked up by college radio stations and was soon being played on major rock stations in Atlanta. The EP *Hints, Allegations, and Things Left Unsaid*, originally intended as a songwriting demo, was re-released by Atlantic Records, and the hastily formed Collective Soul was soon performing at large venues such as Woodstock '94 and various arena tours. "Shine," which was eventually named *Billboard*'s number one Hot Album Rock Track of 1994, exemplified the band's musical approach in several ways: a reliance on guitar-driven riffs, unique changes in textures, and anthemlike melodies, as exemplified in the chorus, "Oh, heaven let your light shine down." A melodic guitar introduction mirrors the vocal line, which then leads into an aggressive distorted guitar riff coupled with the ubiquitous exclamation, "Yeah!" The double-time guitar solo and bridge reveals the influence of 1970s rock, but the song unexpectedly returns to the distorted riff, a strategy that evinces careful attention to structural details.

Collective Soul returned to the recording studio and quickly produced their eponymous second album in 1995. The song "December," with its descending bass progression and harmonic palate, exhibits a relaxed musical approach and highlights the lyrics, which range from the poetic ("Don't throw away your basic needs—ambience and vanity") to the awkward ("December promise," with the emphasis on *December*) The ballad "The World I Know" begins with an acoustic guitar and showcases tasteful string orchestration. The full chorus is withheld until the second iteration, producing a yearning quality that is poignantly reflected in the lyrics.

Collective Soul became embroiled in a lawsuit with their manager, Bill Richardson. After prolonged litigation, the band retreated to Stockbridge, rented a cabin, and began writing songs for their next album. The result of these efforts, *Disciplined Breakdown* (1997), was more pop-oriented, with harmonic progressions that felt awkward and forced. Collective Soul returned to their signature brand of rock in the subsequent albums, *Dosage* (1999) and *Blender* (2000).

Collective Soul forged a sound that embraced guitar-rock with melodic vocal lines. Their songs conjured images of the guitar hero in "Heavy" and evoked 1970s rock groups in "Gel" and "Next Homecoming." Aside from *Disciplined*

Breakdown, Collective Soul largely eschewed the guitar pop embodied by the Spin Doctors or Goo Goo Dolls. In so doing, they crafted songs that expanded formal expectations while maintaining a coherent approach through their economic lyrics and riff-driven structure.

SELECTIVE DISCOGRAPHY: *Hints, Allegations, and Things Left Unsaid* (Atlantic, 1994); *Collective Soul* (Atlantic, 1995); *Disciplined Breakdown* (Atlantic, 1997); *Dosage* (Atlantic, 1999); *Blender* (Atlantic, 2000); *7even Year Itch: The Greatest Hits, 1994–2001* (Atlantic, 2001).

WEBSITE: www.collectivesoul.com.

WYNN YAMAMI

PHIL COLLINS

Born: Phillip Collins; Chiswick, London, England, 31 January 1951

Genre: Rock, Pop

Best-selling album since 1990: *Testify* (2002)

Hit songs since 1990: "Can't Stop Loving You," "Through My Eyes," "You'll Be in My Heart"

With a prolific and successful solo career, singer/drummer Phil Collins transcended the chart and sales triumphs of his former progressive-rock band, Genesis, in the late 1980s. It was a surprise to everyone, including Collins himself. Unlike the complex rock that Genesis specialized in, Collins carved out a niche as a genteel adult-contemporary pop crooner who incorporated R&B and funk influences.

Young Roots

Collins had an early start in entertainment. As a child he was so enamored of playing the drums, his parents bought him a drum kit. Later he appeared in the London West End stage production of *Oliver* (1964) as "the Artful Dodger." Collins was also an extra in the Beatles movie *A Hard Day's Night* (1964). Following minor stints with local bands Hickory and Flaming Youth, Collins broke into the major leagues when he responded to an ad in *Melody Maker* and auditioned for the job as the drummer for Genesis in 1970.

Collins played drums on the band's tours and next five albums: *Nursery Cryme* (1971), *Foxtrot* (1972), *Genesis Live* (1973), *Selling England by the Pound* (1973), and the double album *The Lamb Lies Down on Broadway* (1974). Collins was a major part of the band's evolution as a progressive rock group. The music was increasingly sophisticated, as the lyrics became complex and dark.

But in May 1975, after a show at St. Etienne, France, lead singer Peter Gabriel announced he was leaving the band for personal reasons and launching his own solo career. Although Genesis auditioned hundreds of singers, band members expressed most confidence in Collins.

Though less theatrical than Gabriel, Collins possessed a more soulful voice. With Collins at the helm, the band surprised everyone with its increasing recording and touring success, especially cynics who doubted Genesis sans Gabriel would work. *And Then There Were Three* (1978) went gold, as did *Duke* (1980).

Solo Turns

The next year, Collins released his first solo album, *Face Value* (1981), which was an immediate success. The first single, "In the Air Tonight," shot to number one on the English charts. "I Missed Again" was another hit single.

For Collins the album was more than just his first solo outing. As a first-time songwriter he realized success. "I thought, 'This is a dream, this can't be happening to me.' It was only an album of demos—literally," Collins told the *Washington Post* in 1987. "What's on the record is my demos with just a little bit of tarting up. And the lyrics to 'In the Air' were essentially improvised. I just opened my mouth at home to see what a voice would sound like on top of those chords, and those were the words that came out. I'm constantly being surprised." Collins did not deny that many songs were personal as he was in the process of a divorce.

Collins followed with even more successful albums: *Hello, I Must Be Going!* (1982) and *No Jacket Required* (1985), which has sold more than 12 million copies and won a Grammy for Album of the Year. On the former, the big hit was his cover of the Motown trio Supremes' "You Can't Hurry Love," which proved Collins's appreciation for R&B had not diminished. Again, the album took on personal, sometimes angry themes from Collins's life. He approached several songs from the perspective of looking back on his divorce, including "I Don't Care Anymore," "Do You Know, Do You Care?," and "I Cannot Believe It's True."

Reaching the Top

Collins reached his artistic peak on *No Jacket Required*, fully incorporating the big horn brassy sound into hits like "One More Night," "Sussudio," and "Don't Lose My Number." Collins by now was seemingly everywhere thanks to his work with Genesis and his own chart hits. He won a Grammy Award for the song "Against All Odds" (1984) from the hit movie by the same name.

On . . . *But Seriously* (1989), he downplayed drum machines and keyboards in favor of live instrumentation. The compact disc produced four hit singles including "Hang in Long Enough" and "Find a Way to My Heart." Also notable was Collins's searing, gospel-influenced ballad "I Wish It Would Rain Down," which features guitar hero Eric Clapton.

Collins stayed busy with Genesis albums and tours in the year before his next work, *Both Sides* (1993). With dark tones and somber reflections, the album resembles the wistful *Face Value*. On songs like "There's a Place for Us," "I've Forgotten Everything," and "Can't Turn Back the Years," Collins appeared to be entering a more mature, philosophical period. In 1995 he announced he was leaving Genesis permanently. *Dance into the Light* (1996) is a lighter affair with more R&B, dance-pop influenced material.

Collins kept working at a blistering pace though he began slipping from the pop culture radar. He assembled his Phil Collins Big band to produce *A Hot Night in Paris* (1999) and kept working on other projects including the popular *Tarzan* (1999) soundtrack, which provided a massive boost to Collins's pop resurgence.

Testify (2002) continues the maturing theme in *Both Sides*, with songs about solace and solitude, breakups and fatherhood. Hits include "Can't Stop Loving You" and "Through My Eyes." Collins made a smooth transition from heading the supergroup Genesis in the 1970s to his emergence as a superstar in the 1980s, all while working as a prolific songwriter and producer. While critical praise was moderate, his commercial success was massive (250 million album sales), and insured that his artistic influence would be felt for generations.

SELECTIVE DISCOGRAPHY: *Face Value* (Atlantic, 1981); *Hello, I Must Be Going!* (Atlantic, 1982); *No Jacket Required* (Atlantic, 1985); *. . . But Seriously* (Atlantic, 1989); *Both Sides* (Atlantic, 1993); *Dance into the Light* (Atlantic, 1996); *A Hot Night in Paris* (Atlantic, 1999); *Testify* (Atlantic, 2002). **With Genesis:** *Selling England by the Pound*(Atco, 1973); *The Lamb Lies Down on Broadway* (Atco, 1974); *And Then There Were Three* (Atlantic, 1978); *Abacab* (Atlantic, 1981). **Soundtracks:** *Against All Odds* (Atlantic, 1984); *Tarzan: An Original Walt Disney Records Soundtrack* (Universal/ Walt Disney, 1999).

RAMIRO BURR

SHAWN COLVIN

Born: Vermillion, South Dakota, 10 January 1956

Genre: Folk

Best-selling album since 1990: *A Few Small Repairs* (1996)

Hit songs since 1990: "Steady On," "Sunny Came Home," "Nothin' On Me"

Shawn Colvin is a folk-influenced singer/songwriter who toured the Northeast folk music circuit until she landed a recording deal with Columbia Records in 1987. Her debut album, *Steady On,* earned her fans with both critics and the general public, along with a Grammy Award for Best Contemporary Folk Recording.

The sweet-voiced Colvin is considered a folk-pop musician who became well known with her successful album *A Few Small Repairs* (1996). Co-produced and co-written with her longtime collaborator, the multi-instrumentalist John Leventhal, *A Few Small Repairs* has been called the "breakup album" by critics because Colvin wrote it on the heels of her divorce from her first husband, Simon Tassano. *A Few Small Repairs* won two Grammy Awards, including Record of the Year and Song of the Year for the hit "Sunny Came Home."

Colvin grew up in the big sky country of South Dakota and learned the guitar by age ten. Like many songwriters of her generation, she was influenced by the Beatles, but because of her folk leanings, she also found inspiration in Joni Mitchell and Laura Nyro. She attended college but dropped out and began to pursue a career in music, setting her sights on the folk music scene in the Northeast. In 1987 she signed with Columbia Records and soon after produced her major-label album debut, *Steady On* (1989), which earned her a Grammy in 1990 for Best Contemporary Folk Artist. The acclaim continued with two more Grammy nominations for *Fat City* (1992) and another for *Cover Girl* (1994), a tribute to her apprentice days.

Before the release of *A Few Small Repairs* (1996), Colvin had a small folk music following. Her Grammy-winning album catapulted her into the spotlight and earned her raves. The wise and empowering story-songs examine heartbreak and disappointment and avoid clichés in favor of exploring a full, complex range of emotions. From the rocking, angry "Get Out of This House" to the unfettered self-confidence of "Nothin' on Me" to the smash single "Sunny Came Home," with its irresistible chorus, it is Colvin's best effort.

Colvin took a few years off after *A Few Small Repairs*, remarried after the difficult divorce, and had a baby. *A Whole New You* (2001), another album co-written with and co-produced by John Leventhal, finds Colvin singing with a renewed zest. In the title track's chorus, she marvels, "Go and wish on every star that's fallen / Shake your head in wonder when it's all too good to be true / Like a whole new you." Despite its second-person orientation, it could easily be read as a personal journal entry or a memo to herself, so drastic were the life changes that ensued from the success of *A Few Small Repairs*.

Shawn Colvin has carved a niche for herself as a thoughtful, clear-eyed songwriter with a honeyed voice; she has achieved success in the world of mainstream pop music without losing her integrity or her love of the craft.

SELECTIVE DISCOGRAPHY: *Steady On* (Columbia, 1989); *Fat City* (Columbia, 1992); *Cover Girl* (Columbia, 1994); *A Few Small Repairs* (Columbia, 1996); *Whole New You* (Columbia, 2001).

CARRIE HAVRANEK

SEAN COMBS

Born: Harlem, New York, 4 November 1970

Genre: Rap

Best-selling album since 1990: *No Way Out* (1997)

Hit songs since 1990: "I'll Be Missing You," "It's All about the Benjamins," "I Need a Girl Pt. 1"

Sean "P. Diddy" Combs [AP/WIDE WORLD PHOTOS]

One of hip-hop's most durable and versatile talents, Sean "P. Diddy" Combs (formerly "Puff Daddy"), is a producer, rapper, businessman, and fashion designer. He embodies the entrepreneurial spirit and swagger that has made hip-hop one of entertainment's most profitable industries.

Sean Combs was born in Harlem, in upper Manhattan, to Janice and Melvin Combs. Melvin, a street hustler, was murdered when Combs was three years old, and his mother had to work several jobs to care for him. When Combs was twelve years old, Janice Combs managed to move the family to Mount Vernon, New York, a suburb of Manhattan. Combs played high school football for Mount St. Michael Academy, earning the nickname "Puffy" because he used to "puff" out his chest to make himself appear larger.

Combs became interested in hip-hop and began dancing in music videos. He soon convinced his fellow Mount Vernon resident and rap star Heavy D to secure him an internship at his label, Uptown Records, then run by Andre Harrell. Combs enrolled in Howard University in Washington, D.C., and began interning at Uptown Records. While at Howard, he made a name for himself as a campus party promoter and commuted to his Manhattan internship several times a week on the train.

Combs soon dropped out of Howard to focus on his career. With a knack for promoting, styling, and selecting new talent, Combs vaulted through the company ranks to become vice president of A&R (artist and repertoire) at the age of nineteen. Before Combs most R&B acts were slickly styled and dressed in formal outfits. Combs was one of the first executives to meld hip-hop styling with R&B music. The Uptown Records acts Jodeci and Mary J. Blige wore baggy jeans and backward-turned baseball caps while belting soulful, gospel-influenced vocals over hip-hop beats. The experiment worked. Jodeci and Mary J. Blige's albums went platinum.

Combs has shown as much of a talent for personal and legal controversies as for professional success. His first setback was a celebrity basketball game he and nine other promoters (including Heavy D) oversold at City College of New York in 1991. Fans without seats stampeded the arena, resulting in the deaths of nine young people. In 1999 Combs and Heavy D were found 50 percent responsible for the tragedy, sharing liability with City College of New York.

Professionally the young Combs was becoming too powerful and ambitious for the small Uptown Records. Harrell fired him at the tender age of twenty-one. Combs quickly rebounded, landing a distribution deal for his own label, Bad Boy Entertainment, backed by Arista Records. He signed a gravel-voiced rapper named Craig Mack and a quick-witted MC named Biggie Smalls from Brooklyn. Mack scored a hit in the summer of 1994 with "Flava in Ya Ear" but Smalls, later known as Notorious B.I.G. for trademark reasons, was Combs's first Bad Boy superstar. As executive producer of B.I.G.'s debut album, *Ready to Die* (1994), Combs melded B.I.G.'s storytelling prowess with a smooth R&B sound, sampled from records like the Isley Brothers' "Between the Sheets" and Mtume's "Juicy." B.I.G.'s materialistic lyrics reflected the Clinton-era economic boom and the consummation of the hip-hop dream. The album was a critical and commercial success, helping to establish Bad Boy as a formidable label. Combs's expanded roster included platinum R&B acts Total, 112, Faith Evans, the rap trio the LOX, and a lazy-tongued MC named Ma$e.

In 1996 Combs was named ASCAP's Songwriter of the Year. The success of Bad Boy enabled Combs to bolster his relationship with Arista Records. Bad Boy and Arista formed a joint venture, and Combs pocketed a reported $6 million and secured a $50-million line of credit for the label. Combs was also expanding his artistic horizons. He had already supported B.I.G. onstage as a "hype man," cheering on the crowd and dancing on stage, and was on the verge of becoming a rap star in his own right. B.I.G. became Combs's artist manager, and Puffy rhymed on tracks on B.I.G.'s double disc sophomore album, *Life after Death* (1997). On March 9, 1997, Combs suffered a devastating blow when Notorious B.I.G. was murdered in Los Angeles. Combs released a tribute song, "I'll Be Missing You," based on the Police's "Every Breath You Take." The song hit number one on the pop charts. In 1998 Combs won the Best Rap Performance by a Duo or Group Grammy for the song. The album that spawned that single, *No Way Out* (1997), won the 1998 Grammy for Best Rap Album and confirmed Combs as Bad Boy's new superstar. Combs branched out as a producer beyond the Bad Boy family, helming hits for Mariah Carey ("Honey") and even Aretha Franklin ("Never Leave You Again"). Also that year Bad Boy created its next rap phenomenon when Ma$e's debut album, *Harlem World* (1998), went quadruple platinum.

But just as Bad Boy Records reached its strongest point, the empire began to crack with a string of setbacks. Combs's solo follow-up, *Forever* (1999), sold 1 million copies in the United States, but the media considered it a flop next to the sevenfold platinum run of *No Way Out*. Ma$e relinquished his rap career and moved back to Atlanta to become a preacher. In 1999 Combs faced his second major legal problem for allegedly beating Interscope Records executive Steve Stoute. The conflict centered on a music video of one of Stoute's artists, Nas. Stoute contended in court documents that Combs was angry over his cameo in Nas's "Hate Me Now" video. Combs was convicted of second-degree harassment and was sentenced to a one-day anger-management class.

At the same time his platinum act the LOX were ironically clamoring to be released from Bad Boy, complaining in public forums that Combs's and Bad Boy's image was too tame. Combs released the LOX but gained another highly celebrated rapper, MC Shyne, who was touted as the next Notorious B.I.G. With his slight lisp, he sounded like the late rapper. The music industry saw Shyne as Combs's and Bad Boy's return ticket to greatness.

Instead, Shyne was involved in one of the largest controversies of Combs's life. In December 1999, Combs, Shyne, and Combs's then-girlfriend, actress/singer Jennifer Lopez, were at the Manhattan disco, Club New York. Three people at the nightclub were shot. Police pursued Combs's car and found an unregistered gun. Shyne was convicted and sentenced to fifteen years. Combs, however, was acquitted of all charges. Within days of the decision, Combs announced that he was officially changing his stage moniker from Puff Daddy to P. Diddy.

Combs's career turned around once again. Bad Boy released a hit compilation, *The Saga Continues* (2001). The album includes "Bad Boy for Life," in which Combs defiantly answers criticism that he hires ghostwriters to create his lyrics: "Who cares if I write rhymes? / I write checks." The video, filled with cameos from movie actor Ben Stiller to basketball player Shaquille O'Neal, was an

MTV staple. Bad Boy pulled off another hit with the brazenly titled *We Invented the Remix* (2002). He also re-established himself as a solo artist. Two singles, "I Need a Girl Pt. 1," with R&B star Usher, and the remix "I Need A Girl Pt. 2," featuring Ginuwine, were major successes.

In the midst of this resurgence, Bad Boy experienced more roster and distribution challenges. Arista and Bad Boy severed their relationship, leaving Combs to search for a new partnership. In the process, Faith Evans decided to sign directly with Arista. 112 tried to sign with Def Jam, but Combs worked out a compromise in which Bad Boy and Def Jam shared the group. In 2003 Combs found a new home for Bad Boy, under Universal Records, with a roster that includes the Loon, Black Rob, singer Cherie Dennis, the pop group Dream, 112, rapper Foxy Brown, and the biggest star of all, Combs.

SELECTIVE DISCOGRAPHY: *No Way Out* (Bad Boy, 1997); *Forever* (Bad Boy, 1999).

DARA COOK

COMMON

Born: Lonnie Rashid Lynn; Chicago, Illinois, 13 March 1972

Genre: Hip-Hop

Best-selling album since 1990: *Like Water for Chocolate* (2000)

Hit songs since 1990: "Reminding Me (of Sef)," "One Nine Nine Nine"

Emerging from Chicago in the early 1990s, Common (then known as Common Sense) was an energetic MC who showed that the Midwest could compete with the East Coast and West Coast styles that dominated hip-hop at that time. Over the course of his career, he has developed an increasingly incisive, spiritual, and often poignant writing style, without losing the quick wit and substantial bravado that were the source of his initial appeal.

The son of a schoolteacher (now principal) and a professional basketball player, Common first presented himself as a so-called "battle rapper," an MC who excels in writing rhymes that use creative wordplay to entertainingly insult real and potential rivals. His first album, *Can I Borrow a Dollar?* (1992), was primarily concerned with this theme, as well as with promoting the city of Chicago as an underappreciated center of hip-hop music. His rhymes were delivered to the accompaniment of jazz-influenced rhythms and melodies assembled by producer No I.D. from segments of previously recorded music known as samples.

Common [AP/WIDE WORLD PHOTOS]

Common's second album, *Resurrection* (1994), shows a more political and bohemian bent. It was this album that cemented his reputation with hip-hop listeners, particularly the single, "i used to love h.e.r.," a touchingly detailed first-person reminiscence of the blossoming of a childhood romance into mature love and heartbreak. In the last line of the song, the object of his affection is revealed to be hip-hop itself; "h.e.r." stands for "Hip-hop in its Essence and Reality." "i used to love h.e.r." is considered to be a classic by hip-hop insiders.

The song also created some controversy when Los Angeles rapper Ice Cube took offense at a line that referred to his former group N.W.A. (Niggas with Attitude), which had popularized so-called "Gangsta Rap" in the late 1980s. Ice Cube responded with a few vicious lines in the song "Westside Slaughterhouse" (1995), to which Common replied with a single, "The Bitch in Yoo" (1996). Although the song never saw wide release, its intensely detailed attack on Ice Cube impressed fans of the competitive insult ("dissing") tradition, while startling Common's newer listeners, who had come to see him as a relaxed intellectual.

After dropping the "Sense" from his name due to threatened legal action from a similarly named reggae band, Common released his next album, *One Day It'll All Make Sense* (1997). The album's highlight is the single

"Retrospect for Life," which speaks of his misgivings about the abortion of a child he had fathered. The song is filled with heartbreaking details, such as the fact that he "bought a book of African names / in case our minds changed." The apparent contradictions between this sort of self-conscious poetry and the ego-driven outrageousness of his other songs became more of a factor with the release of this album. He was particularly criticized for his frequent use of homophobic epithets. Unlike other artists who have been subject to similar accusations, however, these critiques largely emerged from his own fan base, who saw this tendency as being out of step with his other, more progressive political views.

This period in Common's career brought many changes. In 1999 he left his record label, Relativity, to sign with MCA, a company that was rapidly developing a reputation as a home for the Philadelphia-based "neo-soul" movement, which looked back to an earlier generation of African-American musicians, such as Stevie Wonder and Donny Hathaway, for its inspiration. The movement is personified by the "hip-hop band" the Roots, who favor the use of live instruments rather than digital sampling. It was largely as a result of his association with the Roots that Common himself began to move away from the sample-based production of his earlier work with No I.D. At this time, he also left his Midwestern home to move to New York, a controversial decision for one who many felt personified Chicago hip-hop.

In a guest appearance on the Roots's song "Act Two (Love of My Life)" (1999), Common seems to sum up these developments in his career, audience, and relationship to hip-hop itself: "Beside God and family, you my life's jewel / Like that, y'all: hip-hop . . . hip-hop . . . hip-hop. . . ."

His literary goals and embrace of live instrumentation continued with his first MCA album, *Like Water for Chocolate* (2000), produced by Roots drummer and bandleader Ahmir "?uestlove" Thompson. On it, he displays his thoughtful, poignant style, particularly on "Song for Assata," dedicated to the Black Liberation Army activist and exile Assata Shakur.

Common's fifth album, *Electric Circus* (2002), demonstrates his ongoing commitment to experimentation. Taking a page from the R&B tradition, the album's lyrics focus on the relationship between romantic love and spirituality. Musically, *Electric Circus* takes full advantage of the opportunities afforded by the use of live instrumentation; it even includes a number of extended instrumental improvisations, a gesture that is totally unprecedented in hip-hop music.

Since the beginning of his career, Common has been recognized as an artist who embraces creativity in his music, lyrics, and public persona. From his early days as an intelligent braggart to his later explorations of spirituality, love, and adulthood, he has always taken it upon himself to explore uncharted territory.

SELECTIVE DISCOGRAPHY: *Can I Borrow a Dollar?* (Relativity, 1992); *Resurrection* (Relativity, 1994); *One Day It'll All Make Sense* (Relativity, 1997); *Like Water for Chocolate* (MCA, 2000); *Electric Circus* (MCA, 2002).

JOE SCHLOSS

HARRY CONNICK JR.

Born: New Orleans, Louisiana, 11 September 1967

Genre: Jazz, Vocal

Best-selling album since 1990: *Music from the Motion Picture When Harry Met Sally . . .* (1989)

Hit songs since 1990: "(I Could Only) Whisper Your Name," "A Wink and a Smile"

Jazz pianist, singer, and actor Harry Connick Jr. emerged from the music scene in New Orleans at the tender age of twenty-two with the voice and physical presence of a jazz singer from a bygone era. With more than a dozen records to his name since his debut in 1987, Connick has become one of the more acclaimed jazz singers and performers of the 1990s. He has released four multiplatinum albums, three platinum albums, and three gold albums. Connick has been awarded two Grammy Awards and has garnered both an Academy Award nomination and Golden Globe nomination for his film roles. Although he initially seemed like just a throwback to the jazz crooner days of Frank Sinatra and the Rat Pack with his love of swing, dreamboat looks, and Sinatra-like voice, Connick has expanded his repertoire to include funk rock, a highly successful Christmas album, and a Tony Award nomination for a Broadway score.

A Prodigy in the Making

Connick puts on a polished, energetic, and entertaining live performance. He is a virtuoso who often trades instruments with his band members, jokes with them, and eggs them on midsong, like an old-school jazz singer. His parents, both music lovers, put themselves through law school by running a record shop in New Orleans. Connick began to learn piano at the young age of three; by the time he turned five he was skilled enough to play "The Star-Spangled Banner" at his father's inauguration as New Orleans district attorney. When he was young, he was able to get into the many clubs and saloons on the legendary

Spot Light | Music from the Motion Picture When Harry Met Sally . . .

When director Rob Reiner asked Harry Connick Jr. to reinterpret a handful of jazz standards to accompany his romantic comedy *When Harry Met Sally . . .* (1989), nobody knew that the film would become a monster hit, both launching actress Meg Ryan's career and earning Connick a Grammy Award for Best Jazz Vocal Performance. From the trill of the woodwinds and the first blast of trumpet on the lead-off tune "It Had to Be You" to his frenzied take on "Stompin' at the Savoy," Connick tapped into America's dormant love of jazz. *When Harry Met Sally . . .* made Connick synonymous with big-band jazz standards and with a vocal style that at times is eerily reminiscent of Frank Sinatra. Connick handled each classic standard with panache and his distinct melodic style.

Bourbon Street, and he often slipped into situations where he could play. Early on he built a reputation as a prodigy and even got the opportunity to study at the New Orleans Center for Creative Arts with accomplished pianist Ellis Marsalis, father of well-respected jazz musicians Wynton and Branford Marsalis.

On his 1987 self-titled, debut album, Connick features a jazz trio with Ron Carter on bass. He released another album, *20* (1998), which introduced the world to his voice. It was the inclusion of his music in the film *When Harry Met Sally . . .* (1989) that put him on the musical map. Director Rob Reiner asked Connick to contribute to the score, and the big-band recording of old classics was a platinum-selling success that turned him into a household name. He followed up the soundtrack with the simultaneous release of two albums, the instrumental *Lofty's Roach Souffle* (1990) and the jazz-influenced *We Are in Love*. The former has sold more than 2 million copies and is replete with ballads such as the tale of slow heartbreak, "Drifting," and upbeat, swinging tunes like "Recipe for Love," which prove he could indeed write his own material. Interspersed between his own material are covers worth noting: a double-time version of Cole Porter's "It's All Right with Me" and a contemplative take on the standard "A Nightingale Sang in Berkeley Square."

Style *and* Substance

Connick had hit his mark with audiences for his keen jazz sensibility. For all his suaveness, slick wardrobe, shiny shoes, and flashy skills in concerts, where he is known to crack jokes and tap dance midsong, Connick is indeed a serious musician. After the success of *When Harry Met Sally . . .* he quickly recorded a few more albums, including the jazz-ragtime-blues mélange of original compositions performed by his stable of musicians, *Blue Light, Red Light* (1991). One year later, *25* followed, a collection of covers of classic blues, folk, and jazz tunes—from Duke Ellington's "Caravan" and the Hoagy Carmichael tune "Stardust" to "Muskrat Ramble"—all performed on solo piano. The early 1990s were a busy time for Connick between touring and releasing a handful of albums, including a smash success Christmas album, *When My Heart Finds Christmas* (1993) and the funk-soul-jazz hybrid *She* (1994), the latter of which peaked in the *Billboard* Top 20. A few years later he followed with *Star Turtle*, an album not nearly as successful as *She*, and a further deviation from his jazz roots. Connick then devoted an entire album to love, *To See You* (1997), on which he wrote, played, and orchestrated all ten ballads. Two years later, perhaps getting an itch to return to his love of jazz, Connick went back into the studio with his big band and recorded a mix of covers and originals, *Come by Me* (1999).

Almost as soon as he gained fame as a singer he began to appear in films. He appeared in *Memphis Belle* (1990), *Little Man Tate* (1991), and as a serial killer in the thriller *Copycat* (1995). He also appeared in the blockbuster hit *Independence Day* (1996) and co-starred with Sandra Bullock in *Hope Floats* (1998). In 2002 he made his television debut as a recurring character on the popular television comedy *Will & Grace*.

Connick is the father of three girls and is married to ex-model Jill Goodacre. His skills as a pianist, singer, and actor showcase his depth and versatility, and his albums have done much to appeal to new audiences who did not grow up with the likes of Frank Sinatra.

SELECTIVE DISCOGRAPHY: *Lofty's Roach Souffle* (Columbia, 1990); *Blue Light, Red Light* (Columbia, 1991); *25* (Columbia, 1992); *When My Heart Finds Christmas* (Columbia 1993); *She* (Columbia, 1994); *Star Turtle* (Columbia 1996); *To See You* (Columbia 1997); *Come by Me* (Columbia, 1999); *Songs I Heard* (Columbia 2001); *30* (Columbia, 2001). **Soundtracks:** *Music from the Motion Picture When Harry Met Sally . . .* (Columbia, 1989).

SELECTIVE FILMOGRAPHY: *Memphis Belle* (1990); *Little Man Tate* (1991); *Copycat* (1995); *Independence Day* (1996); *Hope Floats* (1998).

WEBSITE: www.harryconnickjr.com.

CARRIE HAVRANEK

COOLIO

Born: Artist Ivey Jr.; Los Angeles, California, 1 August 1963

Genre: Rap

Best-selling album since 1990: *Gangsta's Paradise* (1995)

Hit songs since 1990: "Fantastic Voyage," "Gangsta's Paradise," "1,2,3,4 (Sumpin' New)," "All the Way Live (Now)"

Coolio achieved stratospheric album sales in the 1990s, with pop-oriented hip-hop grounded in 1970s funk. Coolio represents a light-hearted alternative to West Coast gangsta rap.

Coolio was born Artis Ivey Jr. in Compton, the gang-saturated section of Los Angeles that eventually spawned the rap group N.W.A. After a teenage affiliation with the Crips gang (the longtime nemesis of the Bloods gang), Ivey devolved into criminal activity and was jailed for larceny at age seventeen. Following his release, he enrolled in community college. He showcased his burgeoning rap skills at talent contests, adopting the stage name Coolio. His gruff, expressive voice landed him an on-air personality position on a Los Angeles rap radio station. Coolio used the platform to help release a local hit "Watcha Gonna Do." But before he could capitalize on the promise of that single, Coolio became addicted to crack cocaine. After completing a rehabiliation program, Coolio reignited his hip-hop career. He secured a cameo on the debut album by WC and the Maad Circle, *Ain't a Damn Thang Changed* (1991).

Finding strength in numbers, Coolio formed a rap group with actual robbers that he dubbed 40 Thievz. Coolio secured a deal with Tommy Boy Records, which had released hits by De La Soul and Naughty by Nature. Coolio's debut album, *It Takes a Thief* (1994), spiraled with the single "Fantastic Voyage." Built on an instantly recognizable funk record of the same name by the group Lakeside, the song offers a cautionary note to the romance of drugs and gangs: "Ain't no Bloodin', ain't no Crippin. . . / Everybody got a stack and it ain't no crack." The song and the album became massive hits, embraced by fans tired of the violent themes emerging from the West Coast.

Bigger success was still to come. Coolio fashioned his next hit single, "Gangsta's Paradise," off another classic, Stevie Wonder's "Pastime Paradise." But his lyrical approach is a stark contrast to "Fantastic Voyage," and he is pessimistic and lamenting: "I'm a loc'ed out gangsta, set-trippin banger. . . . I'm twenty-three now, but will I live to see twenty-four?" Concerned about its divergence from Coolio's well-circumscribed niche, Tommy Boy tried to bury the song on the soundtrack to the film *Dangerous Minds*, about an inner-city school. The song underscored the disillusionment of the movie and struck an international chord. Not only did it rocket to number one on the pop charts in America and England, it became the number one song in 1995. Tommy Boy highlighted it as the title track of Coolio's sophomore album (1995), and it won the 1996 Grammy for Best Rap Solo Performance. The lively *Paradise* sing-along single "1,2,3,4 (Sumpin' New)" went gold, and the album sold more than 2 million copies.

Coolio's subsequent moves eroded his credibility with hardcore hip-hop fans. He recorded the theme song to the Nickelodeon comedy series *Kenan and Kel* and tried acting in movies: He appeared in *Phat Beach* and *Batman and Robin*. Rap fans made Coolio the poster boy for watered-down, commercialized hip-hop. Coolio's third album, *My Soul* (1997) went gold, but only on the strength of Coolio's core fan base. At the same time Coolio began to face a series of legal skirmishes, from a shoplifting charge in Germany to a charge for driving with a concealed weapon and marijuana possession. Coolio seemed to embrace his overly commercial image by moving into television. He appeared in the game show *Hollywood Squares*, notoriously a repository of faded stars, and established himself as a regular contestant on reality TV shows like *Celebrity Fear Factor*. After Tommy Boy folded, Coolio released *El Cool Magnifico* (2002) on the small label Riviera. This effort attained only meager sales.

In 2003 Coolio's place in hip-hop was briefly recognized on VH-1's roster of "50 Greatest Hip-Hop Artists" at number forty-three. His placement on the list above trailblazers Kool Moe Dee and the Sugar Hill Gang rankled many hip-hop purists.

Although Coolio's reputation as a credible rap star seemed on the decline in the latter part of his career, he undeniably minted a formula for creating wildly successful rap-pop records.

SELECTIVE DISCOGRAPHY: *It Takes a Thief* (Tommy Boy, 1994); *Gangsta's Paradise* (Tommy Boy, 1995); *My Soul* (Tommy Boy, 1997); *El Cool Magnifico* (Riviera, 2002).

DARA COOK

THE CORRS

Formed: 1991, Dundalk, Ireland

Members: Andrea Jane Corr, lead vocals, tin whistle (born Dundalk, Ireland, 17 May 1974); Caroline Georgine Corr, drums, bodhran, backing vocals (born Dundalk, Ireland, 17 March 1973); James Steven Corr, acoustic and electric guitars, keyboards, backing vocals (born Dundalk, Ireland, 31 July 1968); Sharon Helga Corr, violin, backing vocals (born Dundalk, Ireland, 24 March 1970)

Genre: Rock

Best-selling album since 1990: *In Blue* (2001)

Hit songs since 1990: "So Young," "Breathless," "When the Stars Go Blue" (duet with Bono)

The impossibly good-looking family band the Corrs, composed of three sisters and a brother, rose to popularity during the mid- to late 1990s with an accessible blend of traditional Irish instruments and splashy, bright pop music. Less politically oriented than their fellow Irish rockers U2 and not as prone to preach as the Cranberries, the Corrs strike a pleasant chord and have sold millions of records worldwide. The Corrs' albums have topped *Billboard*'s U.S. and U.K. record charts.

Growing up in Dundalk, county Louth, the four offspring of Jean and Gerry Corr were a musical lot. Jim took guitar and piano lessons, Andrea studied the penny whistle, Caroline worked at the piano until she switched to drums once the band became seriously ambitious, and Sharon learned the violin, commonly referred to in Irish music as the fiddle. Despite the fact that the family grew up in a town halfway between Belfast and Dublin, near the border of Northern Ireland and home to a branch of the Irish Republican Army, politics rarely surface in their music. Instead, it seems that the Corrs, who write their own material, usually focus on sunny pop songs with touches of their native instruments combined with lovely harmonies.

The band had already hit it big in the U.K., Ireland, Asia, and Australia when it attempted to launch itself on U.S. airwaves. Oddly, its second album, *Talk on Corners*, was a sales dud in America until it was retooled several months later after the group toured with the Rolling Stones. *Talk on Corners: Special Edition* (1997), with its cavernous remixes and glossy production, enjoyed some airplay. The album's sales were buoyed by the danceable pop song "So Young," an ebullient anthem, and the revved-up cover of the Fleetwood Mac song "Dreams." But the first two Corrs albums made nary a mark on the American pop audience. It was not until their third album, *In Blue* (2000), co-produced by Robert Lange and Mitchell Froom, that the Corrs gained their hold on American shores.

The group's fortunes were spurred by the pop radio masterpiece "Breathless," an airy, upbeat celebration of new-found love, in which Andrea sings in her rich, powerful alto, "So go on, go on, come on / Leave me Breathless / Tempt me, tease me, until I can't deny this / Lovin' feeling / Make me long for your kiss." The song landed on a handful of *Billboard* charts, including the number seven position in the Adult Top 40. *In Blue* was not all whistles and fiddles, though, as the Corrs stretched their sound with the country-tinged torch song "All the Love in the World," which could easily have been recorded by the country/pop singer Trisha Yearwood. The Corrs do know how to write beautiful weepers that hold their own against other contemporary Irish bands, although they significantly speed up the tempo of their laments, such as on "Radio" from *In Blue*. Despite the overly cheery tone of the album, there are some darker moments, including the melancholy "All in a Day," which laments a miscarriage.

According to some critics, success in America came at the expense of the Corrs's Irish roots; the band nearly dispensed with the traditional sounds featured so prominently on their prior albums. The criticism did not really harm the band though—*In Blue* went on to top the charts in eighteen different countries. Two years later, the band released a live album and a duet with Bono of U2, a cover of the Ryan Adams song "When the Stars Go Blue"; it hit number eighteen in the Billboard Adult Top 40, signaling their continued appeal.

The Corrs began their career as a family band that took the best of their native country's music and added a high-octane dose of radio-friendly pop music to prove to the rest of the world that Ireland could still produce amazing musical success stories.

SELECTIVE DISCOGRAPHY: *Forgiven Not Forgotten* (Lava/Atlantic, 1995); *Talk on Corners* (Atlantic, 1997); *Unplugged* (Atlantic, 1999); *In Blue* (Atlantic, 2000); *VH-1 Music First Presents the Corrs Live in Dublin* (Atlantic, 2002).

CARRIE HAVRANEK

Elvis Costello [PAUL NATKIN/PHOTO RESERVE]

ELVIS COSTELLO

Born: Declan Patrick MacManus; London, England, 25 August 1954

Genre: Rock, Pop, Country

Best-selling album since 1990: *Painted from Memory* (1998)

Hit songs since 1990: "13 Steps Lead Down," "Toledo," "She"

While Elvis Costello's talents were hardened in the fires of the punk revolution of the mid-1970s, he has managed to spend more than a quarter of a century pursuing numerous projects that have frequently distanced him from that influential era by working in a variety of genres. These include country, middle-of-the-road pop, rock, ballads, political anthems, collaborations with string quartets and orchestras, and compositions for television and movie scores. Wherever

Costello has turned his considerable ability, he has brought a similar level of intensity—a kind of tortured frustration—to the impressive range of work he has produced.

If the emergence of the British punk bands the Sex Pistols and the Clash in 1976 triggered a musical sea change and opened the door for the barbed observations of Costello, he had, in fact, been knocking at it for some time. Although he was born in London, his family had strong connections with Liverpool and Merseyside—he spent time in the port of Birkenhead just over the water from the home of the Beatles—and through his father he had links with the world of show business. Ross MacManus was a vocalist and trumpeter with 1950s dance bands, heard on BBC radio broadcasts of the period. As a result, the young Declan spent his teenage years moving from Birkenhead to the capital and back, but retaining the same Liverpudlian accent that the Beatles had introduced to the United States on their first tour of 1964.

Change of Name, Change of Fortune

It was in London that Costello formed his first significant band, eventually named Flip City, who from 1974 rode on the wave of the pub rock phenomenon. Pub rock was a broad musical school that rejected the increasingly impersonal scale of rock—platinum albums, progressive pretensions, and stadium tours—and returned live popular music to the back rooms and upper floors of bars, particularly in the capital. Flip City were a country-tinged feature in a scene that lay the ground for punk bands to secure early live opportunities. When the group folded, MacManus adopted the name D. P. Costello—his own initials plus his mother's maiden name, emphasising still further the Irish antecedents of his clan.

When Stiff Records, an impetuous young label that had grown out of the pub rock movement, received a hand-delivered demo from Costello, not only did they recognize the young songwriter's potential but they proposed that he adopt the attention-grabbing first name Elvis. His reputation grew rapidly on the strength of his live shows, featuring Costello in his geeky, Buddy Holly eyeglasses that belied a spiky, acerbic stage manner. The music press took instant notice and his first album, *My Aim Is True* (1977), recorded in a single day with the American country rockers Clover, merely confirmed the media hype.

The debut collection unveiled a string of short, sharp shocks. Edgy rock songs like "Blame It on Cain," "(The Angels Want to Wear My) Red Shoes," and "Miracle Man," which connected easily with the angry gestures of punk and the new wave now in full flow, confirmed most of what the critics had been suggesting. The controversial "Less Than Zero," featuring the line, "Hey, Mr Oswald with your swastika tattoo," indicated that Costello was not going to steer clear of difficult topics. Although his ire was probably aimed at Oswald Mosley, the 1930s leader of the British fascists, American listeners assumed that Lee Harvey Oswald was his target. By such means, the artist's aura, as both a serious and challenging contender, was underlined. In addition, in "Alison" he showed that his ability to write a memorable love song was not lacking.

Leader in the New Wave Explosion

With that impressive beginning, Costello then proceeded to strengthen his case. Creating a backing band called the Attractions—bassist Bruce Thomas, drummer Pete Thomas, and keyboardist Steve Nieve—Costello, on guitar and vocals, produced the powerful *This Year's Model* (1978) and then *Armed Forces* (1979). With songs as sensational as "Watching the Detectives," "(I Don't Want to Go to) Chelsea," "Pump It Up," and "Oliver's Army" swelling the group's repertoire, Costello was now established as the premier British solo artist of the new wave explosion that was centered on punk acts but also embraced sharp-witted singer/songwriters like Ian Dury and Joe Jackson. Costello's name began to draw similar plaudits in the United States.

His American adventure was rudely halted, however, when a bar room row in Ohio with established American rock musicians Stephen Stills and Bonnie Bramlett resulted in a fist fight and allegations that Costello had made racist remarks about African-American R&B singer Ray Charles. While Costello claimed he had been merely aiming to enrage representatives of the older musical establishment, his records were removed from playlists and for a couple of years he avoided the U.S. circuit.

The 1980s saw Costello continue an odyssey that would take many twists and turns. His 1980 album *Get Happy!!* paid tribute to the R&B sounds of Stax and Motown—"I Can't Stand Up for Falling Down," the Sam and Dave song, provided the first Attractions cover version—although "New Amsterdam" was a reminder that Costello's talent for a tune remained undiminished. In a string of albums that followed, Costello took a country route on *Almost Blue* (1981), returned to a powerful pop formula on *Punch the Clock* (1983), dabbled in rock and roll influences on *King of America* (1986), where he was joined by T-Bone Burnett and the guitar licks of ex-Presley sideman James Burton, and delved into darker themes on *Blood and Chocolate* (1986).

Collaborations with McCartney, Bacharach, and von Otter

Along the way Costello's personal life shifted—his first marriage collapsed, an experience touched upon on *Goodbye Cruel World* (1984), and he later wed Pogues bassist Cait O'Riordan. He also responded to the policies of Margaret Thatcher's administration with a body of fiercely critical political songs—"Shipbuilding," which questioned the morality of the Falklands War of 1982, "Pills and Soap," issued under the pseudonym of the Imposter in 1983, and "Tramp the Dirt Down," a track from *Spike* (1989). Yet Costello could not be stereotyped as a new politico—the latter album saw him co-write with ex-Beatles member Paul McCartney and produce the upbeat ballad "Veronica."

But if the first decade and a half of Costello's musical career had been rich and varied, the 1990s added a range of further shades to his palette. In 1991 he provided the music for a major U.K. television drama—*GBH* by Liverpool playwright Alan Bleasdale—and penned one of his stronger albums, *Mighty Like a Rose,* before embarking on his most ambitious project to date. Joined by classical chamber group the Brodsky Quartet, he produced *The Juliet Letters* (1993), a marvelously eclectic retelling of the Romeo and Juliet romance, through ballad, rock, and contemporary music. A side project saw him write a whole album, *Now Ain't the Time for Your Tears,* for Wendy James, one-time Transvision Vamp singer.

In 1994 Costello was reunited with the Attractions and the resulting album, *Brutal Youth,* proved a feisty return to basic rock principles, with "13 Steps Lead Down" the stand-out song. The following year he released a collection of covers, *Kojak Variety,* featuring singer/songwriter Bob Dylan's "I Threw It All Away" and Ray Davies's "Days"; he then compiled *All This Useless Beauty* (1996), showcasing original songs he had given to other artists but had never recorded himself.

Most significant perhaps was his major collaboration with Burt Bacharach. Costello had covered a Bacharach/Hal David song, "Please Stay," on his covers album and had always been an admirer of those writers. When Bacharach and Costello co-wrote the song "God Give Me Strength," for *Grace of My Heart,* the movie based on the early 1960s Brill Building, it laid the way for a full-scale recording project involving the pair. *Painted from Memory* (1998) drew on Bacharach's supreme melodic and arranging skills and Costello's lyrical and interpretative talents, and songs like "Toledo" and "This House Is Empty Now" demonstrate a remarkable creative sympathy between the two, despite the generational divide.

Yet *Painted From Memory* enjoyed more critical than commercial success, a recurring theme of Costello's career. Nonetheless the concerts and tours that grew out of the album provided him with a world stage, and international sales of the collection, particularly in Japan, eventually marked it as a triumph. An intriguing companion album also appeared with musician/producer Bill Frisell creating a simultaneous jazz arrangement of the Bacharach/Costello set, an echo of a time when Miles Davis and John Coltrane issued their versions of the standard popular repertoire of the day.

Costello now saw concert action with Steve Nieve, his Attractions pianist, and then the movie *Notting Hill* (1999) saw the singer contribute a hit interpretation of the Charles Aznavour classic "She" to the soundtrack. The big screen beckoned again when *Austin Powers: The Spy Who Shagged Me* (1999) featured cameos by Costello and Bacharach as Carnaby Street buskers.

His quest for experimenting in new fields continued. In 2001 he joined forces with a soprano star of the opera world, Ann Sofie von Otter, directing a collaboration that saw the singer add pop songs to her classical repertoire and include pieces from the Costello catalog on *For the Stars.* But in 2002 he rejoined the Attractions—although now missing Bruce Thomas—to record a new collection, *When I Was Cruel.* His best-received album for many years, perhaps since *Mighty Like a Rose,* it features Costello's acid

wit and raw energy once more, reminiscent at times of his earliest recorded efforts as a newcomer with Stiff.

Elvis Costello's resume frames a variety of pursuits that mark him as a unique figure in the popular music landscape. He has never rested on his laurels; some even suggest that he has acted in reverse, burning boats when he could have settled for an easier life. His restlessness, his yearning for creative tests, has driven him to change horses almost annually. A songwriter who approaches Bob Dylan in terms of the sheer quantity of self-composed material, he has earned a place in the upper echelons of rock musicians.

There is, nonetheless, an argument that if he had plowed a narrower furrow—like Dylan, for example—he could have earned comparison with the greatest of solo troubadours. Instead, he has invariably pushed on from plan to plan, succeeding mostly, falling short occasionally. For that, his loyal fan base is surely grateful: Nearly every year has brought a new Costello to the fore—the punk, the country crooner, the rock and roller, the balladeer, and so on. His obsession with reinvention, coupled with his sheer audacity, makes him one of the most eclectic and invigorating players in the field.

SELECTIVE DISCOGRAPHY: *My Aim Is True* (Rykodisc, 1977); *This Year's Model* (Rykodisc, 1978); *Armed Forces* (Rykodisc, 1979); *Get Happy!!* (Rykodisc, 1980); *Almost Blue* (Rykodisc, 1981) *Imperial Bedroom* (Rykodisc, 1982); *Punch the Clock* (Rykodisc, 1983) *Goodbye Cruel World* (Rykodisc, 1984); *King of America* (Rykodisc, 1986); *Blood and Chocolate* (Rykodisc, 1986) *Spike* (Warner Bros., 1989); *Mighty Like a Rose* (Warner Bros., 1991); *The Juliet Letters* (Warner Bros., 1993); *Brutal Youth* (Warner Bros., 1994); *Kojak Variety* (Warner Bros., 1995); *All This Useless Beauty* (Warner Bros., 1996); *Painted from Memory* (Mercury, 1998); *When I Was Cruel* (Island, 2002). **Soundtracks:** *Notting Hill* (Polygram, 1999); *Austin Powers: The Spy Who Shagged Me* (Warner Bros., 1999).

BIBLIOGRAPHY: D. Gouldstone, *Elvis Costello: God's Comic* (London, 1990).

WEBSITES: www.elviscostello.info; www.elviscostello.com.

SIMON WARNER

COUNTING CROWS

Formed: 1989, San Francisco, California

Members: Adam Duritz, vocals, keyboard (born Baltimore, Maryland, 1 August 1964); David Bryson, guitar (born San Francisco, California, 5 November 1961); Charlie Gillingham, keyboard, accordion (born Torrance, California, 12

January 1960); Matt Malley, bass, guitar (born 4 July 1963); Steve Bowman, drums (born 14 January 1967); Ben Mize, drums (born 2 February 1971).

Genre: Rock

Best-selling album since 1990: *August and Everything After* (1993)

Hit songs since 1990: "Mr. Jones," "Round Here," "A Long December"

Combining the sometimes clashing elements of classic and alternative rock, Counting Crows made a sensational debut in 1993 with their multiplatinum album *August and Everything After*. The hit singles "Mr. Jones" and "Round Here" established the authority of the poetic lyrics and highly emotional vocalism of the lead singer, Adam Duritz. At the height of the grunge movement, with Nirvana and Pearl Jam the bands of the moment, Counting Crows brought to the musical scene a traditional rock sound. At the same time, Duritz's lyrics captured the zeitgeist associated with Generation X but without the nihilism and despair that pervaded Cobain's work. Counting Crows' music was the kind of music that could make it big on both alternative radio and *The Late Show with David Letterman*.

Counting Crows were formed by Duritz and guitarist David Bryson in 1989, when they began performing acoustic arrangements in the coffeehouse circuit of San Francisco. With a name derived from a nursery rhyme, the Crows soon became a larger group, with the addition of bassist Matt Malley, keyboard player Charles Gillingham, and drummer Steve Bowman. After developing a considerable following in the San Francisco area, the group ultimately recorded a demo that caught the attention of DGC Records, which signed them in 1992. *August and Everything After*, issued the following year, with lyrics and music credited to Duritz, shot to number four on the charts and sold more than 6 million copies.

On this album Duritz's lyrics reach a consistently high level, with the density and power of poetry and the authentic note of yearning. Despite their tendency toward grunge-like pessimism, lamenting wasted lives and diminished spirits, these songs end on a note of hope: "All your life is such a shame / All your love is just a dream," the narrator warns in "A Murder of One," the album's final track, but soon adds, "You don't want to waste your life."

The group's second album, *Recovering the Satellites* (1996), was long delayed by what Duritz later described as a block caused by his new-found celebrity, but it was well received upon its release. It carries on many of the same themes as the first album, but the music is often harder-edged. In "Angels of the Silences," the narrator

Spot Light | *August and Everything After*

Certain bands seem to encapsulate the sound of classic rock, even when their songs are in a completely different category. Counting Crows' sensationally successful debut album, *August and Everything After* (1993), is a case in point. At the height of the grunge movement, with Nirvana and Pearl Jam the bands of the moment, lyricist/composer Adam Duritz and his group produced music that echoed the rock of the 1960s and 1970s. This ability to fuse a contemporary sensibility with a traditional sound is one of the reasons Counting Crows became such a popular group. "Round Here," the lead track on the album and a hit single, sets the tone. Its narrator tells of a deeply troubled young woman named Maria, who comes to him seeking a release he can't provide. He lives "In the air between the rain," whereas she seems as if "she's walking on a wire in the circus." In "Mr. Jones," the other hit single, the narrator encounters a Mr. Jones, who, like him, wants to be a rock and roll star: "We all want to be big stars, but we don't know why and we don't know how." With some echoes of the Byrds's "So You Want to Be a Rock and Roll Star" and a reference to Bob Dylan, the song expresses the frustrations of someone on the outside looking in. As a lyrical voice for the outcast and lonely, Duritz's songs on *August and Everything After* provided an eloquent counterpoint to the heavy, occasionally maudlin lamentations of the grunge-rock movement.

yearns to come back to his lover but knows it won't happen: "All my sins— / I said that I would pay for them if I could come back to you."

The title song asks similar questions, asserting that "we only stay in orbit / For a moment of time / And then you're everybody's satellite." "A Long December"—along with "Angels" a hit single from the album—contains laments of much the same kind: "I can't remember all the times I tried to tell myself / To hold on to these moments as they pass." These are songs of loss—lost loves, lost innocence, lost direction. And they are also songs of Los

Angeles. More than in their first album, Duritz makes use of the locale in setting the mood of his lyrics.

Two more albums followed in the nineties. First, the live *Across a Wire: Live in New York City* (1998), which featured acoustic and electric sets recorded in two different venues. This double album reprises songs from the previous albums, giving some of them a new spin. Finally, the following year saw *This Desert Life*, the band's third studio album, and increasing criticism (voiced previously) that Duritz's music was too highly derivative—classic rock in alternative disguise—and too repetitive. Nonetheless, the group remained very popular, received lots of airplay, and retained a considerable following. Beginning in the nineties, they created an enlarged ensemble with a now-familiar sound and a singer/composer whose hopes and yearnings had become staples of the musical scene.

Hard Candy (2002), their most recent album, confirmed their success and made up for the less than enthusiastic reception afforded its predecessor. If the themes of *August and Everything After* and their other earlier albums were yearning and frustration, their later work has stressed memory. Mellower than many tracks from their earlier work, it shows its singer/composer and the group around him in a new and optimistic light.

SELECTIVE DISCOGRAPHY: *August and Everything After* (Geffen, 1993); *Recovering the Satellites* (Geffen, 1996); *Across a Wire: Live in New York* (Geffen, 1998); *This Desert Life* (Interscope, 1999).

BIBLIOGRAPHY: M. Scharfglass, *Counting Crows: This Desert Life* (Milwaukee, 2000).

ARCHIE LOSS

COWBOY JUNKIES

Formed: 1985, Toronto, Ontario

Members: Alan Anton, bass (born Montreal, Quebec, 22 June 1959); Margo Timmins, vocals (born Montreal, Quebec, 27 June 1961); Michael Timmins, guitar (born Montreal, Quebec, 21 April 1959); Peter Timmins, drums (born Montreal, Quebec, 29 October 1965)

Genre: Rock

Best-selling album since 1990: *Lay It Down* (1996)

Hit songs since 1990: "A Common Disaster," "Sun Comes Up, It's Tuesday Morning"

With a sparse, haunting sound rooted in country, folk, and gospel traditions, the Cowboy Junkies enjoyed a devoted cult following throughout the 1990s, particularly on college campuses.

Michael Timmins and Alan Anton first collaborated musically in a band called Hunger Project, formed in Toronto in the late 1970s; the pair later moved to the United Kingdom to form an experimental instrumental group. Returning to Toronto in 1985, Timmins and Anton recruited Timmins's brother Peter and his sister Margo for a new band called the Cowboy Junkies. In 1986 the Junkies released their debut album *Whites Off Earth Now!!* on their own Latent Records label. Two years later the band released *The Trinity Sessions*. Recorded in an abandoned church on a single microphone and a $250 budget, *The Trinity Sessions* featured a whispery cover of the Velvet Underground's "Sweet Jane." College radio stations seized on the track, and a promotional video landed the band in rotation on MTV. RCA signed the Cowboy Junkies to a recording contract, reissuing *The Trinity Sessions* on the RCA label.

The Cowboy Junkies' subsequent major-label recordings did not stray far from the band's core sound: understated twangy guitars coupled with Margo Timmins's detached, ghostly vocals. The band enjoyed another minor radio hit with "Sun Comes Up, It's Tuesday Morning" from *The Caution Horses* (1990). A mournful harmonica and accordion provide the soundtrack for Michael Timmins's postbreakup narrative, moodily articulated by his sister Margo: "I sure do miss the smell of black coffee in the morning / The sound of water splashing all over the bathroom / The kiss that you would give me even though I was sleeping / But I kind of like the feel of this extra few feet in my bed."

Critics showered praise on albums such as *Pale Sun, Crescent Moon*, but positive reviews failed to cement a place for the band outside college radio. The Cowboy Junkies did achieve brief mainstream success with "A Common Disaster" from the album *Lay It Down* (1996). Adult album alternative radio picked up the track, which rocked harder than previous releases by the Junkies. In the chorus of "A Common Disaster," Michael Timmins answers Margo Timmins's plaintive vocal ("Won't you share with me a common disaster?") with a catchy, up-tempo guitar riff not previously heard on Cowboy Junkies releases.

The Cowboy Junkies lost their recording contract in the wake of a record label merger.

The band resurrected its Latent Records label for its next release, the live *Waltz Across America* (2000), which surveyed the group's entire career and captured its intimate performing style. In 2001 the Cowboy Junkies collaborated with the independent label Rounder Records and released *Open*.

Exhibiting their own style of traditional American music, the Cowboy Junkies carved a niche on alternative radio stations in the 1990s and in the process endeared themselves to fans and critics alike.

SELECTIVE DISCOGRAPHY: *The Trinity Sessions* (RCA, 1988); *The Caution Horses* (RCA, 1990);

Black-Eyed Man (RCA, 1992); *Pale Sun, Crescent Moon* (RCA, 1993); *Lay It Down* (Geffen, 1996); *Miles from Our Home* (Geffen, 1998); *Waltz Across America [live]* (Latent, 2000); *Open* (Zoe, 2001).

SCOTT TRIBBLE

CRACKER

Formed: 1991, Richmond, Virginia

Members: Frank Funaro, drums; Johnny Hickman, guitar; David Lowery, vocals (born San Antonio, Texas, 10 October 1960); Brandy Wood, bass. Former members: Davey Faragher, bass; Kenny Margolis, keyboards; Bob Rupe, bass.

Genre: Rock

Best-selling album since 1990: *Kerosene Hat* (1993)

Hit songs since 1990: "Low," "Get Off This," "Teen Angst (What the World Needs Now)"

Cracker enjoyed a short run of commercial success in the early 1990s with a string of eclectic rock hits.

Cracker evolved out of Camper Van Beethoven, a 1980s band. After leaving Camper, vocalist David Lowery began recording demos with guitar player Johnny Hickman and bass player Davey Faragher. In 1991 they signed with Virgin Records and, with the help of a variety of session drummers, released their self-titled debut album the following year. *Cracker* featured the quirky MTV hit "Teen Angst (What the World Needs Now)," an up-tempo folk-rock number that features the memorable hook: "What the world needs now is another folk singer / Like I need a hole in my head."

Cracker refined its sound for the follow-up album, *Kerosene Hat* (1993), offering up a tougher, more traditional electric guitar-based production. The band retained its celebrated lyrical quirkiness, as typified by the lead single "Low." "Low," which features spiraling electric guitars and a sprawling power-chord chorus, poses the memorable question to listeners: "Hey, don't you wanna go down, like some junkie cosmonaut?" The dizzying and drug-themed lyrics reach a climax with the song's main hook: "Being with you girl like being low / Hey, hey, hey / Like being stoned." With its catchy melody and memorable lyrics, "Low" became a staple on MTV and a minor hit on commercial radio. The follow-up "Get Off This" enjoyed similar success. Like "Low," "Get Off This" rocks in a straight-ahead manner and belies a decided funk influence; its jaded lyrics hearken to the band's previous hit "Teen Angst (What the World Needs Now)," with the band challenging idealists to make a difference: "Let's get off this / And get on with it / If you wanna change the world, shut

yer mouth and start to spin it." On the strength of its hit singles, *Kerosene Hat* sold more than 1 million records.

For the remainder of the 1990s, Cracker experienced a number of lineup shifts, including the departure of original member Davey Faragher; Lowery also spent significant time away from Cracker, producing acts such as Joan Osborne, Magnet, and Sparklehorse, while also appearing in various films. On releases such as *Gentleman's Blues* (1998) and *Forever* (2002), Cracker forsook the straight-ahead rock style of *Kerosene Hat* and embraced its musically eclectic roots, mixing blues rock, Southern rock, and Grateful Dead-styled jams into its records. Though the albums were hailed by critics for their musical imagination, none enjoyed the commercial success of *Kerosene Hat*.

Cracker's time in the commercial spotlight was brief. Nevertheless, with its taut rock sound and evocative lyrics, the band offered up some of the memorable pop-rock singles of the mid-1990s.

SELECTIVE DISCOGRAPHY: *Cracker* (Virgin, 1992); *Kerosene Hat* (Virgin, 1993); *The Golden Age* (Virgin, 1996); *Gentleman's Blues* (Virgin, 1998); *Forever* (Back Porch, 2002).

SCOTT TRIBBLE

THE CRANBERRIES

Formed: 1989, Limerick, Ireland

Members: Dolores O'Riordan, vocals, acoustic guitar (born Limerick, Ireland, 6 September 1971); Noel Hogan, guitar, backing vocals (born Limerick, Ireland, 25 December 1974); Michael Hogan, bass (born Limerick, Ireland, 29 April 1973); Feargal Lawler, drums and percussion (born Limerick, Ireland, 4 March 1971).

Genre: Rock

Best-selling album since 1990: *No Need to Argue* (1994)

Hit songs since 1990: "Dreams," "Linger," "Zombie"

The signature sound of the Irish pop group the Cranberries revolves around skillful, clean guitar work and the heavily accented, lilting, yodellike singing of Dolores O'Riordan. The foursome formed in the early 1990s and built up a steady following in their home country, toured in supporting roles, and broke through to the United States thanks to the lovely, melodic single "Dreams" from their multiplatinum debut album, *Everybody's Doing It, So Why Can't We?* (1993).

The Cranberries formed in 1989, and all four members hail from the city of Limerick, Ireland. Every band members endured a hardscrabble childhood. O'Riordan, the youngest of seven children, grew up with a mother who was the family's sole breadwinner. The brothers, Hogan and Lawler, played together in a band called the Cranberry Saw Us; in 1990 their vocalist/songwriter left. O'Riordan heard about the opening, auditioned, and was accepted. The band recorded a couple of demos, and the second one landed at Rough Trade Records, home of their idols, the Smiths. A bidding war ensued, and Island records signed them for their debut album; the legendary producer Stephen Street, who had worked with the Smiths, was at the helm.

Their debut, *Everybody's Doing It, So Why Can't We?* (1993), took off in the United States, which helped spur sales in the United Kingdom and Ireland; the Cranberries toured incessantly. The album is marked by its delicate grace, Dolores O'Riordan's yodeling soprano voice, which is really the centerpiece, and the songwriting of O'Riordan and the guitarist, Noel Hogan. By mid-1994, just a little over a year after its release, the album had sold 2.5 million copies.

The band members owe much of their success to their families—hence the sweet song "Ode to My Family" on the second album, *No Need to Argue* (1994). The songs for *No Need to Argue* were written during the band's tour in support of its debut. The first single, "Zombie," with its angry, crunchy guitar, is essentially a rant against the violence that marks their homeland; bearing little resemblance to the Cranberries' previous recording, it calls to mind the controversial Irish singer Sinéad O'Connor. Nevertheless, *No Need to Argue* has sold more than 7 million copies.

In 1997, reflecting on the grueling demands of their profession, O'Riordan said, "We'd probably be wrecked rock stars without our homes. We found our real happiness, our highs, at home." By this time, the group had recorded, toured, and taken enough breaks to accommodate both their professional lives as a band and the changes in their personal lives, which included O'Riordan's marriage to the Canadian Don Burton in 1994 and the birth of her first child in 1997. By the end of 1998, all four Cranberries were married. The change forced them to rearrange their priorities, and there was a time when their future as a band was cloudy. The release of their fifth album, *Wake Up and Smell the Coffee* (2001), marked a homecoming of sorts as it was produced by Stephen Street again. In it, the band sounds older and wiser, as their single "Analyze" attests. In the chorus O'Riordan advises, "Don't analyze"—just enjoy life.

All of their albums have charted well, despite the inconsistencies in songwriting quality. The Cranberries have sold a staggering number of albums—more than 25 million worldwide. Throughout the Cranberries have managed to balance work, touring, and family and have stayed together even with growing responsibilities in their personal lives. They managed not merely to survive as a band but to evolve artistically: Through the 1990s the Cranberries explored political and religious themes in addition to the stereotypical male-female psychodramas. Their success paved the way for bands such as the Corrs and the Irish teeny-bopper outfit Bewitched. The popularity of the Cranberries demonstrates the impact of Irish music on American and world culture.

SELECTIVE DISCOGRAPHY: *Everybody's Doing It, So Why Can't We* (Island, 1993); *No Need to Argue* (Island, 1994); *To the Faithful Departed* (Island, 1996); *Bury the Hatchet* (1999); *Wake Up and Smell the Coffee* (2001); *The Stars: Best of 1992–2002* (Island).

CARRIE HAVRANEK

ROBERT CRAY

Born: Columbus, Georgia, 1 August 1953
Genre: Blues
Best-selling album since 1990: *Midnight Stroll* (1990)
Hit songs since 1990: "The Forecast (Calls for Pain)," "Just a Loser"

Since the 1980s Robert Cray has brought blues music into the mainstream, giving the idiom a degree of popularity not seen since the early 1970s work of blues master B.B. King. A skilled guitarist as well as singer, Cray's most impressive achievement has been to combine traditional blues forms with more recent styles such as rhythm and blues and soul. The result is an exciting series of albums that capture a modern edge without losing their historical awareness. If Cray has any weakness it is that his music tends to sound overly clean and polished, but even at its slickest it is never less than enjoyable. In the years following the late 1990s Cray moved away from blues to explore a straight-ahead R&B vein, with excellent results.

Cray was born in Columbus, Georgia, but raised in Oregon. As a child his influences included piano and vocal R&B legend Ray Charles as well as lesser-known artists such as searing 1960s soul vocalist O. V. Wright. In 1974 he formed the Robert Cray Blues Band and began playing local engagements around the Oregon city of Eugene. His big break came in 1977, when he was invited to play the San Francisco Blues Festival with legendary artist Albert Collins. Soon after, Cray hooked up with producer Dennis Walker, who arranged for the young performer's initial entry into the studio in 1979. Although several fine albums resulted, Cray's popularity was confined to a small blues audience until the success of *Strong Persuader* (1986). A perfect mixture of tough blues and punchy, horn-driven R&B, the album is distinguished by an excellent selection of material. Hard-driving songs such as "Smoking Gun" and "I Guess I Showed Her" feature classic blues themes of sin and redemption, but Cray fits them into a contemporary matrix of stinging guitar, organ, and swaggering horns. On top of it all is the power of Cray's voice, only slightly less distinctive than those of his idols Wright and B.B. King. While a shouting rasp lay at the center of Wright's voice, Cray's roughness is reserved for the upper edge of his range. His singing is smooth and keening in a manner that recalls 1950s and 1960s R&B great Sam Cooke.

The success of *Strong Persuader* made Cray the only blues artist to place an album on the Top 20 charts in over a decade. His popularity at its peak, he entered the 1990s with a string of albums that, while lacking *Strong Persuader*'s first-rate songs, were fine examples of his unique blues-R&B hybrid. Critics mentioned that occasionally Cray's albums during this period sounded too smooth, lacking the visceral bite that characterized the work of his forebears. Still, Cray's commitment and drive always lent his music credibility. *Midnight Stroll* (1990) features the tough hit "The Forecast (Calls for Pain)," with its opening lyric capturing the essence of blues philosophy: "Coffee for my breakfast / Shot of whisky on the side." *I Was Warned* (1992) is another strong set, highlighted by the simmering ballad "The Price I Pay." Increasingly Cray was showing his skills as a detailed shaper of slow songs, gradually building intensity within a performance. His guitar playing, economical yet incisive, worked hand in hand with his vocals to achieve an exciting synthesis.

As the 1990s progressed Cray began shifting his energies more to singing than playing. Concomitant with this change was a heightened interest in 1960s and 1970s R&B music. On albums such as *Take Your Shoes Off* (1999) the traditional blues influence is still present, but it is overshadowed by the suppleness of his pulsating R&B sound. Rather than diluting the power of his music, this new focus strengthens it. A highlight of the album is the ballad "All the Way," which Cray wrote with his wife, filmmaker Sue Turner-Cray. Set against an inviting bed of bottom-heavy percussion and churchy-sounding organ, Cray's vocal achieves a slow-burning power. The drums and organ recall the deep R&B records created in the early 1970s by master producer Willie Mitchell; *Take Your Shoes Off* honors Mitchell's pioneering sound without resorting to imitation. Cray's release *Shoulda Been Home* (2001) continues in the same style, although songs such as the

stinging "The 12 Year Old Boy" prove that Cray has not lost his sharp blues edge.

Robert Cray's fusion of blues and classic R&B has been so successful that by the late 1990s the two genres were perceived, from a marketing standpoint, as interchangeable. Cray's records and those of his 1960s R&B influences are found side by side in music stores, while the term "R&B" is now reserved for more contemporary artists such as Mary J. Blige and Usher. This development points to Cray's influence and the enduring potency of his soulful blues sound.

SELECTIVE DISCOGRAPHY: *Bad Influence* (Hightone, 1983); *Strong Persuader* (Mercury, 1986); *Midnight Stroll* (Mercury, 1990); *I Was Warned* (Mercury, 1992); *Sweet Potato Pie* (Mercury, 1997); *Take Your Shoes Off* (Rykodisc, 1999); *Shoulda Been Home* (Rykodisc, 2001).

WEBSITE: www.robertcray.com.

DAVID FREELAND

CREED

Formed: 1995, Tallahassee, Florida

Members: Scott Stapp, vocalist (born Orlando, Florida 8 August 1973); Mark Tremonti, guitar (born Orlando, Florida 18 April 1974); Brian Marshall, bass (born Fort Walton Beach, Florida, 24 April 1973); Scott Phillips, drums (born Madison, Florida, 22 February 1973).

Genre: Rock

Best-selling album since 1990: *Human Clay* (1999)

Hit songs since 1990: "My Own Prison," "Torn," "With Arms Wide Open," "Sacrifice"

Creed rose swiftly as a major player in the post-grunge rock world on the strength of direct, sometimes Christian-tinged lyrics, and intense, soaring anthems. But the journey was not smooth. Critics disparaged them as imitative grungers whose overly serious, sometimes spiritual lyrics cast them as a Christian rock group. In time, it became clear that Creed were much more than the sum of their parts as their guitar-heavy rock came to dominate sales and radio charts.

Origins

Creed came together when two Florida high school friends, singer Scott Stapp and guitarist Mark Tremonti, teamed up with bassist Brian Marshall and drummer Scott Phillips in Tallahassee. A son of fundamentalist parents, Stapp grew up in a strict environment where rock music was scorned and punishment sometimes meant having to write Bible verses in longhand.

Over time Stapp rebelled, later experimenting with drugs while studying law at Florida State University. He eventually dropped out to pursue music, a decision that further estranged him from his stringent family. It was during these lean years that Stapp began to pen reflective songs about self-examination, sometimes drawing upon his experience of writing Biblical verses. When he teamed up with Tremonti, they set the lyrics against grunge power chords.

These early compositions made up the bulk of their debut CD, *My Own Prison* (1997), produced by John Kurzweg and released on their label, Blue Collar. It came to the attention of Wind-Up Records, an indie imprint distributed by Sony, where it was remixed and given a brawny sheen. This refurbishing resulted in four number one singles on *Billboard*'s mainstream rock radio charts: the title track, "Torn," "What's This Life For," and "One." Though slightly preachy, Stapp's lyrics captivated fans: "Only in America we kill the unborn / to make ends meet."

The combination of thunderous guitars, direct lyrics, and anthemic songs became Creed's sonic signature.

Taking Off

Creed's ascent began to accelerate, but cynics and other fence riders questioned the band's staying power. The post-grunge world was crowded with sound-alike big-riff guitar bands, and Creed seemed to have molded its sound after Pearl Jam's variation on grunge. It did not help that Stapp's rough vocals were often compared to those of Pearl Jam's Eddie Vedder. But Creed surprised everyone, including the naysayers, when their follow-up, *Human Clay* (1999), debuted at number one on the *Billboard* chart and quickly went multiplatinum, eventually selling more than 10 million copies in two years. "Higher," the first single, spent seventeen weeks at number one on rock radio. Other tracks became chart toppers, including "What If" and the catchy ballad "With Arms Wide Open," which later won a Grammy for Best Rock Song. The song has personal meaning for Stapp. It was written while he awaited the birth of his first son, Jagger. In June 1999 Stapp divorced Jagger's mother, Hillaree Burns, an aspiring model, after a sixteen-month marriage.

In public statements, Stapp said the reason "wasn't infidelity. We were just young and had a baby, and everything happened so fast." The divorce was amicable. "I think in her heart she would like a man who's home every day," he said. "I'm in a rock band and I'm gone a lot. I'll always love her. She gave me one of the greatest gifts in my life, my son." On "With Arms Wide Open," Stapp said he would never tire of singing the song: "It was written about my unborn child. And I have a constant reminder of why I wrote that song in Jagger. The feelings that

inspired that song well up in me every time I sing it." One of the key lines is, "With arms wide open, under the sunlight / Welcome to this place I'll show you everything / With arms wide open."

More muscular and better paced that its predecessor, *Human Clay* featured more accessible, mainstream-leaning guitar rock. For better or for worse, Creed was sounding like the early 1980s power pop band Journey but with more rock muscle and a more passionate singer. Other tunes like "Wrong Way" recalled Led Zeppelin with its Middle Eastern rhythms.

Formula for Success

By the late 1990s, genres like rap/rock, rock metal, and teen boy bands were making major inroads into the market. Creed was going against the grain, producing anthemic guitar-fueled rock complete with angst-filled introspective lyrics and increasingly ruling the charts. From outward appearances, Creed had all the cliches: guitar hooks, soaring choruses, leather pants, messanic poses. It was clear that the group's influences drew from such seminal groups as Black Sabbath, Led Zeppelin, and the Doors, as well as Alice in Chains, Pearl Jam, and Stone Temple Pilots. A VH1 *Behind the Music* special in 2000 touted the band as Orlando's "spiritual band with the thunderous sound." But two elements made Creed distinctive. First, in contrast to the tones of anger and sodden negativity of other grunge bands, Creed seemed comfortable and happy. Second, Stapp's biblically inspired lyrics prompted speculation about Creed's agenda: Were they a Christian band trying to reach rock audiences? Stapp told the Sydney, Australia, *Daily Telegraph* that judgment was in the ears of the beholder: "Everyone has their own background and it affects the way you perceive things. When I make religious or spiritual references in my songs, they don't know the meaning behind what I'm trying to figure out for myself, so when they hear those words, a Christian person will base it on their belief systems," he said. "People of a non-Christian belief hear them in a completely different way. At this point we have no agenda, we're not a professing Christian band, we just write from our hearts about experiences we go through. We don't want to do anything to change how people hear a song because that's what makes a song theirs, makes it personal to them."

By the time Creed went back into the studio in early 2001, the pressure was on to beat the multiplatinum success of the previous CDs. Tremonti took over bass duties in the studio after bassist Brian Marshall left the band, replaced on the tour by Brett Hestla of Virgos Merlot. No official reason was ever given for Marshall's departure. Again, producer Kurzweg was brought in to help hammer out the songs that became *Weathered* in the fall of 2001. Ultimately, there were few surprises. The monster rock anthems were there in "My Sacrifice," and "One Last Breath." Zeppelin's mystical tones were evoked again on "Who's Got My Back Now." The album registered big sales, but not everyone was pleased. Creed demonstrated their proficiency at power rock ballads, but *Weathered* proved that the band could not expand their musical vocabulary. Their messages of hope defy hard rock's gloom and anger, but the band's polished and intense power pop was becoming predictable.

Creed has been an important contributor to rock's evolution. Their radio-friendly hard rock has fused post-grunge elements with spiritual undertones in lyrics that appeal to fans who want more from music than angry alienation.

SELECTIVE DISCOGRAPHY: *My Own Prison* (Wind-Up, 1997); *Human Clay* (Sony, 1999); *Weathered* (Wind-Up, 2001).

RAMIRO BURR

SHERYL CROW

Born: Kennett, Missouri, 11 February 1962

Genre: Rock

Best-selling album since 1990: *The Globe Sessions* (1998)

Hit songs since 1990: "All I Wanna Do," "If It Makes You Happy," "Everyday Is a Winding Road"

Sheryl Crow's debut album came out in 1993, at the height of the popularity of grunge rock and Seattle-based groups like Nirvana. She had started her career as a backup singer for the likes of Michael Jackson, Joe Cocker, and Rod Stewart. She did not find much encouragement moving out on her own as a woman in a field in which the leading talents were either dance mavens like Madonna or urban folkies like Tracy Chapman. She was good-looking but not willing to use those looks in any demeaning way to further her career. She wanted to be her own person musically, and her approach to that goal was thoroughly professional. By the early 2000s, Sheryl Crow had established herself as one of the leading women in rock.

Rural Roots

With a background in rural Missouri and parents who were musicians from the big band era, Crow began piano lessons at the age of six and by her teens was singing in rock groups. At the University of Missouri in the early 1980s, she took a degree in classical piano and then taught music for a short time in a St. Louis elementary school. Soon, however, her musical ambitions took over her life,

Sheryl Crow [PAUL NATKIN/PHOTO RESERVE]

and, in pursuit of her dream, she moved to Los Angeles in 1986, where her first work was as a backup singer.

A Star Is Born

By 1991 she had signed a record contract with A&M, and, after an aborted first effort that she convinced the company not to release, she produced her first album in 1993. On the strength of Crow's musicianship and the popularity of the song "All I Wanna Do," which reached second place on the charts and won a Grammy for best record of the year in 1994, Crow's career was launched. The album *The Tuesday Night Club* (named for the group that gathered on these evenings to make the recording) also features songs that deal with more serious subjects—the kind of material that became characteristic of Crow's subsequent output. "No One Said It Would Be Easy" deals with the end of a relationship—a theme Crow would return to again and again—and "What I Can Do for You" addresses sexual harassment.

The collaborative nature of some of the material in the album led to complaints and criticism from musicians that Crow was taking credit for what was in fact a communal effort. Whatever the validity of the criticism, by her next album Crow made sure that there would be no doubt about who was in charge.

On Her Own

Her self-titled album of 1996 features songs written entirely by Crow. With this release Crow became the singer/songwriter she always wanted to be. Critically, the album was not universally well received. The *Rolling Stone* review, for example, noted the music's blandness and derivativeness. Wal-Mart Corporation objected to something else—the reference, in "Love Is a Good Thing," to guns the giant chain marketed: "Watch our children kill each other / With a gun they bought at a Wal-Mart discount store." As a result, like many other albums with similar socio-political messages, Crow's second effort was removed from the shelves of the chain. Two tracks from the album were radio hits that ended up high on the charts: "If It Makes You Happy" and "Everyday Is a Winding Road." With sales reaching 6 million copies, Crow had reached a seemingly secure niche in the music world.

Crow at the Crest

As if to underscore that success and to win over those who remained skeptical of the originality of her talent, she went on to the sometimes personal, often haunting, semi-confessional album *The Globe Sessions* (1998), which won her her first Grammy for an album.

Of the twelve tracks on this album, eleven are Crow originals, with a wide range of emotional and musical content. The lead track, "My Favorite Mistake," is about a failed love affair: "maybe nothin' lasts forever / Even when you stay together." By now a standard Crow subject, doomed romance recurs in "Anything but Down" later on in the set. "There Goes the Neighborhood" is a walk on the wild side: "the movie of the screenplay of the book about a girl who meets a junkie." "Am I Getting Through" (I and II) strikes a feminist theme by presenting the plight of a young woman who is neither seen nor heard: "I am lovely and weak / I am foul when I speak." Crow also covers a Bob Dylan song, "Mississippi," which Dylan had never released in his own version. ("Sweet Child O' Mine" borrows Axl Rose's title, but the lyrics are Crow's.) With this album Crow achieved a new level of musical accomplishment as a singer/composer.

Her growing stature received another boost with the release of *Sheryl Crow and Friends: Live from Central Park* (1999), which reprises a number of earlier Crow compositions in live performances with the help of friends like Keith Richards, Eric Clapton, Chrissie Hynde, and Stevie Nicks. By the end of the decade, Sheryl Crow had reached the top of her profession.

C'mon C'mon (2002) sustained her success. Crow's special brand of pop-rock, with roots-rock overtones, emerges strongly in this hard-driving set. The title song got wide airplay, and cultish tracks like the opening "Steve McQueen" added to the sense that Crow had a strong sense of cool.

In addition to her recordings, Crow maintains a heavy performance schedule. In the mid-1990s, during one fifteen-month period, she did 542 shows. To this day, live performances are an important part of her schedule. Asked by an interviewer in *Rolling Stone* what advice she would give a woman wanting a musical career today, Crow said, "Learn how to write a song and then don't let anybody tell you what to do or not to do."

SELECTIVE DISCOGRAPHY: *Tuesday Night Club* (A&M, 1993); *Sheryl Crow* (A&M, 1996); *The Globe Sessions* (A&M, 1998); *Sheryl Crow and Friends: Live from Central Park* (A&M, 1999); *C'mon C'mon* (Interscope, 2002).

BIBLIOGRAPHY: R. Buskin, *Sheryl Crow: No Fool to This Game*. (New York, 2002).

ARCHIE LOSS

CELIA CRUZ

Born: Havana, Cuba, 21 October 1924; died Fort Lee, New Jersey, 16 July 2003

Genre: Latin, Tropical, Salsa

Best-selling album since 1990: *La Negra Tiene Tumbao* (2001)

Hit songs since 1990: "La Vida Es un Carnaval," "La Negra Tiene Tumbao"

The undisputed Queen of Salsa entered the twenty-first century still active, exuberant, and on top of the charts. Known for her elaborate costumes, her trademark cry of "Azucar!" (sugar), and her improvisational skills, Celia Cruz influenced three generations of tropical music makers.

Cruz was born in the poor Santa Suarez barrio of Havana, the second oldest of four children. In 1947 Cruz left the teacher's school she was attending to concentrate on her singing career. She studied voice and theory at Cuba's Conservatory of Music from 1947 to 1950.

Her first shot at the big time came in August 1950, when she joined Cuba's legendary Sonora Matancera. Her fifteen-year association with the group would represent the first golden age of her career. The group headlined at the Tropicana nightclub and casino during Havana's final years as a tropical playground for the rich and famous.

Fidel Castro seized power in Cuba's 1959 revolution, and La Sonora Matancera defected to the United States on July 15, 1960, under the pretext of a tour. Cruz settled in New York City for good in 1962. A furious Castro did not let her return to Cuba to visit her ailing mother or attend her father's funeral. Cruz married Matancera trumpeter Pedro Knight on July 15, 1962. In 1965 Knight stepped down from the band to become her personal manager and musical director. Cruz also left La Sonora Matancera that year.

By the early 1970s, young Hispanics looking for identity and roots rediscovered the Afro-Cuban music their

Celia Cruz [AP/WIDE WORLD PHOTOS]

parents listened to. Now dubbed "salsa," the music encompassed rhythms such as mambo, rumba, and guaguanco, and featured piano, a horn section, and a Cuban drum set with congas and timbales. The time was perfect for Cruz to bring her music to a new audience. In 1974 she teamed up with Johnny Pacheco for the landmark *Celia and Johnny*. The album went gold, and Cruz's second golden age had begun. She teamed up with Sonora Matancera one more time in 1982 for *Feliz Encuentro*. She was awarded a Grammy Award in 1989 for *Con Ritmo En El Corazón*, with conga player Ray Barreto. In the 1990s, she ventured into acting, playing nightclub owner Evalina Montoya in the movie *The Mambo Kings* (1992) and making a cameo in *The Perez Family* (1995).

Cruz entered the new millennium winning three straight Latin Grammys—2000 Best Salsa Performance for *Celia Cruz and Friends: A Night of Salsa*, 2001 Traditional Tropical Album for *Siempre Viviré*, and 2002 Best Salsa Album for *La Negra Tiene Tumbao*. But her biggest hit of the early 2000s, "La Vida Es un Carnaval," was not from any of those albums. Included on the album *Mi Vida es Cantar* (1998), it became a hit after being included in the soundtrack of the Mexican movie *Amores Perros* (2000). In keeping with the "carnaval" title, the song features bouncy samba trumpet blasts as Cruz delivers a message of

maintaining defiant optimism in tough times. No one who listened to her weathered but powerful voice could doubt she had experienced, but overcome, her share of heartaches.

In 2001 actress Whoopi Goldberg announced her interest in producing and possibly starring in a Cruz biopic. TV talk show host Cristina Saralegui and husband Marcos Avila were developing the script. Cruz died in her home in Fort Lee, New Jersey, on 16 July 2003 from a brain tumor. She remained an innovative force in salsa music more than fifty years after beginning her career.

SELECTIVE DISCOGRAPHY: *Cuba y Puerto Rico Son* (Tico, 1966); *Mi Vida Es Cantar* (RMM, 1998); *Siempre Viviré* (Sony, 2000); *La Negra Tiene Tumbao* (Sony, 2001). **Soundtrack:** *Amores Perros* (Universal Latino, 2000).

SELECTIVE FILMOGRAPHY: *The Mambo Kings* (1992); *The Perez Family* (1995).

RAMIRO BURR

THE CURE

Formed: 1976, Crawley, England

Members: Perry Bamonte, guitar, keyboard (born London, England, 3 September 1960); Jason Cooper, drums (born

London, England, 31 January 1967); Roger O'Donnell keyboard (born 29 October 1955); Robert Smith, vocals, guitar (born Blackpool, England, 21 April 1959); Porl Thompson, guitar (born Wimbledon, England, 8 November 1957). Former members: Michael Dempsey, bass (born Salisbury, Southern Rhodesia, 29 November 1958); Simon Gallup, bass (born Duxhurst, England, 1 June 1960); Mathieu Hartley, keyboard (born Smallfield, England, 4 February 1960); Laurence Tolhurst, drums, keyboards (born Horley, England, 3 February 1959); Boris Williams, drums (born Versailles, France, 24 April 1957).

Genre: Rock

Best-selling album since 1990: *Wish* (1992)

Hit songs since 1990: "Love Song," "Friday, I'm in Love," "High"

The British alternative rock band the Cure slowly built up a cult following throughout the 1980s in their native United Kingdom and in the United States. The Cure achieved the biggest success of their career in the early 1990s with the albums *Disintegration* (1989) and *Wish* (1992). During their rise to popularity, the guitar-based band struck a chord with alienated teenagers and music fans who were tired of the same old thing.

The driving force behind the band is the songwriter Robert Smith. Because of the many who have found solace in his eccentric punk style and in the band's dark lyrics, the Cure have enjoyed a rabid fan base.

The Early Years

Robert Smith has been one of the few constant members in the lineup of the Cure, a band known for its rapid membership turnover, especially among keyboardists and drummers. Smith grew up in the suburban town of Crawley and started learning the guitar when he was six. A decade later he formed Easy Cure with his school friends Laurence "Lol" Tolhurst on drums and Michael Dempsey on bass. Although they came together with a hardscrabble, scruffy aura that prevailed during the punk explosion in Britain, the band distinguished itself from others with atmospheric touches of keyboards and an unusual vocalist with an unwavering ability to turn private pain into pop songs. The band caught the attention of an A&R man, Chris Parry, with their song "Killing an Arab," inspired by Albert Camus's classic novel *The Stranger*. With this remarkable single, which helped break them through to radio, the Cure found themselves in a similar category of ironic, literate guitar bands such as fellow Brits the Smiths.

Parry signed them to his new record label, Fiction Records, and the band released their follow-up single, "Boys Don't Cry," a midtempo tune with Smith crooning, "I would do most anything to get you back by my side /

But I just keep on laughing hiding the tears in my eyes because / Boys don't cry." The tune, from their album *Three Imaginary Boys* (1979), was well received and helped land them a spot as an opening act for goth punk-rock band Siouxsie and the Banshees.

By the mid-1980s the Cure had released the commercially successful album *The Head on the Door* (1985); at this point the Cure consisted of Smith and Tolhurst. A couple of eccentric hits followed: the jazzy, piano pop song "The Love Cats" and the unusual "The Caterpillar," which featured Smith on violin. The Cure, firmly established as pop oddballs, toured South America and recorded their double album *Kiss Me, Kiss Me, Kiss Me* (1988), which reached the U.S. Top 40 and achieved platinum status. The album catapulted them from cult status in America to arena-filling popularity. The imminently danceable "Why Can't I Be You?" and "Catch" were popular, and the album's "Just Like Heaven" reached the Top 40 in the U.S. All of these tunes exemplified the quality that carried the Cure through the 1990s: offbeat, catchy, slightly eccentric alternative rock with intimations of the macabre.

Disintegration: A Foreshadowing

Before recording their next album, the band took off for a two-year hiatus and reconvened for *Disintegration* (1989), their most downbeat, depressing album to date. However, the album yielded several singles, including the creepy "Lullaby"; the yearning, sad "Pictures of You"; and the hopeless romanticism of "Lovesong." The personnel instability continued, with Tolhurst leaving to form his own band; the Cure then became a band of one, consisting only of Smith, the sole founding member.

Shortly after Tolhurst's departure, Smith announced there would be no more touring of America and went on to release *Mixed Up* (1990), a double album of remixes, reissues, and re-recordings of their singles. By 1992 the band consisted of Smith, Gallup, Perry Bamonte on keyboards and guitar, Porl Thompson, and Boris Williams. They released *Wish* (1992), their most vibrant and uncharacteristically sunny album. The upbeat nature of the singles helped *Wish* become the band's best seller. Reinvigorated, the Cure toured America and scored a series of hits with the giddy, celebratory "Friday I'm in Love" and "High." On *Wish*, the guitars are lighter, sunnier, and chiming rather than heavy, squalling, and laden with effects. There are still elements of bittersweet heartbreak, but overall *Wish* marked a psychological turning point for the band.

Infighting, drinking, and court battles plagued the band in June 1993, when Tolhurst unsuccessfully sued Smith for alleged unpaid royalties. The band staggered on, with Jason Cooper replacing Williams as drummer. The

Cure recorded the unremarkable *Wild Mood Swings* (1996) and then *Bloodflowers* (2000), thus refuting Smith's proclamation that he would disband the Cure by his fortieth birthday. He did, however, declare it to be the band's final album, a statement he later retracted. The Cure played in Europe to much success in 2002 and in 2003 recorded another album, determined to perpetuate a legacy of gloomy beauty unrivaled by any other band of the 1990s.

SELECTIVE DISCOGRAPHY: *Boys Don't Cry* (1980); *Standing on the Beach, Staring at the Sea: The Singles, 1978–1985* (Elektra, 1986); *Kiss Me, Kiss Me, Kiss Me* (Elektra, 1988); *Disintegration* (Elektra, 1989); *Wish* (Elektra, 1992); *Wild Mood Swing* (Elektra, 1996); *Galore: The Singles 1987–1997* (Elektra,1997); *Bloodflowers* (Elektra, 2000).

CARRIE HAVRANEK

CYPRESS HILL

Formed: 1988, Los Angeles, California

Members: B-Real, vocals (Louis Freese, born Los Angeles, California, 2 June 1970); Eric "Bobo" Correa, percussion (born Queens, New York, 27 August 1969); Sen Dog, vocals (Senen Reyes, born Havana, Cuba, 20 November 1965); DJ Muggs, DJ, producer (Lawrence Muggerud, born Queens, New York, 28 January 1968).

Genre: Hip-Hop, Rap-Rock

Best-selling album since 1990: *Black Sunday* (1993)

Hit songs since 1990: "How I Could Just Kill a Man," "The Phuncky Feel One," "Insane in the Brain"

Cypress Hill debuted in 1991 and quickly became hip-hop's first Latino stars, combining Spanish and rap slang and paving the way for other Latino rappers such as Fat Joe and Big Pun. They simultaneously attracted attention with their enthusiastic embrace of marijuana. Echoing frontman B-Real's nasal, pro-pot raps with druggy, eerily distorted beats, producer DJ Muggs forged what became one of the 1990s' most influential sounds, anticipating the work of fellow "Chronic" smoker Dr. Dre and the "trip-hop" of British artists such as Tricky and Portishead. Cypress Hill's increasingly vocal promotion of marijuana culture endeared them to collegiate, alternative rock fans, earning them crossover success at the expense of hip-hop credibility. After a combination of declining sales, internal strife, and DJ Muggs's successful solo career almost led to Cypress Hill's break-up in the mid-1990s, the group returned at the end of the decade with a series of albums that incorporated rock elements into their trademark sound.

The seeds of Cypress Hill were sown in Los Angeles in 1986, when Cuban-born brothers Sen Dog and Mellow Man Ace joined B-Real and New York transplant DJ Muggs to form DVX. By the time Mellow Man Ace left in 1988 to pursue a solo career, DVX had developed a local following with their inventive, Spanish-language-influenced brand of hip-hop. Renaming themselves Cypress Hill after a local street, the remaining three members signed with Ruffhouse/Columbia in 1991. Their self-titled debut appeared in August of that year.

High Achievers

An instant sensation upon its release, *Cypress Hill* gradually emerged as one of the most influential albums of the 1990s. Although marijuana had always had a place in hip-hop culture, never before had a rap group celebrated its use so thoroughly. In fact, *Cypress Hill* seems to take the "blunt" smoking frequently endorsed in its lyrics as its guiding musical principle. Throughout the album, producer DJ Muggs painstakingly employs lazy beats, heavy basslines, disorienting noises, and strangely distorted samples to create the sonic equivalent of being under the influence of the drug. This distinctive production style was a major departure from the denser, more frantic sound of contemporaries such as Public Enemy and N.W.A., and it laid the groundwork for the so-called "G-funk" style that former N.W.A. member Dr. Dre would develop starting with his equally pot-obsessed solo debut, *The Chronic*, a year later. Frontman B-Real complements DJ Muggs's innovation with a nasal, sing-songy delivery that veers from the playful to the menacing, often in the same line. On the album's breakthrough single, "How I Could Just Kill a Man," the narrator recounts pulling a gun on a would-be burglar: "then I watched the rookie pass out. / Didn't have to blast him, but I did anyway / Hahaha . . . that young punk had to pay. / So I just killed a man!" The cartoonish glee with which B-Real raps these lines invests them with a jarring tongue-in-cheek quality that pervades the entire album, rendering its many threats a bit more surreal than the standard "gangsta" rap posturing of the time. *Cypress Hill* also stands out through its frequent nods to the group's Latin heritage. The track "Tres Equis" is performed entirely in Spanish, while tracks such as "Latin Lingo" deftly combine rap slang with Spanish words and phrases.

Cypress Hill soon went platinum, owing much of its sales to the group's presence on college radio and its increasing appeal beyond the traditional hip-hop fan base. In the summer of 1992 Cypress Hill cemented its growing crossover success by appearing in the popular alternative rock festival Lollapalooza. The band's public support of marijuana legalization brought it further publicity, landing it coverage in a number of mainstream national magazines such as *Newsweek* and *Entertainment Weekly*. This

DJ Muggs's Solo Efforts

Much of what made Cypress Hill's debut album so stunning was the production work of DJ Muggs, and he soon parlayed his newfound notoriety into jobs crafting hits for artists such as House of Pain, Ice Cube, and Funkdoobiest. Although Cypress Hill had entered a bit of a slump by 1997, such was DJ Muggs's stature in the hip-hop community that he was able to attract the most prominent emcees of the time to collaborate with him on his solo debut, *Muggs Presents . . . Soul Assassins, Chapter 1* (1997). Featuring artists such as Dr. Dre, Cypress Hill's B-Real, Wu-Tang Clan's GZA and RZA, Goodie Mob, and KRS-One rhyming over Muggs's trippy, menacing beats, *Soul Assassins* was an unqualified critical success. Muggs followed it up with *Juxtapose* (1999), a collaboration with fellow hip-hop producer Grease and British "trip-hop" emcee Tricky. In 2000 Muggs released a sequel to *Soul Assassins* titled *Muggs Presents Soul Assassins II*. The more electronica-oriented *Dust* followed in 2003.

all generated ample anticipation for Cypress Hill's second album, *Black Sunday*, which debuted at number one in the summer of 1993.

Rock Experimentation

Although nowhere near the groundbreaking album as its predecessor, *Black Sunday* skillfully polishes the sound established in *Cypress Hill* and tailors it for mainstream accessibility. The hit single "Insane in the Brain" emphasizes the group's time-tested role as marijuana-puffing outlaws, with B-Real rapping about "hit[ting] that bong" while evading the cops, all in his eerily childish cadences. *Black Sunday* also finds Cypress Hill beginning to incorporate more rock elements into its music, from Black Sabbath samples to the album's vaguely occult cover art. The band further experimented with rock when it recorded two separate collaborations with alternative rock bands Sonic Youth and Pearl Jam for the soundtrack to the movie *Judgment Night* (1993). This new direction prompted a back-

lash from the hip-hop community, with an article in the influential hip-hop magazine *The Source* accusing Cypress Hill of courting a white audience. Undaunted, Cypress Hill continued in this vein, adding percussionist Eric "Bobo" Correa in 1994 and touring with a wide variety of non-hip-hop acts in both the 1994 and 1995 Lollapalooza festivals as well as appearing at the heavily rock-oriented Woodstock festival in 1994.

Cypress Hill's third album, *Cypress Hill III: Temples of Boom* (1995), offers little in the way of innovation. Worse, it offers a far less engaging retread of Cypress Hill's trademark sound than *Black Sunday* does. While reliably warped and druggy, DJ Muggs's production lacks energy, and the lyrics about pot smoking and gun shooting begin to sound tired and self-parodic. Although *Temples of Boom* sold respectably well, after its release Cypress Hill began to fall apart, with DJ Muggs spending time on a successful solo career, and Sen Dog leaving for a period after tiring of playing second fiddle to B-Real. In 1998 Cypress Hill regrouped for the commercially and critically underwhelming *IV*. In late 1999 the group paid homage to their Spanish-speaking fans with a collection of Spanish-language versions of its greatest hits.

Cypress Hill mounted a comeback in 2000 with *Skull & Bones*, a double set consisting of one album of hip-hop and one album of more rock-oriented material. It released both a rap and a rock version of the album's first single, "Superstar," and both versions went on to become significant hits on radio and MTV. In 2001, Cypress Hill continued in this rock-oriented vein with its fifth studio album, *Stoned Raiders*.

Cypress Hill began the 1990s by turning marijuana-inspired lyrics and production into one of the most influential albums of the decade. Although the band itself was never quite able to move beyond the trademark sound it established with its debut, that sound was original and compelling enough to ensure Cypress Hill steady success throughout the 1990s. The band's increasing appeal to rock audiences both contributed to hip-hop's mainstream acceptance and laid the groundwork for the rap-rock that dominated the late 1990s.

SELECTIVE DISCOGRAPHY: *Cypress Hill* (Ruffhouse/Columbia, 1991); *Black Sunday* (Ruffhouse/Columbia, 1993); *Cypress Hill III: Temples of Boom* (Ruffhouse/Columbia, 1995); *IV* (Ruffhouse/Columbia, 1998); *Los Grandes Exitos en Espanol* (Sony, 1999); *Skull & Bones* (Sony, 2000); *Stoned Raiders* (Sony, 2001). **Soundtrack:** *Judgment Night* (Sony, 1993).

WEBSITE: www.cypresshill.com.

MATT HIMES

$$D\left|\frac{d}{D}\right.$$

DAFT PUNK

Formed: 1993, Paris, France

Members: Thomas Bangalter, keyboards (born France, 1 January 1975); Guy-Manuel de Homem-Christo, keyboards (born France, 8 February 1974).

Genre: Electronica, Dance

Best-selling album since 1990: *Discovery* (2001)

Hit songs since 1990: "Da Funk," "Around the World," "Digital Love"

Daft Punk have exploded a longstanding myth that France, the land of the chanson and the chanteur, is incapable of contributing to popular music's cutting edge. Since 1993, this Parisian duo has created an extraordinary collage of disco, funk, hip-hop, and techno on a sequence of remarkably inventive recordings. Not content merely to lay down irrepressible beats, the pair have also put to full use the battery of contemporary studio technology—distortion, compression, sampling—to shape a musical soundtrack that is both rich in tempo and texture but also engagingly intelligent, a rare mixture in a genre more associated with the physical than the thoughtful.

Disc jockeys Thomas Bangalter and Guy-Manuel de Homem-Christo had been influenced by the range of dance styles that emerged in the early 1980s in the United States—house in Chicago, techno in Detroit, go-go in Washington—which were then filtered through the British acid house scene and the influential Mediterranean club scenes like Ibiza in the latter half of the decade. But Bangalter and de Homem-Christo, as they absorbed the bewildering array of hybrids that arose from this transatlantic surge, also clung to an affection for independent ("indie") rock.

Energy of Punk with Pop Twist

Bangalter, the son of Daniel Vangarde, who had written "D.I.S.C.O." for French act Ottowan in 1980, and de Homem-Christo created Darlin', and were quickly signed to Duophonic, a label run by independent stalwarts Stereolab. When a track by Darlin' was included on a compilation tape by U.K. rock weekly *Melody Maker,* the magazine dubbed their sound "daft punk," an innovative sound that married the energy of punk rock with a quirky pop twist, giving the duo a new incarnation.

In 1993, when Bangalter celebrated his eighteenth birthday and received a sampler as a gift, the friends abandoned their guitars and Daft Punk issued their first single, "The New Wave," on the independent Scottish label Soma. "Da Funk" followed to even wider acclaim, and Virgin Records stepped in to sign the group. Their debut album, *Homework* (1997), lived up to their initial promise as the hits "Around the World" and "Burnin'" brought their new sound to an international audience.

Discovery Confirms Duo's Album Credentials

With *Discovery,* their long-delayed second CD, in 2001 Daft Punk truly established themselves as more than mere single maestros. The album, an almost seamless electro concerto, spawned a huge European hit in "One More Time," a stirring dance-floor classic, and laid the way for two other significant singles, "Digital Love," an appealing love song delivered by a disembodied voice, and "Harder, Better, Faster, Stronger," a harsh, metallic grind with an anthemic chorus.

Daft Punk, who issued a live album of earlier work on *Alive 1997* (2001), credit a group of collaborators for the creative concepts surrounding their musical output: album sleeves that are a curious blend of retro and futurism, and their striking videos. The principal pair has also added to their mystique by refusing to present a conventional face to the music media. Bangalter and de Homem-Christo wear robot heads for photo shoots, commenting perhaps on the key part technology plays in the music they craft.

Bangalter has stepped outside that persona to create a series of disco gems that owe something to the Daft Punk style but have a relaxed ebullience that the band's work seems to deliberately avoid. Bangalter issued the underground tune in "Trax on Da Rocks" before assuming the identity of Stardust for a massive mainstream release, "Music Sounds Better with You," in 1998.

Although they have released a relatively modest body of work, Daft Punk musical confections have been hugely inspirational to other French artists like Motorbass and Air and have raised the profile of a nation that previously had contributed little to the development of latterday popular music. The duo have been more than just parochial successes—their finely sculpted dance sound has also inspired U.K. disc jockeys, such as the Chemical Brothers and Kris Needs, to remix a number of their key cuts. While their robotic guises suggest that Daft Punk could be the heirs to Kraftwerk, German groundbreakers in the field of computerized pop in the 1970s, the wit and irony the French duo bring to their recordings mark them as significant innovators in their own right.

SELECTIVE DISCOGRAPHY: *Homework* (Virgin, 1997); *Discovery* (Virgin, 2001); *Alive 1997* (Virgin, 2001).

WEBSITE: www.daftclub.com.

SIMON WARNER

D'ANGELO

Born: Michael Eugene Archer; Richmond, Virginia, 11 February 1974

Genre: R&B

Best-selling album since 1990: *Voodoo* (2000)

Hit songs since 1990: "Brown Sugar," "Untitled (How Does It Feel)"

D'Angelo emerged as the leading artist of the neosoul movement, which favored live instrumentation and classic R&B song structures. Endowed with a voice, writing talent, and sex appeal, he initially attracted attention as a songwriter. He released his first album, *Brown Sugar*, in 1995. His songs suggest the classic R&B style of artists such as Al Green and Marvin Gaye as well as the deep funk of hip-hop. His cult grew slowly, spurred on by the commercial success of like-minded artists such as Erykah Badu, Maxwell, and Lauryn Hill. In the five years between his first and second albums, word of mouth had made D'Angelo a star, as evidenced by the debut of *Voodoo* (2000) at number one on the pop album charts.

D'Angelo took to music at an early age, teaching himself piano while growing up in Richmond, Virginia. Considered something of a local prodigy, he was encouraged to enroll in the weekly amateur talent show at Harlem's Apollo Theater in 1991 and handily won the competition three straight times. Those accolades, along with his songwriting work for the hip-hop group I.D.U., won him a publishing contract with EMI Records. He remained in Virginia for the next few years, working on songs and perfecting his craft. His first noticeable success came as writer and producer of "U Will Know," a song performed by the R&B supergroup Black Men United for the soundtrack of the film *Jason's Lyric* (1994). With a solid hit under his belt, EMI gave D'Angelo the go-ahead to write and produce his own album.

Brown Sugar (1995) was released at a low point for the R&B genre; it pointed both to the future and the past. The record's rich instrumentation and deep, soulful grooves stand in opposition to the shrill production style popularized by R. Kelly and Sean "Puffy" Combs. As a songwriter D'Angelo invokes the balladry of a soul crooner like Stevie Wonder, but he balances that sweetness with the conflicted, confessional style of Prince. His songs are as complicated as they are smooth, exuding retro warmth and hip-hop energy. The title track is an irresistible and nearly psychedelic ode to love. "Me and Those Dreamin' Eyes of Mine" is a soaring ballad that displays the singer's talents in full bloom—its tight structure allows his voice to dance playfully over the groove, creating an emotional experience that recalls the blissful heyday of soul. The album closes on a contemplative note with the atmospheric "Higher."

D'Angelo spent the next few years in relative seclusion, releasing the live set *Live at the Jazz Café* (1998) and a handful of songs for various soundtracks. During this quiet time, however, his popularity grew. *Brown Sugar* was hardly a blockbuster upon release, but it steadily sold more than 2 million copies, fostering a devoted audience and driving intense interest in his work.

After jumping to Virgin Records, D'Angelo began a new album with help from several musicians, including Lauryn Hill and Method Man. The release of *Voodoo* in 2000 ended years of waiting and presented fans with a looser, more experimental set. The album abandons the precise arrangements of *Brown Sugar* for an expansive exploration of deeper tones and textures. On most tracks D'Angelo lets his voice wander over a jammy instrumental, giving the songs an unadorned, live-in-the-studio feel. A less talented artist would have difficulty sustaining such a freewheeling mood over an entire album, but D'Angelo succeeds with confidence and stirring style. "Untitled (How Does It Feel)" provides the template for the record: the singer emotes forcefully over a bare-bones funk guitar riff. "Chicken Grease" and "Spanish Joint" are similarly stripped down, allowing for the delivery of maximum soul with minimal sound and making for an innovative and invigorating interpretation on contemporary R&B.

D'Angelo's neosoul style emanates from his method of operation: He does not rely on well-worn structures, nor does he simply inject hip-hop beats into familiar melodies. He reinvents the genre by applying a hip-hop attitude to an older form; and he follows his own muse rather than chart trends. His work is challenging, often defiant R&B with a rare vibrancy.

SELECTIVE DISCOGRAPHY: *Brown Sugar* (Capitol, 1995); *Live at the Jazz Café* (EMI, 1998); *Voodoo* (Virgin, 2000).

WEBSITE: www.okayplayer.com/dangelo.

SEAN CAMERON

DAVE MATTHEWS BAND

Formed: 1991, Charlottesville, Virginia

Members: Carter Beauford, drums (born Charlottesville, Virginia, 2 November 1958); Stefan Lessard, bass (born Anaheim, California, 4 June 1974); Dave Matthews, vocals, guitar (born Johannesburg, South Africa, 9 January 1967); LeRoi Moore, saxophone, flute (born Durham, North Carolina, 7 September 1961); Boyd Tinsley, violin (born Charlottesville, Virginia, 16 May 1964).

Genre: Rock

Best-selling album since 1990: *Crash* (1996)

Hit songs since 1990: "What Would You Say," "Crash into Me," "The Space Between"

With jazzy chords, theatrical vocals, and impeccable guitar solos, the Dave Matthews Band was one of the most musically masterful groups to make the Top 40 playlists during the 1990s and 2000s.

Lead singer Dave Matthews picked up plenty of musical influences during his childhood. His father was a physicist who performed research in remote locales; the family moved constantly. During his time in South Africa, Matthews absorbed African rhythms but also listened to rock. In the 1980s, he settled in Virginia and began playing small gigs. He formed his band with other local musicians he admired. However, he later expressed regret about naming the band after himself, emphasizing that his band mates influence him more than he influences them.

With three black and two white members, the band is one of the few that is racially integrated. The group attracted label RCA's attention by selling 100,000 copies of independent release *Remember Two Things* (1993). The band's major-label debut, *Under the Table and Dreaming* (1994), followed and it broke through the grunge and neopunk prevalent at modern rock radio with the single "What Would You Say." With a time-signature change and outstanding tenor saxophone solo, it is musically far more challenging than typical radio fare. However, the song's rumbling groove and Matthews's extroverted baritone overcame doubts by nervous program directors, and the group had its first hit.

With the potentially make-or-break sophomore album coming up, the band decided to show more of its personality, figuring that long-term success would only be worthwhile if it reflected the band's true nature. For *Crash* (1996), the band pretested much of the new material on the road and recorded many of the tracks "live in the studio" as a band, instead of one instrument at a time. The first single "Too Much" is a grooving, funk track that skewers gluttony. While its relatively simple hook makes it a logical choice for radio and MTV, that quality makes it seem too blatantly commercial for many diehard fans. For a band with Matthews's reputation, it was not the best choice for a single. Even boosters wondered if the band's 1994–1995 success had been a fluke.

The follow-up single, "So Much to Say," whose midtempo groove, baritone saxophone, and wide-ranging vocals are more representative of the Dave Matthews Band that fans know and love, was another modest hit. It took a third single, "Crash into Me," to both please the old fans and create new ones. The song is a ballad, but the rainy guitar riffs, seductive lyrics, and gentle percussion make it far different from cloying adult contemporary fare. A perfect soundtrack to romantic activities, the song spent fifty-two weeks on the Hot 100 chart. After some tense moments, the gamble on a more authentic sound paid off, and the album went on to sell more than 7 million copies.

For many bands, live albums seem like little more than vanity affairs full of gratuitous applause and frantic

Dave Matthews Band. LR: Carter Beauford, Stefan Lessard, LeRoi Moore, Dave Matthews, Boyd Tinsley [DANNY CLINCH/RCA RECORD LABEL]

postproduction. However, the Dave Matthews Band is in its element on stage. *Live at Red Rocks 8.15.95* (1997) is one of the band's most important albums, showing the group's improvisational prowess.

The stellar success of *Crash* seemed to give the band license to indulge its jam-band tendencies on *Before These Crowded Streets* (1998), many of whose songs clock in at more than seven minutes. Interestingly, the group denies it is a jam band, saying extended solos are common in jazz. The album boasts some interesting guest artists—alternative rock star Alanis Morissette sings on "Spoon" and the Peter Gabriel-esque "Don't Drink the Water" features Bela Fleck on banjo. Matthews opens the album with the world beat groove and scat singing of "Pantala Naga Pampa." The variety continues with the next track, "Rapunzel," one of the group's most R&B-influenced tunes. Steve Lillywhite, one of the top and best-known producers in rock, produced the album, as he did with the previous two studio sets. Although the album was geared more toward die-hard fans and produced no big hits, it sold more than 3 million copies.

By the late 1990s, the Dave Matthews Band had become a phenomenon among college students, young professionals, and so-called bourgeois bohemians. The loyal fans at its concerts prompted comparisons to the Grateful Dead's followers, known as Deadheads; both bands took a relaxed attitude toward home taping of their concerts. Matthews kept the bootleggers from making all the live-recording profits by releasing live albums at a frequent pace, every two years or so.

The band headed back to the studio with Lillywhite in 2000, but management and the label were unhappy with the sessions, which were proceeding under the working title *The Summer So Far*. *Before These Crowded Streets* had been a more self-indulgent effort, and it sold less than half of what *Crash* did. Now the label was getting reports that the band's new material was even less pop-oriented and more introspective. Worried, the band and label agreed to scrap the sessions and start from scratch with proven hit-maker Glen Ballard (Alanis Morissette, No Doubt). Matthews began writing more upbeat material.

The result, *Everyday* (2001), represents a commercial comeback, though naturally some hardcore fans were skeptical of the more mainstream material. Ballard updates the group's sound, bringing electric guitars to the forefront and using echo and reverb to recast Matthews's voice. Matthews sings with a grainier, less twangy tone,

Spot Light | *Busted Stuff*

The Dave Matthews Band stood at a cross-roads in 2002. It was about to release *Busted Stuff,* even though much of the album's material had been circulating around the Internet for more than a year. Nine of the album's eleven songs were originally recorded in 2000 with longtime producer Steve Lillywhite. However, when the project was scrapped in 2001 for seeming too melancholy and the band put out the sunnier *Everyday* instead, fans had a field day sending each other copies of what they dubbed *The Lillywhite Sessions.* Redoing the material with producer Steve Harris in 2002, the band changed some lyrics and added two new songs, "Where Are You Going" and "You Never Know." Many wondered if the release was redundant, since almost every loyal fan already had most of the material. But the band's reworking paid off. The word quickly got around that the arrangements and many of the lyrics were different, and fans also banded together to send a message that they were not trying to pick the band's pocket by avidly trading music. The album easily debuted at number one, selling more than 621,000 copies its first week.

but *Everyday* managed to equal its predecessor's sales of 3 million.

Delighting fans, the group resurrected much of the unreleased 2000 material in 2002, promoting longtime engineer Steve Harris as producer of *Busted Stuff* (2002). Matthews goes back to the acoustic guitar and the tempo slows down a bit. "Grey Street" exemplifies the slightly more melancholy approach, as Matthews croons sympathetic lyrics: "There's an emptiness inside her / and she'd do almost anything to fill it in." However, the group still lets loose—the minor-key "Captain" features some of Stefan Lessard's best bass playing. The album includes a bonus DVD with live footage. Matthews is more lyrically introspective and mellow, perhaps a consequence of his becoming a father. Despite his fame, he continues to live in Charlottesville, Virginia, though he and his wife also have a home in suburban Seattle, Washington.

Long solos, complex chords, and diverse instrumentation are far from the stereotypical makings of a band that regularly conquers the Top 40. Outliving grunge, bubblegum, and skate-rock fads, the eclectic, unpredictable Dave Matthews Band gives idealists faith in an industry where sometimes talent is not as important as looks and demographic trends.

SELECTIVE DISCOGRAPHY: *Under the Table and Dreaming* (RCA, 1994); *Crash* (RCA, 1996); *Live at Red Rocks 8.15.95* (Bama Rags/RCA, 1997); *Before These Crowded Streets* (RCA, 1998); *Everyday* (RCA, 2001); *Busted Stuff* (RCA, 2002).

RAMIRO BURR

and comes across somewhat like Peter Gabriel. He gamely goes along with plugging in his guitar, saying he preferred acoustic guitar in the past because it was what he knew best. "I Did It," a funky confession of sins along the lines of "Too Much," showcases the more compact, slick sound. The group kicks into an uncharacteristically aggressive rock groove on "When the World Ends," which also throws a curve by using layered strings, not just Boyd Tinsley's violin. Ballard brings the drums high in the mix on "So Right," all the better with which to get radio's attention, though Tinsley's colorful violin keeps the song grounded in the band's familiar tradition. Like *Crash,* this album earned its biggest hit with a ballad. "The Space Between" fuses the group's jazzy, sax-fueled, loose-jointed groove with a bright, modern electric guitar riff. Not quite as steamy as *Crash,* it delighted listeners nonetheless. With economic uncertainty and the September 11 terrorist attacks, 2001 was a depressed year for music sales,

CRAIG DAVID

Born: Craig Ashley David; Southampton, England, 5 May 1981.

Genre: R&B

Best-selling album since 1990: *Born to Do It* (2000)

Hit songs since 1990: "Walking Away," "7 Days," "What's Your Flava?"

Craig David, the British-born singer/songwriter, burst upon the American scene in 2001 with his eclectic mix of edgy dance beats and traditional pop song craft. He emerged in Britain as the popular face of U.K. garage, a dance music genre marked by fast-paced, fractured beats and soulful choruses. He won acclaim for his debut album, *Born to Do It* (2000), and became the youngest male artist to top both the singles and album charts in his native country. He continued this success in America, and in 2002 released *Slicker Than Your Average*, in which he ventures further from his garage roots into pop and R&B territory.

Craig David was born in Southampton, a port city in southern England, to an English mother and West Indian father. His multicultural upbringing and love of American pop and soul influenced his first forays into music as a DJ, spinning and mixing records on a local pirate radio station at age fourteen. He soon moved on to club sets, and in 1996 won a national songwriting competition for an original track titled "I'm Ready." The song was recorded by the R&B group Damage and ended up as the B-side of a successful single. "I'm Ready" brought David to the attention of Mark Hill, a member of the popular garage production team Artful Dodger.

The garage style combines quick, clipped beats with rap and R&B-style choruses. The texture of the beats is light and breezy in comparison to the hard, frenetic sound of typical club music. This tonal variation represented a new and engaging sound, and garage caught fire in the U.K. underground dance scene. Hill set David's pop and R&B songs to a garage beat, and the team produced the 1999 U.K. hit single "Rewind." The song is credited with introducing garage to the mainstream, and it set David up for a full album release.

Born to Do It was a hit in Britain upon its release in 2000. Its success was driven by a string of stirring singles, including the sexy "7 Days" and the confessional "Walking Away." Much of the sound is rooted in garage, but what shines through is David's talents as a singer and songwriter. "7 Days" benefits from the novelistic detail of a chance meeting that stretches out over a week. The confident vocals match the smooth arrangements and reveal a real personality usually absent in garage's anonymous producer-driven singles. The following year the album received its American release and garnered significant acclaim and commercial success.

In his second album, *Slicker Than Your Average* (2002), David articulates his love of pop and R&B with a collection of supremely catchy songs. Although some fans regretted his departure from garage, he won wider acclaim for his bold songwriting and ambitious vocals. Dance tracks like "What's Your Flava?" slink with a newfound bravado, and the ballads unfold with assured grace. "Rise & Fall," a ballad recorded with Sting, addresses the perils of fame and the pitfalls of stardom in startlingly open terms: "Now I don't even wanna please the fans, / No autographs, / No interviews, / No pictures, / And less demands."

Craig David stands in a line of pop singers who do not conform to a particular style. Like his heroes Prince and Terence Trent D'Arby, David easily jumps genres with a sound and attitude all his own.

SELECTIVE DISCOGRAPHY: *Born to Do It* (2000, Atlantic); *Slicker Than Your Average* (2002, Atlantic).

WEBSITE: www.craigdavid.com.

SEAN CAMERON

MILES DAVIS

Born: Miles Dewey Davis III; Alton, Illinois, 26 May 1926; died 28 September 1991, Santa Monica, California

Genre: Jazz

Best-selling album since 1990: *Kind of Blue* (1997 re-issue)

Hit songs since 1990: "Time after Time"

Miles Davis has been the missing giant of American popular music since his death in September 1991, little more than two months after his final performances and a session on his posthumously released, Grammy-winning hip-hop effort, *Doo-Bop* (1992). His distinctively spare, introspective, vibratoless style was a marvel of taste and power. An indefatigable innovator, Davis was characterized by Duke Ellington as the jazz Picasso.

Davis's death was rumored to have been related to AIDS. Certainly his constitution was affected by hard living, organic disease, diverse accidents, and self-inflicted knocks. In the year prior to his death, he toured stadiums and festivals with a young electric jazz band featuring the saxophonist Kenny Garrett. He made two major appearances before his death. The first was a one-time-only review at the Montreux Jazz Festival on July 8, 1991, when he played big-band charts written by his late friend Gil Evans and conducted by Quincy Jones. Two days later in Paris, he appeared at a concert along with his longtime associates: saxophonists Jackie McLean and Wayne Shorter; pianists Chick Corea, Herbie Hancock, and Joe Zawinul; guitarists John McLaughlin and John Scofield; bassist Dave Holland; and drummer Jack DeJohnette.

Davis was the son of a prosperous Midwestern oral surgeon and his wife, descendants of accomplished African-Americans and bearers of high cultural standards. They afforded their three children enriching opportunities. Miles started his trumpet studies in sixth grade and took private lessons with a trumpeter from the St. Louis symphony from the age of thirteen, when his father bought him a horn for his birthday. His mother never approved of his musical career.

As a young teen playing local clubs, Davis was encouraged by the trumpeter Clark Terry. Hired as a last-minute substitute on one occasion by balladeer and bandleader

Billy Eckstine, Davis met trumpeter Dizzy Gillespie and alto saxophonist Charlie Parker, the chief proponents of bebop, the virtuosic, small-group jazz movement that flourished after World War II. In 1945 Davis moved to New York City to attend the Juilliard School's Institute of Musical Art, and immediately sought out Parker and Gillespie in the jazz clubs of Fifty-second Street.

Davis was quickly accepted by the boppers, becoming a mainstay of Parker's group in 1947. He also participated in informal jam sessions hosted by Gil Evans, a collaboration that resulted in the short-lived nonet that recorded the groundbreaking album *Birth of the Cool* (1950). The bebop milieu was pervaded by heroin addiction, and Davis fell prey to the drug in 1949, after which his career wobbled as he freelanced erratically with musicians including Eckstine, Stan Getz, and Billie Holiday. After kicking his drug habit by returning to his parents' home and going cold turkey, Davis surged to the fore of the jazz scene, working with J. J. Johnson, Horace Silver, Sonny Rollins, Thelonious Monk, Milt Jackson, and others. After an acclaimed performance at the 1955 Newport Jazz Festival, he never looked back.

The upward trajectory of Davis's career brought him into the leadership of his first quintet, with John Coltrane; a long association with Columbia Records (abandoned in 1985 for Warner Bros.); and the landmark albums *Porgy and Bess* (1959) and *Sketches of Spain* (1960), which drew on the work of the contemporary Spanish composer Joaquín Rodrigo. His band that featured Coltrane, alto saxophonist Cannonball Adderley, and pianist Bill Evans produced the landmark modal take on the blues, *Kind of Blue* (1959), considered by some critics the greatest album in the history of jazz; it remains the best-selling album in the history of the genre.

Nevertheless, reams of criticism has piled up about the music of *Kind of Blue*; among its chief attractions is the mood it sets, and maintains, of relaxed yet alert, soothing but never soporific sweet sadness. The themes are simple (though deceptively so) and repetitious, yet not cloying. The rhythms are mostly soft and mid-tempo, nonetheless propulsive. Davis's improvisations seem casual yet are perfectly phrased; his ideas are never forced, but by turns bold and vulnerable. Each major soloist matches this standard: Adderley, Coltrane, and Evans give performances of their lives, the saxophonists flowing and lucid, the pianist spreading a color spectrum of harmonies. *Kind of Blue* redeems a promise of jazz: to bestow a dollop of grace on those who hear it.

In the early 1960s Davis hired his second great quintet, composed of pianist Hancock, saxophonist Shorter, bassist Ron Carter, and seventeen-year-old drummer Tony Williams, all of whom ably enacted Davis's visionary experiments with elliptical forms, newly available electric instruments, and rhythmic variation. By the late 1960s and early 1970s, the creatively restless Davis was enthralled with the budding progressive rock scene; he gathered guitarist John McLaughlin; bassist Dave Holland; electric keyboardists Joe Zawinul, Chick Corea and Keith Jarrett; electric bassists; sitar players; and drummers Don Alias, Jack DeJohnette, and Lenny White for the suitelike jazz-rock fusion recording (produced by Teo Macero) titled *Bitches Brew* (1970).

That two-LP set announced a revolution in American contemporary instrumental music, fusing grandiose themes and dense orchestrations at high volumes with ferocious improvisation and roiling polyrhythmics. Davis followed with a dozen albums in the same vein—many of them live-in-concert before integrated young audiences—and an international tour of venues that could accommodate his requirements of sound.

Many key members of that ensemble and of other heavily amplified and processed bands Davis maintained until the late 1970s have remained in the forefront of jazz: among them are saxophonists Gary Bartz, Sonny Fortune, Steve Grossman, and David Liebman; tablaist Badal Roy; percussionist Airto Moirea; Brazilian composer Hermeto Pascoal; and guitarist Pete Cosey. After a period of inactivity, Davis rebounded with the album *Man with a Horn* (1981), which features an even younger ensemble in stripped-down productions that did not tax his lapsed trumpet technique.

In the 1980s Davis regained his trumpet technique while continuing to talent-scout and develop material for electronically enhanced, improvising ensembles. He employed guitarists Scofield and Mike Stern; saxophonists Bob Berg, Bill Evans, and Branford Marsalis; bassists Marcus Miller, Darryl Jones, and Foley McCreary; percussionists Alias, Mino Cinelu, and Marilyn Mazur; drummer Al Foster; and a succession of electric keyboardists (including George Duke and Joey DeFrancesco) and synthesizer programmers.

As Davis renewed his career, he extended himself, commercially, artistically, and politically. He was among the first jazz musicians to adapt pop hits of the eighties for his own use, claiming both Cindy Lauper's "Time after Time" and Michael Jackson's "Human Nature" with unique interpretations. He recorded soundtracks—*Siesta* (1987), *The Hot Spot* (1990), and *Djingo* (1990)—for films in which he also acted. He appeared as an icon of cool in advertising campaigns, and began to exhibit his paintings in art galleries. Davis gave pointed titles to his albums: *Tutu* (1986), named for the black archbishop and antiapartheid leader of South Africa, and *Amandla* (1989), meaning "freedom" in Swahili. He also contributed a cameo to the album released by Artists United Against Apartheid, *Sun City* (1985). His personal life, however, remained tempestuous; his fourth marriage, to actress Cicely Tyson, was marked by bursts of violence and ended in divorce.

Davis's gaunt scowl, dramatic clothing, and hoarse voice became legendary, even among those who did not know his music. But they are part of the sensibility that underlay his unforgettable trumpet sound, a gripping evocation of the loneliness, strangeness, exhilaration, and pathos of life in postwar America that rivals the achievement of any artist in any medium of the past fifty years.

SELECTIVE DISCOGRAPHY: *Decoy* (Columbia, 1984); *Tutu* (Warner Bros., 1986); *Original Motion Picture Soundtrack: The Hot Spot* (Antilles, 1990); *Doo-Bop* (1992); *Live Around the World* (Warner Bros. 1996); *The Complete Columbia Studio Recordings of Miles Davis and Gil Evans* (Columbia Legacy, 1996); *Dark Magus* (Columbia reissue, 1997); *Live-Evil* (Columbia reissue, 1997); *Black Beauty* (Columbia reissue, 1997); *Live at the Philharmonic* (Columbia reissue, 1997); *Live at the Fillmore East* Columbia reissue, 1997); *Kind of Blue* (Columbia reissue, 1997); *The Complete Bitches Brew Sessions* Columbia Legacy, 1998); *Birth of the Cool* (Capitol EMI reissue, 2001); *The Complete Miles Davis at Montreux 1973–1991* (Warner Music, 2002).

BIBLIOGRAPHY: J. Szwed, *So What, the Life of Miles Davis* (New York, 2002); B. Kirchner (ed.), *A Miles Davis Reader* (Washington, DC, 1997); P. Tingen, *Miles Beyond: The Electronic Explorations of Miles Davis, 1967–1991* (New York, 2001); M. Davis, *Miles, the Autobiography* (New York, 1989).

WEBSITES: www.milesdavis.com/home.html; www.wam.umd.edu/~losinp/music/miles_ahead.html; servercc.oakton.edu/~larry/miles/milestones.html.

HOWARD MANDEL

DAYS OF THE NEW

Formed: 1996, Louisville, Kentucky

Members: Mike Huettig, bass (born 29 June 1968); Travis Meeks, lead vocals, guitar (born Jeffersonville, Indiana, 27 April 1979); Ray Rizzo, drums (born 19 February 1971). Former members: Chuck Mingis, guitar, vocals (born Louisville, Kentucky, 14 February 1967); Matt Taul, drums (born Jeffersonville, Indiana, 30 August 1978); Jesse Vest, bass (born Jeffersonville, Indiana, 10 May 1977); Todd Whitener, guitar (born Louisville, Kentucky, 25 May 1978).

Genre: Rock

Best-selling album since 1990: *Days of the New* (1997)

Hit songs since 1990: "Touch, Peel and Stand," "Shelf in the Room," "The Down Town"

Days of the New is an ongoing musical exploration by the guitarist, singer, and songwriter Travis Meeks. The group began as an alternative-rock quartet in Louisville, Kentucky, in 1997. Although the group scored several hits from their debut eponymous album, Meeks parted company with the other three members after their first prolonged tour. For subsequent albums, Meeks experimented with different guest vocalists and utilized different instruments, from lush string orchestrations and studio effects to Celtic singing and Native American chants.

In its first incarnation Days of the New was signed to Outpost Records and released their first album in 1997. All of their albums are eponymous and distinguishable only by color. The *Orange* album received favorable reviews and the influence of such alternative pioneers as Pearl Jam and Alice in Chains was duly noted. The first song to be released, "Touch, Peel and Stand," received generous airplay and reached number one on *Billboard*'s Mainstream Rock chart. This song displays their musical economy, with the guitar and bass doubling parts of the melodic line. "Shelf in the Room" is a dark ballad with a pervasive guitar riff and a claustrophobic melodic line that is almost absurd in its simplicity. "The Down Town" reveals a larger harmonic palate and provides a moment of respite from the one-dimensional sound of their first album.

During a tour with Metallica and Jerry Cantrell, frustrations within the band began to escalate. Meeks eventually left the band, and the remaining three members reformulated themselves as Carbon-14 (subsequently, Tantric). Meeks retained the band's moniker and returned to Louisville, immediately working on a second album. The *Green* album (1999) reveals a completely different approach, with varied harmonic progressions and an expanded instrumental sound. Meeks embellishes his hard-rock aesthetic with string and brass orchestrations, textural doublings, and Celtic sounds. The songs overlap the track designations, providing a certain continuity. "I Think" keeps the Metallica-influenced sound of early Days of the New, with its pounding introduction and screaming chorus. "Last One" is an epic song, drawing on the sounds of American Indian chants and the tabla, while "Bring Yourself" begins with an organ and multitracked female voices in a pseudo-Celtic style. Occasionally self-indulgent and sophomoric, *Green* exhibits an ambitious approach to hard rock production techniques and songwriting.

With the third album, *Red* (2001), Meeks struck a balance between the first two albums. Working as a trio with Mike Huettig and Ray Rizzo, Meeks penned straightforward rock songs with a renewed energy. The opening track, "Hang on to This," shows a varied melodic line with a memorable chorus: "Cause I'm doin' what I got to, what I got to hang on." The experimentation found in the *Green* album is evident in the sitar introduction of "Giving In" and the vast orchestrations of "Dirty Road" and "Dancing in the Wind."

The driving force behind Days of the New is undoubtedly the singer and songwriter Travis Meeks. His penchant for experimentation has revealed a creative force deeply rooted in a hard rock aesthetic. Although the *Orange* album strove too hard for a singular sound and the *Green* album overindulged in studio effects, Days of the New seem to be negotiating a natural balance between these two approaches.

SELECTIVE DISCOGRAPHY: *Days of the New— Orange* (Outpost Records, 1997); *Days of the New—Green* (Outpost Records, 1999); *Days of the New—Red* (Outpost Records, 2001).

WEBSITE: www.daysofthenew.com.

WYNN YAMAMI

DE LA SOUL

Formed: 1987, Long Island, New York

Members: P. A. Mase (Vincent Mason; born Amityville, New York, 27 March 1970); Posdnous (Kelvin Mercer; born Bronx, New York, 17 August 1969); Trugoy the Dove (David Joliceur; born Amityville, New York, 21 September 1968).

Genre: Hip-Hop

Hit songs since 1990: "A Roller Skate Named Saturday," "Ring Ring Ring," "Oooh"

When De La Soul emerged in the late 1980s, fans and critics alike embraced them as an alternative to the aggressiveness that dominated much of hip-hop's attitude at the time. Compared to the gold-chain bravado and velour-suit preening exhibited by the likes of LL Cool J, Run-D.M.C., and Big Daddy Kane, De La Soul draped themselves in day-glo colors and flower-child imagery. With the release of their critically lauded *3 Ft. High and Rising* (1989), many labeled De La Soul as the hippies of hip-hop, an association the group itself detested. But their popularity helped create a space for hip-hop's more socially marginal denizens: rap's geeks and nerds, who saw De La Soul as their patron saints.

De La Soul often fought to reconcile the critical praise that was heaped upon them with the lack of the commercial success they craved. One of the outcomes of this struggle was that De La Soul reinvented themselves on almost every album they released. The most dramatic of these transformations was done in literal fashion with the release of their second album, *De La Soul Is Dead* (1991). The cover of the album shows a potted daisy—a symbol from their first album—overturned and broken as the stark lettering of the album's title proclaims the end to De La Soul as we knew them. There are elements on *De La Soul Is Dead* that evince a stark change—what the hip-hop journalist Nelson George argued was a switch from Afrocentrism to ghettocentrism. On "Pease Porridge," Mase can be heard asking, "Why do people think that just because he speak peace we can't throw no joints?" On "Afro Connections at a Hi 5," they lampoon "hoodlum" rap with an aggressive, mocking rhyme style.

The album's darkest song, inexplicably released as a single, is "Millie Pulled a Pistol on Santa," which tells the tale of an incest victim shooting her molester. Although the mood is decidedly less happy-go-lucky on this album than on their previous release, the group is no less inventive or playful. Their club favorite "A Roller Skate Named Saturday" conjures up the rollicking pleasure of a 1970s disco party; the farcical "Bitties in the BK Lounge" and "Hey Love" both deal with the comical complexities of gender relations.

Their next album, *Buhloone Mindstate* (1993), found De La wading even further afield in what many considered their most inventive work, whereas others considered it esoteric and over their heads. Despite likable singles such as the smooth and mellow "Breakadawn," the album produced few hits and has become more of a cult favorite than a mainstream classic. Standout songs include "Stone Age," a collaboration with the always entertaining Biz Markie, and "I Am, I Be," an autobiographical reflection on De La's fears and motivations.

With *Stakes Is High* (1996) De La Soul parted ways with Prince Paul and made new headway with an album that was completely their own. The result was a strong, well-balanced offering that was more lyrically accessible while sacrificing little else. Songs like "The Bizness," "Itzowezee," and the title track itself exhibit the same qualities that graced their previous albums—wit, intelligence, and a commitment to social consciousness. In addition, the group mentors a new generation of talent, with guests like Common, Mos Def, and Truth Enola making cameos.

Their next two albums were meant to be part of a larger triptych named *Art Official Intelligence*, *Mosaic Thump* (2000) and *Bionix* (2001). These works find the group struggling for relevance when they're one of the few hip-hop groups from the 1980s still standing. With singles like "Oooh" (which appears on *Mosaic Thump*), they proved they still had the ability to create hits, but the overall albums failed to resonate with younger audiences.

Throughout their long career, De La Soul proved to be sole survivors, outlasting many peers who were once part of a confederation of artists called the Native Tongues family (A Tribe Called Quest, the Jungle Brothers, Queen Latifah). Though they never matched the success they found with their debut, *3 Ft. High and Rising*, the group was among hip-hop's richest because they never took their artistry for granted. In a genre where consistency and longevity rarely unite, De La Soul managed to build their reputation on both.

SELECTIVE DISCOGRAPHY: *De La Soul Is Dead* (Tommy Boy, 1991); *Buhloone Mindstate* (Tommy Boy, 1993); *Stakes Is High* (Tommy Boy, 1996); *Art Official Intelligence: Mosaic Thump* (Tommy Boy, 2000).

OLIVER WANG

DEF LEPPARD

Formed: 1977, Sheffield, England

Members: Rick Allen, drums (born Derbyshire, England, 1 November 1963); Vivian Campbell, guitar (born Belfast, Northern Ireland, 25 August 1962); Phil Collen, guitar (born London, England, 8 December 1957); Joe Elliott, lead vocals (born Sheffield, England, 1 August 1959); Rick Savage, bass (born Sheffield, England, 2 December 1960). Former members: Steve Clark, guitar (born Sheffield, England, 23 April 1960; d. London, England, 8 January 1991); Pete Willis, guitar (born Sheffield, England, 16 February 1960).

Genre: Rock

Best-selling album since 1990: *Adrenalize* (1992)

Hit songs since 1990: "Let's Get Rocked," "Two Steps Behind"

Def Leppard enjoyed tremendous popularity in the 1980s with their approachable brand of hard rock. Initially inspired by such bands as Judas Priest and AC/DC, Def Leppard soon developed their signature sound of electric guitar riffs and straightforward rock beats augmented with synthesizers and lush vocal backups. Although their lyrics are simplistic and at times banal, Joe Elliot propels each song with his earnest and emotive delivery. The band has weathered hardships during its career, most notably the injury incurred by Rick Allen and the death of Steve Clark. While largely ignored during the 1990s, Def Leppard has continued to produce albums, staunchly retaining their style of arena rock.

Getting Started

Guitarist Pete Willis and bassist Rick "Sav" Savage formed the band Atomic Mass in their hometown of Sheffield, England, in 1977. Singer Joe Eliott soon joined and suggested the name Deaf Leopard, which was refor-

mulated into Def Leppard. With the addition of guitarist Steve Clark and drummer Rick Allen, the group began to perform in various venues and was eventually signed to Phonogram/Mercury in 1978.

Def Leppard toured with Sammy Hagar and AC/DC and garnered some modest radio airplay with their debut album, *On Through the Night* (1980). Working with producer Robert John "Mutt" Lange, the band released their second album, *High 'n' Dry* (1981), which included the hit song "Bringin' on the Heartbreak." Although the song sounded empty at times, with the guitar doubling the bass rather than producing chords and the obvious lack of synthesizer textures, it heralded several key elements of their style, including their reliance on guitar riffs and lithe vocal harmonies. While recording material for their next album, Pete Willis left the group and was replaced by Phil Collen.

With the release of *Pyromania* (1983), Def Leppard gained widespread attention and headlined their own tour. The album rose to *Billboard*'s number two slot and included the power ballad "Foolin'" and the rock anthems "Photograph" and "Rock of Ages." During this time Def Leppard faced their first serious setback. Rick Allen was thrown from his car during an accident on December 31, 1984, and his left arm was completely severed. The band took a hiatus, and Allen slowly taught himself to drum one-armed on a Simmons electronic set. Cautious at first, the band began to perform and record, releasing their hugely successful album *Hysteria* in 1987.

Hysteria includes some of Def Leppard's biggest hits: "Love Bites," "Pour Some Sugar on Me," "Armageddon It," "Hysteria," and "Rocket." The ballad "Love Bites" begins slowly with two full verses and a long transition before presenting the chorus with its soaring melodic line and vocal backups, accompanied by an equally poignant solo guitar riff. "Pour Some Sugar on Me" features a swerving guitar riff and straightforward power chords in the chorus. Although their lyrical style is powerful in its simplicity, at times it veers into banality: "Step inside, walk this way. You and me, babe. Hey hey."

After another round of touring, Def Leppard began working on their next album. On January 8, 1991, Steve Clark died from respiratory failure induced by alcohol and pain killers. Vivian Campbell, previously of Dio and Whitesnake, joined the group, and Def Leppard soon released *Adrenalize* (1992). Although this album rose to *Billboard*'s number one slot, the songs were largely formulaic and uninspired.

The following year, Def Leppard contributed the song "Two Steps Behind" to the film *Last Action Hero*. Surprisingly enough, this B-side became a hit and prompted them to release a full album of unreleased material and alternate versions. *Retro Active* (1993) included the ballad "Miss You in a Heartbeat" and the raucous "She's Too Tough," with Eliott replicating the vocal delivery of AC/DC's Brian Johnson.

In 1995 Def Leppard released the compilation album *Vault*, which included the previously unreleased ballad "When Love and Hate Collide." Showcasing a different approach, Def Leppard introduced piano and strings to the texture, with the electric guitars providing unobtrusive accompaniment. Aside from the ubiquitous guitar solo, the song reveals a pop sensibility far removed from their earlier material.

For their next album, Def Leppard decided to work with the producer Pete Woodroffe rather than their longtime collaborator "Mutt" Lange. Unfortunately *Slang* (1996) was unconvincing and inconsistent. With their next release, however, Def Leppard achieved a balance of new musical styles and signature approaches. *Euphoria* (1999) included the funk-inspired "All Night," the pop song "21st Century Sha La La La Girl," and the straightforward rock songs "Demolition Man" and "Promises."

"Promises" begins with a striking guitar riff that is quickly augmented with a second guitar line. During the chorus, the backup vocals proclaim, "I won't make promises," to which Eliott finishes the thought: "that I can't keep." This technique of sharing the chorus reflects the method in such songs as "Photograph" and "Pour Some Sugar on Me." The funk approach in "All Night," while obviously a stylistic aberration, is surprisingly successful. Def Leppard alters the vocal backups from tight harmonic passages into delineated bass and tenor doublings of the melodic line. While using funk guitar voicings in the verse, they still manage to insert a heavily distorted guitar line in the chorus. With their next release, *X* (2002), the group experimented further with different producers. Although songs such as "You're So Beautiful" and "Now" are promising, the album as a whole is undeveloped and one-dimensional.

Def Leppard developed a popular approach to heavy metal and hard rock in the early 1980s. Along with Van Halen and Mötley Crüe, Def Leppard ushered in the pop-metal movement, which spawned such bands as Bon Jovi, Whitesnake, Poison, and Cinderella. The craftsmanship of their guitar riffs, melodic lines, and vocal harmonies set them above many of their peers, and their rock anthems and earnest power ballads became emblematic of the 1980s. Def Leppard's subsequent albums, particularly those of the late 1990s and early 2000s, seemed like relics of an earlier era and attracted little notice.

SELECTIVE DISCOGRAPHY: *On Through the Night* (Mercury, 1980); *High 'n' Dry* (Mercury, 1981); *Pyromania* (Mercury, 1983); *Hysteria* (Mercury, 1987); *Adrenalize* (Mercury, 1992); *Retro Active* (Mercury, 1993); *Vault: Def Leppard's Greatest Hits* (Mercury, 1995); *Slang* (Mercury, 1996); *Euphoria* (Mercury, 1999); *X* (Mercury, 2002).

WEBSITE: www.defleppard.com.

WYNN YAMAMI

JACK DEJOHNETTE

Born: Chicago, Illinois, 9 August 1942

Genre: Jazz

Best-selling album since 1990: *Parallel Realities* (1998)

Jack DeJohnette is among the most supple, powerful, broadly experienced, and subtle jazz drummers of the past three decades. He is an imaginative bandleader and an anchor for improvisers such as the pianist Keith Jarrett, whom he met when they were both in the Charles Lloyd Quartet from 1966 to 1968 and in whose long-running trio he remains a key member.

DeJohnette was encouraged in his childhood musical interests by his uncle, Roy L. Wood Sr., a popular jazz DJ who later became vice president of the National Network of Black Broadcasters. DeJohnette began piano lessons at age four. He studied classical music for ten years but switched to jazz as a teenager, playing in blues and rock and roll bands while falling under the influence of the pianist Ahmad Jamal. He started playing drums at age eighteen and met musicians with avant-garde interests who later formed the Association for the Advancement of Creative Musicians (AACM), an artists' collective. He also sat in with John Coltrane in Chicago before moving to New York City in 1966.

DeJohnette found more work in New York as a drummer than as a pianist, employed by vocalist Abbey Lincoln, saxophonists Jackie McLean and Charles Lloyd, and pianist Bill Evans, with whom he toured Great Britain. He also worked with saxophonist Stan Getz, and he replaced drummer Tony Williams in Miles Davis's band in 1969, in time to record Davis's groundbreaking double album *Bitches Brew*, which set the direction for jazz-rock-fusion efforts to come. In Davis's group he played with pianists Jarrett and Herbie Hancock, and bassist Dave Holland. He recorded *The DeJohnette Complex* (1969) with his drum mentor Roy Haynes and formed Compost, a jazz-rock band in which he played keyboards with Don Alias as a drummer/percussionist. After considerable freelancing, including the recording of *Ruta and Daitya* (1973), his first album with Keith Jarrett on the ECM label, DeJohnette established the trio Gateway in 1976 with Holland and guitarist John Abercrombie.

DeJohnette has often used his bands—including Directions, formed in 1976, New Directions (1978–1979), and Special Edition—as incubators for new talents, collaborating with trumpeter Lester Bowie; saxophonists David Murray, Arthur Blythe, Gary Thomas, and Greg Osby; and pianists John Hicks and Michael Cain, among others. DeJohnette has been lauded for his compositions for these bands, including lyrical melodies such as "Silver Hollow," "Where or Wayne," "New Orleans Strut," and "Zoot Suite."

DeJohnette has recorded with so many different leaders of ECM sessions that he is considered the label's house drummer; he has worked constantly in Keith Jarrett's trio (with the bassist Gary Peacock) since 1985. He recorded *The Jack DeJohnette Piano Album* (1985), which was well received but has not generated a sequel. He toured with Hancock, Holland, and Pat Metheny in 1990 (the group plans to re-form in 2004) and singer Betty Carter (resulting in the live album *Feed the Fire* [1993]), and he helped introduce Cuban pianist Gonzalo Rubalcaba to audiences in the United States (*The Blessing* [1991]).

Since 1990 DeJohnette has focused on earth studies, ecology, and cultural preservation with his album *Music for the Fifth World* (1992), featuring guitarists Vernon Reid and John Scofield and Native American singers; his meditative releases *Dancing with Nature Spirits* (1995) and *Oneness* (1996); his duets with British reeds virtuoso John Surman in *Invisible Nature* (2002); and participation in Surman's composition for reeds, strings, pianos, and drums, *Free and Equal* (2003). In the summer of 2003 DeJohnette led ensembles in a partial career retrospective over four nights at the Montreal Jazz Festival.

DeJohnette has never won a Grammy Award, but he has been honored innumerable times in *Down Beat* magazine polls, and he is revered by Japanese audiences. Heir to Roy Haynes, Max Roach, and Elvin Jones, DeJohnette is the preeminent living jazz drummer of his generation.

SELECTIVE DISCOGRAPHY: *The DeJohnette Complex* (Milestone, 1969); *Ruta and Daitya* (ECM, 1973); *Cosmic Chicken* (Prestige, 1975); *New Directions* (ECM, 1978); *Tin Can Alley* (ECM, 1980); *Album, Album* (ECM, 1984); *The Jack DeJohnette Piano Album* (Landmark, 1985); *Earthwalk* (Blue Note, 1991); *Music for the Fifth World* (Manhattan, 1992); *Extra Special Edition* (Blue Note, 1994); *Dancing with Nature Spirits* (ECM, 1995); *Oneness* (ECM, 1996); *Parallel Realities* (Universal/GRP, 1998); *Invisible Nature* (ECM, 2002); *Free and Equal* (ECM, 2003).

WEBSITE: www.JackDeJohnette.com.

HOWARD MANDEL

DEPECHE MODE

Formed: 1960, London, England

Members: Andy Fletcher, synthesizers (born Basildon, Essex, England, 8 July 1960); David Gahan, lead vocals (born Epping, Essex, England, 9 May 1962); Martin Gore, synthesizer (born Basildon, Essex, England, 23 July 1961). Former members: Alan Wilder synthesizer (born England, 1 June 1959; Vince Clarke, synthesizer (born South Woodford, London, England, 3 July 1960)

Genre: Rock

Best-selling album since 1990: *Violator* (1990)

Hit songs since 1990: "Enjoy the Silence" "Personal Jesus" "I Feel You"

The music of British electronic synthesizer band Depeche Mode slipped onto American airwaves in the late 1980s and early 1990s, sandwiched between the synthesized sounds of the 1980s New Wave and the guitar-driven sound of grunge rock. Before the release of their seminal album, *Violator* (1990), Depeche Mode (French for "fast fashion") had enjoyed a cult status in the United States throughout the 1980s. The band's music is dark, sensual, and emotional; the chief songwriter Martin Gore composes achingly romantic and heartbreaking love songs that often deal with unhealthy, obsessive relationships. The band has been together for over twenty years, surviving substance abuse, depression, and personnel changes.

Starting Out

The initial trio of Clarke, Fletcher, and Gore debuted in London clubs playing guitars, not synthesizers, but it did not take long for them to switch. When Depeche Mode signed to London's Mute Records in 1980, they were a dance pop band and their debut album, *Speak and Spell* (1981), yielded two hits in the U.K.: "Just Can't Get Enough" and "Dreaming of Me." Their early music was notable for simple electronic dance beats and catchy, rhyming lyrics. By their third album, Depeche Mode began to hit their songwriting stride. With *Some Great Reward* (1984), they had several hits that covered a wide array of subject matter, from religious doubt ("Blasphemous Rumours") to sexual dynamics ("Master and Servant"); the album boasted a massive, transcontinental hit in "People Are People." The follow-up album, *Black Celebration* (1986), features "Strangelove," a song with a typically twisted, self-destructive theme that had become their signature. Its refrain consists of Gahan's deep voice chanting "Pain / Will you return it / I'll say it again / Pain."

Building on the success of 1987's *Music for the Masses*, the band put together a documentary, *Depeche Mode 101*, directed by D. A. Pennebaker, and a companion live double album, culled from years of U.S. tours. *10* is not only an informal greatest hits compilation, but it is also an example of the band's charisma. The documentary captures the band enjoying huge, sold-out success in stadiums and arenas across the United States. Both their music and their lyrics had developed substantially and become more sophisticated, thanks to Martin Gore, their primary songwriter. This trend is evident in the beautiful ballad "Somebody" and a nearly six-minute version of the subversive, double-entendre-laden "Behind the Wheel." "Somebody," with Gore on piano, is especially moving. He sings his plea, accompanied by thousands of fans: "I want somebody to share / Share the rest of my life."

Music for the Masses

With the release of *Violator* (1990), Depeche Mode was poised for their greatest success yet in the United States. *Violator* (1990) is a classic Depeche Mode album: dense, dark, melodic, but with a twist. *Violator* marked a harder-edged sound; its synthesizer pop songs, still melodic and danceable, feature more industrial textures and are suffused with guitars. The unlikely subject matter—religious fanaticism—brought them a number three hit on the *Billboard* Modern Rock chart and inspired several remixes. The video, directed by the renowned photographer Anton Corbijn, known for his super-saturated, sepia-tone processing, is fraught with sexual overtones and enjoyed constant rotation on MTV. The album spawned three hits: "Personal Jesus," "Enjoy the Silence," and "Policy of Truth"; the latter two reached number one on the *Billboard* Modern Rock chart. The album, which examines the ways in which love, trust, sex, and friendship are subject to violation, is the pinnacle of their achievement: nine tracks of spare, sensual, tortured, dark, synthesized rock music. Thematically, it also hints at some manner of chemical dependence with the declarations on "Clean" and the somber, pensive, "Waiting for the Night to Fall."

The band sustained their momentum with the album *Songs of Faith and Devotion* (1993), which debuted at number one on the *Billboard* 200. The album preserves the guitar sounds prevalent in the previous release but introduces something new: real string instruments. The majestic orchestration in love songs such as "One Caress" lends a lush sound to the track and suggested the band was moving in a new direction. The real drums and guitar riff propelling the transcendent lead-off track, "I Feel You," shows a more conventional, rock-and-roll approach.

Change of Heart, Change of Mind

By the mid-1990s the band had began to unravel; Alan Wilder left in 1995 to pursue other musical inter-

ests, and Gahan endured a series of personal crises: In 1996 he divorced, remarried, and redivorced the same American woman and then attempted suicide. By the end of 1996, he was determined to stay clean and he openly discussed his dependency on heroin and his rehabilitation in an interview in the U.K. magazine *New Music Express*. Toward the end of the decade, Depeche Mode recommitted themselves to their music for two more well-received albums, *Ultra* (1997) and *Exciter* (2001); the latter spawned several dance remixes that became popular in both the United States and Canada.

The alternative synth-rock of Depeche Mode wrought a major success out of an unlikely combination of elements: the edgy touches of industrial sound, the melodic sensibility of pop, and offbeat lyrics that probe the dark recesses of the human heart.

SELECTIVE DISCOGRAPHY: *Some Great Reward* (Reprise, 1985); *Black Celebration* (Reprise, 1986); *Music for the Masses* (Reprise, 1987); *Depeche Mode 101* (1989); *Violator* (1990); *Songs of Faith and Devotion* (1993); *Ultra* (Reprise, 1995); *Exciter* (2001).

VIDEOGRAPHY: D. A. Pennebaker, director, *Depeche Mode 101*, VHS. (1989).

CARRIE HAVRANEK

DESTINY'S CHILD

Formed: 1990, Houston, Texas

Members: Beyoncé Knowles (born Houston, Texas, 4 September 1981); Kelly Rowland (born Atlanta, Georgia, 11 February 1981); Michelle Williams (born Rockford, Illinois, 23 July 1980). Former members: Farrah Franklin (born Los Angeles, California, 3 May 1981); LeToya Luckett (born Houston, Texas, 11 March 1981); LaTavia Roberson (born Houston, Texas, 1 November 1981).

Genre: R&B, Pop

Best-selling album since 1990: *Survivor* (2001)

Hit songs since 1990: "Say My Name," "Independent Women, Pt. 1," "Emotion"

The hip, flashy vocal ensemble Destiny's Child became one of the most successful groups of the late 1990s and beyond, maintaining fame despite frequent turnover and internal strife. Building on pop and R&B's long tradition of "girl groups"—from the Supremes in the 1960s to En Vogue in the early 1990s—Destiny's Child performs sweet harmony vocals and a kinetic, well-oiled stage act, adding a contemporary sheen with hits proclaiming female independence and assertiveness. With revealing costumes and

Destiny's Child. L-R: Kelly Rowland, Beyoncé Knowles, Michelle Williams [PAUL NATKIN/PHOTO RESERVE]

songs of romantic one-upmanship Destiny's Child emphasizes sex to an extent unheard of by their genteel girl group predecessors in the 1960s. At the same time the group has preserved its image of wholesomeness and Christianity, never crossing the line into explicitness.

Beginnings and Stardom

Formed in 1990 by two Texas girls after meeting at an audition for a children's singing group, Destiny's Child initially consisted of LaTavia Roberson and Beyoncé Knowles. By 1993 the group had added LeToya Luckett and Knowles's cousin Kelly Rowland, forming a quartet. Managed under the watchful eye of Beyoncé's father,

Matthew Knowles, the group of preteens spent hours practicing and studying performance style through videotapes of famed vocal groups the Supremes and the Jackson 5. Named after a passage from the Book of Isaiah in the Bible, Destiny's Child gradually developed a tight act combining singing and rapping. After an appearance on the television program *Star Search*, the group worked in local Texas clubs and signed a contract with Columbia Records in 1997. Destiny's Child's self-titled debut album, released in 1998, featured the driving hit, "No, No, No, Pt. 2" and a handful of sweet-sounding ballads, although it was otherwise unexceptional.

The next year the group released *The Writing's on the Wall*, a much stronger album in which songs emphasizing female respect and pride were linked through a biblically inspired "thou shalt not" passage spoken before each track. "Say My Name," featuring an off-kilter, jumpy groove supplied by hot producer Rodney Jerkins, was the album's biggest hit, reaching the number one position on the pop and R&B charts. Sporting a catchy melody and insistent, throbbing beat, the song was memorable for eighteen-year-old Knowles's rapid-fire vocals, in which she impressively squeezes a large number of words into a dense, tight rhythm. On other hits, such as the sassy "Bills, Bills, Bills" and "Bug a Boo," Knowles emerges as the star of the group, punctuating her singing with long vocal runs and flamboyant gospel-styled *melisma*, the bending of multiple notes within a syllable. The latter song is notable for its sassy sense of humor, with the young women brushing off an annoying suitor: "You make me wanna throw my pager out the window / Tell MCI to cut the phone poles." If girl groups of the past were somewhat faceless, interchangeably pronouncing the virtues of love, Destiny's Child took a firm stance in life, finding success through a self-determinism that never crossed the line into aggression.

Trouble and Survival

A peak year for the group, 1999 ended on a sour note: Roberson and Luckett tried to break away from manager Knowles, claiming he retained an unfair share of profits and favored daughter Beyoncé and niece Rowland. Matthew Knowles retaliated by replacing the intransigent members with Michelle Williams and Farrah Franklin. Roberson and Luckett, who had never wanted to actually leave the group, in turn sued Knowles. Then, in 2000, new member Franklin was jettisoned from the group, allegedly for missing appearances and concerts. By the end of the year Roberson and Luckett had settled with former manager Knowles but remained ousted from the group. Now reduced to a trio—Knowles, Rowland, and Williams—Destiny's Child struggled to overcome the months of bad press by entering the studio and recording *Survivor* (2001), an allusion to the group's recent history as well as the hit television "reality" program of the same name. The tabloid frenzy proved beneficial for the group, as *Survivor* debuted at number one on the pop and R&B charts and sold 6 million copies worldwide.

Despite solid sales, the album's artistic success is mixed. Critics faulted the album, observing that the female pride and respect of *The Writing's on the Wall* had given way to a cold self-righteousness. In a hypocritical contradiction of their sexy image, the group castigates the protagonist of "Nasty Girl," telling her to "put some clothes on" before asserting that, "everyone knows she's easy." Even the subtly grooving "Fancy" seems designed to leave a bad taste in the mouth, its lyrics marked by pettiness: "You're always trying to steal my shine." Fortunately, the album has its share of peak moments, including "Independent

Women, Pt. 1," a hit from the soundtrack to the film *Charlie's Angels* (2000). Here, the group winningly recaptures its former self-sufficiency: "The shoes on my feet—I bought them . . . I depend on me." On its hit version of the 1970s pop ballad, "Emotion," the group blends voices angelically, spicing its performance with rococo vocal lines. From an artistic standpoint, "Emotion" surges with a distinct emotional current, achieving a depth of feeling absent from the group's earlier work. In 2002 Knowles's profile within the group increased even more dramatically after she starred in the hit comedy film *Austin Powers in Goldmember*. The same year Williams and Rowland released their first solo albums, *Heart to Yours* and *Simply Deep* respectively, under an agreement that allows the members to record individually while remaining part of the group.

Destiny's Child's hits rank among the most enjoyable of the era, combining smooth vocalizing with bold lyrics emphasizing female strength. While adulthood and internal squabbling seemed to thrust a new cynicism upon the group, they retained their hit-making power and gentle harmonic sound.

SELECTIVE DISCOGRAPHY: *Destiny's Child* (Columbia, 1998); *The Writing's on the Wall* (Columbia, 1999); *Survivor* (Columbia, 2001); *8 Days of Christmas* (Columbia, 2001). **Soundtrack:** *Charlie's Angels* (Sony, 2000).

WEBSITE: www.destinyschild.com.

DAVID FREELAND

NEIL DIAMOND

Born: Brooklyn, New York, 24 January 1941
Genre: Pop, Rock, Country
Best-selling album since 1990: *Tennessee Moon* (1996)

A singer/songwriter who has enjoyed a long and varied career, Neil Diamond first achieved recognition during the mid-1960s, writing and recording hits in an exuberant, breezy style associated with the tuneful "Brill Building" sound popular during the era. By the late 1960s and early 1970s he had evolved into a moody rock star, achieving success with powerful songs such as "Holly Holy" (1969) and "Solitary Man" (1970). Never popular among critics, who often lambasted his lack of subtlety and blunt singing style, Diamond gained increased popularity during the 1970s and 1980s, releasing a string of heavily orchestrated pop hits that many writers described as bombastic. Despite critical reservations, Diamond fostered an ardent cult following, its members known informally as "Diamondheads." Always seeking new opportunities as an artist, Diamond in the 1990s made successful forays into country and classic pop standards before returning in 2001 to his former rock-based style.

Raised in Brooklyn, New York, where as a child he was a friend of future music superstar Barbra Streisand, Diamond began writing songs and performing during his midteens. He made his first singles for the small Duel label in 1960 before becoming a full-time songwriter in 1962. After writing pop group the Monkees's number one hit, "I'm a Believer" (1966), Diamond returned to performing, signing with the small Bang label and releasing youth-oriented hits such as the engaging "Cherry Cherry" (1966). In 1968 he moved to Uni Records, a subsidiary of major label MCA, and pursued a tougher, sharper style in the mold of rock stars Paul Simon and Bob Dylan. During this period, he enlisted the services of the American Studio in Memphis, Tennessee, popular with rock and R&B performers such as Dusty Springfield, Wilson Pickett, and, most famously, Elvis Presley. There, he recorded the hits often judged by critics to be his finest: "Sweet Caroline," "Brother Love's Traveling Salvation Show," and the brooding "Holly Holy" (all 1969).

In the 1970s and 1980s, Diamond began to take himself more seriously as an artist, recording songs about poet Henry Wadsworth Longfellow ("Longfellow Serenade," 1974) and scoring the film soundtracks *Jonathan Livingston Seagull* (1973) and *The Jazz Singer* (1980), a film in which he starred. Criticized by music reviewers for his overwrought vocal style and lack of humor, Diamond nonetheless built up a loyal fan base through the strength of his dynamic, entertaining live performances. In 1978 he released one of his biggest hits, "You Don't Bring Me Flowers," a glossy ballad duet with Streisand.

In the 1990s Diamond recorded *Lovescape* (1991), a sophisticated pop album, before returning to his roots on *Up on the Roof—Songs from the Brill Building* (1993). A celebration of the hit music created at the famous edifice in Manhattan, where songwriters such as Carole King and Burt Bacharach crafted pop hits during the 1960s, the album features versions of classic songs such as "Will You Love Me Tomorrow," "Spanish Harlem," and "You've Lost That Lovin' Feelin'," a duet with country star Dolly Parton. While Diamond captures a yearning romantic quality on songs such as "A Groovy Kind of Love," his melodramatic tendencies are often in evidence on other tracks. For instance, in the middle of "Up on the Roof," a hit made famous by the pop and R&B group the Drifters in 1963, he shouts out, "Look at those stars, darlin'!" Aside from moments such as these, Diamond largely retains the phrasing and sound of the original versions, although his new arrangements substitute synthesizers for strings.

Given the nostalgic pop orientation of *Up on the Roof*, Diamond's next move came as a surprise: a legitimate country album, recorded in Nashville, Tennessee, the country capital. Critics inclined to dismiss *Tennessee Moon* (1996) were impressed by Diamond's credible, assured performances of songs such as the romantic "Deep Inside of You" and the breezy title track. Recorded in the streamlined, polished style popular within the world of 1990s country radio, *Tennessee Moon* became a substantial hit, reaching the number three position on the country album charts. Next, Diamond collaborated with legendary film arranger Elmer Bernstein on *The Movie Album: As Time Goes By* (1998), a collection of classic pop songs including "Secret Love" and "Moon River." Despite the effulgence of Bernstein's arrangements, Diamond often sounds unsuited to this type of material, primarily because his gruff vocal style does not translate easily to lush ballads. In 2001 Diamond returned to form with *Three Grand Opera*, an album that comes close to capturing the drive and energy of his late 1960s hits. On songs such as "You Are the Best Part of Me," nicely arranged with steel drums, he achieves power through a new sense of restraint.

Beginning his career in the mid-1960s as a songwriter, Diamond assumed a variety of roles—ranging from hard rocker to dramatic pop belter—as the decades progressed. Although critical acclaim for the most part eluded him, Diamond attained unwavering support from listeners who responded to his heart-on-sleeve brand of romanticism.

SELECTIVE DISCOGRAPHY: *The Feel of Neil Diamond* (Bang, 1966); *Tap Root Manuscript* (Uni, 1970); *Hot August Night* (MCA, 1972); *You Don't Bring Me Flowers* (Columbia, 1978); *Heartlight* (Columbia, 1982); *Lovescape* (Columbia, 1991); *Up On the Roof—Songs from the Brill Building* (Columbia, 1993); *Tennessee Moon* (Columbia, 1996); *The Movie Album: As Time Goes By* (Columbia, 1998); *Three Chord Opera* (Columbia, 2001). **Soundtracks:** *Jonathan Livingston Seagull* (Sony, 1973); *The Jazz Singer* (Sony, 1980).

WEBSITE: www.neildiamond.com.

DAVID FREELAND

DIDO

Born: Dido Armstrong; London, England, 25 December 1971

Genre: Rock

Best-selling album since 1990: *No Angel* (1999)

Hit songs since 1990: "Here with Me," "Thank You"

Arriving at the end of the female singer/songwriter commercial explosion in the late

1990s, Dido brought an electronic flavor and sound to the movement.

Dido was born in London, England, on Christmas Day 1971, into a literary family: Her father was a publisher, her mother a poet. Dido entered London's Guildhall School of Music at the age of six. By the time she was a teenager, Dido had command of the piano, recorder, and violin and was touring the United Kingdom as part of a classical ensemble. She took up singing at the age of sixteen after hearing the records of jazz legend Ella Fitzgerald.

Dido's brother Rollo recruited his sister to join his band Faithless in 1995. Faithless, a trip-hop outfit, combined live instrumentation with electronic beats. Faithless's debut album *Reverence* (1996) was a hit, selling 5 million records worldwide.

Dido's work with Faithless caught the eye of the Arista Records magnate Clive Davis, who signed the young performer to a recording contract in 1997. Two years later, Arista released Dido's debut solo album, *No Angel*. The brooding lead single "Here with Me" achieved some popularity as the theme song to the hit television series *Roswell*. "Here with Me" typifies Dido's unique sound: juxtaposing a simple acoustic guitar with swirling electronic strings and crisp drum machine beats while the singer delivers the lyrics in a ghostly, otherworldly voice.

It was not until controversial rapper Eminem sampled Dido's "Thank You" for his song "Stan" that the English diva won global recognition. In "Thank You" Dido reflects on the solace that a picture of a lover provides during their time apart: "My tea's gone cold, I'm wondering why I got out of bed at all / The morning rain clouds up my window and I can't see at all / And even if I could it'd all be grey, but your picture on my wall / It reminds me that it's not so bad, it's not so bad." In "Stan," Eminem sampled Dido's vocals on the aforementioned lyrics, recasting them in his song about an obsessed fan. The success of "Stan" sparked interest in Dido, who also appeared in the video for "Stan" as the narrator's pregnant wife. "Thank You," which had previously been a minor hit for Dido after appearing in the hit movie *Sliding Doors*, recharted and climbed all the way to number five. *No Angel* went on to sell 3 million copies.

Part of the late-1990s female singer/songwriter movement, Dido expanded the genre's sound and, by means of her affiliation with Eminem, also extended its reach.

SELECTIVE DISCOGRAPHY: *No Angel* (Arista, 1999).

SCOTT TRIBBLE

ANI DIFRANCO

Born: Buffalo, New York, 23 September 1970
Genre: Rock, Folk

Best-selling album since 1990: *Living in Clip* (1997)

Hit songs since 1990: "32 Flavors," "Not a Pretty Girl"

Singer, songwriter, outspoken feminist, and punk-folk prodigy, Ani DiFranco has released more than a dozen albums on her own label, Righteous Babe records. Her impassioned singing, rhythmic approach to playing the acoustic guitar, and incisive political and personal lyrics have inspired a loyal legion of fans. DiFranco has released at least one album a year since the mid-1990s, after the stunning *Not a Pretty Girl* (1995) set the stage for her fame. A true original, DiFranco is punk rock in her approach and in her spiky-haired appearance but folk in her musical preference for confessional and occasionally didactic songs.

Ambition, Purpose, and Will

Ani DiFranco's rise to success is a tale of singularity of purpose. Growing up in a blue-collar town listening to the music of the Beatles and Joni Mitchell, DiFranco picked up the guitar at age nine and started writing her own songs. By the time she was a teenager, she was playing in bars and clubs in upstate New York. At fifteen she moved to New York City, and at nineteen she released her self-titled debut album. DiFranco started touring coffeehouses, bars, college campuses, and music festivals to support each successive album in the early to mid-1990s. She credits her uniquely percussive acoustic guitar style to years of struggling to be heard over the chatty crowds at bars and clubs.

By the time *Out of Range* (1994) came out, DiFranco was starting to attract attention in the folk music circuit, and critics started paying attention to this unique voice. Never one to cow to the tall orders of others, DiFranco defends her right to create her own music, her own image, and her own voice. Throughout *Out of Range* DiFranco mines her acoustic guitar for all its sonic possibilities: furious strumming on the title track, knocking and rapping it on "Buildings and Bridges," and cascading arpeggios on "Hell Yeah."

Success for *Not a Pretty Girl*

In 1995 Ani DiFranco officially hit it big with the release of her album *Not a Pretty Girl*. The album landed on many magazines' top-ten lists, and DiFranco appeared on the cover of *Spin* magazine with spiked-out hair and leather pants. DiFranco's success showed that a female musician did not have to fit into a music-industry pigeonhole; female musicians could contain a multitude of complexities and still be successful. Her next album,

Spot | *Not a Pretty Girl*
Light |

The tongue-in-cheek title of DiFranco's break-through album just barely hints at the firestorm that brews throughout the fourteen thoughtful, polemic, anthemic, and literate punk-folk songs. The saucy leadoff track, "Worthy," spins a relationship on its head in the kiss off in the opening lines: "You think you're not worthy / I'd have to say I'd agree / I'm not worthy of you / You're not worthy of me." But DiFranco is clever and strong and disinclined to let her lover off the hook so easily. *Not a Pretty Girl* also features songs about fame, the death penalty, bisexuality, and abortion. In the title-track manifesto DiFranco defines herself. She starts off with sarcasm and moves to self-assurance, "I am not a pretty girl / That is not what I do / I ain't no damsel in distress." DiFranco then effortlessly moves on to her generation and pop culture, explaining that she is not an angry girl but that "Every time I say something they find hard to hear / They chalk it up to my anger and never to their own fear."

Dilate (1996), was equally progressive, finding DiFranco more comfortable with the range of her voice. *Dilate* features some slightly more edgy sounds of an electric guitar and seems to chronicle a messy relationship and its fallout.

Touring and Recording

DiFranco spent most of the 1990s touring and recording, splitting her time between Buffalo and New York City. She became increasingly productive toward the end of the 1990s, releasing two double albums, one of which, *Living in Clip* (1997), is a live album with the band she had formed. *Living in Clip* is treasured by fans, for it ably captures the energy of her live performances and showcases Ani DiFranco at her best. In 1998 she married her sound engineer, Andrew Gilchrest, and seemed happy to discuss her marital state in interviews. This seemingly conventional act angered fans who felt betrayed by their unorthodox, free-thinking, sexually progressive role model. In 1999 DiFranco released two so-so albums that continued to show her discursive lyrical style, *Up Up Up*

Up Up Up and *To the Teeth*, the former of which spawned the single "Angry Any More."

By the year 2000 Righteous Babe had sold more than 1 million copies of her records, Surprisingly, DiFranco slowed down a bit; she did not release anything in 2000 but made up for it with *Reveling/Reckoning* (2001). A double album that is at times heavy-handed in its polemics, it sold more than 37,000 copies in its debut week, quite a feat for a woman whose music is not embraced by commercial radio. In 2003 DiFranco released *Evolve,* an album that employs a horn section and shows that she has become wiser as a songwriter and as a person in the nearly fifteen years she has been recording music. The political statements never become overwrought diatribes, and the arrangements are spare, raw, and intimate.

Ani DiFranco is a folk poet with the ferocity and spirit of a punk rocker, a woman with an independent mind and a formidable technique on the twelve-string guitar. Having snubbed the corporate overseers to kick-start and master her own career, she is an inspiration to countless singer/songwriters.

SELECTIVE DISCOGRAPHY: *Puddle Dive* (Righteous Babe, 1993); *Out of Range* (Righteous Babe, 1994); *Not a Pretty Girl* (Righteous Babe, 1995); *Dilate* (Righteous Babe, 1996); *Living in Clip* (Righteous Babe, 1997); *Little Plastic Castles* (Righteous Babe, 1998); *Up Up Up Up Up Up* (Righteous Babe, 1999); *To the Teeth* (Righteous Babe, 1999); *Reveling: Reckoning* (Righteous Babe, 2001); *So Much Shouting/ So Much Laughter* (Righteous Babe, 2002); *Evolve* (Righteous Babe, 2003).

WEBSITE: www.righteousbaberecords.com.

CARRIE HAVRANEK

CELINE DION

Born: Charlemagne, Quebec, 30 March 1968

Genre: Rock; Pop

Best-selling album since 1990: *Let's Talk About Love* (1997)

Hit songs since 1990: "My Heart Will Go On," "A New Day Has Come," "Because You Loved Me"

Singer Celine Dion has hurdled language and cultural barriers in her climb to become one of pop music's most recognized divas. Known for her remarkable vocal range and power, the Canadian-born Dion is an international superstar whose recordings have sold more than 150 million copies.

Humble Beginnings

Dion grew up thirty miles east of Montreal in the French-speaking village of Charlemagne, Quebec, the youngest of fourteen children in a family that loved music. Her parents, both musicians, owned a nightclub and the entire family would perform for patrons on the weekends. Dion created a stir early on when, at the age of five, customers of the club would clamor for her to sing. She idolized Ginette Reno and copied many songs from the popular Canadian singer's repertoire. At twelve, she recorded a demo tape of a French song that she had composed with her mother and one of her brothers. The tape was dropped off at the office of a successful Montreal-based agent named Rene Angelil who had once guided Reno's career. After some persuasion by Dion's brother to listen to the tape, Angelil was convinced that she possessed superstar talent. He set aside all other duties to personally manage Dion's career, and at one juncture even mortgaged his house to finance her first album.

By age eighteen, Dion had recorded nine albums—all in French—and toured extensively around the world. She was a major star in Canada and was well established in France where her single, "L'amour ou d'amite," went gold in 1983. Nevertheless, she yearned for American pop music success. Angelil, at this point in complete control of Dion's career, decided that she should disappear from public to regroup and concentrate on her English. She emerged a year later sporting a trendier look and began preliminary work on her first English-language album while continuing to gratify her primary fan base by touring Canada. In the meantime, a romance developed between Dion and Angelil, but it was kept secret primarily over concerns that fans might not accept the twenty-six year difference in their ages.

Dion accomplished her long-awaited foray into the English market by releasing *Unison* (1990). Critics complained that she sang inexpressively, the result of her managing the English language in only its phonetic sense. However, there was no denying her magnificent voice and the album produced four Top Ten singles including "Where Does My Heart Beat Now?" *Unison* sold over 1 million copies, a remarkable feat for a debut album, but it paled in comparison to what was yet to come.

Mainstream Success

She followed *Unison* with a French-language release, *Dion Chante Plamondon* (1991), which was Canada's best-selling French album in 1992. Nevertheless, she received a backlash from some in the French-Canadian music industry who felt slighted by her English-speaking music efforts. Undeterred, Dion charged on to the American pop music scene with *Celine Dion* (1992). The album featured her previously recorded duet with Peabo Bryson of

the title song for Disney's film, *Beauty and the Beast* (1991), and included hits, "If You Asked Me," "Love Can Move Mountains," and "Water from the Moon." *Beauty and the Beast* earned both a Grammy Award and an Academy Award and the album catapulted Dion to global pop music superstardom. She followed the release of *Celine Dion* by headlining her first U.S. concert tour along with Michael Bolton, further launching her with American audiences.

A movie soundtrack theme song, "When I Fall in Love," from the film *Sleepless in Seattle* (1993) was the centerpiece of her next album, *The Colour of My Love* (1993). The album was enormously successful, but it was important for another reason: The album's liner notes announced publicly that she and Angelil were in love. They married the following year in a ceremony that was televised throughout Canada. Incidentally, Dion used the media hype from the wedding to benefit her most important charity. She and Angelil asked—in lieu of wedding gifts—for donations toward the Canadian Cystic Fibrosis Foundation. In 1993 Dion was deeply affected by the death of her niece, Karine, who passed away in her arms. She memorialized Karine with the song "Vole," which was added to her French-language album, *D'euxalbum* (1995). An English translation of the song titled "Fly" appeared on the mega-successful *Falling into You* (1996). Her wedding raised over $200,000 for the charity.

Over the next five years, alternating between French and English recordings, Dion worked nonstop. In 1997 she recorded her most prolific song, "My Heart Will Go On," from the soundtrack to the film *Titanic* (1996). It was included on *Let's Talk About Love* (1997), which also features duets with Barbra Streisand, the Bee Gees, and Luciano Pavarotti. On the strength of "My Heart Will Go On," *Titanic* became the all-time biggest selling orchestral soundtrack and *Let's Talk About Love* sold more than 31 million copies.

Dion began the new millennium by announcing that she was taking a break from performing to start a family and to be with her husband, who had been diagnosed with throat cancer. He later made a full recovery. The hiatus gave her time to reflect on a career that has been showered with awards from all over the world, including six Grammy Awards, two Academy Awards, and countless Juno, Felix, and World Music Awards in Canada and Europe. Dion's record sales and concert appearances made the French-speaking Canadian one of the wealthiest performers in the United States. In January 2001 Dion gave birth to her first child, a boy named Rene-Charles Angelil. The following year she released *A New Day Has Come* (2002), and within two weeks it reached number one in seventeen countries including the United States. Dion drew praise from critics regarding

| Las Vegas Concerts

Celine Dion opened a Las Vegas concert extravaganza on March 25, 2003, at the Colosseum, owned by Caesars Palace. She is under contract to play the four-thousand-seat arena over the next three years for five nights weekly, forty weeks per year. The famous designer, Franco Dragone, the artistic force behind Cirque du Soleil, created the abstract production. *A New Day* rehearsed five months as it combined a variety of multimedia and several stage settings with specialty performers and more than fifty dancers in a concert spectacular where tickets cost up to $200 per seat. Dion performs her concert classics, including "My Heart Will Go On," in an eighteen-song set that mixes in Las Vegas musical fare such as "Fever" and "I've Got the World on a String." Her opening number is "Nature Boy," made famous by the legendary singer Nat King Cole.

Way . . . *A Decade of Song* (Epic, 1999); *The French Love Album* (Empire, 2001); *A New Day Has Come* (Epic, 2002); *One Heart* (Epic, 2003). **Soundtracks:** *Sleepless in Seattle* (Sony, 1993); *Titanic: Music from the Motion Picture* (Sony, 1997).

BIBLIOGRAPHY: N. Z. Lutz, *Celine Dion* (Broomall, PA, 2000); C. Dion, H. Germain, B. Benderson (trans.), *Celine Dion: My Story, My Dream* (New York, 2000).

DONALD LOWE

DIXIE CHICKS

Formed: 1989, Dallas, Texas

Members: Natalie Maines (born Lubbock, Texas, 14 October 1974); Emily Erwin Robison (born Pittsfield, Massachusetts, 16 August 1972); Martie Erwin Seidel (born York, Pennsylvania, 12 October 1969). Former members: Laura Lynch (born Dell City, Texas, 18 November 1958); Robin Lynn Macy (born Sunnyvale, California, 27 November 1958).

Genre: Country

Best-selling album since 1990: *Home* (2002)

Hit songs since 1990: "Wide Open Spaces," "Goodbye Earl," "Travelin' Soldier"

The Dixie Chicks helped redefine country music in the late 1990s and early 2000s, crafting a hip new image for female performers while earning both critical acclaim and popular acceptance. Founded in the late 1980s as a bluegrass band, the group eventually gained mainstream recognition by modifying its sound to better fit the slick pop guidelines of 1990s country radio. At the same time, the group refused to completely abandon its roots, using traditional instruments such as banjo and fiddle to enrich both pop ballads and up-tempo dance songs. As their popularity grew the Dixie Chicks became more comfortable with this dichotomy, returning to a roots-based sound while releasing songs and public statements that challenged country's politically conservative ethos. With close-cropped blonde hair and a chic designer wardrobe, the group also promoted a sex appeal rare in country music. By 2003, after enduring an angry public backlash over its antiwar stance, the band had proven its talent and resilience.

A New Day Has Come for relying less on her relentless five-octave power style, opting instead for a more lilting, subtle vocal sound.

In 2003 Dion and her family relocated to Las Vegas, where she began a three-year commitment to perform her new show, *A New Day*, at Caesars Palace. In conjunction with the opening of the concert spectacular, Dion released *My Heart* (2003).

Renowned in Canada and Western Europe well before her successful crossover into English-language songs, Celine Dion is one of pop music's strongest and most passionate voices. As her English has become more agile, so has her musical styling. Dion is gaining the same comfort with varieties of rock and soul music as she has with the sweeping, emotional ballads that first brought her fame.

SELECTIVE DISCOGRAPHY: *Unison* (Epic, 1990); *Dion Chante Plamondon* (550 Music, 1991); *Celine Dion* (Epic, 1992); *The Christmas Album* (Interscope, 1993); *The Colour of My Love* (550 Music, 1993); *D'eux* (also known as *The French Album* (550 Music, 1995); *Falling into You* (550 Music, 1996); *Let's Talk About Love* (550 Music, 1997); *These Are Special Times* (550 Music, 1998); *All the*

Bluegrass Beginnings

Formed in Dallas, Texas, the group originally consisted of sisters Emily and Martie Erwin, who played the banjo

Dixie Chicks. L-R: Martie Seidel, Natalie Maines, Emily Robison [PAUL NATKIN/PHOTO RESERVE]

and fiddle, respectively, as well as bass player Laura Lynch and guitarist Robin Lynn Macy. In 1989 the group began perfecting its unique brand of bluegrass (a traditional country music style characterized by acoustic guitar playing and banjo picking) on Dallas street corners, reportedly earning $100 during its first hour. Hearing rock group Little Feat's song, "Dixie Chicken," on the radio, the young women named themselves the "Dixie Chicks" and began dressing in cowgirl attire. While the group's first album, *Thank Heavens for Dale Evans* (1990), was recorded in a bluegrass style, successive albums, such as *Little Ol' Cowgirl* (1992), incorporate more of a modern country sound. Unhappy with this change in direction, Macy left the group in 1992. Three years later, thirty-seven-year-old Lynch also left, amid rumors that her age did not fit in with the youthful image the Erwin sisters—then in their twenties—were trying to promote for the group. Lynch's replacement was Natalie Maines, the daughter of noted country guitarist Lloyd Maines. Twenty-one years old in 1995, the powerful-voiced Maines—who spent her childhood singing songs from classic Broadway musicals such as *West Side Story*—perfectly embodied the youthful sensuality the Erwin sisters wanted for the group.

Country and Pop Stardom

The revised lineup now in place, the Dixie Chicks achieved crossover stardom with *Wide Open Spaces* (1998), the band's debut album for a major label. Bearing a sleek, streamlined sound, the album is marked by intelligent song selection and Maines's supple vocals. Exuberant hits such as "I Can Love You Better" and "There's Your Trouble" contribute to the band's confident, likable image, while the expressive title track—detailing the experiences of a girl who leaves home to strike out on her own—speaks to a modern sense of female independence. Although smooth and radio-friendly, the album leaves room for the group's bluegrass roots; "There's Your Trouble," for example, is enlivened by rapid banjo picking, while "Tonight the Heartache's on Me" is a rousing swing number sporting traditional instrumentation of fiddles, drums, and bass guitar.

Winning a Grammy Award in 1998 for Best Country Album, *Wide Open Spaces* paved the way for the Dixie Chicks' second major-label release, *Fly* (1999). Many critics considered the album stronger than its predecessor, noting the new assurance and potency of Maines's vocals and pointing to the boldness of the material. "Goodbye Earl," a song that gave the group its first taste of controversy when it was banned by several male disc jockeys, tells the story of a much-abused wife who, with the help of her best friend, kills her husband. Ironically set against a cheerful backing chorus, the song rails against spousal abuse with an off-kilter sense of humor: "It didn't take 'em long to decide / That Earl had to die." The power and bravado of "Goodbye Earl" are emphasized by Maines's aggressively full-throttle vocal approach. "Sin Wagon," an unrepentant ode to hedonism, likewise breaks new ground for country lyrics, with Maines attesting, "Feel like Delilah lookin' for Samson / Do a little mattress dancing." Then, just in case the listener misses the point, Maines adds humorously, "That's right, I said mattress dancing."

Success and Controversy

By 2000 the Dixie Chicks were engaged in a battle with their record company, Sony, over royalties. Although the legal wrangling kept the group out of the studio for nearly two years, its popularity remained strong. Having settled the case, the group returned in 2002 with *Home*, judged by critics to be its strongest album to date. Inspired perhaps by the surprise commercial success of the film soundtrack, *O Brother Where Art Thou?* (2000)—an album composed entirely of traditional country music—the Dixie Chicks strip down their sound on *Home*, dispensing with drums to achieve a restrained, gentle feel that recalls the roots-based approach of their early work. The songs, including "Travelin' Soldier"—the moving account of a woman in love with a soldier who does not return from the Vietnam War—remain tuneful and accessible, qualities that helped the album reach the number one positions on both the pop and country charts.

Riding the crest of their popularity, the Dixie Chicks risked losing it all in March 2003, when Maines made statements at a concert in England protesting President George Bush and the impending Iraq war: "Just so you know, we're ashamed the president of the United States is from Texas." When news of the comment reached American shores, country radio largely banned the group's music, with several stations setting up trash receptacles in which listeners could dispense of *Home*. Although the Dixie Chicks apologized, stressing that they had meant no disrespect to American troops, the public outcry continued, with rock star Bruce Springsteen and other celebrities eventually coming to the group's defense. By May the fracas, which suggested how conservative the country audience remains at its core, had subsided to an extent, allowing the group to kick off an American tour without major incident. That month *Home* returned to the top of the country album charts.

Combining traditional instrumentation with a fashionable image and sharp, progressive songs, the Dixie Chicks brought a new sensibility to country music in the late 1990s and early 2000s. Aided by the rich lead vocals of Maines, the group displayed the talent and vision to hold onto its success in the midst of controversy.

SELECTIVE DISCOGRAPHY: *Thank Heavens for Dale Evans* (Crystal Clear, 1990); *Little Ol' Cowgirl* (Crystal Clear, 1992); *Wide Open Spaces* (Sony/Monument, 1998); *Fly* (Monument, 1999); *Home* (Open Wide/Sony, 2002).

WEBSITE: www.dixiechicks.com.

DAVID FREELAND

DMX

Born: Earl Simmons; Baltimore, Maryland, 18 December 1970

Genre: Rap

Best-selling album since 1990: *It's Dark and Hell Is Hot* (1998)

Hit songs since 1990: "What's My Name," "Party Up (Up in Here)," "Who We Be"

The hardcore rapper DMX may have seen his first album debut at number one, but he had been laying the groundwork for that feat for nearly a decade. By the early 2000s he was one of the best-selling and most critically respected New York-based rappers, known for emotional cuts that chronicled his inner battles between good and evil.

He began getting notice in the early 1990s on the East Coast and recorded a couple of singles for Sony/Epic in 1993–1994, neither of which charted. However, he continued to build momentum on the live circuit, allying himself with a posse known as Ruff Ryders, which includes Ludacris, Eve, and the producer Swizz Beats. In 1998, he appeared on the LL Cool J hit "4, 3, 2, 1" and got his first taste of Top 40 airplay as part of the LOX's "Money, Respect."

There was plenty of pent-up demand for DMX's debut album, *It's Dark and Hell Is Hot* (1998). It debuted at number one on the *Billboard* 200 and remained on the chart for 101 weeks. With grim, tormented lyrics and slow-to-mid-tempo beats, DMX was speaking to rap's core, urban audience. He punctuated his messages with barking and snarling noises.

On his third album, *And Then There Was X* (1999), DMX inadvertently became the favorite of suburbia with his jock-jam hit "Party Up (Up in Here)." Though the lyrics were laced with implied put-downs of other rappers amid expletive-laden machismo, the "up in here" chorus was made for group chanting. DMX's gruff baritone roared over the minimalist faux-brass synth line and drum pattern. Although he was in no danger of becoming a kid-friendly personality like Nelly, DMX did get enough Top 40 airplay to make number twenty-two on the *Billboard* Hot 100 chart.

DMX takes a more philosophical turn on *The Great Depression* (2001). His first single, "Who We Be," is more of a list than a song; it paints a bleak picture of rampant inner-city crime and accuses "they," the middle class, of not understanding what the underclass goes through.

DMX's flair for vocal drama seems to stand him in good stead on the silver screen. His first film role was in *Belly* (1998), and he followed that up with appearances in *Romeo Must Die*, *Boricua's Bond*, and *Exit Wounds*. He finally got a starring role for the martial-arts flick *Cradle 2 the Grave* (2003), teaming with Jet Li to fight kidnappers and a mad scientist. The pair proved bankable, scoring the number one slot on opening weekend with a $17.1 million gross. The soundtrack features four DMX cuts, including "Go to Sleep" with Eminem and Obie Trice, and "X Gon' Give It to Ya." He also continues to contribute at least one track to the Ruff Ryder CDs, which come out every year or two.

With authentic, gripping tales of underclass, inner-city life, DMX is the rare artist who has expanded his appeal to an audience of millions without diluting his appeal to his original core fans.

SELECTIVE DISCOGRAPHY: *It's Dark and Hell Is Hot* (Def Jam, 1998); *Flesh of My Flesh, Blood of My Blood* (Def Jam, 1998).

RAMIRO BURR

PLÁCIDO DOMINGO

Born: José Plácido Domingo Embil; Madrid, Spain, 21 January 1941

Genre: Classical

Called the "King of Opera," Plácido Domingo is one of the most successful opera artists of the twentieth and early twenty-first centuries. The indefatigable Domingo has carved out careers as one of the leading tenors of his time, as well as an opera conductor and administrator of note.

Domingo was born in Madrid to a family of zarzuela (Spanish popular operetta) stars. When Domingo was nine, his family moved to Mexico City, where his parents founded their own zarzuela company. He first performed in his parents' company at the age of sixteen, but his studies were concentrated in piano and composition at the Mexico City Conservatory, and later in conducting.

Plácido Domingo [SHEILA ROCK/ANGEL RECORDS]

During his teens his big interest was not so much music as soccer, and he even tried bullfighting, until he was thrown by a bull. Musically he got involved in a variety of adventures—he got a small role in the first Mexican production of *My Fair Lady*, played piano and sang in a nightclub, accompanied ballet classes, worked in a local opera house as a *répétiteur*, conducted a zarzuela orchestra, and hosted a music show on Mexican television.

Domingo's opera debut was with the Monterrey Opera as Alfredo in a production of *La traviata*. Then he spent two years at the Israel National Opera, where he got plenty of chances to sing—280 performances in twelve roles. In 1966 he made his American debut in the title role of Argentinean composer Alberto Ginastera's *Don Rodrigo* at the New York City Opera. His Metropolitan Opera debut followed in 1968 as Maurizio in *Adriana Lecouvreur*, when he substituted at the last minute for Franco Corelli, who pulled out of the performance on only thirty-five minutes' notice.

From there Domingo's career took off, and he went on to sing in every major opera house in the world. At the Metropolitan Opera he has sung more than four hundred performances in more than forty roles and has been invited to perform in more season opening nights than any singer, in 1999 surpassing Enrico Caruso's record of seventeen.

Domingo's repertoire is vast. He has sung more than 120 roles, and his repertoire includes everything from Wolfgang Mozart and Giuseppe Verdi to pop songs, from Richard Wagner and Alberto Ginastera to zarzuela. Many of his more than one hundred recordings have been best-sellers, and he has won eleven Grammy Awards. He has made more than fifty videos and starred in three big-screen movies, including Franco Zeffirelli's *La traviata* (1982) and *Otello* (1985), and Francesco Rosi's *Carmen* (1983). More than 1 billion viewers in 117 countries saw a 1992 broadcast of *Tosca*, filmed at actual locations of the opera in Rome.

Arguably Domingo has performed before more people than any singer in history. As a member of the Three Tenors—with Luciano Pavarotti and Jose Carreras—the group's broadcasts, videos, and stadium concerts have been seen by billions of people around the world.

The group the Three Tenors was born in 1990 in a concert at Rome's ancient Baths of Caracalla celebrating the World Cup, and recordings and videos of the concert sold millions. Since then the Tenors have performed in stadiums around the world, and their videos have become a staple of public television. Their three recordings of performances at three World Cups (Rome, 1990; Los Angeles, 1994; and Paris 1998) have sold tens of millions of recordings, making them the biggest-selling classical recordings of all time.

As a conductor Domingo made his professional opera debut in 1974, and he continued to conduct occasionally through the 1970s and 1980s. His conducting career turned serious when he became artistic director of the Washington Opera at the Kennedy Center in 1996. Domingo has energized the company, bringing in major stars and new repertory, and he has established it as an important new player in the opera world. In 2000 he also became artistic director of the Los Angeles Opera.

He is also the founder and director of his own vocal competition Operalia, which he started in 1993 in Paris, and which is held in a different city each year. The competition has attracted more than one thousand young singers, and Domingo personally supervises the proceedings.

In 2000 Domingo received a Kennedy Center Honor, and in 2002 he received the Presidential Medal of Freedom. He has had a rose, a train, and a plane named after him, and in 1993 received a star on the Hollywood Walk of Fame. He is also known for his humanitarian work, helping to raise millions of dollars for relief of the 1985 earthquake in Mexico.

The hallmark of Domingo's art—whether as a tenor, conductor, or administrator—is his amazing energy and sense of musicianship. He never resorts to tricks or gimmicks and seems to have an unending supply of ideas to power his musical interpretations and artistic initiatives.

SELECTIVE DISCOGRAPHY: *La traviata*, with the Bavarian State Orchestra, Carlos Kleiber conducting (Deutsche Grammophon, 1977); *The Plácido Domingo Album* (RCA, 1991).

SELECTIVE FILMOGRAPHY: *La traviata* (Deutsche Grammophon, 1982); *Carmen* (Columbia Tristar, 1983); *Otello* (Cannon, 1985).

BIBLIOGRAPHY: P. Domingo, *My First 40 Years* (New York, 1983).

WEBSITE: www.tenorissimo.com/domingo/pdspot.htm.

DOUGLAS MCLENNAN

DR. DRE

Born: Andre Young; Los Angeles, California, 18 February 1965

Genre: Hip-Hop

Best-selling album since 1990: *The Chronic* (1992)

Hit songs since 1990: "Ain't Nuthin' but a G Thang," "Let Me Ride," "Still D.R.E.," "The Next Episode"

If Phil Spector and Brian Wilson defined the sound of California in the 1960s and 1970s, then Dr. Dre became the next Angelino to seduce the nation with his sonic vision of Southern California. Until the arrival of his album, *The Chronic* (1992), hip-hop had largely followed an East Coast aesthetic shaped by producers such as Marley Marl and the 45 King. Evoking the sonic tempo and texture of the subway cars running throughout New York, the so-called "East Coast sound" pulsed with an edgy, staccato rhythm. Dr. Dre's sound on *The Chronic* (1992) stands in stark contrast.

Dr. Dre began his career in the mid-1980s as the producer and sometime-rapper for the Los Angeles–based rap group the World Class Wrecking Cru. He left the Cru in 1986 to help join the formation of N.W.A., where he, along with his fellow Cru member Yella, were responsible for the production on N.W.A.'s groundbreaking *Straight Outta Compton* (1988). By the late 1980s Dre was the producer of choice for many L.A. rap groups, including Above the Law, the D.O.C., and J.J. Fad. He also continued to produce for N.W.A. until the group disassembled in 1991. Dre then moved onto a solo career, beginning with *The Chronic*.

Inspired by everything from low-rider convertibles to backyard barbecues to Southern California's mythic sun culture, Dre makes music that is about release and hedonism rather than the clenched tension that defines New York's vibe. One of Dr. Dre's main innovations on *The Chronic* is using musicians rather than sampling to interpolate rhythms and melodies throughout the tracks, a technique that gives the album a more organic, vibrant sound yet retains the comfort and familiarity that samples can

Spotlight: "Ain't Nuthin' but a G Thang"

Before the L.A. riots of 1992, the soundtrack to Los Angeles' hip-hop scene had been dominated by loud and aggressive songs like N.W.A.'s "F***the Police" (1988) and Ice Cube's "AmeriKKKa's Most Wanted" (1991). However, with soft keys and a rolling bass line, Dr. Dre's "Ain't Nuthin' but a G Thang" crept onto the airwaves with a quiet ferocity, soon dominating the Southland's musical tempo. Rather than an angry invective against the events leading up to the riots, "G Thang" makes the gangsta's world of money, sex, and violence seem smooth and seductive rather than sinister and dangerous. Though Dr. Dre and his lyrical partner Snoop (Doggy) Dogg may be rapping about murder and mayhem, the song itself is less a call to action and more an affirmation of lifestyle, a soul-soaked road song made for cars cruising along L.A.'s asphalt sea. The most important sonic feature on "G Thang" is Dre's reintroduction of the searing, snaking synthesizers he first used on songs from N.W.A.'s *Efil4zaggin* (1991). A distinctive, signature style that Dre later used on *The Chronic*, "G Thang's" synths soon dominated the so-called "G Funk" sound of L.A. gangsta rap and was incorporated by producers around the country.

provide. The signature style on the album is Dr. Dre's synthesizers, snaking their way through the album's main hits like "Ain't Nuthin' but a G Thang" and "Let Me Ride." These songs are lush, drenched in melodies and harmonies reminiscent of 1970s soul by the likes of Isaac Hayes, Curtis Mayfield, and Gamble and Huff. There is darker fare as well, such as the funk-laden "Escape from Death Row" or the forceful "Lyrical Gangbang," which balance the album's sonic impulses.

As Los Angeles lay smoldering from physical and social fires lit by the riots following the Rodney King verdicts, *The Chronic* stood as an unlikely affirmation and celebration of inner-city life as well as a warning that the age of the gangsta was upon us. Though Dre raps on most of the album's songs, his lack of sophistication as a lyricist led him to bring aboard Snoop (Doggy) Dogg for the

album. With his memorable drawl and sing-song lyrical style, Snoop was an unlikely gangsta icon; his easy-going attitude toward violence and death is made all the more sinister by his relaxed nature. He is the virtuoso, verbal complement to Dre's outstanding soundcraft, and though Snoop's name does not appear on the album's header, it is as much his album as Dre's.

The Chronic was a crowning achievement and instantly inspired an entire generation of followers and copycats. Though Dre never gave up his role of producer and rapper, he spent the rest of the decade learning how to become a kingmaker. His first attempt, *Dr. Dre Presents . . . The Aftermath* (1996), fell short, failing to produce hits or future stars. Dre found more success with *2001* (1999), a well-liked follow-up to *The Chronic* that shows off a sound that is no less soulful for having grown more spare. The project reunited him with Snoop Dogg and a host of other guests. Few new stars, however, emerged from the project.

Dre's main achievement by the turn of the century was not his own work but finding and nurturing new talent. Just as he had promoted Snoop Dogg's early career, Dre took Eminem under his wing. Under his guidance the controversial white rapper emerged in 2000 as one of rap music's biggest new stars. Though Dre did not produce all the songs that appeared on Eminem's albums, his implicit endorsement of Eminem gave the rising rapper a legitimacy among the many fans loyal to Dre. Likewise, in 2003 Dre, along with Eminem, put his credibility and resources behind the rapper 50 Cent, whose debut album, *Get Rich or Die Tryin'* (2003), claimed the biggest-selling debut in pop music history.

Over time, Dr. Dre has attracted his share of admirers and critics, not simply over the amoral lifestyle he champions on his albums, but also for creating such an omnipresent sound that dominated much of hip-hop in the 1990s. Undeniably, though, for those who champion and condemn him, Dr. Dre has become one of the most important and influential figures in hip-hop history.

SELECTIVE DISCOGRAPHY: *The Chronic* (Death Row, 1992).

OLIVER WANG

DRU HILL

Formed: 1992, Baltimore, Maryland

Members: Larry "Jazz," Anthony Jr., vocals (born Baltimore, Maryland, 23 April 1978); Tamir "Nokio" Ruffin, vocals (born Baltimore, Maryland, 21 January 1979); Mark "Sisqó" Andrews, lead vocals (born Baltimore, Maryland, 9 November 1978); James "Woody" Green, vocals (born Baltimore, Maryland, 10 September 1978); Rufus "Scola" Waller, vocals, (born Baltimore, Maryland, 2 March 1979)

Genre: R&B, Hip-Hop

Best-selling album since 1990: *Enter the Dru* (1998)

Hit songs since 1990: "Tell Me," "In My Bed," "How Deep Is Your Love"

Following the template set at the beginning of the 1990s by vocal quartets such as Jodeci and Boyz II Men, Dru Hill became one of the most successful R&B acts of the late 1990s. Although their gospel-influenced harmonizing over hip-hop beats added little innovation to the sound of their predecessors, they exhibited solid talent as singers, songwriters, and instrumentalists. Their skills attracted the industry's top producers and led to an impressive run of number one R&B hits and solo success for lead vocalist, Sisqó.

The four founding members of Dru Hill (Nokio, Jazz, Sisqó, and Woody) met while still in high school in Baltimore, Maryland. In 1992, after a summer spent entertaining tourists with impromptu performances while working at a fudge shop in Baltimore's Inner Harbor, they formed Dru Hill. Their name was inspired by Baltimore's historic Druid Hill Park. Victories at local talent shows earned them a manager, who in 1996 scored them an audience with the Island Records executive Hiriam Hicks. Hicks needed a group to record the song "Tell Me" for the soundtrack to the 1996 movie *Eddie*. Not only did Dru Hill get the job, but the song became a top-five R&B hit, and they released their self-titled debut later that year.

Dru Hill was executive-produced by Keith Sweat, one of the pioneers of New Jack Swing, the late-1980s movement that brought rap rhythms and an edgier, more "street" sound to R&B. The album grounds itself firmly in this tradition, offering a collection of mid-tempo R&B songs that showcase aggressively soulful lead vocals backed by the group's tight harmonizing. "Never Make a Promise" makes sentimental declarations of love, whereas "Tell Me" (re-released on this album) approaches "bedroom ballad" territory. *Dru Hill* also highlights the band's studio and songwriting skills, giving them co-writing and co-producing credits on a number of tracks. *Dru Hill* spawned a string of number one R&B singles and sold more than 1 million copies.

Extensive touring, including a performance at South African president Nelson Mandela's eightieth birthday party, allowed Dru Hill to prove their skills as showmen and instrumentalists while expanding their fan base. Their 1998 sophomore album, *Enter the Dru*, debuted at number two on the *Billboard* album chart and yielded the hits "How Deep Is Your Love" and "These Are the Times," the latter featuring Sisqó delivering the infamous couplet: "Tear you up in little pieces / Swallow you like Reese's Pieces." The album eventually went double platinum.

By this time Sisqó had emerged as the de facto frontman of the group. He sang lead vocals on the majority of Dru Hill's hits, and his platinum blonde-dyed hair, extensive tattoos, and flamboyant clothes further distinguished him from his band mates. In November 1999 he released a solo album, *Unleash the Dragon*. The first single, "Got to Get It," charted respectably, but it was the second single that turned Sisqó into a bona fide superstar. A bombastic, jittery tribute to skimpy beachwear, "The Thong Song" hit the Top 10 pop charts and was proclaimed "the official anthem of Spring Break 2000" by MTV. That summer Sisqó toured with *NSYNC, then at the peak of their popularity. That fall "The Thong Song" won Best Hip-Hop video at the MTV Video Music Awards. *Unleash the Dragon* went quadruple platinum. "The Thong Song" proved to be the apex of Sisqó's solo career, and in 2002 he reteamed with Dru Hill (including a new member, Scola) to release the group's long-awaited third album, *Dru World Order*.

Although scarcely innovators, Dru Hill expertly applied their considerable vocal and songwriting talents to the standard hip-hop-laced R&B of the time. Their succession of hit singles and albums helped push hip-hop toward the mainstream and contributed to its emergence as a major commercial force in the 1990s.

SELECTIVE DISCOGRAPHY: *Dru Hill* (Island, 1996); *Enter the Dru* (Polygram, 1998); *Unleash the Dragon* (Def Soul, 1999).

BIBLIOGRAPHY: L. Furman, *Sisqó: The Man Behind the Thong* (New York, 2001).

WEBSITES: www.defsoul.com/artists/druhill; www.druhilllive.com.

MATT HIMES

TAN DUN

Born: Si Mao, Hunan Province, China, 18 August 1957
Genre: Classical, Soundtrack

Tan Dun, a much-commissioned and much-honored composer originally trained in the Peking Opera, won the 2001 Academy Award for Best Score for his soundtrack to Ang Lee's film *Crouching Tiger, Hidden Dragon*, which received the most nominations for a foreign film in Academy history. During the ceremony at which the award was announced, CoCo Lee sang "A Love Before Time," nominated from the score as Best Song; it was co-composed by Dun and Jorge Calandrelli, with lyrics by James Schamus.

Dun conducted the performance of his score by the Shanghai Symphony Orchestra, the Shanghai National

Orchestra, and the Shanghai Percussion Ensemble; soloists on Chinese instruments such as the erhu, bawu, dizi, rawap, and the cellist Yo-Yo Ma. The *Crouching Tiger, Hidden Dragon Original Motion Picture Soundtrack* was also nominated for honors in the 2001 Golden Globe Awards competition. It won the 2002 Classical Brit Contemporary Music Award and the 2001 Grammy for Best Score Soundtrack Album for a Motion Picture, Television or Other Visual Media. "A Love Before Time" was nominated for a 2001 Grammy as Best Song Written for a Motion Picture, Television or Other Visual Media, and one movement, "The Eternal Vow," was nominated for the Grammy as Best Instrumental Composition. Dun won the Anthony Asquith Award for Achievement in Film Music at the Orange British Academy Film Awards in 2001.

Crouching Tiger, Hidden Dragon was the first film score by Dun, who emigrated to the United States from his native China in 1986. However, his musical accomplishments include *2000 Today: A World Symphony for the Millennium* (1999), commissioned by the BBC, Public Broadcast System Television, and Sony Classical. The piece was heard on fifty-five major television networks during the BBC's live twenty-seven-hour telecast of millennium celebrations around the world on January 1, 2000. Arias from Dun's opera *Peony Pavilion* were recorded by soprano Ying Huang and released on the album *Bitter Love* (1999). His *Ghost Opera* (1994) for string quartet and pipa, with water, stones, paper, and metal, was commissioned by the Brooklyn Academy of Music, the National Endowment for the Arts, and Hancher Auditorium/University of Iowa for the Kronos Quartet, and Wu Man, who recorded it in 1996 for a 1997 release. Dun won the prestigious Grawemeyer Award for his opera *Marco Polo* (libretto by Paul Griffiths), commissioned by the Edinburgh Festival and performed in Munich, Rome, Paris, London, New York, Tokyo, and Hong Kong, among other cities; it was named Opera of the Year in 1996 by the German magazine *Oper*. He has won Japan's Suntory Prize (1992) and the City of Toronto-Glenn Gould Protege Prize in Music and Communication (1996). He also maintains an extraordinary career as a conductor.

Dun is a graduate of Beijing's Central Conservatory and holds a doctoral degree in Music Arts from Columbia University. Raised by his grandmother and exposed as a child to China's rural, shamanistic culture, he was sent during Mao Zedong's Cultural Revolution to a Huangjin commune to harvest rice. Pursuing inherent musical impulses, he began studying local folk music and conducting villagers in musical celebrations and rituals at age seventeen, encouraging them to play whatever sound sources were at hand. When several Beijing Opera musicians on tour drowned in a boating accident, he was inducted as a substitute string-player and in 1978 was one of thirty selected from among thousands of applicants to attend the Central Conservatory. Dun became a leading composer of China's cultural "New Wave" of the 1980s, won recognition at home and abroad for his compositions, but suffered political backlash. He achieved creative breakthroughs in combining the natural sounds of his heritage and personal background with Western symphonic and chamber-music forms. Dun's atonalism is tempered by his command of a vast timbral palette, a sensitivity to dynamics, and a deft use of space and silence, making his music accessible to a wide audience.

SELECTIVE DISCOGRAPHY: *Ghost Dance* (Nonesuch, 1997); *Heaven Earth Mankind: Symphony 1997* (Sony Classical, 1997); *Marco Polo* (Sony Classical, 1997); *Bitter Love* (Sony Classical, 1999); *Crouching Tiger, Hidden Dragon Original Motion Picture Soundtrack* (Sony Classical, 2000); *Silk Road Journeys: When Strangers Meet* (Sony Classical, 2002); *Passion After St. Matthew* (Sony Classical, 2002).

WEBSITE: www.schirmer.com/composers/tan_bio.html.

HOWARD MANDEL

JERMAINE DUPRI

Born: Atlanta, Georgia, 23 September 1972

Genre: R&B

Best-selling album since 1990: *Jermaine Dupri Presents: Life in 1472* (1998)

Hit songs since 1990: "The Party Continues," "Welcome to Atlanta"

Beginning his career in the early 1990s as the driving force behind rap and R&B groups such as Kris Kross and Xscape, Jermaine Dupri quickly built a reputation as one of the most talented, innovative young producers in the music industry, lending his trenchant, hook-laden beats and rhythms to recordings by stars such as Usher, TLC, Mariah Carey, and Aretha Franklin. By the beginning of the twenty-first century Dupri had also established a successful career as a solo artist, releasing two albums that combined his rapping with guest performances by some of the biggest names in R&B. In addition, he became a wealthy music CEO, heading his own label, So So Def, and overseeing its roster of hit-making artists.

The son of an Atlanta-based road manager for touring artists, Dupri began performing by the age of ten, appearing as a dancer in a live concert by pop star Diana Ross in 1982. Spending the next few years dancing onstage with a variety of R&B acts, Dupri moved into production in 1989, overseeing the debut recording of female rap group Silk Tymes Leather. Although the album was a commercial failure, Dupri did not have to wait long for his big break. In 1991 he discovered a pair of thirteen-year-old rappers performing at Atlanta's Greenbriar shopping mall. Dupri named the duo Kris Kross and, displaying an impresario's instinct for gimmick, suggested the young artists wear their clothes backward in public appearances. The subsequent album, *Totally Krossed Out* (1992), features the number one R&B hits "Jump" and "Warm It Up," both written and produced by nineteen-year-old Dupri. Now one of the hottest producers in R&B, Dupri founded his So So Def label and spearheaded the successful careers of female rapper Da Brat and vocal group Xscape. At the same time, he produced tracks for up-and-coming artists such as R&B crooner Usher, who became a pop star when he recorded Dupri's song, "You Make Me Wanna . . ." (1997).

After producing further hits for Mariah Carey, TLC, rapper Lil' Kim, and others, Dupri turned his attentions to a solo project, *Jermaine Dupri Presents: Life in 1472*. Although Dupri raps on each of the album's tracks, he surrounds himself with a host of guest artists, including pop stars Carey and Keith Sweat, as well as rappers Jay-Z, Lil' Kim, and Snoop Dogg. Performed in his characteristically nasal, somewhat sleepy-sounding voice, Dupri's raps take the form of boasts concerning money, success, and women. At times his lyrics evince an exaggerated sense of humor, such as on "Fresh," performed with rap legend Slick Rick: "[I can] even make Salvation Army clothes look good / Don't even wear the same underwear two times." "All That's Got to Go," featuring the vocals of Xscape member LaTocha Scott, is one of the album's most enjoyable tracks, using the melodic riff from Aretha Franklin's 1982 hit "Jump to It" as backdrop for a sharp, profane battle of the sexes.

In 2001 Dupri released a follow-up album, *Instructions*, featuring the tortuous funk groove of the hits, "Welcome to Atlanta" and "Ballin' Out of Control." While Dupri has gained toughness and assurance as a rapper, his lyrical themes—summed up in the song title, "Money, Hoes & Power"—remain the same. Dupri experienced a personal setback in December 2002, when federal agents seized his cars and furniture due to an alleged $2.5 million owed the Internal Revenue Service. Overcoming this crisis, he soon announced a new distribution deal for So So Def with Arista Records, ending a decade-long arrangement with Columbia Records.

Known for a "bouncy" production style in which sinuous rhythms are punctuated by spoken interjections, Dupri was a trendsetter in 1990s rap and R&B. By the end of the decade, Dupri was releasing guest-laden solo albums graced by his verbal wit and rhythmic drive.

SELECTIVE DISCOGRAPHY: *Jermaine Dupri Presents: Life in 1472* (So So Def, 1998); *Instructions* (So So Def, 2001).

WEBSITE: www.jermainedupri.com.

DAVID FREELAND

DURAN DURAN

Formed: 1978, Birmingham, England

Members: Simon Le Bon, lead vocals (born Herfordshire, England, 27 October 1958); Nick Rhodes, keyboards (born Birmingham, England, 8 June 1962). Former members: Simon Colley, bass/clarinet; Warren Cuccurullo (born Brooklyn, New York, 8 December 1956); John Curtis, guitar; Stephen Duffy, lead vocals (born Birmingham, Worcestershire, England, 30 May 1960); Andy Taylor, guitar (born Wolverhampton, England, 16 February 1961); John Taylor, guitar (born Birmingham, England, 20 June 1960); Roger Taylor, drummer (born Birmingham, England, 26 April 1960); Jeff Thomas, lead vocals; Andy Wickett, lead vocals.

Genre: Rock, Pop

Best-selling album since 1990: *Duran Duran: The Wedding Album* (1993)

Hit songs since 1990: "Ordinary World," "Come Undone"

Emerging from the tidal wave of British "new romantic" pop groups, Duran Duran established a reputation in the early 1980s with well-crafted songs coupled with an image-conscious presentation. Borrowing their name from a character in the 1968 science fiction film *Barbarella*, the group charted with a string of hits from their first three albums and became pop icons through their memorable music videos. By the late 1980s their popularity had subsided, and constant personnel changes hindered the quality and consistency of their subsequent albums. Loyal fans (known as "Duranies") assert that Duran Duran is developing into a new type of pop group, one that embraces funk, hip-hop, and, most especially, dance-club sounds and textures.

Nick Rhodes assembled the initial forerunner of Duran Duran in 1978, consisting of Rhodes, Taylor, Simon Colley, and Stephen Duffy. After Colley and Duffy left the group, Roger Taylor was recruited as the drummer, and Andy Wickett took over as the lead vocalist. This lineup recorded several demo tapes, producing the first version of the subsequent hit, "Girls on Film." Further changes ensued: John Taylor moved to bass guitar and John Curtis (guitar) and Jeff Thomas (vocals) joined the group. The lineup eventually stabilized with the introduction of guitarist Andy Taylor and vocalist Simon Le Bon, who soon became the group's primary lyricist.

Duran Duran gained early exposure as the opening act for Hazel O'Connor and was signed by EMI Records in late 1980. Their first single, "Planet Earth," did moderately well in the U.K. charts, but it was their second release, "Girls on Film," accompanied by a racy video directed by Godley & Creme, which brought them widespread acclaim. This emphasis on the visual medium led to a highly successful collaboration with the director Russell Mulchay, who almost single-handedly created the image of Duran Duran. The group traveled to distant locales (Antigua and Sri Lanka) and constructed video narratives that highlighted their sartorial style set against exotic backdrops. This formula was introduced in the colorful videos for "Rio" and "Save a Prayer" and developed further in the animal courtship of "Hungry Like the Wolf." MTV greatly contributed to their success by placing their videos in constant rotation.

Unlike other British pop groups such as the Human League and Spandau Ballet, Duran Duran did not eschew the role of the electric guitar in their songs. Rather they retained the rhythmic and harmonic possibilities of the distorted electric guitar along with the fashionable sounds of the synthesizer. "Is There Something I Should Know?," from *Duran Duran* (1983), displays this balance with a dominant guitar riff in the verse and ascendant synthesizer textures in the chorus. John Taylor's funk-inspired bass lines provided visceral propulsion, evident especially in such songs as the title track from *Rio* (1982) and the bridge section in the extended version of "Hungry Like the Wolf." This unique combination was further integrated in their 1983 album, *Seven and the Ragged Tiger,* which produced three top-ten hits: "The Reflex," "Union of the Snake," and "New Moon on Monday." Le Bon extended his melodic ideas, from syllabic repetition in "The Reflex" to baritone crooning in the beginning of "New Moon on Monday." The melodies were intermittently augmented with backup singers, allowing Rhodes to further weave his melodic and harmonic riffs into the overall texture.

By the end of their 1984 tour and the release of their live album *Arena,* the members of Duran Duran decided to take a break and pursue solo projects. In 1986 the members of Duran Duran came together to record the theme song for the latest James Bond film, *A View to a Kill.*

When Le Bon, Rhodes, and John Taylor attempted to reconvene the group in 1986, they met with resistance from the other two members. Andy Taylor, who was pursuing a solo career, contributed to their next album, *Notorious* (1986), but was replaced for the subsequent tour by Warren Cuccurullo. While Duran Duran attempted new musical ground, most notably in the title-track and the funk-inspired "Skin Trade," the album as a whole was uneven and lacked focus. Most regrettably, the melodic economy and brilliance which had marked their earlier efforts now seemed repetitive and disjunct.

Although Duran Duran continued recording, they garnered little interest until their 1993 eponymous album, known as *The Wedding Album.* With Cuccurollo now a permanent member, the group received wide acclaim for two ballads, "Ordinary World" and "Come Undone." The album seemed at once mindful of their legacy and propelled by fresh energy. Playing on the band's visually driven image of the 1980s, Le Bon now proclaimed in the opening song, "Destroyed by MTV I hate to bite the hand that feeds me so much information."

In 1995 the group released *Thank You,* an album of covers that included a wide variety of songs, from "Crystal Ship" (the Doors) and "Thank You" (Led Zeppelin) to "White Lines" (Grandmaster Flash and the Furious Five) and "911 Is a Joke" (Public Enemy). Although Duran Duran collaborated with Grandmaster Flash and the Furious Five on the album and performed with them on late-night television shows, their appropriation of rap hits invited severe criticism. After this album the longtime member John Taylor left, and the group continued once again as a trio (Le Bon, Rhodes, and Cuccurullo). *Medazzaland* (1997) presented a shockingly new sound with dance-club grooves in "Big Bang Generation" and "Electric Barbarella," and a wry self-assessment in "Undergoing Treatment," which darkly proclaimed, "We are undergoing treatment watching others in the news studying our worst reviews." *Pop Trash* (2000) was equally ambitious, conjuring sonic textures reminiscent of the Beatles, with a renewed emphasis on melodic writing and pop craftsmanship.

Duran Duran has weathered more than two decades in the popular music world, surviving countless personnel changes, shifting public tastes, and a brief, self-imposed name change to Duranduran. While most of their peers from the early 1980s have disbanded and disappeared, Duran Duran continues to explore new musical directions.

SELECTIVE DISCOGRAPHY: *Duran Duran* (EMI, 1981); *Rio* (EMI, 1982); *Seven and the Ragged Tiger* (EMI, 1983); *Arena* (Parlophone, 1984); *Notorious* (EMI, 1986); *Big Thing* (EMI, 1988); *Decade* (EMI, 1989); *Liberty* (Parlophone, 1990); *Duran Duran: The Wedding Album* (Parlophone, 1993); *Thank You* (Capitol, 1995); *Medazzaland* (Capitol, 1997); *Greatest* (EMI, 1998); *Night Versions* (EMI, 1999); *Strange Behaviour* (EMI, 1999); *Pop Trash* (Capitol, 2000).

WYNN YAMAMI

BOB DYLAN

Born: Robert Allen Zimmerman; Duluth, Minnesota, 24 May 1941

Genre: Rock, Folk Rock

Best-selling album since 1990: *Time Out of Mind* (1997)

Bob Dylan [PAUL NATKIN/PHOTO RESERVE]

More than any other single figure of the 1960s and 1970s, Bob Dylan defined the direction of American popular music. Through his influence, the singer as composer became standard, and popular music began to deal with serious matters—war, social injustice, and similar topics—in lyrics that qualified as poetry. With a long and distinguished list of songs to his credit and a record of concertizing equaled by few of his generation, Dylan remains a potent force on the musical scene: respected, even revered, and still musically active.

Born Robert Allen Zimmerman in 1941, Dylan moved to New York in early 1961 after attending the University of Minnesota for three semesters. He took his new name from Welsh poet Dylan Thomas and his musical identity from folk music great Woody Guthrie. In New York, Dylan played the coffeehouse circuit, an important venue for folk artists, especially after the Beat movement of the 1950s. He adopted Guthrie's signature harmonica rack—a metal frame suspended at the neck so the performer can accompany himself—and covered many of his

songs while beginning to create his own. In "a voice that came from you and me" (as late-sixties folk rock musician Don McLean would later describe in his cult song "American Pie"), Dylan soon attracted a following and the attention of John Hammond, a music scout from Columbia Records. Soon afterward, Hammond signed Dylan to his first contract. Hammond's colleagues at Columbia called the young singer "Hammond's Folly." Little did they realize that in a few years Dylan would become the voice of his generation. He expressed the inner feelings of the youth culture of the 1960s, putting them into the words and music of his songs. This was music to be listened to, the message of its lyrics as important as its melody or rhythm.

By the mid-1960s, on the albums *Bringing It All Back Home* (1965), *Highway 61 Revisited* (1965), and *Blonde on Blonde* (1966), Dylan had moved from the folk style that had made him famous to a rock style incorporating certain features of folk music; this style of music became known as folk rock. In the process of undertaking this change, Dylan changed his instrument to electric guitar and his subject matter to intensely personal experiences often rendered in surrealistic imagery and language. "From now on," Dylan told an interviewer during this period, "I want to write from inside me." From then until now, Dylan has always expected his audience to catch up with him. No performer of his stature and achievement has done less to woo fans, more at times to alienate them.

By the 1980s Dylan seemed to have run dry. Then in one of those musical surprises for which he is famous, Dylan ended the decade with the Daniel Lanois-produced *Oh Mercy* (1989), an album of distinctive new material. He had passed through a period of born-again Christianity and musical uncertainty. As if to prove, however, that once a major talent always a major talent, he went on in the 1990s to produce five new albums, two major reissues (one a double album and the other a triple), and a third volume of his greatest hits, reprising past work. Under any circumstances this is a major accomplishment, but all the more so for someone in the fourth decade of his musical career.

Tradition and Individual Talent

What is most notable about Dylan's work since 1990 is its variety. *Under the Red Sky* (1990) is a transitional work, somewhere between the folk rock style of Dylan's earlier work and the albums that follow it. Many tracks have folklike lyrics, but musically lack the folk music sound associated with Dylan. "TV Talkin' Song," for instance, recalls the talking blues style in its lyric, but is up-tempo folk rock in sound. Other lyrics recall nursery songs in their structure and rhythm. "Two by Two" is a retelling of the story of Noah's ark, and "Cat's in the

Well" is a spin-off of the traditional "Pussy's in the Well." The final track on the album, "Wiggle Wiggle," qualifies as nonsense verse. "God Knows," on the other hand, a strong number left out of the *Oh Mercy* album by Dylan's choice, carries on the born-again theme found in Dylan's gospel music of the early 1980s. Uneven, somewhat quirky in effect, *Red Sky* points the way to *Good as I Been to You* (1992) and *World Gone Wrong* (1993), which have a common indebtedness to the folk traditions that informed Dylan's earliest music. In form, content, and instrumentation, they constitute a revisiting of a key part of Dylan's musical roots.

On *Good as I Been to You*, Dylan, accompanying himself Woody Guthrie style on acoustic guitar and harmonica, revises and updates traditional folk songs. They vary from tragic ballads like "Little Maggie," "a-drinkin' down her troubles / Over courtin' some other man," and "Frankie and Albert," about a woman who murders her "man" when he does her wrong, to lighthearted lyrics like "Froggie Went a Courtin'" and "Tomorrow Night." Other tracks—such as "You're Gonna Quit Me"—derive from the blues tradition, in a collection as diverse in its way as the classic, recently reissued Harry Smith anthology of early folk music recordings (for Folkways Records) that inspired Dylan and others in the folk music revival of the early 1960s.

World Gone Wrong continues in the same vein. The songs are adapted from a variety of sources, their performers acknowledged carefully in Dylan's liner notes for the album. He pays tribute to the compositions and arrangements of great folk artists like Blind Willie McTell, Tom Paley (of the New Lost City Ramblers), Frank Hutchinson, the Mississippi Sheiks, and Doc Watson (plus one song by Jerry Garcia of the Grateful Dead). The result is another return to musical roots by an artist who has reached the point in his life where he feels the need to review his past. For a musician like Dylan, that means only one thing—the music he started with, which sustained him at a time in the early 1990s when he was considering giving up recording altogether.

Reprising the Past

Another sign of Dylan's musical life review is the major reissues of the nineties. From early in Dylan's career, pirates of concert, coffeehouse, and private performances circulated widely among his fans. The most famous of these were the so-called *Basement Tapes*, the product of sessions with Dylan and the Band at Woodstock, New York, in 1967, during the hiatus in Dylan's public career following his celebrated motorcycle accident of the preceding year. Ultimately issued commercially by Columbia in 1975 under the same title, these recordings have an important place in the history of American music because they

marked a return to the roots of rock music at a time when psychedelic rock had moved it into outer space.

Dylan has always been more a performance artist than a recording artist. In general, his attitude toward recording sessions has been casual. As a result, many excellent performances—in the form of demos, outtakes, alternative takes, and unreleased concert performances—were available for *The Bootleg Series, vols. 1–3 (Rare & Unreleased), 1961–1991* (1991). Too varied to describe in detail, this collection gives an extraordinary overview of Dylan's long career and increases any listener's appreciation for the sheer diversity of his art.

The third of the *Greatest Hits* series (1994) repackages work already issued commercially in other forms. These range from songs made familiar by their popularity and the frequency with which they are performed in concert by Dylan—"Forever Young," "Tangled Up in Blue," or "Knockin' on Heaven's Door"—to the less familiar but still worthwhile, such as "Dignity" or "Series of Dreams."

Of equal significance to the first three volumes of the *Bootleg Series* is *The Bootleg Series, vol. 4: Bob Dylan LIVE 1966: The "Royal Albert Hall" Concert* (1998), which was recorded in Manchester, England, in the spring of 1966, not at the famous London venue. The previous summer Dylan debuted an electric set at the Newport Folk Festival, provoking a negative response from an audience used to Dylan only as a folk artist. To them, he had betrayed the cause, but their response was mild compared with the Manchester audience of the following spring. This recording, frequently pirated, captures an important moment in Dylan's evolution as an artist. With concerts like this, combined with the very popular recording of the previous year of "Like a Rolling Stone," from *Highway 61 Revisited*, folk rock was born.

Like a number of these reissues, *Bob Dylan Unplugged* (1995), recorded during his appearance on MTV's *Unplugged*, consists almost entirely of material for which Dylan is well known. What makes these interpretations of songs like "Desolation Row" and "Like a Rolling Stone" notable is the spontaneity of their performances on this disk. With so many of Dylan's television appearances uneven or disappointing, this set has a dynamic that sets it apart.

Time Out of Mind

Among the albums of the 1990s, *Time Out of Mind* (1997) occupies a special place. Dylan's second effort with Daniel Lanois as producer would net him several Grammy Awards, including Best Album of the Year. Conceptually, sonically, artistically, it is work on a very high level. In subject matter, the songs Dylan recorded here broke new ground, or at least dug much deeper in certain turf than anything that precedes them in his songbook. And the sessions that produced the album, which took place in Miami, Florida, occurred with a degree of concentration unusual in Dylan's recording history. In fact, the closest approach to what this project involved is probably the Dylan-Lanois combination on *Oh Mercy*, recorded nearly a decade earlier in New Orleans, Louisiana.

In a *Rolling Stone* interview several years after the album's release, Dylan was quick to deny that his own mortality is at the root of some of these tracks but, undeniably, the issues of death, lost love, and disillusionment are addressed here in almost every song. (A serious heart disease nearly took his life as the album was in the editing phase.) "Love Sick," the opening track, became a favorite at Dylan's concerts, with its lament, "I'm sick of love / I wish I'd never met you / I'm sick of love / I'm tryin' to forget you." In "Standin' in the Doorway" Dylan again is left alone: "You left me standin' in the doorway cryin'/ Blues wrapped around my head."

"Not Dark Yet" takes the sense of loneliness one step further, to the edge of the grave: "Sometimes my burden is more than I can bear / It's not dark yet but it's getting there." In "Trying to Get to Heaven," he dreams of reaching the heavenly kingdom before it is too late: "I've been walkin' through the middle of nowhere / Tryin' to get to heaven before they close the door." The same dark imagery enters virtually every song, as in the penultimate "Can't Wait": "I'm strollin' through the lonely graveyard of my mind / I left my life with you."

Only the rambling final track, "Highlands," the record of a conversation between the narrator and a waitress he encounters, seems to lift the mood of the album in closing: "Well, my heart's in the Highlands at the break of day / Over the hills and far away / There's a way to get there, and I'll figure it out somehow / Well, I'm already there in my mind and that's good enough for now." With a title perhaps borrowed from Irish poet William Butler Yeats—his poem of 1910—"Upon a House Shaken by the Land Agitation" begins "How should the world be luckier if this house, / Where passion and precision have been one / Time out of mind . . ."—this album marked a major revival of interest in Dylan, which carried him and his newly widened audience into the new millennium.

In 2001 Dylan released the outstanding *Love and Theft*, yet another revisiting of his musical past. Generically as varied as *Time Out of Mind* is consistent, this album takes Dylan back as far as the 1940s and 1950s, with songs that echo the eras of swing and early rock and roll. Aside from the anthologies, there is little in Dylan's discography with which to compare it.

For Dylan, as for the hobbits of J.R.R. Tolkien's *Lord of the Rings*, the road has gone ever on. From his beginnings as the most influential artist of the folk revival of the sixties, to his creation of the genre of folk rock and his return to the roots of rock music, Dylan has always stayed one step ahead of his audience, urging them on with the certainty, and indifference, of his genius.

SELECTIVE DISCOGRAPHY: *Bringing It All Back Home* (Columbia, 1965); *Highway 61 Revisited* (Columbia, 1965); *Blonde on Blonde* (Columbia, 1966); *Nashville Skyline* (Columbia, 1969); *Planet Waves* (Asylum, 1974); *The Basement Tapes* (Columbia, 1975); *Blood on the Tracks* (Columbia, 1975); *Desire* (Columbia, 1976); *Infidels* (Columbia, 1983); *Oh Mercy* (Columbia, 1989); *Under the Red Sky* (Columbia, 1990); *The Bootleg Series, vols. 1–3 (Rare & Unreleased), 1961–1991* (1991); *Good as I Been to You* (Columbia, 1992); *World Gone Wrong* (Columbia, 1993); *The 30th Anniversary Concert Celebration* (Columbia, 1993); *Bob Dylan Unplugged* (Columbia, 1995); *Time Out of Mind* (Columbia, 1997); *The Bootleg Series, vol. 4: Bob Dylan LIVE 1966: The "Royal Albert Hall" Concert* (Columbia, 1998); *Love and Theft* (Columbia, 2001).

BIBLIOGRAPHY: A. Muir, *The Razor's Edge: Bob Dylan and the Never Ending Tour* (London, 2001); H. Sounes, *Down the Highway: The Life of Bob Dylan* (New York, 2001); D. Hajdu, *Positively 4th Street* (New York, 2002).

ARCHIE LOSS

E e
E

THE EAGLES

Formed: 1971, Los Angeles, California

Members: Glenn Frey, guitar, keyboards, vocals (born Detroit, Michigan, 6 November 1948); Don Henley, drums, vocals (born Gilmer, Texas, 22 July 1947); Timothy B. Schmit, bass (born Sacramento, California, 30 October 1947); Joe Walsh, guitar, vocals (born Wichita, Kansas, 20 November 1947). Former members: Don Felder, guitar, vocals (born Gainesville, Florida, 21 September 1947); Bernie Leadon, guitar, banjo, mandolin, vocals (born Minneapolis, Minnesota, 19 July 1947); Randy Meisner, bass, guitar, vocals (born Scottsbluff, Nebraska, 8 March 1946).

Genre: Rock, Country Rock

Best-selling album since 1990: *Eagles: Hell Freezes Over* (1994)

Although the Eagles called it quits as a band in 1980, the enduring popularity of their hit singles and the emergence of classic rock as a force on FM radio led them to reunite in 1994, turning them into a popular act of the 1990s. Like other bands of their era, their reunion brought their aging fans back to concert arenas and introduced the group's repertoire of classic hits to young fans. Their first anthology, *Eagles: Their Greatest Hits, 1971–1975* (1976), remains the best-selling rock recording of all time. The band is often characterized as emblematic of the excesses of 1970s corporate rock culture, though the group's lyrics reveal their cynicism about the music business and unrestrained 1970s style self-indulgence.

Early Days in California

The Eagles epitomize the laid-back southern California sound of the early 1970s. Drawing on influences such as Crosby, Stills, and Nash, the Byrds, Poco, and the Flying Burrito Brothers, the Eagles blended country rock's twangy banjos and slide guitars with lush vocals, melodic hard rock, and a pop sensibility. The group formed in 1971 when Don Henley and Glenn Frey left singer Linda Ronstadt's backup band. The duo joined forces with Bernie Leadon and Randy Meisner and soon released *The Eagles* (1972). Two successful singles from that album, "Take It Easy" and "Witchy Woman," quickly established the band on the American charts, where they remained during the course of the 1970s. Other Eagles hits, "Best of My Love," "One of These Nights," "New Kid in Town," and "Hotel California," were all number one singles.

From Country Rock to Coliseums

During the course of its career, the band shed its country rock roots for a harder rock edge. Don Felder was added on electric guitar in 1974 and banjo/mandolin player Leadon was replaced with electric guitar rocker Joe Walsh in 1976. *Hotel California* (1976), widely regarded as the band's masterpiece, examines the dark side and moral costs of hedonism. Creative and personal tensions within the band delayed the completion of the group's final studio recording, *The Long Run* (1979). Although the record yielded three successful singles, "Heartache Tonight," "The Long Run," and "I Can't Tell You Why," the band broke up one year later, following the release of a live album. All the band's members pursued solo careers, though only Henley's has been notable.

Since their breakup in 1980, the Eagles' reputation with critics has gradually improved while sales of their albums continue to break records. The titles of several songs such as "Life in the Fast Lane" are part of the American lexicon, and there is increasing nostalgia for the era the band has come to represent. An Eagles tribute album, *Common Thread: The Songs of the Eagles* (1993), including tracks performed by Travis Tritt, Clint Black, and Trisha Yearwood, was a commercial success. The album eventually went to number one on the charts and sold more than 3 million copies in the first six months of its release.

Common Thread's success led Irving Azoff, an executive at Giant Records, to sell the band on the idea of a reunion, which occurred in 1994. The Eagles's first official reunion appearance took place at MTV's studios and was later broadcast. The group played requests from the audience and unveiled four new songs.

Enduring Success

A tour, "Hell Freezes Over," followed the broadcast, as did an album of the same name. In typical Eagles fashion, the record sold more than 7 million copies within months of its release and the accompanying tour in 1994 and 1995 was wildly successful. Despite support from the public, the Eagles have never been a favorite of rock critics. The little critical response generated by the reunion album described it largely as a transparent effort to make cash. The record contains only four new Eagles songs alongside updated versions of their biggest hits, such as "Hotel California" and "Tequila Sunrise." Former band members, such as Meisner, claimed the group re-recorded their classic hits to cheat former members out of royalties. The group's concerts also attracted attention when tour organizers charged and received $115 per ticket, as a means, they claimed, to deter ticket scalpers. Cameron Crowe, a former rock journalist who wrote a *Rolling Stone* cover story on the Eagles in 1975, seems, in part, to have based his screenplay of the popular film *Almost Famous* (2000) on his longtime friendship with the band.

The Eagles were inducted into the Rock and Roll Hall of Fame in 1998. Their brief performance at the induction ceremony included all current and former members of the group. Fittingly, the band (this time Felder, Frey, Henley, Schmit, and Walsh) closed the twentieth century with a New Year's Eve show at Staples Center in Los Angeles. A recording of the concert was included as part of a three-disc retrospective, *Eagles 1972–1999: Selected Works* (2000). In 2002 Felder was suddenly fired from the band and promptly sued his former band for damages. Remaining members planned to release a new studio album in 2003.

The Eagles' reunion album and tour were major events for their legions of fans. It remains clear, however, to crit-

ics and to members of the band that their creative peak reached its zenith in 1976 with the release of *Hotel California*. Eagles members, such as Henley, focus their energy on solo efforts and are content to play the band's classic hits to appreciative crowds during summer reunion tours. The band's impact on American and international popular culture has not lessened since their heyday.

SELECTIVE DISCOGRAPHY: *Eagles* (Asylum, 1972); *Desperado* (Asylum, 1973); *On the Border* (Asylum, 1974); *One of These Nights* (Asylum, 1975); *Eagles: Their Greatest Hits, 1971–1975* (Asylum, 1976); *Hotel California* (Asylum, 1976); *The Long Run* (Asylum, 1979); *Eagles Live* (Asylum, 1980); *Eagles Greatest Hits, Volume 2* (Asylum, 1982); *Hell Freezes Over* (Geffen, 1994); *Eagles 1972–1999: Selected Works* (Elektra/Asylum, 2000).

BIBLIOGRAPHY: M. Shapiro, *The Long Run: The Story of the Eagles* (London, 1995); M. Eliot, *To the Limit: The Untold Story of the Eagles* (New York, 1998).

SHAWN GILLEN

STEVE EARLE

Born: Stephen Fain Earle; Ft. Monroe, Virginia, 17 January 1955

Genre: Country

Best-selling album since 1990: *Transcendental Blues* (2000)

Steve Earle's self-destructive ways nearly ruined a career touted early on to be one of country music's most prolific since Hank Williams Sr. He survived, however, and advanced into the 1990s as a passionate artist whose nimble songwriting has turned increasingly political, at times lending voice to people and issues that unsettled his listeners.

Earle was born in Virginia, where his father, a Texan air-traffic controller, had been temporarily relocated. The eldest child of five children, he grew up less than twenty miles north of San Antonio in the small town of Shertz, Texas. Earle started playing the guitar at age eleven, progressed rapidly, and left home at fourteen to live with his uncle in Houston. Soon thereafter he met a fellow Texan and songwriter, Townes Van Zandt, who became a mentor for Earle in music and fast-track living.

Earle moved to Nashville in 1974 and eventually signed a songwriting deal with a division of RCA Records for seventy-five dollars a week. He played in various bands around Nashville and garnered a reputation as an edgy but talented songwriter/performer. He was slated to have his song "Mustang Love" recorded by Elvis Presley in 1975, but Elvis failed to show up for the session. Carl Perkins recorded it the following year. Earle also appeared in Robert Altman's film *Nashville* (1975).

Backed by his band the Dukes, Earle toured and recorded from 1982 to 1985 with marginal success until he set country music on its ear with the release of *Guitar Town* (1986). The album is a powerful blend of raw country-rocking story songs featuring familiar ill-fated characters. The album earned him two Grammys in 1987 for Best Country Male Vocalist and Best Song for the title track. In 1986 *Rolling Stone* magazine's critic poll hailed Earle as the Country Artist of the Year.

Subsequent recordings were highly acclaimed, but the music industry as a whole was having difficulty defining Earle, whose country-rooted style started to mix with a harder rock sound, particularly on his *Copperhead Road* (1988), an album of self-described "heavy metal bluegrass" that he boasted would shake up the country music establishment.

Earle's personal life shook them up as well. His repeated brushes with the law and longstanding drug problems flew in the face of country music's insistence that its artists maintain squeaky-clean images. By 1991, drugs had torpedoed his career. Driven to poverty by a five-hundred-dollar-a-day drug habit, he took to living on the streets of downtown Nashville, where he was eventually arrested for heroin possession. He served a prison sentence until his parole in 1994 following the completion of a drug-rehabilitation program.

Earle ended a four-year absence from the music scene with a cathartic solo effort, *Train a Comin'* (1995). The album features acoustic versions of older songs that he had written in addition to a few from other artists. It earned a 1996 Grammy nomination for Best Contemporary Folk album. The recording initiated a drug-free comeback that included acting, playwriting, writing a book of short stories and the draft of a novel, ceaseless political activism, and six album releases.

In a style that careers among various genres—country, bluegrass, folk, rock, and Irish—Earle will often write the lyrics in the persona of the song's main character. He has portrayed rednecks, small-town losers, a backwoods marijuana grower, a hometown athletic hero, an old-time bluegrass picker, a death row inmate, and an American Taliban. Prophetic intimations of doom pervade many of these songs.

An avowed borderline Marxist, Earle does not hesitate to write songs that voice his opposition to the political and social status quo. "Good Ol' Boy (Gettin Tough)" from *Guitar Town* was Earle's response to President Ronald Reagan's breaking of the air-traffic controllers strike in 1981. Earle's father lost his job during that chapter in American labor history. "Amerika vs. 6.0 (The Best We Can Do)," from his album *Jerusalem* (2002), railed against the nation's healthcare system. "Ashes to Ashes," another cut off the very political *Jerusalem*, warned of the eventual crumbling of the United States after the events of September 11, 2001. Earle has also been a fervent and outspoken opponent of the death penalty and contributed the song *Ellis Unit One* to the soundtrack of *Dead Man Walking*, a movie about the death penalty. Earle sponsors benefits and protests, appears at Capitol Hill, raises money, visits inmates on death row, and once accompanied and witnessed the execution of a convicted murderer he had counseled. In October 2002 his play *Karla*, about Karla Faye Tucker, the first woman executed in Texas since the 1860s, opened on a Nashville stage.

Another whirlwind of controversy arose from the *Jerusalem* track titled "John Walker's Blues," which reimagines the story of the so-called American Taliban John Walker Lindh. The American media and politicians lambasted Earle for extending sympathies to someone widely regarded as a traitor. Earle contended that he was only doing what he has always done in his songs, which is to let his listeners see a character's particular point of view.

By the year 2000, while many of Earle's contemporaries were winding down, he seemed to be picking up steam. In addition to recording and touring, Earle successfully published a book of eleven short stories titled *Doghouse Roses* (2001), and in 2002 he was working toward the completion of a novel. Earle also took a turn as an actor in 2002, playing a drug counselor in several episodes of the HBO series *The Wire*. In 2002 he was living in Nashville with his fifth wife; he is the father of three children, and his sister, Stacey Earle, is also a successful recording artist.

Earle has emerged from career purgatory with a renewed vigor. He uses his ample talent without apology to speak out on what he believes. This boiling undercurrent of empathy for the oppressed and outcast has landed Earle only on the fringes of music's mainstream, which is about as close as he seems to want to wade.

SELECTIVE DISCOGRAPHY: *Guitar Town* (MCA, 1986); *Early Tracks* (Epic, 1987); *Exit O* (MCA, 1987); *Copperhead Road* (UNI, 1988); *The Hard Way* (MCA, 1990); *Shut Up and Die Like an Aviator* (MCA, 1991); *Train a Comin'* (Winter Harvest, 1995); *I Feel Alright* (E-Squared, 1996); *El Corazon* (E-Squared, 1997); *The Mountain* (E-Squared, 1999); *Transcendental Blues* (E-Squared, 2000); *Jerusalem* (E-Squared, 2002).

BIBLIOGRAPHY: L. St. John, *Hardcore Troubadour: The Life and Near Death of Steve Earle* (New York, 2001).

DONALD LOWE

LINDA EDER

Born: Tucson, Arizona, 3 February 1961

Genre: Vocal

Best-selling album since 1990: *It's No Secret Anymore* (1999)

Hit songs since 1990: "Something to Believe In," "This Is the Moment," "Someone Like You"

Sporting a four-octave range, singer Linda Eder steadily elevated her career from nightclubs in the 1980s to a successful recording career. Along the way, she became a Broadway theater star.

Born in Arizona, Eder (pronounced edd'-er) grew up in the rural lakes region of northern Minnesota on a farm near Brainerd, a town famous for its Paul Bunyan lore. The statuesque soprano (she stands nearly six feet tall) sang continuously in her childhood. Among her influences were Judy Garland, Eileen Farrell, and Barbra Streisand. Overt shyness made Eder reluctant to sing in front of others until she performed a self-composed song at age sixteen on her way to winning the Miss Brainerd beauty pageant. After high school, she and a pianist friend formed a duo that performed in the Minneapolis/St. Paul nightclub circuit where, over the next seven years, Eder seasoned her craft. In 1988, she auditioned for the TV talent competition *Star Search* and won the Best Female Vocalist category, collecting $100,000 in prize money.

In Hollywood, while taping *Star Search*, Eder met up-and-coming composer/songwriter Frank Wildhorn, who had just written the music for a theatrical show called *Jekyll & Hyde*. He cast her in the role of Lucy, one of the leads, and it debuted at the Alley Theatre in Houston, Texas, in 1990. Although the initial version of *Jekyll & Hyde* fared poorly, it brought Eder a recording contract and the release of her first album, an eclectic batch of songs with a slight rock sensibility titled *Linda Eder* (1991). It contained the majestic "Someone Like You" from *Jekyll & Hyde*, although a reworked version of the song would appear on a later recording.

In the meantime, Wildhorn retooled *Jekyll & Hyde* and the show arrived in New York on Broadway in 1997 following a twenty-eight-city tour with Eder again in the role of Lucy. While New York critics largely panned *Jekyll & Hyde*, the audiences loved it. They especially fell for Eder who developed a tremendous, almost cultlike following of adoring fans. She remained in the show until 1998. Eder and Wildhorn married soon after. They live outside of New York in Westchester County and had a son together in 1999.

In the years leading up to and after *Jekyll & Hyde*, Eder continued recording, often singing Wildhorn's pop-influenced compositions. Eder's version of the *Jekyll & Hyde* showstopper "This Is the Moment" became an anthem of sorts for the 1994 Winter Olympics. Her husband, a songwriting machine with over 200 published songs recorded by some of music's biggest stars, credits his wife as the voice he hears when imagining his work being sung. Eder's agile sound mingles power with nuance drawing frequent comparison with Streisand. Although primarily recognized for her Broadway show song renditions, Eder can sing nearly any style effectively, which she has demonstrated on seven solo albums. *It's No Secret Anymore* (1999) is a strong foray into pop music and contains the Broadway version of her now-signature "Someone Like You." Except for Johnny Mercer's "One for My Baby," Wildhorn wrote the album's remaining thirteen songs.

The title song of her release *Gold* (2002) opened the 2002 Olympics Ceremony. *Gold* also has Eder lending her versatile skills to several early 1970s classics including George Harrison's "Here Comes the Sun." She returned to Broadway classics with the release of *Broadway My Way* (2003).

In 2000 Eder fulfilled a personal ambition by performing at New York's Carnegie Hall. Every seat in the esteemed 2,800-seat concert hall was filled and the performance drew tremendous critical acclaim. Eder maintains a concert tour schedule of approximately fifty cities per year and she is slated to star in another Wildhorn-created musical based on the life of French sculptress Camille Claudel in 2003.

Sometimes labeled the "reluctant diva," Eder is content to stay out of the limelight in favor of parenthood and to care for her stable of horses. When the urge to perform or record beckons, her marriage to Wildhorn assures an overflowing fountain of fresh new songs from which to draw.

SELECTIVE DISCOGRAPHY: *Linda Eder* (RCA, 1991); *And So Much More* (Angel, 1994); *It's Time* (Atlantic, 1997); *It's No Secret Anymore* (Atlantic, 1999); *Christmas Stays the Same* (Atlantic, 2000); *Gold* (Atlantic, 2002); *Broadway My Way* (Atlantic, 2003).

DONALD LOWE

DANNY ELFMAN

Born: Los Angeles, California, 29 May 1953

Genre: Film Scores

Best-selling album since 1990: *The Nightmare Before Christmas* (1993)

Danny Elfman, guitarist and co-founder with his brother Richard (an independent film director) of the cult-favorite band Oingo Boingo, became a soundtrack composer in 1985, when he met director Tim Burton and agreed to score *Pee-Wee's Big Adventure*. That film, concerning the surreal, epic search by oddball television kid's show character Pee-Wee Herman (Paul Reubens) for his missing bicycle, established Elfman's metier: the subtle depiction in hyperbolic music of zany and/or peculiar adventures, for thrills and chills and fun.

Elfman has subsequently scored every one of Burton's movies except *Ed Wood* (1994, scored by Howard Shore), collaborating with orchestrator Steve Bartek, another ex-Oingo Boingo member. He has also worked with directors Brian DePalma (*Mission Impossible*, 1996), Sam Raimi (*Darkman*, 1990), Warren Beatty (*Dick Tracy*, 1990), and Wes Craven (*Scream 2*, 1997), among others. He composed the theme for Matt Groening's animated television series *The Simpsons* (1989) and the themes for *The Dilbert Zone* (1999) and *Tales from the Crypt* (1989); he supplied music for television advertising campaigns by Lincoln/Mercury (1998–1999) and Nissan (1996–1997).

Elfman's light touch typically is accompanied by dark undertones, especially in keeping with Burton's chiaroscuro of comic and gothic motifs in films such as *Beetlejuice* (1988), *Batman* (1989), *Edward Scissorhands* (1990), *Batman Returns* (1992), *Mars Attacks!* (1996), *Sleepy Hollow* (1999), *Planet of the Apes* (2001), and *The Nightmare Before Christmas* (1993), which included ten of Elfman's original songs as well as his uninterrupted orchestral score. Elfman has acknowledged the influence of classical composers ranging from Erik Satie through late Russian Romantics (Sergey Prokofiev, Dmitry Shostakovich, Igor Stravinsky) to George Gershwin, and he exhibits a fondness for circus and parade themes, grandiose gestures, xylophone and glockenspiel accents, pizzicato strings, chorales, and cymbal crashes. Around 2000, his projects (including *Spider-Man* [2001], *Red Dragon* [2001], and the supplemental score to the Academy Award-winning Fred Ebb-John Kander musical *Chicago* [2002]) began to exude a renewed rock and roll and minimalist-influenced approach.

Elfman's score to Taylor Hackford's adaptation of Stephen King's novel *Dolores Claiborne* (1995) is perhaps the darkest of Elfman's soundtracks; his writing for *Sommersby* (1993), a drama set after the American Civil War, is probably his most romantic, and his music for *Spy Kids* (2001) may be his sunniest. He has annotated two volumes of his work for diverse films and television projects under the collective title *Music for a Darkened Theater* (1996, 1990).

Elfman received his only Grammy Award in 1989 for the score of Burton's first Batman film, and was accorded two Academy Award nominations in 1998, competing with himself in the category of Best Score for

Good Will Hunting (1997) and *Men in Black* (1997). Even after a career spanning two decades, Elfman considers himself a film and television industry outsider, but that self-image may refer as much to the singularity of the characters in films he has scored than to his own career status.

SELECTIVE DISCOGRAPHY: *Music for a Darkened Theater, Vol. 1* (MCA, 1990); *Edward Scissorhands Soundtrack* (MCA, 1990); *Dick Tracy* (Warner Bros., 1990); *Darkman Soundtrack* (MCA, 1990); *The Nightmare Before Christmas* (Disney, 1993); *Sommersby* (Elektra, 1993); *Dolores Claiborne Soundtrack* (Varese Sarabande, 1994); *Dead Presidents* (Capitol, 1995); *To Die For* (Varese Sarabande, 1995); *Music for a Darkened Theater, Vol. 2* (MCA, 1996); *Good Will Hunting* (EMI/Capitol, 1997); *Men in Black* (Sony, 1997); *Sleepy Hollow* (Hollywood, 2000); *Planet of the Apes* (Sony, 2001); *Spy Kids* (Chapter III, 2001); *Chicago* (Epic/Sony Music Soundtrax, 2002).

WEBSITE: www.elfman.filmmusic.com/news.htm.

HOWARD MANDEL

MISSY ELLIOTT

Born: Melissa Elliott; Portsmouth, Virginia, 1971

Genre: Hip-Hop, R&B

Best-selling album since 1990: *Miss E . . . So Addictive* (2001)

Hit songs since 1990: "The Rain (Supa Dupa Fly)," "Get Ur Freak On," "Work It"

Hip-hop has always relied on outsize personalities to attract an audience, and Missy Elliott is no exception. She differs from many of her peers, however, in the way her individuality informs her music—rather than simply boast about her skills and fame, she employs a comedic and conceptual sophistication that makes her innovative. Since her debut in the mid-1990s, she has produced a string of hits for herself and other artists. They are at once giddy and sexually forceful, and they cut mercilessly through stereotypes. Though first pegged as a female rapper oddity, Missy Elliott has become a hip-hop visionary.

Partners for Success

Missy Elliott endured an abusive upbringing in Portsmouth, Virginia, in which music was her only escape. She instantly took to the new sound of hip-hop, and in her teens she began to write her own lyrics. In the early 1990s she was discovered by DeVante Swing, the Jodeci singer, who signed her to his roster of singers and musicians, which included Timbaland, her future production partner. She released a record with the group Sista titled *4 All the Sistas Around da World* (1994), but the label folded soon after its release. She remained close to Timbaland, who asked her to write lyrics for songs he was producing for R&B singer Aaliyah. The resulting album, *One in a Million* (1996), was a smash hit and led to more work and exposure for the pair as hired guns. Later in 1996 Elektra Records signed Missy Elliott for her solo debut.

Supa Dupa Fly was released in 1997 to outstanding critical acclaim and sales. The interplay of Elliott's bold raps and Timbaland's retro-futuristic beats took radio by storm with a sound that was alternately catchy and disarmingly strange. The first single, "The Rain (Supa Dupa Fly)," floats on Timbaland's "typewriter-funk" beat, creating a charged atmosphere with a smooth Ann Peebles sample and Elliott's lockstep flow. "Hit 'Em Wit da Hee," a funk workout performed with Lil' Kim, expresses Elliott's self-confidence with the line, "It wasn't your car that had me all in love with you / Cause I've got my own ride and a trunk full of tunes." Although she is on the lookout for love, Elliott makes it clear that she refuses to compromise for anyone; the same philosophy applies to the eclectic music. Elliott displays her songwriting and vocal versatility with soulful, sultry R&B tracks like "Friendly Skies" and "Best Friends," recorded with Aaliyah.

So Addictive

After the massive success of *Supa Dupa Fly*, the Elliott/Timbaland sound extended throughout the music industry. The team wrote hits for other artists and rival producers adopted their twisted sonics. By the release of *Da Real World* (1999), their signature sound was dangerously close to feeling dated. They rebounded with an even stronger set of songs, racking up more hits and proving that the true force behind their work was Elliott's gift for songwriting. *Da Real World* is a darker affair; it confronts the stereotypes of rap and females in rap with a firmer hand, especially in the single "She's a Bitch." Missy Elliott's potent sexuality shines through in "Hot Boyz," a gender-twisted take on the typical hip-hop cat-call song. Timbaland's jittery, propulsive beats give each song a futuristic flair, making for deceptively simple soundscapes that elevate both the mind and the body. *Da Real World* established Missy Elliott as the most formidable force in hip-hop.

At the same time Missy Elliott began to appear in TV and print advertisements, further solidifying her position as a rap icon. In a series of music videos, she set herself apart from the typical hip-hop female. She boldly positioned herself as a well-proportioned woman and disarmed naysayers by wearing an inflatable bag suit and robot armor, among other costumes. By moving against the grain, she defined the state of hip-hop and the female viewpoint within it.

This momentum brought great expectations for her third album, *Miss E . . . So Addictive* (2001). A stylistic paean to the sensual joys of the club drug ecstasy (which she describes in the song "X-tasy" as "a place of fulfillment and fantasies / Where your dreams become realities"), the album explores deeper textures, traversing styles from hardcore rap to dance to soulful ballads. Timbaland's sonic design is at its most effective, with nuanced sounds and samples supporting Elliott's vocal and compositional talents. The single "Get Ur Freak On" imagines a crossroads of rap and dance. Its dense and dazzling beat drives Elliott's unmistakable rhyming. She addresses rappers Method Man and Redman in the steamy "Dog in Heat." Her need for love, but demand for respect, crystallize in the line, "When you come home from work, I'm gon' make you do more work." The gorgeous "Take Away," a nearly psychedelic ballad recorded with R&B singer Ginuwine, balances the visceral thrills of those songs with a swirling backing track. The two singers debunk the superficiality of rap in the chorus, "Take away, your gold and platinum chains / Cause I'm gon' love, love you anyway / I'm not in it for, for the love of cash / Cause if you go broke, I gotta make it last." *Miss E . . . So Addictive* is Missy Elliott's warmest album to date.

Back to the Future

Missy Elliott and Timbaland switched gears for *Under Construction* (2002), a retrospective tribute to hip-hop's glory days. The album celebrates the joyous grooves of *Miss E . . . So Addictive* while venerating the simple party atmosphere of golden age rap. The single "Work It" finds Elliott in top form, spinning rhymes about her sexual and artistic prowess ("Let me work it / I put my thing down flip it and reverse it") over a beat loaded with 1980s touchstones like cowbells and dizzy record scratches. She ratchets up the fun with "Gossip Folks," a playful diatribe recorded with the manic Ludacris, and "Nothing Out There for Me," in which she convinces R&B diva Beyoncé Knowles to leave her man at home and party. "Back in the Day" sets the theme of the album: Elliott longingly asks, "What happened to those good old days, when hip-hop was so much fun / those parties in the summer y'all, and no one came through with a gun." The record concludes on a reflective note with "Can You Hear Me," a tribute to deceased singers Aaliyah and Lisa "Left Eye" Lopes.

Missy Elliott's work is consistently engaging. Whereas some rappers choose a demeanor and create songs to reinforce it, Elliott writes lyrics that emanate from a strong, powerful soul.

SELECTIVE DISCOGRAPHY: *Supa Dupa Fly* (1997, Elektra); *Da Real World* (1999, Elektra); *Miss E . . .*

So Addictive (2001, Elektra); *Under Construction* (2002, Elektra).

WEBSITE: www.missy-elliott.com.

SEAN CAMERON

EMERSON STRING QUARTET

Formed: 1976, New York

Members: Eugene Drucker, violin (born Coral Gables, Florida, 17 May 1952); Lawrence Dutton, viola (born New York, New York, 9 May 1954); David Finckel, cello (born Allentown, Pennsylvania, 6 December 1951); Philip Setzer, violin (Cuyahoga County, Ohio, 12 March 1951). Former members: Guillermo Figueroa, viola; Eric Wilson, cello.

Genre: Classical

Known for its penetrating interpretations, technical brilliance, and dynamic sound, the Emerson String Quartet is considered by many to be the world's finest string quartet. Its performances and recordings of the Beethoven, Bartók, and Shostakovich quartet cycles are highly prized, and the quartet has a long history of promoting music of contemporary composers.

Named for American poet and philosopher Ralph Waldo Emerson, the quartet was founded in 1976 while violinists Eugene Drucker, Philip Setzer, violist Guillermo Figueroa, and cellist Eric Wilson were students at the Juilliard School. Unlike most quartets, the Emerson has no first and second violins; Setzer and Drucker trade off playing first and second parts from work to work. This helps keep the music fresh and encourages the players to listen and adapt to one another.

In 1977 violist Lawrence Dutton joined the quartet, and the next year the group won the prestigious Naumburg Award for Chamber Music, launching its international career. Cellist David Finckel joined the quartet in 1978, and the Emersons's current lineup was set. That year the quartet played the first of its annual season of recitals at the Smithsonian Institution in Washington, D.C.

Since then it has worked with some of the world's most prominent musicians, including Menahem Pressler, Mstislav Rostropovich, Isaac Stern, Thomas Hampson, Leon Fleisher, Emanuel Ax, Oscar Shumsky, and Misha Dichter. The quartet has commissioned or premiered work by Edgar Meyer, Ned Rorem, John Harbison, Mario Davidovsky, and Ellen Taaffe Zwilich, among others.

The Emerson Quartet tours relentlessly, giving annual tours at many of the world's most prestigious concert venues and music festivals. The group is also highly committed to teaching and offers master classes in con-

junction with its concerts in many of the cities in which it performs. In 1981 it began teaching at the Hartt School in Hartford, Connecticut, and in 2002 it became quartet-in-residence at the State University of New York, Stony Brook. The Emerson Quartet frequently gives concerts to benefit peace, world hunger, children, the fight against AIDS, and other causes.

The Emerson Quartet has won six Grammy Awards, including two for the *Bartók String Quartets* (1990); one for *American Originals* (1994), featuring music by John Harbison, Richard Wernick, and Gunther Schuller; another for a set of the complete *Beethoven String Quartets* (1998); and two more (Best Chamber Music Performance and Best Classical Album) for the complete *Shostakovich String Quartets* (2000). The Shostakovich set, recorded live over three summers at the Aspen Music Festival, also won *Gramophone* magazine's Record of the Year honors. In 2000 the Emerson Quartet were chosen as *Musical America's* Ensemble of the Year.

Two films have been made about the Emerson Quartet: *In Residence at the Renwick* (1983), produced for public television, which won an Emmy; and *Making Music: The Emerson Quartet*, which won first prize at the National Educational Film Festival (1985).

The 1980s saw a boom in chamber music across America, with hundreds of chamber groups and series springing up. In the 1990s the field contracted considerably, but the Emerson Quartet continued to thrive, building on its claim as one of the top chamber ensembles in the world. Its restless exploration of new repertoire and a seemingly natural affinity for the core of the string quartet literature continue to reinvigorate the quartet's performances. The individuality encouraged in each of the members contributes to the freshness of the quartet's interpretations and its ability to produce highly nuanced performances.

SELECTIVE DISCOGRAPHY: *Bartók String Quartets* (Deutsche Grammophon, 1990); *American Originals* (Deutsche Grammophon, 1994); *Beethoven String Quartets* (Deutsche Grammophon, 1998); *Shostakovich String Quartets* (Deutsche Grammophon, 2000).

WEBSITE: www.emersonquartet.com.

DOUGLAS MCLENNAN

EMINEM

Born: Marshall Bruce Mathers III; Kansas City, Missouri, 17 October 1974

Genre: Rap

Best-selling album since 1990: *The Eminem Show* (2002)

Hit songs since 1990: "The Real Slim Shady," "My Name Is," "Without Me"

Eminem [AP/WIDE WORLD PHOTOS]

A number of rap artists were both controversial and commercially successful throughout the late 1990s and early 2000s. None, however, were as controversial or as successful as Detroit's Marshall Mathers, a.k.a. Eminem. A brash lyricist unafraid to explore and expose his conflicted psyche, Eminem blended elements of explicit humor, misogyny, self-doubt, violence, rage, and homophobia into an undeniably catchy, million-selling formula. Along the way, the bleach-blonde, white rapper went from social pariah to Grammy and Oscar-nominated mainstream music star, actor, and producer.

Breaking Through

Marshall Mathers III was born in Kansas City, Missouri, in 1974 and was raised by his mother, Debbie Mathers-Briggs, who later became fodder for some of his harshest songs. An outcast whose transient lifestyle had made it difficult to make friends, Mathers immersed himself in the cadences of hip-hop, gaining respect for his rhyming skills even as he was flunking out of ninth grade because of his poor attendance record.

The budding rapper worked with a number of local rap crews (Basement Productions, the New Jacks, Sole

Intent), going solo in 1997 with the poorly received *Infinite* album, released through the local FBT Productions label. Though he was ignored on his local scene, the rapper began to gain notice for his skills at freestyle battling—a method of rapping that involves the spontaneous creation of lyrics during a "battle" with another rapper in which each tries to top the other's lyrics with creative insults and rhymes. His notoriety expanded with a second place finish in *Rap Sheet* magazine's 1997 freestyle competition, the "Rap Olympics."

The famed rapper/producer Dr. Dre caught wind of Mathers, rapping as his alter ego, Eminem, and was sufficiently impressed by Eminem's mini album, *The Slim Shady EP* (1997), that he signed him to his Aftermath Entertainment label. By now Mathers had created two distinct characters for his rapping, Eminem and Slim Shady, both of them laced with a dark, often violent and anti-social edge.

Dre famously commented that he did not know or care that the rapper was white, only that he had considerable skills. Rappers had been engaging in violent, misogynist street reportage for more than a decade, but Eminem's resulting album, *The Slim Shady LP*, arrived amidst a firestorm of controversy about its lyrical content.

With songs depicting date rape ("Guilty Conscience"), drug use, violence toward women ("Role Model"), and the murder of his daughter's mother ("'97 Bonnie & Clyde"), the album drew fire for its content, while some critics praised Eminem for his willingness to express his rage, disillusionment, and frustration amid the chaos of his life. In a famous essay late *Billboard* magazine editor-in-chief Timothy White targeted Eminem and his label for "exploiting the world's misery." Though mostly dismissive of the criticism, Mathers claimed in some interviews that he was simply voicing the deviant thoughts of his characters.

Fame, Fortune, and Litigation

The album also raised the ire of Eminem's estranged mother, who filed a $10 million defamation suit in September 1999 against her son for portraying her as a "lawsuit-happy" drug abuser. Though he won a Best New Artist award at MTV's Video Music Awards in September 1999 and that summer married his on-and-off again sweetheart, Kim, the mother of his daughter, the good times did not last. In June 2000 Eminem pleaded not guilty to felony assault charges stemming from a Michigan bar brawl. A month later Kim Mathers attempted suicide and soon filed for divorce.

Following the example of Eminem's mother, his estranged wife filed a $10 million defamation suit against the rapper. In another example of his turbulent home life, Eminem and Kim withdrew their divorce petition in

SpotLight | The Slim Shady LP

Eminem was introduced to the world with the humorous single, "My Name Is," a nasal, comedic performance in which the rapper feigned violence on himself, expressed an interest in impregnating a Spice Girl, and joked about overdosing on drugs. Despite the explicit content, the song from *The Slim Shady LP* was a huge hit but hardly indicative of the rest of the album's content. "Guilty Conscience" featured jokes about robbing convenience stores and date-raping underage girls, couched in terms of conflicted sociopaths whose good and evil sides are at war. Even though women's groups lambasted the rapper for the violence of songs such as "'97 Bonnie & Clyde" (the album's cover featured an image from that song in which a woman's feet protrude from the trunk of a car as Eminem and his daughter peer over a dock), others were impressed by the self-deprecating nature of tracks such as "Rock Bottom," in which Eminem raps about being so poor he does not know how he will afford diapers for his daughter, Hailie. With classic production from his mentor, Dr. Dre, on the album's two singles, *The Slim Shady LP* introduced a stirring new lyrical voice.

December 2000, only to file divorce papers again in March 2001.

Amid the chaos, Eminem released his second album, *The Marshall Mathers LP* (2000), which debuted at number one on the *Billboard* charts and garnered three Grammy nominations. If his debut caused controversy, Eminem's second album poured gasoline on the fire. Musically ambitious and lyrically sophisticated, songs such as "Kill You" ("Slut, think I won't choke no whore until the vocal cords won't work no more?") and "Kim" were laced with bilious lyrics aimed at women and homosexuals, with the threats delivered in a sometimes comical, often angry voice. Women's groups and gay rights groups picketed and spoke out against the rapper, protesting his lyrics.

A groundswell of critical praise for Eminem began to gel around songs such as "Stan," a touching, eerie story/song about an obsessed fan set to the haunting, acoustic strains sampled from a soulful ballad by singer Dido. A commentary on the perils of fame and the danger of hero worship, the song paints a wholly different picture of Eminem: the sensitive artist spooked by the lengths his fans will go to emulate him. Amid furious protests from gay activists, Eminem performed "Stan" on the 2001 Grammy telecast as a duet with the openly gay singer Elton John; they ended the song with a warm embrace. The rapper won the second of three consecutive rap album of the year awards during the broadcast.

After releasing an album with his Detroit posse, D12, *Devil's Night*, Eminem recorded his third album, *The Eminem Show*, which debuted at number one in May 2002. Taking a stronger hand in the production of his songs, Eminem shows a musical dexterity on the album, mixing in elements of classic rock and pop while retaining his me-against-the-world posture on songs such as "White America" and the album's smash single, "Without Me." Still relying on his tortured personal life for inspiration ("Cleaning out My Closet"), Eminem again drew praise from critics for his lyrical prowess and musical creativity.

The soundtrack to his well-received big screen acting debut, the loosely autobiographical *8 Mile*, was also a smash hit, selling more than 5 million copies and launching the biggest single of his career, "Lose Yourself," a gripping story about the struggle to make it in the rap world.

Vilified, protested, and wildly praised, Eminem has undeniably been one of the most riveting forces in contemporary popular music. With his everyman persona, his unchecked id, and his poetic writing skills, he gained respect from both the underground rap world and the mainstream media.

SELECTIVE DISCOGRAPHY: *Infinite* (FBT Productions, 1996); *The Slim Shady EP* (Web, 1997); *The Slim Shady LP* (Interscope/Aftermath, 1999); *The Marshall Mathers LP* (Interscope/Aftermath, 2000); *The Eminem Show* (Interscope/Aftermath, 2002).

SELECTIVE FILMOGRAPHY: *8 Mile* (2002).

GIL KAUFMAN

EN VOGUE

Formed: 1988, Oakland, California

Members: Amanda Cole (born Mississippi, 6 January 1974); Terry Ellis (born Houston, Texas, 5 September 1966); Cindy Herron (born San Francisco, California, 26 September 1965). Former members: Maxine Jones (born Paterson, New Jersey, 16 January 1965); Dawn Robinson (born New London, Connecticut, 28 November 1968).

Genre: R&B, Pop

Best-selling album since 1990: *Funky Divas* (1992)

Hit songs since 1990: "Hold On," "My Lovin' (You're Never Gonna Get It)," "Free Your Mind"

Mixing sweet-sounding harmonies with the grit of hip-hop and adding a dash of old-fashioned glamour, En Vogue became one of the most successful vocal acts of the 1990s, paving the way for later female groups such as TLC and SWV. En Vogue's hits, featuring funky, 1970s-style rhythms overlaid with catchy melodies and clever lyrics, appealed to pop audiences while retaining a toughness favored by R&B and hip-hop fans. The group was most notable, however, for the flashy vocal interplay of its four original members. Switching off on lead vocal parts, frequently embellishing their high soprano notes with sexy growls, the women sounded street-tough and classy at the same time. The group's success was fueled by its glossy, photogenic appearance; attired in sleek designer clothes, En Vogue embodied a 1990s ideal of cool elegance, beauty with an attitude.

Although the group's members—Dawn Robinson, Terry Ellis, Maxine Jones, and Cindy Herron—sounded as if they had been singing together their whole lives, in reality En Vogue was assembled during a series of open auditions held by the production team of Denzil Foster and Thomas McElroy. Aside from Herron, a former Miss Black California, none of the women selected for the group had previous show business experience. At the time of En Vogue's inception Robinson had been working as a grocery store clerk, while Ellis possessed a bachelor's degree in marketing. All four, however, quickly proved their talents on the group's initial album, *Born to Sing* (1990), which features the smash pop and R&B hit, "Hold On." Opening with an a cappella rendition of the Jackson 5's 1969 hit, "Who's Lovin' You," the group effortlessly segues into a hard, funky vamp inspired by the guitar and rhythm track from "The Payback," a 1974 recording by "Godfather of Soul" James Brown. While "Hold On" borrows the sinuous percussion and guitar sound of 1970s funk, its use of a thumping bass line grounds it in the burgeoning hip-hop movement of the 1990s. Vocally, En Vogue's soulful sound recalls pop and R&B "girl groups" of the 1960s such as the Vandellas, but their polished style owes a greater debt to the Andrews Sisters, the 1940s group whose rhythmic swing and angelic harmonies bridged the gap between pop and jazz. In fact, one of *Born to Sing*'s most exciting moments is a one-minute version of the Andrews's "Boogie Woogie Bugle Boy," which the singers perform with a zesty sense of play rarely encountered in 1990s pop music.

Funky Divas

En Vogue's most commercially successful album, marking what rock critic Robert Christgau called "their cultural moment," is *Funky Divas* (1992). Featuring five hit singles and no weak tracks, the album stands as one of the strongest R&B works of the 1990s. Beginning with the exuberant "This Is Your Life" and continuing through the seductive remake of R&B legend Aretha Franklin's "Giving Him Something He Can Feel," the album maintains an undaunted air of optimism and energy. "Free Your Mind," driven by a rock-inspired guitar part, reflects the group's positive approach to fighting prejudice: "I like rap music, wear hip-hop clothes, that doesn't mean that I'm out selling dope." One of the album's most memorable hits is the slick "My Lovin' (You're Never Gonna Get It)." Again borrowing the slinky guitar riff from Brown's "The Payback," the song features one of En Vogue's toughest performances, the women boldly informing a would-be suitor that "you're never gonna get it." "My Lovin'" was the perfect soundtrack to the club and party scene of the early 1990s, an era of bitchy camp humor inspired by the popularity of supermodels, drag queens, and other "divas." En Vogue's harmonized, rhythmic, "Ooh . . . bop," became the perfect accompaniment for a dramatic finger snap, the era's most vaunted gesture of dismissal.

Departures and Regroupings

En Vogue never had another recording as successful as *Funky Divas*, and by the end of the 1990s its popularity had waned. Instead of issuing a follow-up to *Funky Divas*, group members took several years during the middle of the decade to pursue various interests, including solo careers. Although Ellis recorded a satisfying album during this period, *Southern Gal* (1995), the years out of the spotlight had diminished the group's luster by the time of its third outing, *EV3*, in 1997. Prior to the album's release, Robinson, who along with Ellis had been one of the group's most distinctive voices, departed for a solo career. Although the parting was amicable, the remaining members clearly felt dismayed. "We sat down to make plans for [EV3]," Ellis told the *Chicago Tribune* in October 1997, "and Dawn felt it wasn't going to coincide with what she wanted to do. Quite naturally we felt, 'What are we going to do now?'" Reduced to a trio, En Vogue continued to display the assured harmonizing of their previous work, but *EV3* suffers from unfocused production and material. *Masterpiece Theatre* (2000) redresses this problem through a return to the group's former inventiveness. "Love U Crazy," for example, incorporates a famous melody from the classic ballet, *The Nutcracker*. Nonetheless, critics found the material on the whole to be far less distinctive than their best work of the past. Citing the need to spend time with her daughter, Jones left the group in 2002 and was replaced by Mississippi native Amanda Cole.

Sexy and confident, En Vogue defined an early 1990s brand of seductive R&B, balancing class with a solid dose of funkiness. While talented, the group's members relied largely on creative production elements for the uniqueness of their sound. At their best, they fused the multiple musical styles of the past into a heady combination, setting a standard of edgy sophistication for the future.

SELECTIVE DISCOGRAPHY: *Born to Sing* (EastWest, 1990); *Funky Divas* (EastWest, 1992); *EV3* (EastWest, 1997); *Masterpiece Theatre* (EastWest, 2000).

DAVID FREELAND

ENYA

Born: Eithne Ní Bhraonáin; Gweedore, County Donegal, Ireland, 17 May 1961

Genre: New Age

Best-selling album since 1990: *Shepherd Moons* (1991)

Hit songs since 1990: "Orinoco Flow," "Book of Days," "Anywhere Is"

Enya was raised in a musical family: her mother was a musician and her father, Leo Brennan, was the leader of the famous Irish band Slieve Foy. She began her musical training at an early age with a grounding in classical piano. Her uncles, brothers, and sisters formed the famous Irish band Clannad in 1976. Joining Clannad in 1980, Enya gained invaluable musical experience for two years before leaving and working with lyricist Roma Ryan and producer Nicky Ryan. With them she recorded various television and film scores, stints that led to a score for the BBC-TV series, *The Celts*. It was the soundtrack to this film that became her first album, *Enya*, released in 1986.

In 1988 Enya and the Ryans released the album *Watermark*, which became a huge success. The first single, "Orinoco Flow," which is mainly sung in Gaelic, soared to number one in the U.K. and helped sell 8 million copies of the album worldwide. This track captures the essence of Enya's sound, one of undulating, trancelike, melodic themes interwoven with modal harmonies. What is striking in this song is the expanse of layered vocal parts that fuses Celtic themes to a new age style. Engaging in her vocal delivery, Enya was able to find a niche in the pop market with a freshness and sense of personal searching that was unique.

Her next album, *Shepherd Moons* (1991), surpassed the commercial success of her previous album. This album entered the U.S. charts at number seven, remaining there for almost four years and selling more than 10 million copies. Like *Watermark*, this album maintains a romantic Celtic feel through its highly polished production. The folk references are cushioned in waves of hushed vocal parts underpinned by soothing and seductive rhythms. With its mix of ballads, *Shepherd Moons* fuses a variety of popular styles; rock creeps into the best-known song on the album, "Caribbean Blue."

Taking almost four years to complete, her next album, *The Memory of Trees* (1995), entered the U.S. charts at number nine and sold more than 2 million copies in its first year. By this stage in her career, Enya had established herself as a New Age Celtic artist with a contemporary flavor who appealed to a more adult public. With *Memory of Trees*, her style had crystallized into a form of expression that was both sensual and spiritual. This album draws on a range of themes that are at once global, Druidic, and neopagan, with strains of Latin and Gaelic verse woven into the textural fabric of the melodic material. Songs such as "Hope Has a Place" meld simple folk phrases with lush layers of instrumentation. Always at the center of these tracks is Enya's voice, pristine, tranquil, and elegantly pitched.

A greatest hits collection entitled *Paint the Sky with Stars: The Best of Enya* (1997) features two new songs. Consisting of an assortment of Enya's songs, this album captures the spirit of her style, highlighting the consistency of her musical style over more than a decade. Her next album, *A Day Without Rain*, came out at the end of 2000. It lived up to the expectations of millions of fans by delivering an intimate and soothing quality that one associates with Enya. Lasting only thirty-five minutes, this album builds around melancholic phrases and melodramatic gestures that at times overpower her vocal parts, most notably in songs such as "Fallen Embers." Throughout the album Enya not only sings but also plays all the instruments and has insisted in press interviews that none of her material was sampled—hence the time span of five years to produce the album. In many ways this album lives up to the standard of Enya's earlier work and delivers what her fans are looking for: a collection of songs that are beautifully melodious and skilfully arranged and performed.

Fusing strands of traditional Irish folk music with classical and popular elements, Enya's musical idiom has played a major role in shaping the direction of New Age music. Writing and performing much of her material, she was able to find a niche for herself in the pop industry during the 1980s and 1990s, selling millions of records worldwide. As one of the top female artists of her generation, she possesses a warmth in expression that is enchanting and appealing. Enya's inimitably ethereal voice is set within rich arrangements and glossy productions that conjure an aura of calm and peace. She has earned her reputation as a leader in Celtic New Age music.

SELECTIVE DISCOGRAPHY: *Enya (The Celts)* (Atlantic, 1987); *Watermark* (Reprise, 1988); *Shepherd Moons* (Reprise, 1991); *Frog Prince* (Alex,

1995); *The Memory of Trees* (Reprise, 1995); *Paint the Sky with Stars: The Best of Enya* (Reprise, 1997); *Storms in Africa* (WEA, 1998); *A Day Without Rain* (Reprise, 2000).

STAN HAWKINS

GLORIA ESTEFAN

Born: Gloria Fajardo; Havana, Cuba, 1 September 1957

Genre: Latin, Pop

Best-selling album since 1990: *Mi Tierra* (1993)

Hit songs since 1990: "Hold Me, Thrill Me, Kiss Me," "Turn the Beat Around"

Gloria Estefan, the "Queen of Latin Pop," gained prominence in the early 1980s as the singer for the successful Latin disco group, Miami Sound Machine. However, she ultimately outgrew the band and as a solo artist blazed a trail that led the way for other Latin pop stars. Estefan's life story is a testimony of grit and courage and her rags-to-riches success serves as a torch for Cuban Americans.

Life in a New Land

Estefan was born in Havana, Cuba, but fled with her family when she was two years old after Fidel Castro came into power. Her father, Jose Fajardo, was a military man and returned to Cuba in 1961 to take part in the Bay of Pigs invasion where he was captured, reportedly by his own cousin. After eighteen months in prison, President John F. Kennedy secured his release. Shortly after his homecoming, Fajardo enlisted in the service and fought for the United States against North Vietnam. Meanwhile, Estefan's mother forged a life in a new land for herself and two daughters, which grew increasingly more complicated after Fajardo returned from Vietnam with advanced multiple sclerosis. Estefan's preteen years were spent as caregiver to both her invalid father and younger sister while her mother worked. Nevertheless, she managed to achieve excellent grades while attending Catholic school. Socially dormant, her primary source of release was playing guitar and singing pop songs alone in her room.

While attending a wedding dance, Estefan was asked to take the stage and sing with the band. Despite a lingering shyness—which hampered her performing for years to come—she sang and impressed the band's leader, Emilio Estefan. Soon Estefan became their singer and linked romantically with Emilio. The band's name was changed to the Miami Sound Machine and they achieved local success in Miami with a Latin-style disco sound. Estefan performed with them while attending the University of Miami

from which she graduated in 1978 summa cum laude in communications. She and Emilio married in 1978.

In 1980 Emilio Estefan quit his high-paying position as director of Hispanic marketing with Bacardi and began managing the Miami Sound Machine full time. He secured a record deal with an Hispanic division of CBS Records and the band recorded a string of Spanish-language albums with a more effervescent Gloria Estefan slowly shaking the stage fright that plagued her early on. The band's success grew along with Estefan's confidence as a performer and they changed their name to Gloria Estefan and the Miami Sound Machine. They were a major draw in Spanish countries, in Spanish-American neighborhoods, and by 1984 moved into the American pop mainstream with their first English-language album, *Eyes of Innocence* (1984). Subsequent recordings sold well, but Estefan was the main attraction. Although the Miami Sound Machine played on *Cuts Both Ways* (1989), it was principally Estefan's first solo effort and she wrote seven of the hit-filled album's ten songs. Estefan's popularity was soaring, not only in America and surrounding Spanish-speaking countries but in Europe as well. She captivated live audiences with her outgoing stage presence, robust dancing, and intelligent sex appeal. They were fascinated by such a huge voice pouring out from such a petite body and she charmed them with her down-to-earth chatter between songs. *Cuts Both Ways* features equal helpings of ballads, funky dance music, and pop influenced by her native Cuban rhythms—a trend that would continue. Yet it nearly did not.

Dealing with Adversity

During a snowstorm on March 20, 1990, the tour bus carrying a sleeping Estefan and her family was tail-ended by an oncoming semi-truck on a Pennsylvania highway. Emilio and their nine-year-old son, Nayib, were only slightly injured but Estefan's condition was grave. She had broken her back and came frighteningly close to being paralyzed. Doctors inserted two eight-inch steel rods into her back to help fuse the spine, but the recovery was painful and slow. Additionally, the mental picture of herself as an invalid needing care in the same way that her father lived his last days was petrifying for Estefan. She worked tirelessly during an extended rehab and made her remarkable first appearance six months later on Jerry Lewis's Muscular Dystrophy Telethon to a standing ovation.

Estefan's next recording, *Into the Light* (1991), reflects the gravity of the previous year and her rich vocals are full of emotion. The album contains an ode to her son with "Nayib's Song" and a heavy reflection on her accident in the ballad "Coming out of the Dark," which was written by her husband.

Having achieved complete crossover success into English-speaking markets, Estefan paid tribute to her heritage by releasing a Spanish-language album, *Mi Tierra* (1993). The Grammy Award–winning album was surprisingly stellar in all markets, selling over 10 million copies. She demonstrated her bicultural attitude by following with *Hold Me, Thrill Me, Kiss Me* (1994), an album of her favorite American music from the 1950s, 1960s, and 1970s.

Although doctors feared complications from the accident would hinder her ability to have another child, Estefan successfully gave birth to a second, Emily, in 1994. The time off allowed her to reflect on a career that has sold more than 50 million albums worldwide while having been showered with numerous awards, including three Grammy Awards. Additionally, she and Emilio operate Estefan Enterprises. The Miami Beach conglomerate consists of entertainment ventures such as talent management, songwriting, publishing, recording, and film and television studios, in addition to restaurants and hotels. Together they have amassed a fortune estimated to be $250 million.

Estefan finished out the 1990s by continuing to record successful albums including a Spanish album, *Abriendo Puertas* (1995), before returning to her signature Latin-influenced pop and ballads with *Destiny* (1996). *Gloria* (1998), mostly 1970s dance music, was followed by another Spanish effort, *Alma Caribena: Caribbean Soul* (2000).

Through the years, Estefan has increased her interest in politics. She has been embroiled in numerous issues affecting Cuban Americans including the case of Cuban refugee, six-year-old Elian Gonzalez, who entered the United States after his mother drowned while they were fleeing Cuba. Estefan angered some when she lobbied for the boy to remain in the United States as opposed to his being returned to his father in Cuba. After intervention by the United States government, Gonzalez was sent back to his homeland.

Estefan's musical efforts tactfully straddle an allegiance to her Spanish culture while continuing to maintain a global appeal. Her success in the 1980s paved the way for pop stars in the forefront of Latin-influenced music such as Mark Anthony, Ricky Martin, and Jennifer Lopez.

SELECTIVE DISCOGRAPHY: *Cuts Both Ways* (Epic, 1989); *Into the Light* (Epic, 1991); *Mi Tierra* (Epic, 1993); *Hold Me, Thrill Me, Kiss Me* (Epic, 1994); *Abriendo Puertas* (Epic, 1995); *Destiny* (Epic, 1996); *Alma Caribena: Caribbean* (Epic, 2000); *Greatest Hits, Vol. I* (Epic, 1992); *Greatest Hits, Vol. II* (Epic, 2001). **With Miami Sound Machine:** *Eyes of Innocence* (CBS, 1984); *Primitive Love* (Epic, 1985); *Let It Loose* (Epic, 1987).

DONALD LOWE

MELISSA ETHERIDGE

Born: Melissa Lou Etheridge, Leavenworth, Kansas, 29 May 1961

Genre: Rock

Best-selling album since 1990: *Yes I Am* (1993)

Hit songs since 1990: "I'm the Only One," "Come to My Window," "If I Wanted To"

Singer/songwriter Melissa Etheridge is one of rock's most successful female artists of the 1990s, having sold more than 25 million records since her debut in 1988. Etheridge's up-front, blue-collar rock combines gut-wrenching vocals with emotional lyrics straight from her often-broken heart. No lightweight pop-rocker, Etheridge straps on an electric guitar and jams just as hard as the male rockers she admired in her youth. Later in her career Etheridge's personal life sometimes overshadowed her music.

Etheridge grew up in Leavenworth, Kansas, the daughter of a traditional middle-class household in America's heartland. She received her first guitar when she was eight years old and soon began performing at local events. Etheridge would stay up hours into the night listening to her favorite rock artists in AM radio's waning years of eclectic pop music programming. She loved the Allman Brothers Band, Janis Joplin, the Rolling Stones, and other blues/rock-influenced bands.

Etheridge's parents were surprised and pleased to discover that their daughter had a gift for music. Even as a teenager performing at local events, she possessed an effusive stage manner that later marked her professional career. Etheridge moved to Boston in 1980, attended the Berklee College of Music, and began playing regularly in that city's coffeehouses and clubs. After two semesters she left Berklee but stayed in Boston for nearly two years supporting herself as a security guard in the day and performing at night. Etheridge returned to Kansas for several months and worked as a waitress to earn enough money to pursue her musical ambitions in Los Angeles, where she settled in 1982. She built up a steady following in the Los Angeles area, performing her own compositions. She found work as a songwriter for the movie *Weeds* (1987) before catching the attention of Island Records in 1986. Her self-titled debut, *Melissa Etheridge* (1988), was slow to catch on but eventually went gold after she performed the album's hit single, a searing Grammy-nominated rocker called "Bring Me Some Water," at the 1989 Grammy Awards ceremony.

By 1992, after the release of the album *Never Enough* (1992), Etheridge was a star on the rise. *Never Enough* went gold shortly after its release and earned a 1993 Grammy for Best Female Rock Performance. The album was followed by the triumphant *Yes, I Am* (1993), which contained the hits "Come to My Window" and "I'm the Only One." *Yes, I Am* went double platinum before the year was out and scored Etheridge another Grammy Award for Best

Female Rock Performance in 1994. *Yes, I Am* also marked a significant year personally for Etheridge as she publicly acknowledged what the music industry had known for years—she was a lesbian. The album's title put an exclamation point on that announcement, which was a spontaneous decision by Etheridge during a gay and lesbian event in celebration of President Clinton's 1993 inauguration. Since much of Etheridge's fan base consists of blue-collar heterosexual men and women, some feared that the announcement would negatively affect her career. These fears proved groundless, although her personal life began attracting the media's attention. Etheridge's relationship with filmmaker Julie Cypher (they met in 1988) received extra notice when the couple decided to have a family. In 1997 Cypher gave birth to a daughter, and the following year she had a son through artificial insemination. Singer/songwriter David Crosby is the biological father of both children.

Etheridge is often compared to the late rock singer Janis Joplin because of the way she pushes her raspy vocals to their utmost limit. In 1995 she performed Joplin's hit "Piece of My Heart" at the Rock and Roll Hall of Fame ceremonies in honor of Joplin's induction. Etheridge's all-out style also applies to her songwriting, which often consists of heart-on-the-sleeve lyrics about wayward lovers; jealousy is a recurrent theme in Etheridge's music. Her grassroots rock sound has elicited comparisons to Bruce Springsteen and John Mellencamp. However, her next two releases, *Your Little Secret* (1995) and *Breakdown* (1999), contained traces of electronic drumbeats and other techno touches.

Throughout the 1990s Etheridge used her celebrity to advance gay and lesbian causes and dedicated her song "Scarecrow" to the Wyoming gay-bias murder victim, Matthew Shepard. In 2000 Etheridge's personal life made headlines when she and Cypher split up. The separation was extremely difficult for Etheridge, and she cathartically chronicled her feelings about the relationship in the album *Skin* (2001). Except for drums and bass, Etheridge plays every instrument on the album: keyboards, guitars, and harmonicas. The following year she released a two-hour long DVD, *Melissa Etheridge Live . . . and Alone*. The DVD features a twenty-two-song solo concert at Hollywood's Kodak Theater, commentary by Etheridge on her career and personal life, and some rare footage of her early live shows.

Etheridge became the center of the media spotlight again in 2003, when she announced her engagement to actress Tammy Lynn Michaels. She spent much of 2003 juggling motherhood and a full touring schedule. Etheridge has defiantly stood for gay acceptance and has been unafraid throughout her career to express her relationship tribulations in music. Etheridge's popularity is a testament to both her personal and artistic honesty in addition to her passionate performing style.

SELECTIVE DISCOGRAPHY: *Melissa Etheridge* (Polygram, 1988); *Brave and Crazy* (Polygram, 1989); *Never Enough* (Polygram, 1992); *Yes, I Am* (Polygram, 1993); *Your Little Secret* (Polygram, 1995); *Breakdown* (Polygram, 1999); *Skin* (Universal, 2001); *DVD Melissa Etheridge Live . . . and Alone* (Universal, 2002).

BIBLIOGRAPHY: C. Nickson, *Melissa Etheridge: The Only One* (New York, 1997); M. Etheridge with L. Morton, *The Truth Is . . . My Life and Love in Music* (New York, 2002).

DONALD LOWE

FAITH EVANS

Born: Lakeland, Florida, 10 June 1973
Genre: R&B
Best-selling album since 1990: *Keep the Faith* (1998)
Hit songs since 1990: "You Used to Love Me," "Love Like This," "I Love You"

With a popularity ranking second only to that of Mary J. Blige, Faith Evans rose in the 1990s to become one of the most successful female performers in hip-hop. Possessing a strong, supple voice—hushed and intimate in its lower register and powerful on high notes—Evans brings to her performances a personal intensity rare among contemporary R&B artists. Much of her work is tinged with a perceptible sense of loss, a quality likely informed by her turbulent personal history: She is the widow of famed rapper the Notorious B.I.G., who was murdered in 1997. While Evans's career has often threatened to become overshadowed by this tragedy, by the early 2000s she had effectively freed herself from the controversy, releasing acclaimed albums and finding happiness with her new husband, record producer Todd Russaw.

Evans's early life gave little indication of the hardships that would follow in later years. Growing up in Newark, New Jersey, Evans sang gospel music in church and was a high school honor student, singing frequently in her school's plays and concerts. After graduation she earned a full scholarship to study marketing at Fordham University but left college after one year to pursue her dream of becoming a professional musician. By the early 1990s, Evans had found steady work as a backup singer and songwriter, contributing to Mary J. Blige's noted album, *My Life* (1994). Evans's work on the album brought her to the attention of producer Sean "Puff Daddy" Combs, who made her the first female artist signed to his Bad Boy label in 1995. Evans's debut album, *Faith,* appeared the same year and featured hits such as "You Used to Love Me" and "Soon as I Get Home." The album provides the first evidence of Evans's unique style; alternating soft, breathy phrasing with rough-hewn testifying that recalls her gospel upbringing, she infuses hip-hop with a soaring air of spirituality.

In 1995 Evans met the Notorious B.I.G., also known as Biggie Smalls, and married him after a courtship of nine days. Although the couple gave birth to a son, Christopher Wallace Jr., their relations had become tense by mid-1996: Smalls became publicly involved with rapper Lil' Kim, while Evans was rumored to have shared a liaison with Smalls's rival, rapper Tupac Shakur. In September 1996, Shakur was shot to death in a drive-by shooting, and, in an example of the increasingly public nature of violence in the rap world, Smalls met a similar fate just six months later. Although an aggrieved Evans was featured on Combs's hit tribute to Smalls, "I'll Be Missing You" (1997), she otherwise retreated from the spotlight for the next year. In 1998 she returned with her second album, *Keep the Faith,* which includes the infectious dance hits "Love Like This" and "All Night Long." On ballads such as "Never Gonna Let You Go" and "Lately I," Evans displays an impressive ability to build emotion throughout a performance, shaping her songs with honesty and passion. The tender ballad, "My First Love," can be interpreted as a requiem for Smalls: "We never had the chance to make it get better / We never said goodbye."

Evans released a third solo album, *Faithfully,* in 2001, receiving her strongest reviews to date. Like Mary J. Blige's acclaimed *No More Drama* of the same year, *Faithfully* sports a hard, lean sound that emphasizes the tough side of hip-hop. On dance hits such as "Alone in This World," "You Gets No Love," and "Burnin' Up," Evans twists and improvises vocally around sinuous, groove-laden rhythms. Although the album's lyrics often fail to match the inspiration of its sound, *Faithfully* returns Evans to the forefront of contemporary R&B and showcases her new sense of self-respect and peace. On the blues-tinged "Brand New Man," she attests, "I don't have to be alone / Got somebody who understands." As with her finest work in the past, Evans presents an emotional arc within the song, using her flexible, expansive voice to convey liberation and release. By 2001 she had settled into a quiet home life in Georgia with husband and manager Russaw. In addition, she formed her own production company, Pedigree MGI, and earned respect for her active involvement in charity work with inner-city children.

Among the wave of hip-hop stars to emerge in the mid-1990s, Faith Evans was unique; her full-powered voice

and moody, introspective sound brought a new emotional clarity to modern R&B. Displaying personal resilience and a tough spirit, Evans overcame the loss of famous husband Notorious B.I.G. to become an acclaimed artist in her own right.

SELECTIVE DISCOGRAPHY: *Faith* (Bay Boy, 1995); *Keep the Faith* (Bad Boy, 1998); *Faithfully* (Bad Boy, 2001).

WEBSITE: www.faithfullyfaith.com.

DAVID FREELAND

EVE

Born: Eve Jihan Jeffers; Philadelphia, Pennsylvania, 10 November 1978

Genre: Rap

Best-selling album since 1990: *Eve: Ruff Ryders' First Lady* (1999)

Hit songs since 1990: "Gangsta Lovin'," "Let Me Blow Ya Mind"

Female rappers have long had a tougher road to success than men in the male-dominated industry, but the career path of Eve Jeffers was even more difficult given her surroundings. One of the few women in the macho New York rap collective Ruff Ryders, Eve not only rose above the rigors of the rap business, but she also became a superstar with a mixture of street-tough rhymes, soulful singing, and fashion-savvy panache, earning the nickname "pit bull in a skirt."

An award-winning short story writer by the third grade, Philadelphia's Eve Jihan Jeffers performed in local talent shows as a teenager with the all-girl singing group Dope Girl Posse in the mid-1990s, later performing in the female R&B group EDJP (pronounced Egypt). After splitting from the quintet and adopting the name Eve of Destruction, Eve practically dropped out of high school to hone her rapping skills, gaining notice on the local scene for her skills at talent shows and as a warm-up act for local hip-hop concerts. While working briefly as a dancer at an adult club in New York in the late 1990s, Eve was reportedly encouraged by one of the patrons (retired rapper Ma$e) to consider a career in hip-hop.

A short time later a friend arranged for her to have an impromptu audition for the legendary rapper/producer Dr. Dre, who liked Eve's rapping enough to sign her to a one-year contract with his label, Aftermath. Though her contract expired before she was able to record an album for the label, Eve did complete the song "Eve of Destruction" for the soundtrack to the Warren Beatty comedy *Bulworth* (1998). While in Los Angeles working with Dre,

Eve made the acquaintance of the up-and-coming rapper DMX, with whom she kept in touch after her return to Philadelphia, often traveling to New York to spend time with the rapper and his crew, dubbed the Ruff Ryders.

In 1999, Eve became the first female artist signed to the male-dominated, testosterone-heavy label, also named Ruff Ryders, appearing on their first multi-artist compilation, *Ryde or Die Vol. 1* (1999), and releasing her solo debut, *Eve: Ruff Ryders First Lady*, five months later. The number one-charting album mixes gritty, profane, boast-heavy rapping with girlish, sweet pop choruses on the breakout hit "Gotta Man."

Not content to be the token female in a male crew, Eve took control of her career, co-writing all of the album's songs and developing a distinctive style that melded tough-as-nails rapping ("Tried to break us / But we broke through / Got the job done") with controlled, come-hither singing ("Ain't Got No Dough"). The album also features a strong feminist vibe, with Eve vowing to avenge a battered friend in "Love Is Blind," which alternates the rapper's blunt rhymes with her mellifluous R&B singing on the chorus.

The formula was one that Eve would use to great effect, not just in her singing, but also in her appearance. While sporting close-cropped, dyed blonde hair and a pair of menacing tiger paw tattoos above her breasts, Eve was frequently dressed in high fashion ensembles and tasteful makeup, earning her another distinction as "a gangsta and a lady." This image was contrary to such other successful female rappers as Lil' Kim and Foxy Brown, who gained popularity through a mix of sexually explicit lyrics and revealing clothing. Eve's debut went on to sell more than 2 million copies, a bona fide hit for a first album.

Eve Blows Minds with Hit Single

While *Scorpion* (2001) featured a number of raw, biting tracks, it was a duet, "Let Me Blow Ya Mind," with a pop singer, No Doubt's Gwen Stefani, which thrust the rapper into superstar status. Over a slinky funk beat that ranks among Dre's classic productions, Eve raps about people who put on airs, while Stefani adds a sing-songy rhythm and blues chorus. The hit song was accompanied by a very popular music video and gained a wider audience for the rapper.

In "Cowboy," Eve, rapping over a country-western beat, strikes out at people who would denigrate her skills; "You Had Me, You Lost Me" aims for revenge over rock and roll guitars. The album features a wide range of styles (Latin horns, reggae) and guest vocalists, from funk singer Teena Marie to rappers DMX, Da Brat, Drag-On, Trina, the LOX, and reggae singers Damian and Stephen Marley.

Like many hip-hop artists, Eve longed for more than music stardom; she branched out into the movies in 2002

with well-received supporting roles in the action drama *XXX* and the comedy *Barbershop*. Focusing more on smooth R&B than hard-core rapping, *Eve-Olution* (2002) presents a shift in direction for Eve. Though still possessing a stinging, in-your-face rhyme style, Eve embellishes more of her third album's tracks with seductive rhythm and blues beats and choruses, singing as much as rapping and featuring scaled-back cameos from guest rappers.

In the fashion of her hit with Stefani, the alluring hip-hop/pop song "Gangsta Lovin'" is a duet with the hot rhythm and blues performer Alicia Keys singing a seductive chorus to Eve's smoothly delivered boasts. Both "Irresistible Chick" and "Satisfaction" hark back to old-school hip-hop with simple, bouncy rhythms and elemental funk bass and guitar lines. On the latter, Eve sings a bewitching, girlish chorus in which she vows never to go back to her former financially strapped state: "Anything I want, I'ma get it cuz you know I need it / . . . Gotta have it, bet I'm gonna grab it."

With poise and grace the Philadelphia rapper Eve catapulted from struggling musician to world-renowned pop star and high-fashion jet setter in just a few years. Her combination of rough-and-ready lyrics, classic beauty, and spirited feminism proved that although sex can sell, sometimes strength is sexier.

SELECTIVE DISCOGRAPHY: *Eve: Ruff Ryders' First Lady* (Ruff Ryders/Interscope, 1999); *Scorpion* (Ruff Ryders/Interscope, 2001); *Eve-Olution* (Ruff Ryders/Interscope, 2002).

WEBSITES: www.ruffryders.com/eve.

GIL KAUFMAN

EVERCLEAR

Formed: 1992, Portland, Oregon

Members: Art Alexakis, vocals, guitar (born Santa Monica, California, 12 April 1962); Greg Eklund, drums (born Jacksonville, Florida, 18 April 1970); Craig Montoya, bass (born Spokane, Washington, 13 September 1970). Former member: Scott Cuthbert, drums.

Genre: Rock

Best-selling album since 1990: *Sparkle and Fade* (1995)

Hit songs since 1990: "Heroin Girl," "Santa Monica"

An unabashed blast of noisy pop in the midst of the dark, aggressive grunge rock landscape of the mid-1990s, Everclear rose above the din on the power of Art Alexakis's dark tales of drug abuse and dreams of escape.

Raised by a single mother in the housing projects of Culver City, California, Alexakis grew up well acquainted with the seedier side of life. Introduced to drugs by his older brother George, Alexakis was using hard narcotics by age thirteen, but he was later spurred to kick his habit by George's drug-related death. Alexakis turned to music and formed the short-lived punk band Colorfinger after moving to San Francisco in the mid-1980s. The band released one album in 1990 on Alexakis's Shindig label before the singer moved to Portland in 1992, just as the Pacific Northwest's grunge rock scene was exploding onto the mainstream.

After placing an ad in search of musicians to form a band in the local alternative weekly newspaper, Alexakis met bassist Craig Montoya. The pair were soon joined by drummer Scott Cuthbert and quickly recorded a short 1992 album, *Nervous & Weird,* for four hundred dollars for the local Tim/Kerr label.

In a sign of Alexakis's aggressive, hands-on approach, the singer/songwriter took over promotion and distribution of the album from the label, hiring an independent promotions firm when he was unsatisfied with Tim/Kerr's efforts. The songs were folded into a full-length album, *World of Noise* (1993), which bore the signature Alexakis approach: personal tales of struggle voiced by loud, distorted guitars and power pop rhythms. A lengthy slate of touring followed, during which Cuthbert was replaced by drummer Greg Eklund. At this point, Alexakis reacquainted himself with Capitol Records president Gary Gersh, who had been supportive of the singer's music in San Francisco. Gersh signed the group to Capitol Records in 1994. Everclear's major-label debut, *Sparkle and Fade* (1995), distinguished them from the rest of the grunge pack and marked the emergence of a new, powerful songwriting voice in Alexakis's story songs about struggles with drugs, hopes of escaping dead-end lives, and racism.

Painful Memories into Powerful Songs

Tapping into his own early struggles with drugs and poverty, Alexakis is the voice of the struggling everyman on songs such as "The Twistinside," "Summerland," and the album's breakthrough hit, "Santa Monica." Building out of a simply strummed repeating guitar figure, the song grows into a powerful pop confection driven by Alexakis's cigarette-rasp voice. "I don't want to do your sleepwalk dance anymore / I just want to see some palm trees / Go and try and shake away this disease," Alexakis sings, dreaming of a seaside retreat away from his chaotic life.

While many of his peers were using powerful barrages of guitar, ominous lyrics, and bashing rhythm sections to tell similar stories of abuse and alienation, Alexakis seemed to draw more inspiration from the three-part harmonies of the Beatles and the catchy, noisy energy of late-1960s garage bands. Audiences took to the sound in droves, while some in the Northwest's exclusive musical community labeled Alexakis a carpetbagger in the belief that he'd relocated to the area as a career move.

Alexakis's innate sense of melody figured prominently in *So Much for the Afterglow* (1997), on which the band leader indulges his love of the highly produced work of the Beach Boys by layering his energetic pop songs with steel guitar, banjo, mandolin, keyboards, horns, and a string section. Alexakis's ambivalence about success is evident in songs such as the single "Everything to Everyone": "I say they taught you to how to buy and sell / Your own body by the pound / I think you like to be their simple toy / I think you love to play the clown." Again tapping into personal tragedy, Alexakis pines for an absent father in the distorted, hurt-sounding country rock song "Father of Mine," in which he blames his father for giving him a name and then walking away.

Though he contributed the song "Overwhelming" to the soundtrack of the Ben Stiller movie *Permanent Midnight* (1998), Alexakis scrapped his plans for a solo album and instead set to work on what would become a two-CD set from Everclear. *Songs from an American Movie Vol. One: Learning How to Smile* (2000) hop-scotches from songs such as "Here We Go Again"—propelled by a soulful horn section, a drum machine beat, and a sample of the classic Public Enemy rap song "Bring the Noise"—to the first single, "AM Radio," which samples the golden oldie "Mr. Big Stuff" as it lists the cultural hallmarks of Alexakis's youth. The album also features a wistful, grunge pop cover of Van Morrison's "Brown-Eyed Girl."

Songs from an American Movie Vol. Two: Good Time for a Bad Attitude is the id to the first album's ego. Stripped back down to guitar, bass, and drums (and a few programmed drum loops), the second part of the album finds Everclear returning to the formula that first gained them acclaim: forceful, guitar-driven rock songs about lives in turmoil and disarray. This time, though, the songs are told from the point of view of someone who has been to the top and has more to lose. Everclear released a subsequent album, *Slowmotion Daydream,* in February 2003.

Art Alexakis wove his pain and regret into platinum sales, burnishing his grunge rock songs with tenacious pop hooks. Not afraid to experiment, the hands-on rock star added layer upon layer of sound and production to his songs, growing along with his audience and his musical interests.

SELECTIVE DISCOGRAPHY: *World of Noise* (Fire/Tim/Kerr, 1993); *Sparkle and Fade* (Capitol, 1995); *So Much for the Afterglow* (Capitol, 1997); *Songs from an American Movie, Vol. One: Learning How to Smile* (Capitol, 2000); *Songs from an American Movie Vol. Two: Good Time for a Bad Attitude*

(Capitol, 2000); *Slowmotion Daydream* (Capitol, 2003).

WEBSITES: www.everclearonline.com.

GIL KAUFMAN

EVERLAST

Born: Erik Schrody; Hempstead, New York, 18 August 1969

Genre: Rap, Folk, Rock

Best-selling album since 1990: *Whitey Ford Sings the Blues* (1998)

Hit songs since 1990: "What It's Like," "Jump Around"

Only an elite group of rappers has been able to break free of a popular group to attain crossover success as solo artists. Fewer still have been able to do it while reworking their sound to incorporate elements of folk, blues, and country. Former House of Pain rapper Everlast not only reinvented himself on his second solo album, *Whitey Ford Sings the Blues* (1998), but he also opened the doors for other rap artists to broaden their musical horizons with songs such as the smash folk/rap hit "What It's Like."

From the very beginning of his career, Everlast sought to combine his love of blue-collar rock and roll with an equal affection for rap music. He was born in Hempstead, New York, into an Irish family with a construction worker father who constantly moved the family between the East and West coasts in search of work. Everlast eventually landed in the upscale Woodland Hills area of the San Fernando Valley in California.

The clash between his blue-collar roots and white-collar surroundings led the young Erik Schrody to experiment with marijuana and ditch school, often hanging out with a multiracial group of friends who stoked his interest in hip-hop music. A mutual friend passed a demo tape Schrody had made to legendary rapper Ice-T, who asked the seventeen-year-old to join his Rhyme Syndicate Cartel crew of artists in the late 1980s.

Everlast released his poorly received solo debut, *Forever Everlasting* (1990), which apes the pop-inflected hip-hop style of the day. The album was notable mainly for its use of samples of songs by the Knack ("My Sharona") and Steam ("Na Na Hey Hey Kiss Him Goodbye") as source material.

Following the failure of the album, Everlast formed the Irish-themed rap trio House of Pain with MC Danny Boy and DJ Lethal. The group scored a huge hit with their 1992 party anthem "Jump Around," driving their self-titled

debut (1993), which samples old blues songs by Willie Dixon and Albert King, to sales of 3 million. Two subsequent albums failed to reach the same heights, and Everlast quit the group in 1996. The rapper was subsequently sued by his record company, forced to sell his Hollywood Hills home, declared bankruptcy, and placed under house arrest for attempting to carry a gun aboard an airplane. The devout convert to Islam endured a painful breakup with his longtime girlfriend, shunned his former partying ways, moved in with his mother—who was battling cancer at the time—and began five months of writing and recording on his next solo album.

Facing Death, a Rebirth

Just hours after finishing the final vocal track for his second solo album, *Whitey Ford Sings the Blues* (1998), Everlast suffered a nearly fatal heart attack that required bypass surgery. Once he recovered, Everlast emerged with an album that eschewed the tough talk, violence, and boasting of House of Pain in favor of humble, introspective acoustic folk and blues with rap-inspired beats, samples, and scratching.

His voice a low, scratchy rumble now instead of a booming snarl, Everlast reinvents himself in an unprecedented way on the album's smash hit single, "What It's Like." Built around a country blues guitar riff, a lazy, programmed drum beat, and backing from a string section, the song tells sobering tales about homelessness, abortion, and drug dealing without the usual bluster associated with hip-hop. "God forbid you ever had to walk a mile in her shoes / 'Cause then you really might know what it's like to have to choose," Everlast sings of the character facing opposition to her abortion. It marked one of the first times a rap artist had used traditional, blues-based instrumentation to reach not only hip-hop fans but also mainstream rock and pop fans who might never before have listened to a rap record.

Tracks such as the acoustic soul blues "Ends" employ street slang to tell an earnest tale about urban violence and murder, mixing the grim country style of Johnny Cash with hip-hop's cutting-edge production techniques. Chillingly, the album has several songs recorded before Everlast's heart attack that ponder the question of mortality and near-death experiences, including "Painkillers" and "Death Comes Callin'." In the latter, a funky, elastic funk blues number, Everlast raps, "Day to the night / Night to the day / Up around where I stay / We do things this way."

Everlast wrote the song "Put Your Lights On" for the comeback album of the Latin rock legend Santana, *Supernatural* (1999). Here he again explores the dangers of the dark side of life. A second folk-inspired solo album, *Eat at Whitey's* (2000), was not as well received as its predecessor, but came packed with cameos from rap stars (Cee-Lo, Kurupt, Rahzel, B-Real), as well as a return favor from Santana on the meditative acoustic blues "Babylon Feeling."

The rapper is back to some of his boasting ways on tracks such as "Whitey" ("I'm whiter than crack / I'm harder than drugs / I'm smarter than thugs / I'm hotter than slugs"); and he adds a touch of rhythm and blues ("Love for Real") and pop flavor on the single "Black Jesus."

From pop stardom to a near-death experience, the rapper Everlast grew from a boasting, thuggish street tough to a sensitive blues musician over the course of the 1990s, penning introspective songs about redemption, regret, and mortality. Finding a way to integrate Delta blues, acoustic guitars, and folk melodies into the realm of hip-hop, Everlast expanded the horizons of an entire genre while reinventing his sound and image.

SELECTIVE DISCOGRAPHY: *Forever Everlasting* (Warner Bros., 1990); *Whitey Ford Sings the Blues* (Tommy Boy, 1998); *Eat at Whitey's* (Tommy Boy, 2000). **With House of Pain:** *House of Pain* (Tommy Boy, 1992); *Same as It Ever Was* (Tommy Boy, 1994); *Truth Crushed to Earth Shall Rise Again* (1996).

WEBSITE: www.tommyboy.com/ever.

GIL KAUFMAN

EVERYTHING BUT THE GIRL

Formed: 1982, Hull, England

Members: Tracey Thorn, vocals (born Hertfordshire, England, 26 September 1962); Ben Watt, backing vocals, synthesizers, guitars, all instrumentation (born London, England, 6 December 1962).

Genre: Rock

Best-selling album since 1990: *Amplified Heart* (1994)

Hit songs since 1990: "Driving," "Missing," "Wrong"

In the early 1990s, the jazz-influenced pop band Everything but the Girl had a small, devoted following, even though the duo's music verged on the easy-listening genre. In the mid-1990s, with the release of *Amplified Heart* (1994), they crossed over into the mainstream with a carefully constructed mix of acoustic elements and electronic flourishes. With Tracey Thorn as the duo's warm, honeyed vocalist and Ben Watt as the mixing and arranging master, *Amplified Heart* sold more than half a million copies within two years of its release in the United States.

Watt and Thorn began performing together after they met as students at Hull University. In 1984 they signed to Blanco y Negro, a label started by Mike Alway, a friend of Watt's who had produced solo albums for the duo in the early 1980s. The pair released a single, "Each and Everyone," which reached the top thirty in the U.K. Many reporters characterized their collaboration as not only musical but romantic, and though they initially tried to keep the arrangement ambiguous, they eventually revealed their romantic relationship.

After a few releases of jazz-inflected pop (*Eden, The Language of Life, Worldwide*), Thorn began lending vocals to the U.K. trip-hop band Massive Attack, and Watt became more heavily involved in deejaying in London dance clubs. Unsurprisingly, the band's 1994 album *Amplified Heart* began to show evidence of their movement toward electronic music yet remained firmly rooted in strong songwriting. The album's unexpected hit "Missing" hit the charts after Todd Terry remixed it, adding muscular backbeats to what became a top-five hit in Britain and the United States and number one on the *Billboard* dance chart. With its forlorn, pining refrain "And I miss you / Like the deserts miss the rain," the song could be heard on dance floors across the United States and Europe.

Amplified Heart is a landmark album for Everything but the Girl, remarkable because it was recorded after Watt's near-death battle with Churg-Strauss syndrome in 1992 (as recounted in his critically acclaimed book *Patient*). *Amplified Heart* is a personal chronicle of the ups and downs in a romantic relationship, a hopeful testament to love's ability to help people cope through adversity.

Two years later the band released *Walking Wounded*, which found them tinkering further with electronic programming and drum and bass noises, though Thorn's warm vocals prevents it from veering off into a cold, detached direction. The album sold more than 1 million copies in the U.K. In 1999 their ninth release, *Temperamental*, found the band knee-deep in electronic music with an after-hours, jazz-lounge vibe. *Temperamental* shows how the band has honed its sound, undergirding the synthetic patina of electronic music with solid songwriting skills.

SELECTIVE DISCOGRAPHY: *The Language of Life* (Atlantic, 1990); *Amplified Heart* (Atlantic, 1994); *Walking Wounded* (Virgin, 1996); *Temperamental* (Atlantic, 1999); *Back to Mine* (Ultra, 2001); *Like the Deserts Miss the Rain: A Retrospective* (Rhino, 2003).

BIBLIOGRAPHY: B. Watt, *Patient: The True Story of a Rare Illness* (New York, 1997).

CARRIE HAVRANEK

CESARIA EVORA

Born: Mindelo, Sao Vincente, Cape Verde, 27 August 1941

Genre: World

Best-selling album since 1990: *Cesaria* (1995)

Cesaria Evora is the best-known proponent of "morna," a melancholy, cabaret-style poetic music from the impoverished archipelago of Cape Verde in the Atlantic Ocean west of Senegal between Portugal and Brazil. She did not launch her international career until the age of forty-seven. The niece of the composer B. Leza, she started singing professionally at age sixteen and soon was famous in her islands; by the late 1960s her radio air checks were released as albums in the Netherlands and Portugal. Many Cape Verdeans emigrate, but Evora did not leave her home. However, discouraged by a lack of earnings, she gave up singing from the mid 1970s until 1985, when she ventured to Portugal to record two tunes for an anthology of women vocalists from Cape Verde.

A French agent of Cape Verdean descent invited Evora to visit Paris for the first time in 1987 and arranged recording sessions that resulted in the 1988 release of the album *La Diva Aux Pieds Nus* ("The Barefoot Diva"). Her debut performance at the New Morning music club followed, and two more albums were released with limited distribution. She won favorable press attention for her appearance at the 1991 Festival d' Angoulème, which led to radio play, further club engagements in Paris, and the launch of her international renown, which was solidified with the release of the album *Miss Perfumado* (1992).

After sold-out concerts at Paris's prestigious Olympia theatre, Evora embarked on her first international tour in 1993, performing in Spain, Montreal, and Japan. In 1994 the Brazilian vocalist Caetano Veloso joined her onstage in Sao Paolo, and upon her first tour of the United States in 1995, she was hailed by Madonna, David Byrne of Talking Heads, and the saxophonist Branford Marsalis. Her album *Cesaria* (1995), having already sold more than 100,000 copies in France, was nominated for a Grammy when issued in the United States.

Evora's slightly weathered voice, diffident style, romantic failures (she's thrice-wed and thrice-abandoned), and rocky career ascent heightened her image as a tobacco-smoking, cognac-swilling heiress to Billie Holiday.

Mornas and faster-paced, more upbeat coladerias are sung in Kriolu, a mélange of old Portuguese (Cape Verde was a Portuguese colony) and African tongues; they have affinities to Portuguese fado, Brazilian modinha, Argentine tango, British sea chanties, and African percussion.

As Evora intones lyrics by the poets of her homeland, she conveys a world-weariness and hard-earned wisdom reminiscent of Edith Piaf.

A pleasant-looking if no longer beautiful woman with a stocky figure, Evora has a limited range but is capable of compelling, nuanced turns of phrase that communicate to speakers of English as well as Lusaphone listeners. She is typically accompanied by small string ensembles with guitars, the ukelelike cavaquino, bass, an obbligato instrument such as violin or clarinet, sometimes piano or accordion, and a handclapping rhythm section. Since 1995 she has toured worldwide, often with a band led by the string player Bau.

Evora recorded "Besame Mucho" in Spanish for the soundtrack of the film *Great Expectations* (1998), and on *São Vicente* (2001) she collaborated with Cuban musicians, including pianist Chucho Valdes, trumpeter Elipdio Chapotin, and the flute-and-violin band Orquesta Aragon, as well as Veloso and the American blues singer Bonnie Raitt. Whatever she sings seems to proceed at an implacable pace, neither slowing for balladic dramatics nor perking up to dance tempos. In this respect Evora evokes the constancy, if not the heights and depths, of the sea.

SELECTIVE DISCOGRAPHY: *Miss Perfumado* (Melodie, 1993); *Cesaria* (BMG, 1995); *Cabo Verde* (BMG, 1997); *Cafe Atlantico* (RCA, 1999); *Mar Azul* (Melodie, 1999); *São Vicente* (Windham Hill, 2001). **With Salif Keita:** *Moffou* (Universal, 2002); **With Compay Segundo:** *Duets* (Gasa/Warner Bros., 2002); *Original Soundtrack, Great Expectations [Score]* (Atlantic, 1998); **With Caetano Veloso:** *Red Hot + Rio* (BMG, 1996).

HOWARD MANDEL

EXTREME

Formed: 1985, Boston, Massachusetts; Disbanded 1996

Members: Pat Badger, bass (born Boston, Massachusetts, 22 July 1967); Nuno Bettencourt, guitar (born Praia da Vitoria, Terceira, 20 September 1966); Gary Cherone, vocals (born Malden, Massachusetts, 26 July 1961); Mike Mangini, drums (born Newton, Massachusetts, 19 April 1963). Former member: Paul Geary, drums (born Medford, Massachusetts, 2 July 1961).

Genre: Heavy Metal, Rock

Best-selling album since 1990: *Pornograffiti* (1990)

Hit songs since 1990: "More Than Words," "Hole Hearted," "Rest in Peace"

Of all the 1980s pop metal bands influenced by Eddie Van Halen's dazzling guitar work and David Lee Roth's sexually charged attitude, Extreme was originally the most obvious imitator. The ability of guitarist Nuno Bettencourt to take lightning-quick, classically influenced riffs and make them palatable for mainstream rock put him on a par with Van Halen. Yet the group's early, testosterone-fueled lyrics seemed contrived and juvenile. They escaped irrelevance by broadening their musical palette, writing socially and politically conscious concept albums and scoring two Top 10 hits on the *Billboard* Hot 100.

After a local Boston television station claimed the rights to their name, the Dream became Extreme in 1985. The group consisted of vocalist Gary Cherone and drummer Paul Geary. Soon Bettencourt left the band Sinful to join them, and in 1987 he recruited bassist Pat Badger, who had been making custom guitars in a music shop.

Their self-titled debut album was released at the height of the pop metal explosion in 1989. The sexually predatory lyrics of "Little Girls," "Flesh 'n' Blood," and "Teacher's Pet" barely distinguished them from their contemporaries. They did, however, establish themselves as exceptional musicians, particularly Bettencourt. The album's final track, "Play with Me," displayed his blistering speed and technical proficiency on the guitar and was featured in the hit comedy film *Bill and Ted's Excellent Adventure*.

Extreme's sophomore release, *Pornograffiti* (1990), was a daring concept album that challenged many of the genre's norms. Thematically, it addressed the need for genuine love in a decadent society full of greed, corruption, and misogyny. Musically, it incorporated funky horn parts in "Lil' Jack Horny" and "Get the Funk Out," a rap intro in "When I'm President," and piano and strings in the loungelike "When I First Kissed You." The scope of the band's ambition was relatively foreign to their genre.

The album's first single and video, the hard-rocking anthem "Decadence Dance," received modest MTV airplay but failed to generate a mainstream radio buzz. Several months later they released the stripped-down ballad "More Than Words." With only an acoustic guitar to accompany Cherone and Bettencourt's sweet harmonies, it was a commercial smash, peaking at number one on the *Billboard* Hot 100. Though it was commonplace for heavy metal bands of the era to have massive mainstream success with lighter songs, Extreme reached a new audience with "More Than Words." The song crossed over to the Adult Contemporary chart and climbed all the way to number two. This move was unprecedented for a rock band and inherently at odds with their core audience. "Hole Hearted" followed as the album's third single. It, too, was light, acoustic, and a big hit. *Pornograffiti* was their most successful album, selling more than 2 million copies.

III Sides to Every Story (1992) was another bold concept album that tackled the politics of war, philosophy, and spirituality. Though the pro-peace anthem "Rest in Peace" was a strong and successful lead single, the album failed to match the sales of *Pornograffiti*. The rock landscape had changed dramatically, and the bombast of heavy metal had been ousted by the more earnest Seattle grunge sound. The band was tackling heavier topics and was courageously experimenting with their sound, but they still represented an era that had just passed.

Miffed and confused by the public's changing tastes, Extreme struggled with the direction of its fourth album. *Waiting for the Punchline* (1995) was an angrier and simpler effort that attempted to assimilate to current trends. The album's poor showing led to Bettencourt's departure from the band for a solo career. Extreme officially broke up in 1996, and shortly thereafter, Cherone replaced Sammy Hagar in Van Halen, becoming that group's third lead vocalist. He recorded one album with the band before departing in 1999.

Extreme was one of the most talented and ambitious pop metal bands of the late 1980s and early 1990s. Had the group's career started a few years earlier, it is likely they would have sustained a longer run of success. Instead, their rise to fame occurred shortly before the genre fell from prominence, and their time in the spotlight was brief.

SELECTIVE DISCOGRAPHY: *Extreme* (A&M, 1989); *Extreme II: Pornograffitti* (A&M, 1990); *III Sides to Every Story* (A&M, 1992).

WEBSITES: www.nuno-bettencourt.com; www.nunocentral.co.uk.

DAVE POWERS

LARA FABIAN

Born: Etterbeek, Belgium, 9 January 1970

Genre: Rock

Best-selling album since 1990: *Pure* (1997)

Hit songs since 1990: "I Will Love Again"

At home in many languages and cultures, Lara Fabian gives an emotive touch to inoffensive ballads and uplifting disco tunes, making her one of Europe's top divas.

Fabian's mother is from Sicily and her father from Brussels. Her first language was Italian in a childhood spent shuttling between Italy and Belgium. However, she also quickly learned French and later became fluent in English through her studies. From the ages of eight to eighteen, Fabian studied at the prestigious Royal Conservatory of Brussels. There she received a solid classical music foundation and began writing songs. She began performing professionally at the age of fourteen.

Upon graduating, she moved to Montreal and worked with another Brussels expatriate, the writer/producer Rick Allison, on what became her first album, *Lara Fabian* (1991). The CD features French dance pop with the typical electronic beats and perky synths. However, Fabian's plaintive, strong voice and songwriting contributions made it clear that she was more than just another disco clone. The album sold 100,000 copies.

Fabian came into her own on *Carpe Diem* (1994), which still has up-tempo numbers but gives her more room to show off on ballads. The album sold 800,000 copies, further solidifying her status as an up-and-coming diva.

In 1996 Fabian was introduced to English-speaking Canadians in her performance of the orchestral ballad "Que Dieu Aide Les Exclus" ("God Help the Outcast") for the Canadian soundtrack to the Disney animated movie *The Hunchback of Notre Dame*. She also provided the voice of female lead Esmeralda for the movie's French-Canadian release. However, she put English crossover plans on hold in a bid to consolidate her stardom in French-speaking countries. The success of *Pure* (1997), which sold more than 2 million copies in France, proved that she was right to postpone her cross-over debut. She now had even more leverage with record labels looking to ink an English deal, and she was wooed by Sony Music's former chairman Tommy Mottola.

Fabian's English debut, *Lara Fabian* (2000), was given a May 30 release date that gave Sony time to promote the album before the typical pre-Christmas barrage of blockbusters. In an unusual gimmick, Sony even offered a money-back guarantee to dissatisfied listeners. The album's first single, "I Will Love Again," with its piercing, anthemic chorus, serves as a more upscale "I Will Survive" for the recently dumped. The song made number thirty-two on the *Billboard* Hot 100 but got all the way to number one on the dance charts. With swirling synths and busy percussion, it bears the stamp of the producers Mark Taylor and Brian Rawling, who worked with Cher and Enrique Iglesias. She croons seductively in Italian on "Adagio" and exudes class on the piano-based soft-rock tune "Part of Me." However, Fabian sounds a little too much like Celine Dion, making it difficult for casual fans to recognize her. Also, her lyrics suffer from blandness, as the following example shows: "When you look into my eyes / you get what you see." Fabian returned to French with

Nue (2001) and cracked the Spanish-language market the same year with "Quédate," used in the Telemundo comedy/drama *Uga Uga*.

Fabian's clear voice can go from pure fire to a cool whisper as it traverses melodies most singers could only dream of. However, she has faced tough competition in the English-speaking market from other divas like Christina Aguilera, Mariah Carey, and Celine Dion.

SELECTIVE DISCOGRAPHY: *Carpe Diem* (Polydor, 1994); *Pure* (Polydor, 1997); *Lara Fabian* (Sony, 2000); *Nue* (Universal, 2001).

RAMIRO BURR

FAITH NO MORE

Formed: 1982, San Francisco, California; Disbanded 1998

Members: Mike Bordin, drums (born San Francisco, California, 27 November 1962); Roddy Bottum, keyboards (born Los Angeles, California, 1 July 1963); Billy Gould, bass (born Los Angeles, California, 24 April 1963); Mike Patton, vocals (born Eureka, California, 27 January 1968). Former members: Jim Martin, guitar (born Oakland, California, 21 July 1961); Chuck Mosely, vocals (born Hollywood, California, 1960); Preston Lea "Trey" Spruance III, guitar (born Eureka, California, 1969); Dean Menta, guitar; Jon Hudson, guitar.

Genre: Heavy Metal, Rock

Best-selling album since 1990: *The Real Thing* (1989)

Hit songs since 1990: "Epic," "Midlife Crisis"

In the early 1990s Faith No More was one of the most experimental rock bands to achieve mainstream success. The group's ambitious mix of heavy metal, progressive rock, funk, and rap was a precursor to the heavier music that ruled the commercial airwaves in the late 1990s and into the new millennium. Because the group's followers like Korn, Limp Bizkit, Linkin Park, and Incubus reached a much larger audience, Faith No More is an often-forgotten pioneer.

When the short-lived, San Francisco–based Faith No Man disbanded in 1982, drummer Mike Bordin, bassist Billy Gould, and keyboardist Roddy Bottum re-formed as Faith No More. They soon were joined by guitarist Jim Martin, but the group had difficulty finding a singer. Courtney Love, the future wife of Nirvana's Kurt Cobain and the lead singer for Hole, had a brief stint at the helm before Gould's friend and former band mate Chuck Mosely filled the slot.

Mosely's flat vocals wavered in and out of key, but he compensated with attitude. The group released *We Care a Lot* (1985) and *Introduce Yourself* (1987). The latter demonstrated their genre-bending ability to fuse tribal rhythms, funk bass, pounding guitars, and spacey keyboards into a unified sound. The album showed potential for greatness and created a substantial underground buzz, but Mosely's vocals were a drawback. In 1988 he was kicked out because of his erratic behavior. His replacement was Mike Patton, the singer of local band Mr. Bungle. Patton's oddball creativity mixed with his impressive vocal strength and range was the perfect complement to the band's existing sound.

With the release of *The Real Thing* (1989), Patton immediately established himself as one of the most talented and diverse vocalists in rock. From his loungelike crooning on the creepy, piano-driven "Edge of the World" to his throat-splitting, rapid-fire assault on the menacing "Surprise! You're Dead," he proved he could handle a wide array of styles.

It was his ability to rap and sing in the same song, though, that broke Faith No More into the mainstream. Nine months after the initial release of *The Real Thing*, "Epic" found itself in heavy rotation on MTV and eventually peaked at number nine on the *Billboard* Hot 100 in September 1990. It was a strikingly original work, its verses rapped over a jagged bassline and its chorus soaring into a vibrato-heavy hook. The song structure became an archetype for much of the rap/rock and nu-metal of the late 1990s and beyond.

Having Patton from the beginning of the creative process for *Angel Dust* (1992) allowed the band to push the musical boundaries even further and resulted in their finest artistic statement. The album sold a half million copies, received high critical praise, and yielded the number one Modern Rock single "Midlife Crisis." Though a modest success, the public did not embrace it as much as *The Real Thing*. A few years later Korn popularized the most abrasive elements of the record—sludgy, terrorizing rhythms and ominous screams and wails.

While the band was recording their fifth album, original guitarist Jim Martin left because of artistic differences. This marked the end of Faith No More's most prolific era. Three guitarists—Trey Spruance, Dean Menta, and Jon Hudson—worked with the band throughout the recording and touring for its last two albums. *King for a Day . . . Fool for a Lifetime* (1995) and *Album of the Year* (1997) were both respectable, but with altered chemistry Faith No More fell short of the consistency and brilliance of their previous two efforts. With creative friction in the group and each member splitting time with other bands, the inevitable breakup was announced in April 1998.

Faith No More's members soon focused on other projects. Patton worked with Mr. Bungle, which he had never left, and went on to form other bands and his own record label, Ipecac. Bottum concentrated solely on his duties with Imperial Teen, which released its debut album in

Faith No More. L-R: Billy Gould, Jim Martin (former member), Mike Patton, Roddy Bottum, Mike Bordin [PAUL NATKIN/PHOTO RESERVE]

1996. Bordin toured and recorded with several acts, including Ozzy Osbourne, Korn, and former Alice in Chains guitarist Jerry Cantrell. Despite their minimal commercial success, the liberally talented Faith No More turned out to be one of the most influential rock bands of the 1990s.

SELECTIVE DISCOGRAPHY: *Introduce Yourself* (Slash, 1987); *The Real Thing* (Slash/Warner Bros., 1989); *Angel Dust* (Slash/Warner Bros., 1992); *King for a Day . . . Fool for a Lifetime* (Slash/Reprise, 1995).

WEBSITE: www.fnm.com; www.cv.org.

DAVE POWERS

FATBOY SLIM

Born: Norman Cook; Bromley, England, 13 July 1963

Genre: Rap

Best-selling album since 1990: *You've Come a Long Way, Baby* (1998)

Hit songs since 1990: "The Rockafeller Skank," "Praise You"

Though he began his music career as the bassist in a rock band, Norman Cook achieved worldwide acclaim as the anonymous mastermind behind the electronic dance act Fatboy Slim. Cook's adroitness at picking obscure but instantly hummable samples—snippets of previously released songs—to go with his engagingly repetitive dance tracks such as "The Rockafeller Skank" made him one of the most popular DJs and producers of the mid-1990s.

A child of the disco era, Norman Cook was DJing in local Brighton, England, pubs by the time he was fifteen. Less than a year after joining the Housemartins in 1986 as the group's bassist, Cook began to score dance-chart hits and gain notice under a string of aliases. Among the names Cook employed were Beats International, Freakpower, Fried Funk Food, Mighty Dub Katz, and, with producers JC Reid and Tim Jeffery, Pizzaman. Inspired by the acid-house dance scene in England—a boisterous, drug-fueled underground clique that favored hard, driving dance music—Pizzaman scored a number of Top 40 hits in

Fatboy Slim [JILL GREENBERG/ASTRALWERKS]

England in the late 1980s. It was as Fatboy Slim, however, that Cook gained worldwide acclaim with his signature mix of massive, ever-building beats, clever samples, and feel-good slogans.

Along with the Chemical Brothers, Fatboy Slim stood at the vanguard of the British "Big Beat/Electronica" dance music movement. Willfully anonymous, the bald-headed, average-looking Cook let his music do the talking for him on Fatboy's debut, *Better Living Through Chemistry* (1996), recorded in one week in Cook's attic. The album's signature track, "Going Out of My Head," samples the iconic guitar intro to the Who's "Can't Explain," while relying on a vocal cover of the track by 1970s disco diva Yvonne Elliman. By combining these three elements—his own computer-programmed dance track, a vocal line from a disco song, and a segment of the original Who track—Fatboy Slim was able to create a fresh, modern track built on classical elements. The song twists the rock classic into a driving dance anthem, complete with spacey sound effects, insistently programmed drumbeats, and an upwardly cascading drum pattern that became Fatboy Slim's signature effect.

With its mix of obscure and obvious samples, disco beats, thick funk grooves, and mindless repetition, the music became the soundtrack for the Big Beat invasion. Cook continued to remix other artists as well, gaining acclaim for his remix of Jean-Jacques PerrEy's song "Eva" (1960s) and Cornershop's 1998 single, "Brimful of Asha."

His second Fatboy Slim album, *You've Come a Long Way, Baby* (1998), catapulted the shy, perpetually grinning DJ into the stratosphere. With a humorous video directed by acclaimed independent filmmaker Spike Jonze, the surfy, twangy "The Rockafeller Skank" mushroomed into a worldwide hit, buoyed by the same combination of a clever sample (rapper Lord Finesse) and endlessly

repeated beats that built to a peak before starting all over again. In a nod to 1970s soul, "Praise You" sampled an obscure 1975 gospel soul album by the singer Camille Yarborough, another example of the kinds of thrift-store finds Cook was able to spin into gold.

Along with a pair of MTV Video Music Awards and two Grammy nominations, "The Rockafeller Skank" helped elevate Cook to the status of superstar DJ. He performed before tens of thousands at European festivals and at Woodstock '99; his music was featured on a number of television commercials and electronica compilations and even spawned a 2001 album, *A Break from the Norm*, which consisted solely of songs sampled on Fatboy Slim tracks.

While Cook had been happy to remix everyone from the Beastie Boys to James Brown to the African singer Angelique Kidjo in the past, his success and sudden ubiquity caused him to turn down high-profile requests from Madonna and U2, among others. After time off following his marriage to British DJ Zoe Ball in 1998, Cook returned in 2000 with *Halfway Between the Gutter and the Stars*, a more reflective album that relies on the same obscure, dustbin samples but mostly shows a preference for 1970s soul and funk over disco and techno. "Talking About My Baby" samples a bluesy rant from 1970s Southern rockers Wet Willie, while the album's first single, "Sunset (Bird of Prey)," uses a vocal snippet of the late Doors singer Jim Morrison over a shuffling, mid-tempo dance groove.

In addition to sampling, Cook invited guest vocalists to join him on a series of original tracks on which he supplied the music while collaborating with the singers on the lyrics. Among the guest vocalists were the funk legend Bootsy Collins ("Weapon of Choice")—which spawned a widely lauded video featuring actor Willem Dafoe showing off his dancing skills—and the soul singer Macy Gray on two funk-inspired songs ("Love Live," "Demons").

One man's trash was Norman Cook's treasure. The internationally known DJ found gold in the kinds of forgotten records most people would flip by in their local record store, turning them into unforgettable dance hits and creating a star in his Fatboy Slim alter ego.

SELECTIVE DISCOGRAPHY: *Better Living Through Chemistry* (Skint/Astralwerks, 1996); *You've Come a Long Way, Baby* (Skint/Astralwerks, 1998); *Halfway Between the Gutter and the Stars* (Skint/Astralwerks, 2000); *Fatboy Slim/Norman Cook Collection* (Hip-O, 2000); *On the Floor at the Boutique* (Skint/Astralwerks, 2000); *Live on Brighton Beach* (Ministry of Sound/MCA, 2002); *Big Beach Boutique II* (Southern Fried Records, 2002). **With Beats International:** *Let Them Eat Bingo* (Go! Discs, 1990); **With Freakpower:** *Drive Through Booty* (4th and Broadway, 1995); *More of*

Everything for Everybody (4th and Broadway, 1996); **With Pizzaman:** *Pizzamania* (Cowboy Rodeo, 1995). **With Housemartins:** *London 0 Hull 4* (Go! Discs, 1986).

WEBSITE: www.gutterandstars.com.

GIL KAUFMAN

MICHAEL FEINSTEIN

Born: Columbus, Ohio, 7 September 1956

Genre: Vocal

Best-selling album since 1990: *Romance on Film, Romance on Broadway* (2000)

Michael Feinstein was a pioneer among a younger generation of interpreters who have devoted themselves to preserving and proliferating the art of the classic American popular song. With his boyish good looks, warm smile, and gentle personality, Feinstein helped launch a resurgence of interest during the late 1980s and early 1990s in what many had considered a dying art form. Feinstein's extraordinary success has not only inspired many others of his generation to become successful torch singers, but it also did much to rekindle the fading careers of singing stars who had originally been popular during the era of standards. Even contemporary pop stars no longer able to sustain audience interest with their own material now routinely boost sagging careers by turning to American classic popular songs.

The only child of a tap-dancing mother and a barbershop-quartet-singing father, Feinstein began playing piano by ear at the age of five. As a boy he spent hours at a time singing and playing standards he picked up off old 78-rpm records. While his peers were being weaned on the rock and roll of the British Invasion of the 1960s, the Feinstein home was filled with the music of the great American songwriters of yesteryear such as the Gershwins, Irving Berlin, Cole Porter, and Jerome Kern.

When the family moved to the Los Angeles suburb of Canoga Park in the mid-1970s, Feinstein sought out June Levant, the widow of the great Gershwin pianist Oscar Levant, and in 1977 she introduced him to Ira Gershwin himself. For the next six years, until the legendary lyricist's death in 1983, Feinstein immersed himself in the world of the composer/brother songwriting team that he had always idolized: George and Ira Gershwin. While cataloging Gershwin records, music, and memorabilia, and also acting as Ira's surrogate in matters pertaining to the publication and/or performance of Gershwin

works, Feinstein nurtured his calling to preserve the legacy of the Gershwins and their songwriting contemporaries.

Taking his first job as a cabaret pianist in a lounge, Feinstein immediately clashed with the owner about modernizing his repertoire. Gently but firmly sticking to his guns, Feinstein asked for one week for the word to get out about his performances of the classic standards. Word did spread, and a big break came when Feinstein was invited to play at a party hosted by Liza Minnelli. That success led to a triumphant 1986 New York debut at the Algonquin Hotel, which paved the way for Feinstein's one-man Broadway show *Isn't It Romantic?* (1988).

Along with Feinstein's own best-selling recordings and a string of television appearances as both performer and actor, his most valuable contribution to preserving the art of the American popular song has been his series of recorded songbooks, which feature legendary song composers accompanying him at the piano in performances of their own music.

The Gershwin centennial saw Feinstein releasing his third all-Gershwin disc, *Michael & George: Feinstein Sings Gershwin* (1998), which includes a performance of a "lost" number from *Porgy and Bess* (1935), the lullaby "Lonely Boy," discarded before the show's opening. It also afforded Feinstein the opportunity to perform Gershwin's biggest hit, "Swanee" (1919), to the accompaniment of Gershwin himself via piano roll. The September 26, 1998, centennial was the occasion of Feinstein's all-Gershwin concert with a fifty-piece symphony orchestra at the Chicago Theatre, a favorite Gershwin venue before his untimely, sudden death at the age of thirty-eight from a brain hemorrhage during surgery in 1937.

Feinstein's longtime ambition to co-own his own intimate New York City nightclub was realized with the opening of his At the Regency in 1999, a 130-seat Park Avenue showcase for himself and other performers who share Feinstein's devotion to the American standard.

Neither Feinstein's piano technique nor his vocalizing ability is particularly memorable; some find his interpretations banal. Others defend his unadorned approach, his classic repertoire to speak for itself without artistic excess. Yet through his enthusiasm and anecdotes, Feinstein has an uncanny ability to make even an arena audience feel as if he is singing personally to each member in his or her own living room.

The appeal and acceptance of Michael Feinstein remains now what it was from the beginning of his career. Older listeners are blissfully reminded of that musically fertile era of America's cultural past when the nation's best songwriters wrote for the nation's best singers. Likewise, younger listeners, weaned on performers who are expected to be simultaneously singers and songwriters, receive a first taste of an elegant, bygone era where each role was clearly and magnificently delineated, affording each a unique degree of perfection.

SELECTIVE DISCOGRAPHY: *Michael Feinstein Live at the Algonquin* (Elektra, 1987); *Michael Feinstein Sings Irving Berlin* (Elektra, 1987); *Isn't It Romantic?* (Elektra, 1988); *The MGM Album* (Elektra, 1989); *Michael Feinstein Sings the Burton Lane Songbook, Vol. I* (Nonesuch, 1990); *Michael Feinstein Sings the Jule Styne Songbook* (Nonesuch, 1991); *Michael Feinstein Sings the Burton Lane Songbook, Vol. II* (Nonesuch, 1993); *Michael Feinstein Sings the Hugh Martin Songbook* (Nonesuch, 1995); *Nice Work If You Can Get It: Songs from the Gershwins* (Nonesuch, 1996); *George & Michael: Feinstein Sings Gershwin* (Concord, 1998); *Big City Rhythms, with the Maynard Ferguson Big Band* (Concord, 1999); *The Michael Feinstein Anthology* (2 discs, Rhino, 2002); *Michael Feinstein with the Israel Philharmonic* (Concord, 2002); *Livingston & Evans Songbook* (Nonesuch, 2002).

BIBLIOGRAPHY: M. Feinstein, *Nice Work if You Can Get It: My Life in Rhythm and Rhyme* (New York, 1995).

WEBSITE: www.michaelfeinstein.com.

DENNIS POLKOW

VICENTE FERNÁNDEZ

Born: Vicente Fernández; Huentitán El Alto, Jalisco, Mexico, 17 February 1940

Genre: Latin

Best-selling album since 1990: *Entre el Amor y Yo* (1998)

Hit songs since 1990: "Lástima Que Seas Ajena," "Aunque Me Duela el Alma," "Me Voy a Quitar de en Medio"

Known as "El Idolo de Mexico" (the Idol of Mexico) among Spanish speakers for his chart-topping albums and sold-out tours, the ranchera singer Vicente Fernández embodies the valiant Mexican cowboy that figures so largely in the Mexican psyche. Ranchera music is the quintessential Mexican song form, idealizing rural life and drenching tales of love and breakups in unrestrained emotion. Fernández nearly always performs his rancheras with a mariachi backing. His gift for using his voice to plead, to exult, to taunt, and to bare his soul is unmatched. Though not a songwriter, he has a gift for recording songs that speak to Mexico's fatalism, romanticism, and machismo. From the humblest cantinas to family get-togethers to the preppiest discos, Mexicans use his music to heal broken hearts, to bond, to reaffirm their roots. He has inspired hundreds of imitators, but none could match his operatic power and range. His impact in ranchera is comparable to Frank Sinatra's legacy in American pop standards. Despite his many achievements, Fernández remains proud of his humble roots, as Sinatra was.

Born to a rancher, Ramón Fernández, and a homemaker, Paula Gomez de Fernández, Fernández began dreaming of a singing career early. When he was eight, he received a guitar and quickly learned how to play. At fourteen, he entered an amateur contest in Guadalajara, where

---

Spot Light | *Las Clásicas de José Alfredo Jiménez*

Vicente Fernández's defining moment on record came in 1990, when Fernández, Mexico's greatest ranchera singer, released the album *Las Clásicas de José Alfredo Jiménez*, a tribute to Jiménez, Mexico's greatest ranchera songwriter. Like many great composers, Jiménez drew inspiration from the tragedies in his own life. He wrote more than 300 songs in his career, many of which have become classics. His death, on November 23, 1973, plunged Mexico into a period of national mourning. The album resonates with the driving emotional force of Jiménez's words and Fernández's powerful vocals. These are gripping tales, but they are also melodic, lyrical, and richly harmonic set against symphonic-like mariachi arrangements. In "Un Mundo Raro" ("A Rare World"), Jiménez describes surviving an unrequited love to walk away a better man. With his powerful vocals Fernández delivers the message in typical macho swagger: "Better to have loved and lost, than never to have loved." Cascading violins and echoing horns evoke a sentimental mood. In "Viejos Amigos" ("Old Friends"), a gesture so simple as holding hands is made to sound incredibly romantic. In a touching scene Jiménez describes looking into the beautiful, tear-filled face of the woman he loves and has never gotten over: "Let me see you crying, let me be by your side." Even the toughest macho has to be moved.

he won first place. Later relocating to Guadalajara, he performed in a mariachi band that worked the city's streets. He married Maria "Cuca" de Refugio Abarca Villasenor, a neighbor, in 1963. Among their four children are sons Vicente Jr. and Alejandro, who went on to successful solo careers of their own. In late 1965 Fernández traveled to Mexico City, auditioning at record labels. In the summer of 1966, he signed with CBS México (now Sony Discos), recording his first hits: "Perdóname," "Tu Camino y El Mío," and "Cantina del Barrio."

But it was not until 1976 that Fernández became the undisputed ranchera king. The songwriter Fernando Z. Maldonado had penned a ranchera tune with a new twist about a macho who accepted blame and acquiesced in a relationship. The angle may have been new, but the song made an impact. "Volver, Volver" went on to become an anthem in the mariachi ranchera canon. The song pole-vaulted Fernández to international stardom and began his string of unforgettable hits. In the ensuing years Fernández recorded a half dozen other standards, including "La Ley del Monte," "El Rey," and "El Penal."

By the early 1980s the Mexican music press coined a new title for him—"El Ídolo de México"—and it stuck. He continued his streak of hits through the 1990s, with "Aunque Me Duela El Alma" (1995) and "Me Voy a Quitar de En Medio" (1998), the theme song to Univision's popular soap opera *La Mentira*. That year, he received a star on the Hollywood Walk of Fame.

His 2001 studio set *Más Con El Número Uno* produced the hit "El Ayudante," a macho ranchera expressing a mix of resignation and satisfaction about an affair with a married woman. It was written by Manuel Eduardo Toscano, who penned the hit "Sublime Mujer" off Fernández's 1998 CD *Entre el Amor y Yo*.

In 2002 Fernández was named the Latin Recording Academy Person of the Year by the Latin Grammy association for his artistic accomplishments and for donating ticket proceeds to the National Hispanic Scholarship Fund. In addition to the scholarship fund, Fernández helps out his rural fans by waiving his performance fee at small-town Mexican fairs.

SELECTIVE DISCOGRAPHY: *Las Clásicas de José Alfredo Jiménez* (Discos CBS, 1990); *Lástima Que Seas Ajena* (Sony Discos, 1993); *Aunque Me Duela el Alma* (Sony Discos, 1995); *Entre el Amor y Yo* (Sony Discos, 1998); *Más Con el Número Uno* (Sony Discos, 2001).

RAMIRO BURR

---

50 CENT

Born: Curtis Jackson; Queens, New York, 6 July 1976
Genre: Rap

Best-selling album since 1990: *Get Rich or Die Tryin'* (2003)

Hit songs since 1990: "In Da Club," "Wanksta"

In 2003, 50 Cent became the best-selling debut artist in hip-hop history. Although commercially successful hip-hop tends to be lyrically tame and heavily influenced by R&B and pop, 50 Cent has helped prove that street-oriented rap music can be widely embraced.

Curtis Jackson was born and raised in Queens, New York. While many rappers simply rhyme about having a tough upbringing, Jackson actually experienced one. He was born to an estranged father and a teenage mother who sold drugs and was murdered when he was eight years old. Jackson was raised by his grandparents but later followed in his mother's footsteps and began dealing crack cocaine at age twelve. As a teenager he alternated between serving jail time for drug possession and making a fortune selling drugs. He also began to cultivate his greatest love: rapping. He adopted the name 50 Cent as a "metaphor for change." In 1996, a friend introduced him to Run-D.M.C.'s Jam Master Jay. Jay mentored 50 Cent and signed him to his JMJ label. Three years later 50 Cent signed a deal with Columbia Records while maintaining a positive relationship with Jam Master Jay. He scored a hit and some controversy with the song "How to Rob," a clever satire in which he rhymed about stealing from famous rap artists like Jay-Z and Big Pun.

Although 50 Cent was signed to one of the largest labels in the world, he remained in financial straits. Most of his record label advance went to Jam Master Jay, and he continued to peddle crack to support himself. Months before the scheduled release of his debut album *Power of a Dollar*, a rival drug dealer shot him nine times outside his grandmother's house. The assault left him with a bullet fragment in his tongue and a hole in his jaw, which accounts for his signature slur.

Soon after the shooting, Columbia Records dropped 50 Cent from its roster and shelved his album. Nevertheless, 50 Cent continued to record music on his own, supplying songs to DJs who included them on mix tapes. 50 Cent built a grassroots following and attracted the attention of other major record labels and the superstar rappers Eminem and Dr. Dre. Following a fierce bidding war, Eminem and Dr. Dre signed 50 Cent to a joint-label deal, on Eminem's Shady Records and Dre's Aftermath Records, for a reported $1 million. 50 Cent's song "Wanksta," a "dis" record targeted to rapper Ja Rule, appeared on the soundtrack of *8 Mile*, the film featuring Eminem, which was the best-selling soundtrack of 2002. (It went platinum seven times in the United States.) 50 Cent collected many of his mix-tape hits for an independent album, *Guess Who's Back*.

50 Cent's debut album, *Get Rich or Die Trying* (2003), entered the *Billboard* charts at number one and sold more than 2 million copies in its first three weeks of release, making it the fastest-selling debut album from a major label. The album, executive produced by Dr. Dre and Eminem, immediately established 50 Cent as a superstar. The beats are hardcore and the lyrics at times unrelenting and violent, as on the song "Heat," built on a sample of a gun cocking. The dance floor-friendly single "In Da Club" topped the *Billboard* pop charts for many weeks.

The success of 50 Cent proves that hip-hop need not water itself down to sell records and that the American public craves autobiographical authenticity from rap artists.

SELECTIVE DISCOGRAPHY: *Get Rich or Die Trying* (Shady/Aftermath, 2003).

DARA COOK

NEIL FINN

Born: Neil Mullane Finn; Te Awamutu, New Zealand, 27 May 1958

Genre: Rock

Best-selling album since 1990: *Try Whistling This* (1998)

Hit songs since 1990: "Chocolate Cake," "Sinner"

Neil Finn is a singer/songwriter whose compositions bear the mark of his vivid imagination, keen musical intuition, and the tender heart of a true romantic. Finn was the lead singer for the popular New Zealand band Crowded House, which formed in 1984 and released several albums until they finally called it quits in 1996. Finn, who has a warm, crisp, inviting voice, became a solo artist after quitting Crowded House in 1996.

Finn grew up one of four children in Te Awamutu, a small town on New Zealand's North Island where his musical family owned and operated an orchard. Beginning in 1984, Finn acted as the primary songwriter for the pop trio Crowded House, which he formed after his brother Tim left Split Enz to start a solo career. Finn recruited drummer Paul Hester and bassist Nick Seymour, and the band became known for its meticulously detailed lyrics and its knack for irresistible melodies. Finn's solo music showcases the familiar strengths of Crowded House while taking the music a step further to a more adventurous place. His debut solo album, *Try Whistling This* (2000), is moody and textured, and features strings, mellotron, slinky bass, and cello. From the bass-driven, slow, funky tempo of "Sinner," the album's first single, to the redeeming powers of love in the stirring "She Will Have Her Way," *Try Whistling This* is replete with atmospheric layers, sticky melodies, and heartfelt lyrics. With production help from Nigel Goodrich, who worked with the eccentric rock band Radiohead, and Mitchell Froom, the album is ethereal and darkly gothic at times. In the ballad title track, Finn's gift for heartbreakingly romantic lyrics reigns supreme as he sings, "If I can't be with you I would rather have a different face / If I can't be near you I would rather be adrift in space."

Finn toured extensively in support of his debut solo release and even brought along his son Liam, who plays guitar. Between the tour and his second solo album, *One All* (2002), which had a strong debut overseas, Finn scored the music for the Australian drama *Rain* and collaborated with the Australian Chamber Orchestra on musical pieces inspired by the poems of cartoonist Michael Leunig.

Try Whistling This sold well in New Zealand and landed at number five in the United Kingdom the week of its release, but most music fans in the United States know Finn as the lead singer of a band with one bona fide hit song, "Something So Strong." Consequently, much of the American audience overlooks him, to the bewilderment of his fans and critics. If talent shared equivalent rewards with fame, Finn—whose ability to write clean, clever, beautiful pop songs has led to comparisons with Paul McCartney—would have achieved far more success as a solo artist.

SELECTIVE DISCOGRAPHY: *Try Whistling This* (2000); *One All* (Nettwerk, 2002); **With Crowded House:** *Together Alone* (EMI/Capitol,1994); *Woodface* (EMI/Capitol, 1991). **With Tim Finn:** *Finn* (Capitol, 1996). **Soundtrack:** *Rain* (2002).

BIBLIOGRAPHY: N. Finn, *Neil Finn—Once Removed* (London, 2000).

CARRIE HAVRANEK

WILLIAM FINN

Born: Boston, Massachusetts, 28 February 1952

Genre: Musical Theater

Best-selling album since 1990: *Falsettoland* (1990)

William Finn is a prominent Tony Award–winning composer/lyricist in New York's Broadway Theater circles. His best-known work gives a witty, human voice to the challenges and tribulations of American gay life. Somewhat of a theatrical renaissance man, Finn has also worn the hats of director, playwright, and performer.

Finn grew up in the Boston suburb of Natick, Massachusetts, and later studied at Williams College, where he began writing musicals. Known for a magnetic, sometimes eccentric personality, his first production was a failed musical about the executed McCarthy era spies, Ethel and Julius Rosenberg, titled *Sizzle*. In 1976 he moved to New York City and immediately advanced his career by impressing the creative staff of Playwrights Horizons with his show concepts and music. One of Manhattan's most prestigious Off-Broadway theater companies, Playwrights Horizons produced *In Trousers*, Finn's musical about a family man named Marvin who discovers that he is gay. Playwrights Horizons staged Finn's continuing saga of Marvin with *March of the Falsettos* in 1981; in 1990 the same organization produced *Falsettoland* to complete the trilogy. The three plays examined many issues of Marvin's new life, but it was *Falsettoland*, which touched on AIDS, that drew a larger audience to the *Marvin Trilogies*. A decision followed to combine the last two parts of the trilogy into one show simply titled *Falsettos*. It opened on Broadway at the Golden Theatre in 1992 under the direction of James Lapine, who also helped write some of the show's libretto. *Falsettos* ran for 486 performances, and Finn won two Tony Awards, Broadway's highest honor, for Best Original Score and Best Book in a Musical for the 1992 season.

Days after accepting his Tony Awards, Finn was beset with a brain condition that was initially diagnosed as inoperable. Pondering his mortality and all that he had left to accomplish, Finn received a new diagnosis that revealed the condition to be treatable, and he went on to a full recovery. This experience is the basis for his play, *A New Brain*, which opened on Broadway at the Mitzi Newhouse Theatre in Manhattan's Lincoln Center in 1998. Finn composed the music and co-wrote the play's book with Lapine, who was by then a regular collaborator. *A New Brain* did not overwhelm the critics and lasted only seventy-eight performances before closing; however, the cast recording of the show's music still sells well.

In 2001, Finn released *Infinite Joy* (2001), a live recording of twenty-one compositions from *Falsettos*, *A New Brain*, his upcoming *Royal Family*, and some previously unreleased material. *Infinite Joy* was recorded at a popular Broadway talent cabaret venue, *Joe's Pub*, in downtown Manhattan and features Finn's craggy, expressive singing on some of the songs. That year the Pegasus Players in Chicago produced a new musical by Finn called *Muscle*.

A performer at heart, Finn has acted in earlier versions of *In Trousers* in addition to performing in other projects, usually of his creation. He had a small role in the film *Life with Mikey* (1993). In 2002 he directed the *Falsettos* veteran Chip Zien, in Zien's one-man show *Death In Ashtabula*. *Falsettos* returned to the New York stage for six performances in January 2003, featuring members of the original cast in a special program by Playwrights Horizons. Finn's musical *Looking Up*, a revue of his songs, had a lim-

ited one-month run at the Mitzi Newhouse Theatre in March 2003.

Finn is one of a handful of composers and playwrights with the courage to openly address issues affecting the gay experience and bring those issues successfully to a mainstream audience.

SELECTIVE DISCOGRAPHY: *In Trousers: Original Off-Broadway Cast Recording* (Original Cast, 1979); *March of the Falsettos: 1981 Original Off-Broadway Cast Recording* (DRG, 1981); *Falsettoland: 1990 Off-Broadway Cast Recording* (DRG, 1990); *A New Brain: Original Cast Recording* (BMG, 1998); *Infinite Joy: The Songs of William Finn* (RCA Victor, 2001).

DONALD LOWE

THE FLAMING LIPS

Formed: 1983, Oklahoma City, Oklahoma

Members: Wayne Coyne, guitar, vocals (born Pittsburgh, Pennsylvania, 17 March 1965); Steven Drozd, drums, vocals (born Houston, Texas, 6 December 1969); Michael Ivins, bass, vocals (born Omaha, Nebraska, 17 March 1965). Former members: Marc Coyne, vocals, guitar; Jonathan Donahue, guitar; Richard English, drums; Ronald Jones, guitar, vocals (born Angeles, Philippines, 26 November 1970); Nathan Roberts, drums.

Genre: Rock

Best-selling album since 1990: *Transmissions from the Satellite Heart* (1993)

Hit songs since 1990: "She Don't Use Jelly," "Waitin' for a Superman"

For some bands, success is a million seller or a hit single. For Oklahoma's restlessly creative Flaming Lips, success is found in the cracks and creases other bands dare not explore, such as a symphony written for forty automobile tape decks. Over the course of a decade, during which the band toiled in obscurity with the love of a cult audience, the Flaming Lips's often unruly explosion of psychedelia, rock, pop, experimental music, and pure noise shifted and mutated in wholly unexpected, singularly creative, and exciting ways. In the second decade of their career, the Lips grew from an unprincipled band of rank amateurs to studio wizards capable of conjuring masterful symphonies of pop pleasure.

Taking Off

Founded in Oklahoma City in 1983 by singer/guitarists Wayne and Mark Coyne and bassist Michael Ivins, the Flaming Lips were a rock and roll tabula rasa: admittedly amateur musicians who knew nothing about the art of making music. After hiring a string of drummers, the group settled on Richard English and recorded their self-titled debut in 1985, which they released on their own Lovely Sorts of Death label—on green vinyl, no less.

The low-fidelity, dirgelike songs paid homage to such early 1980s gothic rock bands as the Jesus and Mary Chain, while indulging in the echo- and feedback-drenched sound of late 1960s garage rock. Mark Coyne left the group a year later, thrusting his brother Wayne into the spotlight as the lead guitarist, singer, and songwriter. It was his vision that led the band into uncharted waters.

The next year brought *Hear It Is*, which married the psychedelic wanderings of Pink Floyd with folk, punk, and walls of guitar feedback, often in one song, as in the epic freakout, "Jesus Shootin' Heroin." In addition to developing a reputation for their risqué, bizarre song titles and lyrics ("Charlie Manson Blues," "One Million Billionth of a Millisecond on a Sunday Morning") and wild stage shows, the group was slowly progressing from unprincipled amateurs to studio-savvy rockers.

Following the release of *Oh My Gawd!! . . . The Flaming Lips* (1987), another tangled web of meandering, psychedelic rock with druggy lyrics, the group met the concert promoter Jonathan Donahue, who signed on to be their sound technician. English quit the band halfway into the tour in support of *Telepathic Surgery* (1988), forcing Coyne and Ivins to soldier on as a duo with Donahue filling in on guitar. For their final album with Restless Records, Coyne cooked up a bizarre, pseudoreligious epic, *In a Priest-Driven Ambulance* (1990).

Major-Label Success

As a joke, Coyne and Ivins began harassing various A&R (artist and repertoire) scouts at Warner Bros. records in an attempt to land a recording contract. To their surprise, Warner Bros. signed the group, releasing their major-label debut, *Hit to Death in the Future Head*, in 1992; it was yet another passel of psychedelic pop, augmented by trumpets, violins, autoharps, samplers, timpani, flugelhorns, and power tools. Donahue quit the group to focus on his own band, Mercury Rev, and was replaced by guitarist Ronald Jones. The band hooked up with a new collaborator at the same time, producer Dave Fridmann, who helped to expand the group's sound into previously unimaginable shapes.

Despite sharing concert bills with such popular bands as Porno for Pyros and the Stone Temple Pilots, the band's *Transmissions from the Satellite Heart* (1993) garnered little notice upon its release. But a low-budget video for the quirky song "She Don't Use Jelly," in which a helium-voiced Coyne sings about a girl who dyes her hair with

tangerines, slowly gained momentum on MTV and on the radio in 1994. Unafraid to place their music in the strangest of places, the Lips seized on the unexpected hit single's popularity by filming a notorious guest shot as the house band on the Fox teenage soap drama *Beverly Hills 90210*. The album also marked the debut of new drummer, Steven Drozd, who quickly emerged as the yin to Coyne's musical yang.

The success of "She Don't Use Jelly" seemed like even more of a fluke when the band's next album, *Clouds Taste Metallic* (1995), failed to yield a hit single or match the sales of its predecessor. The album, however, is an intriguing blueprint of the band's second life, with sweeping, multilayered, highly melodic pop epics built around Drozd's athletic, bashing drums, Coyne's keening vocals, and swaths of ambient noise, sound effects, and walls of guitars and angelic vocals. It is no wonder, though, that despite beautiful, challenging arrangements, songs such as "Psychiatric Explorations of the Fetus with Needles," "Guy Who Got a Headache and Accidentally Saves the World," and "Placebo Headwound" were not candidates for radio hits.

With an already well-established reputation for energized live concerts featuring confetti canons, thousands of spinning Christmas lights, puppets, and strange films, the group was dealt a double blow: departure of Jones shortly after the album's release and the fracture of Drozd's wrist prior to a tour with the Red Hot Chili Peppers in late 1995.

Rather than take the departure as a setback, Coyne seized on the opportunity. Having mounted several "parking lot experiments" over the previous few years (in which he distributed cassettes of the band's music to forty or more cars in a parking lot and "conducted" a car symphony), Coyne somehow convinced Warner Bros. to release the four-CD *Zaireeka* (1997) set with promises of a more commercial album to follow. Meant to be played simultaneously on four stereos for the full effect, the album was a daring experiment and just a hint of what was to come.

The Soft Bulletin and Beyond

Prior to the release of *The Soft Bulletin* (1999), Drozd nearly lost his hand after being bitten by a spider, Ivins was involved in a nearly fatal car accident, and Coyne's father was dying of cancer. The trio took all the pain, confusion, and suffering and spun it into their most accomplished work to date, dispensing, in Coyne's words, with the spaceships and aliens of the past and focusing on matters of the heart. Featuring an utterly unprecedented style of pop music, the work was many critics' choice for album of the year.

Although the product of just the core trio, the emotional, symphonic pop of the album sounds like the work of several orchestras, anchored by Drozd's thunderous drums, Coyne's plaintive vocals, and sweeping string arrangements. Tracks such as "Race for the Prize," about Coyne's desperation to find a cure for his father's illness, and the album's emotional centerpiece, "Waitin' for a Superman," deal with death and despair without maudlin sentiment. In such songs Coyne transforms his anxiety into celebrations of life and strength. "Is it getting' heavy? / Well, I thought it was already as heavy as can be," Coyne sings in the latter, his helium voice juxtaposed with church bells and a stuttering, soulful, funky drum beat.

Employing a series of drum loops and special effects, the Lips trio took their show on the road in support of the album, adding a number of new oddball aspects to their live show—two dozen audience members in animal costumes, huge rotating disco balls, and madcap films—in time for the release of *Yoshimi Battles the Pink Robots* (2002). Like its predecessor, *Yoshimi* works a startling array of drum loops, orchestral flourishes, and over-the-top arrangements into the band's sound, slightly reversing the turn toward more serious material but still focusing on the healing powers of love. The group served as both the opening act and backing band for the alternative rock hero Beck during his 2002 world tour.

By defying convention and constantly exploring the boundaries of their sound, the Flaming Lips matured from a ragtag group of musical pranksters to envelope-pushing mavericks with one of the most unique sounds in rock.

SELECTIVE DISCOGRAPHY: *The Flaming Lips* (Lovely Sorts of Death/Restless, 1985); *Hear It Is* (Restless/Enigma, 1986); *Oh My Gawd!!! . . . The Flaming Lips* (Restless/Enigma, 1987); *Telepathic Surgery* (Restless/Enigma, 1989); *In a Priest-Driven Ambulance* (Restless/Enigma, 1990); *Hit to Death in the Future Head* (Warner Bros., 1992); *Transmissions from the Satellite Heart* (Warner Bros., 1993); *Clouds Taste Metallic* (Warner Bros., 1995); *Zaireeka* (Warner Bros., 1997); *The Soft Bulletin* (Warner Bros., 1999); *Yoshimi Battles the Pink Robots* (Warner Bros., 2002).

GIL KAUFMAN

BELA FLECK

Born: New York, New York, 10 July 1958

Genre: Bluegrass, Jazz, World

Best-selling album since 1990: *Tales from the Acoustic Planet Vol. 2—The Bluegrass Sessions* (1999)

Bela Fleck is one of the giants in the progressive music scene. His unique prowess on the five-string banjo stretches musical boundaries and

imaginations. Through a passionate fascination for an instrument generally associated with rural music, he is recognized as an affable and innovative performer/composer who utilizes the banjo to fuse bluegrass, jazz, ethnic, funk, and classical music genres into his own distinct style.

Discovering the Banjo

Fleck was born in New York City and raised there by his mother, a schoolteacher. His father, who had a strong interest in classical music, gave him the name Bela (pronounced BAY-lah) after Béla Bartók, the great Hungarian composer. His parents separated when he was one, and Bela has no memories of his father. Fleck's interest in the banjo began as a child, when he heard the theme song for the TV show *The Beverly Hillbillies*. Later he gained entrance into the LaGuardia High School of Music and Art for his abilities on the guitar. However, after hearing the banjo in the film *Deliverance* at age fifteen, he became captivated and completely devoted to the instrument. The high school did not acknowledge the banjo as an appropriate instrument, so Fleck was assigned to study the French horn, which he flunked. He ended up fulfilling his music credits by singing in a choir. Meanwhile, he played the banjo at every opportunity, practicing up to eight hours a day.

There were not many musicians playing the banjo in New York City in the 1970s, and gaining acceptance into any kind of music scene was difficult for Fleck at first. Eventually he found some college musicians for impromptu jam sessions and began studying privately, first with Erik Darling, later with Marc Horowitz, and finally with the banjo veteran Tony Trischka. (Trischka and the legendary Earl Scruggs are Fleck's biggest influences.) After high school graduation in 1976, Fleck moved to Boston to honor a promise to his mother that he attend college. He enrolled in the Julliard Extension School but had already gained a solid reputation as a banjo player and quit to pursue music professionally. His first band was a Boston-based bluegrass group called Tasty Licks, which featured the bluegrass ambassador Jack Tottle on mandolin.

Heading South

By 1979 Fleck had moved to Lexington, Kentucky, where he formed a progressive bluegrass group called Spectrum, which made three albums. He also cut his first solo album, *Crossing the Tracks* (1979), which featured Pat Enright, Sam Bush, and the prodigiously skilled Mark O'Connor. Only twenty-one years old, Fleck had already become one of the beacons of progressive music. As a founder of the progressive supergroup New Grass Revival, he fervently combined the musical base of bluegrass with other styles and creatively expanded the possibilities of the banjo's sound as radically as Charlie Parker had those of the saxophone.

New Grass Revival broke up in 1989, and Fleck created the Flecktones, with Howard Levy on keyboards and the brothers Victor and Roy Wooten on bass and percussion, respectively. The quartet immediately began pushing the musical envelope. Despite the progressive nature of the music, the New Grass Revival albums and most of Fleck's other work generally ended up in the bluegrass and country sections of music stores. However, Bela Fleck and the Flecktone's second album, *Flight of the Cosmic Hippo* (1991), topped the jazz charts. Their fourth album, *Left of Cool (1998)*, gave way to a "blu-bop" sound with more emphasis on horns. It features Dave Matthews on vocals. One special cut from the album is a funky take on one of Fleck's signature compositions, "Big Country." In 2000, the group released *Outbound* and shaded it with Irish and South African sounds and rhythms.

Fleck and his Flecktones captured the essence of their concert performances in *Live at the Quick* (2002). Long known for an accessible and lighthearted quality in his live performances, Fleck will wander through the audience, delighting them with a seemingly endless musical stream of consciousness, playing snippets from classical to bluegrass on his banjo. As a tribute to the first time he heard the banjo, Fleck generally mixes in some musical arrangement from the *The Beverly Hillbillies* theme.

Solo Projects

In between recordings and concerts with the Flecktones, Fleck has ventured several solo projects that have allowed him to work with musicians from different genres. His *Tales from the Acoustic Planet* (1994) is a gathering of musical friends whose talents Fleck holds in highest regard. Contributing to the album is an all-star cast featuring virtuoso jazz keyboardist Chick Corea along with guitar maven Tony Rice and renowned saxophonist Branford Marsalis. In 1999 Fleck recorded *Tales from the Acoustic Planet Vol. 2—The Bluegrass Sessions* (1999) with another amazing guest roster that includes Rice along with longtime playing mates Sam Bush, Mark Schatz, and Jerry Douglas. Vince Gill, Tim O'Brien, Vassar Clements, the late John Hartford, and Ricky Skaggs also appear, but the guest of honor is bluegrass legend and Fleck's most esteemed musical influence—Earl Scruggs. They pay homage to the banjo and each other in a dazzling duet of the traditional "Home Sweet Home." This album features a joyously wide range of musical style, including a polka in "Clarinet Polka," traditional bluegrass in "Ode to Earl" (dedicated to Scruggs), and the stately "Overgrown Waltz."

Classical Banjo

When Fleck inked a five-record deal with Sony in 2000, he became the first banjo player to sign a classical record contract. He explores uncharted banjo territory with *Perpetual Motion* (2001). This album is a solo effort focusing entirely on the works of Bach, Beethoven, Chopin, Scarlatti, and others. It garnered him two Grammy Awards, including Best Classical Crossover Album.

Long considered a studio musician "extraordinaire," Fleck has played on more than 250 albums of various artists. He has been nominated for nineteen Grammy Awards in ten different categories and is a seven-time Grammy winner. His extensive touring schedule included an appearance at the premier bluegrass venue, Merlefest 2003, in Wilkesboro, North Carolina, a celebration of legendary guitarist Doc Watson and his late son, Merle.

By his joyous plunges into any music style of his choice, Fleck and his eclectic banjo skills give fits to critics and others whose job it is to define music. He has redefined the banjo while he carries a torch for the progressive music scene and the fusion of musical genres.

SELECTIVE DISCOGRAPHY: *Crossing the Tracks* (Rounder, 1979); *Fiddle Tunes for Banjo* (Rounder, 1981); *Natural Bridge Suite* (Rounder, 1982); *Double Time* (Rounder, 1984); *Deviation* (Rounder, 1984); *Inroads* (Rounder, 1986); *Drive* (Rounder, 1988); *Places* (Rounder, 1988); *Daybreak* (Rounder,1988); *The Telluride Sessions* (Rounder, 1989); *Bela Fleck and the Flecktones* (Warner Bros., 1990); *Flight of the Cosmic Hippo* (Warner Bros., 1991); *Solo Banjo Works* (Warner Bros., 1992); *UFO TOFU* (Warner Bros., 1992); *Three Flew over the Cuckoos Nest* (Warner Bros., 1993); *Tales from the Acoustic Planet* (Warner Bros., 1995); *Live Art* (Warner Bros., 1996); *Curandero* (Warner Bros., 1996); *Left of Cool* (Warner Bros., 1998); *Tales from the Acoustic Planet Vol. 2* (Warner Bros., 1999); *Outbound* (Sony, 2000); *Perpetual Motion* (Sony, 2001).

DONALD LOWE

FLEETWOOD MAC

Formed: 1967, London, England

Members: Lindsey Buckingham, guitar, vocals (born Palo Alto, California, 3 October 1949); Mick Fleetwood, drums (born Redruth, Cornwall, England, 24 June 1947); Christine McVie, keyboards (Christine Perfect, born Grenodd, Lancashire, England, 12 July 1943); John McVie, bass (born London, England, 26 November 1945); Stevie Nicks, vocals (Stephanie Nicks, born Phoenix, Arizona, 26 May 1948). Former members: Billy Burnette, guitar, vocals (William Beau Burnette III, born Memphis, Tennessee, 8 May 1953); Bekka Bramlett, vocals (born Westwood, California, 19 April 1968); Peter Green, guitar (Peter Allen Greenbaum, born London, England, 29 October 1949); Danny Kirwan, guitar (born London, England, 13 May 1950); Dave Mason, guitar, vocals (Worcester, England, 10 May 1946); Jeremy Spencer, guitar (born Hartlepool, Cleveland, England, 4 July 1948); Rick Vito, guitar, vocals (born Darby, Pennsylvania, 13 October 1949); Dave Walker, vocals (born Birmingham, England); Bob Weston, guitar (born England); Bob Welch, guitar, vocals (Robert Welch, born Los Angeles, California, 31 July 1946).

Genre: Rock

Best-selling album since 1990: *The Dance* (1997)

Hit songs since 1990: "Peacekeeper," "Silver Springs"

Through a tangled web of broken relationships, rotating band members, and musical journeys weaving in and out of five decades, rock group Fleetwood Mac has sold more than 100 million records. The band experienced its greatest success in the 1970s when it focused on a marketable blend of pop rock. That stage of its existence contained the musical lineup most often identified with Fleetwood Mac, and the majority of that lineup reunited to record and tour into the new millennium.

Musical Chairs

When most of its fans think of Fleetwood Mac, they are referring to the band that consisted of singer Stevie Nicks, guitarist/singer Lindsey Buckingham, keyboardist/singer Christine McVie, bassist John McVie, and drummer Mick Fleetwood. However, Fleetwood Mac's roots extend back to 1967 when it was a renowned London blues band. John McVie and Fleetwood were members during that time. The other two original members were guitarist extraordinaire Peter Green and another fine London blues guitarist, Jeremy Spencer. All four core Fleetwood Mac members were refugees from English blues legend John Mayall's group, the Bluesbreakers. By 1970 Christine McVie—Christine Perfect before marrying John McVie—had joined the group. Both Green and Spencer had already left the band to pursue their respective religious beliefs following excessive drug use, and in the case of Green, complications with mental illness. Guitarist Danny Kirwan and guitarist/singer/songwriter Bob Welch replaced them.

Welch, an American from California with pop music roots, began influencing Fleetwood Mac away from the blues and the group made inroads toward a more polished pop rock sound. However, Kirwan's drug problems forced the band's manager at the time, Clifford Davis, to fire him in 1972 and hire ex-Savoy Brown band mates, guitarist Bob Weston and Dave Walker. That move nearly derailed the band as Walker drank heavily and Weston became involved romantically with Christine McVie. At

different junctures, both Walker and Weston were sent packing. Weston's firing closed down the group's U.S. tour prematurely. A series of ensuing legal entanglements resulted in 1974, and the band was, for all practical purposes, disbanded. Eventually, Mick Fleetwood took control of the situation, relieved Davis of his responsibilities, and began managing Fleetwood Mac himself. The band's tumultuous history took its toll on Welch, who left in 1975 to pursue other projects.

In an effort to replace Welch, Fleetwood brought songwriting/performing duo Buckingham and Nicks into the group. Lindsey Buckingham and Stevie Nicks had worked together previously and were lovers. Their soft rock sound, ripe with poignant lyrics coupled between catchy musical phrasing, struck an immediate chord with Fleetwood and greatly impacted the group to form the classic Fleetwood Mac musical lineup. The band's next five years were massively successful as they turned out hits such as "Rhiannon," "Over My Head," "Say You Love Me," "Dreams," "Don't Stop," "Go Your Own Way," and many others. Their album *Rumours* (1977), recorded while the McVies

---

Spot Light | Fleetwood Mac's Farewell for President Clinton

Fleetwood Mac came out of a three-year hiatus to perform a concert in Washington, D.C., in January 2001 for President Bill Clinton, who would soon be leaving office. Organized by President Clinton's staff, it was a surprise farewell party for the president. A favorite band of both the president and the First Lady, Fleetwood Mac's invitation made sense because their song "Don't Stop," used as a theme song for Clinton's 1992 first-term election, helped put him in office. Now they were asked to help him out of office. The impromptu concert marked Fleetwood Mac's first appearance since Christine McVie announced that she would not be performing with the band anymore. Despite major concern within the band about showing rust due to the long layoff and a lack of rehearsal time, the eleven-song set went without a hitch. Fleetwood Mac's impromptu concert included Clinton's campaign theme song, along with other Fleetwood Mac signature fare, such as "Dreams," "Landslide," and "Go Your Own Way."

were divorcing and the Nicks/Buckingham union was landsliding, went on to become one of the top five selling albums in rock history. *Rumours* has sold more than 30 million copies. Fleetwood Mac fired Fleetwood as manager in 1981 and then split up to allow various members to pursue solo careers. Nicks's solo career has become, by a wide margin over the others, the most commercially successful. They soon reunited to record *Mirage* (1982), but broke up again during the promotional tour that followed the album's release. They formed again in 1985 to record *Tango in the Night* (1987), but Buckingham left the band during the ensuing tour.

Breaking Up Is Hard to Do

Fleetwood Mac entered the 1990s with singers/guitarists Rick Vito and Billy Burnette as Buckingham's replacements and the band recorded *Behind the Mask* (1990), which went platinum. At the close of the album's extremely successful tour, Nicks and Vito left Fleetwood Mac. Nicks, a major star on her own merit, stated that she would never return. Meanwhile, Fleetwood fended off rumors of the group's demise by calling it merely a hiatus. In 1992 the band consisted of John McVie, Fleetwood, and Burnette with guitarist Dave Mason and Bekka Bramlett on vocals. Fleetwood Mac received an extra boost when Bill Clinton used one of its hits, "Don't Stop," to theme his 1992 presidential campaign. Burnette officially quit the group in 1992, but joined back up for its 1995 tour and new album release, *Time* (1995). The album did poorly and Fleetwood Mac broke up again. This time, the band reported, it was final.

In 1996 the band re-formed with its mid-1970s classic lineup for a twentieth anniversary tour of *Rumours*. They released *The Dance* (1997), a live recording from an intimate concert in Los Angeles. *The Dance* contains seventeen songs, mostly 1970s hits, with four new releases added. "Landslide," a hit written by Nicks from *Fleetwood Mac* (1975), was released as a single from the album as was a new song, "Silver Springs." *The Dance* went quadruple platinum in sales and earned three Grammy Award nominations, including Best Pop Album. When the album's tour ended in November of that year, Christine McVie announced that she could no longer handle the rigors of touring and recording with the band. Fleetwood Mac entered the Rock and Roll Hall of Fame in 1998.

After another dormant period wherein Nicks and Buckingham resumed their solo careers, Fleetwood Mac regrouped yet again in 2002: this time, however, without Christine McVie but with the rest of the classic formation intact. They released *Say You Will* (2003) and promoted the album with an extensive North American tour. *Say You Will* harks back to the band's glory days with a trademark blend of moody rock, smooth harmonies, and Nicks's emotional vocal work. Many of the album's songs came from Buckingham, who used material he had slated for a solo effort that failed to work out.

No band has ever survived as much fluctuation as Fleetwood Mac and managed to achieve such monumental success. Its songs musically defined both the 1970s and the 1980s. With every effort by the band since the 1990s billed as its final act, fans have learned that, with Fleetwood Mac, never always means maybe.

SELECTIVE DISCOGRAPHY: *Then Play On* (Reprise, 1969); *Kiln House* (Reprise, 1970); *Fleetwood Mac in Chicago* (Blue Horizon, 1971); *Future Games* (Reprise, 1971); *Penguin* (Reprise, 1973); *Mystery to Me* (Reprise, 1973); *Heroes Are Hard to Find* (Reprise, 1974); *Fleetwood Mac* (Reprise, 1975); *Rumours* (Warner Bros., 1977); *Tusk* (Warner Bros., 1979); *Fleetwood Mac Live* (Warner Bros., 1980); *Mirage* (Warner Bros., 1982); *Tango in the Night* (Warner Bros., 1987); *Behind the Mask* (Warner Bros., 1990); *25 Years . . . The Chain* (Warner Bros./WEA, 1992); *Time* (Warner Bros., 1995); *The Dance* (Warner Bros., 1997); *Say You Will* (Warner Bros., 2003).

BIBLIOGRAPHY: B. Brunning, *Fleetwood Mac: The First 30 Years* (London, 1999); L. Furman, *Rumours Exposed: The Unauthorized Biography of Fleetwood Mac* (New York, 1999); E. Wincentsen, *Fleetwood Mac: Through the Years* (New York, 1999).

DONALD LOWE

RENÉE FLEMING

Born: Indiana, Pennsylvania, 14 February 1959
Genre: Classical

Renée Fleming is one of the most versatile and engaging sopranos of the late twentieth and early twenty-first centuries. With a middleweight voice and extended vocal range, she has been able to roam freely over a wide expanse of musical styles and repertoire. Her voice is beautiful in the classic sense, and her dramatic sensibilities make her a favorite with audiences.

The daughter of two vocal teachers, she grew up listening to her parents discuss the art of singing every night at the dinner table. Fleming's parents encouraged her to sing at every turn, and provided plenty of opportunities for her. Deciding on a career in music education, she attended the State University of New York, Potsdam, where she also sang in a jazz trio.

Graduate studies at the Eastman School in Rochester, New York, and at the American Opera Center at the Juilliard School in New York City (1983–1987) helped cement her musical education and set her on a performing career. At Juilliard she began studying with acclaimed voice instructor Beverly Johnson, who helped guide her through her early career.

On her third try, she won the Metropolitan Opera National Council Auditions in 1988. That was also the year of her big break, singing the role of the Countess in Mozart's *Le Nozze de Figaro* at the Houston Grand Opera. In 1989 she made her debuts at the New York City Opera as Mimi in *La Boheme* and at Covent Garden as Glauce in Cherubini's *Medea,* and in 1991 she made her debut at the Metropolitan Opera as the Countess in *Le Nozze de Figaro.* Since then she has been a regular at major opera houses and on concert stages all over the world.

In a profession that likes to typecast its performers, Fleming has resisted sticking to one area of the repertoire. Her early successes were made with Mozart and Richard Strauss, but she has performed and recorded extensively in both operatic and recital literature. A champion of new music, she sang the premieres of John Corigliano's *The Ghosts of Versailles* and the role of Blanche in André Previn's *A Streetcar Named Desire* at San Francisco Opera. In 1997 she was named Musical America's Vocalist of the Year.

A 1998 recording of *Rusalka* (one of the roles most identified with her) with Ben Heppner and the Czech Philharmonic Orchestra, conducted by Charles Mackerras, won wide acclaim, as well as a number of awards, including two Grammophone Awards. Another 1998 album, *The Beautiful Voice,* featuring the works of Gustave Charpentier, Charles Gounod, and Jules Massenet, won a Grammy Award for Best Classical Vocal Performance.

Her success has reached beyond the vocal world. She was named one of *People* magazine's Most Intriguing 25 People in 2000. She has been profiled in the *New Yorker* and on CBS's *60 Minutes,* and was the subject of a *Vogue* photo shoot in 2001. She also appears in Rolex and Anne Klein ads.

Though her career did not start moving until she was almost thirty years old, Fleming connected quickly with audiences, becoming one of the most popular opera stars of the 1990s. Her success derives from the pure tonal beauty of her voice and her innate theatricality.

SELECTIVE DISCOGRAPHY: *Rusalka,* with the Czech Philharmonic, conducted by Charles Mackerras (Polygram, 1998); *The Beautiful Voice,* with the English Chamber Orchestra, conducted by Jeffrey Tate (Polygram, 1998).

WEBSITE: www.renee-fleming.com.

DOUGLAS MCLENNAN

JOHN FOGERTY

Born: Berkeley, California, 28 May 1945
Genre: Country, Rock
Best-selling album since 1990: *Blue Moon Swamp* (1997)

John Fogerty's triumphant solo career has been a puzzling journey. As the celebrated singer/songwriter of the legendary rock group Creedence Clearwater Revival, Fogerty wrote nine Top 10 singles between 1968 and 1972. Yet his success was marred by legal entanglements over the rights to his songs and related stress that forced him into seclusion and nearly into retirement.

In 1959, Fogerty played in his first band with his older brother, Tom Fogerty, while growing up in a suburb outside of the San Francisco Bay area. Along with drummer Doug Clifford and bass player Stu Cook, they formed the Blue Velvets. In 1963 the band took on a British sound, donned blonde wigs, and changed their name to the Golliwogs. They released several singles between 1963 and 1967 as Fogerty began to wrest the lead vocal work from his older brother. In addition to singing, both brothers could play guitar, keyboards, dobro, harmonica, drums, and other instruments, but the younger Fogerty was beginning to emerge as the group's leader. He also played lead guitar while Tom played rhythm guitar. In 1967 they formed Creedence Clearwater Revival (CCR) under the management of Fantasy Records.

CCR scored hit after hit over the next four years with pop/rock standards such as "Proud Mary," "Bad Moon Rising," "Looking Out My Back Door," "Travelin Band," "Who'll Stop The Rain," "Fortunate Son," "Green River," and many other songs whose words and music were written by John. In addition, he arranged the songs, produced the recordings, and even managed the band. Dismayed with their lack of control, the other band members grew disgruntled, and Tom Fogerty quit in 1971 to pursue a solo career. CCR recorded one more album and then disbanded in 1972. CCR entered the Rock and Roll Hall of Fame in 1993, but John opted not to play with his former band mates at the evening's festivities because of his resentment at Clifford and Cook for forming a mid-1990s touring version of CCR that capitalized on what Fogerty felt he had built. Tom Fogerty died of AIDS on September 6, 1990.

The twelve years that followed the break-up of CCR produced only a lukewarm solo project recorded in the midst of a bitter legal quagmire between Fogerty and Fantasy Records that limited the songwriter's ability to concentrate on his music. Fantasy ended up retaining ownership of Fogerty's CCR songs in exchange for his freedom from a long and binding album contract. This result caused him to withdraw from the music business until additional pending legal situations with the record company could be resolved. In 1984 Fogerty began recording what became a hugely successful comeback album, *Centerfield* (1985). The album's title song was inspired by Fogerty's passion for baseball and his memories of watching Willie Mays roam center field in Candlestick Park when he attended San Francisco Giant games in his youth. In a bizarre strategy, Fantasy Records, which now owned all of Fogerty's CCR songs, felt that one song from the album, " The Old Man Down the Road," sounded too much like a CCR hit titled, "Run Through the Jungle." Fantasy sued for the song's profits, making Fogerty the only person in music history to be litigated for plagiarizing his own music. To combat the plagiarizing charges, Fogerty toted a guitar to the witness stand in 1988 and demonstrated his songwriting process for the jury. Fantasy also felt that some of Fogerty's lyrics on the album slandered a top executive in the company, and the company took him to court on that charge as well. The courts finally ruled in favor of Fogerty on all counts in 1995.

Fogerty followed *Centerfield* with a less successful solo effort, *Eye of the Zombie* (1986), and then disappeared once again from the music mainstream.

In 1991 Fogerty married and started a family. Fogerty and his wife, Julie, have four children. This new role as a family man marked a recovery period of sorts for Fogerty. In addition, he was extensively exploring the back roads of the American South in search of the roots of his beloved blues and country music. He returned repeatedly to the Mississippi delta grave sites of some of the legendary blues men. It was there that he felt a musical resurrection. Furthermore, through the help of his wife, he was able to release years of anger over his lost music rights. He began recording the music for his album, *Blue Moon Swamp* (1997). The album represents five years' worth of labor; it is a combination of rock and country pop rooted in Fogerty's blues and country influences. One song, "Joy of My Life," is about his wife, the first standard "love song" that Fogerty has ever recorded. *Blue Moon Swamp* became an immediate success and won a Grammy Award for Best Rock Album of the Year. Instrumentally Fogerty padded his strong vocals and tasteful guitar work with some adept dobro styling. The dobro is an acoustic guitarlike instrument that rests across the lap of its player, who uses a smooth glass or metal bar to create a sliding quality in the notes. The dobro's sound is most often associated with old blues or traditional country music, and Fogerty's only other recording experience with the dobro was twenty-five years earlier on " Looking Out My Backdoor."

Another breakthrough for Fogerty was the release of *Premonition* (1998), a live album that was long awaited by his fans. Although his live performances are highly revered, there had never before been any legitimately released recordings of Fogerty in concert. *Premonition* contains eighteen songs, many of which are from the CCR days, marking the end of Fogerty's reluctance to perform any songs from that period. In 1997, Fogerty earned a Lifetime Achievement Award from the National Association of Songwriters. In the same year, the Orville Gibson Lifetime Achievement Awards honored him as an instrumentalist. He received a star on the Hollywood Walk of Fame in 1998. In 2002 Fogerty was enjoying this resurgence in his career by touring moderately and working on his next solo album with DreamWorks Records.

While not always comfortable with the role, Fogerty is blessed with an ability to write and perform songs that are not just hits, but standards. With his personal life in order and legal troubles off his mind, Fogerty appears poised to return as the classic American singer/songwriter.

SELECTIVE DISCOGRAPHY: *John Fogerty* (Asylum, 1975); *Centerfield* (Warner Bros., 1985); *Eye of the Zombie* (Warner Bros.,1986); *Blue Moon Swamp* (Warner Bros., 1997); *Premonition* (Reprise, 1998).

DONALD LOWE

BEN FOLDS

Born: Winston-Salem, North Carolina; 12 September 1966
Genre: Rock
Best-selling album since 1990: *Whatever and Ever Amen* (1997)

Hit songs since 1990: "Underground," "Brick," "Army"

Piano player Ben Folds surfaced in the mid-1990s with his trio, the curiously named Ben Folds Five. Folds, the group's singer and primary songwriter, backed by Darren Jesse on drums and Robert Sledge on bass, took the idea of a traditional trio and turned it on its head—a pop band with no guitar—with the group's energetic, humorous, self-titled debut on Caroline Records (1995). Their debut album found a home with college-aged Generation Xers, thanks largely to the song "Underground," a tongue-in-cheek skewering of youth culture, specifically nose rings and mosh pits.

Folds, whose initial dabbling with music came through drums and not piano, draws comparisons to Billy Joel, Elton John, and Todd Rundgren. Folds writes pop songs about being a geek, getting picked on growing up, and the pains of adolescence and relationships. Folds and his band were expert live entertainers who thrilled the audience with their dazzling improvisational skills and smart-aleck commentary. Folds often plunked away on the piano with his feet, his head, and other extremities.

Their self-titled debut was a welcome antidote to the guitar-oriented, grunge rock bands popular at the time. The follow-up, *Whatever and Ever Amen* (1997), was no sophomore slump; it went platinum just over a year after its release. A piano/pop masterpiece from start to finish, it runs the gamut sonically and thematically, including three-part vocal harmonies that recall both the British band Queen and the Doobie Brothers. Emotionally, it ranges from a raucous piano on the humorous but angry "Song for the Dumped" to the solemn, poignant "Brick," the unexpected successful single about a lover's abortion. *Whatever and Ever Amen* sets itself up immediately, with the thunderous playing of Folds on the leadoff track, "One Angry Dwarf and 200 Solemn Faces," a sarcasm-fueled, revenge fantasy on being the short guy in gym class who gets picked on. Folds sings, "Now I'm big and important / One angry dwarf and 200 solemn faces are you."

After the disappointing sales of their third release, *The Unauthorized Biography of Reinhold Messner* (1999), the group split up. Folds went solo, and his debut, *Rockin' the Suburbs* (2001), focused on the humility of growing older, perhaps as a result of remarrying for the third time and moving to Australia with his wife Frally Hynes and their twins. Replete with his signature piano bravado and song titles such as "Zak and Sara" and "Annie Waits," *Rockin' the Suburbs* is consistently upbeat. In the fall of 2002, after a year and a half long solo piano tour, Folds released a live album, *Ben Folds Live*.

SELECTIVE DISCOGRAPHY: *Rockin' the Suburbs* (Epic, 2001); *Ben Folds Live* (Epic, 2002). **With Ben Folds Five:** *Ben Folds Five* (Caroline Records, 1995); *Whatever and Ever Amen* (550 Music/Sony, 1997); *The Unauthorized Biography of Reinhold Messner* (550 Music/Sony 1999).

WEBSITE: www.benfolds.com.

CARRIE HAVRANEK

FOO FIGHTERS

Formed: Seattle, Washington, 1995

Members: David Grohl, guitar, vocals (born Warren, Ohio, 14 January 1969); Taylor Hawkins, drums (born El Paso, Texas, 17 February 1972); Nate Mendel, bass (born Seattle, Washington, 2 December 1968); Chris Shiflett, guitar (born Los Angeles, California, 6 May 1971). Former members: William Goldsmith, drums; Pat Smear, guitar (born Georg Ruthenberg, Los Angeles, California, c. 1960); Franz Stahl, guitar.

Genre: Rock

Best-selling album since 1990: *The Colour and the Shape* (1997)

Hit songs since 1990: "This Is a Call," "My Hero"

Although Dave Grohl never intended to have his home demo recordings released, the dissolution of Nirvana following the 1994 suicide of the group's leader, Kurt Cobain, offered the world's most famous drummer an opportunity to step out into the spotlight. The resulting string of power pop/rock albums from Grohl's band, the Foo Fighters, made Grohl a rock star all over again, proving to the world that Cobain had not been the only talented songwriter in Nirvana.

Grohl was raised near Washington, D.C., by a single mother and was steeped in the city's politically charged music scene via a record player he borrowed from the public school where his mother taught. A teenage member of local punk bands such as Dain Bramage and Freakbaby, the seventeen-year-old Grohl quit high school to tour Europe with the group Scream.

Following that band's breakup in 1990, Grohl was introduced to the members of Nirvana, joining the band in the fall of 1990 just as Nirvana prepared to record the album that made them the most lauded rock band of their generation, *Nevermind* (1991). Grohl provided backing vocals and a monster presence behind the drum kit during Nirvana's precipitous rise to fame.

Though Nirvana had been the artistic vision of Cobain, Grohl had been recording his own compositions for several years, working on his own songs during the long spells of enforced idleness resulting from Cobain's struggles with drugs. In 1995, Grohl needed only one week to record the self-titled debut album by his new band, Foo Fighters, with help from his friend Barrett Jones. The Foo Fighters—named after a 1940s-era slang term for flying saucers—were a band in name only, since Grohl sang and played all but a single guitar part on the album. The flying-saucer theme extended to Grohl's label imprint under Capitol Records, Roswell Records, an homage to the New Mexico site where aliens were purported to have crash-landed in 1947.

Foo Fighters is a daring debut from Grohl, harnessing the power and energy of Nirvana's most raucous rock songs while focusing on sunnier, more power pop-oriented music. Though the album bears some of the fuzzed-out power chords of Nirvana's grunge sound along with Grohl's aggressive, athletic drumming, tracks such as "This Is a Call" and "Big Me" are notable for Grohl's slightly hoarse but melodic singing and an occasional evocation of the music of the Beatles.

In order to tour in support of the album, Grohl put together a band that included his Nirvana band mate, guitarist Pat Smear, and two members of the disbanded Seattle group Sunny Day Real Estate, drummer William Goldsmith and bass player Nate Mendel. The group, with Grohl singing and playing lead guitar, undertook a sold-out spring 1995 tour with the former Minutemen member Mike Watt and Hovercraft, an ambient rock project led by the wife of Pearl Jam singer Eddie Vedder.

Fans could not help searching for meaning in the lyrics to songs such as "Alone + Easy Target" ("Tear at the seams / He don't feel so good / Don't feel bad / Not that he should") and "Exhausted" ("If it could be undone / Will it have costed? / It's taught and lost"), but Grohl insisted the words were nonsense. The album sold 1 million copies, and Grohl further demystified his image by appearing in a video for "Big Me," which spoofed the inanely cheery ads for breath mint Mentos.

Though *The Colour and the Shape* (1997) was the first Foo Fighters album recorded by the group, the lineup soon changed. Goldsmith left the band because of creative tensions during the sessions, forcing Grohl back behind the drum kit to finish the remaining rhythm tracks and to re-record many of Goldsmith's parts. Taylor Hawkins, a one-time drummer for Alanis Morissette, replaced Goldsmith after the album was completed, at which time Smear announced his resignation as well. Franz Stahl, a former band mate of Grohl's in Scream, replaced Smear.

The concept album about the death of a relationship coincided with the end of Grohl's marriage to his high school sweetheart. From the fragile ballad "Doll" ("You know in all of the time we've shared / I've never been so scared") to the blast-furnace punk pop of the album's break-out single, "Monkeywrench," *The Colour and the Shape* is a more emotionally engaging, diverse, and slick album. Grohl indulges in his love of the soft/loud musical dynamic made famous by Nirvana, in which the song's verses are calm but explode into furious strumming and singing on the choruses. But he is also unafraid to mix crooning with crunchy guitars on songs such as "Hey, Johnny Park!" and another one of the album's signature hits, the rock ballad "My Hero."

Stahl did not stick around long enough to record *There Is Nothing Left to Lose* (1999), a powerful, dark album that swings from Grohl's guttural screaming ("Stacked Actors"), to sunny crooning on the arena pop single "Learn to Fly." Chris Shiflett, previously a guitarist with No Use for a Name, joined the band after the album's release. During a promotional tour date in Europe, Hawkins was hospitalized in serious condition after what was termed "overindulgence" in substances.

Once healed, the group hit the studio to work on *One by One* (2002), their most cohesive album to date. Unsat-isfied with the songs halfway through, Grohl scrapped the entire album and began the sessions anew after a break. In between, Grohl played drums on an album by the Queens of the Stone Age, later touring the world with them as the group's drummer. *One by One*, the first Foo Fighters album with a returning band, blends the intensity of *The Colour and the Shape* with the clean, straight-ahead pop rock song craft of *There Is Nothing Left to Lose*. Grohl was able to indulge a childhood fantasy by inviting former Queen guitarist Brian May to play a ghostly guitar solo on the ballad "Tired of You."

Through endless personnel shifts and persistent comparisons to his former band, Nirvana, Dave Grohl steered the Foo Fighters through a series of finely crafted power pop albums as he laid to waste the trite jokes about the dim-wittedness of rock drummers. Grohl re-created himself and achieved a rare feat for a rock drummer: coming out from behind the kit and proving himself an adept songwriter and bandleader.

SELECTIVE DISCOGRAPHY: *Foo Fighters* (Roswell/Capitol, 1995); *The Colour and the Shape* (Roswell/ Capitol, 1997); *There Is Nothing Left to Lose* (Roswell/RCA, 1999); *One by One* (Roswell/RCA, 2002).

WEBSITE: foofighters.com.

GIL KAUFMAN

ARETHA FRANKLIN

Born: Memphis, Tennessee, 25 March 1942

Genre: R&B

Best-selling album since 1990: *A Rose Is Still a Rose* (1998)

Hit songs since 1990: "Willing to Forgive," "A Rose Is Still a Rose"

Rock critic Dave Marsh called Aretha Franklin "the greatest female singer of her generation." Revered as "the queen of soul," Franklin has left a deep imprint on popular music, influencing countless younger singers such as Whitney Houston and Mary J. Blige. More than her powerful, three-octave vocal range, sensitive piano playing, and legacy of excellent recordings, Franklin's great contribution lies in helping make rhythm and blues music a popular phenomenon. Her hits of the late 1960s, especially her 1967 signature song, "Respect," tapped into the social and political movements then shaping the nation's consciousness. "Respect" was more than just a great song; it was a summation of the entire era, becoming associated with African-American pride and women's rights. Franklin has also gained renown for her versatility and longevity: Unlike many of her musical peers, she went on making influential records throughout the 1980s and 1990s.

Born to the Rev. C. L. Franklin, a famed minister and recording artist, Franklin was raised in Detroit and immersed in gospel and rhythm and blues music from an early age. As a child she and her sisters Erma and Carolyn became featured performers at their father's New Bethel Baptist Church. By 1959 Franklin had made her first religious recordings for Chess Records and was touring the country as a gospel singer. At seventeen she was already leading a grown-up lifestyle, the single mother of two children.

John Hammond and Columbia

In 1960 Franklin came to the attention of the legendary producer and talent scout John Hammond, who signed her to Columbia Records with the intention of making her a jazz and blues singer. Some excellent work followed, although Columbia soon discarded Hammond's guidance in favor of a more pop-oriented approach. While some of Franklin's Columbia recordings suffer from over-arrangement, her vocals are often warm, full-bodied, and soulful. Hammond explained the situation best, claiming that "Columbia was a white company who misunderstood her genius."

Fame and Fortune at Atlantic

In 1966 Franklin left Columbia and signed with Atlantic Records, a pioneering company in the field of rhythm and blues music, and began recording the work for which she remains best known. Under the production leadership of Atlantic vice president Jerry Wexler, Franklin embarked upon a string of hits that made use of her gospel background and exemplary piano skills. These songs had a harder-edged sound than her Columbia recordings, epitomizing the style of music then becoming known as "soul." Soul evolved from the rock and R&B music of the 1950s, but it added a gospel flavor through vocal devices such as shouting and sermonizing. In addition to the aforementioned "Respect," hits such as "Think," "The House That Jack Built," and "See Saw" (all 1968) used Franklin's emotive singing and piano playing as their musical base. Wexler then added elements such as heavy percussion, darting horns, blues-based guitar playing, and female background vocals, all qualities distinctive to soul music. As Wexler put it, "My idea was to make good tracks, use the best players, put Aretha back on piano, and let the lady wail."

Franklin's hit-making period at Atlantic continued well into the 1970s with softer, more introspective songs such as "Day Dreaming" (1972) and "Until You Come Back to Me" (1973), but by the late 1970s her recorded performances were often listless and unconvincing. She seemed to have difficulty adapting her great talent to the changing trends in popular music.

The Change to Arista

Aware that she needed a change, Franklin ended her fourteen-year association with Atlantic and signed with Arista Records, where she developed a trendier, more pop-oriented approach. At Arista, Franklin climbed back to the top of the charts with bouncy, youth-oriented dance numbers such as "Jump to It" (1982) and "Freeway of Love" (1985).

By the turn of the 1990s, Franklin was widely acknowledged as a living legend. In 1987 she was the first woman inducted into the Rock and Roll Hall of Fame, and was chosen as a recipient of the prestigious Kennedy Center Honors in 1994. That year she moved into the realm of up-tempo dance, or "club," music with "A Deeper Love," a single from the *Sister Act 2* movie soundtrack that once again showcased her remarkable vocal range.

A heavy smoker for most of her life, Franklin gave up cigarettes in the early 1990s, and the change in her voice was noticeable. While she often sounded deep and hoarse during the late 1980s, on "A Deeper Love" her trademark high notes were back with piercing clarity. In 1995 Franklin was one of the highlights of the Kenneth "Babyface" Edmonds–produced soundtrack for the film *Waiting to Exhale*. Babyface, one of the hottest producers of the 1990s, wrote "It Hurts Like Hell" especially for her, and she invests the song with tenderness and depth. Often appearing sad and withdrawn in public interviews throughout her career, Franklin seemed to be singing from personal experience on lines like "Sometimes it hurts to even laugh / There's nothing funny if it's killing you." At times Franklin's voice opens up into glittering high notes, a reminder of how vital the fifty-three-year-old performer still sounded in 1995.

In 1998 Franklin released *A Rose Is Still a Rose,* her first album of all-new material in eight years. Always seeking to be a contemporary artist, Franklin chose to collaborate on the album with some of the hottest young performers of the late 1990s, including Lauryn Hill and Sean "Puffy" Combs. *Rolling Stone* called the album "a miraculous immersion in hip-hop gravity, flow and humor by one of pop music's greatest singers." The title song, penned by Hill, features empowering lyrics that draw upon Franklin's strength and life experience: "He can't lead you and then take you / Make you and then break you / Baby, girl, you hold the power." Other highlights include two fine ballads, "How Many Times" and "In the Morning," as well as the sassy, swaggering "I'll Dip." Taken as a whole, *A Rose Is Still a Rose* proved that Franklin at the turn of the millennium was still a force with which to be reckoned. In 1999 she published her eagerly anticipated autobiography, *From These Roots*. Fans hoping for serious insight into the reclusive star's life were disappointed; the book was mostly a glossed-over treatment of Franklin's complex personality.

During this period Franklin continued to broaden her musical horizons. At the 1998 Grammy Awards, she filled in for the ailing opera star Luciano Pavarotti by agreeing at the last minute to perform "Nessun dorma," Pavarotti's signature aria from the opera *Turandot*. Although Franklin had only eight minutes to rehearse, the audience response was so overwhelming that Pavarotti invited her to perform the aria with him as a duet at a later date. Because of a much-publicized fear of flying, Franklin was unable to accept Pavarotti's offer, but she did announce her intention to record an entire album of opera arias and enroll in classical piano courses at the prestigious Juilliard School of Music in New York. In 2001 Franklin was honored in a special *Divas Live* concert at New York's Radio City Music Hall, and performed for Queen Elizabeth of England at her Fiftieth Jubilee the following year. Although Franklin had planned to fly to the UK for the event, even enrolling in special flight simulation classes to conquer her fear, she eventually decided to perform her tribute in New York via videotape. In late 2002 she announced plans to retire from live performing after undertaking a final U.S. tour in 2003.

Aretha Franklin is one of the few performers legendary enough to be instantly recognized by her first name. For many "Aretha" is synonymous with "soul." She sings with honesty, power, and dedication, making listeners feel as if they are in private communion with her. Her music transcends boundaries of race, sex, and class, speaking to the universality of the human condition. As Franklin has said, "I sing to the realists; people who accept it like it is."

SELECTIVE DISCOGRAPHY: *Aretha* (Columbia, 1961); *I Never Loved a Man (The Way I Love You)* (Atlantic, 1967); *Lady Soul* (Atlantic, 1968); *Spirit in the Dark* (Atlantic, 1970); *Young, Gifted, and Black* (Atlantic, 1972); *Amazing Grace* (Atlantic, 1972); *Jump to It* (Arista, 1982); *Who's Zoomin' Who* (Arista, 1985); *A Rose Is Still a Rose* (Arista, 1998).

BIBLIOGRAPHY: A. Franklin, *From These Roots* (New York, 1999); J. Wexler, *Rhythm and the Blues* (New York, 1993); P. Guralnick, *Sweet Soul Music* (New York, 1986).

DAVID FREELAND

KIRK FRANKLIN

Born: Fort Worth, Texas, 23 January 1970

Genre: Gospel, R&B

Best-selling album since 1990: *Nu Nation Project* (1998)

Hit songs since 1990: "Why We Sing," "Lean on Me"

During the 1990s religious gospel music found increased acceptance within mainstream popular culture, a change spurred largely by the rise of Kirk Franklin. With the possible exception of singer Yolanda Adams, no young gospel artist in the 1990s could match Franklin's degree of commercial success. Franklin updated gospel music by incorporating flashy secular styles such as hip-hop and modern R&B. At the same time, he honored the gospel of the 1940s, 1950s, and 1960s—years known as "the Golden Age of Gospel"—through collaborations with renowned older artists such as Shirley Caesar. Although his attempts at modernization sometimes drew fire from those within the gospel community, Franklin proved that spiritual music could appeal to younger listeners while retaining its resonance and zest.

Abandoned by teenaged parents as a young child, Franklin was raised by his Aunt Gertrude. A devoutly religious woman, she encouraged Franklin's musical abilities within and outside of the Baptist church, at one point collecting aluminum cans so that he could take piano lessons. Franklin's prodigious musical skills were apparent when he began directing the choir at Mt. Rose Baptist Church near Dallas, Texas, at the age of eleven. In his teens he went through a rebellious period, getting expelled from school due to fighting and other behavioral problems. After a friend was shot and killed Franklin decided to reform by returning to the church. By age twenty-two he had assembled his own group, a seventeen-member choir he called "the Family."

Kirk's debut album, *Kirk Franklin & the Family* (1993), was a huge success, spending 100 weeks on the gospel charts and crossing over to become an R&B hit as well. Building on gospel's choir tradition, which achieved prominence in the 1960s with the work of visionary performers such as the late James Cleveland, Franklin arranges the songs using multiple voices singing in unison. The album's biggest hit, "Why We Sing," is structured upon this approach, with voices soaring together in an ode to the emotional release of vocalizing. The downside of the 1960s and 1970s choir movement in gospel, which largely supplanted the popularity of smaller vocal quartets, was that individual voices often got lost in the wash of sound. Franklin anticipates this problem by pulling voices out of the choir for extended solos. "Silver and Gold" and "Call on the Lord," in particular, boast strong female leads that capture the fire and passion of the finest gospel music. Critics note Franklin himself is merely an average singer, but, like Cleveland, he uses his voice to good advantage, exhorting his soloists with the frequently interjected, "Hallelujah" and "C'mon." Several of the tracks spotlight the tough, heavy beats of 1990s hip-hop. Franklin's passion and commitment—qualities inherent within the divine purpose of gospel—give the album a vitality often lacking in the work of his secular hip-hop contemporaries.

Continuing to broaden the appeal of his music, Franklin contracted stars such as hip-hop queen Mary J. Blige and rock singer Bono for his 1998 album, *The Nu Nation Project*. On the album's rousing hit single, which features cameos from Blige and Bono, Franklin opens with a spoken passage that addresses issues such as AIDS and homelessness. The sermon, delivered without heavy-handedness or judgment, underscores gospel's historic commitment to social causes such as civil rights. "Revolution" is a tough hip-hop collaboration with hot R&B producer Rodney Jerkins, while "Riverside" sports a heavy beat that recalls 1970s funk music. Addressing his critics within the gospel community, Franklin allows himself a rare moment of bitterness on "The Verdict." Conceived as a mock courtroom drama, the track besets Franklin with a list of spoken "charges." "Charge number two: making gospel music too secular." Franklin makes a more compelling case when he rebuffs critics through the power of his music, such as on the joyous "My Desire." Here, he proves that gospel can be universal in appeal without losing its message of salvation and redemption. As Franklin noted in a 2000 interview with television network CNN, "I preach Christ . . . in the spirit of love, not in a spirit of hate, for whoever wants to listen—black, white, Jew, or Gentile."

After three years away from the recording spotlight, Franklin returned with *The Rebirth of Kirk Franklin* in 2002. A rewarding blend of traditional and contemporary elements, the album contains a church-wrecking lead vocal by gospel legend Shirley Caesar on "Caught Up." A fiery belter possessing the showmanship of the flamboyant gospel tradition, Caesar breaks the song down and repeats the title in an improvised, exhortatory style known as "testifying." Franklin wisely keeps his own vocal on the track to a minimum, stepping back to let this great performer take control. The album, acknowledging the new while honoring the potency of what has come before, sums up Franklin's invigorating, respectful approach to gospel.

The first performer to successfully merge hip-hop with traditional religious music, Kirk Franklin deserves credit for making gospel accessible to a young audience. While his music often bears the slick surface of modern R&B, the emotion and feeling he imparts have more in common with the passionate gospel of the past. In his work Franklin honors the richness of his heritage while carving a path for gospel in the twenty-first century.

SELECTIVE DISCOGRAPHY: *Kirk Franklin & the Family* (Sparrow, 1993); *Kirk Franklin & the Family Christmas* (Interscope, 1995); *Whatcha Lookin' 4* (GospoCentric, 1995); *God's Property* (B-Rite/Interscope, 1997); *The Nu Nation Project* (Interscope, 1998); *The Rebirth of Kirk Franklin* (GospoCentric, 2002).

WEBSITE: www.nunation.com.

DAVID FREELAND

BILL FRISELL

Born: Baltimore, Maryland, 18 March 1951

Genre: Jazz

Best-selling album since 1990: *Nashville* (1996)

Electric guitarist Bill Frisell has created a broad and personal oeuvre melding aspects of jazz, folk, rock, country, free improvisation, and classical composition, employing sophisticated guitar technique and his reflective personality. Influenced during his teens by 1960s Motown, psychedelia, jazz guitarist Wes Montgomery, and Chicago blues, Frisell has gradually incorporated his experiences of the eclectic New York avant-garde ("downtown") scene with more mainstream modern jazz styles into a music that evokes cultural clashes and mythic U.S. landscapes like the lonesome prairie and the great plains. Although he is naturally shy, Frisell has worked boldly as both leader and sideman with some of the most intense and experimental instrumentalists to arise since the 1980s. In the 1990s he focused his energy on extended ensembles addressing his ambitious but accessible compositions. Whether performing solo, in the trio headed by drummer Paul Motian (featuring saxophonist Joe Lovano), or in front of one of his own bands, Frisell retains a distinctive lyricism.

Frisell studied clarinet while growing up in Denver, Colorado; his father played string bass and tuba, and the family had a piano and Hammond organ. In his early teens he picked up the guitar "for fun" and joined his high school classmates to play dance hits at parties. He entered a purist phase while attending Berklee College of Music in Boston and took private lessons with guitarist Jim Hall, who made him practice Bach violin sonatas. Frisell returned to Denver; subbed in a Los Angeles nightclub show band; returned to Berklee; lived in Belgium for a year, during which he met his wife (who is from a musical family); and recorded with German bassist Eberhard Weber, a stint that led to his debut recording on the ECM label.

Settling in New York City in 1979, Frisell joined a circle of genre-defying musicians anchored by composer/reeds player John Zorn and keyboardist Wayne Horvitz. He remained personally and professionally close with Horvitz after both moved their families to the Seattle area in 1989. While in New York, Frisell was celebrated for the aching, poetic quality of his improvisations, his long, deliberate phrases, and his reverberant sustained notes. Frisell typically juxtaposed such sounds with the explosive use of wildly dissonant electronic effects, and he continues to employ surprising, sometimes extreme shifts of texture and mood in his improvisations. However, his written repertoire, as introduced in the early 1980s by the Bill Frisell Band (with cellist Hank Roberts, electric bassist Kermit Driscoll, and drummer Joey Baron), emphasizes thoughtful melodicism with idiosyncratic twists comparable to but not imitative of those of singular jazz pianist Thelonious Monk.

Frisell established his career trajectory in the 1980s. By mid-decade he was signed to the prestigious Elektra/Nonesuch label, and his coterie of collaborators expanded to include provocative clarinetist Don Byron, producer Hal Willner, and pop-rockers such as guitarist Ry Cooder, bassist/songwriter Nick Lowe, singers Marianne Faithfull and Elvis Costello, and drummers Ginger Baker and Jim Keltner. He continues to work with jazz-associated musicians; since the 1990s, he has performed and/or recorded with bassists Charlie Haden, Dave Holland, Melvin Gibbs, and Marc Johnson (in the quartet Bass Desires, with guitarist John Scofield); and with drummers Ronald Shannon Jackson and Elvin Jones. In the contemporary classical realm Frisell has performed Steve Mackey's "Deal" at Carnegie Hall with the American Composers Orchestra conducted by Dennis Russell Davies. He has also performed in Los Angeles with members of the Los Angeles Philharmonic conducted by Esa-Pekka Salonen.

Frisell wrote an original score for the silent films of the comic Buster Keaton, and his music is heard in films by directors Gus van Sant and Wim Wenders, among others. He has appeared on the TV programs *Night Music*, *The Tonight Show with Jay Leno*, and *Sessions at West 54th Street*. He has formed creative relationships with a new coterie of Pacific Northwest-based musicians and artists, including violin prodigy Eyvind Kang, painter Claude Utley, and cartoonists Jim Woodring and Gary Larson. His albums are sometimes thematic; in 2003, on *The Intercontinentals*, Frisell reached beyond borders to form a band including Brazilian composer/singer/multi-instrumentalist Vinicius Cantuária, Greek-Macedonian oud and bouzouki player Christos Govetas, Malian guitarist Boubacar Traore, and percussionist Sidiki Camara.

SELECTIVE DISCOGRAPHY: *Where in the World* (Elektra, 1991); *Live* (Gramavision, 1991); *Have a*

Little Faith (Elektra/Nonesuch, 1992); *This Land* (Elektra, 1994); *Go West: Music for the Films of Buston Keaton* (Elektra/Nonesuch, 1995); *Nashville* (Elektra/Nonesuch, 1996); *Bill Frisell Quartet* (Nonesuch, 1996); *Gone, Just Like a Train* (Nonesuch, 1997); *Good Dog, Happy Man* (Nonesuch, 1999); *Ghost Town* (Nonesuch, 2000); *Blues Dream* (Elektra/Asylum, 2001). *With Dave Holland and Elvin Jones* (Elektra/Asylum, 2001); *The Intercontinentals* (Nonesuch, 2003). **With Paul Motian Trio:** *Motian in Tokyo* (JMT, 1991); *Trioism* (JMT, 1993); *Fred Hersch, Songs We Know* (Nonesuch, 1998); *Don Byron, Tuskegee Experiments* (Elektra/Musician, 1990); *John Scofield, Grace under Pressure* (Blue Note, 1991); *Jerry Granelli, A Song I Thought I Heard Buddy Sing* (ITM Pacific, 1992).

WEBSITE: www.songtone.com/artists/frisell_link.htm.

HOWARD MANDEL

FUEL

Formed: 1993, Harrisburg, Pennsylvania

Members: Kevin Miller, drums (born Allentown, Pennsylvania, 6 September 1962); Carl Bell, guitar (born Kenton, Tennessee, 9 January 1967); Jeff Abercrombie, bass (born Kenton, Tennessee, 8 January 1969); Brett Scallions, guitar, vocals (born Brownsville, Tennessee, 21 December 1971). Former members: Jody Abbott, drums; Erik Avakian, keyboards.

Genre: Rock

Best-selling album since 1990: *Something Like Human* (2000)

Hit songs since 1990: "Shimmer," "Bittersweet," "Hemorrhage (in My Hands)"

Fuel started out as an irreverent punk-influenced band but gradually added textured alt-rock to its repertoire. By the early 2000s the band had perfected its two sides: the melodic balladry that helped it gain airplay and the hard-rock shouts that made it a formidable live act.

Abercrombie, the main songwriter Bell, and Scallions got together in 1993 in Tennessee but relocated to the more favorable rock climes of Harrisburg, Pennsylvania, 170 miles west of New York. The following year the group released its self-titled debut and began to gain local attention.

The EP *Porcelain* (1996) contains a bouncy but pointed Green Day-like vibe. "Nothing" features two-part vocal harmonies and Scallions's irreverent vocals. But the album's biggest hit was the philosophical, mid-tempo "Shimmer," with its wistful hook: "I've found all that shimmers in this world is sure to fade." The song received regional airplay and helped the band get major-label attention.

Sony 550 released the EP *Hazleton* in 1997; all four tracks except "King for a Day" reappeared on full-length *Sunburn* (1998), which also contains the *Porcelain* track "Shimmer," the group's first single. The two-year hiatus had not sapped the appeal of that song, and it made number two on *Billboard*'s Modern Rock Tracks chart. The second single, "Bittersweet," shows the band's raw, hard-rock side. Scallions shouts the abstract lyrics about ambivalence in the face of decadence as Bell fuses R&B chords with crunching rock guitar. Producer Steve Haigler, whose credits include a bevy of B-level alternative bands, helps maintain a live, no-frills feel. On the harrowing third single, "Jesus or a Gun," Scallions expresses a harrowing desperation: "Tell me now, who's my saving one / Jesus or a gun," he yells over an aggressive guitar riff. The themes of frustration, the band later revealed, had come from their years of laboring in obscurity. With the success of *Sunburn*, those earlier career disappointments began to fade. Nevertheless, critics wondered, would fame dull Bell's tormented muse?

Fuel devoted 1999 to touring and breaking in their new drummer, Kevin Miller. For *Something Like Human* (2000), the band adopts a more polished sound under the supervision of producer Ben Grosse, whose credits include the B-52s, Filter, and Ben Folds. With his help the group sprinkles atmospheric samples and drum loops into the mix. The single "Hemorrhage (in My Hands)" made the hard rockers Top 40 darlings in late 2000; it was also their first number one hit on *Billboard*'s Modern Rock Tracks chart. A melodic, minor-key tune that starts out with acoustic guitar and explodes into full-bore angst, the hit erased the inevitable "sophomore slump" worries. Scallions's slightly twangy, masculine baritone ranges from vulnerable to seething. After keeping a low profile in 2002, Fuel returned to alt-rock play lists in 2003 with "Won't Back Down" from the *Daredevil* soundtrack.

Fuel's rise demonstrated the importance of strong songwriting and a versatile vocalist who could please the punks, the metal heads, and the alt-rock fans in the fragmented rock scene of the 2000s.

SELECTIVE DISCOGRAPHY: *Hazleton* (Epic, 1997); *Sunburn* (Sony, 1998); *Something Like Human* (Epic, 2000).

RAMIRO BURR

FUGAZI

Formed: 1987, Washington, D.C.

Members: Brendan Canty, drums (born Teaneck, New Jersey, 9 March 1966); Joe Lally, bass (born Rockville, Mary-

land, 3 December 1963); Ian MacKaye, vocals, guitar (born Washington, D.C., 16 April 1962); Guy Picciotto, vocals, guitar (born Washington, D.C., 17 December 1965).

Genre: Rock

Best-selling album since 1990: *Repeater* (1990)

Hit songs since 1990: "Waiting Room"

Fugazi bears the gold standard for American independent rock. Its members operate the record label Dischord, offer low prices on albums and concert tickets, and push themselves to make honest and uncompromising music. Their strident anti-sellout stance tends to overshadow their music, which offers a bracing mix of hardcore punk and fearless experimentation. Notwithstanding their politics or allegiances, Fugazi has produced some of the most enthralling music of the postpunk era.

Hardcore Roots

Fugazi took root in two bands from the hardcore punk scene in Washington, D.C., in the 1980s. Hardcore stripped the punk-rock style down to stark anger and aggression, fostering an intense and speedy sound that inspired the politically minded D.C. bands. Ian MacKaye founded Dischord Records in 1980 as a means to distribute work from his band Minor Threat, whose sonically extreme songs preached social and personal awareness. Guy Picciotto fronted Rites of Spring, which married the searing guitars of hardcore rock to more personal songwriting, and thereby established the punk subgenre called emocore. MacKaye recruited drummer Brendan Canty and bassist Joe Lally to form Fugazi in 1987. Picciotto joined the following year. The interplay of MacKaye and Picciotto defined the Fugazi aesthetic: social and personal exploration heightened by angular guitar work. Unlike most hardcore, Fugazi sounded aggressive, but not for the sake of venting testosterone-fueled anger; in fact, the early single "Suggestion" railed against male sexism. Fugazi approached song structures and lyrical themes from a more open perspective than that of the restrictive and insular hardcore scene.

Soon after forming, the band released the EPs *Fugazi* (1988) and *Margin Walker* (1989) to considerable acclaim. (The EPs were later collected on one album as *Thirteen Songs* [1990].) Critics praised the artful take on the hardcore sound, most fully realized by the wildly shifting rhythms of "Waiting Room" and "Suggestion." Canty and Lally provide lockstep backup for MacKaye and Picciotto's anthems, and the songs pulse with blood and fire. The band followed these instantly legendary singles with the full-length album *Repeater* (1990). This recording continues in the tone of the group's first singles, with propulsive

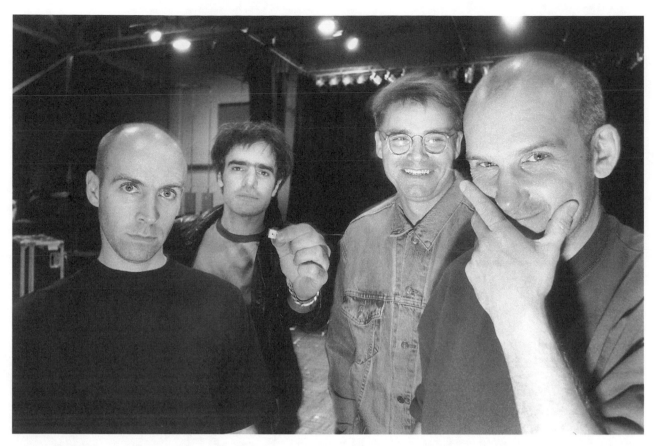

Fugazi. L-R: Joe Lally, Guy Picciotto, Brendan Canty, Ian MacKaye [SHAWN SCALLEN/DISCHORD RECORDS]

rhythms driving political screeds such as "Styrofoam" and "Sieve-Fisted Find." Considered a classic of D.C. hard-core, *Repeater* is Fugazi's most didactic moment, and the clumsy earnestness of lines like "We owe you nothing! / You have no control!" tends to grate. Still, the jittery release of "Repeater" and the contemplative, strangely beautiful closing track "Shut the Door" round out its rough edges.

The band ventured farther away from hardcore with their next album, *Steady Diet of Nothing* (1991). Here, the songwriters stretch out into abstract territory, toning down the political grandstanding of *Repeater* and freeing their guitars from the rigid rhythmical structures of their pre-vious work. The result is dark and textured. "Latin Roots" and "Nice New Outfit" benefit from a combination of wiry noise and reggae-inflected beats. The cerebral *Steady Diet of Nothing* is a visceral album that finds new ways to cre-ate physical, demanding sounds.

Populism and Experimentation

During the tour for *Steady Diet of Nothing*, Fugazi attracted attention from the mainstream media. Press sto-ries focused on their ideological quirks, such as their five-dollar concert tickets and antimoshing stance at the height

of grunge (this stemming more out of concern for the safety of fans than disdain for trend). Concern for their audience, along with a refusal to give interviews to corporate media outlets, kick-started the spread of several Fugazi urban myths that threatened to obscure their music. The most common stories involved the band living in an ascetic commune, subsisting solely on rice. By trying to cultivate equality with their fans, the band found themselves at the center of a legend that made them out to be humorless elitists.

In 1993 Fugazi issued their most vitriolic work, the blis-tering *In on the Killtaker*. Here Fugazi balances intensity and introspection, with a clarity of expression that sets a new standard for postpunk. "Public Witness Program" surges from an anxious march to a cathartic chorus, and the tense Hollywood diatribe "Cassavetes" fuses grinding guitar noise with a supremely catchy verse. Their prowess of noise dynamics complete, the band attacks pulse-pounding anthems like "Smallpox Champion" and "Facet Squared" with maximum authority. The introspective "Last Chance for a Slow Dance" closes the album on a tender note.

Red Medicine (1995) continued the artistic strides of *In on the Killtaker* with a fuller, less dissonant sound. The singers take center stage on this album, delivering lyrics

Spot Light | Instrument

Instrument (1998) is not a documentary about Fugazi; rather, it is a compilation of visual material filmed over the band's first ten years by the noted underground filmmaker and photographer Jem Cohen. This approach allows the director to blend a wide array of sounds and images into a hectic collage of interviews, concert footage, and arresting visuals. For all its scattershot imagery, the film achieves a wholeness and fluidity that evoke Fugazi's arty post-punk aesthetic, thereby providing a dynamic insight into their work. Although the focus of *Instrument* is the music, there are a few scenes that debunk the many myths surrounding the band. In one fascinating sequence Ian MacKaye stops a concert midsong because of the wild flailing of a fan in the front row. MacKaye invites the offender onstage, asks him to apologize to the people he recklessly hit, and then escorts him out of the venue. The message is that Fugazi is not antifun or antidancing but antiviolence and will not tolerate one fan ruining the night of another. Cohen also edits in footage of a music channel interview with a visibly uncomfortable MacKaye, which culminates in MacKaye's statement that Fugazi's seemingly austere methods of operation are simply "about being a band," not a complex public image strategy. *Instrument* is the cinematic equivalent of that statement, a stripped-to-the-essentials portrait of a uniquely demanding and unrelenting band.

with rhythmic and bright inventiveness. Only Fugazi could make a hummable chorus out of "Lockheed, Lockheed / Martin Marietta!" as on "Do You Like Me." The falsetto warble of "Fell, Destroyed" turns into a snaky vamp. *Red Medicine* is a portrait of the band at its most confident. Bashing out invigorating anthems ("Bed for the Scraping") as well as industrial soundscapes ("Version"), the album displays verve and intelligence.

The band soon slowed their breakneck pace of recording and touring, and took three years before the release of *End Hits* (1998), a disjointed, overtly jammy, and experimental album. Talk of a breakup circulated, but the group refuted the rumors with a handful of concert dates. The following year they released the soundtrack for *Instrument*, a documentary that showed their playful side. The accompanying album is a choppy collection of outtakes and live tracks; it displays both musical prowess and a sense of humor.

After another layoff the band bounced back with their most focused work in years, *The Argument* (2001). The album avoids meandering for tight songcraft and expressive melodies. The gut-wrenching surge of "Epic Problem" and the clenched anger of "Full Disclosure" sound like classic Fugazi, but the biggest surprises are the strange twists taken by the soulful "Life and Limb" and the vivid corporate revenge fantasy "Oh." "Argument" builds from a hazy verse to a bright-eyed coda, providing a fine summation to the album's range of styles. *The Argument* mines new terrain with a defiant spirit and hunger.

Fugazi's commitment to the punk do-it-yourself aesthetic is done as much out of practicality as politics—it gives them the freedom to produce their own kind of music. They do not serve a corporate bottom line or retool their image to attract press coverage. In an era of U.S. television programming devoted to the glamour of financial success, this integrity is refreshing.

SELECTIVE DISCOGRAPHY: *Fugazi* (EP) (Dischord, 1988); *Margin Walker* (EP) (Dischord, 1989); *Thirteen Songs* (Dischord, 1990); *Repeater* (Dischord, 1990); *Three Songs* (Dischord, 1990); *Steady Diet of Nothing* (Dischord, 1991); *In on the Killtaker* (Dischord, 1993); *Red Medicine* (Dischord, 1995); *End Hits* (Dischord, 1998); *Instrument* (Dischord, 1999); *The Argument* (Dischord, 2001); *Furniture* (EP) (Dischord, 2001).

SEAN CAMERON

THE FUGEES

Formed: 1992, East Orange, New Jersey

Members: Lauryn Hill, vocals (born South Orange, New Jersey, 25 May 1975); Nelust Wyclef "Clef" Jean, guitar, vocals (born Haiti, 17 October 1972); Prakazrel "Pras" Michel, vocals (born Haiti, 19 October 1972).

Genre: R&B, Hip-Hop

Best-selling album since 1990: *The Score* (1996)

Hit songs since 1990: "Killing Me Softly with His Song"

The Fugees are best known for *The Score* (1996), an album that widened the scope of hip-hop with its fusion of soul, reggae, and Caribbean music. It became the rare hip-hop crossover album, selling more than 8 million copies. Although the album proved to be the group's farewell, it launched the successful solo careers of all three of its members, who continued to follow that album's eclectic blueprint.

Both the sons of preachers, cousins Wyclef Jean and Prakazrel Michel were born in Haiti and raised in Newark, New Jersey, during their teenage years. They met Lauryn Hill during her freshman year of high school. Soon all three christened themselves the Tranzlator Crew, and a local producer helped get them a record deal and release their first album, *Blunted on Reality*. After getting postponed for two years, it saw the light of day in 1994 under the changed band name the Fugees (short for refugees).

The group found itself in limbo after the largely overproduced record failed to make a dent on radio. In the meantime, the group found a new producer and released two singles, "Nappy Heads" and "Vocab." Both remixes became hits on the dance-club circuit. Hill's silky vocals were placed front and center, and buttery horn arrangements harked back to soul music of the late 1960s and early 1970s.

The new direction paved the way for *The Score* (1996), today widely considered the essential Fugees album. By this time Jean and Michel were fully invested in the social consciousness inculcated by their upbringing in the church, and they had adopted the rebel attitude of Jamaican reggae star Bob Marley, whose classic "No Woman, No Cry" they covered. *The Score* became a defining alternative to modern-day hip-hop because it incorporated live instruments and not just programmed samples. It also questioned the use of violent imagery during a time when gangsta rap thrived on stories of gory street violence. ("Another MC loses life tonight, lord / I beg that you pray to Jesus Christ," Jean sang on the song "Zealots.") The music introduced a fresh voice with its sim-plicity, playfulness, and musical embrace of several styles, including soul and reggae. The album's biggest hit, a cover of "Killing Me Softly with His Song," a big hit in 1973 for R&B singer Roberta Flack, crossed over to the pop charts, reaching number one.

The Score won Grammys for best rap album of the year and best R&B performance by a duo or group, and it made the Fugees international stars. The group embraced its Haitian roots by performing a benefit concert for the country's poor before 75,000 people in Port-au-Prince, Haiti, in 1997.

Soon after, the Fugees splintered. They reunited only through cameos on one another's solo projects. Jean was the first to go solo, releasing *The Carnival* (1997) a year after *The Score*. His solo work best fulfilled the eclecticism forged by his old group. He embraced divergent styles from classic rock to country, covering songs by Pink Floyd, the British art rock group, and collaborating with Kenny Rogers, the country singer. In 1998 Michel released his solo debut, *Ghetto Supastar*, under the name Pras, and he enjoyed a Top 40 hit with the title song that summer. Hill became the most commercially successful Fugee. Her solo debut, *The Miseducation of Lauryn Hill* (1998), won five Grammys, including Album of the Year in 1998.

The Fugees never officially announced a breakup, and in the press all three continually discussed the desire to get back together. In the meantime, individually they continued to forge an alternative to hip-hop through music that defies conventional categorization.

SELECTIVE DISCOGRAPHY: *Blunted on Reality* (Columbia/Ruffhouse, 1994); *The Score* (Columbia/Ruffhouse, 1996).

MARK GUARINO

JUAN GABRIEL

Born: Alberto Aguilera Valadez; Parácuaro, Michoacán, Mexico, 7 January 1950
Genre: Latin
Best-selling album since 1990: *Juntos Otra Vez* (1997)
Hit songs since 1990: "Pero Que Necesidad," "Canción 187," "Abrázame Muy Fuerte"

The Mexican chapter of the American Society of Composers, Authors, and Publishers (ASCAP) lists Juan Gabriel as its number one royalties generator. His sentimental, direct lyrics and his marriage of Mexican folk rhythms to pop melodies have made his music legendary and ubiquitous throughout Latin America. His Mexican folkloric songs like "Querida," "Amor Eterno," and "Hasta Que Te Conocí" have become part of the ranchera canon, considered standards by mariachis everywhere.

His parents, Gabriel Aguilera Rodriguez and Victoria Valadez Rojas, were peasants and struggled to support Alberto's nine older siblings. As a young teenager, he lived in the Mexican border city of Juarez, selling tortillas downtown with his sister.

Moving to Mexico City in the late 1960s, he tried to secure a recording contract, but success escaped him until 1971, when Queta "La Prieta Linda" Jimenez introduced him to officials at RCA and recorded his song "Noche a Noche." In late 1971 he recorded his first pop ballad hit "No Tengo Dinero."

Gabriel began writing songs for the Spanish pop/ranchera singer Rocio Durcal, a collaboration that lasted for years. By the early 1980s Gabriel had gained major momentum, expanding his music to include mariachi and disco songs for the label Ariola Discos and scoring ever-bigger hits, including "Costumbres" and "Querida." But it was not all good news. Juan Gabriel was seriously shaken when his mother Victoria died in 1988. He wrote the ode "Amor Eterno" as a tribute to her. The song became another monster hit and was covered by more than a dozen top artists, including Durcal, Ana Gabriel (no relation), and Vicente Fernández.

A dispute with his record company prevented him from releasing any studio albums in the late 1980s and early 1990s. In the interim, however, he reached the pinnacle of his career with the double CD *En Concierto en El Palacio de Bellas Artes* (1990). Hailed critically, the concerts feature backing by the seventy-piece Mexican Symphonic Orchestra, a top-notch mariachi. Juan Gabriel is in impeccable shape. His inspired interpretation of "Querida" elevates the song into a form of worship. On "Amor Eterno," Gabriel plumbs new emotional depths in a song about a dear one gone but not forgotten.

In 1994 Gabriel released his comeback studio album, the synth-driven *Gracias por Esperar,* featuring an uncharacteristic but uplifting first single, the gospel-tinged "Pero Que Necesidad." Gabriel produced an album in 1997 with Durcal, appropriately titled *Juntos Otra Vez* (Together Again). The title track, a duet, got solid airplay.

While a bevy of regional Mexican and Latin pop artists have covered his songs or recorded tribute albums, Gabriel has remained creatively vibrant—witness the orchestral title song to his 2001 album, *Abrázame Muy Fuerte,* which hit number one on *Billboard*'s Hot Latin Tracks. He also performed a duet with the talented young ranchera-pop singer Nydia Rojas on her 2001 CD *Nydia,* which consists entirely of Gabriel songs.

Although his exuberant, sometimes mannered persona makes him an unlikely star in a nation that exalts its singing *charros* (cowboys), Juan Gabriel's direct, poetic lyrics and ingratiating melodies have launched a million serenades in his romantic country.

SELECTIVE DISCOGRAPHY: *Siempre Estoy Pensando en Tí* (RCA, 1978); *Lo Mejor de Juan Gabriel con Mariachi* (RCA, 1983); *Debo Hacerlo* (RCA, 1988); *Gracias Por Esperar* (BMG, 1994); *El México Que Se Nos Fue* (BMG, 1995); *Juntos Otra Vez* (BMG, 1997); *Todo Está Bien* (BMG, 1999); *Abrázame Muy Fuerte* (BMG, 2000).

RAMIRO BURR

PETER GABRIEL

Born: Woking, Surrey, England, 13 February 1950
Genre: Rock
Best-selling album since 1990: *Us* (1992)
Hit songs since 1990: "Steam," "Digging in the Dirt"

One of the most adventurous and provocative artists in modern rock music, Peter Gabriel has been pushing lyrical, thematic, and technological boundaries since the mid-1970s, when he gave up lead vocal duties in the rock band Genesis to pursue a solo career. By the early 1980s Gabriel had developed an ardent cult following, although widespread fame did not arrive until 1986, when his album *So* became a multiplatinum best-seller on the basis of the hit "Sledgehammer." Known for his meticulous attention to detail and bouts with creative block and depression, Gabriel spaces his albums years—even decades—apart. His lyrics are notable for their dark themes, wry humor, raw sexual energy, and a mistrust and horror of modernity. This focus has also informed his personal crusades; among rock artists, he has become an outspoken and dedicated activist on behalf of human rights. Paradoxically, Gabriel's highly conceptual work revels in the technological possibilities offered by the modern studio.

At the age of fifteen, while attending the Charterhouse School in England, Gabriel formed Genesis with his classmates Tony Banks, Michael Rutherford, and Anthony Phillips. Initially recording in a style similar to 1960s pop group the Moody Blues, Genesis gradually sharpened its sound after the addition of drummer Phil Collins in 1970. At the same time Gabriel added theatrical ele-

ments such as masks and props to the group's live performances. In 1975 he left Genesis and two years later released *Peter Gabriel,* the first of three self-titled albums. The third *Peter Gabriel,* released in 1980, is often viewed by critics as his best album, featuring "Biko," a song eulogizing murdered anti-Apartheid poet and activist Steve Biko. The song, incorporating traditional South African funeral music, represented one of the first ventures into the pan-cultural "world music" that became popular in the 1980s. An angry statement against the racism and brutality of Apartheid, "Biko" led to the banning in South Africa of Gabriel's entire catalog. Although "Shock the Monkey" (1982) provided him with a minor hit, the album *So* (1986) made Gabriel an international star. His most upbeat and accessible album, *So* features the R&B-inspired hit "Sledgehammer," packed with sexual allusions, and ballad hits such as the inspirational "Don't Give Up," recorded with the rock performer Kate Bush.

Although he scored the music for the controversial 1988 film *The Last Temptation of Christ,* Gabriel did not release a follow-up album to *So* until 1992, when *Us* appeared. In the intervening years, Gabriel had endured a troublesome divorce and bouts of severe depression—experiences that influence the dark themes explored on *Us.* As evidence of Gabriel's fascination with world music, "Come & Talk to Me" features sonic elements as diverse as bagpipes and African chants. The simmering rhythms of "Love to Be Loved" underscore themes of sadness and loss: "Let it pass, let it go, let it leave / From the deepest place I grieve." "Steam," similar in sound and feel to "Sledgehammer," employs swaggering, R&B-style horns and an insinuating, recurrent guitar lick. One of the album's most moving cuts is the understated "Washing of the Water," driven by a quiet, gentle piano. Gabriel's lyrics, delivered in his hoarse, textured voice, emphasize cleansing and release: "I need something to turn myself around." Unlike his fellow progressive rock artist and world-music proponent David Byrne, who often distances himself emotionally from his material, Gabriel uses the medium of recording to cut to the core of his pain.

During the years following the release of *Us,* Gabriel became involved with various side projects, most notably, the development of a record label devoted to world music. He also spent considerable time in seclusion in the English countryside. As a result fans were forced to wait a long time—ten years—for his next album, *Up* (2002). A typically dense, challenging effort, the album revels in multiple layers of sound and the juxtaposition of contrasting moods, a result of the long, arduous studio hours Gabriel put into its creation. The album's opener, "Darkness," alternates soft, string-laden passages with jarring, slashing bursts of electric guitar, whereas "Growing Up" begins with a somber violin and synthesized piano and then adds varying sonic elements—vocals, light drums. Gabriel augments the song's rhythm with the kind of insistent electronic beat associated with dance or "club" music. Inaccessible and mysterious, *Up* repositions Gabriel as one of rock's most uncompromising artists.

Accorded complete artistic freedom by his record company, Geffen, Peter Gabriel has released albums only sporadically, often spending years in honing and sculpting them. Known for his dark themes and creative boldness, Gabriel has created his own unique place within modern rock music.

SELECTIVE DISCOGRAPHY: *Peter Gabriel [1]* (Atco, 1977); *Peter Gabriel [3]* (Mercury, 1980); *So* (Geffen, 1986); *Passion* (Geffen, 1989); *Us* (Geffen, 1992); *Long Walk Home: Music from the Rabbit-Proof Fence* (EMI, 2002); *Up* (Geffen, 2002).

BIBLIOGRAPHY: S. Bright, *Peter Gabriel: An Authorized Biography* (London, 1988).

WEBSITE: www.petergabriel.com.

DAVID FREELAND

JAMES GALWAY

Born: Belfast, Northern Ireland, 8 December 1939
Genre: Classical

James Galway is second only to Jean-Pierre Rampal as popularizer of the flute in the twentieth century; in the 1990s no flutist was better known than Galway. With impeccable classical credentials, he has ventured frequently into popular idioms with a musical flair and personal charm that have made him an international music celebrity on an instrument that supports few full-time soloists.

Galway started out playing the penny whistle as a small child before taking up the flute. At the age of ten, he won all three classes of the Irish Flute Championships, which got him a radio session on the BBC. After studies at the Royal College of Music, the Guildhall School of Music and Drama in London, and the Paris Conservatory, he won jobs in the orchestras of Sadlers Wells Opera and the Royal Opera Covent Garden. He played piccolo with the BBC Symphony Orchestra and became principal flutist with the London Symphony Orchestra and Royal Philharmonic Orchestra. In 1969 he was appointed principal flutist of the prestigious Berlin Philharmonic.

In 1975 Galway took the unexpected step of resigning from the Berlin Philharmonic to venture out on a solo career. It was a risky decision, but in his first year he performed 120 concerts with some of the world's leading orchestras. Since then he has become a fixture on the international concert circuit and much in demand as a soloist. He has made more than fifty recordings, covering all of the standard repertoire. His recording of the Mozart Concerti earned him the Grand Prix du Disque.

Keenly interested in new music, he has commissioned and premiered dozens of works, both classical and pop, and has freely recorded both. At least some of his appeal is due to his recordings of pop songs. Several of his covers of pop tunes have made the European pop charts, and in 1978 he had an international hit with his recording of John Denver's "Annie's Song." He has had music written for him by Elton John, hosted his own TV series, *James Galway's Music in Time*, and took part in a historic performance of Pink Floyd's "The Wall" in 1991 in Berlin.

He has performed before the queen of England, several times by invitation at the White House, and in 1998 at the ceremony for that year's Nobel Peace Prize, a performance televised to a worldwide audience of millions. In 1997 he was named Musical America's Musician of the Year. In 1999 he became the principal guest conductor of the London Mozart Players and in 2001 was knighted by Queen Elizabeth.

Galway's playing is known for its remarkable tonal range and smooth, clear sound; he's known as "the man with the golden flute." A crowd-pleaser with a showman's sense for the room, he seems to love entertaining as much as playing music; he has been known to pull out his penny whistle for a tune in the middle of a concert. He is unmatched among contemporary flutists for his sound, technical ability, and musicianship.

SELECTIVE DISCOGRAPHY: *Annie's Song* (BMG Classics, 1981); *Flute Sonatas* (BMG Classics, 1997); *The Very Best of James Galway* (RCA Victor, 2002).

BIBLIOGRAPHY: J. Galway, *James Galway: An Autobiography* (New York, 1997).

WEBSITE: www.superflute.com.

DOUGLAS MCLENNAN

GANG STARR

Formed: 1988, Brooklyn, New York
Members: Keith "Guru" Elam, vocals (born Roxbury, Massachusetts, 18 July 1966); Christopher "DJ Premier" Martin, disc jockey, production (born Brooklyn, New York, 3 May 1969).
Genre: Hip-Hop
Best-selling album since 1990: *Moment of Truth* (1998)
Hit songs since 1990: "Take It Personal," "Ex Girl to the Next Girl," "You Know My Steez"

With Guru's self-proclaimed "monotone style" of rapping and DJ Premier's inventive, genre-blending production, Gang Starr emerged as one of hip-hop's most unique and respected groups. Originally noted for incorporating jazz into their sound, they quickly branched out to demonstrate mastery of a wide range of styles. Balancing intelligence and spirituality with a hard street edge, they bridged the gap between "old school," turntable-based DJing, and "new school," studio-concocted production. Though major commercial success eluded them, their legend grew throughout the 1990s.

After graduating from Atlanta's Morehouse College in the mid-1980s, Boston native Keith Elam relocated to New York City. He took the name Guru and began releasing singles as Gang Starr on the independent label Wild Pitch Records. He had no full-time musical partner until he happened upon a demo tape of a Texas-based group called ICP that was produced by Waxmaster C, Christopher Martin. Guru was impressed by his work and eventually convinced Martin to join him.

Martin changed his name to DJ Premier and sought to be the top DJ and producer in hip-hop. At the time, fellow DJs had been sampling abundantly from 1970s funk, especially James Brown, to construct their tracks. Premier wanted to explore new territory, so he began integrating jazz recordings into their music. Though their independent label debut album *No More Mr. Nice Guy* (1989) went widely unnoticed, it contained an homage called "Jazz Music" that caught the attention of filmmaker Spike Lee. Lee asked Gang Starr to update the tribute for his film *Mo' Better Blues* (1990) and "Jazz Thing" landed on the soundtrack. The exposure led to a major label deal with Chrysalis, who planned on marketing them as "jazz rap," like budding contemporaries De La Soul and A Tribe Called Quest.

Uneasy with being pigeonholed, Premier was determined to show the range of Gang Starr's musical palette on *Step in the Arena* (1990). Though horn and piano snippets were prevalent, the musical vocabulary expanded to include both taught rhythmic and spare melodic guitars, orchestrated strings and swirling cosmic sounds. The most divergent endeavor from previous work was the dark, street-tough "Just to Get a Rep." Over a mysterious backdrop, Guru illustrates the motivation behind gang violence and details a chilling narrative ending in murder.

Such commentary on the urban and black situation in America became a widespread part of Guru's agenda. He sought to educate and empower by disseminating knowledge and promoting spiritual wholeness. For balance, he left time for traditional hip-hop topics, too, boasting about his vocal skill and prowess with women. Regardless

of the subject, his delivery is always silky smooth, effortless, and undeniably distinguishable from all other rappers. Though his stage name stands for the acronym Gifted Unlimited Rhymes Universal, the maturity in his voice and wisdom in his lyrics position him as a highly respected teacher, a guru, as his acronym suggests.

Step in the Arena and *Daily Operation* (1992) were heralded by critics and became underground classics. Despite the praise, the camp was divided. Premier still felt there was too much focus on the jazz elements in the group's sound, so Guru launched a solo career to maintain a jazz outlet, releasing *Jazzmatazz, Vol. 1* in 1993.

The following year, Gang Starr returned with their angriest and darkest album, *Hard to Earn*. They remained adamantly noncommercial as stated in their single "Mass Appeal" and maintained the group's lyrical ideology. However, they employed several guest rappers and more of a gangster tone, two trends of the time. Though a solid effort, they seemed confused about their place in the current hip-hop market. The indecision led to a hiatus. Guru released *Jazzmatazz, Vol. 2: The New Reality* in 1995, and Premier went on to produce tracks for several of hip-hop's top names including KRS-One, the Notorious B.I.G., Nas, and Jay-Z.

By the late 1990s Gang Starr's music became essential listening to hip-hop aficionados. When they returned with *Moment of Truth* (1998), their legacy propelled their fifth studio release to become their first gold album. A year later, *Full Clip: A Decade of Gang Starr* (1999) served as a career retrospective. Fans looking for an abbreviated introduction to the group pushed the album to gold sales, as well. After more side projects, Guru and Premier returned again with *The Ownerz* in 2003.

Gang Starr's modernization of hip-hop's original sound—two turntables and a microphone—and preservation of its original mission—positive promotion of change—give their music a timeless quality. Throughout their careers both in and out of the group, Guru and DJ Premier established themselves as inimitable and consummate professionals.

SELECTIVE DISCOGRAPHY: *Step in the Arena* (Chrysalis, 1990); *Daily Operation* (Chrysalis, 1992); *Hard to Earn* (Chrysalis, 1994); *Moment of Truth* (Noo Trybe/Virgin, 1998).

WEBSITES: www.gangstarr.8m.com; www.virgin-records.com/starr/index3.html.

DAVE POWERS

GARBAGE

Formed: 1993, Madison, Wisconsin

Members: Douglas "Duke" Erikson, guitar, keyboards (born 1950); Shirley Manson, vocals (born Edinburgh, Scotland,

26 August 1966); Steve Marker, guitar, keyboards (born Nebraska, 1960); Bryan "Butch" Vig (born Viroqua, Wisconsin, 1957).

Genre: Rock, Pop

Best-selling album since 1990: *Garbage* (1995)

Hit songs since 1990: "Only Happy When It Rains," "Stupid Girl"

When three anonymous Midwestern studio musicians found a flame-haired Irish singer with personality to spare, the result was one of the most inventive pop groups of the 1990s. Garbage, fronted by Shirley Manson, produced a string of meticulously arranged hits such as "Stupid Girl" and "I Think I'm Paranoid," melding Manson's tough-as-nails vocals with electronic-rock soundscapes created by the group's trio of producers, Butch Vig, Steve Marker, and Duke Erikson.

Garbage began as a part-time hobby for three old friends from Wisconsin. Producer/drummer Butch Vig opened the recording studio Smart Studios in Madison, Wisconsin, in 1984 with his friend and future Garbage guitarist/keyboardist Steve Marker. Vig had majored in film at the University of Wisconsin-Madison but spent much of his time composing music, later joining the local rock band Spooner with future Garbage guitarist/keyboardist Duke Erikson. The pair also played together in Firetown, a group formed after Spooner's demise.

During this time Vig and Erikson began producing singles for local punk bands for a hundred dollars apiece, and over the next few years their additional production work for national bands soon changed the rock landscape of the 1990s. Vig, in particular, rose to fame as a much sought-after producer. He helped to form the template for grunge rock with his work on albums by bands such as Tad, Killdozer, Nirvana's *Nevermind*, and the Smashing Pumpkins's *Siamese Dream*.

A native of Edinburgh, Scotland, and the daughter of a jazz singer, Shirley Manson had dropped out of school at age fifteen and spent a frustrating decade in the Irish rock group Goodbye Mr. MacKenzie. By 1993 Manson was fronting an Irish rock band called Angelfish, whose 1994 video for the song "Suffocate Me" made an impression the one time it aired on MTV, a coincidence Garbage chalked up to fate.

Intrigued by Manson's elfin beauty, the trio tracked her down and invited her to Madison to audition. The band's repertoire at this point consisted of leftover samples and tracks the trio had compiled while working on remixes for groups such as U2 and Nine Inch Nails, and none of the men were interested in singing or fronting such an act. Though Manson was nervous about her abilities and had trouble adjusting to the Midwestern sensibilities of her new band mates, the four spent several months at Smart Studios recording and perfecting their self-titled debut (1995).

Not So Trashy

Filled with odd "mistakes" that became the basis of a string of radio hits, *Garbage* is a painstakingly produced symphony of pop. In Manson the group found a poised singer who could swing from seductive to icy within one song. Such darkly alluring songs as "I'm Only Happy When It Rains" and "Queer" are tightly scripted mash-ups of fuzzy rock guitars and bass mixed with cascading keyboards, electronic drums, and futuristic washes of noise. The trio of producers corral it all into perfect three- and four-minute electronic pop nuggets that owe as much to bouncy New Wave as they do to the rhythms of techno dance music.

The album sold more than 1 million copies, earned the group a Best New Artist Grammy nomination, and turned Manson into a bona fide superstar—landing her on the cover of rock and fashion magazines around the globe. Though not intending to tour at first, the group embarked on a grueling two-year road trip to promote the album, working on new material as they traveled.

Despite the amount of exposure the band was getting on the airwaves, Marker, Vig, and Erikson remained relatively anonymous, while Manson quickly developed a public reputation as a strong-willed woman who was not to be taken lightly. Her distinctive singing style became more pronounced on the group's second album, *Version 2.0* (1997). A refinement of the technopop sound of their debut, *Version 2.0* launched yet another string of instantly hummable radio hits, including "Special," "Push It," and "I Think I'm Paranoid." Manson again plays with sexuality and gender roles on the album, taking full control on the raunchy "Sleep Together" and throwing caution to the wind on the driving dance pop track "When I Grow Up": "When I grow up, I'll be stable / When I grow up I'll turn the tables."

The group spent nearly a year, on-and-off, working on their third album. They invited touring bassist Daniel Shulman to contribute to a recording. On *Beautifulgarbage* (2001), the highly polished pop sheen is augmented by techno/new wave, bubble-gum funk ("Shut Your Mouth," "Cherry Lips," "Go Baby Go!"), robotic R&B ("Androgyny"), sweeping, Supremes-style symphonic ballads ("Can't Cry These Tears"), and a bit of dance floor blues ("'Til the Day I Die"). Critics hailed the album as the band's most consistent to date.

With a fierce lead singer, three studio magicians, and a sound that perfectly captured the intensity of 1990s dance music, the crunch of rock, and a timeless pop sensibility, Garbage came blazing out of the Midwest in the mid-1990s. Shirley Manson became an icon to fans around the world, adored by men and women alike for her powerful sense of self and undeniable sensuality.

SELECTIVE DISCOGRAPHY: *Garbage* (Almo Sounds, 1995); *Version 2.0* (Almo Sounds, 1997); *Beautifulgarbage* (Almo Sounds/Interscope, 2001).

WEBSITE: www.garbage.com.

GIL KAUFMAN

DJIVAN GASPARYAN

Born: Solag, Armenia, 1928

Genre: World

Best-selling album since 1990: *Apricots of Eden* (1996)

Djivan Gasparyan introduced the Armenian duduk (wooden oboe) and its ancient repertoire to the world. He has adapted the deceptively simple, double-reed, apricot root instrument to contemporary contexts, and popularized the purest form of its music as an aid to meditation.

Gasparyan was born in a village on the edge of Yerevan, the capital of Armenia, when the country was a member of the Union of Soviet Socialist Republics (USSR). Having heard elder masters of the duduk, the Armenian national instrument, and seen it used in a film, Gasparyan taught himself to play it starting at age six. In 1948 he became a member of the Tatool Altounian National Song and Dance Ensemble, and he was also a duduk soloist with the Yerevan Philharmonic Orchestra.

The duduk, a cylinder-shaped wooden instrument, is hand crafted in three sizes—approximately 11, 13, and 16 inches long, with corresponding mouthpieces 3.5, 5, and 6 inches in length. The density of the apricot root used for its body produces a soft, warm tone, and its large, "split-tube" mouthpiece allows for subtle intonation. A single note, which bears only the slightest timbral edge, may be shaken between the lips for a gentle quavering sound, and a player's ability to manipulate this distinctive sound is highly prized by the instrument's aficionados. Armenian musicologists site evidence of the duduk's use as early as 1200 B.C.E., though Western scholars suggest it is 1,500 years old. Its traditional tunes have a beguiling, often mournful, sentimentality. Its range is only one octave, and it is typically played with one or more other duduk players holding a steady drone against the soloist's melody. Gasparyan sometimes performs unaccompanied.

Gasparyen has been an active professor at the Yerevan Conservatoire, from which he graduated, for more than four decades. He began touring internationally in the late 1950s, holding concerts in Europe, Asia, the Middle East, and the United States. He won Gold Medals in world music competitions sponsored by United Nations Educational, Scientific and Cultural Organization (UNESCO) in 1959, 1962, 1973, and 1980, and is unique in holding the title "People's Artist of Armenia." He is also a singer, and has composed songs based on the love poetry of Vahan Derian. His first album released in the West was *I Will Not Be Sad in This World* (1989).

British rock composer Peter Gabriel featured Gasparyan extensively in the soundtrack to Martin Scorsese's film *The Last Temptation of Christ* (1989). This exposure increased Gasparyan's profile enormously, though the music was not released on an album until 2002, when *The Last Temptation of Christ (Passion)* came out. By then, Gasparyan had released several more albums of Armenian folk and dance songs. He performed with the Kronos Quartet and the Los Angeles Philharmonic Orchestra, and collaborated with Canadian guitarist and ambient music producer Michael Brook on *Black Rock* (1998).

Gasparyan is also prominent on soundtracks of the films *The Russian House* (1990); Atom Egoyan's *Calendar* (1993); *The Crow* (1994); *The Siege* (1998); a Hungarian-American cable television production, *Storm and Sorrow* (1999); *Onegin* (1999); and *Gladiator* (2000). All of these productions depend upon Gasparyan for a sound that seems to acknowledge centuries-worth of sorrow, perseverance, and hope for a better future.

Gasparyan was the winner of a 2002 WOMEX Award, given by the World Music Expo organization, which produces biannual conventions and seminars for activists in world music recording and presentation. The award celebrated a lifetime of "creativity, quality, and success in the name of this world's music."

SELECTIVE DISCOGRAPHY: *Ask Me No Questions* (Traditional Crossroads, 1994); *Apricots from Eden* (Traditional Crossroads, 1996); *Heavenly Duduk* (Network Records, 1999); *The Art of the Armenian Duduk* (Arc, 2001). **With Michael Brook:** *Black Rock* (Real World Records, 1998). **With Magnus Finnes:** *Onegin* (Milan, 1999). **With Peter Gabriel:** *The Last Temptation of Christ (Passion)* (Geffen, 2002). **With Graeme Revell:** *The Seige* (Varese Sarabande, 1998). **With Hans Zimmer/Lisa Gerrard:** *Gladiator* (Decca, 2000). **Soundtracks:** *The Russian House* (MCA, 1990); *The Crow: The Original Motion Picture Score* (Varese Sarabande, 1994); *The Siege* (Varese Sarabande, 1998).

WEBSITES: www.libramusic.gr/artists/nazeli.html; www.traditionalcrossroads.com/pages/4268.html; www.bbc.co.uk/radio3/world/womadgasparyan. shtml.

HOWARD MANDEL

GETO BOYS

Formed: 1986, Houston, Texas

Members: Scarface, vocals (Brad Jordan, born Houston, Texas, 9 November 1969); Bushwick Bill, vocals (Richard Shaw, born Jamaica, 8 December 1966); Willie D, vocals (William Dennis, born Houston, Texas, 11 November 1966); Big Mike, vocals (Michael Banks)

Genre: Hip-Hop

Best-selling album since 1990: *We Can't Be Stopped* (1991)

Hit songs since 1990: "Mind Playing Tricks on Me"

The Geto Boys were the first hip-hop group from Houston, Texas—and one of the first from the southern United States—to achieve national popularity. Their music paints intensely detailed and reflective pictures of drug use, poverty, and psychosis.

Although the name "Geto Boys" had been used by a variety of groups on James Smith's Houston-based Rap-A-Lot label since 1986, their best known and most influential incarnation came together in 1989. The group consisted of three MCs (rappers): Scarface, Willie D, and Bushwick Bill. Willie D provided an energetic, almost hyperactive, militancy, whereas Scarface brought an observant and poetic self-awareness. Bushwick Bill, standing four feet tall, completed the trio with a sense of volatile, barely controlled rage.

The Geto Boys's ascent into the national consciousness began with the album *Grip It! On That Other Level* (1989), later re-released as *Geto Boys* (1990). The album's best-known song, "Mind of a Lunatic," contains a number of first-person depictions of extreme violence, thus creating the impression that rape, murder, and necrophilia were advocated—and possibly committed—by the artists themselves. While such content became commonplace in rap by the middle of the 1990s, at the time it was still troublesome enough to severely restrict their record company's ability to distribute the album to retailers. The album was eventually distributed through Rick Rubin's Def American label and became popular with a nationwide audience.

The popularity of their first album soon led to a second, *We Can't Be Stopped* (1991). Shortly before the album was released, Bushwick Bill, in what he later characterized as a failed suicide attempt, forced his girlfriend to shoot him in the eye. The album's cover is an apparently authentic photo of Bushwick Bill on a hospital gurney following the incident, flanked by band mates Willie D and Scarface.

In addition to its striking cover, the album also contains Geto Boys's only hit single, "Mind Playing Tricks on Me," which reached number one on the *Billboard* Hot Rap Singles chart in 1991, and number twenty-three on the Hot 100 in 1992. The song, now considered a hip-hop classic, features a series of verses in which each MC describes a psychological breakdown that he is undergoing. Far from being exploitative, the song shows the emotional toll created by the drug dealing, violence, and misogyny celebrated in other rap songs. "Day by day it's more impossible to cope / I feel like I'm the one that's doing dope," raps Scarface. The lyrics are supported by a slow, blues-influenced melody that reinforces both the southern identity of the group and the desperation of the song's narrators.

Though all of the Geto Boys eventually embarked upon solo careers, only Willie D left the group to do so. His absence was filled by MC Big Mike before the release of *Uncut Dope* (1992) and *Till Death Do Us Part* (1993), both of which continued the Geto Boys's tradition of slinky beats and intensely personal lyrics.

In 1994 the group disbanded. Only two years later, though, the most popular Geto Boys incarnation, consisting of Scarface, Willie D, and Bushwick Bill, reunited for the appropriately titled albums *The Resurrection* (1996) and *Da Good, Da Bad & Da Ugly* (1998).

The Geto Boys demonstrate that well-crafted, insightful lyricism need not preclude realistic evocations of violence. Their ominous, deep-rooted sound brought attention to the music—and lifestyle—of the southern United States at a time when hip-hop was dominated by groups from the East and West coasts.

SELECTIVE DISCOGRAPHY: *Grip It! On That Other Level* (Rap-A-Lot, 1989); *Geto Boys* (Rap-A-Lot, 1990); *We Can't Be Stopped* (Rap-A-Lot, 1991); *Uncut Dope* (Rap-A-Lot, 1992); *Till Death Do Us Part* (Rap-A-Lot, 1993); *The Resurrection* (Rap-A-Lot, 1996); *Da Good, Da Bad & Da Ugly* (Rap-A-Lot, 1998).

JOE SCHLOSS

GILBERTO GIL

Born: Gilberto Passos Gil Moreira; Salvador, Brazil, 29 June 1942

Genre: World, Tropicalia

Best-selling album since 1990: *Tropicalista 2* (1993)

Hit songs since 1990: "Madalena"

Gilberto Gil regards himself as "the second guy" of Brazilian superstars, behind Caetano Veloso, his longtime friend and collaborator. But Gil's renown as a creative, accessible, and pan-stylistic musician is as appreciated as anyone's worldwide. Besides an acclaimed international recording and performing career, Gil's social

| Gil Named Brazil's
Minister of Culture

Gilberto Gil's political consciousness and
advocacy of the rights and needs of Brazil's
impoverished minority populations have been
central throughout his career. "Politics is a martial art, and I'm more cut out to be a diplomat
than a politician," Gil said, but he already
experienced that martial art as an elected
council member in his native city, Salvador. In
populist president Luiz Inacio Lula da Silva's
administration, Gil manages a $120 million
annual budget, much of it preordained for
departmental costs. His goals include enlisting
artists across disciplines in an antihunger campaign, and promoting Brazilian culture worldwide, including its colonial architectural
heritage, its burgeoning film industry, and the
flora and fauna of its rain forests. Lula's
appointment of two blacks—Gil and Benedita
da Silva (social assistance minister)—to
cabinet-level governmental positions makes an
immediate statement in a country that boasts
of being racially integrated, yet has only had
one previous black minister, the soccer star
Pelé. Gil predicts that his responsibilities will
necessitate the suspension of "at least 80 percent of my professional career." His absence
from the stage and recording studio might dis-
please devotees, but Gil intends to perform on
weekends and holidays, and is following his
28-CD career retrospective release, *Palco*
(2002), with a studio album.

Enthralled by bossa nova singer and guitarist Joao
Gilberto, Gil bought a guitar, taught himself to sing and
play, and earned a living composing television ads until
1964, when he appeared in a Brazilian song review directed
by Veloso (which included other singers, such as Veloso's
sister Maria Bethania, Gal Costa, and Tom Zé). Relocating to Sao Paulo, Brazil's most African-influenced city, Gil
had a hit with singer Elis Regina's rendition of his song
"Louvacao" (1965). First recording under his own name
in 1966, Gil became known as a protest singer and founding member of the artistic circle that established tropicalia,
an esthetic and social movement adapting attitudes of
British and American youth culture.

Tropicalia was, naturally, unpopular with the military
junta that assumed governmental powers through a coup
in 1968; Gil and Veloso suffered censorship, several months
of imprisonment, and voluntary exile in London from early
1969 through 1972. Though Gil's songs continued to be
issued in Brazil (his first hit single was "Aquele Abraco,"
1969), he worked in England with rock artists Pink Floyd,
Yes, the Incredible String Band, and Rod Stewart, among
others, and recorded an album in English.

Back in Brazil, Gil fired up his career with *Expresso
2222* (1972) and subsequent albums, including *Os Doces
Bararos* ("The Sweet Barbarians"; 1976), named after his
band with Brazilian music stars Veloso, Gal Costa, and
Maria Bethania. His most notable fusion of rhythms from
Africa and the Caribbean with those of Brazil was *Refavela*,
which was released in 1977; that year Gil signed an international recording deal with Warner/Elektra/Asylum, leading to United States and European tours.

In 1980 Gil's rendition of Bob Marley's "No Woman,
No Cry," sung with Jimmy Cliff, was a number one hit in
Brazil, selling a reported 700,000 copies. He followed up
a triumph at the Montreux Jazz Festival with Cliff in 1982,
and recorded *Raca Humana* (1984) with Bob Marley's band,
the Wailers. In 1985, Gil celebrated his twentieth career
anniversary with Brazilian musicians Jorge Benjor, Chico
Buarque, Roberto Carlos, Caetano Veloso, Costa, and
Bethania in a Sao Paulo concert titled "Gil 20 Anos Luz."

Even before his late-sixties-early-seventies sojourn in
Europe, Gil had been a spokesperson for the budding black
consciousness movement in Brazil, as well as other humanitarian and ecological issues. After the release of *Gilberto
Gil en Concerto* (1987), he moved to Salvador to become
president of Fundacao Gregorio de Matos, a cultural and
preservationist agency; in 1988 he was elected to the city
council, where he served until 1992. Then, to kick off the
release of *Parabolic* (1992), Gil performed for free to some
80,000 listeners on Rio de Janiero's Copacabana beach.
The track "Madalena" became an important Carnival
anthem, and he toured Europe, the United States, and
Japan.

concerns have led him into politics, and at the
end of 2002 he was named Brazil's minister of culture by president-elect Luiz Inacio Lula da Silva.

As a child in the remote interior of the state of Bahia,
Gil was interested in the improvised musical jousts of street
singers and marketplace guitarists. He returned with his
family to the city of Salvador when he was eight years old;
he heard trio electrico (heavy percussion and electric guitars) and button-accordion star Luiz Gonzago, and he was
inspired to pick up the accordion. As a teenager he played
forros—dance parties—in Os Desafina Dos ("the out-of-
tune ones"), and enrolled in business administration at the
Federal University, where he first met Veloso.

On *Tropicalista 2* (1993), Gil regroups with Veloso to celebrate the twenty-fifth anniversary of tropicalia and thirtieth year of their friendship. Their collaboration is successful; their duets amplify each other's personalities and bring out the best in harmonious comraderie. *Acoustic* (1994) echoes his MTV *Unplugged* video concert; he shines up close, attentive to every nuance of his voice and guitar playing. In *Quanta* (1998), Gil demonstrates the immediacy of his concerns, with lyrics contemplating the Internet's relation to music. In the 1990s, he released some dozen albums, including *Gil and Milton* (2001), a collaboration with vocalist Milton Nascimento, another, but more flamboyant, singer of the Tropicalista generation. Taking chances with his voice, improvising songs without words, and dancing with merriment onstage, Gil exudes playfulness even in his sixties.

Gil's strengths include his inspired blends of Afro-Bahian, rock, soul, reggae, and other Caribbean rhythms, which support lyrics ranging from political issues to songs of seduction. He bears myriad honors, including a Knight of Arts and Letters citation from the French minister of culture, but his greatest rewards are the adoration of an international audience, and the faith his nation's government places in his socio-political integrity.

SELECTIVE DISCOGRAPHY: *O Eterno Deus Mu Dança* (WEA Latina, 1989); *Parabolic* (WEA Latina, 1991); *Tropicalia 2* (Nonesuch, 1993); *Acoustic* (Atlantic, 1994); *Indigo Blue* (Terrascape, 1997); *Quanta* (Atlantic, 1998); *O Sol de Oslo* (Blue Jackel, 1998); *O Viramundo (Ao Vivo)* (Poly-Gram, 1998); *Gil and Milton* (Atlantic, 2001); *Me, You, Them* (Atlantic, 2001); *Kaya N' Gan Daya* (WEA, 2002); *Palco* (WEA, 2002). **With Carlinhos Brown:** *Alfagamabetizado* (1997). **With João Donato:** *João Donato Songbook, Vol. 3* (1999). **With Lalo Guerrero:** *Papa's Dream* (Jarana, 1995). **With Ernie Watts:** *Afoxé* (CTI, 1991).

BIBLIOGRAPHY: C. McGowan and R. Pessanha, *The Brazilian Sound: Samba, Bossa Nova and the Popular Music of Brazil* (New York, 1991).

WEBSITES: www.gilbertogil.com.br; www.thebraziliansound.com/caetano.htm.

HOWARD MANDEL

VINCE GILL

Born: Norman, Oklahoma, 12 April 1957

Genre: Country

Best-selling album since 1990: *When Love Finds You* (1994)

Hit songs since 1990: "I Still Believe in You," "Pocket Full of Gold," "One More Last Chance"

Throughout a long career, Vince Gill has maintained his reputation as one of the most durable performers in country music. Initiating his string of hit singles in the mid-1980s, Gill secured his commercial success during the 1990s and early 2000s. Notable among modern country artists for his ethereal tenor voice and love of traditional music styles, Gill often ignored the slick pop trends that overtook country during the late 1990s. Instead, he pursued his own individualistic style, releasing albums that combine rousing dance numbers with fiddle-drenched ballads of love and heartache. Although critics have noted that Gill's pure, sincere approach can occasionally sound too laid-back, his solid professionalism makes even his lesser work enjoyable. An understated and prolific songwriter, Gill understands how to integrate classic country themes of regret and longing into a modern setting. By the early 2000s, he had exerted his artistic control even further, recording a tribute to his musical hero, country legend Merle Haggard, and acting as his own producer on the 2003 release, *Next Big Thing*.

As a child growing up in Oklahoma, Gill was encouraged to pursue a career in music by his father, a lawyer who performed part time in a country band. In high school Gill joined Mountain Smoke, a student band that performed bluegrass, a traditional country music style characterized by vocal harmonizing and rapid, rhythmic picking on the banjo. Moving to Louisville, Kentucky, at age eighteen, Gill became part of another band, the Bluegrass Alliance, before heading to Los Angeles to pursue a professional music career. In the late 1970s he joined the rock and country band Pure Prairie League, taking lead vocal duties on the group's hit, "I'm Almost Ready" (1980). Shortly after the single's release, Gill left the band to be with his then pregnant wife, bluegrass vocalist Janis Oliver. After the birth of his daughter, Gill became the guitarist for the Cherry Bombs, a band led by country artist Rodney Crowell. Soon, former Cherry Bombs keyboard player Tony Brown had signed Gill to a solo recording contract with RCA Records. Moving to Nashville, Gill scored his first country hit with the up-tempo, bluegrass-influenced, "Victim of Life's Circumstances" (1984). Gill grew in popularity throughout the remainder of the 1980s, earning a Top 5 country hit with "Cinderella" (1987), a song that worked his bluegrass playing into a smooth country-pop context.

1990s Country Star

During the early 1990s Gill reached a new plateau of commercial success, alternating gentle love ballads with tough dance hits such as "Oklahoma Swing" (1990), a duet with fellow country star Reba McEntire. Singing against an energetic backdrop of fast drums and pedal steel guitar, both performers sound assured and powerful, trading vocal lines and harmonizing with a finely tuned sense of play. By the release of *Pocket Full of Gold* (1991), Gill's albums had achieved a successful pattern, combining swing numbers and ballads in equal portions. *Pocket Full of Gold* is highlighted by an updated version of the bluegrass classic "Liza Jane" as well as the aching title track, a classic-styled ballad replete with pedal steel guitar, emotive piano playing by Nashville veteran Hargus "Pig" Robbins, and a lilting melody. Again, Gill proves his talent for writing sharp lyrics with rich thematic imagery. In the song, a man begins an adulterous affair by slipping off his wedding ring. Gill then uses the image of a "pocket full of gold" to represent the price the character must pay: "Some night you're gonna wind up / On the wrong end of a gun . . . what will it say on your tombstone / Here lies a rich man / With a pocket full of gold." During the performance, Gill draws out emotion by climbing higher with his voice, building to a finish that catches the listener off guard with its poignancy. As with much of his finest work, Gill creates an effortless veneer, making his peak emotional moments all the more effective through the use of restraint.

Late 1990s Critical Acclaim

Gill released consistently satisfying albums throughout the 1990s, retaining a traditional sound despite the increased pop formatting of country radio, brought on by the crossover success of artists such as John Michael Montgomery and Shania Twain. After recording two of his most commercially successful albums, *I Still Believe in You* (1992) and *When Love Finds You* (1994), Gill released *High Lonesome Road* (1996), an attempt to survey a wide range of traditional American music styles, including country, rock, and blues. In 1998 he returned with what critics regard as one of his finest efforts, *The Key*. Recorded almost exclusively in a classic country vein, the album is a tribute to Gill's musical heroes, including his late father. "If You Ever Have Forever in Mind" recalls the "countrypolitan" sound popular in the 1960s and 1970s, complete with strings and cooing backup singers, while "Don't Come Crying to Me" is a vigorous, up-tempo swing number. Set against a gentle bed of percolating banjo and guitar, "The Key to Life" is perhaps the album's most affecting moment, a restrained and loving ode to Gill's musician father: "I learned a few chords on the banjo was the key to life." Throughout *The Key* Gill's singing displays a new degree of looseness, spiced with vocal leaps and falsetto twists.

Having divorced his first wife in 1997, Gill married Christian pop star Amy Grant in 2000. Since Grant had likewise divorced her husband after falling in love with Gill, the union created mild controversy within conservative circles. Gill's first album after the marriage was *Let's*

Make Sure We Kiss Goodbye (2000), a collection of love songs inspired by his romance with Grant. Although reviewers criticized the album as too sugary, Gill returned to form with the self-produced *Next Big Thing* (2003). On the guitar-driven title track, Gill sounds reinvigorated, delivering a swaggering groove that suggests brash country-rock artist Delbert McClinton. Proving his voice has not weakened, Gill navigates his tight band through a series of tasteful ballads and rocking dance songs, including the Haggard tribute, "Real Mean Bottle." Opening with an electric guitar line borrowed from Haggard's 1968 classic, "Mama Tried," the song captures the older singer's toughness and honesty: "No man ever sounded so lonesome, no man ever made you feel such pain / Lord, it must've been a real mean bottle, that made you sing that way."

Retaining a sense of musical tradition throughout two decades of country stardom, Gill embodies the spirit of his idol Haggard, who has pursued his own artistic path in defiance of trends. At the same time, Gill has maintained his commercial viability due to unwaveringly pure singing and intelligent songwriting. As a vocalist, Gill's mild-mannered demeanor belies the power he holds in reserve, his consistent taste ensuring that he seldom delivers a weak performance.

SELECTIVE DISCOGRAPHY: *Turn Me Loose* (RCA, 1984); *Pocket Full of Gold* (MCA, 1991); *I Still Believe in You* (MCA, 1992); *When Love Finds You* (MCA, 1994); *High Lonesome Sound* (MCA, 1996); *The Key* (MCA, 1998); *Let's Make Sure We Kiss Goodbye* (MCA, 2000); *Next Big Thing* (MCA, 2003).

WEBSITE: www.vincegill.com.

DAVID FREELAND

JIMMIE DALE GILMORE

Born: Amarillo, Texas, 6 May 1945
Genre: Country, Folk
Best-selling album since 1990: *Spinning Around the Sun* (1993)

Although his recording career has stretched over thirty years, Jimmie Dale Gilmore achieved recognition only at its bookends, with a sixteen-year gap in between. The soothing twang in his voice epitomizes the high and lonesome sound that is the essence of traditional country music. Both country and pop artists have recorded his songs. With his long, stringy hair and Zen-inspired lyrics, the iconoclastic Gilmore operates on country music's fringes, wedding philosophical musings to a honky-tonk sound.

Part Irish and part Native American, Gilmore was raised in Lubbock, Texas, a fertile musical town in West Texas that also gave birth to Buddy Holly. After playing in bands as a teen (Holly's father financed his demos in 1965), he joined in with Lubbock locals and aspiring songwriters Joe Ely and Butch Hancock. Calling themselves the Flatlanders, the group recorded its debut album for a small Nashville label, Plantation Records, in 1972. It was released only on 8-track and was subsequently ignored. The group moved to Austin and ended up launching solo careers.

Although Ely and Hancock immediately poured their energies into music, Gilmore retreated. He studied philosophy at Texas Tech, then dropped out in 1974 and moved to Denver to join an ashram, a secluded religious community led by the Indian guru Maharaj Ji. In those six years of study, his music leaked out. Ely recorded his songs, particularly "Dallas" and "Treat Me Like a Saturday Night," which later became staples of Gilmore's live performances.

Gilmore returned to Austin in 1980. In the years that followed, he refined his songwriting, creating rich emotions from simple images. After performing around town for years, he finally released his solo debut album, *Fair and Square*, in 1988. A second album followed the next year; around that time he attracted the attention of Natalie Merchant, the lead singer with the folk/pop group 10,000 Maniacs. She helped get him signed to Elektra, a major label that released *After Awhile* in 1991.

Gilmore's breakthrough came with *Spinning Around the Sun* in 1993. Combining traditional country songs, a few Hancock covers, and his originals, the album was a crosscurrent of American musical styles: country, swing, rock, folk, and bluegrass. Rather than sell the music hard as most contemporary country stars do, Gilmore sang the songs with the sweet but mournful twang of an earlier era. The album's success gave Gilmore a level of exposure he had never experienced. He was soon playing to capacity crowds, appearing on television and on the covers of magazines, and even briefly collaborating with the Seattle grunge rock group Mudhoney.

A more commercial album, *Braver Newer World*, arrived three years later. Its atmospheric production and rockabilly songs made it a departure from his earlier work. Gilmore was later dropped from Elektra and ended up releasing *One Endless Night*, a collection of covers of Texas songwriters on the Windcharger Music imprint.

Meanwhile, throughout the 1990s, Gilmore, Ely, and Hancock experienced an unexpected bit of serendipity. The album they made in the early 1970s began circulating a decade later, and by 1990, the Massachusetts roots music label Rounder Records re-released it with the fitting title *More a Legend Than a Band*. It became the holy grail for a younger generation of rock fans who were beginning to discover country music giants like Hank Williams and Johnny Cash. The building buzz around the Flatlanders led them to record the song "South Wind of Summer" for the soundtrack for the Robert Redford film *The Horse Whisperer* in 1997. They began touring together again, and in 2002—thirty years after their debut—the Flatlanders recorded a second album, *Now Again*, to critical acclaim.

His sublime vocal style and subtle, philosophical lyrics helped to make Jimmie Dale Gilmore a leading voice in the 1990s resurgence of traditional country music.

SELECTIVE DISCOGRAPHY: *Fair and Square* (HighTone, 1988); *Jimmie Dale Gilmore* (HighTone, 1989); *After Awhile* (American Explorer/Elektra, 1991); *Spinning Around the Sun* (Elektra, 1993); *Braver Newer World* (Elektra, 1996); *One Endless Night* (Windcharger Music/Rounder, 2000). **With the Flatlanders:** *More a Legend Than a Band* (Rounder, 2000); *Now Again* (New West, 2002). **With Butch Hancock:** *Two Roads* (Caroline, 1993).

WEBSITE: www.jimmiedalegilmore.com.

MARK GUARINO

GIN BLOSSOMS

Formed: 1987, Tempe, Arizona

Members: Scott Johnson, guitar (born 12 May 1952); Bill Leen, bass (born 1 March 1962); Jesse Valenzuela, guitar (born 22 May 1962); Robin Wilson, vocals (born Detroit, Michigan, 12 July 1965). Former members: Doug Hopkins, guitar (born 11 April 1971; died Tempe, Arizona, 5 December 1993); Phillip Rhodes, drums (born 26 May 1968).

Genre: Rock

Best-selling album since 1990: *New Miserable Experience* (1992)

Hit songs since 1990: "Hey Jealousy," "Found Out about You," "Til I Hear It from You"

The Gin Blossoms enjoyed a minor run of success in the early 1990s, commercializing the guitar-oriented, power-pop sound of 1980s college radio.

Bass player Bill Leen and guitarist Doug Hopkins, longtime friends, formed the Gin Blossoms in 1987; the band endured a number of personnel shifts before settling on a permanent lineup that included Robin Wilson (vocals), Jesse Valenzuela (guitar), and Phillip Rhodes (drums). The Gin Blossoms recorded a self-released album in 1989, and the following year A&M Records picked up the promising band.

Gin Blossoms. L-R: Jesse Valenzuela, Scott Johnson, Bill Leen, Robin Wilson, Phillip Rhodes (former member) [PAUL NATKIN/PHOTO RESERVE]

"Hey Jealousy," the lead single from the band's A&M debut, *New Miserable Experience* (1992), quickly bounded from the college radio charts and onto mainstream radio. "Hey Jealousy" opens with a simple, honest lyrical request ("Tell me do you think it'd be all right / If I could just crash here tonight? / You can see I'm in no shape for driving / And anyway I've got no place to go") and proceeds to chronicle the narrator's quest for meaning: "The past is gone but something might be found to take its place / Hey, jealousy." Wilson's soft, melodic vocal neatly

contrasts the band's garage-style musical romp fueled by mildly distorted guitars.

The band's second single, "Found Out about You," achieved similar crossover success, with its alternative-lite sound. A moody, midtempo track punctuated by the jangling guitars of Valenzuela and Hopkins, "Found Out about You" springs from the same roots as contemporary college radio favorites R.E.M. and the Replacements, but offers a more pop-oriented production and a memorable, anthem-like chorus: "Whispers at the bus stop / I heard about nights out in the schoolyard / I found out about you."

The Gin Blossoms's crossover formula earned the band extensive airplay on both college and mainstream radio, and *New Miserable Experience* proceeded to sell 3 million copies. In 1993, tragedy befell the Gin Blossoms, as guitarist and founding member Hopkins committed suicide. The Gin Blossoms were in the unique position of having lost their primary songwriter at the height of the band's success.

The band called upon pop craftsman Marshall Crenshaw to co-write its first post-Hopkins tune, "Til I Hear It from You," which appeared in the movie *Empire Records* (1995). With its fluid guitars, sugary melody, and wistful vocal, "Til I Hear It from You" strays little from the band's established style. Though never officially released as a single, "Til I Hear It from You" was a radio smash, hooking listeners with its easy-to-remember chorus: "Well, baby, I don't want to take advice from fools / I'll just figure everything is cool / Until I hear it from you."

With Scott Johnson taking over for Hopkins on guitar, the Gin Blossoms released their second album, *Congratulations . . . I'm Sorry*, in 1996. The album initially charted well and featured the hit "Follow You Down," but the album disappeared from the charts within six months. Following the tour in support of the album, the Gin Blossoms chose to disband.

The Gin Blossoms sans Rhodes reunited for a New Year's Eve show in 2001, and the band subsequently entered the studio to record its first new music since *Congratulations . . . I'm Sorry*. In part because of unexpected tragedy, the Gin Blossoms failed to convert their initial chart successes into a long-lasting career, but the band's legacy includes a few of the familiar pop-rock hits of the early 1990s.

SELECTIVE DISCOGRAPHY: *New Miserable Experience* (A&M, 1992); *Congratulations . . . I'm Sorry* (A&M, 1996). **Soundtrack:** *Empire Records* (A&M, 1995).

SCOTT TRIBBLE

GINUWINE

Born: Elgin Baylor Lumpkin; Washington, D.C., 15 October 1975

Genre: R&B

Best-selling album since 1990: *100% Ginuwine* (1999)

Hit songs since 1990: "Pony," "Only When U R Lonely," "So Anxious"

Young crooner Ginuwine became the heartthrob of the moment when he entered the music scene in 1996. His understated vocals, creative sexual euphemisms, and collaboration with some of the most inventive songwriters and one of the most inventive producers of the decade established him as more than just another flash-in-the-pan R&B "loverman." Although his later work increasingly neglected innovation in favor of a more commercial sound, he ended the 1990s having made a significant impact on pop music and with a promising career still ahead of him.

Washington, D.C., native Elgin Lumpkin began his music career at age twelve, performing in local hip-hop groups and working as a Michael Jackson impressionist. In 1996 he went solo under the name "Ginuwine," simultaneously studying to be a paralegal as a backup career. That year he met fledgling producer Tim "Timbaland" Mosley. The two recorded the song "Pony," which helped Ginuwine land a deal with 550 Music, a New York–based subsidiary of Sony. In October 1996 it released his debut album, *Ginuwine . . . the Bachelor*, executive produced by Timbaland.

Ginuwine . . . the Bachelor finds the singer delivering traditional R&B proclamations of devotion, heartbreak, and sexual desire on a series of slow-tempo songs. Although Ginuwine's vocals often forsake the earnest, gospel-tinged melodrama of contemporaries such as Dru Hill and Jodeci for a cooler, more laid-back approach, they clearly ground him in the pop/R&B territory charted by his earliest musical influences, Michael Jackson and Prince. *Ginuwine . . . the Bachelor* directly acknowledges the debt to the latter by including a version of Prince's 1983 hit "When Doves Cry"; this cover's clever execution is indicative of the way the album updates Ginuwine's influences for the 1990s. Slowing down the song's tempo, Timbaland subtracts the original's guitars, adds a hip-hop beat, and laces the track with video game bleeps and an eerie sample of doves cooing. "Pony" is equally innovative, pitting a minimalist and distorted start-and-stop groove against Ginuwine's playfully suggestive metaphor: "My saddle's waiting / Come and jump on it." Released as the album's first single, "Pony" went to number one on the R&B charts and became a crossover pop hit. The hit singles "Tell Me Do U Wanna," "I'll Do Anything / I'm Sorry," "Holler," and "Only When U R Lonely" followed, and *Ginuwine . . . the Bachelor* went double platinum. Ginuwine became a star, and the album's stripped-down, futuristic, yet simultaneously soulful sound made Timbaland one of the most sought-after producers in hip-hop and R&B.

Tours supporting artists such as Aaliyah and Bone Thugs-N-Harmony secured Ginuwine's newfound stardom, and in 1999 he reteamed with Timbaland for his second album, *100% Ginuwine*. Largely building upon the successful formula pioneered with *Ginuwine . . . the*

Bachelor, the album entered the pop charts at number five. Including a cover of Michael Jackson's "She's Out of My Life," and spawning hit singles such as "So Anxious," "What's So Different," and "None of Ur Friends Business," it too went double platinum.

Ginuwine parted ways with Timbaland for his third album, *The Life,* which debuted in April 2001 at number three on the pop charts. Less concerned with innovative production than with cementing Ginuwine's appeal to his legions of female fans, the album yielded his biggest pop hit to date, the ode to newfound commitment "Differences."

Backing up his sex appeal with vocal talent and shrewd pop instincts, Ginuwine made a semi-successful bid to be the 1990s heir to 1980s crossover R&B artists such as Michael Jackson and Prince. Although he never equaled his predecessors' commercial success, his debut album revitalized R&B and launched the career of producer Timbaland, who went on to help create some of the decade's most innovative popular music.

SELECTIVE DISCOGRAPHY: *Ginuwine . . . the Bachelor* (550 Music, 1996); *100% Ginuwine* (550 Music, 1999); *The Life* (550 Music, 2001).

WEBSITE: www.ginuwine.com.

MATT HIMES

THE GIPSY KINGS

Formed: 1979, Arles, France

Members: Diego Baliardo, guitar (Maurice Victor Baliardo); Paco Baliardo, guitar (Jacques Baliardo); Tonino Baliardo, solo guitar (born Arles, France); Jon Carin, programmed percussion (born New York, New York, 21 October 1964); Pino Palladino, bass guitar (born Arles, France); Nicolas Reyes, lead vocals, palmas (born Arles, France); Andre Reyes, harmony vocals, palmas, guitar (born Arles, France); Canut Reyes, guitar, background vocals (François Reyes, born Arles, France). Former members: Chico Bouchikhi, guitar, background vocals (Djeloul Bouchikhi).

Genre: World

Best-selling album since 1990: *Gipsy Kings* (1988)

Hit songs since 1990: "Vamos a Bailar," "Bamboleo," "Volare"

The interfamily, traveling flamenco guitarists and singers who make up the Gipsy Kings are responsible for bringing their uniquely rhythmic guitar playing and exuberant, multi-harmonied singing to the rest of the world through a dozen or so widely selling albums and the commercial licensing of their songs. The band is world renowned for its joyful, pop-infused flamenco music.

The Gipsy Kings derive their name from the group's two co-founders, brothers Nicolas and Andre Reyes (*rey* means "king" in Spanish), sons of flamenco artist Jose Reyes. The Reyes brothers initially started playing in the family band in the late 1970s with their father and cousins, who are all from Arles, a village in southern France, close to the Spanish border. In 1976 Nicolas and Andre teamed up with another family of Gypsy musicians from France, Paco, Diego, and Tonino Baliardo, and Chico Bouchikhi, all of whom are either cousins or brothers-in-law to the Reyes brothers, and called themselves Los Reyes. They started out as a gypsy band, traveling to play at weddings, at parties, at festivals, and in the streets, playing a style of celebratory flamenco music (Spanish folk music) that reflects their caravan upbringing. In 1982 Los Reyes changed their name to Gipsy Kings to reflect their traveling nature. The Gipsy Kings released their first two albums in Europe to much success, but did not reach an American audience until 1988 with their self-titled U.S. debut, produced by Claude Martinez, who eventually became their manager.

Gipsy Kings was well received in the United States and although it barely squeaked into the *Billboard* 200, at number 199, it managed to sell approximately 150,000 copies. The album was a huge success in Europe. The band followed up the album with *Allegria* (1989), full of traditional Spanish folk tunes sung in the band's native tongue called gitane, which is a mixture of Spanish, French, and gypsy languages, along with instrumentals. "Pena Penita" and "Solituda" are joyous, multiguitar tunes replete with syncopated hand claps and foot stomps. They provide good examples of how the Gipsy Kings's music is literally moving; its tempo, rhythms, and happy tone bring people to their feet. The space between each track is punctuated by informal conversation and encouraging shouts among and between musicians, imparting a familial, laid-back, and folksy feel.

With the help of producer Martinez, the band experimented with different world music elements from the Middle East, Latin America, North Africa, and even a little bit of rock thrown in for good measure. Building on the success of their first few U.S. releases, the Gipsy Kings collaborated with Cuban musician Ruben Blades on *Mosaique* (1989), bridging their own flamenco sounds with jazz, and reached for a more contemporary sound by incorporating electronic and acoustic percussion. The album, a smashing success, reached the number one slot of *Billboard*'s Top World Music Albums chart.

Immediately successive albums fared reasonably well, with Middle East influences on *Este Mundo* (1991) and a live album in 1992. By the mid-1990s the personnel had shuffled slightly, and their album *Compas* (1997) reached number one on *Billboard*'s World Music chart.

Toward the end of the 1990s, the Gipsy Kings amassed a loyal, diverse following, appealing equally to college-aged fans and adults. In 1997, they appeared on a Public Broadcasting Service television series, *Sessions at West 54th*, that brought together a small studio audience for an intimate recording. Things perked up for the Kings with *Cantos de Amor* (1998), a collection of classic Spanish love ballads.

The music of the Gipsy Kings is transcendent and melodic, and eloquently expresses the sadness of life with a beauty that few bands, world, pop, or otherwise, can match.

SELECTIVE DISCOGRAPHY: *Gipsy Kings* (Elektra, 1988); *Allegria* (Elektra, 1989): *Mosaique* (Elektra 1989); *Este Mundo* (Elektra, 1991); *Live!* (Elektra, 1992); *Compas* (Nonesuch, 1997); *Cantos de Amor* (Nonesuch, 1998); *Somos Gitanos* (Nonesuch, 2001).

CARRIE HAVRANEK

PHILIP GLASS

Born: Baltimore, Maryland, 31 January 1937
Genre: Classical, Soundtrack
Best-selling album since 1990: *The Hours* (2002)

Philip Glass is the most prolific, successful, and emulated American composer of the last quarter of the twentieth century. Although he dislikes the term, Glass is considered one of the founding fathers of Minimalism, a style of music characterized by static—though slightly shifting—repetitious traditional rhythmic and harmonic patterns. Although Minimalism has roots in La Monte Young's experiments with repeated and sustained tones, Terry Riley's *In C* (1964) is widely recognized as the first Minimalist composition. Steve Reich's use of multitracked tape loops that would gradually go further and further out of phase as his music progressed is another pioneering use of Minimalism. Glass, however, achieved a level of success and attention with his distinctive and multimedia use of the style, which became something of a pop culture phenomenon, and which went on to influence a wide variety of musicians across musical boundaries.

A Shift of Styles

Glass's father ran a Baltimore, Maryland, radio repair shop that also carried records, which he often brought home for his three children to listen to when they would

not sell. Thus, Glass was exposed to a wide variety of music at an early age, and began playing the violin at six and the flute at eight. While majoring in mathematics and philosophy at the University of Chicago, Glass practiced avant-garde piano scores by Charles Ives and Anton Webern and began composing pieces in the atonal and complex twelve-tone system that had been developed by Arnold Schoenberg in the early twentieth century. Determined to become a composer, Glass headed for New York and attended the Juilliard School, where he studied with Vincent Persichetti and William Bergsma. Upon graduation in 1964, Glass felt he still had not found his own compositional voice, and went to Paris for two years of intense study with legendary composition teacher Nadia Boulanger.

Although Glass has always credited Boulanger for opening his ears and teaching him how to hear music from the inside out, it was his encounter with Indian music while he was in Paris that brought about a total transformation of his music. Asked to transcribe film music written by Indian music master and sitar player Ravi Shankar to Western notation for French musicians to perform, Glass became obsessed with Indian notions of musical form and rhythm and began incorporating these ideas into his own pieces when he returned to New York.

Having renounced his previous works and the then-academic fascination with twelve-tone music and atonality, Glass formed the Philip Glass Ensemble in 1968 to begin performing his new style of reductive and tonal music. Glass incorporated electronic organs and synthesizers because of the portability of the instruments, amplified sound, intense volume, and steady, rhythmic drive of the ensemble, which gave his music instantaneous appeal with young rock audiences of the day. Driving a taxicab by day and performing to small, but dedicated Soho club, gallery, and loft audiences by night, Glass was an underground sensation throughout the late 1960s and early 1970s.

Two Trilogies

Theater collaborations with the Mabou Mines led to the groundbreaking Glass collaboration with theater director Robert Wilson, the unconventional opera *Einstein on the Beach* (1976). *Einstein* premiered in France in 1976, toured Europe, and ended up at New York's Metropolitan Opera the following fall. Glass's swirling score and singers intoning syllables and numbers alongside Wilson's staging of abstract aspects of Albert Einstein's interests and influences—including a finale in a spaceship—became a significant dividing line between traditionalists and those seeking out a new late-twentieth-century aesthetic. Glass's follow-up opera, *Satyagraha* (1980), based on the nonviolent struggles and influence of Mahatma

Gandhi, was far more conventional and was written for traditional operatic voices and forces. A third opera, *Akhnaten* (1984), based on the pharaoh who revolutionized ancient Egyptian religion, completed the *Trilogy*, as Glass referred to his first three "portrait" operas that had historical figures as their subject matter.

In the late 1970s Glass was asked by filmmaker Godfrey Reggio to score a nonnarrative film of images showing the effect of technology on the natural environment. Their careful collaboration, which took three years to complete, became *Koyaanisqatsi* (1982), after the Native American Hopi word for "life out of balance." Like the climax of director Stanley Kubrick's *2001: A Space Odyssey* (1968), *Koyaanisqatsi* became a cinematic experience that its cult of admirers went to see repeatedly. The sped-up images of traffic patterns set to Glass's relentless repetitions would become a multimedia cliché for those seeking to represent life at the end of the century as monotonous and meaningless. Glass and Reggio would go on to collaborate on the sequels *Powaqqatsi* (1988) and *Naqoyqatsi* (2002) as well as *A Brief History of Time* (1992), based on the book of the same name by revolutionary physicist Stephen Hawking.

Having been increasingly emulated by film composers, Glass himself began scoring more conventional films in the 1980s such as *Hamburger Hill* (1987) and *The Thin Blue Line* (1988), and remains one of the most prolific and sought-after film composers in the industry. The most satisfying of these have been those with Eastern themes such as *Mishima* (1984) and director Martin Scorsese's film biography of the Dalai Lama, *Kundun* (1997). The relationship between Eastern culture and Minimalism, in fact, is vital. Glass himself has spent a great deal of time studying Eastern music and thought and is a practicing Buddhist. While the West tends to view repetition on a literal level, the East often uses repetition as a means to an end. In the case of a mantra, a phrase is repeated over and over again as the basis of meditation so that the participant may achieve a higher level of awareness; the repetition becomes a conscious way to move beyond consciousness. Many who have become virtually addicted to Glass's music report similar experiences, while detractors hear only tedious and trivial repetition.

Here, There, and Everywhere

By the late 1980s and early 1990s, Glass's music seemed to be everywhere, even on television and radio commercials. Glass even released a pop album, *Songs from Liquid Days* (1986), which included collaborations with Paul Simon, David Byrne, Linda Ronstadt, Laurie Anderson, and Suzanne Vega. Glass's brand of Minimalism was already revealing itself in an entire generation of jazz, New

Age, film, theater, dance, opera, pop and rock performers, found most commercially in the post-*Unforgettable Fire* (1984) sound of Irish rock band U2, produced by Velvet Underground co-founder and Glass devotee Brian Eno. Glass himself would tour with the Philip Glass Ensemble in larger spaces, often offering live accompaniment to films he had scored, as well as give more intimate solo piano recitals of his own pieces. In 1988 the Metropolitan Opera offered Glass more than $300,000, the most expensive opera commission ever, to write a work to celebrate the 500th anniversary of Columbus's journey to America. *The Voyage* (1992) premiered on Columbus Day 1992, and was such a smash that it was revived there in 1996. *Galileo Galilei* (2002) was commissioned by and premiered at the Goodman Theatre in Chicago, and subsequently came to New York and London.

Although Glass had been a stranger to the traditional symphonic genre, he would take up the form in his late 1950s and write two symphonies based on musical themes of David Bowie and Brian Eno: the *Low Symphony* (1993), after the Bowie/Eno album *Low* (1977), and the *Heroes Symphony* (1997), based on their album *Heroes* (1977). When some classical critics attacked him for incorporating rock themes into a symphony, Glass was quick to point out that composers from Haydn to Copland had incorporated folk material and popular tunes of their day into their works. By the time of his Symphony No. 5: *Requiem, Bardo, Nirmanakaya* (2000), a millennium commission from the Salzburg Festival, Glass was back to exploring the kind of religious themes that had characterized *Satyagraha* and *Akhnaten*; the Fifth Symphony is a work that powerfully explores the great, timeless issues of humanity—creation, love, evil, suffering, death, and afterlife, among others—by offering inspiring quotes from such diverse world scriptures of the past and present as the Hindu Vedas, Shinto epics, Mayan Popul Voh, Hebrew Bible, and Muslim Qur'an, among others. Glass's sixty-fifth birthday was marked in 2002 with the world premiere of his Symphony No. 6: *Plutonian Ode* (2002), after poet Allen Ginsburg, at Carnegie Hall. A tribute to Glass's ongoing influence on popular culture can also be seen in the satirical presence of a character on the *South Park* animated television series called Glass, who likes to write pieces based on a single note.

SELECTIVE DISCOGRAPHY: *Einstein on the Beach* (Sony re-release, 1990); *Satyagraha* (Sony re-release, 1990); *Akhnaten* (Sony re-release, 1990); *Glassworks* (Sony re-release, 1990); *The Photographer* (Sony re-release, 1990); *Songs from Liquid Days* (Nonesuch re-release, 1990); *1,000 Airplanes on the Roof* (Virgin re-release, 1992); *Low Symphony* (Nonesuch, 1993); *Itaipu/The Canyon* (Sony, 1993); *Einstein on the Beach* (Nonesuch re-recording,

1993); *Music with Changing Parts* (Nonesuch re-release, 1994); *Kronos Quartet Plays Philip Glass* (Nonesuch, 1995); *Music in Twelve Parts* (Nonesuch 1996); *Heroes Symphony* (Nonesuch, 1997); *Symphony No. 2/Concerto for Saxophone Quartet and Orchestra* (Nonesuch, 1998); *the CIVIL warS* (Nonesuch, 1999); *Concerto for Violin and Orchestra* (Deutsche Grammaphon re-release, 1999); *Symphony No. 3* (Nonesuch, 2000); *Symphony No. 5: Requiem, Bardo, Nirmanakaya* (Nonesuch, 2000); *Glass Cage* (Arabesque, 2000); *Early Voice* (Orange Mountain, 2002); *A Descent into the Maelström* (Orange Mountain, 2002). **With Ravi Shankar:** *Passages* (Private Music, 1990). **Soundtracks:** *Koyaanisqatsi* (Polygram re-release, 1990); *The Thin Blue Line* (Nonesuch re-release, 1990); *Mishima* (Nonesuch re-release, 1990); *Anima Mundi* (Nonesuch, 1993); *La Belle et la Bête* (Nonesuch, 1995); *North Star* (EMI re-release, 1995); *The Secret Agent* (Nonesuch, 1996); *Kundun* (Nonesuch, 1997); *Koyaanisqatsi* (Nonesuch re-recording, 1998); *The Truman Show* (Milan Records,1998); *Dracula* (Nonesuch, 1999); *Powaqqatsi* (Nonesuch re-release, 1990); *The Music of Candyman* (Orange Mountain, 2001); *Naqoyqatsi* (Nonesuch, 2002); *The Hours* (Nonesuch, 2002); *Music from the Thin Blue Line* (Orange Mountain, 2003).

BIBLIOGRAPHY: P. Glass with R. T. Jones, *Music by Philip Glass* (New York, 1987); R. Kostelanetz and R. Flemming, *Writings on Glass: Essays, Interviews, Criticism* (New York, 1997); R. Maycock, *Glass: A Biography of Philip Glass* (London, 2002).

WEBSITE: www.philipglass.com.

DENNIS POLKOW

GODSMACK

Formed: 1995, Boston, Massachusetts

Members: Salvatore "Sully" Erna, vocals (born Lawrence, Massachusetts, 7 February 1968); James "Shannon" Larkin, drums (born Chicago, Illinois, 24 April 1967); Robbie Merrill, bass (born Lawrence, Massachusetts, 13 June 1964); Tony Rombola, guitar (born Norwood, Massachusetts, 24 November 1964). Former member: Tommy Stewart, drums (born Flint, Michigan, 26 May 1966)

Genre: Rock

Best-selling album since 1990: *Godsmack* (1997)

Hit songs since 1990: "Whatever," "Awake," "I Stand Alone"

This loud foursome delivered meat-and-potatoes heavy metal with typically angry lyrics and better-than-average hooks.

Godsmack. L-R: Tony Rombola, Tommy Stewart, Sully Erna, Robbie Merrill [CLAY PATRICK MCBRIDE/UNIVERSAL MUSIC AND GLOBAL ARTISTS MANAGEMENT]

Sully Erna grew up in the working-class town of Lawrence, Massachusetts. His father was a professional trumpet player who would jam with his jazz buddies in the basement. However, his parents divorced, and his father was dismissive of his musical dreams. Nevertheless, Erna began playing in cover bands as a teen, influenced by the Doobie Brothers, Aerosmith, and Black Sabbath. In the early 1990s he joined Stripmined. The band signed with Sire/Reprise but lacked the maturity to put an album together.

He gamely tried again with Godsmack, which fortunately boasted better band chemistry. In fact, its name comes from some rehearsal banter between Erna and Rombola. Erna was teasing the group's original drummer, Tommy Stewart, about a cold sore, but the next day Erna showed up with one. Rombola quipped that Erna had been "God-smacked."

For their debut album, *Godsmack* (1998), the band goes for atmospheric rock that's hard enough for head bangers but melodic enough for the radio. The first single from the album, "Whatever," began to garner airplay with its get-off-my-case lyrics and a stuttering, macho guitar groove. Rombola cranks out rhumbalike stairstep guitar riffs on "Moon Baby," while Erna creates a sinister feel by stretching out the vowels. However, he enunciates more clearly than most vocalists in his genre. Identifying himself as a follower of the Wiccan creed, Erna adds mystical touches to some of the lyrics but he does not put his beliefs front and center. A back-to-basics rock album in a scene that was tending toward hip-hop fusions, *Godsmack* sold more than 4 million copies in the United States.

Their next album, *Awake* (2000), is even more aggressive, pounding out arena-rock bombast on "Bad Magick" and giving Merrill a chance to deliver an almost-funky bass line on the midtempo "Goin' Down." On their headlining

"Wake the F*** Up" tour (2001), the members casually referred to drinking before going onstage and talked about fighting hangovers with the antidehydration infant drink Pedialyte. However, alcohol was causing the band to fray at the edges, and the members ended up bringing in counselors to help them kick the habit.

The group previewed new material with "I Stand Alone," a contribution to the soundtrack of the film *The Scorpion King* (2002). Erna sounds more like Metallica's James Hetfield than ever on this midtempo, minor-key song with ominous cymbal hisses. The tune is a good lead-in to the album *Faceless* (2003), which contains several songs cut from the same cloth. The CD kicks off with the aggressive "Straight Out of Line," with searing but expansive guitars that create desolate soundscapes. The album eases off on the nihilism of past works—Erna had become a father, and the band had beaten the bottle. "Make Me Believe" and "I Am" deal with the group's struggle to stay clean. But musically, *Faceless* finds Godsmack beginning to chase its tail, having done about as much as it could with its toolbox of minor-key motifs, primeval shouts, and bashing drums. Though the album debuted at number one on the *Billboard* 200 album chart, it lacked the staying power of its predecessors, tumbling to number thirteen the following week.

Competent rockers who expertly melded their many influences, Godsmack never blazed new trails. They specialized in mixing energetic musicianship, bleak opuses, and anthemic melodies into occasional flashes of brilliance.

SELECTIVE DISCOGRAPHY: *Godsmack* (Republic/Universal, 1998); *Awake* (Republic/Universal, 2000); *Faceless* (Universal, 2003).

RAMIRO BURR

JERRY GOLDSMITH

Born: Los Angeles, California, 10 February 1929
Genre: Soundtrack

Jerry Goldsmith is one of the few remaining exemplars of the old school of movie music composition. He studied piano, composition, theory, and counterpoint seriously as an early adolescent and attended film composition classes held by Miklos Rozsa at the University of Southern California. He began his professional life as a clerk typist in the music department at CBS in 1950, writing one score each week for live performance and immediate transmission on radio shows, including *Romance* and *CBS Radio Workshop*.

Goldsmith switched to television and composed the unforgettable theme of Rod Serling's innovative series *The*

Twilight Zone and for *Gunsmoke, Perry Mason,* and *Have Gun Will Travel*. Goldsmith left CBS in 1960 to work at a smaller studio and drew the attention of the famed film composer Alfred Newman, who hired him to score *Lonely Are the Brave* (1963). This was not Goldsmith's first major studio film—that distinction belongs to *The Black Patch* (1957)—but along with the score for John Huston's *Freud* (1962), his work on *Lonely Are the Brave* was his career breakthrough.

Since then Goldsmith has been a first-call composer for producers and directors interested in professionalism and innovation. He pioneered unconventional treatments of conventional instruments, such as horns blown without mouthpieces or fingered without being blown. He was also an early adopter of electronic sound sources, using them extensively on *The Omen* (1976), his one Academy Award–winning soundtrack. Goldsmith's subsequent scores, including his Academy Award–nominated works for *Star Trek: The Motion Picture, Under Fire, Hoosiers,* and *Poltergeist,* have made extensive use of synthesizers as a sound source.

Goldsmith's first Academy Award nomination was for his score to *The Sand Pebbles* (1965), a military epic set in China, and his name is associated with an impressive number of films that feature military action and/or travel in outer space, including *A Gathering of Eagles* (1963), *Seven Days in May* (1964), *Von Ryan's Express* (1965), *In Harm's Way* (1965), *Morituri* (1965), *The Blue Max* (1966), *Planet of the Apes* (1968), *Tora, Tora, Tora* (1970), *Patton* (1970), *The Wind and the Lion* (1975), *Twilight's Last Gleaming* (1977), *MacArthur* (1977), *Damnation Alley* (1977), *Capricorn One* (1978), *The Final Conflict* (1981), *Supergirl* (1984), *Rambo: First Blood Part II* (1985), *Lionheart* (1987), *Extreme Prejudice* (1987), *Rambo III* (1988), *Total Recall* (1990), *Executive Decision* (1996), *Air Force One* (1997), the animated *Mulan* (1998; for which he was again nominated for an Oscar), *The Last Castle* (2001), and five *Star Trek* films (he also wrote themes for three series of the television franchise). Goldsmith is known for his bold dramatic strokes—his bold brass fanfares and electronic episodes, his broad, thick harmonies, and his use of seamlessly shifting and building motifs. He is sometimes credited with developing the movie-music genre Militaria, which evokes aspirations to glory several steps beyond martial marches.

Goldsmith has also been commissioned to write for many science fiction, horror, and fantasy films such as *Gremlins 2: The New Batch* (1990), *The Mummy* (1999), and *The Haunting* (1999). He also writes against type, as he did for the police drama *L.A. Confidential* (1997), the shaggy dog spy story *The Russia House* (1990), the slapstick *Dennis the Menace* (1993), the sophisticated treatment of John Guare's stage play *Six Degrees of Separation*

(1993), and the literate Steve Martin comedy *Picasso at the Lapin Agile* (2003). Goldsmith has an active English fan club with its own website. His most avid fans claim that his sensitivity to details of human interactions has allowed him to elevate laughable situations and bad writing in wretchedly realized films to watchable—or at least listenable—levels. (*The Swarm* [1974] may qualify as one such example.)

Nearly all of Jerry Goldsmith's film scores have been released as commercial recordings, and his work has frequently been re-recorded in expanded editions, but not all of his music remains in print. One compilation of his work—produced in an edition of 500 by the Society for the Preservation of Film Music as a party favor for its annual dinner in 1993—is said to have become "one of the most collectable soundtrack-related CDs of all time," fetching bids of more than $500 on the open market.

When he is not composing film soundtracks, Goldsmith tours with a concert ensemble that performs excerpts from his oeuvre. He also teaches a graduate course in music composition at the University of Southern California School of Music.

SELECTIVE DISCOGRAPHY: *The Russia House Soundtrack* (MCA, 1990); *Sleeping with the Enemy* (Columbia, 1990); *Total Recall* (Varese Sarabande, 1990); *Basic Instinct* (Varese Sarabande, 1992); *Dennis the Menace Soundtrack* (Big Screen, 1993); *Goldsmith Society for the Preservation of Film Music Tribute* (1993); *Six Degrees of Separation* (Nonesuch, 1994); *First Knight* (Epic Soundtrax, 1995); *L.A. Confidential* (Restless, 1997); *Star Trek VIII: First Contact* (GNP Crescendo, 1996); *Frontiers* (Varese Sarabande, 1997); *The Omen: The Essential Jerry Goldsmith Collection* (Silva, 1998); *Mulan* (Disney, 1998); *The Mummy* (Decca, 1999); *The Last Castle* (Decca, 2001); *The Film Music of Jerry Goldsmith* (Telarc, 2001); *Star Trek X: Nemesis* (Varese Sarabande, 2002).

WEBSITES: www.jerrygoldsmithonline.com; www.filmtracks.com/composers/goldsmith.shtml; www.mfiles.co.uk/Composers/Jerry-Goldsmith.htm.

HOWARD MANDEL

THE GOO GOO DOLLS

Formed: 1985, Buffalo, New York

Members: Mike Malinin, drums (born Washington, D.C., 10 October 1967); John Rzeznik, guitar, vocals (born Buffalo, New York, 5 December 1965); Robby Takac, bass, vocals (born Buffalo, New York, 30 September 1964). Former member: George Tutuska, drums (born Buffalo, New York).

Genre: Rock

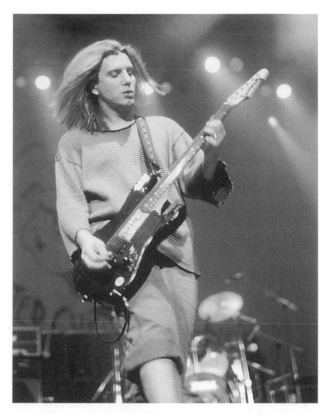

John Rzeznik of the Goo Goo Dolls [PAUL NATKIN/PHOTO RESERVE]

Best-selling album since 1990: *Dizzy Up the Girl* (1998)

Hit songs since 1990: "Name," "Iris," "Slide"

The three-piece Goo Goo Dolls made a seamless transition from raucous postpunk rockers in the 1980s to Top 40 pop rockers in the 1990s. In just fifteen years the arc of their career encompassed regional popularity with crowds of drunken head bangers to national exposure on the children's television show *Sesame Street* in 2000.

The Sex Maggots was the first name that guitarist/singer/songwriter John Rzeznik, bassist Robby Takac, and drummer George Tutuska chose for their band. Soon after, these natives of Buffalo, New York, traded that name for one they discovered while paging through an issue of *True Detective* magazine: the Goo Goo Dolls. They quickly gained local fame as a good-time alternative rock band with intense chops and a sense of humor. One of their goals was to emulate the success and style of their favorite group, the popular postpunk pop rockers the Replacements. In the meantime they covered versions of various classic rock songs from bands such as Blue Oyster Cult, Cream, Creedence Clearwater Revival, and even Prince while creating their own material.

Their first album, *Goo Goo Dolls* (1987), recorded with a small independent label, gained regional attention and gave them enough confidence to land a record-label deal in Los Angeles. Their momentum increased with the release of the album *Jed* (1989), which preceded their signing with Metal Blade, a division of Warner Bros. Records. Both albums contain a raw, slashing energy, reminiscent of the Ramones or a tamer Sex Pistols. Their next two releases, *Hold Me Up* (1990) and *Superstar Car Wash* (1993), made use of Rzeznik's maturing songwriting skills in adding catchier melodies and lyrics to their ripping sound. The Goo Goo Dolls were beginning to reach a more mainstream audience, yet each member of the band still held down a second job to make ends meet.

A *Boy Named Goo* (1995)—an allusion to Johnny Cash's offbeat hit "A Boy Named Sue"—was the band's major breakthrough into the mass market. The album contains "Name," a power ballad that became a huge hit. Sales of *A Boy Named Goo* quickly rose to double platinum. Rzeznik had somehow survived ten years of punkish blaring to emerge as a classic radio rock voice in the mode of Bryan Adams or the 1980s pop rocker Eddie Money. The rest of the songs on the album are driving rockers with appealing hooks that fulfilled the band's goal of emulating their heroes, the Replacements.

Nevertheless, the triumph arrived with its slings and arrows. Their first hurdle was to reap some of the profit that an album producing millions of dollars is expected to bring. Unfortunately, the Goo Goo Dolls—young, naïve, and eager to make a record deal—had signed away most of their royalty rights to Metal Blade Records and thus saw very little money from the album's sales. Although they were rock superstars, the Goo Goo Dolls had to go back to a familiar place—the road—just to survive. During their two-year concert tour to support legal bills, a judge ruled in their favor to break the contract with Metal Blade. Metal Blade's parent company, Warner Bros., signed them to a more lucrative deal, but trouble still loomed. The drummer, Tutuska, left over a money dispute within the band and had to be replaced by Mike Malinin.

The previous year's events and the pressures of the ensuing record deal gave Rzeznik a severe case of writer's block, which lasted nearly three years. Eventually he came up with "Iris" for the soundtrack to the film *City of Angels*. The song became a Top 40 staple that opened up the creative floodgates for Rzeznik, who quickly went back to work writing new material. The Goo Goo Dolls put "Iris" on their next release, *Dizzy Up the Girl* (1998). The album contains three other singles that charted: "Broadway," "Black Balloon," and "Slide." It went triple platinum, confirming that the boys from Buffalo were truly superstars and not ready to languish in the annals of pop/rock history as "one-hit wonders."

This ascension was not completely good news for some of their fans, however, especially those from the Buffalo area, who had developed a cult love for the band's earlier punk ways. They greeted the Goo Goo Dolls with criticism for "selling out." Nevertheless, the band—which for the first time in their existence was making ends meet financially—continued moving forward in a commercial vein. In 2000 they even appeared on the children's television show *Sesame Street* and performed a parody of their hit "Slide," retitled by *Sesame Street*'s Elmo as "Pride."

The Goo Goo Dolls released a unique compilation album, *What I Learned About Ego, Opinion, Art and Commerce* (2001), which includes a twenty-two-song retrospective of their career. Noticeably absent on the release are any of their commercial hits. They followed with a much-anticipated seventh studio recording, *Gutterflowers* (2002). The album reinforced Rzeznik's abilities as an agile, poetic songwriter and followed in much the same commercial rock style as found on *Dizzy Up the Girl*.

While the band's initial name was quickly discarded, Rzeznik later came to rue their chosen name, Goo Goo Dolls, believing that it probably hurts them commercially. This concern for popularity reflects the change in the band's focus as they take their place as new kids on pop rock's block.

SELECTIVE DISCOGRAPHY: *Goo Goo Dolls* (Celluloid, 1987); *Jed* (Death/Enigma, 1989); *Hold Me Up* (Metal Blade/Warner Bros., 1990); *Superstar Car Wash* (Metal Blade/Warner Bros., 1993); *A Boy Named Goo* (Metal Blade/Warner Bros., 1995); *Dizzy Up the Girl* (Warner Bros., 1998); *What I Learned about Ego, Opinion, Art, and Commerce* (Warner Bros., 2001); *Gutterflower* (Warner Bros., 2002).

DONALD LOWE

HENRYK MIKOŁAJ GÓRECKI

Born: Czernica, Poland, 6 December 1933
Genre: Classical

It is tempting to classify the composer Henryk Mikołaj Górecki as a one-hit wonder, and, by the definition of the popular music world, he is one. But classical composers are not usually judged by the sales standards of the pop music world; Górecki's outsized and unexpected success in 1992–1993 with his Symphony no. 3, op. 36 (*Symphony of Sorrowful Songs*), was unprecedented for a living classical composer.

The work was written in 1976, and though it became fairly well known in Poland, not until it was recorded on Elektra Nonesuch by the American singer Dawn Upshaw and the London Sinfonietta, conducted by David Zinman, did it become a sensation. The recording sold more than 1.2 million copies internationally, took up residence on both the American and English pop charts, and was the first (only) recording featuring music by a living classical composer ever to top the *Billboard* charts. By listener request, excerpts were played day and night on the English station Classic FM, and it was *Gramophone's* Best-selling CD in 1993.

Certainly the performance helped make the symphony a hit. Upshaw's long, clear notes are translucent, and the performance is ripe with gravitas. But the composer seems to have tapped into a combination of mysticism and simple musical textures that resonated with a great many people. The music gets some of its inspiration from Polish music of the thirteenth and sixteenth centuries, mixes in fragments of texts gathered from a variety of sources, and tethers it all to a musical structure that makes it seem like the music is slowly, inevitably unwrapping itself. The tone is melancholy, contemplative, and, in the end, oddly reassuring. Even listeners not normally given to responding to classical music seemed to form a bond with the Symphony. But Symphony no. 3 is not representative of most of Górecki's work. Indeed, earlier in his career, Górecki had a reputation as a rebel more likely to pitch musical fits than write a simple melody.

Górecki studied with Boleslaw Szabelski at the State Higher School of Music (PWSM) in Katowice from 1955 to 1960, and, after some postgraduate study in Paris, came back to teach at the State School, becoming Rector from 1975 to 1979. Although he has traveled, Górecki has spent most of his career in southern Poland.

In the 1950s and 1960s he was considered among the most adventurous and difficult of the Polish avant-garde composers. Along with Penderecki and Serocki, the group tried to incorporate as much dissonance and harsh sound as possible. Their style became known as "sound mass composition" a process that stripped away traditional musical elements of rhythm and pitch in favor of pure sound. Górecki's *Genesis* cycle op. 19, written in 1962–1963, and *Scontri* op. 17 (1960) feature aggressive clashes of sounds piled up against one another. Yet the music was tightly and rigorously planned out.

In the 1970s Górecki moved away from such raw aggression and began exploring spirituality as an element, trying to draw emotional and spiritual links through his music. His work became more tonal and melodic, less dissonant. This turn to a mellower sensibility is evident in his Symphony no. 2, op. 31 (*Copernican*)(1972).

After surprising his colleagues in the 1970s by radically simplifying his work, Górecki began expanding his compositional material in the 1980s and 1990s, introducing contrasts of tempo, dynamics, and harmonic language that took him far away from Symphony no. 3. He builds on spiritual themes in works such as his *Kleines Requiem fur eine Polka,* op. 66 (1993) for fourteen instruments; the works echo composers such as Chopin and Szymanowski as well as traditional Polish and Czech music.

Górecki has written more than seventy works, including pieces for orchestra, orchestra and voice, chamber music, choral music, and solo instruments. Despite his success with Symphony no. 3 and a general shift in the compositional world away from dissonance, Górecki is considered somewhat outside the mainstream of contemporary music.

SELECTIVE DISCOGRAPHY: *Symphony no. 3, "Symphony of Sorrowful Songs," Opus 36* (Nonesuch 1992); *Kleines Requiem fur eine Polka, Opus 66; Lerchenmusik, Opus 53* (Philips, 1995).

SELECTIVE WORKS: *Monologhi,* op. 16 (1960); *Scontri,* op. 17 (1960); Symphony no. 2, op. 31, *Copernican* (1972); Symphony no. 3, op. 36, *Symphony of Sorrowful Songs* (1976); *Lerchenmusik,* op. 53 (1984); *Kleines Requiem fur eine Polka* (1993).

DOUGLAS MCLENNAN

AMY GRANT

Born: Augusta, Georgia, 25 November 1960
Genre: Rock
Best-selling album since 1990: *Heart in Motion* (1991)
Hit songs since 1990: "Baby Baby," "That's What Love Is For," "Every Heartbeat"

One of the most celebrated and influential Christian music artists, Amy Grant added "pop star" to her resume in the 1990s, crossing over to mainstream radio with hits such as "Baby Baby."

Grant released her first record at the age of fifteen. Her soaring vocals and inspiring songs of faith and devotion quickly established her as a leading artist in the Christian music community. Her 1982 album *Age to Age* sold more than 1 million copies and earned Grant a Grammy Award for Best Female Gospel Performance.

Grant's affinity for pop sounds led to her discovery by mainstream audiences. Her 1985 album *Unguarded* spawned two crossover pop singles: "Find a Way" and "Wise Up." She also topped the *Billboard* pop charts in 1986 with "The Next Time I Fall," a duet with Peter Cetera. Sensing Grant's potential for massive mainstream appeal, A&M Records signed Grant to a major distribution deal.

In 1991 Grant released *Heart in Motion,* her best-selling album and her most controversial. While *Heart in*

Motion continued Grant's foray into pop music, the album was less explicitly Christian, with fewer direct references to Scripture; conservative elements of the Christian music community criticized Grant for "selling out" her faith. The lead single "Baby Baby" was a flashpoint for the controversy. Though the lyrics were generally sweet and wholesome ("Baby, baby / I'm taken with the notion / To love you with the sweetest of devotion / Baby, baby / My tender love will flow from / The bluest sky to the deepest ocean"), the song's promotional video depicted Grant frolicking around with a male model—a visual that some of Grant's traditionalist fans refused to accept. Despite the controversy, "Baby Baby" was a major hit and exposed Grant to entirely new pop audiences.

In 1991 and 1992, Grant was omnipresent on pop radio; the follow-up singles—"Every Heartbeat," "That's What Love Is For," and "Good for Me"—were all Top 10 hits. Grant's singles all flowed from the same basic crossover strategy: light synthesizer-based pop sounds with broadly devotional lyrics that could be interpreted in a spiritual manner by many of her traditional fans while not alienating non-Christian listeners; the serene ballad "That's What Love Is For" typifies this approach, with its celebration of love, spiritual or otherwise: "Sometimes I wonder if we really feel the same / Why we can be unkind / Questioning the strongest of hearts / That's when we must start / Believing in the one thing that has gotten us this far." On the strength of such crossover hits as "That's What Love Is For," *Heart in Motion* spent fifty-two weeks on the *Billboard* album charts and sold more than 4 million records.

For the rest of the decade, Grant remained entrenched in the pop scene. *House of Love*, released in 1994, did not spawn any major hit singles along the lines of "Baby Baby," but it did broaden Grant's mainstream sound; the album included a duet with the country star Vince Gill and a cover of Joni Mitchell's folk-pop classic "Big Yellow Taxi." *Behind the Eyes* (1997) also registered with pop audiences, debuting at number eight on the *Billboard* album charts and selling 1 million copies; *Behind the Eyes* also featured the minor hit "Takes a Little Time," a track that finds Grant delving into bluesy rock.

Grant's tenuous relationship with the Christian music community was further strained in 1999, when she divorced Gary Chapman, her husband of sixteen years, and married her duet partner Gill. Musically, Grant returned to her roots with the release of *Legacy . . . Hymns and Faith* (2002), a collection of sacred and secular recordings; the album features Gill as an arranger and includes standards such as "My Jesus, I Love Thee."

Though it earned her the enmity of traditionalists, Grant was the first and most successful crossover act from the contemporary Christian music scene.

SELECTIVE DISCOGRAPHY: *Amy Grant* (Reunion, 1977); *My Father's Eyes* (Reunion, 1979); *Never Alone* (Reunion, 1980); *Age to Age* (Reunion, 1982); *Straight Ahead* (Reunion, 1984); *Unguarded* (Reunion, 1985); *Lead Me On* (A&M, 1988); *Heart in Motion* (A&M, 1991); *Home for Christmas* (A&M, 1992); *House of Love* (A&M, 1994); *Behind the Eyes* (A&M, 1997); *A Christmas to Remember* (Interscope, 1999); *Legacy . . . Hymns and Faith* (Universal, 2002).

SCOTT TRIBBLE

THE GRATEFUL DEAD

Formed: 1965, San Francisco, California; Disbanded 1995

Members: Jerry Garcia, guitar, vocals (Jerome John Garcia, born San Francisco, California, 1 August 1942; died Forest Knolls, California, 9 August 1995); Michael "Mickey" Hart, drums (born Brooklyn, New York, 11 September 1943); William "Bill" Kreutzmann, drums (born Palo Alto, California, 7 June 1946); Phil Lesh, bass (Philip Chapman, born Berkeley, California, 15 March 1940); Bob Weir, guitar, vocals (Robert Hall, born San Francisco, California, 16 October 1947); Vincent Leo "Vince" Welnick, keyboards (born Phoenix, Arizona, 21 February 1951). Former members: Tom Constanten, keyboards (Thomas Charles Sture Hills, born Long Branch, New Jersey, 19 March 1949); Donna Godchaux, vocals (born San Francisco, California, 22 August 1947); Keith Godchaux, keyboards (born San Francisco, California, 19 July 1948; died Marin County, California, 22 July 1980); Ronald C. "Pigpen" McKernan, keyboards, vocals, harmonica (born San Bruno, California, 8 September 1946; died Corte Madera, California, 8 March 1973); Brent Mydland, keyboards (born Munich, West Germany, 21 October 1952; died Lafayette, California, 26 July 1990).

Genre: Rock

Best-selling album since 1990: *Ladies and Gentlemen . . . The Grateful Dead: Fillmore East New York April 1971* (2000)

The Grateful Dead was the longest-running major American rock act that came to prominence in the 1960s and performed continuously throughout its three-decade career. Only the death of its unofficial leader, Jerry Garcia, in 1995 succeeded in pulling the plug on the thirty-year party that the band had hosted with its legions of followers—called "Deadheads"—virtually nonstop since late 1965.

Origins, Acid Tests, and Early Recordings

In 1963 bluegrass banjo and guitar player Jerry Garcia, blues vocalist and harmonica player Ron "Pigpen" McKernan, and washtub bass and jug blower Bob Weir formed Mother McCree's Uptown Jug Champions in East Palo Alto, California. Constantly recruiting new players, the group was looking to be more improvisational and spontaneous than the highly structured and formulaic bluegrass San Francisco Bay area bands of the era. Group attitudes and early attempts at lyrics were influenced by the cynicism of the poets and authors of the 1950s Beat generation that were still hanging around San Francisco clubs. After the British Invasion of 1964, however, McKernan suggested that the acoustic band should go electric and get a rhythm section. Both Garcia and Weir picked up electric guitars, McKernan obtained a portable electronic organ, and drummer Bill Kreutzmann and an electric bassist were added. When the original bass player did not work out, Garcia friend and avant-garde composer Phil Lesh was recruited for the spot. Called the Warlocks until Lesh discovered that another band was already using the name, some early demos were recorded under the name Emergency Crew; the name Grateful Dead was found by Garcia in a dictionary.

Having moved into a single house in the Haight-Ashbury district of San Francisco, the group was introduced to the hallucinogenic powers of LSD (lysergic acid diethyl amide) by author friend Ken Kesey and his Merry Pranksters, as his party group was known. Early Grateful Dead appearances were as a house band for Kesey's infamous "acid test" challenges, where audience members were encouraged—along with the band, of course—to share a common exploration of "inner space" together. This psychedelic phenomenon peaked in early 1966 with an audience of five thousand tripping along with the Dead and other Bay area acts at the Trips Festival. Such spectacles helped contribute to LSD's becoming illegal, however, and by late 1966 whatever official or unofficial acid tests might accompany future Dead gigs were left unspoken.

A Warner Bros. record executive heard the group in San Francisco and persuaded it to come down to Los Angeles to record its first album, *The Grateful Dead* (1967). Recorded in three days with the band nervous and away from home, the record failed to convey the full sense of wonder and excitement that accompanied the group's live performances. This, in fact, would be a common observation from the band and from Deadheads throughout its long career, which is why there is such an uneven ratio of "live" over studio Dead albums. An audience was not simply a sounding board for the Dead: It was the synergistic component necessary for completing its improvisational sound sculptures. The group's second effort, *Anthem of the Sun* (1968), was a collage of studio and live performances and by *Live Dead* (1969), the entire album was recorded live, a rare occurrence at the time.

Personnel Changes and Band Losses

In late 1967, Garcia friend and Beat generation poet Robert Hunter began collaborating with Garcia on lyrics and Kreutzmann drummer and percussionist friend Mickey Hart sat in with the band and was added to the lineup. Hunter's lyrics gave Garcia's music a profundity and introspection that had been lacking and Hart's presence added a polyrhythmic vitality and groove to the Dead sound. Lesh composer and pianist friend Tom Constanten was brought into the lineup in 1968, playing John Cage–inspired prepared piano and adding other avant-garde touches until his 1970 departure, when keyboardist Keith Godchaux and his wife and vocalist Donna joined the band. The Dead's best-known studio albums of the time—*Workingman's Dead* and *American Beauty* (both 1970)—saw a return to acoustic instruments and brought a Crosby, Stills, Nash and Young sense of vocal harmonization to such highly polished and radio-friendly songs as "Uncle John's Band" and "Truckin'" that would become timeless band classics.

By the time of the Dead's first tour of Europe that would be documented on the three-disc *Europe '72* (1972) set, McKernan's alcohol abuse was catching up with him, and his participation was limited; he would die of a stomach hemorrhage in 1973 at age twenty-six, the band releasing *History of the Grateful Dead, Vol. 1 (Bear's Choice)* (1973) in his memory. Meanwhile, Hart had departed from the band in 1971 in embarrassment after his father, who upon his son's recommendation became the band's business manager, disappeared to Mexico with a large Dead recording company advance; Hart would return in 1974.

The formation of Grateful Dead Records in 1973 was a group attempt to have more artistic control over its recorded product, but the experiment was a financial disaster and in 1975 the company needed to be bailed out by United Artists. The Dead signed with Arista Records in 1977, but stopped recording altogether in 1980 after being dissatisfied with Arista's overproducing and undermarketing of *Terrapin Station* (1977), *Shakedown Street* (1978), and *Go to Heaven* (1980). The Godchauxs were planning to leave the Dead in 1980 when Keith Godchaux was killed in a car accident and was replaced by German keyboardist Brent Mydland. Garcia's health was also deteriorating with increased substance abuse, and when he fell into a diabetic coma in 1986, there seemed little hope of his emerging. When he did, Garcia was able to recover and put his near-death experience into perspective with "Touch of Grey," recorded for *In the Dark* (1987), the first new Dead album in seven years. "Touch of Grey" became the Dead's first-ever Top 10 single, and *In the Dark* the best-selling album of its long career. By 1991 the Dead had become—to its own amazement as well as that of industry observers—the highest-grossing touring attraction in the music business. After twenty-two years, the Dead had finally become something it never had been before: mainstream.

Following in the footsteps of McKernan and Keith Godchaux, Mydland became the third Dead keyboardist to die prematurely when he was found dead in his home from a drug overdose in July 1990. Bruce Hornsby sat in for gigs as he was able, but it was Vince Welnick, keyboardist for the Tubes, who would join the band later that year and remain with the Dead for the final five years of its existence.

The End of an Era

Garcia himself would continue to experience health problems in the early 1990s, but Deadheads had become used to this by now. When Garcia could not make it to the band's induction into the Rock and Roll Hall of Fame in 1994, the group brought along a cardboard cutout of him to stand alongside band members while they accepted the award, and even for the extended jam session that followed. By the record-breaking hot summer of 1995, the Dead were getting more media attention for the raucous behavior of Deadheads than for Garcia's health. Traffic jams and halted highways had always been routine accompaniments to Dead concerts, but when three thousand ticketless fans crashed the gate of a concert in Indiana and caused a riot, the band posted a scolding message on its Internet site and cancelled its next day's show at the same venue in protest of the behavior. After performing what would be its final concert on July 9, 1995, at Soldier Field, Chicago, the group took a hiatus while Garcia went to a rehabilitation center in Forest Knolls, California. It was there that Garcia was found dead in his room on August 9, 1995, having celebrated his fifty-third birthday just days before; the cause of death was heart failure.

The standard line that was used in reporting Garcia's death was the much overused yet apt cliché that it represented "the end of an era." Such insights would be expected from MTV and *Rolling Stone*, but it was unprecedented to see CNN offer hours of coverage of a rock performer's death and to see veteran network news anchors pontificating about that performer's "cultural significance." Surviving band members reminded fans that Garcia would have been the first one to say not to read anything into his death, except that people should take better care of themselves. That was the message that President Bill Clinton, a longtime Dead admirer who used to sport Garcia-designed ties, publicly read into the death. Given Garcia's drive to keep playing even in the wake of no less than three band deaths over the years—including that of the group's then-frontman in 1973—it was surprising that surviving group members made a formal announcement in December 1995 that the Grateful Dead would be no more.

Legacy and Future of the Dead

With the Grateful Dead having passed into history, Dead-inspired jam-based bands that had emerged in the 1990s such as the Dave Matthews Band and Phish became more popular than ever. With the Dead's liberal policy of allowing fans to tape record its live shows, die-hard Deadheads had more recordings to trade and pore over than most could possibly fully absorb in a lifetime. And now that the party really was over, the overall meaning and significance of that party could be pored over in books, documentaries, and recording compilations: The 1960s had finally passed into memory.

With the Grateful Dead, it was never about the music in and of itself; it was music being used as a rallying point for a common experience. What died with Garcia was a thirty-year continuum of a shared experience of musicians and audiences bonding together to be part of something bigger than they were individually. Neither the band nor its legions of followers forgot this aspect of 1960s counterculture, and both became the torchbearers of this ongoing tradition, passing it on to entire new generations of fans as time went on. Encountering the Dead live was, above all, an experience, and an experience that became an obsession for many who had to keep on having it. This remained true right through the band's final 1995 performances in a way that was not true of the handful of 1960s acts that were still performing in the 1990s. The Rolling Stones, for instance, toured infrequently even into the 1990s, and always needed a new album to promote to do so. Even so, the big hits were the bread and butter of these tours, and most went to see the Stones for nostalgia. Audiences would look back, with fondness and a smile, at a time when they were young and happy, and then most would go back home to the present. Not Deadheads. They were not recalling anything: Most had never left the 1960s. Many still had lava lamps and colored light organs, black lights and bell-bottoms tucked away, along with rubber bands and blocks of dye.

In 1998 surviving Dead members Lesh, Weir, and Hart, along with keyboardist Hornsby, saxophonist Dave Ellis, and guitarists Mark Karan and Steve Kimock, made appearances billed as the Other Ones. A double live CD called *The Strange Remain* (1999) was subsequently released, which includes favorites from the Dead canon along with five new songs. During the summer of 2002, Lesh, Weir, Hart, and Kreutzmann reunited for two concerts in Wisconsin along with guitarist Jimmy Herring and keyboardists Rob Barraco and Jeff Chimenti. Called "Terrapin Station: A Grateful Dead Family Reunion," thirty thousand fans descended on the event. That success saw the group embark on a national tour of seventeen venues during the late fall of 2002. The enthusiastic response from Deadheads and the media was so overwhelming that the band announced it would re-form on a permanent basis. After a seven-year hiatus, however, and without Garcia, it would not be called the Grateful Dead; henceforth, the group would be formally known by the nickname that had been applied to it for years: the Dead.

SELECTIVE DISCOGRAPHY: *Built to Last* (Arista, 1989); *Without a Net* (Arista, 1990); *Steal Your Face* (Arista re-release, 1990); *Terrapin Station* (Arista re-release, 1990); *Shakedown Street* (Arista re-release, 1990); *Go to Heaven* (Arista re-release, 1990); *In the Dark* (Arista re-release, 1990); *Reckoning* (Arista re-release, 1990); *Wake of the Flood* (Arista re-release, 1995); *Grateful Dead from the Mars Hotel* (Arista re-release, 1995); *Blues for Allah* (Arista re-release, 1995); *Infrared Roses* (Arista re-release, 1995); *Dozin' at the Knick* (Arista, 1996); *Dick's Picks, Vol. 9: Madison Square Garden, New York, NY, 9/16/90* (Arista, 1997); *Mother McCree's Uptown Jug Champions* (Grateful Dead Records, 1999); *So Many Roads (1965–1995)* (Arista, 1999); *Dick's Picks, Vol. 17: Boston Garden, Boston, MA, 9/25/91* (Arista, 2000); *View from the Vault* (Grateful Dead Records, 2000); *Ladies and Gentlemen . . . The Grateful Dead: Fillmore East New York April 1971* (Arista, 2000); *View from the Vault II* (Grateful Dead Records, 2001); *Grateful Dead: The Golden Road (1965–1973)*. (Warner Bros./Rhino, 2001); *Steppin' Out with the Grateful Dead: England '72* (Arista, 2002); *Go to Nassau* (Arista, 2002); *Postcards of the Edge: Grateful Dead Perform the Songs of Bob Dylan* (Arista, 2002); *Birth of the Dead* (Rhino, 2003); *The Grateful Dead* (Warner Bros./Rhino re-release, 2003); *Anthem of the Sun* (Warner Bros./Rhino re-release, 2003); *Aoxomoxoa* (Warner Bros./Rhino re-release, 2003); *Live Dead* (Warner Bros./Rhino re-release, 2003); *Workingman's Dead* (Warner Bros./Rhino re-release, 2003); *American Beauty* (Warner Bros./Rhino re-release, 2003); *Grateful Dead (Skull and Roses)* (Warner Bros./Rhino re-release, 2003); *Europe '72* (Warner Bros./Rhino re-release, 2003); *History of the Grateful Dead, Vol. 1 (Bear's Choice)* (Warner Bros./Rhino re-release, 2003).

BIBLIOGRAPHY: D. Brook, *The Book of the Dead* (London, 1972); H. Harrison, *The Dead Book* (New York, 1973); B. Jackson, *Grateful Dead: The Music Never Stopped* (New York, 1983); P. and J. Grushkin, C. Bassett, *Grateful Dead: The Official Book of the Deadheads* (New York, 1983); D. Shank and S. Silberman, *Skeleton Key: A Dictionary for Deadheads* (New York, 1994); M. M. Getz and J. R. Dwork, *The Deadhead's Taping Compendium* (New York, 1998); M. M. Getz and J. R. Dwork, *The Deadhead's Taping Compendium, Volume II* (New York, 1999); S. Peters, *What a Long, Strange Trip: The Stories Behind Every Grateful Dead Song 1965–1995* (Berkeley, CA, 1999); M. M. Getz and

J. R. Dwork, *The Deadhead's Taping Compendium, Volume III* (New York, 2000); D. Gans, *Conversations with the Dead: The Grateful Dead Interview Book* (New York, 2002); D. McNally, *A Long, Strange Trip: The Inside History of the Grateful Dead* (New York, 2002); D. McNally, *Grateful Dead: The Illustrated Trip* (New York, 2003).

WEBSITE: www.dead.net.

DENNIS POLKOW

DAVID GRAY

Born: Manchester, England, 1970
Genre: Rock
Best-selling album since 1990: *White Ladder* (2000)
Hit songs since 1990: "Babylon," "Please Forgive Me," "The Other Side"

After toiling in relative obscurity and slowly building a fan base over three albums during the 1990s, singer/songwriter David Gray broke through in 1998 with the European release of his homegrown recording *White Ladder*. With an ingenious sonic backdrop for beautiful melodies and insightful, emotional lyrics, *White Ladder* is a carefully crafted, seamless work.

At the age of nine, Gray moved with his family to Pembrokeshire, Wales, where he spent the remainder of his childhood. As a teen, Gray played in various local punk bands, and his interest in music continued when he returned to England to study at the Liverpool School of Art, once attended by John Lennon. He released several albums and developed a small following, but was by no means a huge success. Although his earlier albums such as *Sell, Sell, Sell* and *Flesh* did not feature the marriage of folk and electronic so prominently on *White Ladder*, it was clear that Gray had a lyrical talent that elicited comparisons to the folk legends Bob Dylan and Van Morrison. The folksinger Joan Baez has said that Gray writes "the best lyrics since young Bob Dylan." Despite the kudos, EMI dropped him shortly after its release of *Sell, Sell, Sell*.

Determined to keep making music, Gray decided to do it himself. *White Ladder* was recorded in Gray's London flat and released on his own IHT label with his collaborator Clune, who plays drums and sings backup vocals. The album is a brilliant meeting of electronic and folk music; the light and airy touch of programmed synthesizers and drum machines provide a perfect match for the organic earthiness of piano and acoustic guitar. After its European release in 1998, *White Ladder* became a huge success in Ireland and the United Kingdom. *White Ladder* was

David Gray [STEPHANIE PFRIENDER/BIG HASSLE MEDIA]

brought to a wider audience after it caught the attention of the singer and guitarist Dave Matthews, who offered Gray a deal on his label ATO Records. *White Ladder* was released in the United States in March 2000, and within less than a year it reached platinum status. As of the fall of 2002, the album had sold more than 5 million copies worldwide.

Gray toured extensively to sold-out crowds in support of *White Ladder*. He took some time off between 2001 and 2002 to spend time with his lawyer wife, Olivia, whom he had married in 1995, and to record his 2002 fall release *A New Day at Midnight*.

From the ambling chord changes in "Dead in the Water," the lead-off track, to the chilling, soul-searching of "The Other Side," Gray somehow remains optimistic on *A New Day at Midnight*, an otherwise somber album that no doubt reflects the emotional impact of his father's death in the previous year. In the album's press release Gray says, "There's a vividness to life even at the bleakest moments. Those are the times when you get the most out of other people." The sentiment seems to sum up Gray's overall attitude toward songwriting, and it is what keeps his music consistently hopeful, even in the face of adversity.

SELECTIVE DISCOGRAPHY: *Sell, Sell, Sell* (EMI, 1996; re-released on Nettwerk America, 2001); *White Ladder* (ATO/MCA, 2000); *Lost Songs:*

95–98 (ATO/RCA, 2001); *A New Day at Midnight* (ATO/MCA, 2002).

WEBSITE: www.davidgray.com.

CARRIE HAVRANEK

MACY GRAY

Born: Natalie McIntyre; Canton, Ohio, c. 1970
Genre: R&B, Pop
Best-selling album since 1990: *On How Life Is* (1999)
Hit songs since 1990: "I Try," "Sexual Revolution"

Possessed of an unusual, high-pitched, immediately distinctive singing voice and an almost cartoonishly freewheeling personality, the Ohio-born Macy Gray emerged, after years of music-industry frustration, as one of the most arresting new voices of rhythm and blues and soul in the late 1990s.

Born Natalie McIntyre in the industrial city of Canton, Ohio, to a steelworker father and teacher mother, Macy Gray was self-conscious about her voice as a child. A grainy, high-pitched whine of an instrument, Gray's voice manages to sound raspy and helium-high at the same time, mixing the range of jazz singer Billie Holiday with the raw power of the 1960s rock singer Janis Joplin. Although exposed to classic 1970s soul and R&B by her African-American parents, Gray also learned an appreciation for everything from rock to classical music while attending an all-white prep school as a teenager and studying classical piano for seven years.

Gray was asked to leave the school after making an unkind comment about one of its deans (though, despite her good grades, the school said it was a performance-based assessment), Gray moved to Los Angeles to attend film school at the University of Southern California and soon began writing lyrics. She made her performance debut when a friend for whom she'd written lyrics failed to show up to a recording session. The tape of those sessions circulated, and Gray was asked to join a local jazz band as its vocalist.

Working as a secretary at a pair of movie studios and as a hostess at the hot underground Hollywood rap and R&B club, We Ours, Gray honed her stage presence on the coffee shop/club's small stage. After landing a recording contract with Atlantic Records in 1994, the former Natalie McIntyre took the stage name Macy Gray as an homage to a pool-playing pal of her father's, who had assured her that she was going to be famous some day.

Gray gave birth to two children in 1995 and was dropped by Atlantic after completing her debut album just before the birth of her third child and her 1997 divorce from Tracy Hinds, a mortgage collector. Dejected, the singer left Los Angeles and moved back to Canton. Inspired to give it another shot by the music publishing executive Jeff Blue, Gray wrote an album about her experiences under the pseudonym "Mushroom," which landed her a deal with Epic Records.

Life Is Good

Gray's debut, *On How Life Is* (1999), garnered acclaim for its lyrical sophistication and classic soul sound, with critics lauding Gray's distinctive, wholly original singing voice. The soaring, gospel-tinged soul ballad "I Try" became the album's signature single, built around Gray's clear-eyed lyrics about romantic obsession: "I try to say goodbye and I choke / I try to walk away and I stumble / Though I try to hide it, it's clear / My world crumbles when you are not near."

In addition to songs about drug abuse and violent relationships, the album has a healthy, funk-inspired dose of another one of Gray's favorite topics: sex. With a worldview that owes much to the free-love ideal of 1960s hippies, Gray expresses her sexual liberation on the aptly titled grinding funk tune "Caligula" and the self-explanatory "Sex-O-Matic Venus Freak."

In 2000 Gray took home an MTV Video Music Award for Best New Artist, an *LA Weekly* Music Award for Best New Artist, and two BRIT Awards for Best International Newcomer and Best International Female Artist. In 2001 she won the Grammy Award for Best Female Pop Vocal Performance for "I Try," besting such competitors as Madonna and Britney Spears.

Gray recorded two guest vocals for the 2000 album by the techno artist Fatboy Slim, *Halfway Between the Gutter and the Stars*, and appeared on albums by the Black Eyed Peas and Stevie Nicks. She played a drug dealer's wife in the Denzel Washington film *Training Day* (2001) and appeared as herself in the 2002 blockbuster *Spider Man*. At the 2001 MTV Video Music Awards, the singer famously wore a dress with the release date of her second album, *The Id*, emblazoned across the front.

Though it failed to connect with critics and audiences as much as her debut, *The Id* (2001) is a daring experiment in genre-hopping soul. Piled high with layers of backing vocals, drum machines, burbling guitar solos, tape loops and retro keyboard sounds, the album is the sound of 1960s soul and funk brought into a modern setting.

The anthemic, Technicolor dance song "Sexual Revolution" is the high point of the album, encouraging people to liberate their sexual being: "I got to be . . . the freak that God made me / So many thangz that I want to try / Got to do them before I die." Also included is the hip-

hop inspired song "Hey Young World Part 2," featuring rapper Slick Rick, the sweeping R&B ballad "Sweet Baby" with Erykah Badu, and the reggae-inspired slow burn "Gimme All Your Lovin' or I Will Kill You." Gray's third album, *The Trouble with Being Myself*, was released in mid-2003.

Combining a seemingly constant altered state with a bizarre style, Macy Gray became one of the most unpredictable, exciting soul divas of the late 1990s.

SELECTIVE DISCOGRAPHY: *On How Life Is* (Epic, 1999); *The Id* (Epic, 2001); *The Trouble with Being Myself* (Epic, 2003).

WEBSITE: www.macygray.com.

GIL KAUFMAN

GREEN DAY

Formed: 1989, Berkeley, California

Members: Billie Joe Armstrong, guitar, vocals (born San Pablo, California, 17 February 1972); Mike Dirnt, bass (Mike Pritchard, born California, 4 May 1972); Tre Cool, drums (Frank Edwin Wright, III, born Germany, 9 December 1972); Former member: John Kiftmeyer (aka Al Sobrante), drums.

Genre: Rock, Pop

Best-selling album since 1990: *Dookie* (1993)

Hit songs since 1990: "Longview," "Time of Your Life"

Over the course of the 1990s, Green Day grew from an underground trio beloved by their local punk community to a worldwide pop phenomenon reviled by that same community for "selling out." Along the way, the trio created some of the decade's most tuneful, inspired punk anthems about teenage isolation, insecurity, and apathy. Growing from bratty rebels into mature, polished pop songwriters, they inspired a legion of similar acts such as Blink-182 and Sum 41 and became the best-selling punk band in history.

When ten-year-old Billie Joe Armstrong met Michael Pritchard, the two boys with chaotic home lives bonded over their love of music. Born in the bleak refinery town of Rodeo, California (just north of Berkeley), Armstrong was dejected over the recent death of his jazz musician father; Pritchard—who later changed his last name to Dirnt—was born to a heroin-addicted mother and was a child of divorce when his adopted parents split when he was seven.

In 1987 the two formed the group Sweet Children with the drummer John Kiftmeyer (also known as Al Sobrante), with Dirnt on bass. They spent every weekend

Green Day. L-R: Mike Dirnt, Tre Cool, Billie Joe Armstrong [AP/WIDE WORLD PHOTOS]

at the popular punk hangout/club Gilman Street Project in Berkeley. After changing their name to Green Day, they independently recorded an EP, *1,000 Hours*, and soon after were signed by the Berkeley punk label Lookout Records, which released their full-length debut, *39/Smooth* (1990), ten blistering tracks recorded in a single day. Both albums bear the group's distinct voice: a mix of classic late-1970s punk attitude and snarl spiked with an aggressively catchy sensibility.

Kiftmeyer quit the band after Green Day's first major tour in 1990, and the Lookout chief Larry Livermore suggested his neighbor and Kiftmeyer's drum teacher, Frank Edwin Wright (Tre Cool), as a replacement. Although *39/Smooth* helped gain the group national attention and packed houses across the United States, it was their next album, *Kerplunk!* (1992), that shattered Lookout's sales records and paved the way for the band's ascension to rock stardom.

Seeking a label that would give them wider tour support and promotion, Green Day signed a contract with Reprise Records, a division of Warner Bros. Records. With Rob Cavallo on board as a producer, the group released *Dookie* (1993) (a slang for excrement), which provided a soundtrack to the media-hyped Generation X cohort of disaffected teens and twenty-somethings already primed for the music through the popularity of Nirvana. Their first professional, big-budget production, *Dookie* refined the group's catchy, speedy three-chord punk revivalist sound and brought out the inherent tunefulness of the songs.

Hits such as "Longview," "Basketcase," and "Burnout" chronicle the lives of drug-addicted, bored, and uninspired punks. The band's sound is classic punk (The Jam, Buzzcocks) slathered with the same joy of pop beloved by the Ramones. Armstrong's lyrics are blunt, as in "Welcome to Paradise": "Some call it the slums / Some call it nice / I want to take you through / A wasteland I like to call my home / Welcome to Paradise."

The group graced the covers of countless music magazines and performed a legendary, career-making set at Woodstock '94. Meawhile, the album was flying out of stores, eventually selling more than 8 million copies. A 1994 Best Alternative Music Performance Grammy followed, although the prosperity and accolades failed to cushion the cries of betrayal emanating from their erstwhile fellow denizens of rock's underground.

A Dark Follow Up

Though all three were married with children at this point, *Insomniac* (1995)—again produce by Cavallo—shows no signs of leaving behind the adolescent concerns of *Dookie*. This darker album, although not nearly as popular as *Dookie*, further refined the band's sound, telling the stories of confused teens ("Armatage Shanks") and bored kids awaiting their inheritance ("Brat"). The singles "Geek Stink Breath" and "Brain Stew"—both chronicling the hell of addiction to methamphetamine—add a more deliberate, heavy bass-end sound to Green Day's repertoire, with the latter featuring a choppy, big riff guitar sound similar to AC/DC.

After canceling a 1996 European tour, claiming exhaustion, the band took a year off to catch up with their families. They returned to the studio with *Nimrod* (1997) another step forward in the expansion of the group's sound that is best remembered for the least predictable songs: the rockabilly punk thumper "Hitchin' a Ride" and "Good Riddance (Time of Your Life)." The latter, a string-laced ballad about taking time to appreciate your life, shows signs of punkers reluctantly growing up: "It's something unpredictable / But in the end is right / I hope you had the time of your life."

By the time of *Warning* (2000), Green Day had taken over the production reins from Cavallo and recorded an album of swinging pop songs that were, in some ways, worlds away from their Gilman Street punk roots. Though Armstrong's jaded view of the world remains, songs such as the plucky acoustic rocking title track, "Church on Sunday," and "Misery" bear the imprint of pop craftsmen, not punks aiming for light speed.

Though their punk peers from the old days abandoned them, Green Day never forgot their roots on the way to pop stardom. Their influential 1990s albums inspired a whole generation of punk groups (Good Charlotte, New Found Glory) to find ways to fuse pop and punk.

SELECTIVE DISCOGRAPHY: *1,000 Hours* (Lookout!, 1987); *39/Smooth* (Lookout!, 1990); *Kerplunk!*, (Lookout!, 1992); *Dookie* (Reprise, 1993); *Insomniac* (Reprise, 1995); *Nimrod* (Reprise, 1997);

Warning (Reprise, 2000); *International Superhits!* (Reprise, 2001); *Shenanigans* (Reprise, 2002).

WEBSITE: www.greenday.com.

GIL KAUFMAN

NANCI GRIFFITH

Born: Nanci Caroline Griffith; Austin, Texas, 6 July 1953
Genre: Country, Folk, Rock
Best-selling album since 1990: *Flyer* (1994)

Like fellow performer Mary Chapin Carpenter, Nanci Griffith straddles the line between country and folk music, her quiet, girlish voice finding an outlet in her confessional songwriting. Unlike Carpenter, however, Griffith failed to make a significant impact on the country charts, perhaps because her literate material and intellectual demeanor did not translate easily into the smooth conventions of mainstream radio. After scoring with several small country hits in the late 1980s, Griffith spent the early 1990s recording pop and rock-oriented music before returning to her folk roots with the acclaimed album, *Other Voices, Other Rooms* (1993). A consistently challenging artist, Griffith continued to expand her horizons in the late 1990s and beyond, recording an album of her best-known songs with the London Symphony Orchestra and releasing another set of original material, *Clock without Hands*, in 2001.

Raised in Austin, Texas, Griffith cultivated her early love of music through the influence of her mother, an amateur actress, and her father, a singer in a barbershop quartet. Although Griffith began performing in Austin-area clubs at the age of fourteen, she later decided upon a career in education, receiving her undergraduate degree from the University of Texas and spending several years in the mid-1970s as a kindergarten teacher. In 1977 she returned to performing, enlisting a small local label to release *There's a Light Beyond These Woods* (1978), a folk-influenced album of her own material. Recording for the small Philo label during the 1980s, Griffith released fine albums such as *The Last of the True Believers* (1986). A set of acoustic songs recorded with gentle, sensitive accompaniment, the album features several songs that would become regarded by fans as Griffith classics, particularly "Love at the Five and Dime," later recorded by country star Kathy Mattea. Like much of Griffith's finest work, the song boasts a strong narrative line, lilting melody, and lyrics that mine themes of love, regret, and loneliness: "Dance a little closer to me, 'cause it's closing time / And love's on sale tonight at this five and dime."

In 1987 Griffith signed with the country division of MCA Records, where she enjoyed minor hits such as "Lone Star State of Mind" (1987) and "I Knew Love" (1988). With the albums *Storms* (1989) and *Late Night Grande Hotel* (1991), Griffith moved in a rock and pop direction, diminishing her limited country recognition but building a strong fan base among a young, urban audience. With its flowing string arrangement, soulful organ, and assertive backup vocals, the title track of *Late Night Grande Hotel* imparts a pop and R&B feel representative of this phase of Griffith's career. Moving to the Elektra label, she revisited her early influences on *Other Voices, Other Rooms*, a faithful, affectionate homage to folk legends such as Woody Guthrie and Malvina Reynolds. On songs such as "Across the Great Divide" and "Tecumseh Valley," Griffith uses her quavering voice and sensitive guitar playing to create a mood of warm intimacy. Featuring guest appearances by folk and country legends Odetta, Arlo Guthrie, and Chet Atkins, the album was applauded by critics as a noteworthy attempt to honor the sincerity and truthfulness of classic folk music.

Throughout the 1990s Griffith continued to release personal albums that resisted musical categorization. *Flyer* (1994), a collection of original material, sports a rock-oriented sound through the use of electric guitar and drums, while *Blue Roses from the Moons* (1997) is marked by slick production from Don Gehman, the producer for successful 1990s rock band Hootie & the Blowfish. After releasing another album of folk material, *Other Voices, Too (A Trip Back to Bountiful)* in 1998, Griffith revisited some of her previous material on *The Dust Bowl Symphony* (1999), an album recorded with the London Symphony Orchestra. Despite the sophisticated orchestral backing, Griffith retains her air of quiet introspection, proving the adaptability of her unique style. While she is arguably more effective when utilizing the muted, sparse background of earlier albums, Griffith succeeds in capturing on *The Dust Bowl Symphony* a new, intriguing setting for her talents. Always a prolific artist, Griffith returned to the studio for *Clock without Hands*, her final album for Elektra, before releasing *Winter Marquee* in 2002. Recorded for Rounder Records, the parent company of her former label, Philo, *Winter Marquee* is a live set containing intelligent versions of songs Griffith initially released on previous albums.

A sensitive performer whose restrained voice and intelligent songwriting found limited success on country radio, Griffith has pursued her own musical path, frequently adapting her folk-imbued style to rock and pop formats. Never attaining the far-reaching stardom of some of her country and rock peers, Griffith has nonetheless built up a loyal following over the course of a long and distinguished career.

SELECTIVE DISCOGRAPHY: *The Last of the True Believers* (Philo, 1986); *Little Love Affairs* (MCA, 1988); *Late Night Grande Hotel* (MCA, 1991); *Other Voices, Other Rooms* (Elektra, 1993); *Flyer* (Elektra, 1994); *The Dust Bowl Symphony* (Elektra, 1999); *Clock without Hands* (Elektra/Asylum, 2001).

WEBSITE: www.nancigriffith.com.

DAVID FREELAND

GRUPO LÍMITE

Formed: 1995, Monterrey, Nuevo León, Mexico

Members: Alicia Villarreal, bandleader, vocals (Martha Alicia Villarreal Esparza, born Monterrey, Mexico, 31 August 1974); Gerardo Padilla, keyboards, accordion; Sergio Ponce, guitar; Johnny Cantú, bass; Carlos Ramírez, percussion; Frank García, drums.

Genre: Latin

Best-selling album since 1990: *Partiéndome el Alma* (1996)

Hit songs since 1990: "Te Aprovechas," "El Príncipe," "Sentimientos"

With sing-along choruses, energized cumbia rhythms, and photogenic appeal, Grupo Límite helped modernize norteño music and popularize it with Mexico's middle class. Norteño ensembles, which represent the rural musical folklore of northern Mexico, traditionally comprise a vocalist, accordionist, bajo sexto (twelve-string guitar) player, and a drummer. Límite added keyboards and electric guitar. The group's sound and look sparked a wave of imitators in the Tejano and norteño camps when they emerged in 1995. Other ingredients of Límite's success were the childlike vocals of the singer/songwriter Alicia Villarreal and the novelty of a female-led norteño act. Villarreal even has her own catch phrase, a flirtatious "*ah*-hah" that quickly became part of the Límite mystique, as did her blond braids.

Villarreal began singing in hotel lobby bars while still in high school in Monterrey. Eventually, she teamed with Padilla and Cantú to form the nucleus of what became Grupo Límite. After recording a demo, the band approached all the labels in Monterrey, but it was during a trip to Mexico City that Límite attracted serious attention from PolyGram (now Universal).

In 1995 Límite produced their debut album, *Por Puro Amor*. It came just months after the untimely death of Selena, who, at age twenty-three, was the best-selling artist in the musically similar Texas-Mexican genre known as

Tejano. The album's bouncy style and female lead vocals drew inevitable comparisons to Selena. In fact, Límite is one of the few Mexico-based groups to be embraced by Tejano fans, who generally prefer their music made in Texas. Yet the group's original songwriting and accordion-rooted norteño vibe helped it stand on its own. The album produced "Te Aprovechas," Límite's signature hit, plus the cumbia singles "Esta Vez" and "Con La Misma Piedra."

The sophomore album *Partiéndome el Alma* (1996) kept the momentum going with the *Billboard* chart singles "El Príncipe" and "Solo Contigo." Límite's ingratiating approach helped spread norteño, often considered working-class music, to new upscale audiences in Monterrey. The group's impact on Mexico's pop scene was evident on *De Corazón al Corazón* (1998), which contained Villarreal-penned "Pasión," a duet with the preppy young crooner Cristián Castro.

Villarreal married the ruggedly handsome soccer player Arturo Carmona in 1998. The couple had a daughter, Melanie Aidee, but split in 2001. That year Villarreal took a chance with a mariachi solo album, *Soy Lo Prohibido*. The album rose to number three on *Billboard*'s Top Latin Albums chart, largely on the strength of the antimacho torch song "Te Quedó Grande la Yegua," which tells off an unfaithful lover.

Límite underwent a makeover in 2002. Villarreal undid the braids, and the group threw out the cowboy look in favor of a mall-rat wardrobe. *Soy Así* (2002) was produced by A. B. Quintanilla and Cruz Martinez, leaders of Texas-based cumbia-rap group Kumbia Kings. Featuring the rhythmic jam "Papacito," the album updated Límite's sound with overdubbed vocals and touches of funk.

One of the driving forces behind the resurgence of norteño music of the late 1990s and early 2000s, Límite has done much to urbanize and update Mexico's beloved rural-rooted genre.

SELECTIVE DISCOGRAPHY: *Por Puro Amor* (Polygram, 1995); *Partiéndome el Alma* (Polygram, 1996); *Sentimientos* (Polygram, 1997); *De Corazón al Corazón* (Polygram, 1998); *Por Encima de Todo* (Universal, 2000); *Soy Así* (Universal, 2002).

RAMIRO BURR

GUIDED BY VOICES

Formed: 1983, Dayton, Ohio

Members: Robert Pollard; born Dayton, Ohio, 31 October 1957

Genre: Pop, Rock

Best-selling album since 1990: *Isolation Drills* (2001)

Hit songs since 1990: "I Am a Scientist"

Guided By Voices is the namesake of Robert Pollard, a former elementary-school teacher whose prolific songwriting skills, obsession with the Beatles, and relentless onstage beer swilling made him one of the most unusual pop figures of the 1990s. Reportedly, more than forty musicians have served at one time or another in Guided By Voices, making the group less a band and more of a union brotherhood.

Before Pollard received national attention in 1993, he was busy cranking out volumes of music regionally for twelve years. His homemade method of recording—on four-track tape machines with little attention to overdubs—defined the noisy and unkempt "low-fi" sound that influenced the leading independent rock bands of the 1990s like Pavement, the Breeders, and Sonic Youth. Guided By Voices never reached the commercial heights of those bands, but by the end of the decade, it had amassed a devoted cult following and was recognized as a vital influence by its peers.

Robert Pollard started Guided By Voices as a hobby in 1983. At the time he worked as a fourth-grade schoolteacher in Dayton, Ohio. In the beginning he focused just on recording and neglected playing live. In the years that followed, Pollard released a dozen EPs, six full-length albums, and a wide assortment of bootlegs and live albums, all released independently or on small local Ohio labels. Pollard made it clear he was seeking pop perfection at the level of the Beatles and wanted to write more songs than they did.

Pollard began singing in a fake English accent. His early recordings reflected his unique transformation of his two greatest influences: the psychedelic pop melodies of the Beatles and the dark and cerebral heaviness of early 1970s arena rock outfits like Genesis and Blue Oyster Cult. When Pollard siphoned both through the noisy aesthetic of basement recording, he created his band's signature sound.

Pollard scored his first record deal in 1993, releasing *Vampire on Titus* on Cleveland's Scat Records. The label had wide distribution, and Guided By Voices started touring for the first time in years at the same time it began receiving major kudos from high profile peers like Thurston Moore of the acclaimed New York art punk band Sonic Youth. The next year, Scat entered a distribution deal with Matador Records. With the release of *Bee Thousand* in 1994, Guided By Voices finally reached the masses, receiving national press, MTV airplay, and extensive touring opportunities. That year Pollard quit teaching.

To curb his stage fright, Pollard took to drinking beer before and during shows, usually setting up a cooler of longnecks on the stage. His high kicks and stage rancor were soon part of the act. Unlike his more cerebral peers in the indie rock underground, Pollard made it clear that it was essential for rock and roll to teeter on the brink of danger.

Soon enough Guided By Voices was an official Matador band. It re-released its output from the 1980s on *Box*, a five-disc compilation. The band briefly jumped to TVT Records for two albums. The first, *Do the Collapse* (1999), was produced by Ric Ocasek, former leader of the 1980s pop group the Cars. It was the most polished and accessible album of their career. By 2002 the group was back on Matador and released *Universal Truths and Cycles*.

Throughout the band's success in the 1990s, Pollard was releasing twenty-six solo albums on his own Fading Captain label, most limited editions. In 1999 he told the *Onion* newspaper he had "an addiction to songwriting" and tries to write a song a day, no matter where they end up. "My solo career is Guided by Voices, it's all Guided by Voices," he said. "I write so many songs, and it's hard at the sales level we're at to be able to market and promote them. It's hard for us to put out albums less than a year apart."

Robert Pollard founded Guided By Voices as a passionate outlet for his music making and ended up a voice for independent artists in the 1990s. His prodigious recording output, sharp pop instincts, do-it-yourself production style, and exorbitant stage personality made him an iconoclast who helped to break the barrier between rock fan and rock star.

SELECTIVE DISCOGRAPHY: *Devil Between My Toes* (Schwa, 1987); *Sandbox* (Halo, 1989); *Self-Inflicted Aerial Nostalgia* (Halo, 1989); *Same Place the Fly Got Smashed* (Rocket #9, 1990); *Propeller* (Rockathon, 1992); *Vampire on Titus* (Scat, 1993); *Bee Thousand* (Scat/Matador, 1994); *Crying Your Knife Away* (Lo-Fi, 1994); *Alien Lanes* (Matador, 1995); *Box* (Scat, 1995); *Jellyfish Reflector* (Jellyfish, 1996); *Under the Bushes under the Stars* (Matador, 1996); *Mag Earwig!* (Matador, 1997); *Tonics and Twisted Chasers* (Rockathon, 1997); *Do the Collapse* (TVT, 1999); *Suitcase: Failed Experiments and Trashed Aircraft* (Fading Captain, 2000); *Isolation Drills* (TVT, 2001); *Universal Truth and Cycles* (Matador, 2002).

WEBSITE: www.guidedbyvoices.com.

MARK GUARINO

GUNS N' ROSES

Formed: Los Angeles, California, 1984

Members: Brian "Buckethead" Carroll, guitar (born Marietta, Georgia, 1969); Robin Finck, guitar; Brian "Brain"

Mantia, drums (born Cupertino, California, 7 November 1971); Chris Pittman, keyboards (born Independence, Missouri, 25 February 1976); Dizzy Reed, keyboards (Darren Reed, born Hinsdale, Illinois, 18 June 1963); Axl Rose, vocals (William Bailey, born Lafayette, Indiana, 6 February 1962); Tommy Stinson, bass (born Minneapolis, Minnesota, 6 October 1966). Former members: Steven Adler, drums (born Cleveland, Ohio, 22 January 1965); Gilby Clarke, guitar (born Cleveland, Ohio, 17 August 1962); Josh Freese, drums; Paul Huge, guitar (Paul Tobias, born Indianapolis, Indiana, 1962); Duff McKagan, bass (Michael McKagan, born Seattle, Washington, 5 February 1964); Slash, guitar (Saul Hudson, born Stoke-on-Trent, Staffordshire, England, 23 July 1965); Matt Sorum (born Mission Viejo, California, 19 November 1960); Izzy Stradlin, guitar (Jeffery Isbell, born Lafayette, Indiana, 8 April 1962).

Genre: Rock

Best-selling album since 1990: *Use Your Illusion I* (1991)

Hit songs since 1990: "Don't Cry," "November Rain," "You Could Be Mine"

The most controversial hard rock band of the 1980s spent much of the 1990s trying to recapture their former glory amidst internal turmoil, lawsuits, and the departures of all but one of the group's original members.

Rapid Rise, Gradual Decline

Guns N' Roses exploded onto the rock scene in the mid-1980s with their incendiary debut, *Appetite for Destruction* (1987), heralding the arrival of a blues-influenced heavy metal band on a par with the Rolling Stones and Aerosmith. But volatile personalities, self-destructive behavior, and creative conflicts led to the slow dissolution of the original band slowly after the release of their two-album epic, *Use Your Illusion* (1991), never to recapture their former glory.

Guns N' Roses ended the 1980s with one of the most successful debut albums of the decade; *Appetite for Destruction* (1987) sold more than 20 million copies. In just three short years, the group had established a reputation for unpredictability, volatility, and loutishness, resulting in part from the deaths of two fans during crowd disturbances at a festival show in England in 1988 and in part from the controversial lyrics to the song "One in a Million" (from their 1989 mini-album, *G n' R Lies*), widely criticized for their homophobic and racist sentiments.

The 1990s proved even more chaotic. The singer Axl Rose faced tabloid rumors that he had abused his wife; he also faced charges of attacking an audience member following a riot at a St. Louis show. The controversy faded from headlines in September with the release of the band's eagerly awaited double-album set, *Use Your Illusion I* and *Use Your Illusion II*.

The albums were a triumph for the group, occupying the two top positions of the *Billboard* album charts—the first time that feat had been accomplished since 1974—and winning critical praise for the more mature, ambitious songwriting and arrangements. The three-year process of recording the work proved to be the band's undoing, however; the creative tensions and the artistic split within the group was audible on several of the album's tracks.

While Rose was enamored of the baroque rock and pop of groups such as Queen and Elton John, the guitarists Slash and Izzy Stradlin had more meat-and-potatoes rock and roll tastes, favoring hard rock and blues in the manner of the Rolling Stones and Aerosmith. *I* is the more up-tempo, rock-oriented of the albums, featuring some of Stradlin's most blues-influenced hard rock songs such as "Dust N' Bones," "Double Talkin' Jive," and "You Ain't the First." Rose explores his more progressive rock tendencies on the sprawling, piano-laden hit ballads "November Rain" and "Don't Cry."

II is packed with longer songs—four run over six minutes—that hint at Rose's more pretentious, overindulgent tendencies, such as the antiwar "Civil War" and the nearly ten-minute epic "Estranged." Not surprisingly, Rose also drew fire for "Get in the Ring," on which he threatens a number of rock journalists by name for giving poor reviews to his group. The album also features a cover of Bob Dylan's rock standard "Knockin' on Heaven's Door," delivered in Rose's strangulated, piercing scream of a voice. The albums went on to sell more than 4 million copies each.

In late 1993 after several defections, what was left of the original lineup of the group released its swan song, the covers album, *The Spaghetti Incident?* With covers of songs by groups such as the Misfits, Fear, the New York Dolls, and the Stooges, the ferocious album reveals the punk-rock roots that underlay the heavy-metal influences of bands such as Nazareth.

The Beginning of the End

The band recorded a cover of the Rolling Stones's "Sympathy for the Devil" for the 1994 soundtrack to the Tom Cruise film *Interview with a Vampire.* Though Stradlin was invited back in May 1995, the group was unable to move forward with the recording of new material because of creative disputes between Rose and Slash.

Five years after the release of their first album of new material, the group had been eclipsed by the more punk-oriented, less bombastic sound of grunge rock bands such as Alice in Chains, Nirvana, and Pearl Jam, which eschewed the flashy dress and public excess that had made Guns N' Roses stars a decade before.

In November 1996 Slash announced that Rose had left the band, but Rose quickly retorted with a fax to MTV

Spot Light | Chinese Democracy

From 1997 through 2003, Rose worked with a string of producers on the next Guns N' Roses album, including Mike Clink, techno artist Moby, Sean Beavan, Pink Floyd producer Bob Ezrin, and former Killing Joke bassist Youth. Rumors of a new album came and went, fueled in July of 1999 by a bizarre MTV report that the new lineup of the band made a secret debut in the Adam Sandler film *Big Daddy.* The end credits of the film feature an old version of "Sweet Child 'O Mine" with the original lineup that morphs into a new version of the band's biggest hit with the band's new members: guitarist Robin Finck, drummer Josh Freese, bassist Tommy Stinson, and lone holdover from the original group, keyboardist Reed. Rose reportedly recorded hundreds of tracks with the new members between 1997 and 2003 for the album, dubbed *Chinese Democracy,* constantly tweaking the songs, with more than half a dozen alleged release dates passing without any new material. A handful of new songs were performed during the band's concerts in 2000 and 2002, but after more than a decade in the works, the album remained unreleased, and many wondered how many of the group's fans would still care enough to buy it if it ever did see the light of day.

in which he said that Slash had been fired from the group and that he had purchased the rights to the band's name. At the time Rose promised to deliver a new album from the group by the next summer. Soon after, Rose became a recluse, earning the title "rock and roll Howard Hughes." He broke the silence in February 1998 with an arrest in the Phoenix airport for disorderly conduct.

Rose unveiled the band's new lineup with a New Year's Day concert in Las Vegas in 2001, taking the stage hours late before a crowd of 1,800. Several weeks later the band played a well-received set at the Rock in Rio festival in Rio de Janeiro and announced a European tour, which was canceled and rescheduled within two weeks in April. It was canceled once more in November.

In August 2002 the revamped group made an appearance at the MTV Video Music Awards, performing two classics and a new ballad from an album in the works, *Chinese Democracy*. The performance set tongues wagging, as Rose sounded off key and out of breath and appeared to have had cosmetic surgery. Despite an almost entirely new membership, the group was up to its old tricks when it launched its first North American tour in nearly a decade in November. The Vancouver kickoff date was canceled at the last minute, inspiring irate fans to riot, smash windows, and clash with police, who resorted to pepper spray to subdue the fans. Less than a month later, the tour was canceled after Rose failed to appear for a show in Philadelphia. By early 2003 *Chinese Democracy* remain unreleased.

Guns N' Roses rose to prominence in the late 1980s thanks to a volatile combination of cynicism, belligerence, arrogance, self-destruction, violence, and reckless disregard for society's rules. When the band failed to agree on a musical direction, that reckless energy turned to torpor and career limbo in the early 1990s. The enigmatic, eccentric leader Axl Rose then began a nearly decade-long exile in the studio with an all-new group, working on an album that would have to make a spectacular impression to reflect the band's sunken fortunes.

SELECTIVE DISCOGRAPHY: *Live Like a Suicide* (Geffen, 1986); *Appetite for Destruction* (Geffen, 1987); *G n' R Lies* (Geffen, 1988); *Use Your Illusion I* (Geffen, 1991); *Use Your Illusion II* (Geffen, 1991); *The Spaghetti Incident?* (Geffen, 1993).

GIL KAUFMAN

BUDDY GUY

Born: George Guy; Lettsworth, Louisiana, 30 July 1936
Genre: Blues
Best-selling album since 1990: *Damn Right, I've Got the Blues* (1991)

Effervescent guitarist/vocalist Buddy Guy is a post–World War II blues pioneer who helped move blues into the electric guitar era, ultimately opening the door for the rock/blues explosion of the 1970s. One of the few remaining players with lineage to Chicago's blues heyday, Guy is an energetic ambassador who generously passes his music's culture down to others just as older bluesmen passed theirs down to him. Guy's performance style is uniquely robust and many consider him the greatest living blues guitarist.

From Cotton Fields to Chicago Blues Clubs

Guy grew up in rural Louisiana. He taught himself to play guitar from listening to recordings of old bluesmen that he purchased with money he had earned from picking cotton. As a teenager, he moved to Baton Rouge and began playing gigs with local groups. He traveled to Chicago in 1957 and finally broke into the Chicago blues scene with the help of blues icon Muddy Waters who graciously took the talented guitarist under his wing. Soon Guy was in the mix with other hot blues players such as B.B. King, Otis Rush, and Magic Sam. In an effort to gain notoriety among Chicago's logjam of talented blues guitarists, Guy purchased the longest guitar chord possible—about 150 feet—and began wandering among the audience, even meandering outside the club and into the street while playing his ferocious guitar solos. Most guitarists of that time generally sat when they performed. Considered a consummate showman, Guy still incorporates the trademark guitar-playing stroll during his live shows.

On the strength of his guitar skills, Guy managed a record contract and became a notable studio musician, playing on records for many of the blues legends. He also recorded solo albums but they failed to catch the excitement generated by his live performances. In 1972 he formed an enduring musical alliance with harmonica great Junior Wells that lasted until 1993. Although blues is an American art form, Guy and most of his contemporaries went virtually unnoticed in the American music landscape, garnering much more attention overseas, particularly in London. In the 1970s, English rock/blues guitar giants Eric Clapton and Jeff Beck, in addition to the Rolling Stones, all pointed to Guy as their major influence. Clapton asserted that Guy was the best guitar player in the world. American guitar superstars Jimi Hendrix and Stevie Ray Vaughn also hailed Guy as a primary inspiration.

Acclaim and Appreciation

However, by the 1980s, Guy was having trouble securing a record label and survived mostly on the strength of his live shows. In 1990 Clapton asked Guy to perform with him at his Royal Albert Hall concerts in London. Guy's performance and appearance on Clapton's album of the concerts, *24 Nights,* received enthusiastic acclaim and Silvertone Records offered Guy a recording contract. They released, *Damn Right, I've Got the Blues* (1991) and finally Guy was allowed to create in the studio a sound that matched the zeal of his live performances. The Grammy Award–winning album featured special guests, Clapton, Beck, and Mark Knopfler joining Guy's pleading guitar and all-out singing. Hardcore blues fans resented the rock and R&B presence on *Damn Right, I've Got the Blues* but Guy appreciated the long-awaited and much-deserved trip to the limelight and he intended to stay there. He released *Feels Like Rain* (1993), which again mixed his blues sound with a slight commercial crossover into rock and R&B. The title song is a Hendrix-like ballad, and he adds his blues touch to the pop rock "Some Kind of Wonderful."

Feels Like Rain also won a Grammy Award and it features an impressive guest list that includes Bonnie Raitt, Travis Tritt, and Paul Rodgers.

Blues fans were thrilled with Guy's following recording, *Slippin'* (1994), because it captures, without any guest artists, his unbridled energy. The album is a good example of Guy's brand of power blues and James Brown–styled vocals.

Guy can also deliver a mellow blues, the kind of pre-electric sound associated with the Mississippi Delta. The re-released *Alone and Acoustic* (1991), recorded with Junior Wells and first released as *Going Back* in 1981, offers a dramatic contrast to his high-powered, frenzied blues. This straightforward recording displays Guy's tasteful acoustic guitar skills accompanying his more subdued vocals.

Guy enjoys promoting his music's culture to younger players and he has toured with blues-influenced musicians such as Kenny Wayne Shepherd, Susan Tedeschi, and the young blues phenomenon, Jonny Lang. He included Lang on the rocking blues release, *Heavy Love* (1998). Guy owns a downtown Chicago nightclub dedicated to the blues called Buddy Guy's Legends. *Sweet Tea* (2001), recorded in the heart of Mississippi, recreates the early blues sound and it might well be the sound Guy remembers hearing as part of the Chicago blues fraternity in the late 1950s. The album starts out with a solo acoustic lament, "Done Got Old," and the raw power of the remaining eight songs make the listener forget that Guy is past middle age. His musician friends call him an "ageless wonder" as he carries the persona of a man in his twenties. Guy's younger brother Phil Guy is also a noted Chicago blues guitar player and he often appears at Buddy's nightclub. Guy's daughter performs in the hip-hop group Infamous Syndicate.

After giving so much to so many for so many years, it is poetic justice that Guy is reaping the rewards of music stardom. He tours the world and records, enjoying his role as one of the elder statesmen of blues.

SELECTIVE DISCOGRAPHY: *Crazy Music* (Chess, 1965); *This Is Buddy Guy* (Chess, 1968); *Blues Today* (Chess, 1968); *Coming at You* (Chess, 1968); *Buddy & the Juniors* (BGO, 1970); *Hold That Plane* (Vanguard, 1972); *Live in Montreux* (Evidence, 1977); *Pleading the Blues* (Evidence, 1979); *Stone Crazy!* (Alligator, 1981); *DJ Play My Blues* (JSP, 1982); *Original Blues Brothers Live* (Blue Moon, 1983); *I Left My Blues in San Francisco* (MCA, 1987); *Live at the Checkerboard Lounge* (JSP, 1988); *Damn Right, I've Got the Blues* (Jive, 1991); *The Very Best of Buddy Guy* (Rhino, 1992); *My Time after Awhile* (Vanguard, 1992); *Feels Like Rain* (Jive, 1993); *Slippin' In* (Jive, 1994); *Buddy Guy Live! The Real Deal* (Jive 1996); *As Good As It Gets* (Vanguard, 1998); *Buddy's Blues: The Best of the JSP Sessions* (Jive, 1998); *Heavy Love* (Jive, 1998); *Sweet Tea* (Jive, 2001). **With Junior Wells:** *I Was Walking through the Woods* (MCA, 1970); *Buddy Guy and Junior Wells Play the Blues* (Vanguard, 1972); *Drinkin' TNT 'n' Smokin' Dynamite* (Blind Pig, 1982); *Alone & Acoustic* (Alligator, 1991); *Last Time Around: Live at Legends* (Jive, 1998).

DONALD LOWE

H

CHARLIE HADEN

Born: Shenandoah, Iowa, 6 August 1937

Genre: Jazz

Best-selling album since 1990: *Beyond the Missouri Sky (Short Stories)* (1996)

Charlie Haden is known by jazz aficionados worldwide for his deep tone on the double bass and his supportive, unadorned improvisational style, which emphasizes the harmonic fundamentals of the various jazz, folk, political, and film musical styles he addresses.

Having begun his career as "Cowboy Charlie," a two-year-old singer in the Haden Family Band performing hillbilly music daily on an Ozark radio station, Haden took up piano after an attack of bulbar polio in his throat; he picked up his older brother's bass when he was fourteen. In the mid-1950s, Haden moved to Los Angeles to study at Westlake College of Modern Music, where he roomed with the innovative bassist Scot LaFaro (who died in a car crash in 1961). Soon Haden was playing in jam sessions and with West Coast leaders, including the saxophonist Art Pepper and pianists Hampton Hawes and Paul Bley, in whose quintet he met the iconoclastic saxophonist and composer Ornette Coleman.

Haden enjoyed a career breakthrough in Coleman's quartet, performing at a legendary booking at the Five Spot in New York City in 1959, but he left the band in 1960 because of heroin addiction, for which he underwent treatment at Synanon House in California. Returning to New York in 1966, he restarted his career in earnest, working with jazz traditionalists and avant-gardists alike. The father of triplets, he recorded at every opportunity and rejoined Coleman, whom he regards as a genius and mentor. When Coleman reorganized his ensemble around electric guitars in the early 1970s, Haden and Coleman's other ex-band members formed Old and New Dreams to regroup in their acoustic performance mode.

Haden's first album as a leader, *Liberation Music Orchestra* (1969), was a critical success, notable for arrangements by the pianist Carla Bley and the trombonist Roswell Rudd depicting the riots at the Democratic National Convention of 1968; the album also includes the Civil Rights anthem "We Shall Overcome." Highly outspoken, Haden was arrested while performing in Portugal in 1971 for his onstage support of the Angolan liberation movement. In the early 1970s he was a founding member of the quartet led by the pianist Keith Jarrett. In the middle of that decade, he recorded two albums of duets with his closest associates, an unprecedented project.

In the early 1980s Haden was named the director of jazz studies at California Institute of the Arts and reached out internationally, recording with the Norwegian saxophonist Jan Gabarek and the Brazilian guitarist Egberto Gismonti for the German-based ECM label, and with Chet Baker and the pianist Enrico Pieranunzi for the Italian Soul Note label. He recorded two further albums with the Liberation Music Orchestra, one backed by Japanese producers. In 1986 Haden established Quartet West, a saxophone-piano-bass-drums band performing conventional jazz repertoire and themes from film noir soundtracks of the 1940s and 1950s, albeit with a lyrical, sometimes nostalgic air. Through 1999 the band released six albums,

Haden in Montreal

In 1989 the Festival International de Jazz de Montreal staged an eight-night Charlie Haden retrospective, the documentation of which has come out since 1990. Verve Records offers four volumes of *The Montreal Tapes,* featuring the bassist with his pianist protégés Geri Allen and Gonzalo Rubalcaba, his mid-1950s California colleague Paul Bley (Paul Motian, the drum partner of Haden's tragically killed friend Scott LaFaro, appears on all three albums), and his former Ornette Coleman band mates Don Cherry and Edward Blackwell. In 2001 ECM Records put out *In Montreal,* Haden's festival set with Brazilian guitarist-pianist Egberto Gismonti. *Charlie Haden at the Montreal Jazz Festival,* a sixty-minute DVD, features the Liberation Music Orchestra with the saxophone soloist Joe Lovano performing traditional Latin American songs and "Nkosi Sikelel-I Afrika," the African National Congress anthem. Radio Canada also recorded Haden's concerts with saxophonist Joe Henderson and drummer Al Foster, and with guitarist Pat Metheny and drummer Jack DeJohnette, but these recordings have not been released.

David Sanchez, and Havana-born musicians Rubalcaba, Ignacio Berroa (drums), and Federico Britos Ruiz (violin).

Haden suffers from severe hyperacusis—a reduced tolerance to loudness—which requires him to wear earplugs while performing. Yet he seldom shirks opportunities to perform. He has guest-starred with sophisticated pop musicians, including Bruce Hornsby and Rickie Lee Jones. He understands that abstract improvisations, folk airs, and complex songs alike are rooted in profound bass notes, which he can unerringly discover and articulately express.

SELECTIVE DISCOGRAPHY: *Montreal Tapes with Geri Allen* (Verve, 1990); *Montreal Tapes with Gonzalo Rubalcaba* (Verve, 1990); *In Montreal* (ECM, 2001); *Montreal Tapes, Vol. 1* (Verve, 1990); *Dialogues* (Antilles, 1991); *Dream Keeper* (Blue Note, 1991); *First Song* (Soul Note, 1991); *Haunted Heart* (Verve, 1992); *Always Say Goodbye* (Verve, 1994); *Steal Away* (Verve, 1995); *Now Is the Hour* (Verve, 1996); *Night and the City* (Verve, 1997); *Beyond the Missouri Sky (Short Stories)* (Verve, 1996); *The Art of the Song* (Polygram, 1999); *Nocturne* (Verve, 2001); *American Dreams* (Verve, 2002).

WEBSITE: http://interjazz.com/haden.

HOWARD MANDEL

HERBIE HANCOCK

Born: Chicago, Illinois, 12 April 1940
Genre: Jazz, Fusion, Electronica
Best-selling album since 1990: *Gershwin's World* (1998)

Keyboardist Herbie Hancock has the past, present, and future much on his mind. Since 1990 he has reimagined the pre–World War II contexts of George Gershwin, revisited the 1960s jazz of John Coltrane and Miles Davis, kept up with hip-hop rhythms, turntable disc jockeys, and the latest keyboard technology, and looked for new standards among popular songs of rock, pop, and soul genres.

Hancock has the experience to justify such a range of interests. A piano prodigy who performed a Mozart concerto movement with the Chicago Symphony Orchestra at age eleven and had his own high school jazz band, Hancock studied electrical engineering at Grinnell College in Iowa before switching to composition. He left school in 1960, one course short of graduation, to accompany saxophonist Coleman Hawkins in a Chicago engagement. By 1962 he was in New York City with a contract from Blue Note Records, and with challenging work as a pianist for avant-garde reeds player Eric Dolphy.

including *Always Say Goodbye* (1994), a Grammy nominee and *Down Beat* Critics Poll Album of the Year. Haden's ability to enhance a breadth of repertoire performed by a wide range of musicians—newcomers and veterans alike—has been a lifetime boon. He has become an enthusiastic Americanist, collaborating on spirituals, hymns, and folk songs with pianist Hank Jones on *Steal Away* (1995); on standards such as "Body and Soul" with pianist Kenny Barron; and with the Midwestern guitarist Pat Metheny on the Grammy-winning *Beyond the Missouri Sky (Short Stories)* (1997). He evoked a majestic "America the Beautiful" with saxophonist Michael Brecker, the young pianist Brad Mehldau, and a thirty-four-piece orchestra on *American Dreams* (2001). But Haden is also an ardent internationalist, exploring indigenous fado repertoire with Portuguese lutist Carlos Paredes on *Dialogues* (1990) and playing Cuban boleros on *Nocturnes* (2001) in an ensemble that included Metheny, the Liberation Music Orchestra saxophonist Joe Lovano, Panamanian saxophonist

Herbie Hancock [PAUL NATKIN/PHOTO RESERVE]

Hancock is as accessible as he is advanced. He had his first hit song almost by accident with the gospel-inflected "Watermelon Man" (1963), covered by Afro-Cuban congero Mongo Santamaria. Besides leading his own albums, he was the highly regarded house pianist of the Blue Note label through 1968, recording with trumpeters Donald Byrd, Lee Morgan, and Freddie Hubbard; saxophonists Jackie McLean, Hank Mobley, Sam Rivers, and Wayne Shorter; vibist Bobby Hutcherson; guitarist Grant Green; and drummers Billy Higgins and Elvin Jones. In 1963 Hancock joined Miles Davis's quintet. With bassist Ron Carter and drummer Tony Williams, he developed a jazz rhythm section concept that was elastic in regard to time and dynamics.

At Davis's direction, Hancock became the first musician in jazz to adapt electric pianos to regular stage performance and was the keyboard anchor of the electric jazz revolution. In 1969 Hancock converted his acoustic octet into an electrically amplified and processed band—Mwandishi—in which he employed the most advanced electric synthesizers and keyboards as they evolved. Hancock had his first crossover fusion hit with "Chameleon" introduced by his band Headhunters (their debut self-titled recording was the first jazz album to sell platinum). Han-

cock was also the first fusion star to reassert his straight-ahead acoustic background with fellow refugees from Davis-inspired amplification—Carter, Williams, and Shorter—in the quintet V.S.O.P., from 1976 to 1979.

Throughout the 1970s and 1980s Hancock kept a hand in two camps, as street-smart future funkster, recording the breakthrough hip-hop hit "Rockit," as well as acoustic trio albums, in large part for Japanese and European markets. He hosted two television series: *Rock School*, a music education program on Public Broadcasting Service, and cable network Showtime's *Coast to Coast*, featuring in-concert performances and interviews. He won an Academy Award for *Round Midnight* (1986), excelling at the soundtrack sideline he began with Michelangelo Antonioni's counterculture film *Blow-Up* (1966).

Hancock has won eight Grammy Awards, including Best Instrumental Jazz Performance, Individual or Group for *A Tribute to Miles* (1994), and Best Traditional Jazz Album for *Gershwin's World* (1998). In that project, Hancock, with Shorter, Chick Corea, Stevie Wonder, Joni Mitchell, Kathleen Battle, and the Orpheus Chamber Orchestra, interprets Gershwin's Roaring 1920s and depression-era milieu.

Hancock's works have been endlessly sampled and licensed. "Cantaloop (Flip Fantasia)" from the British turntablists US3 became a Top 20 radio success on the basis of thirty-five signature seconds of Hancock's composition and recording of "Cantaloupe Island" (1964). Rather than be historified by younger musicians, Hancock rejoined the fray, producing *Dis Is Da Drum* (1994), a disappointing release that wore its electronic percussion and street credibility too heavily. He followed with a contrasting tack, *The New Standard* (1995), for which he convened an all-star band to perform repertoire associated with pop songs from the 1970s through the 1990s. This album was better received—one track, "Manhattan (Island of Lights and Love)," won a Grammy Award for Best Instrumental Composition—and it gave rise to Hancock's *Directions in Music: Live at Massey Hall* (2002), a collaboration with saxophonist Michael Brecker and trumpeter Roy Hargrove. True to form, between those albums Hancock released an austere program of spontaneous duets with Shorter, *1+1* (1997). After *Directions in Music* he and Bill Laswell produced another electro-jazz-pop-fusion effort, *Future2Future* (2001).

In a project co-sponsored by Berklee College of Music, he has been a Distinguished Artist in Residence at Jazz Aspen Snowmass (Colorado) since 1991, mentoring promising young jazz musicians selected from worldwide applicants. He is a member of the Board of Trustees of the Thelonious Monk Institute, and established his Rhythm of Life Foundation in 1996, aiming to "narrow the gap between those technologically empowered and those who are not; and to find ways to help technology improve humanity." Hancock is a full partner in Transparent Music, a multimedia company that produced his concert DVD, even while he records larger projects under contract with Universal Music/Verve. Whether interpreting the past or doing something new in the present, Hancock contributes to jazz's future.

SELECTIVE DISCOGRAPHY: *Takin' Off* (Blue Note, 1962); *Maiden Voyage* (Blue Note, 1965); *Head-hunters* (Columbia, 1973); *V.S.O.P.* (Columbia, 1977); *Future Shock* (Columbia, 1983); *Mwandishi: The Complete Warner Bros. Recordings* (Warner Bros., 1994); *A Tribute to Miles* (Qwest, 1994); *Dis Is Da Drum* (Mercury, 1994); *1+1* (Verve, 1997); *Gershwin's World* (1998); *Future2Future* (Transparent, 2001); *The Herbie Hancock Box* (Columbia, 2002). **With Michael Brecker and Roy Hargrove:** *Directions in Music: Live at Massey Hall* (Verve, 2002). **With Miles Davis:** *E.S.P.* (Columbia, 1965); *Bitches Brew* (Columbia, 1970). **Soundtracks:** *Blow-Up* (MGM, 1966); *Death Wish* (One Way, 1974); *Round Midnight* (Columbia, 1986).

WEBSITE: www.herbiehancock.com.

HOWARD MANDEL

HANSON

Formed: 1992, Tulsa, Oklahoma

Members: Clarke Isaac Taylor, guitar, vocals (born Tulsa, Oklahoma, 17 November 1980); Jordan Taylor, singer, keyboards (born Tulsa, Oklahoma, 14 March 1983); Zachary Walker Taylor, drums, vocals (born Tulsa, Oklahoma, 22 October 1985).

Genre: Rock, Pop

Best-selling album since 1990: *Middle of Nowhere* (1997)

Hit songs since 1990: "MMMBop," "Weird"

Before the pop sensations Britney Spears, *NSYNC, the Backstreet Boys, and Christina Aguilera, there was Hanson. The trio of brothers from Tulsa, Oklahoma, unwittingly opened the floodgates for the teen pop revolution in 1996 with their irresistible pop confection, "MMM-Bop," setting the stage for the resurgence of bubble-gum pop in the late 1990s.

The home-schooled Hanson boys began harmonizing as children around their family dinner table in Tulsa, graduating to writing and performing their original songs at local venues in the early 1990s. On the road in places such as Trinidad and Venezuela with their father, Walker, then

an international financier for an oil-drilling concern, the young boys listened to a well-worn *Time/Life* collection of classic pop hits from 1957–1969 featuring the likes of Bobby Darin, the Beach Boys, Otis Redding, and Chuck Berry. The music and their feeling of being "in the middle of nowhere" became their template, as the boys developed a style that fused the boyish harmonies of the Jackson 5 with the milk-fed image of the Osmonds and the Partridge Family.

Sensing that they were destined for greater success than local school functions, the brothers and their parents approached the music attorney Christopher Sabec in 1992 in hopes of procuring a recording contract. Sabec signed on as the trio's manager and shopped them around to music labels, five of which passed on the Hanson brothers between 1992 and 1995. Frustrated, Hanson independently released a pair of records locally, including *Boomerang* (1995), which hinted at their radio-ready pop sound. Around this time the Hanson brothers began playing their own instruments and working on the song that later made them superstars, "MMMBop." When "MMMBop" finally caught the ears of the music industry in Los Angeles, their dreams of pop stardom seemed within reach.

Out of Nowhere

The pinup-handsome, blonde-haired thirteen-year-old Taylor was the singer/keyboardist, the sixteen-year-old "serious" Isaac was lead guitarist, and the high-energy eleven-year-old Zac played the drums. The act earned a contract with Mercury Records in 1996, by which time they had already amassed a catalog of 100 original songs.

The entire family moved to Hollywood in July 1996 as the trio recorded their debut, *Middle of Nowhere*, produced by the Dust Brothers (Beck, Beastie Boys) and Steve Lironi (Black Grape). All thirteen songs were written by the brothers, some with help from such renowned songwriters as Cynthia Weil and Barry Mann, Desmond Child, and Mark Hudson.

Just six weeks after the release of the "MMMBop" single in March 1997, the song jumped to number one on the *Billboard* charts, setting the stage for the album's release in May. With its combination of classic pop, soul, gospel, and sunny lyrics, *Middle of Nowhere* was the antidote to the gloomy rock that had dominated the airwaves for so long. With a metronomic drumbeat, soaring three-part harmonies, turntable scratches, and a nonsense lyric in the chorus, "MMMBop" was the perfect summer hit. *Middle of Nowhere* beguiles with a mixture of joyous love songs ("Thinking of You," "Lucy"), torch songs ("Weird," "I Will Come to You"), and a healthy helping of funky Motown-style soul ("Speechless," "Where's the Love").

The boys became instant superstars, touring the world and appearing on countless magazine covers and televi-

Spot Light | "MMMBop"

It was the shot heard round the world: "Mmm bop, ba duba dop / Ba du bop, ba duba dop." With those nonsense lyrics from their break-through 1996 hit "MMMBop," Hanson single-handedly launched the teen pop revolution in the United States. Released at a time when the predominant grunge rock sound was on the wane, the Hanson brothers' major-label debut, *Middle of Nowhere,* was issued after the debuts of fellow pop bands the Spice Girls and Backstreet Boys, but it was not until the smash success of "MMMBop" that the musical sea change began in earnest. With their squeaky clean, approachable good looks and relent-lessly hooky songs, the Hanson boys were an antidote to the brooding imagery and dark music of the early 1990s. Within a year of its release, their debut was followed by smash albums from the Backstreet Boys, *NSYNC, and, later, Britney Spears, Christina Aguilera, and dozens of similar harmonizing boy and girl groups who never made it out of the starting gate.

sion shows. Not taking any chances on the group losing heat, Mercury released a Christmas album in late 1997, *Snowed In,* followed by a reissue of the boy's early record-ings, *Three Car Garage: The Independent Recordings '95–'96* (1998), and, later that year, a live album, *Live from Albertane* (1998).

As Hanson regrouped to work on their second album, the *Billboard* charts exploded with teen pop acts of every stripe. By the time *This Time Around* was released in the spring of 2000, the trio had been nearly forgotten in favor of groups such as the Backstreet Boys and *NSYNC. Not surprisingly, the album is a stab at maturity, with more soul-inflected vocals, guitar solos, rock-oriented arrange-ments, and noticeably lower-register vocals from Taylor, whose voice had deepened in between albums.

The album features guest guitar playing from the prodigy Jonny Lang, a harmonica solo from the Blues Trav-eler leader John Popper, string arrangements, and solo writ-ing credits for the boys on all of the songs. The album gently steps away from the sound the trio perfected on their debut, instead going for the grittier, gospel-inspired blues-rock sound of such bands as the Black Crowes.

Though the first single of the album, "If Only," fea-tures the same mixture of poppy arrangement, turntable scratching, and a soaring, repetitive chorus, it was not as successful as "MMMBop." Taylor Hanson was sanguine about the group's prospects in an interview with MTV.com in 2001. "I think we're in a really weird place as a band because we are a band, and we always have been, but a lot of people don't realize that. I want people to hear the name Hanson and think credible, musical, creative music. That's what people should think 'cause that's what it is—it's just about the music."

The Hanson brothers began work on a third album in late 2001, tentatively titled *Underneath,* due in the spring of 2003. The singer/songwriter Michelle Branch was slated to appear on the song "Deeper." In 2002, nineteen-year-old Taylor Hanson married eighteen-year-old Natalie Anne Bryant, who gave birth to the couple's first son, Jor-dan Ezra Hanson, five months later.

With their combination of boyish good looks and prodigious songwriting talent, Hanson helped spark a pop music revolution in 1997. Though their subsequent efforts did not reach the pinnacle of their major-label debut, the brothers continued to hone their craft and attempted to achieve the hardest music business trick of all: maturing in the spotlight.

SELECTIVE DISCOGRAPHY: *Middle of Nowhere* (Mer-cury, 1997); *Snowed In* (Mercury, 1997); *Live from Albertane* (Mercury, 1998); *Three Car Garage: Indie Recordings '95–'96* (Mercury, 1998); *This Time Around* (Island, 2000).

WEBSITES: www.hanson.net; www.hansononline.com.

GIL KAUFMAN

BEN HARPER

Born: Pomona, California, 28 October 1969

Genre: Rock

Best-selling album since 1990: *Burn to Shine* (1999)

Hit songs since 1990: "Steal My Kisses"

A restless singer/songwriter, Ben Harper has cre-ated original, distinctively American fusions by drawing on blues, folk-rock, country, reggae, and gospel. As a child, Harper often hung out at his grandparents' record store in Claremont, Cal-ifornia. There he got an eclectic musical educa-tion listening to Little Feat's blues, the Allman Brothers' rock, Otis Redding's soul, and Stevie Wonder's R&B. Surrounded by the sounds of his heroes, he decided he wanted to pursue a music career, too.

He was discovered by Taj Mahal, the world-beat blues fusionist who saw his own eclecticism and curiosity reflected in Harper. Signed to Virgin Records in 1992, Harper started out as a twangy, acoustic-heavy folk balladeer. He even had a signature instrument: the Weissenhorn, a 1920s slide guitar played in the lap. Despite the fact that he had to play it seated, his lyrical fire and soulful vocals worked audiences into a frenzy, and he became an underground favorite among folk-music lovers, activists, and urban sophisticates.

His debut album, *Welcome to the Cruel World* (1994), makes ample use of his slide guitar. The album begins with a couple of acoustic ballads, "The Three of Us" and "Whipping Boy," but catches fire with the up-tempo "Breakin' Down," where his sweet falsetto channels Aaron Neville. He reveals his liberal politics on the midtempo "Don't Take That Attitude to the Grave," delivering fire and brimstone to law-and-order conservatives. "You're gonna reap what you sow," he scolds. But he is more effective at delivering honey than fire—"Waiting on an Angel" is pure seduction, a waltz where he uses his gentle baritone to convincingly plead to a lover. While not a big seller in the United States, the album created some buzz in Europe, where Harper appeared on bills with John Lee Hooker, Ray Charles, and Neneh Cherry.

His next effort, *Fight for Your Mind* (1995), is one of those critically acclaimed, commercially ignored efforts that new fans rediscover years later, after the artist has finally broken into the mainstream. Here he maintains his acoustic framework, but adds some energetic blues and a powerful rhythm section, featuring the nineteen-year-old drummer Oliver Charles. The album kicks off with the political "Oppression," another slide-guitar-centered song with a meandering melody and quietly determined lyrics: "oppression / you shall learn to fear me." Harper picks up the energy on the swampy, shuffling "Ground on Down," where he turns his Weissenhorn into an unlikely funk instrument. He ventures even further into rootsy, Delta blues on "Gold to Me," where he conjures the genre's raw pain, pleading for redemption. He again shines on the ballads, singing soft and low and somehow making time stop on the deceptively up-tempo "Another Lonely Day." Almost dropping to a whisper on "Please Me Like You Want To," he sings, "you're with somebody / but you don't want to be."

Always on the move, Harper veered into Hendrix-inspired alt-rock for *The Will to Live* (1997). "Faded" demonstrates Harper's lingering awkwardness with heavier music, as his subtle vocals don't match the amped-up sound. Recalling the country-blues fusions of his mentor Taj Mahal, Harper combines a Western-swing two-step with bluesman

vocals on "Homeless Child," which also features Harper's spot-on falsetto. The more electric, rock tendencies of *The Will to Live* helped push it to number eighty-nine on the *Billboard* 200 album chart, making it his first chart album in the United States. The album also marks the debut of his regular backing band, the Innocent Criminals.

Though his albums were not big moneymakers, Virgin continued to support him without the usual label meddling; his critical acclaim represented a feather in the label's cap, as did his road-warrior's willingness to perform 200 to 300 dates a year.

The efforts finally paid off commercially with *Burn to Shine*, a more confident sequel to *The Will to Live*. He garnered significant Top 40 airplay with the single "Steal My Kisses," a cute ditty that does not dilute Harper's essence, combining modern funk rhythms with stripped-down arrangements. The rest of the album is also more commercial. The rocker "Alone" uses Red Hot Chili Peppers-like bass and an ominous, minor-key melody. "Less" is a bombastic, cymbal-heavy rock anthem that despairs over a jaded, demanding partner. He flirts with hard rock on "Two Hands of a Prayer" and "Please Bleed." While fans who expected him to continue his roots-revival ways forever were disappointed, Harper's many facets and interests kept him from settling on any style for too long.

Harper summed up the best of his 1990s material with a double-live set *Live from Mars* in 2001. That year he fathered a child with his actress girlfriend Laura Dern (her first, his third). He was also the subject of a low-budget documentary, *Pleasure and Pain* (2002), co-directed by the music photographer Danny Clinch.

Diamonds on the Inside (2003) displays his most ambitious world-music vibe yet. The African spiritual "Picture of Jesus" features the famed South African vocal group Ladysmith Black Mambazo. "With My Own Two Hands" is Marley-esque reggae, while the ethereal, almost prayerful "When She Believes" uses a Caribbean-style accordion. The album did not produce any more crossover hits, but no one could fault its creative heft or inspired fusions.

While flying below the pop-star radar, Harper has delighted music connoisseurs with his ability to make modern, relevant pop informed by multicultural American and world traditions.

SELECTIVE DISCOGRAPHY: *The Will to Live* (Virgin, 1997); *Burn to Shine* (Virgin, 1999); *Live from Mars* (Virgin, 2001); *Diamonds on the Inside* (Virgin, 2003).

RAMIRO BURR

EMMYLOU HARRIS

Born: Birmingham, Alabama, 2 April 1947
Genre: Folk, Country

Best-selling album since 1990: *Wrecking Ball* (1995)

Hit songs since 1990: "Long May You Run"

Although Emmylou Harris was a country music hit maker in the 1970s, she strayed from the music's mainstream, evolving into a traditionalist who deliberately blurred the lines between country, folk, and rock. Praised for her angelic soprano voice, Harris is a consummate harmony singer, collaborating with musicians inside and outside country music circles. After the release of *Wrecking Ball* (1995), her comeback album that won her an entirely new audience of young rock fans, Harris championed the legacy of her mentor and former harmony partner Gram Parsons. Harris became a sort of godmother to a new generation of country rock musicians who campaigned to record with her and who connected with her eclectic vision of country music.

Harris was raised in a military family and spent her teenage years in a suburb of Washington, D.C. After graduating from high school, she pursued a music career in Greensboro, North Carolina, and later moved to New York City, and Nashville, Tennessee, before returning to the D.C. area, where she became active on the city's folk music circuit. She soon met Gram Parsons, a Harvard-educated southerner who taught Harris how to sing country-music harmony. She ended up joining his band and recorded two albums with him, *GP* (1973) and *Grievous Angel* (1974), before he died at age twenty-six of an overdose of morphine and tequila. Through his solo work and brief stints influencing bands like the Byrds, the Flying Burrito Brothers, and the Rolling Stones, Parsons was a pioneer in the cross-pollination of country and rock.

Harris produced several country hits throughout the 1970s and 1980s, recorded the country opera *The Ballad of Sally Rose* (1985), and collaborated with the country stars Dolly Parton and Linda Ronstadt on the album *Trio* (1987). She was perceived as a risk-taking traditional country artist who recorded and performed with bluegrass musicians, seasoned Nashville session players, old-time country stars, and rock stars like Bob Dylan, Roy Orbison, and Neil Young. Her repertoire included covers of the songs of country pioneers like Buck Owens, the Louvin Brothers, and Patsy Cline as well as the Beatles and the disco queen Donna Summer. Notwithstanding this ecumenical impulse, Harris often reverted to an old-fashioned acoustic style, a penchant that helped to earn her a term as the president of the Country Music Foundation.

By the 1990s mainstream country music had lost its twang and rural character. With new mass-appeal stars like Garth Brooks and Brooks and Dunn, the country music industry embraced pop hooks and the flashy sensation of stadium rock. Harris's old-time sensibilities were suddenly out of fashion, and she publicly lamented the music's high-gloss makeover. "The reason modern country audiences miss out is that they haven't heard the music's true roots outside its boot-kickin', hat-wearin', bronco-ridin' stereotypes," she told a reporter in 1997. "It's crazy. A lot of them think country music started in 1982."

Harris cut her ties with her longtime label, Warner Bros./Reprise, and recorded *Wrecking Ball* (1995) with the producer Daniel Lanois, acclaimed for his work with U2, Peter Gabriel, and Bob Dylan. The twelve-track album highlighted Harris's ethereal voice, surrounding it with hypnotic percussion and atmospheric beauty. She reinterpreted songs by the rock artists Jimi Hendrix, Neil Young, and Steve Earle, and she transformed them into ghostly spirituals of regret and redemption. It was a bold musical departure that opened the door to a broad new audience of younger fans.

Harris was a beacon for rock artists who identified with country music's classic soulfulness and rebellious impulses, but who shunned the slick formulas that held sway over its commercial mainstream. Harris sang harmony on hundreds of albums, and she executive-produced a tribute to Parsons that featured his songs performed by alternative rockers including Beck, Wilco, and Whiskeytown. She was pivotal in keeping alive Parson's legacy: that of a venturesome maverick who seeks to redeem country music from its commercial leanings with stirring reminders of its roots in the yearnings of the human heart.

SELECTIVE DISCOGRAPHY: *Gliding Bird* (Jubilee, 1970); *Pieces of the Sky* (Reprise, 1975); *Elite Hotel* (Reprise, 1976); *Luxury Liner* (Warner Bros., 1977); *Quarter Moon in a Ten-Cent Town* (Warner Bros., 1978); *Profile: The Best of Emmylou Harris* (Warner Bros., 1978); *Blue Kentucky Girl* (Warner Bros., 1979); *Roses in the Snow* (Warner Bros., 1980); *The Ballad of Sally Rose* (Warner Bros., 1985); *Thirteen* (Warner Bros., 1986); *Angel Band* (Warner Bros., 1987); *Bluebird* (Warner Bros., 1989); *Duets* (Warner Bros., 1990); *Brand New Dance* (Warner Bros., 1990); *At the Ryman* (Warner Bros., 1992); *Cowgirl's Prayer* (Asylum, 1993); *Wrecking Ball* (Asylum, 1995); *Portraits* (Warner Bros., 1996); *Spyboy* (Eminent, 1998); *Red Dirt Girl* (Nonesuch, 2000); *Anthology: The Warner/Reprise Years* (Warner Archives/Reprise/Rhino, 2001).

WEBSITE: www.emmylou.net.

MARK GUARINO

GEORGE HARRISON

Born: Liverpool, England, 25 February 1943; died Los Angeles, California, 29 November 2001

Genre: Rock

Best-selling album since 1990: *Brainwashed* (2002)

George Harrison was the lead guitarist of the Beatles, the twentieth century's most influential pop group. Tagged "the quiet Beatle" in the early days of Beatles stardom, he maintained a low profile throughout his four-decade career, sidestepping the calculated moves typical of a rock star of his stature. Instead, Harrison chose to make music that was a path to personal enlightenment. His rock mysticism opened the door for future musical journeymen. The youngest Beatle, Harrison became a world music pioneer by introducing Eastern rhythms, instrumentation, and philosophy to a generation of Westerners. By organizing the Concert for Bangladesh, rock's first benefit concert, he demonstrated on a mass scale how rock culture can serve as a vehicle for raising social awareness.

Harrison worked outside the Beatles primary songwriting partnership of John Lennon and Paul McCartney, but he contributed songs to successive albums that were equal to theirs. In his role as lead guitarist, Harrison broke new ground and his introduction of the sitar to a Western pop group was unprecedented. Although Harrison made songwriting contributions to earlier Beatles albums, his breakthrough was the song "Love You To" on the band's landmark album *Revolver* (1966). With several Indian musicians playing the opening chord flourishes on sitars, the song erupts into a bustling rhythm accented by heavy Indian percussion.

Harrison continued to play the sitar all his life—he last recorded with it on his 1987 comeback album *Cloud Nine*. But when he was still with the Beatles, he further expanded the group's boundaries. On songs like "Within You Without You," "Fool on the Hill" and "Long Long Long," he demonstrated how pop music can be a conduit for meditative bliss. His songs reflected on death and God. Harrison's contemplative side was also paired with a scorching pessimism. Songs like "Taxman," "Piggies," and "I Me Mine" railed against social hypocrisy, and he joined Lennon as the group's most outspoken critics of fame.

When the Beatles broke up, Harrison recorded solo. The result was the three-vinyl collection "All Things Must Pass" (1970), a sprawling, twenty-three-track masterpiece that aimed for transcendence through country-tinged pop songs.

Harrison created his own label, Dark Horse Records, and quietly released eight solo albums, many not selling well. He also produced films and in 1979 released an autobiography. But besides a high-profile, two-album tenure

Spot Light | Brainwashed

A year after his death came the album George Harrison fans had waited fourteen years for. *Brainwashed* (2002) was mostly at the demo stage when Harrison died, but he reportedly left instructions of his intentions to his son Dhani and producer and past collaborator Jeff Lynne. Some of the notes were specific—Harrison hummed string arrangements to tape and even listed the song sequence. Harrison's vocals and slide guitar playing are at the forefront while all additional work—background vocals, drums—is seamlessly woven in behind. Harrison was no austere mystic and *Brainwashed* is proof. He zips along playing a ukulele on a cover of composer Hoagy Carmichael's standard "Between the Devil and the Deep Blue Sea" and later makes Hawaiian beach music and the blues unlikely cousins in "Rocking Chair in Hawaii." The title song is the most revealing. Over several segments, a meditation is quoted by page number, along with a joke about his granny, a choice expletive, a chorus that rings "God, God, God," and an ending featuring Vedic chants. As contradictory as it all sounds, the new songs show Harrison was hardly afraid of dying. Created in the final stages of his life, it resonates with the same themes he explored in all of his music—that life is eternal and the material world is a meaningless cage. It is a perfect swan song summing up who Harrison was: a cranky spiritual seeker who played guitar so very sweetly.

with the Traveling Wilburys—a supergroup featuring Bob Dylan, Tom Petty, Roy Orbison, and Jeff Lynne—Harrison retreated from public life.

In 1987 he broke his seclusion and released *Cloud Nine*, which yielded a number one hit, "Got My Mind Set on You." He briefly returned to touring in 1991, playing a few dates in Japan with guitarist Eric Clapton. Harrison returned to his seclusion in the 1990s, helping contribute to *The Beatles Anthology*, an officially sanctioned video and compact disc series documenting the group. He recorded two new Beatles songs with band mates McCartney and Ringo Starr. In 1998 he announced he had throat cancer and a year later was stabbed and nearly killed in his home by a deranged intruder who was later found not guilty for reasons of insanity. Harrison died of cancer. His album *Brainwashed* was released posthumously in 2002.

SELECTIVE DISCOGRAPHY: *All Things Must Pass* (Apple, 1970); *Concert for Bangladesh* (Apple, 1972); *Living in the Material World* (Apple, 1973); *Dark Horse* (Apple, 1974); *Somewhere in England* (Dark Horse, 1981); *Cloud Nine* (Dark Horse, 1987); *Brainwashed* (Capitol, 2002).

WEBSITE: www.thebeatles.com.

MARK GUARINO

PJ HARVEY

Born: Polly Jean Harvey; Yeovil, England, 9 October 1969

Genre: Rock

Best-selling album since 1990: *To Bring You My Love* (1995)

Hit songs since 1990: "Down by the Water," "Good Fortune"

British singer, guitarist, and songwriter PJ Harvey began recording in the early 1990s. Her first albums, recorded with a small band also called PJ Harvey, combined powerful, punk-influenced rock with brash, confrontational lyrics. With her 1995 release, *To Bring You My Love*, Harvey smoothed some of her music's rough edges. She exchanged the brutal honesty of her earlier lyrics for an expanded sense of storytelling and fantasy. In 2001 Harvey was awarded Britain's Mercury Music Prize (the first woman to win since its inception in 1991), confirming her status as one of England's most respected performers and songwriters.

Polly Jean Harvey grew up on a sheep farm in the Dorset village Yeovil. Both her quarryman father and artist mother were music aficionados who supported her musical education: first saxophone and later guitar. In Yeovil, Harvey played in a series of bands, including Automatic Dlamini with longtime collaborator John Parish. She eventually founded PJ Harvey in 1991 with bassist Steve Vaughn and drummer Robert Ellis. Two albums later she parted ways with Vaughn and Ellis and she has picked up additional collaborators over the years, including bassist Mick Harvey (also of Nick Cave and the Bad Seeds). She and Parish continue to work together, a relationship that culminated in their joint release *Dance Hall at Louse Point* (1996). Harvey maintains a home near Yeovil, returning there after extended absences, and continues to describe herself as a country girl. Many find her persona in interviews—polite, charming, and quick to laugh—radically different from the characters she inhabits in her music.

The PJ Harvey Trio

The stripped-down textures of PJ Harvey's first album, *Dry* (1992), cannot hide the ensemble's tight rhythmic center, propelled by Ellis's often polyrhythmic drumming. The song "Dress" is one of several tracks to feature Harvey playing cello. In her hands, the instrument, generally used in rock to offer a mellow bass line, adds to the music's agitation and forward momentum. Harvey did not shy away from displaying her body on album covers early in her career—a tactic she later characterized as a publicity stunt. Song lyrics on *Dry* also focus on the female body, as in "Sheela Na Gig," which begins "look at these my child-bearing hips, look at these my ruby-red ruby lips."

PJ Harvey's second album, *Rid of Me* (1993), continues to explore the musical terrain established with *Dry*. *Rid of Me* was produced by American Steve Albini (best known for recording rock group Nirvana's *In Utero*) whose intense dynamics focus the trio's sparse instrumentation. His precise use of microphones on the drums accentuates Ellis's work. The first track, "Rid of Me," alternates frenetically between intense whispers and ferocious guitar outbursts. It concludes with Harvey demanding "lick my legs, I'm on fire, lick my legs, of desire." Her lyrical focus on the body reappears throughout *Rid of Me*, including "50ft Queenie," where Harvey establishes her power by declaring herself "fifty-inches long."

From Dorset to the Big Apple

After the supporting tours for *Rid of Me*, Harvey shed her band, and has since reconstituted it in a variety of forms. The cover of her next album, *To Bring You My Love* (1995), announces Harvey's new incarnation as a heavily made-up vixen in a red satin dress. Whereas *Dry* and *Rid of Me* made Harvey a critic's darling but not a financial success, this album found a larger audience, and the single "Down by the Water" was nominated for a Grammy Award. In this song Harvey becomes a mother drowning her daughter, singing, "I heard her holler, I heard her moan, my lovely daughter, I took her home." Harshly plucked violins in the background add to the creepy and stylized experience of the song. In the album's relatively lush arrangements, Harvey develops and explores her characters in greater depth.

Following the success of *To Bring You My Love*, Harvey returned to Dorset for an extended self-exile. Her next creative project was her collaboration with Parish, *Dance Hall at Louse Point*. Both Parish and Harvey contributed creatively to the album, which successfully deflected critical attention from Harvey's follow-up to *To Bring You My Love*. Two years later she released the cryptic *Is This Desire?*

| *To Bring You My Love*

PJ Harvey initiated a major change in her music (and image) with the release of *To Bring You My Love* (1995). Formerly a rough, punk woman on stage, she became a torch singer. Like other torch singers before her, the new Harvey sang of relationships gone dangerously sour, and of holding onto hope beyond any chance of redemption. She appeared in concert made up much as she looks on the album: deep-red lipstick, red satin dress and an elaborate hair-do. Although Harvey's lyrics have always explored other characters and narrative positions, *To Bring You My Love* further destabilizes Harvey's position as the speaker. Indeed, Harvey fills the record with mothers abandoned by their lovers and children. In "C'mon Billy" she assumes the role of a woman pleading the father of her child to return. "C'mon Billy," she sings, "you're the only one, don't you think its time now, you met your only son?" Harvey's musical language also deepened with *To Bring You My Love*. She abandoned the pure rhythmic intensity of her earlier albums. Instead, songs acquire their drive and intensity from Harvey's vocal lines and her sense of musical form. Despite the central role of her singing in these songs, Harvey often distorts or otherwise estranges her voice, further distancing herself from the music she sings. Her consistent use of organ throughout adds a new timbre already culturally marked as serious and sad. This musical language expresses Harvey's new persona in ways unavailable in the terse rock songs of *Dry* and *Rid of Me*.

natown and the Empire State Building. Ellis plays on many tracks, reuniting Harvey with the pounding rhythms that gave her earliest albums their rhythmic ferocity. The video for "Good Fortune" (perhaps her most optimistic song) features a chic Harvey rapidly progressing through the city's streets, embracing yet distinct from the world around her. *Stories from the City, Stories from the Sea* radiates a happiness absent from earlier albums. Even its darker ballads, such as "The Mess We're In," sung by Radiohead's Thom Yorke, maintain an element of hope.

While none of Harvey's records have made it into *Billboard*'s Top 40 in the United States, many know and admire her work as a singer and songwriter. She has fared better on the charts in Britain. Her first two records remain visceral landmarks of female expression, while *To Bring You My Love* established her range and brought her voice to a larger audience. Her millennial release, *Stories from the City, Stories from the Sea*, assures the listener that everything could end up okay, in the end. Harvey has produced few direct musical ancestors, she has never belonged to a scene, but she has profoundly altered the rock landscape with her powerful songwriting and performances.

SELECTIVE DISCOGRAPHY: *Dry* (Too Pure, 1992); *Rid of Me* (Island, 1993); *To Bring You My Love* (Island, 1995); *Is This Desire?* (Island, 1998); *Stories from the City, Stories from the Sea* (Island, 2000). **With John Parish:** *Dance Hall at Louse Point* (1996).

CAROLINE POLK O'MEARA

HEAVY D

Born: Dwight Myers; Kingston, Jamaica, 21 May 1967
Genre: Rap
Best-selling album since 1990: *Nuttin' but Love* (1994) with Heavy D and the Boyz
Hit songs since 1990: "Now That We Found Love," "Nuttin' but Love," "Big Daddy/Keep It Coming"

Heavy D is one of the most well-balanced artists in hip-hop. Lyrically, he combines fun and romance with social awareness. Musically, he mixes elements of pop, reggae, and R&B for an accessible yet grounded sound. He has been a producer, actor, and music executive. He is also largely responsible for the career of Sean "P. Diddy" Combs.

Myers was born in Jamaica. His family moved to the New York City suburb of Mount Vernon. Myers began to rhyme as a child and asked friend Eddie F. to help him write songs. He adopted the name Heavy D as a reference to his large frame. He linked up with three dancers named

(1998) whose illusive songs turn so deeply inward the listener must struggle to find its narrative and musical center.

After years in the English countryside, Harvey briefly relocated to New York City in 1999. The result was her release *Stories from the City, Stories from the Sea* (2000), which reflects her experiences of living in both New York and Dorset. Many songs on the album reproduce the rapid tempo and excitement of booming late-1990s New York City. Lyrics are full of references to the city, including Chi-

Eddie, G-Wiz, and Trouble T-Roy, collectively called the Boyz, and in 1986 signed to the fledgling rap label Uptown Records. Heavy D and the Boyz's debut album, *Living Large* (1987), includes the danceable "The Overweight Lover's in the House," a remake of the Jean Knight hit "Mr. Big Stuff," the early rap ballad "Don't You Know," and a Teddy Rile–produced hometown homage "Moneyearnin' Mount Vernon." Heavy D also showcases his early production skills by co-piloting the tracks. Heavy D's rap style is colorful and lighthearted. The Boyz's buoyant dancing on stage and in their video intensifies the electric energy.

Fortified by the success of the debut, Heavy D and the Boyz' second album, *Big Tyme* (1989), boasts a variety of musical styles and big-name collaborators. The group scored crossover success with "Somebody for Me," the masterful dance-hall song "Mood for Love," and the New Jack Swing–influenced "We Got Our Own Thang." Around this time another Mount Vernon teenager named Sean Combs was badgering Heavy D to give him an internship at Uptown Records. Heavy D eventually obliged, thus starting Combs's legendary ascent through the music industry. *Big Tyme* went on to sell more than 1 million copies, establishing the group as a hip-hop juggernaut.

In 1990 Heavy D and the Boyz suffered a devastating blow when Boyz member Troy Dixon, aka T-Roy, fell off a stage to his death. T-Roy's passing influenced the sound of the group's third album, *Peaceful Journey* (1991). It is a calm often introspective album, as evidenced by the missive "Letter to the Future." The tribute record to T-Roy, "Now That We Found Love," became the group's best-selling single, earning a gold plaque. The entire album went platinum, and Heavy D catapulted to stardom. In 1990 he became the first rapper to record with Janet Jackson when he lent his vocals to the remix of her hit song "Alright." Soon after, Heavy D scored another pop slam dunk when he rhymed on Michael Jackson's song "Jam," from Jackson's album *Dangerous* (1992). Heavy D was the first rapper to record with the self-proclaimed King of Pop.

Balancing out these high-profile collaborations, Heavy D returned to his pure hip-hop roots on *Blue Funk* (1992). Gone are the R&B producers of past. This time he employs underground rap track-masters like DJ Premier of Gang Starr and Pete Rock (who is also Heavy D's cousin). Nevertheless, the album's most remembered hit is "Truthful," airy with an R&B melody. It is one of the few times a rap artist, typically concerned with maintaining a Teflon image, rhymes honestly about heartbreak.

Heavy D and the Boyz tipped the scales again with the rap/R&B triumph *Nuttin' but Love* (1994). Heavy D had become a well-entrenched hip-hop heavyweight, and this album is slick and well packaged. The hit title song, the female-directed "Black Coffee," and "Keep Waiting"

(based on a smooth Luther Vandross sample) helped Heavy D and the Boyz score another platinum plaque.

In the ensuing years Heavy D began to expand his career horizons. He received a 1995–1996 Drama Desk award for his performance in the New York play *Riff Raff*, starring Laurence Fishburne, who also wrote and directed it. In 1996 Heavy D succeeded André Harrell and was named president of Uptown Records. He discovered and developed R&B acts like the successful Soul For Real and Monifah. Soon after, he relinquished the title, and the label folded. Heavy D decided to focus on acting, obtaining recurring roles on the TV show *Living Single* and parts in the films *The Cider House Rules*, *Life*, *New Jersey Drive*, and *Big Trouble*.

Taking a break from the Boyz, Heavy released a solo album, *Waterbed Hev* (1997), which features the gold-selling single "Big Daddy/Keep It Coming." His sophomore solo album, *Heavy*, became his first to sell fewer than 500,000 copies since his debut album with the Boyz.

Nevertheless, Heavy D had built a strong career behind the sound boards. He produced a hit single, "Summer Rain," and album track "Hey Now" for the R&B singer Carl Thomas, from his debut album, *Emotional* (2000). He tracked the daring, rock charged Jay-Z/Lenny Kravitz collaboration "Guns & Roses" for Jay-Z's album *The Blueprint 2: The Gift and the Curse* (2002). He also produced "Call Me," a song for the album *Street Dreams* (2003) by the rapper Fabolous.

SELECTIVE DISCOGRAPHY: *Living Large* (Uptown, 1987); *Big Tyme* (Uptown, 1989); *Peaceful Journey* (Uptown, 1991); *Blue Funk* (Uptown, 1992); *Nuttin' but Love* (Uptown, 1994); *Waterbed Hev* (Uptown/Universal, 1997); *Heavy* (Uptown/Universal, 1999).

DARA COOK

DON HENLEY

Born: Gilmer, Texas, 22 July 1947
Genre: Rock
Best-selling album since1990: *Inside Job* (2000)
Hit songs since 1990: "Taking You Home"

Singer/songwriter Don Henley first came into prominence as a core member of the Eagles, a 1970s supergroup for whom he was the drummer and singer. The Eagles broke up in 1981, and, while all of the band's members went on to solo careers, Henley's post-Eagles career became the most commercially successful. Never afraid to voice his opinion, Henley uses his celebrity status to champion and raise money for such causes as the environment, copyright infringement, and corporate greed.

Don Henley grew up in Linden, Texas, located in the northeast corner of the state. He first developed a passion for music when his mother brought him home a record of Elvis Presley's "Hound Dog." He was also influenced by the country music that his parents enjoyed, and he was an avid fan of the Beatles all through high school. Henley attended Stephen F. Austin University and North Texas State, earning a degree in English. Along the way he played in a band made up of friends from high school called Shiloh. With the help of fellow Texan, the singer/songwriter Kenny Rogers, Shiloh cut one album, but it barely reached the public. Henley ventured to Los Angeles in 1969, where he became part of Linda Ronstadt's backup band. He and a fellow Ronstadt band mate, guitarist/singer Glen Frey, formed the Eagles in 1972, with Henley on drums and vocals. In addition, Henley wrote many of the band's songs. Before their high-profile breakup, the Eagles emerged as one of rock music's most popular bands and ended up selling some 85 million records. Only Led Zeppelin and the Beatles have sold more.

Henley's first non-Eagles foray into recording was a duet with Stevie Nicks in 1981 titled "Leather and Lace," which became a Top 10 hit. He released three albums in the 1980s, each of which spawned several hits. *I Can't Stand Still* (1982) contains "Dirty Laundry"; *Building the Perfect Beast* (1984) features "Sunset Grill" and "The Boys of Summer" (which won a 1985 Grammy for Best Rock Vocal on a Single); the most successful of the trio, *The End of the Innocence* (1989) (which earned Henley a 1989 Grammy for Best Rock Vocal on an Album), contains the hits "The Heart of the Matter," "The End of the Innocence," "The Last Worthless Evening," and "New York Minute."

These albums evinced the political bent of much of Henley's work. He does not hesitate to advance his views outside the recording studio. In the 1990s he began to raise money to protect portions of Massachusetts' Walden Woods, the setting that inspired much of the best writing of the nineteenth-century author and naturalist Henry David Thoreau. Henley helped raise $25 million to purchase one hundred acres of the forest, and his efforts were honored with a National Humanities Medal from President Clinton in 1997. In 1999 he opposed Clinton's signing into law the "Work for Hire" amendment of the Copyright Act, giving record companies sole ownership of an artist's work forever. Henley has been an impassioned voice for the repeal of this amendment.

In 1994 Henley rejoined the Eagles for their self-effacingly titled "Hell Freezes Over" reunion tour. Their breakup in 1981 was bitter, and members of the band stated publicly that they would regroup only "when hell freezes over." They released a live album from the tour, and it features Henley playing drums on a few of the cuts, an instrument that he abandoned in his solo career because of the strain it put on his back. As a solo performer Henley has focused mostly on vocals although he does play guitar. Henley pushes his high-pitched, penetrating tone to its limit; it is one of rock music's strongest voices.

He waited eleven years to release his next solo effort, *Inside Job* (2000), a typical blend of personal and political songs. The title track is a scathing comment on the "Work for Hire" amendment, "Goodbye to a River" is an environmental anthem, and "Working It" is a satire on corporate greed. Large conglomerates, lawyers, and America's propensity for lawsuits have all provided fodder for Henley's scorn. A ballad from the album, "Taking You Home," was first slated to be part of the soundtrack for the film, *Double Jeopardy* (1999). When it was yanked at the last minute, Henley, a multimillionaire, immediately sued for the profits lost.

Henley reunited with the Eagles again for a short tour in 2003, ironically titled "Farewell Tour I." In 2003 the Eagles were planning to release a studio album—their first in twenty-three years. Henley's solo projects come slowly; he remains one of rock music's most meticulous songwriters, working into his lyrics an array of vivid images and messages.

SELECTIVE DISCOGRAPHY: *I Can't Stand Still* (Asylum, 1982); *Building the Perfect Beast* (Geffen, 1985); *The End of the Innocence* (Geffen, 1989); *Inside Job* (Warner Bros., 2000).

DONALD LOWE

JOHN HIATT

Born: Indianapolis, Indiana, 20 August 1952
Genre: Rock
Best-selling album since 1990: *Perfectly Good Guitar* (1993)
Hit songs since 1990: "Perfectly Good Guitar"

Although John Hiatt has been one of America's most prolific singer/songwriters since the early 1970s, it was not until the 1990s that he began to earn widespread acclaim. Growing up in Indianapolis, Hiatt found himself drawn to the music of the Rolling Stones and Bob Dylan. Later, after having become a successful, established artist, Hiatt often told the story of hearing Dylan's "Like a Rolling Stone" as a youngster for the first time on the car radio while waiting for his mother to return; he recalled worrying that his mother would not recognize him upon her return.

Hiatt moved to Nashville in 1971 and began his musical career, writing hits for Three Dog Night and Conway Twitty, among other artists. In 1974 he released his debut album, *Hangin' Around the Observatory*, which established his folk-rock sound and his wry, lyrical humor. After Hiatt's first two albums failed to garner much public attention, Hiatt tried his hand at a new-wave audience with *Slug Line* (1979); although critics continued to applaud his inventive work, Hiatt had yet to reach a broad record-buying audience.

In the 1980s Hiatt recorded albums at a torrid pace, releasing nearly an album a year. His efforts culminated in the masterpiece *Bring the Family* (1986). As an indication of his growing reputation among his peers, Hiatt assembled an ensemble cast to serve as his backing band on the album; he was joined by musical luminaries Ry Cooder (guitar), Nick Lowe (bass), and Jim Keltner (drums). *Bring the Family* expanded Hiatt's sound to incorporate blues and country influences. A cult favorite, the album was Hiatt's first to chart, peaking at 107 on the *Billboard* album listings. *Rolling Stone* magazine recognized the album as one of the Top 100 of the decade.

Hiatt's profile rose quickly when other artists began scoring hits with his songs. In 1988 the Jeff Healey band enjoyed Top 40 success with a cover of the bluesy ballad "Angel Eyes" from *Bring the Family*. The blues-rocker Bonnie Raitt used "Thing Called Love," also from *Bring the Family*, as the springboard for her comeback in 1989. During the 1990s a diverse array of artists covered Hiatt, including Bob Dylan, Ronnie Milsap, Iggy Pop, Jewel, and Counting Crows. In 1993 Rhino Records paid tribute to Hiatt by releasing *Love Gets Strange: The Songs of John Hiatt*, an anthology of Hiatt songs recorded by other artists. Hiatt put his solo career in the early 1990s on hiatus to join much-ballyhooed supergroup Little Village. Essentially, a reunion of the band that recorded *Bring the Family*, the album was a critical and commercial disappointment. During the tour supporting the album, conflicting egos sealed the band's fate; when the tour concluded, the band split up.

Hiatt returned to the solo fold in 1993 with *Perfectly Good Guitar*. Recorded in two weeks with members of the alternative bands School of Fish and Wire Train, *Perfectly Good Guitar* remains Hiatt's most commercially successful album and features one of his most-beloved songs, "Perfectly Good Guitar," in which Hiatt wittily jabs at the grunge acts who had recently renewed the rock tradition of beating up their guitars onstage: "There ought to be a law with no bail / Smash a guitar and you'll go to jail / With no chance for early parole / You don't get out till you get some soul." The pounding music reaches a crescendo with the memorable chorus, a Hiatt classic: "It breaks my heart to see those stars smashing a perfectly good guitar."

In keeping with Hiatt's enhanced critical and commercial cachet, his albums of the late 1990s were star-studded affairs; in addition to Bonnie Raitt, members of the Jayhawks, Cracker, and Counting Crows appeared on Hiatt albums such as *Walk On* (1995) and *Crossing Muddy Waters* (2000). The latter album, Hiatt's first for Vanguard Records, was a predominantly acoustic album with an organic, back-porch feel; it features only Hiatt and the multi-instrumentalists Davey Faragher (Cracker) and David Immergluck (Counting Crows). For the acclaimed *Crossing Muddy Waters* Hiatt received the Artist/Songwriter of the Year Award at the Nashville Music Awards in 2000. That same year Hiatt also had the distinction of having rock legends Eric Clapton and B.B. King cover his song "Ridin' with the King" in their long-anticipated duets album, which they also titled *Ridin' with the King*.

Hiatt returned to electric music on *The Tiki Bar Is Open* (2002), reuniting with his backing band the Goners for the first time since *Slow Turning* (1988). The critically acclaimed album includes musical nods to Hiatt influences such as the Band, the Beatles, and Little Feat. Always unpredictable, Hiatt resurfaced in 2002 as the producer of the soundtrack of the Disney movie *The Country Bears*. In addition to performing songs himself, Hiatt also wrote new songs for the soundtrack performers, Krystal Marie Harris and Jennifer Paige.

Prolific and versatile, John Hiatt has earned the respect of critics, peers, and a small segment of the record-buying public with an enduring collection of roots-oriented American songs.

SELECTIVE DISCOGRAPHY: *Hangin' Around the Observatory* (Epic Records, 1974); *Slug Line* (Universal Records, 1979); *Two Bit Monsters* (MCA Records, 1980); *Riding with the King* (Geffen Records, 1983); *Bring the Family* (A&M Records, 1987); *Slow Turning* (A&M Records, 1988); *Stolen Moments* (A&M Records, 1990); *Perfectly Good Guitar* (A&M Records, 1993); *Walk On* (Capitol Records, 1995); *Crossing Muddy Waters* (Vanguard Records, 2000); *The Tiki Bar Is Open* (Vanguard Records, 2001).

SCOTT TRIBBLE

FAITH HILL

Born: Audrey Faith Perry Hill; Jackson, Mississippi, 21 September 1967

Genre: Country

Best-selling album since 1990: *Breathe* (1999)

Faith Hill [PAUL NATKIN/PHOTO RESERVE]

Hit songs since 1990: "Breathe," "This Kiss," "The Way You Love Me"

In the late 1990s, crossover sensation Faith Hill turned heads with her powerful string of singles that topped both the country and pop charts.

Raised in the aptly named Star, Mississippi, Hill began singing at an early age; her musical influences included Elvis Presley, Tammy Wynette, George Strait, and Reba McEntire. Hill performed publicly for the first time at a 4-H luncheon when she was seven years old. While in school, Hill was involved in sports as well as drama, but singing remained her first passion. During her high school years, Hill began singing with a local band, which performed at a variety of community events and festivals, including the infamous Raleigh, Mississippi, Tobacco Spit.

Hill enrolled at Hinds Community College in Mississippi, but dropped out after a semester and moved to Nashville to pursue a career in music. After selling t-shirts in her first job, Hill became a receptionist at a music publishing company. Her singing along to the radio caught the attention of her co-workers, who convinced Hill to cut a demo. Hill soon after began performing around town with local singer Gary Burr. During one performance with

Burr, Hill caught the attention of a scout from Warner Bros. Records, which subsequently signed her to a recording contract.

Warner Bros. released Hill's debut album, *Take Me As I Am*, in 1994. The lead single "Wild One" was an instant sensation, its mild, finger-snapping beat and twanging steel guitars pleasing country traditionalists, who pegged Hill as the next Reba McEntire. On the strength of its memorable chorus ("She's a wild one / With an angel's face / She's a woman-child / In a state of grace"), "Wild One" topped the country singles charts for four weeks; Hill was the first female country singer to achieve that milestone on her debut single in more than thirty years. The rollicking follow-up "Piece of My Heart," a cover of the Janis Joplin rock classic, also hit number one on the charts. *Take Me As I Am* ultimately sold 2 million copies and established Hill as a rising star in the country world.

Hill's follow-up album, *It Matters to Me* (1995), outdid its predecessor, selling an additional 1 million records. While touring in support of the album, Hill became romantically involved with tourmate Tim McGraw, one of country music's leading male performers. After an intense courtship, the pair married on October 6, 1996, in Rayville, Louisiana. Soon after, the newlyweds collaborated on "It's Your Love" for McGraw's studio album *Everywhere* (1997). The duet spent six weeks at number one on the country charts and became *Billboard*'s most-played country single to date.

Hill appealed to an entirely new fan base with her album *Faith* (1998). A major crossover success, *Faith* reached the Top 10 of both the country and pop album charts and sold 5 million copies. The album's success stemmed in large part from the hit single "This Kiss," which climbed all the way to number seven on the pop singles charts. While featuring some traditional country instrumentation such as steel guitars, Hill forsakes her vocal twang on "This Kiss" in favor of a more bubbly, pop-influenced singing style, suitable for the song's exuberant, cosmopolitan feel: "It's the way you love me / It's a feeling like this / It's centrifugal motion / It's perpetual bliss." Hill further enhanced her burgeoning celebrity by signing an endorsement deal with Cover Girl makeup, who anointed Hill one of its leading spokeswomen.

Hill's follow-up album *Breathe* (1999) further embraces the pop world and outdid its predecessor in sales, debuting at number one on the pop charts and ultimately selling over 7 million copies. The title track peaked at number two on the pop charts and was the most-played single of the year. A lush ballad, "Breathe" at once posits Hill as vulnerable, seductive, and emotive and features a soaring, inspiring chorus: "'Cause I can feel you breathe / It's washing over me / Suddenly, I'm melting into you." Hill also scored Top 10 hits with "The Way You Love Me" and "There You'll Be," the latter of which appeared on the soundtrack to the movie *Pearl Harbor* (2001) and was nominated for Best Original Song at the Academy Awards.

Hill took a brief hiatus to care for her daughters, but returned in 2002 with the album *Cry*. The album finds Hill further refining her pop sound, incorporating R&B and soul influences into her country-pop mix. The album's title track was a Top 40 hit and earned Hill a Grammy Award for Best Female Country Vocal Performance.

By the end of the 1990s, Hill had surpassed fellow crossover sensation Shania Twain as mainstream radio's leading country-pop act and became Nashville's most recognizable contribution to pop culture.

SELECTIVE DISCOGRAPHY: *Take Me As I Am* (Warner Bros., 1993); *It Matters to Me* (Warner Bros., 1995); *Faith* (Warner Bros., 1998); *Breathe* (Warner Bros., 1999); *Cry* (Warner Bros., 2002). **Soundtrack:** *Pearl Harbor* (Warner Bros., 2001).

SCOTT TRIBBLE

LAURYN HILL

Born: South Orange, New Jersey, 25 May 1975

Genre: R&B, Rap

Best-selling album since 1990: *The Miseducation of Lauryn Hill* (1998)

Hit songs since 1990: "Doo Wop (That Thing)," "Ex-Factor"

Lauryn Hill launched a solo career just a year after her hip-hop group, the Fugees, had rocketed to international stardom with their second album, *The Score* (1996). *The Miseducation of Lauryn Hill* (1998) was hailed as a masterpiece, fusing timeless Motown soul and R&B with a hip-hop sensibility and the sound of a strong female voice. While the photogenic Hill became a star all over again, her group splintered, and she struggled with the price of fame, dropping out of the music business only to return four years later with a confounding two-CD set of new material that lacked the polish of her earlier work.

Born in 1975 in South Orange, New Jersey, Lauryn Hill grew up in the shadow of public housing, surrounded by the sounds of old-school R&B from her parents' vast record collection. Her father, Mal, was a computer analyst and former professional singer; her mother, Valerie, was a teacher in nearby Newark. Hill made her performing debut at the age of thirteen on *Showtime at the Apollo*, singing Smokey Robinson's "Who's Lovin' You." A track star in school, Hill had also been stealing off to the city

to audition for acting parts, landing a recurring role on the CBS daytime drama *As the World Turns* in the early 1990s and a bit part in the 1993 Whoopi Goldberg movie *Sister Act II: Back in the Habit.*

Both Lauryn and her brother, Malaney, were sent to an academically challenging high school, Columbia High, where Hill met Prakazrel "Pras" Michel, a budding rapper, who asked Hill to join his rap group, the Fugees-Tranzlator Crew. With the addition of Michel's cousin, Wyclef Jean, the trio came together as the Fugees, and Hill deferred full-time college study in order to attend Columbia University part time and concentrate on her career.

The trio released their debut album, *Blunted on Reality* (1993), which met disappointing sales and poor critical response. Two remixed tracks became underground hits, highlighting Hill's combination singing/rapping style, which became the centerpiece of the group's breakthrough album, *The Score* (1996). With a smash hit cover of the 1973 Roberta Flack hit "Killing Me Softly with His Song" and the hit "Ready or Not," the album became the best-selling rap album in history.

The group was saddled with resentments and tension, much of it caused by the focus on Hill and persistent rumors that she would split to go solo. By late 1996 Hill was pregnant with a son sired by Rohan Marley, the offspring of late reggae great Bob Marley; although she continued to deny rumors of a solo career, Hill recorded a solo gospel track with CeCe Winans, "The Sweetest Thing," for the soundtrack to the film *Love Jones* and began work on the songs that would appear on her solo debut. Both Jean and Michel recorded solo albums during this period.

A Record-Breaking Solo Debut

The Miseducation of Lauryn Hill (1998), Hill's solo debut, took the soul/hip-hop mix of the Fugees's album to a new level, debuting with sales of 400,000 copies in its first week, a record for a black female artist. The album is a seamless mix of Hill's socially conscious lyrics, confident rapping, and soulful alto singing over hip-hop, gospel, reggae, and doo-wop backing; it quickly sold 1 million copies and landed Hill on the cover of *Time* magazine. The chanting, reggae-inspired "Lost Ones" appears to lash out at her former band mates and their materialism ("It's funny how money change a situation / Miscommunication leads to complication / My emancipation don't fit your equation"), though, on a whole, the album eschews confrontation in favor of notes of conciliation and peace. Tracks such as the slow-rolling ballad "Ex-Factor" and the Latin-tinged "To Zion" expand Hill's musical palette in previously unexplored directions while making social and political statements on subjects such as racism, sexism, the loss of community, and the wonders of motherhood. The alluring single and video for the hip-hop soul anthem "Doo

Wop (That Thing)" were inescapable for many months, helping to further integrate the sound of hip-hop onto mainstream pop radio and MTV.

When Jean and Michel's solo albums weren't as well received, rumors constantly swirled that the group would be getting back together. Nominated for eleven Grammys, Hill—who produced, wrote, and arranged the album—was awarded five, beating Carole King's 1971 record of four for her album *Tapestry*. *Spin* magazine named her "Artist of the Year" and Hill wrote, produced, and directed the video for the track "A Rose Is a Rose" for Aretha Franklin's 1998 album of the same name, garnering two more Grammy nominations.

With the birth of her daughter, Selah, in 1999 and a lawsuit (later settled) by a quartet of songwriters claiming they had helped write and produce songs on the album, Hill retreated from the limelight. A long silence ensued, broken periodically by rumors of a new album by Hill or by the occasional comment by Jean—by now a successful solo artist and producer—that he would welcome a Fugees reunion.

When Hill took tentative steps back into the spotlight in early 2000 and 2001, it was alone with her acoustic guitar, performing new songs during which she invariably broke down in tears. During her break, Hill told interviewers she had undergone a paralyzing identity crisis that had led her to reconnect with God and shed most of her entourage and star trappings. The evidence is in the spiritually based songs on *MTV Unplugged 2.0* (2002), a two-CD set of live versions of new material from an MTV special recorded nearly a year earlier. Stripped-down, emotionally raw songs such as "Mr. Intentional," "Freedom Time," and "Mystery of Iniquity" feature just Hill and her guitar, eschewing traditional pop structures in favor of often rambling, folk-rock-like tales of redemption spiked with Biblical imagery and vignettes of self-doubt and confusion. Hill had also traded her former high-fashion look in favor of jeans, a T-shirt, and a head scarf over her nearly bald pate. The new sincerity is summed up in the lyrics to "I Gotta Find Peace of Mind": "Please don't be mad with me, I have no identity / All that I've known is gone, all I was building on."

After breaking free from the Fugees, Lauryn Hill became an acclaimed female hip-hop artist with a solo debut that sold more than 15 million copies. The acclaim was short-lived, however, as her baffling follow-up album confounded critics and painted a portrait of an artist who had been so overwhelmed by fame that she shed not only the trappings of stardom but also the very musical elements that had made her a star just a few years earlier.

SELECTIVE DISCOGRAPHY: *The Miseducation of Lauryn Hill* (Ruffhouse/Columbia, 1998); *MTV Unplugged 2.0* (Sony, 2002).**With the Fugees:**

Blunted on Reality (Ruffhouse/Columbia, 1993); *The Score* (Ruffhouse/Columbia, 1996).

SELECTIVE FILMOGRAPHY: *King of the Hill* (1993); *Sister Act 2: Back in the Habit* (1993); *Rhyme & Reason* (1997); *Hav Plenty* (1997); *Restaurant* (1998).

WEBSITE: www.laurynhill.com.

GIL KAUFMAN

HOLE

Formed: 1989, Los Angeles, California; Disbanded 2002

Members: Melisssa Auf Der Maur, bass (born Montreal, 17 March 1972); Eric Erlandson, guitar (born Los Angeles, California, 9 January 1963); Courtney Love, vocals, guitar (Love Michelle Harrison, born San Francisco, California, 9 July 1965); Samantha Maloney, drums (born New York, 11 December 1975). Former members: Jill Emery, bass (born Covina, California, late 1960s); Kristen Pfaff, bass (born Amherst, New York, 26 May 1967; died 16 June 1994); Caroline Rue, drums (born San Pedro, California, late 1960s); Patty Schemel, drums (born Seattle, Washington, 28 April 1967).

Genre: Rock

Best-selling album since 1990: *Live through This* (1994)

Hit songs since 1990: "Doll Parts," "Violet," "Malibu"

Hole, the alternative punk rock band, was largely the vehicle of its lead singer and principal songwriter Courtney Love, one of the most difficult and troubled popular musicians to emerge in the 1990s. Hole gained success with their angry but melodic rock music and with lyrics that vacillated between feminist manifesto and self-destructive melodrama. The band grabbed the spotlight a few weeks after the suicide of Love's husband, Kurt Cobain, the enigmatic lead singer of Nirvana, in April 1994.

Formed in Los Angeles in 1989, Hole's signature sound revolves around Eric Erlandson's distinct raucous guitar playing style, tight rhythms, and Love's emotionally charged singing. By the time of their debut on Caroline Records, *Pretty on the Inside* (1991), produced by Sonic Youth's Kim Gordon, Hole had developed a following in Seattle and the Pacific Northwest. They also gained attention internationally as a riot grrl band known for wedding punk rock's do-it-yourself ethos with the polemics and power of political feminism. Hole, however, did not really make their mark until their major label debut on Geffen Records, mere weeks after Cobain's death.

Hole gained platinum sales with *Live through This* (1994). In this album Love's lyrics are often aggressive,

Spot Light | "Doll Parts"

The hard-rocking, aggression of *Live through This* (1994) includes a song with which Courtney Love and the riot grrl phenomena came to be associated. Her lyrics are usually straightforward and leave little to the imagination, and in "Doll Parts" Love clearly plays with the ideas of femininity. It is up for debate whether or not she is being ironic when she declares that she is made of doll parts—in essence, that she is not real. Or perhaps she is pointing the finger of blame at a pop culture that focuses so exclusively and reverentially on women's body parts through repeated exposure on television, in films, and in music videos. Either way, "Doll Parts" offers a window into Love's tortured soul. The song marked a turning point; Love sings, "I want to be the girl with the most cake / I love him so much it just turns to hate / I fake it so real I am beyond fake / And someday you will ache like I ache," repeating the lyrics several times until they build to a scream. The song depicts a woman torn between what she wants to be, who she is, and what society expects from her.

polished sheen, or perhaps because of it, *Celebrity Skin* sold more than 1 million copies and it eventually went platinum. Through their short tenure as a band, Hole endured more than their fair share of drug problems and personality clashes. The band went through several personnel changes, and lost bassist Kristen Pfaff to a heroin overdose in 1996. After *Celebrity Skin*'s release, their replacement bassist Melissa Auf Der Maur departed to join grunge band Smashing Pumpkins.

When Love and Erlandson mutually agreed to dissolve Hole in 2002, they were the sole remaining original members, mostly because Love dictated the terms of the band's creativity and direction, and Erlandson was agreeable to her whims. In early 2001 Love filed a lawsuit against her label, Universal Music Group, seeking for release from what she termed an unfair recording contract. From 2001 to 2002, Love spent a good portion of her time in court, in a legal wrangling with former Nirvana members over rights to unreleased Nirvana material.

Hole made their mark as an outlet for Love's powerful demons. By promoting unabashed, aggressive guitar playing, the group created a new paradigm for female bands, but not without leaving a succession of lawsuits, controversy, and notoriety behind them.

SELECTIVE DISCOGRAPHY: *Pretty on the Inside* (Caroline, 1991); *Live through This* (Geffen, 1994); *Celebrity Skin* (Geffen, 1998).

BIBLIOGRAPHY: P. Z. Brite, *Courtney Love: The Real Story* (New York, 1997).

CARRIE HAVRANEK

shouted, and hollered rather than sung. She confronts controversial topics like rape in "Asking for It." She presents a swaggering disturbed bravado in "Miss World," in which she sings "I'm Miss World / Somebody kill me." Another single, "Violet," adapts the sonic structure popularized by Nirvana, with quieter and tension-filled verses building to a furiously loud paroxysm in the chorus. Through her no-holds-barred vocal style, Love did much to legitimize the expression of female anger. *Live through This* struck a chord with frustrated youth and female fans who empathized with Love's complexity and saw her as a real personality unapologetically capable of expressing the range of female experience.

In between *Live through This* and their follow-up, Hole toured. Love managed to undergo a Hollywood makeover and appeared in the movie *The People vs. Larry Flynt* (1996). In 1998, the band released the eagerly awaited *Celebrity Skin*, a mainstream, slickly produced album of pop tune craft that is markedly less depressing and confrontational than their previous recordings. Despite the

JOHN LEE HOOKER

Born: Clarksdale, Mississippi, 22 August 1917; died Los Altos, California, 21 June 2001

Genre: Blues

Best-selling album since 1990: *Don't Look Back* (1997)

John Lee Hooker was one of the most prolific and influential artists in blues history. His up-and-down career survived nearly sixty years of music industry tastes and changes, ending when it had reached its zenith. Many of his songs live as blues standards, and he is a major influence on numerous rock/blues artists who recorded Hooker's songs and borrowed from his distinctive style. In contrast to the twelve-bar, three-chord blues played by most of his contemporaries, Hooker's unique brand of blues was often based upon a simple melody wrapped around a one-chord riff, accompanied by the rhythmic stomp of his foot and the rich tones of his mesmerizing voice.

Accounts of Hooker's year of birth vary: 1915, 1917, and 1920 crop up, but most scholars hold with 1917. He was one of eleven children born to Minnie and William Hooker, Mississippi Delta sharecroppers. His mother separated from his father when Hooker was very young, and she married a farmer named Will Moore, who played the blues locally and became a prominent influence in Hooker's musical development. Moore gave Hooker his first guitar and taught his stepson a mix of 1920s country Delta and one-chord Louisiana blues. Hooker also sang gospel music locally before leaving rural Mississippi when he was fifteen for the bright lights of Memphis to start a music career.

By the 1940s, Hooker had settled in Detroit, hoping to pick up some work in the expanding automobile trade. It was there that he gained a reputation as a top-notch performer and recorded the famous blues anthem "Boogie Chillen," whose familiar riff has been borrowed by various artists, most notably, ZZ Top on their first hit, "La Grange." Hooker sang the song into a penny arcade vending machine, a novelty of its day that recorded for the price of a quarter. He presented the crude demo to a small Detroit record company, and the owner, Bernie Besman, was amazed at what he heard. He immediately began recording Hooker's songs, and "Boogie Chillen" became a number one hit across the country on R&B charts.

Over the next four years, Besman recorded Hooker's music, capturing his sound by equipping a microphone inside Hooker's acoustic guitar and placing a recording microphone inside a toilet. He rested the speaker on the lid. In this way, Hooker's forceful guitar, relentless foot-stomping rhythm, and gospel-style singing received a reverberating echo that shaped his trademark hypnotic blues sound, which was just as compelling when recorded in later years with better technology.

Hooker had several other hits, including "I'm in the Mood," "Dimples," and the frequently borrowed "Boom, Boom." However, his discography is complicated—he recorded for more than two dozen record labels under a variety of pseudonyms because of contractual problems, usually pertaining to disputes over song royalties. Hooker's popularity waxed and waned in the United States in proportion to the popularity of blues music in general; hence he was delighted to learn of his rising status in the 1960s in the British rock scene. Bands such as the Animals, the Yardbirds, John Mayall's Bluesbreakers, and many others began recording his music. He toured both Europe and the United States, becoming a legend and an inspiration for stars such as Eric Clapton, Bob Dylan, Van Morrison, Bonnie Raitt, and Carlos Santana. Hooker continued to record throughout the 1970s and 1980s, but it was mostly a recy-

cling of his past material. His career momentum began to slow by the end of the 1970s. Although he appeared in the film *The Blues Brothers* (1980) and recorded a song for another film, *The Color Purple* (1986), by the mid-1980s his career was on the verge of collapse.

Hooker rebounded, however, with the 1989 album *The Healer,* which featured guest appearances by Bonnie Raitt, Santana, Robert Cray, and George Thorogood. It earned him a 1990 Grammy Award for Best Blues Recording and sold more than 1 million copies. A string of successful recordings followed, all of them featuring contributions by big-name musical admirers. *Mr. Lucky* (1991) garnered critical raves and a Grammy nomination; among those featured on the album are Keith Richards, Ry Cooder, and Johnny Winter. That same year, Hooker was inducted into the Rock and Roll Hall of Fame.

His next album, *Boom Boom* (1992), a reprise of many of his old hits, was buoyed by the contributions of the Texas blues veterans Jimmie Vaughn and Albert Collins. Van Morrison, a longtime friend, played on *Chill Out* (1995), which won a Grammy for Best Traditional Blues Recording. Santana, on the verge of his own remarkable comeback, played on the title track. Hooker's next release, *Don't Look Back* (1997), also won a Grammy in that same category. Van Morrison produced the album, and it contains some of the last songs that Hooker wrote along with Jimi Hendrix's "Red House." Hooker had promised Hendrix's father and sister that he would put the slow twelve-bar blues on the album in homage to the renowned rock guitarist, who counted Hooker as one of his leading influences.

Hooker's last recording was *The Best of Friends* (1998). Just as the title implies, the album hosts an all-star cast of well-wishers who contributed to the album's songs, many of which are again reworked versions of Hooker's old hits. In a poetic turn the guitarist Eric Clapton, whose musical development owes as much to Hooker as anyone, plays on "Boogie Chillen." At the 2000 Grammy Awards, Hooker received a Lifetime Achievement Award for musical excellence. He continued to perform, sometimes teaming with blues legend B.B. King, on light concert tours until he died in his sleep on the morning of June 21, 2001, at his home near San Francisco. Hooker's passing marked the loss of one of the last direct links to the original Mississippi Delta blues.

SELECTIVE DISCOGRAPHY: *Boogie Chillen* (Sensation, 1949); *I'm John Lee Hooker* (Vee Jay, 1959); *House of the Blues* (Chess, 1960); *The Folklore of John Lee Hooker* (Vee Jay, 1961); *Burnin'* (Vee Jay, 1962); *The Big Soul of John Lee Hooker* (Vee Jay, 1963); *Moanin' and Stompin' the Blues* (King, 1970); *Endless Boogie* (ABC, 1970); *Hooker n' Heat* (Liberty, 1971); *Johnny Lee* (Greene Bottle, 1972); *Mad Man Blues* (Chess, 1973); *Free Beer and*

Chicken (ABC Records, 1974); *Never Get Out of These Blues Alive* (Pickwick, 1978); *The Best of John Lee Hooker* (Crescendo, 1987); *Real Folk Blues* (MCA, 1987); *Simply The Truth* (One Way, 1988); *The Healer* (Chameleon, 1989); *Mr. Lucky* (Silvertone, 1991); *The Country Blues of John Lee Hooker* (Riverside, 1991); *John Lee Hooker: The Ultimate Collection 1948-1990* (Rhino, 1991); *Boom Boom* (Pointblank/Virgin, 1992); *Chill Out* (Pointblank/Virgin, 1995); *Alone* (Blues Alliance, 1996); *His Best* (Chess/MCA, 1997); *Don't Look Back* (Pointblank/Virgin, 1997); *The Best of Friends* (Pointblank/Virgin, 1998).

BIBLIOGRAPHY: C. Murray, *Boogie Man: The Adventures of John Lee Hooker in the American Twentieth Century* (New York, 2000).

DONALD LOWE

HOOTIE & THE BLOWFISH

Formed: 1989, Columbia, South Carolina

Members: Mark Bryan, guitar (born Silver Spring, Maryland, 6 May 1967); Dean Felber, bass (born Bethesda, Maryland, 9 June 1967); Darius Rucker, vocals, guitar (born Charleston, South Carolina, 13 May 1966); Jim Sonefeld, drums (born Lansing, Michigan, 20 October 1964).

Genre: Rock

Best-selling album since 1990: *Cracked Rear View* (1994)

Hit songs since 1990: "Hold My Hand," "Let Her Cry," "Only Wanna Be with You"

With a feel-good rock style appealing to all ages, Hootie & the Blowfish enjoyed one of the most successful debuts ever. Unfortunately it set the band up for what would be one of the biggest falls from mainstream prominence.

Named after two eccentric friends of the band, Hootie & the Blowfish formed in 1989 at South Carolina University. The band slowly built a following by playing bars and colleges throughout the Southeast. Hootie & the Blowfish released two independent albums before attracting the attention of JRS Records in 1992. The relationship with JRS failed, and the band had no choice but to return to self-release for its third album, *Kootchypop* (1991); the band sold a remarkable 50,000 copies of *Kootchypop*, largely on the strength of sales at the band's concerts. Atlantic Records took stock of Hootie & the Blowfish's grassroots appeal and signed the band to a recording contract in 1993.

Hootie & the Blowfish's fourth album and first major label release, *Cracked Rear View* (1994), did not make an immediate chart impression. Ultimately, the single "Hold

<table>
<tr><td>Spot Light</td><td>Cracked Rear View</td></tr>
</table>

In commercial terms, Hootie & the Blowfish's *Cracked Rear View* (1994) was as remarkable a debut as they come. The album was the fastest-selling debut album in Atlantic Records history. It spent eight weeks at number one on the Billboard album charts and fifty-five weeks in the Top 10. *Cracked Rear View* ultimately sold 16 million units, tying rock group Boston's self-titled album from 1976 as the biggest-selling major-label debut in history. In so doing, the unassuming South Carolina quartet outperformed the massively successful debuts of many well-known artists, including Guns N' Roses (15 million), Meatloaf (14 million), Backstreet Boys (14 million), Whitney Houston (13 million), Britney Spears (13 million), matchbox twenty (12 million), and Carole King (10 million). Not surprisingly, given such sales numbers, *Cracked Rear View* also ranked among the top-selling albums of the 1990s. According to SoundScan (an information system that tracks sales of music and music video products throughout the United States and Canada and acts as a sales source for *Billboard*), the album charted sixth behind albums by mainstream luminaries Alanis Morissette, Shania Twain, Metallica, Whitney Houston, and Celine Dion.

My Hand" became a major hit through word-of-mouth; the band received a huge boon when talk-show host David Letterman pronounced the heretofore-unknown rockers to be his "favorite new band." A slow-building rocker, "Hold My Hand" features Darius Rucker's trademark soulful vocals. The song soars to memorable heights on the chorus, when seminal rocker David Crosby appears to lend a hand with background vocals; while Crosby and the other band members wail the "Hold my hand" refrain, Rucker jumps in with husky lyrical exclamation points: "I want you to hold my hand" and "'Cause I want to love you the best that I can." "Hold My Hand" reached the Top 10 on the *Billboard* singles chart.

The band also scored hits with the follow-up singles "Let Her Cry" and "Only Wanna Be with You." The former, a mournful ballad, allows Rucker ample room to emote in his trademark soulful style, while the latter returns the band to familiar, feel-good environs. The rollicking acoustic-guitar-driven "Only Wanna Be with You" won over many male fans with its memorable hook about football-watching frustrations: "And you wonder why I'm such a baby / 'Cause the Dolphins make me cry." Miami quarterback Dan Marino lent his star power to the band by appearing in the promotional video for "Only Wanna Be with You."

Its nonthreatening classic rock sound appealing to older fans and its catchy pop melodies ensnaring the young, *Cracked Rear View* ultimately sold an astounding 16 million copies—a record performance for a band's major label debut. Despite the public acclaim, critics savaged the group for what they considered punchless soft rock. Critics also predicted the band's ultimate chart demise, charging that they were incapable of a follow-up album anywhere as successful as *Cracked Rear View.*

Though the follow-up album *Fairweather Johnson* (1996) debuted at number one and sold a respectable 2 million copies, the Hootie & the Blowfish phenomenon clearly had begun to dissipate. The album spawned a couple of minor hits, but none came close to approaching the popularity of "Let Her Cry" or "Hold My Hand." A third major-label release, *Musical Chairs* (1998), was a commercial flop, confirming the band's fall from grace.

Despite the bottoming out of the band's mainstream appeal, Hootie & the Blowfish continued to tour and play to enthusiastic, if small, crowds. In 2000 the band returned to its bar-band roots by releasing a collection of cover songs titled *Scattered, Smothered and Covered.*

SELECTIVE DISCOGRAPHY: *Cracked Rear View* (Atlantic, 1994); *Fairweather Johnson* (Atlantic, 1996); *Musical Chairs* (Atlantic, 1998); *Scattered, Smothered and Covered* (Atlantic, 2000).

SCOTT TRIBBLE

JAMES HORNER

Born: Los Angeles, California, 14 August 1953

Genre: Soundtrack

Best-selling album since 1990: *Music from the Motion Picture Titanic* (1997)

Hit songs since 1990: "My Heart Will Go On (Love Theme from *Titanic*)"

James Horner is one of Hollywood's most successful soundtrack composers, having won Academy Awards for Best Original Dramatic Score and Best Original Song for the huge commercial smash *Titanic* (1997). A prolific composer equally comfortable with epic and personal emo-

tions, period and futuristic settings, romances, horror movies and music for children's stories, he has also been honored with nominations for *Apollo 13, Braveheart, Field of Dreams, Aliens,* and *A Beautiful Mind.*

In more than one hundred films that Horner has scored since late 1979, he has demonstrated mastery of both conventional symphony instrumentation and synthesizers. He delights in spicing his works with traditional Irish colors and references, and favors strong melodic motifs with dramatic counterthemes or contrasting backdrops. He has forged an especially productive creative relationship with the filmmaker Ron Howard.

Horner grew up in London, began studying piano at age five, and attended the Royal Academy of Music. Relocating to California in the early 1970s, he earned a B.A. degree in music from the University of Southern California and then a Ph.D. in music composition and theory at UCLA. While teaching music theory there, he was offered the job of scoring a film by the American Film Institute. He took to scoring as an opportunity to have his compositions heard and continued collaborating on AFI projects until being lured by horror movie-maker Roger Corman to his New World Pictures.

Horner's first several pictures—including two *Star Trek* movies of a series he inherited briefly from the veteran composer Jerry Goldsmith—depended on his use of electronics to enhance and amplify live musicians. Horner has credited music friends such as Ian Underwood, a former member of Frank Zappa's Mothers of Invention, as sources of inspiration on his efforts. But he proved equal to full symphony orchestras with his scores for *Willow* (1988) and *Land Before Time* (1988).

The next year, the commercial success of *Field of Dreams* (1989) and critical acclaim for *Glory* (1989) brought new attention to Horner's contributions. His theme for the latter, a Civil War drama, was licensed several times for commercial use. Horner's songwriting abilities came to the fore with *An American Tail* (1986), an animated musical about a Jewish mouse immigrating to the United States, and its sequel, *An American Tail: Fievel Goes West* (1991). He had a banner year in 1995, producing Academy Award–nominated scores for *Apollo 13* and *Braveheart*, as well as soundtracks for the animated films *Casper* and *Balto,* and the Robin Williams vehicle *Jumanji.*

Horner's score for *Titanic* (1997) secured his future. The love theme, a ballad sung grandly by Celine Dion, is countered by ghostly pipes and percussion, lush but not cloying string sections, choirs, and harps. He had employed similar Irish touches in previous soundtracks, most notably *Patriot Games* (1992) and *Braveheart* (1995). After *Titanic* Horner exhibited a new interest in cinematic personal portraits, such as those of the writer Iris Murdoch in *Iris* (2001) and mathematician John Forbes Nash Jr. in *A Beautiful Mind* (2001). Horner's music for *Windtalkers* (2002) depicts a Marine's crisis of conscience guarding a Navajo code-talker in the Pacific threater during World War II.

Nothing succeeds in the movie business like success, and it seems that Horner's past accomplishments will provide him with further opportunities to exploit his favorite tropes—especially his use of Irish motifs—while also giving him the chance to expand his array of devices and source materials.

SELECTIVE DISCOGRAPHY: *Star Trek II: The Wrath of Khan* (GNP Crescendo, 1982); *Star Trek III: The Search for Spock* (GNP Cresendo, 1984); *Cocoon* (Polydor, 1985); *An American Tail* (MCA Records, 1986); *Willow* (Virgin, 1988); *The Land Before Time* (MCA, 1988); *Field of Dreams* (Novus/RCA, 1989); *Glory* (Virgin, 1989); *An American Tail: Fievel Goes West* (MCA, 1991); *Patriot Games* (Milan, 1992); *Thunderheart* (Intrada, 1993); *Legends of the Fall* (Epic Soundtrax, 1994); *Apollo 13* (MCA, 1995); *Braveheart* (London, 1995); *Casper* (MCA, 1995); *Jumanji* (Epic Soundtrax, 1995); *Titanic* (Sony Classical, 1997); *The Devil's Own* (Beyond Music, 1997); *The Mask of Zorro* (Sony Classical, 1998); *How the Grinch Stole Christmas* (Interscope, 2000); *The Perfect Storm* (Sony Classical, 2000); *Iris* (Sony Classical, 2001); *A Beautiful Mind* (Decca, 2001); *Windtalkers* (RCA Victor, 2002).

HOWARD MANDEL

WHITNEY HOUSTON

Born: Newark, New Jersey, 9 August 1963

Genre: R&B, Pop

Best-selling album since 1990: *The Bodyguard* (1992)

Hit songs since 1990: "I Will Always Love You," "Exhale (Shoop Shoop)," "It's Not Right but It's Okay"

During the 1980s and 1990s, Whitney Houston set new standards for vocal artistry in pop and rhythm and blues music. Her magnificent voice—powerful, wide-ranging, and pitch-perfect—was the key ingredient in a remarkable string of hits featuring sudden, dramatic swoops into her upper register and liberal use of *melisma*, the singing of multiple notes within a single syllable. In the 1990s Houston's style was so influential that it inspired a generation of pop singers, including major stars such as Toni Braxton, Celine Dion, and Mariah Carey. In the words of a critic

for *The Los Angeles Times*, "No other female pop star—not Mariah Carey, not Celine Dion, not even Barbra Streisand—quite rivals Houston in her exquisite vocal fluidity and purity of tone."

Gospel Roots and Meteoric Rise

The daughter of the legendary gospel and pop singer Cissy Houston, Whitney was raised in a religious household and spent much of her childhood performing in church and singing with her mother in New York nightclubs. By the age of fourteen, when she sang on her mother's album *Think It Over* (1978), Houston already sounded startlingly mature. By the early 1980s Houston was modeling for teen-oriented magazines and acting on television shows.

In 1983 the president of Arista Records, Clive Davis, heard Houston and immediately offered her a recording contract. Her self-titled first album was released in 1985 and became the biggest-selling debut album by a female artist in pop history. The album's big ballads "The Greatest Love of All" and "Saving All My Love for You" were played so often that they became indelible parts of the era's musical consciousness. Heavily orchestrated showcases for Houston's flamboyant vocals, the songs were the musical equivalent of the glossy nighttime soap operas so popular during the 1980s. Like *Falcon Crest* and *Dynasty*, Houston's songs exuded an aura of class and glamour. A follow-up album, *Whitney* (1987), was just as successful, selling more than 9 million copies.

Success in Films

By now Houston was an established superstar, one of the most recognizable voices of her generation. Soon Houston turned her attentions to acting, earning the starring role in the 1992 film *The Bodyguard*. For much of the 1990s, Houston eschewed solo albums in favor of performing on soundtracks to films in which she also starred, such as *The Preacher's Wife* (1997).

After the success of "I Will Always Love You" (1992) from the soundtrack to *The Bodyguard*, it seemed that Houston could do no wrong commercially, although some critics complained that her music was long on style and short on substance. Reviewing a CD compilation of her greatest hits, a reviewer for *Entertainment Weekly* observed in 2000, "So much has been made of Houston's R&B lineage, it bears observing that her singing, for all its power and agility, suffers from a crucial lack of soulfulness."

Maturing as an Artist

Notwithstanding the criticism, Houston's performance on the soundtrack to the film *Waiting to Exhale* (1995) was a turning point. The album features performances by some of the greatest female voices in rhythm and blues, among

"I Will Always Love You"

When the actor Kevin Costner chose Whitney Houston to co-star with him in the 1992 film *The Bodyguard,* a Hollywood barrier was broken. The film marked one of the first instances of a love interest between a Caucasian man and an African-American woman in which race was not depicted as an issue. It was Houston's first starring movie role after seven years of success as a recording artist. For the film's big ballad, Costner persuaded Houston to record a 1974 country hit by Dolly Parton, "I Will Always Love You." Bolstered by its inclusion in *The Bodyguard's* television ad campaign, "I Will Always Love You" became one of the biggest singles in pop music history, selling 5 million copies. In the song's intro, Houston sings without any orchestral accompaniment—an unusual tactic for a contemporary pop song. Soon these soft opening lines became famous around the world: "If I should stay / I would only be in your way. . ." The restrained opening hooks listeners into the song's drama, which Houston builds with dazzling vocal flourishes. Later in the song, after a dramatic key change, Houston bursts forth with a loud, full-bodied repetition of the chorus: "And I . . . will always love you. . . ." "I Will Always Love You" displays the full range of Houston's vocal talent and leaves no doubt that she was a notable pop voice of the 1990s.

some of the hottest producers and artists in the industry, among them Fugees group members Lauryn Hill and Wyclef Jean, Houston had never sounded so adult or contemporary. Although the album sports a few old-fashioned ballads that recall Houston's 1980s music, its most startling moments are assertive midtempo songs such as the hit "It's Not Right but It's Okay" and the reggae-infused title track. The former in particular is one of the peak moments in Houston's career. Singing against a jittery, complex rhythm devised by her producer, Rodney Jerkins, Houston creates a sinuous vocal groove, giving listeners a glimpse of her sharp rhythmic skills and timing. The lyrics are far removed from her girlish image of the past: "It's not right, but it's okay / I'm gonna make it anyway / Pack your bags, up and leave / Don't you dare come running back to me." Houston's masterful voice has deepened with age, grittier and tougher than it was in the 1980s. With its streetwise sound, *My Love Is Your Love* gives listeners the impression that they are finally hearing the "real" Whitney Houston in what many consider to be her finest work. Critics responded positively to the new direction Houston's music was taking. Writing in *The Village Voice,* Vince Aletti commented, "We have a record that is Whitney's sharpest and most satisfying so far. If we still come away from it wondering, who is this person? at least we've got a few more solid clues. . . . Whitney remains a mystery, but she's opening doors."

Personal Turmoil

By the end of 1998, Houston's troubled personal life was making more headlines than her music. She married the singer Bobby Brown in 1992 and gave birth to a daughter the following year, but the union was a volatile one, giving rise to rumors of spousal abuse and indulgence in drugs. Furthermore, Houston gained a reputation for erratic behavior and canceled engagements. In 1999 she startled fans by appearing on a Michael Jackson tribute concert looking alarmingly thin, and in 2000 she failed to appear on an Oscar Awards ceremony due to rumored vocal problems. Early that year she was stopped at a Hawaii airport for possession of marijuana, and in 2001 she was forced to dispel widespread rumors that she had died of a drug overdose.

Amid the continuing tabloid frenzy, Houston released *Just Whitney* in 2002, her first album of new material in over four years. This release marked a return to more conventional territory, with little of the risk-taking that characterized her previous album. Overall the critical response was lukewarm and disappointing. In December 2002, Houston granted a much-publicized network television interview to Diane Sawyer; alternately tearful and defensive, she discussed the rumors surrounding her life and career, addressing her past drug use for the first time in public. When Sawyer asked which drug was "the biggest devil" for her, she responded, "That would be me . . .

them Aretha Franklin and Toni Braxton. It is Houston, however, who makes the strongest impression, singing lead on three of the sixteen songs. On the hit single, "Exhale (Shoop Shoop)," she exhibits a new sensitivity. In lines such as, "Life never tells us / the whens or whys," there is an emotional pull in Houston's voice, as if, in her decade of stardom, she had gained life experience and wanted to share it with her fans. There was now an artist of intelligence and depth discernible beneath the high gloss of Houston's public persona. Overall, the *Exhale* soundtrack showcased an older, more restrained Houston, suggesting that her best years lay ahead of her.

Houston's next nonsoundtrack album, *My Love Is Your Love* (1998), substantiated this impression. Teaming with

nobody makes me do anything I don't want to do. It's my decision. So the biggest devil is me."

In spite of Houston's personal troubles and the erratic quality of her albums, she remains one of the most formidable singers in contemporary music. Throughout her evolution from wide-eyed teenager to mature, complex artist, her vocal powers have never flagged, attesting to the continued vitality of an artist who redefined pop singing in the 1980s and 1990s.

SELECTIVE DISCOGRAPHY: *Whitney Houston* (Arista, 1985); *Whitney* (Arista, 1987); *I'm Your Baby Tonight* (Arista, 1990); *My Love Is Your Love* (Arista, 1998); *Just Whitney* (Arista, 2002).

SELECTIVE FILMOGRAPHY: *The Bodyguard* (1992); *Waiting to Exhale* (1995); *The Preacher's Wife* (1996); *Cinderella* (TV, 1997).

WEBSITE: www.whitneyhouston.com.

DAVID FREELAND

HUUN-HUUR-TU

Formed: 1992, Kyzyl, Tuva (as Kungurtuk)

Members: Alexander Bapa, Tuvan percussion; Sayan Bapa, voice, igil, Tuvan percussion (born 1962); Kaigal-ool Khovalyg, voice, igil, doshpuluur, chanzy (born 1960); Albert Kuvezin, voice, guitar; Anatoli Kuular, mouth harp (xomuz), byzaanchi (born Chadan, Tuva, 1965); Alexei Saryglar, percussionist, singer, string instrumentalist (born 1966).

Genre: World

Huun-Huur-Tu is a group of musicians who combine the ancient musical traditions of their Central Asian, southern Siberian Tuva peoples (who still labor as sheep and reindeer herders) with contemporary performance practices and selected electronic instruments.

A male quartet originally organized to preserve and highlight unique repertoire from a remote region, the members of what became Huun-Huur-Tu were discovered by a Boston-based ethnomusicologist, Ted Levin, on a field expedition in 1987 to an area which the Soviet government had formerly forbidden to tourists. The area is populated by some 150,000 people, mostly in rural areas. The musicians were working separately in state-run folkloric ensembles, and Levin helped bring them to the United States for the first time in 1993. Since then Huun-Huur-Tu has toured the United States, Europe, Japan, and Australia and has recorded five albums under its own name along with several collaborations with an array of musicians across genres and geographic boundaries, including Frank Zappa, Ry Cooder, the Chieftains, Johnny "Guitar"

Watson, the Kronos Quartet, the Indian violinist L. Shankar, the Scottish-Canadian Niall MacAulay, Angelite, and the Bulgarian Women's Choir.

The members of Huun-Huur-Tu excel at the traditional solo practice of xoomei (throat-singing), in which two distinct pitches are produced, sustained and shaped simultaneously; some of their recordings capture them throat-singing while riding horses. They also employ instruments indigenous to their region of grasslands, forests, and mountain ranges. These instruments include the two-string igil, a "horsehead fiddle"; the bowed, three-string chanzy; the banjolike, plucked doshpuluur; the tungur frame drum; the khomuz jew's harp; the dazhaanning khavy, a rattle made of bull scrotum and sheep kneebones; the deer-horn amarga; dried horses' hooves used as clappers; and the birch-bark bird-whistle ediski.

Huun-Huur-Tu's lyrics recount stories, prayers, descriptions of personal relationships, and mythic incidents. The musicians imitate natural ambient sounds and the noises of animals, to cohere as sonic maps of physical landscapes; a primary purpose of Tuvan music seems to be to detail topography. The name "Huun-Huur-Tu" refers to the quality of light on open countryside at dawn and dusk. The band's spare, string-dominated arrangements suggest African-American blues as well as Eastern Asian folk forms; Huun-Huur-Tu has also explored the kinship of Tuvan and early Russian music (Moscow is approximately 2,500 miles west of Tuva).

The founding member Albert Kuvezin left Huun-Huur-Tu to establish the pop-oriented group Yat-Kha, and the founding percussionist Alexander Bapa departed for Moscow to concentrate on record production and music group management. Anatoli Kuular and Alexei Saryglar replaced them in 1993 and 1995, respectively, with no noticeable loss of virtuosity or authenticity.

Throat-singing is practiced by the Inuit of Alaska and Canada; the Tuvan vocalist Sainkho Namchylak has employed throat-singing in avant-garde improvisations with the Moscow Composers Orchestra. But Huun-Huur-Tu has succeeded like no other ensemble or individual in keeping an age-old vocal technique alive and adapting it to contemporary circumstances without diffusing its essence.

SELECTIVE DISCOGRAPHY: *Best *Live* (JARO, 2001); *Where Young Grass Grows* (Shanachie, 1999); *If I'd Been Born an Eagle* (Shanachie, 1997); *Fly Fly My Sadness* (Shanachie, 1996); *The Orphan's Lament* (Shanachie, 1994); *Sixty Horses in My Herd: Old Songs and Tunes of Tuva* (Shanachie, 1993).

BIBLIOGRAPHY: T. Levin, *The Hundred Thousand Fools of God: Musical Travels in Central Asia (and Queens, New York)* (Bloomington, 1997).

WEBSITE: www.huunhuurtu.com.

HOWARD MANDEL

ICE CUBE

Born: O'Shea Jackson; Los Angeles, California, 15 June 1969

Genre: Rap

Best-selling album since 1990: *The Predator* (1992)

Hit songs since 1990: "It Was a Good Day," "Check Yo Self," "Bop Gun (One Nation)"

Ice Cube was one of the most talented, successful, and controversial gangsta rappers of the late 1980s and early 1990s. As a member of N.W.A. (Niggaz With Attitude), his substantial writing and vocal contributions helped make them the seminal group of their genre. After leaving for a solo career, he recorded some of the most incendiary and articulate music ever to deal with racial and social issues in America. His bigoted stance was divisive, but his incisiveness brought critical praise and consistent platinum sales. By the mid-1990s and beyond, his burgeoning film career took precedence over music.

Despite growing up in the tumultuous South Central area of Los Angeles, California, Ice Cube (born O'Shea Jackson) was not involved in the heavy gang violence eventually portrayed in his lyrics. He was an above average student with parents who strongly encouraged his educational development. Though he was widely exposed to funk and soul music during his childhood, it was the advent of rap in the late 1970s that truly sparked his musical interest.

In high school, he began writing rap lyrics and formed a duo called CIA with Sir Jinx. During this time, he met

Dr. Dre, who was creating music for a local group called the World Class Wrecking Cru, and Eazy-E, who had recently formed his own record label, Ruthless Records. The three of them formed N.W.A., a side project for them to make dirty party records for fun. Audience interest in their first three singles, though, made the group a bigger priority.

Inspired by the noisy and confrontational rhythms of innovative political rappers Public Enemy, the group revamped their sound, added MC Ren to the roster, and released the landmark album *Straight Outta Compton* (1988). By promoting misogyny, glamorizing gang violence, and advocating the murder of police officers as a reaction to brutality and racial profiling, the group ignited controversy and elicited condemnation from the Federal Bureau of Investigation. Despite minimal support from mainstream radio or MTV, the album was an enormous underground hit that launched the gangsta rap genre.

Since Ice Cube had been involved in writing ten out of thirteen tracks on the multiplatinum-selling album and toured the country in support of it, he felt his contributions were worth more than the $30,000 he received. His dispute with manager Jerry Heller led to his unceremonious departure from the group.

Going Solo

Ice Cube went to New York and recorded his solo debut, *AmeriKKKa's Most Wanted* (1990), with Public Enemy's production team, the Bomb Squad, and his new supporting cast, Da Lench Mob. With a more cacophonous rhythmic assault than N.W.A., and an equally profane lyrical palette, he positions himself as the hostile voice of change in an urban, black community oppressed by white-dominated America. As a diversion, though, he offers tracks like the darkly comedic and misogynistic anecdote about a sexual partner inaccurately claiming his paternity in "You Can't Fade Me," and the incorporation of classic fairy-tale characters into a life of gun wielding and promiscuous sex in "A Gangsta's Fairytale." The album was an immediate success with many critics and consumers, attaining platinum sales within a few months of its release and establishing Ice Cube as a premiere solo entity.

Naturally Ice Cube's expanding appeal raised fear and objections from many moral watchdogs and conservative groups, but when he raised the racial invective on *Death Certificate* (1991), he drew many more detractors. The songs "Black Korea" and "No Vaseline" garnered the largest backlash. The former issues a threat to burn down all Korean-owned liquor stores nationwide if the owners do not stop profiling black customers. The latter blames white, Jewish, N.W.A. manager Heller for breaking up the group and is full of homophobic and anti-Semitic references. The controversy only fueled quicker sales though, as the album debuted at number two on the *Billboard* 200 and went platinum in a month. Though chastised for its bigotry, the work was lauded for directly dealing with current black economic, social, and health care issues, without the gangster posturing of his previous efforts.

In 1991 Ice Cube also received praise for his role as Doughboy in the John Singleton–directed movie *Boyz N the Hood*. The critically acclaimed film was an unflinching and sobering portrayal of Los Angeles' inner-city problems. With his role as ghetto spokesman reaching a second medium, interest in Ice Cube's commentary became even more prominent on April 29, 1992, when riots broke out in Los Angeles after the announcement of the acquittal of three of the four policemen accused of beating black motorist Rodney King. His response was released in the form of his third album, *The Predator*, later that year.

With its dark and anxious tone, news sound bites relating to the riots and its aftermath, and Ice Cube discussing his prophecy of the riots, the album is an urgent document of its time. It debuted at number one on the *Billboard* 200 and Top R&B Albums charts simultaneously and immediately went platinum. Surprisingly, it also contains his catchiest material and yielded his only two Top 20 pop hits on the *Billboard* Hot 100, the day-in-the-life reflection "It Was a Good Day" and the cautionary dance jam "Check Yo Self."

Going Hollywood

Though *Lethal Injection* (1993) was another strong commercial success, its laid-back vibe made it less vital than his previous efforts and foreshadowed his five-year hiatus between solo albums. By 1994 he was married with

children and following the beliefs of the Nation of Islam. These events in his personal life had a calming effect and led to a new chapter in his professional life: film. Throughout the rest of the decade, he acted in several successful feature films, including *Higher Learning* (1995), *Anaconda* (1997), and *Three Kings* (1999). He also wrote, produced, and starred in the hit comedies *Friday* (1995), *Next Friday* (2000), and *Friday After Next* (2002) and directed *The Player's Club* (1998).

Though his film career began to eclipse his musical output, Ice Cube did stay busy by producing albums for artists like his former partners Da Lench Mob and Mack 10 and WC, with whom he formed the Westside Connection and released an album. He also directed several music videos and returned to his solo career with the release of *War & Peace Volume 1 (The War Disc)* (1998) and *War & Peace Volume 2 (The Peace Disc)* (2000). Both albums generated hits, sold well, and boasted solid production, but lacked the raw fury of his earlier work. Lyrically, he was still articulate, but his continuing Hollywood success, including starting his own film company, Cubevision, reduced his credibility as the underprivileged voice of the streets. In the new millennium his most promising musical prospect was a potential N.W.A. reunion.

Ice Cube's intentionally confrontational and racially biased recordings were some of the most objectionable and frightening statements ever recorded. At his peak, though, his ability to identify and promote awareness of the social problems plaguing America's ghettos made him one of the most important voices of the late 1980s and early 1990s. His sharp-witted intelligence, candor, and business sense bolstered his ascent from underground revolutionary to mainstream celebrity.

SELECTIVE DISCOGRAPHY: *AmeriKKKa's Most Wanted* (Priority, 1990); *Kill at Will* EP (Priority, 1990); *Death Certificate* (Priority, 1991); *The Predator* (Priority, 1992); *Lethal Injection* (Priority, 1993). **With N.W.A.:** *Straight Outta Compton* (Priority/Ruthless, 1988). **With Westside Connection:** *Bow Down* (Priority, 1996).

SELECTIVE FILMOGRAPHY: *Boyz N the Hood* (1991); *Higher Learning* (1995); *Friday* (1995); *Anaconda* (1997); *The Player's Club* (1998); *Three Kings* (1999); *Next Friday* (2000); *Barbershop* (2002); *Friday After Next* (2002).

BIBLIOGRAPHY: J. McIver, *Ice Cube Attitude* (London, 2002).

WEBSITE: www.icecubemusic.com.

DAVE POWERS

ENRIQUE IGLESIAS

Born: Madrid, Spain, 8 May 1975

Genre: Latin Pop

Best-selling album since 1990: *Enrique* (1999)

Hit songs since 1990: "Hero," "Rhythm Divine," "Esperanza"

Enrique Iglesias, the son of the famous Spanish singer Julio Iglesias, was born in Madrid, Spain, where he lived with his mother, brother, and sister until 1982 when the children moved to live with their father in Miami, Florida. At a private school in Miami Iglesias's interest in music was nurtured, and he took part in school musicals.

Embarking on a singing career in the mid-1990s, Iglesias decided to conceal his ambitions from his parents and pursued music under the pseudonym Enrique Martinez. It was only after he had clinched his first record deal that he told them about his intentions to pursue music professionally, and at that time reverted back to his family name. His first album, *Enrique Iglesias*, was released in 1996 and sold more than 6 million copies worldwide, with the United States as the largest part of the market. This album comprises a mix of pop ballads and easily memorable tunes. In this album the first signs of Iglesias's wailing and deeply sentimental vocal technique came to characterize a sound that surfaces in all his later albums. In songs such as "Por Amarte," the yearning and earnest mood of his vocal style is drawn out to its fullest in a manner that capitalizes on the Latin American genre to which he aspires.

His follow-up album, *Vivir*, was released in 1997 and became an instant success, winning him a Grammy Award, and by the end of this year he had topped more than 8 million sales of both albums. The album *Vivir* displays greater versatility in musical style than its forerunner, with Iglesias turning to a mix of styles such as rock on the track "Volveré," reggae on "Lluvia Cae," and pop ballad on "Miente." However, there is a sense that his performance on this album could be pushed even further to achieve a greater depth and degree of personal reflection. Most of the songs, which consist of a mix of Latin, dance-pop, and ballads, laced with seductive vocals, were written when Iglesias was only seventeen years old.

The release of *Cosas del Amor* in 1998 brought clear evidence that Iglesias had matured. Dealing with themes of love and romance, the songs in this work are highly polished in their production. Notable are the musical arrangements, with their melodramatic gestures and lush scoring. In the tuneful ballads "Cosas del Amor" and "Esperanza," Iglesias uses catchy rhythms and percussion parts to draw out the songs' strong melodic lines. In "Para de Jugar," he turns to funk with a rhythm and blues flavor that brings the track alive.

In 1999 the album *Enrique* became the singer's biggest global success, selling more than 23 million copies, with gold and platinum sales in thirty-two countries. Including a cover of rocker Bruce Springsteen's "Sad Eyes" and a duet with pop icon Whitney Houston, this glossy production offers a variety of songs that blend Iglesias's emotional delivery with a strong, rhythmic Latin undertow. In the same year, the album *Bailamos: Greatest Hits* signified a colossal breakthrough for Iglesias in the Latin world and topped the *Billboard* Hot 100.

By the time he released *Escape* in 2001, Iglesias had sold more than 23 million albums and reached superstar status all around the world. Together with other pop stars such as Ricky Martin, Jennifer Lopez, Selena, and Christina Aguilera, he played a major part in the international Latin pop boom.

SELECTIVE DISCOGRAPHY: *Enrique Iglesias* (Fonovisa, 1995); *Version en Italiano* (Fonovisa, 1996); *Master Pistas* (Spartacus, 1997); *Vivir* (Fonovisa, 1997); *Cosas del Amor* (Fonovisa, 1998); *Enrique* (Interscope, 1999); *Bailamos: Greatest Hits* (Fonovisa, 1999); *Escape* (Interscope, 2001); *Quizás* (Universal, 2002).

BIBLIOGRAPHY: E. Furman and L. Furman, *Enrique Iglesias* (New York, 2000).

STAN HAWKINS

INCUBUS

Formed: 1991, Calabasas, California

Members: Brandon Boyd, vocals (born Van Nuys, California, 15 February 1976); Michael Einziger; guitar (born Los Angeles, California, 21 June 1976); Alex Katunich, bass (a.k.a. "Dirk Lance," born 18 August 1976); Chris "DJ" Kilmore, turntable (born Pittsburgh, Pennsylvania, 21 January 1973); Jose Pasillas, drums (born 26 April 1976). Former member: DJ Lyfe (Gavin Koppel).

Genre: Rock

Best-selling album since 1990: *Morning View* (2001)

Hit songs since 1990: "Drive," "Pardon Me"

With songs such as "Nice to Know You" and "Wish You Were Here" from *Morning View* (2001) Incubus was a ten-year overnight success story. Buoyed by a photogenic lead singer, tireless touring, and jubilant anthems, the group's mixture of turntable culture and peaceful, easy feeling California rock provided a mellow antidote to such hard-charging brethren as Korn and Limp Bizkit. They were a rare 1990s example of a rock group given time to find their audience and mature over the course of several albums.

Incubus started life as a funk-metal band formed in 1991 by three fifteen-year-old elementary school buddies:

Brandon Boyd (vocals), Jose Pasillas (drums), and Mike Einziger (guitar). They had to wait until the tenth grade, however, to meet their future bassist, Alex Katunich. The boys were primed to launch their rock star dreams, playing an endless succession of house parties, all-ages clubs and, despite their age, a 1992 gig at the Roxy on Hollywood's famed Sunset Strip. As legend has it, the pay-to-play show was booked after Einziger found a hundred-dollar bill on the ground and bought the necessary number of tickets to secure the group a show at the venue.

Presaging the soon-to-be-ubiquitous sight of rock bands with DJs, Incubus agreed to let the rapper DJ Lyfe (Gavin Koppel) join the group in 1995 after a single jam session. They independently released the ten-track album *Fungus Amongus* (1995), which features such early funk-metal tracks as "You Will Be a Hot Dancer" and "Shaft," which owe a heavy debt to the frantic, genre-blurring early works of Los Angeles' Red Hot Chili Peppers.

The combination of Boyd's exhilarating stage presence and energy and the group's unique rock/hip-hop sound caught the attention of several record labels. Immortal/Epic Records signed the band in 1996 and a year later released their debut EP, *Enjoy Incubus*, which contains six professionally remixed versions of demos the band had been peddling at their live shows.

A full-length album, *S.C.I.E.N.C.E.*, was released in September 1997, again fusing the band's love of heavy metal and funk with a childlike sense of studio experimentation (among the instruments employed were children's walkie-talkies) with Boyd's positive, hippie-esque lyrics. Two years of touring with like-minded bands such as Korn, 311, Sugar Ray, Black Sabbath, Limp Bizkit, and the Urge followed the album's release. The band's song "Familiar," recorded with DJ Greyboy, is featured on the soundtrack to the 1997 film, *Spawn*. DJ Lyfe was replaced by another hip-hop fanatic, DJ Kilmore, in 1998. Following Lyfe's pattern, Kilmore was interested in integrating his scratching into the sonic palette of the band rather than interjecting jarring scratching and mixing into their songs.

Success, at Last

During their two-year stint on the road, Incubus not only amassed a larger audience, but their expanding sound—a fusion of jazz, funk, rock, rap, metal, and ska—was now primed to mine chart gold thanks to the success of friends such as Limp Bizkit, the Deftones, and Korn. After an eight-week writing stint, the band spent nine weeks during the summer of 1999 recording *Make Yourself*, an album that illustrates their growing maturity with a mix of heavy, melodic, thought-provoking songs such as "Consequence" and their career-making hits, "Pardon Me" and "Drive."

The album offers a bit of something for everyone, from the hip-hop/funk turntable scratchfest "Battlestar Scralatchtica," with guests DJ Cut Chemist and DJ NuMark, to "Nowhere Fast," which melds smooth jazz with drum-and-bass-style techno percussion.

A limited edition EP of rarities, acoustic, and live songs, *When Incubus Attacks, Vol. 1* was released in the fall of 2000, followed by the reissue of *Fungus Amongus*. Again teaming with former R.E.M. producer Scott Litt, the band released *Morning View* in the fall of 2001. The album is their most refined to date, melding Japanese instruments with sunny California grooves and spinning out the expansive arena rock hits "Wish You Were Here" and "Nice to Know You." While the former retains a shadow of hard rock with a heavy backbeat, "Nice to Know You" is the apex of the band's radio-friendly experimentation, melding off-kilter techno rhythms with turntable noises and rock guitars. With his lean, muscular, tattooed, and pierced body, shoulder-length brown hair, and wide, expressive eyes, Boyd became a new kind of teen pin-up: sensitive with a dark side. By the middle of 2002, the group was burned out from nearly a decade of nonstop touring and announced an indefinite break before beginning their next studio effort.

Besieged by file sharing and illegal song swapping, by the late 1990s major record labels were desperate to find pop groups that, like Incubus, could spin instant gold with hit singles from their debut albums. Through a combination of hard work, savvy marketing, and a unique sound, Incubus was able to buck the trend by steadily building a worldwide audience in their own way, at their own pace.

SELECTIVE DISCOGRAPHY: *Fungus Amongus* (Uson Red Eye, 1995); *Enjoy Incubus* (Immortal/Epic, 1997); *S.C.I.E.N.C.E.* (Immortal/Epic, 1997); *Make Yourself* (Sony, 1999); *Morning View* (Sony, 2001).

WEBSITES: www.enjoyincubus.com.

GIL KAUFMAN

INDIGO GIRLS

Formed: 1983, Athens, Georgia

Members: Amy Ray, guitar, vocals (born Decatur, Georgia, 12 April 1964); Emily Saliers, guitar, vocals (born New Haven, Connecticut, 22 July 1963).

Genre: Rock

Best-selling album since 1990: *Indigo Girls* (1989)

Hit songs since 1990: "Closer to Fine," "Galileo," "Least Complicated"

In 2003 the idea of two guitar-slinging, harmonizing female singer/songwriters making a go at the music business as a duo hardly seems revolu-

Indigo Girls. L-R: Amy Ray, Emily Saliers [PAUL NATKIN/PHOTO RESERVE]

tionary, but that is just what the Indigo Girls were when they caught the attention of fans, radio, and Christian conservatives in the early 1990s. After their formation, the Indigo Girls, who are up front about their homosexuality, went on to write scores of folk rock hits. They performed at sell-out arenas, joined Sarah McLachlan's Lilith Fair tour in the late 1990s, and released a handful of platinum-selling albums. The Indigo Girls melded the personal and the political without sacrificing one for the other, without succumbing to didacticism, and without losing their musicality.

The pair met when Amy was ten and Emily eleven, at school in Decatur, Georgia. They formed a musical partnership early on, and released a cassette of mostly cover songs called *Tuesday's Children* under the name Saliers and Ray. They went to college together at Emory University and changed their name to the Indigo Girls.

The Seamless Blending of Opposites

Saliers, with fair skin and blonde hair, possesses a wispy, velvety voice, and usually writes the more introspective, contemplative ballads. Ray is often full of fire and has a raspier, more earthy voice. They do not usually write a song together—they will compose separately and play together, working out guitar parts and harmonies when they combine it all to form a song.

Their breakthrough album, the self-titled *Indigo Girls* (1989), was their second release but their first for Epic Records, which signed them in 1988. With production help from Scott Litt, who worked with fellow Georgians and superstars R.E.M., and guest vocals from Michael Stipe and the Irish group Hothouse Flowers, the work is a collection of folk rock songs about coming to terms with yourself, your world, and your relationships. The spiritual quest

"Closer to Fine," written by Saliers, was the album's first single, and it climbed up the charts to peak at number twenty-two on the *Billboard* 200. Listeners were impressed with "Kid Fears," with vocal help from Michael Stipe. The album's territory, ruminations on faith, love, and religion, whether in passionate ballads such as Ray's "Blood and Fire" or Saliers's heartfelt ballad "History of Us," marked the duo as intelligent musicians with a keen command of melody and harmony. As a result, the Indigo Girls were asked by Neil Young and R.E.M. to tour as an opening act. By September 1989 *Indigo Girls* reached gold and the pair won a Grammy Award for Best Contemporary Folk Group of 1989.

Confession, reflection, and instigation are qualities of a good Indigo Girls song. On their earlier albums, they stuck with an acoustic approach and sometimes fleshed out their sound with the addition of bass, drums, and other instruments. In 1990, they issued *Nomads Indians Saints*, which was not a critical success although it was nominated for a Grammy.

The Rites of Success

By this point, the Indigo Girls began to release an album approximately every two years and were beginning to hit their stride as songwriters. *Rites of Passage* (1992) fared better, with the rousing "Galileo," which finds the Girls questioning themselves, the solar system, and invoking the spirit of Galileo to sort things out for them. On *Rites of Passage* they tackle everything from governmental misbehavior to Native American rights to romantic disappointment without loss of hope, energy, or passion, as in *Love Will Come to You*. Other standout tracks include the rambunctious, mandolin-fueled "Joking," and their cover of the Dire Straits song "Romeo and Juliet," which, as a duet between two women, adds a completely different feel to the impassioned love song. The album also boasts appearances from singer/songwriter Jackson Browne, bassist Edgar Meyer, fiddler Lisa Germano, and Celtic instruments such as bouzouki, bodhrán, and uillean pipes.

Showing their reliability as solid, skilled songwriters and performers, the Indigo Girls followed up with *Swamp Ophelia* (1994), which peaked at number nine on the *Billboard* 200. A turning point for them, it reaches beyond the comfort zone of weepy ballads and anthemic rock. It offers a close look at their relationships, particularly in "Least Complicated" and "Power of Two." *Swamp Ophelia* is not as murky or maudlin as the title might suggest.

The Indigo Girls spent part of their summers in the late 1990s touring with Sarah McLachlan's all-female Lilith Fair, and produced a live album along the way. In 2003 they released the understated *Become You*, which features the subtle use of horns, piano, and organ. Their ninth album, *Become You*, shows the wisdom of their years as a musical partnership. With "Yield," written by Ray, they sing "It takes a lot to keep it going / It takes a lot to keep it real / It takes a lot to learn to yield." *Become You* also finds the pair willing to explore relationship issues more directly, specifically in the Saliers-penned "She's Saving Me" and the lilting strings of ballad "Hope Alone."

As the Indigo Girls, Ray and Saliers proved to radio and record label executives that two women with guitars can indeed make a mark on pop music. Through their years together the Girls have been honest, to themselves and to their music, and their voices have resonated with fans and critics alike.

SELECTIVE DISCOGRAPHY: *Strange Fire* (Indigo Records, 1987); *Indigo Girls* (Epic, 1989); *Nomads Indians Saints* (Epic, 1990); *Rites of Passage* (Epic, 1992); *Swamp Ophelia* (Epic, 1994); *1200 Curfews* (Epic, 1995); *Shaming of the Sun* (Epic, 1997); *Come on Now Social* (Sony, 1999); *Become You* (Sony, 2001).

CARRIE HAVRANEK

INTOCABLE

Formed: 1993, Zapata, Texas

Members: Juan Hernández, MC, percussion; René Martínez, drums; Ricardo "Ricky" Muñoz, vocals, accordion; Félix Salinas, bass; Daniel Sánchez, backing vocals, bajo sexto; Sergio Serna, percussion.

Genre: Latin

Best-selling album since 1990: *Contigo* (1999)

Hit songs since 1990: "Coqueta," "Y Todo Para Qué," "El Amigo Que Se Fue"

When Tejano music's popularity was peaking in the early 1990s, Intocable took a left-of-center approach by playing a new norteño/Tejano hybrid. Norteño is the regional Mexican genre from northern Mexico; its primary instruments are the accordion and bajo sexto (a twangy twelve-string guitar), and its signature rhythm is the polka. The genre began to incorporate the tropical Colombian rhythm known as cumbia. Tejano, Spanish for "from Texas," is influenced by norteño but also incorporates American traditions such as rock and jazz. The group injected a freshness into the increasingly predictable Tejano sound with norteño cumbias and polkas and took a fresh approach on songs like "Dónde Estás?" and "La Mentira." At a time when many Tejano labels were pressuring groups to get easy airplay by recording quickie covers of beloved old songs, Intocable insisted on seeking out original mate-rial, though the members themselves do little songwriting.

Intocable was formed when Muñoz and friends he had known since junior high school came together in the tiny border town of Zapata. Ricky Muñoz, René Martínez, and Sergio Serna forged the sound that used raw norteño cumbias and upbeat Tejano polkas as the foundation, and topped it with a rock sensibility and Beatles-like vocal harmonies. They also added congas, not a typical norteño instrument, to add a bit of danceable tropical flavor.

The band signed with EMI in 1993 and released their major-label debut album, *Fuego Eterno*, the following year. Their breakthrough album was *Otro Mundo*, from 1995, which contained hits "La Mentira" and "Coqueta." An ode to a flirtatious girlfriend, "Coqueta" creatively juxtaposes Mexican cumbia with twelve-bar blues. The song was written by the young Mexican composer Luis Padilla, whose success with Intocable helped make him Tejano/norteño music's most in-demand songwriter by the late 1990s. *Otro Mundo* was produced by Jose Luis Ayala, whose brother Ramón Ayala had also brought Tejano and norteño together in the 1960s with his group Los Relámpagos del Norte.

By 1996 Intocable had become a major player, attracting full houses and ecstatic crowds with the band's almost constant touring. In 1997 the group released *Llévame Contigo*. It produced two *Billboard* Hot Latin Tracks hits: the title cut and the ranchera "No Te Vayas." In late 1997 internal conflicts led to the departure of the bajo sexto player Johnny Lee Rosas and the bass player Albert Ramírez Jr. (who were replaced by Danny Sánchez and Silvestre Rodriguez Jr., respectively). Rosas and Ramírez went on to form Masizzo. Muñoz and Intocable lost no momentum, releasing the already complete *Intocable IV* (1997), which generated the hit rancheras "Eres Mi Droga" and "Vivir sin Ellas." The latter track explores infidelity from the bad boy's point of view—he loves both his girlfriends so much that he just can't choose between them.

On January 31, 1999, the stage MC José Ángel Farias, twenty-three, and the bass player Rodriguez, twenty-six, were killed in a car crash outside Monterrey, Mexico. Despite taking time off to mourn and regroup, Intocable somehow managed to keep up its one-album-per-year pace, releasing *Contigo* in July. It features a tribute to Farias and Rodriguez, "El Amigo Que Se Fue."

Intocable's 2002 release, *Sueños*, debuted at number one on *Billboard*'s Top Latin Albums chart and was certified platinum by the Recording Industry Association of America for sales exceeding 200,000 units. Padilla, known for his carnally themed lyrics, adopted a loftier tone this time for the inspirational singles "El Poder de tus Manos" and "Sueña," both of which hit number one on *Billboard*'s Regional Mexican Airplay chart.

Intocable has spawned a musical movement that is sometimes known as norteño romántico. Centered on Texas's Rio Grande Valley, the genre eschews corrido story-songs and drug ballads but sticks to traditional norteño instrumentation. New groups that follow Intocable's template to some extent include La Costumbre, Duelo, Iman, and Palomo.

SELECTIVE DISCOGRAPHY: *Fuego Eterno* (EMI Latin, 1994); *Otro Mundo* (EMI Latin, 1995); *Llévame Contigo* (EMI Latin, 1996); *Intocable IV* (EMI Latin, 1997); *Intocable* (EMI Latin, 1998); *Contigo* (EMI Latin, 1999); *Es Para Tí* (EMI Latin, 2000); *Sueños* (EMI Latin, 2002).

RAMIRO BURR

INXS

Formed: 1977, Sydney, Australia; Disbanded 1997; Reformed 2001

Members: Garry Gary Beers, bass (born Sydney, Australia, 22 June 1957); Andrew Farriss, keyboard, guitars (born Sydney, Australia, 27 March 1959); Jon Farriss, drums (born Sydney, Australia, 18 August 1961); Tim Farriss, guitar (born Sydney, Australia, 16 August 1957); Kirk Pengilly, saxophone, guitar, vocals (born Sydney, Australia, 4 July 1958); Jon Stevens, vocals (born Upper Hut, New Zealand). Former member: Michael Hutchence, vocals (born Sydney, Australia, 22 January 1960; died Australia, 22 November 1997).

Genre: Rock

Best-selling album since 1990: *Kick* (1987)

Hit songs since 1990: "Suicide Blonde," "Disappear," "Beautiful Girl"

The Australian band INXS (pronounced in-excess) toiled away for ten years with moderate success throughout the 1980s, and made its biggest impact on the pop music landscape with its album *Kick* (1987). Thanks to the band's strong guitar-based sound, danceable sensibility, sultry appeal of its lead singer Michael Hutchence, and quirky, jazzy touch, *Kick* went on to sell more than 9 million albums worldwide. INXS approached the 1990s after having already launched a successful album, and spent much of the 1990s trying to keep its rock-based act relevant in the changing musical landscape that began to favor alternative music. The band continued on, despite a decline in sales toward the mid-1990s and personal troubles of lead singer Hutchence. The album X (1990) brought the band on a tour around the world and it eventually disbanded in 1997 after the tragic suicide of Hutchence, who hung himself in his Sydney, Australia, hotel room. Though INXS officially broke up shortly thereafter, in 2002, band members decided to carry on, and added vocalist Jon Stevens of the Australian band Noiseworks. INXS once again set upon a world tour that, despite its success, appeared a little distasteful and disrespectful in the eyes of some fans; Hutchence, as the lead singer, was the essence of the band.

Few bands rival INXS's longevity and success, and the fact that all six members remained committed to the music and their mission up until the untimely death of their lead singer is remarkable. The band formed in the late 1970s with three brothers, Tim, Jon, and Andrew Farriss, in Perth, Australia, and at first called themselves the Farriss Brothers. After Jon graduated high school, the three teamed up with schoolmates Kirk Pengilly, Michael Hutchence, and Garry Beers, moved to Sydney, and renamed themselves INXS. At the time of its emergence, INXS rivaled bands such as Irish rockers U2 and the U.S. rock band R.E.M. The sonic palette of INXS is a mix of the swagger and rock-star guitar stylings of the Rolling Stones, the synthetic dance beats of the 1980s New Wave trend, and its own personal imprint of layered guitars, slinky bass lines, and the slithering, smoldering vocals of Hutchence.

INXS developed a loyal following in its native Australia, starting off with placement in the Top 40 with "Underneath the Colors," and then with its third album, *Shabooh Shoobah*, which reached the Australian Top 5. However, *The Swing*, a sassy, guitar-driven album, brought the band the breakthrough hit "Original Sin" that landed it at the top of the Australian charts. Throughout the early and mid-1980s, INXS laid the foundation for a big breakthrough in 1987, with the October release of *Kick*.

Thanks in part to the sultry good looks and hushed vocals of Hutchence, "Need You Tonight" soared to the number one slot in the United States and helped propel *Kick* to number three on the *Billboard* 200. The video for the complete song "Need You Tonight/Mediate" was also prominent and garnered the band much attention. The "Mediate" portion of the song, which operates kind of like a postscript, recreates scenes from legendary rocker Bob Dylan's documentary *Don't Look Back*. Throughout the video band members take turns flipping cue cards with select lyrics as the song progresses. The video certainly caught people's attention and established an association between INXS and the iconic political voice of Dylan. At the end of the video, Pengilly wails away on an empty, dirty street. Part of what made the band so popular and unusual at the time was its liberal use of saxophone, heretofore nonexistent. Other tracks from *Kick*, such as the Rolling

Stones-like riffs on "Devil Inside," the adrenaline-fueled "New Sensation," and the jazzy rocker "Mystify," became hits in the United States and helped expand the group's audience.

After the unprecedented sales of *Kick*, the band took about a year off and reconvened for *X*, which abandoned the band's previous synthesizer-dance-pop tendencies and adopted a more liberal use of guitars. The sassy, unusual "Suicide Blonde" continued their trademark hooks, deft combination of guitar and saxophone. After *Kick*, *X* is INXS's best album—the albums the band released after *X* did not fare as well with fans or critics. *X* has been certified multiplatinum.

Tragic Finish

The release of the band's fourteenth album, *Elegantly Wasted* (1997), turned out to be oddly prescient with its hedonistic dance-rock vibe that curried little favor with fans and critics alike. On the heels of the album's release, band members planned to rehearse in their hometown, Sydney, when tragic events intervened. In November 1997, Hutchence was discovered dead in his hotel room. After his death it was revealed that Hutchence had been at odds with his girlfriend, Paula Yates, for some months; there were also rumors circulating of drug abuse. The band broke up, more or less, but reconvened in 2001.

Overall, INXS scored seven Top 10 hits in the United States from the 1980s through the mid-1990s. Part of its success can be attributed to the fact that the band brought on a different producer for every album, which insured that its sound would never become stale; it also toured the world in support of each release. Oddly, although the band won scores of awards in its native country, in the United Kingdom, and from magazines such as *Rolling Stone*, it never earned a Grammy Award in the United States, though it was nominated three times. INXS had a sizable impact on the transformation of 1980s new wave music into a more full-fledged rock sound, complete with guitars and keyboards, and the occasional blast from a saxophone.

SELECTIVE DISCOGRAPHY: *Listen Like Thieves* (Atlantic,1985); *Kick* (Atlantic, 1987); *X* (Atlantic, 1990); *Live Baby Live* (1991); *Welcome to Wherever You Are* (Atlantic, 1992); *Full Moon, Dirty Hearts* (Atlantic, 1993); *Elegantly Wasted* (Mercury, 1997); *Shine Like It Does: The Anthology (1979–1997)* (Rhino, 2001).

CARRIE HAVRANEK

CHRIS ISAAK

Born: Stockton, California, 26 June 1956
Genre: Rock

Best-selling album since 1990: *Forever Blue* (1995)
Hit songs since 1990: "Wicked Game," "Somebody's Crying," "Baby Did a Bad Bad Thing"

A throwback inspired by 1950s rock, country, and rockabilly, Chris Isaak became a distinctive and enduring male solo artist in the 1990s while also carving a career in film and television. The son of a forklift operator, Isaak received his first guitar at the age of fifteen. Isaak and his brother Nick performed frequently for their parents, specializing in country ballads as well as the classic tunes of 1950s crooner Roy Orbison. Isaak attended the University of the Pacific and held down a variety of jobs, including movie-studio tour guide, film extra, and boxer, which left him with his noticeably flattened nose.

In college Isaak became enthralled by *Sun Sessions* (1976), the seminal collection of Elvis Presley's 1954 and 1955 recordings. He relocated to San Francisco and formed his first band, a rockabilly outfit named the Silvertones. At this stage Isaak, a struggling artist, began wearing retro country-and-western outfits, courtesy of his local thrift store.

Isaak attracted the attention of Warner Bros. Records, which signed the young singer to a recording contract in 1985 and released his debut album, *Silvertone*, that same year, and its follow-up, *Chris Isaak* (1986). Both albums invoked a variety of time-honored sounds, from country blues to more modern R&B, but neither album thrived commercially.

In 1989 Isaak released his third album, *Heart-Shaped World*. Like its predecessors, the album was initially a commercial disappointment. The following year the director David Lynch used an instrumental version of the haunting track "Wicked Game" in his movie *Wild at Heart* (1990). An Atlanta DJ sought out the full track and started a radio frenzy that sent the song to number six on the *Billboard* charts in 1991. "Wicked Game" was one of the more unusual radio hits of the 1990s. A sparse ballad with moody country guitars, it features Isaak sexily drawling lines such as "The world was on fire, and no one could save me but you / It's strange what desire will make foolish people do," reaching a crescendo on the chorus with the falsetto-delivered, "No, I don't want to fall in love."

Isaak's unique features, especially his flat nose and greased-up, rockabilly haircut, attracted the attention of Hollywood, which gave him bit parts in movies such as *The Silence of the Lambs* (1991) and *Twin Peaks: Fire Walk with Me* (1992). Isaak also scored a leading role in *Little Buddha* (1993).

In 1993 Isaak released *San Francisco Days*, which featured the minor hit "Can't Do a Thing (To Stop Me)."

The follow-up album, *Forever Blue* (1995), was Isaak's most popular of the decade, selling 1 million copies. A concept album centered on his breakup with a longtime girlfriend, *Forever Blue* runs the gamut of emotions, from extreme melancholy to raw anger. The album features the wistful hit "Somebody's Crying," with its simple plea: "Please, return the love you took from me." *Forever Blue* also features a dark boogie-rocker entitled "Baby Did a Bad Bad Thing." "Baby Did a Bad Bad Thing" presents Isaak at his most emotionally raw; over a snakelike guitar, a tense Isaak seethes with anger at his former lover: "You ever toss and turn your lying awake and thinking about the one you love?/ I don't think so." "Baby Did a Bad Bad Thing" enjoyed a second life when the director Stanley Kubrick featured the song in his 1999 movie *Eyes Wide Shut.*

Isaak's subsequent albums, *Baja Sessions* (1996) and *Speak of the Devil* (1996), each sold more than 500,000 copies, further establishing Isaak as a commercially viable artist. Isaak continued to delve into acting on the side, scoring roles in the movies *Grace of My Heart* (1996) and *That Thing You Do!* (1996) as well as the HBO series *From the Earth to the Moon* (1998). In 2001 the Showtime cable network launched *The Chris Isaak Show*, an irreverent comedy series about the life of a rock star; the show gave him the opportunity to act and perform musically. In 2002 Isaak released *Always Got Tonight*, his eighth studio album, which features the minor hit "Let Me Down Easy." During the 1990s Chris Isaak carved a unique niche in pop culture, parlaying his affection for the 1950s into a distinctive style that led to multimedia celebrity.

SELECTIVE DISCOGRAPHY: *Silvertone* (Warner, 1985); *Chris Isaak* (Warner, 1986); *Heart-Shaped World* (Reprise, 1989); *San Francisco Days* (Reprise, 1993); *Forever Blue* (Reprise, 1995); *Baja Sessions* (Reprise, 1996); *Speak of the Devil* (Reprise, 1998); *Always Got Tonight* (Reprise, 2002).

SCOTT TRIBBLE

MARK ISHAM

Born: New York, New York, 7 September 1951
Genre: Soundtrack, Jazz, New Age
Best-selling album since 1990: *Mark Isham* (1990)

Mark Isham, a trumpeter and a prolific, adaptable soundtrack composer, has insinuated his sounds into American culture through movies, television, advertising, featured solos in other artists' productions, and ambitious recordings under his own name.

Isham's father was a music and history teacher, and his mother was a violinist; he studied violin and piano before settling on trumpet, with which he began his career playing in Bay Area classical orchestras. He also freelanced in jazz, rock, and soul bands in the late 1960s and early 1970s. In this period he fell under the influence of the late jazz trumpeter Miles Davis. Isham's signature sound is a devotee's emulation of Davis's fragile, muted jazz style. Isham also evokes Davis in his movie and television themes, jingles, straightforward album tributes, and live concerts.

During the early 1970s Isham toured with the Beach Boys, Van Morrison, and jazz saxophonists Pharoah Sanders and Charles Lloyd. His interests in mid-1970s ambient music experiments by British rocker Brian Eno and guitarist Robert Fripp inform his recordings with the Seattle-based pianist Art Lande in the quartet *Rubisa Patrol* (1976). Together, Isham and Lande designed a limpid jazz distillation whose attention to engineered acoustics foreshadowed New Age music. Isham refined this style with his album *Group 87* (1980). His solo debut, *Vapor Drawings* (1983), was one of the first albums on Windham Hill Records, the premiere New Age label.

Isham's music has seldom been entirely meditative. He does not shirk challenges: His first film score for Disney's *Never Cry Wolf* (1983) was followed by a second, his most acclaimed, for the Academy Award–nominated documentary *The Times of Harvey Milk* (1984), a film about the assassinated gay alderman of San Francisco. Isham received early acclaim in the form of Grammy nominations in the Best New Age Performance category for *Castalia* (1988) and *Tibet* (1989), and won for his eponymous 1990 release, his first album under a new contract with Virgin Records.

Isham has written scores for films featuring major stars such as the Jodie Foster vehicles *Little Man Tate* (1991) and *Nell* (1994), but he has also worked with innovative, sound-oriented directors such as Robert Altman on *Short Cuts* (1993) or Alan Rudolph on *Trouble in Mind* (1986). Additionally, Isham contributed music to several Rabbit Ears Productions albums of classic stories for children told by comics and actors.

As Isham turned forty, he addressed new goals. In 1992 he premiered *Five Stories for Trumpet and Orchestra*, his first commissioned orchestral work, and did a stint as soloist with the St. Louis Symphony. He was nominated for an Academy Award for his score for the fisherman's epic, *A River Runs through it* (1992). He played more jazz live, establishing a touring band to support *Blue Sun* (1995), his first Columbia album of original tunes, and Duke Ellington's "In A Sentimental Mood," arranged for a relatively conventional quintet. He set himself amid his former employer Charles Lloyd, jazz vibist Gary Burton, pianist Geri Allen, and drummer Billy Higgins for the score to Alan Rudolph's film *Afterglow* (1998), and he won numerous nominations and occasional awards, including a 1996 Emmy, for his scoring of the television series *EZ Streets*. His 2003 projects range from an album of duets with female singer/songwriters to remixes of Peggy Lee and Ella Fitzgerald recordings for a Revlon cosmetics commercial campaign.

Musicians such as Mark Isham, who are adept at disseminating their sounds broadly, sometimes remain faceless. But when he steps up to deliver his own inspiration, Isham summons up Miles Davis's 1980s format of electric keyboards and/or guitars and bass with measured rock/soul drumming. Isham does a respectable job at reconstruction but is at a fatal disadvantage when his derivative trumpet playing is compared to the original Davis. This problem disappears when he operates as a composer of soundtracks, creating musical cues that appropriately reflect and/or comment upon action on-screen.

SELECTIVE DISCOGRAPHY: *Film Music* (Windham Hill, 1985); *Trouble in Mind* (Island, 1986); *Everybody Wins* (Virgin U.K., 1990); *The Emperor's New Clothes* (BMG Kidz, 1990); *Mark Isham* (Virgin Records, 1990); *Little Man Tate* (Varese Sarabande, 1991); *Billy Bathgate* (Milan America, 1991); *A River Runs through It* (Milan America, 1992); *Of Mice and Men* (Varese Sarabande, 1992); *Short Cuts* (Imago, 1993); *Quiz Show* (Hollywood Records, 1994); *Nell* (Fox, 1994); *Afterglow* (Columbia, 1997); *Mark Isham: A Windham Hill Retrospective* (Windham Hill, 1998); *Miles Remembered: The Silent Way Project* (Columbia Records, 1999); *October Sky* (Sony Classical, 1999); *Men of Honor* (Motown Records, 2000); *The Majestic* (Warner Bros., 2001); *Moonlight Mile* (Epic Soundtrax, 2002).

HOWARD MANDEL

THE ISLEY BROTHERS

Formed: 1954, Cincinnati, Ohio

Members: Ronald Isley, vocals (born Cincinnati, Ohio, 21 May 1941); Rudolph Isley, vocals (born Cincinnati, Ohio, 1 April 1939). Former members: O'Kelly Isley, vocals (born Cincinnati, Ohio, 25 December 1937; died Alpine, New Jersey, 31 March 1986); Vernon Isley, vocals (born Cincinnati, Ohio; died Cincinnati, Ohio, 1954); Ernie Isley, guitar (born Cincinnati, Ohio, 7 March 1952); Marvin Isley, bass (born Cincinnati, Ohio, 18 August 1953); Chris Jasper, keyboards (born Cincinnati, Ohio, 30 December 1951).

Genre: R&B

Best-selling album since 1990: *Eternal* (2001)

Hit songs since 1990: "Let's Lay Together"

For their powers of endurance alone the Isley Brothers qualify as one of the most important acts in African-American music. But their achievement is about far more than mere longevity. A significant group in at least three different versions, the Isleys's momentous tale spans the history of post-Presley popular music. The Isley Brothers have been a powerful and influential presence for half a century: They began as a gospel quartet in the mid-1950s, trimmed to a soul trio in the 1960s, expanded to a full-fledged funk band in the early 1970s, and continued their work in the 1980s and 1990s in various incarnations connected to the family unit. Along the way, they have suffered some keenly felt tragedies—two of the original brothers have died—that have lent a further dimension of intensity to the group's style.

Formed in the brothers' home city of Cincinnati, Ohio, as the rock and roll revolution was beginning to filter through the American airwaves, they initially sang gospel and developed a call-and-response style typical of evangelical worship, with Ronald's imposing tenor supported by his brothers' backing work. Hailing from a musical family—their father was a professional vocalist and their mother a church pianist—they had the right springboard from which to progress. They suffered a serious setback, however, in 1955, when the singer Vernon was killed in a cycling accident.

First Hits, Then Motown

Two years later, the remaining trio decided to move to New York City and recorded a number of failed doo-wop singles. But in 1959 they composed and released "Shout" and, although it failed to reach the Top 40, the song became a much-covered, much-recorded classic. The 1964 version by the Scottish singer Lulu was a major U.K. hit. In 1962 the brothers did score a hit with "Twist and Shout," and their arrangement was reproduced not long after by the Beatles. Numerous white acts, including the Yardbirds and the Human Beinz, struck gold with Isley R&B selections.

In 1964, frustrated with their inability to break into the big time, the Isley Brothers took an unprecedented step among black performers: They formed their own record company, T-Neck. The first release, "Testify," was ahead of its time, showcasing the instrumental talents of a young guitarist called Jimmy James, later known as Jimi Hendrix.

A move to the Motown label followed, resulting in a string of hit songs during the mid- to late 1960s. Teamed with the songwriting team of Holland/Dozier/Holland, the Isleys released "This Old Heart of Mine (Is Weak for You)" and enjoyed further successes with "Behind a Painted Smile" and "I Guess I'll Always Love You" in the United Kingdom.

After Motown

In 1969 "It's Your Thing" gave the Isleys a huge U.S. hit and reactivated the T-Neck label. They also said good-bye to the mohair suits that had typified their soulful Motown period and began to assume a more casual, funky wardrobe. Adding three younger relatives—their brothers Ernie on guitar and Marvin on bass and their cousin Chris Jasper on keyboards—they extended the group and the vision, adding layers of bass-driven rhythm and soaring lead guitar work that was reminiscent of instrumental elements that Hendrix had added years before.

After the release of their albums *3+3* (1973), *Live It Up* (1974), *The Heat Is On* (1975), and *Harvest for the World* (1976), the group had produced a body of work as potent as any R&B act of the period, including James Brown, Sly Stone, and Stevie Wonder. Songs like "That Lady," "Highways of My Life," "Fight the Power," and "Harvest for the World" blended the distinctive vocal interplay of Ronald, Rudolph, and O'Kelly with the contemporary funk attack of the new musical ensemble. The group made regular appearances on the U.S. and U.K. charts during the decade and gained a reputation as an outstanding live combo.

For more than ten years, the resurrected Isleys plowed this profitable furrow, but in 1984 the more recent recruits, Ernie and Marvin Isley and Chris Jasper, departed to form Isley/Jasper/Isley. The older Isleys seemed set to return to their former vocal format, but in 1986 the death of O'Kelly of a heart attack struck a shattering blow to those plans. Nonetheless, *Smooth Sailin'* (1986), a tribute to their departed brother, saw Ronald and Rudolph still in impressive form. A key figure in the Isley circle now was the singer/songwriter Angela Winbush, soon to be Ronald's wife. She contributed heavily to the first post-O'Kelly album and then wrote and produced the 1989 release *Spend the Night*.

In the 1990s the Isleys continued to make their creative mark in a variety of ways. In 1990 Roland guested on Rod Stewart's remake of "This Old Heart of Mine." In 1992 *Tracks of My Life* saw Ronald team up with Marvin and Ernie; they remained together on *Live!* (1993). The same lineup then released *Mission to Please* in 1996, with a string of leading black producers: Angela Wimbush, R. Kelly, Babyface, and Keith Sweat. The album yielded the hit song "Let's Lay Together."

"Let's Lay Together" was included in the soundtrack of the Wayans Brothers' movie *Don't Be a Menace to South Central While Drinking Your Juice in the Hood*. Other movie soundtrack work by the Isleys includes a contribution to *Friday* (1995), with the song "Tryin' to See Another Day." Ice Cube had earlier drawn on the Isley catalog, sampling "Footsteps in the Dark" from the brothers' 1977 album *Go for Your Guns* for his 1993 hit "It Was a Good Day."

In 2001 Ronald and Ernie joined forces on *Eternal*, featuring songs with artists such as R. Kelly and Jill Scott, Jimmy Jam and Terry Lewis, and Raphael Saadiq. On the album Ronald introduces his alter ego, Mr. Biggs; Ernie shows his undiminished instrumental abilities on the track "Ernie's Jam." Furthermore, Ronald has made guest appearances with leading R&B performers such as Foxy Brown, Ja Rule, and Keith Sweat.

The Isley Brothers, in all their diverse incarnations, have been an enduring and important presence not only on the R&B scene but also among white rock bands as significant as the Beatles and black rock performers such as Jimi Hendrix and Prince. By the time they found their own funk voice, they had become leading lights in a ground-breaking genre, forging a coherent relationship between funk and rock styles at a time when black and white musical expressions rarely crossed over.

SELECTIVE DISCOGRAPHY: *Shout* (Collectables, 1959); *Twist and Shout* (Sundazed, 1962); *This Old Heart of Mine* (Motown, 1966); *In the Beginning* (T-Neck, 1970); *3+3* (T-Neck, 1973); *Live It Up* (T-Neck, 1974); *The Heat Is On* (T-Neck, 1975); *Harvest for the World* (T-Neck, 1976); *Go for Your Guns* (T-Neck, 1977); *Forever Gold* (T-Neck, 1977); *Timeless* (T-Neck, 1979); *Smooth Sailin'* (Warner, 1986); *Spend the Night* (Warner, 1989); *Tracks of My Life* (Warner, 1992); *Live!* (Elektra, 1993); *Mission to Please* (T-Neck/Island, 1996); *Eternal* (Dreamworks, 2001).

SIMON WARNER

JA RULE

Born: Jeff Atkins; Queens, New York, 29 February 1976
Genre: Rap
Best-selling album since 1990: *Pain Is Love* (2001)
Hit songs since 1990: "Holla Holla," "Between Me and You," "Always on Time"

With a winning smile, a gravelly voice, and a facility for unforgettable hooks, Ja Rule became one of the most successful rappers on the hip-hop scene in the late 1990s. Releasing albums at a torrid clip of one per year, as well as appearing in major motion pictures, the Queens, New York, native launched hit after hit with songs such as "Holla Holla" and "Between You and Me," often juxtaposing his gruff vocals with the smooth vocals of a female singer. Rule was the rare hip-hop artist who appealed to both male and female listeners with a combination of street anthems and bad boy sensitivity.

Born Jeff Atkins, Ja Rule began rapping at age sixteen, making his debut on Mic Geronimo's 1995 single, "Time to Build." The song gained Rule the attention of the TVT label, which signed his trio, the Cash Money Click, to a recording contract. Their single "Get the Fortune" (1995) gained some airplay on Hot 97, one of New York's leading rap/R&B stations. Soon after, producer and later benefactor, Irv Gotti, introduced Rule to Def Jam Records president Lyor Cohen. The latter was so impressed with Gotti's street savvy that he hired the producer as an A&R (artist and repertoire) scout and asked him to make Rule his first signing.

With a rough, in-your-face baritone growl that drew immediate comparisons to one of hip-hop's most revered voices, that of late rapper Tupac Shakur, Rule immediately gained notice with his solo debut single, "Story to Tell," from the soundtrack to the film *Belly* (1998). After a lauded appearance on Jay-Z's 1998 club hit "Can I Get A . . ." on which he wrote the "hook"—the melodic, repeated chorus—Rule was ready to release his debut, *Venni, Vetti, Vecci* (1999), translated, "He came, he saw, he conquered." Like many late 1990s hip-hop albums, the record was available in bootleg versions on the streets of New York prior to its release, but thanks to the hit single "Holla Holla," it debuted at number three on the *Billboard* 200 chart.

With an elastic funk groove and party atmosphere, "Holla Holla" is typical of Rule's early work, with a lyric about yearning for sex, partying with friends, and making money. Rule pays frequent homage to his label, Murder Inc., with songs such as "It's Murda," "Murda 4 Life," and "The Murderers." According to label lore, the deadly name has nothing to do with violence, but rather is a reference to how Murder Inc.'s artists "murder," or top, all other artists with their rapping. The grim, violent work is not unlike hit albums by another gruff-voiced New York rapper, DMX, with whom Rule performs a duet on "It's Murda," and with whom he would later feud over the similarity of their styles. By year's end, the album had sold 1 million copies. It was quickly followed by a collaboration between Rule and the Murderers—Blackchild, 0-1, Vita, and Tah Murdah—called *Irv Gotti Presents the Murderers* (2000), which was decried for its lyrics about violence toward police and homosexuals.

On his second solo album, *Rule 3:36* (2000), Rule does not drastically alter his style, though the album features a mix of more positive songs along with harsh, violent ones over spare, percussion heavy tracks. The addition of female vocalists helped the rapper reach a whole new audience. Rule is a thuggish street tough haunted by spirituality. "Between Me and You" is a straight-ahead sexual romp about infidelity over a slinky keyboard track that has a touch of Asian strings and a booming drum beat.

Similarly, on the hit "gangsta and a lady" duet with female rapper Vita, "Put It on Me," Rule—who is married to his high school sweetheart, with whom he has two children—sings, "What would I be without my baby / The thought alone might break me / And I don't want to go crazy / But every thug needs a lady," showing a sensitive side not normally seen in street-tough rappers. The album sold 3 million copies by year's end.

Rule Branches out in Acting as the Hits Keep Coming

With his good looks and affable charm, Rule was a natural for film work, appearing with rapper Pras in *Turn It Up* (2000) and as street racer Edwin Bishop in the hit movie *The Fast and the Furious* (2001); Rule also contributed songs to the soundtracks of both films. Rule released his third album, *Pain Is Love*, in October 2001; it debuted at number one with sales of 360,000, earning Rule his second top debut in less than a year. The album sold more than 1 million copies within a month.

Pain Is Love follows the same pattern as its predecessor, mixing hard core anthems about the violent life on the street with duets with girlish singers. The pop-oriented "I'm Real," with actress/singer Jennifer Lopez and "Always on Time," with rising Murder Inc. star Ashanti, established Rule as an unparalleled rap hit maker, uncovering his facility with gruff, but melodic singing alongside his burr-voiced rapping.

Rule appeared in the film *Half Past Dead* (2002) with action star Steven Seagal, and in May 2002 he announced that he would release two more albums before retiring from recording to concentrate on acting. *The Last Temptation* (2002) is purportedly a return to Rule's grittier ghetto anthems, but the singer continues to mix sweet and sour on the album. Troubled R&B singer Bobby Brown provides the mellifluous chorus to the hit single "Thug Lovin'," while Ashanti drops in for the sexy duet "Mesmerize." In November 2002, Rule and Ashanti announced that they would co-star in urban-themed sequels to the films *Sparkle* and *Grease*.

Ja Rule often drew fire from peers for embracing pop hooks and radio-friendly fare, but in a genre where credibility is paramount, the Queens rapper had the last laugh with a string of hit albums. Bringing an unparalleled melody to mainstream hip-hop, Rule proved that even thugs need love.

SELECTIVE DISCOGRAPHY: *Venni Vetti Vecci* (Def Jam/Murder Inc., 1999); *Rule 3:36* (Def Jam/Murder Inc., 2000); *Pain Is Love* (Def Jam/Murder Inc., 2001); *The Last Temptation* (Def Jam/Murder Inc., 2002).

SELECTIVE FILMOGRAPHY: *Turn It Up* (2000); *The Fast and the Furious* (2001); *Half Past Dead* (2002).

GIL KAUFMAN

ALAN JACKSON

Born: Newnan, Georgia, 17 October 1958
Genre: Country
Best-selling album since 1990: *Drive* (2002)
Hit songs since 1990: "Here in the Real World," "Chattahoochee," "Little Bitty"

The music writer Alanna Nash has called Alan Jackson "the last of Nashville's pure traditionalists." Unlike contemporary country performers such as Tim McGraw and Faith Hill, whose styles often resemble pop music, Jackson harks back to the country feel of the 1950s and 1960s, mining traditional country themes of heartbreak and loneliness. With basic instrumentation of guitar, piano, and fiddles, Jackson pays tribute to older, hard-living country singers such as George Jones and Merle Haggard. Jackson's voice, although less distinctive than the keening tones of those performers, is flexible and warm, an ideal vehicle for the sensitive songs he writes.

Jackson's modest early life and long struggle to the top are the stuff of country legend. One of five children born to an auto-mechanic father in the small Georgia town of Newnan, Jackson spent his childhood singing gospel music in church and listening to the music of his idol, Hank Williams. As an adult, Jackson worked as a forklift operator, car salesman, construction worker, and, after his move to Nashville with wife Denise in 1985, mail sorter at the cable network TNN, all the while honing his singing and songwriting.

A chance meeting at an airport between Denise, a flight attendant, and the veteran country singer Glen Campbell led to Jackson's official introduction to the music business. Although signed with Campbell's management company, Jackson was rejected by one record label after another during the latter part of the 1980s. Many Nashville executives felt the mild-mannered singer lacked star quality and stage presence. Fortunately, Arista Records, a label known mostly for its pop and rhythm and blues artists, announced in 1989 its intention to open a Nashville office and subsequently signed Jackson as its first country artist.

The next year Jackson released his debut album, *Here in the Real World*, and became a hot commodity with the title track, a melodic ballad built around the theme of romantic fantasy in movies versus the hard reality of love "in the real world." Although the song features strong lyrics and melody, its most memorable aspect is Jackson himself. Virile but gentle, his voice carries an emotional authority that draws listeners into the lovelorn story.

Jackson's third album, *A Lot about Livin' (And a Little 'bout Love)* (1992), is one of his finest works. Adhering to the short Nashville format of ten songs per disc, Jackson fills the album with nothing but first-rate material, most of which he wrote himself. "Chattahoochee," one of the album's six hit singles, is a charming up-tempo number featuring a loping rhythm that suggests the Cajun style of Louisiana dance music. On the lovelorn ballad, "(Who Says) You Can't Have It All," Jackson proves himself a master of lyrical irony, a country music hallmark. On the line, "I'm lord and master of a fool's Taj Mahal," he achieves the careful balance between humor and self-pity that marked the work of Jackson's forebears Jones and Haggard. Adding to the dramatic atmosphere is the heavy, supple piano playing of Hargus "Pig" Robbins, whose flowery style was featured on numerous country records of the 1960s and 1970s. The album's song titles—"She's Got the Rhythm (And I Got the Blues)" and "Up to My Ears in Tears"—sum up Jackson's woebegone but lighthearted persona.

Jackson went on to release five more albums during the decade, each containing multiple country hits. During an era in which country artists such as Garth Brooks incorporated rock elements into their repertoire, Jackson's consistency and adherence to country formula were unique. His down-home image also stayed the same. Tall, wearing tight blue jeans and a cowboy hat that partially covered his long, blond hair, Jackson came off as a self-effacing hunk, a family man with sex appeal.

Behind the scenes, however, stardom was taking a toll on his marriage, forcing a temporary separation from wife Denise in 1998. The pair later reconciled, and Jackson's stance on his life and music remained humble. In 1997 he told a reporter, "I listen to my records and don't know why they're so popular." A decade into his recording career his homespun message was evident in the lyrics to his 2001 hit "Where I Come From": "Where I come from, it's cornbread and chicken / Where I come from a lot of front porch sittin'." Beneath Jackson's simple persona, however, lay a sophisticated musician with a sharp intellect.

As it turned out, Jackson's biggest fame was still ahead of him. During late 2001, in the wake of the September 11 attacks on the World Trade Center and the Pentagon, he wrote "Where Were You (When the World Stopped Turning)," a song that summed up what many Americans were feeling on that frightening day. Against a sparse, restrained musical arrangement, Jackson considers the range of reactions to the horror: "Did you shout out in anger and fear for your neighbor / Or did you just sit down and cry." Written quickly during the middle of the night, the song comes across as an artist's attempt to grasp the extent of human cruelty rather than a commercialized exploitation of tragedy. The single proved enormously popular, pushing the album that contained it, *Drive* (2002), to the number one position on the pop album charts. Despite his new stature as pop star, Jackson remained true to his country roots. Reviewing a 2002 concert performance, a critic for *The Louisville Courier-Journal* called him "one of the few superstars in country music to actually sing country music."

Alan Jackson's success proves that, no matter how much modern country music embraces pop, older, more traditional approaches to country still find an audience. Although gentler in image than the hell-raising singers of the past, Jackson conveys emotional resonance through music that is humorous, probing, and likable.

SELECTIVE DISCOGRAPHY: *Here in the Real World* (Arista, 1990); *A Lot About Livin' (And a Little 'Bout Love)* (Arista, 1992); *Who I Am* (Arista, 1994); *Everything I Love* (Arista, 1996); *When Somebody Loves You* (Arista, 2000); *Drive* (Arista, 2002).

WEBSITE: www.alanjackson.com.

DAVID FREELAND

JANET JACKSON

Born: Janet Damita Jackson; Gary, Indiana, 16 May 1966

Genre: R&B, Pop

Best-selling album since 1990: *The Velvet Rope* (1997)

Hit songs since 1990: "Love Will Never Do (without You)," "When I Think of You," "That's the Way Love Goes"

Janet Jackson comes from one of the most famous families in pop history. She was the eighth member of the Jackson family to produce records and gain superstar status. Her father, Joseph Jackson, managed the careers of all his children. By the early 1960s the Jackson children—Tito, Jermaine, and Jackie—had started performing around Gary, Indiana, and were known as the Jackson family. In 1964, when Marlon and Michael joined the troupe, they became known as the Jackson 5.

The youngest of the nine Jackson children, Janet made her first performance appearance at seven years of age in Los Angeles with her brothers. By 1982 with Michael's success soaring, Joseph turned his attention to La Toya's and Janet's first albums. In 1982 Janet signed a contract with A&M Records and released her first album, *Janet Jackson,* which was not a huge success. This effort was followed two years later by a second album, *Dream Street,* which did not sell that well either. It was only in 1986, when she insisted on artistic independence from her father, that her first major breakthrough came with the release of the album *Control,* which sold more than 4 million copies in the Unites States alone. The songs on this album were better crafted than those on the previous two albums, with a shift in style to a more contemporary dance-pop and funk feel. This blend appealed instantly to a generation on the brink of the house movement scene. With this album also came a change of attitude and image, as Jackson traded her "nice girl" image for a more aggressive role, dressing in black and leather and singing about control over her boyfriends. Hit singles from this album include "What Have You Done for Me Lately," "Nasty," "When I Think of You," "Control," and "Let's Wait Awhile."

Another quadruple platinum album followed in 1989, *Rhythm Nation 1814.* In contrast to the songs from *Control,* those from this album are brighter, with a more romantic pull and evidence of social and political awareness. The poignant track "Living in a World (They Didn't Make)" addresses the issue of suffering and the exposure of children to violence. Musically, the sentiments of this song are extracted through a vocal style that draws on thin tones and restricted register control. In contrast the influence of Prince is evident in the more raucous, funk-derived tracks, such as "Miss You Much" and "Alright," in which Jackson pulls together all her vocal forces to deliver a brashly energetic, celebratory, and stylish performance. The success of this dance album, with its blend of social-protest songs and heart-rending ballads, helped secure Jackson a position on par with Madonna as she went on her Rhythm of the Nation tour in 1990.

In 1991 Jackson left the A&M label and signed a historic two-album deal with Virgin for a reported $50 million. In one of the biggest promotional campaigns ever, Jackson's first album for Virgin, *Janet* (1993), was ushered in by a full revamp of her image. On a provocative *Rolling Stone* cover inspired by the album, Jackson appears topless, with her breasts covered by a pair of hands. The sexiness and erotic quality of this cover is reflected in the songs on the album, the most famous one being "That's the Way Love Goes," a grinding sexual number that remained at the top of the charts for eight weeks. The groove of this song is hypnotic and slow, transporting Jackson's vocal sentiments in a melodic phrase that is easy to remember. The song's strength lies in both its performance and production, which is slick, glossy, and sophisticated for its time. There is a wealth of stylistic changes from one track to

the next, as Jackson includes everything from dance-based material to funk, jazz, and big-band swing. In a rendition of Lionel Hampton's "I'm in the Mood for Swing" from 1938, Jackson demonstrates her high quality of musicianship by delivering a convincingly zappy performance.

In 1996 A&M released a compilation album of Jackson's years with them, *Design of the Decade, 1986–1996.* This followed a collaboration with her brother, Michael, on the hit single "Scream," which was released together with a hi-tech, space-age promo video in 1995. This video was rumored to be the most costly ever produced.

In 1996 Jackson suffered a nervous breakdown with severe bouts of depression. This setback preceded the release of her next album, *The Velvet Rope* (1997), which consists of twenty-two songs with a running time of over seventy minutes. Themes of sexual yearning and self-discovery pervade the album, reflecting the influence of Madonna. Often the songs deal explicitly with themes of perversity, sexual difference (bisexuality, gay, lesbian, transsexual), and fetishism (body piercing and bondage) as Jackson attempts to push forward the boundaries of sexual tolerance. One song that stands out in this respect is her arrangement of Rod Stewart's "Tonight's the Night," to which she imparts a lesbian inflection. The singing style on this album builds on that of her earlier album, *Janet,* with a polished, innovative, and reflective performance. The collection of songs is a reminder of Jackson's talent for combining a diverse range of traditions within African-American popular music; her delivery of compelling dance grooves is both seductive and playful.

In 1999 Jackson went on another international tour and hit the pop charts again with the Busta Rhymes's hit "What's It Gonna Be?!" Over seventy minutes in duration, her next album, *All for You* (2001), consists of a collection of sensual tracks that are less overtly erotic than those on *The Velvet Rope.* The songs, mostly bittersweet in flavor, are confidently performed and stylishly arranged. The album employs sampling of artists whom Jackson admires. On the track "Sun of a Gun," for example, she samples Carly Simon's hit "You're So Vain" in a manner that blends rock with rap into her groove-based musical material. The two main hits from this album were the title track and "Someone to Call My Lover," which helped pave the way for the collection's enormous success worldwide.

Despite the album's success, Jackson's stature had dimmed somewhat by the end of the 1990s. She was unable to sustain the superstardom she had achieved earlier in her career. Sexy, provocative, and soulful in her performance style, Jackson was one of the leading pop divas of the 1990s. She is a magnetic star whose career trajectory was a testament to her family's standing as one of the most legendary and commercially successful generators of African-American pop music.

SELECTIVE DISCOGRAPHY: *Janet Jackson* (A&M, 1982); *Dream Street* (A&M, 1984); *Control* (A&M, 1986); *Rhythm Nation 1814* (A&M, 1989); *Janet* (Virgin, 1993); *The Velvet Rope* (Virgin, 1997); *All for You* (Virgin, 2001).

BIBLIOGRAPHY: D. L. Mabery, *Janet Jackson* (Minneapolis, 1992); B. Andres and H. R. Taborelli, *Out of the Madness: The Strictly Unauthorised Biography of Janet Jackson* (London, 1994); C. Dyson, *Janet Jackson* (Philadelphia, 2000); K. Garcia, *Janet Jackson* (Real Life Reader Biography) (Bear, DE, 2003).

STAN HAWKINS

MICHAEL JACKSON

Born: Gary, Indiana, 29 August 1958

Genre: Rock, Pop, R&B

Best-selling album since 1990: *Dangerous* (1991)

Hit songs since 1990: "Remember the Time," "Black or White," "You Rock My World"

Since his first years as a performer, singing with his brothers in the 1970s pop outfit the Jackson 5, Michael Jackson has ranked as one of the most distinguished and innovative voices in popular music. A naturally talented singer, with the inbred ability to draw upon a rich legacy of R&B and pop vocalizing, Jackson had revealed himself as an intuitive stylist by the age of eleven. On his first hit single with the Jackson 5, "I Want You Back," he displayed an indebtedness to great R&B vocalists such as Smokey Robinson and Jackie Wilson, while forging his own energetic, charismatic style. As an adult, Jackson continued to define trends and break down barriers, releasing *Thriller* (1982), the best-selling album in recorded history, and pioneering the development of music videos. Although Jackson's albums have proved extremely influential, they have been issued years apart; his prolificacy is low for an artist of such importance. Also, his work since the mid-1990s has been overshadowed by scandal and controversy, to the point where the press has depicted his life and career as a grotesque joke. This development does not detract, however, from the vast contribution Jackson has made to modern pop music.

With the Jackson 5

The fifth son of Joe and Katherine Jackson, Michael was raised in Gary, Indiana. His father's harsh disciplinary tactics and the devout Jehovah's Witness beliefs of his mother contributed to what he would later describe as a sad, difficult childhood. By 1962 Joe, a steelworker and former musician, had organized his three eldest sons into a family singing group. Soon, young Michael joined the lineup, his mature vocals augmented by an uncanny ability to mimic the nimble-footed dance moves popularized by R&B star James Brown. By 1969 the Jackson 5 had signed with Detroit's famed Motown Records and released the number one pop and R&B hit "I Want You Back." The single was backed with a version of R&B group Smokey Robinson & the Miracles' 1960 song, "Who's Lovin' You," on which eleven-year-old Michael bends and twists his vocals in homage to the R&B vocal tradition.

Throughout the early 1970s the Jackson 5 scored major hits, including "The Love You Save," "Never Can Say Goodbye," and "Dancing Machine," before moving to Epic Records in 1976. Now known as the Jacksons, the group released *Destiny* (1978), an acclaimed album they largely wrote and produced. The success of *Destiny* allowed Michael to pursue his solo career while remaining with the group. Working with producer and arranger Quincy Jones, he gained renewed stardom with *Off the Wall* (1979), a classic collection of pop, R&B, and disco that spawned four Top 10 singles.

1980s Superstardom

Thriller (1982) cemented Jackson's status as the biggest pop star of the 1980s. Defining the decade in the same way that the music of Elvis Presley represented the 1950s, the album remained on the pop charts for more than two years, selling 25 million copies in the United States alone. Sporting dense, insistent production by Jones, *Thriller* contains instantly identifiable hits such as "Beat It," "Billie Jean," and the title track, featuring a ghoulish spoken part by horror movie star Vincent Price. The music videos for *Thriller* set the songs within cinematic narratives, thereby altering the way music would be marketed; after *Thriller*, a song's video would become as important as the song itself. Videos for "Beat It," "Billie Jean," and "Thriller" were wildly popular, making Jackson the first African-American artist played with regularity by cable network MTV. Although it took five years to deliver, *Thriller*'s follow-up, *Bad* (1987), was nearly as successful, spawning four number one pop hits, including "Man in the Mirror" and "The Way You Make Me Feel." By this point, the media had begun to speculate upon Jackson's eccentricities: his rumored nose jobs, attempts to lighten his skin, and his development of Neverland, a large personal ranch in California that he filled with exotic animals and rides. In late 1991, after another nearly five-year hiatus, Jackson released *Dangerous*.

Turmoil in the 1990s

In 1993 Jackson was accused of molesting a thirteen-year-old boy who had made frequent visits to the Neverland

Spot Light | *Dangerous*

By the end of 1991 Michael Jackson had not released an album in nearly five years. His previous album, *Bad* (1987), was a hit that nonetheless suffered by comparison with the overwhelming success of *Thriller* (1982). For *Dangerous*, released in December 1991, Jackson hired producer Teddy Riley, known for the bouncy, rhythmic "New Jack Swing" sound he developed with artists such as Keith Sweat. Riley's aggressive, funky approach revitalizes Jackson; singing against a matrix of tricky, unpredictable beats and rhythmic hooks, Jackson brings a new degree of vocal toughness to "Why You Wanna Trip on Me," "She Drives Me Wild," and the hit, "Remember the Time." Despite the high-tech production, Jackson's basic approach has not changed from his earlier work. On "Remember the Time," he builds his performance gradually, layering vocal parts with each rhythmic shift in the arrangement. By the song's end, he is sparring vocally with the propulsive background, employing a complex set of shouts and trills. "Black or White" features a bright, rock-influenced guitar part and lyrics that emphasize racial acceptance. The song's positive message was undercut by controversy arising from its video, the end of which features Jackson breaking car windows and grabbing his crotch. Balancing this depiction of violence is "Heal the World," a highly orchestrated tribute to children that critics found syrupy and trite. Despite these inconsistencies, *Dangerous* preserved Michael Jackson's status as the "King of Pop," a title he would hold until scandal unhinged his career later in the 1990s.

greatest hits and another of original material. On songs such as "Tabloid Junkie," Jackson lashes out at the press: "With your pen you torture men / you'd crucify the Lord." Similarly angry songs such as "They Don't Care about Us" give the "Present" section of *HIStory* an unsettling air of paranoia. Near the end of 1996, Jackson married nurse Debbie Rowe. Although he would have two children with Rowe, the union dissolved in 1999.

In 2001 Jackson released *Invincible*, his first album of all-new material in a decade. Proving his ability to change his sound with the times, Jackson enlisted the services of trendy R&B producer Rodney Jerkins, who imbues tracks such as "Unbreakable" and "Heartbreaker" with a flashy modern edge. While *Invincible* scored high on the album charts, debuting at the number one position, its singles did not perform as well, with only one song, the thumping "You Rock My World," reaching the Top 10. The album features some of Jackson's toughest rhythm tracks to date, but critics observed that none of the songs are particularly distinctive or memorable, a factor contributing to its disappointing commercial impact.

By the summer of 2002 Jackson was waging an acrimonious battle with his record label, Sony. In interviews, Jackson charged Sony with not promoting *Invincible*, claiming the company had asked him for a $200 million reimbursement in marketing costs. The fight became more heated once Jackson described Sony chairman Tommy Mottola in a press conference as "racist" and "devilish." As evidence of Jackson's declining importance, many music stars—including Mariah Carey and Ricky Martin—rushed to defend Mottola. In the following months, the press continued to scrutinize Jackson's unusual behavior, giving special attention to an incident at a German hotel in which he dangled one of his children over a balcony while greeting fans. In 2003 Jackson was the subject of a British Broadcasting Company documentary, *Living with Michael Jackson*, that he later denounced as an inaccurate and distorted portrayal.

Despite the public speculation upon his ever-diminishing nose and unconventional personal life, Jackson remains a seminal figure in the development of contemporary pop music. Epitomizing the former child performer unable to grasp the reality of the adult world, Jackson has channeled his personal troubles into a rich and enduring body of work.

SELECTIVE DISCOGRAPHY: *Got to Be There* (Motown, 1972); *Forever, Michael* (Motown, 1975); *Off the Wall* (Epic, 1979); *Thriller* (Epic, 1982); *Bad* (Epic, 1987); *Dangerous* (Epic, 1991); *HIStory: Past, Present, and Future, Book 1* (Epic, 1995); *Invincible* (Epic, 2001). **With the Jackson 5:** *Diana Ross Presents the Jackson 5* (Motown, 1969); *ABC* (Motown, 1970); *Lookin' through the Windows*

Ranch. Although he eventually settled the case out of court for an estimated $18 to $20 million, the negative publicity—combined with escalating reports of his plastic surgery and skin lightening—damaged Jackson's reputation. The next year, he married Elvis Presley's daughter Lisa Marie, although the union dissolved after nineteen months. In 1995 Jackson released the sprawling *HIStory: Past, Present, and Future, Book 1* containing one compact disc of

(Motown, 1972). **With the Jacksons:** *Destiny* (1978).

WEBSITE: www.michaeljackson.com.

DAVID FREELAND

JAGGED EDGE

Formed: 1996, Atlanta, Georgia

Members: Brandon Casey (born Hartford, Connecticut, 13 October 1977); Brian Casey (born Hartford, Connecticut, 13 October 1977); Kyle "Quick" Norman (born Atlanta, Georgia, 26 February 1977); Richard Wingo (born Atlanta, Georgia, 3 September 1977).

Genre: R&B

Best-selling album since 1990: *J. E. Heartbreak* (2000)

Hit songs since 1990: "I Gotta Be," "Let's Get Married," "Where the Party At"

Of the numerous male vocal groups that formed in the wake of Boyz II Men's 1990s stardom, Jagged Edge was one of the most successful, using insistent harmonies to flavor both love ballads and dance tracks with gospel-style urgency. On songs ranging from the devotional "Let's Get Married" to the high-spirited "Where the Party At," Jagged Edge proved adept at a range of styles. More forceful than Boyz II Men but less overtly sexual than the R&B group Next, Jagged Edge enjoyed an impressive string of hits but failed to establish a distinctive vocal identity.

The band is a quartet composed of identical twin brothers Brandon and Brian Casey, Kyle Norman, and Richard Wingo. They came together in Atlanta, Georgia, having met through their frequent performances with local church choirs. Enlisting the help of their friend Kandi Burruss, a member of the female R&B group Xscape, Jagged Edge sent a demo recording to the producer Jermaine Dupri, who quickly signed the group to his So So Def label. Jagged Edge's debut album, *A Jagged Era*, was released in early 1998 and features the hit "I Gotta Be," a love ballad hoisted by the group's gently pleading vocals. Although *A Jagged Era* includes several additional songs recorded in the lush, romantic style of Boyz II Men, the group proved equally at ease with sharp dance numbers such as "The Way That You Talk."

The group's fame was secured with their follow-up recording, *J. E. Heartbreak*, released in 2000. The album's biggest hits, "Let's Get Married" and "Promise," are gentle ballads extolling the virtues of matrimony and commitment, although the group's pleading harmonies imbue both songs with a sensuousness absent in the lyrics. On "Let's Get Married," the singers exchange lead vocal parts

with flamboyant energy, spicing their performance with gospel-influenced growls and shouts. Like its predecessor, *J. E. Heartbreak* left plenty of room for funky dance tracks such as "Girl Is Mine," which features a tough guest spot by rap artist Ja Rule. *Jagged Little Thrill*, sparked by the exuberant hit, "Where the Party At," followed in 2001. Similar in format to the group's previous albums, the album veers from the sinuous funk of "Driving Me to Drink" to ballads such as "Respect," which speaks out against domestic abuse: "Don't matter how strong she is for a woman / A man should never attempt to lay his hands on her." Despite the new commitment to social issues, Jagged Edge's sound on the album remains unchanged. Unlike Boyz II Men or Next, however, none of the lead singers have truly distinctive voices, a handicap that lends a faceless quality to the group's albums, despite their undeniable verve and energy.

Jagged Edge used the gospel techniques of its members to craft lively, engaging R&B hits in the late 1990s and early 2000s. Although the group's harmony sound is not pioneering, Jagged Edge is nonetheless a successful modern representative of the group vocal tradition in R&B.

SELECTIVE DISCOGRAPHY: *A Jagged Era* (So So Def/Columbia, 1998); *J. E. Heartbreak* (So So Def/Columbia, 2000); *Jagged Little Thrill* (So So Def/Columbia, 2001).

DAVID FREELAND

ETTA JAMES

Born: Jamesetta Hawkins; Los Angeles, California, 25 January 1938

Genre: R&B, Jazz

Best-selling album since 1990: *Mystery Lady: Songs of Billie Holiday* (1994)

The remarkable career of Etta James has encompassed five decades of rhythm and blues music. Blessed with a powerful, "church-wrecking" voice, James is known for her soulfulness and versatility. She can sing a sophisticated ballad or rocking blues song with equal ease and never loses track of the emotion underlying her material. In performance she wrings every ounce of meaning from her songs, often crying as she sings the ballads. It is this commitment to emotional truth that has endeared James to her fans.

Born to an African-American mother and an Italian-American father, James sang in church from an early age. Her first hit was "Roll with Me, Henry" (1955), a song that had to be retitled "The Wallflower" because of its raunchy theme. In 1960 she began recording a series of hits for Chess Records in Chicago, including "All I Could Do Was Cry" (1960) and "At Last" (1961). By that point, James's style had fully developed: She sang with maturity and depth, shouting one minute and then softly purring the next. On the ballad "At Last," for example, she imbues the line "My heart was wrapped up in clover," with a girlish tenderness that brings out the poetry of the lyric.

James's years at Chess Records reached an artistic peak in 1967, when she recorded "Tell Mama" and the classic ballad "I'd Rather Go Blind." By this time, however, James was battling heroin addiction, a struggle that slowed her career down until the mid-1970s. Nevertheless, she continued recording excellent music, never fully leaving the spotlight. In 1978, after kicking heroin, she released *Deep in the Night* on Warner Bros. Records. Working with the legendary producer Jerry Wexler, James sounds relaxed and assured, ranging with customary ease over a variety of genres: rock, pop, and rhythm and blues.

By 1988, James was back in full force. That year she released *Seven Year Itch,* one of her finest albums. The production is clean and tight, the songs are all first-rate, and James sings with a ferocity that recalls her best 1960s work. Always developing as an artist, James fulfilled a lifelong dream in 1994 when she released *Mystery Lady,* a collection of songs associated with the great jazz singer Billie Holiday. It was one of the most mature albums of James's career, one in which her tremendous talents finally found a wider audience. James wisely chooses not to mimic Holiday's improvisational vocal style; instead she delivers each song in a straight-ahead manner, singing with sultry directness. On "Don't Explain" and "Lover Man" she lets her husky, seasoned voice float over the restrained arrangements, lingering on phrases like "Right or wrong don't matter / When you're with me sweet" to bring out deep shades of meaning. By turns passionate, graceful, and seductive, *Mystery Lady* is one of the most intimate recordings of the 1990s and won James a Grammy Award for Best Jazz Vocal Performance. As a result of the Grammy and her 1993 induction into the Rock and Roll Hall of Fame, James was receiving the popular recognition she had long been due.

Later in the 1990s James continued to broaden her horizons, recording another fine jazz album, *Time after Time,* in 1995. Although the album features the same low-key ambience as *Mystery Lady,* James is less restrained, belting songs such as "Don't Go to Strangers" and "Teach Me Tonight" with the full power of her voice. In 1995 James also published an acclaimed autobiography, *Rage to Survive,* in which she chronicles her troubled life in honest, sometimes brutal detail. In 1997 James released *Love's Been Rough on Me,* an uneven but heartfelt album featuring material by top country songwriters. On "If I Had Any Pride Left at All," previously recorded by country singer John Berry, she imbues the line "I wouldn't be here now . . . not ashamed to crawl" with palpable ache.

Since *Love's Been Rough on Me,* James's albums have been less artistically fulfilling, sometimes hampered by trite musical arrangements and production. Still, she remains capable of powerful work—witness her fine live album from 2002, *Burnin' Down the House.* Here, James wraps her diminished but still potent voice around songs that have defined her career, including "At Last," "I'd Rather Go Blind," and the raunchy "Come to Mama." Her longtime backup group, the Roots Band, provides tight support with a fire that matches James's own.

One of the most moving and profound singers in rhythm and blues, Etta James has legitimately secured the overused honorific "legend." After decades of hard work and struggle, she has earned a lasting place in the annals of American music.

SELECTIVE DISCOGRAPHY: *Miss Etta James* (Crown, 1961); *At Last* (Argo, 1961); *Etta James Sings for Lovers* (Argo, 1962); *Tell Mama* (Cadet, 1968); *Come a Little Closer* (Chess, 1974); *Deep in the Night* (Warner Bros., 1978); *Seven Year Itch* (Island, 1988); *Mystery Lady: Songs of Billie Holiday* (Private Music, 1994); *Time after Time* (Private Music, 1995); *Love's Been Rough on Me* (Private Music, 1997); *Matriarch of the Blues* (Private Music, 2000); *Burnin' Down the House* (RCA Victor, 2002).

BIBLIOGRAPHY: E. James, *Rage to Survive* (New York, 1995).

DAVID FREELAND

JAMIROQUAI

Formed: 1992, London, England

Members: Sola Akingbola, percussion (born Lagos, Nigeria, 1965); Nick Fyffe, bass (born Reading, England, 14 October 1972); Rob Harris, guitar (born Cambridgeshire, England, 27 August 1971); Matt Johnson, keyboards; Jason Kay, vocals (born Stretford, Manchester, England, 30 December 1969); Derrick McKenzie, drums (born Islington, North London, England, 27 March 1962). Former members: Wallis Buchanan, vibraphone (born 29 November 1965); Toby Smith, keyboards (born London, England, 29 October 1970); Nick Van Gelder, drums; Stuart Zender, bass (born Sheffield, England, 18 March 1974).

Genre: Rock, R&B

Best-selling album since 1990: *Travelling without Moving* (1996)

Hit songs since 1990: "Virtual Insanity," "Cosmic Girl"

With a celebrated, eye-popping promotional video for its hit "Virtual Insanity," the

British band Jamiroquai fused modern sounds with a 1970s rhythm and blues vibe and gained international commercial attention.

The son of a jazz singer, John Kay spent his teenage years involved in petty crime, landing in jail on one occasion and almost losing his life in a stabbing incident. Kay turned to music as a refuge and conceived of a project called "Jamiroquai," the combination of "jam," the free-flowing musical style that he hoped to pursue, with "Iroquois," the name of a Native-American tribe. Kay's home demos attracted the attention of the Acid Jazz label in London, which subsequently issued a Jamiroquai single. Kay recruited several London-area musicians and launched a full-scale band in 1992; Jamiroquai's lineup would shift throughout the 1990s, though Kay would remain the focal point and de facto leader of the band.

Jamiroquai's first two albums, *Emergency on Planet Earth* (1993) and *The Return of the Space Cowboy* (1995), were sizable hits in Europe as well as in Japan. The albums established Jamiroquai's patented sound, with the band fusing 1970s funk and jazz with hip-hop rhythms and Kay crooning in a smooth, silky voice that hearkened to pop music icon Stevie Wonder.

Jamiroquai finally gained a foothold in America with the hit single "Virtual Insanity" from the album *Travelling without Moving* (1996). The midtempo "Virtual Insanity" grooves along effortlessly, giving Kay plenty of room to bob and weave in and out of the mix, at times tossing in stirring, soulful pleas for global change: "While we're livin' in oh, oh virtual insanity / Oh, this world, has got to change / 'Cos I just, I just can't keep going on." While critics and the listening public equally praised the band's music, "Virtual Insanity" garnered more attention for its promotional video. Directed by Jonathan Glazer, the video employs eye-popping special effects; as Kay sings and dances in front of the camera, the walls and floors of an all-white room rotate around him, making his dance moves seem to defy gravity. "Virtual Insanity" won MTV's Video of the Year Award in 1997 and introduced the band to completely new audiences.

Kay and his band waited three years before releasing a follow-up to *Travelling without Moving*, during which time original bass player Stuart Zender left to pursue other ventures. *Synkronized*, released in 1999, was a hit in Europe, but the band's absence from the spotlight in the intervening years stalled Jamiroquai's momentum in the United States; *Synkronized* quickly fell off the charts. *A Funk Odyssey*, released in 2001, suffered the same fate, despite critical plaudits for its adventurous sound.

Though one of pop's unique-sounding bands in the late 1990s, Jamiroquai's legacy remains its groundbreaking "Virtual Insanity" video.

SELECTIVE DISCOGRAPHY: *Emergency on Planet Earth* (Columbia Records, 1993); *The Return of the Space Cowboy* (Work Records, 1995); *Travelling without Moving* (Work Records, 1996); *Synkronized* (Work Records, 1999); *A Funk Odyssey* (Epic Records, 2001).

SCOTT TRIBBLE

JANE'S ADDICTION

Formed: 1986, Los Angeles, California; Disbanded 1991; Re-formed 1997

Members: Eric Avery, bass (born Los Angeles, California, 25 April 1965); Perry Farrell, vocals (Perry Bernstein, born Queens, New York, 29 March 1959); Dave Navarro, guitar (David Michael Navarro, born Santa Monica, California, 6 June 1967); Stephen Perkins, drums (born Los Angeles, California, 13 September 1967).

Genre: Punk, Rock

Best-selling album since 1990: *Ritual de lo Habitual* (1990)

Hit songs since 1990: "Been Caught Stealing," "Ain't No Right"

One of the most influential and progressive rock bands of the 1990s was also one of the few that quit while they were ahead. Fusing classic rock bombast with tribal drumming, shamanistic visuals, punk aggression, and a healthy dose of cosmic spirituality, Jane's Addiction almost single-handedly created the notion of "alternative" rock, launched the pioneering Lollapalooza traveling music and fringe culture festival, and producing two classic albums of psychedelic punk before disbanding in 1991.

Jane's Addiction formed in Los Angeles in 1986 when former Psi Com leader Perry Farrell recruited guitarist Dave Navarro, bass player Eric Avery, and drummer Stephen Perkins to join his new band. Farrell—who had changed his name from Bernstein to the pun-worthy variation on "peripheral"—the son of a New York diamond merchant, moved to California to attend college in 1980. After suffering a nervous breakdown and dropping out, Farrell lived in his car with his girlfriend on the streets of Los Angeles and danced at an adult bar for a time. The untrained musician fronted the gothic rock band Psi Com in the early 1980s before forming Jane's Addiction, named after a drug-addicted prostitute with whom he was friendly.

The band quickly became one of the most buzzed-about on the Los Angeles club scene through their unique fusion of arty rock with thundering Led Zeppelin–style drums and heavy metal guitar solos, as well as their unabashedly hedonistic lifestyle and look. Farrell, with his

Jane's Addiction. L-R: Dave Navarro, Perry Farrell, Eric Avery, Stephen Perkins [PAUL NATKIN/PHOTO RESERVE]

pinched, quavering vocals, made to sound echoey and ominous through on-stage effects machines, was a stunning front man, all Day-Glo braids, mismatched thrift store chic clothes, vinyl bodysuits, and quivering, nervous energy.

Next to the preening, hair-sprayed, makeup-wearing heavy metal bands such as Poison and Mötley Crüe that populated Los Angeles' clubs at the time, bondage wearing, dread-locked, pierced, and eyeliner-wearing Jane's Addiction looked like rock and roll aliens. Their outsider look and sound would prove prescient, giving voice and style to a disaffected youth nation soon to be labeled "Generation X" by the media. It was an age cohort born into a bleak economic time, with little hope for finding jobs in a slumping, war-focused economy, but in need of an outlet for their aggression and angst.

A Promising Debut

The band captured the raw, postmodern sound of their live shows on their self-titled 1987 debut, recorded at the Roxy nightclub in Los Angeles. With typically provocative cover art from Farrell—a watercolor of the singer in a girdle—the album has all the shades of the group's sound: furious jazz punk ("Trip Away," "Pigs in Zen"), profane Led Zeppelin-esque heavy metal art rock ("Whores," "1%"), and tender psychedelic folk ballads ("I Would for You," "Jane Says"), the latter about their patron saint of drug-addicted prostitutes. The album set off a fierce bidding war among record labels, won by Warner Bros. Records, which

released *Nothing's Shocking* in 1988. Farrell had insisted on artistic control from Warner Bros., and he exercised it immediately, creating a nude sculpture of his future wife, Casey Niccoli, for the album's cover.

The tactic worked, as several national retail chains refused to stock the album. With a proper studio in which to record, the band flourished. The irony of the title can be found in the numerous references to heroin—which was the drug of choice for all but drummer Perkins—and a song about Ted Bundy ("Ted, Just Admit It"). In the latter, Farrell growls the lyrics, "Showed me everybody / Naked and disfigured / Nothing's shocking," before breaking into the disturbing chorus, "Sex is violent."

The songs are expansive, even indulgent at times, but undeniable in their vastness and power, with a tension that progresses through multiple moods and dynamic shifts. "Ocean Size" begins as a gentle acoustic meditation before, literally, exploding into a heavy rock dirge, with Navarro spinning out unabashedly heavy metal solos over Perkins's aggressive, off-kilter drumming and Avery's steady bass playing. The lurid debauchery is perverse, yet alluring, escaping the sometimes comical darkness of more traditional heavy metal bands. Though sales were not brisk, critics almost universally lauded the album and the typically conservative Academy of Recording Arts and Sciences nominated it in the newly formed Best Heavy Metal Album Grammy Awards category.

A Classic Album, Lollapalooza Launch, and the Surprise Break Up

The band toured as the opening act for punk legend Iggy Pop, followed by the release of their third album, *Ritual de lo Habitual* (1990). The album's artwork launched another controversy and threats of bans at major retail chains due to a Farrell-created collage depicting the naked singer with two nude women amidst a collage of icons from the Mexican spiritual sect, Santeria. The band responded by creating an alternate cover with the text of the First Amendment. The combination of the controversy and heavy rotation on MTV for the humorous video to the single, "Been Caught Stealing," helped the album chart at number nineteen and eventually sell more than 1 million copies.

"Been Caught Stealing" is the perfect song to introduce the band to the masses, as it is the most commercial, poppy track in the group's oeuvre. Over a bouncy, funk bass and syncopated drumming, Farrell gleefully brags about shoplifting ("When we want something / We don't want to pay for it / We walk right through the door"). It was, however, the exception to the rule on an album that has a depth, complexity, and nuance that the group had not achieved to date.

The album's centerpiece is a pair of ten-minute epics, "Three Days" and "Then She Did . . ." in which the band employ all of their musical arsenal: ebbing and flowing tempos, fiery guitar solos, Perkins's athletic, tribal drumming, Farrell's whining, haunted falsetto vocals, and Avery's funky bass. In the latter, Farrell also alludes to his mother, an artist who committed suicide when he was four ("Will you say hello to my ma? / Will you pay a visit to her? / She was an artist, just as you were").

Ritual de lo Habitual features a small Novena card insert addressed to "the mosquitoes," in which Farrell writes, "We have more influence over your children than you do, but we love your children." With the launch of Farrell's brainchild in the summer of 1991, the traveling Lollapalooza rock festival/circus sideshow, the singer would give ample proof of his statement. With three stages and a midway with circus freaks, political booths, art galleries, and Internet connections, as well as a lineup that included some of the most promising and varied rock, rap, and punk acts of the day, Lollapalooza was a smash success. It was also a major factor in the commercial rise of such alternative rock stars as the Smashing Pumpkins, Soundgarden, and Nine Inch Nails.

Though it lived on for six more years, Lollapalooza was also Jane's Addiction's swan song. Farrell announced that the group would break up following the conclusion of the tour in order to go out on a high note. Farrell was arrested for drug possession in October 1991 and the band folded after a final show in Hawaii, during which Farrell performed the final half of their set in the nude. Farrell and Perkins joined to form Porno for Pyros in 1992, while Navarro joined Avery in the short-lived band Deconstruction. Navarro went on to briefly join the Red Hot Chili Peppers.

In 1997 Farrell dissolved Porno for Pyros, Navarro quit the Chili Peppers, and Jane's Addiction was reunited—deemed a "relapse" by Farrell—with Chili Peppers bassist Flea filling in for Avery for a well-regarded tour and the recording of two new songs for the outtakes collection, *Kettle Whistle* (1997). After poorly received 2001 solo albums from Farrell and Navarro, Jane's Addiction reunited again to tour in 2001 with Porno for Pyros bassist Martyn Lenoble filling in for Avery. The band recorded a new album in 2002, *Hypersonic*, with bassist Chris Chaney, which was slated for release in mid-2003.

Jane's Addiction succeeded in making the depressingly ugly into the luridly beautiful on their three late 1980s-early 1990s albums. With a look that was shocking, lyrics that chronicled the seamy underbelly of marginal lives, and an artistic vision that refused to be compromised, the group influenced a generation of bands and fans to follow their muse, no matter into what bizarre corner she takes you.

SELECTIVE DISCOGRAPHY: *Jane's Addiction* (Triple X, 1987); *Nothing's Shocking* (Warner Bros., 1988); *Ritual de lo Habitual* (Warner Bros., 1990); *Kettle Whistle* (Warner Bros., 1997); *Hypersonic* (Virgin, 2003).

GIL KAUFMAN

KEITH JARRETT

Born: Allentown, Pennsylvania, 8 May 1945

Genre: Jazz, Classical

Best-selling album since 1990: *The Melody at Night, with You* (1999)

A pianist of refined technique and outspoken attitude, Keith Jarrett has been lauded by critics and audiences alike for his virtuosic purity, demonstrated in fully improvised solo concerts, classical recitals, and programs highlighting his longstanding trio's exceptional empathy.

Jarrett was a child prodigy, learning piano from age three, presenting a public program by age seven, and, during his teens, touring for a season as the piano soloist with Fred Waring's Pennsylvanians, a dance band for businessmen. After studying on scholarship at the Berklee College of Music from 1962 to 1963, Jarrett moved to New York, where he gained attention for his short stint in Art Blakey's Jazz Messengers. Although Jarrett objected to commercialism in jazz, he became an international star not only for his musicality but also for the intense physicality of his appearances in the youth-oriented quartet headed by the saxophonist Charles Lloyd from 1967 to 1970. Jarrett would often stand up from his piano bench while improvising, dance or stomp in rhythm, affect dramatic facial expressions, and hum along with his parts.

As a member of Miles Davis's band for nineteen months and in his own work of 1972, Jarrett experimented with electric keyboards and overdubbing; he also played soprano saxophone. However, upon establishing his quartet with bassist Charlie Haden, drummer Paul Motian, and saxophonist Dewey Redman, he turned exclusively to the acoustic piano. Jarrett's ensemble focused on his compositions, usually ruminative and impressionistic melodies set over repetitive ostinato patterns or simple chordal vamps—essentially lyricism atop a backbeat. They also performed pieces by Ornette Coleman, with whom both Haden and Redman were associated; Paul Bley, with whom Motian had played; and Bill Evans, a towering figure among postwar jazz pianists.

In 1970 Jarrett met Manfred Eicher, the principal of ECM Records. He released *Facing You*, his first solo piano album, on Eicher's label in 1971. In 1972 Jarrett initiated spontaneously improvised concerts of thirty to forty-five minutes uninterrupted, using no preplanned music. ECM has issued more than half a dozen recordings of these solo concerts, including the ten-LP (six-CD) *Sun Bear Concerts* (1976), performed in five Japanese cities. He has also recorded original, classically oriented compositions involving string sections, chamber groups, and, on one occasion, a string orchestra with the saxophonist Jan Gabarek.

Jarrett disbanded his first quartet in 1976 but continued to work in similar formats with first-rate European musicians. He founded a trio with bassist Gary Peacock and drummer DeJohnette in 1983, ostensibly to interpret jazz standards. He also turned his attention to classical repertoire, recording Barber's Piano Concerto; works by Mozart, Handel, and Bach; and hymns by the mystic G. I Gurdjieff. He suffered criticism in the 1980s, accused of arrogance and pretension—charges he invited by complaining about critics from the concert stage and chastising audiences for noises that interfered with his inspiration.

By 1990, Jarrett had regained equanimity and critical regard. He slightly slowed his recording schedule and celebrated his origins with a return to the site of his first significant jazz job, *At the Deer Head Inn* (1992). His neo-classical album, *Bridge of Light* (1993), was well received. His solo recordings, *Vienna Concert* (1991) and *La Scala* (1995), were welcomed by reviewers as a return to form, and he released a six-CD box set fully documenting six complete sets of his trio, recorded in New York's Blue Note jazz club over three consecutive nights.

In 1996 Jarrett put his career on hold because of an attack of "chronic fatigue syndrome." He remained in retirement and seclusion in his New Jersey home for three years, during which time he occasionally granted interviews in which he expressed his disagreement with the conservative vision of jazz propounded by Wynton Marsalis.

Jarrett marked his comeback with *The Melody at Night, with You* (1999), which features solo renditions of American classics, including "My Wild Irish Rose," "Shenandoah," and songs by Gershwin, all recorded in his living room and dedicated to his wife. His first postsyndrome performance, with Peacock and DeJohnette, inaugurated the New Jersey Performing Arts Center in Newark.

His stamina restored, Jarrett continues to record jazz standards with his trio, displaying a fleet, elegant touch and sweeping two-handed technique. In 2002 he issued a two-CD set of spontaneous trio improvisations. Jarrett retains his fan base, appearing at major concert venues. In January 2003 he became the first jazz musician to receive the Royal Swedish Academy of Music's $117,000 Polar Music Award, cited for "effortlessly cross[ing] boundaries in the world of music."

SELECTIVE DISCOGRAPHY: *The Cure* (ECM, 1990); *Vienna Concert* (ECM, 1991); *Bye Bye Blackbird* (ECM, 1991); *At the Dear Head Inn* (ECM, 1992); *Bridge of Light* (ECM, 1993); *Keith Jarrett at the Blue Note: The Complete Recordings* (ECM, 1994); *La Scala* (ECM, 1995); *Tokyo '96* (ECM, 1996); *The Melody at Night, with You* (ECM,1999); *Whisper Not* (ECM, 1999); *Inside Out* (ECM, 2000); *Always Let Me Go* (ECM, 2002).

WEBSITES: www.eecs.umich.edu/~lnewton/music/JarrettSketch.html; www.northwestern.edu/jazz/artists/jarrett.keith/; www.ecmrecords.com/ecm/artists/bio/47.html.

HOWARD MANDEL

JAY-Z

Born: Sean Carter; Brooklyn, New York, 4 December 1971
Genre: Hip-Hop
Hit songs since 1990: "Hard Knock Life (Ghetto Anthem)," "Can I Get a . . ."

Jay-Z began his career in the early 1990s as a sideman to more prominent artists and ended the decade as one of hip-hop's most popular rappers. He has replaced the violence and poverty associated with his childhood home—the Marcy Projects in Brooklyn, New York—with a self-made image of opulent excess and material wealth. Though talented as a lyricist, both in his evocative story-telling abilities and in his clever writing skills, Jay-Z's greatest asset has been his charisma. Like his peer, the Notorious B.I.G., the alternately seductive and sinister Jay-Z exudes confidence and charm in his music.

While still in his teens, Sean Carter was mentored by a Brooklyn MC, Jaz, who gave the younger artist the moniker of Jay-Z as a diminutive of his own name. Jaz's own career stalled out by the early 1990s, despite modest hits such as "Hawaiian Sophie," which features Jay-Z. For the first half of the 1990s, Jay-Z appeared as a cameo guest on other artists' songs, most prominently Original Flavor's "Can I Get Open?" and Mic Geronimo's "Train of Thought," but it was not until 1995 that Jay-Z released his own single, "In My Lifetime." However, the song was not a success, and Jay-Z languished in industry invisibility until his decision to start his own label, Roc-A-Fella, and restart his career as an independent artist.

The first single Roc-A-Fella released was "Dead Presidents" (1996). The song was a modest success, but it was the single's b-side, "Ain't No Nigga," which included a then-unknown Foxy Brown, that became Jay-Z's runaway

Spot Light

"Hard Knock Life (Ghetto Anthem)"

Few could have predicted it, but one of the major summer smashes of 1998 featured a Broadway musical chorus mixed into a hip-hop hit. Unlike previous rap songs that sampled from well-known soul or funk songs, "Hard Knock Life (Ghetto Anthem)" drew from the unlikely source of *Annie: The Musical*. Producer 45 King looped part of the piano melody from *Annie*, but he also used the song's main chorus, making "Hard Knock Life (Ghetto Anthem)" instantly recognizable and memorable. Jay-Z uses this playful platform as a backdrop for lyrics that both praise his own greatness but also give a nod to all the hard luck cases out there, from "All my niggas / locked down in the ten by four," to "Chicks wishin', they ain't have to strip to pay tuition." On the strength of its wide-ranging appeal, the song quickly catapulted its way up the pop charts. Combined with Jay-Z's other memorable anthems of the time, "Can I get a . . ." and "Money Ain't a Thing," the song made *Hard Knock Life (Ghetto Anthem)* one of Jay-Z's best-selling albums. An altered version of the song appears in the 2002 movie *Austin Powers in Goldmember*.

hit. "Ain't No Nigga" interpolates two elements already familiar to fans of R&B and hip-hop: the bass line from the Whole Darn Family's "Seven Minutes of Funk" and a chorus based on the R&B hit "Ain't No Woman." Rather than sing platitudes to his paramour, Jay-Z turns "Ain't No Nigga" into a celebration of sex, money, and fashion with lines such as "Fresh to def in Moschino, Coach bag / Lookin' half black and Filipino."

First Albums

The immense success of "Ain't No Nigga" led to the release of Jay-Z's debut album, *Reasonable Doubt* (1996). Though *Reasonable Doubt* is not Jay-Z's best-selling album, critics laud it as his most compelling. The key to that critical praise lies in how Jay-Z simultaneously celebrates his material success while moralizing on his excess.

For example, like his peer, the Notorious B.I.G., Jay-Z plays up his past as a drug pusher, celebrating the lifestyle

on the album's "Can't Knock the Hustle." At the same time, songs like "D'Evils" and "Regrets" reflect Jay-Z's awareness of the spiritual cost of his underworld aspirations. This duality imbues Jay-Z's music with a complexity that distinguishes him from other rappers who also rhyme about their wealth but do not admit the price paid.

Jay-Z's next two albums, *In My Lifetime Vol. 1* (1997) and *Vol. 2: Hard Knock Life* (1998), were commercial successes but were coolly received by critics. These works were criticized for containing formulaic pop hits rather than career-advancing material save for the unlikely hit title track from *Hard Knock Life (Ghetto Anthem)*, which samples the chorus from the Broadway musical *Annie*.

It took until *Vol. 3: The Life and Times of S. Carter* (1999) for Jay-Z to return to form. Unlike the previous two albums, *The Life and Times of S. Carter* finds Jay-Z lording over his competition with sweeping street narratives and outrageous displays of bravado. Producer Timbaland makes a prominent contribution to the album thanks to his funky minimalism, and Jay-Z does his part by minting another pop anthem with the exotically flavored "Big Pimpin." He attacks with fierce braggadocio on songs like "Come and Get Me": "Ignorant bastard, I'm takin' it back to day one / No kids, but trust me I know how to raise a gun."

In 2001 Jay-Z released *The Blueprint* (2001), which was both a financial and critical triumph. Lyrically, *The Blueprint* covers familiar ground for Jay-Z—weapons, women, wealth—but his production team, led by Just Blaze and Kayne West, engineered one of the best-sounding hip-hop albums of the year.

Tapping into soul music samples from the 1970s, Blaze and West create a soundtrack that is comforting and familiar, an unintentionally appropriate tone given the macabre coincidence that *The Blueprint* was released on September 11, 2001, the day of the terrorist attacks on the Pentagon and the World Trade Center.

Public Controversies

The Blueprint coincided with Jay-Z's growing popularity and attendant coverage in the mass media, fueled by interest in an alleged stabbing incident involving Jay-Z and a rap industry executive. Jay-Z made a great deal of this situation, even building it into *The Blueprint*'s major hit, "Izzo," "Not guilty / ya'll got to feel me." Ironically, in 2002 Jay-Z pled guilty to the charge and was given probation. During this time Jay-Z also carried on a public battle with the rival rapper Nas, both of whom drafted songs and made radio appearances in which they attacked each other.

Rather than stemming his popularity, these incidents only inflated Jay-Z's public prominence, which was further enhanced by an August 2001 profile in *The New*

Yorker and a November 2002 appearance on *60 Minutes II*. The same month Jay-Z released *The Blueprint 2: The Gift and the Curse*, his first double-album. Despite its aspirations to match the excellence of its predecessor, *The Blueprint 2* is a bloated affair of anemic production and grating martyrdom.

For most of his career, Jay-Z has lived in the shadow of the Notorious B.I.G. Had Biggie not been murdered in 1997, it is quite possible that the two would have ended up as rivals for the title of Brooklyn's finest, but Biggie's death vacated a throne to which Jay-Z has paid homage. At times, Jay-Z's stature as one of rap's greatest talents has seemed secure. However, artistic inconsistencies and a penchant for public controversy have shadowed his legacy.

SELECTIVE DISCOGRAPHY: *Reasonable Doubt* (Roc-A-Fella/Priority, 1996), *Vol. 3: The Life and Times of S. Carter* (Roc-A-Fella, 1999); *The Blueprint* (Roc-A-Fella, 2001).

OLIVER WANG

THE JAYHAWKS

Formed: 1985, Minneapolis, Minnesota

Members: Gary Louris, vocals, guitar, cofounder, songwriter (born Toledo, Ohio, 10 March 1955); Tim O'Reagan, drums, vocals, percussion (born Chandler, Arizona, 1 October 1958); Marc Perlman, bass (born St. Petersburg, Florida, 28 July 1961); Stephen McCarthy, pedal steel, lap steel guitar, banjo, vocals (born Richmond, Virginia, 12 February 1958). Former members: Ken Callahan, drums; Karen Grotberg, keyboards; Jen Gunderman, keyboards/organ; Don Heffington, drums; Kraig Johnson, guitar, vocals; Mark Olson, vocals, guitar, co-founder; Norm Rogers, drums; Thad Spencer, drums.

Genre: Rock

Best-selling album since 1990: *Tomorrow the Green Grass* (1995)

Hit songs since 1990: "Waiting for the Sun," "Blue," "I'm Gonna Make You Love Me"

A little bit country, a little bit rock and roll, and a little bit folk is probably the best way to describe the music of the Jayhawks, an alternative country band that hit its stride in the mid- to late 1990s with their album *Tomorrow the Green Grass* (1995). The Jayhawks have been compared to Gram Parsons, the Flying Burrito Brothers, and other arbiters of a worn-out, lonesome country-rock songwriting style.

The Jayhawks formed in Minneapolis, Minnesota, in 1985 but did not really make an impact until the mid-

1990s. Mark Olson had been playing in a rockabilly band and began his solo career by enlisting the help of Marc Perlman, a guitarist whom Olson persuaded to learn bass. The two added the drummer Norm Rogers and debuted at a club with a crowd of fewer than a dozen people. But they got lucky: Guitarist Gary Louris was in the audience, and, by the end of the night, he joined the not-yet-named Jayhawks. The band garnered accolades and a consistent local following. Their eponymous, independently released debut album sold a respectable few thousand copies. Eventually, the Minnesota independent label Twin/Tone issued a few demos and released it as *Blue Earth* (1989). After the departure of Rogers and the addition of new drummer, Ken Callahan, the Jayhawks geared up for a national tour.

The Jayhawks were signed to American Records after producer George Drakoulias heard *The Blue Earth* playing while placing a phone call to Twin/Tone's offices. Drakoulias produced their breakthrough album, *Hollywood Town Hall*, which became a fixture on the year-end critics lists in 1991. Building on that success, the band released more albums with the twangy honeyed harmonizing of its lead singers, Olson and Louris, serving as the band's unmistakable centerpiece. Their fourth album, *Tomorrow the Green Grass*, is a country-rock gem and features the heartbreaking, woe-is-me love song "Blue."

Despite their success, the group underwent several personnel changes: Olson left the band in 1996 to spend more time with his wife, the singer Victoria Williams, and play with his country rock band the Original Harmony Ridge Creek Dippers. Callahan exited prior to the release of the record and was replaced by the session drummer Don Heffington; tour drumming duties were handled by Tim O'Reagan. Unsurprisingly, the Jayhawks's subsequent album, *Sound of Lies* (1997), was a more melancholy affair, but they followed it up with a pop-oriented approach in the critically hailed *Smile* (2000).

Though the Jayhawks spent a good deal of time shifting personnel and record labels, Louris, Perlman, and O'Reagan have remained in the lineup. The band formed an integral part of the alternative country trend of the 1990s. Despite the accessibility and beauty of the Jayhawks' music, they have yet to achieve the combined commercial and critical success achieved by bands such as Wilco.

SELECTIVE DISCOGRAPHY: *The Jayhawks* (Bunkhouse, 1986); *Blue Earth* (Twin/Tone, 1989); *Hollywood Town Hall* (American, 1992); *Tomorrow the Green Grass* (American, 1995); *Sound of Lies* (Columbia, 1997); *Smile* (American, 2000); *Rainy Day Music* (American, 2003).

CARRIE HAVRANEK

WYCLEF JEAN

Born: Nelust Wyclef Jean; Croix-des-Bouquets, Haiti, 17 October 1972

Genre: R&B

Best-selling album since 1990: *Masquerade* (2002)

Hit songs since 1990: "Gone Till November," "We Trying to Stay Alive," "Two Wrongs"

As a driving member of the group the Fugees, Wyclef Jean established a reputation in the 1990s as one of the most distinctive, visionary talents in hip-hop, rap, and R&B. Following the success of the Fugees's groundbreaking 1996 album, *The Score*, Jean was the first group member to pursue a solo career, releasing three ambitious albums that fused hip-hop rhythms with reggae, Latin music, pop, and even country. Within the tough world of rap and hip-hop, Jean's music is notable for its humanitarian core. His lyrics often advocate social responsibility and rail against social injustice. Critics note that, while never particularly impressive as a rapper or singer, Jean succeeds in orchestrating a rich palette of sound, pulling together disparate musical influences to create cohesive and satisfying works.

The son of a minister, Jean was born in Haiti and moved with his family to Brooklyn, New York, at the age of nine. Later settling in New Jersey, Jean began studying jazz and guitar during his high school years. In 1987 he joined a rap group with his cousin Prakazrel Michel (Pras) and his classmate Lauryn Hill. First calling themselves the Tranzlator Crew and then the Fugees (a term used to describe Haitian refugees), the group in 1994 released a hardcore rap album that attracted little attention. But the group's second album, *The Score* (1996), was immediately recognized by critics and fans as a classic. Combining hip-hop beats with social commentary on songs such as "The Beast," which attacks racial profiling among police, *The Score* inaugurated a new, "alternative" style of hip-hop. The success of the album, which also features the pop hit "Killing Me Softly with His Song," allowed Jean and Hill to work on solo albums while remaining part of the Fugees.

In its broad survey of musical styles, Jean's solo debut, *Presents the Carnival Featuring the Refugee Allstars* (1997), was more adventurous than his earlier work with the Fugees. An uncompromising attempt to break down musical barriers, the album scored a hit with its first single, "We Trying to Stay Alive." Sampling the disco rhythms of "Stayin' Alive," the Bee Gees 1978 hit, the song gains power through its incorporation of a tough, driving hip-hop beat. Moving across the stylistic spectrum, "Gone Till November," recorded with the New York Philharmonic Orchestra, is richly orchestrated with soaring strings, while "Mona Lisa," performed with legendary R&B group the Neville Brothers, sports the complex, delayed rhythms of New Orleans–style funk. Jean's commitment to social issues is evident in the antiviolence message of "Gunpowder," which recalls the spirit of reggae legend Bob Marley through the use of Marley's former backing group, the I-Threes. "Jaspora" and "Yele," both performed in Creole, speak to Jean's Haitian roots and became hits in his native country. Despite its eclectic range of influences, *Carnival* achieves a sense of unity through Jean's clear-headed artistic vision.

With the Fugees remaining separated because of internal divisions, Jean released a second solo album, *The Ecleftic*, in 2000. The album pushes its predecessor's stylistic boundaries even further. It features guest appearances from the wrestling star the Rock and the country artist Kenny Rogers. The album expresses Jean's commitment to social equality. "Diallo," for example, is a stirring eulogy for Amadou Diallo, the unarmed West African immigrant who was shot by police forty-one times outside his apartment in the Bronx, New York, in 1999: "You guys are vampires / In the middle of the night / Sucking on human blood / Is that your appetite?" Jean's third solo album, *Masquerade*, appeared in 2002. This time, however, critics felt that the album's guest appearances, including those from the 1960s pop stars Tom Jones and Frankie Valli, sounded random and unnecessary. Still, Jean captures his familiar excitement on the hit "Two Wrongs," a sweet-tempered track featuring a gentle rhythm and the warm vocals of R&B singer Claudette Ortiz.

Following the crossover pop success of the Fugees in the late 1990s, Wyclef Jean began a career as a challenging solo artist, releasing albums that confounded expectations of musical genre and style. Repudiating the violence that characterizes much contemporary hip-hop, Jean has created highly personal work with a life-affirming message.

SELECTIVE DISCOGRAPHY: *Presents the Carnival Featuring the Refugee Allstars* (Columbia, 1997); *The Ecleftic: 2 Sides II a Book* (Columbia, 2000); *Masquerade* (Columbia, 2002). **With the Fugees:** *Blunted on Reality* (Ruffhouse/Columbia, 1994); *The Score* (Ruffhouse/Columbia, 1996).

WEBSITE: www.wyclef.com.

DAVID FREELAND

JEWEL

Born: Jewel Kilcher; Payson, Utah, 23 May 1974

Genre: Rock

Best-selling album since 1990: *Pieces of You* (1995)

Hit songs since 1990: "Who Will Save Your Soul," "You Were Meant for Me," "Hands"

An idiosyncratic performer who rose from humble beginnings to become a multimedia star, Jewel helped bring the female singer/songwriter back into commercial fashion.

Humble Beginnings

Jewel spent much of her childhood in remote Homer, Alaska, on an 800-acre homestead lacking in television, telephone lines, and indoor plumbing. Her parents were itinerant musicians, performing regularly in bars, in Eskimo villages, and at tourist attractions across the state. Jewel got in on the act at the age of six, accompanying her father with her precocious yodeling.

While performing represented a source of happiness for the young Jewel, her childhood was filled with mental and emotional strain. Schoolmates ridiculed Jewel for her dyslexia as well as for her parents' simple lifestyle. When Jewel was eight, her parents divorced. She turned to song and poetry for an escape, writing naïvely optimistic verses to cope with the emotional trauma she was experiencing—an approach that would form the basis of many of her adult compositions.

A San Diego Sensation

Jewel left Alaska to study at the prestigious Interlochen Fine Arts Academy in Michigan. Upon graduation, she joined her impoverished mother in San Diego, California. Jewel initially worked a variety of jobs to support herself while pursuing a career in music. Frustrated by a lack of progress and faced with mounting expenses, Jewel moved into her 1969 Volkswagen bus and began working on her music full time. Soon thereafter, she landed a regular gig at the Innerchange, a San Diego coffeehouse. Jewel's unique style quickly earned her a following. Accompanying herself on acoustic guitar, Jewel sang in a disarmingly child-like voice; alternatively, she could summon up a sexy drawl or even throw in a yodel for good measure. Her songs ranged in content from sunny pleas for global unity to angry dismissals of racism, from hopelessly romantic odes to despairing ruminations on lost love. No matter the subject, Jewel's songs stood to reach far beyond the folk community. Her pop-like melodies were exceedingly accessible—much more so than those of earlier mainstream folk artists such as Joni Mitchell. Atlantic Records, having noted the buzz on Jewel around San Diego and sensing her potential for mass appeal, signed her to a recording contract in 1993.

In 1995 Jewel released her debut album *Pieces of You*. The sparse recording, much of it done live at the Inner-

change, did not immediately impress radio. Not until Jewel re-recorded a number of songs for release as singles did she begin to garner widespread airplay. The single version of "You Were Meant for Me" epitomizes Jewel's formula for success. Backed by a full pop production, Jewel jauntily delivers a fresh perspective on the time-honored breakup song with lines like, "Got my eggs and my pancakes too / Got my maple syrup, everything but you." "You Were Meant for Me" climbed all the way to number two on the *Billboard* singles charts. With her seemingly fairytale rise to stardom, Jewel was embraced by critics and public alike; she received two Grammy Award nominations and sold more than 10 million copies of *Pieces of You*.

Jewel's success also ushered in an unparalleled commercial period for female singer/songwriters. These artists not only began topping the singles and album charts, but also sold out concert pavilions across the country. The highly successful and influential Lilith Fair tour, which paired Jewel with other successful female artists such as Sarah McLachlan and the Indigo Girls, was a clear sign that female singer/songwriters were once again commercially viable.

Jewel's follow-up album *Spirit*, released in 1998, was another commercial smash, selling 6 million copies. Like the singles from *Pieces of You*, *Spirit* marries Jewel's quirky delivery with more standard pop arrangements. Critics were less enthused with *Spirit*, charging that Jewel's lyrics had become increasingly naïve and self-important. The single "Hands," in particular, drew the ire of critics for lines such as, "If I could tell the world just one thing / It would be that we're all OK / And not to worry 'cause worry is wasteful / And useless in times like these."

As Jewel grew more commercially successful, she began to make forays into other creative realms. In 1998 Harper Collins published *A Night without Armor*, a collection of Jewel's poems. Though savaged by critics for its amateurish verse, *A Night without Armor* sold more than 2 million copies in the United States. Jewel released a second book in 2000, *Chasing Down the Dawn*, which chronicles her 1998 tour in support of *Spirit* and contains stories and images from her childhood. Jewel also starred alongside Tobey Maguire and Skeet Ulrich in Ang Lee's 1999 film *Ride with the Devil*. Though the film was a disappointment at the box office, Jewel earned plaudits from critics such as Roger Ebert, who hailed her for being "an actress . . . not a pop star trying out a new hobby."

Jewel returned her focus to music in 2001, releasing *This Way*. The album finds Jewel straying even further from her folk roots, forgoing her quirky individualism in favor of a more refined delivery and experimenting sonically with jazz, country, and hard rock sounds. The album yielded the hit "Standing Still," but failed to achieve the sales standards set by *Pieces of You* and *Spirit*.

With *This Way*, Jewel had completed another stage in her remarkable evolution from artist on the commercial fringe to mainstream pop princess. Though her album sales have declined over the years, she remains one of pop music's leading female artists.

SELECTIVE DISCOGRAPHY: *Pieces of You* (Atlantic, 1995); *Spirit* (Atlantic, 1998); *Joy: A Holiday Collection* (Atlantic, 1999); *This Way* (Atlantic, 2001); *0304* (Atlantic, 2003).

SELECTIVE FILMOGRAPHY: *Ride with the Devil* (1999).

BIBLIOGRAPHY: Jewel, *A Night without Armor* (New York, 1998); Jewel, *Chasing Down the Dawn* (New York, 2000).

SCOTT TRIBBLE

JODECI

Formed: 1990, Tiny Grove, North Carolina

Members: Dalvin DeGrate, vocals (born Hampton, Virginia, 23 July 1971); Donald "Devante Swing" DeGrate, vocals (born Hampton, Virginia, 29 September 1969); Cedric "K-Ci" Hailey, vocals (born Tiny Grove, North Carolina, 2 September 1969); Joel "Jo-Jo" Hailey, vocals (born Tiny Grove, North Carolina, 10 June 1971).

Genre: R&B

Best-selling album since 1990: *Forever My Lady* (1991)

Hit songs since 1990: "Come and Talk to Me," "Cry for You," "Freek 'n You"

Gospel-trained vocal quartet Jodeci was one of the emblematic groups of the "New Jack Swing" era of the late 1980s/early 1990s, during which hip-hop production techniques and rhythms began to be applied to R&B. While finding success with a number of sentimental love ballads, the group also dwelt increasingly on sexual themes, cultivating a wild, "bad boy" image that distinguished them from more clean-cut contemporaries such as Boyz II Men. Jodeci dominated early 1990s R&B with a succession of platinum albums, and paved the way for band members K-Ci and Jo-Jo's equally successful career as a duo in the latter half of the decade.

Jodeci was formed in 1990 by two sets of brothers, Dalvin and Donald DeGrate, and Cedric and Joel Hailey. From a young age, the DeGrates had been touring and recording with their father's gospel group, Reverend DeGrate and the DeGrate Delegation. The Haileys were also members of a family gospel group, Little Cedric and the Hailey Singers. Familiar with each other from the southern gospel circuit, the brothers finally met when Joel

discovered that he and Dalvin were dating the same girl. Recognizing their shared musical ambition, they quickly overcame their initial animosity and began singing together in the DeGrates's hometown, Tiny Grove, North Carolina. Combining Donald, Cedric, and Joel's nicknames to form the name Jodeci, they went to New York in 1991 with a demo tape of songs written by Donald. A chance intercession by rapper Heavy D led them to Uptown Records president Andre Harrell, who promptly signed them.

In May 1991 Jodeci released their debut album *Forever My Lady*. The album shows its New Jack roots in club-oriented songs like the up-tempo "Playthang" and "Gotta Love," the lyrics of which hint at the carnality and sexual bravado the band would later fully embrace. It was the album's series of love ballads, however, that established Jodeci's reputation as master of the contemporary "baby-makin'" song. On *Forever My Lady*'s first single, "Come and Talk to Me," the foursome's passionate gospel flourishes inject a sultry urgency into even the tamest of come-ons: "I'm a single man / I hope that you are single too." And on the album's title track they praise fidelity and starting a family with vocals oozing seduction. *Forever My Lady* ultimately went triple platinum, and announced Jodeci as heirs to the tradition of earlier bedroom balladeers such as Barry White.

Jodeci's latent raunchiness comes to the forefront on their second album, *Diary of a Mad Band* (1993). Tracks such as "Slide 'n Ride," "Alone," and "Sweaty" are unabashed sexual propositions, in which the protagonist sells his skill at sexually gratifying females in explicit detail. The hit single "Cry for You" counterbalances the prevailing sexual swagger with the frank vulnerability of its lament to a departed lover: "Sometimes my pillow gets so wet with tears / I don't have no one to call my own." Although critically praised as at least the equal of *Forever My Lady*, the album received lackluster promotion, prompting a public dispute between Jodeci and their label. Further controversy dogged the band when K-Ci and Devante Swing were charged with sexually assaulting a woman they met in a New Jersey nightclub. Sales of *Diary of a Mad Band* leveled off at 2 million, 1 million less than its predecessor.

In 1995 they followed up *Diary of a Mad Band* with *The Show, the After-Party, The Hotel*, a concept album purporting to show a typical hedonistic night in the life of Jodeci. Although the album produced a number of Top 40 singles, it sold only 1 million copies, marking the group's second consecutive failure to match its previous success.

In 1996 the members of Jodeci began focusing on solo projects, the most notable of which were Devante's work as a producer and K-Ci and Jo-Jo's career as a duo. Although Jodeci never formally dissolved, the 1990s ended without a fourth album from the group.

Jodeci drew upon their gospel training to invest even the most innocuous love songs with sincerity, passion, and a hint of menace. They struck a balance between vulnerability and toughness that set the template for 1990s hip-hop soul and paved the way for later artists such as Dru Hill and their spin-off group, K-Ci & Jo-Jo.

SELECTIVE DISCOGRAPHY: *Forever My Lady* (Uptown/MCA, 1991); *Diary of a Mad Band* (Uptown/MCA, 1993); *The Show, the After-Party, the Hotel* (Uptown/MCA, 1995).

WEBSITE: www.rockonthenet.com.

MATT HIMES

BILLY JOEL

Born: William Martin Joel; Bronx, New York, 9 May 1949
Genre: Pop
Best-selling album since 1990: *River of Dreams* (1993)
Hit songs since 1990: "River of Dreams"

Singer/songwriter Billy Joel grabbed America's attention in 1973 and never let it go. His songs, as sung in his expressive tenor, combine a pop music touch with a rock and roll energy and offer compelling lyrics that seem always in step with the common people. When the new millennium began, Joel had sold over 100 million records. Remarkably, he remains an artist unimpressed with the past and in perpetual forward motion to learn and achieve new things, musical and otherwise.

The Making of a Piano Man

Billy Joel was born the only son of Howard Joel, a survivor of the Nazi concentration camp Dachau who immigrated to the United States and found work as an electrical engineer for General Electric. When Joel was a toddler, his father moved the family to Levittown, Long Island. His parents divorced when he was seven and his mother, Rosalind, and older sister, Judy, raised Joel. Although money was never plentiful, Joel's mother insisted that he take piano lessons and he showed promise immediately. In this way, Joel received a strong classical music foundation that would serve him well later. However, like many boys his age, he disliked practicing. When asked to perform classical pieces that he was to have learned, Joel was skilled enough as a preteen to improvise on the spot, sometimes fooling his teacher and musically educated mother that he was playing Mozart, Beethoven, or Chopin.

Around this time, he also became enthralled with rock and R&B music. Among his early influences were Ray

Charles, Sam Cooke, Otis Redding, the Rolling Stones, and the Beatles. His mother could not afford a television so Joel became an avid reader, a trait he carried into adulthood. The works of Ernest Hemingway, Mark Twain, F. Scott Fitzgerald, Franz Kafka, and many others fascinated him and this literate underpinning formed the basis of Joel's ability to create song lyrics. While attending high school, Joel played keyboards in a band called the Echoes, which later changed their name to the Lost Souls. They played church and school dances and Joel was beginning to garner quite a bit of attention locally for his playing and songwriting talent. Ironically, despite his passion and knowledge for music and literature, Joel was not allowed to graduate. He had missed too many classes. At that point, in 1967, he decided to pursue music professionally.

After a variety of musical pursuits including screeching hard rock, Joel signed with a Long Island–based record company, Family Records, and recorded his first solo album, *Cold Spring Harbor* (1972). Now a valuable collector's item, this disastrously produced record features Joel singing his well-crafted songs in a speeding high vocal register because of a recording studio blunder. Additionally, Joel had signed over his music rights to the struggling record company. In order to escape the legal and financial entanglements created by this mistake, he disappeared to the West Coast and began making a living in Los Angeles piano bars, playing under the pseudonym Bill Martin. Despite efforts to remain incognito, Columbia Records discovered Joel after hearing a bootlegged version of the song "Captain Jack" over the radio. The song—a sweeping ballad about teenage lethargy spinning into drug abuse with the song's antagonist a drug dealer named Captain Jack ("Captain Jack can get you high tonight . . .")—was recorded from a live performance Joel had given for a Philadelphia radio station. Columbia Records signed him, freed him from his financial snares with Family Records, and released the album *Piano Man* (1973). It went gold and the title song became an instant hit. Chronicling his nights in Los Angeles piano bars, "Piano Man" contains lyrics such as, "they sit at the bar and put bread in my jar, and say, 'man what are you doing here?'" The song became a signature song of sorts for Joel, although he rejected the Piano Man image as too restricting.

Suddenly thrust in the forefront of American contemporary music, Joel released fourteen albums over the next sixteen years in an impressive and diverse catalog of music that includes everything from pop ballads such as "New York State of Mind," "Honesty," and "Just the Way You Are" to story songs such as "Scenes from an Italian Restaurant." Joel's fascination with 1950s be-bop is heard in "The Longest Time" and "Keeping the Faith," among others. He flirts with the dum-de-dum of new wave rock in "It's Just a Fantasy" and "It's Still Rock and Roll to Me." He rocks hard with "Big Shot," a song describing a disastrous date with a high-profile New York socialite, "you had the Dom Perignon in your hand, and a spoon up your nose." Yet Joel's songs about common people most endear him to his vast audience. He wrote "Allentown" after playing a concert in the Pennsylvania town and becoming impressed with the work ethic of a town so completely dependent on the steel industry. Another such effort is "The Downeaster *Alexa*," a tribute to the remaining survivors of the dwindling Long Island fishermen's trade. Joel's passion for the Atlantic Ocean is renowned.

Reflecting on an Ocean of Hits

After *Storm Front* (1989), Joel waited four years before releasing *River of Dreams* (1993). The album received four Grammy Award nominations in 1994 including nominee for Best Song with the title track "River of Dreams," another foray into be-bop shuffle. Joel has earned twenty-three Grammy Award nominations and five Grammy Awards in his career. August of 1994 also marked a change in Joel's personal life as his high-profile marriage to supermodel Christie Brinkley ended in divorce. They have one daughter, Alexa. The song, "Lullabye (Goodnight, My Angel)" from *River of Dreams*, is a softly sung, poetic response to his daughter's inquiries regarding the uncertainty of life. The same summer Joel began a wildly successful stadium tour with fellow superstar Elton John. The two piano-playing singer/songwriters would often start the show by playing together on each other's songs, then take turns on the stage solo and finish the concert by once again combining talents and dueling on each other's material. They have toured together many times since, including in 2002.

With a volume of musical work to his credit, Joel began taking time in the 1990s to reflect on neglected passions and give something back to those he could help. In 1996 he donated his time to lecture and teach master's classes at various universities. This was part of an ongoing effort by Joel to teach music education to young musicians around the world. He also followed his lifelong love for the ocean by designing a boat, the 38-foot Shelter Island Runabout, and forming a company to produce them called the Long Island Boat Company. Musically, Joel was working on a collection of classical pieces. In the meantime, he rounded out a trilogy of greatest hits collections with the seventeen-song, *Greatest Hits, Vol. III* (1997).

Joel brought in the new millennium by performing a landmark concert at New York's Madison Square Garden, released on May 2, 2000, as a live album called *2000 Years—The Millennium Concert* (2000). The previous year, Joel gained induction into the Rock and Roll Hall of Fame. He had entered the Songwriters Hall of Fame in 1992 and the organization presented him with its highest honor, the Johnny Mercer Award, in 2001. Joel has received many

---

Spot Light | *Movin' Out*

Movin' Out, which opened on Broadway at the Richard Rogers Theater in New York City in 2002, features preexisting Billy Joel music put to dance by the legendary choreographer Twyla Tharp. Tharp conceived the show, which borrows characters from well-known Joel songs such as Brenda and Eddie from "Scenes from an Italian Restaurant" and Tony from "Movin' Out." The show's narrative is communicated solely through dance and features an exquisite cast of ballet and modern concert dancers in addition to some of Broadway's finest as Tharp's mutinously lyrical choreography takes them through twenty-seven popular Joel songs. Singer/pianist Matt Cavanaugh sings them and members of Joel's touring band are part of the live band that accompanies the dancers on stage. The story concerns a twenty-year arc in the lives of the play's characters, following them from high school, through the Vietnam War, the war's aftermath, and their recovery from the loss of innocence.

---

awards from the American Society of Composers, Authors and Publishers (ASCAP) and Broadcast Music, Inc. (BMI) and he holds four honorary doctorates in music.

When the United States was reeling from the terrorist attacks of September 11, 2001, Joel was in the forefront of those in the music industry who raised money and spirits by performing music. He played a poignant "New York State of Mind" on the TV special *America: A Tribute to Heroes*, which aired ten days after the attacks and featured the country's biggest entertainment industry names in an effort to raise money for the victims' families. He also received wild applause from an audience of New York City firefighters and police officers during the Concert for New York City held on October 20, 2001; the money raised went to the September 11 Relief Fund.

That autumn Joel released his first classical album, the long-awaited *Fantasies and Delusions* (2001). For followers of Joel's music this came as no surprise as he had been offering snippets of classical work throughout his previous releases. Pianist Richard Joo performs the twelve compositions and the album held the number one spot on the classical charts for many weeks. At nearly the same time, Joel released a thirty-six-song collection titled *The Essential Billy Joel* (2001).

Another project brewing inside of Joel was a Broadway show. This dream was realized when *Movin' Out* opened at the Richard Rogers Theater in New York City in 2002. Directed and choreographed by Twyla Tharp, *Movin' Out* received spectacular reviews and was a hit of the 2002 Broadway season. It earned Joel a 2003 Tony Award for Best Orchestrations, which he shared with Stuart Malina.

With talents that divert in many successful directions, it will be interesting to see where Joel's path takes him next. He has traveled a long distance from his humble beginnings, although his strong connections to those days certainly shape the foundation for what inspires and drives him.

SELECTIVE DISCOGRAPHY: *Cold Spring Harbor* (Family, 1972); *Piano Man* (Columbia, 1973); *Streetlife Serenade* (Columbia, 1974); *Turnstiles* (Columbia, 1976); *The Stranger* (CBS, 1977); *52nd Street* (CBS, 1978); *Glass Houses* (Columbia, 1980); *Songs in the Attic* (Columbia, 1981); *The Nylon Curtain* (CBS, 1982); *An Innocent Man* (CBS, 1983); *Greatest Hits, Vols. I & II* (Columbia, 1985); *The Bridge* (Columbia, 1986); *Kohuept in Concert* (Columbia, 1987); *Storm Front* (Columbia, 1989); *Live at Yankee Stadium* (Columbia, 1990); *River of Dreams* (Columbia, 1993); *Greatest Hits, Vol. III* (Columbia, 1997); *2000 Years—The Millennium Concert* (Columbia, 2000); *The Essential Billy Joel* (Columbia, 2001); *Fantasies and Delusions* (Columbia, 2001), *Movin Out: Original Broadway Cast Recording* (Columbia, 2002).

BIBLIOGRAPHY: J. Tamarkin, *Billy Joel: From Hicksville to Hitsville* (Port Chester, NY, 1985); D. Geller and T. Hibbert, *Billy Joel: An Illustrated Biography* (New York, 1985); M. McKenzie, *Billy Joel* (New York, 1985).

DONALD LOWE

ELTON JOHN

Born: Reginald Kenneth Dwight; Pinner, England, 25 March 1947

Genre: Rock, Pop

Best-selling album since 1990: *Made in England* (1995)

Hit songs since 1990: "Don't Let the Sun Go Down on Me," "Can You Feel the Love Tonight," "Candle in the Wind 1997"

From 1976 into the 1990s, Elton John managed to get a single into the Top 40 chart every year.

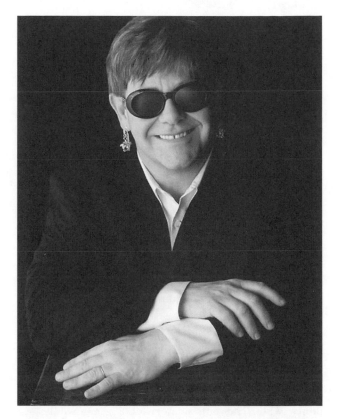

Elton John [GREG GORMAN/ROGERS AND COWAN AND UNIVERSAL RECORDS]

His superb songwriting skills, charismatic performance techniques, and stylistic versatility have made him a leading pop superstar for three decades. Like most pop artists with that kind of longevity, he has endured his share of career peaks and slumps. Through the 1990s he gained back much of the popularity he had lost in the 1980s. For many his fame peaked when he responded to the tragic death of Princess Diana in 1997 with a re-recording of "Candle in the Wind," originally recorded on the death of another close friend. The success of this hit was overwhelming. It registered the quickest sales of any single ever released in the United Kingdom or the United States, where it sold more than 3 million copies in its first week of release.

Rising Star

Elton John's career as singer/songwriter started in the early 1960s, when he won a piano scholarship to the Royal Academy of Music in London at the age of eleven. Two weeks before his final exams, he abandoned his studies to pursue a career in show business, starting off as a messenger boy for a music publishing company. At the same time he earned extra money by performing with his band Bluesology, which backed up soul artists such as Patti LaBelle and Doris Troy. As early as 1967 his first success came with the chart single "Let the Heartaches Begin," sung by R&B singer Long John Baldry and backed by Bluesology.

Following this hit, John teamed up with lyricist Bernie Taupin to write pop songs for the Dick James Music (DJM) label. Their song, "I've Been Loving You," was performed by Lulu as her U.K. entry for the 1969 Eurovision Song Contest. Although this song did not win, it led to a contract with Columbia Records for singles such as "Skyline Pigeon." While this song would become a classic later, it sold poorly in the beginning and Gus Dudgeon, who produced his records through *Blue Moves*, was brought in. At this point, John turned to a style of writing that blended rock and gospel into ballads with spectacular arrangements.

In 1970, backed by former members of the Spencer Davis Group, with Dee Murray on bass and Nigel Olsson on drums, John broke into the U.S. scene in a live concert in Los Angeles. His flamboyant style of performance, with direct references to Jerry Lee Lewis, was an instant success and catapulted his album, *Tumbleweed Connection*, into the U.S. Top 10. The song "Your Song" contributed to the fast album sales. Before long, John had four albums in the U.S. Top 10 simultaneously, the first time this had happened since the Beatles.

Following the release of *Madman Across the Water* (1971), he formed his own group, the Elton John group, which included Olsson, Murray, and guitarist Davey Johnstone. In 1972 they released *Honky Chateau*, and from this point onward John's singles dominated the Top 10. Notably this album was the first of eight number one albums.

During the early to mid-1970s, it seemed that Elton John's success would never falter. His spectacular concerts became so legendary that they reached a peak when he invited John Lennon to appear with him at Madison Square Garden on Thanksgiving Day in 1974. John's songwriting collaboration with Taupin resulted in a string of Top 20 hits, including "Rocket Man," "Crocodile Rock," "Bennie and the Jets," "Daniel," "The Bitch Is Back," and "Philadelphia Freedom." All of these songs are in a rock and roll style accompanied by John's expressive and energetic piano playing. His eighth album, *Honky Chateau*, was the first of seven albums that reached number one and went platinum.

Career Detours

By 1977 the exhausting pace of John's concert tour, along with negative publicity surrounding his sexual preferences, prompted the singer to announce that he would retire from live performing. In 1978 he released the album *A Single Man* with Gary Osborne. Through the 1980s his musical output continued at a brisk pace, with one album released each year and each spawning a series of hits. At the same time he battled against drug addiction, bulimia, and alcohol abuse.

Comeback

By the beginning of the 1990s, John was able to turn around his personal problems. He also took a greater interest in public service with the establishment of the Elton John AIDS Foundation and a commitment to AIDS research. The album *The One*, released in 1992, became an instant success and helped lead to a publishing deal with Warner/Chappell music, a twelve-year agreement that involved the highest cash advance in the music industry until Robbie Williams surpassed it in a deal he signed in 2002. John's singing style throughout *The One* is warmly expressive, demonstrating a sensitivity for the lyrical sentiments through a control of register that is always reliable and convincing. Musically, the style on this album is laid back within an adult-oriented rock genre that affords the singer the opportunity to reflect. John claimed that this album was the first he released without alcohol or drugs, a circumstance that might account for the measured and poignant mood of all the songs.

A memorable event was John's performance at the Freddie Mercury Memorial and AIDS concert at Wembley Stadium in London in 1992, where he performed Queen's "Bohemian Rhapsody" with Axl Rose of Guns N' Roses. His duet with George Michael in the revival of "Don't Let the Sun Go Down on Me" also proved a major highlight at this event. A collaboration with Tim Rice led to the release of songs for Disney's *The Lion King*. The song "Can You Feel the Love Tonight" became a huge success. Beautifully arranged, with padded out orchestration and cushy harmonies, this song demonstrates John's mastery at singing ballads. Not surprisingly, it won the Academy Award for Best Original Song and the Grammy for Best Male Pop Vocal Performance in 1994.

In 1995 the album *Made in England* sold well in the United States and Britain. With a style strongly influenced by John Lennon's solo ballads, Elton John again demonstrates his superb control of melodic flow against the backdrop of laid-back lyrics set to one-word titles such as "Cold," "Pain," "Blessed," and "Believe." The album's material is enhanced by the inclusion of musicians with whom John had previously worked, such as guitarist Davey Johnstone, percussionist Ray Cooper, and arranger/orchestrator Paul Buckmaster. There is a strong sense of thematic progression in the journey undertaken through all the songs, which are performed in a medley style that culminates in the upbeat final track, "Blessed." Following this album was *The Big Picture*, released in 1997, featuring the Top 10 hit "Something about the Way You Look Tonight." In 2002 John released *Songs from the West Coast*, a limited-edition collection. Featuring a range of familiar tracks, including John's three most recent hits, this album thrilled fans by including both songs and videos.

John's influence on pop artists is significant. Not only has he written songs for others, but he has also performed extensively on recordings by artists such as Bon Jovi, Rod Stewart, Tom Jones, Jackson Browne, Ringo Starr, Kevin Ayers, Rick Astley, the Hollies, and Blue Feat.

Elton John's flamboyant personality, glam-rock image, and soulful performance style have inspired generations of musicians working in the pop industry. In 1996, he was awarded a CBE (Commander of the Most Excellent Order of the British Empire), and he was knighted two years later, a testament to his iconic stature.

SELECTIVE DISCOGRAPHY: *Empty Sky* (Rocket/Island, 1969); *Elton John* (Rocket/Island, 1970); *Tumbleweed Connection* (Rocket/Island, 1971); *Madman Across the Water* (Rocket/Island, 1971); *Honky Chateau* (Rocket/Island, 1972); *Don't Shoot Me I'm Only the Piano Player* (Rocket/Island, 1973); *Goodbye Yellow Brick Road* (Rocket/Island, 1973), *Captain Fantastic & the Brown Dirt Cowboy* (Rocket/Island, 1975); *A Single Man* (MCA, 1978); *The Fox* (MCA, 1981); *Jump Up!* (MCA, 1982); *Too Low for Zero* (MCA, 1983); *Ice on Fire* (MCA, 1985); *Sleeping with the Past* (MCA, 1989); *Duets* (MCA, 1993); *Made in England* (Rocket/Island, 1995); *The Muse* (Polygram, 1999); *Prologue* (MF, 2001); *Songs from the West Coast* (Universal, 2001).

BIBLIOGRAPHY: B. Toberman, *Elton John: A Biography* (London, 1989); E. John and B. Taupin, *Two Rooms: A Celebration of Elton John and Bernie Taupin* (London, 1991); P. Norman, *Sir Elton: The Definitive Biography of Elton John* (London, 2000).

STAN HAWKINS

GEORGE JONES

Born: Saratoga, Texas, 12 September 1931

Genre: Country

Best-selling album since 1990: *Cold Hard Truth* (1999)

Hit songs since 1990: "A Good Year for the Roses," "Choices," "Beer Run"

Writers and critics often describe George Jones as the finest living country singer. In his book, *In the Country of Country* (1997), writer Nicolas Dawidoff accurately sums up Jones's vocal appeal: "It's the way he lingers on a word, kneading it for a sadness you didn't know was there." This overriding air of sadness is a fundamental aspect of Jones's art; his pinched, constricted singing and wide vocal range imbue his performances with a sense of longing and despair. Throughout a career that began in the early 1950s, Jones's self-destructive bouts with drinking, drugs, and lawlessness have found expression in his music. Although he has enjoyed some success in an up-tempo vein, Jones is at heart a ballad singer. On slow tearjerkers such as "A Good Year for the Roses" and "He Stopped Loving Her Today," Jones pulls listeners into his pain, expressing sorrow through small details—a dated photograph, half-smoked cigarettes in an ashtray—that speak to the larger realm of human experience. By the 1980s and 1990s, Jones had inspired an entire generation of younger singers; modern country stars such as Randy Travis, Alan Jackson, and Kenny Chesney frequently proclaim his influence. Overcoming personal demons, Jones continued to perform and record in the new millennium, cementing his position as an elder statesman of country music.

Jones grew up near the East Texas town of Beaumont, the son of an alcoholic, bullying father and devoutly religious mother. As a child, he would often be woken up in the middle of the night by his drunken father, who insisted Jones perform for him. Jones's interest in country deepened once his family purchased a radio when he was seven. Soon after, his father bought him a guitar, encouraging him to perform on the streets of Beaumont for money. By the early 1950s, after an unsuccessful first marriage and a stint with the U.S. Marines, Jones was performing in clubs and bars, his singing influenced by the flowing vocal style of country balladeer Lefty Frizzell. Spotted by producer Pappy Dailey in 1953, Jones signed with Texas-based Starday Records and released his first single, "No Money in This Deal" (1954). Recording for a succession of labels during the 1950s and 1960s, Jones first performed in a hard-rocking, "honky-tonk" style before refining his vocal approach on string-laden ballads such as "She Thinks I Still Care" and "Walk through This World with Me."

Achieving Fame in the 1970s

In 1971 Jones moved to Epic Records, where Billy Sherrill, a producer largely responsible for the heavily orchestrated "countrypolitan" sound popular during the era, helmed his career. At Epic, Jones achieved his greatest degree of fame, the tear and ache in his voice informing hits such as "A Picture of Me (without You)" (1972) and "The Grand Tour" (1974). During this period Jones also recorded hits with his third wife, country star Tammy Wynette, who later wrote frankly about their tormented relationship. Establishing what writer Peter Guralnick described as "a reality-based framework for [his] art," Jones recorded "The Battle" (1976), a song that sets his marriage to Wynette within a military theme: "her soft satin armor lying on the far side of the bed / wounded and heartbroken and scarred by the killing words I said." By the end of the 1970s Jones was often homeless, addicted to alcohol and cocaine. Further, he became known as "No-show Jones," due to the frequency of his missed performances. Nonetheless, he managed to record what many critics consider his finest album, *I Am What I Am* (1980). The album features "He Stopped Loving Her Today," a dramatic tale of unrequited love that became one of Jones's signature hits.

Going Strong in the 1990s

Married to fourth wife Nancy Sepulvada, Jones had succeeded in shaking most of his demons by the late 1980s. Always a prolific artist, he recorded with undiminished energy in the 1990s, although his singles no longer hit the upper reaches of the country charts. Ironically, Jones had been ousted by singers—Travis, Jackson, and others—who modeled their vocal styles after his own. Still, Jones's professionalism was unwavering. In 1994 he scored a minor hit with a new version of "A Good Year for the Roses," recorded as a duet with Jackson. Although Jackson performs with characteristic sensitivity, he is largely obscured once Jones begins singing. Jones's voice tells a story, its lived-in, burnished edge imbuing each detail with sadness: "a lip-print on a half-filled cup of coffee that you poured and didn't drink / But at least you thought you wanted it / That's so much more than I can say for me." With his trademark ability to highlight words for emphasis, Jones extends "roses" across six syllables, singing certain lyrics powerfully while growing hushed on others. The effect for the listener is one of being drawn into Jones's world as an intimate witness. Pitching the final "roses" at the top of his range, supported by a sympathetic arrangement of guitar and steel pedal, Jones ends the performance on a note of loss and resignation.

In 1999 Jones released *Cold Hard Truth*, touted as a return to his tough country roots. An anomaly within the slick, radio-groomed world of late 1990s country, the album was hailed by critics as his finest in over a decade. Featuring clean, restrained instrumentation, songs such as "Our Bed of Roses" and the biting title track capture Jones's emotional honesty and renegade spirit. Although Jones sounds rushed and tired on the album's follow-up, *Live with the Possum* (1999), he rebounded for *The Rock: Stone Cold Country 2001* (2001), his first album for the BNA label. A solid collection of contemporary material, Jones proves that his weathered voice still bears potency at the age of seventy. While most of his troubles lay behind him, these years were not without signs of Jones's former recklessness. In 1999 he was seriously injured in Nashville after his car crashed into a bridge. Although he recov-

ered, an investigation showed that he had been drinking while driving.

Legendary pop vocalist Frank Sinatra once referred to Jones as "the second best male singer in America." Over the course of a fifty-year career, Jones has balanced such praise with ongoing commercial success, continuing to record minor hits in the 1990s and 2000s. More than any other singer, Jones is cited by contemporary country vocalists as a primary influence, not only for his keening vocal style but also for the heart and soul he pours into his work.

SELECTIVE DISCOGRAPHY: *The Grand Ole Opry's New Star* (Starday, 1957); *My Favorites of Hank Williams* (United Artists, 1962); *Sings the Songs of Dallas Frazier* (Musicor, 1968); *George Jones with Love* (Musicor, 1971); *A Picture of Me (without You)* (Epic, 1972); *I Am What I Am* (Epic, 1980); *Walls Can Fall* (MCA, 1992); *The Bradley Barn Sessions* (MCA, 1994); *Cold Hard Truth* (Elektra, 1999); *The Rock: Stone Cold Country 2001* (BNA, 2001).

BIBLIOGRAPHY: B. Allen, *George Jones: The Saga of an American Singer* (New York, 1988).

WEBSITE: www.georgejones.com.

DAVID FREELAND

NORAH JONES

Born: New York, New York, 30 March 1979

Genre: Jazz

Best-selling album since 1990: *Come Away with Me* (2002)

Hit songs since 1990: "Come Away with Me," "Don't Know Why"

Norah Jones's calling cards are her soothing material and unassuming stage presence, which form a stark counterpoint to her meteoric rise to stardom. The daughter of the concert producer Sue Jones and the Grammy-winning classical sitarist Ravi Shankar, Jones was raised almost exclusively by her mother. Her parents had a nine-year relationship, but Shankar subsequently married another woman. Sue and Norah Jones moved to the Dallas area in 1984.

Influenced by two towering jazz artists—singer Billie Holiday and pianist Bill Evans—Norah Jones displayed songwriting and piano skills at an early age. She enrolled in the University of North Texas's respected jazz program, remaining for two years. While studying there, she was asked to pick up the Ferdinandos, a visiting band from New York City, at the airport. She got along well with one of the members, Jesse Harris, who invited her to visit during the summer of 1998. She joined his band and, although she was living in a seedy neighborhood and struggling to make ends meet, she fell in love with her new life and decided to stay.

Jones's commercial potential was a compound of smoky, mature vocals—reminiscent of Bonnie Raitt and Rickie Lee Jones—formidable songwriting talent, and striking good looks. From December 1999 to December 2000, she performed with Wax Poetic, a jazz-funk band. She continued to work on her own material, however, and in October 2000 recorded a six-song demo that includes future hits "Come Away with Me," written by Jones, and "Don't Know Why," written by Harris.

The jazz label Blue Note signed her in 2001, and she set out to record her debut album, produced by the great Arif Mardin, whose credits include Aretha Franklin and the Bee Gees. The finished product, *Come Away with Me* (2002), comprises jazz-tinged soft rock with touches of blues and country. Jones's supple voice gives the acoustic-framed album its signature stamp. Mostly originals by Harris, Jones, and her boyfriend, the bassist Lee Alexander, the album also contains covers of Hank Williams's "Cold, Cold Heart" and Hoagy Carmichael's "The Nearness of You."

The album built slowly during 2002, as "Come Away with Me" and "Don't Know Why" garnered adult contemporary and smooth-jazz airplay, appealing to an audience at least a decade older than Jones herself. Constant touring and appearances on *The Tonight Show with Jay Leno* and *Saturday Night Live* helped her gain momentum as 2002 ended. Jones was a favorite at the 2003 Grammys, but she and her CD surprised even her biggest boosters by winning eight awards, including Album of the Year, Record of the Year ("Don't Know Why"), and Best New Artist. In her acceptance speeches she thanked her mother but pointedly left out any mention of her father.

The Grammy boost finally helped Jones garner Top 40 airplay for "Don't Know Why," even though the youth-dominated format warmed to the track slowly. Meanwhile, the album hit number one more than a year after its release, becoming a must-have for the baby-boomer intelligentsia. Critics debate the significance of her Grammy and chart triumphs: Some praise her success as heralding the return of authentic personal songwriting with acoustic instruments, whereas others insist that her music is snoozy soft rock sweetened by a beautiful face. Although the idea of a young artist becoming successful by appealing to older audiences is an anomaly in the modern pop scene, Jones's triumphs have reminded audiences of the less-is-more power of simple, intimate music.

SELECTIVE DISCOGRAPHY: *First Sessions* (Blue Note, 2001); *Come Away with Me* (Blue Note, 2002).

RAMIRO BURR

QUINCY JONES

Born: Chicago, Illinois, 14 March 1933
Genre: R&B, Pop, Jazz
Best-selling album since 1990: *Q's Jook Joint* (1995)
Hit songs since 1990: "I'll Be Good to You," "You Put a Move on My Heart"

In a diverse career ranging through six decades of African-American musical styles, from 1950s jazz to hip-hop of the 1990s and 2000s, Quincy Jones has earned his reputation as an American institution, excelling as an arranger, producer, instrumentalist, songwriter, film composer, and solo artist. The key ingredient of Jones's lasting success, apart from far-reaching talent, has been his breadth of vision. Viewing music as a multi-colored tapestry, Jones has repeatedly transcended categorical limitations, infusing his work with a wide array of elements: classical, pop, jazz, blues, and R&B. At the same time he has become one of the top businesspeople within the record industry, proving that art and commerce can reside side by side peaceably. In the 1990s, after health and personal problems threatened a setback, Jones remained active in music, film, and television production, running his own record label and recording all-star albums that reflected his catholic taste.

Young Arranger and Producer

Jones spent his early years on Chicago's South Side, an African-American neighborhood rich with a palette of music during the 1930s and 1940s. Although she suffered bouts of mental illness, Jones's mother was a learned and intelligent woman who instilled in him a love of music. In 1943 the family moved to Seattle, Washington, where Jones learned to play a variety of instruments before focusing on the trumpet. While still a teenager he performed with future R&B star Ray Charles, and after graduation from high school won a scholarship to study music at the prestigious Schillinger House in Boston. In the early 1950s Jones moved to New York City and began working as a musical arranger, overseeing recording sessions for artists such as jazz singer Helen Merrill, trumpeter Clifford Brown, and famed "Queen of the Blues," Dinah Washington. Jones spent a large portion of the 1950s in Europe, where he organized a jazz musical theater play in 1959.

Deeply in debt after continuing to pay the musicians' salaries once the show had dissolved, Jones returned to the United States, where he joined Chicago-based Mercury Records as vice president in 1961. The first African American to hold a senior position within a large record company, Jones produced his biggest pop hit at Mercury with "It's My Party," a 1963 smash by teen star Lesley Gore. At the same time, Jones began releasing his own albums and composing musical scores for Hollywood films such as *In Cold Blood* and *In the Heat of the Night* (both 1967). Like his solo albums, Jones's film scores were lush, hip, and atmospheric, appealing to pop listeners while retaining a jazz-based groove.

New Directions in the 1970s and 1980s

Jones continued to work steadily throughout the 1960s and 1970s, although a brain aneurysm nearly killed him in 1974. Given a one-in-one-hundred chance of recovering, Jones rebounded with energy and strength, producing some of the most successful work of his career. On albums such as *Body Heat* (1974), Jones merges his jazz sensibility with 1970s R&B and funk. In the late 1970s he began collaborating with pop star Michael Jackson, overseeing production on *Thriller* (1982), the best-selling album in recorded history. For *Thriller*, Jones constructed a thick, dense series of beats that found a winning middle ground between R&B and pop. "We Are the World" (1985), a single that Jones produced for the relief organization USA for Africa, brought him further acclaim on the basis of its all-star vocal cast and humanitarian message.

By this time, Jones possessed the clout to assemble diverse groups of performers under one roof, a testament to his stature within the music industry. Released on his own Qwest label, *Back on the Block* (1989) was one such effort, a collection of jazzy R&B featuring guest artists such as Ray Charles, rapper Kool Moe Dee, and keyboardist Herbie Hancock. In 1985 Jones again turned his energies to Hollywood, producing the film *The Color Purple*, starring actors Whoopi Goldberg and Danny Glover. The heavy responsibilities of Jones's new endeavor took a toll: In 1986 he suffered an emotional breakdown, followed by divorce from his wife, actress Peggy Lipton, in 1990. After taking time to refocus on a quiet island in Tahiti, Jones bounced back by founding *Vibe*, a magazine devoted to hip-hop and rap culture, in 1992. He also produced the hit television series *The Fresh Prince of Bel-Air*, which starred rapper and actor Will Smith and ran from 1990 to 1996.

1990s Diversity

Jones continued to record during the 1990s, his work displaying more of a contemporary R&B feel than the swinging jazz arrangements he created in the past. As cultural critic Gerald Early noted for PBS television network's *American Masters* program in 2001, Jones is a "culminator," rather than an innovator. Rarely inaugurating new styles, Jones instead assembles the finest work of the past into a new, exciting brew. *Q's Jook Joint* (1995) is an attempt to fit a range of twentieth-century African-American music, from 1940s vocal jazz to 1970s disco, within the context of a modern R&B album. Again Jones gathers an all-star lineup, including R&B singer Brian McKnight and jazz flutist Hubert Laws.

Despite Jones's historical jazz sensibility, the album is weighted toward the contemporary. "You Put a Move on My Heart," featuring young R&B singer Tamia, is a strong ballad, informed with the slow-building passion of religious gospel music, while Michael Jackson's 1979 hit "Rock with You" is updated with an electronic funk arrangement by teenage R&B star Brandy. Critics note that other songs are less successful: The jazz-styled funk of "Cool Joe, Mean Joe (Killer Joe)" is a bit too clean-sounding, and vocal group Take 6 is unable to handle the tricky phrasing on the jazz standard, "Moody's Mood for Love." The disappointment of such tracks points to the down side of Jones's eclecticism. His familiarity with so many different styles sometimes prevents him from digging into the emotional core of his material. As a result, critics have observed that *Q's Jook Joint* has the feel of a discursive survey, rather than a detailed exploration. On the whole, however, the album emerges as a worthy effort, informed by Jones's vast knowledge and discernment.

While Jones continued to score films during the late 1990s, working on the hit movie *Austin Powers: International Man of Mystery* (1997), he also devoted time to more personal projects. In 2000 he released *Basie and Beyond*, a tribute to great jazz bandleader Count Basie. One of the few pure jazz works of Jones's later career, the album features a large orchestra consisting of top players such as percussionist Paulinho Da Costa. Although only one of the songs, "For Lena and Lennie," is actually associated with Basie, Jones and arranger Sammy Nestico capture Basie's gently swinging rhythmic style. Like Jones's R&B albums, *Basie and Beyond* is more pleasant than trenchant, the music gliding on a feathery bed of sound. On "Grace," an elegiac mood is created through trilling woodwinds and dark-sounding brass, but the arrangement never attains the level of complexity that would make it truly memorable. Still, *Basie and Beyond* qualifies as a laudable attempt to bypass mainstream pop audiences in favor of reaching a loyal jazz base.

Since the 1950s Jones has continuously sought to balance his various influences and instincts, creating music that looks to the past while staying rooted in the present. Defining the range of possibilities for the contemporary African-American musical artist, Jones excels in every field of entertainment. Regardless of style, his work is informed with unerring professionalism and taste.

SELECTIVE DISCOGRAPHY: *The Birth of a Band* (Mercury, 1959); *Walking in Space* (A&M, 1969); *Body Heat* (A&M, 1974); *The Dude* (A&M, 1981);

Back on the Block (Qwest, 1989); *Q's Jook Joint* (Qwest, 1995); *Basie and Beyond* (Warner, 2000).

BIBLIOGRAPHY: Q. Jones, *Q: The Autobiography of Quincy Jones* (New York, 2002).

DAVID FREELAND

RICKIE LEE JONES

Born: Chicago, Illinois, 8 November 1954
Genre: Rock, Pop
Best-selling album since 1990: *Traffic from Paradise* (1993)

Identified primarily by the success of her 1979 hit, "Chuck E.'s in Love," singer/songwriter Rickie Lee Jones has made an indelible mark as a musical adventurer whose literate songs combine post–beat era poetry with jazz, folk, rock, and even trip-hop exploration. In addition, Jones is unafraid to impose her artistry on classic songs of all genres.

Jones was born the third of four children to a struggling family rife with numerous dysfunctional elements. Her father was an aspiring actor/musician who worked mostly as a waiter, and her mother became a nurse after her brother lost a leg and suffered partial paralysis from a motorcycle accident. Both parents were products of orphanage upbringings and their marriage was volatile at best. The family lived a nomadic lifestyle, uprooting from one city to the next. Jones escaped the turmoil by creating musical imaginary friends and later, at age fourteen, by running away.

After some time spent drifting around, Jones finished high school in Olympia, Washington, before taking off alone to live in Los Angeles where she worked as a waitress while singing in clubs and coffeehouses for several years. Jones resided in West Hollywood's famed artist bunkhouse, the Tropicana Motel, and took up friendships with musicians Tom Waits and Los Angeles eccentric, Chuck E. Weiss, the subject of her hit "Chuck E.'s in Love." On the strength of that song, her debut album, *Rickie Lee Jones* (1979), scored six 1979 Grammy Award nominations and she won for Best New Artist. Her second album, *Pirates* (1981), also received high acclaim and the free-spirited Jones was likened to singer/songwriter Joni Mitchell. Jones's idiosyncratic, often blues-influenced songs come off as flippant, but are laced with emotional intensity. She sings—sometimes speaks—her music with a voice that ranges wide and she is as comfortable with raw sexuality as delicate jazz phrasing. Jones reached her pinnacle fast and the pop music world was hers for the taking. However, Jones's next two recordings, artistic experiments,

fared poorly and she struggled with substance abuse for the latter half of the 1980s, disappearing from music for almost five years.

After touring with Lyle Lovett throughout 1990, Jones reestablished her forte as a song stylist by releasing *Pop Pop* (1991), a musically spare album of jazz standards interpreted by her flexible vocal dynamics. Two years later, Jones released *Traffic from Paradise*, a mercurial change in style more reminiscent of her debut. Except for David Bowie's "Rebel, Rebel," the album is her first collection of original material since *Pirates*. Ripe with Jones's unique combination of ethereal melodies and vivid lyrics, *Traffic from Paradise* features several guest artists, such as Lyle Lovett singing back up and Leo Kottke on acoustic guitar.

After an acoustic live solo release, *Naked Songs* (1995), Jones, one of music's most organic artists, turned heads when she delved into the industrial-funk sounds of trip-hop (a more produced, electronic cousin to hip-hop) on *Ghostyhead* (1997). Her manipulated vocals fade in and out while studio special effects transform her music into a dreamy club beat sound.

Jones received a Grammy nomination for Best Traditional Pop Recording with *It's Like This* (2000), an album of pop music standards crossing into a variety of genres. She lends her vocal agility, including scat style jazz, to songs by the Beatles, Traffic, Steely Dan, Marvin Gaye, and Ira Gershwin, among others, and even includes her rendition of a Charlie Chaplin composition, "Smile." In 2001 she released a live album of twelve songs called *Red Rocks Live*. Although Jones detoured from a once promising pop music career, she has found a comfortable niche as one of music's foremost song stylists.

SELECTIVE DISCOGRAPHY: *Rickie Lee Jones* (Warner Bros., 1979); *Pirates* (Warner Bros., 1981); *Girl at Her Volcano* (Warner Bros., 1983); *The Magazine* (Warner Bros., 1984); *Flying Cowboys* (Geffen, 1989); *Pop Pop* (Geffen, 1991); *Traffic from Paradise* (Geffen, 1993); *Naked Songs* (Reprise, 1995); *Ghostyhead* (Warner Bros., 1997); *It's Like This* (Artemis, 2000); *Red Rocks Live* (Artemis, 2001).

DONALD LOWE

WYNONNA JUDD

Born: Christina Ciminella; Ashland, Kentucky, 30 May 1964
Genre: Country
Best-selling album since 1990: *Wynonna* (1992)
Hit songs since 1990: "She Is His Only Need," "I Saw the Light"

As half of the popular duo the Judds, Wynonna Judd released some of the most commercially successful country singles of the 1980s, including the 1984 hits "Mama He's Crazy" and "Why Not Me?" As a solo artist Judd became increasingly adventurous as the 1990s progressed, incorporating elements of rhythm and blues, gospel, and hard rock into her work. Regardless of style, the quality that most distinguishes Judd's music is her remarkable voice: Bold, full-bodied, and expressive, it recalls soulful country singers of the past such as Patsy Cline.

Although they lived for several years in Los Angeles, the Judd family—Wynonna, mother Naomi, and younger sister Ashley—later returned to their home state of Kentucky, where they lived in rural surroundings with no television or phone. Their main form of entertainment was listening to famed country program *The Grand Ole Opry* on the radio. Moving to Nashville in 1979, Naomi and Wynonna began making demo tapes on a thirty-dollar recorder purchased at K-Mart. After an audition in which Wynonna accompanied herself on acoustic guitar, the duo landed a contract with RCA Records. With Wynonna singing lead and Naomi supplying harmony, the Judds had a warm, distinctive sound that inspired a long string of number one country hits. While fans responded to mother Naomi's youthful, beautiful appearance, it was Wynonna who received the greatest attention. With her nimble guitar skills and tough, growling voice, she fit in perfectly with the 1980s "neo-traditionalist" movement, which overturned the heavily produced, pop-oriented country of the 1970s in favor of a subtler, gently rocking approach. When Naomi contracted life-threatening hepatitis in 1990 and the Judds were forced to disband, it made sense that Wynonna would strike out as a solo artist.

Judd's first album on her own, *Wynonna*, was released in 1992 and more than lived up to the artist's commercial promise, spawning three number one singles and going triple platinum. With its even mixture of hard-rocking numbers and ballads *Wynonna* is a fairly conventional country album, although Judd's unique style shines through. The gospel-influenced "Live with Jesus" showcases her sensuous vocal growl while "It's Never Easy to Say Goodbye" is a moving ballad. Opening with a scene of a mother crying as she puts her young son on a school bus, the song might have sounded corny in other hands, but Judd makes it believable through her heartfelt sincerity. Judd's follow-up album, *Tell Me Why* (1993), gave the first indication of a widening stylistic range, featuring a more diverse sound than the previous album. "That Was Yesterday," for example, is a bluesy number pointing to Judd's increasing interest in R&B music. "It's finally over, and I can't even cry," Judd sings darkly, her voice carrying a new depth and authority. The song features a guitar solo by

Steve Cropper, whose haunting playing was featured on many great rhythm and blues records of the 1960s.

By the time of her fifth studio album, *New Day Dawning* (2000), Judd had matured into a performer who could take any kind of material and make it her own. From the hard rock–influenced "Chain Reaction" to the breathy cover of rock and folk singer Joni Mitchell's "Help Me," Judd sounds assured, her voice gaining command through years of experience. By this time, however, Judd was no longer hitting the country charts with regularity, a situation over which she voiced much public frustration. "I'm finding myself sort of overlooked," she told *Country Music International* in September 2000, adding that, "Country radio just doesn't play me because they really don't know what to do with me right now." While ranking as one of her finest albums, *New Day Dawning* was perhaps too eclectic for popular acceptance. Furthermore, in an age dominated by athletic, sexy country singers such as Shania Twain and Faith Hill, the heavy, big-haired Judd seemed out of date, relying on talent rather than image to get her message across. Never publicity shy, Judd focused on nurturing fans outside of the country mainstream, including a devoted lesbian following that embraced her tough but vulnerable performance style. In the meantime, public attention shifted to sister Ashley, who became a successful Hollywood actress.

As country music edged closer in the 1990s to the pop mainstream, Wynonna Judd was an anomaly, her soulful, full-bodied vocal style reminiscent of female country performers of the past such as Patsy Cline and Tammy Wynette. Like those vocalists, Judd delves into the emotional life of her songs to draw up pain and heartache. At the same time, her experiments with rock, R&B, and gospel make her one of country music's most innovative artists.

SELECTIVE DISCOGRAPHY: *Wynonna* (MCA, 1992); *Tell Me Why* (MCA, 1993); *Revelations* (MCA, 1996); *New Day Dawning* (MCA, 2000).

WEBSITE: www.wynonna.com.

DAVID FREELAND

JURASSIC 5

Formed: 1993, Los Angeles, California

Members: Akil, MC; Chali 2na, MC; Cut Chemist, DJ; Marc 7, MC; Nu-Mark, DJ; Zaakir (Soup) MC.

Genre: Hip-Hop

Best-selling album since 1990: *Quality Control* (2000)

Jurassic 5 is a collective of six individuals who together helped bring back hip-hop to its early roots by employing the basic formula of vocal interplay and turntable beats.

Although its debut album was not released until 2000, the group came together in 1993 when members met at the Good Life Café, an open microphone venue in South Central Los Angeles. During the early to mid-1990s, the club was the epicenter of the underground hip-hop movement in the city. At the time, gangsta rap was shaking up the mainstream. Featuring stars like Tupac Shakur and groups like N.W.A., gangsta rap ignited controversy for its brutal portrayal of inner-city street life. As the 1990s wore on and the hardcore images of gangsta rap faded, mainstream hip-hop became filled with stars like Sean "P. Diddy" Combs and Shawn Carter, also known as Jay-Z. In real life, these artists doubled as corporate moguls and their music became less about the travails of street life and more about women, jewelry, and the enjoyments of living the high life.

As mainstream hip-hop went from guns and gangs to rhinestones and luxury cars, the underground concentrated on keeping it simple. Taking cues from early hip-hop innovators like De La Soul and Kool Moe Dee, Jurassic 5's music was about harmony and the simplest production possible. Its members originated from two hip-hop groups, Rebels of Rhythm and Unity Committee. After releasing the single "Unified Rebelution" under both names in 1993, they ended up forming a new group. Four years later, they independently released the self-titled album *Jurassic 5* (1997), which ended up selling tens of thousands of copies and sparking the interest of Interscope, a major label. (Interscope released the album in 2000.)

Unlike their gangsta rap peers, Jurassic 5's music emphasizes peace and social justice and also pays tribute to their hip-hop heroes. With the backing beats of its two DJs, the four MCs combine the harmonic interplay of doo-wop singing with the individual freestyle rhyming of contemporary rap. Their debut, *Quality Control* (2000), was hailed by critics who declared it one of the freshest albums of recent years and a return to the playfulness, economic production values, and memorable melodies of hip-hop's roots. The group quickly became associated with other like-minded groups of the alternative hip-hop movement including the Roots and Dilated Peoples.

As with those groups, Jurassic 5 found they played to a mostly white audience—exactly the kind of fans who felt alienated from the ghetto tales of gangsta rap or the pimp fantasies portrayed in latter-day hip-hop. Jurassic 5 toured with singer/songwriter Fiona Apple and later shared the stage with Dilated Peoples, the Beat Junkies, and MC Supernatural for the "Word of Mouth" tour. The group returned two years later with its second album, *Power in Numbers* (2002). Once again breaking stereotypes, the

album presents a variety of styles including soul, jazz, and pop, with songs ranging from political to party jams.

In 2002, Jurassic 5 joined the "Smokin' Grooves" tour featuring Lauryn Hill and the Roots. The group remained an alternative in the larger hip-hop picture, emphasizing group unity rather than individual braggadocio.

SELECTIVE DISCOGRAPHY: *Jurassic 5* (Rumble/Pickininny, 1997); *Quality Control* (Interscope, 2000); *Power in Numbers* (Interscope, 2002).

MARK GUARINO

JUVENILE

Born: Terius Gray; New Orleans, Louisiana, 26 March 1975
Genre: Hip-Hop
Best-selling album since 1990: *400 Degreez* (1998)
Hit songs since 1990: "Ha," "Back That Thang Up," "Follow Me Now"

New Orleans–based Juvenile was one of the most prominent southern rappers to win mainstream exposure in the second half of the 1990s. He helped to define the sound of the so-called "Dirty South" and to establish it as a force in hip-hop. Juvenile's success with his group, the Hot Boys, and as a solo artist helped turn the New Orleans label Cash Money Records from a regional success into a national powerhouse.

Terius Gray began rapping in his teens while growing up in New Orleans' infamous Magnolia Housing projects. In 1995 he released his debut album, *Being Myself*, on the Warlock label. It made enough of an impact locally to attract the attention of Ronald "Suga Slim" Williams and his brother Brian "Baby" Williams, co-owners of the local Cash Money Records label. The Williams brothers had started their label in the early 1990s with one artist, the teenage B.G., whose regional success had given Cash Money the funds to expand. They signed Juvenile and in May 1997 released his album *Soulja Rags*.

Soulja Rags finds Juvenile and the Cash Money house producer Mannie Fresh developing the sound they later perfected on *400 Degreez*. It presents Juvenile's tightly constructed rhyming over a collection of synth-heavy, bouncy, club-friendly tracks typical of southern hip-hop. Also typical are the album's "gangsta" lyrics. On track after track Juvenile boasts in gleeful, vivid detail of a hedonistic life of crime, sex, and violence. The above-average skill with which *Solja Rags* delivers standard-issue Southern hip-hop made it an underground sensation, selling some 200,000 copies throughout the South. This success set the stage for the Cash Money "supergroup," the Hot Boys, which paired Juvenile and the increasingly popular B.G.

with two new rappers, Lil Wayne and Turk. The Hot Boys' debut album, *Get It How U Live*, was released in October 1997. Like B.G. and Juvenile's solo albums, it concerns itself mainly with typical "gangsta" boasts of guns, drugs, sex, and money. Again, however, the exceptional talent of the artists involved managed to distinguish the album from its many competitors, with the four rappers trading rhymes in compellingly varied yet complementary styles over Mannie Fresh's original take on the "dirty south" production style. With almost no commercial airplay *Get It How U Live* sold almost 400,000 copies throughout the South and the Midwest. This phenomenal success scored Cash Money a distribution deal with Universal Records in the summer of 1998.

While the deal with Universal was a great step forward for Cash Money, it was Juvenile's third album, released around the same time, that ultimately turned the label into a major commercial force. Again produced entirely by Mannie Fresh, *400 Degreez* is the culmination of the producer's career. He takes the bass-heavy, skittering beats typical of southern hip-hop and layers them with keyboards, strings, and off-the-wall sound effects to create a fresh yet extremely catchy and accessible backdrop for Juvenile's rapping. If *400 Degreez* represents the pinnacle of the Cash Money sound, it also represents the ultimate expression of the Cash Money philosophy of the over-the-top, conspicuous flaunting of wealth. Track after track flirts with absurdity in its loving descriptions of jewelry, cars, and other symbols of "the good life." Juvenile is also in top form, particularly on the album's two popular singles. On "Ha" Juvenile lays down a rapid-fire series of lines describing a typical high-flying day in the life of a "gangsta," punctuating each with a final "Ha": "When you broke you drove—ha / When you paid you got bookoo places to go—Ha." This simple device, coupled with Juvenile's aggressive delivery and spaced-out keyboards, makes for an almost hypnotically compelling track. Although "Ha" became a big hit, it was surpassed by the album's second single, "Back That Thang Up," a gleefully explicit come-on set to an infectious, club-friendly beat. These two singles eventually drove sales of *400 Degreez* to the 4 million mark, making Cash Money Records a household name.

Two subsequent Juvenile releases, *Tha G-Code* (1999) and *Project English* (2001), competently returned to the sound that had made *400 Degreez* such a success. While neither album squanders the artistic or commercial legacy of *400 Degreez*, they fail to attain the breakthrough quality that makes *400 Degreez* one of the landmark albums of 1990s hip-hop.

Juvenile's southern-accented delivery and uniquely New Orleans slang combined with Mannie Fresh's party-oriented yet idiosyncratic production to create a fresh take on an already regionally successful sound. The success of *400 Degreez* transformed hip-hop in the 1990s by turning Cash Money into a major industry force and spawning numerous imitators working in the "dirty south" style.

SELECTIVE DISCOGRAPHY: *Being Myself* (Warlock, 1995); *Solja Rags* (Cash Money, 1997); *400 Degreez* (Cash Money, 1998); *Being Myself* (remixed) (Warlock, 1999); *Tha G-Code* (Cash Money, 1999); *Project English* (Cash Money, 2001).

WEBSITE: www.cashmoney-records.com.

MATT HIMES

K $\left.\frac{\text{k}}{\text{K}}\right|$

MICHAEL KAMEN

Born: New York, New York, 15 April 1948
Genre: Soundtrack

Schooled as a classical oboist and armed with a Juilliard education, composer Michael Kamen has carved out a career as a prolific writer of movie soundtracks. He has also collaborated with pop groups such as Pink Floyd and Metallica, experimenting with fusing classical techniques with rock and pop.

Born in New York City, Kamen studied at the High School of Music and Art before entering Juilliard as an oboist. While at Juilliard he formed a rock/classical fusion band called the New York Rock and Roll Ensemble. The band included two oboists and a cellist, making for an odd combination of instruments for a rock band. The group was invited by Leonard Bernstein to perform on one of the New York Philharmonic's Young People's concerts and by Arthur Fiedler to perform on a Boston Pops program.

Kamen's early compositions were ballet scores—for the Joffrey Ballet, Alvin Ailey, and La Scala in Milan. In 1976 Kamen wrote his first film score, for *The Next Man*, starring Sean Connery. His big break in pop music came with Pink Floyd, collaborating on arrangements for the group's hit album *The Wall* (1979).

Kamen regards his score for the 1983 Terry Gilliam movie *Brazil* as his first big movie soundtrack success. He has gone on to write the soundtracks for more than seventy movies and TV projects, picking up Golden Globe and Academy Award nominations for *Robin Hood: Prince of Thieves* (1991) and *Don Juan DeMarco* (1995) and an Emmy nomination for *From the Earth to the Moon* (1998). Other well-known movie projects include the *Lethal Weapon* and *Die Hard* series, *Mr. Holland's Opus* (1995), *X-Men* (2000), *101 Dalmations* (1996), and *Fear and Loathing in Las Vegas* (1998).

In pop music Kamen has created hit songs for Bryan Adams—"Everything I Do, I Do It for You" (from *Robin Hood*) and "Have You Ever Really Loved a Woman" (from *Don Juan de Marco*), both of which won Grammys, and for Sting ("It's Probably Me"). He has also collaborated with David Bowie, the Eurythmics, Aerosmith, and Eric Clapton, among others. Additionally, Kamen created music for the closing ceremonies of the 1996 Olympic Summer Games in Atlanta, Georgia.

A musical fusionist, Kamen has worked to incorporate diverse genres into his scores, experimenting with classical, jazz, world music, rock, and pop. He has written concertos for guitar and for saxophone. He has collaborated with David Sanborn, Herbie Hancock, and Eric Clapton on symphonic projects and has written a piece for the band Metallica and the San Francisco Symphony called *S&M*. In 2000 he wrote and recorded an orchestral piece for conductor Leonard Slatkin and the National Symphony Orchestra in Washington, D.C., called *The Old Moon in the New Moon's Arms*, which was derisively reviewed by *The Washington Post*.

Kamen was one of the most prolific and well-known film score composers of the 1990s. He well understands the ability of music to convey in a few notes the tone of a scene or underscore and foreshadow its emotional tenor. He writes music that aims for an emotional response from a listener, and his romantic scores work well in the visual medium of film.

SELECTIVE DISCOGRAPHY: *Adventures of Baron Munchausen* (1988); *Concerto for Saxophone* (Warner Bros., 1990); *Let Him Have It* (Virgin Movie, 1992); *Last Action Hero* (1993); *The Three Musketeers* (Hollywood, 1993); *101 Dalmations* (Walt Disney, 1996); *Event Horizon* (London, 1997); *Michael Kamen's Opus* (London, 1998); *The Iron Giant* (Varese, 1999); *Die Hard* (Varese, 2002).

DOUGLAS MCLENNAN

KANDER AND EBB

Formed: 1962, New York, New York

Members: Fred Ebb, lyricist (born New York, New York, 18 March 1932); John Harold Kander, composer (born Kansas City, Missouri, 18 March 1927).

Genre: Musical Theater

Best-selling album since 1990: *Chicago: Music from the Miramax Motion Picture* (2002)

Since collaborating on the first of a long string of musicals in the early 1960s, composer John Kander and lyricist Fred Ebb became Broadway's most notable songwriting team. Their work specializes in spotlighting social and political themes in period settings. Kander and Ebb gained increased recognition when their signature stage musical, *Chicago*, was transformed into an Oscar-winning film and best-selling movie soundtrack. They are the longest-running music-and-lyric partnership in Broadway theater history.

Although Kander and Ebb's talents and sensibilities complement one another perfectly—only rarely have they worked separately since meeting in 1962—their backgrounds differ greatly. Kander grew up in the Midwest where his parents worked in the poultry business. He received piano lessons at an early age, continued his studies at Oberlin College, and in 1954 received a master's degree in fine arts from Columbia University. By the mid-1950s, Kander worked consistently in New York as a pianist, often playing at Broadway auditions and helping with other preshow production. His first significant work came in 1960 when choreographer/director Jerome Robbins hired him to score dances for the Broadway show *Gypsy*. Kander had impressed the impulsive Robbins while accompanying performers during the show's auditions. In 1962 Kander scored the music for his first Broadway show, *A Family Affair*, which fared poorly but garnered Kander excellent notices within the industry.

Ebb was born and raised in New York City by a family with little interest in music or the arts. His father died suddenly when Ebb was fourteen years old, leaving his mother and him in financial straights. However, Ebb did well in school (he was the valedictorian of DeWitt Clinton High School) and went on to both New York University and Columbia in literary pursuits. After failing to get his short stories optioned for Hollywood movies, Ebb returned to New York and started writing for nightclub revues and a television show titled *That Was the Week That Was*. He also wrote lyrics for composer Phil Springer. Their most notable songs were "Heartbroken," recorded by Judy Garland, and "Santa Baby," which actress Eartha Kit turned into a hit. Prior to meeting Kander, Ebb had just written the lyrics for his first show, an off-Broadway musical called *Morning Sun*. Like Kander's first effort, it failed miserably.

Kander and Ebb's first Broadway show was *Flora, the Red Menace* (1965) with seventeen-year-old Liza Minnelli in the lead and making her Broadway debut. The show did poorly, but Minnelli received a Tony Award for her performance and the cast album sold well. Not only were Kander and Ebb cemented as a team, but they also formed a professional and congenial relationship with Minnelli that still exists. They went on to create stellar songs for other female stars such as Barbra Streisand, Lauren Bacall, Gwen Verdon, and Chita Rivera. Their next Broadway show, *Cabaret* (1966), set in Berlin, Germany, during the rise of Nazism, elevated Kander and Ebb as Broadway's premier songwriting team. Directed by Harold Prince, the show was a smash success that ran for 1,166 performances. Adapted into a hit film by Bob Fosse in 1972, it won eight Academy Awards. *Cabaret* was revived on Broadway in 1998, and the new production continued its successful, award-winning run into the new millennium.

Kander and Ebb proceeded to write the songs for many Broadway shows, including *The Happy Time* (1968), *Zorba* (1968), *70 Girls 70* (1971), *Chicago* (1975), *The Act* (1977), *Woman of the Year* (1981), *The Rink* (1984), *Kiss of the Spider Woman* (1992), and *Steel Pier* (1997). They also composed for films, television specials, and off-Broadway productions. Their "New York, New York," written for the film *New York, New York* (1976), starring Liza Minnelli and Robert De Niro, became a signature song for legendary crooner Frank Sinatra.

In 1996 one of their most cherished musicals, *Chicago*, a play about celebrity-seeking murderesses in prohibition-era Chicago, was revived on Broadway to rave reviews. Due to high-profile court cases such as the O. J. Simpson murder case in 1994–1995, *Chicago's* cynical look at the American justice system played far better in 1996 than it did in 1975. The play's success—it entered its seventh year on Broadway in November 2002—rekindled late-1970s plans to adapt the show into a film. *Chicago* (the film) opened in late 2002 to resounding praise. It won six

Oscars at the 2003 Academy Awards, including the coveted award for Best Picture. Additionally, Kander and Ebb's soundtrack to the film sold extremely well. Along with the same songs from the Broadway production ("Class" was cut from the film, but included on the soundtrack), the film soundtrack also includes an extra Kander and Ebb composition, "I Move On," sung as a duet by the film's leading ladies, Catherine Zeta-Jones and Renee Zellweger. Chicago's catchy melodies and clever, often wry lyrics encompass much of what is special about Kander and Ebb's work.

Their much-hyped *Steel Pier* (1997) closed after a disappointingly short run of seventy-six performances. However, Kander and Ebb, veterans of the fickle ways of Broadway theater, simply moved on to the next project. In 1999 they staged a presentation of *Over and Over* at the Signature Theatre in Arlington, Virginia, a new musical based on the play *The Skin of Our Teeth*, by Thornton Wilder. They are currently preparing the music for the upcoming premier of the Broadway musical *The Visit*, scheduled to premier in 2004.

Kander and Ebb were honored in 1998 with a Lifetime Achievement Award at the Kennedy Center Honors. As Broadway leans more toward revivals or adaptations of hit film and television shows, Kander and Ebb remain vestiges of an earlier era when musicals were created by an original idea from the ground up.

SELECTIVE DISCOGRAPHY: *Flora, the Red Menace* (RCA Victor, 1965); *Cabaret* (Columbia, 1967); *Zorba* (Capitol, 1969); *70 Girls 70* (Sony, 1971); *Chicago* (Arista, 1975); *Woman of the Year* (Arista, 1981); *The Rink* (TER, 1984); *And the World Goes 'Round* (RCA Victor, 1991); *An Evening with Kander and Ebb* (DRG, 1992); *Kiss of the Spider Woman* (RCA Victor, 1993); *Steel Pier* (RCA Victor, 1997). **Soundtracks:** *New York, New York* (EMI, 1977); *Chicago: Music from the Miramax Motion Picture* (Sony, 2002).

DONALD LOWE

SALIF KEITA

Born: Salifou Keita; Djoliba, Mali, 25 August 1949
Genre: World
Best-selling album since 1990: *Soro* (re-release 1990)

Nicknamed the "Golden Voice of Mali," Salif Keita is the artist most responsible for arousing international interest in the music of his native Mali by casting it in the conventions of Western rock and pop music. In doing so, Keita created a formula that was emulated by other

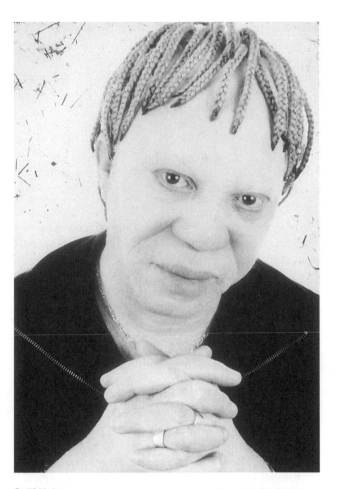

Salif Keita [LUCILLE REYBOZ/BLUE NOTE RECORDS]

African artists seeking to popularize the music of their respective traditions and cultures.

Born in the heart of Mali, Salif Keita was an albino in a rural West African culture so filled with superstitions about being black but having white skin that his own family was afraid of him. Growing up hidden away and isolated, in part because of his lack of natural protection against the region's tropical climate and hot sun, Keita turned inward and developed deep passions for reading, study, and music. He studied to become a schoolteacher, but the increasingly poor eyesight that was a symptom of albinism kept him from being able to teach for a living. Enormously moved by encounters with jelis or griots, the professional class of troubadours who would sing powerfully of the region's royal history, family sagas, and oral traditions, Keita began developing his own voice in the jeli tradition. One needed to be a jeli by birth, however, and so Keita would go out by himself deep into his father's fields and practice and mold his singing prowess by serenading the area wildlife until he developed an enormously distinctive and dynamic vocal instrument. At eighteen Keita left home and set off for the Mali capital of Bamako and began singing on the streets, making his way into clubs. Heard by Tidiane Koné, the founder and leader of the government-sponsored sixteen-piece Rail Band du Buffet Hôtel de la Gare (later known as the Super Rail Band de Bamako), Keita became a star attraction in one of the country's most revered and innovative bands. After traveling abroad for a short time in 1972, Keita returned to Bamako to find the rising Guinean singer Mory Kanté singing his lead repertoire with the Rail Band and felt so snubbed that he joined the act's biggest rival, Les Ambassadeurs du Motel (later called Les Ambassadeurs Internationales).

After over a decade with the Ambassadeurs, Keita left the band and moved to Paris in 1984 and began secretly recording *Soro* (1987) with French keyboardist Jean-Philippe Rykriel and Senegalese producer Ibrahima Sylla. *Soro* ignited enormous international interest in Keita and the music of his beloved Mali.

Keita had left behind Afro-Cuban influences so indelibly associated with his work with the Ambassadeurs and began aggressively mixing traditional music of Mali with Western rock and pop. This same, widely emulated formula marked the majority of Keita's releases of the 1990s: Keita would soulfully wail away like a warning siren—usually in his native Bambara language—over soundscapes made up of Western synthesizers, guitars, and brass instruments alongside African polyrhythms, choruses, and the traditional kora, a cross between a harp and a lute. The Afro-pop *Amen* (1990), produced by Weather Report's Joe Zawinul, is Keita's most Western and commercial album to date. *Sosie* (1997) marks an unusual departure for Keita as it is made up of repertoire made famous by French singers such as Serge Gainsbourg, Michel Legrand, and Bernard Lavilliers. The album *Papa* (1999) includes a duet with Grace Jones and is an intensely melancholy and personal one for Keita. It marks a musical coming-to-terms of sorts with the 1995 death of his father, who had rejected Keita as a boy because of his albinism and had later disowned him when he left home to go into music; the two had long since reconciled, however. *Moffou* (2002) is named after the small, shrill traditional West African flute and is also the name of the nightclub that Keita opened in Bamako in 2002 to spotlight the ever-burgeoning West African music scene. Whereas the all-acoustic *Moffou* opens with an upbeat duet with Cesaria Evora, the heart of the album is a welcome, unadulterated return to Keita's roots: soulful ballads of Mali sung by an artist at the peak of his interpretive powers.

SELECTIVE DISCOGRAPHY: *Soro* (Mango/Island re-release, 1990); *Amen* (Mango/Island, 1991); *The Mansa of Mali . . . A Retrospective* (Mango/Island, 1994); *Folon: The Past* (Mango/Island, 1995); *Seydou Bathili* (Sonodisc re-release, 1997); *Papa* (Blue Note, 1999); *1969-1980* (Sonodisc, 2000); *Sosie* (Mellemfolkeligt re-release, 2001); *Moffou* (Decca/Universal, 2002); *Ko-yan* (Palm/Island re-release, 2003). **With Les Ambassadeurs Internationales:** *Les Ambassadeurs Internationales with Salif Keita* (Rounder re-release, 1992). **With Super Rail Band de Bamako:** *Rail Band* (Melodie re-release, 1996); *Mansa* (Indigo/Harmonia Mundi re-release, 1996); *Mory Kanté & Salif Keita* (Sonodisc, 2000); *De Bamako* (Indigo/Harmonia Mundi re-release, 2001). **Soundtracks:** *Baobab* (Polygram, 1992); *Besieged* (Milan Records, 1999); *Twice Upon a Yesterday* (Narada, 1999); *Ali* (Universal, 2001).

WEBSITE: www.salifkeita.net.

DENNIS POLKOW

TOBY KEITH

Born: Clinton, Oklahoma, 8 July 1961
Genre: Country
Best-selling album since 1990: *Unleashed* (2002)
Hit songs since 1990: "Courtesy of the Red, White, and Blue (The Angry American)," "Should've Been a Cowboy," "Who's That Man"

A relaxed vocalist with a deep, powerful baritone, Toby Keith came on the country scene in the early 1990s sporting a tough, neotraditionalist sound built upon classic country instrumentation of drums, guitar, and fiddles. Changing his basic style little as the 1990s progressed, Keith proved himself a capable songwriter with the ability to probe the psychological underpinnings of his characters. While songs such as "Boomtown" (1995) reveal Keith to be a sharp chronicler of working-class social history, he also succeeds when exploring more conventional country themes of love and loss. The quality of Keith's work has been overshadowed by his controversial 2002 hit "Courtesy of the Red, White and Blue (The Angry American)," a jingoistic response to the terrorist attacks of September 11, 2001.

Born in Oklahoma, Keith developed a love of country music while listening to the musicians who performed in his grandmother's nightclub as a child. After losing his job working in the Oklahoma oil industry, Keith gravitated toward a performing career, playing in local rock and country bands and recording for small labels. In the early 1990s Harold Shedd, a top Nashville producer who had worked with the hit 1980s country band Alabama, heard one of Keith's demo tapes and flew to Oklahoma to hear his band. Impressed, Shedd offered Keith a recording contract with Mercury Records. Keith's self-titled debut album appeared in 1993 and features the energetic, up-tempo hit, "I Should've Been a Cowboy." Like many of Keith's later songs, "Cowboy" expresses a longing for the past, finding comfort in lost traditions: "I should've been a cowboy / I should've learned to rope and ride." Keith's lyrical astuteness was further developed on his second album, *Boomtown* (1995), which, in addition to the social realism of the title track, features incisive ballads such as "Victoria's Secret." Narrating the story of a reputable housewife in the midst of an extramarital affair, Keith displays a talent for fashioning strong characters with distinct points of view. A gifted storyteller, he draws listeners into the woman's life: "Her husband's always working and he's never home / When he's there with her he's still gone."

Although Keith's rowdy sense of humor and detailed songwriting contributed to a long series of country hits during the 1990s and early 2000s, his career became identified with a single recording, "Courtesy of the Red, White, and Blue," subtitled "The Angry American" (2002). One of the most aggressively patriotic recordings to have surfaced in the wake of the terrorist attacks of September 11, 2001, the song drew widespread criticism for its right-wing slant and vulgarity: "We'll put a boot in your ass / It's the American way." Unlike Alan Jackson's more sensitively rendered "Where Were You When the World Stopped Turning," "Red, White, and Blue" depicts an unsettling image of American bellicosity. The extensive popularity of the single helped make the album containing it, *Unleashed* (2002), Keith's biggest commercial success, although the remainder of the album's songs are marked by a subtler approach more in keeping with his earlier work.

Along with Mark Chesnutt and Collin Raye, Toby Keith was part of a wave of 1990s neotraditionalists who sought a return to country's tough-sounding roots. More than his contemporaries, who shifted their sound toward pop as country music became slicker in the late 1990s, Keith largely retained his rough-and-tumble style and flinty personality.

SELECTIVE DISCOGRAPHY: *Toby Keith* (Mercury, 1993); *Boomtown* (Mercury, 1995); *Dream Walkin'* (Mercury, 1997); *How Do You Like Me Now?* (DreamWorks, 1999); *Pull My Chain* (Dream-Works, 2001); *Unleashed* (DreamWorks, 2002).

WEBSITE: www.tobykeith.com.

DAVID FREELAND

R. KELLY

Born: Robert S. Kelly; Chicago, Illinois, 8 January 1967

Genre: R&B, Pop
Best-selling album since 1990: *R. Kelly* (1995)
Hit songs since 1990: "Bump N Grind," "I Believe I Can Fly," "Ignition"

R. Kelly is frequently cited by critics as one of the most talented hip-hop and R&B artists of the 1990s, his work informed with intelligence and breadth of vision. Excelling as a producer, arranger, and instrumentalist, Kelly creates deep, supple music with dense rhythmic grooves. Although his skills as a vocalist are arguably less impressive, he possesses the taste and ability to imbue his performances with a range of influences—notably great R&B singers of the 1960s and 1970s such as Al Green and Marvin Gaye. Like these vocalists, Kelly infuses his material with sexual and religious imagery, emphasizing the carnal and spiritual in equal measure. Attracting controversy during the early 1990s for explicit hits such as "Bump n' Grind," Kelly toned down his image in the mid-1990s to record his best-known song, the inspirational "I Believe I Can Fly." By the early 2000s, Kelly's artistic achievements were overshadowed by a sex-related scandal that threatened to topple his career. Fortunately, he rebounded with *Chocolate Factory* (2003), viewed by critics as one of his finest albums.

Commercial Breakthroughs

Raised in a tough neighborhood on Chicago's South Side, Kelly was no stranger to violence, having been shot during a mugging at an early age. With the support of his mother and a sympathetic teacher, Kelly developed a love for basketball and music, spending his free time performing for money on the streets of Chicago. By 1990 he had put together an R&B group, MGM, and won a talent contest on the television program *Big Break*, hosted by pop and R&B singer Natalie Cole. MGM having disbanded, Kelly met manager Barry Hankerson while auditioning for a play in Chicago. With Hankerson's assistance, Kelly signed with Jive Records in 1991, working initially with the supporting band Public Announcement. After Kelly's first album, *Born into the 90s* (1992), scored with the R&B smash hits, "Honey Love" and "Slow Dance (Hey Mr. DJ)," Kelly returned with his commercial breakthrough, *12 Play* (1993). On the album's biggest hits, "Bump n' Grind" and "Sex Me (Parts I & II)," he cultivated his reputation for erotic themes that pushed boundaries of acceptability within mainstream radio. On "Bump n' Grind," Kelly's gruff, full-bodied vocals—recalling the spirit and tradition of gospel music—are set against a relaxed, seductive groove and lyrics that promote a guilt-free attitude toward sex.

Spot Light | "I Believe I Can Fly"

By 1996 R. Kelly had established a reputation as an R&B craftsperson of the highest order, producing hits for himself as well as for other performers; however, he had yet to fully cross over into the lucrative pop market. The success of "I Believe I Can Fly," recorded as part of the soundtrack for the film *Space Jam* (1996), changed the course of Kelly's career, transforming him from a raunchy specialist in erotic-tinged R&B into a family-friendly balladeer. The song's overwhelming success—it hit number two on the pop and number one on the R&B charts—is due to its uplifting approach, using a surging choir to incorporate the sound of gospel music without making specific reference to divinity. Building upon a long tradition in pop music of "inspirational" songs—"You'll Never Walk Alone," from the 1945 Broadway musical *Carousel,* stands as one example—Kelly emphasizes strength and triumph over challenge: "I was on the verge of breaking down . . . if I can see it, then I can be it / If I just believe it, there's nothing to it." What makes "I Believe I Can Fly" truly memorable, however, is the sincerity of Kelly's singing, which elevates the lyrics into the realm of personal experience. Writing in rock magazine *Rolling Stone*, Rob Sheffield attested, "For the five minutes of 'I Believe,' you hear seasons change, tides turn, and colts grow into stallions." By 1998 when the song won three Grammy Awards, Kelly had not only solidified his career he had created one of the few popular song "standards" of the hip-hop era.

By the mid-1990s, Kelly had also established a reputation as a skilled producer for other artists, including the gospel group the Winans and R&B singers Janet Jackson and Aaliyah. In 1994 Kelly experienced his first taste of controversy when it was revealed that he had married fifteen-year-old Aaliyah, although the union was quickly annulled. In 1995 he returned to his solo career with *R. Kelly*, which tones down the explicit nature of his previous album in favor of "slow jams" that emphasize the romantic side of sex. On the album's opening track, "The

Sermon," Kelly depicts himself as a gospel preacher, defending himself against accusations that his music is excessively lascivious. Elsewhere, he appeals to past musical styles by performing the hit duet, "Down Low (Nobody Has to Know)" with R&B legends the Isley Brothers. Like many contemporary R&B singers, Kelly's singing tends to sound thin, sometimes wavering off-pitch; at the same time, his assured phrasing successfully captures the gentle, pleading style of his R&B forebears. The same deep understanding of R&B and gospel tradition informs his most famous recording, the 1996 smash hit, "I Believe I Can Fly."

Artistic Triumph and Personal Trouble

On the heels of the success of "I Believe I Can Fly," Kelly released *R.* (1998), a two-CD set that stands as one of his most ambitious albums. Ranging from slick pop to gritty R&B—and including a short track where Kelly mimics operatic vocalizing—*R.* is the first album to present Kelly's musical vision in its entirety. In 2000 he returned to more traditional musical territory with *TP-2.Com*, an album composed largely of up-tempo party anthems and ballads. While the album's smooth sound, however, is meant to recall *12 Play*, Kelly takes risks with lyric and theme. Defying traditional hip-hop standards of masculinity, "A Woman's Threat" is a biting track sung from a female point of view: "My man, my lover, my king . . . if you don't stop, someone's gonna lay in your bed." On "I Wish," Kelly struggles with the death of his mother and a close friend, imbuing the song with a sense of loss and conscience. At the same time, songs such as "Feelin' on Yo Booty" threaten to turn his sex-god persona into caricature.

Kelly's career derailed in early 2002, when videotapes surfaced that purportedly depict him engaging in sexual activity with a fourteen-year-old girl. Soon, reports of past settlements for similar suits with underage girls, as well as additional videotapes, came to the fore, prompting a ban by some radio stations on Kelly's music. In June 2002, Kelly was charged with twenty-one counts of child pornography after the girl on the tape was identified as the niece of his former protégée, singer Sparkle. Kelly's career was dealt further blows when his duet album, *The Best of Both Worlds* (2002), recorded with rapper Jay-Z, sold poorly, and his attempts to release another solo recording—to be titled *Loveland*—were hampered by Internet piracy and bootlegging.

In 2003 Kelly regained his reputation and commercial footing with *Chocolate Factory*, an album that hit the top position on both the R&B and pop charts. Hailed by critics as one of his strongest works, the album features "Ignition," a hit that creates an erotic atmosphere through a seductive rhythm and aggressive, full-voiced backup vocalists. Like many of Kelly's best records, "Ignition" stirs a dollop of sexuality into a brew of traditional R&B, capturing a warmth and personality absent from the work of many of his hip-hop peers. Certain editions of *Chocolate Factory* feature a bonus compact disc of selections scrapped from the *Loveland* project. Of these songs, "Heaven I Need a Hug" is a compelling response to the sex allegations Kelly was facing. Singing against a delicate, flowing string arrangement, Kelly captures a disarming poignancy: "Heaven I need a hug / Is there anybody out there willing to embrace a thug?" The song stands out within Kelly's body of work as a striking moment of vulnerability, rare in contemporary R&B.

A multitalented artist who received both acclaim and criticism for his forays into sexual explicitness, Kelly modified his style in the mid-1990s, creating an inspirational, accessible sound with the hit ballad, "I Believe I Can Fly." Exploring many different channels for his talent—production, songwriting, arranging, singing—Kelly maintained his popularity during the 1990s and early 2000s. In the process, he proved his capacity to withstand scandals that would have ended the careers of lesser performers.

SELECTIVE DISCOGRAPHY: *12 Play* (Jive, 1993); *R. Kelly* (Jive, 1995); *R.* (Jive, 1998); *TP-2.Com* (Jive, 2000); *Chocolate Factory* (Jive, 2003). **Soundtracks:** *Space Jam* (Atlantic, 1996).

WEBSITE: www.r-kelly.com.

DAVID FREELAND

KENNY G

Born: Kenny Gorelick; Seattle, Washington, 6 July 1956
Genre: Jazz, Easy Listening
Best-selling album since 1990: *Breathless* (1992)

Kenny G is the best-selling instrumentalist in recording history. His fans have snapped up some 70 million recordings since the release of his debut album, *Kenny G* (1982). He reached the peak of his popularity in the 1990s, selling more than 15 million copies of *Breathless* (1992) worldwide and more than 12 million in the United States. Though he was born and raised Jewish, Kenny G recorded the all-time best-selling Christmas album, *Miracles: The Holiday Album* (1995), which retailed 13 million copies. Playing the high-pitched soprano sax in a dependably mellow, sweet, midtempo manner, the slender, long-haired Kenny G was not the instigator of the enduring "smooth jazz" or "pop instrumental" genre, but he has established himself at the pinnacle of the form, with a legion of fans and imitators far outnumbering the vocal critics who decry his music as cloyingly sweet, banal, and invariably unimaginative.

Of his upbringing, Kenny G told an interviewer in 1997, "I was lucky; my family was fairly well off. I didn't need to have an after-school job when I was in high school. I could spend my time practicing, and by the time I was 21, 22 years old I was making enough through music to pay all my bills." A childhood saxophone student, he toured Europe with his Franklin High School band in 1974, and in 1976 worked his first professional job in Seattle with Barry White's Love Unlimited Orchestra. Kenny G studied accounting at the University of Washington and recorded with Cold, Bold & Together, a funk band that backed up visiting singing acts. Following graduation in 1979, he joined Jeff Lorber Fusion, led by one of the era's reigning electric keyboardists, and then, in 1981, signed a solo contract with Arista Records.

His first three albums—*Kenny G* (1981), *G Force* (1983), and *Gravity* (1985)—were commercially successful; the latter two attained platinum status. *Duotones* (1986), produced by Preston Glass and Narada Michael Walden, was Kenny G's breakthrough, selling more than 500,000, in part on the strength of the hit track "Songbird." *Silhouette* (1988) and *Kenny G Live* (1989) proved that Kenny G's approach—easily played and digested melodic phrases, repeated with slight variation yet suffused with sentiment, over unobtrusive, often-synthesized backgrounds—had staying power. Kenny G was also in demand as a guest soloist with numerous R&B singers. His frequent touring included an appearance at the Newport Jazz Festival in 1987.

In 1990 the newly elected, saxophone-playing President Bill Clinton claimed Kenny G as his favorite jazz musician. *Breathless* (1992) was embraced by an international audience, though it was reviled by jazz aficionados as soporific schlock and was no better received by mainstream rock fans. The recording industry has not been generous in honoring him, either; he's won only one Grammy, in 1993, for Best Instrumental Composition for the track "Forever in Love." Nevertheless, Kenny G remains undaunted. *Miracles: The Holiday Album* (1994), the first of his three holiday albums, features Kenny G's renditions of seasonal staples, including "Winter Wonderland," "Silver Bells," "Away in a Manger," and "Brahms's Lullaby," with his personal stamp on each piece.

The Moment (1996), another multiplatinum recording, was produced by the soul artist Babyface using the elaborate process of studio overdubbing (as opposed to live-in-the-studio collaborations) through which all Kenny G's albums have been created. Babyface sings "Every Time I Close My Eyes," and the vocalist Toni Braxton, with whom Kenny G shared a tour bill in the mid-1990s, sings "That Somebody Was You." Notwithstanding the guest appearances by soul singers and occasional Latin rhythm accents, Kenny G's sound appeals largely to listeners who have little exposure to or taste for original music with venturesome qualities. His album *Classics in the Key of G* raises this point to a height of controversy; in this collection he covers beloved songs such as Sam Cooke's "You Send Me," with Michael Bolton providing the vocal, and "What a Wonderful World," the last recording by Louis Armstrong, into which Kenny G overdubs a saxophone solo.

Kenny G's contrivance of a posthumous duet with Armstrong, a major pioneer of the jazz trumpet and vocalization, was the crowning outrage for legions of serious music devotees. The guitarist Pat Metheny said, "Kenny G plays the dumbest music on the planet—something that all 8- to 11-year-[old] kids on the planet already intrinsically know." Asked on his website to express himself more fully, the characteristically mild-mannered Metheny accused Kenny G of "musical necrophilia" and stated, "By disrespecting Louis, his legacy and by default, everyone who has ever tried to do something positive with improvised music and what it can be, Kenny G has created a new low point in modern culture—something that we all should be totally embarrassed about—and afraid of."

Such indictments do not concern Kenny G, who continues to record and tour, garnering high fees and unprecedented sales. *Faith: A Holiday Album* (1999) repeated the success of *Miracles*; it features "Eternal Light (A Chanukah Song)" and "Ave Maria." During celebrations of the millennium in January 2000, Kenny G had a U.S. Top 10 single with his version of "Auld Lang Syne." *Paradise* (2002) features Chante Moore singing "One More Time" and Brian McKnight singing "All the Way," two tracks that received considerable airplay on radio stations following Adult Contemporary, New Adult Contemporary, and Urban Adult Contemporary formats. *Wishes: A Holiday Album* (2002) features G's interpretations of "Joy to the World" and the medley "Rudolph the Rednose Reindeer/Frosty the Snowman."

The split decision on Kenny G's music persists. The hearty disdain of the relatively small community of serious musicians and critics and the adulation of a vast public raise the question: Can 70 million record and CD buyers be wrong?

SELECTIVE DISCOGRAPHY: *Breathless* (Arista, 1992); *Miracles: The Holiday Album* (Arista, 1994); *The Moment* (Arista, 1996); *Greatest Hits* (Arista, 1997); *Classics in the Key of G* (Arista, 1999); *Faith: A Holiday Album* (Arista 1999); *Paradise* (Arista, 2002); *Wishes: A Holiday Album* (Arista 2002).

WEBSITES: www.vh1.com/artists/az/g_kennyParadise; www.vh1.com/artists/az/g_kenny/bio.jhtml;

www.bmi.com/musicworld/features/200210/kenny_g.asp.

HOWARD MANDEL

ALICIA KEYS

Born: Alicia Augello Cook; New York, New York, 4 January 1981

Genre: R&B

Best-selling album since 1990: *Songs in A Minor* (2001)

Hit songs since 1990: "Fallin'," "A Woman's Worth"

Alicia Keys is a pop phenomenon. The classically trained, piano-playing R&B prodigy was carefully groomed for success by the music industry legend Clive Davis, whose smarts paid off when Keys's 2001 debut album, *Songs in a Minor*, became one of the breakout hits of the year. Songs such as "Fallin'" and "A Woman's Worth" rocketed Keys to the top of the pop heap with their combination of timeless 1970s soul, classical piano, and hip-hop sensibility.

A native of New York's rough-and-tumble Hell's Kitchen neighborhood, Keys was born to an Italian-American mother, Terri Augello, and African-American father, Craig Cook. She began piano lessons at age five, and, after her parents split, her mother, a paralegal and part-time actress, was left to raise Keys alone in sometimes difficult circumstances.

Her mother's record collection, which included such diverse artists as Beethoven, Roberta Flack, U2, Miles Davis, and Ella Fitzgerald, prodded Keys to keep up her piano playing, no matter the cost. By the age of seven, Keys was proficient in classical piano, and by eleven she began writing original songs. (She penned the song "Butterflyz" at age fourteen; it ended up on *Songs in A Minor*.) Keys majored in choir at the Professional Performing Arts School of Manhattan as a teen, graduating early at age sixteen, having already signed and rescinded a 1995 deal with Capitol Records.

Her manager, Jeff Robinson, had begun booking Keys at important music industry events during her senior year, leading to a hectic life of studying, practicing, and performing. Though she entered Columbia University on a full scholarship in 1995, the allure of the music business was too great, and Keys dropped out after just four weeks to focus on her just-signed recording contract with Columbia Records.

While Columbia pushed Keys to model herself on such established stars as Mariah Carey and Whitney Houston, the singer was not interested in fitting into an established mold, and the deal faltered after producing only one

Alicia Keys [JOSHUA JORDAN/J-RECORDS-BIFF WARREN]

song, "Dah Dee Dah (Sexy Thing)," for the soundtrack of the 1997 film *Men in Black*. Just a few months later the president of Arista Records, Clive Davis, caught a showcase performance by the seventeen-year-old singer and signed her on the spot.

Just as Keys finished *Songs in A Minor*, Davis was ousted from his position in 1998, and Keys's career went on hold. Davis took Keys with him to his new label, J Records, formed in 1999. While waiting for her debut to be released, Keys appeared on Jermaine Dupri's *Jermaine Dupri Presents: 12 Soulful Nights*, Jimmy Cozier's self-titled debut, and Da Brat's *Unrestricted*. She also contributed the songs "Rock Wit U" to the *Shaft (2000)* soundtrack and "Rear View Mirror" to the *Dr. Doolittle 2* soundtrack.

After months of Davis-secured appearances on BET and MTV, and *The Oprah Winfrey Show* (courtesy of a personal plea to Winfrey from Davis), *Songs in A Minor* was released in June 2001, debuting at number one on the *Billboard* 200 album chart and selling nearly 3 million copies within three weeks.

Although Keys wrote most of its songs while still in her teens, *Songs In A Minor* carries an old soul wisdom, sagacity, and heartache that belies her age. Written and co-produced almost entirely by Keys, the album blends clas-

sical, jazz, R&B, and hip-hop influences on tracks such as "Fallin'," the album's first single, which pervaded pop, R&B, and video outlets upon release. It is a pop-gospel song with a classical piano feel about a failed romance, conveyed by a voice that is strong, sexy, confident yet vulnerable. Songs about failed romance, respect, and independence earned Keys comparisons to R&B artists such as Roberta Flack and Aretha Franklin, while her love of hip-hop style and attitude pegged Keys as thoroughly modern. The combination was a breath of fresh air amid a sea of prepackaged female artists whose images and performances were typically directed by their male collaborators. Keys cemented her crossover appeal by collaborating with the rapper Eve on her hit 2002 single, "Gangsta Lovin'." During her live concerts, Keys often led her twelve-piece band through medleys that incorporated Beethoven and bits of songs by rapper Notorious B.I.G., pop star Michael Jackson, 1960s rockers the Doors, and soul legend Marvin Gaye, synthesizing the diverse influences of her youth.

In addition to hundreds of appearances, magazine covers, and interviews, Keys gained critical acceptance for her work in 2002, garnering an MTV Video Music Award for Best New Artist, two *Billboard* Awards, two American Music Awards, two NAACP Image Awards, three Soul Train Awards, and five Grammys. In late 2002 Keys began developing talent for her own company, Krucial Keys Enterprise, and began work on her second album, scheduled for a 2003 release. Keys was also expected to make her film debut in late 2003.

Although it was the flavor of the day, Alicia Keys knew she was not destined to be a choreographed, belly-baring teen music queen. With the help of Clive Davis, the prodigiously talented singer/songwriter exploded onto the R&B scene in 2001 with *Songs in A Minor*, the multimillion-selling first chapter in what is sure to be a long career.

SELECTIVE DISCOGRAPHY: *Songs in A Minor* (J Records, 2001).

WEBSITE: www.aliciakeys.net.

GIL KAUFMAN

NUSRAT FATEH ALI KHAN

Born: Lyallpur (now Faisalabad), Pakistan, 13 October 1948; died London, England, 16 August 1997

Genre: World

Best-selling album since 1990: *Mustt Mustt* (1991)

Nusrat Fateh Ali Khan, son of the revered *qawwali* (a professional singer of mystical Sufi poetry) Ustad Fateh Ali Khan, took over his father's Party (male-only ensemble) in 1971, and by the end of his life he had popularized a specifically spiritual genre as a music of ecstatic release among non-Sufi Westerners, even adapting the style's ancient tenets to pop-oriented song forms and arrangements.

Qawwali is a modal music performed by one or two improvising vocalists over and in alternation with a vocal chorus, supported by vigorous percussion, handclapping, and a harmonium (portable pump-organ) that underscores the melody. Sung in Farsi, Hindi, and Urdu, the lyrics of qawwali draw on both Islamic and Hindu poetic traditions, usually repeating a few lines that employ subjects such as romantic love and alcoholic intoxication as metaphors for the adoration of God and inner enlightenment. Nusrat Fateh Ali Khan, an overweight, heavily sweating performer with a beaklike nose, was not conventionally charismatic but sang with enormous drive and passion in a slightly hoarse voice that was capable of elaborate, seemingly inspired phrases. The late singer/songwriter Jeff Buckley likened Khan's voice to "a velvet fire," and his utterances do indeed seem to rise and singe the air like flame.

Khan first performed to a predominantly Western audience in 1985, at Peter Gabriel's WOMAD (World of Music, Arts, and Dance) festival at Mersea Island, Essex, England. Besides introducing qawwali to young white audiences in Great Britain and the United States, he de-emphasized the music's devotional content (but not its inherent energy) to establish it as a soundtrack staple in the Bollywood Indian and Pakistani film industries and as a feature of soundtracks for some American-made movies, including *Dead Man Walking* (1995), in which he duetted in qawwali style with Eddie Vedder of Pearl Jam; *Passion*, the Peter Gabriel–produced soundtrack to Martin Scorsese's *Last Temptation of Christ* (1988); and Oliver Stone's *Natural Born Killers* (1995).

Ustad Fateh Ali Khan discouraged his son's interest in qawwali despite their family's six-century heritage of musicianship, urging him to study medicine, but as a child Khan eavesdropped on music lessons his father gave to gain an understanding of the fundamentals of the genre. Shortly after his father's death in 1964, Khan sang for the first time in public and then commenced serious study of the qawwali form with his uncle Ustad Salamat Ali Khan. He joined his uncle Ustad Marbarik Ali Khan's qawwali party. He gained personal recognition and popularity upon speeding up the tempo of the music, and when Ustad Marbarik fell ill in 1971, Khan claimed leadership of his group. In 1979 he realized his recurring vision to become the first qawwali to sing at the Muslim shrine Hazrat Khwaja Moin-ud-Din Chisti in Ajmer, India, where neither qawwalis nor Pakistanis had previously been welcome.

First recording in 1973, Khan became prolific, recording more than fifty albums for Pakistani, British,

American, European, and Japanese labels by 1993. Don Heckman, a music journalist for the *Los Angeles Times*, has proposed that Khan's "Western reputation was built through live performance." Nonetheless, Khan actively courted a crossover audience by recording the album *Musst Musst* (1991) with the experimental composer Michael Brook. Khan and Brook cut typically expansive qawwali performances to pop-song length, employed vocal exercises rather than words as the basis of the vocals, and underscored everything with Western rhythms. Massive Attack's remix of the title track was a surprise club hit throughout the United Kingdom.

Khan died of natural causes accelerated by general ill health and exhaustion brought on by continuous world touring. Lacking a male heir, he passed his musical legacy on to a nephew, Rahat Nusrat Fateh Ali Khan. Posthumously, his own voice continues to burn in remix collections, especially by Asian-British musicians such as those in the Asian Dub Foundation.

SELECTIVE DISCOGRAPHY: *Rough Guide to Nusrat Fateh Ali Khan* (World Music Network, 2002); *The Final Studio Recordings* (American Recording Company, 2001); *Bandit Queen* (Milan, 2000); *The Supreme Collection Vol. 1* (Caroline, 1997); *Greatest Hits Vol. 2* (Shanchie Records, 1998); *Greatest Hits Vol. 1* (Shanachie, 1997); *Mustt Mustt* (Real-World/CEMA 1991); *The Day, the Night, the Dawn, the Dusk* (Shanchie, 1991). **With Peter Gabriel:** *Passion* (Universal Music, 2002). **With Eddie Vedder:** *Dead Man Walking Soundtrack* (Columbia, 1996); *Natural Born Killers Soundtrack* (Interscope, 1994); *Asian Dub Foundation remix: Community Music* (London, 2001).

HOWARD MANDEL

KID ROCK

Born: Robert James Ritchie; Romeo, Michigan, 15 January 1971

Genre: Rock, Rap

Best-selling album since 1990: *Devil without a Cause* (1998)

Hit songs since 1990: "Bawitdaba," "Cowboy," "Devil without a Cause"

It took Bob Ritchie nearly a decade to become an overnight sensation. But when the rapper known as Kid Rock finally hit the big time with his 1998 major-label debut, *Devil without a Cause*, the Hank Williams–loving hip-hop outlaw turned millions of heads with his utterly unique amalgam of profane sexual boasting, old school hip-hop bragging, country blues and rock, heavy metal, and Detroit funk. With a brash, bad-boy persona that shamelessly glorifies blue collar/white trash American culture, Kid Rock rivaled only fellow Detroit native Eminem for mainstream popularity and notoriety in the late 1990s, selling millions of records and gaining respect from his African-American rap peers for his prowess on the microphone and skills as a producer.

Born in rural Romeo, Michigan, unlike many rappers from the inner cities, Kid Rock grew up in a well-adjusted, middle-class household with his stay-at-home mother, Susan, and successful businessman father, Bill. Kid Rock often butted heads with his demanding dad—he later titled a song "My Oedipus Complex"—who had wanted his son to take over his car dealership. A fan of classic rocker Bob Seger, as well as country artists such as Hank Williams Jr., Kid Rock became enthralled with hip-hop upon receiving his first set of turntables at age thirteen. Shortly after, Kid Rock attended a dance party in Detroit and took his first shot at working two turntables in front of an audience. The spur-of-the-moment performance landed him a regular gig at a club in the Detroit suburb of Mt. Clemens, where he played to an all-black, urban crowd.

The notoriety led to a recording contract with New York–based Jive Records, which released his debut, *Grits Sandwiches for Breakfast* (1990). The album, produced by Kid Rock and rapper Too $hort, features the ode to oral sex, "Yo-Da-Lin in the Valley," which drew the ire of the Federal Communications Commission and a $23,000 fine—later rescinded—after a college disc jockey played the song on the air. Though crudely produced, the album has a hint of the style that would make Kid Rock successful: a mixture of ceaseless boasting, swatches of funk and classic rock, and an obvious love and respect for classic hip-hop music.

Jive Can't Jibe with Rock

The still relatively unknown eighteen-year-old white rapper—who had already begun honing his Beastie Boys–inspired combination of hard rock and rap—managed to get an opening slot on a twenty-city tour with rap legends Ice Cube and Too $hort. The controversy over the song resulted in some national press for Kid Rock, but Jive had had enough of the rapper's antics and dropped him from their roster.

Kid Rock then signed a deal with the small Continuum label and explored an even harder combination of rock, rap, and a touch of country on his second album, *The Polyfuse Method* (1993). A short, more rock/rap-oriented album, *Fire It Up* followed a year later on Kid Rock's own Top Dog imprint, but neither album gained Kid Rock the national audience he sought.

Despondent, he returned to Detroit and began recording his third album, *Early Mornin' Stoned Pimp* (1996), which he produced and released on Top Dog. The album is the finest example of the rapper's signature sound: thick, funk-inspired bass and guitar ("Paid"), 1960s soul ("Detroit Thang"), and plenty of Kid Rock's shouted/rapped bragging over a mix of programmed beats and squealing guitar solos ("My Name Is Rock"). Also contributing to the album are Black Crowes keyboard player Eddie Harsch and Detroit soul singer Thornetta Davis.

Around the same time, Kid Rock put together a live band consisting of Detroit musicians to help perform the album's more elaborate songs live. The group, Twisted Brown Trucker, featured diminutive rapper Joe C., guitarists Kenny Olson and Jason Krause, keyboardist Jimmie Bones, drummer Stefanie Eulinberg, DJ/turntablist Uncle Kracker (who had been with Kid Rock since the early 1990s), and backing vocalists Misty Love and Shirley Hayden. The album—financed with a loan from Kid Rock's father—caught the attention of Atlantic Records, which signed him to a recording deal.

Under Intense Pressure, Kid Rock Produces a Classic

Crippled by a bout of writer's block and pressure from his new label to produce an album with more rock and less rap, Kid Rock foundered in his initial attempts to record *Devil without a Cause* (1998). Recorded in just one week, the album shows no sign of a difficult birth, however. In fact, against the wishes of his label, Kid Rock boasts "I'm going platinum" on the album's title track, a presumptuous statement given that he had never sold more than several thousand copies of his previous records.

The boast would prove prophetic, however, as the unique combination of soulful southern rock/rap ("Wasting Time," "Cowboy"), metal-infused hip-hop ("Bawitdaba," "Roving Gangster"), and classic hip-hop ("Welcome 2 the Party") reached stores just as the combination of rock and rap was beginning to explode on the charts thanks to bands such as Limp Bizkit. Few were using the vast resources employed by Kid Rock, which ranged from a live band to samples of groups such as Fleetwood Mac ("Wastin' Time") and hip-hop classics from Whodini and his early benefactor, Too $hort. Kid Rock also revived an older song, "Black Chic, White Guy," a true story of interracial dating from his past, which includes the lyrics, "He came from a family of middle class / Where everything he did he always had to ask / She came from a place that was so alone / You know the same old tale of a broken home."

The album sold slowly at first, but with the help of flashy videos for songs such as "Bawitdaba" and "Devil without a Cause," Kid Rock became a staple on MTV and the album eventually sold 10 million copies. In his signature felt hat, white undershirt, baggy pants, and white fur coat, Kid Rock was one of the star attractions at the ill-fated Woodstock '99 concert in July. In September, Kid Rock took the stage with hip-hop legends Run-D.M.C. and classic rockers Aerosmith at the MTV Video Music Awards, uniting the old friends for a version of the hit 1980s Aerosmith/Run-D.M.C. collaboration, "Walk This Way."

A bona fide star, Kid Rock indulged in his penchant for partying in the company of adult film stars, but also spent 2000 producing the debut from Uncle Kracker and collaborating with artists such as Sheryl Crow and Run-D.M.C., releasing a career retrospective, *The History of Rock* and touring with Metallica all summer. November 16 brought the death of sidekick Joe C. from a chronic intestinal disorder.

Kid Rock returned to the studio, amidst the distracting din of attention paid to his high-profile relationship with actress Pamela Anderson, and emerged with the new studio album *Cocky* (2001). With cameos from Crow and rapper Snoop Dogg, *Cocky* has even more of a rock and country edge than Kid Rock's previous albums, especially on songs such as the first single, the heavy metal/rap anthem "Forever." Over wailing guitars, Kid Rock rhymes "I make punk rock / And I mix it with the hip-hop." Never at a loss for swaggering words of self-confidence, the album features a number of paeans to Kid Rock's newfound riches and trophy girlfriend, but fans did not connect with the songs as they did with his smash breakthrough.

Kid Rock took to the road with his heroes in Run-D.M.C. and Aerosmith for a summer 2002 tour and followed it up with a role in the film *Biker Boyz*. Even after selling millions of albums with his rock/rap/country hybrid, Kid Rock maintained a home in a Detroit suburb, expressed his love for recreational vehicles and alcohol, and dressed like an extra in a circa 1975 country music video. Rock reached the pinnacle of pop success in the late 1990s by sticking to his guns and creating an outsized outlaw style and image that was unique, and, perhaps more importantly, believable.

SELECTIVE DISCOGRAPHY: *Grits Sandwiches for Breakfast* (Jive/Novus, 1990); *The Polyfuze Method* (Continuum, 1993); *Fire It Up* (Continuum, 1994); *Early Mornin' Stoned Pimp* (Top Dog, 1996); *Devil without a Cause* (Lava/Atlantic, 1998); *The History of Rock* (Lava/Atlantic, 2000); *Cocky* (Atlantic, 2001).

SELECTIVE FILMOGRAPHY: *Biker Boyz* (2003).

GIL KAUFMAN

ANGÉLIQUE KIDJO

Born: Cotonou, Benin, 14 June 1960

Genre: World

Best-selling album since 1990: *Keep on Moving: The Best of Angélique Kidjo* (2001)

Angélique Kidjo is the most popular and successful African female vocalist to have emerged since the heyday of South African singer Miriam Makeba in the 1960s. Kidjo has managed to successfully create her own unique style of Afropop that is characterized by funky, African-based dance rhythms topped off by contagious Western pop-inspired melodic hooks sung with a rich, contralto voice so evocative and beautiful that Dave Matthews describes it as the "voice of God."

A native of Benin, located between Togo and Nigeria in West Africa, Kidjo was one of nine children born into a performing family. Her mother, a director and a choreographer, ran a local theater troupe in Ouidah, where Kidjo learned to dance, sing, and act from the age of six. Her father and brothers were guitarists and helped Kidjo master traditional Benin and Indian music as well as Western pop and rock music with the Kidjo Brothers Band as a teenager before she struck out on her own to perform on radio broadcasts and in music festivals throughout Benin.

A woman performing alone was still looked down upon in Benin culture; however, when government repression made it clear that Kidjo could not freely express herself, she fled the country and in 1983 moved to Paris to study law. While in Paris she met other exiled African and Caribbean musicians as well as French and American artists, all of whom helped her to learn and cross-fertilize the wide variety of international styles that would become part of her performing arsenal when she decided to pursue a music career. Kidjo joined the Afro-funk group Alafia before singing and recording Afro-jazz-rock fusion with Pili Pili. Then, in 1987, she formed her own band with French bassist, composer, and producer Jean Hebrail, who also became her husband. Together they recorded her first album in the West, *Parakou* (1990), as well as follow-ups.

Loganzo (1991) gave Kidjo her first commercial airplay with her first dance hit, "Batonga"; the album included a nod to her idol and role model Miriam Makeba, the Swahili ballad "Malaika," which Makeba had made famous. Joining Kidjo on her first major American tour as part of the 1992 African Fete were Branford Marsalis, who had performed on *Loganzo*, and Peter Gabriel.

The hit single "Agolo" from *Ayé* (1994) and its colorful Grammy Award–nominated music video further established Kidjo as an international star and as a staple of the dance club scene. *Fifa* (1996) is a salute to Kidjo's Benin roots and features the guitar work of Carlos Santana on "Naïma." Kidjo's dynamic voice has also been a regular presence on soundtracks of movies that have included a string of unrelated singles. The most popular of these was Kidjo's performance of "We Are One" for *The Lion King II: Simba's Pride* (1998).

Oremi (1998) ("my friends") is the first in a trilogy of albums that are part of a Kidjo-led guided tour of the music of the black diaspora. As a cultural ambassador Kidjo offers a statement of her own African roots but also seeks to demonstrate how African music has both influenced and been influenced by African-American musicians, especially those of the R&B variety. *Oremi* opens with an African send-up of Jimi Hendrix's "Voodoo Child." Guest performers on the album include Robbie Nevil, Cassandra Wilson, Branford Marsalis, and Kelly Price. *Black Ivory Soul* (2002) moves Kidjo's tour into South America; it is a festive exploration of the kinship between African and Brazilian music. Performing guests include Roots drummer Ahmir Thompson and Dave Matthews. The third album of the completed trilogy will explore the African connection to music of Haiti, Cuba, and New Orleans.

Kidjo mostly sings in Fon, Benin's primary language, but she also sings in Yoruba, French, and English. Part of Kidjo's unique ability to bond with her audiences while she performs is that singing was always a vital part of everyday life personally and publicly in Benin. The vital importance of dancing, a natural expression of Benin culture and of the voodoo religion that originated there, is also obvious as Kidjo contagiously gyrates her way through her concerts, often inspiring audience members to join with her in joyous jubilation.

SELECTIVE DISCOGRAPHY: *Parakou* (Aye, 1990); *Loganzo* (Mango/Island, 1991); *Ayé* (Mango/Island, 1994); *Fifa* (Mango/Island, 1996); *Amazing Grace* (Island, 1997); *Oremi* (Mango/Island, 1998); *Lilith Fair: A Celebration of Women in Music, Volume 2* (Arista, 1999); *Keep on Moving: The Best of Angélique Kidjo* (Wrasse Columbia, 2001); *Black Ivory Soul* (Columbia, 2002); *Cover the World: World Music Versions of Classic Pop Hits* (Putumayo World Music, 2003). **Soundtracks:** *Street Fighter* (MCA, 1994); *Ace Ventura: When Nature Calls* (MCA, 1995); *Lion King II: Simba's Pride* (Disney, 1998); *The Wild Thornberrys Movie* (Jive, 2002); *The Truth About Charlie* (Sony, 2002); *People I Know* (Universal, 2003).

BIBLIOGRAPHY: A. McGovern, *Musichound World: The Essential Album Guide* (New York, 2000).

WEBSITE: www.angeliquekidjo.com.

DENNIS POLKOW

B.B. KING

Born: Riley King; Indianola, Mississippi, 16 September 1925
Genre: Blues
Best-selling album since 1990: *Blues Summit* (1993)

Known worldwide as the undisputed "King of the Blues," B.B. King ranks as one of the most important figures in popular music. His inventive yet straightforward guitar playing, which fuses jazz and gospel elements with blues, has influenced not only younger blues performers but also rock artists such as Eric Clapton and the late Jimi Hendrix. In addition, he is a tough, bellowing vocalist who delves into the emotional core of his songs. Beyond King's flexible, conversational guitar style and powerful singing, his great contribution lies in bringing blues music to a mainstream audience. Performing live between two hundred and three hundred nights per year, recording albums well into his seventies, King is a formidable presence whose work has become part of the American cultural fabric.

Roots and Blues Stardom

Raised in the Mississippi Delta, an area of northern Mississippi rich in blues history, King worked the land as a sharecropper from an early age, living alternately with his mother, grandmother, and father. In 1946 he traveled to nearby Memphis, Tennessee, to seek out his cousin, Bukka White, a well-known practitioner of blues music. King studied with his cousin for ten months, gaining invaluable instruction in guitar playing. By 1949 King had become a popular disc jockey on Memphis radio station WDIA, the first station in the country to adopt an all-black programming format. It was at WDIA that King came up with his distinctive initials, short for "Blues Boy." In 1951 he recorded his first national hit, "Three O' Clock Blues," in Memphis for the Los Angeles–based RPM label. King remained with RPM, later known as Kent, until moving to the larger ABC label in 1962. At ABC he released a number of fine albums, including the classic *Live at the Regal* (1965), the first recording to capture the energy and charisma of King's live shows. In 1969 his version of the blues song, "The Thrill Is Gone," became a pop and R&B hit on the strength of a haunting string arrangement and his searing vocals. The success of the single brought King a new degree of prominence in nightclubs, on television, and on college campuses. During this period, many up-and-coming rock musicians were influenced by King's trademark guitar style, which features a distinctive *tremolo*, or trilling sound. Rock performers of the 1970s also borrowed his technique of playing extended guitar solos without vocal accompaniment, a practice stemming from King's inability to play and sing at the same time.

A Nontraditional Career

By the 1990s King was regarded as the nation's leading ambassador of the blues, given the kind of reverence shown to jazz legend Louis Armstrong decades earlier. At an age when many performers retire, King pushed himself even further, recording the acclaimed *Blues Summit* album in 1993. The album, in which King duets with well-known blues artists such as Robert Cray and Etta James, creates an infectious party atmosphere with the enthusiasm of respected colleagues working together. The collaboration with Cray, "Playing with My Friends," is a highlight, with King and his younger disciple trading vocals and dexterous guitar licks in a spirit of mutual admiration. *Blues Summit* won a Grammy Award for Best Traditional Blues Album in 1993, with jazz magazine *Down Beat* calling it "just plain, raw, sweaty, down-home blues with a sense of humor and a lot of spontaneous interaction in the studio, the way records ought to be made."

As the 1990s progressed King continued to record challenging, rewarding albums. Nowhere is his vitality better displayed than on *Blues on the Bayou* (1998). Recorded with his touring band in a small Louisiana studio, the album features a rich, full sound that captures the exuberant spirit of his live shows. On his composition, "Blues Man," he begins with simplicity and directness, singing "I'm a blues man, but I'm a good man—understand," pouring into the short line a lifetime of sadness and resignation. As the song progresses he slowly builds to a burning rage, shouting, "I would be all right, people, just give me a break." The track displays one of King's greatest strengths as a singer: finding the peak emotional moments in a song and emphasizing them with all the power of his voice. As a vocalist King understands how the balance between power and restraint affects a listener's response, and he manipulates this balance with a master's skill.

In 1999 King released one of his most personal albums, a tribute to great 1940s and 1950s bandleader Louis Jordan titled *Let the Good Times Roll*. The album emphasizes the light-hearted side of the blues, with titles from the Jordan canon including "Ain't Nobody Here but Us Chickens" and "Saturday Night Fish Fry." On "I'm Gonna Move to the Outskirts of Town," the song that made Jordan a rhythm and blues star in 1942, King plays with delicate precision, milking the lines for their risqué humor: "It may seem funny, honey / Funny as funny can be / But if we have any children / I want them *all* to look like me." While Jordan's style was flashier and more exuberant than King's, the two artists share much in common. Chiefly, Jordan was one of the great musical show

B.B. King [PAUL NATKIN/PHOTO RESERVE]

personalities of his day, his entertaining stage presence influencing King's own shows. In live performance, the environment longtime fans believe represents King at his best, he incorporates humor into the hardest, most biting blues, singing to the audience with mock sobs, "Nobody loves me but my mother—sometimes I think she could be jiving too." In the 1990s, although health problems forced him to perform sitting down, King remained a fascinating presence onstage: Telling jokes and closing his eyes as he played stinging riffs on his guitar (affectionately named "Lucille"), critics confirm he created an aura of high-spirited excitement.

For many music fans and performers, B.B. King represents the standard by which other blues artists are judged. His emotive singing and guitar playing have won him lasting respect among fellow musicians. Most importantly, his prolific recorded output and engaging live shows made the blues popular with a mainstream audience. Without King's lasting influence, the blues as an art form might otherwise have been neglected.

SELECTIVE DISCOGRAPHY: *Singin' the Blues* (Crown, 1956); *Live at the Regal* (ABC, 1965); *Completely Well* (Bluesway, 1969); *Live in Cook County Jail* (ABC, 1971); *There Must Be a Better World Somewhere* (MCA, 1981); *Blues Summit* (MCA, 1993); *Blues on the Bayou* (MCA, 1998); *Let the Good Times Roll: The Music of Louis Jordan* (MCA, 1999); *Riding with the King* (with Eric Clapton; Reprise, 2000); *Makin' Love Is Good for You* (MCA, 2000).

WEBSITE: www.bbking.com.

DAVID FREELAND

KISS

Formed: 1973, New York, New York

Members: Peter Criss, drums, vocals (George Peter John Criscoula; born Brooklyn, New York, 20 December 1945); Ace Frehley, guitar, vocals (Paul Daniel Frehley; born Bronx, New York, 27 April 1951); Gene Simmons, bass, vocals (Chaim Witz, changed to Gene Klein; born Haifa, Israel, 25 August 1949); Paul Stanley, guitar, vocals (Stanley Harvey Eisen; born Queens, New York, 20 January 1952). Former members: Eric Carr, drums (Paul Charles Caravello; born Brooklyn, New York, 12 July 1950; died New York, New York, 24 November 1991); Bruce Kulick, guitar (Bruce Howard Kulick; born Brooklyn, New York, 12 December 1953); Eric Singer, drums (Eric D. Mensinger; born Cleveland, Ohio, 12 May 1958); Mark St. John, guitar (Mark Norton; born Hollywood, California, 7 February 1956); Vinnie Vincent, guitar (Vincent John Cusano; born Bridgeport, Connecticut, 6 August 1952).

Genre: Rock

Best-selling album since 1990: *Unplugged* (1996)

Despite what critics say about them musically, the extravagant rock group KISS will forever occupy an exalted corner of rock history as one of those rare bands responsible for expanding the boundaries of formulaic image, stage demeanor, and aggressive marketing. Illustrious for a ten-year commitment to shielding their identities with elaborate stage makeup, KISS refined the showy theatrical rock styles of David Bowie and Alice Cooper into a choreographed rock and roll circus. The original members of the band reunited in the 1990s and achieved album sales success with slightly less hype and more attention to their music.

Standing in six-inch platform shoes, clad in shiny shoulder-padded costumes, and faces caked with Japanese Kabuki-styled makeup, the four-piece KISS took the rock and roll world by storm in the mid-1970s. It began when Queens, New York, natives, bassist Chiam Witz (Gene Simmons) and guitarist Stan Eisen (Paul Stanley), decided to form a new group after their band, Wicked Lester, folded. They added fellow New Yorkers, guitarist Paul Frehley (Ace Frehley) and drummer George Criscoula (Peter Criss), and embarked on a journey to play hard rock music and garner as much attention as possible by donning costumes and makeup in order to transform themselves into maniacal characters. Simmons came naturally equipped with an unusually long tongue, which he wagged relentlessly, that added perfectly to his demon character. He was also infamous for blowing fire out of his mouth onstage. Stanley was a hunky lothario with lush lips and a star on one eye. Criss, with his painted-on whiskers, looked like a futuristic cat as he beat away on the drums, and Frehley, in a silver and black spacesuit, resembled an outer space creature manipulating the guitar. As they rehearsed material in a Manhattan loft, a choreographer guided them toward a well-rehearsed stage show replete with an extensive light show and exploding flash pots.

KISS cut a record deal with Casablanca Records and toured extensively in 1973 and 1974, gaining fan recognition at every stop. However, as audiences from all across North America were enthralled with KISS's walloping rock and flashy stage show, critics showed great disdain for their music. Not yet introduced to punk rock or to the heavy metal soon to come, critics labeled KISS's music simplistic and vapid. None of the commentary stopped people from buying their records or attending shows and by the release of their live album, *Alive* (1975), the members of KISS were bona fide rock superstars, and no one knew who they were. With makeup hiding their faces, the members of KISS kept their identities a closely guarded secret by staying in full regalia at all times in public. They recorded a massive amount of records, sometimes releasing several in one year. In 1978 each member of KISS released a separate solo album. They scored a hit with the rock standard "Rock and Roll All Nite," and another with the power ballad "Beth." They became adept marketers and managed to get their KISS label on virtually everything, providing extra royalty money when their popularity began to wane in the 1980s.

KISS went through several band member changes and finally abandoned their makeup in 1983. The late 1980s saw an increased popularity in heavy metal hair bands and KISS managed to rise with the tide. They entered the 1990s having sold nearly 70 million records. They had released more than forty albums, many of them various compilations that recycled song after song. In 1996 the original four members gathered to perform on MTV's live acoustic venue, *Unplugged*. The subsequent album from that session went platinum.

In 1997 KISS released their first studio album in five years and one of their most intriguing, *Carnival of Souls*. The band's lineup consisted of Simmons, Stanley, guitarist Bruce Kulick, and Eric Singer on drums. *Carnival of Souls* contains a deeper grunge sound more associated with bands like Nirvana. The album sold poorly as years of driving, one-dimensional power rock conditioned KISS's massive fan base into expecting a certain signature sound. The original members gathered again to record *Psycho Circus* (1998), an effort that duplicates their work from the 1970s. One of the highlights for KISS fans on *Psycho Circus* is the energetic, "I Pledge Allegiance to the State of Rock and Roll." Another favorite is Criss singing the power ballad, "I Finally Found My Way Home." KISS promoted the album with a successful tour as they performed decked out in full costume and the makeup of their 1970s concert days.

KISS continues to release a wide variety of compilation albums and they have taken advantage of the Internet to expand their barefaced marketing shrewdness. KISS goes light years beyond selling T-shirts, posters, and buttons to hawk items as diverse as condoms, credit cards, children's lunch boxes, school supplies, action figures, paper goods, home décor, and monthly memberships to a XXX website, to name a few. They even have a portion of their website dedicated to female fans, featuring them as KISS Girls by having a provocative picture of them displayed.

In 2003 the original members of KISS toured in full costume and makeup with the legendary rock group Aerosmith. Individually, each member of KISS has attempted solo careers with varying measures of success. Due to their flamboyant and innovative presentation, KISS will always tend to be more closely associated with their show than their music.

SELECTIVE DISCOGRAPHY: *KISS* (Casablanca, 1974); *Hotter Than Hell* (Casablanca, 1974); *Dressed to Kill* (Casablanca, 1975); *Alive* (Casablanca, 1975); *Destroyer* (Casablanca, 1976); *KISS—The Originals* (Casablanca, 1976); *Rock and Roll Over* (Casablanca, 1976); *Love Gun* (Casablanca, 1977); *Alive 2* (Casablanca, 1977); *Dynasty* (Casablanca, 1979); *KISS Unmasked* (Casablanca, 1980); *Creatures of the Night* (Casablanca, 1982); *Lick It Up* (Mercury, 1983); *Animalize* (Mercury, 1984); *Asylum* (Mercury, 1985); *Crazy Nights* (Mercury, 1987); *Hot in the Shade* (Mercury, 1989); *Revenge* (Mercury, 1992); *Unplugged* (Mercury, 1996); *Carnival of Souls* (Mercury, 1997), *Psycho Circus* (Mercury, 1998); *The Very Best of KISS* (Mercury, 2002).

BIBLIOGRAPHY: P. Elliot, *KISS Hotter Than Hell: The Stories Behind Every Song* (New York, 2002); C. Gooch and J. Suhs, *KISS Alive Forever: The Complete Touring History* (New York, 2002); G. Simmons and P. Stanley, *KISS: The Early Years* (New York, 2002).

DONALD LOWE

MARK KNOPFLER

Born: Glasgow, Scotland, 12 August 1949
Genre: Rock, Pop
Best-selling album since 1990: *Golden Heart* (1996)

British guitarist Mark Knopfler is best known as the leader of Dire Straits, one of the most popular stadium rock bands in the late 1980s. He is a virtuoso guitarist renowned for his subtle fingerpicking style and also for his laid-back demeanor and cool, understated vocals. Although Dire Straits was responsible for many hits during the heyday of MTV, Knopfler pursued many low-key side projects including the country band Notting Hillbillies and a Grammy Award–winning collaboration with country music guitar master Chet Atkins. After abandoning Dire Straits in the early 1990s, Knopfler pursued life as a solo artist, which resulted in quieter albums of acoustic folk blues. Knopfler is also a successful film composer.

Knopfler formed Dire Straits with his brother David in the late 1970s. After a demo of their song "Sultans of Swing" became a hit in London, they got a record contract to record their debut album, which ended up selling 11 million copies worldwide in 1979. The group continued to make best-selling albums that culminated with *Brothers in Arms* (1985), the group's biggest seller that yielded many smash hit singles including "Walk of Life" and "Money for Nothing" (a song skewering MTV, but whose video was considered groundbreaking). The album—which ended up selling 26 million copies—defined the band's sound: wry lyrics, Knopfler's husky vocals, sly guitar leads, and a rock steady groove.

Dire Straits made its last album, *On Every Street*, in 1991. It failed to generate the sales of its previous album and the group disbanded. Knopfler was already involved with side projects. He produced albums for singer/songwriters Randy Newman and Bob Dylan, wrote "Private Dancer," the comeback hit for pop diva Tina Turner, scored films such as *Local Hero* (1983), *The Princess Bride* (1987), and many others, and actively pursued an interest in country music. Under the group name the Notting Hillbillies, he released a traditional country album in 1990. He also collaborated with country music guitar virtuoso Chet Atkins whose fingerpicking style he idolized.

The first album released under Knopfler's own name was *Golden Heart* (1996). It was recorded with Nashville session players as well as members of the Chieftains and Beausoleil, two groups known as worldwide ambassadors for Celtic and Cajun music respectively. The album moved further in the direction of Knopfler's side interests than the rock sound he established with Dire Straits. Melancholy and mostly acoustic, the album has touches of Celtic, Cajun, and country music tastefully arranged and complemented by Knopfler's sparse and melodic guitar lines. Not selling anywhere near the numbers he was used to with Dire Straits, the album did receive stellar reviews. It ultimately helped Knopfler end his career as a stadium rocker and begin a new chapter as a serious singer/songwriter.

Knopfler returned to a full rock band sound on his next album, *Sailing to Philadelphia* (2000). Songs like "What It Is" and "Speedway at Nazareth" had the same epic drive of Dire Straits. With each song featuring his signature guitar flourishes, Knopfler once again returned to the themes he explored in his previous band: the perversity of the powerful and the flawed charm of American success.

Two years later, Knopfler toned down his guitar god stature with *The Ragpicker's Dream* (2002). Sounding less the rock warrior of his early days and more a country gentleman just discovering some dusty old 78 records in his farmhouse attic, this quiet, frisky, and often eloquent set of acoustic songs is an exploration of American roots music. The intimate album glows with whispering blues ("Fare Thee Well"), jazz noir ("A Place Where We Used to Live"), and classic country from the golden age of Nashville. Knopfler bypasses grand lyrical statements in favor of scenarios about circus freaks, shoe salesmen, hoof and mouth disease, and cartoons. But his husky cool voice is seductive enough to make it sound as important as Shakespeare.

Even though he sold millions of records in the 1980s, Mark Knopfler played to a much smaller audience the decade following. His reputation as a remarkable guitarist and a compelling singer transcends the fact that his solo career did not yield the mass commercial hits he enjoyed before. Knopfler remained an Englishman enamored of American roots music as well as American themes in his music. He is respected as an eloquent craftsman who does not believe in excess, but instead makes the simplest musical statements resonate.

SELECTIVE DISCOGRAPHY: *Golden Heart* (Warner Bros., 1996); *Sailing to Philadelphia* (Warner Bros., 2000); *The Ragpicker's Dream* (Warner Bros., 2002). **With Dire Straits:** *Dire Straits* (Warner Bros., 1978); *Communique* (Warner Bros., 1979); *Making Movies* (Warner Bros., 1980); *Love Over Gold* (Warner Bros., 1982); *Brothers in Arms* (Warner Bros., 1985); *On Every Street* (Warner Bros., 1991).

WEBSITE: www.mark-knopfler.com.

MARK GUARINO

KORN

Formed: 1992, Bakersfield, California

Members: Reginald "Fieldy Snuts" Arzivu, bass (born Bakersfield, California, 2 November 1969); Jonathan Davis, lead vocals, bagpipes (born Bakersfield, California, 18 January 1971); James "Munky" Shaffer, guitar (born Rosedale, California, 6 June 1970); David Silveria, drums (born Bakersfield, California, 21 September 1972); Brian "Head" Welch, guitar (born Torrance, California, 19 June 1970).

Genre: Heavy Metal, Rock

Best-selling album since 1990: *Follow the Leader* (1998)

Hit songs since 1990: "Freak on a Leash," "Got the Life," "Falling Away from Me"

One of the most distinctive and controversial heavy metal bands of the decade, Korn ascended from mid-1990s cult favorite to late-1990s popular phenomenon. Blending rhythmic elements of funk and hip-hop into an effects-laden stew of eerie, sludgy terror, the group dug deep into a host of adolescent scars with the brutal passion and rage of personal experience. At the forefront of the decade's rap-metal and nu-metal movements, they took a page from their predecessors, Faith No More, but also set trends that others followed.

The band formed in 1992, at a time when the serious Seattle grunge of Nirvana, Pearl Jam, Alice in Chains, and Soundgarden pushed the more shallow 1980s pop metal bands—the likes of Mötley Crüe, Poison, Warrant, and Skid Row—out of the mainstream. From this shift heavier and more substantive bands emerged. Guitarists James "Munky" Shaffer and Brian "Head" Welch, bassist Reginald "Fieldy Snuts" Arzivu, and drummer David Silveria played in a Bakersfield, California, band named LAPD when they met Jonathan Davis. Davis was a mortuary science student who also sang lead vocals in another local band, Sexart. LAPD soon asked Davis to join their band, and Korn was born.

Davis added a substantial measure of childhood trauma to Korn's lyrics and vocals. As a youth he often donned dresses and makeup, behavior that brought him much verbal ridicule and physical harm. Throughout the band's 1994 self-titled debut, he vents his frustrations with menacing ferocity. On "Faget," he moans about sexual confusion: "I'm just a pretty boy / Whatever you call it / You wouldn't know a real man if you saw it." On "Clown" he growls with pent-up anger: "Throw your hate at me with all your might / Hit me 'cause I'm strange, hit me!" And on "Daddy," he cathartically relives memories of molestation: "You've raped! / I feel dirty / It hurt! / As a child / Tied down! / That's a good boy." These candid, angst-ridden themes of abuse and neglect at school and at home became staples of late 1990s and turn-of-the millennium rock. This was the "new" facet of nu-metal incorporated by Staind, Linkin Park, Papa Roach, and other bands that followed Korn's lead.

Despite little publicity, radio play, or MTV exposure, the band's music slowly reached an audience. Handfuls of adolescent males could relate and found Korn to be a crutch and a release. The band began to develop a sizable underground following that caused their 1996 sophomore album *Life Is Peachy* to rise to number three on the *Billboard* 200 album chart within weeks of its release.

"Freak on a Leash" Video

Korn's music video for "Freak on a Leash" was wildly popular and received several awards, despite its controversial imagery and unfortunate timing. The video, directed by Jonathan Dayton, Valerie Faris, and Todd McFarlane, features a bullet flying through scenes of everyday American life. The shot originates from the accidental firing of a security guard's gun in an animated world, and it is thrust into reality. The bullet eventually reaches Korn performing. Finally, it returns to the animated world, where a young girl catches it and gives it to the officer.

It became an instant success on MTV's *Total Request Live,* and viewer votes pushed it to number one on February 25, 1999. The video stayed on or near the top spot until its obligatory retirement after sixty-five days on the countdown. It received little airtime, though, during the last three weeks of its impressive run. The massacre at Columbine High School in Littleton, Colorado, occurred on April 20 of that year. Showing sensitivity to the incident and responsibility toward its viewers, MTV decided to edit out all scenes that include the bullet, which left little to air. Though it was essentially hidden from viewers for the remainder of the year, it was nominated for eight MTV Video Music Awards and won for Best Rock Video and Best Editing. The following year the Grammy Awards also recognized it as Best Music Video (Short Form).

wide, band members autographed Korn paraphernalia and had lengthy question-and-answer sessions with fans. Much of their core audience considered the stunt to be a conscious push toward the mainstream.

Whether calculated or considerate, the band's new celebrity paid enormous dividends. MTV put the group in heavy rotation, and their videos for "Got the Life" and "Freak on a Leash" became mainstays on MTV's Total Request Live, a teen-targeted daily video countdown. With fellow heavier acts Limp Bizkit and Kid Rock, Korn balanced out the sugary pop of boy bands such as *NSYNC and the Backstreet Boys and teen idols Britney Spears and Christina Aguilera.

Follow the Leader debuted at number one on the *Billboard* 200, went on to multiplatinum success, and became their best-selling album. *Issues* followed in December 1999, debuting atop the album chart as well. Although Korn never again matched the honesty and intensity of their debut album, the group maintained a consistent, signature sound. Musically, they compromised little to achieve their mainstream success. It was not until *Untouchables* (2002) that they began to add more melody to their music and even recorded their first version of a ballad, "Alone I Break." The band released the song in 2002 as the third single from the album. This mainstream-minded move once again tested its core fan base. But throughout Korn's career the dependability of the consistent, throbbing pulse, gloomy atmosphere, and intensely personal lyrics captured the allegiance of frustrated youth.

SELECTIVE DISCOGRAPHY: *Korn* (Immortal/Epic, 1994); *Life Is Peachy* (Immortal/Epic, 1996); *Follow the Leader* (Immortal/Epic, 1998); *Issues* (Immortal/Epic, 1999).

BIBLIOGRAPHY: L. Furman and E. Furman, *Korn: Life in the Pit* (New York, 2000).

WEBSITES: www.korn.com; www.kornweb.com; www.korntv.com.

DAVE POWERS

In 1998, while recording their third album, *Follow the Leader,* Korn received national headlines when a student in Zeeland, Michigan, was suspended for wearing a T-shirt with the group's logo. The school's principal claimed their music was "indecent, vulgar, and obscene." The band responded by giving away free T-shirts outside the school and obtaining a cease-and-desist order against the school district. This publicity massively expanded their fan base.

The band built on its higher profile by launching the Korn Kampaign to coincide with the release of *Follow the Leader.* On this promotional tour of record stores nation-

DIANA KRALL

Born: Nanaimo, British Columbia, 16 November 1964

Genre: Jazz, Pop

Best-selling album since 1990: *The Look of Love* (2001)

Hit songs since 1990: "When I Look in Your Eyes," "The Look of Love"

Smoky-voiced singer and pianist Diana Krall captured the admiration of the jazz world in the 1990s, earning praise from critics and musicians before casting her sights on a mainstream pop audience. By the end of the decade she had become contemporary jazz's most successful crossover artist, recording the multimillion-selling album *When I Look in Your Eyes* (1999). While it would be easy to explain her appeal on the basis of sultry good looks, Krall is a gifted musician with the ability to create a mood so intimate that it often feels like private conversation. Her quiet husky voice is no match for the deft, whimsical quality of her playing, but on her best recordings voice and piano merge in a warm, inviting style completely her own.

Raised in British Columbia, Krall's early appreciation for music came through the influence of her father, an avid record collector who also played piano. Enrolling in piano lessons by the age of four and performing professionally at fifteen, Krall was influenced by the swinging, flexible style of great 1920s and 1930s pianist Fats Waller. In the early 1980s she attended California's prestigious Berklee College of Music on a scholarship, then moved to Los Angeles where she studied under the tutelage of master pianist Jimmy Rowles. Rowles, famed for his sensitive accompaniment behind the greatest twentieth-century jazz vocalists, encouraged Krall to sing while playing, although the shy performer initially demurred. Moving to New York in 1990, Krall released her first album for a small label in 1993 and a year later signed with GRP Records, a well-known company in the jazz genre. In 1995 she released *All for You*, an acclaimed tribute to legendary vocalist and pianist Nat "King" Cole. Recorded with simple accompaniment of guitar, piano, and bass, the album garnered positive reviews for its charming, laid-back ambience. Krall informs the album with her winning musical personality, performing rapid, dexterous piano runs on "I'm an Errand Girl for Rhythm" and singing the nonsense lyrics of "Frim Fram Sauce" with just the right amount of humor. While proficient on ballads, critics note that Krall really shines on up-tempo numbers, where her snappy, engaging playing and easygoing vocals fall into an infectious groove.

In an effort to reach a wider pop audience, Krall began to sing more and play less as the 1990s progressed. The effort paid off: *When I Look in Your Eyes* (1999), an album built largely around Krall's vocals, made a sizable impact on the pop charts and won the music industry's Grammy Award for Best Jazz Vocal Performance. Compared to veteran jazz vocalist Carole Sloane's breathtaking 1994 rendition, however, critics found Krall's performance of the title track lacking in sufficient depth, and her vocal style too even-keeled and mellow to make ballads such as "Let's Face the Music and Dance" sound interesting. She is impressive on the faster songs, however, using her piano to lead "I Can't Give You Anything but Love" through

multiple tempo shifts. On the insouciant "Devil May Care" and "Let's Fall in Love" she displays an acute sense of rhythm and swing.

By the late 1990s, Krall was a ubiquitous presence on soundtracks for television programs and films, her easy-on-the-ears style leading the *Calgary Sun* to crown her in 2001, rather sardonically, "the reigning queen of soft jazz." Krall's next album, *The Look of Love* (2001) features a sexy cover photograph, large orchestral arrangements, and even less of her distinctive piano playing. Buoyed by savvy marketing it became Krall's most commercially successful release, reaching the Top 10 of the pop album charts. In 2002 she released *Live in Paris*, a restrained, well-structured set showcasing her almost hypnotic power over an audience. While Krall is in fine form throughout, critics make special note of the album's biggest surprise: an emotive version of rock and folk singer Joni Mitchell's "A Case of You." Here, it has been observed that Krall exhibits a more evolved sense of vocal dynamics, the power in her voice bearing a new urgency. While her past vocal performances have resembled the hushed, breathy sound of 1950s singer Julie London, on "A Case of You" Krall sings harder and louder, suggesting that she has been holding much in reserve.

Diana Krall carried 1990s jazz music into the mainstream, giving it a degree of popular acceptance not seen in decades. Although critics note her talent is best showcased on up-tempo songs, which she performs with a carefree sense of play, she has found great commercial success through her ballad performances. On her finest recordings, she conveys excitement and vitality through the sincere warmth of her sound.

SELECTIVE DISCOGRAPHY: *Steppin' Out* (Justin Time, 1993); *Only Trust Your Heart* (GRP, 1994); *All for You* (Impulse!, 1995); *Love Scenes* (Impulse!, 1997); *When I Look in Your Eyes* (GRP, 1999); *The Look of Love* (Verve, 2001); *Live in Paris* (Verve, 2002). **Soundtracks:** *Midnight in the Garden of Good and Evil* (Warner Bros., 1997); *Melrose Place Jazz: Upstairs at MP* (Windham Hill, 1998); *Kissing Jessica Stein* (Verve, 2002).

WEBSITE: www.dianakrall.com.

DAVID FREELAND

ALISON KRAUSS

Born: Decatur, Illinois, 23 July 1971

Genre: Country, Bluegrass

Best-selling album since 1990: *Now That I've Found You: A Collection* (1995)

Hit songs since 1990: "I've Got That Old Feelin'," "Looking into the Eyes of Love," "The Lucky One"

Often called "the first lady of bluegrass," fiddler and sweet-voiced soprano Alison Krauss, with her band Union Station, helped bring bluegrass music to a wider audience by blending it with country and folk music. Unlike her country counterparts such as Shania Twain and Faith Hill, Krauss relies heavily on her tradition, through instrumentation choices such as steel guitar, fiddle, banjo, and mandolins, and her recordings are produced in such a way that the music's warmth and sincerity easily shine through.

Krauss started playing classical violin at age five, but she soon grew tired of its limitations and she began to experiment with a more country and bluegrass style. She had success early and quickly, winning an Illinois State Fiddle Championship at age twelve in 1983. That same year, Krauss was named the Most Promising Fiddler in the Midwest by the Society for the Preservation of Bluegrass in America. A few years later, in 1987, she signed to the prestigious traditional music label Rounder Records and, at just sixteen years old, released her first album, *Too Late to Cry*, with the band Union Station.

But it was *Now That I've Found You: A Collection* (1995) that made Krauss a star, selling over 1 million copies, reaching number two on the country charts, and, more remarkably, charting in *Billboard*'s Pop Top 10. Its success suggested that bluegrass music had a far wider appeal than any musician in the genre had expected. Fans were somehow taken with this compilation, which spans Krauss's ten-year recording career with Rounder Records up to that point and features a cover of the Beatles song "I Will," in addition to more traditional bluegrass tunes.

In 2000 Krauss and Union Station benefited from an unlikely source: a movie soundtrack. Collectively and individually, band members appeared on the award-winning soundtrack to the film *O Brother, Where Art Thou?* The success of the album raised Krauss and her band's profile so that when *New Favorite* (2001) was released, Krauss and her band had officially crossed over to the mainstream. The themes running through *New Favorite*—regret, redemption, and resolution—are illustrated in the title track, a sorrowful ballad in which Krauss sings, "I know you've got a new favorite." The album won a Grammy Award for Best Bluegrass Album. Krauss and Union Station have garnered countless music awards; she herself has thirteen Grammys.

SELECTIVE DISCOGRAPHY: *Too Late to Cry* (Rounder, 1987); *I've Got That Old Feeling* (Rounder, 1990); *Now That I've Found You: A Collection* (Rounder, 1995); *Forget About It* (Rounder, 1999). **With Union Station:** *Two Highways* (Rounder, 1989); *Every Time You Say Goodbye* (Rounder, 1992); *So Long So Wrong* (Rounder,

Spot Light | O Brother, Where Art Thou?

The motion picture *O Brother, Where Art Thou?* (2000), by filmmakers Joel and Ethan Coen, was a surprise hit, thanks in large part to its music. The soundtrack, with contributions from Ralph Stanley, Emmylou Harris, Alison Krauss, and Gillian Welch, sold over 6 million copies and spawned a mainstream interest in bluegrass, country, gospel, and traditional roots music. Krauss contributed several tunes, including "Down to the River to Pray" and the chilling, a cappella "Didn't Leave Nobody But the Baby" performed with Emmylou Harris and Gillian Welch. As of fall 2002, the album had spent 105 weeks on *Billboard*'s Top Country chart, and it won five Grammy Awards, including an upset victory for Album of the Year. The soundtrack also received eleven bluegrass awards from the International Bluegrass Music Association in 2001. The success of the soundtrack helped buoy the success of the group's next album, *New Favorite* (2001), which was certified gold in 2002.

1997); *New Favorite* (Rounder, 2001); *Blue Trail of Sorrow* (Rounder, 2001); *Alison Krauss and Union Station Live* (Rounder, 2002). **Soundtrack:** *O Brother, Where Art Thou?* (Universal, 2000).

CARRIE HAVRANEK

LENNY KRAVITZ

Born: New York, New York, 26 May 1964

Genre: Rock

Best-selling album since 1990: *Are You Gonna Go My Way* (1993)

Hit songs since 1990: "Fly Away," "Stand by My Woman," "Let Love Rule"

Lenny Kravitz grew up in Los Angeles in a show-business family; his father was a top television producer and his mother was a well-known actress. From a young age he came in contact with a range of music celebrities who were friends of his parents. Some of his peers at Beverly Hills High School also became big names in the rock and pop world. His early enthusiasm for performing and recording led him to produce a number of demos, which he completed in 1987.

Kravitz's career as one of America's leading rock artists began at the end of the 1980s with a recording contract from Virgin and a debut album, *Let Love Rule* (1989), which sold half a million copies in the United States and then reached the Top 60 in the United Kingdom By 1990 the hit single "Let Love Rule" had become successful in the United Kingdom. On the album, Kravitz's style is retro with blatant quotations from the music of Curtis Mayfield, John Lennon, and Jimi Hendrix. Kravitz makes no attempt to conceal his longtime admiration of these stars, whose influence struck many critics as the reason for the derivative sound of his work.

Following a successful tour, he went on to produce his next album, *Mama Said*, released in 1991. This album instantly placed him in a different category from the first. The songs are bolder and more passionately performed, in part because of his collaboration with the guitarist Slash from Guns N' Roses on the funk-rock track "Always on the Run." The influence of other artists such as Curtis Mayfield is evident on this album, especially in the soul ballad "It Ain't Over Til It's Over." This is a warmly intimate love song with a gentle melody that Kravitz milks to the fullest. His abundant musical talent radiates through the polished production.

All eleven songs on Kravitz's third album, *Are You Gonna Go My Way* (1993), became hits, with every song charting. The three songs that stand out are "Heaven Help," "Believe," and "Are You Gonna Go My Way." Aside from drawing directly on the work of many 1960s artists, Kravitz also shapes a fresh contemporary rock sound with a vocal expression that is inimitable and instantly recognizable. The album spent six months on the U.K. charts while gaining him his first gold disc in the United States.

Almost two years later the album *Circus* elicited a lukewarm critical reaction. For many it was a disappointment, with Kravitz's performance too imitative and unfocused. As a result he attempted to experiment more in his next album, *5* (1998), by turning to digital technology and electronic dance styles. More funk-oriented than his previous material, the album is an exercise in showmanship. The hit "Fly Away" is one of his most successful songs to date, a favorite cover song for bands and singers all over the world. In addition to the superb production and arrangement, the musical performance, instrumentally and vocally, is brashly compelling. It is worth noting that most of the work invested in this song and the others is all Kravitz, who often writes all the songs and plays all the instruments on the recording. With the

huge success of "Fly Away," Virgin reissued *5* with a number of bonus tracks. This release was directly followed by the "best of" set, *Greatest Hits*, in 2000, and, one year later, his sixth album, *Lenny*. Kravitz has worked with numerous artists, as a producer, songwriter, and musician, including Madonna, Mick Jagger, Aerosmith, and the French singer Vanessa Paradis.

His 2001 release, *Lenny*, consists of songs skillfully performed and produced in a blend of classic rock, soul, and hipster pop. The gracefulness of his ballad writing, along with his lyrical control and deft instrumental textures, places this album on a level with the best of his earlier work. The following year he released *If I Could Fall in Love* (2002).

Kravitz's musical style is a pastiche composed of the influences of his most-admired forerunners. In particular, his adoration of Prince is obvious in his musical idiom, which centers on tightly controlled rhythmic and harmonic riffs that define funk and rock. Despite the strong influence of his predecessors, Kravitz has managed to shape his own musical identity.

SELECTIVE DISCOGRAPHY: *Let Love Rule* (Virgin, 1989); *Mama Said* (Virgin, 1991); *Are You Gonna Go My Way?* (Virgin, 1993); *Circus* (Virgin, 1995); *5* (Virgin, 1998); *Lenny* (Virgin, 2001); *If I Could Fall in Love* (Virgin, 2002).

BIBLIOGRAPHY: M. Seliger, *Lenny Kravitz* (Santa Fe, NM, 2001).

STAN HAWKINS

KRONOS QUARTET

Formed: 1978, San Francisco, California

Members: Jennifer Culp, cello; Hank Dutt, viola (born Muscatine, Iowa, 4 November 1952); David Harrington, violin (born Oregon, 9 September 1949); John Sherba, violin (born Milwaukee, Wisconsin, 10 December 1954). Former member: Joan Jeanrenaud, cello (born Memphis, Tennessee, 25 January 1956).

Genre: Classical

Best-selling album since 1990: *Pieces of Africa* (1992)

Since its founding in 1973 by violinist David Harrington, the Kronos Quartet has become one of the United States' premier chamber groups. With the help of its eclectic repertoire, featuring works by composers from Astor Piazzolla to John Zorn, Kronos Quartet has attracted a diverse audience. It has brought the music of the twentieth century to the attention of a large public and opened the art music establishment to the sounds of rock, tango, and other popular genres.

Kronos Quartet began in the early 1970s when Harrington started assembling string quartets dedicated to performing new music in his native Seattle, Washington. Harrington settled in San Francisco in 1978, and obtained a residency for his string quartet at Mills College. It was in the early days at Mills that the Kronos Quartet settled into its first lineup, with violinists John Sherba and Hank Dutton and cellist Joan Jeanrenaud. After more than twenty years with the group, Jeanrenaud left in 1999. She was replaced by cellist Jennifer Culp.

The Kronos Quartet established itself in new music circles with its expert playing of difficult twentieth-century works. In the early 1980s, the group made a larger name for itself through extensive touring and several well-received recordings. Kronos Quartet's concerts include works by established twentieth-century composers like Anton Webern and new works from modern composers. Encores famously included Kronos Quartet's string quartet arrangement of Jimi Hendrix's "Purple Haze" (originally for electric guitar and rock bands), which was later released on *Kronos Quartet* (1986). The Kronos Quartet's 1989 recording of Steve Reich's *Different Trains* helped the composer win the Grammy Award for Best Classical Contemporary Composition. Thus the group entered the 1990s as one of the biggest names in American chamber music.

Kronos Quartet continued to push classical music forward throughout the 1990s, with a combination of innovative performances and commissions. In 1990 Kronos Quartet premiered a fully staged version of George Crumb's string quartet *Black Angels*. Two years later, it released *Pieces of Africa* on which it performs a selection of African songs arranged for string quartet. Over the decade, Kronos Quartet increasingly added instruments to its concerts and recordings. For example, performances of Steven Mackey's "Physical Property," released on *Short Stories* (1993), includes the composer playing his electric guitar alongside the quartet. *Howl, U.S.A.* (1996) made it to the top of the classical charts and includes a reading of Allen Ginsberg's poem *Howl*. Kronos Quartet has also redefined the boundaries of "new music," as in its 1997 release *Early Music,* which contains thirteenth-century music that sounds strange and new to modern ears.

In 1998 the Kronos Quartet celebrated its twenty-five-year anniversary. It released a ten-disc box set to celebrate this landmark, which includes works representing the wide range and arcane nature of the group's repertoire. Once the bad boys of the classical recording world, Kronos Quartet has become one of the most well-established and highly regarded American chamber ensembles. And while the Kronos Quartet may no longer represent classical music's most cutting edge, it played a pivotal role in bringing American art music into the twenty-first century.

SELECTIVE DISCOGRAPHY: *Black Angels* (Atlantic, 1990); *Pieces of Africa* (Elektra/Nonesuch, 1992); *Short Stories* (Nonesuch, 1993); *Howl, U.S.A.* (Nonesuch, 1996); *Early Music* (Elektra/Nonesuch, 1997); *25 Years* (Nonesuch, 1998); *Nuevo* (Elektra/Asylum, 2002).

WEBSITE: www.kronosquartet.org.

CAROLINE POLK O'MEARA

KRS-ONE

Born: Laurence Krisna Parker; Brooklyn, New York, 20 August 1965
Genre: Rap
Best-selling album since 1990: *KRS-One* (1995)
Hit songs since 1990: "Out of Here," "Do or Die," "Black Cop"

In a hip-hop world in which rappers typically brag about the thug life of mistreating hos and tramps and driving fancy cars, KRS-One, nicknamed the Teacher, stands apart for his philosophical views. A study in contradictions, he went from rapping about New York's tough ghettos to guest-lecturing at Yale University. For a while he worked as a Warner Bros. A&R executive while railing against mainstream rap. He lived the gangsta lifestyle but also studied theology and preached the word of God.

KRS-One, an acronym for Knowledge Reigns Supreme over Nearly Everyone, grew up close to Brooklyn's lush Prospect Park. At thirteen he left home to live in the park and nearby subways. Eventually he was arrested as part of a drug bust in the city's shelter system. After a two-month stint at the Brooklyn House of Detention, he was shuffled between shelters and foster homes and the street. It was while living at the Franklin Avenue shelter in the South Bronx that he ran across the counselor Scott Sterling, aka DJ Scott LaRock. They found common ground in their love of music and formed Boogie Down Productions.

Boogie Down Productions released a duet album, *Criminal Minded* (1987), a work eventually recognized as the foundation of hardcore rap. The CD cover features the men holding automatic weapons, something no rapper had ever done before. There were other hardcore rappers, but Boogie Down Productions stood apart for their hard-edged music, explicit lyrics dealing with inner-city drugs and crime, and KRS-One's deep baritone vocals.

As they began to prepare to record their next album, LaRock was murdered on August 26, 1987, in a dispute over a woman. KRS-One pressed forward with another

370 Baker's Biographical Dictionary of Popular Musicians Since 1990

album, *By All Means Necessary* (1988), but he had been clearly transformed by LaRock's death. Now he questioned, as much as he boasted, challenged as much as he criticized. Songs like "Stop the Violence" and "Illegal Business" examine the growing crack and crime problem. On "My Philosophy," KRS-One took the first step as the Teacher, as he would later call himself, by decrying the social and economic conditions that drive people to desperate measures.

KRS-One continues in this vein on *Ghetto Music: The Blueprint of Hip Hop* (1989), *Edutainment* (1990), and *Sex and Violence* (1992), exploring black history and condemning police brutality, racism, ignorance, and homelessness with lucid and insightful lyrics. But by now, fans were tiring of KRS-One's increasingly preachy stance, and sales slowed dramatically.

KRS-One made an attempt for street credibility on *KRS-One* (1995) by incorporating a fuller sound and working with a younger crew that include several guest artists—Das EFX, Fat Joe, and Mad Lion. His momentum continued with *I Got Next* (1997) and *The Sneak Attack* (2001), but by this point KRS-One was past his peak. Through it all he remained a philosopher, and he tackled premarital sex and the struggle for absolution in *Spiritual Minded* (2002). Essentially a gospel album with the requisite Christian messages of confession and salvation, the CD lacked the slick production values of his previous works.

With his thundering voice and socially conscious music, KRS-One became a lone voice of reason in the macho world of rap and helped shape the evolution of the genre in the late 1990s.

SELECTIVE DISCOGRAPHY: *Criminal Minded* (Sugar Hill, 1987); *By All Means Necessary* (Jive, 1988); *KRS-One* (Jive, 1995); *I Got Next* (Jive, 1997); *The Sneak Attack* (Koch, 2001); *Spiritual Minded* (Koch, 2002).

RAMIRO BURR

L¹L

LADYSMITH BLACK MAMBAZO

Formed: 1964, Durban, South Africa

Members: Jabulani Dubazana (born South Africa, 25 April 1954); Abednego Mazibuko (born Ladysmith, South Africa, 12 March 1954); Albert Mazibuko (born Ladysmith, South Africa, 16 April 1948); Geophrey Mdletshe (born South Africa, 23 January 1960); Russel Mthembu (born South Africa, 12 March 1947); Inos Phungula (born South Africa, 31 March 1945); Ben Shabalala (born Ladysmith, South Africa, 30 November 1957); Jockey Shabalala (born Ladysmith, South Africa, 4 November 1944); Joseph Shabalala (born Ladysmith, South Africa, 28 August 1940). Former member: Headman Shabalala (born Ladysmith, South Africa, 9 October 1945; died Durban, South Africa, 11 December 1991).

Genre: World

Best-selling album since 1990: *The Star and the Wise Man* (1998)

Ladysmith Black Mambazo, the colorful men's choral ensemble led by Joseph Shabalala, is a musical diplomatic corps representing postapartheid South Africa and the liberation of black traditions from repressive policies reaching back to the nineteenth century. Their greatest international renown resulted from their collaboration with Paul Simon, the American singer/songwriter, on the album *Graceland* (1985).

Ladysmith Black Mambazo were big sellers in South Africa even before Paul Simon featured them on "Homeless" and "Diamonds on the Soles of Her Shoes" on *Graceland* and in his subsequent tours and television appearances on shows ranging from *Saturday Night Live* to *Sesame Street*. But Ladysmith Black Mambazo were far from an overnight success. Ladysmith Black Mambazo's director, Joseph Shabalala, is the oldest son of eight children of tenant farmers living near the South African town Ladysmith. As a teenager he played guitar and sang, eventually joining the Devan Choir, an *Iscathamiya* ("tiptoe guys") singing group that performed the music South African migrant laborers developed in the late 1800s—"tiptoeing" for fear of being punished if their parties became too loud.

Shabalala established his own band in Durban in 1960 but in 1964 claimed to have heard new harmonies in a dream. Consequently he converted to Christianity and induced his brothers Headman and Jockey and their cousins the Mazibuko brothers into joining Ladysmith (for the name of their hometown) Black (referring to black oxen) Mambazo (axe, meaning they cut the competition).

Their first album, *Amabutho* (1973), was the first African LP to go gold (sales of 25,000). The ensemble steadily issued other highly successful records in Africa into the mid-1980s. But they gained worldwide renown when Simon discovered them on pirated cassette tapes, visited South Africa to find Shabalala, signed Ladysmith Black Mambazo to Warner Bros., and produced their first U.S. album, the Grammy-winning *Shaka Zulu* (1987). In a controversial move Simon toured with the ensemble during the global boycott of South Africa prior to apartheid's fall. Simon and Shabalala believed it better to express South Africa's black culture than to silence themselves to shame the white government.

The group's thick, warm tenor-baritone-bass harmonies answering Shamabala's leads are derived from

Anglican hymns and three major sounds from Zulu singing, characterized by Shabalala as "a high keening ululation; a grunting, puffing sound that we make when we stomp our feet; and a certain way of singing melody." Shabalala also cites an affinity for the blues; his arrangements suggest African-American spirituals, too. The music bespeaks his Christian faith, including forbearance in the face of pain. When in 1991 his brother Headman was shot dead on a highway near Durban by a white South African security guard (who was convicted of manslaughter), Joseph's response was, "Keep singing."

Ladysmith Black Mambazo enjoyed the endorsement of Nelson Mandela prior to singing at his inauguration in 1994; at his request the group sang at the Oslo ceremony for the Nobel Peace Prize he shared with F. W. de Klerk, former president of South Africa, in 1993. In 1996 Mandela invited Ladysmith Black Mambazo to accompany him to London to meet Queen Elizabeth.

The ensemble returned to London for a triumphant concert that was recorded and released as an album and video, *Live at the Royal Albert Hall* (1999). At Mandela's behest they also represented South Africa in celebrations of the Queen's fifty-year reign in 2002, singing "Hey Jude" and "All You Need Is Love" with Paul McCartney, Eric Clapton, Rod Stewart, Joe Cocker, and Phil Collins.

Ladysmith Black Mambazo has performed in Rome for the pope, on Muhammad Ali's sixtieth-birthday television special, and at the 1999 Nobel Peace Prize Concert honoring Doctors Without Borders. They have recorded with Stevie Wonder and Dolly Parton, among others. They are heard on Michael Jackson's *MoonWalker* (1988) video and on soundtracks of various films, including Disney's *The Lion King II: Simba's Pride* (1999), *Coming to America* (1988), *A Dry White Season* (1989), and *Cry, the Beloved Country* (1995).

Ladysmith Black Mambazo's a capella purity translates well to the stage. The group developed the musical play *The Song of Jacob Zulu* (1992) with Chicago's Steppenwolf Theater Company. The Broadway production, with Ladysmith Black Mambazo members acting and singing, earned six Tony Award nominations and a Drama Desk Award for original score. The group developed another musical, *Nomathemba* (1995), with writer Ntozake Shange. Based on the story behind Shabalala's first Ladysmith Black Mambazo song, the play enjoyed well-received runs in Chicago, Boston, and Washington, D.C. Eric Simonson directed both plays and co-directed *On Tip Toe: Gentle Steps to Freedom* (2000), a documentary on Ladysmith Black Mambazo that was nominated for a 2001 Academy Award and a 2002 Emmy Award.

Ladysmith Black Mambazo maintains a full concert and touring schedule despite Joseph Shabalala's academic positions as an associate professor of ethnomusicology at the University of Nepal and at UCLA in California. He also directs the Mambazo Foundation for South African Music and Culture, which was founded in 1999 "to promote fund-raising efforts to devise a proper academic syllabus to teach South African students about their indigenous culture." Few listeners in the United States would have any awareness of South Africa's indigenous male vocal culture were it not for Ladysmith Black Mambazo.

SELECTIVE DISCOGRAPHY: *Shaka Zulu* (Warner Bros., 1987); *Two Worlds One Heart* (Warner Bros., 1991); *Liph' Iqiniso* (Shanachie, 1994); *Gift of the Tortoise* (Warner Bros., 1994); *Thuthukani Ngoxolo* (Shanachie, 1996); *Heavenly* (Shanachie, 1997); *Star & the Wise Man* (Shanachie, 1998); *Live at Royal Albert Hall* (Shanachie, 1999); *In Harmony* (Polygram, 2001). **With Dolly Parton:** *Peace Train* (RCA, 1996). **With Paul Simon:** *Graceland* (Warner Bros., 1985); *Rhythm of the Saints* (Warner Bros., 1990). **With Andreas Vollenweider:** *Book of Roses* (Columbia, 1992); *Kryptos* (Sony Classical, 1998). **With Stevie Wonder:** *Conversation Peace* (Motown, 1995).

WEBSITE: www.mambazo.com.

HOWARD MANDEL

JONNY LANG

Born: Jonathon Langseth; Fargo, North Dakota, 29 January 1981

Genre: Blues, Rock

Best-selling album since 1990: *Lie to Me* (1996)

Hit songs since 1990: "Lie to Me"

Jonny Lang's sudden emergence onto the blues scene in 1995 was a deviation from the seasoned path customarily blazed by other well-known blues artists. Hailed as a guitar prodigy, Lang was already touring with major acts such as B.B. King, the Rolling Stones, and Aerosmith by age sixteen, earning raves for his tasteful guitar skills and spirited vocal work. Lang's age is not the only anomaly: His childhood was spent in a North Dakota farm town, Casselton, which rests on the fertile soil of the Red River Valley—not exactly a renowned cornerstone of the blues. Further breaking the mold are his throaty vocals that bring to mind the burden of a seventy-five-year-old man, not the muse of a skinny Scandinavian kid with a teen idol's face. However, as soon as his second album, *Lie to Me* (1996), gained national release,

Lang's standing in the blues community rose from novelty performer to an accepted and serious artist. *Lie to Me* has sold over 1 million copies.

Lang began playing the guitar at the age of thirteen after his father took him to a concert of local blues bands in Fargo, North Dakota. Inspired by one of the guitarists, Ted Larsen of the group Bad Medicine, Lang dropped an earlier notion to become a saxophonist and sought the guitarist out for private lessons. Soon thereafter he was fronting Bad Medicine, renamed Jonny Lang and the Big Bang, as lead guitarist/singer. Lang's band moved to Minneapolis/St. Paul and recorded an independently released album titled *Smokin'* (1995), which sold over 25,000 copies on first release—a major success for an independent label. *Smokin'* caught the attention of major record companies and after a bidding war A&M Records promptly signed him. *Lie to Me* was released a day before Lang's sixteenth birthday.

After receiving highly favorable reviews for *Lie to Me*, Lang was selected Best New Guitarist in *Guitar Magazine's* readers poll. He appeared with guitar legend Jeff Beck at the 1997 Rock and Roll Hall of Fame induction ceremony and can be seen performing the song "6345789" with Wilson Pickett and Eddie Floyd in the film *Blues Brothers 2000* (1998). In 1998 Lang released his third album, *Wander This World*, and again received praise from critics. *Wander This World* features R&B and rock ballad textures in lieu of the straight blues from his earlier recordings. Heavily influenced by the Motown records that he sang along with as a child, Lang has indicated that his future music ventures might incorporate even more R&B and funk.

Distinguished by an effusive "no holds barred" style of performing, Lang growls out his vocals, contorts his face, and twists his body, seemingly "wringing out" the blues when he plays. The sense of incongruity created by the difference between his grown-up sound and his adolescent look continues to fascinate an audience that ranges from preteen idol worshipers to veteran fans of classic blues. Lang's commitment to the blues has turned skeptics into believers and garnered praise from venerable blues artists such as B.B. King, Buddy Guy, and the late Luther Allison—all of whom he has shared the stage with at various junctures. In 2002, while other musicians his age were focusing on varieties of fad-driven alternative rock, Lang remained faithful to his blues roots, giving certain assurance that the blues would be carried into future generations.

SELECTIVE DISCOGRAPHY: *Smokin'* (independent release, 1995); *Lie to Me* (A&M, 1996); *Wander This World* (A&M, 1998); *Smokin'* (re-release, 2002).

DONALD LOWE

K.D. LANG

Born: Katherine Dawn Lang; Consort, Alberta, 2 November 1961

Genre: Pop

Best-selling album since 1990: *Ingenue* (1992)

Hit songs since 1990: "Constant Craving"

Singer k.d. lang left behind her country music aspirations in the early 1990s to make forays into a variety of adult contemporary pop music, including jazz. Despite recording and concert success, country music's establishment rejected lang for her atypical look, fringe politics, and upfront homosexuality. She is a unique artist who upholds a respect for music's traditional aspects, yet harbors a counterculturist's personification.

Katherine Dawn Lang (she uses the lowercase k.d. lang) grew up in Consort, Alberta (population 700), where her father ran the drugstore and her mother, a schoolteacher, would drive more than an hour for lang's singing and dancing lessons. In high school, she excelled in volleyball and worked one summer driving a grain truck in the agriculturally based region. She attended Red Deer College and began a passionate interest in traditional country music, particularly the works of country legend Patsy Cline. She left college early and formed a band, the Reclines, named in homage to Cline.

As the Reclines toured Canada, they developed a reputation as an offbeat country band with a punk sensibility and a crazy female lead singer. Roaming the stage dressed cross-sexually, lang wore odd rhinestone glasses frames with no lenses, and belted country or rockabilly songs. In the band's beginnings, listeners thought lang was parodying country music, although it became apparent that she was sincere. After a dismal selling debut album, *A Truly Western Experience* (1984), lang dropped some of the stage histrionics in an effort to be taken more seriously and released *Angel with a Lariat* (1987), a mixture of country classics and her own songs. That year lang arrived on the Nashville scene after a much-heralded duet with the late Roy Orbison. They sang his hit "Crying," which earned lang a 1988 Grammy Award for Best Country Collaboration. She and the Reclines followed with two more country albums, *Shadowland* (1988) and *Absolute Torch and Twang* (1989), both of which went gold. *Absolute Torch and Twang* garnered lang a 1990 Grammy Award for Best Country Female Vocal Performance, which should have put her on top of the country music saddle, but it was a rough ride. Nashville had little tolerance for lang's androgynous appearance or her fringe politics, such as the support she gave lobbyist group PETA (People for the Ethical Treatment of Animals). In 1992 lang ended what little speculation might have remained about her sexuality by announcing publicly that she was a lesbian.

She released her first non-country album, *Ingenue* (1992), a collection of ten thematically based songs written by lang and her guitarist, Ben Mink, that deal with introspection and personal longing. The album went platinum and produced the only hit single of lang's career, "Constant Craving," which gave lang a third Grammy for Best Pop Female Vocal. In addition, the song's video was honored with a 1993 MTV Video Music Award for Best Female Video.

The singer continued her androgyny mystique by dressing publicly in upscale male clothing and slicking her hair back in a tight masculine wave. However, lang's voice is unmistakably female with its pure tones and wide, expressive range. It is a fluid sound, tranquil, subtle and rich with emotion, possessing tremendous power when called upon. *Ingenue* amazed listeners by showing no trace of the country twang so evident in lang's previous recordings.

All You Can Eat (1995), lang's follow-up, was another journey into the arty pop sound that identified lang through the success of *Ingenue*. She and Mink wrote the album's material that is, once again, centered on a theme, this time love. Her next recording, *Drag* (1997), was lang's first foray into jazz styling. *Drag* features renditions of a variety of cabaret-styled torch songs in addition to some current pop. Curiously, all of the songs relate in some way to smoking. Under these guidelines, her dreamy versions of "Don't Smoke in Bed" and "My Last Cigarette" are quite apropos, as is her unique take on Steve Miller's chestnut, "The Joker." She purrs, "I'm a joker, I'm a smoker, I'm a midnight toker." In gallows humor, she added the Hollies hit, "The Air That I Breathe."

After *Drag*, lang went into a reclusive period, somewhat disillusioned by high-profile fame. She re-emerged with another album of unique pop styling, her first album of original material in five years, *Invincible Summer* (2000). She wrote all the songs except "The Consequences of Falling."

Her enigmatic career took another interesting twist in 2001 as lang toured throughout the year with crooner extraordinaire, Tony Bennett. Sometimes coined "the odd couple" because of their diverse backgrounds, musical eras, and styles, the duo became close friends and recorded *A Wonderful World* (2002). The album, a collection of twelve of Louis Armstrong's best-known love songs, went gold. It contains standards such as "What a Wonderful World" and "La Vie En Rose."

Among her most acclaimed efforts, lang performed the classic "Leavin' on Your Mind" for MCA Record's tribute album, *Remembering Patsy Cline* (2003). The album features various artists singing the songs of the ill-fated singer who died in a plane crash in 1963.

Throughout her career, lang has identified with Cline's singing, and empathized with the boundaries Cline faced in the male-oriented world of country music. The brave steps lang has taken toward breaking boundaries have opened doors for other performers—professionally, artistically, and personally.

SELECTIVE DISCOGRAPHY: *A Truly Western Experience* (Bumstead, 1984); *Angel with a Lariat* (Warner Bros., 1987); *Shadowland* (Warner Bros., 1988); *Absolute Torch and Twang* (Warner Bros., 1989); *Ingenue* (Warner Bros., 1992); *All You Can Eat* (Warner Bros., 1995); *Drag* (Warner Bros., 1997); *Invincible Summer* (Warner Bros., 2000); *A Wonderful World* (Sony, 2002). **Soundtrack:** *Even Cowgirls Get the Blues* (Warner Bros., 1993).

BIBLIOGRAPHY: W. Robertson, *k.d. lang: Carrying the Torch* (Toronto, 1993); R. Collis, *k.d. lang* (London, 1999).

DONALD LOWE

JONATHAN LARSON

Born: White Plains, New York, 4 February 1960; died New York, New York, 25 January 1996

Genre: Musical Theater

Best-selling album since 1990: *Rent: Original Broadway Cast Record* (1996)

Although his reputation rests solely on one work—the groundbreaking 1996 musical *Rent*—Jonathan Larson is widely credited with revitalizing Broadway, infusing the commercial theater with an immediacy and freshness that drew in a new generation of young fans. What made *Rent* different was its musical and social relevance. In the 1990s, the majority of Broadway musicals were either "revivals"—remounted versions of classic shows from the past—or new, "family-friendly" shows designed to capitalize on mainstream films such as *Beauty and the Beast* and *Footloose*. With its flashy, rock-based sound and exploration of contemporary issues such as AIDS, drug addiction, and the struggle for artistic integrity, *Rent* captured the uncertainty, confusion, and optimism of audiences in their twenties and thirties. Tragically, Larson—who labored long and hard on *Rent* for seven years—died the night prior to the show's first performance.

Larson grew up in the New York City suburb of White Plains, where he was active in his high school's music and drama departments. Attending Adelphi University on

Long Island, he helped write nine musical theater shows while pursuing his love of acting. He moved to New York after graduation, setting his sights upon a professional theatrical career. During the next fourteen years Larson supported himself by working as a waiter and taking on occasional writing assignments for children's television shows such as *Sesame Street*. In the late 1980s and early 1990s he developed small-scale, or "workshop," productions of his musicals *Superbia*, *J.P. Morgan Saves the Nation*, and *tick, tick . . . BOOM!* During this period, Larson earned the support of legendary musical theater composer Stephen Sondheim, who offered the young artist valuable feedback and guidance.

In 1994 *Rent* had its first workshop production at New York Theatre Workshop, a noted off-Broadway theater company. Based loosely on the classic Puccini opera *La Bohème*, the musical tells the story of a band of struggling artists living in the East Village section of Manhattan. The characters, including Roger, an HIV-positive musician, Daphne, a drug addict, and Angel, a drag queen, represent a cross-section of young people who are set apart from mainstream society. In songs such as "Seasons of Love," which effectively combines rock rhythms with the emotiveness of gospel music, Larson comments on the insecurity of human existence: "How do you measure the life / Of a woman or a man? / In truths that she learned / Or in times that he cried?" Writing in the *New York Times*, drama critic Frank Rich praised the show's boldness: "[Larson] takes the very people whom politicians now turn into scapegoats for our woes—the multi-cultural, the multi-sexual, the homeless, the sick . . . and lets them revel in their joy, their capacity for love and, most important, their tenacity, all in a ceaseless outpouring of melody."

On January 25, 1996, the night before *Rent's* scheduled opening at New York Theatre Workshop (the success of the workshop two years prior had encouraged the company to mount a full-scale production), Larson died in his apartment of an aortic aneurysm. Lacking health insurance or the money to visit a private doctor, he had complained of chest pains and fever during the previous week, but was sent home by emergency rooms at two different hospitals. Within a month of his death, *Rent* became a national sensation, transferring to a larger theater on Broadway and earning coverage in magazines such as *Time* and *Newsweek*. In 2001, Larson's earlier musical, *tick, tick . . . BOOM!*, opened in a new production off-Broadway.

Ultimately, *Rent* did not transform Broadway to the extent that many critics and fans had hoped. By the early 2000s, the Broadway scene was still dominated by revivals and Hollywood adaptations, with little attention given to the cultivation of new, exciting theatrical voices. Nonetheless, Larson breathed life into what many considered a threatened art form—the musical—and helped spur Broadway to a period of economic growth in the late 1990s.

SELECTIVE DISCOGRAPHY: *Rent: Original Broadway Cast Recording* (DreamWorks, 1996).

DAVID FREELAND

AVRIL LAVIGNE

Born: Napanee, Ontario, 27 September 1984
Genre: Rock, Pop
Best-selling album since 1990: *Let Go* (2002)
Hit songs since 1990: "Complicated," "Sk8ter Boi"

Tomboy pop superstar Avril Lavigne quickly made a name for herself in 2002 with her platinum debut album *Let Go*. Her rock-tinged sound and punk-influenced image helped distinguish her from many of the male and female teen pop acts of the previous years. *Let Go* features rock and hip-hop sounds mixed in with more standard pop production, but what sets Lavigne apart from many other teen pop acts is the songwriting credits she shares with professional songwriters on each track.

The middle child of a phone company employee and a homemaker, Lavigne spent her first sixteen years in Napanee, Ontario, a small town two hundred miles northeast of Toronto. She began singing country music publicly at an early age, including a performance with fellow Canadian Shania Twain. Her flexible and expressive alto voice betrays this early experience with country singing. Lavigne began writing her own songs at the age of twelve and soon set her sights on a record contract, signing a deal with New York–based Arista Records in 2000. With a highly publicized move from New York to Los Angeles prior to the completion of *Let Go*, Lavigne took an active role in her career development. In Los Angeles she met up with producer/songwriter Clif Magness, who sculpted the final sound of *Let Go*.

The first two singles from *Let Go*, "Complicated" and "Sk8ter Boi," represent the album's two stylistic poles: medium tempo ballads and more upbeat, pop-rock songs. On "Complicated," which begins characteristically with her solo voice accompanied by acoustic guitar, Lavigne's catchy chorus showcases the strengths of her husky voice. Throughout *Let Go*, her confident singing stands out as the most defining and engaging element of the musical texture. "Sk8ter Boi," with its simple, guitar-heavy texture, borrows from the bratty but highly accessible punk songs made popular by male bands like Blink-182. Lavigne adds a distinctively female point of view, but in the end she aspires merely to be the rock star's girlfriend rather than taking his side either on stage or on a skateboard.

Most of her lyrics are rooted in teen experiences, including the autobiographical "My World."

After years in which the question of authenticity faded from the pop landscape with the popularity of acts like Britney Spears and *NSYNC, Lavigne has successfully placed herself as an alternative to alleged pop superficiality. As Lavigne stresses her guitar playing and songwriting abilities, detractors point to her roots in country and the use of professional songsmiths. They criticize her for jumping on the punk bandwagon in order to sell more records. Her supporters point out that Lavigne has situated herself outside the mainstream—and by implication pop conformity—in interviews and songs like "Anything but Ordinary." Because of this, many of Lavigne's teenage fans find that her music speaks to them more directly than that of the pop princesses who preceded her.

SELECTIVE DISCOGRAPHY: *Let Go* (Arista, 2002).

WEBSITE: www.avril-lavigne.com.

CAROLINE POLK O'MEARA

UTE LEMPER

Born: Munster, Germany, 4 July 1963
Genre: Vocal
Best-selling album since 1990: *Punishing Kiss* (2000)

Ute Lemper is a Bavarian-voiced cabaret stylist whose work, despite an edgy defiance of the mainstream, has somehow trickled into the pop music scene. Never one to follow the pack, the statuesque singer evolved from a theater background, is proficient in a variety of art forms, and renowned for her bold one-person shows. Lemper is the foremost living performer of German composer Kurt Weill's music.

While growing up in Munster, Germany, Ute (pronounced Oo'-tah) Lemper's parents sent her to classical singing, ballet, and piano training at an early age and she worked professionally in jazz bars and nightclubs by age fifteen. Shortly after, she joined a punk rock band but left to study classical and musical theater at the Max Reinhardt Seminary in Vienna. Andrew Lloyd Webber placed Lemper in his 1983 Viennese production of *Cats* and she played the characters Grizabella and Bombalurina over the course of that year. In 1986, her career quickly picked up momentum as the European theater world took notice of her portrayal of Sally Bowles in the European tour of *Cabaret*. She won the Moliere Award for best actress in a musical during the Paris leg of the tour. New York City audiences were introduced to Lemper in 1987 when she performed a musical repertoire of Weill in a one-person show. A subsequent world tour and an album, *Ute Lemper Sings Kurt Weill* (1989),

were widely acclaimed. Lemper also began working extensively as a film actress and portrayed Lola in the German film, *Blue Angel*. Continually at odds with her German heritage, she left her native country in the early 1990s and began living in Paris, London, and New York where she centered her eclectic interest in a variety of art forms. Lemper wrote political articles for European publications, published two books, displayed her paintings in Paris exhibits and danced as a principal in the ballet, *La Mort Subite*.

Often compared to Edith Piaf and Marlene Dietrich from her already extensive recording career, Lemper made a first foray into popular music with *Crimes of the Heart* (1991). The album contains songs in English, French, and German and only hints at mainstream pop, as Lemper's flexible soprano possesses a rich, timeless quality that recurrently conjures up smoky German nightclubs. The album's title song is a ballad laced with Lemper's trademark irony. In 1995, she recorded *City of Strangers* (1995) and lent her breathy interpretations to the works of Stephen Sondheim and popular French poet/songwriter, Jacques Prevert. One of the highlights from *City of Strangers* is the silky, aching "Losing My Mind."

Lemper stepped into the world of Bob Fosse in 1998 when she joined the Broadway cast of the already-running hit show, *Chicago*, to play one of the leads, Velma Kelly. More accustomed to the flexibility of one-person shows and other self-created projects, Lemper found performing in *Chicago* somewhat stifling. Her stylized performance confounded critics, but the notoriety gained from the show in addition to a recording, *All That Jazz: The Best of Ute Lemper,* whose title song came from *Chicago,* expanded her cult following. She built on that by releasing *Punishing Kiss* (2000), a collection of songs written by notable artists such as Elvis Costello, Tom Waits, Nick Cave, Philip Glass, and many others. Songs from *Punishing Kiss* began to overcome reluctant radio airplay and its sales increased.

Never one to stray far from the music of despair, Lemper's *But One Day* (2002) revisits the work of Weill and other cabaret/art songs, including Jacques Brel's musically gorgeous but forlorn tale, "Amsterdam." It also features five songs written by Lemper. A concert tour of *But One Day* kicked off in Germany following the album's release and she continues to perform concerts and one-woman shows all around the world. Lemper is married to American comedian/actor David Tabatsky and they reside in New York City.

Lemper is a maverick who possesses diverse talents, a fearless heart, and a true artist's soul. Strikingly beautiful, her astonishing insistence to pursue only projects that stir her passion has kept her from becoming a more mainstream star.

SELECTIVE DISCOGRAPHY: *Life Is a Cabaret* (CBS, 1987); *Ute Lemper Sings Kurt Weill* (Decca, 1988); *I*

Dreamed a Dream (CBS, 1988); *Crimes of the Heart* (Polygram, 1991); *Ute Lemper Sings Kurt Weill, Vol. 2* (Decca, 1993); *Espace Indecent* (Polydor, 1993); *City of Strangers* (Decca, 1995); *Berlin Cabaret Songs* (Decca, 1997); *All That Jazz: The Best of Ute Lemper* (Decca, 1998); *Punishing Kiss* (Decca, 2000); *But One Day* (Decca, 2003).

DONALD LOWE

ANNIE LENNOX

Born: Aberdeen, Scotland, 25 December 1954

Genre: Rock

Best-selling album since 1990: *Diva* (1992)

Hit songs since 1990: "Why," "Walking on Broken Glass," "No More I Love You"

The Eurythmics stood out as one of the most colorful groups of the 1980s; they were a slick, synth pop group with a strong international following thanks to the efforts of Dave Stewart and Annie Lennox. The latter's appearances in music videos were groundbreaking for their time, provoking strong reactions from the media and public. For many, however, her teasing displays of sexual ambiguity were confusing. At the 1984 Grammy Awards, MTV demanded her birth certificate as proof that she was a woman when she appeared disguised as Elvis Presley with greased black hair and fake sideburns. Lennox's impersonations of both men and women demonstrated how a female pop artist could seek new forms of representation within the apparatus of music television. Following the release of the album *We Too Are One* (1989), which was a commercial letdown, Lennox announced that she would be leaving the group to have a child. In 1991 the Eurythmics quietly disbanded.

From an early age Lennox played flute and piano and advanced so well that she got into the Royal Academy of Music in London. However, the pressures and demands of a classical training became too much, and she left just prior to her final exams. More inspired by popular music, especially the sounds of Motown, she directed her energies to session singing. This led to the formation of a group, the Catch, in 1977, which later became the Tourists, whose members included Dave Stewart and Peet Coombes. They released three albums before breaking up on tour in Bangkok in 1980. It was at this stage that Lennox and Stewart formed the Eurythmics.

In the early 1990s after the breakup of the Eurythmics, Lennox embarked on a solo career with work on her debut album, *Diva* (1992). The material on this album caters to a more adult contemporary public. With the success of two singles from the album, "Walking on Broken Glass" and "Why," the *Diva* album sold millions of copies internationally and was nominated for three Grammy Awards. While "Walking on Broken Glass" is an up-tempo, aggressive, rock-driven number, "Why" is pensive and balladlike, with Lennox pouring her emotions into beautifully shaped, tuneful lyrics. These songs marked Lennox's arrival at a more mature and reflective style. Tapping into the synth-based pop and rock styles of the time, Lennox fashioned a sound that appealed to a wide audience. Above all, her powerful voice encompassed an extensive range of expressive nuances. The album's blend of electropop, rock, and R&B is testimony to Lennox's assuredness and versatility.

In promoting the album, Lennox continued to experiment with gender roles and to question notions of traditional femininity and masculinity through androgynous display. The image of her on the album cover—heavily made up, with feather plumage—challenges the domain of male drag, suggesting that gender should take a backseat to talent in pop music. In the promotional videos accompanying the album, the issue of gender-bending is central. Lennox masquerades as the character she actually seeks to reject. She draws on a range of characterizations, from the pretty little girl to the smirking femme fatale diva. These visual reference points help to draw out the musical expression and stylistic resources of her performances with Lennox breaking out of the constraints of traditional femininity to journey into a world of guises and masks.

The 1995 release of Lennox's second solo album, *Medusa*, was preceded by the hit single from the album, "No More I Love You." Lennox's voice gracefully strains and swells in this touching ballad. The accompanying video, which received high exposure on MTV, also challenges gender roles with men dressed up as female ballet dancers in a lampoon of the ballet *Swan Lake*. Like her first album, *Medusa* offers electropop with smatterings of other pop and rock styles, and the quality of the mix and production stand out. Musical allegiances to artists and groups such as the Clash, Neil Young, and Al Green are evident. Lennox adapts the Clash's song "Train in Vain" and Young's "Don't Let It Bring You Down" in renditions that work best if one does not know the original. Her delivery of the classic "A Whiter Shade of Pale" is an emotional tour de force. Much of the artistic merit of *Medusa* is attributable to the well-crafted and poignant charts of Lennox's arranger, Anne Dudley.

In 1996 Lennox released a limited-edition live album, *Live in Central Park*, and, much to everyone's surprise, teamed up with Stewart two years later to re-form the Eurythmics. The reunion proved successful enough to warrant the release of a new album, *Peace* (1999). In 2000 Lennox's video compilation, *Totally Diva*, was released on DVD with two additional tracks, "Precious" and "Remember." Included on this compilation is "Why," the track that won the MTV Video Award for Best Female Video in 1992. Although Lennox's output is not extensive, she stands as a major female artist in the MTV era.

SELECTIVE DISCOGRAPHY: *Diva* (Arista, 1992); *Medusa* (Arista, 1995); *Train in Vain* (RCA, 1995); *Bare* (J-Records, 2003).

BIBLIOGRAPHY: L. Ellis and B. Sutherland, *Annie Lennox: The Biography* (New York, 2002); S. Hawkins, *Settling the Pop Score* (Aldershot, England, 2002).

STAN HAWKINS

JAMES LEVINE

Born: Cincinnati, Ohio, 23 June 1943
Genre: Classical

It was said by some in the 1990s that the best orchestra in America was the Metropolitan Opera Orchestra. If it was, credit goes to James Levine, who became the orchestra's principal conductor in 1973 and the opera company's music director in 1976. In 1986 the company showed its approval of Levine by making him its first-ever artistic director. He is credited with developing the Met orchestra and chorus to its highest level ever and securing the Met's status as America's top opera company.

Levine's accomplishments at the Met are in part due to an expansive conducting style and solid musicianship. But they are also the result of his level of commitment to working with the company—he spends more than seven months of every season at the Met, which is unusual in an era of jet-setting maestros. By 2000 he had conducted almost 2,000 performances of seventy operas at the Met. He also grants players in the orchestra an unusually high level of autonomy in managing their own affairs, and his collaborative style has attracted some of the best musicians in America.

One sign of the Met orchestra's high standing is the extent of its performances outside its home opera house. Levine and the orchestra began performing concerts away from the Met in 1991 and have toured Japan, Europe, and the United States, including annual performances at Carnegie Hall.

Though Levine's biggest accomplishments have been as a conductor, his musical talent was first obvious as a pianist. He was a child prodigy and made his pianistic debut at the age of ten as a soloist with the Cincinnati

Symphony Orchestra. He studied piano and conducting at the Juilliard School in New York and in 1963 was named assistant conductor of the Cleveland Orchestra under George Szell—at twenty-one, the youngest assistant in the orchestra's history. He stayed in Cleveland for five years, but his real career break came in 1971, when he first guest-conducted at the Met.

Levine established the *Metropolitan Opera Presents* series of live public television broadcasts and founded the Young Artist Development Program. He has also broadened the company's repertoire by including premieres of operas by Mozart, Verdi, Schoenberg, Rossini, Weill, Berg, Stravinsky, Gershwin, and new commissions from John Corigliano, John Harbison, and Philip Glass.

In addition to his Met duties, Levine is a busy guest conductor and has conducted nearly every major orchestra in the world. He has had close relationships with the Vienna and Berlin Philharmonics, the Dresden Staatskapelle, and London's Philharmonic Orchestra; he has also been a regular guest artist at the festivals in Salzburg and Bayreuth. For twenty-five years (1971–1995) he was music director of the Chicago Symphony's summer Ravinia Festival. In 1999 he became chief conductor of the Munich Philharmonic and was appointed music director of the Boston Symphony beginning in 2004.

Since 1996 Levine has often been conductor of the lucrative *Three Tenors* stadium shows, and in 1999 he conducted the soundtrack for Disney's *Fantasia 2000*. He is also a much-admired piano accompanist and chamber musician, and he performs frequently in recital with some of the world's best vocalists and instrumental soloists. He has made more than 200 recordings with some of the best soloists and orchestras in the world.

As a conductor, artistic administrator, pianist, and music personality, Levine has established himself as one of the most important figures on the American classical music scene. Among his many awards and honors are the National Medal of Arts (1997), Austria's Gold Cross of Honor, and a Kennedy Center Honor (2002).

SELECTIVE DISCOGRAPHY: *James Levine's 25th Anniversary Gala* (Deutsche Grammophon, 1996); *Mahler Symphony No. 7* with the Chicago Symphony (RCA, 1980); *Maestro at the Met* (Deutsche Grammophon, 1995).

BIBLIOGRAPHY: R. Marsh, *Dialogues and Discoveries: James Levine: His Life and His Music* (New York, 1998).

DOUGLAS McLENNAN

OTTMAR LIEBERT

Born: Cologne, Germany, 1963
Genre: New Age, Flamenco Rock

Best-selling album since 1990: *Nouveau Flamenco* (1990)

Hit songs since 1990: "Santa Fe," "Rosa Negra," "Barcelona Nights"

Born to a Chinese-German father and a Hungarian mother, Ottmar Liebert was exposed to a wide variety of music while growing up. Early on, he learned to play guitar, a gift from his father, and his love of the instrument led to studies in classical guitar at Germany's Rheinische Musikhochschule. At age eighteen, he began to travel through Russia and Asia, studying traditional music of the region.

While he was fascinated with the indigenous rhythms he was discovering, including flamenco, he was eventually disappointed to find very few outlets for this music. In Germany, and later in Boston, Massachusetts, where he moved, Liebert played guitar in a few jazz/funk bands. When the last of these bands broke up in 1985, Liebert moved to Santa Fe, New Mexico.

Perhaps it was the move away from the concentrated music industry where the pressure to "make it" was high, or the comfort in the more laid-back ambience of New Mexico, but Liebert found himself relaxed in Santa Fe where the artistic community was thriving. Playing in restaurants, Liebert developed a style that incorporated the influences he ran across in Europe and Asia. By 1988 he formed his band, Luna Negra. It was here that Liebert began to hone his fusion of rock, pop, folk, and flamenco, a hybrid that eventually wound up on his self-released debut *Marita: Shadows and Storms* (1988). Liebert had originally teamed up with local artist Frank Howell, producing the compact discs (CDs) that would be distributed along with Howell's drawings. Copies of the CD found their way to Los Angeles smooth jazz station KTWV (the Wave) in 1989. Several CD songs were added to the playlist and after label reps from Higher Octave took note, they signed Liebert, and eventually re-released the CD as *Nouveau Flamenco* (1990).

Liebert's sonic signature features the mixture of synthesizer and electric bass around the basic flamenco form. Alternately sultry and ambient, the CD attracted new fans to flamenco, but the CD also draws on influences from R&B and jazz to Asia and the Middle East. Tracks like "Barcelona Nights" and "Santa Fe" mix spicy grooves with lush New Agey synthesizer washes.

Liebert further sharpens his vision on subsequent albums. *Solo Para Ti* (1992) features contributions by rock guitarist Carlos Santana. Liebert expands his palette with soul and blues standards on *The Hours between Night and Day* (1993). Impressive is his new reading on "Ten Piedad de Mi," a Spanish cover of soulmaster Marvin Gaye's classic "Mercy Mercy Me."

Electronic fans found plenty to enjoy on Liebert's *Euphoria* (1995). Although essentially remixes of material from *The Hours between Night and Day*, the album features mix masters Steve Hillage and Aki Nawaz of England. *Little Wing* (2001) features Liebert tackling classic rock by interpreting Led Zeppelin's "Kashmir," Jimi Hendrix's "Little Wing," and the Rolling Stones' "Paint It Black." Cynics may carp that Liebert's recent records contain too many remixes, compilations, or covers with little original material. But in the larger picture, Liebert, through his masterful compositions and virtuosity, helped bring flamenco and his various fusions to a wider audience.

SELECTIVE DISCOGRAPHY: *Nouveau Flamenco* (Higher Octave, 1990); *The Hours between Night and Day* (Epic, 1993); *Euphoria* (Epic, 1995); *Opium* (Epic, 1996); *Little Wing* (Epic, 2001).

RAMIRO BURR

LIL' KIM

Born: Kimberly Jones; New York, New York, 11 July 1977

Genre: Hip-Hop

Best-selling album since 1990: *The Notorious K.I.M.* (2000)

Hit songs since 1990: "No Time," "Not Tonight," "How Many Licks"

Diminutive hip-hop queen Lil' Kim became one of the most distinctive female voices in late 1990s rap music. In contrast to pro-women rappers from the 1980s like Queen Latifah, Lil' Kim's explicit, sexual raps use the language of unquenchable male sexual desire to describe her own sexuality. She thus turns rap's misogyny against itself. In the four-year lapse between her first two albums, during which her lover and mentor Biggie Smalls was murdered, Lil' Kim established herself as one of hip-hop's prime cultural icons.

Lil' Kim, born Kimberly Jones, grew up in Brooklyn, New York. Her parents divorced when Jones was nine years old, and she soon found herself in her father's custody. By Jones's account her father, a bus driver and member of the Air Force Reserve, was a strict disciplinarian. She ran away in her early teens and for a handful of years lived an itinerant lifestyle, staying with a series of boyfriends or on the streets. This ended when she was discovered by up-and-coming rapper Biggie Smalls, also called the Notorious B.I.G. (born Christopher Wallace). Jones quickly became the lone female member of the Junior M.A.F.I.A. (Masters at Finding Intelligent Attitudes), a group assembled by Smalls. It was here that 4-foot-11 Jones became Lil' Kim.

Lil' Kim launched her solo career following the success of the Junior M.A.F.I.A. release *Conspiracy* (1995) and their single "Player's Anthem." Her debut album, *Hard Core* (1996), was released on Smalls's Undeas Recordings, and recorded by a group of producers that included Sean "Puff Daddy" (later "P. Diddy") Combs. At the time, *Hard Core* was the best-selling debut rap album by a woman, and its first single, "No Time," charted. The lyrics on *Hard Core* depict a sexually liberated, confident woman. The song "Dreams" begins with a group of women sitting around discussing which R&B singer they find most sexually desirable, turning the tables on a popular hip-hop trope.

The murder of Smalls in 1997 hit Lil' Kim hard. This, combined with the theft of several tracks from her new album, pushed her sophomore release back two years. In the interval Lil' Kim stayed in the public eye. When it was finally released, *The Notorious K.I.M.* (2000) confirmed Lil' Kim's reputation as one of the most explicit rappers around. On the single "How Many Licks," she describes her many lovers. Whereas *Hard Core* was an explicit celebration of female sexuality, *The Notorious K.I.M.* finds the artist in charge, demanding oral sex, multiple orgasms and, above all, control. Her star continued to rise—along with pop artists Pink, Christina Aguilera, and Mya she released a remake of the 1970s classic "Lady Marmalade," whose sexy video won MTV's Video of the Year in 2001.

Critics maintain it is difficult to determine whether Lil' Kim's explicit raps mark the heights of female sexual liberation or the depths of self-objectification. While other female rappers, including her arch-rival Foxy Brown, write sexually graphic lyrics, Lil' Kim has distinguished herself by accentuating the discord between her small body and larger than life voice.

SELECTIVE DISCOGRAPHY: *Hard Core* (Atlantic, 1996); *The Notorious K.I.M.* (Atlantic, 2000).

WEBSITE: www.lilkim.com.

CAROLINE POLK O'MEARA

LIMP BIZKIT

Formed: 1994, Jacksonville, Florida

Members: Fred Durst, vocals (William Frederick Durst, born Jacksonville, Florida, 20 August 1971); DJ Lethal, turntables (Leor DiMant, born Latvia, 18 December 1972); John Otto, drums (born Jacksonville, Florida); Sam Rivers, bass (born Jacksonville, Florida, 21 September 1977). Former member: Wes Borland, guitar (born Richmond, Virginia, 7 February 1975).

Genre: Rock

Best-selling album since 1990: *Significant Other* (1999)
Hit songs since 1990: "Counterfeit," "Nookie," "My Way"

In the late 1990s, Limp Bizkit started a musical rebellion. Though not the first group to meld the attitude and style of hip-hop with hard rock and funk, Limp Bizkit were among the most successful. They helped to launch a raft of imitators in a category dubbed "nu-metal" for its contemporary spin on heavy metal. Under the inspiration of Fred Durst, a former tattoo artist-turned-record-mogul and their singer/rapper and visionary, the group released a string of hit albums. With cathartic hits such as "Nookie" and "Counterfeit," they developed a reputation for loutish, misogynist behavior, volatile fans, and outrageous live shows.

A native of Gaston County, North Carolina, Fred Durst, the son of a police officer and social worker, grew up listening to rap and break dancing in local competitions while also feeding his hunger for the hard rock of bands such as Nirvana and Soundgarden. Durst began pursuing a career in tattooing when, in 1994, he saw the bassist Sam Rivers performing with his heavy metal band and convinced Rivers to join him in a new group.

The group got an early break when the California hard rockers Korn performed their first show in Jacksonville in 1995. When Korn returned to Jacksonville the next year, Durst gave them Limp Bizkit's demo tape, which was passed on to the rising hard rock producer Ross Robinson. In 1996 the band signed with up-and-coming independent label Flip Records. The lineup was completed that year by DJ Lethal.

Their debut, *Three Dollar Bill, Y'all* (1997), failed to make an impression on the charts when first released. In the first of many controversies to follow, Limp Bizkit found themselves at the center of a media firestorm when it was revealed that Flip's distributor, Interscope Records, had paid a Portland, Oregon, station to play the thrashing single "Counterfeit" fifty times. Although technically legal—the song was prefaced by a voice-over announcing the sponsor, making it a paid ad—the move was frowned upon by the music press and industry insiders.

Limp Bizkit's debut signaled a shift in rock music. Ushering in a new genre of rock variously called "rapcore" or "nu-metal," the album blends hard rock with funk bass and Durst's screamed lyrics about low self-worth and anger at the world ("Pollution," "Nobody Loves Me"). Critics, though, faulted the group for their one-dimensional sound and the misogynist lyrics of "Stuck."

In 1998 Limp Bizkit performed an energetic set on MTV's *Spring Break Fashion Show*; that appearance led to more support from the channel and a very important slot

| Nu-Metal Explosion

For a generation of young men with rock-star dreams in the 1990s, the rhythms and attitude of hip-hop were just as vital a part of their musical education as the posturing and guitar slinging of rock gods past. Combining their love of rapping and programmed drum beats with crunching guitar chords and pent-up aggression, Limp Bizkit led the charge for a new genre of bands that came to be known as nu-metal, a moniker that signified their embrace of fresh styles over the traditionally bombastic attack of heavy metal. The successors to the noisy grunge mantle of the early 90s, these nu-metal bands tended to vent their spleen about dysfunctional childhoods over the scratching of turntables and distorted guitars. With the success of their 1997 debut, Limp Bizkit provided the formula for the success of dozens of other platinum nu-metal acts such as Linkin Park, Sevendust, Disturbed, P.O.D., Saliva, and Staind.

At their peak Limp Bizkit became embroiled in yet another controversy. Durst was roundly criticized for inciting fans to follow the edict of a *Significant Other* song, "Break Stuff," during the group's set at the disastrous Woodstock '99 concert, which ended the next day in fiery riots and several alleged sexual assaults. Following Durst's exhortation, the crowd in the teeming mosh pit near the front of the stage became frenzied, leading to dozens of injuries and an alleged rape in the swirling pit. The band's set was cut short because of the chaos.

In the fall of 1999, the group released their third album, *Chocolate Starfish and the Hot Dog Flavored Water*, which sold more than 1 million copies its first week, a new record for a rock group. Along with Durst's profane lyrics, delivered in his pinched, nasal style, the album features the standard array of crunching metal chords from Borland and deep, throbbing rhythms from John Otto and Sam Rivers. In songs such as "My Generation," Durst also enters into the time-honored tradition of grousing about how, in light of his success, nobody understands him.

Citing creative differences, Borland split with the group in October. An album of remixes, *New Old Songs*, sans Borland's contributions, was released in December. In January 2002 Durst launched a heavily hyped, twenty-two-city talent contest in search of a fresh face to replace Borland. The stunt did not yield the expected results, and Durst made a public plea to Borland to return in May 2002, a plea that Borland shunned. The group recorded their fourth album, *Bipolar* (2003), with no lead guitarist in place.

Limp Bizkit were not the first nu-metal band, but they were certainly among the genre's most popular and controversial groups. Critics lambasted the band for what was termed their "mook rock" attitude—denigrating and objectifying women—while mostly male fans eagerly embraced their antiestablishment, testosterone-driven lyrics and music.

SELECTIVE DISCOGRAPHY: *Three Dollar Bill, Y'all* (Flip/Interscope, 1997); *Significant Other* (Flip/Interscope, 1999); *Chocolate Starfish and the Hot Dog Flavored Water* (Flip/Interscope, 2000); *New Old Songs* (Flip/Interscope, 2001); *Less Is More* (Flip/Interscope, 2003).

GIL KAUFMAN

on that summer's inaugural Family Values tour, headlined by Korn. The group also performed on the Ozzfest tour.

Shortly after the debut of the rap/metal song "Nookie," the first single from the band's second album, *Significant Other* (1999), Limp Bizkit had become rock superstars. Durst's signature look, a red backwards baseball cap, black work pants, and a white T-shirt, had become the outfit of choice for both the band's male and female fans. The album debuted at number one on the *Billboard* album charts and sold more than 635,000 copies in its first week, a stunning achievement for a relatively new rock band. The testosterone-laden lyrics and aggressive music is augmented here with a string section, coupled with more cathartic lyrics from Durst.

The album features even more hip-hop attitude and music than earlier releases, with Lethal's turntable scratching and rap-style beats moving to the fore along with improved, fluid rapping from Durst. Guest rapping from Method Man and production by the revered hip-hopper DJ Premier also helped the group gain credibility within the hip-hop community, while Wes Borland's guitar keeps them firmly rooted in heavy metal.

LINKIN PARK

Formed: 1996, Los Angeles, California
Members: Chester Bennington, vocals (born 20 March 1976); Rob Bourdon, drums (born Calabasas, California, 20 January 1979); Brad Delson, guitar (born 1 December 1977); Darren "Phoenix" Farrell, bass (born Plymouth, Massachusetts, 8 February 1977); Joseph Hahn, turntables (born 15 March 1977); Mike Shinoda, bass (born 11 February 1977).

Genre: Rock

Best-selling album since 1990: *Hybrid Theory* (2000)

Hit songs since 1990: "Crawling," "One Step Closer"

The members of Linkin Park were as shocked as anyone when their debut album *Hybrid Theory* (2000) became the biggest-selling album of 2001. This was, after all, a rap-rock outfit whose nu-metal sound, a blend of turntable scratching, hard rock guitars, rapping, and singing, was allegedly on its way out. Instead, the six-man Los Angeles band that could barely get meetings with executives at record labels just a few years before became the surprise success story of the year.

Linkin Park began life in 1996 as a Los Angeles high school heavy metal band named Xero. Guitarist Brad Delson and drummer Rob Bourdon had performed in a high school band called Relative Degree, which had set the single goal of performing a show at the Los Angeles club, the Roxy, which they did, then promptly broke up.

Vocalist Mike Shinoda, another friend of Delson's, had attended a few Relative Degree practices, developing a songwriting partnership with the guitarist. The two began the messy experiment of mixing Delson's love of hard rock with Shinoda's appreciation for hip-hop. The pair recruited DJ Joseph Hahn after he and Shinoda met while studying in the same painting course at the Pasadena Arts Center.

Xero's first recordings were created in Shinoda's cramped bedroom studio. Delson also asked fellow UCLA student and roommate Darren "Phoenix" Farrell to join the group; Farrell would leave the band in 2000 to join Tasty Snax, returning in 2002. The budding band decided they needed a proper singer, which they found in transplanted Arizona native Chester Bennington, who completed the lineup in 1999. When Bennington's impassioned singing melded with Shinoda's streetwise rapping, Linkin Park's signature sound was born: a unique mix of old school hip-hop rapping and turntable scratching, classic rock guitar riffs, and a subtle underpinning of electronic dance music beats and ambience. Before they had a recording contract, the group secured a publishing deal from Zomba Recordings in 1999 after their first showcase at Los Angeles' famed bar, the Whisky-a-Go-Go. They used the money to record an album of songs to play for record labels and sell at shows.

A Slow Crawl to the Top

Though in 1999 three different labels rebuffed the group—now known as Linkin Park—Warner Bros. Records offered them a deal with the artistic control they craved and they began work on *Hybrid Theory* with pro-

ducers the Dust Brothers (Beck) and Don Gilmore (Eve 6, Pearl Jam). The album was released in the fall of 2000, debuting at number sixteen on the *Billboard* charts. Once the singles "Crawling" and the cathartic "One Step Closer" ("Everything you say to me / Takes me one step closer to the edge / And I'm about to break / I need a little room to breathe") gained increased radio play, the album began a march up the charts into the Top 10, where it would reside, on and off, for nearly a year.

Tours with Family Values 2001, featuring a lineup that, like Linkin Park, favored mixing heavy metal with hip-hop, and Projekt: Revolution, featuring rappers Cypress Hill, kept the group on the road for 324 days in 2001, paying off in January 2002 with three Grammy Award nominations. The group took home one Grammy Award for Best Hard Rock Performance for "Crawling." With more than 6 million copies in sales, *Hybrid Theory* was named the top-selling album of 2001, a huge accomplishment for a group's debut. Hahn and Shinoda lent their voices to a hit single, "It's Going Down," for the hip-hop group the X-Ecutioners in early 2002.

The achievements were a testament to the group's hard work and artistic vision, which extends to all aspects of their imagery and style. Bennington designs clothing for the Replicant Company, Hahn directed the "Crawling" video, as well as five other clips, and Shinoda designed the cover art for the group's albums, which he also co-produced.

Eager to keep their momentum flowing, the group entered a studio in summer 2002 to record the twenty-track remix album *Reanimated*. An amalgamation of ambient passages and radical reworkings of their songs, the album features new tracks and guest vocals from rappers Rasco & Planet Asia, Aceyalone, Pharoahe Monch, and Black Thought, as well as Staind singer Aaron Lewis, Korn singer Jonathan Davis, and Orgy singer Jay Gordon. For songs such as the hit "Crawling"—renamed "Krwlng" for this album—the group has completely reimagined the track, adding classical violin and cello in place of crunching guitars for a majestic sound that is more chamber music than hard rock. Aaron Lewis's haunting vocals float over the string section, layered with stuttering samples, a faint drum machine beat, and rapping.

Though their mix-and-match style of music was believed to be on the wane following a period in which many rock bands had added superfluous DJs or rappers to their lineups, Linkin Park's combination of arresting visuals and tightly produced rap-rock tracks made them the breakout success story of the early 2000s. Linkin Park's third album, *Meteora*, was released in 2003.

SELECTIVE DISCOGRAPHY: *Hybrid Theory* (Warner Bros., 2000); *Reanimation* (Warner Bros., 2002); *Meteora* (Warner Bros., 2003).

WEBSITE: www.linkinpark.com.

GIL KAUFMAN

LIVE

Formed: 1984, York, Pennsylvania

Members: Patrick Dahlheimer, bass (born York, Pennsylvania, 30 May 1971); Chad Gracey, drums, background vocals (born York, Pennsylvania, 23 July 1971); Edward Kowalczyk, vocals, guitar (born York, Pennsylvania, 16 July 1971); Chad Taylor, guitar, background vocals (born Lancaster, Pennsylvania, 24 November 1970).

Genre: Rock

Best-selling album since 1990: *Throwing Copper* (1994)

Hit songs since 1990: "Selling the Drama," "I Alone," "Lightning Crashes"

The rock band Live (pronounced with a long *i*) was formed in the band members' hometown of York, Pennsylvania, in the mid-1980s as an after-school project of four middle-school students: Chad Gracey, Patrick Dahlheimer, Edward Kowalczyk, and Chad Taylor. Theirs is a stereotypical rock and roll story: A small-town band is discovered and signed by a record label's representative and then goes on to international fame and fortune. Their second album for Radioactive, *Throwing Copper* (1994), resulted in overnight success; with the popularity of "Selling the Drama" and "I Alone," Live found an audience thirsty for idealistic, honest rock music with a message.

Live's debut album, *Mental Jewelry* (1991), is notable for singer Kowalczyk's propulsive, passionate tenor and the stellar, steady rhythm section of Gracey on bass and Dahlheimer on drums. On *Throwing Copper*, Live manages to keep their raw sound while smoothing it out with a clean, glossy layer. *Throwing Copper* landed near the top of the charts and earned the band a spot on the popular Lollapalooza tour.

In many respects, Live is an unlikely rock band because of its preoccupations with religion, spirituality, mortality, and hot-button issues. The powerful, muscular *Throwing Copper* features some hit singles, including the passionate "I Alone," "Selling the Drama," and the moving crescendo of "Lightning Crashes," whose elliptical lyrics tell the story of a classmate who was killed by a drunk driver in 1993.

Unfortunately, even though their next albums—*Secret Samadhi* (1997), which debuted at number one on the *Billboard* 200 album chart and *The Distance to Here* (1999), which debuted at number four—sold reasonably well, critics dismissed them as dry, joyless, and didactic, earnestly

retreading the same thematically sanctimonious turf. Toward the end of the 1990s, renewed by the energy of popular nu-metal bands such as Limp Bizkit, Live went back into the studio to record their fifth album, appropriately titled *V*. On *V*, Live's anthems are delivered with a heavy hand and offer little inspiration despite the fervor of their message.

Live has yet to equal or surpass the majesty and power of *Throwing Copper*. Nevertheless, they continue to create rock music that aspires to grapple with serious social issues.

SELECTIVE DISCOGRAPHY: *Mental Jewelry* (Radioactive, 1991); *Throwing Copper* (Radioactive, 1994); *Secret Samadhi* (Radioactive, 1997); *The Distance to Here* (Radioactive, 1999); *V* (Radioactive, 2001).

CARRIE HAVRANEK

LL COOL J

Born: James Todd Smith; Long Island, New York, 17 January 1968

Genre: Hip-Hop, Rap

Best-selling album since 1990: *Mama Said Knock You Out* (1990)

Hit songs since 1990: "Mama Said Knock You Out," "Hey Lover," "Luv U Better"

As one of the first rappers to achieve mainstream success, LL Cool J helped to define the brash but playful style of 1980s hip-hop. As other acts from the era began to fade, he retained his commercial and artistic clout through a signature mix of streetwise rhyming and engaging humor.

Rapping Young

James Todd Smith witnessed the birth of hip-hop while growing up in Queens, New York, during the 1970s. He started composing and performing raps before the age of ten under the stage name LL Cool J (which stands for "Ladies Love Cool James"). After receiving a DJ system as a birthday present, he recorded a series of demo tapes and distributed them to major record companies. He attracted the attention of the fledgling hip-hop label Def Jam, which signed the young rapper and released his first single, "I Need a Beat," in 1984. The single was a modest success and led to the recording of the album *Radio* (1985). The consciously stripped-down production gives *Radio* a harsh and aggressive tone, but LL Cool J's clever rhymes and penchant for pop-song structure lend the album an unmistakable personality. He followed the work with *Bigger and Deffer* (1986), which features two significant hit singles: the incendiary boast track "I'm Bad" and the tender ballad "I Need Love." The effort sealed his reputation as hip-hop's resident lover. His next album, *Walking with a Panther* (1989), found him in an even more playful mood with the dynamic and witty singles "I'm That Type of Guy" and "Jingling Baby."

Don't Call It a Comeback

While *Walking with a Panther* was a mainstream hit, LL Cool J faced disapproval from the hip-hop mainstream for embracing the pop audience. He responded to his critics with the blistering *Mama Said Knock You Out* (1990), a hard-edged but catchy affair that ranks among the best hip-hop albums of the 1990s. The title track delivers a punishing mission statement, from its opening line ("Don't call it a comeback!") to the dense, bass-heavy production. The complex beats and layered samples, a mix of hard funk and pop hooks, make for a full-bodied sound. The album appeals to hip-hop fans with hard, rolling jams ("The Boomin' System") and to pop listeners with spirited love songs ("Around the Way Girl"). *Mama Said Knock You Out* proved that rap could be commercial and stay true to its roots.

The staggering success of the album led to a number of career detours. LL Cool J performed with a full acoustic band on MTV's popular program *Unplugged*, delivering a raucous and utterly unique performance of "Mama Said Knock You Out" that drove even more interest in the album. He also began an acting career, winning minor parts in Hollywood films, and he performed at the inauguration of President Bill Clinton in 1993. He returned to recording that year with *14 Shots to the Dome*. The album brought a more focused attempt to win the respect of the hip-hop community with even harder beats and rhymes than those of *Mama Said Knock You Out*. But because LL Cool J neglected his gift for pop songcraft, the album produced no major hits. There are good songs, including the cheeky love anthem "Backseat" and the provocative opener "How I'm Comin'," but the work does not give full reign to LL Cool J's distinctive personality.

As *14 Shots to the Dome* fell from the charts, LL Cool J took the lead role in a television sitcom titled *In the House*. The show returned him to mainstream exposure and led to the unexpected success of the album *Mr. Smith* (1995). The record provided the blueprint for the next phase of his career with its emphasis on mature love songs and witty rhymes backed by smooth, well-produced R&B beats. "Hey Lover," a confessional ballad performed with the R&B vocal group Boyz II Men, placed LL Cool J back at the top of the pop charts, once again proving his tenacity. Each song is a portrait of a different LL Cool J persona, from boastful lover ("Doin' It") to streetwise firebrand ("God Bless") to pop powerhouse ("Loungin'"). Far from

distracting him, his career as an actor taught him how to bring subtle details to his stock musical characters.

Phenomenon followed in 1997 with the same basic structure of party jams and smooth soul ballads. Despite its unabashed appeal to the pop audience, the album actually thrust LL Cool J back into the center of the world of rap thanks to the track "4, 3, 2, 1." The song features turns by the hardcore rappers Redman, Method Man, and DMX, as well as the newcomer Canibus. Shortly after the album's release, Canibus engaged LL Cool J in a rap battle with the single "2nd Round KO," in which he accuses the older rapper of stealing his rhymes. LL Cool J responded with "The Ripper Strikes Back," an unrelenting track marked by a string of one-liners and put-downs not seen since his early days. Once again, LL Cool J blurred the lines of hardcore and commercial rap, proving himself to be the most versatile MC in the business.

G.O.A.T. Featuring James T. Smith: The Greatest of All Time (2000) and *10* (2002) find LL Cool J as comfortable as ever with his dual lover-man/hardcore rapper demeanor. While many hip-hop artists follow his formula of alternating sensitivity and brutishness, few can pull it off with similar charisma and technical verve. LL Cool J has demonstrated that personality can win out over trendiness and that it is possible to sustain a long and successful career.

SELECTIVE DISCOGRAPHY: *Radio* (Def Jam, 1985); *Bigger and Deffer* (Def Jam, 1987); *Walking with a Panther* (Def Jam, 1989); *Mama Said Knock You Out* (Def Jam, 1990); *14 Shots to the Dome* (Def Jam, 1993); *Mr. Smith* (Def Jam, 1995); *All World: Greatest Hits* (Def Jam, 1996); *Phenomenon* (Def Jam, 1997); *G.O.A.T. Featuring James T. Smith: The Greatest of All Time* (Def Jam, 2000); *10* (Def Jam, 2002).

WEBSITE: www.llcoolj.com.

SEAN CAMERON

ANDREW LLOYD WEBBER

Born: London, England, 22 March 1948

Genre: Musical Theater

Best-selling album since 1990: *Andrew Lloyd Webber: The Greatest Songs* (1995)

Composer Andrew Lloyd Webber epitomized the type of lavish, heavily produced musical theater works—often called "mega musicals"—popular in the 1980s and early 1990s. Lloyd Webber's most successful creations—*Evita, Cats, The Phantom of the Opera*—found a popularity that went far beyond the main theater arteries of

Broadway in New York and London's West End. Setting records for longevity among musicals, they became worldwide phenomena, translated and performed in many languages. Lloyd Webber borrowed melodic ideas from great classical composers such as Giacamo Puccini, pairing tuneful hooks with the blaring electrics of modern rock music. At the same time he spent millions of dollars on breathtaking stage effects that combined modern technology with an old-fashioned sense of razzle-dazzle. By the mid-1990s, with the mega-musical being supplanted by cheaper, more restrained productions, Lloyd Webber's predominance began to erode. Even in his less successful productions, however, he displayed an acute understanding of the power of stagecraft.

Beginnings and 1970s Hits

Born in England to musician parents, Lloyd Webber began writing plays for school as a boy. Attending college at prestigious Oxford University he met lyricist Tim Rice, with whom he wrote his first musical, *Joseph and the Amazing Technicolor Dreamcoat* (1968), based on a story in the Bible. Turning to the same source, Lloyd Webber and Rice next composed *Jesus Christ Superstar* (1971), which became a pop hit when released as an album prior to its stage production. One of the first "rock operas"—musicals that captured a young audience through the use of electric guitars and other rock elements—*Superstar* invigorated Broadway and the West End with a bold, fresh spirit. *Evita* (1978) was the duo's next triumph, a bio-musical based on the life of Argentine ruler Eva Peron. Graced with tuneful, romantic songs such as "Don't Cry for Me Argentina," *Evita* was Lloyd Webber's biggest success to date, making a star out of actress Patti LuPone when it opened on Broadway in 1979.

Greatest Successes

Parting ways from Rice, Lloyd Webber paired with English producer Cameron Mackintosh for *Cats* (1982), based on the work of great twentieth-century poet T. S. Eliot. *Cats* made up for its lack of plot with an abundance of style. With actors dressed in whiskers, tails, and full body costumes, a hit song, "Memory," based on the dramatic style of Puccini, and a striking visual gimmick—the entire theater was transformed into a massive junkyard—*Cats* virtually defined musical theater in the 1980s, becoming the longest-running show in Broadway history. Lloyd Webber's next musical, *The Phantom of the Opera* (1986), adapted from French author Gaston Leroux's novel about a disfigured man haunting the Paris Opera House, rivaled *Cats* in popularity. By this point, fans had learned to expect high-tech production effects from Lloyd Webber's musicals. *Phan-*

tom, featuring a giant glass chandelier designed to give the illusion of crashing down upon the audience, did not disappoint. While critics expressed disdain for Lloyd Webber's lowbrow style—in 2001 the U.K. *Guardian* described his musicals as "unspeakable attempts to send the audience out whistling the scenery"—he displayed his talent as a serious classical composer with *Requiem* (1985). Written after the death of his father, *Requiem* was an attempt to unify rock and classical styles through the theme of mortality.

Sunset Boulevard

With *Phantom* and *Cats* drawing record crowds, Lloyd Webber was at his commercial peak in the early 1990s. However, rocky times lay ahead. The 1989 show *Aspects of Love* had been a rare misfire, closing on Broadway after only two years—a short run by Lloyd Webber's standards. A dissertation on love from various perspectives, the show's theme was perhaps too abstract for mainstream audiences. Lloyd Webber returned to well-known source material for his next musical, *Sunset Boulevard* (1993), based on the classic 1950 film by legendary director and writer Billy Wilder. The story of Norma Desmond, a lonely, aging movie queen who latches onto a struggling young writer, *Sunset Boulevard* was full of the rich dramatic potential that Lloyd Webber had so often used to his advantage. But despite its promise, the musical was plagued by trouble from the beginning. After New York critics panned the original West End production, Lloyd Webber fired its star LuPone, who had already been contracted to transfer her role to the forthcoming Broadway run. The ensuing bad press only intensified after Lloyd Webber gave the Broadway role to film star Glenn Close, who had received good reviews in the U.S. premiere of the show in Los Angeles. Actress Faye Dunaway was hired as the Los Angeles replacement, but dismissed just days before her scheduled opening. Lloyd Webber went on to engage in heated, much-publicized battles with LuPone and Dunaway, eventually settling with them after a lengthy series of lawsuits.

Despite its tumultuous beginnings, *Sunset Boulevard* had some memorable elements. This time the visual gimmick was Desmond's ornate mansion, which descended slowly onto the stage as Norma herself walked down a grand staircase. The score, however, is unmemorable save for two songs, "With One Look" and "As If We Never Said Goodbye." The latter ranks as one of Lloyd Webber's finest moments. The once-famous Desmond, under the false impression that she has been called back to work, visits the studio lot where thirty years prior she made her greatest films. After Desmond walks onto the set, blinking her eyes against the bright lights, she looks around, trying to discern something familiar in the updated equipment that surrounds her. This woman, who has seemed so impervious throughout the evening, suddenly appears small and vulnerable. Lloyd Webber and stage director Trevor Nunn allow the silence to linger as the poignant irony of the scene sets in. The music then swells gently as Desmond sings the first lines: "I don't know why I'm frightened / I know my way around here." The song and its placement within the show demonstrate Lloyd Webber's talent for finding the human within the grandiose. On one level, "As If We Never Said Goodbye" works as a tuneful, emotive ballad, but it is also an aching portrayal of memory, association, and the enduring power of fame.

Unfortunately, *Sunset Boulevard* fell victim to changing trends in musical theater. By 1994, when it opened on Broadway, the popularity of the mega-musical was declining. Due to increasingly prohibitive costs, theater producers began mounting smaller-scale productions with less elaborate sets. Concurrently, the rise in ticket prices to ninety dollars or more made Broadway audiences less willing to try new and untested shows. As a result, producers largely devoted their energies in the late 1990s and early 2000s to "revivals"—updated versions of familiar musicals of the past such as *Oklahoma!* and *Annie Get Your Gun*. After *Sunset Boulevard* none of Lloyd Webber's shows, including *Bombay Dreams* (2002), a musical about the Indian film industry, moved to Broadway following their initial West End premieres. Always resourceful, Lloyd Webber responded to the changing climate by cutting back on expenses and reducing staff at his company, Really Useful Productions.

Andrew Lloyd Webber changed the face of musical theater through elaborate productions that combined rock music, classical melodies, and technological wizardry. Beneath the high gloss of his work was a human core that appealed to a broad range of audiences. While Lloyd Webber had difficulty sustaining his popularity past the mid-1990s, his innovations left a lasting imprint on the theatrical world.

SELECTIVE DISCOGRAPHY: *Jesus Christ Superstar* (Decca, 1971); *Evita: Original Broadway Cast Recording* (MCA, 1979); *Cats: Original Broadway Cast Recording* (Polygram, 1982); *The Phantom of the Opera: Original Broadway Cast Recording* (Polygram, 1986); *Sunset Boulevard: 1994 Los Angeles Cast Recording* (Polygram, 1994); *Requiem* (Polygram, 1995).

WEBSITE: www.reallyuseful.com.

DAVID FREELAND

LOS LOBOS

Formed: 1973, Los Angeles, California

Members: Steven "Steve" Berlin, saxophone, keyboards (born Philadelphia, Pennsylvania, 14 September, 1955); David Hidalgo, lead vocals, guitar (born Los Angeles, California, 6 October 1954); Conrad Lozano, bass, vocals (born Los Angeles, California, 21 March 1951); Luis "Louie" Pérez, drums, guitar, vocals (born Los Angeles, California, 29 January 1953); Cesar Rosas, lead vocals, guitar (born Los Angeles, California, 26 September 1954).

Genre: Rock, World

Best-selling album since 1990: *Good Morning Aztlán* (1990)

Los Lobos is the most innovative and successful band to have combined elements of rock music with the traditional folk music of Mexico. The band came out of East Los Angeles, a center of Hispanic culture for decades. Ritchie Valens was the first East L.A. artist to become nationally known, but he was killed at the height of his popularity along with Buddy Holly and the Big Bopper in a 1959 plane crash that would be memorialized by Don McLean's "American Pie" as "the day the music died." Ironically, it took a film about Valens's brief career, *La Bamba* (1987), to bring Los Lobos into mainstream prominence with the number one hit single "La Bamba"—despite the fact that the group had been together almost a decade and a half prior to their smash number one hit version of the movie's title track. The single's extraordinary success exceeded Valens's original, which had only reached number twenty-two in 1958.

Rock Roots and Mexican Influence

The founding members of the group—David Hidalgo, Cesar Rosas, Conrad Lozano, and Louie Pérez—met in the late 1960s while attending Garfield High School in East Los Angeles. The earliest group musical efforts were based in the sound and approach of the British Invasion, complete with electric guitars. By the early 1970s the quartet had gone acoustic and become interested in performing norteño, the traditional folk music of Northern Mexico. Incorporating traditional instruments such as the bajo sexto, the guitarrón, the jaran requinto and the button accordion, the quartet dubbed itself Los Lobos del Este (de Los Angeles) ("The Wolves of the East [Los Angeles]") in a satirical nod to the Tex-Mex band Los Lobos del Norte ("The Wolves of the North.") They were in the unique position of bridging both sides of the Hispanic generation gap by appealing to both older audiences seeking to recapture their Mexican heritage and younger audiences in search of cultural roots and identity.

Although Los Lobos had appeared on the compilation album *Sí Se Puede* (*Yes, It Can Be Done*) (1976), it was the group's own independently produced *Del Este De Los Angeles* (1978) that became the group's first recorded statement of purpose. Each of the album's eleven tracks highlights the folk music of a different region of Mexico. The title is a whimsical wink to an album by Frank Zappa and the Mothers of Invention, *Just Another Band from L.A.* (1972). By the late 1970s the group began to reelectrify and reincorporate elements of the rock music that the band had played together as teenagers. Los Lobos was soon playing up and down the Sunset Strip, and they were asked to record a Spanish-language version of "Devil with a Blue Dress On" for the cult comedy film *Eating Raoul* (1982). That soundtrack also features the group's original "How Much Can I Do?"

Saxophonist and percussionist Steve Berlin of the Blasters was so taken with Los Lobos that he joined up as a fifth member in 1983. Berlin also co-produced the group's album *. . . And a Time to Dance* (1983), which features the group's Grammy Award–winning track "Anselma." The band's first full-length album for the new Warner Bros. Slash label, *How Will the Wolf Survive?* (1984), was a huge critical success, if not a commercial one; Los Lobos tied with Bruce Springsteen and the E Street Band for the *Rolling Stone* critics' poll "Band of the Year" award.

By the mid-1980s, Los Lobos had become an underground sensation. Appearances in Europe as part of Peter Gabriel's WOMAD (World of Music of Dance) Festival and on Paul Simon's smash album *Graceland* (1986) contributed to their 1987 emergence into the mainstream in *La Bamba*. In defiance of its newfound success, the group decided to return to an acoustic emphasis with the album *La Pistola y El Corazón* (The Pistol and the Heart) (1988), reestablishing the group's identity as emissaries of traditional Mexican folk music and winning Los Lobos its second Grammy Award.

Finding a Group Voice with Kiko

The early 1990s saw Los Lobos going electric again with *The Neighborhood* (1990) and *Kiko* (1992), the latter the most experimental of the band's albums to date and generally considered to be the group's masterpiece. Under the careful ears of producer Mitchell Froom and engineer Tchad Blake, *Kiko* epitomizes Los Lobos' uncanny ability to take diverse and seemingly irreconcilable influences and combine them into something truly new, exciting, and forward-looking. The Hidalgo-Pérez songwriting team had evolved to an extraordinary degree by *Kiko*; the lyrics reflect the dreamlike influence of the Latin magic-realist writers Jorge Luis Borges and Gabriel Garcia Márquez; the band's arrangements are adventuresome and ethereal sonic collages. *Kiko* was chosen "Album of the Year" by many critics and remains an influential album across musical boundaries.

The hallucinatory freedom of *Kiko* inspired Hidalgo, Pérez, Froom, and Blake to continue to work together outside of the Los Lobos moniker as the Latin Playboys and to release the much-heralded *Latin Playboys* (1994) and *Dose* (1999). Hidalgo and Rosas also formed Los Super Seven to collaborate in summit sessions with other Latin artists on the Grammy Award–winning *Los Super Seven* (1998) and *Canto* (2001).

With the album *This Time* (1999) the band reunited with the *Kiko* producer and engineer team of Froom and Blake, and brought considerable acclaim to Hollywood Records, which finally reissued the group's long out-of-print, self-produced debut album. The legendary producer John Leckie (his client roster includes the Beatles individually, Pink Floyd, Radiohead, and XTC) came aboard to produce Los Lobos' Mammoth Records release *Good Morning Aztlán* (2002). Neither exclusively traditional acoustic Mexican folk music nor experimental, Latin-flavored, blues-tinged electric rock, the album straddles these polarities with ease on studio tracks and live bonus cuts.

Los Lobos has continued to contribute to major Hollywood soundtracks, including *Desperado* (1995), which won Los Lobos its third Grammy Award, *From Dusk Till Dawn* (1996), *Feeling Minnesota* (1996), and *The Mambo Kings* (2000). The group also received El Primio *Billboard*, a lifetime achievement award, at the 2001 *Billboard* Latin Music Awards, where Los Lobos was honored as the most enduring bicultural and bilingual band in the nation.

Having been together for over three decades, Los Lobos remains a fresh experience for both its members and audiences largely because the group is able to maintain the same spontaneity that it had when the group was playing neighborhood parties back in East Los Angeles. Indeed, for many, Los Lobos continues to embody the spirit of the rock and roll party band, albeit the thinking person's rock and roll party band.

SELECTIVE DISCOGRAPHY: *How Will the Wolf Survive?* (Warner Bros., 1984); *By the Light of the Silvery Moon* (Warner Bros., 1987); *La Pistola y El Corazón* (Warner Bros., 1988); *The Neighborhood* (Warner Bros., 1990); *Kiko* (Warner Bros., 1992); *Colossal Head* (Warner Bros., 1996); *This Time* (Hollywood Records, 1999); *Del Este De Los Angeles* (Hollywood, 2000 re-release); *El Cancionero: Mas e Mas* (Rhino, 2000); *Good Morning Aztlán* (Mammoth, 2002). **With the Chieftains:** *Santiago* (RCA, 1996). **With Lalo Guerrero:** *Papa's Dream* (Music Little People, 1995). **Soundtracks:** *La Bamba* (Warner Bros., 1987); *Desperado* (Sony, 1995); *From Dusk till Dawn* (Sony, 1996); *Feeling Minnesota* (Atlantic, 1996); *The Mambo Kings* (Sony, 2000).

WEBSITE: www.loslobos.org.

DENNIS POLKOW

LONDON SYMPHONY ORCHESTRA

Formed: 1904, London, England
Genre: Classical

In one of the world's great cities, which boasts no less than five professional symphony orchestras, the London Symphony Orchestra stands out—not only for the high quality of its musicianship but also for the entrepreneurial spirit that has made it one of the most recorded orchestras in the world.

The orchestra was founded in 1904, and is owned, directed, and operated by its players. Unlike American orchestras, the London Symphony is self-governing, and musicians determine business and work policies. The orchestra has attracted first-rate players who appreciate the flexibility of being able to pursue solo and chamber careers outside the orchestra. For its first forty years the orchestra survived by hiring itself out to conductors who wanted to perform in London, accompanying choruses, and making itself available for outside projects. Since its earliest days the orchestra has toured extensively; it was the first British orchestra to visit Europe (1906), America (1912), and Japan (1963), and it now regularly performs and records with top soloists.

The orchestra has been led by some of the most distinguished conductors of the twentieth century: Hans Richter (1904–1911), Sir Edward Elgar (1911–1912), Artur Nikisch (1912–1914), Sir Thomas Beecham (1915–1917), Albert Coates (1919–1922), Willem Mengelberg (1930–1931), Sir Hamilton Harty (1932–1935), Josef Krips (1951–1954), Pierre Monteux (1961–1964), André Previn (1968–1979), Claudio Abbado (1979–1987), Michael Tilson Thomas (1987–1995), and Sir Colin Davis (1995–present).

The London Symphony has been prolific in recording the symphonic repertoire: It has released almost 100 albums in the 1990s alone. The orchestra has also had a long career in the movies. As early as the 1920s, the LSO began accompanying silent movies. In 1922 the orchestra was hired by the head of United Artists to accompany a season of movies at the Royal Opera House; the first movie was *The Three Musketeers*, starring Douglas Fairbanks, Sr.

In 1934 the LSO recorded its first soundtrack—a science fiction epic called *Things to Come*, based on a story by H. G. Wells. That project launched the orchestra into the movie business, and it has recorded soundtracks for hundreds of movies since then. Its film-score business has been so successful that by the 1990s it was one of the most-recorded and most widely heard orchestras in the world. In the 1970s, 1980s, and 1990s the LSO recorded scores for some of the biggest movies in Hollywood: *Raiders of the Lost Ark*, *Superman*, and all of the *Star Wars* movies. The original *Star Wars* soundtrack sold more than 3 million copies. The orchestra also recorded extensively with popular artists in the 1990s—including Tony Bennett,

Metallica, Deep Purple, and Diana Krall—and recorded classical works by popular artists including Paul McCartney, Elvis Costello, and Frank Zappa.

As the 1990s came to a close, the classical music recording business collapsed, and major labels canceled most orchestras' recording contracts. The LSO responded with typical entrepreneurial resourcefulness and started its own recording company in 1999. The orchestra records its live performances and releases the best of them commercially. Not one of the soloists, players, or conductors is paid until the recordings start earning money.

One of the first of the new recordings on the LSO Live label—Berlioz's *Les Troyens*, recorded in 2000—won two Grammy Awards for Best Classical Recording and Best Opera Recording. The orchestra has also entered into a partnership with the on-line music producer Andante to produce audio streaming webcasts and archive recordings. As orchestras struggle to reinvent themselves for new audiences, the London Symphony Orchestra is better positioned than most because of its film work and willingness to take risks on new ventures.

SELECTIVE DISCOGRAPHY: *Star Wars Trilogy: The Original Soundtrack Anthology* (Arista, 1993); *Berlioz: Les Troyens* (LSO Live, 2001); *Elgar—Symphony no. 1* (LSO Live, 2001).

WEBSITE: www.lso.co.uk.

DOUGLAS MCLENNAN

LONESTAR

Formed: 1992, Nashville, Tennessee

Members: Michael Britt, guitar (born Fort Worth, Texas, 15 June 1966); Richie McDonald, vocals (born Lubbock, Texas, 6 February 1962); Keech Rainwater, drums (born Plano, Texas, 24 January 1963); Dean Sams, keyboards (born Garland, Texas, 3 August 1966). Former member: John Rich (born Amarillo, Texas, 7 January 1974).

Genre: Country, Pop

Best-selling album since 1990: *Lonely Grill* (1999)

Hit songs since 1990: "No News," "Amazed," "I'm Already There"

Lonestar emerged in the mid-1990s as a traditional-sounding country band with pop leanings, achieving renown through adept musicianship and a strong pair of lead vocalists. As the decade progressed, the group gradually incorporated a harder rock edge into its work, an approach resulting in the 1999 smash crossover hit, "Amazed." By 2001 Lonestar's country sound had largely vanished, although classic country instruments such as pedal steel guitar still appeared on a few songs. Never known for grittiness in sound or message, Lonestar's later work is largely notable for its unabashed sentimentality.

Although all five original band members hailed from Texas, Lonestar formed in the country music capital of Nashville, Tennessee, in 1992. Most of the members carried years of experience performing with previous bands; however, lead singer John Rich, an eighteen-year-old bluegrass enthusiast who had forsaken college to pursue a career in music, was a novice. Lonestar became known for its unyielding professionalism as it toured the country in a Jeep Cherokee, promoting a self-produced live CD and performing more than 500 shows from 1993 to 1994. In 1995 the hard work paid off when the band secured a recording contract with BNA Records, a division of music conglomerate BMG. Lonestar's self-titled debut album appeared that year and featured the gentle hit, "Tequila Talkin'," a charming, midtempo song that mines time-proven themes of love and regret while featuring a lyrical hook built upon tequila's reputation for promoting verbal indiscretion. The album's most enduring hit, however, is the sharp, danceable, "No News," a guitar-driven shuffle recalling the work of modern blues artist Robert Cray.

Crazy Nights (1997), Lonestar's second album, largely sanded down the few rough edges the first album had possessed. The result is a pleasant release that relies on easy melodies with little instrumental or lyrical surprise. After *Crazy Nights* the band lost Rich, who departed to pursue a solo career. Beginning with *Lonely Grill* (1999), member Richie McDonald assumed lead duties on all vocals, ushering the band into its most commercially successful phase. By now Lonestar's sound resembled that of 1980s "arena-rock" bands such as Journey or REO Speedwagon, complete with blaring electric guitars and heavy, thudding drums. The group's giant hit single, "Amazed," which climbed to the number one position on both the country and pop charts, recalls the loud power ballads of the 1980s, with devotional lyrics and a dramatic modulation before the final choral repetition. The fleeting presence of a pedal steel guitar sounds like an afterthought, added in acknowledgment of the group's country origins. In 2001 Lonestar released *I'm Already There*, similar in spirit to the rock sound of "Amazed." Picking up on a salient trend in country of the early 2000s, the hit title track radiates feel-good sentiment. After a little boy, speaking on long-distance telephone, asks his father when he will come home from a business trip, the father replies, "I'm already there / Take a look around / I'm the sunshine in your hair."

Beginning as a raucous, if clean-cut, country outfit in the 1990s, Lonestar slowly achieved stardom by adopting a blunter-edged rock sound. In the process the group became a polished example of country's late 1990s assimilation into the pop mainstream, bringing country music a new level of recognition.

SELECTIVE DISCOGRAPHY: *Lonestar* (BNA, 1995); *Crazy Nights* (BNA, 1997); *Lonely Grill* (BNA, 1999); *This Christmas Time* (BNA, 2000); *I'm Already There* (BNA, 2001).

DAVID FREELAND

JENNIFER LOPEZ

Born: Bronx, New York, 24 July 1970
Genre: Pop, R&B
Best-selling album since 1990: *J.Lo* (2001)
Hit songs since 1990: "If You Had My Love," "Waiting for Tonight," "Jenny from the Block"

Jennifer Lopez, actor/dancer/singer, and one of the most versatile and driven stars of the late 1990s, became Hollywood's highest-paid Latina actress the same year she released an album that entered the charts at number one. Lopez, who is of Puerto Rican descent, is the most successful member of a 1990s wave of Latin pop stars that includes Ricky Martin and Enrique Iglesias. Her enduring success is due in large measure to her memorable videos, frequent appearances in films and tabloids, and careful recording production techniques that veil the limitations of her singing.

Lopez has pursued a career in acting since her childhood. At sixteen she appeared in the film *My Little Girl* (1986), though other early credits were limited to stage appearances. Her major break came in 1990, when she became a "Fly Girl" on *In Living Color*, a groundbreaking, controversial comedy show written primarily for African-American audiences. As a Fly Girl, Lopez's role was to dance between comedy sets and between commercial breaks. The dancers' gyrating moves brought hip-hop culture into mainstream American living rooms as Lopez became the group's most prominent face.

After Fox Television canceled *In Living Color*, Lopez appeared in a number of television shows and films. The most significant musically was her starring role in *Selena* (1997), a biopic about the murdered Latina pop sensation Selena Quintanilla. Lopez's notable star turn assured her emergence as the Latina star of the 1990s. A year later she starred alongside George Clooney in *Out of Sight* (1998), a well-regarded film that cemented her status as a serious actor in Hollywood.

Two years after *Selena*, Lopez launched her career as a pop star. Her first album, *On the 6* (1999), was named

Jennifer Lopez [KEVIN MAZUR/WIREIMAGE.COM]

after the train line that Lopez rode into Manhattan from the Bronx early in her career. The album was an immense success, yielding two singles, "If You Had My Love" and "Waiting for Tonight." "If You Had My Love" topped the American charts for over a month. The quality of *On the 6*, like that of Lopez's follow-ups, was boosted by high-profile producers such as Sean "Puff Daddy" Combs, Track Masters, and Emilio Estefan Jr. It also includes cameo raps by Fat Joe and Big Punisher and a duet with Marc Anthony on "No Me Ames." The album's combination of genres—R&B, rap, and Latina pop—makes it difficult to identify a distinctive Lopez sound, an advantage in her cannily commercial crossover strategy. Lopez has labeled her sound "Latin Soul."

The album's success coincided with the tabloid sensation over Lopez's relationship with Combs. A New York native like Lopez, Combs was responsible for producing some of the 1990s' most successful R&B and rap acts. On December 27, 1999, Combs and Lopez were together at a Manhattan nightclub when three people were injured during a shooting. Combs and Lopez were arrested with two members of Combs's entourage. Lopez was released almost immediately, and Combs was later acquitted, but the incident's fallout led Lopez to guard her public image more carefully.

Lopez's second album, *J.Lo* (2001), is essentially a remake of *On the 6*. The recording lacks the freshness and sense of play of its predecessor but still contains a few hit singles, most notably "Love Don't Change a Thing." The video from that track, along with hits such as "I'm Real" and "Play," helped the album reach the top spot on U.S. album charts. Lopez's climb to the top spot coincided with her starring role in the film *The Wedding Planner* (2001).

Let's Get Loud, Lopez's first musical television special, aired on NBC on November 25, 2001. It was the number one program in its time slot in the United States and also found a huge international audience. The forty-four-minute performance was recorded in Puerto Rico and featured all of Lopez's best songs performed with expensive props, elaborate costumes, and high-energy dancing.

This Is Me . . . Then (2002) finds Lopez attempting to get back to her musical roots as she belts out love songs to her fiancé, movie actor Ben Affleck. The record attempts to invoke the fun that marked *On the 6*, but it lacks that recording's marriage of edgy production and pop

| On the 6

Jennifer Lopez once described her sound as "Latin Soul," but, at their best, Lopez's pop albums draw on a wider, distinctly 1990s range of influences. *On the 6,* her first and best album, is a highly-polished mix of ballads, raps, high-energy dance songs, and rhythmically dense "tropical remixes." Although Lopez takes writing credits on a few tracks, *On the 6,* like all her subsequent recordings, features an all star lineup of writers and producers, including Sean "Puff Daddy" Combs, Gloria Estefan, and Emilio Estefan, Jr. A few tracks feature lyrics sung in Spanish to Latin rhythms. Lopez's music is at its best when her songs are upbeat and soar beyond the limits of her passable voice. The smash hit "Waiting for Tonight," has remained a staple on dance floors. It begins with Latin-inspired drumming and soon takes off into an infectious and updated disco beat. Less successful are Lopez's ballads such as "Should've Never" and "Could This Be Love." On these tracks her thin vocals only expose the songs' sugary, trite lyrics. Nevertheless, *On the 6* remains an example of 1990s pop at its most infectious and versatile.

SELECTIVE FILMOGRAPHY: *My Little Girl* (1986); *Selena* (1997); *Out of Sight* (1998); *The Wedding Planner* (2001); *Maid in Manhattan* (2002).

WEBSITE: www.jenniferlopez.com.

SHAWN GILLEN

LYLE LOVETT

Born: Klein, Texas, 1 November 1957
Genre: Country
Best-selling album since 1990: *The Road to Ensenada* (1996)

Singer/songwriter Lyle Lovett inadvertently riled the Nashville music establishment by embroidering his country-rooted sound with a literate fusion of big-band swing, jazz, blues, and gospel. Unclaimed by any musical genre in particular, Lovett possesses a style of his own design and is one of the craftiest songwriters in contemporary music.

Motorcycles and music received most of Lovett's attention growing up on his parents' horse ranch near Houston, Texas, in a town called Klein, which was founded by his great-great-grandfather, Adam Klein. He was his parents' only child, and as a teenager, worked in a motorcycle shop and raced competitively. Songwriters also fascinated Lovett and Texas has a rich history of them. At any opportunity, the teenaged Lovett would slip off to Houston to see his favorites play. Among them were fellow Texas natives Guy Clark, Townes Van Vandt, and Willis Alan Ramsay; all became huge influences on Lovett's music. While attending college at Texas A&M, he organized the hiring of talent for the campus coffeehouse and began writing his own songs, performing them in local venues. After graduating college with a degree in journalism—which he never used—Lovett traveled around Germany where he met a musician named Buffalo Wayne. Wayne asked Lovett to play in a country-western event that he had organized and Lovett went on to achieve modest musical success while in Europe.

The Next Country Music Star

Bolstered by his European experience, he returned to the United States in 1983 and settled in Nashville, Tennessee, to shop his musical wares in the country music capitol of the world. Singer/songwriter and fellow Texan Nanci Griffith remembered Lovett from an interview he did with her at college and recorded one of his songs, "If I Were the Woman You Wanted." (Lovett's original title was a male gender-specific "If I Were the Man You Wanted.") Lovett also sang backup on two of her albums and was able

surfaces. The first single from the album, "All I Have," featuring rapper LL Cool J, was a smash international hit and a popular video. Like her previous album, the release of *This Is Me . . . Then* coincided with the premiere of *Maid in Manhattan* (2002), a successful movie starring Lopez. Other tracks on *This Is Me . . . Then* such as "Jenny from the Block," "I'm Glad," and "Still" made less of an impression on listeners and fans.

Jennifer Lopez emerged in the mid-1990s as a promising actor and dancer. Her career as a singer started in 1999 and quickly propelled her to celebrity heights never achieved by a U.S. Latina performer. Her music and sexually charged videos capture what so many fans find captivating about Lopez: her combination of sweet soulfulness and Latin urban rhythms.

SELECTIVE DISCOGRAPHY: *On the 6* (Work, 1999); *J.Lo* (Epic, 2001); *This Is Me . . . Then* (Epic, 2002); *J to Tha L-O!: The Remixes* (Epic, 2002).

to get a demo tape of his own songs to her label, MCA. They signed Lovett, and his debut album *Lyle Lovett* (1986) met glowing reviews and five songs from it made the country charts.

Lovett's highly acclaimed second release, *Pontiac* (1988), firmly set his reputation as a top-notch songwriter with a yen for the avant-garde. On the album, he explores the big band sound and defines his style of jazz-influenced honky-tonk shuffles, black-humored sometimes spoken blues, and offbeat ballads. Lovett gained the ground that he was losing in traditional country music as a wider audience, including pop, jazz, and rock fans, listened to *Pontiac*. On his next album, *Lyle Lovett and His Large Band* (1989), Lovett rattled Nashville with his rendition of Tammy Wynette's ode to female devotion, "Stand By Your Man." (Lovett did not change the gender.) With Lovett's rascally wit already a trademark, critics listened carefully, certain that Lovett was lampooning the country music icon's signature song. However, no parody was evident and Lovett's effort appears earnest. Nevertheless, the country music establishment, already flummoxed by his penchant for accompanying himself with a twenty-plus piece jazz band, unofficially disowned Lovett.

Lyle Lovett and His Large Band brought him his first of four Grammy Awards, this time for Best Male Vocalist of 1989. In addition to his off-the-wall songwriting, Lovett's appearance and performance style added further intrigue and cemented a cultlike following. His rail thin body and long, angular face is exaggerated by elevated hair that rests scruffy and out-of-kilter to the right—more the look of a French painter than that of a country-western singer. His performance style is discernible by shy politeness, Zen stillness, and a deadpan delivery with humor that catches its listener off guard. Lovett's country tenor is a pleasing mix of restraint tinged by a bluesy grind mysteriously emerging from a mouth that barely moves. Lovett generally accompanies himself on acoustic guitar and approaches his work with a theatrical bearing, mixing spoken lyrics, scripted monologues, and stories into his musical interplay.

Music and Movies

He left Nashville for Los Angeles in 1990 and during the recording of another well-received album, *Joshua Judges Ruth* (1992), Lovett received a call from film director Robert Altman. He asked if Lovett was interested in appearing in his new film, *The Player* (1991). Critics commended Lovett's honest, subtle acting performance, making his screen debut a success. Additionally, the movie was notable because he met superstar actress Julia Roberts during the filming. Their romance and subsequent marriage in 1993 received an excessively high level of media attention, as did their divorce in 1995—reportedly brought on by the pressure of constant media scrutiny. Lovett

appeared as an actor in three more Altman films, *Short Cuts* (1993), *Ready to Wear* (1995), and *Cookie's Fortune* (1999), in addition to roles in several other films including *The Opposite of Sex* (1998), and *The New Guy* (2001).

However, Lovett's forays into acting have not interfered with his music career. He released three more successful studio albums in the 1990s including, *Step Inside This House* (1998), a twenty-one song, double-CD tribute to Texas songwriters. The album contains songs from Guy Clark, Walter Hyatt, Robert Earl Keen, and many other songwriters that have influenced his work. He followed that by recapping his own songwriting and music career with *Live in Texas* (1999), a live recording featuring many of his classic songs. Included is the wistful ballad, "Nobody Knows Me" about a man's guilt over cheating on his girl and another ballad, "If I had a Boat" where Lovett absurdly declares his dedication to a horse. He sings, "Go out on the ocean, me upon my pony on my boat." He humorously explores a bad choice in a marriage partner in "She's No Lady" (written well before his failed union to Roberts). It is a blues shuffle on which he sings, "And the preacher said, I pronounce you ninety-nine to life. Son, that's no lady, she's your wife."

Lovett scored the music to the Robert Altman film, *Dr. T & The Women* (2000), and released *Smile* (2003), a collection of twelve songs that he has performed on various movie soundtracks. It includes a duet with fellow songwriter extraordinaire, Randy Newman, "You've Got a Friend in Me," from the popular children's hit film *Toy Story* (1995).

While his unusual style, eclectic music, and cross-media jaunts offer intrigue and perplexities, Lovett is primarily a storyteller whose song lyrics inspire his listeners to examine issues—comic or otherwise—in an honest light.

SELECTIVE DISCOGRAPHY: *Lyle Lovett* (MCA, 1986); *Pontiac* (MCA, 1988); *Lyle Lovett and His Large Band* (MCA, 1989); *Joshua Judges Ruth* (MCA, 1992); *I Love Everybody* (MCA, 1994); *The Road to Ensenada* (MCA, 1996); *Step Inside This House* (MCA, 1998); *Live in Texas* (MCA, 1999); *Smile* (MCA, 2003). **Soundtrack:** *Dr. T & The Women* (MCA, 2000).

SELECTIVE FILMOGRAPHY: *The Player* (1991); *Short Cuts* (1993); *Ready to Wear* (1995); *Cookie's Fortune* (1999); *The Opposite of Sex* (1998); *The New Guy* (2001).

DONALD LOWE

THE LOX

Formed: 1996, Yonkers, New York

Members: Jayson "Jadakiss" Phillip (born Yonkers, New York, 27 May 1975); Sean "Sheek" Jacobs (born Yonkers, New York, 30 September 1974); David Styles (born Corona, New York, 28 November 1974).

Genre: Rap

Best-selling album since 1990: *Money, Power & Respect* (1998)

Hit songs since 1990: "Money, Power & Respect," "Wild Out"

The LOX are a resilient hardcore rap trio. They survived the changing tastes of hip-hop and a public face-off with Sean "Puffy" Combs, the powerful impresario. Their lyrics are gritty and street-oriented, enhanced with wit and a no-nonsense delivery.

Members of the LOX hail from Yonkers, New York, a lower-middle-class suburb of New York City. As preteens, the neighborhood friends started rapping together. They formed a rap group called the Warlocks and made tapes to sell at their high school. The trio entered Westchester Community College but soon dropped out to pursue rap careers. Fellow Yonkers native Mary J. Blige eventually heard their homemade mix tapes and introduced them to Combs, who signed them to his Bad Boy Records and suggested they shorten their name to the LOX, an acronym for Living Off Experience. The group started ghostwriting for Puffy, providing his verses on Notorious B.I.G.'s "Victory" and the remix to Ma$e's "Can't Nobody Hold Me Down."

Puffy introduced the LOX to the rap world, giving them cameos on hit songs "It's All About the Benjamins" and the remix of Mariah Carey's "Honey." Their ode to the late Biggie Smalls, "We'll Always Love Big Poppa," was the b-side of Puffy's runaway hit, "I'll Be Missing You." Although the LOX's debut album, *Money, Power & Respect* (1998), peaked at number three on the pop album charts, it presents a confusing image of the group. The single "If You Think I'm Jiggy," built off a sample of the Rod Stewart hit "Do Ya Think I'm Sexy," portrays them as flashy and materialistic, while the title track, featuring Lil' Kim and DMX, underscores their harder side.

The LOX preferred the harder side. Uncomfortable with the glossy image of Combs and the largely R&B Bad Boy roster (Faith Evans, Total, 112), the LOX sought a label with a rougher image. They began a dialogue with Ruff Ryders Records, home of DMX and Eve. Combs refused to release them, and the LOX appealed publicly, wearing "Free the LOX" T-shirts at appearances and asking Combs to sign their release papers during radio interviews.

Finally, in 1999, Combs granted the LOX their wish while retaining a portion of their future publishing rights.

The LOX's Ruff Ryders album debut, *We Are the Streets* (2000), is brash and unabashed. No R&B hooks and pop samples mitigate it. The title track is a diatribe directed at Combs. The gold success of *Streets* enabled the members to release single projects.

Jadakiss, often renowned for his wordplay and hailed as the group's best lyricist, was the first out of the gate with *Kiss tha Game Goodbye* (2001). It was a solid release, featuring the superstar collaborators Nas, DMX, and Snoop Dogg on the rapping end and Timbaland, the Neptunes, and Ruff Ryders producer Swizz Beats on the production side. The solo effort further raised his profile. He contributed to a remix of Mary J. Blige's number one pop hit "Family Affair" and a Reebok running shoes television commercial. Styles followed, scoring a hit with "My Life" featuring Pharoahe Monche and the marijuana tribute "Good Times." His album *A Gangster and a Gentleman* (2002) was critically acclaimed.

Sheek, known for a more buoyant and rambunctious style, has also broken off as a solo artist. Nevertheless, the LOX maintains a group identity and plans to record more albums as a trio. As a group and as individual members, the LOX caters to die-hard hip-hop fans and occasionally to a wider commercial audience.

SELECTIVE DISCOGRAPHY: *Money, Power & Respect* (Bad Boy, 1998); *We Are the Streets* (Ruff Ryders/Interscope, 2000).

DARA COOK

LUDACRIS

Born: Chris Bridges; Champaign, Illinois, 11 September 1977

Genre: Rap

Best-selling album since 1990: *Word of Mouf* (2001)

Hit songs since 1990: "Rollout (My Business)," "Area Codes," "What's Your Fantasy?"

For successful rappers in the late 1990s and early 2000s, there were typically two surefire ways to reach the top: amiable pop/rap songs about cars, women, and jewels or aggressive, hardcore rhymes expressing toughness with attacking verses boasting about lyrical unassailability. Atlanta rapper Ludacris became a superstar nearly overnight thanks to his blend of these styles on albums such as *Word of Mouf* (2001), in which the good-natured, but gleefully foul-mouthed rapper obsesses about sex and material possessions in his elastic, cartoony voice. Ludacris's larger-than-life personality also made him a favorite guest on other artists' songs and a budding movie star, rocketing him from obscurity to near ubiquity in less than two years.

In the rap equivalent of being discovered at the soda fountain, Atlanta rapper Ludacris got his big break when he scored a job recording between-song tidbits for local urban radio station Hot 97.5 in 1998. The humorous, one-minute raps quickly established Ludacris's name in the thriving Atlanta music community.

It was the culmination of a dream that began when toddler Chris Bridges began attending house parties with his college-age parents, during which he soaked up the sounds of old school funk and soul. At twelve years old, Ludacris joined the Chicago-based rap collective Loud-mouth Hooligans, leaving the group when his family relocated to Atlanta in the early 1990s. Battle rapping in the lunchroom at College Park's Banneker High School led to talent shows in clubs, which, eventually, led to the radio gig. A small cameo on legendary rap producer Timbaland's *Tim's Bio* (1998) helped the developing rapper learn more about recording albums and set the stage for the brash move that would put him on the hip-hop map. With a rap moniker derived from a combination of his given name, Chris, and his self-described tendency to sometimes act ridiculous, Ludacris began his rapping career in a time-honored tradition: He released a self-financed debut album, *Incognegro* (1999), on his own Disturbing the Peace label.

"Fantasy" Turns into a Reality

When the bouncy, flirtatious sex rhyme "What's Your Fantasy"—an explicit duet with Disturbing the Peace member Shawna about sexual fantasies from a man's and a woman's perspective—became a regional hit and the album sold 30,000 copies in three months, the rapper caught the attention of Scarface, the president of the record label Def Jam South.

The former Geto Boys member, now a label boss, made Ludacris the first act signed to the southern offshoot of the venerable New York hip-hop label and re-released *Incognegro* as *Back for the First Time* (2000). Padded out with three new tracks, the album is a celebration of the "dirty South" sound pioneered by artists such as Outkast and the Goodie Mob: a combination of thick, bass-heavy beats and raucous sex rhymes. Scarface also polished up the album's tracks with additional production from such notable rap producers as Organized Noize, Jermaine Dupri, and Timbaland.

With the hiccoughing "What's Your Fantasy" now a national hit, the album sold more than 2 million copies and Ludacris became a favorite guest star on songs by other rappers and R&B artists, including Missy Elliott ("One Minute Man"), Method Man, Jermaine Dupri ("Welcome to Atlanta"), Ginuwine, LL Cool J, Mariah Carey, Three 6 Mafia, Jagged Edge, and 112.

Branching out into Movies, Raising the Ire of Conservative Commentators

Featuring influences that range from classic Philadelphia funk and soul to the blue comedy of such African-American comedians as Redd Foxx and Rudy Ray Moore, Ludacris's second album, *Word of Mouf*, is highlighted by such raunchy songs as "Area Codes" (a hit from the *Rush Hour 2* [2001] soundtrack), "Move Bitch," and "Freaky Thangs." The songs are mostly stereotypical male fantasies writ large, in which Ludacris indulges in his imagined status as a lothario without equal. With strong beats and production from such renowned producers as Swizz Beatz, Timbaland, and Organized Noize, the album again boasts an insistent set of pop rap hits, most memorably "Rollout (My Business)." The album also features the uncharacteristically sentimental "Growing Pains," a wistful, guitar-inflected soul song about childhood antics and dreams that samples the Stax classic "I Forgot to Be Your Lover" by William Bell.

Ludacris joined the Eminem-headlined "Anger Management" tour in the summer of 2002 and began work on his headlining debut in the film *Radio*, in which he was to play a radio disc jockey. He also announced plans to executive produce and star in the high school comedy *Skip Day*, and he began filming his part in the sequel to the hit film, *The Fast and the Furious*.

In the first hint of controversy in his career, Ludacris was dropped as a spokesperson for Pepsi in early September 2002, one day after conservative Fox News Channel ranter Bill O'Reilly aired his view that Ludacris was a "thug rapper" who "espouses violence, intoxication, and degrading conduct toward women." Two weeks later, the rapper oversaw the release of *Golden Grain*, a compilation of songs by his Disturbing the Peace crew, which includes Shawna, I-20, Infamous 2-0, and Fate Wilson. A third album, tentatively titled *Chicken and Beer*, was slated for a spring 2003 release.

With a combination of moxie, charisma, and a flair for infectious choruses, rapper Ludacris established himself as a reliable hit-maker in just a few short years in the late 1990s. From unknown to superstar, Ludacris took his rise in stride, recording his raunchy sex rhymes and plotting a film career as if he had been a pop star his entire life.

SELECTIVE DISCOGRAPHY: *Incognegro* (Disturbing the Peace, 1999); *Back for the First Time* (Def Jam South/Disturbing the Peace, 2000); *Word of Mouf* (Def Jam South/Disturbing the Peace, 2001).

GIL KAUFMAN

PATTI LUPONE

Born: Northport, New York, 21 April 1949
Genre: Vocal
Best-selling album since 1990: *Heatwave* (1995)

A leading Broadway stage performer of the 1980s and 1990s, Patti LuPone is a versatile singer whose torchy style encompasses rock, pop, and jazz. Infusing her performances with her larger-than-life personality, LuPone conveys a winning mixture of tartness and vulnerability. Her voice is powerful and wide-ranging, moving effortlessly from a rich bellow to a breathy soprano. A skilled actress, she is adept at shifting the dramatic emphasis within a song, altering the texture of her voice to communicate a breadth of emotional experience.

Descended from Adelina Patti, a popular opera singer of the 1880s, LuPone began performing at the age of four. In 1972 she graduated from the prestigious Juilliard School of Drama in New York, where she gained solid training in drama as well as musical theater. In 1979 LuPone created the role for which she remains best known, that of glamorous Argentine ruler Eva Peron in *Evita*, a musical written by hit Broadway composer Andrew Lloyd Webber. LuPone's charismatic performance, highlighted by her yearning treatment of the song, "Don't Cry for Me Argentina," won Broadway's annual Tony Award in 1980. In 1985 she starred in the original London production of the musical *Les Miserables*, belting one of the show's standout numbers, "I Dreamed a Dream," with heart-rending conviction.

Although she spent the late 1980s and early 1990s acting in the television drama "Life Goes On," LuPone returned to the stage in the London production of Lloyd Webber's musical *Sunset Boulevard* (1993), based on the classic 1950 film of the same name. Portraying faded movie star Norma Desmond, LuPone found an aching humanity beneath the character's bravado, transforming the show's finest song, "As if We Never Said Goodbye," into a beguiling treatise on the lingering power of fame. Unfortunately, LuPone's triumph was short-lived: After the show received mostly negative reviews from American critics, Lloyd Webber replaced her with film star Glenn Close for the Broadway opening in 1994. Although recalling that she was "deeply burned" in a 1997 interview with the U.K.'s *Daily Telegraph*, she rebounded, performing a one-woman show on Broadway in 1995 and appearing in several films. In 1995 she recorded *Heatwave*, a live album with the Hollywood Bowl Orchestra.

In 1999 LuPone released *Matters of the Heart*, her first in-studio, as opposed to live, recording. Tackling a diverse array of material, she is alternately sensitive and comedic, contemplative and raucous. On "Shattered Illusions," for example, she details the disappointments of love in boisterous fashion: "But the thing that caused the final rift / Was when his toupee started to drift." Her rendition of "Air That I Breathe," on the other hand, is subtle and direct, bearing a winning simplicity absent from the hit 1974 version by pop group the Hollies. The album's restrained moments, such as the tender "My Son," evince the depth of LuPone's artistic maturation. On the more aggressive numbers, such as a belting treatment of composer Stephen Sondheim's "Not a Day Goes By," she tends to slur the words, her brassy delivery carrying a nasal ring. Nonetheless, even when singing too fervently she succeeds on the strength of her personality. In 2001 LuPone returned to Broadway in a nonmusical role, performing in the farcical play *Noises Off*.

Patti LuPone's expressive dramatic range and finely honed acting skills contributed to some of the most memorable musical theater portrayals of the 1980s and 1990s. While known for her forcefulness and humor, beginning in the late 1990s she revealed a softer, more introspective side, infusing an eclectic repertoire with subtle intelligence.

SELECTIVE DISCOGRAPHY: *Patti LuPone Live* (RCA Victor, 1993); *Heatwave* (Philips, 1995); *Matters of the Heart* (LayZLay, 1999).

WEBSITE: www.pattilupone.net.

DAVID FREELAND

LUSCIOUS JACKSON

Formed: 1991, New York, New York; Disbanded 2000
Members: Jill Cunniff, bass, vocals, songwriter (born New York, New York, 17 August 1966); Gabby Glaser, guitar, vocals, songwriter (born New York, New York, 12 December 1965); Kate Schellenbach, drums (born New York, New York, 5 January 1966). Former member: Vivien Trimble, keyboards (born New York, New York, 24 May 1963).
Genre: Rock
Best-selling album since 1990: *Fever in Fever Out* (1996)
Hit songs since 1990: "Naked Eye," "Under Your Skin," "Nervous Breakthrough"

Luscious Jackson, the funky all-female foursome, derives its name from the athlete Luscious Jackson, who played basketball for the Philadelphia 76ers in the 1970s. The music group Luscious Jackson, which emerged in the early 1990s, takes its inspiration from the funk and soul of the 1970s, and mixes it with the rhymes, rhythms, and samples found in hip-hop and rap. Streetwise, stylish, and sassy, the New York–based band often earns comparisons to the Beastie Boys, a similar all-white, all-male, rap-inspired trio based in New York City; the press initially dubbed them "the Beastie Girls." The band enjoyed a few successful albums, most notably their second release, *Fever in Fever Out* (1996), but eventually disbanded amicably in March 2000 to pursue other interests, both personal and professional.

The future band mates met at various punk clubs when they were teens. Kate Schellenbach, a friend of Mike D from the Beastie Boys, was the original drummer for his then-hardcore band. The threesome went off to college, with Schellenbach remaining in New York and Jill Cunniff and Gabby Glaser heading to San Francisco for art school. They officially reconvened in 1991, recruited Cunniff's classically trained friend Vivien Trimble, and started off by playing opening gigs for the Beastie Boys around the New York City area, an association that landed them an EP, *In Search of Manny* (1992), on the Boys' label Grand Royal. In 1994 they released *Natural Ingredients*, which brought them to the attention of many college students immersed in indie rock and in search of female role models. The album explores a young woman's coming of age. *Natural Ingredients* is a dance album, uneven at times and generous in its use of different genres, but the band's third effort, *Fever in Fever Out* (1996), moved them out of indie rock and into the mainstream.

Primarily produced by Daniel Lanois, noted for his esteemed work with U2 and Bob Dylan, and largely written by Cunniff, *Fever in Fever Out* has a smooth sound. It marks a clear advance in the band's songwriting, performing, and producing skills; the songs are fully developed, offering clearly defined choruses and melodies rather than a smattering of disjointed samples and loops. With the smash radio hit "Naked Eye," which peaked at number twenty-four on the *Billboard* Top 40 chart, the album was propelled to gold status in 1997, within a year of its release. Cunniff sings in the first chorus with rapid-fire, articulate delivery: "Wearing nothing is divine / Naked is a state of mind / I take things off to clear my head / To say the things I haven't said."

In 1998 keyboardist Trimble quit the band to pursue other interests. The remaining trio released what proved to be their final and most critically acclaimed work, *Electric Honey* (1999). On this recording the band is at its most accomplished and mature, having assumed greater production and mixing duties. The songs explore themes of self-acceptance and satisfaction. Nevertheless, the album did not sell as well as *Fever in Fever Out*.

SELECTIVE DISCOGRAPHY: *In Search of Manny* (EP; Grand Royal, 1992); *Natural Ingredients* (Grand Royal/Capitol 1994); *Fever in Fever Out* (Grand Royal/Capitol, 1996); *Electric Honey* (Grand Royal/Capitol, 1999).

CARRIE HAVRANEK

SHELBY LYNNE

Born: Shelby Lynne Moorer; Quantico, Virginia, 22 October 1968
Genre: Country, Pop
Best-selling album since 1990: *I Am Shelby Lynne* (2000)
Hit songs since 1990: "Life Is Bad," "Gotta Get Back," "Killin' Kind"

Shelby Lynne is a big-voiced singer who blends country, blues, rock, and pop and whose soulful voice conveys years of pain, loneliness, and heartbreak. Sometimes compared to the rootsy and successful rock artist Sheryl Crow, Lynne had huge success with her sixth album, *I Am Shelby Lynne* (2000). She spent years toiling away in Nashville's songwriting system, writing and recording five albums for three different labels, including an album of big band music that, due to financial pitfalls, was never released.

Lynne's fame was hard-won. In the press release for *I Am Shelby Lynne*, she says, "I wanted to include more of my soul and pop influences," something that was not possible in the pigeonholing constraints of the Nashville country scene.

Lynne sought out producer Bill Bottrell, who also produced Sheryl Crow's breakthrough album *Tuesday Night Music Club*. Bottrell had been living, semi-retired, in northern California. The two bonded over music business bitterness and personal tragedy. The bitterness, loneliness, and self-determination that permeates *I Am Shelby Lynne*, an album that jumps from down-and-out blues to pop to twangy country, comes from a real place. Between the ages of seventeen and nineteen, Lynne witnessed her father shoot her mother to death and then take his own life. She raised her younger sister Alison Moorer, also a singer; she married and then divorced. Lynne's straightforwardly titled song "Life Is Bad," a bluesy rock song, conjures a picture of a worldly but hardened woman by combining images of an "inner descending hell" and the "stench of livin' on thin dimes," with a twang worthy of country singer Lucinda Williams. In the song's chorus, she drawls, "Oh, life is bad. Oh no, worst I ever had." The album reached number six on *Billboard*'s Heatseekers chart and won her a belated Grammy Award for Best New Artist in 2000.

The attention from *I Am Shelby Lynne* brought her into a film project the following year. She wrote "Killin'

Kind," a pop song reminiscent of the 1960s, for the soundtrack to the film adaptation of Helen Fielding's *Bridget Jones's Diary* (2001). After extensive touring, Lynne returned to the studio for her more rock-oriented follow-up, *Love, Shelby* (2001), which she wrote and co-produced with Glen Ballard.

Though she wins comparisons to country legend Patsy Cline for her gutsy emotionalism, Lynne is her own woman. She is at her best when her tales of overcoming adversity mix the cry-in-your-beer tendencies of country with the swagger and sorrow of blues and a rock-and-roll reverence for electric guitar.

SELECTIVE DISCOGRAPHY: *I Am Shelby Lynne* (Mercury, 2000); *Love, Shelby* (Island, 2001). **Soundtrack:** *Bridget Jones's Diary* (Universal, 2001).

CARRIE HAVRANEK

LYNYRD SKYNYRD

Formed: 1964, Jacksonville, Florida
Members: Michael Cartellone, drums; Ean Evans, bass; Rickey Medlocke, guitar; Billy Powell, keyboards (born 3 June 1952); Gary Rossington, guitar (born Jacksonville, Florida, 4 December 1951); Hughie Thomasson, guitar; Johnny Van-Zant, lead vocals. Former members: Bob Burns, drums; Allen Collins, guitar (born Jacksonville, Florida, 19 July 1952; died 23 January 1990); Steve Gaines, guitar (born Seneca, Missouri, 14 September 1949; died Gillsburg, Mississippi, 20 October 1977); Randall Hall, guitar; Larry Jungstrom, bass; Edward King, guitar, Artimus Pyle, drums (born Spartanburg, South Carolina, 15 July 1948); Ronnie Van Zant, lead vocals (born Jacksonville, Florida, 15 January 1948; died Gillsburg, Mississippi, 20 October 1977); Leon Wilkeson, bass (born 2 April 1952; died Ponte Vedra Beach, Florida, 28 July 2001).
Genre: Rock
Best-selling album since 1990: *All Time Greatest Hits* (2000)
Hit songs since 1990: "You Got That Right," "Red, White and Blue"

Lynyrd Skynyrd's driving three-guitar boogie attack made them the most prominent southern rock band of the 1970s. Although they dissolved in 1977 after a plane crash killed two core members, Lynyrd Skynyrd reunited ten years later. Lynyrd Skynrd has had to revamp their musical lineup several times, but their signature sound remains virtually untouched as they continue recording and performing into the new millennium.

Southern Rockin' Freebirds

After trying many other names, guitarists Gary Rossington and Allen Collins took fellow founding member, singer Ronnie Van Zant's suggestion to use Lynyrd Skynyrd. The name was a sarcastic homage to a notorious and despised high school gym teacher named Leonard Skinner. Following the success of the Allman Brothers Band, a prolific southern group who found fame in 1970, Lynyrd Skynyrd quickly gained a regional reputation as a freewheeling southern rock act. In 1972 they added a third guitarist, Ed King, which rounded out the band's initial foundation that included Billie Powell on keyboards, Leon Wilkeson on bass, and Bob Burns on drums. Their debut album contains "Free Bird," a tribute to legendary guitarist Duane Allman, who died in a motorcycle crash in 1971. Lynyrd Skynyrd would soon grapple with similar misfortunes. "Free Bird" became one of rock's classic anthems, thanks mostly to a spirited live version on their multiplatinum-selling live release, *One More for the Road* (1976).

However, it was the band's hit song "Sweet Home Alabama" from the follow-up album *Second Helping* (1974) that defined their image as swaggering country boys who stood fiercely protective of their southern roots. They wrote "Sweet Home Alabama" in response to singer/songwriter Neil Young's "Southern Man" and "Alabama," which were interpreted as slights against southern life. In one of the verses Van Zant belted, "I hope Neil Young will remember, Southern man don't need him around anyhow, oh, sweet home Alabama." In actuality, the band's aura as rednecks was somewhat overblown. Closer inspection of several songs finds them siding on issues more in tune with liberal mind-sets, such as environmental preservation, gun control, and desegregation. Regardless, an undeniable aspect to their image was as hard-partying rogues. The wreckage that Lynyrd Skynyrd left in the wake of their 1970s substance abuse is legendary.

After scoring hits such as "Saturday Night Special," "Gimme Three Steps," "That Smell," and "What's Your Name?" and releasing their fifth studio album, *Street Survivors* (1977), the band's fate took a tragic twist. On October 20, 1977, en route to a concert in Baton Rouge, Louisiana, a fuel miscalculation on their private jet caused the aircraft to crash in a marshy swamp near Gillsburg, Mississippi. Van Zant and guitarist Steve Gaines (who had recently joined the band while Rossington recovered from injuries sustained in a serious car accident) were killed, as was Gaines's sister, Cassie, a backup singer for the group. Also killed were the band's road manager and the aircraft's pilot and co-pilot. Almost every other member of Lynyrd Skynyrd was severely injured. Without Van Zant, the band dissipated. An offshoot featuring guitarists Rossington and Collins, called the Rossington-Collins Band, formed from 1980 to 1983. A car accident in which he was the driver paralyzed Collins from the chest down in 1986. His girlfriend died in the accident and Collins died of complications from pneumonia in 1990.

New Southern Faces, Same Sweet Sound

In 1987, the tenth anniversary of the crash, members of Lynyrd Skynyrd reunited for a tribute tour. After some legal haggling with Van Zant's widow, wherein she relinquished use of the band's name as long as at least three founding members of Lynyrd Skynyrd remained, the band re-formed. Johnny Van Zant, Ronnie's younger brother (and the only one who hyphenates his surname), took over on vocals. The younger Van Zant looks and sounds eerily identical to the prolific Ronnie Van Zant, who was a headstrong, free-spirited individual with an earthy blues voice. Although the rest of their musical lineup frequently changed hands, it remained true to its roots by sticking with a trio of lead guitarists. For the most part, the band's lineup has Ricky Medlocke and Hughie Thomasson joining Rossington in their trademark style where, at times, all three guitarists solo simultaneously, trading and feeding guitar licks off one another. Another guitar arrangement in Lynyrd Skynyrd is having one guitarist chugging rhythms while the other two play note-for-note harmonies. All three get their due in every song. However, even on long "jams" like the relentless "Free Bird" where the temptation to freely improvise is immediate, the new guitarists, for the most part, stay close to the note patterns set in the solos of original creators. This is a characteristic differentiating Lynyrd Skynyrd from their southern counterparts, the duel guitar-driven Allman Brothers Band, who thrive on free improvisation.

Their first "reunion" album release, *Lynyrd Skynyrd 1991* (1991), offers more of the lively blues boogie characteristic of southern rock in general and specific to the band's original sound. Lynyrd Skynyrd does not attempt to reinvent themselves in any of their following six studio releases, with the exception of an all-acoustic album, *Endangered Species* (1994), which contains softer reworkings of past hits.

Interspersed between new studio albums and concert appearances, Lynyrd Skynyrd has released a plethora of compilation albums. Wilkeson died in his sleep in 2001 and King retired due to recurring heart failure in 1995, leaving the band with only two founding members, Powell and Rossington. (Rossington underwent triple-bypass surgery in early 2003, but toured later that year.) Nevertheless, they continue playing and their release *Vicious Circle* (2003) includes their first big hit in years, "Red White and Blue," a patriotic paean in support of the United States' post–September 11 activities. Lynyrd Skynyrd's identity and sound is so well defined that it would be difficult—even if they wanted to—for the band to change musical directions. Hence, they seem most at ease rehashing the music of their past, which makes up a large share of their concert material.

SELECTIVE DISCOGRAPHY: *Pronounced Leh-Nerd Skin-Nerd* (Sounds of the South/MCA, 1973); *Second Helping* (Sounds of the South/MCA, 1974); *Nuthin' Fancy* (MCA, 1975); *Gimme Back My Bullets* (MCA, 1976); *One More from the Road* (MCA, 1976); *Street Survivors* (MCA, 1977); *Skynyrd's First . . . and Last* (MCA, 1978); *Southern by the Grace of God/Lynyrd Skynyrd Tribute Tour—1987* (MCA, 1988); *Lynyrd Skynyrd 1991* (Atlantic, 1991); *The Last Rebel* (Atlantic, 1993); *Endangered Species* (Capricorn, 1994); *Southern Knights* (CBH, 1996); *Twenty* (CMC/SPV, 1997); *Lyve* (CMC/SPV, 1998); *Skynyrd's First: The Complete Muscle Shoals Album* (MCA, 1998); *Edge of Forever* (CMC/SPV, 1999); *Then and Now* (CMC, 2000); *Christmas Time Again* (CMC, 2000); *Collectybles* (MCA, 2000); *Vicious Circle* (Sanctuary, 2003).

BIBLIOGRAPHY: M. Brant, *Freebirds* (New York, 2001); G. Odom, *Lynyrd Skynyrd: The Free Birds of Southern Rock* (New York, 2003).

DONALD LOWE